THE OXFORD

GERMAN
DICTIONARY

Also available

THE OXFORD DESK DICTIONARY AND THESAURUS
THE OXFORD DICTIONARY OF AMERICAN USAGE AND STYLE
THE OXFORD ESSENTIAL GUIDE FOR PUZZLE SOLVERS
THE OXFORD ESSENTIAL GUIDE TO THE U.S. GOVERNMENT
THE OXFORD ESSENTIAL GUIDE TO WRITING
THE OXFORD ESSENTIAL QUOTATIONS DICTIONARY
THE OXFORD ESSENTIAL SPELLING DICTIONARY
THE OXFORD ESSENTIAL THESAURUS
THE OXFORD ESSENTIAL BIOGRAPHICAL DICTIONARY
THE OXFORD ESSENTIAL GEOGRAPHICAL DICTIONARY
THE OXFORD ESSENTIAL DICTIONARY OF FOREIGN TERMS IN ENGLISH
THE OXFORD FRENCH DICTIONARY
THE OXFORD GREEK DICTIONARY
THE OXFORD ITALIAN DICTIONARY
THE OXFORD PORTUGUESE DICTIONARY
THE OXFORD RUSSIAN DICTIONARY
THE OXFORD SPANISH DICTIONARY
THE OXFORD NEW SPANISH DICTIONARY

Most Berkley Books are available at special quantity discounts for bulk purchases for sales promotions, premiums, fund-raising or educational use. Special books, or book excerpts, can also be created to fit specific needs.

For details, write: Special Markets, The Berkley Publishing Group, 375 Hudson Street, New York, New York 10014.

THE OXFORD GERMAN DICTIONARY

German–English Deutsch–Englisch
English–German Englisch–Deutsch

Gunhild Prowe
Jill Schneider

BERKLEY BOOKS, NEW YORK

If you purchased this book without a cover, you should be aware that this book is stolen property. It was reported as "unsold or destroyed" to the publisher, and neither the author nor the publisher has received any payment for this "stripped book."

THE OXFORD GERMAN DICTIONARY

A Berkley Book / published in mass-market paperback by arrangement with by arrangement with Oxford University Press, Inc.

PRINTING HISTORY
Oxford University Press edition published 1994
Berkley edition / August 1997

Copyright © 1993, 1997 by Oxford University Press, Inc.
First published in 1993 as *The Oxford German Minidictionary*.
First published in 1994 as *The Oxford Paperback German Dictionary*.
Oxford is a registered trademark of Oxford University Press, Inc.
All rights reserved. No part of this publication may be reproduced, stored in a retrieval system, or transmitted, in any form or by any means, electronic, mechanical, photocopying, recording, or otherwise, without the prior written permission of Oxford University Press, Inc.
For information contact: Oxford University Press, Inc., 198 Madison Avenue, New York, New York 10016.

The Penguin Putnam Inc. World Wide Web site address is
http://www.penguinputnam.com

ISBN: 0-425-16011-4

BERKLEY®
Berkley Books are published by
The Berkley Publishing Group, a division of Penguin Putnam Inc.,
375 Hudson Street, New York, New York 10014.
BERKLEY and the "B" design are trademarks
belonging to Penguin Putnam Inc.

PRINTED IN THE UNITED STATES OF AMERICA

15 14 13 12 11 10 9 8 7

Preface

This dictionary is designed for both English and German users. It provides a handy and comprehensive reference work for students, tourists and business people.

We should like to express our thanks to Dr Michael Clark of Oxford University Press for his advice and support, and to Roswitha and Neil Morris for reading the proofs.

G.P. & J.S.

Introduction

A swung dash ~ represents the headword or that part of the headword preceding a vertical bar |. The initial letter of a German headword is given to show whether or not it is a capital.

The vertical bar | follows the part of the headword which is not repeated in compounds or derivatives.

Square brackets [ ] are used for optional material.

Angled brackets ⟨ ⟩ are used after a verb translation to indicate the object; before a verb translation to indicate the subject; before an adjective to indicate a typical noun which it qualifies.

Parentheses ( ) are used for field or style labels (see list on page x) and for explanatory matter.

A ● indicates a new part of speech within an entry.

od (oder) and *or* denote that words or portions of a phrase are synonymous. An oblique stroke / is used where there is a difference in usage or meaning.

≈ is used where no exact equivalent exists in the other language.

A dagger † indicates that a German verb is irregular and that the parts can be found in the verb table on page 555. Compound verbs are not listed there as they follow the pattern of the basic verb.

The stressed vowel is marked in a German headword by – (long) or · (short). A phonetic transcription is only given for words which do not follow the normal rules of pronunciation. These rules can be found on page 551.

Phonetics are given for all English headwords and for derivatives where there is a change of pronunciation or stress. In blocks of compounds, if no stress is shown, it falls on the first element.

A change in pronunciation or stress shown within a block of compounds applies only to that particular word (subsequent entries revert to the pronunciation and stress of the headword).

German headword nouns are followed by the gender and, with the exception of compound nouns, by the genitive and plural. These are only given at compound nouns if they present some difficulty. Otherwise the user should refer to the final element.

Nouns that decline like adjectives are entered as follows: **-e(r)** *m/f,* **-e(s)** *nt.*

Adjectives which have no undeclined form are entered in the feminine form with the masculine and neuter in brackets **-e(r,s)**.

The reflexive pronoun **sich** is accusative unless marked (*dat*).

Note on proprietary status

This dictionary includes some words which have, or are asserted to have, proprietary status as trademarks or otherwise. Their inclusion does not imply that they have acquired for legal purposes a non-proprietary or general significance, nor any other judgment concerning their legal status. In cases where the editorial staff have some evidence that a word has proprietary status this is indicated by the symbol ® in the entry, but no judgment concerning the legal status of such words is made or implied thereby.

Abbreviations · Abkürzungen

adjective	a	Adjektiv
abbreviation	abbr	Abkürzung
accusative	acc	Akkusativ
Administration	Admin	Administration
adverb	adv	Adverb
American	Amer	amerikanisch
Anatomy	Anat	Anatomie
Archaeology	Archaeol	Archäologie
Architecture	Archit	Architektur
Astronomy	Astr	Astronomie
attributive	attrib	attributiv
Austrian	Aust	österreichisch
Automobile	Auto	Automobil
Aviation	Aviat	Luftfahrt
Biology	Biol	Biologie
Botany	Bot	Botanik
Chemistry	Chem	Chemie
collective	coll	Kollektivum
Commerce	Comm	Handel
conjunction	conj	Konjunktion
Cooking	Culin	Kochkunst
dative	dat	Dativ
definite article	def art	bestimmter Artikel
demonstrative	dem	Demonstrativ-
dialect	dial	Dialekt
Electricity	Electr	Elektrizität
something	etw	etwas
feminine	f	Femininum
familiar	fam	familiär
figurative	fig	figurativ
genitive	gen	Genitiv
Geography	Geog	Geographie
Geology	Geol	Geologie
Geometry	Geom	Geometrie
Grammar	Gram	Grammatik
Horticulture	Hort	Gartenbau
impersonal	impers	unpersönlich
indefinite article	indef art	unbestimmter Artikel

indefinite pronoun	indef pron	unbestimmtes Pronomen
infinitive	inf	Infinitiv
inseparable	insep	untrennbar
interjection	int	Interjektion
invariable	inv	unveränderlich
irregular	irreg	unregelmäßig
someone	jd	jemand
someone	jdm	jemandem
someone	jdn	jemanden
someone's	jds	jemandes
Journalism	Journ	Journalismus
Law	Jur	Jura
Language	Lang	Sprache
literary	liter	dichterisch
masculine	m	Maskulinum
Mathematics	Math	Mathematik
Medicine	Med	Medizin
Meteorology	Meteorol	Meteorologie
Military	Mil	Militär
Mineralogy	Miner	Mineralogie
Music	Mus	Musik
noun	n	Substantiv
Nautical	Naut	nautisch
North German	N Ger	Norddeutsch
nominative	nom	Nominativ
neuter	nt	Neutrum
or	od	oder
Proprietary term	P	Warenzeichen
pejorative	pej	abwertend
Photography	Phot	Fotografie
Physics	Phys	Physik
plural	pl	Plural
Politics	Pol	Politik
possessive	poss	Possessiv-
past participle	pp	zweites Partizip
predicative	pred	prädikativ
prefix	pref	Präfix
preposition	prep	Präposition
present	pres	Präsens
present participle	pres p	erstes Partizip

pronoun	pron	Pronomen
Psychology	Psych	Psychologie
past tense	pt	Präteritum
Railroad	Rail	Eisenbahn
reflexive	refl	reflexiv
regular	reg	regelmäßig
relative	rel	Relativ-
Religion	Relig	Religion
see	s.	siehe
School	Sch	Schule
separable	sep	trennbar
singular	sg	Singular
South German	S Ger	Süddeutsch
slang	sl	Slang
someone	s.o.	jemand
something	sth	etwas
Technical	Techn	Technik
Telephone	Teleph	Telefon
Textiles	Tex	Textilien
Theater	Theat	Theater
Television	TV	Fernsehen
Typography	Typ	Typographie
University	Univ	Universität
auxiliary verb	v aux	Hilfsverb
intransitive verb	vi	intransitives Verb
reflexive verb	vr	reflexives Verb
transitive verb	vt	transitives Verb
vulgar	vulg	vulgär
Zoology	Zool	Zoologie

Pronunciation of the alphabet
Aussprache des Alphabets

English/Englisch		*German/Deutsch*
eɪ	a	a:
bi:	b	be:
si:	c	tse:
di:	d	de:
i:	e	e:
ef	f	ɛf
dʒi:	g	ge:
eɪtʃ	h	ha:
aɪ	i	i:
dʒeɪ	j	jɔt
keɪ	• k	ka:
el	l	ɛl
em	m	ɛm
en	n	ɛn
o:	o	o:
pi:	p	pe:
kju:	q	ku:
a:(r)	r	ɛr
es	s	ɛs
ti:	t	te:
ju:	u	u:
vi:	v	faʊ
'dʌblju:	w	ve:
eks	x	ɪks
waɪ	y	'ʏpsilɔn
zi:	z	tsɛt
eɪ umlaut	ä	ɛ:
əʊ umlaut	ö	ø:
ju: umlaut	ü	y:
long es	ß	ɛs'tsɛt

GERMAN–ENGLISH

DEUTSCH–ENGLISCH

A

Aal *m* -[e]s,-e eel. **a~en (sich)** *vr* laze; (*ausgestreckt*) stretch out

Aas *nt* -es carrion; (*sl*) swine

ab *prep* (+ *dat*) from; **ab Montag** from Monday ● *adv* off; (*weg*) away; (*auf Fahrplan*) departs; **von jetzt ab** from now on; **ab und zu** now and then; **auf und ab** up and down

abändern *vt sep* alter; (*abwandeln*) modify

abarbeiten *vt sep* work off; **sich a~** slave away

Abart *f* variety. **a~ig** *a* abnormal

Abbau *m* dismantling; (*Kohlen-*) mining; (*fig*) reduction. **a~en** *vt sep* dismantle; mine (*Kohle*); (*fig*) reduce, cut

abbeißen† *vt sep* bite off

abbeizen *vt sep* strip

abberufen† *vt sep* recall

abbestellen *vt sep* cancel; **jdn a~** put s.o. off

abbiegen† *vi sep* (*sein*) turn off; **[nach] links a~** turn left

Abbild *nt* image. **a~en** *vt sep* depict, portray. **A~ung** *f* -,-en illustration

Abbitte *f* **A~ leisten** apologize

abblättern *vi sep* (*sein*) flake off

abblend|en *vt/i sep* (*haben*) **[die Scheinwerfer]** *a~* dip one's headlights. **A~licht** *nt* dipped headlights *pl*

abbrechen† *v sep* ● *vt* break off; (*abreißen*) demolish ● *vi* (*sein/haben*) break off

abbrennen† *v sep* ● *vt* burn off; (*niederbrennen*) burn down; let off (*Feuerwerkskörper*) ● *vi* (*sein*) burn down

abbringen† *vt sep* dissuade (**von** from)

Abbruch *m* demolition; (*Beenden*) breaking off; **etw** (*dat*) **keinen A~ tun** do no harm to sth

abbuchen *vt sep* debit

abbürsten *vt sep* brush down; (*entfernen*) brush off

abdank|en *vi sep* (*haben*) resign; (*Herrscher:*) abdicate. **A~ung** *f* -,-en resignation; abdication

abdecken *vt sep* uncover; (*abnehmen*) take off; (*zudecken*) cover; **den Tisch a~** clear the table

abdichten *vt sep* seal

abdrehen *vt sep* turn off

Abdruck *m* (*pl* ¨e) impression; (*Finger-*) print; (*Nachdruck*) reprint. **a~en** *vt sep* print

abdrücken *vt/i sep* (*haben*) fire; **sich a~** leave an impression

Abend *m* -s,-e evening; **am A~** in the evening. **a~** *adv* **heute a~** this evening, tonight; **gestern a~** yesterday evening, last night. **A~brot** *nt* supper. **A~essen** *nt* dinner; (*einfacher*) supper. **A~kurs[us]** *m* evening class. **A~mahl** *nt* (*Relig*) [Holy] Communion. **a~s** *adv* in the evening

Abenteuer *nt* -s,- adventure; (*Liebes-*) affair. **a~lich** *a* fantastic; (*gefährlich*) hazardous

Abenteurer *m* -s,- adventurer

aber *conj* but; **oder a~** or else ● *adv* (*wirklich*) really; **a~ ja!** but of course! **Tausende und a~ Tausende** thousands upon thousands

Aber|glaube *m* superstition. **a~gläubisch** *a* superstitious

abermals *adv* once again

abfahr|en† *v sep* ● *vi* (*sein*) leave; (*Auto:*) drive off ● *vt* take away; (*entlangfahren*) drive along; use (*Fahrkarte*); **abgefahrene Reifen** worn tyres. **A~t** *f* departure; (*Talfahrt*) descent; (*Piste*) run; (*Ausfahrt*) exit

Abfall *m* refuse, rubbish, (*Amer*) garbage; (*auf der Straße*) litter;

(Industrie-) waste. **A~eimer** *m* rubbish-bin; litter-bin

abfallen† *vi sep (sein)* drop, fall; *(übrigbleiben)* be left **(für** for); *(sich neigen)* slope away; *(fig)* compare badly **(gegen** with); **vom Glauben a~** renounce one's faith. **a~d** *a* sloping

Abfallhaufen *m* rubbish-dump

abfällig *a* disparaging, *adv* -ly

abfangen† *vt sep* intercept; *(beherrschen)* bring under control

abfärben *vi sep (haben)* ⟨*Farbe:*⟩ run; ⟨*Stoff:*⟩ not be colour-fast; **a~ auf** *(+ acc) (fig)* rub off on

abfassen *vt sep* draft

abfertigen *vt sep* attend to; *(zollamtlich)* clear; **jdn kurz a~** *(fam)* give s.o. short shrift

abfeuern *vt sep* fire

abfind|en† *vt sep* pay off; *(entschädigen)* compensate; **sich a~en mit** come to terms with. **A~ung** *f* -,-**en** compensation

abflauen *vi sep (sein)* decrease

abfliegen† *vi sep (sein)* fly off; ⟨*Aviat*⟩ take off

abfließen† *vi sep (sein)* drain *or* run away

Abflug *m* ⟨*Aviat*⟩ departure

Abfluß *m* drainage; *(Öffnung)* drain. **A~rohr** *nt* drain-pipe

abfragen *vt sep* jdn *od* jdm **Vokabeln a~** test s.o. on vocabulary

Abfuhr *f* - removal; *(fig)* rebuff

abführ|en *vt sep* take *or* lead away. **a~end** *a* laxative. **A~mittel** *nt* laxative

abfüllen *vt sep* **auf** *od* **in Flaschen a~** bottle

Abgabe *f* handing in; *(Verkauf)* sale; *(Fußball)* pass; *(Steuer)* tax

Abgang *m* departure; *(Theat)* exit; *(Schul-)* leaving

Abgase *ntpl* exhaust fumes

abgeben† *vt sep* hand in; *(abliefern)* deliver; *(verkaufen)* sell; *(zur Aufbewahrung)* leave; *(Fußball)* pass; *(ausströmen)* give off; *(abfeuern)* fire; *(verlauten lassen)* give; cast *(Stimme)*; **jdm etw a~** give s.o. a share of sth; **sich a~ mit** occupy oneself with

abgedroschen *a* hackneyed

abgehen† *v sep* ● *vi (sein)* leave; *(Theat)* exit; *(sich lösen)* come off; *(abgezogen werden)* be deducted; *(abbiegen)* turn off; *(verlaufen)* go off; **ihr geht jeglicher Humor ab** she totally lacks a sense of humour ● *vt* walk along

abgehetzt *a* harassed. **abgelegen** *a* remote. **abgeneigt** *a* etw *(dat)* **nicht a~ sein** not be averse to sth. **abgenutzt** *a* worn. **Abgeordnete(r)** *m/f* deputy; *(Pol)* Member of Parliament. **abgepackt** *a* pre-packed. **abgerissen** *a* ragged

abgeschieden *a* secluded. **A~heit** *f* - seclusion

abgeschlossen *a (fig)* complete; ⟨*Wohnung*⟩ self-contained. **abgeschmackt** *a (fig)* tasteless. **abgesehen** *prep* apart (from **von**). **abgespannt** *a* exhausted. **abgestanden** *a* stale. **abgestorben** *a* dead; ⟨*Glied*⟩ numb. **abgetragen** *a* worn. **abgewetzt** *a* threadbare

abgewinnen† *vt sep* win **(jdm** from s.o.); **etw** *(dat)* **Geschmack a~** get a taste for sth

abgewöhnen *vt sep* jdm/sich das Rauchen a~ cure s.o. of/give up smoking

abgezehrt *a* emaciated

abgießen† *vt sep* pour off; drain ⟨*Gemüse*⟩

abgleiten† *vi sep (sein)* slip

Abgott *m* idol

abgöttisch *adv* **a~ lieben** idolize

abgrenz|en *vt sep* divide off; *(fig)* define. **A~ung** *f* - demarcation

Abgrund *m* abyss; *(fig)* depths *pl*

abgucken *vt sep (fam)* copy

Abguß *m* cast

abhacken *vt sep* chop off

abhaken *vt sep* tick off

abhalten† *vt sep* keep off; *(hindern)* keep, prevent **(von** from); *(veranstalten)* hold

abhanden *adv* **a~ kommen** get lost

Abhandlung *f* treatise

Abhang *m* slope

abhängen¹ *vt sep (reg)* take down; *(abkuppeln)* uncouple

abhäng|en²† *vi sep (haben)* depend **(von** on). **a~ig** *a* dependent **(von** on). **A~igkeit** *f* - dependence

abhärten *vt sep* toughen up

abhauen† *v sep* ● *vt* chop off ● *vi (sein) (fam)* clear off

abheben† *v sep* ● *vt* take off; *(vom Konto)* withdraw; **sich a~** stand out **(gegen** against) ● *vi (haben)* ⟨*Cards*⟩ cut [the cards]; ⟨*Aviat*⟩ take off; ⟨*Rakete:*⟩ lift off

abheften *vt sep* file

abhelfen† *vt sep* (+ *dat*) remedy

Abhilfe f remedy; **A~ schaffen** take [remedial] action

abholen vt sep collect; call for ⟨Person⟩; **jdn am Bahnhof a~** meet s.o. at the station

abhorchen vt sep (Med) sound

abhör|en vt sep listen to; (überwachen) tap; **jdn** od **jdm Vokabeln a~en** test s.o. on vocabulary. **A~gerät** nt bugging device

Abitur nt -s ≈ A levels pl. **A~ient(in)** m -en,-en (f -,-nen) pupil taking the 'Abitur'

abkanzeln vt sep (fam) reprimand

abkaufen vt sep buy (dat from)

abkehren (sich) vr sep turn away

abkette[l]n vt/i sep (haben) cast off

abklingen† vi sep (sein) die away; (nachlassen) subside

abkochen vt sep boil

abkommen† vi sep (sein) **a~ von** stray from; (aufgeben) give up; **vom Thema a~** digress. **A~** nt -s,- agreement

abkömmlich a available

Abkömmling m -s,-e descendant

abkratzen v sep ● vt scrape off ● vi (sein) (sl) die

abkühlen vt/i sep (sein) cool; **sich a~** cool [down]; ⟨Wetter:⟩ turn cooler

Abkunft f - origin

abkuppeln vt sep uncouple

abkürz|en vt sep shorten; abbreviate ⟨Wort⟩. **A~ung** f short cut; (Wort) abbreviation

abladen† vt sep unload

Ablage f shelf; (für Akten) tray

ablager|n vt sep deposit; **sich a~n** be deposited. **A~ung** f -,-en deposit

ablassen† v sep ● vt drain [off]; let off ⟨Dampf⟩; (vom Preis) knock off ● vi (haben) **a~ von** give up; **von jdm a~** leave s.o. alone

Ablauf m drain; (Verlauf) course; (Ende) end; (einer Frist) expiry. **a~en†** v sep ● vi (sein) run or drain off; (verlaufen) go off; (enden) expire; ⟨Zeit:⟩ run out; ⟨Uhrwerk:⟩ run down ● vt walk along; (absuchen) scour (nach for); (abnutzen) wear down

ableg|en v sep ● vt put down; discard ⟨Karte⟩; (abheften) file; (ausziehen) take off; (aufgeben) give up; sit, take ⟨Prüfung⟩; **abgelegte Kleidung** cast-offs pl ● vi (haben) take off one's coat; (Naut) cast off. **A~er** m -s,- (Bot) cutting; (Schößling) shoot

ablehn|en vt sep refuse; (mißbilligen) reject. **A~ung** f -,-en refusal; rejection

ableit|en vt sep divert; **sich a~en** be derived (**von/aus** from). **A~ung** f derivation; (Wort) derivative

ablenk|en vt sep deflect; divert ⟨Aufmerksamkeit⟩; (zerstreuen) distract. **A~ung** f -,-en distraction

ablesen† vt sep read; (absuchen) pick off

ableugnen vt sep deny

ablicht|en vt sep photocopy. **A~ung** f photocopy

abliefern vt sep deliver

ablös|en vt sep detach; (abwechseln) relieve; **sich a~en** come off; (sich abwechseln) take turns. **A~ung** f relief

abmach|en vt sep remove; (ausmachen) arrange; (vereinbaren) agree; **abgemacht!** agreed! **A~ung** f -,-en agreement

abmager|n vi sep (sein) lose weight. **A~ungskur** f slimming diet

abmarschieren vi sep (sein) march off

abmelden vt sep cancel ⟨Zeitung⟩; **sich a~** report that one is leaving; (im Hotel) check out

abmess|en† vt sep measure. **A~ungen** fpl measurements

abmühen (sich) vr sep struggle

abnäh|en vt sep take in. **A~er** m -s,- dart

Abnahme f - removal; (Kauf) purchase; (Verminderung) decrease

abnehm|en† v sep ● vt take off, remove; pick up ⟨Hörer⟩; **jdm etw a~en** take/(kaufen) buy sth from s.o. ● vi (haben) decrease; (nachlassen) decline; ⟨Person:⟩ lose weight; ⟨Mond:⟩ wane. **A~er** m -s,- buyer

Abneigung f dislike (**gegen** of)

abnorm a abnormal, adv -ly

abnutz|en vt sep wear out; **sich a~en** wear out. **A~ung** f - wear [and tear]

Abon|nement /abonə'mã:/ nt -s,-s subscription. **A~nent** m -en,-en subscriber. **a~nieren** vt take out a subscription to

Abordnung f -,-en deputation

abpassen vt sep wait for; **gut a~** time well

abprallen vi sep (sein) rebound; ⟨Geschoß:⟩ ricochet

abraten† vi sep (haben) **jdm von etw a~** advise s.o. against sth

abräumen vt/i (haben) clear away; clear ⟨Tisch⟩

abrechn|en v sep ● vt deduct ● vi (haben) settle up; (fig) get even. **A~ung** f settlement [of accounts]; (Rechnung) account

Abreise f departure. **a~n** vi sep (sein) leave

abreißen† v sep ● vt tear off; (demolieren) pull down ● vi (sein) come off; (fig) break off

abrichten vt sep train

abriegeln vt sep bolt; (absperren) seal off

Abriß m demolition; (Übersicht) summary

abrufen† vt sep call away; (Computer) retrieve

abrunden vt sep round off; **nach unten/oben a~** round down/up

abrupt a abrupt, adv -ly

abrüst|en vi sep (haben) disarm. **A~ung** f disarmament

abrutschen vi sep (sein) slip

Absage f -,-n cancellation; (Ablehnung) refusal. **a~n** v sep ● vt cancel ● vi (haben) [jdm] a~n cancel an appointment [with s.o.]; (auf Einladung) refuse [s.o.'s invitation]

absägen vt sep saw off; (fam) sack

Absatz m heel; (Abschnitt) paragraph; (Verkauf) sale

abschaff|en vt sep abolish; get rid of ⟨Auto, Hund⟩. **A~ung** f abolition

abschalten vt/i sep (haben) switch off

abschätzig a disparaging, adv -ly

Abschaum m (fig) scum

Abscheu m - revulsion

abscheulich a revolting; (fam) horrible, adv -bly

abschicken vt sep send off

Abschied m -[e]s,-e farewell; (Trennung) parting; **A~ nehmen** say goodbye (**von** to)

abschießen† vt sep shoot down; (abtrennen) shoot off; (abfeuern) fire; launch ⟨Rakete⟩

abschirmen vt sep shield

abschlagen† vt sep knock off; (verweigern) refuse; (abwehren) repel

abschlägig a negative; **a~e Antwort** refusal

Abschlepp|dienst m breakdown service. **a~en** vt sep tow away. **A~seil** nt tow-rope. **A~wagen** m breakdown vehicle

abschließen† v sep ● vt lock; (beenden, abmachen) conclude; make ⟨Wette⟩; balance ⟨Bücher⟩; **sich a~** (fig) cut oneself off ● vi (haben) lock up; (enden) end. **a~d** adv in conclusion

Abschluß m conclusion. **A~prüfung** f final examination. **A~zeugnis** nt diploma

abschmecken vt sep season

abschmieren vt sep lubricate

abschneiden† v sep ● vt cut off; **den Weg a~** take a short cut ● vi (haben) **gut/schlecht a~** do well/badly

Abschnitt m section; (Stadium) stage; (Absatz) paragraph; (Kontroll-) counterfoil

abschöpfen vt sep skim off

abschrauben vt sep unscrew

abschreck|en vt sep deter; (Culin) put in cold water ⟨Ei⟩. **a~end** a repulsive, adv -ly; **a~endes Beispiel** warning. **A~ungsmittel** nt deterrent

abschreib|en† v sep ● vt copy; (Comm & fig) write off ● vi (haben) copy. **A~ung** f (Comm) depreciation

Abschrift f copy

Abschuß m shooting down; (Abfeuern) firing; (Raketen-) launch

abschüssig a sloping; (steil) steep

abschwächen vt sep lessen; **sich a~** lessen; (schwächer werden) weaken

abschweifen vi sep (sein) digress

abschwellen† vi sep (sein) go down

abschwören† vi sep (haben) (+ dat) renounce

abseh|bar a **in a~barer Zeit** in the foreseeable future. **a~en†** vt/i sep (haben) copy; (voraussehen) foresee; **a~en von** disregard; (aufgeben) refrain from; **es abgesehen haben auf** (+ acc) have one's eye on; (schikanieren) have it in for

absein† vi sep (sein) (fam) have come off; (erschöpft) be worn out

abseits adv apart; (Sport) offside ● prep (+ gen) away from. **A~** nt - (Sport) offside

absend|en† vt sep send off. **A~er** m sender

absetzen v sep ● vt put or set down; (ablagern) deposit; (abnehmen) take off; (absagen) cancel; (abbrechen) stop; (entlassen) dismiss; (verkaufen) sell; (abziehen) deduct; **sich a~** be deposited; (fliehen) flee ● vi (haben) pause

Absicht f -,-en intention; **mit A~** intentionally, on purpose

absichtlich *a* intentional, *adv* -ly, deliberate, *adv* -ly

absitzen† *v sep* ● *vi (sein)* dismount ● *vt (fam)* serve ⟨*Strafe*⟩

absolut *a* absolute, *adv* -ly

Absolution /-'tsio:n/ *f* - absolution

absolvieren *vt* complete; (*bestehen*) pass

absonderlich *a* odd

absonder|n *vt sep* separate; (*ausscheiden*) secrete; **sich a~n** keep apart (**von** from). **A~ung** *f* -,-en secretion

absor|bieren *vt* absorb. **A~ption** /-'tsio:n/ *f* - absorption

abspeisen *vt sep* fob off (**mit** with)

abspenstig *a* **a~ machen** take (**jdm** from s.o.)

absperr|en *vt sep* cordon off; (*abstellen*) turn off; (*SGer*) lock. **A~ung** *f* -,-en barrier

abspielen *vt sep* play; (*Fußball*) pass; **sich a~** take place

Absprache *f* agreement

absprechen† *vt sep* arrange; **sich a~** agree; **jdm etw a~** deny s.o. sth

abspringen† *vi sep (sein)* jump off; (*mit Fallschirm*) parachute; (*abgehen*) come off; (*fam: zurücktreten*) back out

Absprung *m* jump

abspülen *vt sep* rinse; (*entfernen*) rinse off

abstamm|en *vi sep (haben)* be descended (**von** from). **A~ung** *f* - descent

Abstand *m* distance; (*zeitlich*) interval; **A~ halten** keep one's distance; **A~ nehmen von** (*fig*) refrain from

abstatten *vt sep* **jdm einen Besuch a~** pay s.o. a visit

abstauben *vt sep* dust

abstech|en† *vi sep (haben)* stand out. **A~er** *m* -s,- detour

abstehen† *vi sep (haben)* stick out; **a~ von** be away from

absteigen† *vi sep (sein)* dismount; (*niedersteigen*) descend; (*Fußball*) be relegated

abstell|en *vt sep* put down; (*lagern*) store; (*parken*) park; (*abschalten*) turn off; (*fig: beheben*) remedy. **A~gleis** *nt* siding. **A~raum** *m* box-room

absterben† *vi sep (sein)* die; (*gefühllos werden*) go numb

Abstieg *m* -[e]s,-e descent; (*Fußball*) relegation

abstimm|en *v sep* ● *vi (haben)* vote (**über**+*acc* on) ● *vt* coordinate (**auf**+*acc* with). **A~ung** *f* vote

Abstinenz /-st-/ *f* - abstinence. **A~ler** *m* -s,- teetotaller

abstoßen† *vt sep* knock off; (*abschieben*) push off; (*verkaufen*) sell; (*fig: ekeln*) repel. **a~d** *a* repulsive, *adv* -ly

abstrakt /-st-/ *a* abstract

abstreifen *vt sep* remove; slip off ⟨*Kleidungsstück, Schuhe*⟩

abstreiten† *vt sep* deny

Abstrich *m* (*Med*) smear; (*Kürzung*) cut

abstufen *vt sep* grade

Absturz *m* fall; (*Aviat*) crash

abstürzen *vi sep (sein)* fall; (*Aviat*) crash

absuchen *vt sep* search; (*ablesen*) pick off

absurd *a* absurd

Abszeß *m* -sses,-sse abscess

Abt *m* -[e]s,-̈e abbot

abtasten *vt sep* feel; (*Techn*) scan

abtauen *vt/i sep (sein)* thaw; (*entfrosten*) defrost

Abtei *f* -,-en abbey

Abteil *nt* compartment

abteilen *vt sep* divide off

Abteilung *f* -,-en section; (*Admin, Comm*) department

abtragen† *vt sep* clear; (*einebnen*) level; (*abnutzen*) wear out; (*abzahlen*) pay off

abträglich *a* detrimental (*dat* to)

abtreib|en† *v sep* ● *vt (Naut)* drive off course; **ein Kind a~en lassen** have an abortion ● *vi (sein)* drift off course. **A~ung** *f* -,-en abortion

abtrennen *vt sep* detach; (*abteilen*) divide off

abtret|en† *v sep* ● *vt* cede (**an**+*acc* to); **sich** (*dat*) **die Füße a~en** wipe one's feet ● *vi (sein)* (*Theat*) exit; (*fig*) resign. **A~er** *m* -s,- doormat

abtrocknen *vt/i sep (haben)* dry; **sich a~** dry oneself

abtropfen *vi sep (sein)* drain

abtrünnig *a* renegade; **a~ werden** (+*dat*) desert

abtun† *vt sep (fig)* dismiss

abverlangen *vt sep* demand (*dat* from)

abwägen† *vt sep (fig)* weigh

abwandeln *vt sep* modify

abwandern *vi sep (sein)* move away

abwarten *v sep* ● *vt* wait for ● *vi (haben)* wait [and see]

abwärts *adv* down[wards]

Abwasch *m* -[e]s washing-up; (*Geschirr*) dirty dishes *pl*. **a~en†** *v sep* ● *vt* wash; wash up (*Geschirr*); (*entfernen*) wash off ● *vi* (*haben*) wash up. **A~lappen** *m* dishcloth

Abwasser *nt* -s,- sewage. **A~kanal** *m* sewer

abwechseln *vi/r sep* (*haben*) [sich] **a~** alternate; (*Personen:*) take turns. **a~d** *a* alternate, *adv* -ly

Abwechslung *f* -,-en change; **zur A~** for a change. **a~sreich** *a* varied

Abweg *m* **auf A~e geraten** (*fig*) go astray. **a~ig** *a* absurd

Abwehr *f* - defence; (*Widerstand*) resistance; (*Pol*) counter-espionage. **a~en** *vt sep* ward off; (*Mil*) repel; (*zurückweisen*) dismiss. **A~system** *nt* immune system

abweich|en† *vi sep* (*sein*) deviate/ (*von Regel*) depart (**von** from); (*sich unterscheiden*) differ (**von** from). **a~end** *a* divergent; (*verschieden*) different. **A~ung** *f* -,-en deviation; difference

abweis|en† *vt sep* turn down; turn away (*Person*); (*abwehren*) repel. **a~end** *a* unfriendly. **A~ung** *f* -,-en rejection; (*Abfuhr*) rebuff

abwenden† *vt sep* turn away; (*verhindern*) avert; **sich a~** turn away; **den Blick a~** look away

abwerfen† *vt sep* throw off; throw (*Reiter*); (*Aviat*) drop; (*Kartenspiel*) discard; shed (*Haut, Blätter*); yield (*Gewinn*)

abwert|en *vt sep* devalue. **a~end** *a* pejorative, *adv* -ly. **A~ung** *f* -,-en devaluation

abwesen|d *a* absent; (*zerstreut*) absent-minded. **A~heit** *f* - absence; absent-mindedness

abwickeln *vt sep* unwind; (*erledigen*) settle

abwischen *vt sep* wipe; (*entfernen*) wipe off

abwürgen *vt sep* stall (*Motor*)

abzahlen *vt sep* pay off

abzählen *vt sep* count

Abzahlung *f* instalment

abzapfen *vt sep* draw

Abzeichen *nt* badge

abzeichnen *vt sep* copy; (*unterzeichnen*) initial; **sich a~** stand out

Abzieh|bild *nt* transfer. **a~en†** *v sep* ● *vt* pull off; take off (*Laken*); strip (*Bett*); (*häuten*) skin; (*Phot*) print; run off (*Kopien*); (*zurückziehen*) withdraw; (*abrechnen*) deduct ● *vi* (*sein*) go away; (*Rauch:*) escape

abzielen *vi sep* (*haben*) **a~ auf** (+ *acc*) (*fig*) be aimed at

Abzug *m* withdrawal; (*Abrechnung*) deduction; (*Phot*) print; (*Korrektur-*) proof; (*am Gewehr*) trigger; (*A~söffnung*) vent; **A~e** *pl* deductions

abzüglich *prep* (+ *gen*) less

Abzugshaube *f* [cooker] hood

abzweig|en *v sep* ● *vi* (*sein*) branch off ● *vt* divert. **A~ung** *f* -,-en junction; (*Gabelung*) fork

ach *int* oh; **a~ ja!** oh dear! **a~ so** I see; **mit A~ und Krach** (*fam*) by the skin of one's teeth

Achse *f* -,-n axis; (*Rad-*) axle

Achsel *f* -,-n shoulder; **die A~n zucken** shrug one's shoulders. **A~höhle** *f* armpit. **A~zucken** *nt* -s shrug

acht[1] *inv a*, **A~** *f* -,-en eight; **heute in a~ Tagen** a week today

acht[2] **außer a~ lassen** disregard; **sich in a~ nehmen** be careful

acht|e(r,s) *a* eighth. **a~eckig** *a* octagonal. **A~el** *nt* -s,- eighth. **A~elnote** *f* quaver; (*Amer*) eighth note

achten *vt* respect ● *vi* (*haben*) **a~ auf** (+ *acc*) pay attention to; (*aufpassen*) look after; **darauf a~, daß** take care that

ächten *vt* ban; ostracize (*Person*)

Achter|bahn *f* roller-coaster. **a~n** *adv* (*Naut*) aft

achtgeben† *vi sep* (*haben*) be careful; **a~ auf** (+ *acc*) look after

achtlos *a* careless, *adv* -ly

achtsam *a* careful, *adv* -ly

Achtung *f* - respect (**vor** + *dat* for); **A~!** look out! (*Mil*) attention! **'A~ Stufe'** 'mind the step'

acht|zehn *inv a* eighteen. **a~zehnte(r,s)** *a* eighteenth. **a~zig** *a* *inv* eighty. **a~zigste(r,s)** *a* eightieth

ächzen *vi* (*haben*) groan

Acker *m* -s,- field. **A~bau** *m* agriculture. **A~land** *nt* arable land

addieren *vt/i* (*haben*) add; (*zusammenzählen*) add up

Addition /-'tsio:n/ *f* -,-en addition

ade *int* goodbye

Adel *m* -s nobility

Ader *f* -,-n vein; **künstlerische A~** artistic bent

Adjektiv *nt* -s,-e adjective

Adler *m* -s,- eagle

adlig *a* noble. **A~e(r)** *m* nobleman

Administration /-'tsio:n/ f - administration

Admiral m -s,-e admiral

adop|tieren vt adopt. **A~tion** /-'tsio:n/ f -,-en adoption. **A~tiv-eltern** pl adoptive parents. **A~tiv-kind** nt adopted child

Adrenalin nt -s adrenalin

Adres|se f -,-n address. **a~sieren** vt address

adrett a neat, adv -ly

Adria f - Adriatic

Advent m -s Advent. **A~skranz** m Advent wreath

Adverb nt -s,-ien /-jən/ adverb

Affäre f -,-n affair

Affe m -n,-n monkey; (Menschen-) ape

Affekt m -[e]s,-e im A~ in the heat of the moment

affektiert a affected. **A~heit** f - affectation

affig a affected; (eitel) vain

Afrika nt -s Africa

Afrikan|er(in) m -s,- (f -,-nen) African. **a~isch** a African

After m -s,- anus

Agen|t(in) m -en,-en (f -,-nen) agent. **A~tur** f -,-en agency

Aggres|sion f -,-en aggression. **a~siv** a aggressive, adv -ly. **A~sivi-tät** f - aggressiveness

Agitation /-'tsio:n/ f - agitation

Agnostiker m -s,- agnostic

Ägypt|en /ɛ'gyptən/ nt -s Egypt. **Ä~er(in)** m -s,- (f -,-nen) Egyptian. **ä~isch** a Egyptian

ähneln vi (haben) (+ dat) resemble; sich ä~ be alike

ahnen vt have a presentiment of; (vermuten) suspect

Ahnen mpl ancestors. **A~forschung** f genealogy. **A~tafel** f family tree

ähnlich a similar, adv -ly; jdm ä~ sehen resemble s.o.; (typisch sein) be just like s.o. **Ä~keit** f -,-en similarity; resemblance

Ahnung f -,-en premonition; (Vermutung) idea, hunch; keine A~ (fam) no idea. **a~slos** a unsuspecting

Ahorn m -s,-e maple

Ähre f -,-n ear [of corn]

Aids /e:ts/ nt - Aids

Akademie f -,-n academy

Akadem|iker(in) m -s,- (f -,-nen) university graduate. **a~isch** a academic, adv -ally

akklimatisieren (sich) vr become acclimatized

Akkord m -[e]s,-e (Mus) chord; im A~ arbeiten be on piece-work. **A~arbeit** f piece-work

Akkordeon nt -s,-s accordion

Akkumulator m -s,-en /-'to:rən/ (Electr) accumulator

Akkusativ m -s,-e accusative. **A~objekt** nt direct object

Akrobat|(in) m -en,-en (f -,-nen) acrobat. **a~isch** a acrobatic

Akt m -[e]s,-e act; (Kunst) nude

Akte f -,-n file; **A~n** documents. **A~ndeckel** m folder. **A~nkoffer** m attaché case. **A~nschrank** m filing cabinet. **A~ntasche** f briefcase

Aktie /'aktsiə/ f -,-n (Comm) share. **A~ngesellschaft** f joint-stock company

Aktion /ak'tsio:n/ f -,-en action; (Kampagne) campaign. **A~är** m -s,-e shareholder

aktiv a active, adv -ly. **a~ieren** vt activate. **A~ität** f -,-en activity

Aktualität f -,-en topicality; **A~en** current events

aktuell a topical; (gegenwärtig) current; nicht mehr a~ no longer relevant

Akupunktur f - acupuncture

Akust|ik f - acoustics pl. **a~isch** a acoustic, adv -ally

akut a acute

Akzent m -[e]s,-e accent

akzept|abel a acceptable. **a~ieren** vt accept

Alarm m -s alarm; (Mil) alert; **A~ schlagen** raise the alarm. **a~ieren** vt alert; (beunruhigen) alarm. **a~ie-rend** a alarming

albern a silly ● adv in a silly way ● vi (haben) play the fool

Album nt -s,-ben album

Algebra f - algebra

Algen fpl algae

Algerien /-jən/ nt -s Algeria

Alibi nt -s,-s alibi

Alimente pl maintenance sg

Alkohol m -s alcohol. **a~frei** a non-alcoholic

Alkohol|iker(in) m -s,- (f -,-nen) alcoholic. **a~isch** a alcoholic. **A~ismus** m - alcoholism

all inv pron all das/mein Geld all the/my money; all dies all this

All nt -s universe

alle *pred a* finished, (*fam*) all gone;
a~ machen finish up

all|e(r,s) *pron* all; (*jeder*) every; **a~es**
everything, all; (*alle Leute*) everyone;
a~e *pl* all; **a~es Geld** all the money;
a~e meine Freunde all my friends;
a~e beide both [of them/ us]; **wir a~e**
we all; **a~e Tage** every day; **a~e drei
Jahre** every three years; **in a~er Unschuld** in all innocence; **ohne a~en
Grund** without any reason; **vor a~em**
above all; **a~es in a~em** all in all;
a~es aussteigen! all change! **a~e-
dem** *pron* **bei/trotz a~edem** with/
despite all that

Allee *f -,-n* avenue

Alleg|orie *f -,-n* allegory. **a~orisch** *a*
allegorical

allein *adv* alone; (*nur*) only; **a~ der
Gedanke** the mere thought; **von a~[e]**
of its/(*Person*) one's own accord; (*automatisch*) automatically; **einzig und a~**
solely ● *conj* but. **A~erziehende(r)**
m/f single parent. **a~ig** *a* sole. **A~
stehend** *a* single; **A~stehende** *pl*
single people

allemal *adv* every time; (*gewiß*) certainly; **ein für a~** once and for all

allenfalls *adv* at most; (*eventuell*)
possibly

aller|beste(r,s) *a* very best; **am
a~besten** best of all. **a~dings**
adv indeed; (*zwar*) admittedly.
a~erste(r,s) *a* very first

Allergie *f -,-n* allergy

allergisch *a* allergic (**gegen** to)

aller|hand *inv a* all sorts of ● *pron* all
sorts of things; **das ist a~hand!** that's
quite something! (*empört*) that's a bit
much! **A~heiligen** *nt* -s All Saints
Day. **a~höchstens** *adv* at the very
most. **a~lei** *inv a* all sorts of ● *pron*
all sorts of things. **a~letzte(r,s)** *a*
very last. **a~liebst** *a* enchanting.
a~liebste(r,s) *a* favourite ● *adv* **am
a~liebsten** for preference; **am a~
liebsten haben** like best of all. **a~
meiste(r,s)** *a* most ● *adv* **am
a~meisten** most of all. **A~seelen** *nt*
-s All Souls Day. **a~seits** *adv* generally; **guten Morgen a~seits!** good
morning everyone! **a~wenigste(r,s)**
a very least ● *adv* **am a~wenigsten**
least of all

alle|s *s.* **alle(r,s)**. **a~samt** *adv* all.
A~swisser *m -s, -* (*fam*) know-all

allgemein *a* general, *adv* -ly; **im
a~en** in general. **A~heit** *f* - community; (*Öffentlichkeit*) general public

Allheilmittel *nt* panacea

Allianz *f -,-en* alliance

Alligator *m -s,-en /-'to:rən/* alligator

alliiert *a* allied; **die A~en** *pl* the Allies

all|jährlich *a* annual, *adv* -ly. **a~
mächtig** *a* almighty; **der A~
mächtige** the Almighty. **a~mählich** *a*
gradual, *adv* -ly

Alltag *m* working day; **der A~** (*fig*)
everyday life

alltäglich *a* daily; (*gewöhnlich*)
everyday; (*Mensch*) ordinary ● *adv*
daily

alltags *adv* on weekdays

allzu *adv* [far] too; **a~ vorsichtig**
over-cautious. **a~bald** *adv* all too
soon. **a~oft** *adv* all too often.
a~sehr *adv* far too much. **a~viel**
adv far too much

Alm *f -,-en* alpine pasture

Almosen *ntpl* alms

Alpdruck *m* nightmare

Alpen *pl* Alps. **A~veilchen** *nt*
cyclamen

Alphabet *nt* -[e]s,-e alphabet.
a~isch *a* alphabetical, *adv* -ly

Alptraum *m* nightmare

als *conj* as; (*zeitlich*) when; (*mit Komparativ*) than; **nichts als** nothing but;
als ob as if *or* though; **so tun als ob**
(*fam*) pretend

also *adv & conj* so; **a~ gut** all right
then; **na a~!** there you are!

alt *a* (**älter, ältest**) old; (*gebraucht*)
second-hand; (*ehemalig*) former; **alt
werden** grow old; **alles beim a~en
lassen** leave things as they are

Alt *m* -s (*Mus*) contralto

Altar *m -s,¨e* altar

Alt|e(r) *m/f* old man/woman; **die
A~en** old people. **A~eisen** *nt* scrap
iron. **A~enheim** *nt* old people's
home

Alter *nt* -s,- age; (*Bejahrtheit*) old age;
im A~ von at the age of; **im A~** in old
age

älter *a* older; **mein ä~er Bruder** my
elder brother

altern *vi* (*sein*) age

Alternative *f -,-n* alternative

Alters|grenze *f* age limit. **A~heim**
nt old people's home. **A~rente** *f* old-
age pension. **a~schwach** *a* old and
infirm; (*Ding*) decrepit

Alter|tum *nt* -s,¨er antiquity. **a~
tümlich** *a* old; (*altmodisch*) old-
fashioned

ältest|e(r,s) *a* oldest; **der ä~e Sohn** the eldest son

althergebracht *a* traditional

altklug *a* precocious, *adv* -ly

ältlich *a* elderly

alt|modisch old-fashioned ● *adv* in an old-fashioned way. **A~papier** *nt* waste paper. **A~stadt** *f* old [part of a] town. **A~warenhändler** *m* second-hand dealer. **A~weibermärchen** *nt* old wives' tale. **A~weibersommer** *m* Indian summer; (*Spinnfäden*) gossamer

Alufolie *f* [aluminium] foil

Aluminium *nt* -s aluminium, (*Amer*) aluminum

am *prep* = **an dem**; **am Montag** on Monday; **am Morgen** in the morning; **am besten/meisten** [the] best/ most; **am teuersten sein** be the most expensive

Amateur /-'tø:ɐ/ *m* -s,-e amateur

Ambition /-'tsjo:n/ *f* -,-en ambition

Amboß *m* -sses,-sse anvil

ambulan|t *a* out-patient ... ● *adv* **a~t behandeln** treat as an out-patient. **A~z** *f* -,-en out-patients' department; (*Krankenwagen*) ambulance

Ameise *f* -,-n ant

amen *int*, **A~** *nt* -s amen

Amerika *nt* -s America

Amerikan|er(in) *m* -s,- (*f* -,-nen) American. **a~isch** *a* American

Ami *m* -s,-s (*fam*) Yank

Ammoniak *nt* -s ammonia

Amnestie *f* -,-n amnesty

amoralisch *a* amoral

Ampel *f* -,-n traffic lights *pl*; (*Blumen-*) hanging basket

Amphib|ie /-jə/ *f* -,-n amphibian. **a~isch** *a* amphibious

Amphitheater *nt* amphitheatre

Amput|ation /-'tsjo:n/ *f* -,-en amputation. **a~ieren** *vt* amputate

Amsel *f* -,-n blackbird

Amt *nt* -[e]s,-̈er office; (*Aufgabe*) task; (*Teleph*) exchange. **a~ieren** *vi* (*haben*) hold office; **a~ierend** acting. **a~lich** *a* official, *adv* -ly. **A~s-zeichen** *nt* dialling tone

Amulett *nt* -[e]s,-e [lucky] charm

amüs|ant *a* amusing, *adv* -ly. **a~ieren** *vt* amuse; **sich a~ieren** be amused (**über** + *acc* at); (*sich vergnügen*) enjoy oneself

an *prep* (+ *dat/acc*) at; (*haftend, berührend*) on; (*gegen*) against; (+ *acc*) ⟨*schicken*⟩ to; **an der/die Uni-**versität at/to university; **an dem Tag** on that day; **es ist an mir** it is up to me; **an [und für] sich** actually; **die Arbeit an sich** the work as such ● *adv* (*angeschaltet*) on; (*auf Fahrplan*) arriving; **an die zwanzig Mark/Leute** about twenty marks/ people; **von heute an** from today

analog *a* analogous; (*Computer*) analog. **A~ie** *f* -,-n analogy

Analphabet *m* -en,-en illiterate person. **A~entum** *nt* -s illiteracy

Analy|se *f* -,-n analysis. **a~sieren** *vt* analyse. **A~tiker** *m* -s,- analyst. **a~tisch** *a* analytical

Anämie *f* - anaemia

Ananas *f* -,-[se] pineapple

Anarch|ie *f* - anarchy. **A~ist** *m* -en,-en anarchist

Anat|omie *f* - anatomy. **a~omisch** *a* anatomical, *adv* -ly

anbahnen (sich) *vr sep* develop

Anbau *m* cultivation; (*Gebäude*) extension. **a~en** *vt sep* build on; (*anpflanzen*) cultivate, grow

anbehalten† *vt sep* keep on

anbei *adv* enclosed

anbeißen† *v sep* ● *vt* take a bite of ● *vi* (*haben*) ⟨*Fisch:*⟩ bite; (*fig*) take the bait

anbelangen *vt sep* = **anbetreffen**

anbellen *vt sep* bark at

anbeten *vt sep* worship

Anbetracht *m* in **A~** (+ *gen*) in view of

anbetreffen† *vt sep* **was mich/das anbetrifft** as far as I am/that is concerned

Anbetung *f* - worship

anbiedern (sich) *vr sep* ingratiate oneself (**bei** with)

anbieten† *vt sep* offer; **sich a~** offer (**zu** to)

anbinden† *vt sep* tie up

Anblick *m* sight. **a~en** *vt sep* look at

anbrechen† *v sep* ● *vt* start on; break into ⟨*Vorräte*⟩ ● *vi* (*sein*) begin; ⟨*Tag:*⟩ break; ⟨*Nacht:*⟩ fall

anbrennen† *v sep* ● *vt* light ● *vi* (*sein*) burn; (*Feuer fangen*) catch fire

anbringen† *vt sep* bring [along]; (*befestigen*) fix

Anbruch *m* (*fig*) dawn; **A~ des Tages/der Nacht** daybreak/nightfall

anbrüllen *vt sep* (*fam*) bellow at

Andacht *f* -,-en reverence; (*Gottesdienst*) prayers *pl*

andächtig *a* reverent, *adv* -ly; (*fig*) rapt, *adv* -ly

andauern *vi sep* (*haben*) last; (*anhalten*) continue. **a~d** *a* persistent, *adv* -ly; (*ständig*) constant, *adv* -ly

Andenken *nt* -s,- memory; (*Souvenir*) souvenir; **zum A~ an** (+ *acc*) in memory of

ander|e(r,s) *a* other; (*verschieden*) different; (*nächste*) next; **ein a~er, eine a~e** another ● *pron* **der a~e/die a~en** the other/others; **ein a~er** another [one]; (*Person*) someone else; **kein a~er** no one else; **einer nach dem a~en** one after the other; **alles a~e/nichts a~es** everything/nothing else; **etwas ganz a~es** something quite different; **alles a~e als** anything but; **unter a~em** among other things. **a~enfalls** *adv* otherwise. **a~erseits** *adv* on the other hand. **a~mal** *adv* **ein a~mal** another time

ändern *vt* alter; (*wechseln*) change; **sich ä~** change

andernfalls *adv* otherwise

anders *pred a* different; **a~ werden** change ● *adv* differently; (*riechen, schmecken*) different; (*sonst*) else; **jemand/niemand/irgendwo a~** someone/no one/somewhere else

anderseits *adv* on the other hand

anders|herum *adv* the other way round. **a~wo** *adv* (*fam*) somewhere else

anderthalb *inv a* one and a half; **a~ Stunden** an hour and a half

Änderung *f* -,-en alteration; (*Wechsel*) change

anderweitig *a* other ● *adv* otherwise; (*anderswo*) elsewhere

andeut|en *vt sep* indicate; (*anspielen*) hint at. **A~ung** *f* -,-en indication; hint

andicken *vt sep* (*Culin*) thicken

Andrang *m* rush (**nach** for); (*Gedränge*) crush

andre *a & pron* = **andere**

andrehen *vt sep* turn on; **jdm etw a~** (*fam*) palm sth off on s.o.

andrerseits *adv* = **andererseits**

androhen *vt sep* **jdm etw a~** threaten s.o. with sth

aneignen *vt sep* **sich** (*dat*) **a~** appropriate; (*lernen*) learn

aneinander *adv & pref* together; (*denken*) of one another; **a~ vorbei** past one another. **a~geraten†** *vi sep* (*sein*) quarrel

Anekdote *f* -,-n anecdote

anekeln *vt sep* nauseate

anerkannt *a* acknowledged

anerkenn|en† *vt sep* acknowledge, recognize; (*würdigen*) appreciate. **a~end** *a* approving, *adv* -ly. **A~ung** *f* - acknowledgement, recognition; appreciation

anfahren† *v sep* ● *vt* deliver; (*streifen*) hit; (*schimpfen*) snap at ● *vi* (*sein*) start; **angefahren kommen** drive up

Anfall *m* fit, attack. **a~en†** *v sep* ● *vt* attack ● *vi* (*sein*) arise; (*Zinsen:*) accrue

anfällig *a* susceptible (**für** to); (*zart*) delicate. **A~keit** *f* - susceptibility (**für** to)

Anfang *m* -s,ˉe beginning, start; **zu od am A~** at the beginning; (*anfangs*) at first. **a~en†** *vt/i sep* (*haben*) begin, start; (*tun*) do

Anfäng|er(in) *m* -s,- (*f* -,-nen) beginner. **a~lich** *a* initial, *adv* -ly

anfangs *adv* at first. **A~buchstabe** *m* initial letter. **A~gehalt** *nt* starting salary. **A~gründe** *mpl* rudiments

anfassen *v sep* ● *vt* touch; (*behandeln*) treat; tackle (*Arbeit*); **jdn a~** take s.o.'s hand; **sich a~** hold hands; **sich weich a~** feel soft ● *vi* (*haben*) **mit a~** lend a hand

anfechten† *vt sep* contest; (*fig: beunruhigen*) trouble

anfeinden *vt sep* be hostile to

anfertigen *vt sep* make

anfeuchten *vt sep* moisten

anfeuern *vt sep* spur on

anflehen *vt sep* implore, beg

Anflug *m* (*Aviat*) approach; (*fig: Spur*) trace

anforder|n *vt sep* demand; (*Comm*) order. **A~ung** *f* demand

Anfrage *f* enquiry. **a~n** *vi sep* (*haben*) enquire, ask

anfreunden (sich) *vr sep* make friends (**mit** with); (*miteinander*) become friends

anfügen *vt sep* add

anfühlen *vt sep* feel; **sich weich a~** feel soft

anführ|en *vt sep* lead; (*zitieren*) quote; (*angeben*) give; **jdn a~en** (*fam*) have s.o. on. **A~er** *m* leader. **A~ungszeichen** *ntpl* quotation marks

Angabe *f* statement; (*Anweisung*) instruction; (*Tennis*) service; (*fam: Angeberei*) showing-off; **nähere A~n** particulars

angeb|en† *v sep* ● *vt* state; give (*Namen, Grund*); (*anzeigen*) indicate; set (*Tempo*) ● *vi* (*haben*) (*Tennis*) serve; (*fam: protzen*) show off. **A~er(in)** *m -s,- (f -,-nen)* (*fam*) show-off. **A~erei** *f - (fam)* showing-off

angeblich *a* alleged, *adv* -ly

angeboren *a* innate; (*Med*) congenital

Angebot *nt* offer; (*Auswahl*) range; **A~ und Nachfrage** supply and demand

angebracht *a* appropriate

angebunden *a* **kurz a~** curt

angegriffen *a* worn out; (*Gesundheit*) poor

angeheiratet *a* (*Onkel, Tante*) by marriage

angeheitert *a* (*fam*) tipsy

angehen† *v sep* ● *vi* (*sein*) begin, start; (*Licht, Radio:*) come on; (*anwachsen*) take root; **a~ gegen** fight ● *vt* attack; tackle (*Arbeit*); (*bitten*) ask (**um** for); (*betreffen*) concern; **das geht dich nichts an** it's none of your business. **a~d** *a* future; (*Künstler*) budding

angehör|en *vi sep* (*haben*) (+ *dat*) belong to. **A~ige(r)** *m/f* relative; (*Mitglied*) member

Angeklagte(r) *m/f* accused

Angel *f -,-n* fishing-rod; (*Tür-*) hinge

Angelegenheit *f* matter; **auswärtige A~en** foreign affairs

Angel|haken *m* fish-hook. **a~n** *vi* (*haben*) fish (**nach** for); **a~n gehen** go fishing ● *vt* (*fangen*) catch. **A~rute** *f* fishing-rod

angelsächsisch *a* Anglo-Saxon

angemessen *a* commensurate (*dat* with); (*passend*) appropriate, *adv* -ly

angenehm *a* pleasant, *adv* -ly; (*bei Vorstellung*) **a~!** delighted to meet you!

angenommen *a* (*Kind*) adopted; (*Name*) assumed

angeregt *a* animated, *adv* -ly

angesehen *a* respected; (*Firma*) reputable

angesichts *prep* (+ *gen*) in view of

angespannt *a* intent, *adv* -ly; (*Lage*) tense

Angestellte(r) *m/f* employee

angetan *a* **a~ sein von** be taken with

angetrunken *a* slightly drunk

angewandt *a* applied

angewiesen *a* dependent (**auf** + *acc* on); **auf sich selbst a~** on one's own

angewöhnen *vt sep* **jdm etw a~** get s.o. used to sth; **sich** (*dat*) **etw a~** get into the habit of doing sth

Angewohnheit *f* habit

Angina *f* - tonsillitis

angleichen† *vt sep* adjust (*dat* to)

Angler *m -s,-* angler

anglikanisch *a* Anglican

Anglistik *f* - English [language and literature]

Angorakatze *f* Persian cat

angreif|en† *vt sep* attack; tackle (*Arbeit*); (*schädigen*) damage; (*anbrechen*) break into; (*anfassen*) touch. **A~er** *m -s,-* attacker; (*Pol*) aggressor

angrenzen *vi sep* (*haben*) adjoin (**an etw** *acc* sth). **a~d** *a* adjoining

Angriff *m* attack; **in A~ nehmen** tackle. **a~slustig** *a* aggressive

Angst *f -,¨e* fear; (*Psych*) anxiety; (*Sorge*) worry (**um** about); **A~ haben** be afraid (**vor** + *dat* of); (*sich sorgen*) be worried (**um** about) ● **jdm a~ machen** frighten s.o.; **mir ist a~** I am frightened; I am worried (**um** about)

ängstigen *vt* frighten; (*Sorge machen*) worry; **sich ä~** be frightened; be worried (**um** about)

ängstlich *a* nervous, *adv* -ly; (*scheu*) timid, *adv* -ly; (*verängstigt*) frightened, scared; (*besorgt*) anxious, *adv* -ly. **Ä~keit** *f* - nervousness; timidity; anxiety

angstvoll *a* anxious, *adv* -ly; (*verängstigt*) frightened

angucken *vt sep* (*fam*) look at

angurten (sich) *vr sep* fasten one's seat-belt

anhaben† *vt sep* have on; **er/es kann mir nichts a~** (*fig*) he/it cannot hurt me

anhalt|en† *v sep* ● *vt* stop; hold (*Atem*); **jdn zur Arbeit/Ordnung a~en** urge s.o. to work/be tidy ● *vi* (*haben*) stop; (*andauern*) continue. **a~end** *a* persistent, *adv* -ly; (*Beifall*) prolonged. **A~er(in)** *m -s,- (f -,-nen)* hitch-hiker; **per A~er fahren** hitch-hike. **A~spunkt** *m* clue

anhand *prep* (+ *gen*) with the aid of

Anhang *m* appendix; (*fam: Angehörige*) family

anhängen[1] *vt sep* (*reg*) hang up; (*befestigen*) attach; (*hinzufügen*) add

anhäng|en[2]†*vi* (*haben*) be a follower of. **A~er** *m* -s,- follower; (*Auto*) trailer; (*Schild*) [tie-on] label; (*Schmuck*) pendant; (*Aufhänger*) loop. **A~erin** *f* -,-nen follower. **A~erschaft** *f* - following, followers *pl*. **a~lich** *a* affectionate. **A~sel** *nt* -s,- appendage

anhäufen *vt sep* pile up; **sich a~** pile up, accumulate

anheben† *vt sep* lift; (*erhöhen*) raise

Anhieb *m auf* **A~** straight away

Anhöhe *f* hill

anhören *vt sep* listen to; **mit a~** overhear; **sich gut a~** sound good

animieren *vt* encourage (**zu** to)

Anis *m* -es aniseed

Anker *m* -s,- anchor; **vor A~ gehen** drop anchor. **a~n** *vi* (*haben*) anchor; (*liegen*) be anchored

anketten *vt sep* chain up

Anklage *f* accusation; (*Jur*) charge; (*Ankläger*) prosecution. **A~bank** *f* dock. **a~n** *vt sep* accuse (*gen* of); (*Jur*) charge (*gen* with)

Ankläger *m* accuser; (*Jur*) prosecutor

anklammern *vt sep* clip on; peg on the line (*Wäsche*); **sich a~** cling (**an**+ *acc* to)

Anklang *m* **bei jdm A~ finden** meet with s.o.'s approval

ankleben *v sep* ● *vt* stick on ● *vi* (*sein*) stick (**an**+ *dat* to)

Ankleide|kabine *f* changing cubicle; (*zur Anprobe*) fitting-room. **a~n** *vt sep* dress; **sich a~n** dress

anklopfen *vi sep* (*haben*) knock

anknipsen *vt sep* (*fam*) switch on

anknüpfen *v sep* ● *vt* tie on; (*fig*) enter into (*Gespräch, Beziehung*) ● *vi* (*haben*) refer (**an**+ *acc* to)

ankommen *vi sep* (*sein*) arrive; (*sich nähern*) approach; **gut a~** arrive safely; (*fig*) go down well (**bei** with); **nicht a~ gegen** (*fig*) be no match for; **a~ auf** (+ *acc*) depend on; **es a~ lassen auf** (+ *acc*) risk; **das kommt darauf an** it [all] depends

ankreuzen *vt sep* mark with a cross

ankündig|en *vt sep* announce. **A~ung** *f* announcement

Ankunft *f* - arrival

ankurbeln *vt sep* (*fig*) boost

anlächeln *vt sep* smile at

anlachen *vt sep* smile at

Anlage *f* -,-n installation; (*Industrie-*) plant; (*Komplex*) complex; (*Geld-*) investment; (*Plan*) layout; (*Beilage*) enclosure; (*Veranlagung*) aptitude; (*Neigung*) predisposition; **[öffentliche] A~n** [public] gardens; **als A~** enclosed

Anlaß *m* -sses,-̈sse reason; (*Gelegenheit*) occasion; **A~ geben zu** give cause for

anlass|en† *vt sep* (*Auto*) start; (*fam*) leave on (*Mantel*); **sich gut/schlecht a~en** start off well/ badly. **A~er** *m* -s,- starter

anläßlich *prep* (+ *gen*) on the occasion of

Anlauf *m* (*Sport*) run-up; (*fig*) attempt. **a~en**† *v sep* ● *vi* (*sein*) start; (*beschlagen*) mist up; (*Metall:*) tarnish; **rot a~en** go red; (*erröten*) blush; **angelaufen kommen** come running up ● *vt* (*Naut*) call at

anlegen *v sep* ● *vt* put (**an**+ *acc* against); put on (*Kleidung, Verband*); lay back (*Ohren*); aim (*Gewehr*); (*investieren*) invest; (*ausgeben*) spend (**für** on); (*erstellen*) build; (*gestalten*) lay out; draw up (*Liste*); **[mit] Hand a~** lend a hand; **es darauf a~** (*fig*) aim (**zu** to); **sich a~ mit** quarrel with ● *vi* (*haben*) (*Schiff:*) moor; **a~ auf** (+ *acc*) aim at

anlehnen *vt sep* lean (**an**+ *acc* against); **sich a~** lean (**an**+ *acc* on); **eine Tür angelehnt lassen** leave a door ajar

Anleihe *f* -,-n loan

anleinen *vt sep* put on a lead

anleit|en *vt sep* instruct. **A~ung** *f* instructions *pl*

anlernen *vt sep* train

Anliegen *nt* -s,- request; (*Wunsch*) desire

anlieg|en† *vi sep* (*haben*) [eng] **a~en** fit closely; [eng] **a~end** close-fitting. **A~er** *mpl* residents; **'A~er frei'** 'access for residents only'

anlocken *vt sep* attract

anlügen† *vt sep* lie to

anmachen *vt sep* (*fam*) fix; (*anschalten*) turn on; (*anzünden*) light; (*Culin*) dress (*Salat*)

anmalen *vt sep* paint

Anmarsch *m* (*Mil*) approach

anmaß|en *vt sep* **sich** (*dat*) **a~en** presume (**zu** to); **sich** (*dat*) **ein Recht a~en** claim a right. **a~end** *a* presumptuous, *adv* -ly; (*arrogant*) arrogant, *adv* -ly. **A~ung** *f* - presumption; arrogance

anmeld|en vt sep announce; (Admin) register; **sich a~en** say that one is coming; (Admin) register; (Sch) enrol; (im Hotel) check in; (beim Arzt) make an appointment. **A~ung** f announcement; (Admin) registration; (Sch) enrolment; (Termin) appointment

anmerk|en vt sep mark; **sich** (dat) **etw a~en lassen** show sth. **A~ung** f -,-en note

Anmut f - grace; (Charme) charm

anmuten vt sep **es mutet mich seltsam/vertraut an** it seems odd/familiar to me

anmutig a graceful, adv -ly; (lieblich) charming, adv -ly

annähen vt sep sew on

annäher|nd a approximate, adv -ly. **A~ungsversuche** mpl advances

Annahme f -,-n acceptance; (Adoption) adoption; (Vermutung) assumption

annehm|bar a acceptable. **a~en†** vt sep accept; (adoptieren) adopt; acquire (Gewohnheit); (sich zulegen, vermuten) assume; **sich a~en** (+gen) take care of; **angenommen, daß** assuming that. **A~lichkeiten** fpl comforts

annektieren vt annex

Anno adv **A~** 1920 in the year 1920

Annon|ce /a'nõ:sə/ f -,-n advertisement. **a~cieren** /-'si:-/ vt/i (haben) advertise

annullieren vt annul; cancel (Flug)

anöden vt sep (fam) bore

Anomalie f -,-n anomaly

anonym a anonymous, adv -ly

Anorak m -s,-s anorak

anordn|en vt sep arrange; (befehlen) order. **A~ung** f arrangement; order

anorganisch a inorganic

anormal a abnormal

anpacken v sep ● vt grasp; tackle (Arbeit, Problem) ● vi (haben) **mit a~** lend a hand

anpass|en vt sep try on; (angleichen) adapt (dat to); **sich a~en** adapt (dat to). **A~ung** f - adaptation. **a~ungsfähig** a adaptable. **A~ungsfähigkeit** f adaptability

Anpfiff m (Sport) kick-off; (fam: Rüge) reprimand

anpflanzen vt sep plant; (anbauen) grow

Anprall m -[e]s impact. **a~en** vi sep (sein) strike (**an etw** acc sth)

anprangern vt sep denounce

anpreisen† vt sep commend

Anprob|e f fitting. **a~ieren** vt sep try on

anrechnen vt sep count (**als** as); (berechnen) charge for; (verrechnen) allow (Summe); **ich rechne ihm seine Hilfe hoch an** I very much appreciate his help

Anrecht nt right (**auf**+acc to)

Anrede f [form of] address. **a~n** vt sep address; (ansprechen) speak to

anreg|en vt sep stimulate; (ermuntern) encourage (**zu** to); (vorschlagen) suggest. **a~end** a stimulating. **A~ung** f stimulation; (Vorschlag) suggestion

anreichern vt sep enrich

Anreise f journey; (Ankunft) arrival. **a~n** vi sep (sein) arrive

Anreiz m incentive

anrempeln vt sep jostle

Anrichte f -,-n sideboard. **a~n** vt sep (Culin) prepare; (garnieren) garnish (**mit** with); (verursachen) cause

anrüchig a disreputable

Anruf m call. **A~beantworter** m -s,- answering machine. **a~en†** v sep ● vt call to; (bitten) call on (**um** for); (Teleph) ring ● vi (haben) ring (**bei jdm** s.o.)

anrühren vt sep touch; (verrühren) mix

ans prep = **an das**

Ansage f announcement. **a~n** vt sep announce; **sich a~n** say that one is coming. **A~r(in)** m -s,- (f -,-nen) announcer

ansamm|eln vt sep collect; (anhäufen) accumulate; **sich a~eln** collect; (sich häufen) accumulate; (Leute:) gather. **A~lung** f collection; (Menschen-) crowd

ansässig a resident

Ansatz m beginning; (Haar-) hairline; (Versuch) attempt; (Techn) extension

anschaff|en vt sep [**sich** dat] **etw a~en** acquire/(kaufen) buy sth. **A~ung** f -,-en acquisition; (Kauf) purchase

anschalten vt sep switch on

anschau|en vt sep look at. **a~lich** a vivid, adv -ly. **A~ung** f -,-en (fig) view

Anschein m appearance; **den A~ haben** seem. **a~end** adv apparently

anschicken (sich) *vr sep* be about (**zu to**)

anschirren *vt sep* harness

Anschlag *m* notice; (*Vor-*) estimate; (*Überfall*) attack (**auf** + acc on); (*Mus*) touch; (*Techn*) stop; **240 A~e in der Minute** ≈ 50 words per minute. **A~brett** *nt* notice board. **a~en†** (*v sep* ● *vt* put up (*Aushang*); strike (*Note, Taste*); cast on (*Masche*); (*beschädigen*) chip ● *vi* (*haben*) strike/ (*stoßen*) knock (**an** + acc against); (*Hund:*) bark; (*wirken*) be effective ● *vi* (*sein*) knock (**an** + acc against); **mit dem Kopf a~en** hit one's head. **A~zettel** *m* notice

anschließen† *v sep* ● *vt* connect (**an** + acc to); (*zufügen*) add; **sich a~ an** (+ acc) (*anstoßen*) adjoin; (*folgen*) follow; (*sich anfreunden*) become friendly with; **sich jdm a~** join s.o. ● *vi* (*haben*) **a~ an** (+ acc) adjoin; (*folgen*) follow. **a~d** *a* adjoining; (*zeitlich*) following ● *adv* afterwards; **a~d an** (+ acc) after

Anschluß *m* connection; (*Kontakt*) contact; **A~ finden** make friends; **im A~ an** (+ acc) after

anschmieg|en (sich) *vr sep* snuggle up/(*Kleid:*) cling (**an** + acc to). **a~sam** *a* affectionate

anschmieren *vt sep* smear; (*fam: täuschen*) cheat

anschnallen *vt sep* strap on; **sich a~** fasten one's seat-belt

anschneiden† *vt sep* cut into; broach (*Thema*)

anschreiben† *vt sep* write (**an** + acc on); (*Comm*) put on s.o.'s account; (*sich wenden*) write to; **bei jdm gut/schlecht angeschrieben sein** be in s.o.'s good/ bad books

anschreien† *vt sep* shout at

Anschrift *f* address

anschuldig|en *vt sep* accuse. **A~ung** *f* -,-en accusation

anschwellen† *vi sep* (*sein*) swell

anschwemmen *vt sep* wash up

anschwindeln *vt sep* (*fam*) lie to

ansehen† *vt sep* look at; (*einschätzen*) regard (**als** as); [**sich** *dat*] **etw a~** look at sth; (*TV*) watch sth. **A~** *nt* -**s** respect; (*Ruf*) reputation

ansehnlich *a* considerable

ansetzen *v sep* ● *vt* join (**an** + acc to); (*festsetzen*) fix; (*veranschlagen*) estimate; **Rost a~** get rusty; **sich a~**

form ● *vi* (*haben*) (*anbrennen*) burn; **zum Sprung a~** get ready to jump

Ansicht *f* view; **meiner A~ nach** in my view; **zur A~** (*Comm*) on approval. **A~s[post]karte** *f* picture postcard. **A~ssache** *f* matter of opinion

ansiedeln (sich) *vr sep* settle

ansonsten *adv* apart from that

anspannen *vt sep* hitch up; (*anstrengen*) strain; tense (*Muskel*)

anspiel|en *vi sep* (*haben*) **a~en auf** (+ acc) allude to; (*versteckt*) hint at. **A~ung** *f* -,-en allusion; hint

Anspitzer *m* -**s**,- pencil-sharpener

Ansporn *m* (*fig*) incentive. **a~en** *vt sep* spur on

Ansprache *f* address

ansprechen† *v sep* ● *vt* speak to; (*fig*) appeal to ● *vi* (*haben*) respond (**auf** + acc to). **a~d** *a* attractive

anspringen† *v sep* ● *vt* jump at ● *vi* (*sein*) (*Auto*) start

Anspruch *m* claim/(*Recht*) right (**auf** + acc to); **A~ haben** be entitled (**auf** + acc to); **in A~ nehmen** make use of; (*erfordern*) demand; take up (*Zeit*); occupy (*Person*); **hohe A~e stellen** be very demanding. **a~slos** *a* undemanding; (*bescheiden*) unpretentious. **a~svoll** *a* demanding; (*kritisch*) discriminating; (*vornehm*) up-market

anspucken *vt sep* spit at

anstacheln *vt sep* (*fig*) spur on

Anstalt *f* -,-en institution; **A~en/ keine A~en machen** prepare/make no move (**zu** to)

Anstand *m* decency; (*Benehmen*) [good] manners *pl*

anständig *a* decent, *adv* -ly; (*ehrbar*) respectable, *adv* -bly; (*fam: beträchtlich*) considerable, *adv* -bly; (*richtig*) proper, *adv* -ly

Anstands|dame *f* chaperon. **a~los** *adv* without any trouble; (*bedenkenlos*) without hesitation

anstarren *vt sep* stare at

anstatt *conj* & *prep* (+ *gen*) instead of; **a~ zu arbeiten** instead of working

anstechen† *vt sep* tap (*Faß*)

ansteck|en *v sep* ● *vt* pin (**an** + acc to/ on); put on (*Ring*); (*anzünden*) light; (*in Brand stecken*) set fire to; (*Med*) infect; **sich a~en** catch an infection (**bei** from) ● *vi* (*haben*) be infectious. **a~end** *a* infectious, (*fam*) catching. **A~ung** *f* -,-en infection

anstehen† *vi sep* (*haben*) queue, (*Amer*) stand in line

ansteigen† *vi sep* (*sein*) climb; ⟨*Gelände, Preise:*⟩ rise

anstelle *prep* (+ *gen*) instead of

anstell|en *vt sep* put, stand (**an** + *acc* against); (*einstellen*) employ; (*anschalten*) turn on; (*tun*) do; **sich a~en** queue [up], (*Amer*) stand in line; (*sich haben*) make a fuss. **A~ung** *f* employment; (*Stelle*) job

Anstieg *m* -[e]s,-e climb; (*fig*) rise

anstifte|n *vt sep* cause; (*anzetteln*) instigate; **jdn a~n** put s.o. up (**zu** to). **A~r** *m* instigator

Anstoß *m* (*Anregung*) impetus; (*Stoß*) knock; (*Fußball*) kick-off; **a~erregen/nehmen** give/take offence (**an** + *dat* at). **a~en†** *v sep* ● *vt* knock; (*mit dem Ellbogen*) nudge ● *vi* (*sein*) knock (**an** + *acc* against) ● *vi* (*haben*) adjoin (**an etw** *acc* sth); [**mit den Gläsern**] **a~en** clink glasses; **a~en auf** (+ *acc*) drink to; **mit der Zunge a~en** lisp

anstößig *a* offensive, *adv* -ly

anstrahlen *vt sep* floodlight; (*anlachen*) beam at

anstreiche|n† *vt sep* paint; (*anmerken*) mark. **A~r** *m* -s,- painter

anstreng|en *vt sep* strain; (*ermüden*) tire; **sich a~en** exert oneself; (*sich bemühen*) make an effort (**zu** to). **a~end** *a* strenuous; (*ermüdend*) tiring. **A~ung** *f* -,-en strain; (*Mühe*) effort

Anstrich *m* coat [of paint]

Ansturm *m* rush; (*Mil*) assault

Ansuchen *nt* -s,- request

Antagonismus *m* - antagonism

Antarktis *f* - Antarctic

Anteil *m* share; **A~ nehmen** take an interest (**an** + *dat* in); (*mitfühlen*) sympathize. **A~nahme** *f* - interest (**an** + *dat* in); (*Mitgefühl*) sympathy

Antenne *f* -,-n aerial

Anthologie *f* -,-n anthology

Anthropologie *f* - anthropology

Anti|alkoholiker *m* teetotaller. **A~biotikum** *nt* -s,-ka antibiotic

antik *a* antique. **A~e** *f* - [classical] antiquity

Antikörper *m* antibody

Antilope *f* -,-n antelope

Antipathie *f* - antipathy

Anti|quariat *nt* -[e]s,-e antiquarian bookshop. **a~quarisch** *a & adv* second-hand

Antiquitäten *fpl* antiques. **A~händler** *m* antique dealer

Antisemitismus *m* - anti-Semitism

Antisept|ikum *nt* -s,-ka antiseptic. **a~isch** *a* antiseptic

Antrag *m* -[e]s,-e proposal; (*Pol*) motion; (*Gesuch*) application. **A~steller** *m* -s,- applicant

antreffen† *vt sep* find

antreiben† *v sep* ● *vt* urge on; (*Techn*) drive; (*anschwemmen*) wash up ● *vi* (*sein*) be washed up

antreten† *v sep* ● *vt* start; take up ⟨*Amt*⟩ ● *vi* (*sein*) line up; (*Mil*) fall in

Antrieb *m* urge; (*Techn*) drive; **aus eigenem A~** of one's own accord

antrinken† *vt sep* **sich** (*dat*) **einen Rausch a~** get drunk; **sich** (*dat*) **Mut a~** give oneself Dutch courage

Antritt *m* start; **bei A~ eines Amtes** when taking office. **A~srede** *f* inaugural address

antun† *vt sep* **jdm etw a~** do sth to s.o.; **sich** (*dat*) **etwas a~** take one's own life; **es jdm angetan haben** appeal to s.o.

Antwort *f* -,-en answer, reply (**auf** + *acc* to). **a~en** *vt/i* (*haben*) answer (**jdm** s.o.)

anvertrauen *vt sep* entrust/(*mitteilen*) confide (**jdm** to s.o.); **sich jdm a~** confide in s.o.

anwachsen† *vi sep* (*sein*) take root; (*zunehmen*) grow

Anwalt *m* -[e]s,-e, **Anwältin** *f* -,-nen lawyer; (*vor Gericht*) counsel

Anwandlung *f* -,-en fit (**von** of)

Anwärter(in) *m*(*f*) candidate

anweis|en† *vt sep* assign (*dat* to); (*beauftragen*) instruct. **A~ung** *f* instruction; (*Geld-*) money order

anwend|en† *vt sep* apply (**auf** + *acc* to); (*gebrauchen*) use. **A~ung** *f* application; use

anwerben† *vt sep* recruit

Anwesen *nt* -s,- property

anwesen|d *a* present (**bei** at); **die A~den** those present. **A~heit** *f* - presence

anwidern *vt sep* disgust

Anwohner *mpl* residents

Anzahl *f* number

anzahl|en *vt sep* pay a deposit on; pay on account ⟨*Summe*⟩. **A~ung** *f* deposit

anzapfen *vt sep* tap

Anzeichen *nt* sign

Anzeige f -,-n announcement; (*Inserat*) advertisement; **A~ erstatten gegen jdn** report s.o. to the police. **a~n** vt sep announce; (*inserieren*) advertise; (*melden*) report [to the police]; (*angeben*) indicate, show. **A~r** m indicator

anzieh|en† vt sep ● vt attract; (*festziehen*) tighten; put on ⟨Kleider, Bremse⟩; draw up ⟨Beine⟩; (*ankleiden*) dress; **sich a~en** get dressed; **was soll ich a~en?** what shall I wear? **gut angezogen** well-dressed ● vi (*haben*) start pulling; ⟨Preise:⟩ go up. **a~end** a attractive. **A~ung** f - attraction. **A~ungskraft** f attraction; (*Phys*) gravity

Anzug m suit; **im A~ sein** (*fig*) be imminent

anzüglich a suggestive; ⟨Bemerkung⟩ personal

anzünden vt sep light; (*in Brand stecken*) set fire to

anzweifeln vt sep question

apart a striking, adv -ly

Apathie f - apathy

apathisch a apathetic, adv -ally

Aperitif m -s,-s aperitif

Apfel m -s,⁻ apple. **A~mus** nt apple purée

Apfelsine f -,-n orange

Apostel m -s,- apostle

Apostroph m -s,-e apostrophe

Apothek|e f -,-n pharmacy. **A~er(in)** m -s,- (f -,-nen) pharmacist, [dispensing] chemist

Apparat m -[e]s,-e device; (*Phot*) camera; (*Radio, TV*) set; (*Teleph*) telephone; **am A~!** speaking! **A~ur** f -,-en apparatus

Appell m -s,-e appeal; (*Mil*) rollcall. **a~ieren** vi (*haben*) appeal (**an** + acc **to**)

Appetit m -s appetite; **guten A~!** enjoy your meal! **a~lich** a appetizing, adv -ly

applaudieren vi (*haben*) applaud

Applaus m -es applause

Aprikose f -,-n apricot

April m -[s] April; **in den A~ schicken** (*fam*) make an April fool of

Aquarell nt -s,-e water-colour

Aquarium nt -s,-ien aquarium

Äquator m -s equator

Ära f - era

Araber(in) m -s,- (f -,-nen) Arab

arabisch a Arab; (*Geog*) Arabian; ⟨Ziffer⟩ Arabic

Arbeit f -,-en work; (*Anstellung*) employment, job; (*Aufgabe*) task; (*Sch*) [written] test; (*Abhandlung*) treatise; (*Qualität*) workmanship; **bei der A~** at work; **zur A~ gehen** go to work; **an die A~ gehen, sich an die A~ machen** set to work; **sich** (*dat*) **viel A~ machen** go to a lot of trouble. **a~en** v sep ● vi (*haben*) work (**an** + dat **on**) ● vt make; **einen Anzug a~en lassen** have a suit made; **sich durch etw a~en** work one's way through sth. **A~er(in)** m -s,- (f -,-nen) worker; (*Land-, Hilfs-*) labourer. **A~erklasse** f working class

Arbeit|geber m -s,- employer. **A~nehmer** m -s,- employee. **a~sam** a industrious

Arbeits|amt nt employment exchange. **A~erlaubnis, A~genehmigung** f work permit. **A~kraft** f worker; **Mangel an A~kräften** shortage of labour. **a~los** a unemployed; **a~los sein** be out of work. **A~lose(r)** m/f unemployed person; **die A~losen** the unemployed pl. **A~losenunterstützung** f unemployment benefit. **A~losigkeit** f - unemployment

arbeitsparend a labour-saving

Arbeits|platz m job. **A~tag** m working day. **A~zimmer** nt study

Archäo|loge m -n,-n archaeologist. **A~logie** f - archaeology. **a~logisch** a archaeological

Arche f - **die A~** Noah Noah's Ark

Architek|t(in) m -en,-en (f -,-nen) architect. **a~tonisch** a architectural. **A~tur** f - architecture

Archiv nt -s,-e archives pl

Arena f -,-nen arena

arg a (ärger, ärgst) bad; (*groß*) terrible; **sein ärgster Feind** his worst enemy ● adv badly; (*sehr*) terribly

Argentin|ien /-jən/ nt -s Argentina. **a~isch** a Argentinian

Ärger m -s annoyance; (*Unannehmlichkeit*) trouble. **ä~lich** a annoyed; (*leidig*) annoying; **ä~lich sein** be annoyed. **ä~n** vt annoy; (*necken*) tease; **sich ä~n** get annoyed (**über jdn/etw** with s.o./about sth). **Ä~nis** nt -ses,-se annoyance; **öffentliches Ä~nis** public nuisance

Arglist f - malice. **a~ig** a malicious, adv -ly

arglos *a* unsuspecting; (*unschuldig*) innocent, *adv* -ly

Argument *nt* -[e]s,-e argument. **a~ieren** *vi* (*haben*) argue (**daß** that)

Argwohn *m* -s suspicion

argwöhn|en *vt* suspect. **a~isch** *a* suspicious, *adv* -ly

Arie /'a:rjə/ *f* -,-n aria

Aristo|krat *m* -en,-en aristocrat. **A~kratie** *f* - aristocracy. **a~kratisch** *a* aristocratic

Arithmetik *f* - arithmetic

Arkt|is *f* - Arctic. **a~isch** *a* Arctic

arm *a* (**ärmer, ärmst**) poor; **arm und reich** rich and poor

Arm *m* -[e]s,-e arm; **jdn auf den Arm nehmen** (*fam*) pull s.o.'s leg

Armaturenbrett *nt* instrument panel; (*Auto*) dashboard

Armband *nt* (*pl* **-bänder**) bracelet; (*Uhr*-) watch-strap. **A~uhr** *f* wristwatch

Arm|e(r) *m/f* poor man/woman; **die A~en** the poor *pl*; **du A~e** *od* **Ärmste!** you poor thing!

Armee *f* -,-n army

Ärmel *m* -s,- sleeve. **Ä~kanal** *m* [English] Channel. **ä~los** *a* sleeveless

Arm|lehne *f* arm. **A~leuchter** *m* candelabra

ärmlich *a* poor, *adv* -ly; (*elend*) miserable, *adv* -bly

armselig *a* miserable, *adv* -bly

Armut *f* - poverty

Arom|a *nt* -s,-men & -mas aroma; (*Culin*) essence. **a~atisch** *a* aromatic

Arran|gement /arãʒə'mã:/ *nt* -s,-s arrangement. **a~gieren** /-'ʒi:rən/ *vt* arrange; **sich a~gieren** come to an arrangement

Arrest *m* -[e]s (*Mil*) detention

arrogan|t *a* arrogant, *adv* -ly. **A~z** *f* -arrogance

Arsch *m* -[e]s,̈-e (*vulg*) arse

Arsen *nt* -s arsenic

Art *f* -,-en manner; (*Weise*) way; (*Natur*) nature; (*Sorte*) kind; (*Biol*) species; **auf diese Art** in this way. **a~en** *vi* (*sein*) **a~en nach** take after

Arterie /-jə/ *f* -,-n artery

Arthritis *f* - arthritis

artig *a* well-behaved; (*höflich*) polite, *adv* -ly; **sei a~!** be good!

Artikel *m* -s,- article

Artillerie *f* - artillery

Artischocke *f* -,-n artichoke

Artist(in) *m* -en,-en (*f* -,-nen) [circus] artiste

Arznei *f* -,-en medicine. **A~mittel** *nt* drug

Arzt *m* -[e]s,̈-e doctor

Ärzt|in *f* -,-nen [woman] doctor. **ä~lich** *a* medical

As *nt* -ses,-se ace

Asbest *m* -[e]s asbestos

Asche *f* - ash. **A~nbecher** *m* ashtray. **A~rmittwoch** *m* Ash Wednesday

Asiat|(in) *m* -en,-en (*f* -,-nen) Asian. **a~isch** *a* Asian

Asien /'a:zjən/ *nt* -s Asia

asozial *a* antisocial

Aspekt *m* -[e]s,-e aspect

Asphalt *m* -[e]s asphalt. **a~ieren** *vt* asphalt

Assistent(in) *m* -en,-en (*f* -,-nen) assistant

Ast *m* -[e]s,̈-e branch

ästhetisch *a* aesthetic

Asth|ma *nt* -s asthma. **a~matisch** *a* asthmatic

Astro|loge *m* -n,-n astrologer. **A~logie** *f* - astrology. **A~naut** *m* -en,-en astronaut. **A~nom** *m* -en,-en astronomer. **A~nomie** *f* - astronomy. **a~nomisch** *a* astronomical

Asyl *nt* -s,-e home; (*Pol*) asylum. **A~ant** *m* -en,-en asylum-seeker

Atelier /-'lje:/ *nt* -s,-s studio

Atem *m* -s breath; **tief A~ holen** take a deep breath. **a~beraubend** *a* breath-taking. **a~los** *a* breathless, *adv* -ly. **A~pause** *f* breather. **A~zug** *m* breath

Atheist *m* -en,-en atheist

Äther *m* -s ether

Äthiopien /-jən/ *nt* -s Ethiopia

Athlet|(in) *m* -en,-en (*f* -,-nen) athlete. **a~isch** *a* athletic

Atlant|ik *m* -s Atlantic. **a~isch** *a* Atlantic; **der A~ische Ozean** the Atlantic Ocean

Atlas *m* -lasses,-lanten atlas

atmen *vt/i* (*haben*) breathe

Atmosphär|e *f* -,-n atmosphere. **a~isch** *a* atmospheric

Atmung *f* - breathing

Atom *nt* -s,-e atom. **a~ar** *a* atomic. **A~bombe** *f* atom bomb. **A~krieg** *m* nuclear war

Atten|tat *nt* -[e]s,-e assassination attempt. **A~täter** *m* [would-be] assassin

Attest *nt* -[e]s,-e certificate

Attrak|tion /-'tsjo:n/ *f* -,-en attraction. **a~tiv** *a* attractive, *adv* -ly

Attrappe *f* -,-n dummy

Attribut *nt* -[e]s,-e attribute. **a~iv** *a* attributive, *adv* -ly

ätzen *vt* corrode; (*Med*) cauterize; (*Kunst*) etch. **ä~d** *a* corrosive; (*Spott*) caustic

au *int* ouch; **au fein!** oh good!

Aubergine /obɛr'ʒi:nə/ *f* -,-n aubergine

auch *adv & conj* also, too; (*außerdem*) what's more; (*selbst*) even; **a~ wenn** even if; **ich mag ihn—ich a~** I like him—so do I; **ich bin nicht müde—ich a~ nicht** I'm not tired—nor *or* neither am I; **sie weiß es a~ nicht** she doesn't know either; **wer/wie/was a~ immer** whoever/however/whatever; **ist das a~ wahr?** is that really true?

Audienz *f* -,-en audience

audiovisuell *a* audio-visual

Auditorium *nt* -s,-ien (*Univ*) lecture hall

auf *prep* (+ *dat*) on; (+ *acc*) on [to]; (*bis*) until, till; (*Proportion*) to; **auf deutsch/englisch** in German/English; **auf einer/eine Party** at/to a party; **auf der Straße** in the street; **auf seinem Zimmer** in one's room; **auf einem Ohr taub** deaf in one ear; **auf einen Stuhl steigen** climb on [to] a chair; **auf die Toilette gehen** go to the toilet; **auf ein paar Tage verreisen** go away for a few days; **auf 10 Kilometer zu sehen** visible for 10 kilometres ● *adv* open; (*in die Höhe*) up; **auf und ab** up and down; **sich auf und davon machen** make off; **Tür auf!** open the door!

aufarbeiten *vt sep* do up; **Rückstände a~** clear arrears [of work]

aufatmen *vi sep* (*haben*) heave a sigh of relief

aufbahren *vt sep* lay out

Aufbau *m* construction; (*Struktur*) structure. **a~en** *v sep* ● *vt* construct, build; (*errichten*) erect; (*schaffen*) build up; (*arrangieren*) arrange; **sich a~en** (*fig*) be based (**auf** + *dat* on) ● *vi* (*haben*) be based (**auf** + *dat* on)

aufbäumen (sich) *vr sep* rear [up]; (*fig*) rebel

aufbauschen *vt sep* puff out; (*fig*) exaggerate

aufbehalten† *vt sep* keep on

aufbekommen† *vt sep* get open; (*Sch*) be given [as homework]

aufbessern *vt sep* improve; (*erhöhen*) increase

aufbewahr|en *vt sep* keep; (*lagern*) store. **A~ung** *f* - safe keeping; storage; (*Gepäck-*) left-luggage office

aufbieten† *vt sep* mobilize; (*fig*) summon up

aufblas|bar *a* inflatable. **a~en**† *vt sep* inflate; **sich a~en** (*fig*) give oneself airs

aufbleiben† *vi sep* (*sein*) stay open; (*Person:*) stay up

aufblenden *vt/i sep* (*haben*) (*Auto*) switch to full beam

aufblicken *vi sep* (*haben*) look up (**zu** at / (*fig*) to)

aufblühen *vi sep* (*sein*) flower; (*Knospe:*) open

aufbocken *vt sep* jack up

aufbraten† *vt sep* fry up

aufbrauchen *vt sep* use up

aufbrausen *vi sep* (*sein*) (*fig*) flare up. **a~d** *a* quick-tempered

aufbrechen† *v sep* ● *vt* break open ● *vi* (*sein*) (*Knospe:*) open; (*sich aufmachen*) set out, start

aufbringen† *vt sep* raise (*Geld*); find (*Kraft*); (*wütend machen*) infuriate

Aufbruch *m* start, departure

aufbrühen *vt sep* make (*Tee*)

aufbürden *vt sep* **jdm etw a~** (*fig*) burden s.o. with sth

aufdecken *vt sep* (*auflegen*) put on; (*abdecken*) uncover; (*fig*) expose

aufdrängen *vt sep* force (*dat* on); **sich jdm a~** force one's company on s.o.

aufdrehen *vt sep* turn on

aufdringlich *a* persistent

aufeinander *adv* one on top of the other; (*schießen*) at each other; (*warten*) for each other. **a~folgen** *vi sep* (*sein*) follow one another. **a~folgend** *a* successive; (*Tage*) consecutive

Aufenthalt *m* stay; **10 Minuten A~ haben** (*Zug:*) stop for 10 minutes. **A~serlaubnis, A~sgenehmigung** *f* residence permit. **A~sraum** *m* recreation room; (*im Hotel*) lounge

auferlegen *vt sep* impose (*dat* on)

aufersteh|en† *vi sep* (*sein*) rise from the dead. **A~ung** *f* - resurrection

aufessen† *vt sep* eat up

auffahr|en† *vi sep* (*sein*) drive up; (*aufprallen*) crash, run (**auf** + *acc* into); (*aufschrecken*) start up; (*aufbrausen*) flare up. **A~t** *f* drive; (*Autobahn-*) access road, slip road; (*Bergfahrt*) ascent

auffallen† *vi sep* (*sein*) be conspicuous; **unangenehm a~** make a bad impression; **jdm a~** strike s.o. **a~d a** striking, *adv* -ly

auffällig *a* conspicuous, *adv* -ly; (*grell*) gaudy, *adv* -ily

auffangen† *vt sep* catch; pick up ⟨*Funkspruch*⟩

auffass|en *vt sep* understand; (*deuten*) take; **falsch a~en** misunderstand. **A~ung** *f* understanding; (*Ansicht*) view. **A~ungsgabe** *f* grasp

aufforder|n *vt sep* ask; (*einladen*) invite; **jdn zum Tanz a~n** ask s.o. to dance. **A~ung** *f* request; invitation

auffrischen *v sep* ⚫ *vt* freshen up; revive (*Erinnerung*); **seine Englischkenntnisse a~** brush up one's English

aufführ|en *vt sep* perform; (*angeben*) list; **sich a~en** behave. **A~ung** *f* performance

auffüllen *vt sep* fill up; **[wieder] a~** replenish

Aufgabe *f* task; (*Rechen-*) problem; (*Verzicht*) giving up; **A~n** (*Sch*) homework *sg*

Aufgang *m* way up; (*Treppe*) stairs *pl*; (*Astr*) rise

aufgeben† *v sep* ⚫ *vt* give up; post ⟨*Brief*⟩; send ⟨*Telegramm*⟩; place ⟨*Bestellung*⟩; register ⟨*Gepäck*⟩; put in the paper ⟨*Annonce*⟩; **jdm eine Aufgabe/ein Rätsel a~** set s.o. a task/ a riddle; **jdm Suppe a~** serve s.o. with soup ⚫ *vi* (*haben*) give up

aufgeblasen *a* (*fig*) conceited

Aufgebot *nt* contingent (**an** + *dat* of); (*Relig*) banns *pl*; **unter A~ aller Kräfte** with all one's strength

aufgebracht *a* (*fam*) angry

aufgedunsen *a* bloated

aufgehen† *vi sep* (*sein*) open; (*sich lösen*) come undone; ⟨*Teig, Sonne:*⟩ rise; ⟨*Saat:*⟩ come up; (*Math*) come out exactly; **in Flammen a~** go up in flames; **in etw** (*dat*) **a~** (*fig*) be wrapped up in sth; **ihm ging auf** (*fam*) he realized (**daß** that)

aufgelegt *a* **a~ sein zu** be in the mood for; **gut/schlecht a~ sein** be in a good/ bad mood

aufgelöst *a* (*fig*) distraught; **in Tränen a~** in floods of tears

aufgeregt *a* excited, *adv* -ly; (*erregt*) agitated, *adv* -ly

aufgeschlossen *a* (*fig*) open-minded

aufgesprungen *a* chapped

aufgeweckt *a* (*fig*) bright

aufgießen† *vt sep* pour on; (*aufbrühen*) make ⟨*Tee*⟩

aufgreifen† *vt sep* pick up; take up ⟨*Vorschlag, Thema*⟩

aufgrund *prep* (+*gen*) on the strength of

Aufguß *m* infusion

aufhaben† *v sep* ⚫ *vt* have on; **den Mund a~** have one's mouth open; **viel a~** (*Sch*) have a lot of homework ⚫ *vi* (*haben*) be open

aufhalsen *vt sep* (*fam*) saddle with

aufhalten† *vt sep* hold up; (*anhalten*) stop; (*abhalten*) keep, detain; (*offenhalten*) hold open; hold out ⟨*Hand*⟩; **sich a~** stay; (*sich befassen*) spend one's time (**mit** on)

aufhäng|en *vt/i sep* (*haben*) hang up; (*henken*) hang; **sich a~en** hang oneself. **A~er** *m* **-s,-** loop. **A~ung** *f* - (*Auto*) suspension

aufheben† *vt sep* pick up; (*hochheben*) raise; (*aufbewahren*) keep; (*beenden*) end; (*rückgängig machen*) lift; (*abschaffen*) abolish; (*Jur*) quash ⟨*Urteil*⟩; repeal ⟨*Gesetz*⟩; (*ausgleichen*) cancel out; **sich a~** cancel each other out; **gut aufgehoben sein** be well looked after. **A~ nt -s viel A~s machen** make a great fuss (**von** about)

aufheitern *vt sep* cheer up; **sich a~** ⟨*Wetter:*⟩ brighten up

aufhellen *vt sep* lighten; **sich a~** ⟨*Himmel:*⟩ brighten

aufhetzen *vt sep* incite

aufholen *v sep* ⚫ *vt* make up ⚫ *vi* (*haben*) catch up; (*zeitlich*) make up time

aufhorchen *vi sep* (*haben*) prick up one's ears

aufhören *vi sep* (*haben*) stop; **mit der Arbeit a~, a~ zu arbeiten** stop working

aufklappen *vt/i sep* (*sein*) open

aufklär|en *vt sep* solve; **jdn a~en** enlighten s.o.; (*sexuell*) tell s.o. the facts of life; **sich a~en** be solved; ⟨*Wetter:*⟩ clear up. **A~ung** *f* solution; enlightenment; (*Mil*) reconnaissance; **sexuelle A~ung** sex education

aufkleb|en *vt sep* stick on. **A~er** *m* **-s,-** sticker

aufknöpfen *vt sep* unbutton

aufkochen *v sep* ● *vt* bring to the boil ● *vi (sein)* come to the boil

aufkommen† *vi sep (sein)* start; ⟨*Wind:*⟩ spring up; ⟨*Mode:*⟩ come in; **a~ für** pay for

aufkrempeln *vt sep* roll up

aufladen† *vt sep* load; *(Electr)* charge

Auflage *f* impression; *(Ausgabe)* edition; *(Zeitungs-)* circulation; *(Bedingung)* condition; *(Überzug)* coating

auflassen† *vt sep* leave open; leave on ⟨*Hut*⟩

auflauern *vi sep (haben)* **jdm a~** lie in wait for s.o.

Auflauf *m* crowd; *(Culin)* ≈ soufflé. **a~en†** *vi sep (sein) (Naut)* run aground

auflegen *v sep* ● *vt* apply (**auf** + *acc* to); put down ⟨*Hörer*⟩; **neu a~** reprint ● *vi (haben)* ring off

auflehn|en (sich) *vr sep (fig)* rebel. **A~ung** *f -* rebellion

auflesen† *vt sep* pick up

aufleuchten *vi sep (haben)* light up

aufliegen† *vi sep (haben)* rest (**auf** + *dat* on)

auflisten *vt sep* list

auflockern *vt sep* break up; *(entspannen)* relax; *(fig)* liven up

auflös|en *vt sep* dissolve; close ⟨*Konto*⟩; **sich a~en** dissolve; ⟨*Nebel:*⟩ clear. **A~ung** *f* dissolution; *(Lösung)* solution

aufmach|en *v sep* ● *vt* open; *(lösen)* undo; **sich a~en** set out (**nach** for); *(sich schminken)* make oneself up ● *vi (haben)* open; **jdm a~en** open the door to s.o. **A~ung** *f -,-en* get-up; *(Comm)* presentation

aufmerksam *a* attentive, *adv* -ly; **a~ werden auf** (+ *acc*) notice; **jdn a~ machen auf** (+ *acc*) draw s.o.'s attention to. **A~keit** *f -,-en* attention; *(Höflichkeit)* courtesy

aufmucken *vi sep (haben)* rebel

aufmuntern *vt sep* cheer up

Aufnahme *f -,-n* acceptance; *(Empfang)* reception; *(in Klub, Krankenhaus)* admission; *(Einbeziehung)* inclusion; *(Beginn)* start; *(Foto)* photograph; *(Film-)* shot; *(Mus)* recording; *(Band-)* tape recording. **a~fähig** *a* receptive. **A~prüfung** *f* entrance examination

aufnehmen† *vt sep* pick up; *(absorbieren)* absorb; take ⟨*Nahrung, Foto*⟩; *(fassen)* hold; *(annehmen)* accept; *(leihen)* borrow; *(empfangen)* receive; *(in Klub, Krankenhaus)* admit; *(beherbergen, geistig erfassen)* take in; *(einbeziehen)* include; *(beginnen)* take up; *(niederschreiben)* take down; *(filmen)* film, shoot; *(Mus)* record; **auf Band a~** tape[-record]; **etw gelassen a~** take sth calmly; **es a~ können mit** *(fig)* be a match for

aufopfer|n *vt sep* sacrifice; **sich a~n** sacrifice oneself. **a~nd** *a* devoted, *adv* -ly. **A~ung** *f* self-sacrifice

aufpassen *vi sep (haben)* pay attention; *(sich vorsehen)* take care; **a~ auf** (+ *acc*) look after

aufpflanzen (sich) *vr sep (fam)* plant oneself

aufplatzen *vi sep (sein)* split open

aufplustern (sich) *vr sep* ⟨*Vogel:*⟩ ruffle up its feathers

Aufprall *m* -[e]s impact. **a~en** *vi sep (sein)* **a~en auf** (+ *acc*) hit

aufpumpen *vt sep* pump up, inflate

aufputsch|en *vt sep* incite; **sich a~en** take stimulants. **A~mittel** *nt* stimulant

aufquellen† *vi sep (sein)* swell

aufraffen *vt sep* pick up; **sich a~** pick oneself up; *(fig)* pull oneself together; *(sich aufschwingen)* find the energy (**zu** for)

aufragen *vi sep (sein)* rise [up]

aufräumen *vt/i sep (haben)* tidy up; *(wegräumen)* put away; **a~ mit** *(fig)* get rid of

aufrecht *a & adv* upright. **a~erhalten†** *vt sep (fig)* maintain

aufreg|en *vt sep* excite; *(beunruhigen)* upset; *(ärgern)* annoy; **sich a~en** get excited; *(sich erregen)* get worked up. **a~end** *a* exciting. **A~ung** *f* excitement

aufreiben† *vt sep* chafe; *(fig)* wear down; **sich a~** wear oneself out. **a~d** *a* trying, wearing

aufreißen† *v sep* ● *vt* tear open; dig up ⟨*Straße*⟩; open wide ⟨*Augen, Mund*⟩ ● *vi (sein)* split open

aufreizend *a* provocative, *adv* -ly

aufrichten *vt sep* erect; *(fig: trösten)* comfort; **sich a~** straighten up; *(sich setzen)* sit up

aufrichtig *a* sincere, *adv* -ly. **A~keit** *f -* sincerity

aufriegeln *vt sep* unbolt

aufrollen vt sep roll up; (entrollen) unroll

aufrücken vi sep (sein) move up; (fig) be promoted

Aufruf m appeal (an + dat to). **a~en†** vt sep call out (Namen); jdn a~en call s.o.'s name; (fig) call on s.o. (zu to)

Aufruhr m -s,-e turmoil; (Empörung) revolt

aufrühr|en vt sep stir up. **A~er** m -s,- rebel. **a~erisch** a inflammatory; (rebellisch) rebellious

aufrunden vt sep round up

aufrüsten vi sep (haben) arm

aufs prep = auf das

aufsagen vt sep recite

aufsammeln vt sep gather up

aufsässig a rebellious

Aufsatz m top; (Sch) essay

aufsaugen† vt sep soak up

aufschauen vi sep (haben) look up (zu at/(fig) to)

aufschichten vt sep stack up

aufschieben† vt sep slide open; (verschieben) put off, postpone

Aufschlag m impact; (Tennis) service; (Hosen-) turn-up; (Ärmel-) upturned cuff; (Revers) lapel; (Comm) surcharge. **a~en†** v sep ● vt open; crack (Ei); (hochschlagen) turn up; (errichten) put up; (erhöhen) increase; cast on (Masche); **sich** (dat) das Knie a~en cut [open] one's knee ● vi (haben) hit (auf etw acc/dat sth); (Tennis) serve; (teurer werden) go up

aufschließen† v sep ● vt unlock ● vi (haben) unlock the door

aufschlitzen vt sep slit open

Aufschluß m A~ geben give information (über + acc on). **a~reich** a revealing; (lehrreich) informative

aufschneid|en† v sep ● vt cut open; (in Scheiben) slice; carve (Braten) ● vi (haben) (fam) exaggerate. **A~er** m -s,- (fam) show-off

Aufschnitt m sliced sausage, cold meat [and cheese]

aufschrauben vt sep screw on; (abschrauben) unscrew

aufschrecken v sep ● vt startle ● vi† (sein) start up; **aus dem Schlaf a~** wake up with a start

Aufschrei m [sudden] cry

aufschreiben† vt sep write down; (fam: verschreiben) prescribe; jdn a~ (Polizist:) book s.o.

aufschreien† vi sep (haben) cry out

Aufschrift f inscription; (Etikett) label

Aufschub m delay; (Frist) grace

aufschürfen vt sep sich (dat) das Knie a~ graze one's knee

aufschwatzen vt sep jdm etw a~ talk s.o. into buying sth

aufschwingen† (sich) vr sep find the energy (zu for)

Aufschwung m (fig) upturn

aufsehen† vi sep (haben) look up (zu at/(fig) to). **A~** nt -s A~ erregen cause a sensation. **a~erregend** a sensational

Aufseher(in) m -s,- (f -,-nen) supervisor; (Gefängnis-) warder

aufsein† vi sep (sein) be open; (Person:) be up

aufsetzen vt sep put on; (verfassen) draw up; (entwerfen) draft; **sich a~** sit up

Aufsicht f supervision; (Person) supervisor. **A~srat** m board of directors

aufsitzen† vi sep (sein) mount

aufspannen vt sep put up

aufsparen vt sep save, keep

aufsperren vt sep open wide

aufspielen v sep ● vi (haben) play ● vr sich a~ show off; **sich als Held a~** play the hero

aufspießen vt sep spear

aufspringen† vi sep (sein) jump up; (aufprallen) bounce; (sich öffnen) burst open; (Haut:) become chapped; **a~ auf** (+ acc) jump on

aufspüren vt sep track down

aufstacheln vt sep incite

aufstampfen vi sep (haben) **mit dem Fuß a~** stamp one's foot

Aufstand m uprising, rebellion

aufständisch a rebellious. **A~e(r)** m rebel, insurgent

aufstapeln vt sep stack up

aufstauen vt sep dam [up]

aufstehen† vi sep (sein) get up; (offen sein) be open; (fig) rise up

aufsteigen† vi sep (sein) get on; (Reiter:) mount; (Bergsteiger:) climb up; (hochsteigen) rise [up]; (fig: befördert werden) rise (zu to); (Sport) be promoted

aufstell|en vt sep put up; (Culin) put on; (postieren) post; (in einer Reihe) line up; (nominieren) nominate; (Sport) select (Mannschaft); make out (Liste); lay down (Regel); make (Behauptung); set up (Rekord); **sich**

a~en rise [up]; (*in einer Reihe*) line up. **A~ung** *f* nomination; (*Liste*) list

Aufstieg *m* ascent; (*fig*) rise; (*Sport*) promotion

aufstöbern *vt sep* flush out; (*fig*) track down

aufstoßen† *v sep* ● *vt* push open ● *vi* (*haben*) burp; **a~ auf** (+ *acc*) strike. **A~ nt -s** burping

aufstrebend *a* (*fig*) ambitious

Aufstrich *m* [sandwich] spread

aufstützen *vt sep* rest (**auf** + *acc* on); **sich a~** lean (**auf** + *acc* on)

aufsuchen *vt sep* look for; (*besuchen*) go to see

Auftakt *m* (*fig*) start

auftauchen *vi sep* (*sein*) emerge; ⟨U-Boot:⟩ surface; (*fig*) turn up; ⟨Frage:⟩ crop up

auftauen *vt/i sep* (*sein*) thaw

aufteil|en *vt sep* divide [up]. **A~ung** *f* division

auftischen *vt sep* serve [up]

Auftrag *m* -[e]s, ⸚e task; (*Kunst*) commission; (*Comm*) order; **im A~** (+ *gen*) on behalf of. **a~en†** *v sep* ● *vt* apply; (*servieren*) serve; (*abtragen*) wear out; **jdm a~en** instruct s.o. (**zu** to) ● *vi* (*haben*) **dick a~en** (*fam*) exaggerate. **A~geber** *m* -s, - client

auftreiben† *vt sep* distend; (*fam: beschaffen*) get hold of

auftrennen *vt sep* unpick, undo

auftreten† *v sep* ● *vi* (*sein*) tread; (*sich benehmen*) behave, act; (*Theat*) appear; (*die Bühne betreten*) enter; (*vorkommen*) occur ● *vt* kick open. **A~ nt -s** occurrence; (*Benehmen*) manner

Auftrieb *m* buoyancy; (*fig*) boost

Auftritt *m* (*Theat*) appearance; (*auf die Bühne*) entrance; (*Szene*) scene

auftun† *vt sep* **jdm Suppe a~** serve s.o. with soup; **sich** (*dat*) **etw a~** help oneself to sth; **sich a~** open

aufwachen *vi sep* (*sein*) wake up

aufwachsen† *vi sep* (*sein*) grow up

Aufwand *m* -[e]s expenditure; (*Luxus*) extravagance; (*Mühe*) trouble; **A~ treiben** be extravagant

aufwärmen *vt sep* heat up; (*fig*) rake up; **sich a~** warm oneself; (*Sport*) warm up

Aufwartefrau *f* cleaner

aufwärts *adv* upwards; (*bergauf*) uphill. **a~gehen†** *vi sep* (*sein*) **es geht a~ mit jdm/etw** s.o./sth is improving

Aufwartung *f* - cleaner; **jdm seine A~ machen** call on s.o.

aufwaschen† *vt/i sep* (*haben*) wash up

aufwecken *vt sep* wake up

aufweichen *v sep* ● *vt* soften ● *vi* (*sein*) become soft

aufweisen† *vt sep* have, show

aufwend|en† *vt sep* spend; **Mühe a~en** take pains. **a~ig** *a* lavish, *adv* -ly; (*teuer*) expensive, *adv* -ly

aufwerfen† *vt sep* (*fig*) raise

aufwert|en *vt sep* revalue. **A~ung** *f* revaluation

aufwickeln *vt sep* roll up; (*auswickeln*) unwrap

aufwiegeln *vt sep* stir up

aufwiegen† *vt sep* compensate for

Aufwiegler *m* -s, - agitator

aufwirbeln *v sep* **Staub a~** stir up dust; (*fig*) cause a stir

aufwisch|en *vt sep* wipe up; wash ⟨Fußboden⟩. **A~lappen** *m* floorcloth

aufwühlen *vt sep* churn up; (*fig*) stir up

aufzähl|en *vt sep* enumerate, list. **A~ung** *f* list

aufzeichn|en *vt sep* record; (*zeichnen*) draw. **A~ung** *f* recording; **A~ungen** notes

aufziehen† *v sep* ● *vt* pull up; hoist ⟨Segel⟩; (*öffnen*) open; draw ⟨Vorhang⟩; (*auftrennen*) undo; (*großziehen*) bring up; rear ⟨Tier⟩; mount ⟨Bild⟩; thread ⟨Perlen⟩; wind up ⟨Uhr⟩; (*arrangieren*) organize; (*fam: necken*) tease ● *vi* (*sein*) approach

Aufzucht *f* rearing

Aufzug *m* hoist; (*Fahrstuhl*) lift, (*Amer*) elevator; (*Prozession*) procession; (*Theat*) act; (*fam: Aufmachung*) get-up

Augapfel *m* eyeball

Auge *nt* -s, -n eye; (*Punkt*) spot; **vier A~n werfen** throw a four; **gute A~n** good eyesight; **unter vier A~n** in private; **aus den A~n verlieren** lose sight of; **im A~ behalten** keep in sight; (*fig*) bear in mind

Augenblick *m* moment; **im/jeden A~** at the/at any moment; **A~!** just a moment! **a~lich** *a* immediate; (*derzeitig*) present ● *adv* immediately; (*derzeit*) at present

Augen|braue *f* eyebrow. **A~höhle** *f* eye socket. **A~licht** *nt* sight. **A~lid** *nt* eyelid. **A~schein** *m* in **A~schein**

nehmen inspect. **A~zeuge** *m* eye-witness

August *m* -[s] August

Auktion /-'tsjo:n/ *f* -,-en auction. **A~ator** *m* -s,-en /-'to:rən/ auctioneer

Aula *f* -,-len ⟨*Sch*⟩ [assembly] hall

Au-pair-Mädchen /o'pɛːr-/ *nt* au-pair

aus *prep* (+ *dat*) out of; ⟨*von*⟩ from; ⟨*bestehend*⟩ [made] of; **aus Angst** from *or* out of fear; **aus Spaß** for fun ● *adv* out; ⟨*Licht, Radio*⟩ off; **aus und ein** in and out; **nicht mehr aus noch ein wissen** be at one's wits' end; **von ... aus** from ...; **von sich aus** of one's own accord; **von mir aus** as far as I'm concerned

ausarbeiten *vt sep* work out

ausarten *vi sep (sein)* degenerate (**in** + *acc* into)

ausatmen *vt/i sep (haben)* breathe out

ausbaggern *vt sep* excavate; dredge ⟨*Fluß*⟩

ausbauen *vt sep* remove; ⟨*vergrößern*⟩ extend; ⟨*fig*⟩ expand

ausbedingen† *vt sep* **sich** (*dat*) **a~** insist on; ⟨*zur Bedingung machen*⟩ stipulate

ausbesser|n *vt sep* mend, repair. **A~ung** *f* repair

ausbeulen *vt sep* remove the dents from; ⟨*dehnen*⟩ make baggy

Ausbeut|e *f* yield. ● **a~en** *vt sep* exploit. **A~ung** *f* - exploitation

ausbild|en *vt sep* train; ⟨*formen*⟩ form; ⟨*entwickeln*⟩ develop; **sich a~en** train (**als/zu** as); ⟨*entstehen*⟩ develop. **A~er** *m* -s,- instructor. **A~ung** *f* training; ⟨*Sch*⟩ education

ausbitten† *vt sep* **sich** (*dat*) **a~** ask for; ⟨*verlangen*⟩ insist on

ausblasen† *vt sep* blow out

ausbleiben† *vi sep (sein)* fail to appear/⟨*Erfolg:*⟩ materialize; ⟨*nicht heimkommen*⟩ stay out; **es konnte nicht a~** it was inevitable. **A~** *nt* -s absence

Ausblick *m* view

ausbrech|en† *vi sep (sein)* break out; ⟨*Vulkan:*⟩ erupt; ⟨*fliehen*⟩ escape; **in Tränen a~en** burst into tears. **A~er** *m* runaway

ausbreit|en *vt sep* spread [out]; **sich a~en** spread. **A~ung** *f* - spread

ausbrennen† *v sep* ● *vt* cauterize ● *vi (sein)* burn out; ⟨*Haus:*⟩ be gutted [by fire]

Ausbruch *m* outbreak; ⟨*Vulkan-*⟩ eruption; ⟨*Wut-*⟩ outburst; ⟨*Flucht*⟩ escape, break-out

ausbrüten *vt sep* hatch

Ausbund *m* **A~ der Tugend** paragon of virtue

ausbürsten *vt sep* brush; ⟨*entfernen*⟩ brush out

Ausdauer *f* perseverance; ⟨*körperlich*⟩ stamina. **a~nd** *a* persevering; ⟨*unermüdlich*⟩ untiring; ⟨*Bot*⟩ perennial ● *adv* with perseverance; untiringly

ausdehn|en *vt sep* stretch; ⟨*fig*⟩ extend; **sich a~en** stretch; ⟨*Phys & fig*⟩ expand; ⟨*dauern*⟩ last. **A~ung** *f* expansion; ⟨*Umfang*⟩ extent

ausdenken† *vt sep* **sich** (*dat*) **a~** think up; ⟨*sich vorstellen*⟩ imagine

ausdrehen *vt sep* turn off

Ausdruck *m* expression; ⟨*Fach-*⟩ term; ⟨*Computer*⟩ printout. **a~en** *vt sep* print

ausdrück|en *vt sep* squeeze out; squeeze ⟨*Zitrone*⟩; stub out ⟨*Zigarette*⟩; ⟨*äußern*⟩ express; **sich a~en** express oneself. **a~lich** *a* express, *adv* -ly

ausdrucks|los *a* expressionless. **a~voll** *a* expressive

auseinander *adv* apart; ⟨*entzwei*⟩ in pieces. **a~falten** *vt sep* unfold. **a~gehen†** *vi sep (sein)* part; ⟨*Linien, Meinungen:*⟩ diverge; ⟨*Menge:*⟩ disperse; ⟨*Ehe:*⟩ break up; ⟨*entzweigehen*⟩ come apart. **a~halten†** *vt sep* tell apart. **a~nehmen†** *vt sep* take apart *or* to pieces. **a~setzen** *vt sep* explain (**jdm** to s.o.); **sich a~setzen** have it out (**mit jdm** with s.o.); come to grips (**mit einem Problem** with a problem). **A~setzung** *f* -,-en discussion; ⟨*Streit*⟩ argument

auserlesen *a* select, choice

ausfahr|en† *v sep* ● *vt* take for a drive; take out ⟨*Baby*⟩ [in the pram] ● *vi (sein)* go for a drive. **A~t** *f* drive; ⟨*Autobahn-, Garagen-*⟩ exit

Ausfall *m* failure; ⟨*Absage*⟩ cancellation; ⟨*Comm*⟩ loss. **a~en†** *vi sep (sein)* fall out; ⟨*versagen*⟩ fail; ⟨*abgesagt werden*⟩ be cancelled; **gut/ schlecht a~en** turn out to be good/poor

ausfallend, ausfällig *a* abusive

ausfertig|en *vt sep* make out. **A~ung** *f* -,-en in doppelter/dreifacher **A~ung** in duplicate/triplicate

ausfindig *a* **a~ machen** find

ausflippen *vi (sein)* freak out

Ausflucht *f -,-̈e* excuse

Ausflug *m* excursion, outing

Ausflügler *m -s,-* [day-]tripper

Ausfluß *m* outlet; *(Abfluß)* drain; *(Med)* discharge

ausfragen *vt sep* question

ausfransen *vi sep (sein)* fray

Ausfuhr *f -,-en (Comm)* export

ausführ|en *vt sep* take out; *(Comm)* export; *(durchführen)* carry out; *(erklären)* explain. **a~lich** *a* detailed ● *adv* in detail. **A~ung** *f* execution; *(Comm)* version; *(äußere)* finish; *(Qualität)* workmanship; *(Erklärung)* explanation

Ausgabe *f* issue; *(Buch-)* edition; *(Comm)* version

Ausgang *m* way out, exit; *(Flugsteig)* gate; *(Ende)* end; *(Ergebnis)* outcome, result; **A~ haben** have time off. **A~spunkt** *m* starting-point. **A~ssperre** *f* curfew

ausgeben† *vt sep* hand out; issue ⟨*Fahrkarten*⟩; spend ⟨*Geld*⟩; buy ⟨*Runde Bier*⟩; **sich a~ als** pretend to be

ausgebeult *a* baggy

ausgebildet *a* trained

ausgebucht *a* fully booked; ⟨*Vorstellung*⟩ sold out

ausgedehnt *a* extensive; *(lang)* long

ausgedient *a* worn out; ⟨*Person*⟩ retired

ausgefallen *a* unusual

ausgefranst *a* frayed

ausgeglichen *a* [well-]balanced; *(gelassen)* even-tempered

ausgeh|en† *vi sep (sein)* go out; ⟨*Haare:*⟩ fall out; ⟨*Vorräte, Geld:*⟩ run out; *(verblassen)* fade; *(herrüh- ren)* come **(von** from); *(abzielen)* aim **(auf** + *acc* at); **gut/schlecht a~en** end well/badly; **leer a~en** come away empty-handed; **davon a~en, daß** assume that. **A~verbot** *nt* curfew

ausgelassen *a* high-spirited; **a~ sein** be in high spirits

ausgelernt *a* [fully] trained

ausgemacht *a* agreed; *(fam: vollkommen)* utter

ausgenommen *conj* except; **a~ wenn** unless

ausgeprägt *a* marked

ausgerechnet *adv* **a~ heute** today of all days; **a~ er/Rom** he of all people/ Rome of all places

ausgeschlossen *pred a* out of the question

ausgeschnitten *a* low-cut

ausgesprochen *a* marked ● *adv* decidedly

ausgestorben *a* extinct; **[wie] a~** ⟨*Straße:*⟩ deserted

Ausgestoßene(r) *m/f* outcast

ausgewachsen *a* fully-grown

ausgewogen *a* [well-]balanced

ausgezeichnet *a* excellent, *adv* -ly

ausgiebig *a* extensive, *adv* -ly; *(ausgedehnt)* long; **a~ Gebrauch machen von** make full use of; **a~ frühstücken** have a really good breakfast

ausgießen† *vt sep* pour out; *(leeren)* empty

Ausgleich *m -[e]s* balance; *(Entschädigung)* compensation. **a~en†** *v sep* ● *vt* balance; even out ⟨*Höhe*⟩; *(wettmachen)* compensate for; **sich a~en** balance out ● *vi (haben) (Sport)* equalize. **A~sgymnastik** *f* keep-fit exercises *pl*. **A~streffer** *m* equalizer

ausgleiten† *vi sep (sein)* slip

ausgrab|en† *vt sep* dig up; *(Archaeol)* excavate. **A~ung** *f -,-en* excavation

Ausguck *m -[e]s,-e* look-out post; *(Person)* look-out

Ausguß *m* [kitchen] sink

aushaben† *vt sep* have finished ⟨*Buch*⟩; **wann habt ihr Schule aus?** when do you finish school?

aushalten† *v sep* ● *vt* bear, stand; hold ⟨*Note*⟩; *(Unterhalt zahlen für)* keep; **nicht auszuhalten, nicht zum A~** unbearable ● *vi (haben)* hold out

aushandeln *vt sep* negotiate

aushändigen *vt sep* hand over

Aushang *m* [public] notice

aushängen¹ *vt sep (reg)* display; take off its hinges ⟨*Tür*⟩

aushäng|en²† *vi sep (haben)* be displayed. **A~eschild** *nt* sign

ausharren *vi sep (haben)* hold out

ausheben† *vt sep* excavate; take off its hinges ⟨*Tür*⟩

aushecken *vt sep (fig)* hatch

aushelfen† *vi sep (haben)* help out **(jdm** s.o.)

Aushilf|e *f* [temporary] assistant; **zur A~e** to help out. **A~skraft** *f* temporary worker. **a~sweise** *adv* temporarily

aushöhlen *vt sep* hollow out

ausholen *vi sep (haben)* **[zum Schlag]** **a~** raise one's arm [ready to strike]

aushorchen *vt sep* sound out

auskennen† **(sich)** *vr sep* know one's way around; **sich mit/in etw** (*dat*) **a~** know all about sth

auskleiden *vt sep* undress; (*Techn*) line; **sich a~** undress

ausknipsen *vi sep* switch off

auskommen† *vi sep (sein)* manage (**mit/ohne** with/without); (*sich vertragen*) get on (**gut** well). **A~** *nt* **-s sein** **A~/ein gutes A~** haben get by/be well off

auskosten *vt sep* enjoy [to the full]

auskugeln *vt sep* **sich** (*dat*) **den Arm** **a~** dislocate one's shoulder

auskühlen *vt/i sep (sein)* cool

auskundschaften *vt sep* spy out; (*erfahren*) find out

Auskunft *f* **-,-̈e** information; (*A~stelle*) information desk/ (*Büro*) bureau; (*Teleph*) enquiries *pl*, **eine A~** a piece of information. **A~sbüro** *nt* information bureau

auslachen *vt sep* laugh at

ausladen† *vt sep* unload; (*fam: absagen*) put off (*Gast*). **a~d** *a* projecting

Auslage *f* [window] display; **A~n** expenses

Ausland *nt* **im/ins A~** abroad

Ausländ|er(in) *m* **-s,-** (*f* **-,-nen**) foreigner. **a~isch** *a* foreign

Auslandsgespräch *nt* international call

auslass|en† *vt sep* let out; let down (*Saum*); (*weglassen*) leave out; (*versäumen*) miss; (*Culin*) melt; (*fig*) vent (*Ärger*) (**an** + *dat* on); **sich a~en** **über** (+ *acc*) go on about. **A~ungszeichen** *nt* apostrophe

Auslauf *m* run. **a~en†** *vi sep (sein)* run out; (*Farbe:*) run; (*Naut*) put to sea; (*leerlaufen*) run dry; (*enden*) end; (*Modell:*) be discontinued

Ausläufer *m* (*Geog*) spur; (*Bot*) runner, sucker

ausleeren *vt sep* empty [out]

ausleg|en *vt sep* lay out; display (*Waren*); (*bedecken*) cover/(*auskleiden*) line (**mit** with); (*bezahlen*) pay; (*deuten*) interpret. **A~ung** *f* **-,-en** interpretation

ausleihen† *vt sep* lend; **sich** (*dat*) **a~** borrow

auslernen *vi sep (haben)* finish one's training

Auslese *f* - selection; (*fig*) pick; (*Elite*) elite. **a~n†** *vt sep* finish reading (*Buch*); (*auswählen*) pick out, select

ausliefern *vt sep* hand over; (*Jur*) extradite; **ausgeliefert sein** (+ *dat*) be at the mercy of. **A~ung** *f* handing over; (*Jur*) extradition; (*Comm*) distribution

ausliegen† *vi sep (haben)* be on display

auslöschen *vt sep* extinguish; (*abwischen*) wipe off; (*fig*) erase

auslosen *vt sep* draw lots for

auslös|en *vt sep* set off, trigger; (*fig*) cause; arouse (*Begeisterung*); (*einlösen*) redeem; pay a ransom for (*Gefangene*). **A~er** *m* **-s,-** trigger; (*Phot*) shutter release

Auslosung *f* draw

auslüften *vt/i sep (haben)* air

ausmachen *vt sep* put out; (*abschalten*) turn off; (*abmachen*) arrange; (*erkennen*) make out; (*betragen*) amount to; (*darstellen*) represent; (*wichtig sein*) matter; **das macht mir nichts aus** I don't mind

ausmalen *vt sep* paint; (*fig*) describe; **sich** (*dat*) **a~** imagine

Ausmaß *nt* extent; **A~e** dimensions

ausmerzen *vt sep* eliminate

ausmessen† *vt sep* measure

Ausnahm|e *f* **-,-n** exception. **A~ezustand** *m* state of emergency. **a~slos** *adv* without exception. **a~sweise** *adv* as an exception

ausnehmen† *vt sep* take out; gut (*Fisch*); draw (*Huhn*); (*ausschließen*) exclude; (*fam: schröpfen*) fleece; **sich gut a~** look good. **a~d** *adv* exceptionally

ausnutz|en, ausnütz|en *vt sep* exploit; make the most of (*Gelegenheit*). **A~ung** *f* exploitation

auspacken *v sep* ●*vt* unpack; (*auswickeln*) unwrap ●*vi (haben)* (*fam*) talk

auspeitschen *vt sep* flog

auspfeifen *vt sep* whistle and boo

ausplaudern *vt sep* let out, blab

ausplündern *vt sep* loot; rob (*Person*)

ausprobieren *vt sep* try out

Auspuff *m* **-s** exhaust [system]. **A~gase** *ntpl* exhaust fumes. **A~rohr** *nt* exhaust pipe

auspusten *vt sep* blow out

ausradieren *vt sep* rub out

ausrangieren *vt sep (fam)* discard

ausrauben *vt sep* rob

ausräuchern *vt sep* smoke out; fumigate ⟨*Zimmer*⟩

ausräumen *vt sep* clear out

ausrechnen *vt sep* work out, calculate

Ausrede *f* excuse. **a~n** *v sep* • *vi* (*haben*) finish speaking; **laß mich a~n!** let me finish! • *vt jdm etw a~n* talk s.o. out of sth

ausreichen *vi sep* (*haben*) be enough; **a~ mit** have enough. **a~d** *a* adequate, *adv* -ly; (*Sch*) ≈ pass

Ausreise *f* departure [from a country]. **a~n** *vi sep* (*sein*) leave the country. **A~visum** *nt* exit visa

ausreiß|en† *v sep* • *vt* pull *or* tear out • *vi* (*sein*) (*fam*) run away. **A~er** *m* (*fam*) runaway

ausrenken *vt sep* dislocate; **sich** (*dat*) **den Arm a~** dislocate one's shoulder

ausrichten *vt sep* align; (*bestellen*) deliver; (*erreichen*) achieve; **jdm a~** tell s.o. (**daß** that); **kann ich etwas a~?** can I take a message? **ich soll Ihnen Grüße von X a~** X sends [you] his regards

ausrotten *vt sep* exterminate; (*fig*) eradicate

ausrücken *vi sep* (*sein*) (*Mil*) march off; (*fam*) run away

Ausruf *m* exclamation. **a~en†** *vt sep* exclaim; call out ⟨*Namen*⟩; (*verkünden*) proclaim; call ⟨*Streik*⟩; **jdn a~en lassen** have s.o. paged. **A~ezeichen** *nt* exclamation mark

ausruhen *vt/i sep* (*haben*) rest; **sich a~** have a rest

ausrüst|en *vt sep* equip. **A~ung** *f* equipment; (*Mil*) kit

ausrutschen *vi sep* (*sein*) slip

Aussage *f* -,-n statement; (*Jur*) testimony, evidence; (*Gram*) predicate. **a~n** *vt/i sep* (*haben*) state; (*Jur*) give evidence, testify

Aussatz *m* leprosy

Aussätzige(r) *m/f* leper

ausschachten *vt sep* excavate

ausschalten *vt sep* switch *or* turn off; (*fig*) eliminate

Ausschank *m* sale of alcoholic drinks; (*Bar*) bar

Ausschau *f* - **A~ halten nach** look out for. **a~en** *vi sep* (*haben*) (*SGer*) look; **a~en nach** look out for

ausscheiden† *v sep* • *vi* (*sein*) leave; (*Sport*) drop out; (*nicht in Frage kommen*) be excluded; **aus dem Dienst a~** retire • *vt* eliminate; (*Med*) excrete

ausschenken *vt sep* pour out; (*verkaufen*) sell

ausscheren *vi sep* (*sein*) (*Auto*) pull out

ausschildern *vt sep* signpost

ausschimpfen *vt sep* tell off

ausschlachten *vt sep* (*fig*) exploit

ausschlafen† *v sep* • *vi/r* (*haben*) [**sich**] **a~** get enough sleep; (*morgens*) sleep late; **nicht ausgeschlafen haben** *od* **sein** be still tired • *vt* sleep off ⟨*Rausch*⟩

Ausschlag *m* (*Med*) rash; **den A~ geben** (*fig*) tip the balance. **a~en†** *v sep* • *vi* (*haben*) kick [out]; (*Bot*) sprout; ⟨*Baum:*⟩ come into leaf • *vt* knock out; (*auskleiden*) line; (*ablehnen*) refuse. **a~gebend** *a* decisive

ausschließ|en† *vt sep* lock out; (*fig*) exclude; (*entfernen*) expel. **a~lich** *a* exclusive, *adv* -ly

ausschlüpfen *vi sep* (*sein*) hatch

Ausschluß *m* exclusion; expulsion; **unter A~ der Öffentlichkeit** in camera

ausschmücken *vt sep* decorate; (*fig*) embellish

ausschneiden† *vt sep* cut out

Ausschnitt *m* excerpt, extract; (*Zeitungs-*) cutting; (*Hals-*) neckline

ausschöpfen *vt sep* ladle out; (*Naut*) bail out; exhaust ⟨*Möglichkeiten*⟩

ausschreiben† *vt sep* write out; (*ausstellen*) make out; (*bekanntgeben*) announce; put out to tender ⟨*Auftrag*⟩

Ausschreitungen *fpl* riots; (*Exzesse*) excesses

Ausschuß *m* committee; (*Comm*) rejects *pl*

ausschütten *vt sep* tip out; (*verschütten*) spill; (*leeren*) empty; **sich vor Lachen a~** (*fam*) be in stitches

ausschweif|end *a* dissolute. **A~ung** *f* -,-en debauchery; **A~ungen** excesses

ausschwenken *vt sep* rinse [out]

aussehen† *vi sep* (*haben*) look; **es sieht nach Regen aus** it looks like rain; **wie sieht er/es aus?** what does he/it look like? **A~** *nt* -s appearance

aussein† *vi sep* (*sein*) be out; ⟨*Licht, Radio:*⟩ be off; (*zu Ende sein*) be over; **a~ auf** (+ *acc*) be after; **mit ihm ist es aus** he's had it

außen *adv* [on the] outside; **nach a~** outwards. **A~bordmotor** *m* outboard motor. **A~handel** *m* foreign trade. **A~minister** m Foreign Minister. **A~politik** f foreign policy. **A~seite** f outside. **A~seiter** m -s,- outsider; (fig) misfit. **A~stände** mpl outstanding debts. **A~stehende(r)** m/f outsider

außer prep (+ dat) except [for], apart from; (außerhalb) out of; **a~ Atem/ Sicht** out of breath/sight; **a~ sich** (fig) beside oneself ● conj except; **a~ wenn** unless. **a~dem** adv in addition, as well ● conj moreover

äußer|e(r,s) a external; ⟨Teil, Schicht⟩ outer. **Ä~e(s)** nt exterior; ⟨Aussehen⟩ appearance

außer|ehelich a extramarital. **a~ gewöhnlich** a exceptional, adv -ly. **a~halb** prep (+ gen) outside ● adv **a~halb wohnen** live outside town

äußer|lich a external, adv -ly; (fig) outward, adv -ly. **ä~n** vt express; **sich ä~n** comment; (sich zeigen) manifest itself

außerordentlich a extraordinary, adv -ily; (außergewöhnlich) exceptional, adv -ly

äußerst adv extremely

außerstande adv unable (**zu** to)

äußerste|(r,s) a outermost; (weiteste) furthest; (höchste) utmost, extreme; (letzte) last; (schlimmste) worst; **am ä~n Ende** at the very end; **aufs ä~** extremely. **Ä~(s)** nt **das Ä~** the limit; ⟨Schlimmste⟩ the worst; **sein Ä~s tun** do one's utmost

Äußerung f -,-en comment; (Bemerkung) remark

aussetzen v sep ● vt expose (dat to); abandon ⟨Kind, Hund⟩; launch ⟨Boot⟩; offer ⟨Belohnung⟩; **etwas auszusetzen haben an** (+ dat) find fault with ● vi (haben) stop; ⟨Motor:⟩ cut out

Aussicht f -,-en view/(fig) prospect (**auf** + acc of); **in A~ stellen** promise; **weitere A~en** (Meteorol) further outlook sg. **a~slos** a hopeless, adv -ly. **a~sreich** a promising

aussöhnen vt sep reconcile; **sich a~** become reconciled

aussortieren vt sep pick out; (ausscheiden) eliminate

ausspann|en v sep ● vt spread out; unhitch ⟨Pferd⟩; (fam: wegnehmen) take (dat from) ● vi (haben) rest. **A~ung** f rest

aussperr|en vt sep lock out. **A~ung** f -,-en lock-out

ausspielen v sep ● vt play ⟨Karte⟩; (fig) play off (**gegen** against) ● vi (haben) (Kartenspiel) lead

Aussprache f pronunciation; (Sprechweise) diction; (Gespräch) talk

aussprechen† v sep ● vt pronounce; (äußern) express; **sich a~** talk; come out (**für/gegen** in favour of/against) ● vi (haben) finish [speaking]

Ausspruch m saying

ausspucken v sep ● vt spit out ● vi (haben) spit

ausspülen vt sep rinse out

ausstaffieren vt sep (fam) kit out

Ausstand m strike; **in den A~ treten** go on strike

ausstatt|en vt sep equip; **mit Möbeln a~en** furnish. **A~ung** f -,-en equipment; (Innen-) furnishings pl; (Theat) scenery and costumes pl; (Aufmachung) get-up

ausstehen† v sep ● vt suffer; **Angst a~** be frightened; **ich kann sie nicht a~** I can't stand her ● vi (haben) be outstanding

aussteig|en† vi sep (sein) get out; (aus Bus, Zug) get off; (fam: ausscheiden) opt out; (aus einem Geschäft) back out; **alles a~en!** all change! **A~er(in)** m -s,- (f -,-nen) (fam) drop-out

ausstell|en vt sep exhibit; (Comm) display; (ausfertigen) make out; issue ⟨Paß⟩. **A~er** m -s,- exhibitor. **A~ung** f exhibition; (Comm) display. **A~ungsstück** nt exhibit

aussterben† vi sep (sein) die out; (Biol) become extinct. **A~** nt -s extinction

Aussteuer f trousseau

Ausstieg m -[e]s,-e exit

ausstopfen vt sep stuff

ausstoßen† vt sep emit; utter ⟨Fluch⟩; heave ⟨Seufzer⟩; (ausschließen) expel

ausstrahl|en vt/i sep (sein) radiate, emit; (Radio, TV) broadcast. **A~ung** f radiation; (fig) charisma

ausstrecken vt sep stretch out; put out ⟨Hand⟩; **sich a~** stretch out

ausstreichen† vt sep cross out

ausstreuen vt sep scatter; spread ⟨Gerüchte⟩

ausströmen v sep ● vi (sein) pour out; (entweichen) escape ● vt emit; (ausstrahlen) radiate

aussuchen vt sep pick, choose

Austausch *m* exchange. **a~bar** *a* interchangeable. **a~en** *vt sep* exchange; (*auswechseln*) replace

austeilen *vt sep* distribute; (*ausgeben*) hand out

Auster *f* -,-*n* oyster

austoben (sich) *vr sep* ⟨*Sturm:*⟩ rage; ⟨*Person:*⟩ let off steam; ⟨*Kinder:*⟩ romp about

austragen† *vt sep* deliver; hold ⟨*Wettkampf*⟩; play ⟨*Spiel*⟩

Austral|ien /-jən/ *nt* -s Australia. **A~ier(in)** *m* -s,- (*f* -,-nen) Australian. **a~isch** *a* Australian

austreiben† *v sep* ● *vt* drive out; (*Relig*) exorcize ● *vi* (*haben*) (*Bot*) sprout

austreten† *v sep* ● *vt* stamp out; (*abnutzen*) wear down ● *vi* (*sein*) come out; (*ausscheiden*) leave (**aus etw** sth); [**mal**] **a~** (*fam*) go to the loo; (*Sch*) be excused

austrinken† *vt/i sep* (*haben*) drink up; (*leeren*) drain

Austritt *m* resignation

austrocknen *vt/i sep* (*sein*) dry out

ausüben *vt sep* practise; carry on ⟨*Handwerk*⟩; exercise ⟨*Recht*⟩; exert ⟨*Druck, Einfluß*⟩; have ⟨*Wirkung*⟩

Ausverkauf *m* [clearance] sale. **a~t** *a* sold out; **a~tes Haus** full house

auswachsen† *vt sep* outgrow

Auswahl *f* choice, selection; (*Comm*) range; (*Sport*) team

auswählen *vt sep* choose, select

Auswander|er *m* emigrant. **a~n** *vi sep* (*sein*) emigrate. **A~ung** *f* emigration

auswärt|ig *a* non-local; (*ausländisch*) foreign. **a~s** *adv* outwards; (*Sport*) away; **a~s essen** eat out; **a~s arbeiten** not work locally. **A~sspiel** *nt* away game

auswaschen† *vt sep* wash out

auswechseln *vt sep* change; (*ersetzen*) replace; (*Sport*) substitute

Ausweg *m* (*fig*) way out. **a~los** *a* (*fig*) hopeless

ausweich|en† *vi sep* (*sein*) get out of the way; **jdm/etw a~en** avoid/⟨*sich entziehen*⟩ evade s.o./sth. **a~end** *a* evasive, *adv* -ly

ausweinen *vt sep* **sich** (*dat*) **die Augen a~** cry one's eyes out; **sich a~** have a good cry

Ausweis *m* -es,-e pass; (*Mitglieds-, Studenten-*) card. **a~en†** *vt sep* deport; **sich a~en** prove one's identity. **A~papiere** *ntpl* identification papers. **A~ung** *f* deportation

ausweiten *vt sep* stretch; (*fig*) expand

auswendig *adv* by heart

auswerten *vt sep* evaluate; (*nutzen*) utilize

auswickeln *vt sep* unwrap

auswirk|en (sich) *vr sep* have an effect (**auf** + *acc* on). **A~ung** *f* effect; (*Folge*) consequence

auswischen *vt sep* wipe out; **jdm eins a~** (*fam*) play a nasty trick on s.o.

auswringen *vt sep* wring out

Auswuchs *m* excrescence; **Auswüchse** (*fig*) excesses

auszahlen *vt sep* pay out; (*entlohnen*) pay off; (*abfinden*) buy out; **sich a~** (*fig*) pay off

auszählen *vt sep* count; (*Boxen*) count out

Auszahlung *f* payment

auszeichn|en *vt sep* (*Comm*) price; (*ehren*) honour; (*mit einem Preis*) award a prize to; (*Mil*) decorate; **sich a~en** distinguish oneself. **A~ung** *f* honour; (*Preis*) award; (*Mil*) decoration; (*Sch*) distinction

ausziehen† *v sep* ● *vt* pull out; (*auskleiden*) undress; take off ⟨*Mantel, Schuhe*⟩; **sich a~** take off one's coat; (*sich entkleiden*) undress ● *vi* (*sein*) move out; (*sich aufmachen*) set out

Auszubildende(r) *m/f* trainee

Auszug *m* departure; (*Umzug*) move; (*Ausschnitt*) extract, excerpt; (*Bank-*) statement

authentisch *a* authentic

Auto *nt* -s,-s car; **A~ fahren** drive; (*mitfahren*) go in the car. **A~bahn** *f* motorway, (*Amer*) freeway

Autobiographie *f* autobiography

Auto|bus *m* bus. **A~fähre** *f* car ferry. **A~fahrer(in)** *m*(*f*) driver, motorist. **A~fahrt** *f* drive

Autogramm *nt* -s,-e autograph

autokratisch *a* autocratic

Automat *m* -en,-en automatic device; (*Münz-*) slot-machine; (*Verkaufs-*) vending-machine; (*Fahrkarten-*) machine; (*Techn*) robot. **A~ik** *f* - automatic mechanism; (*Auto*) automatic transmission

Auto|mation /-'tsjo:n/ *f* - automation. **a~matisch** *a* automatic, *adv* -ally

autonom *a* autonomous. **A~ie** *f* - autonomy

Autonummer *f* registration number

Autopsie *f* -,-n autopsy
Autor *m* -s,-en /-'to:rən/ author
Auto|reisezug *m* Motorail. **A~
rennen** *nt* motor race
Autorin *f* -,-nen author[ess]
Autori|sation /-'tsjo:n/ *f* - author-
ization. **a~sieren** *vt* authorize. **a~
tär** *a* authoritarian. **A~tät** *f*
-,-en authority
Auto|schlosser *m* motor mechanic.
A~skooter /-sku:tɐ/ *m* -s,- dodgem.
A~stopp *m* -s per **A~stopp fahren**
hitch-hike. **A~verleih** *m* car hire
[firm]. **A~waschanlage** *f* car wash
autsch *int* ouch
Aversion *f* -,-en aversion (**gegen** to)
Axt *f* -,¨e axe

B

B, b /be:/ *nt* - (*Mus*) B flat
Baby /'be:bi/ *nt* -s,-s baby. **B~aus-
stattung** *f* layette. **B~sitter** /-sɪtɐ/
m -s,- babysitter
Bach *m* -[e]s,¨e stream
Backbord *nt* -[e]s port [side]
Backe *f* -,-n cheek
backen *v* ● *vt/i* † (*haben*) bake;
(*braten*) fry ● *vi* (*reg*) (*haben*)
(*kleben*) stick (**an** + *dat* to)
Backenzahn *m* molar
Bäcker *m* -s,- baker. **B~ei** *f* -,-en,
B~laden *m* baker's shop
Back|form *f* baking tin. **B~obst** *nt*
dried fruit. **B~ofen** *m* oven.
B~pfeife *f* (*fam*) slap in the face.
B~pflaume *f* prune. **B~pulver** *nt*
baking-powder. **B~rohr** *nt* oven.
B~stein *m* brick. **B~werk** *nt* cakes
and pastries *pl*
Bad *nt* -[e]s,¨er bath; (*im Meer*) bathe;
(*Zimmer*) bathroom; (*Schwimm-*) pool;
(*Ort*) spa
Bade|anstalt *f* swimming baths *pl.*
B~anzug *m* swim-suit. **B~hose** *f*
swimming trunks *pl.* **B~kappe** *f*
bathing-cap. **B~mantel** *m* bathrobe.
B~matte *f* bath-mat. **B~mütze** *f*
bathing-cap. **b~n** *vi* (*haben*) have a
bath; (*im Meer*) bathe ● *vt* bath; (*waschen*) bathe. **B~ort** *m* seaside resort; (*Kurort*) spa. **B~tuch** *nt* bath-
towel. **B~wanne** *f* bath[-tub].
B~zimmer *nt* bathroom
Bagatelle *f* -,-n trifle; (*Mus*) bagatelle

Bagger *m* -s,- excavator; (*Naß-*)
dredger. **b~n** *vt/i* (*haben*) excavate;
dredge. **B~see** *m* flooded gravel-pit
Bahn *f* -,-en path; (*Astr*) orbit; (*Sport*)
track; (*einzelne*) lane; (*Rodel-*) run;
(*Stoff-, Papier-*) width; (*Rock-*) panel;
(*Eisen-*) railway; (*Zug*) train; (*Straßen-*)
tram; **auf die schiefe B~ kommen**
(*fig*) get into bad ways. **b~brechend**
a (*fig*) pioneering. **b~en** *vt sich* (*dat*)
einen Weg b~en clear a way (**durch**
through). **B~hof** *m* [railway] station.
B~steig *m* -[e]s,-e platform. **B~
übergang** *m* level crossing, (*Amer*)
grade crossing
Bahre *f* -,-n stretcher; (*Toten-*) bier
Baiser /bɛ'ze:/ *nt* -s,-s meringue
Bajonett *nt* -[e]s,-e bayonet
Bake *f* -,-n (*Naut, Aviat*) beacon
Bakterien /-jən/ *fpl* bacteria
Balance /ba'lã:sə/ *f* - balance; **die
B~e halten/verlieren** keep/lose one's
balance. **b~ieren** *vt/i* (*haben/sein*)
balance
bald *adv* soon; (*fast*) almost; **b~ …
b~…** now … now …
Baldachin /-xi:n/ *m* -s,-e canopy
bald|ig *a* early; (*Besserung*) speedy.
b~möglichst *adv* as soon as poss-
ible
Balg *nt* & *m* -[e]s,¨er (*fam*) brat. **b~en**
(**sich**) *vr* tussle. **B~erei** *f* -,-en tussle
Balkan *m* -s Balkans *pl*
Balken *m* -s,- beam
Balkon /bal'kõ:/ *m* -s,-s balcony;
(*Theat*) circle
Ball[1] *m* -[e]s,¨e ball
Ball[2] *m* -[e]s,¨e (*Tanz*) ball
Ballade *f* -,-n ballad
Ballast *m* -[e]s ballast. **B~stoffe** *mpl*
roughage *sg*
ballen *vt* **die** [**Hand zur**] **Faust b~**
clench one's fist; **sich b~** gather, mass.
B~ *m* -s,- bale; (*Anat*) ball of the hand/
(*Fuß-*) foot; (*Med*) bunion
Ballerina *f* -,-nen ballerina
Ballett *nt* -s,-e ballet
Balletttänzer(in) *m*(*f*) ballet dancer
ballistisch *a* ballistic
Ballon /ba'lõ:/ *m* -s,-s balloon
Ball|saal *m* ballroom. **B~ungs-
gebiet** *nt* conurbation. **B~wechsel**
m (*Tennis*) rally
Balsam *m* -s balm
Balt|ikum *nt* -s Baltic States *pl.*
b~isch *a* Baltic
Balustrade *f* -,-n balustrade
Bambus *m* -ses,-se bamboo

banal *a* banal. **B~ität** *f* -,-en banality
Banane *f* -,-n banana
Banause *m* -n,-n philistine
Band[1] *nt* -[e]s,¨er ribbon; (*Naht-, Ton-, Ziel-*) tape; (*Anat*) ligament; **auf B~ aufnehmen** tape; **laufendes B~** conveyor belt; **am laufenden B~** (*fam*) non-stop
Band[2] *m* -[e]s,¨e volume
Band[3] *nt* -[e]s,-e (*fig*) bond; **B~e der Freundschaft** bonds of friendship
Band[4] /bɛnt/ *f* -,-s [jazz] band
Bandag|e /ban'da:ʒə/ *f* -,-n bandage. **b~ieren** *vt* bandage
Bande *f* -,-n gang
bändigen *vt* control, restrain; (*zähmen*) tame
Bandit *m* -en,-en bandit
Band|maß *nt* tape-measure. **B~nudeln** *fpl* noodles. **B~scheibe** *f* (*Anat*) disc. **B~scheibenvorfall** *m* slipped disc. **B~wurm** *m* tapeworm
bang|[e] *a* (**bänger, bängst**) anxious; **jdm b~e machen** frighten s.o. **B~e** *f* **B~e haben** be afraid. **b~en** *vi* (*haben*) fear (**um** for); **mir b~t davor** I dread it
Banjo *nt* -s,-s banjo
Bank[1] *f* -,¨e bench
Bank[2] *f* -,-en (*Comm*) bank. **B~einzug** *m* direct debit
Bankett *nt* -s,-e banquet
Bankier /baŋ'kje:/ *m* -s,-s banker
Bank|konto *nt* bank account. **B~note** *f* banknote
Bankrott *m* -s,-s bankruptcy; **B~ machen** go bankrupt. **b~** *a* bankrupt
Bankwesen *nt* banking
Bann *m* -[e]s,-e (*fig*) spell; **in jds B~** under s.o.'s spell. **b~en** *vt* exorcize; (*abwenden*) avert; [**wie**] **gebannt** spellbound
Banner *nt* -s,- banner
Baptist(in) *m* -en,-en (*f* -,-nen) Baptist
bar *a* (*rein*) sheer; ⟨*Gold*⟩ pure; **b~es Geld** cash; [**in**] **b~ bezahlen** pay cash; **etw für b~e Münze nehmen** (*fig*) take sth as gospel
Bar *f* -,-s bar
Bär *m* -en,-en bear; **jdm einen B~en aufbinden** (*fam*) pull s.o.'s leg
Baracke *f* -,-n (*Mil*) hut
Barb|ar *m* -en,-en barbarian. **b~arisch** *a* barbaric
bar|fuß *adv* barefoot. **B~geld** *nt* cash
Bariton *m* -s,-e /-'to:nə/ baritone

Barkasse *f* -,-n launch
Barmann *m* (*pl* -männer) barman
barmherzig *a* merciful. **B~keit** *f* - mercy
barock *a* baroque. **B~** *nt* & *m* -[s] baroque
Barometer *nt* -s,- barometer
Baron *m* -s,-e baron. **B~in** *f* -,-nen baroness
Barren *m* -s,- (*Gold-*) bar, ingot; (*Sport*) parallel bars *pl*. **B~gold** *nt* gold bullion
Barriere *f* -,-n barrier
Barrikade *f* -,-n barricade
barsch *a* gruff, *adv* -ly; (*kurz*) curt, *adv* -ly
Barsch *m* -[e]s,-e (*Zool*) perch
Barschaft *f* - **meine ganze B~** all I have/had on me
Bart *m* -[e]s,¨e beard; (*der Katze*) whiskers *pl*
bärtig *a* bearded
Barzahlung *f* cash payment
Basar *m* -s,-e bazaar
Base[1] *f* -,-n [female] cousin
Base[2] *f* -,-n (*Chem*) alkali, base
Basel *nt* -s Basle
basieren *vi* (*haben*) be based (**auf** + *dat* on)
Basilikum *nt* -s basil
Basis *f* -,**Basen** base; (*fig*) basis
basisch *a* (*Chem*) alkaline
Bask|enmütze *f* beret. **b~isch** *a* Basque
Baß *m* -sses,¨sse bass; (*Kontra-*) doublebass
Bassin /ba'sɛ̃:/ *nt* -s,-s pond; (*Brunnen-*) basin; (*Schwimm-*) pool
Bassist *m* -en,-en bass player; (*Sänger*) bass
Baßstimme *f* bass voice
Bast *m* -[e]s raffia
basta *int* [**und damit**] **b~!** and that's that!
bast|eln *vt* make ● *vi* (*haben*) do handicrafts; (*herum-*) tinker (**an** + *dat* with). **B~ler** *m* -s,- amateur craftsman; (*Heim-*) do-it-yourselfer
Bataillon /batal'jo:n/ *nt* -s,-e battalion
Batterie *f* -,-n battery
Bau[1] *m* -[e]s,-e burrow; (*Fuchs-*) earth
Bau[2] *m* -[e]s,-ten construction; (*Gebäude*) building; (*Auf-*) structure; (*Körper-*) build; (*B~stelle*) building site; **im Bau** under construction. **B~arbeiten** *fpl* building work *sg*;

(*Straßen-*) roadworks. **B~art** *f* design; (*Stil*) style

Bauch *m* -[e]s, Bäuche abdomen, belly; (*Magen*) stomach; (*Schmer-*) paunch; (*Bauchung*) bulge. **b~ig** *a* bulbous. **B~nabel** *m* navel. **B~redner** *m* ventriloquist. **B~schmerzen** *mpl* stomach-ache *sg*. **B~speicheldrüse** *f* pancreas. **B~weh** *nt* stomach-ache

bauen *vt* build; (*konstruieren*) construct; (*an-*) grow; **einen Unfall b~** (*fam*) have an accident ● *vi* (*haben*) build (**an etw** *dat* sth); **b~ auf** (+ *acc*) (*fig*) rely on

Bauer[1] *m* -s, -n farmer; (*Schach*) pawn
Bauer[2] *nt* -s, - [bird]cage
Bäuer|in *f* -, -nen farmer's wife. **b~lich** *a* rustic
Bauern|haus *nt* farmhouse. **B~hof** *m* farm

bau|fällig *a* dilapidated. **B~genehmigung** *f* planning permission. **B~gerüst** *nt* scaffolding. **B~jahr** *nt* year of construction; **B~jahr 1989** (*Auto*) 1989 model. **B~kasten** *m* box of building bricks; (*Modell-*) model kit. **B~klotz** *m* building brick. **B~kunst** *f* architecture. **b~lich** *a* structural, *adv* -ly. **B~lichkeiten** *fpl* buildings

Baum *m* -[e]s, Bäume tree

baumeln *vi* (*haben*) dangle; **die Beine b~ lassen** dangle one's legs

bäumen (sich) *vr* rear [up]

Baum|schule *f* [tree] nursery. **B~stamm** *m* tree-trunk. **B~wolle** *f* cotton. **b~wollen** *a* cotton

Bauplatz *m* building plot

bäurisch *a* rustic; (*plump*) uncouth

Bausch *m* -[e]s, Bäusche wad; **in B~ und Bogen** (*fig*) wholesale. **b~en** *vt* puff out; **sich b~en** billow [out]. **b~ig** *a* puffed [out]; ⟨*Ärmel*⟩ full

Bau|sparkasse *f* building society. **B~stein** *m* building brick; (*fig*) element. **B~stelle** *f* building site; (*Straßen-*) roadworks *pl*. **B~unternehmer** *m* building contractor. **B~werk** *nt* building. **B~zaun** *m* hoarding

Bayer|(in) *m* -s, -n (*f* -, -nen) Bavarian. **B~n** *nt* -s Bavaria

bay[e]risch *a* Bavarian

Bazillus *m* -, -len bacillus; (*fam: Keim*) germ

beabsichtig|en *vt* intend. **b~t** *a* intended; (*absichtlich*) intentional

beacht|en *vt* take notice of; (*einhalten*) observe; (*folgen*) follow; **nicht b~en** ignore. **b~lich** *a* considerable. **b~ung** *f* - observance; (*dat*) **keine B~ung schenken** take no notice of sth

Beamte(r) *m*, **Beamtin** *f* -, -nen official; (*Staats-*) civil servant; (*Schalter-*) clerk

beängstigend *a* alarming

beanspruchen *vt* claim; (*erfordern*) demand; (*brauchen*) take up; (*Techn*) stress; **die Arbeit beansprucht ihn sehr** his work is very demanding

beanstand|en *vt* find fault with; (*Comm*) make a complaint about. **B~ung** *f* -, -en complaint

beantragen *vt* apply for

beantworten *vt* answer

bearbeiten *vt* work; (*weiter-*) process; (*behandeln*) treat (**mit** with); (*Admin*) deal with; (*redigieren*) edit; (*Theat*) adapt; (*Mus*) arrange; (*fam: bedrängen*) pester; (*fam: schlagen*) pummel

Beatmung *f* **künstliche B~** artificial respiration. **B~sgerät** *nt* ventilator

beaufsichtig|en *vt* supervise. **B~ung** *f* - supervision

beauftrag|en *vt* instruct; commission ⟨*Künstler*⟩; **jdn mit einer Arbeit b~en** assign a task to s.o. **B~te(r)** *m/f* representative

bebauen *vt* build on; (*bestellen*) cultivate

beben *vi* (*haben*) tremble

bebildert *a* illustrated

Becher *m* -s, - beaker; (*Henkel-*) mug; (*Joghurt-, Sahne-*) carton

Becken *nt* -s, - basin; (*Schwimm-*) pool; (*Mus*) cymbals *pl*; (*Anat*) pelvis

bedacht *a* careful; **b~ auf** (+ *acc*) concerned about; **darauf b~** anxious (**zu** to)

bedächtig *a* careful, *adv* -ly; (*langsam*) slow, *adv* -ly

bedanken (sich) *vr* thank (**bei jdm** s.o.)

Bedarf *m* -s need/(*Comm*) demand (**an** + *dat* for); **bei B~** if required. **B~sartikel** *mpl* requisites. **B~shaltestelle** *f* request stop

bedauer|lich *a* regrettable. **b~licherweise** *adv* unfortunately. **b~n** *vt* regret; (*bemitleiden*) feel sorry for; **bedaure!** sorry! **B~n** *nt* -s regret; (*Mitgefühl*) sympathy. **b~nswert** *a* pitiful; (*bedauerlich*) regrettable

bedeck|en *vt* cover; **sich b~en** ⟨*Himmel.*⟩ cloud over. **b~t** *a* covered; ⟨*Himmel*⟩ overcast

bedenken† *vt* consider; (*überlegen*) think over; **jdn b~** give s.o. a present; **sich b~** consider. **B~** *pl* misgivings; **ohne B~** without hesitation. **b~los** *a* unhesitating, *adv* -ly

bedenklich *a* doubtful; (*verdächtig*) dubious; (*bedrohlich*) worrying; (*ernst*) serious

bedeut|en *vi* (*haben*) mean; **jdm viel/nichts b~en** mean a lot/nothing to s.o.; **es hat nichts zu b~en** it is of no significance. **b~end** *a* important; (*beträchtlich*) considerable. **b~sam** *a* = **b~ungsvoll**. **B~ung** *f* -,-en meaning; (*Wichtigkeit*) importance. **b~ungslos** *a* meaningless; (*unwichtig*) unimportant. **b~ungsvoll** *a* significant; (*vielsagend*) meaningful, *adv* -ly

bedien|en *vt* serve; (*betätigen*) operate; **sich [selbst] b~en** help oneself. **B~ung** *f* -,-en service; (*Betätigung*) operation; (*Kellner*) waiter; (*Kellnerin*) *f* waitress. **B~ungsgeld** *nt*, **B~ungszuschlag** *m* service charge

bedingt *a* conditional; (*eingeschränkt*) qualified

Bedingung *f* -,-en condition; **B~en** conditions; (*Comm*) terms. **b~slos** *a* unconditional, *adv* -ly; (*unbedingt*) unquestioning, *adv* -ly

bedrängen *vt* press; (*belästigen*) pester

bedroh|en *vt* threaten. **b~lich** *a* threatening. **B~ung** *f* threat

bedrück|en *vt* depress. **b~end** *a* depressing. **b~t** *a* depressed

bedruckt *a* printed

bedürf|en† *vi* (*haben*) (+ *gen*) need. **B~nis** *nt* -ses,-se need. **B~nisanstalt** *f* public convenience. **b~tig** *a* needy

Beefsteak /'bi:fste:k/ *nt* -s,-s steak; **deutsches B~** hamburger

beeilen (sich) *vr* hurry; hasten (**zu** to); **beeilt euch!** hurry up!

beeindrucken *vt* impress

beeinflussen *vt* influence

beeinträchtigen *vt* mar; (*schädigen*) impair

beend[ig]en *vt* end

beengen *vt* restrict; **beengt wohnen** live in cramped conditions

beerben *vt* **jdn b~** inherit s.o.'s property

beerdig|en *vt* bury. **B~ung** *f* -,-en funeral

Beere *f* -,-n berry

Beet *nt* -[e]s,-e bed

Beete *f* -,-n **rote B~** beetroot

befähig|en *vt* enable; (*qualifizieren*) qualify. **B~ung** *f* - qualification; (*Fähigkeit*) ability

befahr|bar *a* passable. **b~en†** *a* drive along; **stark b~ene Straße** busy road

befallen† *vt* attack; ⟨*Angst.*⟩ seize

befangen *a* shy; (*gehemmt*) self-conscious; (*Jur*) biased. **B~heit** *f* - shyness; self-consciousness; bias

befassen (sich) *vr* concern oneself/ (*behandeln*) deal (**mit** with)

Befehl *m* -[e]s,-e order; (*Leitung*) command (**über** + *acc* of). **b~en†** *vt* **jdm etw b~en** order s.o. to do sth ● *vi* (*haben*) give the orders. **b~igen** *vt* (*Mil*) command. **B~sform** *f* (*Gram*) imperative. **B~shaber** *m* -s,- commander

befestig|en *vt* fasten (**an** + *dat* to); (*stärken*) strengthen; (*Mil*) fortify. **B~ung** *f* -,-en fastening; (*Mil*) fortification

befeuchten *vt* moisten

befind|en† (**sich**) *vr* be. **B~** *nt* -s [state of] health

beflecken *vt* stain

beflissen *a* assiduous, *adv* -ly

befolgen *vt* follow

beförder|n *vt* transport; (*im Rang*) promote. **B~ung** *f* -,-en transport; promotion

befragen *vt* question

befrei|en *vt* free; (*räumen*) clear (**von** of); (*freistellen*) exempt (**von** from); **sich b~en** free oneself. **B~er** *m* -s,- liberator. **b~t** *a* (*erleichtert*) relieved. **B~ung** *f* - liberation; exemption

befremd|en *vt* disconcert. **B~en** *nt* -s surprise. **b~lich** *a* strange

befreunden (sich) *vr* make friends; **befreundet sein** be friends

befriedig|en *vt* satisfy. **b~end** *a* satisfying; (*zufriedenstellend*) satisfactory. **B~ung** *f* - satisfaction

befrucht|en *vt* fertilize. **B~ung** *f* - fertilization; **künstliche B~ung** artificial insemination

Befug|nis *f* -,-se authority. **b~t** *a* authorized

Befund *m* result

befürcht|en vt fear. **B~ung** f -,-en fear

befürworten vt support

begab|t a gifted. **B~ung** f -,-en gift, talent

begatten (sich) vr mate

begeben† **(sich)** vr go; (liter: geschehen) happen; **sich in Gefahr b~** expose oneself to danger. **B~heit** f -,-en incident

begegn|en vi (sein) jdm/etw b~en meet s.o./sth; **sich b~en** meet. **B~ung** f -,-en meeting; (Sport) encounter

begehen† vt walk along; (verüben) commit; (feiern) celebrate

begehr|en vt desire. **b~enswert** a desirable. **b~t** a sought-after

begeister|n vt jdn b~n arouse s.o.'s enthusiasm; **sich b~n** be enthusiastic (für about). **b~t** a enthusiastic, adv -ally; (eifrig) keen. **B~ung** f - enthusiasm

Begier|de f -,-n desire. **b~ig** a eager (auf + acc for)

begießen† vt water; (Culin) baste; (fam: feiern) celebrate

Beginn m -s beginning; **zu B~** at the beginning. **b~en†** vt/i (haben) start, begin; (anstellen) do

beglaubigen vt authenticate

begleichen† vt settle

begleit|en vt accompany. **B~er** m -s,-, **B~erin** f -,-nen companion; (Mus) accompanist. **B~ung** f -,-en company; (Gefolge) entourage; (Mus) accompaniment

beglück|en vt make happy. **b~t** a happy. **b~wünschen** vt congratulate (zu on)

begnadig|en vt (Jur) pardon. **B~ung** f -,-en (Jur) pardon

begnügen (sich) vr content oneself (mit with)

Begonie /-jə/ f -,-n begonia

begraben† vt bury

Begräbnis n -ses,-se burial; (Feier) funeral

begreif|en† vt understand; **nicht zu b~en** incomprehensible. **b~lich** a understandable; **jdm etw b~lich machen** make s.o. understand sth. **b~licherweise** adv understandably

begrenz|en vt form the boundary of; (beschränken) restrict. **b~t** a limited. **B~ung** f -,-en restriction; (Grenze) boundary

Begriff m -[e]s,-e concept; (Ausdruck) term; (Vorstellung) idea; **für meine**

B~e to my mind; **im B~ sein** od **stehen** be about (**zu** to); **schwer von B~** (fam) slow on the uptake. **b~sstutzig** a obtuse

begründ|en vt give one's reason for; (gründen) establish. **b~et** a justified. **B~ung** f -,-en reason

begrüß|en vt greet; (billigen) welcome. **b~enswert** a welcome. **B~ung** f - greeting; welcome

begünstigen vt favour; (fördern) encourage

begutachten vt give an opinion on; (fam: ansehen) look at

begütert a wealthy

begütigen vt placate

behaart a hairy

behäbig a portly; (gemütlich) comfortable, adv -bly

behag|en vi (haben) please (jdm s.o.). **B~en** nt -s contentment; (Genuß) enjoyment. **b~lich** a comfortable, adv -bly. **B~lichkeit** f - comfort

behalten† vt keep; (sich merken) remember; **etw für sich b~** (verschweigen) keep sth to oneself

Behälter m -s,- container

behand|eln vt treat; (sich befassen) deal with. **B~lung** f treatment

beharr|en vi (haben) persist (auf + dat in). **b~lich** a persistent, adv -ly; (hartnäckig) dogged, adv -ly. **B~lichkeit** f - persistence

behaupt|en vt maintain; (vorgeben) claim; (sagen) say; (bewahren) retain; **sich b~en** hold one's own. **B~ung** f -,-en assertion; claim; (Äußerung) statement

beheben† vt remedy; (beseitigen) remove

behelf|en† **(sich)** vr make do (mit with). **b~smäßig** a makeshift ● adv provisionally

behelligen vt bother

behende a nimble, adv -bly

beherbergen vt put up

beherrsch|en vt rule over; (dominieren) dominate; (meistern, zügeln) control; (können) know; **sich b~en** control oneself. **b~t** a self-controlled. **B~ung** f - control; (Selbst-) self-control; (Können) mastery

beherz|igen vt heed. **b~t** a courageous, adv -ly

behilflich a jdm b~ **sein** help s.o.

behinder|n vt hinder; (blockieren) obstruct. **b~t** a handicapped;

(*schwer*) disabled. **B~te(r)** *m/f* handicapped/disabled person. **B~ung** *f* **-,-en** obstruction; (*Med*) handicap; disability

Behörde *f* **-,-n** [public] authority

behüten|n *vt* protect; **Gott behüte!** heaven forbid! **b~t a** sheltered

behutsam *a* careful, *adv* -ly; (*zart*) gentle, *adv*-ly

bei *prep* (+ *dat*) near; (*dicht*) by; at ⟨*Firma, Veranstaltung*⟩; **bei der Hand nehmen** take by the hand; **bei sich haben** have with one; **bei mir** at my place; (*in meinem Fall*) in my case; **Herr X bei Meyer** Mr X c/o Meyer; **bei Regen** when/(*falls*) if it rains; **bei Feuer** in case of fire; **bei Tag/Nacht** by day/night; **bei der Ankunft** on arrival; **bei Tisch/der Arbeit** at table/work; **bei guter Gesundheit** in good health; **bei der hohen Miete** [what] with the high rent; **bei all seiner Klugheit** for all his cleverness

beibehalten† *vt sep* keep

beibringen† *vt sep* **jdm etw b~** teach s.o. sth; (*mitteilen*) break sth to s.o.; (*zufügen*) inflict sth on s.o.

Beicht|e *f* **-,-n** confession. **b~en** *vt/i* (*haben*) confess. **B~stuhl** *m* confessional

beide *a & pron* both; **die b~n Brüder** the two brothers; **b~s** both; **dreißig b~** (*Tennis*) thirty all. **b~rseitig** *a* mutual. **b~rseits** *adv & prep* (+ *gen*) on both sides of

beidrehen *vi sep* (*haben*) heave to

beieinander *adv* together

Beifahrer|(in) *m*(*f*) [front-seat] passenger; (*Lkw*) driver's mate; (*Motorrad*) pillion passenger. **B~sitz** *m* passenger seat

Beifall *m* **-[e]s** applause; (*Billigung*) approval; **B~ klatschen** applaud

beifällig *a* approving, *adv* -ly

beifügen *vt sep* add; (*beilegen*) enclose

beige /bɛːʒ/ *inv a* beige

beigeben† *v sep* ● *vt* add ● *vi* (*haben*) **klein b~** give in

Beigeschmack *m* [slight] taste

Beihilfe *f* financial aid; (*Studien*-) grant; (*Jur*) aiding and abetting

beikommen† *vi sep* (*sein*) **jdm b~** get the better of s.o.

Beil *nt* **-[e]s,-e** hatchet, axe

Beilage *f* supplement; (*Gemüse*) vegetable; **als B~ Reis** (*Culin*) served with rice

beiläufig *a* casual, *adv*-ly

beilegen *vt sep* enclose; (*schlichten*) settle

beileibe *adv* **b~ nicht** by no means

Beileid *nt* condolences *pl*. **B~sbrief** *m* letter of condolence

beiliegend *a* enclosed

beim *prep* = **bei dem; b~ Militär** in the army; **b~ Frühstück** at breakfast; **b~ Lesen** when reading; **b~ Lesen sein** be reading

beimessen† *vt sep* (*fig*) attach (*dat* to)

Bein *nt* **-[e]s,-e** leg; **jdm ein B~ stellen** trip s.o. up

beinah[e] *adv* nearly, almost

Beiname *m* epithet

beipflichten *vi sep* (*haben*) agree (*dat* with)

Beirat *m* advisory committee

beirren *vt* **sich nicht b~ lassen** not let oneself be put off

beisammen *adv* together. **b~sein†** *vi sep* (*sein*) be together. **B~sein** *nt* **-s** get-together

Beisein *nt* presence

beiseite *adv* aside; (*abseits*) apart; **b~ legen** put aside; (*sparen*) put by; **Spaß** *od* **Scherz b~** joking apart

beisetz|en *vt sep* bury. **B~ung** *f* **-,-en** funeral

Beispiel *nt* example; **zum B~** for example. **b~haft** *a* exemplary. **b~los** *a* unprecedented. **b~sweise** *adv* for example

beispringen† *vi sep* (*sein*) **jdm b~** come to s.o.'s aid

beiß|en† *vt & i* (*haben*) bite; (*brennen*) sting; **sich b~en** ⟨*Farben:*⟩ clash. **b~end** *a* (*fig*) biting; ⟨*Bemerkung*⟩ caustic. **B~zange** *f* pliers *pl*

Bei|stand *m* **-[e]s** help; **jdm B~stand leisten** help s.o. **b~stehen†** *vi sep* (*haben*) **jdm b~stehen** help s.o.

beisteuern *vt sep* contribute

beistimmen *vi sep* (*haben*) agree

Beistrich *m* comma

Beitrag *m* **-[e]s,ᵉe** contribution; (*Mitglieds*-) subscription; (*Versicherungs*-) premium; (*Zeitungs*-) article. **b~en†** *vt/i sep* (*haben*) contribute

beitreten† *vi sep* (*sein*) (+ *dat*) join. **B~tritt** *m* joining

beiwohnen *vi sep* (*haben*) (+ *dat*) be present at

Beize *f* **-,-n** (*Holz*-) stain; (*Culin*) marinade

beizeiten *adv* in good time

beizen vt stain ⟨Holz⟩

bejahen vt answer in the affirmative; ⟨billigen⟩ approve of

bejahrt a aged, old

bejubeln vt cheer

bekämpf|en vt fight. **B∼ung** f - fight ⟨gen against⟩

bekannt a well-known; ⟨vertraut⟩ familiar; **jdm b∼ sein** be known to s.o.; **jdn b∼ machen** introduce s.o. **B∼e(r)** m/f acquaintance; ⟨Freund⟩ friend. **B∼gabe** f announcement. **b∼geben†** vt sep announce. **b∼lich** adv as is well known. **b∼machen** vt sep announce. **B∼machung** f -,-en announcement; ⟨Anschlag⟩ notice. **B∼schaft** f - acquaintance; ⟨Leute⟩ acquaintances pl; ⟨Freunde⟩ friends pl. **b∼werden†** vi sep (sein) become known

bekehr|en vt convert; **sich b∼en** become converted. **B∼ung** f -,-en conversion

bekenn|en† vt confess; profess ⟨Glauben⟩; **sich [für] schuldig b∼** admit one's guilt; **sich b∼en zu** confess to ⟨Tat⟩; profess ⟨Glauben⟩; ⟨stehen zu⟩ stand by. **B∼tnis** nt -ses,-se confession; ⟨Konfession⟩ denomination

beklag|en vt lament; ⟨bedauern⟩ deplore; **sich b∼en** complain. **b∼enswert** a unfortunate. **B∼te(r)** m/f ⟨Jur⟩ defendant

beklatschen vt applaud

bekleid|en vt hold ⟨Amt⟩. **b∼et** a dressed (**mit** in). **B∼ung** f clothing

Beklemmung f -,-en feeling of oppression

beklommen a uneasy; ⟨ängstlich⟩ anxious, adv -ly

bekommen† vt get; have ⟨Baby⟩; catch ⟨Erkältung⟩; **Angst/Hunger b∼** get frightened/hungry; **etw geliehen b∼** be lent sth ● vi (sein) **jdm gut b∼** do s.o. good; ⟨Essen:⟩ agree with s.o.

bekömmlich a digestible

beköstig|en vt feed; **sich selbst b∼en** cater for oneself. **B∼ung** f - board; ⟨Essen⟩ food

bekräftigen vt reaffirm; ⟨bestätigen⟩ confirm

bekreuzigen (sich) vr cross oneself

bekümmert a troubled; ⟨besorgt⟩ worried

bekunden vt show; ⟨bezeugen⟩ testify

belächeln vt laugh at

beladen† vt load ● a laden

Belag m -[e]s,∸e coating; ⟨Fußboden-⟩ covering; ⟨Brot-⟩ topping; ⟨Zahn-⟩ tartar; ⟨Brems-⟩ lining

belager|n vt besiege. **B∼ung** f -,-en siege

Belang m **von/ohne B∼** of/of no importance; **B∼e** pl interests. **b∼en** vt ⟨Jur⟩ sue. **b∼los** a irrelevant; ⟨unwichtig⟩ trivial. **B∼losigkeit** f -,-en triviality

belassen† vt leave; **es dabei b∼** leave it at that

belasten vt load; ⟨fig⟩ burden; ⟨beanspruchen⟩ put a strain on; ⟨Comm⟩ debit; ⟨Jur⟩ incriminate

belästigen vt bother; ⟨bedrängen⟩ pester; ⟨unsittlich⟩ molest

Belastung f -,-en load; ⟨fig⟩ strain; ⟨Last⟩ burden; ⟨Comm⟩ debit. **B∼smaterial** nt incriminating evidence. **B∼szeuge** m prosecution witness

belaufen (sich) vr amount (**auf** + acc to)

belauschen vt eavesdrop on

beleb|en vt ⟨fig⟩ revive; ⟨lebhaft machen⟩ enliven; **sich b∼en** revive; ⟨Stadt:⟩ come to life. **b∼t** a lively; ⟨Straße⟩ busy

Beleg m -[e]s,-e evidence; ⟨Beispiel⟩ instance ⟨**für** of⟩; ⟨Quittung⟩ receipt. **b∼en** vt cover/⟨garnieren⟩ garnish ⟨**mit** with⟩; ⟨besetzen⟩ reserve; ⟨Univ⟩ enrol for; ⟨nachweisen⟩ provide evidence for; **den ersten Platz b∼en** ⟨Sport⟩ take first place. **B∼schaft** f -,-en work-force. **b∼t** a occupied; ⟨Zunge⟩ coated; ⟨Stimme⟩ husky; **b∼te Brote** open sandwiches; **der Platz ist b∼t** this seat is taken

belehren vt instruct; ⟨aufklären⟩ inform

beleibt a corpulent

beleidig|en vt offend; ⟨absichtlich⟩ insult. **B∼ung** f -,-en insult

belesen a well-read

beleucht|en vt light; ⟨anleuchten⟩ illuminate. **B∼ung** f -,-en illumination; ⟨elektrisch⟩ lighting; ⟨Licht⟩ light

Belg|ien /-jən/ nt -s Belgium. **B∼ier(in)** m -s,- (f -,-nen) Belgian. **b∼isch** a Belgian

belicht|en vt ⟨Phot⟩ expose. **B∼ung** f - exposure

Belieb|en nt -s **nach B∼en** [just] as one likes; ⟨Culin⟩ if liked. **b∼ig** a **eine b∼ige Zahl/Farbe** any number/ colour you like ● adv **b∼ig lange/oft** as

long/often as one likes. **b~t** *a* popular.
B~theit *f* - popularity
beliefern *vt* supply (**mit** with)
bellen *vi* (*haben*) bark
belohn|en *vt* reward. **B~ung** *f* -,-en
reward
belüften *vt* ventilate
belügen† *vt* lie to; **sich [selbst] b~**
deceive oneself
belustig|en *vt* amuse. **B~ung** *f* -,-en
amusement
bemächtigen (sich) *vr* (+ *gen*) seize
bemalen *vt* paint
bemängeln *vt* criticize
bemannt *a* manned
bemerk|bar *a* **sich b~bar machen**
attract attention; ⟨*Ding:*⟩ become noticeable. **b~en** *vt* notice; (*äußern*) remark. **b~enswert** *a* remarkable,
adv -bly. **B~ung** *f* -,-en remark
bemitleiden *vt* pity
bemittelt *a* well-to-do
bemüh|en *vt* trouble; **sich b~en** try
(**zu** to; **um etw** to get sth); (*sich kümmern*) attend (**um** to); **b~t sein** endeavour (**zu** to). **B~ung** *f* -,-en effort;
(*Mühe*) trouble
bemuttern *vt* mother
benachbart *a* neighbouring
benachrichtig|en *vt* inform; (*amt-
lich*) notify. **B~ung** *f* -,-en notification
benachteilig|en *vt* discriminate
against; (*ungerecht sein*) treat un-
fairly. **B~ung** *f* -,-en discrimination
(*gen* against)
benehmen† (**sich**) *vr* behave. **B~** *nt*
-s behaviour
beneiden *vt* envy (**um etw** sth).
b~swert *a* enviable
Bengel *m* -s,- boy; (*Rüpel*) lout
benommen *a* dazed
benötigen *vt* need
benutz|en, (*SGer*) **benütz|en** *vt* use;
take ⟨*Bahn*⟩. **B~er** *m* -s,- user. **b~er-
freundlich** *a* user-friendly. **B~ung** *f*
use
Benzin *nt* -s petrol, (*Amer*) gasoline.
B~tank *m* petrol tank
beobacht|en *vt* observe. **B~er** *m* -s,-
observer. **B~ung** *f* -,-en observation
bepacken *vt* load (**mit** with)
bepflanzen *vt* plant (**mit** with)
bequem *a* comfortable, *adv* -bly;
(*mühelos*) easy, *adv* -ily; (*faul*) lazy.
b~en (**sich**) *vr* deign (**zu** to). **B~
lichkeit** *f* -,-en comfort; (*Faulheit*)
laziness

berat|en† *vt* advise; (*überlegen*) dis-
cuss; **sich b~en** confer; **sich b~en
lassen** get advice ● *vi* (*haben*) discuss
(**über etw** *acc* sth); (*beratschlagen*)
confer. **B~er** *m* -s,-, **B~erin** *f* -,-nen
adviser. **b~schlagen** *vi* (*haben*) confer. **B~ung** *f* -,-en guidance; (*Rat*)
advice; (*Besprechung*) discussion; (*Med,
Jur*) consultation. **B~ungsstelle** *f* advice centre
berauben *vt* rob (*gen* of)
berauschen *vt* intoxicate. **b~d** *a*
intoxicating, heady
berechn|en *vt* calculate; (*anrechnen*)
charge for; (*abfordern*) charge.
b~end *a* (*fig*) calculating. **B~ung** *f*
calculation
berechtig|en *vt* entitle; (*befugen*)
authorize; (*fig*) justify. **b~t** *a*
justified, justifiable. **B~ung** *f* -,-en
authorization; (*Recht*) right; (*Rechtmä-
ßigkeit*) justification
bered|en *vt* talk about; (*klatschen*)
gossip about; (*überreden*) talk round;
sich b~en talk. **B~samkeit** *f* - elo-
quence
beredt *a* eloquent, *adv* -ly
Bereich *m* -[e]s,-e area; (*fig*) realm;
(*Fach-*) field
bereichern *vi* enrich; **sich b~** grow
rich (**an** + *dat* on)
Bereifung *f* - tyres *pl*
bereinigen *vt* (*fig*) settle
bereit *a* ready. **b~en** *vt* prepare;
(*verursachen*) cause; give ⟨*Über-
raschung*⟩. **b~halten†** *vt sep* have/
(*ständig*) keep ready. **b~legen** *vt sep*
put out [ready]. **b~machen** *vt sep* get
ready; **sich b~machen** get ready. **b~s**
adv already
Bereitschaft *f* -,-en readiness;
(*Einheit*) squad. **B~sdienst** *m* **B~s-
dienst haben** (*Mil*) be on stand-by;
⟨*Arzt:*⟩ be on call; ⟨*Apotheke:*⟩ be open for
out-of-hours dispensing. **B~s-
polizei** *f* riot police
bereit|stehen† *vi sep* (*haben*) be
ready. **b~stellen** *vt sep* put out
ready; (*verfügbar machen*) make
available. **B~ung** *f* - preparation.
b~willig *a* willing, *adv* -ly. **B~
willigkeit** *f* - willingness
bereuen *vt* regret
Berg *m* -[e]s,-e mountain; (*Anhöhe*)
hill; **in den B~en** in the mountains.
b~ab *adv* downhill. **b~an** *adv* uphill. **B~arbeiter** *m* miner. **b~auf**

adv uphill; **es geht b~auf** (*fig*) things are looking up. **B~bau** *m* -[e]s mining
bergen† *vt* recover; (*Naut*) salvage; (*retten*) rescue
Berg|führer *m* mountain guide. **b~ig** *a* mountainous. **B~kette** *f* mountain range. **B~mann** *m* (*pl* -leute) miner. **B~steigen** *nt* -s mountaineering. **B~steiger(in)** *m* -s,- (*f* -,-nen) mountaineer, climber. **B~-und-Talbahn** *f* roller-coaster
Bergung *f* - recovery; (*Naut*) salvage; (*Rettung*) rescue
Berg|wacht *f* mountain rescue service. **B~werk** *nt* mine
Bericht *m* -[e]s,-e report; (*Reise-*) account; **B~ erstatten** report (**über** + *acc* on). **b~en** *vt/i* (*haben*) report; (*erzählen*) tell (**von** of). **B~erstatter(in)** *m* -s,- (*f* -,-nen) reporter; (*Korrespondent*) correspondent
berichtig|en *vt* correct. **B~ung** *f* -,-en correction
beriesel|n *vt* irrigate. **B~ungsanlage** *f* sprinkler system
beritten *a* (*Polizei*) mounted
Berlin *nt* -s Berlin. **B~er** *m* -s,- Berliner; (*Culin*) doughnut ● *a* Berlin . . .
Bernhardiner *m* -s,- St Bernard
Bernstein *m* amber
bersten† *vi* (*sein*) burst
berüchtigt *a* notorious
berückend *a* entrancing
berücksichtig|en *vt* take into consideration. **B~ung** *f* - consideration
Beruf *m* profession; (*Tätigkeit*) occupation; (*Handwerk*) trade. **b~en†** *vt* appoint; **sich b~en** refer (**auf** + *acc* to); (*vorgeben*) plead (**auf etw** *acc* sth) ● *a* competent; **b~en sein** be destined (**zu** to). **b~lich** *a* professional; (*Ausbildung*) vocational ● *adv* professionally; **b~lich tätig sein** work, have a job. **B~saussichten** *fpl* career prospects. **B~sberater(in)** *m*(*f*) careers officer. **B~sberatung** *f* vocational guidance. **b~smäßig** *adv* professionally. **B~sschule** *f* vocational school. **B~ssoldat** *m* regular soldier. **b~stätig** *a* working; **b~stätig sein** work, have a job. **B~stätige(r)** *m/f* working man/woman. **B~sverkehr** *m* rush-hour traffic. **B~ung** *f* -,-en appointment; (*Bestimmung*) vocation; (*Jur*) appeal; **B~ung einlegen** appeal. **B~ungsgericht** *nt* appeal court

beruhen *vi* (*haben*) be based (**auf** + *dat* on); **eine Sache auf sich b~ lassen** let a matter rest
beruhig|en *vt* calm [down]; (*zuversichtlich machen*) reassure; **sich b~en** calm down. **b~end** *a* calming; (*tröstend*) reassuring; (*Med*) sedative. **B~ung** *f* - calming; reassurance; (*Med*) sedation. **B~ungsmittel** *nt* sedative; (*bei Psychosen*) tranquillizer
berühmt *a* famous. **B~heit** *f* -,-en fame; (*Person*) celebrity
berühr|en *vt* touch; (*erwähnen*) touch on; (*beeindrucken*) affect; **sich b~en** touch. **B~ung** *f* -,-en touch; (*Kontakt*) contact
besag|en *vt* say; (*bedeuten*) mean. **b~t** *a* [afore]said
besänftigen *vt* soothe; **sich b~** calm down
Besatz *m* -es,ˉe trimming
Besatzung *f* -,-en crew; (*Mil*) occupying force
besaufen† (**sich**) *vr* (*sl*) get drunk
beschädig|en *vt* damage. **B~ung** *f* -,-en damage
beschaffen *vt* obtain, get ● *a* **so b~ sein, daß** be such that; **wie ist es b~ mit?** what about? **B~heit** *f* - consistency; (*Art*) nature
beschäftig|en *vt* occupy; (*Arbeitgeber:*) employ; **sich b~en** occupy oneself. **b~t** *a* busy; (*angestellt*) employed (**bei** at). **B~te(r)** *m/f* employee. **B~ung** *f* -,-en occupation; (*Anstellung*) employment. **b~ungslos** *a* unemployed. **B~ungstherapie** *f* occupational therapy
beschäm|en *vt* make ashamed. **b~end** *a* shameful; (*demütigend*) humiliating. **b~t** *a* ashamed; (*verlegen*) embarrassed
beschatten *vt* shade; (*überwachen*) shadow
beschau|en *vt* (*SGer*) [**sich** (*dat*)] **etw b~en** look at sth. **b~lich** *a* tranquil; (*Relig*) contemplative
Bescheid *m* -[e]s information; **jdm B~ sagen** *od* **geben** let s.o. know; **B~ wissen** know
bescheiden *a* modest, *adv* -ly. **B~heit** *f* - modesty
bescheinen† *vt* shine on; **von der Sonne beschienen** sunlit
bescheinig|en *vt* certify. **B~ung** *f* -,-en [written] confirmation; (*Schein*) certificate

beschenken vt give a present/presents to

bescher|en vt jdm b~en give s.o. presents; **jdm etw b~en** give s.o. sth. **B~ung** f -,-en distribution of Christmas presents; (fam: Schlamassel) mess

beschießen† vt fire at; (mit Artillerie) shell, bombard

beschildern vt signpost

beschimpf|en vt abuse, swear at. **B~ung** f -,-en abuse

beschirmen vt protect

Beschlag m in **B~ nehmen, mit B~ belegen** monopolize. **b~en†** vt shoe ● vi (sein) steam or mist up ● a steamed or misted up; (erfahren) knowledgeable (in + dat about). **B~nahme** f -,-n confiscation; (Jur) seizure. **b~nahmen** vt confiscate; (Jur) seize; (fam) monopolize

beschleunig|en vt hasten; (schneller machen) speed up; quicken ⟨Schritt, Tempo⟩; **sich b~en** speed up; quicken ● vi (haben) accelerate. **B~ung** f - acceleration

beschließen† vt decide; (beenden) end ● vi (haben) decide (**über** + acc about)

Beschluß m decision

beschmieren vt smear/(bestreichen) spread (**mit** with)

beschmutzen vt make dirty; **sich b~** get [oneself] dirty

beschneid|en† vt trim; (Hort) prune; (fig: kürzen) cut back; (Relig) circumcise. **B~ung** f - circumcision

beschneit a snow-covered

beschnüffeln, beschnuppern vt sniff at

beschönigen vt (fig) gloss over

beschränken vt limit, restrict; **sich b~ auf** (+ acc) confine oneself to; ⟨Sache:⟩ be limited to

beschrankt a ⟨Bahnübergang⟩ with barrier[s]

beschränk|t a limited; (geistig) dullwitted; (borniert) narrow-minded. **B~ung** f -,-en limitation, restriction

beschreib|en† vt describe; (schreiben) write on. **B~ung** f -,-en description

beschuldig|en vt accuse. **B~ung** f -,-en accusation

beschummeln vt (fam) cheat

Beschuß m -sses (Mil) fire; (Artillerie-) shelling

beschütz|en vt protect. **B~er** m -s,- protector

Beschwer|de f -,-n complaint; **B~den** (Med) trouble sg. **b~en** vt weight down; **sich b~en** complain. **b~lich** a difficult

beschwichtigen vt placate

beschwindeln vt cheat (**um** out of); (belügen) lie to

beschwingt a elated; (munter) lively

beschwipst a (fam) tipsy

beschwören† vt swear to; (anflehen) implore; (herauf-) invoke

besehen† vt look at

beseitig|en vt remove. **B~ung** f - removal

Besen m -s,- broom. **B~ginster** m (Bot) broom. **B~stiel** m broomstick

besessen a obsessed (**von** by)

besetz|en vt occupy; fill ⟨Posten⟩; (Theat) cast ⟨Rolle⟩; (verzieren) trim (**mit** with). **b~t** a occupied; ⟨Toilette, Leitung⟩ engaged; ⟨Zug, Bus⟩ full up; **der Platz ist b~t** this seat is taken; **mit Perlen b~t** set with pearls. **B~t-zeichen** nt engaged tone. **B~ung** f -,-en occupation; (Theat) cast

besichtig|en vt look round ⟨Stadt, Museum⟩; (prüfen) inspect; (besuchen) visit. **B~ung** f -,-en visit; (Prüfung) inspection; (Stadt-) sightseeing

besiedelt a **dünn/dicht b~** sparsely/ densely populated

besiegeln vt (fig) seal

besieg|en vt defeat; (fig) overcome. **B~te(r)** m/f loser

besinn|en† (sich) vr think, reflect; (sich erinnern) remember (**auf jdn/ etw** s.o./sth); **sich anders b~en** change one's mind. **b~lich** a contemplative; (nachdenklich) thoughtful. **B~ung** f - reflection; (Bewußtsein) consciousness; **bei/ohne B~ung** conscious/unconscious; **zur B~ung kommen** regain consciousness; (fig) come to one's senses. **b~ungslos** a unconscious

Besitz m possession; (Eigentum, Land-) property; (Gut) estate. **b~an-zeigend** a (Gram) possessive. **b~en†** vt own, possess; (haben) have. **B~er(in)** m -s,- (f -,-nen) owner; (Comm) proprietor. **B~ung** f -,-en [landed] property; (Gut) estate

besoffen a (sl) drunken; **b~ sein** be drunk

besohlen vt sole

besold|en vt pay. **B~ung** f - pay

besonder|e(r,s) a special; (bestimmt) particular; (gesondert) separate; **nichts B~es** nothing special. **B~heit** f -,-en peculiarity. **b~s** adv [e]specially, particularly; (gesondert) separately

besonnen a calm, adv -ly

besorg|en vt get; (kaufen) buy; (erledigen) attend to; (versorgen) look after. **B~nis** f -,-se anxiety; (Sorge) worry. **b~niserregend** a worrying. **b~t** a worried-/(bedacht) concerned (**um** about). **B~ung** f -,-en errand; **B~ungen machen** do shopping

bespielt a recorded

bespitzeln vt spy on

besprech|en† vt discuss; (rezensieren) review; **sich b~en** confer; **ein Tonband b~en** make a tape recording. **B~ung** f -,-en discussion; review; (Konferenz) meeting

bespritzen vt splash

besser a & adv better. **b~n** vt improve; **sich b~n** get better, improve. **B~ung** f - improvement; **gute B~ung!** get well soon! **B~wisser** m -s,- know-all

Bestand m -[e]s,ˆe existence; (Vorrat) stock (**an** + dat of); **B~ haben, von B~ sein** last

beständig a constant, adv -ly; (Wetter) settled; **b~ gegen** resistant to

Bestand|saufnahme f stock-taking. **B~teil** m part

bestärken vt (fig) strengthen

bestätig|en vt confirm; acknowledge (Empfang); **sich b~en** prove to be true. **B~ung** f -,-en confirmation

bestatt|en vt bury. **B~ung** f -,-en funeral. **B~ungsinstitut** nt [firm of] undertakers pl, (Amer) funeral home

bestäuben vt pollinate

bestaubt a dusty

Bestäubung f - pollination

bestaunen vt gaze at in amazement; (bewundern) admire

best|e(r,s) a best; **b~en Dank!** many thanks! **am b~en sein** be best; **zum b~en geben** recite (Gedicht); tell (Geschichte, Witz); sing (Lied); **jdn zum b~en halten** (fam) pull s.o.'s leg. **B~e(r,s)** m/f/nt best; **sein B~es tun** do one's best; **zum B~en der Armen** for the benefit of the poor

bestech|en† vt bribe; (bezaubern) captivate. **b~end** a captivating.

b~lich a corruptible. **B~ung** f - bribery. **B~ungsgeld** nt bribe

Besteck nt -[e]s,-e [set of] knife, fork and spoon; (coll) cutlery

bestehen† vi (haben) exist; (fortdauern) last; (bei Prüfung) pass; **b~ aus** consist-/(gemacht sein) be made of; **b~ auf** (+ dat) insist on ● vt pass (Prüfung). **B~** nt -s existence

bestehlen† vt rob

besteig|en† vt climb; (einsteigen) board; (aufsteigen) mount; ascend (Thron). **B~ung** f ascent

bestell|en vt order; (vor-) book; (ernennen) appoint; (bebauen) cultivate; (ausrichten) tell; **zu sich b~en** send for; **b~t sein** have an appointment; **kann ich etwas b~en?** can I take a message? **b~en Sie Ihrer Frau Grüße von mir** give my regards to your wife. **B~schein** m order form. **B~ung** f order; (Botschaft) message; (Bebauung) cultivation

besten|falls adv at best. **b~s** adv very well

besteuer|n vt tax. **B~ung** f - taxation

bestialisch /-st-/ a bestial

Bestie /ˈbɛstjə/ f -,-n beast

bestimm|en vt fix; (entscheiden) decide; (vorsehen) intend; (ernennen) appoint; (ermitteln) determine; (definieren) define; (Gram) qualify ● vi (haben) be in charge (**über** + acc of). **b~t** a definite, adv -ly; (gewiß) certain, adv -ly; (fest) firm, adv -ly. **B~theit** f - firmness; **mit B~theit** for certain. **B~ung** f fixing; (Vorschrift) regulation; (Ermittlung) determination; (Definition) definition; (Zweck) purpose; (Schicksal) destiny. **B~ungsort** m destination

Bestleistung f (Sport) record

bestraf|en vt punish. **B~ung** f -,-en punishment

bestrahl|en vt shine on; (Med) treat with radiotherapy; irradiate (Lebensmittel). **B~ung** f radiotherapy

Bestreb|en nt -s endeavour; (Absicht) aim. **b~t** a **b~t sein** endeavour (**zu** to). **B~ung** f -,-en effort

bestreichen† vt spread (**mit** with)

bestreikt a strike-hit

bestreiten† vt dispute; (leugnen) deny; (bezahlen) pay for

bestreuen vt sprinkle (**mit** with)

bestürmen vt (fig) besiege

bestürz|t *a* dismayed; (*erschüttert*) stunned. **B~ung** *f* - dismay, consternation

Bestzeit *f* (*Sport*) record [time]

Besuch *m* -[e]s,-e visit; (*kurz*) call; (*Schul-*) attendance; (*Gast*) visitor; (*Gäste*) visitors *pl*; **B~ haben** have a visitor/visitors; **bei jdm zu** *od* **auf B~ sein** be staying with s.o. **b~en** *vt* visit; (*kurz*) call on; (*teilnehmen*) attend; go to ⟨*Schule, Ausstellung*⟩; **gut b~t** well attended. **B~er(in)** *m* -s,- (*f* -,-nen) visitor; caller; (*Theat*) patron. **B~szeit** *f* visiting hours *pl*

betagt *a* aged, old

betasten *vt* feel

betätig|en *vt* operate; **sich b~en** work (**als** as); **sich politisch b~en** engage in politics. **B~ung** *f* -,-en operation; (*Tätigkeit*) activity

betäub|en *vt* stun; ⟨*Lärm:*⟩ deafen; (*Med*) anaesthetize; (*lindern*) ease; deaden ⟨*Schmerz*⟩; **wie b~t** dazed. **B~ung** *f* - daze; (*Med*) anaesthesia; **unter örtlicher B~ung** under local anaesthetic. **B~ungsmittel** *nt* anaesthetic

Bete *f* -,-n **rote B~** beetroot

beteilig|en *vt* give a share to; **sich b~en** take part (**an**+*dat* in); (*beitragen*) contribute (**an**+*dat* to). **b~t** *a* **b~t sein** take part/(*an Unfall*) be involved/(*Comm*) have a share (**an**+*dat* in); **alle B~ten** all those involved. **B~ung** *f* -,-en participation; involvement; (*Anteil*) share

beten *vi* (*haben*) pray; (*bei Tisch*) say grace ● *vt* say

beteuer|n *vt* protest. **B~ung** *f* -,-en protestation

Beton /be'tɔŋ/ *m* -s concrete

betonen *vt* stress, emphasize

betonieren *vt* concrete

beton|t *a* stressed; (*fig*) pointed, *adv* -ly. **B~ung** *f* -,-en stress, emphasis

betören *vt* bewitch

betr., Betr. *abbr* (*betreffs*) re

Betracht *m* **in B~ ziehen** consider; **außer B~ lassen** disregard; **nicht in B~ kommen** be out of the question. **b~en** *vt* look at; (*fig*) regard (**als** as)

beträchtlich *a* considerable, *adv* -bly

Betrachtung *f* -,-en contemplation; (*Überlegung*) reflection

Betrag *m* -[e]s,¨e amount. **b~en†** *vt* amount to; **sich b~en** behave. **B~en** *nt* -s behaviour; (*Sch*) conduct

betrauen *vt* entrust (**mit** with)

betrauern *vt* mourn

betreff|en† *vt* affect; (*angehen*) concern; **was mich betrifft** as far as I am concerned. **b~end** *a* relevant; **der b~ende Brief** the letter in question. **b~s** *prep* (+*gen*) concerning

betreiben† *vt* (*leiten*) run; (*ausüben*) carry on; (*vorantreiben*) pursue; (*antreiben*) run (**mit** on)

betreten† *vt* step on; (*eintreten*) enter; **'B~ verboten'** 'no entry'; (*bei Rasen*) 'keep off [the grass]' ● *a* embarrassed ● *adv* in embarrassment

betreu|en *vt* look after. **B~er(in)** *m* -s,- (*f* -,-nen) helper; (*Kranken-*) nurse. **B~ung** *f* - care

Betrieb *m* business; (*Firma*) firm; (*Treiben*) activity; (*Verkehr*) traffic; **in B~** working; (*in Gebrauch*) in use; **außer B~** not in use; (*defekt*) out of order

Betriebs|anleitung, B~anweisung *f* operating instructions *pl*. **B~ferien** *pl* firm's holiday; **'B~ferien'** 'closed for the holidays'. **B~leitung** *f* management. **B~rat** *m* works committee. **B~ruhe** *f* **'montags B~ruhe'** 'closed on Mondays'. **B~störung** *f* breakdown

betrinken† (sich) *vr* get drunk

betroffen *a* disconcerted; **b~ sein** be affected (**von** by); **die B~en** those affected ● *adv* in consternation

betrüb|en *vt* sadden. **b~lich** *a* sad. **b~t** *a* sad, *adv* -ly

Betrug *m* -[e]s deception; (*Jur*) fraud

betrüg|en† *vt* cheat, swindle; (*Jur*) defraud; (*in der Ehe*) be unfaithful to; **sich selbst b~en** deceive oneself. **B~er(in)** *m* -s,- (*f* -,-nen) swindler. **B~erei** *f* -,-en fraud. **b~erisch** *a* fraudulent; ⟨*Person*⟩ deceitful

betrunken *a* drunken; **b~ sein** be drunk. **B~e(r)** *m* drunk

Bett *nt* -[e]s,-en bed; **im B~** in bed; **ins** *od* **zu B~ gehen** go to bed. **B~couch** *f* sofa-bed. **B~decke** *f* blanket; (*Tages-*) bedspread

bettel|arm *a* destitute. **B~ei** *f* - begging. **b~n** *vi* (*haben*) beg

bett|en *vt* lay, put; **sich b~en** lie down. **b~lägerig** *a* bedridden. **B~laken** *nt* sheet

Bettler(in) *m* -s,- (*f* -,-nen) beggar

Bettpfanne *f* bedpan

Bettuch *nt* sheet

Bett|vorleger *m* bedside rug. **B~wäsche** *f* bed linen. **B~zeug** *nt* bedding

betupfen *vt* dab (**mit** with)

beug|en *vt* bend; ⟨*Gram*⟩ decline; conjugate ⟨*Verb*⟩; **sich b~en** bend; (*lehnen*) lean; (*sich fügen*) submit (*dat* to). **B~ung** *f* -,-en (*Gram*) declension; conjugation

Beule *f* -,-n bump; (*Delle*) dent

beunruhig|en *vt* worry; **sich b~en** worry. **B~ung** *f* - worry

beurlauben *vt* give leave to; (*des Dienstes entheben*) suspend

beurteil|en *vt* judge. **B~ung** *f* -,-en judgement; (*Ansicht*) opinion

Beute *f* - booty, haul; ⟨*Jagd-*⟩ bag; (*B~tier*) quarry; (*eines Raubtiers*) prey

Beutel *m* -s,- bag; (*Geld-*) purse; (*Tabak-& Zool*) pouch. **B~tier** *nt* marsupial

bevölker|n *vt* populate. **B~ung** *f* -,-en population

bevollmächtig|en *vt* authorize. **B~te(r)** *m/f* [authorized] agent

bevor *conj* before; **b~ nicht** until

bevormunden *vt* treat like a child

bevorstehen† *vi sep* (*haben*) approach; (*unmittelbar*) be imminent; **jdm b~** be in store for s.o. **b~d** *a* approaching, forthcoming; **unmittelbar b~d** imminent

bevorzug|en *vt* prefer; (*begünstigen*) favour. **b~t** *a* privileged; ⟨*Behandlung*⟩ preferential; (*beliebt*) favoured

bewachen *vt* guard; **bewachter Parkplatz** car park with an attendant

bewachsen *a* covered (**mit** with)

Bewachung *f* - guard; **unter B~** under guard

bewaffn|en *vt* arm. **b~et** *a* armed. **B~ung** *f* - armament; (*Waffen*) arms *pl*

bewahren *vt* protect (**vor** + *dat* from); (*behalten*) keep; **die Ruhe b~** keep calm; **Gott bewahre!** heaven forbid!

bewähren (sich) *vr* prove one's/ ⟨*Ding:*⟩ its worth; (*erfolgreich sein*) prove a success

bewahrheiten (sich) *vr* prove to be true

bewähr|t *a* reliable; (*erprobt*) proven. **B~ung** *f* - (*Jur*) probation. **B~ungsfrist** *f* [period of] probation. **B~ungsprobe** *f* (*fig*) test

bewaldet *a* wooded

bewältigen *vt* cope with; (*überwinden*) overcome; (*schaffen*) manage

bewandert *a* knowledgeable

bewässer|n *vt* irrigate. **B~ung** *f* - irrigation

bewegen[1] *vt* (*reg*) move; **sich b~** move; (*körperlich*) take exercise

bewegen[2]† *vt* **jdn dazu b~,** **etw zu tun** induce s.o. to do sth

Beweg|grund *m* motive. **b~lich** *a* movable, mobile; (*wendig*) agile. **B~lichkeit** *f* - mobility; agility. **b~t** *a* moved; (*ereignisreich*) eventful; ⟨*See*⟩ rough. **B~ung** *f* -,-en movement; (*Phys*) motion; (*Rührung*) emotion; (*Gruppe*) movement; **körperliche B~ung** physical exercise; **sich in B~ung setzen** [start to] move. **B~ungsfreiheit** *f* freedom of movement/(*fig*) of action. **b~ungslos** *a* motionless

beweinen *vt* mourn

Beweis *m* -es,-e proof; (*Zeichen*) token; **B~e** evidence *sg*. **b~en†** *vt* prove; (*zeigen*) show; **sich b~en** prove oneself/⟨*Ding:*⟩ itself. **B~material** *nt* evidence

bewenden *vi* **es dabei b~ lassen** leave it at that

bewerb|en† (**sich**) *vr* apply (**um** for; **bei** to). **B~er(in)** *m* -s,- (*f* -,-nen) applicant. **B~ung** *f* -,-en application

bewerkstelligen *vt* manage

bewerten *vt* value; (*einschätzen*) rate; (*Sch*) mark, grade

bewilligen *vt* grant

bewirken *vt* cause; (*herbeiführen*) bring about; (*erreichen*) achieve

bewirt|en *vt* entertain. **B~ung** *f* - hospitality

bewohn|bar *a* habitable. **b~en** *vt* inhabit, live in. **B~er(in)** *m* -s,- (*f* -,-nen) resident, occupant; (*Einwohner*) inhabitant

bewölk|en (sich) *vr* cloud over; **b~t** cloudy. **B~ung** *f* - clouds *pl*

bewunder|n *vt* admire. **b~nswert** *a* admirable. **B~ung** *f* - admiration

bewußt *a* conscious (*gen* of); (*absichtlich*) deliberate, *adv* -ly; (*besagt*) said; **sich** (*dat*) **etw** (*gen*) **b~ sein/ werden** be/become aware of sth. **b~los** *a* unconscious. **B~losigkeit** *f* - unconsciousness. **B~sein** *n* -s consciousness; (*Gewißheit*) awareness; **bei [vollem] B~sein** [fully] conscious; **mir kam zum B~sein** I realized (**daß** that)

bez. *abbr* (**bezahlt**) paid; (**bezüglich**) re

bezahl|en *vt/i (haben)* pay; pay for ⟨*Ware, Essen*⟩; **sich b∼t machen** (*fig*) pay off. **B∼ung** *f* - payment; (*Lohn*) pay

bezähmen *vt* control; (*zügeln*) restrain; **sich b∼** restrain oneself

bezaubern *vt* enchant. **b∼d** *a* enchanting

bezeichn|en *vt* mark; (*bedeuten*) denote; (*beschreiben, nennen*) describe (**als** as). **b∼end** *a* typical. **B∼ung** *f* marking; (*Beschreibung*) description (**als** as); (*Ausdruck*) term; (*Name*) name

bezeugen *vt* testify to

bezichtigen *vt* accuse (*gen* of)

bezieh|en† *vt* cover; (*einziehen*) move into; (*beschaffen*) obtain; (*erhalten*) get, receive; take ⟨*Zeitung*⟩; (*in Verbindung bringen*) relate (**auf** + *acc* to); **sich b∼en** (*bewölken*) cloud over; **sich b∼en auf** (+ *acc*) refer to; **das Bett frisch b∼en** put clean sheets on the bed. **B∼ung** *f* -,-en relation; (*Verhältnis*) relationship; (*Bezug*) respect; **in dieser B∼ung** in this respect; [**gute**] **B∼ungen haben** have [good] connections. **b∼ungsweise** *adv* respectively; (*vielmehr*) or rather

beziffern (sich) *vr* amount (**auf** + *acc* to)

Bezirk *m* -[e]s,-e district

Bezug *m* cover; (*Kissen-*) case; (*Beschaffung*) obtaining; (*Kauf*) purchase; (*Zusammenhang*) reference; **B∼e** *pl* earnings; **B∼ nehmen** refer (**auf** + *acc* to); **in b∼ auf** (+ *acc*) regarding, concerning

bezüglich *prep* (+ *gen*) regarding, concerning ● *a* relating (**auf** + *acc* to); (*Gram*) relative

bezwecken *vt* (*fig*) aim at

bezweifeln *vt* doubt

bezwingen† *vt* conquer

BH /beːˈhaː/ *m* -[s],-[s] bra

bibbern *vi* (*haben*) tremble; (*vor Kälte*) shiver

Bibel *f* -,-n Bible

Biber¹ *m* -s,- beaver

Biber² *m* & *nt* -s flannelette

Biblio|graphie *f* -,-n bibliography. **B∼thek** *f* -,-en library. **B∼thekar(in)** *m* -s,- (*f* -,-nen) librarian

biblisch *a* biblical

bieder *a* honest, upright; (*ehrenwert*) worthy; (*einfach*) simple

bieg|en† *vt* bend; **sich b∼en** bend; **sich vor Lachen b∼en** (*fam*) double up with laughter ● *vi* (*sein*) curve (**nach**

to); **um die Ecke b∼en** turn the corner. **b∼sam** *a* flexible, supple. **B∼ung** *f* -,-en bend

Biene *f* -,-n bee. **B∼nhonig** *m* natural honey. **B∼nstock** *m* beehive. **B∼nwabe** *f* honeycomb

Bier *nt* -s,-e beer. **B∼deckel** *m* beer-mat. **B∼krug** *m* beer-mug

Biest *nt* -[e]s,-er (*fam*) beast

bieten† *vt* offer; (*bei Auktion*) bid; (*zeigen*) present; **das lasse ich mir nicht b∼** I won't stand for that

Bifokalbrille *f* bifocals *pl*

Biga|mie *f* - bigamy. **B∼mist** *m* -en,-en bigamist

bigott *a* over-pious

Bikini *m* -s,-s bikini

Bilanz *f* -,-en balance sheet; (*fig*) result; **die B∼ ziehen** (*fig*) draw conclusions (**aus** from)

Bild *nt* -[e]s,-er picture; (*Theat*) scene; **jdn ins B∼ setzen** put s.o. in the picture

bilden *vt* form; (*sein*) be; (*erziehen*) educate; **sich b∼** form; (*geistig*) educate oneself

Bild|erbuch *nt* picture-book. **B∼ergalerie** *f* picture gallery. **B∼fläche** *f* screen; **von der B∼fläche verschwinden** disappear from the scene. **B∼hauer** *m* -s,- sculptor. **B∼hauerei** *f* - sculpture. **b∼hübsch** *a* very pretty. **b∼lich** *a* pictorial; (*figurativ*) figurative, *adv* -ly. **B∼nis** *nt* -ses,-se portrait. **B∼schirm** *m* (*TV*) screen. **B∼schirmgerät** *nt* visual display unit, VDU. **b∼schön** *a* very beautiful

Bildung *f* - formation; (*Erziehung*) education; (*Kultur*) culture

Billard /ˈbɪljart/ *nt* -s billiards *sg*. **B∼tisch** *m* billiard table

Billett /bɪlˈjɛt/ *nt* -[e]s,-e & -s ticket

Billiarde *f* -,-n thousand million million

billig *a* cheap, *adv* -ly; (*dürftig*) poor; (*gerecht*) just; **recht und b∼** right and proper. **b∼en** *vt* approve. **B∼ung** *f* - approval

Billion /bɪlˈjoːn/ *f* -,-en million million, billion

bimmeln *vi* (*haben*) tinkle

Bimsstein *m* pumice stone

bin *s.* **sein; ich bin** I am

Binde *f* -,-n band; (*Verband*) bandage; (*Damen-*) sanitary towel. **B∼hautentzündung** *f* conjunctivitis. **b∼n**† *vt* tie (**an** + *acc* to); make

⟨Strauß⟩; bind ⟨Buch⟩; ⟨fesseln⟩ tie up; ⟨Culin⟩ thicken; **sich b~n** commit oneself. **b~nd** a ⟨fig⟩ binding. **B~strich** m hyphen. **B~wort** nt (pl -wörter) ⟨Gram⟩ conjunction

Bind|faden m string; **ein B~faden** a piece of string. **B~ung** f -,-en ⟨fig⟩ tie, bond; ⟨Beziehung⟩ relationship; ⟨Verpflichtung⟩ commitment; ⟨Ski-⟩ binding; ⟨Tex⟩ weave

binnen prep (+ dat) within; **b~ kurzem** shortly. **B~handel** m home trade

Binse f -,-n ⟨Bot⟩ rush. **B~nwahrheit, B~nweisheit** f truism

Bio- pref organic

Bio|chemie f biochemistry. **b~dynamisch** m organic

Biographie f -,-n biography

Bio|hof m organic farm. **B~laden** m health-food store

Biolog|e m -n,-n biologist. **B~ie** f - biology. **b~isch** a biological, adv -ly; **b~ischer Anbau** organic farming; **b~isch angebaut** organically grown

Birke f -,-n birch [tree]

Birm|a nt -s Burma. **b~anisch** a Burmese

Birn|baum m pear-tree. **B~e** f -,-n pear; ⟨Electr⟩ bulb

bis prep (+ acc) as far as, [up] to; ⟨zeitlich⟩ until, till; ⟨spätestens⟩ by; **bis zu** up to; **bis jetzt** up to now, so far; **bis dahin** until/⟨spätestens⟩ by then; **bis auf** (+ acc) ⟨einschließlich⟩ [down] to; ⟨ausgenommen⟩ except [for]; **drei bis vier Mark** three to four marks; **bis morgen!** see you tomorrow! ● conj until

Bischof m -s,̈-e bishop

bisher adv so far, up to now. **b~ig** attrib a ⟨Präsident⟩ outgoing; **meine b~igen Erfahrungen** my experiences so far

Biskuit|rolle /bɪsˈkviːt-/ f Swiss roll. **B~teig** m sponge mixture

bislang adv so far, up to now

Biß m -sses,-sse bite

bißchen inv pron **ein b~** a bit, a little; **ein b~ Brot** a bit of bread; **kein b~** not a bit

Biss|en m -s,- bite, mouthful. **b~ig** a vicious; ⟨fig⟩ caustic

bist s. sein; **du b~** you are

Bistum nt -s,̈-er diocese, see

bisweilen adv from time to time

bitt|e adv please; ⟨nach Klopfen⟩ come in; ⟨als Antwort auf 'danke'⟩ don't mention it, you're welcome; **wie b~e?** pardon? ⟨empört⟩ I beg your pardon? **möchten Sie Kaffee?—ja b~e** would you like some coffee?—yes please. **B~e** f -,-n request/⟨dringend⟩ plea (**um** for). **b~en†** vt/i (haben) ask/⟨dringend⟩ beg (**um** for); ⟨einladen⟩ invite, ask; **ich b~e dich!** I beg [of] you! ⟨empört⟩ I ask you! **b~end** a pleading, adv -ly

bitter a bitter, adv -ly. **B~keit** f - bitterness. **b~lich** adv bitterly

Bittschrift f petition

bizarr a bizarre, adv -ly

bläh|en vt swell; puff out ⟨Vorhang⟩; **sich b~en** swell; ⟨Vorhang, Segel:⟩ billow ● vi (haben) cause flatulence. **B~ungen** fpl flatulence sg, ⟨fam⟩ wind sg

Blamage /blaˈmaːʒə/ f -,-n humiliation; ⟨Schande⟩ disgrace

blamieren vt disgrace; **sich b~** disgrace oneself; ⟨sich lächerlich machen⟩ make a fool of oneself

blanchieren /blãˈʃiːrən/ vt ⟨Culin⟩ blanch

blank a shiny; ⟨nackt⟩ bare; **b~ sein** ⟨fam⟩ be broke. **B~oscheck** m blank cheque

Blase f -,-n bubble; ⟨Med⟩ blister; ⟨Anat⟩ bladder. **B~balg** m -[e]s,̈-e bellows pl. **b~n†** vt/i (haben) blow; play ⟨Flöte⟩. **B~nentzündung** f cystitis

Bläser m -s,- ⟨Mus⟩ wind player; **die B~** the wind section sg

blasiert a blasé

Blas|instrument nt wind instrument. **B~kapelle** f brass band

Blasphemie f - blasphemy

blaß a (**blasser, blassest**) pale; ⟨schwach⟩ faint; **b~ werden** turn pale

Blässe f - pallor

Blatt nt -[e]s,̈-er ⟨Bot⟩ leaf; ⟨Papier⟩ sheet; ⟨Zeitung⟩ paper; **kein B~ vor den Mund nehmen** ⟨fig⟩ not mince one's words

blätter|n vi (haben) **b~n in** (+ dat) leaf through. **B~teig** m puff pastry

Blattlaus f greenfly

blau a, **B~** nt -s,- blue; **b~er Fleck** bruise; **b~es Auge** black eye; **b~ sein** ⟨fam⟩ be tight; **Fahrt ins B~e** mystery tour. **B~beere** f bilberry. **B~licht** nt blue flashing light. **b~machen** vi sep (haben) ⟨fam⟩ skive off work

Blech nt -[e]s,-e sheet metal; ⟨Weiß-⟩ tin; ⟨Platte⟩ metal sheet; ⟨Back-⟩ baking sheet; (*Mus*) brass; (*fam: Unsinn*) rubbish. **b~en** *vt/i* (*haben*) (*fam*) pay. **B~[blas]instrument** *nt* brass instrument. **B~schaden** *m* (*Auto*) damage to the bodywork

Blei *nt* -[e]s lead

Bleibe *f* - place to stay. **b~n†** *vi* (*sein*) remain, stay; (*übrig-*) be left; **ruhig b~n** keep calm; **bei etw b~n** (*fig*) stick to sth; **b~n Sie am Apparat** hold the line. **b~nd** *a* permanent; (*anhaltend*) lasting. **b~nlassen†** *vt sep* **etw b~nlassen** not do sth; (*aufhören*) stop doing sth

bleich *a* pale. **b~en†** *vi* (*sein*) bleach; (*ver-*) fade ● *vt* (*reg*) bleach. **B~mittel** *nt* bleach

blei|ern *a* leaden. **b~frei** *a* unleaded. **B~stift** *m* pencil. **B~stiftabsatz** *m* stiletto heel. **B~stiftspitzer** *m* -s,- pencil-sharpener

Blende *f* -,-n shade, shield; (*Sonnen-*) [sun] visor; (*Phot*) diaphragm; (*Öffnung*) aperture; (*an Kleid*) facing. **b~n** *vt* dazzle, blind. **b~nd** *a* (*fig*) dazzling; (*prima*) marvellous, *adv* -ly

Blick *m* -[e]s,-e look; (*kurz*) glance; (*Aussicht*) view; **auf den ersten B~** at first sight; **einen B~ für etw haben** (*fig*) have an eye for sth. **b~en** *vi* (*haben*) look/(*kurz*) glance (**auf** + *acc* at). **B~punkt** *m* (*fig*) point of view

blind *a* blind; (*trübe*) dull; **b~er Alarm** false alarm; **b~er Passagier** stowaway. **B~darm** *m* appendix. **B~darmentzündung** *f* appendicitis. **B~e(r)** *m/f* blind man/woman; **die B~en** the blind *pl*. **B~enhund** *m* guide-dog. **B~enschrift** *f* braille. **B~gänger** *m* -s,- (*Mil*) dud. **B~heit** *f* - blindness. **b~lings** *adv* (*fig*) blindly

blink|en *vi* (*haben*) flash; (*funkeln*) gleam; (*Auto*) indicate. **B~er** *m* -s,- (*Auto*) indicator. **B~licht** *nt* flashing light

blinzeln *vi* (*haben*) blink

Blitz *m* -es,-e [flash of] lightning; (*Phot*) flash; **ein B~ aus heiterem Himmel** (*fig*) a bolt from the blue. **B~ableiter** *m* lightning-conductor. **b~artig** *a* lightning ... ● *adv* like lightning. **B~birne** *f* flashbulb. **b~en** *vi* (*haben*) flash; (*funkeln*) sparkle; **es hat geblitzt** there was a flash of lightning. **B~gerät** *nt* flash [unit]. **B~licht** *nt* (*Phot*) flash. **b~sauber** *a*

spick and span. **b~schnell** *a* lightning ... ● *adv* like lightning. **B~strahl** *m* flash of lightning

Block *m* -[e]s,ᵉe block ● -[e]s,-s & ᵉe (*Schreib-*) [note-]pad; (*Häuser-*) block; (*Pol*) bloc

Blockade *f* -,-n blockade

Blockflöte *f* recorder

blockieren *vt* block; (*Mil*) blockade

Blockschrift *f* block letters *pl*

blöd[e] *a* feeble-minded; (*dumm*) stupid, *adv* -ly

Blödsinn *m* -[e]s idiocy; (*Unsinn*) nonsense. **b~ig** *a* feeble-minded; (*verrückt*) idiotic

blöken *vi* (*haben*) bleat

blond *a* fair-haired; (*Haar*) fair. **B~ine** *f* -,-n blonde

bloß *a* bare; (*alleinig*) mere; **mit b~em Auge** with the naked eye ● *adv* only, just; **was mache ich b~?** whatever shall I do?

Blöße *f* -,-n nakedness; **sich** (*dat*) **eine B~ geben** (*fig*) show a weakness

bloß|legen *vt sep* uncover; **b~stellen** *vt sep* compromise; **sich b~stellen** show oneself up

Bluff *m* -s,-s bluff. **b~en** *vt/i* (*haben*) bluff

blühen *vi* (*haben*) flower; (*fig*) flourish. **b~d** *a* flowering; (*fig*) flourishing, thriving; (*Phantasie*) fertile

Blume *f* -,-n flower; (*vom Wein*) bouquet. **B~nbeet** *nt* flower-bed. **B~ngeschäft** *nt* flower-shop, florist's [shop]. **B~nkohl** *m* cauliflower. **B~nmuster** *nt* floral design. **B~nstrauß** *m* bunch of flowers. **B~ntopf** *m* flowerpot; (*Pflanze*) [flowering] pot plant. **B~nzwiebel** *f* bulb

blumig *a* (*fig*) flowery

Bluse *f* -,-n blouse

Blut *nt* -[e]s blood. **b~arm** *a* anaemic. **B~bahn** *f* bloodstream. **b~befleckt** *a* blood-stained. **B~bild** *nt* blood count. **B~buche** *f* copper beech. **B~druck** *m* blood pressure. **b~dürstig** *a* bloodthirsty

Blüte *f* -,-n flower, bloom; (*vom Baum*) blossom; (*B~zeit*) flowering period; (*Baum-*) blossom time; (*fig*) flowering; (*Höhepunkt*) peak, prime; (*fam: Banknote*) forged note, (*fam*) dud

Blut|egel *m* -s,- leech. **b~en** *vi* (*haben*) bleed

Blüten|blatt *nt* petal. **B~staub** *m* pollen

Blut|er *m* -s,- haemophiliac. **B~erguß** *m* bruise. **B~gefäß** *nt* blood-vessel. **B~gruppe** *f* blood group. **B~hund** *m* bloodhound. **b~ig** *a* bloody. **b~jung** *a* very young. **B~körperchen** *nt* -s,- [blood] corpuscle. **B~probe** *f* blood test. **b~rünstig** *a* (*fig*) bloody, gory; ⟨*Person*⟩ bloodthirsty. **B~schande** *f* incest. **B~spender** *m* blood donor. **B~sturz** *m* haemorrhage. **B~s-verwandte(r)** *m/f* blood relation. **B~transfusion**, **B~übertragung** *f* blood transfusion. **B~ung** *f* -,-en bleeding; (*Med*) haemorrhage; (*Regel-*) period. **b~unterlaufen** *a* bruised; ⟨*Auge*⟩ bloodshot. **B~vergießen** *nt* -s bloodshed. **B~vergiftung** *f* blood-poisoning. **B~wurst** *f* black pudding

Bö *f* -,-en gust; (*Regen-*) squall

Bob *m* -s,-s bob[-sleigh]

Bock *m* -[e]s,¨e buck; (*Ziege*) billy goat; ⟨*Schaf*⟩ ram; (*Gestell*) support; **einen B~ schießen** (*fam*) make a blunder. **b~en** *vi* (*haben*) ⟨*Pferd:*⟩ buck; ⟨*Kind:*⟩ be stubborn. **b~ig** *a* (*fam*) stubborn. **B~springen** *nt* leap-frog

Boden *m* -s,¨ ground; (*Erde*) soil; (*Fuß-*) floor; (*Grundfläche*) bottom; (*Dach-*) loft, attic. **B~kammer** *f* attic [room]. **b~los** *a* bottomless; (*fam*) incredible. **B~satz** *m* sediment. **B~schätze** *mpl* mineral deposits. **B~see (der)** Lake Constance

Bogen *m* -s,- & ¨ curve; (*Geom*) arc; (*beim Skilauf*) turn; (*Archit*) arch; (*Waffe, Geigen-*) bow; (*Papier*) sheet; **einen großen B~ um jdn/etw machen** (*fam*) give s.o./sth a wide berth. **B~gang** *m* arcade. **B~schießen** *nt* archery

Bohle *f* -,-n [thick] plank

Böhm|en *nt* -s Bohemia. **b~isch** *a* Bohemian

Bohne *f* -,-n bean; **grüne B~n** French beans. **B~nkaffee** *m* real coffee

bohner|n *vt* polish. **B~wachs** *nt* floor-polish

bohr|en *vt/i* (*haben*) drill (**nach** for); drive ⟨*Tunnel*⟩; sink ⟨*Brunnen*⟩; ⟨*Insekt:*⟩ bore; **in der Nase b~en** pick one's nose. **B~er** *m* -s,- drill. **B~insel** *f* [off-shore] drilling rig. **B~maschine** *f* electric drill. **B~turm** *m* derrick

Boje *f* -,-n buoy

Böllerschuß *m* gun salute

Bolzen *m* -s,- bolt; (*Stift*) pin

bombardieren *vt* bomb; (*fig*) bombard (**mit** with)

bombastisch *a* bombastic

Bombe *f* -,-n bomb. **B~nangriff** *m* bombing raid. **B~nerfolg** *m* huge success. **B~r** *m* -s,- (*Aviat*) bomber

Bon /bɔŋ/ *m* -s,-s voucher; (*Kassen-*) receipt

Bonbon /bɔŋ'bɔŋ/ *m* & *nt* -s,-s sweet

Bonus *m* -[sses],-[sse] bonus

Boot *nt* -[e]s,-e boat. **B~ssteg** *m* landing-stage

Bord[1] *nt* -[e]s,-e shelf

Bord[2] *m* (*Naut*) **an B~** aboard, on board; **über B~** overboard. **B~buch** *nt* log[-book]

Bordell *nt* -s,-e brothel

Bord|karte *f* boarding-pass. **B~stein** *m* kerb

borgen *vt* borrow; **jdm etw b~** lend s.o. sth

Borke *f* -,-n bark

borniert *a* narrow-minded

Börse *f* -,-n purse; (*Comm*) stock exchange. **B~nmakler** *m* stockbroker

Borst|e *f* -,-n bristle. **b~ig** *a* bristly

Borte *f* -,-n braid

bösartig *a* vicious; (*Med*) malignant

Böschung *f* -,-en embankment; (*Hang*) slope

böse *a* wicked, evil; (*unartig*) naughty; (*schlimm*) bad, *adv* -ly; (*zornig*) cross; **jdm** *od* **auf jdn b~ sein** be cross with s.o. **B~wicht** *m* -[e]s,-e villain; (*Schlingel*) rascal

bos|haft *a* malicious, *adv* -ly; (*gehässig*) spiteful, *adv* -ly. **B~heit** *f* -,-en malice; spite; (*Handlung*) spiteful act/(*Bemerkung*) remark

böswillig *a* malicious, *adv* -ly. **B~keit** *f* -malice

Botani|k *f* - botany. **B~ker(in)** *m* -s,- (*f* -,-nen) botanist. **b~sch** *a* botanical

Bot|e *m* -n,-n messenger. **B~engang** *m* errand. **B~schaft** *f* -,-en message; (*Pol*) embassy. **B~schafter** *m* -s,- ambassador

Bottich *m* -[e]s,-e vat; (*Wasch-*) tub

Bouillon /bʊl'jɔŋ/ *f* -,-s clear soup. **B~würfel** *m* stock cube

Bowle /'boːlə/ *f* -,-n punch

box|en *vi* (*haben*) box ● *vt* punch. **B~en** *nt* -s boxing. **B~er** *m* -s,- boxer. **B~kampf** *m* boxing match; (*Boxen*) boxing

Boykott *m* -[e]s,-s boycott. **b~ieren** *vt* boycott; (*Comm*) black

brachliegen† vi sep (haben) lie fallow

Branche /'brãːʃə/ f -,-n [line of] business. **B~nverzeichnis** nt (Teleph) classified directory

Brand m -[e]s,-̈e fire; (Med) gangrene; (Bot) blight; **in B~ geraten** catch fire; **in B~ setzen** od **stecken** set on fire. **B~bombe** f incendiary bomb

branden vi (haben) surge; (sich brechen) break

Brand|geruch m smell of burning. **b~marken** vt (fig) brand. **B~stifter** m arsonist. **B~stiftung** f arson

Brandung f - surf. **B~sreiten** nt surfing

Brand|wunde f burn. **B~zeichen** nt brand

Branntwein m spirit; (coll) spirits pl. **B~brennerei** f distillery

bras|ilianisch a Brazilian. **B~ilien** /-jən/ nt -s Brazil

Brat|apfel m baked apple. **b~en**† vt/i (haben) roast; (in der Pfanne) fry. **B~en** m -s,- roast; (B~stück) joint. **B~ensoße** f gravy. **b~fertig** a oven-ready. **B~hähnchen, B~huhn** nt roast/(zum Braten) roasting chicken. **B~kartoffeln** fpl fried potatoes. **B~klops** m rissole. **B~pfanne** f frying-pan

Bratsche f -,-n (Mus) viola

Brat|spieß m spit. **B~wurst** f sausage for frying; (gebraten) fried sausage

Brauch m -[e]s, Bräuche custom. **b~bar** a usable; (nützlich) useful. **b~en** vt need; (ge-, verbrauchen) use; take (Zeit); **er b~t es nur zu sagen** he only has to say; **du b~st nicht zu gehen** you needn't go

Braue f -,-n eyebrow

brau|en vt brew. **B~er** m -s,- brewer. **B~erei** f -,-en brewery

braun a, **B~** nt -s,- brown; **b~ werden** (Person:) get a tan

Bräune f - [sun-]tan. **b~n** vt/i (haben) brown; (in der Sonne) tan

braungebrannt a [sun-]tanned

Braunschweig nt -s Brunswick

Brause f -,-n (Dusche) shower; (an Gießkanne) rose; (B~limonade) fizzy drink. **b~n** vi (haben) roar; (duschen) shower ● vi (sein) rush [along] ● vr **sich b~n** shower. **b~nd** a roaring; (sprudelnd) effervescent

Braut f -,-̈e bride; (Verlobte) fiancée

Bräutigam m -s,-e bridegroom; (Verlobter) fiancé

Brautkleid nt wedding dress

bräutlich a bridal

Brautpaar nt bridal couple; (Verlobte) engaged couple

brav a good, well-behaved; (redlich) honest ● adv dutifully; (redlich) honestly

bravo int bravo!

BRD abbr (**Bundesrepublik Deutschland**) FRG

Brech|eisen nt jemmy; (B~stange) crowbar. **b~en**† vt break; (Phys) refract (Licht); (erbrechen) vomit; **sich b~en** (Wellen:) break; (Licht:) be refracted; **sich** (dat) **den Arm b~en** break one's arm ● vi (sein) break ● vi (haben) vomit, be sick; **mit jdm b~en** (fig) break with s.o. **B~er** m -s,- breaker. **B~reiz** m nausea. **B~stange** f crowbar

Brei m -[e]s,-e paste; (Culin) purée; (Grieß-) pudding; (Hafer-) porridge. **b~ig** a mushy

breit a wide; (Schultern, Grinsen) broad ● adv **b~ grinsen** grin broadly. **b~beinig** a & adv with legs apart. **B~e** f -,-n width; breadth; (Geog) latitude. **b~en** vt spread (über + acc over). **B~engrad** m [degree of] latitude. **B~enkreis** m parallel. **B~seite** f long side; (Naut) broadside

Bremse[1] f -,-n horsefly

Bremse[2] f -,-n brake. **b~n** vt slow down; (fig) restrain ● vi (haben) brake

Bremslicht nt brake-light

brenn|bar a combustible; **leicht b~bar** highly [in]flammable. **b~en**† vi (haben) burn; (Licht:) be on; (Zigarette:) be alight; (weh tun) smart, sting; **es b~t in X** there's a fire in X; **darauf b~en, etw zu tun** be dying to do sth ● vt burn; (rösten) roast; (im Brennofen) fire; (destillieren) distil. **b~end** a burning; (angezündet) lighted; (fig) fervent ● adv **ich würde b~end gern . . .** I'd love to . . . **B~erei** f -,-en distillery

Brennessel f -,-n stinging nettle

Brenn|holz nt firewood. **B~ofen** m kiln. **B~punkt** m (Phys) focus; **im B~punkt des Interesses stehen** be the focus of attention. **B~spiritus** m methylated spirits. **B~stoff** m fuel

brenzlig a (fam) risky; **b~er Geruch** smell of burning

Bresche f -,-n (fig) breach
Bretagne /bre'tanjə/ (die) - Brittany
Brett nt -[e]s,-er board; (im Regal) shelf; **schwarzes B~** notice board. **B~chen** nt -s,- slat; (Frühstücks-) small board (used as plate). **B~spiel** nt board game
Brezel f -,-n pretzel
Bridge /brɪtʃ/ nt - (Spiel) bridge
Brief m -[e]s,-e letter. **B~beschwerer** m -s,- paperweight. **B~block** m writing pad. **B~freund(in)** m(f) pen-friend. **B~kasten** m letter-box, (Amer) mailbox. **B~kopf** m letter-head. **b~lich** a & adv by letter. **B~marke** f [postage] stamp. **B~öffner** m paper-knife. **B~papier** nt notepaper. **B~porto** nt letter rate. **B~tasche** f wallet. **B~träger** m postman, (Amer) mailman. **B~umschlag** m envelope. **B~wahl** f postal vote. **B~wechsel** m correspondence
Brigade f -,-n brigade
Brikett nt -s,-s briquette
brillant /brɪl'jant/ a brilliant, adv -ly. **B~t** m -en,-en [cut] diamond. **B~z** f -brilliance
Brille f -,-n glasses pl, spectacles pl; (Schutz-) goggles pl; (Klosett-) toilet seat
bringen† vt bring; (fort-) take; (ein-) yield; (veröffentlichen) publish; (im Radio) broadcast; show (Film); **ins Bett b~** put to bed; **jdn nach Hause b~** take/(begleiten) see s.o. home; **an sich (acc) b~** get possession of; **mit sich b~** entail; **um etw b~** deprive of sth; **etw hinter sich (acc) b~** get sth over [and done] with; **jdn dazu b~, etw zu tun** get s.o. to do sth; **es weit b~** (fig) go far
brisant a explosive
Brise f -,-n breeze
Brite m -n,-n, **B~in** f -,-nen Briton. **b~isch** a British
Bröckchen nt -s,- (Culin) crouton. **b~elig** a crumbly; (Gestein) friable. **b~eln** vt/i (haben/sein) crumble
Brocken m -s,- chunk; (Erde, Kohle) lump; **ein paar B~ Englisch** (fam) a smattering of English
Brokat m -[e]s,-e brocade
Brokkoli pl broccoli sg
Brombeer|e f blackberry. **B~strauch** m bramble [bush]
Bronchitis f - bronchitis
Bronze /'brõːsə/ f -,-n bronze
Brosch|e f -,-n brooch. **b~iert** a paperback. **B~üre** f -,-n brochure; (Heft) booklet

Brösel mpl (Culin) breadcrumbs
Brot n -[e]s,-e bread; **ein B~** a loaf [of bread]; (Scheibe) a slice of bread; **sein B~ verdienen** (fig) earn one's living (mit by)
Brötchen n -s,- [bread] roll
Brot|krümel m breadcrumb. **B~verdiener** m breadwinner
Bruch m -[e]s,-e break; (Brechen) breaking; (Rohr-) burst; (Med) fracture; (Eingeweide-) rupture, hernia; (Math) fraction; (fig) breach; (in Beziehung) break-up
brüchig a brittle
Bruch|landung f crash-landing. **B~rechnung** f fractions pl. **B~stück** nt fragment. **b~stückhaft** a fragmentary. **B~teil** m fraction
Brücke f -,-n bridge; (Teppich) rug
Bruder m -s,- brother
brüderlich a brotherly, fraternal
Brügge nt -s Bruges
Brüh|e f -,-n broth; (Knochen-) stock; **klare B~e** clear soup. **b~en** vt scald; (auf-) make (Kaffee). **B~würfel** m stock cube
brüllen vt/i (haben) roar; (Kuh:) moo; (fam: schreien) bawl
brumm|eln vt/i (haben) mumble. **b~en** vi (haben) (Insekt:) buzz; (Bär:) growl; (Motor:) hum; (murren) grumble ● vt mutter. **B~er** m -s,- (fam) bluebottle. **b~ig** a (fam) grumpy, adv -ily
brünett a dark-haired. **B~e** f -,-n brunette
Brunnen m -s,- well; (Spring-) fountain; (Heil-) spa water. **B~kresse** f watercress
brüsk a brusque, adv -ly. **b~ieren** vt snub
Brüssel nt -s Brussels
Brust f -,-e chest; (weibliche, Culin: B~stück) breast. **B~bein** nt breastbone. **B~beutel** m purse worn round the neck
brüsten (sich) vr boast
Brust|fellentzündung f pleurisy. **B~schwimmen** nt breast-stroke
Brüstung f -,-en parapet
Brustwarze f nipple
Brut f -,-en incubation; (Junge) brood; (Fisch-) fry
brutal a brutal, adv -ly. **B~ität** f -,-en brutality
brüten vi (haben) sit (on eggs); (fig) ponder (über + dat over); **b~de Hitze** oppressive heat

Brutkasten m (Med) incubator
brutto adv, **B~-** pref gross
brutzeln vi (haben) sizzle ● vt fry
Bub m -en,-en (SGer) boy. **B~e** m -n,-n
(Karte) jack, knave
Bubikopf m bob
Buch nt -[e]s,-̈er book; **B~ führen** keep
a record (**über**+ acc of); **die B~̈er
führen** keep the accounts. **B~drucker**
m printer
Buche f -,-n beech
buchen vt book; (Comm) enter
Bücher|bord, B~brett nt book-
shelf. **B~ei** f -,-en library. **B~regal**
nt bookcase, bookshelves pl. **B~
schrank** m bookcase. **B~wurm** m
bookworm
Buchfink m chaffinch
Buch|führung f bookkeeping.
B~halter(in) m -s,- (f -,-nen) book-
keeper, accountant. **B~haltung** f
bookkeeping, accountancy; (Abteilung) accounts department. **B~händ-
ler(in)** m(f) bookseller. **B~hand-
lung** f bookshop. **B~macher** m -s,-
bookmaker. **B~prüfer** m auditor
Büchse f -,-n box; (Konserven-) tin, can;
(Gewehr) [sporting] gun. **B~nmilch** f
evaporated milk. **B~nöffner** m tin
or can opener
Buch|stabe m -ns,-n letter. **b~sta-
bieren** vt spell [out]. **b~stäblich** adv
literally
Buchstützen fpl book-ends
Bucht f -,-en (Geog) bay
Buchung f -,-en booking, reservation;
(Comm) entry
Buckel m -s,- hump; (Beule) bump;
(Hügel) hillock; **einen B~ machen**
(Katze.) arch its back
bücken (sich) vr bend down
bucklig a hunchbacked. **B~e(r)** m/f
hunchback
Buckling m -s,-e smoked herring;
(fam: Verbeugung) bow
buddeln vt/i (haben) (fam) dig
Buddhis|mus m - Buddhism. **B~t(in)**
m -en,-en (f -,-nen) Buddhist. **b~t-
isch** a Buddhist
Bude f -,-n hut; (Kiosk) kiosk; (Markt-)
stall; (fam: Zimmer) room; (Studen-
ten-) digs pl
Budget /by'dʒe:/ nt -s,-s budget
Büfett nt -[e]s,-e sideboard; (Theke)
bar; **kaltes B~** cold buffet
Büffel m -s,- buffalo. **b~n** vt/i
(haben) (fam) swot
Bug m -[e]s,-e (Naut) bow[s pl]

Bügel m -s,- frame; (Kleider-) coat-
hanger; (Steig-) stirrup; (Brillen-) side-
piece. **B~brett** nt ironing-board.
B~eisen nt iron. **B~falte** f crease.
b~frei a non-iron. **b~n** vt/i (haben)
iron
bugsieren vt (fam) manœuvre
buhen vi (haben) (fam) boo
Buhne f -,-n breakwater
Bühne f -,-n stage. **B~nbild** nt set.
B~neingang m stage door
Buhrufe mpl boos
Bukett nt -[e]s,-e bouquet
Bulette f -,-n [meat] rissole
Bulgarien /-iən/ nt -s Bulgaria
Bull|auge nt (Naut) porthole.
B~dogge f bulldog. **B~dozer**
/-do:zɐ/ m -s,- bulldozer. **B~e** m -n,-n
bull; (sl: Polizist) cop
Bummel m -s,- (fam) stroll. **B~lant**
m -en,-en (fam) dawdler; (Faulenzer)
loafer. **B~lei** f - (fam) dawdling;
(Nachlässigkeit) carelessness
bummel|ig a (fam) slow; (nach-
lässig) careless. **b~n** vi (sein) (fam)
stroll ● vi (haben) (fam) dawdle.
B~streik m go-slow. **B~zug** m (fam)
slow train
Bums m -es,-e (fam) bump, thump
Bund¹ nt -[e]s,-e bunch; (Stroh-) bundle
Bund² m -[e]s,-̈e association; (Bündnis)
alliance; (Pol) federation; (Rock-,
Hosen-) waistband; **im B~e sein** be in
league (**mit** with); **der B~** the Federal
Government; (fam: Bundeswehr) the
[German] Army
Bündel nt -s,- bundle. **b~n** vt bundle
[up]
Bundes|- pref Federal. **B~genosse**
m ally. **B~kanzler** m Federal Chan-
cellor. **B~land** nt [federal] state;
(Aust) province. **B~liga** f German
national league. **B~rat** m Upper
House of Parliament. **B~regierung**
f Federal Government. **B~republik**
f **die B~republik Deutschland** the
Federal Republic of Germany.
B~straße f ≈ A road. **B~tag** m
Lower House of Parliament.
B~wehr f [Federal German] Army
bünd|ig a & adv **kurz und b~ig** short
and to the point. **B~nis** nt -sses,-sse
alliance
Bunker m -s,- bunker; (Luftschutz-)
shelter
bunt a coloured; (farbenfroh) colourful; (grell) gaudy; (gemischt)
varied; (wirr) confused; **b~er Abend**

social evening; **b~e Platte** assorted cold meats ● *adv* **b~ durcheinander** higgledy-piggledy; **es zu b~ treiben** (*fam*) go too far. **B~stift** *m* crayon

Bürde *f* -,-n (*fig*) burden

Burg *f* -,-en castle

Bürge *m* -n,-n guarantor. **b~n** *vi* (*haben*) **b~n für** vouch for; (*fig*) guarantee

Bürger|(in) *m* -s,- (*f* -,-nen) citizen. **B~krieg** *m* civil war. **b~lich** *a* civil; (*Pflicht*) civic; (*mittelständisch*) middle-class; **b~liche Küche** plain cooking. **B~liche(r)** *m/f* commoner. **B~meister** *m* mayor. **B~rechte** *npl* civil rights. **B~steig** *m* -[e]s,-e pavement, (*Amer*) sidewalk

Burggraben *m* moat

Bürgschaft *f* -,-en surety; **B~ leisten** stand surety

Burgunder *m* -s,- (*Wein*) Burgundy

Burleske *f* -,-n burlesque

Büro *nt* -s,-s office. **B~angestellte(r)** *m/f* office-worker. **B~klammer** *f* paper-clip. **B~krat** *m* -en,-en bureaucrat. **B~kratie** *f* -,-n bureaucracy. **b~kratisch** *a* bureaucratic

Bursch|e *m* -n,-n lad, youth; (*fam: Kerl*) fellow. **b~ikos** *a* hearty; (*männlich*) mannish

Bürste *f* -,-n brush. **b~n** *vt* brush. **B~nschnitt** *m* crew cut

Bus *m* -ses,-se bus; (*Reise-*) coach. **B~bahnhof** *m* bus and coach station

Busch *m* -[e]s,¨e bush

Büschel *nt* -s,- tuft

buschig *a* bushy

Busen *m* -s,- bosom

Bussard *m* -s,-e buzzard

Buße *f* -,-n penance; (*Jur*) fine

büßen *vt/i* (*haben*) [**für**] **etw b~** atone for sth; (*fig: bezahlen*) pay for sth

buß|fertig *a* penitent. **B~geld** *nt* (*Jur*) fine

Büste *f* -,-n bust; (*Schneider-*) dummy. **B~nhalter** *m* -s,- bra

Butter *f* - butter. **B~blume** *f* buttercup. **B~brot** *nt* slice of bread and butter. **B~brotpapier** *nt* greaseproof paper. **B~faß** *nt* churn. **B~milch** *f* buttermilk. **b~n** *vi* (*haben*) make butter ● *vt* butter

b.w. *abbr* (**bitte wenden**) PTO

bzgl. *abbr s.* **bezüglich**

bzw. *abbr s.* **beziehungsweise**

C

ca. *abbr* (**circa**) about

Café /ka'fe:/ *nt* -s,-s café

Cafeteria /kafete'ri:a/ *f* -,-s cafeteria

camp|en /'kɛmpən/ *vi* (*haben*) go camping. **C~ing** *nt* -s camping. **C~ingplatz** *m* campsite

Cape /ke:p/ *nt* -s,-s cape

Caravan /'ka[:]ravan/ *m* -s,-s (*Auto*) caravan; (*Kombi*) estate car

Cassette /ka'sɛta/ *f* -,-n cassette. **C~nrecorder** /-rekɔrdɐ/ *m* -s,-cassette recorder

CD /tse:'de:/ *f* -,-s compact disc, CD

Cell|ist(in) /tʃɛ'lɪst(ɪn)/ *m* -en,-en (*f* -,-nen) cellist. **C~o** /'tʃɛlo/ *nt* -s,-los & -li cello

Celsius /'tsɛlzjʊs/ *inv* Celsius, centigrade

Cembalo /'tʃɛmbalo/ *nt* -s,-los & -li harpsichord

Champagner /ʃam'panjɐ/ *m* -s champagne

Champignon /'ʃampɪnjɔŋ/ *m* -s,-s [field] mushroom

Chance /'ʃã:s[ə]/ *f* -,-n chance

Chaos /'ka:ɔs/ *nt* - chaos

chaotisch /ka'o:tɪʃ/ *a* chaotic

Charakter /ka'raktɐ/ *m* -s,-e /-'te:rə/ character. **c~isieren** *vt* characterize. **c~istisch** *a* characteristic (**für** of), *adv* -ally

Charism|a /ka'rɪsma/ *nt* -s charisma. **c~atisch** *a* charismatic

charm|ant /ʃar'mant/ *a* charming, *adv* -ly. **C~e** /ʃarm/ *m* -s charm

Charter|flug /'tʃ-, 'ʃartɐ-/ *m* charter flight. **c~n** *vt* charter

Chassis /ʃa'si:/ *nt* -,- /-'si:[s], -'si:s/ chassis

Chauffeur /ʃo'fø:ɐ̯/ *m* -s,-e chauffeur; (*Taxi-*) driver

Chauvinis|mus /ʃovi'nɪsmʊs/ *m* -chauvinism. **C~t** *m* -en,-en chauvinist

Chef /ʃɛf/ *m* -s,-s head; (*fam*) boss

Chem|ie /çe'mi:/ *f* - chemistry. **C~ikalien** /*fpl* chemicals

Chem|iker(in) /'çe:-/ *m* -s,- (*f* -,-nen) chemist. **c~isch** *a* chemical, *adv* -ly; **c~ische Reinigung** dry-cleaning; (*Geschäft*) dry-cleaner's

Chicorée /'ʃikore:/ *m* -s chicory

Chiffr|e /'ʃɪfə, 'ʃɪfrə/ *f* -, **-n** cipher; (*bei Annonce*) box number. **c~iert** *a* coded

Chile /'çi:le/ *nt* **-s** Chile

Chin|a /'çi:na/ *nt* **-s** China. **C~ese** *m* **-n,-n**, **C~esin** *f* -, **-nen** Chinese. **c~esisch** *a* Chinese. **C~esisch** *nt* **-[s]** (*Lang*) Chinese

Chip /tʃɪp/ *m* **-s,-s** [micro]chip. **C~s** *pl* crisps, (*Amer*) chips

Chirurg /çi'rʊrk/ *m* **-en,-en** surgeon. **C~ie** /-'gi:/ *f* - surgery. **c~isch** /-g-/ *a* surgical, *adv* -ly

Chlor /kloːɐ̯/ *nt* **-s** chlorine. **C~oform** /kloro'fɔrm/ *nt* **-s** chloroform

Choke /tʃoːk/ *m* **-s,-s** (*Auto*) choke

Cholera /'koːlera/ *f* - cholera

cholerisch /koˈleːrɪʃ/ *a* irascible

Cholesterin /ço-, koleste'riːn/ *nt* **-s** cholesterol

Chor /koːɐ̯/ *m* **-[e]s,ˆe** choir; (*Theat*) chorus; **im C~** in chorus

Choral /koˈraːl/ *m* **-[e]s,ˆe** chorale

Choreographie /koreograˈfiː/ *f* -,**-n** choreography

Chor|knabe /'koːɐ̯-/ *m* choirboy. **C~musik** *f* choral music

Christ /krɪst/ *m* **-en,-en** Christian. **C~baum** *m* Christmas tree. **C~entum** *nt* **-s** Christianity. **C~in** *f* -,**-nen** Christian. **C~kind** *nt* Christ-child; (*als Geschenkbringer*) ≈ Father Christmas. **c~lich** *a* Christian

Christus /'krɪstʊs/ *m* **-ti** Christ

Chrom /kroːm/ *nt* **-s** chromium

Chromosom /kromo'zoːm/ *nt* **-s,-en** chromosome

Chronik /'kroːnɪk/ *f* -,**-en** chronicle

chron|isch /'kroːnɪʃ/ *a* chronic, *adv* -ally. **c~ologisch** *a* chronological, *adv* -ly

Chrysantheme /kryzan'teːmə/ *f* -,**-n** chrysanthemum

circa /'tsɪrka/ *adv* about

Clique /'klɪkə/ *f* -,**-n** clique

Clou /kluː/ *m* **-s,-s** highlight, (*fam*) high spot

Clown /klaʊn/ *m* **-s,-s** clown. **c~en** *vi* (*haben*) clown

Club /klʊp/ *m* **-s,-s** club

Cocktail /'kɔkteːl/ *m* **-s,-s** cocktail

Code /koːt/ *m* **-s,-s** code

Cola /'koːla/ *f* -,- (*fam*) Coke (P)

Comic-Heft /'kɔmɪk-/ *nt* comic

Computer /kɔm'pjuːtɐ/ *m* **-s,-** computer. **c~isieren** *vt* computerize

Conférencier /kõferã'sje:/ *m* **-s,-s** compère

Cord /kɔrt/ *m* **-s**, **C~samt** *m* corduroy. **C~[samt]hose** *f* cords *pl*

Couch /kaʊtʃ/ *f* -,**-es** settee. **C~tisch** *m* coffee-table

Coupon /ku'põː/ *m* **-s,-s** = **Kupon**

Cousin /ku'zɛ̃:/ *m* **-s,-s** [male] cousin. **C~e** /-'ziːnə/ *f* -,**-n** [female] cousin

Creme /kreːm/ *f* **-s,-s** cream; (*Speise*) cream dessert. **c~farben** *a* cream

cremig /'kreːmɪç/ *a* creamy

Curry /'kari, 'kœri/ *nt & m* **-s** curry powder ● *nt* **-s,-s** (*Gericht*) curry

D

da *adv* there; (*hier*) here; (*zeitlich*) then; (*in dem Fall*) in that case; **von da an** from then on ● *conj* as, since

dabehalten† *vt sep* keep there

dabei (*emphatic:* **dabei**) *adv* nearby; (*daran*) with it; (*eingeschlossen*) included; (*hinsichtlich*) about it; (*während*) during this; (*gleichzeitig*) at the same time; (*doch*) and yet; **dicht d~** close by; **d~ bleiben** (*fig*) remain adamant; **was ist denn d~?** (*fam*) so what? **d~sein†** *vi sep* (*sein*) be present; (*mitmachen*) be involved; **d~sein, etw zu tun** be just doing sth

dableiben† *vi sep* (*sein*) stay there

Dach *nt* **-[e]s,ˆer** roof. **D~boden** *m* loft. **D~gepäckträger** *m* roof-rack. **D~kammer** *f* attic room. **D~luke** *f* skylight. **D~rinne** *f* gutter

Dachs *m* **-es,-e** badger

Dach|sparren *m* **-s,-** rafter. **D~ziegel** *m* [roofing] tile

Dackel *m* **-s,-** dachshund

dadurch (*emphatic:* **dadurch**) *adv* through it/them; (*Ursache*) by it; (*deshalb*) because of that; **d~, daß** because

dafür (*emphatic:* **dafür**) *adv* for it/them; (*anstatt*) instead; (*als Ausgleich*) but [on the other hand]; **d~, daß** considering that. **d~können†** *vi sep* (*haben*) **ich kann nichts dafür** it's not my fault

dagegen (*emphatic:* **dagegen**) *adv* against it/them; (*Mittel, Tausch*) for it; (*verglichen damit*) by comparison; (*jedoch*) however; **hast du was d~?** do you mind? **d~halten†** *vt sep* argue (*daß* that)

daheim *adv* at home

daher (*emphatic:* **daher**) *adv* from there; (*deshalb*) for that reason; **das**

kommt d~, weil that's because; d~ meine Eile hence my hurry ● *conj* that is why

dahin (*emphatic:* **dahin**) *adv* there; **bis d~** up to there; (*bis dann*) until/(*Zukunft*) by then; **jdn d~ bringen, daß er etw tut** get s.o. to do sth; **d~ sein** (*fam*) be gone. **d~gehen†** *vi sep* (*sein*) walk along; (*Zeit:*) pass. **d~gestellt** *a* **d~gestellt lassen** (*fig*) leave open; **das bleibt d~gestellt** that remains to be seen

dahinten *adv* back there

dahinter (*emphatic:* **dahinter**) *adv* behind it/them. **d~kommen†** *vi sep* (*sein*) (*fig*) get to the bottom of it

Dahlie /-jə/ *f -,-n* dahlia

dalassen *vt sep* leave there

daliegen† *vi sep* (*haben*) lie there

damalig *a* at that time; **der d~e Minister** the then minister

damals *adv* at that time

Damast *m -es,-e* damask

Dame *f -,-n* lady; (*Karte, Schach*) queen; (*D~spiel*) draughts *sg*, (*Amer*) checkers *sg*, (*Doppelstein*) king. **D~n-pref** ladies'/lady's ... **d~nhaft** *a* ladylike

damit (*emphatic:* **damit**) *adv* with it/them; (*dadurch*) by it; **hör auf d~!** stop it! ● *conj* so that

dämlich *a* (*fam*) stupid, *adv* -ly

Damm *m -[e]s,-̈e* dam; (*Insel-*) causeway; **nicht auf dem D~** (*fam*) under the weather

dämmer|ig *a* dim; **es wird d~ig** dusk is falling. **D~licht** *nt* twilight. **d~n** *vi* (*haben*) (*Morgen:*) dawn; **der Abend d~t** dusk is falling; **es d~t** it is getting light/(*abends*) dark. **D~ung** *f -* dawn; (*Abend-*) dusk

Dämon *m -s,-en* /-'mo:nən/ demon

Dampf *m -[e]s,-̈e* steam; (*Chem*) vapour. **d~en** *vi* (*haben*) steam

dämpfen *vt* (*Culin*) steam; (*fig*) muffle (*Ton*); lower (*Stimme*); dampen (*Enthusiasmus*)

Dampf|er *m -s,-* steamer. **D~kochtopf** *m* pressure-cooker. **D~maschine** *f* steam engine. **D~walze** *f* steamroller

Damwild *nt* fallow deer *pl*

danach (*emphatic:* **danach**) *adv* after it/them; (*suchen*) for it/them; (*riechen*) of it; (*später*) afterwards; (*entsprechend*) accordingly; **es sieht d~ aus** it looks like it

Däne *m -n,-n* Dane

daneben (*emphatic:* **daneben**) *adv* beside it/them; (*außerdem*) in addition; (*verglichen damit*) by comparison. **d~gehen†** *vi sep* (*sein*) miss; (*scheitern*) fail

Dän|emark *nt -s* Denmark. **D~in** *f -,-nen* Dane. **d~isch** *a* Danish

Dank *m -es* thanks *pl*; **vielen D~!** thank you very much! **d~** *prep* (+ *dat or gen*) thanks to. **d~bar** *a* grateful, *adv* -ly; (*erleichtert*) thankful, *adv* -ly; (*lohnend*) rewarding. **D~barkeit** *f -* gratitude. **d~e** *adv* **d~e** [**schön** *od* **sehr**]! thank you [very much]! [**nein**] **d~e!** no thank you! **d~en** *vi* (*haben*) thank (**jdm** s.o.); (*ablehnen*) decline; **ich d~e!** no thank you! **nichts zu d~en!** don't mention it!

dann *adv* then; **d~ und wann** now and then; **nur/selbst d~, wenn** only/even if

daran (*emphatic:* **daran**) *adv* on it/them; at it/them; (*denken*) of it; **nahe d~** on the point (**etw zu tun** of doing sth); **denkt d~!** remember! **d~gehen†** *vi sep* (*sein*), **d~machen** (**sich**) *vr sep* set about (**etw zu tun** doing sth). **d~setzen** *vt sep* **alles d~setzen** do one's utmost (**zu** to)

darauf (*emphatic:* **darauf**) *adv* on it/them; (*warten*) for it; (*antworten*) to it; (*danach*) after that; (*d~hin*) as a result; **am Tag d~** the day after. **d~folgend** *a* following. **d~hin** *adv* as a result

daraus (*emphatic:* **daraus**) *adv* out of or from it/them; **er macht sich nichts d~** he doesn't care for it; **was ist d~ geworden?** what has become of it?

Darbietung *f -,-en* performance; (*Nummer*) item

darin (*emphatic:* **darin**) *adv* in it/them

darlegen *vt sep* expound; (*erklären*) explain

Darlehen *nt -s,-* loan

Darm *m -[e]s,-̈e* intestine; (*Wurst-*) skin. **D~grippe** *f* gastric flu

darstell|en *vt sep* represent; (*bildlich*) portray; (*Theat*) interpret; (*spielen*) play; (*schildern*) describe. **D~er** *m -s,-* actor. **D~erin** *f -,-nen* actress. **D~ung** *f* representation; interpretation; description; (*Bericht*) account

darüber (*emphatic:* **darüber**) *adv* over it/them; (*höher*) above it/them; (*sprechen, lachen, sich freuen*) about it;

(*mehr*) more; (*inzwischen*) in the meantime; **d~ hinaus** beyond [it]; (*dazu*) on top of that

darum (*emphatic:* **darum**) *adv* round it/them; (*bitten, kämpfen*) for it; (*deshalb*) that is why; **d~, weil** because

darunter (*emphatic:* **darunter**) *adv* under it/them; (*tiefer*) below it/them; (*weniger*) less; (*dazwischen*) among them

das *def art & pron s.* **der**

dasein† *vi sep (sein)* be there/(*hier*) here; (*existieren*) exist; **wieder d~** be back; **noch nie dagewesen** unprecedented. **D~** *nt* **-s** existence

dasitzen† *vi sep (haben)* sit there

dasjenige *pron s.* **derjenige**

daß *conj* that; **daß du nicht fällst!** mind you don't fall!

dasselbe *pron s.* **derselbe**

dastehen† *vi sep (haben)* stand there; **allein d~** (*fig*) be alone

Daten|sichtgerät *nt* visual display unit, VDU. **D~verarbeitung** *f* data processing

datieren *vt/i (haben)* date

Dativ *m* **-s,-e** dative. **D~objekt** *nt* indirect object

Dattel *f* **-,-n** date

Datum *nt* **-s,-ten** date; **Daten** (*Angaben*) data

Dauer *f* - duration, length; (*Jur*) term; **von D~** lasting; **auf die D~** in the long run. **D~auftrag** *m* standing order. **d~haft** *a* lasting, enduring; (*fest*) durable. **D~karte** *f* season ticket. **D~lauf** *m* **im D~lauf** at a jog. **D~milch** *f* long-life milk. **d~n** *vi (haben)* last; **lange d~n** take a long time. **d~nd** *a* lasting; (*ständig*) constant, *adv* -ly; **d~nd fragen** keep asking. **D~stellung** *f* permanent position. **D~welle** *f* perm. **D~wurst** *f* salami-type sausage

Daumen *m* **-s,-** thumb; **jdm den D~ drücken** *od* **halten** keep one's fingers crossed for s.o.

Daunen *fpl* down *sg.* **D~decke** *f* [down-filled] duvet

davon (*emphatic:* **davon**) *adv* from it/ them; (*dadurch*) by it; (*damit*) with it/them; (*darüber*) about it; (*Menge*) of it/them; **die Hälfte d~** half of it/ them; **das kommt d~!** it serves you right! **d~kommen†** *vi sep (sein)* escape (**mit dem Leben** with one's life). **d~laufen†** *vi sep (sein)* run away. **d~machen (sich)** *vr sep (fam)* make

off. **d~tragen†** *vt sep* carry off; (*erleiden*) suffer; (*gewinnen*) win

davor (*emphatic:* **davor**) *adv* in front of it/them; (*sich fürchten*) of it; (*zeitlich*) before it/them

dazu (*emphatic:* **dazu**) *adv* to it/them; (*damit*) with it/them; (*dafür*) for it; **noch d~** in addition to that; **jdn d~ bringen, etw zu tun** get s.o. to do sth; **ich kam nicht d~** I didn't get round to [doing] it. **d~gehören** *vi sep (haben)* belong to it/them; **alles, was d~gehört** everything that goes with it. **d~kommen†** *vi sep (sein)* arrive [on the scene]; (*hinzukommen*) be added; **d~ kommt, daß er krank ist** on top of that he is ill. **d~rechnen** *vt sep* add to it/them

dazwischen (*emphatic:* **dazwischen**) *adv* between them; in between; (*darunter*) among them. **d~fahren†** *vi sep (sein)* (*fig*) intervene. **d~kommen†** *vi sep (sein)* (*fig*) crop up; **wenn nichts d~kommt** if all goes well. **d~reden** *vi sep (haben)* interrupt. **d~treten†** *vi sep (sein)* (*fig*) intervene

DDR *f* - *abbr* (**Deutsche Demokratische Republik**) GDR

Debatte *f* **-,-n** debate; **zur D~te stehen** be at issue. **d~tieren** *vt/i (haben)* debate

Debüt /de'by:/ *nt* **-s,-s** début

dechiffrieren /deʃi'fri:rən/ *vt* decipher

Deck *nt* **-[e]s,-s** (*Naut*) deck; **an D~** on deck. **D~bett** *nt* duvet

Decke *f* **-,-n** cover; (*Tisch-*) table-cloth; (*Bett-*) blanket; (*Reise-*) rug; (*Zimmer-*) ceiling; **unter einer D~ stecken** (*fam*) be in league

Deckel *m* **-s,-** lid; (*Flaschen-*) top; (*Buch-*) cover

decken *vt* cover; tile (*Dach*); lay (*Tisch*); (*schützen*) shield; (*Sport*) mark; meet (*Bedarf*); **jdn d~** (*fig*) cover up for s.o.; **sich d~** (*fig*) cover oneself (**gegen** against); (*übereinstimmen*) coincide

Deck|mantel *m* (*fig*) pretence. **D~name** *m* pseudonym

Deckung *f* - (*Mil*) cover; (*Sport*) defence; (*Mann-*) marking; (*Boxen*) guard; (*Sicherheit*) security; **in D~ gehen** take cover

Defekt *m* **-[e]s,-e** defect. **d~** *a* defective

defensiv *a* defensive. **D~e** *f* - defensive

defilieren *vi (sein/haben)* file past

defin|ieren *vt* define. **D~ition** /-'tsjo:n/ *f* -,-en definition. **d~itiv** *a* definite, *adv* -ly

Defizit *nt* -s,-e deficit

Deflation /-'tsjo:n/ *f* - deflation

deformiert *a* deformed

deftig *a (fam) ⟨Mahlzeit⟩* hearty; *⟨Witz⟩* coarse

Degen *m* -s,- sword; *(Fecht-)* épée

degenerier|en *vi (sein)* degenerate. **d~ta** *(fig)* degenerate

degradieren *vt (Mil)* demote; *(fig)* degrade

dehn|bar *a* elastic. **d~en** *vt* stretch; lengthen *⟨Vokal⟩*; **sich d~en** stretch

Deich *m* -[e]s,-e dike

Deichsel *f* -,-n pole; *(Gabel-)* shafts *pl*

dein *poss pron* your. **d~e(r,s)** *poss pron* yours; **die D~en** *pl* your family *sg*. **d~erseits** *adv* for your part. **d~etwegen** *adv* for your sake; *(wegen dir)* because of you, on your account. **d~etwillen** *adv* **um d~etwillen** for your sake. **d~ige** *poss pron* **der/die/das d~ige** yours. **d~s** *poss pron* yours

Deka *nt* -[s],- *(Aust)* = **Dekagramm**

dekaden|t *a* decadent. **D~z** *f* - decadence

Dekagramm *nt (Aust)* 10 grams; **10 D~** 100 grams

Dekan *m* -s,-e dean

Deklin|ation /-'tsjo:n/ *f* -,-en declension. **d~ieren** *vt* decline

Dekolleté /dekɔl'te:/ *nt* -s,-s low neckline

Dekor *m* & *nt* -s decoration. **D~ateur** /-'tø:ɐ/ *m* -s,-e interior decorator; *(Schaufenster-)* window-dresser. **D~ation** /-'tsjo:n/ *f* -,-en decoration; *(Schaufenster-)* window-dressing; *(Auslage)* display; **D~ationen** *(Theat)* scenery *sg*. **d~ativ** *a* decorative. **d~ieren** *vt* decorate; dress *⟨Schaufenster⟩*

Deleg|ation /-'tsjo:n/ *f* -,-en delegation. **d~ieren** *vt* delegate. **D~ierte(r)** *m/f* delegate

delikat *a* delicate; *(lecker)* delicious; *(taktvoll)* tactful, *adv* -ly. **D~esse** *f* -,-n delicacy. **D~essengeschäft** *nt* delicatessen

Delikt *nt* -[e]s,-e offence

Delinquent *m* -en,-en offender

Delirium *nt* -s delirium

Delle *f* -,-n dent

Delphin *m* -s,-e dolphin

Delta *nt* -s,-s delta

dem *def art & pron s*. **der**

Dement|i *nt* -s,-s denial. **d~ieren** *vt* deny

dem|entsprechend *a* corresponding; *(passend)* appropriate ● *adv* accordingly; *(passend)* appropriately. **d~gemäß** *adv* accordingly. **d~nach** *adv* according to that; *(folglich)* consequently. **d~nächst** *adv* soon; *(in Kürze)* shortly

Demokrat *m* -en,-en democrat. **D~ie** *f* -,-n democracy. **d~isch** *a* democratic, *adv* -ally

demolieren *vt* wreck

Demonstr|ant *m* -en,-en demonstrator. **D~ation** /-'tsjo:n/ *f* -,-en demonstration. **d~ativ** *a* pointed, *adv* -ly; *(Gram)* demonstrative. **D~ativpronomen** *nt* demonstrative pronoun. **d~ieren** *vt/i (haben)* demonstrate

demontieren *vt* dismantle

demoralisieren *vt* demoralize

Demoskopie *f* - opinion research

Demut *f* - humility

demütig *a* humble, *adv* -bly. **d~en** *vt* humiliate; **sich d~en** humble oneself. **D~ung** *f* -,-en humiliation

demzufolge *adv* = **demnach**

den *def art & pron s*. **der**. **d~en** *pron s*. **der**

denk|bar *a* conceivable. **d~en†** *vt/i (haben)* think **(an**+ *acc* of); *(sich erinnern)* remember **(an etw** *acc* sth); **für jdn gedacht** meant for s.o.; **das kann ich mir d~en** I can imagine [that]; **ich d~e nicht daran** I have no intention of doing it; **d~t daran!** don't forget! **D~mal** *nt* memorial; *(Monument)* monument. **d~würdig** *a* memorable. **D~zettel** *m* **jdm einen D~zettel geben** *(fam)* teach s.o. a lesson

denn *conj* for; **besser/mehr d~ je** better/more than ever ● *adv* **wie/wo d~?** but how/where? **warum d~ nicht?** why ever not? **es sei d~ [, daß]** unless

dennoch *adv* nevertheless

Denunz|iant *m* -en,-en informer. **d~ieren** *vt* denounce

Deodorant *nt* -s,-s deodorant

deplaciert /-'tsi:ɐt/ *a (fig)* out of place

Deponie *f* -,-n dump. **d~ren** *vt* deposit

deportieren vt deport

Depot /de'po:/ nt -s,-s depot; (Lager) warehouse; (Bank-) safe deposit

Depression f -,-en depression

deprimieren vt depress. **d~d** a depressing

Deputation /-'tsio:n/ f -,-en deputation

der, die, das, pl **die** def art (acc **den, die, das,** pl **die**; gen **des, der, des,** pl **der**; dat **dem, der, dem,** pl **den**) the; **der Mensch** man; **die Natur** nature; **das Leben** life; **das Lesen/Tanzen** reading/dancing; **sich** (dat) **das Gesicht/die Hände waschen** wash one's face/hands; **5 Mark das Pfund** 5 marks a pound ● pron (acc **den, die, das,** pl **die**; gen **dessen, deren, dessen,** pl **deren**; dat **dem, der, dem,** pl **denen**) ● dem pron that; (pl) those; (substantivisch) he, she, it; (Ding) it; (betont) that; (d~jenige) the one; (pl) they, those; (Dinge) those; (diejenigen) the ones; **der und der** such and such, **um die und die Zeit** at such and such a time; **das waren Zeiten!** those were the days! ● rel pron who; (Ding) which, that

derart adv so; (so sehr) so much. **d~ig** a such ● adv = **derart**

derb a tough; (kräftig) strong; (grob) coarse, adv -ly; (unsanft) rough, adv -ly

deren pron s. **der**

dergleichen inv a such ● pron such a thing/such things; **nichts d~** nothing of the kind; **und d~** and the like

der-/die-/dasjenige, pl **diejenigen** pron the one; (Person) he, she; (Ding) it; (pl) those, the ones

dermaßen adv = **derart**

der-/die-/dasselbe, pl **dieselben** pron the same; **ein- und dasselbe** one and the same thing

derzeit adv at present

des def art s. **der**

Desert|eur /-'tø:ɐ/ m -s,-e deserter. **d~ieren** vi (sein/haben) desert

desgleichen adv likewise ● pron the like

deshalb adv for this reason; (also) therefore

Designer(in) /di'zaɪnɐ, -nərɪn/ m -s,- (f-,-nen) designer

Desin|fektion /dɛs?ɪnfɛk'tsio:n/ f - disinfecting. **D~fektionsmittel** nt disinfectant. **d~fizieren** vt disinfect

Desodorant nt -s,-s deodorant

Despot m -en,-en despot

dessen pron s. **der**

Dessert /dɛ'se:ɐ/ nt -s,-s dessert, sweet. **D~löffel** m dessertspoon

Destill|ation /-'tsio:n/ f - distillation. **d~ieren** vt distil

desto adv je mehr/eher, **d~** besser the more/sooner the better

destruktiv a (fig) destructive

deswegen adv = **deshalb**

Detail /de'taɪ/ nt -s,-s detail

Detektiv m -s,-e detective. **D~roman** m detective story

Deton|ation /-'tsio:n/ f -,-en explosion. **d~ieren** vi (sein) explode

deut|en vt interpret; predict (Zukunft) ● vi (haben) point (**auf**+ acc at/(fig) to). **d~lich** a clear, adv -ly; (eindeutig) plain, adv -ly. **D~lichkeit** f - clarity

deutsch a German; **auf d~** in German. **D~** nt -[s] (Lang) German. **D~e(r)** m/f German. **D~land** nt -s Germany

Deutung f -,-en interpretation

Devise f -,-n motto. **D~n** pl foreign currency or exchange sg

Dezember m -s,- December

dezent a unobtrusive, adv -ly; (diskret) discreet, adv -ly

Dezernat nt -[e]s,-e department

Dezimal|system nt decimal system. **D~zahl** f decimal

dezimieren vt decimate

dgl. abbr s. **dergleichen**

d.h. abbr (**das heißt**) i.e.

Dia nt -s,-s (Phot) slide

Diabet|es m - diabetes. **D~iker** m -s,- diabetic

Diadem nt -s,-e tiara

Diagnos|e f -,-n diagnosis. **d~tizieren** vt diagnose

diagonal a diagonal, adv -ly. **D~e** f -,-n diagonal

Diagramm nt -s,-e diagram; (Kurven-) graph

Diakon m -s,-e deacon

Dialekt m -[e]s,-e dialect

Dialog m -[e]s,-e dialogue

Diamant m -en,-en diamond

Diameter m -s,- diameter

Diapositiv nt -s,-e (Phot) slide

Diaprojektor m slide projector

Diät f -,-en (Med) diet. **d~** adv **d~ leben** be on a diet. **D~assistent(in)** m(f) dietician

dich pron (acc of **du**) you; (refl) yourself

dicht a dense; (dick) thick; (undurchlässig) airtight; (wasser-) watertight ● adv densely; thickly; (nahe)

close (**bei** to). **D~e** f - density. **d~en¹**
vt make watertight; (ab-) seal

dicht|en² vi (haben) write poetry. ● vt
write, compose. **D~er(in)** m -s,- (f
-,-nen) poet. **d~erisch** a poetic.
D~ung f -,-en poetry; (Gedicht) poem

Dichtung² f -,-en seal; (Ring) washer;
(Auto) gasket

dick a thick, adv -ly; (beleibt) fat; (geschwollen) swollen; (fam: eng) close;
d~ werden get fat; **d~ machen** be
fattening; **ein d~es Fell haben** (fam)
be thick-skinned. **D~e** f -,-n thick-
ness; (D~leibigkeit) fatness. **d~fellig**
a (fam) thick-skinned. **d~flüssig**
a thick; (Phys) viscous. **D~kopf**
m (fam) stubborn person; **einen
D~kopf haben** be stubborn. **d~-
köpfig** a (fam) stubborn

didaktisch a didactic

die def art & pron s. **der**

Dieb|(in) m -[e]s,-e (f -,-nen) thief.
d~isch a thieving; ⟨Freude⟩ malicious. **D~stahl** m -[e]s,ˆe theft;
(geistiger) plagiarism

diejenige pron s. **derjenige**

Diele f -,-n floorboard; (Flur) hall

dien|en vi (haben) serve. **D~er** m -s,-
servant; (Verbeugung) bow. **D~erin** f
-,-nen maid, servant. **d~lich** a helpful

Dienst m -[e]s,-e service; (Arbeit)
work; (Amtsausübung) duty; **außer D~**
off duty; (pensioniert) retired; **D~
haben** be on duty; ⟨Soldat, Arzt:⟩ be on duty;
jdm einen schlechten D~ erweisen
do s.o. a disservice

Dienstag m Tuesday. **d~s** adv on
Tuesdays

Dienst|alter nt seniority. **d~bereit**
a obliging; ⟨Apotheke⟩ open. **D~bote**
m servant. **d~eifrig** a zealous, adv -
ly. **d~frei** a; **~freier Tag** day off;
d~frei haben have time off; ⟨Soldat,
Arzt:⟩ be off duty. **D~grad** m rank.
d~habend a duty ... **D~leistung** f
service. **d~lich** a official ● adv
d~lich verreist away on business.
D~mädchen nt maid. **D~reise** f
business trip. **D~stelle** f office.
D~stunden fpl office hours.
D~weg m official channels pl

dies inv pron this. **d~bezüglich** a
relevant ● adv regarding this
matter. **d~e(r,s)** pron this; (pl)
these; (substantivisch) this [one];
(pl) these; **d~e Nacht** tonight; (letzte)
last night

Diesel m -[s],- (fam) diesel

dieselbe pron s. **derselbe**

Diesel|kraftstoff m diesel [oil].
D~motor m diesel engine

diesig a hazy, misty

dies|mal adv this time. **d~seits** adv
& prep (+ gen) this side (of)

Dietrich m -s,-e skeleton key

Diffam|ation /-'tsjo:n/ f - defama-
tion. **d~ierend** a defamatory

Differential /-'tsja:l/ nt -s,-e
differential

Differenz f -,-en difference. **d~ieren**
vt/i (haben) differentiate (zwischen
+ dat between)

Digital- pref digital. **D~uhr** f digital
clock/watch

Dikt|at nt -[e]s,-e dictation. **D~ator**
m -s,-en /-'to:rən/ dictator. **d~a-
torisch** a dictatorial. **D~atur** f -,-en
dictatorship. **d~ieren** vt/i (haben)
dictate

Dilemma nt -s,-s dilemma

Dilettant|(in) m -en,-en (f -,-nen)
dilettante. **d~isch** a amateurish

Dill m -s dill

Dimension f -,-en dimension

Ding nt -[e]s,-e & (fam) -er thing;
guter D~e sein be cheerful; **vor allen
D~en** above all

Dinghi /'dıŋgi/ nt -s,-s dinghy

Dinosaurier /-ie/ m -s,- dinosaur

Diözese f -,-en diocese

Diphtherie f - diphtheria

Diplom nt -s,-e diploma; (Univ) degree

Diplomat m -en,-en diplomat. **D~ie** f
- diplomacy. **d~isch** a diplomatic,
adv -ally

dir pron (dat of du) [to] you; (refl)
yourself; **ein Freund von dir** a friend of
yours

direkt a direct ● adv directly;
(wirklich) really. **d~ion** /-'tsjo:n/ f -
management; (Vorstand) board of directors. **D~or** m -s,-en /-'to:rən/,
D~orin f -,-nen director; (Bank-,
Theater-) manager; (Sch) head; (Gefängnis) governor. **D~übertragung** f live
transmission

Dirig|ent m -en,-en (Mus) conductor.
d~ieren vt direct; (Mus) conduct

Dirndl nt -s,- dirndl [dress]

Dirne f -,-n prostitute

Diskant m -s,-e (Mus) treble

Diskette f -,-n floppy disc

Disko f -,-s (fam) disco. **D~thek** f
-,-en discothèque

Diskrepanz f -,-en discrepancy

diskret *a* discreet, *adv* -ly. **D~ion**
/-'tsjo:n/ *f* - discretion
diskriminier|en *vt* discriminate
against. **D~ung** *f* - discrimination
Diskus *m* -,-se & **Disken** discus
Disku|ssion *f* -,-en discussion. **d~
tieren** *vt/i (haben)* discuss
disponieren *vi (haben)* make ar-
rangements; **d~ [können] über**
(+ *acc*) have at one's disposal
Disput *m* -[e]s,-e dispute
Disqualifi|kation /-'tsjo:n/ *f* dis-
qualification. **d~zieren** *vt* dis-
qualify
Dissertation /-'tsjo:n/ *f* -,-en dissertation
Dissident *m* -en,-en dissident
Dissonanz *f* -,-en dissonance
Distanz *f* -,-en distance. **d~ieren
(sich)** *vr* dissociate oneself **(von**
from). **d~iert** *a* aloof
Distel *f* -,-n thistle
distinguiert /dıstıŋ'gi:ɐt/ *a* distinguished
Disziplin *f* -,-en discipline. **d~arisch**
a disciplinary. **d~iert** *a* disciplined
dito *adv* ditto
diverse *attrib a pl* various
Divid|ende *f* -,-n dividend. **d~ieren**
vt divide **(durch** by)
Division *f* -,-en division
DJH *abbr* **(Deutsche Jugend-
herberge)** [German] youth hostel
DM *abbr* **(Deutsche Mark)** DM
doch *conj & adv* but; *(dennoch)* yet;
(trotzdem) after all; **wenn d~ ...!** if
only ...! **nicht d~!** don't [do that]! **er
kommt d~?** he is coming, isn't he?
kommst du nicht?— d~! aren't you
coming?—yes, I am!
Docht *m* -[e]s,-e wick
Dock *nt* -s,-s dock. **d~en** *vt/i (haben)*
dock
Dogge *f* -,-n Great Dane
Dogm|a *nt* -s,-men dogma. **d~atisch**
a dogmatic, *adv* -ally
Dohle *f* -,-n jackdaw
Doktor *m* -s,-en /-'to:rən/ doctor.
D~arbeit *f* [doctoral] thesis.
D~würde *f* doctorate
Doktrin *f* -,-en doctrine
Dokument *nt* -[e]s,-e document.
D~arbericht *m* documentary.
D~arfilm *m* documentary film
Dolch *m* -[e]s,-e dagger
doll *a (fam)* fantastic; *(schlimm)*
awful ● *adv* beautifully; *(sehr)* very;
(schlimm) badly

Dollar *m* -s,- dollar
dolmetsch|en *vt/i (haben)* inter-
pret. **D~er(in)** *m* -s,- *(f* -,-nen) inter-
preter
Dom *m* -[e]s,-e cathedral
domin|ant *a* dominant. **d~ieren** *vi*
(haben) dominate; *(vorherrschen)*
predominate
Domino *nt* -s,-s dominoes *sg*.
D~stein *m* domino
Dompfaff *m* -en,-en bullfinch
Donau *f* - Danube
Donner *m* -s thunder. **d~n** *vi (haben)*
thunder
Donnerstag *m* Thursday. **d~s** *adv*
on Thursdays
Donnerwetter *nt (fam)* telling-off;
(Krach) row ● *int* /'--'--/ wow! *(Fluch)*
damn it!
doof *a (fam)* stupid, *adv* -ly
Doppel *nt* -s,- duplicate; *(Tennis)*
doubles *pl*. **D~bett** *nt* double bed.
D~decker *m* -s,- double-decker [bus].
d~deutig *a* ambiguous. **D~gänger**
m -s,- double. **D~kinn** *nt* double chin.
D~name *m* double-barrelled name.
D~punkt *m (Gram)* colon. **D~
schnitte** *f* sandwich. **d~sinnig** *a*
ambiguous. **D~stecker** *m* two-way
adaptor. **d~t** *a* double; *(Boden)* false;
in d~ter Ausfertigung in duplicate;
die d~te Menge twice the amount
● *adv* doubly; *(zweimal)* twice; **d~t so
viel** twice as much. **D~zimmer** *nt*
double room
Dorf *nt* -[e]s,¨er village. **D~be-
wohner** *m* villager
dörflich *a* rural
Dorn *m* -[e]s,-en thorn. **d~ig** *a*
thorny
Dörrobst *nt* dried fruit
Dorsch *m* -[e]s,-e cod
dort *adv* there; **d~ drüben** over there.
d~her *adv* [von] **d~her** from there.
d~hin *adv* there. **d~ig** *a* local
Dose *f* -,-n tin, can; *(Schmuck-)* box
dösen *vi (haben)* doze
Dosen|milch *f* evaporated milk.
D~öffner *m* tin or can opener
dosieren *vt* measure out
Dosis *f* -, **Dosen** dose
Dotter *m & nt* -s,- [egg] yolk
Dozent(in) *m* -en,-en *(f* -,-nen) *(Univ)*
lecturer
Dr. *abbr* **(Doktor)** Dr
Drache *m* -n,-n dragon. **D~n** *m* -s,-
kite; *(fam: Frau)* dragon. **D~nfliegen**

nt hang-gliding. **D~nflieger** *m* hang-glider

Draht *m* -[e]s,̈-e wire; **auf D~** (*fam*) on the ball. **d~ig** *a* (*fig*) wiry. **D~seilbahn** *f* cable railway

drall *a* plump; (*Frau*) buxom

Dram|a *nt* -s,-men drama. **D~atik** *f* - drama. **D~atiker** *m* -s,- dramatist. **d~atisch** *a* dramatic, *adv* -ally. **d~atisieren** *vt* dramatize

dran *adv* (*fam*) = **daran**; **gut/schlecht d~ sein** be well off/in a bad way; **ich bin d~** it's my turn

Dränage /-'na:ʒə/ *f* - drainage

Drang *m* -[e]s urge; (*Druck*) pressure

dräng|eln *vt/i* (*haben*) push; (*bedrängen*) pester. **d~en** *vt* push; (*bedrängen*) urge; **sich d~en** crowd (**um** round) ● *vi* (*haben*) push; (*eilen*) be urgent; (*Zeit:*) press; **d~en auf** (+*acc*) press for

dran|halten† (**sich**) *vr sep* hurry. **d~kommen†** *vi sep* (*sein*) have one's turn; **wer kommt dran?** whose turn is it?

drapieren *vt* drape

drastisch *a* drastic, *adv* -ally

drauf *adv* (*fam*) = **darauf**; **d~ und dran sein** be on the point (**etw zu tun** of doing sth). **D~gänger** *m* -s,- daredevil. **d~gängerisch** *a* reckless

draus *adv* (*fam*) = **daraus**

draußen *adv* outside; (*im Freien*) out of doors

drechseln *vt* (*Techn*) turn

Dreck *m* -s dirt; (*Morast*) mud; (*fam: Kleinigkeit*) trifle; **in den D~ ziehen** (*fig*) denigrate. **d~ig** *a* dirty; muddy

Dreh *m* -s (*fam*) knack; **den D~ heraushaben** have got the hang of it. **D~bank** *f* lathe. **D~bleistift** *m* propelling pencil. **D~buch** *nt* screenplay, script. **d~en** *vt* turn; (*im Kreis*) rotate; (*verschlingen*) twist; roll ⟨*Zigarette*⟩; shoot ⟨*Film*⟩; **lauter/leiser d~en** turn up/down; **sich d~en** turn; (*im Kreis*) rotate; (*schnell*) spin; ⟨*Wind:*⟩ change; **sich d~en um** revolve around; (*sich handeln*) be about ● *vi* (*haben*) turn; ⟨*Wind:*⟩ change; **an etw** (*dat*) **d~en** turn sth. **D~orgel** *f* barrel organ. **D~stuhl** *m* swivel chair. **D~tür** *f* revolving door. **D~ung** *f* -,-en turn; (*im Kreis*) rotation. **D~zahl** *f* number of revolutions

drei *inv a*, **D~** *f* -,-en three; (*Sch*) ≈ pass. **D~eck** *nt* -[e]s,-e triangle. **d~eckig** *a* triangular. **D~einigkeit** *f* - **die** [**Heilige**] **D~einigkeit** the [Holy] Trinity. **D~erlei** *inv a* three kinds of ● *pron* three things. **d~fach** *a* triple; **in d~facher Ausfertigung** in triplicate. **D~faltigkeit** *f* - = **D~einigkeit. d~mal** *adv* three times. **D~rad** *nt* tricycle

dreißig *inv a* thirty. **d~ste(r,s)** *a* thirtieth

dreist *a* impudent, *adv* -ly; (*verwegen*) audacious, *adv* -ly. **D~igkeit** *f* - impudence; audacity

dreiviertel *inv a* three-quarter. **D~stunde** *f* three-quarters of an hour

dreizehn *inv a* thirteen. **d~te(r,s)** *a* thirteenth

dreschen† *vt* thresh

dress|ieren *vt* train. **D~ur** *f* - training

dribbeln *vi* (*haben*) dribble

Drill *m* -[e]s (*Mil*) drill. **d~en** *vt* drill

Drillinge *mpl* triplets

drin *adv* (*fam*) = **darin**; (*drinnen*) inside

dring|en† *vi* (*sein*) penetrate (**in** + *acc* into; **durch etw** sth); (*heraus-*) come (**aus** out of); **d~en auf** (+ *acc*) insist on. **d~end** *a* urgent, *adv* -ly. **d~lich** *a* urgent. **D~lichkeit** *f* - urgency

Drink *m* -[s],-s [alcoholic] drink

drinnen *adv* inside; (*im Haus*) indoors

dritt *adv* **zu d~** in threes; **wir waren zu d~** there were three of us. **d~e(r,s)** *a* third; **ein D~er** a third person. **D~el** *nt* -s,- third. **d~ens** *adv* thirdly. **d~rangig** *a* third-rate

Drog|e *f* -,-n drug. **D~enabhängige(r)** *m/f* drug addict. **D~erie** *f* -,-n chemist's shop, (*Amer*) drugstore. **D~ist** *m* -en,-en chemist

drohen *vi* (*haben*) threaten (**jdm** s.o.). **d~d** *a* threatening; ⟨*Gefahr*⟩ imminent

dröhnen *vi* (*haben*) resound; (*tönen*) boom

Drohung *f* -,-en threat

drollig *a* funny; (*seltsam*) odd

Drops *m* -,- [fruit] drop

Droschke *f* -,-n cab

Drossel *f* -,-n thrush

drosseln *vt* (*Techn*) throttle; (*fig*) cut back

drüb|en *adv* over there. **d~er** *adv* (*fam*) = **darüber**

Druck¹ *m* -[e]s,̈-e pressure; **unter D~ setzen** (*fig*) pressurize

Druck² *m* -[e]s,-e printing; (*Schrift, Reproduktion*) print. **D~buchstabe** *m* block letter

Drückeberger *m* -s,- shirker

drucken *vt* print

drücken *vt/i* (*haben*) press; (*aus-*) squeeze; (*Schuh:*) pinch; (*umarmen*) hug; (*fig: belasten*) weigh down; **Preise d~** force down prices; (*an Tür*) **d~** push; **sich d~** (*fam*) make oneself scarce; **sich d~ vor** (+ *dat*) (*fam*) shirk. **d~d** *a* heavy; (*schwül*) oppressive

Drucker *m* -s,- printer

Drücker *m* -s,- push-button; (*Tür-*) door knob

Druckerei *f* -,-en printing works

Druck|fehler *m* misprint. **D~knopf** *m* press-stud; (*Drücker*) push-button. **D~luft** *f* compressed air. **D~sache** *f* printed matter. **D~schrift** *f* type; (*Veröffentlichung*) publication; **in D~schrift** in block letters *pl*

drucksen *vi* (*haben*) hum and haw

Druck|stelle *f* bruise. **D~taste** *f* push-button. **D~top~** ~pressure-cooker

drum *adv* (*fam*) = **darum**

drunter *adv* (*fam*) = **darunter**; **alles geht d~ und drüber** (*fam*) everything is topsy-turvy

Drüse *f* -,-n (*Anat*) gland

Dschungel *m* -s,- jungle

du *pron* (*familiar address*) you; **auf du und du** on familiar terms

Dübel *m* -s,- plug

duck|en *vt* duck; (*fig: demütigen*) humiliate; **sich d~en** duck; (*fig*) cringe. **D~mäuser** *m* -s,- moral coward

Dudelsack *m* bagpipes *pl*

Duell *nt* -s,-e duel

Duett *nt* -s,-e [vocal] duet

Duft *m* -[e]s,ˇe fragrance, scent; (*Aroma*) aroma. **d~en** *vi* (*haben*) smell (**nach** of). **d~ig** *a* fine; (*zart*) delicate

duld|en *vt* tolerate; (*erleiden*) suffer ● *vi* (*haben*) suffer. **d~sam** *a* tolerant

dumm *a* (**dümmer, dümmst**) stupid, *adv* -ly; (*unklug*) foolish, *adv* -ly; (*fam: lästig*) awkward; **wie d~!** what a nuisance! **der D~e sein** (*fig*) be the loser. **d~erweise** *adv* stupidly; (*leider*) unfortunately. **D~heit** *f* -,-en stupidity; (*Torheit*) foolishness; (*Handlung*) folly. **D~kopf** *m* (*fam*) fool.

dumpf *a* dull, *adv* -y; (*muffig*) musty. **d~ig** *a* musty

Düne *f* -,-n dune

Dung *m* -s manure

Düng|emittel *nt* fertilizer. **d~en** *vt* fertilize. **D~er** *m* -s,- fertilizer

dunk|el *a* dark; (*vage*) vague, *adv* -ly; (*fragwürdig*) shady; **d~les Bier** brown ale; **im D~eln** in the dark

Dünkel *m* -s conceit

dunkel|blau *a* dark blue. **d~braun** *a* dark brown

dünkelhaft *a* conceited

Dunkel|heit *f* - darkness. **D~kammer** *f* dark-room. **d~n** *vi* (*haben*) get dark. **d~rot** *a* dark red

dünn *a* thin, *adv* -ly; (*Buch*) slim; (*spärlich*) sparse; (*schwach*) weak

Dunst *m* -es,ˇe mist, haze; (*Dampf*) vapour

dünsten *vt* steam

dunstig *a* misty, hazy

Dünung *f* - swell

Duo *nt* -s,-s [instrumental] duet

Duplikat *nt* -[e]s,-e duplicate

Dur *nt* - (*Mus*) major [key]; **in A-Dur** A major

durch *prep* (+ *acc*) through; (*mittels*) by; [**geteilt**] **d~** (*Math*) divided by ● *adv* **die Nacht d~** throughout the night; **sechs Uhr d~** (*fam*) gone six o'clock; **d~ und d~ naß** wet through

durcharbeiten *vt sep* work through; **sich d~** work one's way through

durchaus *adv* absolutely; **d~ nicht** by no means

durchbeißen† *vt sep* bite through

durchblättern *vt sep* leaf through

durchblicken *vi sep* (*haben*) look through; **d~ lassen** (*fig*) hint at

Durchblutung *f* circulation

durchbohren *vt insep* pierce

durchbrechen¹† *vt/i sep* (*haben*) break [in two]

durchbrechen²† *vt insep* break through; break (*Schallmauer*)

durchbrennen† *vi sep* (*sein*) burn through; (*Sicherung:*) blow; (*fam: weglaufen*) run away

durchbringen† *vt sep* get through; (*verschwenden*) squander; (*versorgen*) support; **sich d~ mit** make a living by

Durchbruch *m* breakthrough

durchdacht *a* **gut d~** well thought out

durchdrehen *v sep* ● *vt* mince ● *vi* (*haben/sein*) (*fam*) go crazy

durchdringen[1]† vt insep penetrate

durchdringen[2]† vi sep (sein) penetrate; (sich durchsetzen) get one's way. **d~d** a penetrating; ⟨Schrei⟩ piercing

durcheinander adv in a muddle; ⟨Person⟩ confused. **D~** nt -s muddle. **d~bringen**† vt sep muddle [up]; confuse ⟨Person⟩. **d~geraten**† vi sep (sein) get mixed up. **d~reden** vi sep (haben) all talk at once

durchfahren[1]† vi sep (sein) drive through; ⟨Zug:⟩ go through

durchfahren[2]† vt insep drive/go through; **jdn d~** ⟨Gedanke:⟩ flash through s.o.'s mind

Durchfahrt f journey/drive through; **auf der D~** passing through; **'D~ verboten'** 'no thoroughfare'

Durchfall m diarrhoea; (fam: Versagen) flop. **d~en**† vi sep (sein) fall through; (fam: versagen) flop; (bei Prüfung) fail

durchfliegen[1]† vi sep (sein) fly through; (fam: durchfallen) fail

durchfliegen[2]† vt insep fly through; (lesen) skim through

durchfroren a frozen

Durchfuhr f - (Comm) transit

durchführ|bar a feasible. **d~en** vt sep carry out

Durchgang m passage; (Sport) round; **'D~ verboten'** 'no entry'. **D~sverkehr** m through traffic

durchgeben† vt sep pass through; (übermitteln) transmit; (Radio, TV) broadcast

durchgebraten a gut **d~** well done

durchgehen† v sep ● vi (sein) go through; (davonlaufen) run away; ⟨Pferd:⟩ bolt; **jdm etw d~ lassen** let s.o. get away with sth ● vt go through. **d~d** a continuous, adv -ly; **d~d geöffnet** open all day; **d~der Wagen/ Zug** through carriage/train

durchgreifen† vi sep (haben) reach through; (vorgehen) take drastic action. **d~d** a drastic

durchhalte|n† v sep (fig) ● vi (haben) hold out ● vt keep up. **D~vermögen** nt stamina

durchhängen† vi sep (haben) sag

durchkommen† vi sep (sein) come through; (gelangen, am Telefon) get through; (bestehen) pass; (überleben) pull through; (finanziell) get by (**mit** on)

durchkreuzen vt insep thwart

durchlassen† vt sep let through

durchlässig a permeable; (undicht) leaky

durchlaufen[1]† v sep ● vi (sein) run through ● vt wear out

durchlaufen[2]† vt insep pass through

Durchlauferhitzer m -s, - geyser

durchleben vt insep live through

durchlesen† vt sep read through

durchleuchten vt insep X-ray

durchlöchert a riddled with holes

durchmachen vt sep go through; (erleiden) undergo; have ⟨Krankheit⟩

Durchmesser m -s, - diameter

durchnäßt a wet through

durchnehmen† vt sep (Sch) do

durchnumeriert a numbered consecutively

durchpausen vt sep trace

durchqueren vt insep cross

Durchreiche f -, -n [serving] hatch. **d~n** vt sep pass through

Durchreise f journey through; **auf der D~** passing through. **d~n** vi sep (sein) pass through

durchreißen† vt/i sep (sein) tear

durchs adv = durch das

Durchsage f -, -n announcement. **d~n** vt sep announce

durchschauen vt insep (fig) see through

durchscheinend a translucent

Durchschlag m carbon copy; (Culin) colander. **d~en**[1]† v sep ● vt (Culin) rub through a sieve; **sich d~en** (fig) struggle through ● vi (sein) ⟨Sicherung:⟩ blow

durchschlagen[2]† vt insep smash

durchschlagend a (fig) effective; ⟨Erfolg⟩ resounding

durchschneiden† vt sep cut

Durchschnitt m average; **im D~** on average. **d~lich** a average ● adv on average. **D~s-** pref average

Durchschrift f carbon copy

durchsehen† v sep ● vi (haben) see through ● vt look through

durchseihen vt sep strain

durchsetzen[1] vt sep force through; **sich d~** assert oneself; ⟨Mode:⟩ catch on

durchsetzen[2] vt insep intersperse; (infiltrieren) infiltrate

Durchsicht f check

durchsichtig a transparent

durchsickern vi sep (sein) seep through; ⟨Neuigkeit:⟩ leak out

durchsprechen† vt sep discuss

durchstehen† *vt sep* ⟨*fig*⟩ come through

durchstreichen† *vt sep* cross out

durchsuch|en *vt insep* search. **D∼ung** *f* -,-en search

durchtrieben *a* cunning

durchwachsen *a* ⟨*Speck*⟩ streaky; ⟨*fam: gemischt*⟩ mixed

durchwacht *a* sleepless ⟨*Nacht*⟩

durchwählen *vi sep* ⟨*haben*⟩ ⟨*Teleph*⟩ dial direct

durchweg *adv* without exception

durchweicht *a* soggy

durchwühlen *vt insep* rummage through; ransack ⟨*Haus*⟩

durchziehen† *v sep* ● *vt* pull through ● *vi* ⟨*sein*⟩ pass through

durchzucken *vt insep* ⟨*fig*⟩ shoot through; **jdn d∼** ⟨*Gedanke:*⟩ flash through s.o.'s mind

Durchzug *m* through draught

dürfen† *vt & v aux etw* [tun] **d∼** be allowed to do sth; **darf ich?** may I? **sie darf es nicht sehen** she must not see it; **ich hätte es nicht tun/sagen d∼** I ought not to have done/said it; **das dürfte nicht allzu schwer sein** that should not be too difficult

dürftig *a* poor; ⟨*Mahlzeit*⟩ scanty

dürr *a* dry; ⟨*Boden*⟩ arid; ⟨*mager*⟩ skinny. **D∼e** *f* -,-n drought

Durst *m* -[e]s thirst; **D∼ haben** be thirsty. **d∼en** *vi* ⟨*haben*⟩ be thirsty. **d∼ig** *a* thirsty

Dusche *f* -,-n shower. **d∼n** *vi/r* ⟨*haben*⟩ [sich] **d∼n** have a shower

Düse *f* -,-n nozzle. **D∼nflugzeug** *nt* jet

düster *a* gloomy, *adv* -ily; ⟨*dunkel*⟩ dark

Dutzend *nt* -s,-e dozen. **d∼weise** *adv* by the dozen

duzen *vt* jdn **d∼** call s.o. 'du'

Dynam|ik *f* - dynamics *sg*; ⟨*fig*⟩ dynamism. **d∼isch** *a* dynamic; ⟨*Rente*⟩ index-linked

Dynamit *nt* -es dynamite

Dynamo *m* -s,-s dynamo

Dynastie *f* -,-n dynasty

D-Zug /'de:-/ *m* express [train]

E

Ebbe *f* -,-n low tide

eben *a* level; ⟨*glatt*⟩ smooth; **zu e∼er Erde** on the ground floor ● *adv* just; ⟨*genau*⟩ exactly; **e∼ noch** only just;

⟨*gerade vorhin*⟩ just now; **das ist es e∼!** that's just it! [na] **e∼!** exactly! **E∼bild** *nt* image. **e∼bürtig** *a* equal; **jdm e∼bürtig sein** be s.o.'s equal

Ebene *f* -,-n ⟨*Geog*⟩ plain; ⟨*Geom*⟩ plane; ⟨*fig: Niveau*⟩ level

eben|falls *adv* also; **danke, e∼falls** thank you, [the] same to you. **E∼holz** *nt* ebony. **e∼mäßig** *a* regular, *adv* -ly. **e∼so** *adv* just the same; ⟨*ebensosehr*⟩ just as much; **e∼so gut/teuer** just as good/expensive. **e∼sogut** *adv* just as well. **e∼sosehr** *adv* just as much. **e∼soviel** *adv* just as much/many. **e∼sowenig** *adv* just as little/few; ⟨*noch*⟩ no more

Eber *m* -s,- boar. **E∼esche** *f* rowan

ebnen *vt* level; ⟨*fig*⟩ smooth

Echo *nt* -s,-s echo. **e∼en** *vt/i* ⟨*haben*⟩ echo

echt *a* genuine, real; ⟨*authentisch*⟩ authentic; ⟨*Farbe*⟩ fast; ⟨*typisch*⟩ typical ● *adv* ⟨*fam*⟩ really; typically. **E∼heit** *f* - authenticity

Eck|ball *m* ⟨*Sport*⟩ corner. **E∼e** *f* -,-n corner; **um die E∼e bringen** ⟨*fam*⟩ bump off. **e∼ig** *a* angular; ⟨*Klammern*⟩ square; ⟨*unbeholfen*⟩ awkward. **E∼stein** *m* corner-stone. **E∼stoß** *m* = **E∼ball**. **E∼zahn** *m* canine tooth

Ecu, ECU /e'ky:/ *m* -[s],-[s] ecu

edel *a* noble, *adv* -bly; ⟨*wertvoll*⟩ precious; ⟨*fein*⟩ fine. **E∼mann** *m* ⟨*pl* -leute⟩ nobleman. **E∼mut** *m* magnanimity. **e∼mütig** *a* magnanimous, *adv* -ly. **E∼stahl** *m* stainless steel. **E∼stein** *m* precious stone

Efeu *m* -s ivy

Effekt *m* -[e]s,-e effect. **E∼en** *pl* securities. **e∼iv** *a* actual, *adv* -ly; ⟨*wirksam*⟩ effective, *adv* -ly. **e∼voll** *a* effective

EG *f* - *abbr* (Europäische Gemeinschaft) EC

egal *a* **das ist mir e∼** ⟨*fam*⟩ it's all the same to me ● *adv* **e∼ wie/wo** no matter how/where. **e∼itär** *a* egalitarian

Egge *f* -,-n harrow

Ego|ismus *m* - selfishness. **E∼ist(in)** *m* -en,-en ⟨*f* -,-nen⟩ egoist. **e∼istisch** *a* selfish, *adv* -ly. **e∼zentrisch** *a* egocentric

eh *adv* ⟨*Aust fam*⟩ anyway; **seit eh und je** from time immemorial

ehe *conj* before; **ehe nicht** until

Ehe *f* -,-n marriage. **E∼bett** *nt* double bed. **E∼bruch** *m* adultery. **E∼frau** *f*

wife. E∼leute pl married couple sg.
e∼lich a marital; ⟨Recht⟩ conjugal;
⟨Kind⟩ legitimate

ehemal|ig a former. e∼s adv formerly

Ehe|mann m (pl -männer) husband.
E∼paar nt married couple

eher adv earlier, sooner; (lieber,
vielmehr) rather; (mehr) more

Ehering m wedding ring

ehr|bar a respectable. E∼e f -,-n
honour; jdm E∼e machen do credit to
s.o. e∼en vt honour. e∼enamtlich a
honorary ● adv in an honorary
capacity. E∼endoktorat nt
honorary doctorate. E∼engast m
guest of honour. e∼enhaft a honourable, adv -bly. E∼enmann m (pl
-männer) man of honour. E∼enmitglied nt honorary member. e∼enrührig a defamatory. E∼enrunde
f lap of honour. E∼ensache f point
of honour. e∼enwert a honourable.
E∼enwort nt word of honour. e∼erbietig a deferential, adv -ly. E∼erbietung f - deference. E∼furcht f
reverence; ⟨Scheu⟩ awe. e∼fürchtig
a reverent, adv -ly. E∼gefühl nt
sense of honour. E∼geiz m ambition.
e∼geizig a ambitious. e∼lich a
honest, adv -ly; e∼lich gesagt to be
honest. E∼lichkeit f - honesty. e∼los
a dishonourable. e∼sam a respectable. e∼würdig a venerable;
(als Anrede) Reverend

Ei nt -[e]s,-er egg

Eibe f -,-n yew

Eiche f -,-n oak. E∼l f -,-n acorn.
E∼lhäher m -s,- jay

eichen vt standardize

Eichhörnchen nt -s,- squirrel

Eid m -[e]s,-e oath

Eidechse f -,-n lizard

eidlich a sworn ● adv on oath

Eidotter m & nt egg yolk

Eier|becher m egg-cup. E∼kuchen
m pancake; ⟨Omelett⟩ omelette. E∼schale f eggshell. E∼schnee m
beaten egg-white. E∼stock m ovary.
E∼uhr f egg-timer

Eifer m -s eagerness; ⟨Streben⟩ zeal.
E∼sucht f jealousy. e∼süchtig a
jealous, adv -ly

eiförmig a egg-shaped; (oval) oval

eifrig a eager, adv -ly; (begeistert)
keen, adv -ly

Eigelb nt -[e]s,-e [egg] yolk

eigen a own; (typisch) characteristic
(dat of); (seltsam) odd, adv -ly;
(genau) particular. E∼art f peculiarity. e∼artig a peculiar, adv -ly;
(seltsam) odd. E∼brötler m -s,- crank.
e∼händig a personal, adv
-ly; ⟨Unterschrift⟩ own. E∼heit f -,
-en peculiarity. e∼mächtig a highhanded; (unbefugt) unauthorized
● adv high-handedly; without authority. E∼name m proper name.
E∼nutz m self-interest. e∼nützig a
selfish, adv -ly. e∼s adv specially.
E∼schaft f -,-en quality; ⟨Phys⟩ property; (Merkmal) characteristic;
(Funktion) capacity. E∼schaftswort
nt (pl -wörter) adjective. E∼sinn m
obstinacy. e∼sinnig a obstinate,
adv -ly

eigentlich a actual, real; (wahr) true
● adv actually, really; (streng genommen) strictly speaking; wie geht es
ihm e∼? by the way, how is he?

Eigen|tor nt own goal. E∼tum nt
-s property. E∼tümer(in) m -s,- (f
-,-nen) owner. e∼tümlich a odd, adv
-ly; (typisch) characteristic. E∼tumswohnung f freehold flat. e∼willig a self-willed; ⟨Stil⟩ highly
individual

eign|en (sich) vr be suitable. E∼ung
f - suitability

Eil|brief m express letter. E∼e f -
hurry; E∼e haben be in a hurry;
⟨Sache:⟩ be urgent. e∼en vi (sein)
hurry ● (haben) (drängen) be urgent.
e∼ends adv hurriedly. e∼ig a hurried, adv -ly; (dringend) urgent, adv -
ly; es e∼ig haben be in a hurry. E∼zug m semi-fast train

Eimer m -s,- bucket; (Abfall-) bin

ein[1] adj one; e∼es Tages/Abends
one day/evening; mit jdm in einem
Zimmer schlafen sleep in the same
room as s.o. ● indef art a, (vor Vokal)
an; so ein such a; was für ein (Frage)
what kind of a? (Ausruf) what a!

ein[2] adv ein und aus in and out; nicht
mehr ein noch aus wissen (fam) be at
one's wits' end

einander pron one another

einarbeiten vt sep train

einäscher|n vt sep reduce to ashes;
cremate ⟨Leiche⟩. E∼ung f -,-en
cremation

einatmen vt/i sep (haben) inhale,
breathe in

ein|äugig *a* one-eyed. **E~bahnstraße** *f* one-way street

einbalsamieren *vt sep* embalm

Einband *m* binding

Einbau *m* installation; (*Montage*) fitting. **e~en** *vt sep* install; (*montieren*) fit. **E~küche** *f* fitted kitchen

einbegriffen *pred a* included

einberuf|en† *vt sep* convene; (*Mil*) call up, (*Amer*) draft. **E~ung** *f* call-up, (*Amer*) draft

Einbettzimmer *nt* single room

einbeulen *vt sep* dent

einbeziehen† *vt sep* [mit] **e~** include; (*berücksichtigen*) take into account

einbiegen† *vi sep* (*sein*) turn

einbild|en *vt sep* sich (*dat*) etw **e~en** imagine sth; **sich** (*dat*) **viel e~en** be conceited. **E~ung** *f* imagination; (*Dünkel*) conceit. **E~ungskraft** *f* imagination

einblenden *vt sep* fade in

einbleuen *vt sep* **jdm etw e~** (*fam*) drum sth into s.o.

Einblick *m* insight

einbrech|en† *vi sep* (*haben/sein*) break in; **bei uns ist eingebrochen worden** we have been burgled ● (*sein*) set in; (*Nacht:*) fall. **E~er** *m* burglar

einbring|en† *vt sep* get in; bring in (*Geld*); **das bringt nichts ein** it's not worth while. **e~lich** *a* profitable

Einbruch *m* burglary; **bei E~ der Nacht** at nightfall

einbürger|n *vt sep* naturalize; **sich e~n** become established. **E~ung** *f* - naturalization

Ein|buße *f* loss (**an** + *dat* of). **e~büßen** *vt sep* lose

einchecken /-tʃɛkən/ *vt/i sep* (*haben*) check in

eindecken (sich) *vr sep* stock up

eindeutig *a* unambiguous; (*deutlich*) clear, *adv* -ly

eindicken *vt sep* (*Culin*) thicken

eindring|en† *vi sep* (*sein*) **e~en in** (+ *acc*) penetrate into; (*mit Gewalt*) force one's/(*Wasser:*) its way into; (*Mil*) invade; **auf jdn e~en** (*fig*) press s.o.; (*bittend*) plead with s.o. **e~lich** *a* urgent, *adv* -ly. **E~ling** *m* -s,-e intruder

Eindruck *m* impression; **E~ machen** impress (**auf jdn** s.o.)

eindrücken *vt sep* crush

eindrucksvoll *a* impressive

ein|e(r,s) *pron* one; (*jemand*) someone; (*man*) one, you; **e~er von uns** one of us; **es macht e~en müde** it makes you tired

einebnen *vt sep* level

eineiig *a* (*Zwillinge*) identical

eineinhalb *inv a* one and a half; **e~ Stunden** an hour and a half

Einelternfamilie *f* one-parent family

einengen *vt sep* restrict

Einer *m* -s,- (*Math*) unit. **e~** *pron s.* **eine(r,s)**. **e~lei** *inv a* ● *attrib a* one kind of; (*eintönig, einheitlich*) the same ● *pred a* (*fam*) immaterial; **es ist mir e~lei** it's all the same to me. **E~lei** *nt* -s monotony. **e~seits** *adv* on the one hand

einfach *a* simple, *adv* -ly; (*Essen*) plain; (*Faden, Fahrt, Fahrkarte*) single; **e~er Soldat** private. **E~heit** *f* - simplicity

einfädeln *vt sep* thread; (*fig: arrangieren*) arrange; **sich e~** (*Auto*) filter in

einfahr|en† *v sep* ● *vi* (*sein*) arrive; (*Zug:*) pull in ● *vt* (*Auto*) run in; **die Ernte e~en** get in the harvest. **E~t** *f* arrival; (*Eingang*) entrance, way in; (*Auffahrt*) drive; (*Autobahn-*) access road; **keine E~t** no entry

Einfall *m* idea; (*Mil*) invasion. **e~en†** *vi sep* (*sein*) collapse; (*eindringen*) invade; (*einstimmen*) join in; **jdm e~en** occur to s.o.; **sein Name fällt mir nicht ein** I can't think of his name; **was fällt ihm ein!** what does he think he is doing! **e~sreich** *a* imaginative

Einfalt *f* - naïvety

einfältig *a* simple; (*naiv*) naïve

Einfaltspinsel *m* simpleton

einfangen† *vt sep* catch

einfarbig *a* of one colour; (*Stoff, Kleid*) plain

einfass|en *vt sep* edge; set (*Edelstein*). **E~ung** *f* border, edging

einfetten *vt sep* grease

einfinden† (**sich**) *vr sep* turn up

einfließen† *vi sep* (*sein*) flow in

einflößen *vt sep* **jdm etw e~** give s.o. sips of sth; **jdm Angst e~** (*fig*) frighten s.o.

Einfluß *m* influence. **e~reich** *a* influential

einförmig *a* monotonous, *adv* -ly. **E~keit** *f* - monotony

einfried[ig]|en *vt sep* enclose. **E~ung** *f* -,-en enclosure

einfrieren† *vt/i sep* (*sein*) freeze

einfügen vt sep insert; (einschieben) interpolate; **sich e~** fit in

einfühl|en (sich) vr sep empathize (in + acc with). **e~sam** a sensitive

Einfuhr f -,-en import

einführ|en vt sep introduce; (einstecken) insert; (einweisen) initiate; (Comm) import. **e~end** a introductory. **E~ung** f introduction; (Einweisung) initiation

Eingabe f petition; (Computer) input

Eingang m entrance, way in; (Ankunft) arrival

eingebaut a built-in; (Schrank) fitted

eingeben† vt sep hand in; (einflößen) give (jdm s.o.); (Computer) feed in

eingebildet a imaginary; (überheblich) conceited

Eingeborene(r) m/f native

Eingebung f -,-en inspiration

eingedenk prep (+ gen) mindful of

eingefleischt a **e~er Junggeselle** confirmed bachelor

eingehakt adv arm in arm

eingehen† v sep ● vi (sein) come in; (ankommen) arrive; (einlaufen) shrink; (sterben) die; (Zeitung, Firma:) fold; **auf etw** (acc) **e~** go into sth; (annehmen) agree to sth ● vt enter into; contract (Ehe); make (Wette); take (Risiko). **e~d** a detailed; (gründlich) thorough, adv -ly

eingelegt a inlaid; (Culin) pickled; (mariniert) marinaded

eingemacht a (Culin) bottled

eingenommen pred a (fig) taken (von with); prejudiced (gegen against); **von sich e~** conceited

eingeschneit a snowbound

eingeschrieben a registered

Einge|ständnis nt admission. **e~stehen†** vt sep admit

eingetragen a registered

Eingeweide pl bowels, entrails

eingewöhnen (sich) vr sep settle in

eingießen† vt sep pour in; (einschenken) pour

eingleisig a single-track

einglieder|n vt sep integrate. **E~ung** f integration

eingraben† vt sep bury

eingravieren vt sep engrave

eingreifen† vi sep (haben) intervene. **E~** nt -s intervention

Eingriff m intervention; (Med) operation

einhaken vt/r sep jdn **e~** od **sich bei jdm e~** take s.o.'s arm

einhalten† v sep ● vt keep; (befolgen) observe ● vi (haben) stop

einhändigen vt sep hand in

einhängen v sep ● vt hang; put down (Hörer); **sich bei jdm e~** take s.o.'s arm ● vi (haben) hang up

einheimisch a local; (eines Landes) native; (Comm) home-produced. **E~e(r)** m/f local; native

Einheit f -,-en unity; (Maß-, Mil) unit. **e~lich** a uniform, adv -ly; (vereinheitlicht) standard. **E~spreis** m standard price; (Fahrpreis) flat fare

einhellig a unanimous, adv -ly

einholen vt sep catch up with; (aufholen) make up for; (erbitten) seek; (einkaufen) buy; **e~ gehen** go shopping

einhüllen vt sep wrap

einhundert inv a one hundred

einig a united; [**sich** (dat)] **e~ werden/sein** come to an/be in agreement

einig|e(r,s) pron some; (ziemlich viel) quite a lot of; (substantivisch) **e~e** pl some; (mehrere) several; (ziemlich viele) quite a lot; **e~es** sg some things; **vor e~er Zeit** some time ago. **e~emal** adv a few times

einigen vt unite; unify (Land); **sich e~** come to an agreement; (ausmachen) agree (auf + acc on)

einigermaßen adv to some extent; (ziemlich) fairly; (ziemlich gut) fairly well

Einig|keit f - unity; (Übereinstimmung) agreement. **E~ung** f - unification; (Übereinkunft) agreement

einjährig a one-year-old; (ein Jahr dauernd) one year's ...; **e~e Pflanze** annual

einkalkulieren vt sep take into account

einkassieren vt sep collect

Einkauf m purchase; (Einkaufen) shopping; **Einkäufe machen** do some shopping. **e~en** vt sep buy; **e~en gehen** go shopping. **E~skorb** m shopping/(im Geschäft) wire basket. **E~stasche** f shopping bag. **E~swagen** m shopping trolley. **E~szentrum** nt shopping centre

einkehren vi sep (sein) [**in einem Lokal**] **e~** stop for a meal/drink [at an inn]

einklammern vt sep bracket

Einklang m harmony; **in E~ stehen** be in accord (**mit** with)

einkleben vt sep stick in

einkleiden vt sep fit out

einklemmen vt sep clamp; **sich** (dat) **den Finger in der Tür e~** catch one's finger in the door

einkochen v sep ● vi (sein) boil down ● vt preserve, bottle

Einkommen nt **-s** income. **E~[s]-steuer** f income tax

einkreisen vt sep encircle; **rot e~** ring in red

Einkünfte pl income sg; (Einnahmen) revenue sg

einlad|en† vt sep load; (auffordern) invite; (bezahlen für) treat. **e~end** a inviting. **E~ung** f invitation

Einlage f enclosure; (Schuh-) arch support; (Zahn-) temporary filling; (Programm-) interlude; (Comm) investment; (Bank-) deposit; **Suppe mit E~** soup with noodles/ dumplings

Ein|laß m **-sses** admittance. **e~lassen†** vt sep let in; run (Bad, Wasser); **sich auf etw** (acc)/**mit jdm e~lassen** get involved in sth/with s.o.

einlaufen† vi sep (sein) come in; (ankommen) arrive; (Wasser:) run in; (schrumpfen) shrink; **[in den Hafen] e~** enter port

einleben (sich) vr sep settle in

Einlege|arbeit f inlaid work. **e~n** vt sep put in; lay in (Vorrat); lodge (Protest, Berufung); (einfügen) insert; (Auto) engage (Gang); (verzieren) inlay; (Culin) pickle; (marinieren) marinade; **eine Pause e~n** have a break. **E~sohle** f insole

einleit|en vt sep initiate; (eröffnen) begin. **e~end** a introductory. **E~ung** f introduction

einlenken vi sep (haben) (fig) relent

einleuchten vi sep (haben) be clear (dat to). **e~d** a convincing

einliefer|n vt sep take (**ins Krankenhaus** to hospital). **E~ung** f admission

einlösen vt sep cash (Scheck); redeem (Pfand); (fig) keep

einmachen vt sep preserve

einmal adv once; (eines Tages) one or some day; **noch/schon e~** again/ before; **noch e~ so teuer** twice as expensive; **auf e~** at the same time; (plötzlich) suddenly; **nicht e~** not even; **es geht nun e~ nicht** it's just not possible. **E~eins** nt - [multiplication]

tables pl. **e~ig** a single; (einzigartig) unique; (fam: großartig) fantastic, adv -ally

einmarschieren vi sep (sein) march in

einmisch|en (sich) vr sep interfere. **E~ung** f interference

einmütig a unanimous, adv -ly

Einnahme f **-,-n** taking; (Mil) capture; **E~n** pl income sg; (Einkünfte) revenue sg; (Comm) receipts; (eines Ladens) takings

einnehmen† vt sep take; have (Mahlzeit); (Mil) capture; take up (Platz); (fig) prejudice (**gegen** against); **jdn für sich e~** win s.o. over. **e~d** a engaging

einnicken vi sep (sein) nod off

Einöde f wilderness

einordnen vt sep put in its proper place; (klassifizieren) classify; **sich e~** fit in; (Auto) get in lane

einpacken vt sep pack; (einhüllen) wrap

einparken vt sep park

einpauken vt sep jdm etw e~ (fam) drum sth into s.o.

einpflanzen vt sep plant; implant (Organ)

einplanen vt sep allow for

einpräg|en vt sep impress (jdm [up]on s.o.); **sich** (dat) **etw e~en** memorize sth. **e~sam** a easy to remember; (Melodie) catchy

einquartieren vt sep (Mil) billet (**bei** on); **sich in einem Hotel e~** put up at a hotel

einrahmen vt sep frame

einrasten vi sep (sein) engage

einräumen vt sep put away; (zugeben) admit; (zugestehen) grant

einrechnen vt sep include

einreden v sep ● vt jdm/sich (dat) etw e~ persuade s.o./oneself of sth ● vi (haben) **auf jdn e~** talk insistently to s.o.

einreib|en† vt sep rub (**mit** with). **E~mittel** nt liniment

einreichen vt sep submit; **die Scheidung e~** file for divorce

Einreih|er m **-s,** - single-breasted suit. **e~ig** a single-breasted

Einreise f entry. **e~n** vi sep (sein) enter (**nach Irland** Ireland). **E~visum** nt entry visa

einreißen† v sep ● vt tear; (abreißen) pull down ● vi (sein) tear; (Sitte:) become a habit

einrenken *vt sep (Med)* set

einricht|en *vt sep* fit out; *(möblieren)* furnish; *(anordnen)* arrange; *(Med)* set *(Bruch)*; *(eröffnen)* set up; **sich e~en** furnish one's home; *(sich einschränken)* economize; *(sich vorbereiten)* prepare **(auf** + *acc* for). **E~ung** *f* furnishing; *(Möbel)* furnishings *pl*; *(Techn)* equipment; *(Vorrichtung)* device; *(Eröffnung)* setting up; *(Institution)* institution; *(Gewohnheit)* practice. **E~ungsgegenstand** *m* piece of equipment/*(Möbelstück)* furniture

einrollen *vt sep* roll up; put in rollers *(Haare)*

einrosten *vi sep (sein)* rust; *(fig)* get rusty

einrücken *v sep* ● *vi (sein) (Mil)* be called up; *(einmarschieren)* move in ● *vt* indent

eins *inv* a & *pron* one; **noch e~** one other thing; **mir ist alles e~** *(fam)* it's all the same to me. **E~** *f* -,-**en** one; *(Sch)* ≈ A

einsam a lonely; *(allein)* solitary; *(abgelegen)* isolated. **E~keit** *f* - loneliness; solitude; isolation

einsammeln *vt sep* collect

Einsatz *m* use; *(Mil)* mission; *(Wett-)* stake; *(E~teil)* insert; **im E~** in action. **e~bereit** a ready for action

einschalt|en *vt sep* switch on; *(einschieben)* interpolate; *(fig: beteiligen)* call in; **sich e~en** *(fig)* intervene. **E~quote** *f* *(TV)* viewing figures *pl*; ≈ ratings *pl*

einschärfen *vt sep* **jdm etw e~** impress sth [up]on s.o.

einschätz|en *vt sep* assess; *(bewerten)* rate. **E~ung** *f* assessment; estimation

einschenken *vt sep* pour

einscheren *vi sep (sein)* pull in

einschicken *vt sep* send in

einschieben† *vt sep* push in; *(einfügen)* insert; *(fig)* interpolate

einschiff|en (sich) *vr sep* embark. **E~ung** *f* -embarkation

einschlafen† *vi sep (sein)* go to sleep; *(aufhören)* peter out

einschläfern *vt sep* lull to sleep; *(betäuben)* put out; *(töten)* put to sleep. **e~d** a soporific

Einschlag *m* impact; *(fig: Beimischung)* element. **e~en†** *v sep* ● *vt* knock in; *(zerschlagen)* smash; *(einwickeln)* wrap; *(falten)* turn up;

(drehen) turn; take *(Weg)*; take up *(Laufbahn)* ● *vi (haben)* hit/*(Blitz:)* strike **(in etw** *acc* sth); *(zustimmen)* shake hands [on a deal]; *(Erfolg haben)* be a hit; **auf jdn e~en** beat s.o.

einschlägig a relevant

einschleusen *vt sep* infiltrate

einschließ|en† *vt sep* lock in; *(umgeben)* enclose; *(einkreisen)* surround; *(einbeziehen)* include; **sich e~en** lock oneself in; **Bedienung eingeschlossen** service included. **e~lich** *adv* inclusive ● *prep* (+ *gen*) including

einschmeicheln (sich) *vr sep* ingratiate oneself **(bei** with)

einschnappen *vi sep (sein)* click shut; **eingeschnappt sein** *(fam)* be in a huff

einschneiden† *vt/i sep (haben)* **[in] etw** *acc* cut into sth. **e~d** a *(fig)* drastic, *adv* -ally

Einschnitt *m* cut; *(Med)* incision; *(Lücke)* gap; *(fig)* decisive event

einschränk|en *vt sep* restrict; *(reduzieren)* cut back; **sich e~en** economize. **E~ung** *f* -,-en restriction; *(Reduzierung)* reduction; *(Vorbehalt)* reservation

Einschreib|[e]brief *m* registered letter. **e~en†** *vt sep* enter; register *(Brief)*; **sich e~en** put one's name down; *(sich anmelden)* enrol. **E~en** *nt* registered letter/packet; **als** *od* **per E~en** by registered post

einschreiten† *vi sep (sein)* intervene

einschüchter|n *vt sep* intimidate. **E~ung** *f* - intimidation

einsegn|en *vt sep (Relig)* confirm. **E~ung** *f* -,-en confirmation

einsehen† *vt sep* inspect; *(lesen)* consult; *(begreifen)* see. **E~** *nt* -s **ein E~ haben** show some understanding; *(vernünftig sein)* see reason

einseitig a one-sided; *(Pol)* unilateral ● *adv* on one side; *(fig)* onesidedly; *(Pol)* unilaterally

einsenden† *vt sep* send in

einsetzen *v sep* ● *vt* put in; *(einfügen)* insert; *(verwenden)* use; put on *(Zug)*; call out *(Truppen)*; *(Mil)* deploy; *(ernennen)* appoint; *(wetten)* stake; *(riskieren)* risk; **sich e~ für** support ● *vi (haben)* start; *(Winter, Regen:)* set in

Einsicht *f* insight; *(Verständnis)* understanding; *(Vernunft)* reason; **zur E~ kommen** see reason. **e~ig** a understanding; *(vernünftig)* sensible

Einsiedler *m* hermit

einsilbig *a* monosyllabic; ⟨Person⟩ taciturn

einsinken† *vi sep (sein)* sink in

einspannen *vt sep* harness; **jdn e~** *(fam)* rope s.o. in; **sehr eingespannt** *(fam)* very busy

einsparen *vt sep* save

einsperren *vt sep* shut/*(im Gefängnis)* lock up

einspielen (sich) *vr sep* warm up; **gut aufeinander eingespielt sein** work well together

einsprachig *a* monolingual

einspringen† *vi sep (sein)* step in (**für** for)

einspritzen *vt sep* inject

Einspruch *m* objection; **E~ erheben** object; *(Jur)* appeal

einspurig *a* single-track; *(Auto)* single-lane

einst *adv* once; *(Zukunft)* one day

Einstand *m (Tennis)* deuce

einstecken *vt sep* put in; post ⟨Brief⟩; *(Electr)* plug in; *(fam: behalten)* pocket; *(fam: hinnehmen)* take; suffer ⟨Niederlage⟩; **etw e~** put sth in one's pocket

einstehen† *vi sep (haben)* **e~ für** vouch for/answer for ⟨Folgen⟩

einsteigen† *vi sep (sein)* get in; *(in Bus/Zug)* get on

einstell|en *vt sep* put in; *(anstellen)* employ; *(aufhören)* stop; *(regulieren)* adjust, set; *(Optik)* focus; tune ⟨Motor, Zündung⟩; tune to ⟨Sender⟩; **sich e~en** turn up; *(ankommen)* arrive; *(eintreten)* occur; *(Schwierigkeiten:)* arise; **sich e~en auf** (+ *acc*) adjust to; *(sich vorbereiten)* prepare for. **E~ung** *f* employment; *(Aufhören)* cessation; *(Regulierung)* adjustment; *(Optik)* focusing; *(TV, Auto)* tuning; *(Haltung)* attitude

Einstieg *m* -[e]s, -e entrance

einstig *a* former

einstimmen *vi sep (haben)* join in

einstimmig *a* unanimous, *adv* -ly. **E~keit** *f* - unanimity

einstöckig *a* single-storey

einstudieren *vt sep* rehearse

einstufen *vt sep* classify

Ein|sturz *m* collapse. **e~stürzen** *vi sep (sein)* collapse

einstweil|en *adv* for the time being; *(inzwischen)* meanwhile. **e~ig** *a* temporary

eintasten *vt sep* key in

eintauchen *vt/i sep (sein)* dip in; *(heftiger)* plunge in

eintauschen *vt sep* exchange

eintausend *inv a* one thousand

einteil|en *vt sep* divide (**in** + *acc* into); *(Biol)* classify; **sich** *(dat)* **seine Zeit gut e~en** organize one's time well. **e~ig** *a* one-piece. **E~ung** *f* division; classification

eintönig *a* monotonous, *adv* -ly. **E~keit** *f* - monotony

Eintopf *m*, **E~gericht** *nt* stew

Ein|tracht *f* - harmony. **e~trächtig** *a* harmonious ● *adv* in harmony

Eintrag *m* -[e]s, -̈e entry. **e~en**† *vt sep* enter; *(Admin)* register; *(einbringen)* bring in; **sich e~en** put one's name down

einträglich *a* profitable

Eintragung *f* -,-en registration; *(Eintrag)* entry

eintreffen† *vi sep (sein)* arrive; *(fig)* come true; *(geschehen)* happen. **E~nt** -s arrival

eintreiben† *vt sep* drive in; *(einziehen)* collect

eintreten† *v sep* ● *vi (sein)* enter; *(geschehen)* occur; **in einen Klub e~** join a club; **e~ für** *(fig)* stand up for ● *vt* kick in

Eintritt *m* entrance; *(zu Veranstaltung)* admission; *(Beitritt)* joining; *(Beginn)* beginning. **E~s-karte** *f* [admission] ticket

eintrocknen *vi sep (sein)* dry up

einüben *vt sep* practise

einundachtzig *inv a* eighty-one

einverleiben *vt sep* incorporate *(dat* into); **sich** *(dat)* **etw e~** *(fam)* consume sth

Einvernehmen *nt* -s understanding; *(Übereinstimmung)* agreement; **in bestem E~** on the best of terms

einverstanden *a* **e~ sein** agree

Einverständnis *nt* agreement; *(Zustimmung)* consent

Einwand *m* -[e]s, -̈e objection

Einwander|er *m* immigrant. **e~n** *vi sep (sein)* immigrate. **E~ung** *f* immigration

einwandfrei *a* perfect, *adv* -ly; *(untadelig)* impeccable, *adv* -bly; *(eindeutig)* indisputable, *adv* -bly

einwärts *adv* inwards

einwechseln *vt sep* change

einwecken *vt sep* preserve, bottle

Einweg- *pref* non-returnable; ⟨Feuerzeug⟩ throw-away

einweichen vt sep soak

einweih|en vt sep inaugurate; (Relig) consecrate; (einführen) initiate; (fam) use for the first time; **in ein Geheimnis e~en** let into a secret. **E~ung** f -,-en inauguration; consecration; initiation

einweisen† vt sep direct; (einführen) initiate; **ins Krankenhaus e~** send to hospital

einwenden† vt sep **etwas e~** object (**gegen** to); **dagegen hätte ich nichts einzuwenden** (fam) I wouldn't say no

einwerfen† vt sep insert; post (Brief); (Sport) throw in; (vorbringen) interject; (zertrümmern) smash

einwickeln vt sep wrap [up]

einwillig|en vi sep (haben) consent, agree (**in** + acc to). **E~ung** f - consent

einwirken vi sep (haben) **e~ auf** (+ acc) have an effect on; (beeinflussen) influence

Einwohner|(in) m -s,- (f -,-nen) inhabitant. **E~zahl** f population

Einwurf m interjection; (Einwand) objection; (Sport) throw-in; (Münz-) slot

Einzahl f (Gram) singular

einzahl|en vt sep pay in. **E~ung** f payment; (Einlage) deposit

einzäunen vt sep fence in

Einzel nt -s,- (Tennis) singles pl. **E~bett** nt single bed. **E~fall** m individual/(Sonderfall) isolated case. **E~gänger** m -s,- loner. **E~haft** f solitary confinement. **E~handel** m retail trade. **E~händler** m retailer. **E~haus** nt detached house. **E~heit** f -,-en detail. **E~karte** f single ticket. **E~kind** nt only child

einzeln a single, adv -gly; (individuell) individual, adv -ly; (gesondert) separate, adv -ly; odd (Handschuh, Socken); **e~e Fälle** some cases. **e~e(r,s)** pron **der/die e~e** the individual; **ein e~er** a single one; **jeder e~e** every single one; **im e~en** in detail; **e~e** pl some

Einzel|person f single person. **E~teil** nt [component] part. **E~zimmer** nt single room

einziehen† v sep ● vt pull in; draw in (Atem, Krallen); (Zool, Techn) retract; indent (Zeile); (aus dem Verkehr ziehen) withdraw; (beschlagnahmen) confiscate; (eintreiben) collect; make (Erkundigungen); (Mil) call up;

(einfügen) insert; (einbauen) put in; **den Kopf e~** duck [one's head] ● vi (sein) enter; (umziehen) move in; (eindringen) penetrate

einzig a only; (einmalig) unique; **eine/keine e~e Frage** a/not a single question; **ein e~es Mal** only once ● adv only; **e~ und allein** solely. **e~artig** a unique; (unvergleichlich) unparalleled. **e~e(r,s)** pron **der/die/das e~e** the only one; **ein/kein e~er** a/not a single one; **das e~e, was mich stört** the only thing that bothers me

Einzug m entry; (Umzug) move (**in** + acc into). **E~sgebiet** nt catchment area

Eis nt -es ice; (Speise-) ice-cream; **Eis am Stiel** ice lolly. **E~bahn** f ice rink. **E~bär** m polar bear. **E~becher** m ice-cream sundae. **E~bein** nt (Culin) knuckle of pork. **E~berg** m iceberg. **E~diele** f ice-cream parlour

Eisen nt -s,- iron. **E~bahn** f railway. **E~bahner** m -s,- railwayman

eisern a iron; (fest) resolute, adv -ly; **e~er Vorhang** (Theat) safety curtain; (Pol) Iron Curtain

Eis|fach nt freezer compartment. **e~gekühlt** a chilled. **e~ig** a icy. **E~kaffee** m iced coffee. **e~kalt** a ice cold; (fig) icy, adv -ily. **E~kunstlauf** m figure skating. **E~lauf** m skating. **e~laufen†** vi sep (sein) skate. **E~läufer(in)** m(f) skater. **E~pickel** m ice-axe. **E~scholle** f ice-floe. **E~schrank** m refrigerator. **E~vogel** m kingfisher. **E~würfel** m ice-cube. **E~zapfen** m icicle. **E~zeit** f ice age

eitel a vain; (rein) pure. **E~keit** f - vanity

Eiter m -s pus. **e~n** vi (haben) discharge pus

Eiweiß nt -es,-e egg-white; (Chem) protein

Ekel¹ m -s disgust; (Widerwille) revulsion

Ekel² nt -s,- (fam) beast

ekel|erregend a nauseating. **e~haft** a nauseating; (widerlich) repulsive. **e~n** vt/i (haben) **mich** od **mir e~t [es] davor** it makes me feel sick ● vr **sich e~n vor** (+ dat) find repulsive

eklig a disgusting, repulsive

Eksta|se f - ecstasy. **e~tisch** a ecstatic, adv -ally

Ekzem nt -s,-e eczema

elasti|sch *a* elastic; (*federnd*) springy; (*fig*) flexible. **E~zität** *f* - elasticity; flexibility

Elch *m* -[e]s,-e elk

Elefant *m* -en,-en elephant

elegan|t *a* elegant, *adv* -ly. **E~z** *f* - elegance

elektrifizieren *vt* electrify

Elektri|ker *m* -s,- electrician. **e~sch** *a* electric, *adv* -ally

elektrisieren *vt* electrify; **sich e~** get an electric shock

Elektrizität *f* - electricity. **E~swerk** *nt* power station

Elektr|oartikel *mpl* electrical appliances. **E~ode** *f* -,-n electrode. **E~oherd** *m* electric cooker. **E~on** *nt* -s,-en /-'tro:nən/ electron. **E~onik** *f* - electronics *sg*. **e~onisch** *a* electronic

Element *nt* -[e]s,-e element; (*Anbau-*) unit. **e~ar** *a* elementary

Elend *nt* -s misery; (*Armut*) poverty. **e~** *a* miserable, *adv* -bly, wretched, *adv* -ly; (*krank*) poorly; (*gemein*) contemptible; (*fam: schrecklich*) dreadful, *adv* -ly. **E~sviertel** *nt* slum

elf *inv a*, **E~** *f* -,-en eleven

Elfe *f* -,-n fairy

Elfenbein *nt* ivory

Elfmeter *m* (*Fußball*) penalty

elfte(r,s) *a* eleventh

eliminieren *vt* eliminate

Elite *f* -,-n élite

Elixier *nt* -s,-e elixir

Ell[en]bogen *m* elbow

Ellip|se *f* -,-n ellipse. **e~tisch** *a* elliptical

Elsaß *nt* - Alsace

elsässisch *a* Alsatian

Elster *f* -,-n magpie

elter|lich *a* parental. **E~n** *pl* parents. **E~nhaus** *nt* [parental] home. **e~nlos** *a* orphaned. **E~nteil** *m* parent

Email /e'maɪ/ *nt* -s,-s, **E~le** /e'maljə/ *f* -,-n enamel. **e~lieren** /ema[l]'ji:rən/ *vt* enamel

Emanzi|pation /-'tsɪo:n/ *f* - emancipation. **e~piert** *a* emancipated

Embargo *nt* -s,-s embargo

Emblem *nt* -s,-e emblem

Embryo *m* -s,-s embryo

Emigr|ant(in) *m* -en,-en (*f* -,-nen) emigrant. **E~ation** /-'tsɪo:n/ *f* - emigration. **e~ieren** *vi* (*sein*) emigrate

eminent *a* eminent, *adv* -ly

Emission *f* -,-en emission; (*Comm*) issue

Emotion /-'tsɪo:n/ *f* -,-en emotion. **e~al** *a* emotional

Empfang *m* -[e]s,ˆe reception; (*Erhalt*) receipt; **in E~ nehmen** receive; (*annehmen*) accept. **e~en†** *vt* receive; (*Biol*) conceive

Empfäng|er *m* -s,- recipient; (*Post-*) addressee; (*Zahlungs-*) payee; (*Radio, TV*) receiver. **e~lich** *a* receptive/ (*Med*) susceptible (**für** to). **E~nis** *f* - (*Biol*) conception

Empfängnisverhütung *f* contraception. **E~smittel** *nt* contraceptive

Empfangs|bestätigung *f* receipt. **E~chef** *m* reception manager. **E~dame** *f* receptionist. **E~halle** *f* [hotel] foyer

empfehl|en† *vt* recommend; **sich e~en** be advisable; (*verabschieden*) take one's leave. **e~enswert** *a* to be recommended; (*ratsam*) advisable. **E~ung** *f* -,-en recommendation; (*Gruß*) regards *pl*

empfind|en† *vt* feel. **e~lich** *a* sensitive (**gegen** to); (*zart*) delicate; (*wund*) tender; (*reizbar*) touchy; (*hart*) severe, *adv* -ly. **E~lichkeit** *f* - sensitivity; delicacy; tenderness; touchiness. **e~sam** *a* sensitive; (*sentimental*) sentimental. **E~ung** *f* -,-en sensation; (*Regung*) feeling

emphatisch *a* emphatic, *adv* -ally

empor *adv* (*liter*) up[wards]

empören *vt* incense; **sich e~** be indignant; (*sich auflehnen*) rebel. **e~d** *a* outrageous

Empor|kömmling *m* -s,-e upstart. **e~ragen** *vi sep* (*haben*) rise [up]

empör|t *a* indignant, *adv* -ly. **E~ung** *f* - indignation; (*Auflehnung*) rebellion

emsig *a* busy, *adv* -ily

Ende *nt* -s,-n end; (*eines Films, Romans*) ending; (*fam: Stück*) bit; **E~ Mai** at the end of May; **zu E~ sein/ gehen** be finished/come to an end; **etw zu E~ schreiben** finish writing sth; **am E~** at the end; (*schließlich*) in the end; (*fam: vielleicht*) perhaps; (*fam: erschöpft*) at the end of one's tether

end|en *vi* (*haben*) end. **e~gültig** *a* final, *adv* -ly; (*bestimmt*) definite, *adv* -ly

Endivie /-jə/ *f* -,-n endive

end|lich *adv* at last, finally; (*schließlich*) in the end. **e~los** *a* endless,

adv -ly. **E~resultat** *nt* final result.
E~spiel *nt* final. **E~spurt** *m* **-[e]s**
final spurt. **E~station** *f* terminus.
E~ung *f* -,-en (*Gram*) ending

Energie *f* - energy

energisch *a* resolute, *adv* -ly;
(*nachdrücklich*) vigorous, *adv* -ly;
e~ werden put one's foot down

eng *a* narrow; (*beengt*) cramped;
(*anliegend*) tight; (*nah*) close, *adv* -ly

Enga|gement /ãgaʒə'mã:/ *nt* **-s,-s**
(*Theat*) engagement; (*fig*) commitment.
e~gieren /-'ʒi:rən/ *vt* (*Theat*) engage; **sich e~gieren** become involved;
e~giert committed

eng|anliegend *a* tight-fitting. **E~e** *f*
- narrowness; **in die E~e treiben** (*fig*)
drive into a corner

Engel *m* **-s,-** angel. **e~haft** *a* angelic

engherzig *a* petty

England *nt* **-s** England

Engländer *m* **-s,-** Englishman; (*Techn*)
monkey-wrench; **die E~** the English *pl*.
E~in *f* -,-nen Englishwoman

englisch *a* English; **auf e~** in English. **E~** *nt* **-[s]** (*Lang*) English

Engpaß *m* (*fig*) bottle-neck

en gros /ã'gro:/ *adv* wholesale

engstirnig *a* (*fig*) narrow-minded

Enkel *m* **-s,-** grandson; **E~** *pl* grandchildren. **E~in** *f* -,-nen granddaughter. **E~kind** *nt* grandchild.
E~sohn *m* grandson. **E~tochter** *f*
granddaughter

enorm *a* enormous, *adv* -ly; (*fam:
großartig*) fantastic

Ensemble /ã'sã:bəl/ *nt* **-s,-s** ensemble; (*Theat*) company

entart|en *vi* (*sein*) degenerate. **e~et**
a degenerate

entbehr|en *vt* do without; (*ver-
missen*) miss. **e~lich** *a* dispensable;
(*überflüssig*) superfluous. **E~ung** *f*
-,-en privation

entbind|en† *vt* release (**von** from);
(*Med*) deliver (**von** of) ● *vi* (*haben*) give
birth. **E~ung** *f* delivery. **E~ungs-
station** *f* maternity ward

entblöß|en *vt* bare. **e~t** *a* bare

entdeck|en *vt* discover. **E~er** *m* **-s,-**
discoverer; (*Forscher*) explorer.
E~ung *f* -,-en discovery

Ente *f* -,-n duck

entehren *vt* dishonour

enteignen *vt* dispossess; expro-
priate (*Eigentum*)

enterben *vt* disinherit

Enterich *m* **-s,-e** drake

entfachen *vt* kindle

entfallen† *vi* (*sein*) not apply; **jdm
e~** slip from s.o.'s hand; (*aus dem Gedächtnis*) slip s.o.'s mind; **auf jdn e~** be
s.o.'s share

entfalt|en *vt* unfold; (*entwickeln*) de-
velop; (*zeigen*) display; **sich e~en** unfold; develop. **E~ung** *f* - development

entfern|en *vt* remove; **sich e~en**
leave. **e~t** *a* distant; (*schwach*)
vague, *adv* -ly; **2 Kilometer e~t** 2 kilometres away; **e~t verwandt** distantly
related; **nicht im e~testen** not in
the least. **E~ung** *f* -,-en removal;
(*Abstand*) distance; (*Reichweite*) range.
E~ungsmesser *m* range- finder

entfesseln *vt* (*fig*) unleash

entfliehen† *vi* (*sein*) escape

entfremd|en *vt* alienate. **E~ung** *f* -
alienation

entfrosten *vt* defrost

entführ|en *vt* abduct, kidnap; hijack
⟨*Flugzeug*⟩. **E~er** *m* abductor,
kidnapper; hijacker. **E~ung** *f* abduction, kidnapping; hijacking

entgegen *adv* towards ● *prep*
(+ *dat*) contrary to. **e~gehen**† *vi sep*
(*sein*) (+ *dat*) go to meet; (*fig*) be
heading for. **e~gesetzt** *a* opposite;
(*gegensätzlich*) opposing. **e~
halten**† *vt sep* (*fig*) object. **e~
kommen**† *vi sep* (*sein*) (+ *dat*) come
to meet; (*zukommen auf*) come
towards; (*fig*) oblige. **E~kommen**
nt **-s** helpfulness; (*Zugeständnis*)
concession. **e~kommend** *a* approaching; ⟨*Verkehr*⟩ oncoming; (*fig*)
obliging. **e~nehmen**† *vt sep* accept.
e~sehen† *vi sep* (*haben*) (+ *dat*)
(*fig*) await; (*freudig*) look forward to.
e~setzen *vt sep* **Widerstand e~
setzen** (+ *dat*) resist. **e~treten**† *vi
sep* (*sein*) (+ *dat*) (*fig*) confront; (*bekämpfen*) fight. **e~wirken** *vi sep* (*haben*) (+ *dat*) counteract; (*fig*) oppose

entgegn|en *vt* reply (**auf** + *acc* to).
E~ung *f* -,-en reply

entgehen† *vi sep* (*sein*) (+ *dat*) escape; **jdm e~** (*unbemerkt bleiben*) escape s.o.'s notice; **sich** (*dat*) **etw e~
lassen** miss sth

entgeistert *a* flabbergasted

Entgelt *nt* **-[e]s** payment; **gegen E~**
for money. **e~en** *vt* **jdn etw e~en
lassen** (*fig*) make s.o. pay for sth

entgleis|en *vi* (*sein*) be derailed;
(*fig*) make a gaffe. **E~ung** *f* -,-en de-
railment; (*fig*) gaffe

entgleiten† *vi (sein)* jdm e~ slip from s.o.'s grasp

entgräten *vt* fillet, bone

Enthaarungsmittel *nt* depilatory

enthalt|en† *vt* contain; **in etw** *(dat)* e~en sein be contained/*(eingeschlossen)* included in sth; **sich der Stimme e~en** *(Pol)* abstain. **e~sam** *a* abstemious. **E~samkeit** *f* - abstinence. **E~ung** *f (Pol)* abstention

enthaupten *vt* behead

entheben† *vt* jdn seines Amtes e~ relieve s.o. of his post

enthüll|en *vt* unveil; *(fig)* reveal. **E~ung** *f* -,-en revelation

Enthusias|mus *m* - enthusiasm. **E~t** *m* -en,-en enthusiast. **e~tisch** *a* enthusiastic, *adv* -ally

entkernen *vt* stone; core *(Apfel)*

entkleid|en *vt* undress; **sich e~en** undress. **E~ungsnummer** *f* striptease [act]

entkommen† *vi (sein)* escape

entkorken *vt* uncork

entkräft|en *vt* weaken; *(fig)* invalidate. **E~ung** *f* - debility

entkrampfen *vt* relax; **sich e~** relax

entladen† *vt* unload; *(Electr)* discharge; **sich e~** discharge; *(Gewitter:)* break; *(Zorn:)* explode

entlang *adv & prep* (+ *preceding acc or following dat*) along; **die Straße e~, e~ der Straße** along the road; **an etw** *(dat)* e~ along sth. **e~fahren**† *vi sep (sein)* drive along. **e~gehen**† *vi sep (sein)* walk along

entlarven *vt* unmask

entlass|en† *vt* dismiss; *(aus Krankenhaus)* discharge; *(aus der Haft)* release; **aus der Schule e~en werden** leave school. **E~ung** *f* -,-en dismissal; discharge; release

entlast|en *vt* relieve the strain on; ease *(Gewissen, Verkehr)*; relieve **(von** of); *(Jur)* exonerate. **E~ung** *f* - relief; exoneration. **E~ungszug** *m* relief train

entlaufen† *vi (sein)* run away

entledigen (sich) *vr* (+ *gen)* rid oneself of; *(ausziehen)* take off; *(erfüllen)* discharge

entleeren *vt* empty

entlegen *a* remote

entleihen† *vt* borrow **(von** from)

entlocken *vt* coax *(dat* from)

entlohnen *vt* pay

entlüft|en *vt* ventilate. **E~er** *m* -s,- extractor fan. **E~ung** *f* ventilation

entmündigen *vt* declare incapable of managing his own affairs

entmutigen *vt* discourage

entnehmen† *vt* take *(dat* from); *(schließen)* gather *(dat* from)

Entomologie *f* - entomology

entpuppen (sich) *vr (fig)* turn out **(als etw** to be sth)

entrahmt *a* skimmed

entreißen† *vt* snatch *(dat* from)

entrichten *vt* pay

entrinnen† *vi (sein)* escape

entrollen *vt* unroll; unfurl *(Fahne)*; **sich e~** unroll; unfurl

entrüst|en *vt* fill with indignation; **sich e~en** be indignant **(über** + *acc* at). **e~et** *a* indignant, *adv* -ly. **E~ung** *f* - indignation

entsaft|en *vt* extract the juice from. **E~er** *m* -s,- juice extractor

entsag|en *vi (haben)* (+ *dat)* renounce. **E~ung** *f* - renunciation

entschädig|en *vt* compensate. **E~ung** *f* -,-en compensation

entschärfen *vt* defuse

entscheid|en† *vt/i (haben)* decide; **sich e~en** decide; *(Sache:)* be decided. **e~end** *a* decisive, *adv* -ly; *(kritisch)* crucial. **E~ung** *f* decision

entschieden *a* decided, *adv* -ly; *(fest)* firm, *adv* -ly

entschlafen† *vi (sein) (liter)* pass away

entschließen† **(sich)** *vr* decide, make up one's mind; **sich anders e~** change one's mind

entschlossen *a* determined; *(energisch)* resolute, *adv* -ly; **kurz e~** without hesitation; *(spontan)* on the spur of the moment. **E~heit** *f* - determination

Entschluß *m* decision; **einen E~ fassen** make a decision

entschlüsseln *vt* decode

entschuld|bar *a* excusable. **e~igen** *vt* excuse; **sich e~igen** apologize **(bei** to); **e~igen Sie [bitte]!** sorry! *(bei Frage)* excuse me. **E~igung** *f* -,-en apology; *(Ausrede)* excuse; **[jdn] um E~igung bitten** apologize [to s.o.]; **E~igung!** sorry! *(bei Frage)* excuse me

entsetz|en *vt* horrify. **E~en** *nt* -s horror. **e~lich** *a* horrible, *adv* -bly; *(schrecklich)* terrible, *adv* -bly. **e~t** *a* horrified

entsinnen† **(sich)** *vr* (+ *gen)* remember

Entsorgung *f* - waste disposal

entspann|en *vt* relax; **sich e~en** relax; ⟨*Lage:*⟩ ease. **E~ung** *f* - relaxation; easing; (*Pol*) détente

entsprech|en† *vi (haben)* (+*dat*) correspond to; (*übereinstimmen*) agree with; (*nachkommen*) comply with. **e~end** *a* corresponding; (*angemessen*) appropriate; (*zuständig*) relevant ● *adv* correspondingly; appropriately; (*demgemäß*) accordingly ● *prep* (+*dat*) in accordance with. **E~ung** *f* -,-en equivalent

entspringen† *vi (sein)* ⟨*Fluß:*⟩ rise; (*fig*) arise, spring (*dat* from); (*entfliehen*) escape

entstammen *vi (sein)* come/(*abstammen*) be descended (*dat* from)

entsteh|en† *vi (sein)* come into being; (*sich bilden*) form; (*sich entwickeln*) develop; ⟨*Brand:*⟩ start; (*stammen*) originate/(*sich ergeben*) result (**aus** from). **E~ung** *f* - origin; formation; development; (*fig*) birth

entsteinen *vt* stone

entstell|en *vt* disfigure; (*verzerren*) distort. **E~ung** *f* disfigurement; distortion

entstört *a* (*Electr*) suppressed

enttäusch|en *vt* disappoint. **E~ung** *f* disappointment

entvölkern *vt* depopulate

entwaffnen *vt* disarm. **e~d** *a* (*fig*) disarming

Entwarnung *f* all-clear [signal]

entwässer|n *vt* drain. **E~ung** *f* - drainage

entweder *conj & adv* either

entweichen† *vi (sein)* escape

entweih|en *vt* desecrate. **E~ung** *f* - desecration

entwenden *vt* steal (*dat* from)

entwerfen† *vt* design; (*aufsetzen*) draft; (*skizzieren*) sketch

entwert|en *vt* devalue; (*ungültig machen*) cancel. **E~er** *m* -s,- ticket-cancelling machine. **E~ung** *f* devaluation; cancelling

entwick|eln *vt* develop; **sich e~eln** develop. **E~lung** *f* -,-en development; (*Biol*) evolution. **E~lungsland** *nt* developing country

entwinden† *vt* wrench (*dat* from)

entwirren *vt* disentangle; (*fig*) unravel

entwischen *vi (sein)* **jdm e~** (*fam*) give s.o. the slip

entwöhnen *vt* wean (*gen* from); cure ⟨*Süchtige*⟩

entwürdigend *a* degrading

Entwurf *m* design; (*Konzept*) draft; (*Skizze*) sketch

entwurzeln *vt* uproot

entzie|hen† *vt* take away (*dat* from); **jdm den Führerschein e~hen** disqualify s.o. from driving; **sich e~hen** (+*dat*) withdraw from; (*entgehen*) evade. **E~hungskur** *f* treatment for drug/alcohol addiction

entziffern *vt* decipher

entzücken *vt* delight. **E~** *nt* -s delight. **e~d** *a* delightful

Entzug *m* withdrawal; (*Vorenthaltung*) deprivation. **E~serscheinungen** *fpl* withdrawal symptoms

entzünd|en *vt* ignite; (*anstecken*) light; (*fig: erregen*) inflame; **sich e~en** ignite; (*Med*) become inflamed. **e~et** *a* (*Med*) inflamed. **e~lich** *a* inflammable. **E~ung** *f* (*Med*) inflammation

entzwei *a* broken. **e~en (sich)** *vr* quarrel. **e~gehen†** *vi sep (sein)* break

Enzian *m* -s,-e gentian

Enzyklo|pädie *f* -,-en encyclopaedia. **e~pädisch** *a* encyclopaedic

Enzym *nt* -s,-e enzyme

Epidemie *f* -,-n epidemic

Epi|lepsie *f* - epilepsy. **E~leptiker(in)** *m* -s,- (*f* -,-nen) epileptic. **e~leptisch** *a* epileptic

Epilog *m* -s,-e epilogue

episch *a* epic

Episode *f* -,-n episode

Epitaph *nt* -s,-e epitaph

Epoche *f* -,-n epoch. **e~machend** *a* epoch-making

Epos *nt* -,**Epen** epic

er *pron* he; (*Ding, Tier*) it

erachten *vt* consider (**für nötig** necessary). **E~** *nt* -s **meines E~s** in my opinion

erbarmen (sich) *vr* have pity/⟨*Gott:*⟩ mercy (*gen* on). **E~** *nt* -s pity; mercy

erbärmlich *a* wretched, *adv* -ly; (*stark*) terrible, *adv* -bly

erbarmungslos *a* merciless, *adv* -ly

erbau|en *vt* build; (*fig*) edify; **sich e~en** be edified (**an**+*dat* by); **nicht e~t von** (*fam*) not pleased about. **e~lich** *a* edifying

Erbe¹ *m* -n,-n heir

Erbe² *nt* -s inheritance; (*fig*) heritage. **e~n** *vt* inherit

erbeuten *vt* get; (*Mil*) capture

Erbfolge *f (Jur)* succession
erbieten† *(sich) vr* offer *(zu* to)
Erbin *f -,-nen* heiress
erbitten† *vt* ask for
erbittert *a* bitter; *(heftig)* fierce, *adv* -ly
erblassen *vi (sein)* turn pale
erblich *a* hereditary
erblicken *vt* catch sight of
erblinden *vi (sein)* go blind
erbost *a* angry, *adv* -ily
erbrechen† *vt* vomit ● *vi/r* [sich] e~ vomit. E~ *nt* -s vomiting
Erbschaft *f -,-en* inheritance
Erbse *f -,-n* pea
Erb|stück *nt* heirloom. **E~teil** *nt* inheritance
Erd|apfel *m (Aust)* potato. **E~beben** *nt* -s,- earthquake. **E~beere** *f* strawberry. **E~boden** *m* ground
Erde *f -,-n* earth; *(Erdboden)* ground; *(Fußboden)* floor; **auf der E~** on earth; *(auf dem Boden)* on the ground/floor. **e~n** *vt (Electr)* earth
erdenklich *a* imaginable
Erd|gas *nt* natural gas. **E~geschoß** *nt* ground floor, *(Amer)* first floor. **e~ig** *a* earthy. **E~kugel** *f* globe. **E~kunde** *f* geography. **E~nuß** *f* peanut. **E~öl** *nt* [mineral] oil. **E~reich** *nt* soil
erdreisten (sich) *vr* have the audacity (**zu** to)
erdrosseln *vt* strangle
erdrücken *vt* crush to death. **e~d** *a (fig)* overwhelming
Erd|rutsch *m* landslide. **E~teil** *m* continent
erdulden *vt* endure
ereifern (sich) *vr* get worked up
ereignen (sich) *vr* happen
Ereignis *nt* -ses,-se event. **e~los** *a* uneventful. **e~reich** *a* eventful
Eremit *m* -en,-en hermit
ererbt *a* inherited
erfahr|en† *vt* learn, hear; *(erleben)* experience ● *a* experienced. **E~ung** *f -,-en* experience; **in E~ung bringen** find out
erfassen *vt* seize; *(begreifen)* grasp; *(einbeziehen)* include; *(aufzeichnen)* record; **von einem Auto erfaßt werden** be struck by a car
erfind|en† *vt* invent. **E~er** *m* -s,-inventor. **e~erisch** *a* inventive. **E~ung** *f -,-en* invention
Erfolg *m* -[e]s,-e success; *(Folge)* result; **E~ haben** be successful. **e~en**

vi (sein) take place; *(geschehen)* happen. **e~los** *a* unsuccessful, *adv* -ly. **e~reich** *a* successful, *adv* -ly. **e~versprechend** *a* promising
erforder|lich *a* required, necessary. **e~n** *vt* require, demand. **E~nis** *nt* -ses,-se requirement
erforsch|en *vt* explore; *(untersuchen)* investigate. **E~ung** *f* exploration; investigation
erfreu|en *vt* please; **sich guter Gesundheit e~en** enjoy good health. **e~lich** *a* pleasing, gratifying; *(willkommen)* welcome. **e~licherweise** *adv* happily. **e~t** *a* pleased
erfrier|en† *vi (sein)* freeze to death; ⟨Glied:⟩ become frostbitten; ⟨Pflanze:⟩ be killed by the frost. **E~ung** *f -,-en* frostbite
erfrisch|en *vt* refresh; **sich e~en** refresh onself. **e~end** *a* refreshing. **E~ung** *f -,-en* refreshment
erfüll|en *vt* fill; *(nachkommen)* fulfil; serve ⟨Zweck⟩; discharge ⟨Pflicht⟩; **sich e~en** come true. **E~ung** *f* fulfilment; **in E~ung gehen** come true
erfunden invented; *(fiktiv)* fictitious
ergänz|en *vt* complement; *(nachtragen)* supplement; *(auffüllen)* replenish; *(vervollständigen)* complete; *(hinzufügen)* add; **sich e~en** complement each other. **E~ung** *f* complement; supplement; *(Zusatz)* addition. **E~ungsband** *m* supplement
ergeb|en† *vt* produce; *(zeigen)* show, establish; **sich e~en** result; ⟨Schwierigkeit:⟩ arise; *(kapitulieren)* surrender; *(sich fügen)* submit; **es ergab sich** it turned out (**daß** that) ● *a* devoted, *adv* -ly; *(resigniert)* resigned, *adv* -ly. **E~enheit** *f* - devotion
Ergebnis *nt* -ses,-se result. **e~los** *a* fruitless, *adv* -ly
ergehen† *vi (sein)* be issued; **etw über sich** *(acc)* **e~ lassen** submit to sth; **wie ist es dir ergangen?** how did you get on? ● *vr* **sich e~ in** (+ *dat*) indulge in
ergiebig *a* productive; *(fig)* rich
ergötzen *vt* amuse
ergreifen† *vt* seize; take ⟨Maßnahme, Gelegenheit⟩; take up ⟨Beruf⟩; *(rühren)* move; **die Flucht e~** flee. **e~d** *a* moving
ergriffen *a* deeply moved. **E~heit** *f* - emotion

ergründen vt (fig) get to the bottom of

erhaben a raised; (fig) sublime; **über etw** (acc) **e~ sein** (fig) be above sth

Erhalt m -[e]s receipt. **e~en†** vt receive, get; (gewinnen) obtain; (bewahren) preserve, keep; (instandhalten) maintain; (unterhalten) support; **am Leben e~en** keep alive ● **a gut/schlecht e~en** in good/ bad condition; **e~en bleiben** survive

erhältlich a obtainable

Erhaltung f - (s. **erhalten**) preservation; maintenance

erhängen (sich) vr hang oneself

erhärten vt (fig) substantiate

erheb|en† vt raise; levy ⟨Steuer⟩; charge ⟨Gebühr⟩; **Anspruch e~en** lay claim (**auf** + acc to); **Protest e~en** protest; **sich e~en** rise; (Frage:) arise; (sich empören) rise up. **e~lich** a considerable, adv -bly. **E~ung** f -,-en elevation; (Anhöhe) rise; (Aufstand) uprising; (Ermittlung) survey

erheiter|n vt amuse. **E~ung** f - amusement

erhitzen vt heat; **sich e~** get hot; (fig) get heated

erhoffen vt **sich** (dat) **etw e~** hope for sth

erhöh|en vt raise; (fig) increase; **sich e~en** rise, increase. **E~ung** f -,-en increase. **E~ungszeichen** nt (Mus) sharp

erhol|en (sich) vr recover (**von** from); (nach Krankheit) convalesce, recuperate; (sich ausruhen) have a rest. **e~sam** a restful. **E~ung** f - recovery; convalescence; (Ruhe) rest. **E~ungsheim** nt convalescent home

erhören vt (fig) answer

erinner|n vt remind (**an** + acc of); **sich e~n** remember (**an jdn/etw** s.o./sth). **E~ung** f -,-en memory; (Andenken) souvenir

erkält|en (sich) vr catch a cold; **e~et sein** have a cold. **E~ung** f -,-en cold

erkenn|bar a recognizable; (sichtbar) visible. **e~en†** vt recognize; (wahrnehmen) distinguish; (einsehen) realize. **e~tlich** a **sich e~tlich zeigen** show one's appreciation. **E~tnis** f -,-se recognition; realization; (Wissen) knowledge; **die neuesten E~tnisse** the latest findings

Erker m -s,- bay

erklär|en vt declare; (erläutern) explain; **sich bereit e~en** agree (**zu** to);

ich kann es mir nicht e~en I can't explain it. **e~end** a explanatory. **e~lich** a explicable; (verständlich) understandable. **e~licherweise** adv understandably. **e~t** attrib a declared. **E~ung** f -,-en declaration; explanation; **öffentliche E~ung** public statement

erklingen† vi (sein) ring out

erkrank|en vi (sein) fall ill; be taken ill (**an** + dat with). **E~ung** f -,-en illness

erkunden vt explore; (Mil) reconnoitre

erkundig|en (sich) vr enquire (**nach jdm/etw** after s.o./about sth). **E~ung** f -,-en enquiry

erlahmen vi (sein) tire; ⟨Kraft, Eifer:⟩ flag

erlangen vt attain, get

Erlaß m -sses,-ˇsse (Admin) decree; (Befreiung) exemption; (Straf-) remission

erlassen† vt (Admin) issue; **jdm etw e~** exempt s.o. from sth; let s.o. off ⟨Strafe⟩

erlauben vt allow, permit; **sich e~, etw zu tun** take the liberty of doing sth; **ich kann es mir nicht e~** I can't afford it

Erlaubnis f - permission. **E~schein** m permit

erläuter|n vt explain. **E~ung** f -,-en explanation

Erle f -,-n alder

erleb|en vt experience; (mit-) see; have ⟨Überraschung, Enttäuschung⟩; **etw nicht mehr e~en** not live to see sth. **E~nis** nt -ses,-se experience

erledig|en vt do; (sich befassen mit) deal with; (beenden) finish; (entscheiden) settle; (töten) kill; **e~t sein** be done/settled/(fam: müde) worn out/(fam: ruiniert) finished

erleichter|n vt lighten; (vereinfachen) make easier; (befreien) relieve; (lindern) ease; **sich e~n** (fig) unburden oneself. **e~t** a relieved. **E~ung** f - relief

erleiden† vt suffer

erlernen vt learn

erlesen a exquisite; (auserlesen) choice, select

erleucht|en vt illuminate; **hell e~et** brightly lit. **E~ung** f -,-en (fig) inspiration

erliegen† vi (sein) succumb (dat to); **seinen Verletzungen e~** die of one's injuries

erlogen *a* untrue, false

Erlös *m* -es proceeds *pl*

erlöschen† *vi (sein)* go out; *(verge-hen)* die; *(aussterben)* die out; *(un-gültig werden)* expire; **erloschener Vulkan** extinct volcano

erlös|en *vt* save; *(befreien)* release *(von* from); *(Relig)* redeem. **e~t** *a* relieved. **E~ung** *f* release; *(Erleichterung)* relief; *(Relig)* redemption

ermächtig|en *vt* authorize. **E~ung** *f* -,-en authorization

ermahn|en *vt* exhort; *(zurecht-weisen)* admonish. **E~ung** *f* ex-hortation; admonition

ermäßig|en *vt* reduce. **E~ung** *f* -,-en reduction

ermatt|en *vi (sein)* grow weary ● *vt* weary. **E~ung** *f* - weariness

ermessen† *vt* judge; *(begreifen)* ap-preciate. **E~** *nt* -s discretion; *(Urteil)* judgement; **nach eigenem E~** at one's own discretion

ermitt|eln *vt* establish; *(heraus-finden)* find out ● *vi (haben)* in-vestigate *(gegen jdn* s.o.). **E~lungen** *fpl* investigations. **E~lungs-verfahren** *nt (Jur)* preliminary in-quiry

ermöglichen *vt* make possible

ermord|en *vt* murder. **E~ung** *f* -,-en murder

ermüd|en *vt* tire ● *vi (sein)* get tired. **E~ung** *f* - tiredness

ermunter|n *vt* encourage; **sich e~n** rouse oneself. **E~ung** *f* - encouragement

ermutigen *vt* encourage. **e~d** *a* encouraging

ernähr|en *vt* feed; *(unterhalten)* sup-port, keep; **sich e~en von** live/ *(Tier:)* feed on. **E~er** *m* -s,- breadwinner. **E~ung** *f* - nourishment; nutrition; *(Kost)* diet

ernenn|en† *vt* appoint. **E~ung** *f* -,-en appointment

erneu|ern *vt* renew; *(auswechseln)* replace; change *(Verband)*; *(renovieren)* renovate. **E~erung** *f* re-newal; replacement; renovation. **e~t** *a* renewed; *(neu)* new ● *adv* again

erniedrig|en *vt* degrade; **sich e~en** lower oneself. **e~end** *a* degrading. **E~ungszeichen** *nt (Mus)* flat

ernst *a* serious, *adv* -ly; **e~ nehmen** take seriously. **E~** *m* -es seriousness;

im E~ seriously; **mit einer Drohung E~ machen** carry out a threat; **ist das dein E~?** are you serious? **E~fall** *m* **im E~fall** when the real thing happens. **e~haft** *a* serious, *adv* -ly. **e~lich** *a* serious, *adv* -ly

Ernte *f* -,-n harvest; *(Ertrag)* crop. **E~dankfest** *nt* harvest festival. **e~n** *vt* harvest; *(fig)* reap, win

ernüchter|n *vt* sober up; *(fig)* bring down to earth; *(enttäuschen)* dis-illusion. **e~nd** *a (fig)* sobering. **E~ung** *f* - disillusionment

Erober|er *m* -s,- conqueror. **e~n** *vt* conquer. **E~ung** *f* -,-en conquest

eröffn|en *vt* open; **jdm etw e~en** announce sth to s.o.; **sich jdm e~en** *(Aussicht:)* present itself to s.o. **E~ung** *f* opening; *(Mitteilung)* an-nouncement. **E~ungsansprache** *f* opening address

erörter|n *vt* discuss. **E~ung** *f* -,-en discussion

Erosion *f* -,-en erosion

Erot|ik *f* - eroticism. **e~isch** *a* erotic

Erpel *m* -s,- drake

erpicht *a* **e~ auf** *(+ acc)* keen on

erpress|en *vt* extort; blackmail *(Person)*. **E~er** *m* -s,- blackmailer. **E~ung** *f* - extortion; blackmail

erprob|en *vt* test. **e~t** *a* proven

erquicken *vt* refresh

erraten† *vt* guess

erreg|bar *a* excitable. **e~en** *vt* ex-cite; *(hervorrufen)* arouse; **sich e~en** get worked up. **e~end** *a* exciting. **E~er** *m* -s,- *(Med)* germ. **e~t** *a* agit-ated; *(hitzig)* heated. **E~ung** *f* - ex-citement; *(Erregtheit)* agitation

erreich|bar *a* within reach; *(Ziel)* attainable; *(Person)* available. **e~en** *vt* reach; catch *(Zug)*; live to *(Alter)*; *(durchsetzen)* achieve

erretten *vt* save

errichten *vt* erect

erringen† *vt* gain, win

erröten *vi (sein)* blush

Errungenschaft *f* -,-en achievement; *(fam: Anschaffung)* acquisition; **E~en der Technik** technical advances

Ersatz *m* -es replacement, substitute; *(Entschädigung)* compensation. **E~dienst** *m* = **Zivildienst**. **E~reifen** *m* spare tyre. **E~spieler(in)** *m(f)* sub-stitute. **E~teil** *nt* spare part

ersäufen† *vt* drown

erschaffen† *vt* create

erschallen† *vi (sein)* ring out

erschein|en† *vi (sein)* appear; ⟨*Buch:*⟩ be published; **jdm merkwürdig e~en** seem odd to s.o. **E~en** *nt* -s appearance; publication. **E~ung** *f* -,-en appearance; (*Person*) figure; (*Phänomen*) phenomenon; (*Symptom*) symptom; (*Geist*) apparition

erschieß|en† *vt* shoot [dead]. **E~ungskommando** *nt* firing squad

erschlaffen *vi (sein)* go limp; ⟨*Haut, Muskeln:*⟩ become flabby

erschlagen† *vt* beat to death; (*tödlich treffen*) strike dead; **vom Blitz e~ werden** be killed by lightning ● *a* (*fam*) (*erschöpft*) worn out; (*fassungslos*) stunned

erschließen† *vt* develop; (*zugänglich machen*) open up; (*nutzbar machen*) tap

erschöpf|en *vt* exhaust. **e~end** *a* exhausting; (*fig: vollständig*) exhaustive. **e~t** *a* exhausted. **E~ung** *f* - exhaustion

erschreck|en† *vi (sein)* get a fright ● *vt (reg)* startle; (*beunruhigen*) alarm; **du hast mich e~t** you gave me a fright ● *vr (reg & irreg)* **sich e~en** get a fright. **e~end** *a* alarming, *adv* -ly

erschrocken *a* frightened; (*erschreckt*) startled; (*bestürzt*) dismayed

erschütter|n *vt* shake; (*ergreifen*) upset deeply. **E~ung** *f* -,-en shock

erschweren *vt* make more difficult

erschwinglich *a* affordable

ersehen† *vt* (*fig*) see (**aus** from)

ersetzen *vt* replace; make good ⟨*Schaden*⟩; refund ⟨*Kosten*⟩; **jdm etw e~** compensate s.o. for sth

ersichtlich *a* obvious, apparent

erspar|en *vt* save; **jdm etw e~en** save/(*fernhalten*) spare s.o. sth. **E~nis** *f* -,-se saving; **E~nisse** savings

erst *adv* (*zuerst*) first; (*noch nicht mehr als*) only; (*nicht vor*) not until; **e~ dann** only then; **eben** *od* **gerade e~** [only] just; **das machte ihn e~ recht wütend** it made him all the more angry

erstarren *vi (sein)* solidify; (*gefrieren*) freeze; (*steif werden*) go stiff; (*vor Schreck*) be paralysed

erstatten *vt* (*zurück-*) refund; **Bericht e~** report (**jdm** to s.o.)

Erstaufführung *f* first performance, première

erstaun|en *vt* amaze, astonish. **E~en** *nt* amazement, astonishment.

e~lich *a* amazing, *adv* -ly. **e~licherweise** *adv* amazingly

Erst|ausgabe *f* first edition. **e~e(r,s)** *a* first; (*beste*) best; **E~e Hilfe** first aid; **er kam als e~er** he arrived first; **als e~es** first of all; **fürs e~e** for the time being; **der e~e beste** the first one to come along; (*fam*) any Tom, Dick or Harry. **E~e(r)** *m/f* best; **er ist der/sie ist die E~e in Latein** he/she is top in Latin

erstechen† *vt* stab to death

erstehen† *vt* buy

ersteigern *vt* buy at an auction

erst|ens *adv* firstly, in the first place. **e~ere(r,s)** *a* the former; **der/die/das e~ere** the former

ersticken *vt* suffocate; smother ⟨*Flammen*⟩; (*unterdrücken*) suppress ● *vi (sein)* suffocate. **E~** *nt* -s suffocation; **zum E~** stifling

erst|klassig *a* first-class. **e~mals** *adv* for the first time

erstreben *vt* strive for. **e~swert** *a* desirable

erstrecken (sich) *vr* stretch; **sich e~ auf** (+*acc*) (*fig*) apply to

ersuchen *vt* ask, request. **E~** *nt* -s request

ertappen *vt* (*fam*) catch

erteilen *vt* give (**jdm** s.o.)

ertönen *vi (sein)* sound; (*erschallen*) ring out

Ertrag *m* -[e]s, ⁻e yield. **e~en†** *vt* bear

erträglich *a* bearable; (*leidlich*) tolerable

ertränken *vt* drown

ertrinken† *vi (sein)* drown

erübrigen (sich) *vr* be unnecessary

erwachen *vi (sein)* awake

erwachsen *a* grown-up. **E~e(r)** *m/f* adult, grown-up

erwäg|en† *vt* consider. **E~ung** *f* -,-en consideration; **in E~ung ziehen** consider

erwähn|en *vt* mention. **E~ung** *f* -,-en mention

erwärmen *vt* warm; **sich e~** warm up; (*fig*) warm (**für** to)

erwart|en *vt* expect; (*warten auf*) wait for. **E~ung** *f* -,-en expectation. **e~ungsvoll** *a* expectant, *adv* -ly

erwecken *vt* (*fig*) arouse; give ⟨*Anschein*⟩

erweichen *vt* soften; (*fig*) move; **sich e~ lassen** (*fig*) relent

erweisen† *vt* prove; (*bezeigen*) do ⟨*Gefallen, Dienst, Ehre*⟩; **sich e~ als** prove to be

erweitern vt widen; dilate ⟨*Pupille*⟩; (*fig*) extend, expand

Erwerb m -[e]s acquisition; (*Kauf*) purchase; (*Brot-*) livelihood; (*Verdienst*) earnings pl. **e~en†** vt acquire; (*kaufen*) purchase; (*fig: erlangen*) gain. **e~slos** a unemployed. **e~s-tätig** a [gainfully] employed. **E~ung** f -,-en acquisition

erwider|n vt reply; return ⟨*Besuch, Gruß*⟩. **E~ung** f -,-en reply

erwirken vt obtain

erwischen vt (*fam*) catch

erwünscht a desired

erwürgen vt strangle

Erz nt -es,-e ore

erzähl|en vt tell (**jdm** s.o.) ● vi (haben) talk (**von** about). **E~er** m -s,- narrator. **E~ung** f -,-en story, tale

Erzbischof m archbishop

erzeug|en vt produce; (*Electr*) generate; (*fig*) create. **E~er** m -s,- producer; (*Vater*) father. **E~nis** nt -ses, -se product; **landwirtschaftliche E~nisse** farm produce sg. **E~ung** f - production; generation

Erz|feind m arch-enemy. **E~herzog** m archduke

erzieh|en† vt bring up; (*Sch*) educate. **E~er** m -s,- [private] tutor. **E~erin** f -,-nen governess. **E~ung** f - upbringing; education

erzielen vt achieve; score ⟨*Tor*⟩

erzogen a **gut/schlecht e~** well/badly brought up

erzürnt a angry

erzwingen† vt force

es pron it; (*Mädchen*) she; (*acc*) her; *impers* **es regnet** it is raining; **es gibt** there is/(*pl*) are; **ich hoffe es** I hope so

Esche f -,-n ash

Esel m -s,- donkey; (*fam: Person*) ass. **E~sohr** nt **E~sohren haben** ⟨*Buch:*⟩ be dog-eared

Eskal|ation /-'tsjo:n/ f - escalation. **e~ieren** vt/i (haben) escalate

Eskimo m -[s],-[s] Eskimo

Eskort|e f -,-n (*Mil*) escort. **e~ieren** vt escort

eßbar a edible. **Eßecke** f dining area

essen† vt/i (haben) eat; **zu Mittag/Abend e~** have lunch/supper; **[aus-wärts] e~ gehen** eat out; **chinesisch e~** have a Chinese meal. **E~** nt -s,- food; (*Mahl*) meal; (*festlich*) dinner

Essenz f -,-en essence

Esser(in) m -s,- (f -,-nen) eater

Essig m -s vinegar. **E~gurke** f [pickled] gherkin

Eßkastanie f sweet chestnut. **Eßlöffel** m ≈ dessertspoon. **Eßstäbchen** ntpl chopsticks. **Eßtisch** m dining-table. **Eßwaren** fpl food sg; (*Vorräte*) provisions. **Eßzimmer** nt dining-room

Estland nt -s Estonia

Estragon m -s tarragon

etablieren (sich) vr establish one-self/⟨*Geschäft:*⟩ itself

Etage /e'ta:ʒə/ f -,-n storey. **E~nbett** nt bunk-beds pl. **E~nwohnung** f flat, (*Amer*) apartment

Etappe f -,-n stage

Etat /e'ta:/ m -s,-s budget

etepetete a (*fam*) fussy

Eth|ik f - ethic; (*Sittenlehre*) ethics sg. **e~isch** a ethical

Etikett nt -[e]s,-e[n] label; (*Preis-*) tag. **E~e** f -,-n etiquette; (*Aust*) = **Etikett**. **e~ieren** vt label

etlich|e(r,s) pron some; (*mehrere*) several; **e~es** a number of things; (*ziemlich viel*) quite a lot. **e~emal** adv several times

Etui /e'tvi:/ nt -s,-s case

etwa adv (*ungefähr*) about; (*zum Beispiel*) for instance; (*womöglich*) perhaps; **nicht e~, daß . . .** not that . . . ; **denkt nicht e~ . . .** don't imagine . . . ; **du hast doch nicht e~ Angst?** you're not afraid, are you? **e~ig** a possible

etwas pron something; (*fragend/verneint*) anything; (*ein bißchen*) some, a little; **ohne e~ zu sagen** without saying anything; **sonst noch e~?** anything else? **noch e~ Tee?** some more tea? **so e~ Ärgerliches!** what a nuisance! ● adv a bit

Etymologie f - etymology

euch pron (acc of **ihr** pl) you; (dat) [to] you; (refl) yourselves; (einander) each other; **ein Freund von e~** a friend of yours

euer poss pron pl your. **e~e**, **e~t-** s. **eure**, **euret-**

Eule f -,-n owl

Euphorie f - euphoria

eur|e poss pron pl your. **e~e(r,s)** poss pron yours. **e~erseits** adv for your part. **e~etwegen** adv for your sake; (*wegen euch*) because of you, on your account. **e~etwillen** adv **um e~et-willen** for your sake. **e~ige** poss pron **der/die/das e~ige** yours

Euro- *pref* Euro-

Europa *nt* -s Europe. **E~-** *pref* European

Europä|er(in) *m* -s,- (*f* -,-nen) European. **e~isch** *a* European; **E~ische Gemeinschaft** European Community

Euro|paß *m* Europassport. **E~scheck** *m* Eurocheque

Euter *nt* -s,- udder

evakuier|en *vt* evacuate. **E~ung** *f* - evacuation

evan|gelisch *a* Protestant. **E~gelist** *m* -en,-en evangelist. **E~gelium** *nt* -s,-ien gospel

evaporieren *vt/i* (*sein*) evaporate

Eventu|alität *f* -,-en eventuality. **e~ell** *a* possible ● *adv* possibly; (*vielleicht*) perhaps

Evolution /-'tsjo:n/ *f* - evolution

evtl. *abbr s.* **eventuell**

ewig *a* eternal, *adv* -ly; (*fam: ständig*) constant, *adv* -ly; (*endlos*) never-ending; **e~ dauern** (*fam*) take ages. **E~keit** *f* - eternity; **eine E~keit** (*fam*) ages

exakt *a* exact, *adv* -ly. **E~heit** *f* - exactitude

Examen *nt* -s,- & -mina (*Sch*) examination

Exekutive *f* - (*Pol*) executive

Exempel *nt* -s,- example; **ein E~ an jdm statuieren** make an example of s.o.

Exemplar *nt* -s,-e specimen; (*Buch*) copy. **e~isch** *a* exemplary

exerzieren *vt/i* (*haben*) (*Mil*) drill; (*üben*) practise

exhumieren *vt* exhume

Exil *nt* -s exile

Existenz *f* -,-en existence; (*Lebensgrundlage*) livelihood; (*pej: Person*) individual

existieren *vi* (*haben*) exist

exklusiv *a* exclusive. **e~e** *prep* (+ *gen*) excluding

exkommunizieren *vt* excommunicate

Exkremente *npl* excrement *sg*

exotisch *a* exotic

expan|dieren *vt/i* (*haben*) expand. **E~sion** *f* - expansion

Expedition /-'tsjo:n/ *f* -,-en expedition

Experiment *nt* -[e]s,-e experiment. **e~ell** *a* experimental. **e~ieren** *vi* (*haben*) experiment

Experte *m* -n,-n expert

explo|dieren *vi* (*sein*) explode. **E~sion** *f* -,-en explosion. **e~siv** *a* explosive

Export *m* -[e]s,-e export. **E~teur** /-'tø:ɐ/ *m* -s,-e exporter. **e~tieren** *vt* export

Expreß *m* -sses,-sse express

extra *adv* separately; (*zusätzlich*) extra; (*eigens*) specially; (*fam: absichtlich*) on purpose

Extrakt *m* -[e]s,-e extract

Extras *npl* (*Auto*) extras

extravagan|t *a* flamboyant, *adv* -ly; (*übertrieben*) extravagant. **E~z** *f* -,-en flamboyance; extravagance; (*Überspanntheit*) folly

extravertiert *a* extrovert

extrem *a* extreme, *adv* -ly. **E~** *nt* -s,-e extreme. **E~ist** *m* -en,-en extremist. **E~itäten** *fpl* extremities

Exzellenz *f* - (*title*) Excellency

Exzentr|iker *m* -s,- eccentric. **e~isch** *a* eccentric

Exzeß *m* -sses,-sse excess

F

Fabel *f* -,-n fable. **f~haft** *a* (*fam*) fantastic, *adv* -ally

Fabrik *f* -,-en factory. **F~ant** *m* -en,-en manufacturer. **F~at** *nt* -[e]s,-e product; (*Marke*) make. **F~ation** /-'tsjo:n/ *f* - manufacture

Facette /fa'sɛtə/ *f* -,-n facet

Fach *nt* -[e]s,ˆer compartment; (*Schub-*)drawer; (*Gebiet*) field; (*Sch*) subject. **F~arbeiter** *m* skilled worker. **F~arzt** *m*, **F~ärztin** *f* specialist. **F~ausdruck** *m* technical term

fäch|eln (sich) *vr* fan oneself. **F~er** *m* -s,- fan

Fach|gebiet *nt* field. **f~gemäß, f~gerecht** *a* expert, *adv* -ly. **F~hochschule** *f* ≈ technical university. **f~kundig** *a* expert, *adv* -ly. **f~lich** *a* technical, *adv* -ly; (*beruflich*) professional. **F~mann** *m* (*pl* -leute) expert. **f~männisch** *a* expert, *adv* -ly. **F~schule** *f* technical college. **f~simpeln** *vi* (*haben*) (*fam*) talk shop. **F~werkhaus** *nt* half-timbered house. **F~wort** *nt* (*pl* -wörter) technical term

Fackel *f* -,-n torch. **F~zug** *m* torchlight procession

fade *a* insipid; (*langweilig*) dull

Faden m -s,- thread; (Bohnen-) string; (Naut) fathom. **f~scheinig** a threadbare; (Grund) flimsy

Fagott nt -[e]s,-e bassoon

fähig a capable (**zu**/gen of); (tüchtig) able, competent. **F~keit** f -,-en ability; competence

fahl a pale

fahnd|en vi (haben) search (**nach** for). **F~ung** f -,-en search

Fahne f -,-n flag; (Druck-) galley [proof]; **eine F~ haben** (fam) reek of alcohol. **F~nflucht** f desertion. **f~nflüchtig** a **f~nflüchtig werden** desert

Fahr|ausweis m ticket. **F~bahn** f carriageway; (Straße) road. **f~bar** a mobile

Fähre f -,-n ferry

fahr|en† vi (sein) go, travel; (Fahrer:) drive; (Radfahrer:) ride; (verkehren) run; (ab-) leave; (Schiff:) sail; **mit dem Auto/Zug f~en** go by car/train; **in die Höhe f~en** start up; **in die Kleider f~en** throw on one's clothes; **mit der Hand über etw** (acc) **f~en** run one's hand over sth; **was ist in ihn gefahren?** (fam) what has got into him? ● vt drive; ride (Fahrrad); take (Kurve). **f~end** a moving; (f~bar) mobile; (nicht seßhaft) travelling, itinerant. **F~er** m -s,- driver. **F~erflucht** f failure to stop after an accident. **F~erhaus** nt driver's cab. **F~erin** f -,-nen woman driver. **F~gast** m passenger; (im Taxi) fare. **F~geld** nt fare. **F~gestell** nt chassis; (Aviat) undercarriage. **f~ig** a nervy; (zerstreut) distracted. **F~karte** f ticket. **F~kartenausgabe** f, **F~kartenschalter** m ticket office. **f~lässig** a negligent, adv -ly. **F~lässigkeit** f - negligence. **F~lehrer** m driving instructor. **F~plan** m timetable. **f~planmäßig** a scheduled ● adv according to/(pünktlich) on schedule. **F~preis** m fare. **F~prüfung** f driving test. **F~rad** nt bicycle. **F~schein** m ticket

Fährschiff nt ferry

Fahr|schule f driving school. **F~schüler(in)** m(f) learner driver. **F~spur** f [traffic] lane. **F~stuhl** m lift; (Amer) elevator. **F~stunde** f driving lesson

Fahrt f -,-en journey; (Auto) drive; (Ausflug) trip; (Tempo) speed; **in voller F~** at full speed. **F~ausweis** m ticket

Fährte f -,-n track; (Witterung) scent; **auf der falschen F~** (fig) on the wrong track

Fahr|tkosten pl travelling expenses. **F~werk** nt undercarriage. **F~zeug** nt -[e]s,-e vehicle; (Wasser-) craft, vessel

fair /fɛːɐ̯/ a fair, adv -ly. **F~neß** f - fairness

Fakten pl facts

Faktor m -s,-en /-'toːrən/ factor

Fakul|tät f -,-en faculty. **f~tativ** a optional

Falke m -n,-n falcon

Fall m -[e]s,ᵉe fall; (Jur, Med, Gram) case; **im F~[e]** in case (gen of); **auf jeden F~, auf alle F~e** in any case; (bestimmt) definitely; **für alle F~e** just in case; **auf keinen F~** on no account

Falle f -,-n trap; **eine F~ stellen** set a trap (dat for)

fallen† vi (sein) fall; (sinken) go down; **[im Krieg] f~** be killed in the war; **f~ lassen** drop

fällen vt fell; (fig) pass (Urteil); make (Entscheidung)

fallenlassen† vt sep (fig) drop; make (Bemerkung)

fällig a due; (Wechsel) mature; **längst f~** long overdue. **F~keit** f - (Comm) maturity

Fallobst nt windfalls pl

falls conj in case; (wenn) if

Fallschirm m parachute. **F~jäger** m paratrooper. **F~springer** m parachutist

Falltür f trapdoor

falsch a wrong; (nicht echt, unaufrichtig) false; (gefälscht) forged; (Geld) counterfeit; (Schmuck) fake ● adv wrongly; falsely; (singen) out of tune; **f~ gehen** (Uhr:) be wrong

fälsch|en vt forge, fake. **F~er** m -s,- forger

Falsch|geld nt counterfeit money. **F~heit** f - falseness

fälschlich a wrong, adv -ly; (irrtümlich) mistaken, adv -ly. **f~erweise** adv by mistake

Falsch|meldung f false report; (absichtlich) hoax report. **F~münzer** m -s,- counterfeiter

Fälschung f -,-en forgery, fake; (Fälschen) forging

Falte f -,-n fold; (Rock-) pleat; (Knitter-) crease; (im Gesicht) line; (Runzel) wrinkle

falten vt fold; **sich f~** ⟨Haut:⟩ wrinkle.
   F~rock m pleated skirt
Falter m -s,- butterfly; ⟨Nacht-⟩ moth
faltig a creased; ⟨Gesicht⟩ lined;
   ⟨runzlig⟩ wrinkled
familiär a family ...; ⟨vertraut, zu-
   dringlich⟩ familiar; ⟨zwanglos⟩ informal
Familie /-jə/ f -,-n family. **F~n-
   anschluß** m **F~nanschluß haben** live
   as one of the family. **F~nforschung** f
   genealogy. **F~nleben** nt family life.
   F~nname m surname. **F~n-
   planung** f family planning. **F~n-
   stand** m marital status
Fan /fɛn/ m -s,-s fan
Fana|tiker m -s,- fanatic. **f~tisch** a
   fanatical, adv -ly. **F~tismus** m - fan-
   aticism
Fanfare f -,-n trumpet; ⟨Signal⟩ fanfare
Fang m -[e]s,ˀe capture; ⟨Beute⟩ catch;
   F~e ⟨Krallen⟩ talons; ⟨Zähne⟩ fangs.
   F~arm m tentacle. **f~en†** vt catch;
   ⟨ein-⟩ capture; **sich f~en** get caught
   (in + dat in); ⟨fig⟩ regain one's balance/
   ⟨seelisch⟩ composure. **F~en** nt -s **F~en
   spielen** play tag. **F~frage** f catch
   question. **F~zahn** m fang
fantastisch a = phantastisch
Farb|aufnahme f colour photo-
   graph. **F~band** nt ⟨pl -bänder⟩ typewriter ribbon. **F~e** f -,-n colour;
   ⟨Maler-⟩ paint; ⟨zum Färben⟩ dye;
   ⟨Karten⟩ suit. **f~echt** a colour-fast
färben vt colour; dye ⟨Textilien,
   Haare⟩; ⟨fig⟩ slant ⟨Bericht⟩; **sich [rot]
   f~** turn [red] ● vi ⟨haben⟩ not be colour-
   fast
farb|enblind a colour-blind. **f~en-
   froh** a colourful. **F~fernsehen** nt
   colour television. **F~film** m colour
   film. **F~foto** nt colour photo. **f~ig**
   a coloured ● adv in colour. **F~ige(r)**
   m/f coloured man/woman. **F~-
   kasten** m box of paints. **f~los** a
   colourless. **F~stift** m crayon. **F~-
   stoff** m dye; ⟨Lebensmittel-⟩ colouring. **F~ton** m shade
Färbung f -,-en colouring; ⟨fig: An-
   strich⟩ bias
Farce /'farsə/ f -,-n farce; ⟨Culin⟩
   stuffing
Farn m -[e]s,-e, **F~kraut** nt fern
Färse f -,-n heifer
Fasan m -[e]s,-e[n] pheasant
Faschierte(s) nt ⟨Aust⟩ mince
Fasching m -s ⟨SGer⟩ carnival

Faschis|mus m - fascism. **F~t** m
   -en,-en fascist. **f~tisch** a fascist
faseln vt/i ⟨haben⟩ ⟨fam⟩ [Unsinn] f~
   talk nonsense
Faser f -,-n fibre. **f~n** vi ⟨haben⟩ fray
Faß nt -sses,ˀsser barrel, cask; **Bier
   vom Faß** draught beer; **Faß ohne
   Boden** ⟨fig⟩ bottomless pit
Fassade f -,-n façade
faßbar a comprehensible; ⟨greifbar⟩
   tangible
fassen vt take [hold of], grasp; ⟨er-
   greifen⟩ seize; ⟨fangen⟩ catch; ⟨ein-⟩
   set; ⟨enthalten⟩ hold; ⟨fig: begreifen⟩
   take in, grasp; conceive ⟨Plan⟩; make
   ⟨Entschluß⟩; **sich f~** compose oneself;
   sich kurz/in Geduld f~ be brief/
   patient; **in Worte f~** put into words;
   nicht zu f~ ⟨fig⟩ unbelievable ● vi
   ⟨haben⟩ **f~ an** (+ acc) touch; **f~ nach**
   reach for
faßlich a comprehensible
Fasson /fa'sõ:/ f - style; ⟨Form⟩ shape;
   ⟨Weise⟩ way
Fassung f -,-en mount; ⟨Edelstein-⟩ setting; ⟨Electr⟩ socket; ⟨Version⟩ version;
   ⟨Beherrschung⟩ composure; **aus der
   F~ bringen** disconcert. **f~slos** a
   shaken; ⟨erstaunt⟩ flabbergasted.
   F~svermögen nt capacity
fast adv almost, nearly; **f~ nie** hardly
   ever
fast|en vi ⟨haben⟩ fast. **F~enzeit**
   f Lent. **F~nacht** f Shrovetide;
   ⟨Karneval⟩ carnival. **F~nachts-
   dienstag** m Shrove Tuesday. **F~-
   tag** m fast-day
Faszin|ation /-'tsjo:n/ f - fascination.
   f~ieren vt fascinate; **f~ierend** fascinating
fatal a fatal; ⟨peinlich⟩ embarrassing. **F~ismus** m - fatalism. **F~ist**
   m -en,-en fatalist
Fata Morgana f - -/- -nen mirage
fauchen vi ⟨haben⟩ spit, hiss ● vt
   snarl
faul a lazy; ⟨verdorben⟩ rotten, bad;
   ⟨Ausrede⟩ lame; ⟨zweifelhaft⟩ bad;
   ⟨verdächtig⟩ fishy
Fäule f - decay
faul|en vi ⟨sein⟩ rot; ⟨Zahn:⟩ decay;
   ⟨verwesen⟩ putrefy. **f~enzen** vi
   ⟨haben⟩ be lazy. **F~enzer** m -s,- lazy-
   bones sg. **F~heit** f - laziness. **f~ig** a
   rotting; ⟨Geruch⟩ putrid
Fäulnis f - decay
Faulpelz m ⟨fam⟩ lazy-bones sg
Fauna f - fauna

Faust f -, **Fäuste** fist; **auf eigene F~** (fig) off one's own bat. **F~handschuh** m mitten. **F~schlag** m punch

Fauxpas /fo'pa/ m -, -/-[s],-s/ gaffe

Favorit(in) /favo'ri:t(ɪn)/ m -en,-en (f -,-nen) (Sport) favourite

Fax nt -,-[e] fax. **f~en** vt fax

Faxen fpl (fam) antics; **F~ machen** fool about; **F~ schneiden** pull faces

Faxgerät nt fax machine

Feber m -s,- (Aust) February

Februar m -s,-e February

fecht|en† vi (haben) fence. **F~er** m -s,- fencer

Feder f -,-n feather; (Schreib-) pen; (Spitze) nib; (Techn) spring. **F~ball** m shuttlecock; (Spiel) badminton. **F~busch** m plume. **f~leicht** a as light as a feather. **F~messer** nt penknife. **f~n** vi (haben) be springy; (nachgeben) give; (hoch-) bounce; **f~nd** springy; (elastisch) elastic. **F~ung** f - (Techn) springs pl; (Auto) suspension

Fee f -,-n fairy

Fegefeuer nt purgatory

fegen vt sweep ● vi (sein) (rasen) tear

Fehde f -,-n feud

fehl a **f~ am Platze** out of place. **F~betrag** m deficit. **f~en** vi (haben) be missing/(Sch) absent; (mangeln) be lacking; **es f~t an** (+dat) there is a shortage of; **mir f~t die Zeit** I haven't got the time; **sie/es f~t mir sehr** I miss her/it very much; **was f~t ihm?** what's the matter with him? **es f~te nicht viel und er ...** he very nearly ...; **das hat uns noch gefehlt!** that's all we need! **f~end** a missing; (Sch) absent

Fehler m -s,- mistake, error; (Sport & fig) fault; (Makel) flaw. **f~frei** a faultless, adv -ly. **f~haft** a faulty. **f~los** a flawless, adv -ly

Fehl|geburt f miscarriage. **f~gehen**† vi sep (sein) go wrong; (Schuß:) miss; (fig) be mistaken. **F~griff** m mistake. **F~kalkulation** f miscalculation. **F~schlag** m failure. **f~schlagen**† vi sep (sein) fail. **F~start** m (Sport) false start. **F~tritt** m false step; (fig) [moral] lapse. **F~zündung** f (Auto) misfire

Feier f -,-n celebration; (Zeremonie) ceremony; (Party) party. **F~abend** m end of the working day; **F~abend machen** stop work, (fam) knock off; **nach F~abend** after work. **f~lich** a solemn, adv -ly; (förmlich) formal, adv -ly. **F~lichkeit** f -,-en solemnity;

F~lichkeiten festivities. **f~n** vt celebrate; hold (Fest); (ehren) fête ● vi (haben) celebrate; (lustig sein) make merry. **F~tag** m [public] holiday; (kirchlicher) feast-day; **erster/zweiter F~tag** Christmas Day/Boxing Day. **f~tags** adv on public holidays

feige a cowardly; **f~ sein** be a coward ● adv in a cowardly way

Feige f -,-n fig. **F~nbaum** m fig tree

Feig|heit f - cowardice. **F~ling** m -s,-e coward

Feile f -,-n file. **f~n** vt/i (haben) file

feilschen vi (haben) haggle

Feilspäne mpl filings

fein a fine, adv -ly; (zart) delicate, adv -ly; (Strümpfe) sheer; (Unterschied) subtle; (scharf) keen; (vornehm) refined; (elegant) elegant; (prima) great; **sich f~ machen** dress up. **F~arbeit** f precision work

Feind|(in) m -es,-e (f -,-nen) enemy. **f~lich** a enemy; (f~selig) hostile. **F~schaft** f -,-en enmity. **f~selig** a hostile. **F~seligkeit** f -,-en hostility

fein|fühlig a sensitive. **F~gefühl** nt sensitivity; (Takt) delicacy. **F~heit** f -,-en (s. fein) fineness; delicacy; subtlety; keenness; refinement; **F~heiten** subtleties. **F~kostgeschäft** nt delicatessen [shop]. **F~schmecker** m -s,- gourmet

feist a fat

feixen vi (haben) smirk

Feld nt -[e]s,-er field; (Fläche) ground; (Sport) pitch; (Schach-) square; (auf Formular) box. **F~bau** m agriculture. **F~bett** nt camp-bed, (Amer) cot. **F~forschung** f fieldwork. **F~herr** m commander. **F~marschall** m Field Marshal. **F~stecher** m -s,- field-glasses pl. **F~webel** m (Mil) sergeant. **F~zug** m campaign

Felge f -,-n [wheel] rim

Fell nt -[e]s,-e (Zool) coat; (Pelz) fur; (abgezogen) skin, pelt; **ein dickes F~ haben** (fam) be thick-skinned

Fels m -en,-en rock. **F~block** m boulder. **F~en** m -s,- rock. **f~enfest** a (fig) firm, adv -ly. **f~ig** a rocky

feminin a feminine; (weibisch) effeminate

Femininum nt -s,-na (Gram) feminine

Feminist|(in) m -en,-en (f -,-nen) feminist. **f~isch** a feminist

Fenchel m -s fennel

Fenster *nt* -s,- window. **F~brett** *nt* window-sill. **F~laden** *m* [window] shutter. **F~leder** *nt* chamois [-leather]. **F~putzer** *m* -s,- window-cleaner. **F~scheibe** *f* [window-]pane

Ferien /'fe:rjən/ *pl* holidays; (*Univ*) vacation *sg*; **F~ haben** be on holiday. **F~ort** *m* holiday resort

Ferkel *nt* -s,- piglet

fern *a* distant; **der F~e Osten** the Far East ● *adv* far away; **von f~** from a distance ● *prep* (+ *dat*) far [away] from. **F~bedienung** *f* remote control. **f~bleiben†** *vi sep* (*sein*) stay away (*dat* from). **F~e** *f* - distance; **in/aus der F~e** in the/from a distance; **in weiter F~e** far away; (*zeitlich*) in the distant future. **f~er** *a* further ● *adv* (*außerdem*) furthermore; (*in Zukunft*) in future. **f~gelenkt** *a* remote-controlled; ⟨*Rakete*⟩ guided. **F~gespräch** *nt* long-distance call. **f~gesteuert** *a* = **f~gelenkt**. **F~glas** *nt* binoculars *pl*. **f~halten†** *vt sep* keep away; **sich f~halten** keep away. **F~kopierer** *m* -s,- fax machine. **F~kurs[us]** *m* correspondence course. **F~lenkung** *f* remote control. **F~licht** *nt* (*Auto*) full beam. **F~meldewesen** *nt* telecommunications *pl*. **F~rohr** *nt* telescope. **F~schreiben** *nt* telex. **F~schreiber** *m* -s,- telex [machine]

Fernseh|apparat *m* television set. **f~en†** *vi sep* (*haben*) watch television. **F~en** *nt* -s television. **F~er** *m* -s,- [television] viewer; (*Gerät*) television set. **F~gerät** *nt* television set

Fernsprech|amt *nt* telephone exchange, (*Amer*) central. **F~er** *m* telephone. **F~nummer** *f* telephone number. **F~zelle** *f* telephone box

Fernsteuerung *f* remote control

Ferse *f* -,-n heel. **F~ngeld** *nt* **F~ngeld geben** (*fam*) take to one's heels

fertig *a* finished; (*bereit*) ready; (*Comm*) ready-made; ⟨*Gericht*⟩ ready-to-serve; **f~ werden mit** finish; (*bewältigen*) cope with; **f~ sein** have finished; (*fig*) be through (**mit jdm** with s.o.); (*fam: erschöpft*) be all in/(*seelisch*) shattered ● *adv* **f~ essen/lesen** finish eating/reading. **F~bau** *m* (*pl* -bauten) prefabricated building. **f~bringen†** *vt sep* manage to do; (*beenden*) finish; **ich bringe es nicht f~** I can't bring myself to do it. **f~en** *vt* make. **F~gericht** *nt* ready-to-serve meal.

F~haus *nt* prefabricated house. **F~keit** *f* -,-en skill. **f~kriegen** *vt sep* (*fam*) = **f~bringen**. **f~machen** *vt sep* finish; (*bereitmachen*) get ready; (*fam: erschöpfen*) wear out; (*seelisch*) shatter; (*fam: abkanzeln*) carpet; **sich f~machen** get ready. **f~stellen** *vt sep* complete. **F~stellung** *f* completion. **F~ung** *f* - manufacture

fesch *a* (*fam*) attractive; (*flott*) smart; (*Aust: nett*) kind

Fessel *f* -,-n ankle

fesseln *vt* tie up; tie (**an** + *acc* to); (*fig*) fascinate; **ans Bett gefesselt** confined to bed. **F~** *fpl* bonds. **F~d** *a* (*fig*) fascinating; (*packend*) absorbing

fest *a* firm; (*nicht flüssig*) solid; (*erstarrt*) set; (*haltbar*) strong; (*nicht locker*) tight; (*feststehend*) fixed; (*ständig*) steady; ⟨*Anstellung*⟩ permanent; ⟨*Schlaf*⟩ sound; ⟨*Blick, Stimme*⟩ steady; **f~ werden** harden; ⟨*Gelee*⟩ set; **f~e Nahrung** solids *pl* ● *adv* firmly; tightly; steadily; soundly; (*kräftig, tüchtig*) hard; **f~ schlafen** be fast asleep

Fest *nt* -[e]s,-e celebration; (*Party*) party; (*Relig*) festival; **frohes F~!** happy Christmas!

fest|angestellt *a* permanent. **f~binden†** *vt sep* tie (**an** + *dat* to). **f~bleiben†** *vi sep* (*sein*) (*fig*) remain firm. **f~e** *adv* (*fam*) hard. **F~essen** *nt* = **F~mahl**. **f~fahren†** *vi/r sep* (*sein*) [**sich**] **f~fahren** get stuck; ⟨*Verhandlungen*⟩ reach deadlock. **f~halten†** *v sep* ● *vt* hold on to; (*aufzeichnen*) record; **sich f~halten** hold on ● *vi* (*haben*) **f~halten an** (+ *dat*) (*fig*) stick to; cling to ⟨*Tradition*⟩. **f~igen** *vt* strengthen; **sich f~igen** grow stronger. **F~iger** *m* -s,- styling lotion/(*Schaum-*) mousse. **F~igkeit** *f* - (*s.* **fest**) firmness; solidity; strength; steadiness. **f~klammern** *vt sep* clip (**an** + *dat* to); **sich f~klammern** cling (**an** + *dat* to). **F~land** *nt* mainland; (*Kontinent*) continent. **f~legen** *vt sep* fix, settle; lay down ⟨*Regeln*⟩; tie up ⟨*Geld*⟩; **sich f~legen** commit oneself

festlich *a* festive, *adv* -ly. **F~keiten** *fpl* festivities

fest|liegen† *vi sep* (*haben*) be fixed, settled. **f~machen** *v sep* ● *vt* fasten/ (*binden*) tie (**an** + *dat* to); (*f~legen*) fix, settle ● *vi* (*haben*) (*Naut*) moor.

F~**mahl** nt feast; (Bankett) banquet.
F~**nahme** f -,-n arrest. f~**nehmen**†
vt sep arrest. F~**ordner** m steward.
f~**setzen** vt sep fix, settle; (inhaftieren) gaol; **sich f~setzen** collect.
f~**sitzen**† vi sep (haben) be firm/
⟨Schraube:⟩ tight; (haften) stick;
(nicht weiterkommen) be stuck. F~
spiele npl festival sg. f~**stehen**† vi
sep (haben) be certain. f~**stellen** vt
sep fix; (ermitteln) establish; (bemerken) notice; (sagen) state.
F~**stellung** f establishment; (Aussage) statement; (Erkenntnis) realization. F~**tag** m special day

Festung f -,-en fortress

Fest|zelt nt marquee. f~**ziehen**† vt
sep pull tight. F~**zug** m [grand] procession

Fete /'fe:tə, 'fɛ:tə/ f -,-n party

fett a fat; (f~reich) fatty; (fettig)
greasy; (üppig) rich; ⟨Druck⟩ bold.
F~ nt -[e]s,-e fat; (flüssig) grease.
f~**arm** a low-fat. f~**en** vt grease ● vi
(haben) be greasy. F~**fleck** m grease
mark. f~**ig** a greasy. f~**leibig** a
obese. f~**näpfchen** nt ins F~**näpfchen treten** (fam) put one's foot in it

Fetzen m -s,- scrap; (Stoff) rag; **in F~**
in shreds

feucht a damp, moist; ⟨Luft⟩ humid.
f~**heiß** a humid. F~**igkeit** f - damp-
ness; (Nässe) moisture; (Luft-) humid-
ity. F~**igkeitscreme** f moisturizer

feudal a (fam: vornehm) sumptuous,
adv -ly. F~**ismus** m - feudalism

Feuer nt -s,- fire; (für Zigarette) light;
(Begeisterung) passion; F~ **machen**
light a fire; F~ **fangen** catch fire; (fam:
sich verlieben) be smitten; **jdm F~
geben** give s.o. a light. F~**alarm**
m fire alarm. F~**bestattung** f
cremation. f~**gefährlich** a [in]
flammable. F~**leiter** f fire-escape.
F~**löscher** m -s,- fire extinguisher.
F~**melder** m -s,- fire alarm. f~**n** vi
(haben) fire (auf + acc on) ● vt (fam)
(schleudern) fling; (entlassen) fire.
F~**probe** f (fig) test. f~**rot** a crimson. f~**speiend** a f~**speiender Berg**
volcano. F~**stein** m flint. F~**stelle** f
hearth. F~**treppe** f fire-escape.
F~**wache** f fire station. F~**waffe**
f firearm. F~**wehr** f -,-en fire brigade. F~**wehrauto** nt fire-engine.
F~**wehrmann** m (pl -männer &
-leute) fireman. F~**werk** nt firework

display, fireworks pl. F~**werkskör-
per** m firework. F~**zeug** nt lighter

feurig a fiery; (fig) passionate

Fiaker m -s,- (Aust) horse-drawn cab

Fichte f -,-n spruce

fidel a cheerful

Fieber nt -s [raised] temperature; F~
haben have a temperature. f~**haft** a
(fig) feverish, adv -ly. f~**n** vi (haben)
be feverish. F~**thermometer** nt
thermometer

fiebrig a feverish

fies a (fam) nasty, adv -ily

Figur f -,-en figure; (Roman-, Film-)
character; (Schach-) piece

Fik|tion /-'tsjo:n/ f -,-en fiction. f~**tiv**
a fictitious

Filet /fi'le:/ nt -s,-s fillet

Filial|e f -,-n, F~**geschäft** nt (Comm)
branch

Filigran nt -s filigree

Film m -[e]s,-e film; (Kino-) film, (Amer)
movie; (Schicht) coating. f~**en** vt/i
(haben) film. F~**kamera** f cine/(für
Kinofilm) film camera

Filt|er m & (Techn) nt -s,- filter;
(Zigaretten-) filter-tip. f~**ern** vt filter.
F~**erzigarette** f filter-tipped cigar-
ette. f~**rieren** vt filter

Filz m -es felt. f~**en** vi (haben) become
matted ● vt (fam) (durch- suchen)
frisk; (stehlen) steal. F~**schreiber** m
-s,-, F~**stift** m felt-tipped pen

Fimmel m -s,- (fam) obsession

Fina|le nt -s,- (Mus) finale; (Sport) final.
F~**list(in)** m -en,-en (f -,-nen) finalist

Finanz f -,-en finance. F~**amt** nt tax
office. f~**iell** a financial, adv -ly.
f~**ieren** vt finance. F~**minister** m
minister of finance

find|en† vt find; (meinen) think; **den
Tod f~en** meet one's death; **wie f~est
du das?** what do you think of that?
f~**est du?** do you think so? **es wird
sich f~en** it'll turn up; (fig) it'll be all
right ● vi (haben) find one's way. F~**er**
m -s,- finder. F~**erlohn** m reward.
f~**ig** a resourceful. F~**ling** m -s,-e
boulder

Finesse f -,-n (Kniff) trick; F~**n**
(Techn) refinements

Finger m -s,- finger; **die F~ lassen von**
(fam) leave alone; **etw im kleinen
F~ haben** (fam) have sth at one's
fingertips. F~**abdruck** m finger-
mark; (Admin) fingerprint. F~**hut**
m thimble. F~**nagel** m finger-nail.

F~ring m ring. **F~spitze** f finger-tip. **F~zeig** m -[e]s,-e hint

fingier|en vt fake. **f~t** a fictitious

Fink m -en,-en finch

Finn|e m -n,-n, **F~in** f -,-nen Finn. **f~isch** a Finnish. **F~land** nt -s Finland

finster a dark; (düster) gloomy; (unheildrohend) sinister; **im F~n** in the dark. **F~nis** f - darkness; (Astr) eclipse

Finte f -,-n trick; (Boxen) feint

Firma f -,-men firm, company

firmen vt (Relig) confirm

Firmen|wagen m company car. **F~zeichen** nt trade mark, logo

Firmung f -,-en (Relig) confirmation

Firnis m -ses,-se varnish. **f~sen** vt varnish

First m -[e]s,-e [roof] ridge

Fisch m -[e]s,-e fish; **F~e** (Astr) Pisces. **F~dampfer** m trawler. **f~en** vt/i (haben) fish; **aus dem Wasser f~en** (fam) fish out of the water. **F~er** m -s,- fisherman. **F~erei** f -, **F~fang** m fishing. **F~gräte** f fishbone. **F~händler** m fishmonger. **F~otter** m otter. **F~reiher** m heron. **F~stäbchen** nt -s,- fish finger. **F~teich** m fish-pond

Fiskus m - der **F~** the Treasury

Fisole f -,-n (Aust) French bean

fit a fit. **F~neß** f - fitness

fix a (fam) quick, adv -ly; (geistig) bright; **f~e Idee** obsession; **fix und fertig** all finished; (bereit) all ready; (fam: erschöpft) shattered. **F~er** m -s,- (sl) junkie

fixieren vt stare at; (Phot) fix

Fjord m -[e]s,-e fiord

FKK abbr (Freikörperkultur) naturism

flach a flat; (eben) level; (niedrig) low; (nicht tief) shallow; **f~er Teller** dinner plate; **die f~e Hand** the flat of the hand

Fläche f -,-n area; (Ober-) surface; (Seite) face. **F~nmaß** nt square measure

Flachs m -es flax. **f~blond** a flaxen-haired; (Haar) flaxen

flackern vi (haben) flicker

Flagg|e f -,-n flag

flagrant a flagrant

Flair /flɛ:ɐ/ nt -s air, aura

Flak f -,-[s] anti-aircraft artillery/(Geschütz) gun

flämisch a Flemish

Flamme f -,-n flame; (Koch-) burner; **in F~n** in flames

Flanell m -s (Tex) flannel

Flank|e f -,-n flank. **f~ieren** vt flank

Flasche f -,-n bottle. **F~nbier** nt bottled beer. **F~nöffner** m bottle-opener

flatter|haft a fickle. **f~n** vi (sein/haben) flutter; (Segel:) flap

flau a (schwach) faint; (Comm) slack; **mir ist f~** I feel faint

Flaum m -[e]s down. **f~ig** a downy; **f~ig rühren** (Aust Culin) cream

flauschig a fleecy; (Spielzeug) fluffy

Flausen fpl (fam) silly ideas; (Ausflüchte) silly excuses

Flaute f -,-n (Naut) calm; (Comm) slack period; (Schwäche) low

fläzen (sich) vr (fam) sprawl

Flechte f -,-n (Med) eczema; (Bot) lichen; (Zopf) plait. **f~n†** vt plait; weave (Korb)

Fleck m -[e]s,-e[n] spot; (größer) patch; (Schmutz-) stain, mark; **blauer F~** bruise; **nicht vom F~ kommen** (fam) make no progress. **f~en** vi (haben) stain. **F~en** m -s,- =**Fleck**; (Ortschaft) small town. **f~enlos** a spotless. **F~entferner** m -s,- stain remover. **f~ig** a stained; (Haut) blotchy

Fledermaus f bat

Flegel m -s,- lout. **f~haft** a loutish. **F~jahre** npl (fam) awkward age sg. **f~n (sich)** vr loll

flehen vi (haben) beg (um for). **f~tlich** a pleading, adv -ly

Fleisch nt -[e]s flesh; (Culin) meat; (Frucht-) pulp. **F~er** m -s,- butcher. **F~erei** f -,-en, **F~erladen** m butcher's shop. **f~fressend** a carnivorous. **F~fresser** m -s,- carnivore. **F~hauer** m -s,- (Aust) butcher. **f~ig** a fleshy. **f~lich** a carnal. **F~wolf** m mincer. **F~wunde** f flesh-wound

Fleiß m -es diligence; **mit F~** diligently; (absichtlich) on purpose. **f~ig** a diligent, adv -ly; (arbeitsam) industrious, adv -ly

flektieren vt (Gram) inflect

fletschen vt **die Zähne f~** (Tier:) bare its teeth

flex|ibel a flexible; (Einband) limp. **F~ibilität** f - flexibility. **F~ion** f -,-en (Gram) inflexion

flicken vt mend; (mit Flicken) patch. **F~** m -s,- patch

Flieder m -s lilac. **f~farben** a lilac

Fliege f -,-n fly; (Schleife) bow-tie; **zwei F~n mit einer Klappe schlagen** kill two birds with one stone. **f~t** *vi* (*sein*) fly; (*geworfen werden*) be thrown; (*fam: fallen*) fall; (*fam: entlassen werden*) be fired/(*von der Schule*) expelled; **in die Luft f~n** blow up ● *vt* fly. **f~nd** *a* flying; (*Händler*) itinerant; **in f~nder Eile** in great haste. **F~r** *m* -s,- airman; (*Pilot*) pilot; (*fam: Flugzeug*) plane. **F~rangriff** *m* air raid

flieh|en† *vi* (*sein*) flee (**vor** + *dat* from); (*entweichen*) escape ● *vt* shun. **f~end** *a* fleeing; (*Kinn, Stirn*) receding. **F~kraft** *f* centrifugal force

Fliese *f* -,-n tile

Fließ|band *nt* assembly line. **f~en†** *vi* (*sein*) flow; (*aus Wasserhahn*) run. **f~end** *a* flowing; (*Wasser*) running; (*Verkehr*) moving; (*geläufig*) fluent, *adv* -ly. **F~heck** *nt* fastback. **F~wasser** *nt* running water

flimmern *vi* (*haben*) shimmer; (*TV*) flicker; **es flimmert mir vor den Augen** everything is dancing in front of my eyes

flink *a* nimble, *adv* -bly; (*schnell*) quick, *adv* -ly

Flinte *f* -,-n shotgun

Flirt /flœrt/ *m* -s,-s flirtation. **f~en** *vi* (*haben*) flirt

Flitter *m* -s sequins *pl*; (*F~schmuck*) tinsel. **F~wochen** *fpl* honeymoon *sg*

flitzen *vi* (*sein*) (*fam*) dash; (*Auto:*) whizz

Flock|e *f* -,-n flake; (*Wolle*) tuft. **f~ig** *a* fluffy

Floh *m* -[e]s,-e flea. **F~markt** *m* flea market. **F~spiel** *nt* tiddly-winks *sg*

Flor *m* -s gauze; (*Trauer-*) crape; (*Samt-, Teppich-*) pile

Flora *f* - flora

Florett *nt* -[e]s,-e foil

florieren *vi* (*haben*) flourish

Floskel *f* -,-n [empty] phrase

Floß *nt* -es,-e raft

Flosse *f* -,-n fin; (*Seehund-, Gummi-*) flipper; (*sl: Hand*) paw

Flöt|e *f* -,-n flute; (*Block-*) recorder. **f~en** *vi* (*haben*) play the flute/recorder; (*fam: pfeifen*) whistle ● *vt* play on the flute/recorder. **F~ist(in)** *m* -en,-en (*f* -,-nen) flautist

flott *a* quick, *adv* -ly; (*lebhaft*) lively; (*schick*) smart, *adv* -ly; **f~ leben** live it up

Flotte *f* -,-n fleet

flottmachen *vt sep* **wieder f~** (*Naut*) refloat; get going again (*Auto*); put back on its feet (*Unternehmen*)

Flöz *nt* -es,-e [coal] seam

Fluch *m* -[e]s,-e curse. **f~en** *vi* (*haben*) curse, swear

Flucht¹ *f* -,-en (*Reihe*) line; (*Zimmer-*) suite

Flucht² *f* - flight; (*Entweichen*) escape; **die F~ ergreifen** take flight. **f~artig** *a* hasty, *adv* -ily

flücht|en *vi* (*sein*) flee (**vor** + *dat* from); (*entweichen*) escape ● *vr* **sich f~en** take refuge. **f~ig** *a* fugitive; (*kurz*) brief, *adv* -ly; (*Blick, Gedanke*) fleeting; (*Bekanntschaft*) passing; (*oberflächlich*) cursory, *adv* -ily; (*nicht sorgfältig*) careless, *adv* -ly; (*Chem*) volatile; **f~ig sein** be on the run; **f~ig kennen** know slightly. **F~igkeitsfehler** *m* slip. **F~ling** *m* -s,-e fugitive; (*Pol*) refugee

Fluchwort *nt* (*pl* -wörter) swearword

Flug *m* -[e]s,-e flight. **F~abwehr** *f* anti-aircraft defence. **F~ball** *m* (*Tennis*) volley. **F~blatt** *nt* pamphlet

Flügel *m* -s,- wing; (*Fenster-*) casement; (*Mus*) grand piano

Fluggast *m* [air] passenger

flügge *a* fully-fledged

Flug|gesellschaft *f* airline. **F~hafen** *m* airport. **F~lotse** *m* air-traffic controller. **F~platz** *m* airport; (*klein*) airfield. **F~preis** *m* air fare. **F~schein** *m* air ticket. **F~schneise** *f* flight path. **F~schreiber** *m* -s,- flight recorder. **F~schrift** *f* pamphlet. **F~steig** *m* -[e]s,-e gate. **F~wesen** *nt* aviation. **F~zeug** *nt* -[e]s,-e aircraft, plane

Fluidum *nt* -s aura

Flunder *f* -,-n flounder

flunkern *vi* (*haben*) (*fam*) tell fibs; (*aufschneiden*) tell tall stories

Flunsch *m* -[e]s,-e pout

fluoreszierend *a* fluorescent

Flur *m* -[e]s,-e [entrance] hall; (*Gang*) corridor

Flusen *fpl* fluff *sg*

Fluß *m* -sses,-sse river; (*Fließen*) flow; **im F~** (*fig*) in a state of flux. **f~abwärts** *adv* downstream. **f~aufwärts** *adv* upstream. **F~bett** *nt* river-bed

flüssig *a* liquid; (*Lava*) molten; (*fließend*) fluent, *adv* -ly; (*Verkehr*) freely moving. **F~keit** *f* -,-en liquid; (*Anat*) fluid

Flußpferd *nt* hippopotamus

flüstern *vt/i* (*haben*) whisper

Flut *f* -,-en high tide; (*fig*) flood; **F~en** waters. **F~licht** *nt* floodlight. **F~welle** *f* tidal wave

Föderation /-'tsio:n/ *f* -,-en federation

Fohlen *nt* -s,- foal

Föhn *m* -s föhn [wind]

Folg|e *f* -,-n consequence; (*Reihe*) succession; (*Fortsetzung*) instalment; (*Teil*) part; **F~e leisten** (+ *dat*) accept (*Einladung*); obey (*Befehl*). **f~en** *vi* (*sein*) follow (**jdm/etw** s.o./sth); (*zuhören*) listen (*dat* to); **daraus f~t, daß** it follows that; **wie f~t** as follows ● (*haben*) (*gehorchen*) obey (**jdm** s.o.). **f~end** *a* following; **f~endes** the following. **f~endermaßen** *adv* as follows

folger|n *vt* conclude (**aus** from). **F~ung** *f* -,-en conclusion

folg|lich *adv* consequently. **f~sam** *a* obedient, *adv* -ly

Folie /'fo:liə/ *f* -,-n foil; (*Plastik-*) film

Folklore *f* - folklore

Folter *f* -,-n torture; **auf die F~ spannen** (*fig*) keep on tenterhooks. **f~n** *vt* torture

Fön (**P**) *m* -s,-e hair-drier

Fonds /fõ:/ *m* -,- /-[s],-s/ fund

fönen *vt* [blow-]dry

Fontäne *f* -,-n jet; (*Brunnen*) fountain

Förder|band *nt* (*pl* **-bänder**) conveyor belt. **f~lich** *a* beneficial

fordern *vt* demand; (*beanspruchen*) claim; (*zum Kampf*) challenge; **gefordert werden** (*fig*) be stretched

fördern *vt* promote; (*unterstützen*) encourage; (*finanziell*) sponsor; (*gewinnen*) extract

Forderung *f* -,-en demand; (*Anspruch*) claim

Förderung *f* - (*s.* fördern) promotion; encouragement; (*Techn*) production

Forelle *f* -,-n trout

Form *f* -,-en form; (*Gestalt*) shape; (*Culin, Techn*) mould; (*Back-*) tin; [**gut**] **in F~** in good form

Formalität *f* -,-en formality

Format *nt* -[e]s,-e format; (*Größe*) size; (*fig: Bedeutung*) stature

Formation /-'tsio:n/ *f* -,-en formation

Formel *f* -,-n formula

formell *a* formal, *adv* -ly

formen *vt* shape, mould; (*bilden*) form; **sich f~** take shape

förmlich *a* formal, *adv* -ly; (*regelrecht*) virtual, *adv* -ly. **F~keit** *f* -,-en formality

form|los *a* shapeless; (*zwanglos*) informal, *adv* -ly. **F~sache** *f* formality

Formular *nt* -s,-e [printed] form

formulier|en *vt* formulate, word. **F~ung** *f* -,-en wording

forsch *a* brisk, *adv* -ly; (*schneidig*) dashing, *adv* -ly

forsch|en *vi* (*haben*) search (**nach** for). **f~end** *a* searching. **F~er** *m* -s,- research scientist; (*Reisender*) explorer. **F~ung** *f* -,-en research. **F~ungsreisende(r)** *m* explorer

Forst *m* -[e]s,-e forest

Förster *m* -s,- forester

Forstwirtschaft *f* forestry

Forsythie /-tsiə/ *f* -,-n forsythia

Fort *nt* -s,-s (*Mil*) fort

fort *adv* away; **f~ sein** be away; (*gegangen/verschwunden*) have gone; **und so f~** and so on; **in einem f~** continuously. **f~bewegen** *vt sep* move; **sich f~bewegen** move. **F~bewegung** *f* locomotion. **F~bildung** *f* further education/training. **f~bleiben†** *vi sep* (*sein*) stay away. **f~bringen†** *vt sep* take away. **f~fahren†** *vi sep* (*sein*) go away ● (*haben/sein*) continue (**zu** to). **f~fallen†** *vi sep* (*sein*) be dropped/ (*ausgelassen*) omitted; (*entfallen*) no longer apply; (*aufhören*) cease. **f~führen** *vt sep* continue. **F~gang** *m* departure; (*Verlauf*) progress. **f~gehen†** *vi sep* (*sein*) leave, go away; (*ausgehen*) go out; (*andauern*) go on. **f~geschritten** *a* advanced; (*spät*) late. **F~geschrittene(r)** *m/f* advanced student. **f~gesetzt** *a* constant, *adv* -ly. **f~jagen** *vt sep* chase away. **f~lassen†** *vt sep* let go; (*auslassen*) omit. **f~laufen†** *vi sep* (*sein*) run away; (*sich f~setzen*) continue. **f~laufend** *a* consecutive, *adv* -ly. **f~nehmen†** *vt sep* take away. **f~pflanzen (sich)** *vr sep* reproduce; (*Ton, Licht:*) travel. **F~pflanzung** *f* - reproduction. **F~pflanzungsorgan** *nt* reproductive organ. **f~reißen†** *vt sep* carry away; (*entreißen*) tear away. **f~schaffen** *vt sep* take away. **f~schicken** *vt sep* send away; (*abschicken*) send off. **f~schreiten†** *vi sep* (*sein*) continue; (*Fortschritte machen*) progress, advance. **f~schreitend** *a* progressive; (*Alter*) advancing. **F~schritt** *m* progress; **F~schritte machen** make progress.

f~schrittlich *a* progressive. **f~setzen** *vt sep* continue; **sich f~setzen** continue. **F~setzung** *f* -,-en continuation; *(Folge)* instalment. **f~setzung folgt** to be continued. **F~setzungsroman** *m* serialized novel, serial. **f~während** *a* constant, *adv* -ly. **f~werfen†** *vt sep* throw away. **f~ziehen†** *v sep* ● *vt* pull away ● *vi (sein)* move away

Fossil *nt* -,-ien /-jən/ fossil

Foto *nt* -s,-s photo. **F~apparat** *m* camera. **f~gen** *a* photogenic

Fotograf|(in) *m* -en,-en *(f* -,-nen) photographer. **F~ie** *f* -,-n photography; *(Bild)* photograph. **f~ieren** *vt* take a photo[graph] of; **sich f~ie-ren lassen** have one's photo[graph] taken ● *vi (haben)* take photographs. **f~isch** *a* photographic

Fotokopie *f* photocopy. **f~ren** *vt* photocopy. **F~rgerät** *nt* photocopier

Fötus *m* -,-ten foetus

Foul /faul/ *nt* -s,-s *(Sport)* foul. **f~en** *vt* foul

Foyer /foa'je:/ *nt* -s,-s foyer

Fracht *f* -,-en freight. **F~er** *m* -s,- freighter. **F~gut** *nt* freight. **F~schiff** *nt* cargo boat

Frack *m* -[e]s,ⁿe & -s tailcoat; **im F~** in tails *pl*

Frage *f* -,-n question; **eine F~ stellen** ask a question; **etw in F~ stellen** question sth; *(ungewiß machen)* make sth doubtful; **ohne F~** undoubtedly; **nicht in F~ kommen** be out of the question. **F~bogen** *m* questionnaire. **f~n** *vt/i (haben)* ask; **sich f~n** wonder *(ob* whether). **f~nd** *a* questioning, *adv* -ly; *(Gram)* interrogative. **F~zeichen** *nt* question mark

frag|lich *a* doubtful; *(Person, Sache)* in question. **f~los** *adv* undoubtedly

Fragment *nt* -[e]s,-e fragment. **f~a-risch** *a* fragmentary

fragwürdig *a* questionable; *(verdächtig)* dubious

fraisefarben /'frɛ:s-/ *a* strawberry-pink

Fraktion /-'tsjo:n/ *f* -,-en parliamentary party

Franken¹ *m* -s,- *(Swiss)* franc

Franken² *nt* -s Franconia

Frankfurter *f* -,- frankfurter

frankieren *vt* stamp, frank

Frankreich *nt* -s France

Fransen *fpl* fringe *sg*

Franz|ose *m* -n,-n Frenchman; **die F~osen** the French *pl*. **F~ösin** *f* -,-nen Frenchwoman. **f~ösisch** *a* French. **F~ösisch** *nt* -[s] *(Lang)* French

frapp|ant *a* striking. **f~ieren** *vt (fig)* strike; **f~ierend** striking

fräsen *vt (Techn)* mill

Fraß *m* -es feed; *(pej: Essen)* muck

Fratze *f* -,-n grotesque face; *(Grimasse)* grimace; *(pej: Gesicht)* face; **F~n schneiden** pull faces

Frau *f* -,-en woman; *(Ehe-)* wife; **F~ Thomas** Mrs/*(unverheiratet)* Miss/*(Admin)* Ms Thomas; **Unsere Liebe F~** *(Relig)* Our Lady. **F~chen** *nt* -s,- mistress

Frauen|arzt *m*, **F~ärztin** *f* gynaecologist. **F~rechtlerin** *f* -,-nen feminist. **F~zimmer** *nt* woman

Fräulein *nt* -s,- single woman; *(jung)* young lady; *(Anrede)* Miss

fraulich *a* womanly

frech *a* cheeky, *adv* -ily; *(unverschämt)* impudent, *adv* -ly. **F~dachs** *m (fam)* cheeky monkey. **F~heit** *f* -,-en cheekiness; impudence; *(Äußerung, Handlung)* impertinence

frei *a* free; *(freischaffend)* freelance; *(Künstler)* independent; *(nicht besetzt)* vacant; *(offen)* open; *(bloß)* bare; **f~er Tag** day off; **sich (dat) f~ nehmen** take time off; **f~ machen** *(räumen)* clear; vacate *(Platz)*; *(entkleiden)* bare; **f~ lassen** leave free; **jdm f~e Hand lassen** give s.o. a free hand; **ist dieser Platz f~?** is this seat taken? **'Zimmer f~'** 'vacancies' ● *adv* freely; *(ohne Notizen)* without notes; *(umsonst)* free

Frei|bad *nt* open-air swimming pool. **f~bekommen†** *vt sep* get released; **einen Tag f~bekommen** get a day off. **f~beruflich** *a & adv* freelance. **F~e** *nt* im **F~en** in the open air, out of doors. **F~frau** *f* baroness. **F~gabe** *f* release. **f~geben†** *v sep* ● *vt* release; *(eröffnen)* open; **jdm einen Tag f~geben** give s.o. a day off ● *vi (haben)* **jdm f~geben** give s.o. time off. **F~gebig** *a* generous, *adv* -ly. **F~gebigkeit** *f* - generosity. **f~haben†** *v sep* ● *vt* **eine Stunde f~haben** have an hour off; *(Sch)* have a free period ● *vi (haben)* be off work/*(Sch)* school; *(beurlaubt sein)* have time off. **f~halten†** *vt sep* keep clear; *(belegen)* keep; **einen Tag/sich f~halten** keep a day/

oneself free; **jdn f∼halten** treat s.o. [to a meal/ drink]. **F∼handelszone** *f* free-trade area. **f∼händig** *adv* without holding on

Freiheit *f* -,-en freedom, liberty; **sich** (*dat*) **F∼en erlauben** take liberties. **F∼sstrafe** *f* prison sentence

freiheraus *adv* frankly

Frei|herr *m* baron. **F∼karte** *f* free ticket. **F∼körperkultur** *f* naturism. **f∼lassen†** *vt sep* release, set free. **F∼lassung** *f* - release. **F∼lauf** *m* free-wheel. **f∼legen** *vt sep* expose. **f∼lich** *adv* admittedly; (*natürlich*) of course. **F∼lichttheater** *nt* open-air theatre. **f∼machen** *v sep* ● *vt* (*frankieren*) frank ● *vi/r* (*haben*) [**sich**] **f∼machen** take time off. **F∼marke** *f* [postage] stamp. **F∼maurer** *m* Freemason. **f∼mütig** *a* candid, *adv* -ly. **F∼platz** *m* free seat; (*Sch*) free place. **f∼schaffend** *a* freelance. **F∼schwimmen†** (**sich**) *vr sep* pass one's swimming test. **f∼setzen** *vt sep* release; (*entlassen*) make redundant. **f∼sprechen†** *vt sep* acquit. **F∼spruch** *m* acquittal. **f∼stehen†** *vi sep* (*haben*) stand empty; **es steht ihm f∼** (*fig*) he is free (**zu** to). **f∼stellen** *vt sep* exempt (**von** from); **jdm etw f∼stellen** leave sth up to s.o. **f∼stempeln** *vt sep* frank. **F∼stil** *m* freestyle. **F∼stoß** *m* free kick. **F∼stunde** *f* (*Sch*) free period

Freitag *m* Friday. **f∼s** *adv* on Fridays

Frei|tod *m* suicide. **F∼übungen** *fpl* [physical] exercises. **F∼umschlag** *m* stamped envelope. **f∼weg** *adv* freely; (*offen*) openly. **f∼willig** *a* voluntary, *adv* -ily. **F∼willige(r)** *m/f* volunteer. **F∼zeichen** *nt* ringing tone; (*Rufzeichen*) dialling tone. **F∼zeit** *f* free *or* spare time; (*Muße*) leisure; (*Tagung*) [weekend/holiday] course. **F∼zeit-** *pref* leisure ... **F∼zeitbekleidung** *f* casual wear. **f∼zügig** *a* unrestricted; (*großzügig*) liberal; (*moralisch*) permissive

fremd *a* foreign; (*unbekannt, ungewohnt*) strange; (*nicht das eigene*) other people's; **ein f∼er Mann** a stranger; **f∼e Leute** strangers; **unter f∼em Namen** under an assumed name; **jdm f∼ sein** be unknown/ (*wesens-*) alien to s.o.; **ich bin hier f∼** I'm a stranger here. **f∼artig** *a* strange, *adv* -ly; (*exotisch*) exotic.

F∼e *f* - **in der F∼e** away from home; (*im Ausland*) in a foreign country. **F∼e(r)** *m/f* stranger; (*Ausländer*) foreigner; (*Tourist*) tourist. **F∼enführer** *m* [tourist] guide. **F∼enverkehr** *m* tourism. **F∼enzimmer** *nt* room [to let]; (*Gäste-*) guest room. **f∼gehen†** *vi sep* (*sein*) (*fam*) be unfaithful. **F∼körper** *m* foreign body. **f∼ländisch** *a* foreign; (*exotisch*) exotic. **F∼ling** *m* -s,-e stranger. **F∼sprache** *f* foreign language. **F∼wort** *nt* (*pl* -wörter) foreign word

frenetisch *a* frenzied

frequen|tieren *vt* frequent. **F∼enz** *f* -,-en frequency

Freske *f* -,-n, **Fresko** *nt* -s,-ken fresco

Fresse *f* -,-n (*sl*) (*Mund*) gob; (*Gesicht*) mug; **halt die F∼!** shut your trap! **f∼n†** *vt/i* (*haben*) eat. **F∼n** *nt* -s feed; (*sl: Essen*) grub

Freßnapf *m* feeding bowl

Freud|e *f* -,-n pleasure; (*innere*) joy; **mit F∼en** with pleasure; **jdm eine F∼e machen** please s.o. **f∼ig** *a* joyful, *adv* -ly; **f∼iges Ereignis** (*fig*) happy event. **f∼los** *a* cheerless; (*traurig*) sad

freuen *vt* please; **sich f∼** be pleased (**über** + *acc* about); **sich f∼ auf** (+ *acc*) look forward to; **es freut mich, ich freue mich** I'm glad *or* pleased (**daß** that)

Freund *m* -es,-e friend; (*Verehrer*) boyfriend; (*Anhänger*) lover (*gen* of). **F∼in** *f* -,-nen friend; (*Liebste*) girlfriend; (*Anhängerin*) lover (*gen* of). **f∼lich** *a* kind, *adv* -ly; (*umgänglich*) friendly; (*angenehm*) pleasant; **wären Sie so f∼lich?** would you be so kind? **f∼licherweise** *adv* kindly. **F∼lichkeit** *f* -,-en kindness; friendliness; pleasantness

Freundschaft *f* -,-en friendship; **F∼ schließen** become friends. **f∼lich** *a* friendly

Frevel /'fre:fəl/ *m* -s,- (*liter*) outrage. **f∼haft** *a* (*liter*) wicked

Frieden *m* -s peace; **F∼ schließen** make peace; **im F∼** in peacetime; **laß mich in F∼!** leave me alone! **F∼srichter** *m* ≈ magistrate. **F∼svertrag** *m* peace treaty

fried|fertig *a* peaceable. **F∼hof** *m* cemetery. **f∼lich** *a* peaceful, *adv* -ly; (*verträglich*) peaceable. **f∼liebend** *a* peace-loving

frieren† *vi* (*haben*) 〈*Person:*〉 be cold; *impers* **es friert/hat gefroren** it is freezing/there has been a frost; **frierst du? friert [es] dich?** are you cold? ● (*sein*) (*gefrieren*) freeze

Fries *m* -es,-e frieze

Frikadelle *f* -,-n [meat] rissole

frisch *a* fresh; (*sauber*) clean; (*leuchtend*) bright; (*munter*) lively; (*rü- stig*) fit; **sich f~ machen** freshen up ● *adv* freshly, newly; **f~ gelegte Eier** new-laid eggs; **ins Bett f~ beziehen** put clean sheets on a bed; **f~ gestrichen!** wet paint! **F~e** *f* - freshness; brightness; liveliness; fitness. **F~haltepackung** *f* vacuum pack. **F~käse** *m* ≈ cottage cheese. **f~weg** *adv* freely

Fri|seur /fri'zø:ɐ/ *m* -s,-e hairdresser; (*Herren-*) barber. **F~seursalon** *m* hairdressing salon. **F~seuse** /-'zø:zə/ *f* -,-n hairdresser

frisier|en *vt* jdn/sich **f~en** do s.o.'s/ one's hair; **die Bilanz/einen Motor f~en** (*fam*) fiddle the accounts/soup up an engine. **F~kommode** *f* dressing-table. **F~salon** *m* = Friseursalon. **F~tisch** *m* dressing-table

Frisör *m* -s,-e = Friseur

Frist *f* -,-en period; (*Termin*) deadline; (*Aufschub*) time; **drei Tage F~** three days' grace. **f~en** *vt* **sein Leben f~en** eke out an existence. **f~los** *a* instant, *adv* -ly

Frisur *f* -,-en hairstyle

fritieren *vt* deep-fry

frivol /fri'vo:l/ *a* frivolous, *adv* -ly; (*schlüpfrig*) smutty

froh *a* happy; (*freudig*) joyful; (*erleichtert*) glad; **f~e Ostern!** happy Easter!

fröhlich *a* cheerful, *adv* -ly; (*vergnügt*) merry, *adv* -ily; **f~e Weihnachten!** merry Christmas! **F~keit** *f* - cheerfulness; merriment

frohlocken *vi* (*haben*) rejoice; (*schadenfroh*) gloat

Frohsinn *m* - cheerfulness

fromm *a* (**frömmer, frömmst**) devout, *adv* -ly; (*gutartig*) docile, *adv* -ly; **f~er Wunsch** idle wish

Frömm|igkeit *f* - devoutness, piety. **f~lerisch** *a* sanctimonious, *adv* -ly

frönen *vi* (*haben*) indulge (*dat* in)

Fronleichnam *m* Corpus Christi

Front *f* -,-en front. **f~al** *a* frontal; (*Zusammenstoß*) head-on ● *adv* from the front; (*zusammenstoßen*) head-on. **F~alzusammenstoß** *m* head-on collision

Frosch *m* -[e]s,-̈e frog. **F~laich** *m* frog-spawn. **F~mann** *m* (*pl* -männer*) frogman

Frost *m* -[e]s,-̈e frost. **F~beule** *f* chilblain

frösteln *vi* (*haben*) shiver; **mich fröstelte [es]** I shivered/(*fror*) felt chilly

frost|ig *a* frosty, *adv* -ily. **F~schutzmittel** *nt* antifreeze

Frottee *nt* & *m* -s towelling

frottier|en *vt* rub down. **F~[hand]tuch** *nt* terry towel

frotzeln *vt/i* (*haben*) [über] jdn **f~** make fun of s.o.

Frucht *f* -,-̈e fruit; **F~ tragen** bear fruit. **f~bar** *a* fertile; (*fig*) fruitful. **F~barkeit** *f* - fertility. **f~en** *vi* (*haben*) **wenig/nichts f~en** have little/ no effect. **F~ig** *a* fruity. **f~los** *a* fruitless, *adv* -ly. **F~saft** *m* fruit juice

frugal *a* frugal, *adv* -ly

früh *a* early ● *adv* early; (*morgens*) in the morning; **heute/gestern/morgen f~** this/yesterday/tomorrow morning; **von f~ an** from an early age. **f~auf** *adv* **von f~auf** from an early age. **F~aufsteher** *m* -s,- early riser. **F~e** *f* - **in aller F~e** bright and early; **in der F~e** (*SGer*) in the morning. **f~er** *adv* earlier; (*eher*) sooner; (*ehemals*) formerly; (*vor langer Zeit*) in the old days; **f~er oder später** sooner or later; **ich wohnte f~er in X** I used to live in X. **f~ere(r,s)** *a* earlier; (*ehemalig*) former; (*vorige*) previous; **in f~eren Zeiten** in former times. **f~estens** *adv* at the earliest. **F~geburt** *f* premature birth/(*Kind*) baby. **F~jahr** *nt* spring. **F~jahrsputz** *m* spring-cleaning. **F~kartoffeln** *fpl* new potatoes. **F~ling** *m* -s,-e spring. **f~morgens** *adv* early in the morning. **f~reif** *a* precocious

Frühstück *nt* breakfast. **f~en** *vi* (*haben*) have breakfast

frühzeitig *a* & *adv* early; (*vorzeitig*) premature, *adv* -ly

Frustr|ation /-'tsjo:n/ *f* -,-en frustration. **f~ieren** *vt* frustrate; **f~ierend** frustrating

Fuchs *m* -es,-̈e fox; (*Pferd*) chestnut. **f~en** *vt* (*fam*) annoy

Füchsin *f* -,-nen vixen

fuchteln *vi* (*haben*) **mit etw f~** (*fam*) wave sth about

Fuder *nt* -s,- cart-load

Fuge[1] *f* -,-n joint; **aus den F~n gehen** fall apart

Fuge² *f -,-n* (*Mus*) fugue

füg|en *vt* fit (**in**+*acc* into); (*an-*) join (**an**+*acc* on to); (*dazu-*) add (**zu** to); (*fig: bewirken*) ordain; **sich f~en** fit (**in**+*acc* into); adjoin/(*folgen*) follow (**an etw** *acc* sth); (*fig: gehorchen*) submit (*dat* to); **sich in sein Schicksal f~en** resign oneself to one's fate; **es f~te sich** it so happened (**daß** that). **f~sam** *a* obedient, *adv* -ly. **F~ung** *f -,-en* eine F~ung des Schicksals a stroke of fate

fühl|bar *a* noticeable. **f~en** *vt/i* (*haben*) feel; **sich f~en** feel (**krank/ einsam** ill/lonely); (*fam: stolz sein*) fancy oneself; **sich [nicht] wohl f~en** [not] feel well. **F~er** *m -s,-* feeler. **F~ung** *f -,-* contact; **F~ung aufnehmen** get in touch

Fuhre *f -,-n* load

führ|en *vt* lead; guide 〈*Tourist*〉; (*geleiten*) take; (*leiten*) run; (*befehligen*) command; (*verkaufen*) stock; bear 〈*Namen, Titel*〉; keep 〈*Liste, Bücher, Tagebuch*〉; **bei** *od* **mit sich f~en** carry; **sich gut/schlecht f~en** conduct oneself well/badly ● *vi* (*haben*) lead; (*verlaufen*) go, run; **zu etw f~en** lead to sth. **f~end** *a* leading. **F~er** *m -s,-* leader; (*Fremden-*) guide; (*Buch*) guide[book]. **F~erhaus** *nt* driver's cab. **F~erschein** *m* driving licence; **den F~erschein machen** take one's driving test. **F~erscheinentzug** *m* disqualification from driving. **F~ung** *f -,-en* leadership; (*Leitung*) management; (*Mil*) command; (*Betragen*) conduct; (*Besichtigung*) guided tour; (*Vorsprung*) lead; **in F~ung gehen** go into the lead

Fuhr|unternehmer *m* haulage contractor. **F~werk** *nt* cart

Fülle *f -,-n* abundance, wealth (**an**+*dat of*); (*Körper-*) plumpness. **f~n** *vt* fill; (*Culin*) stuff; **sich f~n** fill [up]

Füllen *nt -s,-* foal

Füll|er *m -s,-* (*fam*), **F~federhalter** *m* fountain pen. **f~ig** *a* plump; 〈*Busen*〉 ample. **F~ung** *f -,-en* filling; (*Kissen-, Braten-*) stuffing; (*Pralinen-*) centre

fummeln *vi* (*haben*) fumble (**an**+*dat* with)

Fund *m -[e]s,-e* find

Fundament *nt -[e]s,-e* foundations *pl.* **f~al** *a* fundamental

Fund|büro *nt* lost-property office. **F~grube** *f* (*fig*) treasure trove. **F~sachen** *fpl* lost property *sg*

fünf *inv a,* **F~** *f -,-en* five; (*Sch*) ≈ fail mark. **F~linge** *mpl* quintuplets. **f~te(r,s)** *a* fifth. **f~zehn** *inv a* fifteen. **f~zehnte(r,s)** *a* fifteenth. **f~zig** *inv a* fifty. **F~ziger** *m -s,-* man in his fifties; (*Münze*) 50-pfennig piece. **f~zigste(r,s)** *a* fiftieth

fungieren *vi* (*haben*) act (**als** as)

Funk *m -s* radio; **über F~** over the radio. **F~e** *m -n,-n* spark. **f~eln** *vi* (*haben*) sparkle; 〈*Stern:*〉 twinkle. **f~elnagelneu** *a* (*fam*) brand-new. **F~en** *m -s,-* spark. **f~en** *vt* radio. **F~er** *m -s,-* radio operator. **F~sprechgerät** *nt* walkie-talkie. **F~spruch** *m* radio message. **F~streife** *f* [police] radio patrol

Funktion /-'tsio:n/ *f -,-en* function; (*Stellung*) position; (*Funktionieren*) working; **außer F~** out of action. **F~är** *m -s,-e* official. **f~ieren** *vi* (*haben*) work

für *prep* (+*acc*) for; **Schritt für Schritt** step by step; **was für [ein]** what [a]! (*fragend*) what sort of [a]? **für sich** by oneself/〈*Ding:*〉 itself. **Für** *nt* **das Für und Wider** the pros and cons *pl.* **F~bitte** *f* intercession

Furche *f -,-n* furrow

Furcht *f -* fear (**vor**+*dat* of). **f~bar** *a* terrible, *adv* -bly

fürcht|en *vt/i* (*haben*) fear; **sich f~en** be afraid (**vor**+*dat* of); **ich f~e, das geht nicht** I'm afraid that's impossible. **f~erlich** *a* dreadful, *adv* -ly

furcht|erregend *a* terrifying. **f~los** *a* fearless, *adv* -ly. **f~sam** *a* timid, *adv* -ly

füreinander *adv* for each other

Furnier *nt -s,-e* veneer. **f~t** *a* veneered

fürs *prep* = **für das**

Fürsorg|e *f* care; (*Admin*) welfare; (*fam: Geld*) ≈ social security. **F~er(in)** *m -s,-* (*f -,-nen*) social worker. **f~lich** *a* solicitous

Fürsprache *f* intercession; **F~ einlegen** intercede

Fürsprecher *m* (*fig*) advocate

Fürst *m -en,-en* prince. **F~entum** *nt -s,-̈er* principality. **F~in** *f -,-nen* princess. **f~lich** *a* princely; (*üppig*) lavish, *adv* -ly

Furt *f -,-en* ford

Furunkel *m -s,-* (*Med*) boil

Fürwort *nt* (*pl* -**wörter**) pronoun

Furz *m -es,-e* (*vulg*) fart. **f~en** *vi* (*haben*) (*vulg*) fart

Fusion *f* -,-en fusion; (*Comm*) merger.
f~ieren *vi* (*haben*) (*Comm*) merge
Fuß *m* -es,¨e foot; (*Aust: Bein*) leg;
(*Lampen-*) base; (*von Weinglas*) stem; **zu
Fuß** on foot; **zu Fuß gehen** walk; **auf
freiem Fuß** free; **auf freundschaft-
lichem/großem Fuß** on friendly
terms/in grand style. **F~abdruck** *m*
footprint. **F~abtreter** *m* -s,- door-
mat. **F~bad** *nt* foot-bath. **F~ball** *m*
football. **F~ballspieler** *m* footballer.
F~balltoto *nt* football pools *pl*.
F~bank *f* footstool. **F~boden** *m*
floor. **F~bremse** *f* footbrake
Fussel *f* -,-n & *m* -s,-[n] piece of fluff;
F~n fluff *sg*. **f~n** *vi* (*haben*) shed fluff
fuß|en *vi* (*haben*) be based (**auf** + *dat*
on). **F~ende** *nt* foot
Fußgänger|(in) *m* -s,- (*f* -,-nen) ped-
estrian. **F~brücke** *f* footbridge.
F~überweg *m* pedestrian crossing.
F~zone *f* pedestrian precinct
Fußgeher *m* -s,- (*Aust*) = **F~gänger.**
F~gelenk *nt* ankle. **F~hebel** *m*
pedal. **F~nagel** *m* toenail. **F~note** *f*
footnote. **F~pflege** *f* chiropody.
F~pfleger(in) *m(f)* chiropodist.
F~rücken *m* instep. **F~sohle** *f* sole
of the foot. **F~stapfen** *pl* in jds
F~stapfen treten (*fig*) follow in s.o.'s
footsteps. **F~tritt** *m* kick. **F~weg** *m*
footpath; **eine Stunde F~weg** an
hour's walk
futsch *pred a* (*fam*) gone
Futter¹ *nt* -s feed; (*Trocken-*) fodder
Futter² *nt* -s,- (*Kleider-*) lining
Futteral *nt* -s,-e case
füttern¹ *vt* feed
füttern² *vt* line
Futur *nt* -s (*Gram*) future; **zweites F~**
future perfect. **f~istisch** *a* futuristic

G

Gabe *f* -,-n gift; (*Dosis*) dose
Gabel *f* -,-n fork. **g~n (sich)** *vr* fork.
G~stapler *m* -s,- fork-lift truck.
G~ung *f* -,-en fork (*in road*)
gackern *vi* (*haben*) cackle
gaffen *vi* (*haben*) gape, stare
Gag /gɛk/ *m* -s,-s (*Theat*) gag
Gage /'ga:ʒə/ *f* -,-n (*Theat*) fee
gähnen *vi* (*haben*) yawn. **G~** *nt* -s
yawn; (*wiederholt*) yawning
Gala *f* - ceremonial dress
galant *a* gallant, *adv* -ly

Galavorstellung *f* gala performance
Galerie *f* -,-n gallery
Galgen *m* -s,- gallows *sg*. **G~frist** *f*
(*fam*) reprieve
Galionsfigur *f* figurehead
Galle *f* - bile; (*G~nblase*) gall-bladder.
G~nblase *f* gall-bladder. **G~nstein**
m gallstone
Gallert *nt* -[e]s,-e, **Gallerte** *f* -,-n
[meat] jelly
Galopp *m* -s gallop; **im G~** at a gallop.
g~ieren *vi* (*sein*) gallop
galvanisieren *vt* galvanize
gamm|eln *vi* (*haben*) (*fam*) loaf
around. **G~ler(in)** *m* -s,- (*f* -,-nen)
drop-out
Gams *f* -,-en (*Aust*) chamois
gang *pred a* **g~ und gäbe** quite usual
Gang *m* -[e]s,¨e walk; (*G~art*) gait;
(*Boten-*) errand; (*Funktionieren*) running; (*Verlauf, Culin*) course; (*Durch-*)
passage; (*Korridor*) corridor; (*zwischen
Sitzreihen*) aisle, gangway; (*Anat*) duct;
(*Auto*) gear; **in G~ bringen/halten**
get/keep going; **in G~ kommen** get
going/(*fig*) under way; **im G~e/in vol-
lem G~e sein** be in progress/in full
swing; **Essen mit vier G~en** four-
course meal. **G~art** *f* gait
gängig *a* common; (*Comm*) popular
Gangschaltung *f* gear change
Gangster /'gɛŋstɐ/ *m* -s,- gangster
Gangway /'gɛŋweː/ *f* -,-s gangway
Ganove *m* -n,-n (*fam*) crook
Gans *f* -,¨e goose
Gänse|blümchen *nt* -s,- daisy.
G~füßchen *ntpl* inverted commas.
G~haut *f* goose-pimples *pl*. **G~
marsch** *m* im **G~marsch** in single file.
G~rich *m* -s,-e gander
ganz *a* whole, entire; (*vollständig*)
complete; (*fam: heil*) undamaged, intact; **die g~e Zeit** all the time, the
whole time; **eine g~e Weile/Menge**
quite a while/lot; **g~e zehn Mark** all
of ten marks; **meine g~en Bücher** all
my books; *inv* **g~ Deutschland** the
whole of Germany; **g~ bleiben** (*fam*)
remain intact; **wieder g~ machen**
(*fam*) mend; **im g~en** in all, altogether; **im großen und g~en** on the
whole ● *adv* quite; (*völlig*) completely,
entirely; (*sehr*) very; **nicht g~** not
quite; **g~ allein** all on one's own; **ein
g~ alter Mann** a very old man; **g~ wie
du willst** just as you like; **es war g~**

nett it was quite nice; **g~ und gar** completely, totally; **g~ und gar nicht** not at all. **G~e(s)** *nt* whole; **es geht ums G~e** it's all or nothing. **g~jährig** *adv* all the year round

gänzlich *adv* completely, entirely

ganz|tägig *a & adv* full-time; *(geöffnet)* all day. **g~tags** *adv* all day; *(arbeiten)* full-time

gar¹ *a* done, cooked

gar² *adv* **gar nicht/nichts/niemand** not/nothing/no one at all; **oder gar** or even

Garage /ga'ra:ʒə/ *f* -,-n garage

Garantie *f* -,-n guarantee. **g~ren** *vt/i* *(haben)* **[für] etw g~ren** guarantee sth; **er kommt g~rt zu spät** *(fam)* he's sure to be late. **G~schein** *m* guarantee

Garbe *f* -,-n sheaf

Garderobe *f* -,-n *(Kleider)* wardrobe; *(Ablage)* cloakroom, *(Amer)* checkroom; *(Flur-)* coat-rack; *(Künstler-)* dressing-room. **G~nfrau** *f* cloakroom attendant

Gardine *f* -,-n curtain. **G~nstange** *f* curtain rail

garen *vt/i* *(haben)* cook

gären† *vi* *(haben)* ferment; *(fig)* seethe

Garn *nt* -[e]s,-e yarn; *(Näh-)* cotton

Garnele *f* -,-n shrimp; *(rote)* prawn

garnieren *vt* decorate; *(Culin)* garnish

Garnison *f* -,-en garrison

Garnitur *f* -,-en set; *(Wäsche)* set of matching underwear; *(Möbel-)* suite; **erste/zweite G~ sein** *(fam)* be first-rate/second best

garstig *a* nasty

Garten *m* -s,-̈ garden; **botanischer G~** botanical gardens *pl*. **G~arbeit** *f* gardening. **G~bau** *m* horticulture. **G~haus** *nt*, **G~laube** *f* summerhouse. **G~lokal** *nt* open-air café. **G~schere** *f* secateurs *pl*

Gärtner|(in) *m* -s,- *(f* -,-nen*)* gardener. **G~ei** *f* -,-en nursery; *(fam: Gartenarbeit)* gardening

Gärung *f* - fermentation

Gas *nt* -es,-e gas; **Gas geben** *(fam)* accelerate. **G~herd** *m* gas cooker. **G~maske** *f* gas mask. **G~pedal** *nt* *(Auto)* accelerator

Gasse *f* -,-n alley; *(Aust)* street

Gast *m* -[e]s,-̈e guest; *(Hotel-, Urlaubs-)* visitor; *(im Lokal)* patron; **zum Mittag G~e haben** have people to lunch; **bei**

jdm zu G~ sein be staying with s.o. **G~arbeiter** *m* foreign worker. **G~bett** *nt* spare bed

Gäste|bett *nt* spare bed. **G~buch** *nt* visitors' book. **G~zimmer** *nt* [hotel] room; *(privat)* spare room; *(Aufenthaltsraum)* residents' lounge

gast|frei, g~freundlich *a* hospitable, *adv* -bly. **G~freundschaft** *f* hospitality. **G~geber** *m* -s,- host. **G~geberin** *f* -,-nen hostess. **G~haus** *nt*, **G~hof** *m* inn, hotel

gastieren *vi* *(haben)* make a guest appearance; *(Truppe, Zirkus:)* perform *(in + dat* in*)*

gastlich *a* hospitable, *adv* -bly. **G~keit** *f* - hospitality

Gastro|nomie *f* - gastronomy. **g~nomisch** *a* gastronomic

Gast|spiel *nt* guest performance. **G~spielreise** *f* *(Theat)* tour. **G~stätte** *f* restaurant. **G~stube** *f* bar; *(Restaurant)* restaurant. **G~wirt** *m* landlord. **G~wirtin** *f* landlady. **G~wirtschaft** *f* restaurant

Gas|werk *nt* gasworks *sg*. **G~zähler** *m* gas-meter

Gatte *m* -n,-n husband

Gatter *nt* -s,- gate; *(Gehege)* pen

Gattin *f* -,-nen wife

Gattung *f* -,-en kind; *(Biol)* genus; *(Kunst)* genre. **G~sbegriff** *m* generic term

Gaudi *f* - *(Aust, fam)* fun

Gaul *m* -[e]s, Gäule *m* [old] nag

Gaumen *m* -s,- palate

Gauner *m* -s,- crook, swindler. **G~ei** *f* -,-en swindle

Gaze /'ga:zə/ *f* - gauze

Gazelle *f* -,-n gazelle

geachtet *a* respected

geädert *a* veined

geartet *a* **gut g~** good-natured; **anders g~** different

Gebäck *nt* -s [cakes and] pastries *pl*; *(Kekse)* biscuits *pl*

Gebälk *nt* -s timbers *pl*

geballt *a* *(Faust)* clenched

Gebärde *f* -,-n gesture. **g~n (sich)** *vr* behave *(wie* like*)*

Gebaren *nt* -s behaviour

gebär|en† *vt* give birth to, bear; **geboren werden** be born. **G~mutter** *f* womb, uterus

Gebäude *nt* -s,- building

Gebeine *ntpl* -[mortal] remains

Gebell *nt* -s barking

geben† vt give; (tun, bringen) put; (Karten) deal; (aufführen) perform; (unterrichten) teach; **etw verloren g~** give sth up as lost; **von sich g~** utter; (fam: erbrechen) bring up; **viel/ wenig g~ auf** (+acc) set great/little store by; **sich g~** (nachlassen) wear off; (besser werden) get better; (sich verhalten) behave; **sich geschlagen g~** admit defeat ● impers **es gibt** there is/ are; **was gibt es Neues/ zum Mittag/ im Kino?** what's the news/for lunch/ on at the cinema? **es wird Regen g~** it's going to rain; **das gibt es nicht** there's no such thing ● vi (haben) (Karten) deal

Gebet nt -[e]s,-e prayer

Gebiet nt -[e]s,-e area; (Hoheits-) territory; (Sach-) field

gebieten† vt command; (erfordern) demand ● vi (haben) rule. **G~er** m -s,- master; (Herrscher) ruler. **g~erisch** a imperious, adv -ly; (Ton) peremptory

Gebilde nt -s,- structure

gebildet a educated; (kultiviert) cultured

Gebirg|e nt -s,- mountains pl. **g~ig** a mountainous

Gebiß nt -sses,-sse teeth pl; (künstliches) false teeth pl, dentures pl; (des Zaumes) bit

geblümt a floral, flowered

gebogen a curved

geboren a born; **g~er Deutscher** German by birth; **Frau X, g~e Y** Mrs X, née Y

geborgen a safe, secure. **G~heit** f - security

Gebot nt -[e]s,-e rule; (Relig) commandment; (bei Auktion) bid

gebraten a fried

Gebrauch m use; (Sprach-) usage; **Gebräuche** customs; **in G~** in use; **G~ machen von** make use of. **g~en** vt use; **ich kann es nicht/gut g~en** I have no use for/can make good use of it; **zu nichts zu g~en** useless

gebräuchlich a common; (Wort) in common use

Gebrauch|sanleitung, G~sanweisung f directions pl for use. **g~t** a used; (Comm) secondhand. **G~twagen** m used car

gebrechlich a frail, infirm

gebrochen a broken ● adv **g~ Englisch sprechen** speak broken English

Gebrüll nt -s roaring; (fam: Schreien) bawling

Gebrumm nt -s buzzing; (Motoren-) humming

Gebühr f -,-en charge, fee; **über G~** excessively. **g~en** vi (haben) **ihm g~t Respekt** he deserves respect; **wie es sich g~t** as is right and proper. **g~end** a due, adv duly; (geziemend) proper, adv -ly. **g~enfrei** a free ● adv free of charge. **g~enpflichtig** a & adv subject to a charge; **g~enpflichtige Straße** toll road

gebunden a bound; (Suppe) thickened

Geburt f -,-en birth; **von G~** by birth. **G~enkontrolle, G~enregelung** f birth-control. **G~enziffer** f birthrate

gebürtig a native (aus of); **g~er Deutscher** German by birth

Geburts|datum nt date of birth. **G~helfer** m obstetrician. **G~hilfe** f obstetrics sg. **G~ort** m place of birth. **G~tag** m birthday. **G~urkunde** f birth certificate

Gebüsch nt -[e]s,-e bushes pl

Gedächtnis nt -ses memory; **aus dem G~** from memory

gedämpft a (Ton) muffled; (Stimme) hushed; (Musik) soft; (Licht, Stimmung) subdued

Gedanke m -ns,-n thought (an+acc of); (Idee) idea; **sich** (dat) **G~n machen** worry (über+acc about). **G~nblitz** m brainwave. **G~nlos** a thoughtless, adv -ly; (zerstreut) absent-minded, adv -ly. **G~nstrich** m dash. **G~nübertragung** f telepathy. **g~nvoll** a pensive, adv -ly

Gedärme ntpl intestines; (Tier-) entrails

Gedeck nt -[e]s,-e place setting; (auf Speisekarte) set meal; **ein G~ auflegen** set a place. **g~t** a covered; (Farbe) muted

gedeihen† vi (sein) thrive, flourish

gedenken† vi (haben) propose (etw zu tun to do sth); **jds/etw g~** remember s.o./sth. **G~** nt -s memory; **zum G~ an** (+acc) in memory of

Gedenk|feier f commemoration. **G~gottesdienst** m memorial service. **G~stätte** f memorial. **G~tafel** f commemorative plaque. **G~tag** m day of remembrance; (Jahrestag) anniversary

Gedicht nt -[e]s,-e poem

gediegen *a* quality . . .; (*solide*) well-made; ⟨*Charakter*⟩ upright; ⟨*Gold*⟩ pure ● *adv* **g~ gebaut** well built

Gedräng|e *nt* -s crush, crowd. **g~t** *a* (*knapp*) concise ● *adv* **g~t voll** packed

gedrückt *a* depressed

gedrungen *a* stocky

Geduld *f* - patience; **G~ haben** be patient. **g~en (sich)** *vr* be patient. **g~ig** *a* patient, *adv* -ly. **G~[s]spiel** *nt* puzzle

gedunsen *a* bloated

geehrt *a* honoured; **Sehr g~er Herr X** Dear Mr X

geeignet *a* suitable; **im g~en Moment** at the right moment

Gefahr *f* -,-en danger; **in/außer G~** in/out of danger; **auf eigene G~** at one's own risk; **G~ laufen** run the risk (**etw zu tun** of doing sth)

gefähr|den *vt* endanger; (*fig*) jeopardize. **g~lich** *a* dangerous, *adv* -ly; (*riskant*) risky

gefahrlos *a* safe

Gefährt *nt* -[e]s,-e vehicle

Gefährte *m* -n,-n, **Gefährtin** *f* -,-nen companion

gefahrvoll *a* dangerous, perilous

Gefälle *nt* -s,- slope; (*Straßen-*) gradient

gefallen† *vi* (*haben*) **jdm g~** please s.o.; **er/es gefällt mir** I like him/it; **sich** (*dat*) **etw g~ lassen** put up with sth

Gefallen[1] *m* -s,- favour

Gefallen[2] *nt* -s pleasure (**an**+ *dat* in); **G~ finden an** (+ *dat*) like; **dir zu G~** to please you

Gefallene(r) *m* soldier killed in the war

gefällig *a* pleasing; (*hübsch*) attractive, *adv* -ly; (*hilfsbereit*) obliging; **jdm g~ sein** do s.o. a good turn; **[sonst] noch etwas g~?** will there be anything else? **G~keit** *f* -,-en favour; (*Freundlichkeit*) kindness. **g~st** *adv* (*fam*) kindly

Gefangen|e(r) *m/f* prisoner. **g~halten†** *vt sep* hold prisoner; keep in captivity ⟨*Tier*⟩. **G~nahme** *f* - capture. **g~nehmen†** *vt sep* take prisoner. **G~schaft** *f* - captivity; **in G~schaft geraten** be taken prisoner

Gefängnis *nt* -ses,-se prison; (*Strafe*) imprisonment. **G~strafe** *f* imprisonment; (*Urteil*) prison sentence. **G~wärter** *m* [prison] warder, (*Amer*) guard

Gefäß *nt* -es,-e container, receptacle; (*Blut-*) vessel

gefaßt *a* composed; (*ruhig*) calm, *adv* -ly; **g~ sein auf** (+ *acc*) be prepared for

Gefecht *nt* -[e]s,-e fight; (*Mil*) engagement; **außer G~ setzen** put out of action

gefedert *a* sprung

gefeiert *a* celebrated

Gefieder *nt* -s plumage. **g~t** *a* feathered

Geflecht *nt* -[e]s,-e network; (*Gewirr*) tangle; (*Korb-*) wickerwork

gefleckt *a* spotted

geflissentlich *adv* studiously

Geflügel *nt* -s poultry. **G~klein** *nt* -s giblets *pl*. **g~t** *a* winged; **g~tes Wort** familiar quotation

Geflüster *nt* -s whispering

Gefolg|e *nt* -s retinue, entourage. **G~schaft** *f* - followers *pl*, following; (*Treue*) allegiance

gefragt *a* popular; **g~ sein** be in demand

gefräßig *a* voracious; ⟨*Mensch*⟩ greedy

Gefreite(r) *m* lance-corporal

gefrier|en† *vi* (*sein*) freeze. **G~fach** *nt* freezer compartment. **G~punkt** *m* freezing-point. **G~schrank** *m* upright freezer. **G~truhe** *f* chest freezer

gefroren *a* frozen. **G~e(s)** *nt* (*Aust*) ice-cream

Gefüge *nt* -s,- structure; (*fig*) fabric

gefügig *a* compliant; (*gehorsam*) obedient

Gefühl *nt* -[e]s,-e feeling; (*Empfindung*) sensation; (*G~sregung*) emotion; **im G~ haben** know instinctively. **g~los** *a* insensitive; (*herzlos*) unfeeling; (*taub*) numb. **g~sbetont** *a* emotional. **g~skalt** *a* (*fig*) cold. **g~smäßig** *a* emotional, *adv* -ly; (*instinktiv*) instinctive, *adv* -ly. **G~sregung** *f* emotion. **g~voll** *a* sensitive, *adv* -ly; (*sentimental*) sentimental, *adv* -ly

gefüllt *a* filled; (*voll*) full; (*Bot*) double; (*Culin*) stuffed; ⟨*Schokolade*⟩ with a filling

gefürchtet *a* feared, dreaded

gefüttert *a* lined

gegeben *a* given; (*bestehend*) present; (*passend*) appropriate; **zu g~er Zeit** at the proper time. **g~enfalls** *adv* if need be. **G~heiten** *fpl* realities, facts

gegen *prep* (+ *acc*) against; (*Sport*) versus; (*g~über*) to[wards]; (*Vergleich*) compared with; (*Richtung, Zeit*) towards; (*ungefähr*) around; **ein Mittel g~** a remedy for ● *adv* **g~ 100 Leute** about 100 people. **G~angriff** *m* counter-attack

Gegend *f* -,-en area, region; (*Umgebung*) neighbourhood

gegeneinander *adv* against/ (*gegenüber*) towards one another

Gegen|fahrbahn *f* opposite carriageway. **G~gift** *nt* antidote. **G~leistung** *f* als **G~leistung** in return. **G~maßnahme** *f* countermeasure. **G~satz** *m* contrast; (*Widerspruch*) contradiction; (*G~teil*) opposite; **im G~satz zu** unlike. **g~sätzlich** *a* contrasting; (*widersprüchlich*) opposing. **g~seitig** *a* mutual, *adv* -ly; **sich g~seitig hassen** hate one another. **G~spieler** *m* opponent. **G~sprechanlage** *f* intercom. **G~stand** *m* object; (*Gram, Gesprächs-*) subject. **g~standslos** *a* unfounded; (*überflüssig*) irrelevant; (*abstrakt*) abstract. **G~stück** *nt* counterpart; (*G~teil*) opposite. **G~teil** *nt* opposite, contrary; **im G~teil** on the contrary. **g~teilig** *a* opposite

gegenüber *prep* (+ *dat*) opposite; (*Vergleich*) compared with; **jdm g~ höflich sein** be polite to s.o. ● *adv* opposite. **G~** *nt* -s person opposite. **g~liegen†** *vi sep* (*haben*) be opposite (etw *dat* sth). **g~liegend** *a* opposite. **g~stehen†** *vi sep* (*haben*) (+ *dat*) face; **feindlich g~stehen** (+ *dat*) be hostile to. **g~stellen** *vt sep* confront; (*vergleichen*) compare. **g~treten†** *vi sep* (*sein*) (+ *dat*) face

Gegen|verkehr *m* oncoming traffic. **G~vorschlag** *m* counter-proposal. **G~wart** *f* - present; (*Anwesenheit*) presence. **g~wärtig** *a* present ● *adv* at present. **G~wehr** *f* - resistance. **G~wert** *m* equivalent. **G~wind** *m* head wind. **g~zeichnen** *vt sep* countersign

geglückt *a* successful

Gegner|(in) *m* -s,- (*f* -,-nen) opponent. **g~isch** *a* opposing

Gehabe *nt* -s affected behaviour

Gehackte(s) *nt* mince, (*Amer*) ground meat

Gehalt[1] *m* -[e]s content

Gehalt[2] *nt* -[e]s,-̈er salary. **G~serhöhung** *f* rise, (*Amer*) raise

gehaltvoll *a* nourishing

gehässig *a* spiteful, *adv* -ly

gehäuft *a* heaped

Gehäuse *nt* -s,- case; (*TV, Radio*) cabinet; (*Schnecken-*) shell; (*Kern-*) core

Gehege *nt* -s,- enclosure

geheim *a* secret; **im g~en** secretly. **G~dienst** *m* Secret Service. **g~halten†** *vt sep* keep secret. **G~nis** *nt* -ses,-se secret. **g~nisvoll** *a* mysterious, *adv* -ly. **G~polizei** *f* secret police

gehemmt *a* (*fig*) inhibited

gehen† *vi* (*sein*) go; (*zu Fuß*) walk; (*fort-*) leave; (*funktionieren*) work; (*Teig:*) rise; **tanzen/einkaufen g~** go dancing/shopping; **an die Arbeit g~** set to work; **in Schwarz [gekleidet] g~** dress in black; **nach Norden g~** (*Fenster:*) face north; **wenn es nach mir ginge** if I had my way; **über die Straße g~** cross the road; **was geht hier vor sich?** what is going on here? **das geht zu weit** (*fam*) that's going too far; *impers* **wie geht es [Ihnen]?** how are you? **es geht mir gut/ besser** I am well/better; **es geht nicht/nicht anders** it's impossible/there is no other way; **es ging ganz schnell** it was very quick; **es geht um** it concerns; **es geht ihr nur ums Geld** she is only interested in the money; **es geht [so]** (*fam*) not too bad ● *vt* walk. **g~lassen† (sich)** *vr sep* lose one's self-control; (*sich vernachlässigen*) let oneself go

geheuer *a* **nicht g~** eerie; (*verdächtig*) suspicious; **mir ist nicht g~** I feel uneasy

Geheul *nt* -s howling

Gehilfe *m* -n,-n, **Gehilfin** *f* -,-nen trainee; (*Helfer*) assistant

Gehirn *nt* -s brain; (*Verstand*) brains *pl*. **G~erschütterung** *f* concussion. **G~hautentzündung** *f* meningitis. **G~wäsche** *f* brainwashing

gehoben *a* (*fig*) superior; (*Sprache*) elevated

Gehöft *nt* -[e]s,-e farm

Gehölz *nt* -es,-e coppice, copse

Gehör *nt* -s hearing; **G~ schenken** (+ *dat*) listen to

gehorchen *vi* (*haben*) (+ *dat*) obey

gehören *vi* (*haben*) belong (*dat* to); **zu den Besten g~** be one of the best; **dazu gehört Mut** that takes courage;

sich g~ be [right and] proper; **es gehört sich nicht** it isn't done

gehörig *a* proper, *adv* -ly; **jdn g~ verprügeln** give s.o. a good hiding

gehörlos *a* deaf

Gehörn *nt* -s,-e horns *pl*; (*Geweih*) antlers *pl*

gehorsam *a* obedient, *adv* -ly. **G~** *m* -s obedience

Geh|steig *m* -[e]s,-e pavement, (*Amer*) sidewalk. **G~weg** *m* = **Gehsteig**; (*Fußweg*) footpath

Geier *m* -s,- vulture

Geig|e *f* -,-n violin. **g~en** *vi* (*haben*) play the violin ● *vt* play on the violin. **G~er(in)** *m* -s,- (*f* -,-nen) violinist

geil *a* lecherous; (*fam*) randy; (*fam: toll*) great

Geisel *f* -,-n hostage

Geiß *f* -,-en (*SGer*) [nanny-]goat. **G~blatt** *nt* honeysuckle

Geißel *f* -,-n scourge

Geist *m* -[e]s,-er mind; (*Witz*) wit; (*Gesinnung*) spirit; (*Gespenst*) ghost; **der Heilige G~** the Holy Ghost *or* Spirit; **im G~** in one's mind. **g~erhaft** *a* ghostly

geistes|abwesend *a* absentminded, *adv* -ly. **G~blitz** *m* brainwave. **G~gegenwart** *f* presence of mind. **g~gegenwärtig** *adv* with great presence of mind. **g~gestört** *a* [mentally] deranged. **g~krank** *a* mentally ill. **G~krankheit** *f* mental illness. **G~wissenschaften** *fpl* arts. **G~zustand** *m* mental state

geist|ig *a* mental, *adv* -ly; (*intellektuell*) intellectual, *adv* -ly; **g~ige Getränke** spirits. **g~lich** *a* spiritual, *adv* -ly; (*religiös*) religious; ⟨*Musik*⟩ sacred; ⟨*Tracht*⟩ clerical. **G~liche(r)** *m* clergyman. **G~lichkeit** *f* - clergy. **g~los** *a* uninspired. **g~reich** *a* clever; (*witzig*) witty

Geiz *m* -es meanness. **g~en** *vi* (*haben*) be mean (**mit** with). **G~hals** *m* (*fam*) miser. **g~ig** *a* mean, miserly. **G~kragen** *m* (*fam*) miser

Gekicher *nt* -s giggling

geknickt *a* (*fam*) dejected, *adv* -ly

gekonnt *a* accomplished ● *adv* expertly

Gekrakel *nt* -s scrawl

gekränkt *a* offended, hurt

Gekritzel *nt* -s scribble

gekünstelt *a* affected, *adv* -ly

Gelächter *nt* -s laughter

geladen *a* loaded; (*fam: wütend*) furious

Gelage *nt* -s,- feast

gelähmt *a* paralysed

Gelände *nt* -s,- terrain; (*Grundstück*) site. **G~lauf** *m* cross-country run

Geländer *nt* -s,- railings *pl*; (*Treppen-*) banisters *pl*; (*Brücken-*) parapet

gelangen *vi* (*sein*) reach/(*fig*) attain (**zu etw/an etw** *acc* sth); **in jds Besitz g~** come into s.o.'s possession

gelassen *a* composed; (*ruhig*) calm, *adv* -ly. **G~heit** *f* - equanimity; (*Fassung*) composure

Gelatine /ʒela-/ *f* - gelatine

geläufig *a* common, current; (*fließend*) fluent, *adv* -ly; **jdm g~ sein** be familiar to s.o.

gelaunt *a* **gut/schlecht g~ sein** be in a good/bad mood

gelb *a* yellow; (*bei Ampel*) amber; **g~e Rübe** (*SGer*) carrot; **das G~e vom Ei** the yolk of the egg. **G~** *nt* -s,- yellow; **bei G~** (*Auto*) on [the] amber. **g~lich** *a* yellowish. **G~sucht** *f* jaundice

Geld *nt* -es,-er money; **öffentliche G~er** public funds. **G~beutel** *m*, **G~börse** *f* purse. **G~geber** *m* -s,- backer. **g~lich** *a* financial, *adv* -ly. **G~mittel** *ntpl* funds. **G~schein** *m* banknote. **G~schrank** *m* safe. **G~strafe** *f* fine. **G~stück** *nt* coin

Gelee /ʒe'le:/ *nt* -s,-s jelly

gelegen *a* situated; (*passend*) convenient; **jdm sehr g~ sein** *od* **kommen** suit s.o. well; **mir ist viel/wenig daran g~** I'm very/not keen on it; (*es ist wichtig*) it matters a lot/little to me

Gelegenheit *f* -,-en opportunity; chance; (*Anlaß*) occasion; (*Comm*) bargain; **bei G~** some time. **G~sarbeit** *f* casual work. **G~sarbeiter** *m* casual worker. **G~skauf** *m* bargain

gelegentlich *a* occasional ● *adv* occasionally; (*bei Gelegenheit*) some time ● *prep* (+ *gen*) on the occasion of

gelehrt *a* learned. **G~e(r)** *m/f* scholar

Geleise *nt* -s,- = **Gleis**

Geleit *nt* -[e]s escort; **freies G~** safe conduct. **g~en** *vt* escort. **G~zug** *m* (*Naut*) convoy

Gelenk *nt* -[e]s,-e joint. **g~ig** *a* supple; (*Techn*) flexible

gelernt *a* skilled

Geliebte(r) *m/f* lover; (*liter*) beloved

gelieren /ʒe-/ vi (haben) set

gelinde a mild, adv -ly; **g~ gesagt** to put it mildly

gelingen† vi (sein) succeed, be successful; **es gelang ihm, zu entkommen** he succeeded in escaping. **G~ nt -s** success

gell int (SGer) = **gelt**

gellend a shrill, adv -y

geloben vt promise [solemnly]; **sich** (dat) **~** vow (**zu** to); **das Gelobte Land** the Promised Land

Gelöbnis nt -ses, -se vow

gelöst a (fig) relaxed

Gelse f -,-n (Aust) mosquito

gelt int (SGer) **das ist schön, g~?** it's nice, isn't it? **ihr kommt doch, g~?** you are coming, aren't you?

gelten† vi (haben) be valid; ⟨Regel:⟩ apply; **g~ als** be regarded as; **etw nicht g~ lassen** not accept sth; **wenig/ viel g~** be worth/(fig) count for little/a lot; **jdm g~** be meant for s.o.; **das gilt nicht** that doesn't count. **g~d** a valid; ⟨Preise⟩ current; ⟨Meinung⟩ prevailing; **g~d machen** assert ⟨Recht, Forderung⟩; bring to bear ⟨Einfluß⟩

Geltung f - validity; ⟨Ansehen⟩ prestige; **G~ haben** be valid; **zur G~ bringen/kommen** set off/show to advantage

Gelübde nt -s,- vow

gelungen a successful

Gelüst nt -[e]s,-e desire/(stark) craving (**nach** for)

gemächlich a leisurely ● adv in a leisurely manner

Gemahl m -s,-e husband. **G~in** f -,-nen wife

Gemälde nt -s,- painting. **G~galerie** f picture gallery

gemäß prep (+ dat) in accordance with ● a **etw** (dat) **g~ sein** be in keeping with sth

gemäßigt a moderate; ⟨Klima⟩ temperate

gemein a common; ⟨unanständig⟩ vulgar; ⟨niederträchtig⟩ mean; **g~er Soldat** private; **etw g~ haben** have sth in common ● adv shabbily; ⟨fam: schrecklich⟩ terribly

Gemeinde f -,-n [local] community; ⟨Admin⟩ borough; ⟨Pfarr-⟩ parish; ⟨bei Gottesdienst⟩ congregation. **G~rat** m local council/(Person) councillor. **G~wahlen** fpl local elections

gemein|gefährlich a dangerous. **G~heit** f -,-en (s. gemein) commonness; vulgarity; meanness; ⟨Bemerkung, Handlung⟩ mean thing [to say/do]; **so eine G~heit!** how mean! ⟨wie ärgerlich⟩ what a nuisance! **G~kosten** pl overheads. **g~nützig** a charitable. **G~platz** m platitude. **g~sam** a common; **etw g~sam haben** have sth in common ● adv together

Gemeinschaft f -,-en community. **g~lich** a joint; ⟨Besitz⟩ communal ● adv jointly; ⟨zusammen⟩ together. **G~sarbeit** f team-work

Gemenge nt -s,- mixture

gemessen a measured; ⟨würdevoll⟩ dignified

Gemetzel nt -s,- carnage

Gemisch nt -[e]s,-e mixture. **g~t** a mixed

Gemme f -,-n engraved gem

Gemse f -,-n chamois

Gemurmel nt -s murmuring

Gemüse nt -s,- vegetable; ⟨coll⟩ vegetables pl. **G~händler** m greengrocer

gemustert a patterned

Gemüt nt -[e]s,-er nature, disposition; ⟨Gefühl⟩ feelings pl; ⟨Person⟩ soul

gemütlich a cosy; ⟨gemächlich⟩ leisurely; ⟨zwanglos⟩ informal; ⟨Person⟩ genial; **es sich** (dat) **g~ machen** make oneself comfortable ● adv cosily; in a leisurely manner; informally. **G~keit** f - cosiness; leisureliness

Gemüts|art f nature, disposition. **G~mensch** m ⟨fam⟩ placid person. **G~ruhe** f **in aller G~ruhe** ⟨fam⟩ calmly. **G~verfassung** f frame of mind

Gen nt -s,-e gene

genau a exact, adv -ly, precise, adv -ly; ⟨Waage, Messung⟩ accurate, adv -ly; ⟨sorgfältig⟩ meticulous, adv -ly; ⟨ausführlich⟩ detailed; **nichts G~es wissen** not know any details; **es nicht so g~ nehmen** not be too particular; **g~!** exactly! **g~genommen** adv strictly speaking. **G~igkeit** f - exactitude; precision; accuracy; meticulousness

genauso adv just the same; ⟨g~sehr⟩ just as much; **g~ gut/teuer** just as good/expensive. **g~gut** adv just as well. **g~sehr** adv just as much. **g~viel** adv just as much/many.

g~wenig *adv* just as little/few; (*noch*) no more

Gendarm /ʒãˈdarm/ *m* **-en,-en** (*Aust*) policeman

Genealogie *f* - genealogy

genehmig|en *vt* grant; approve ⟨*Plan*⟩. **G~ung** *f* **-,-en** permission; (*Schein*) permit

geneigt *a* sloping, inclined; (*fig*) well-disposed (*dat* towards); [**nicht**] **g~ sein** (*fig*) [not] feel inclined (**zu** to)

General *m* **-s,ⁿe** general. **G~direktor** *m* managing director. **g~isieren** *vi* (*haben*) generalize. **G~probe** *f* dress rehearsal. **G~streik** *m* general strike. **g~überholen** *vt insep* (*inf & pp only*) completely overhaul

Generation /-ˈtsɪoːn/ *f* **-,-en** generation

Generator *m* **-s,-en** /-ˈtoːrən/ generator

generell *a* general, *adv* -ly

genes|en† *vi* (*sein*) recover. **G~ung** *f* - recovery; (*Erholung*) convalescence

Genet|ik *f* - genetics *sg*. **g~isch** *a* genetic, *adv* -ally

Genf *nt* **-s** Geneva. **G~er** *a* Geneva . . . ; **G~er See** Lake Geneva

genial *a* brilliant, *adv* -ly; **ein g~er Mann** a man of genius. **G~ität** *f* - genius

Genick *nt* **-s,-e** [back of the] neck; **sich** (*dat*) **das G~ brechen** break one's neck

Genie /ʒeˈniː/ *nt* **-s,-s** genius

genieren /ʒeˈniːrən/ *vt* embarrass; **sich g~** feel *or* be embarrassed

genieß|bar *a* fit to eat/drink. **g~en†** *vt* enjoy; (*verzehren*) eat/drink. **G~er** *m* **-s,-** gourmet. **g~erisch** *a* appreciative ● *adv* with relish

Genitiv *m* **-s,-e** genitive

Genosse *m* **-n,-n** (*Pol*) comrade. **G~nschaft** *f* **-,-en** co-operative

Genre /ˈʒãːrə/ *nt* **-s,-s** genre

Gentechnologie *f* genetic engineering

genug *inv a* & *adv* enough

Genüge *f* **zur G~** sufficiently. **g~n** *vi* (*haben*) be enough; **jds Anforderungen g~n** meet s.o.'s requirements. **g~nd** *inv a* sufficient, enough; (*Sch*) fair ● *adv* sufficiently, enough

genügsam *a* frugal, *adv* -ly; (*bescheiden*) modest, *adv* -ly

Genugtuung *f* - satisfaction

Genuß *m* **-sses,ⁿsse** enjoyment; (*Vergnügen*) pleasure; (*Verzehr*) consumption. **genüßlich** *a* pleasurable ● *adv* with relish

geöffnet *a* open

Geo|graphie *f* - geography. **g~graphisch** *a* geographical, *adv* -ly. **G~loge** *m* **-n,-n** geologist. **G~logie** *f* - geology. **g~logisch** *a* geological, *adv* -ly. **G~meter** *m* **-s,-** surveyor. **G~metrie** *f* - geometry. **g~metrisch** *a* geometric[al]

geordnet *a* well-ordered; (*stabil*) stable; **alphabetisch g~** in alphabetical order

Gepäck *nt* **-s** luggage, baggage. **G~ablage** *f* luggage-rack. **G~aufbewahrung** *f* left-luggage office. **G~schalter** *m* luggage office. **G~schein** *m* left-luggage ticket; (*Aviat*) baggage check. **G~stück** *nt* piece of luggage. **G~träger** *m* porter; (*Fahrrad-*) luggage carrier; (*Dach-*) roof-rack. **G~wagen** *m* luggage-van

Gepard *m* **-s,-e** cheetah

gepflegt *a* well-kept; ⟨*Person*⟩ well-groomed; ⟨*Hotel*⟩ first-class

Gepflogenheit *f* **-,-en** practice; (*Brauch*) custom

Gepolter *nt* **-s** [loud] noise

gepunktet *a* spotted

gerade *a* straight; (*direkt*) direct; (*aufrecht*) upright; (*aufrichtig*) straightforward; ⟨*Zahl*⟩ even ● *adv* straight; directly; (*eben*) just; (*genau*) exactly; (*besonders*) especially; **nicht g~ billig** not exactly cheap; **g~ erst** only just; **g~ an dem Tag** on that very day. **G~** *f* **-,-n** straight line. **g~aus** *adv* straight ahead/on

gerade|biegen† *vt sep* straighten; (*fig*) straighten out. **g~halten†** (**sich**) *vr sep* hold oneself straight. **g~heraus** *adv* (*fig*) straight out. **g~sitzen†** *vi sep* (*haben*) sit [up] straight. **g~so** *adv* just the same; **g~so gut** just as good. **g~sogut** *adv* just as well. **g~stehen†** *vi sep* (*haben*) stand up straight; (*fig*) accept responsibility (**für** for). **g~wegs** *adv* directly, straight. **g~zu** *adv* virtually; (*wirklich*) absolutely

Geranie /-jə/ *f* **-,-n** geranium

Gerät *nt* **-[e]s,-e** tool; (*Acker-*) implement; (*Küchen-*) utensil; (*Elektro-*) appliance; (*Radio-, Fernseh-*) set;

(*Turn-*) piece of apparatus; (*coll*) equipment

geraten† *vi (sein)* get; **in Brand g~** catch fire; **in Wut g~** get angry; **in Streit g~** start quarrelling; **gut/ schlecht g~** turn out well/badly; **nach jdm g~** take after s.o.

Geratewohl *nt* **aufs G~** at random

geräuchert *a* smoked

geräumig *a* spacious, roomy

Geräusch *nt* **-[e]s,-e** noise. **g~los** *a* noiseless, *adv* -ly. **g~voll** *a* noisy, *adv* -ily

gerben *vt* tan

gerecht *a* just, *adv* -ly; (*fair*) fair, *adv* -ly; **g~ werden** (+ *dat*) do justice to. **g~fertigt** *a* justified. **G~igkeit** *f* -justice; fairness

Gerede *nt* **-s** talk; (*Klatsch*) gossip

geregelt *a* regular

gereift *a* mature

gereizt *a* irritable, *adv* -bly. **G~heit** *f* - irritability

gereuen *vt* **es gereut mich nicht** I don't regret it

Geriatrie *f* - geriatrics *sg*

Gericht[1] *nt* **-[e]s,-e** (*Culin*) dish

Gericht[2] *nt* **-[e]s,-e** court [of law]; **vor G~** in court; **das Jüngste G~** the Last Judgement; **mit jdm ins G~ gehen** take s.o. to task. **g~lich** *a* judicial; ⟨*Verfahren*⟩ legal ● *adv* **g~lich vorgehen** take legal action. **G~sbarkeit** *f* - jurisdiction. **G~shof** *m* court of justice. **G~smedizin** *f* forensic medicine. **G~ssaal** *m* courtroom. **G~svollzieher** *m* **-s,-** bailiff

gerieben *a* grated; (*fam: schlau*) crafty

gering *a* small; (*niedrig*) low; (*g~fügig*) slight. **g~achten** *vt sep* have little regard for; (*verachten*) despise. **g~fügig** *a* slight, *adv* -ly. **g~schätzig** *a* contemptuous, *adv* -ly; ⟨*Bemerkung*⟩ disparaging. **g~ste(r,s)** *a* least; **nicht im g~sten** not in the least

gerinnen† *vi (sein)* curdle; ⟨*Blut:*⟩ clot

Gerippe *nt* **-s,-** skeleton; (*fig*) framework

gerissen *a* (*fam*) crafty

Germ *m* **-[e]s** & (*Aust*) *f* - yeast

German|e *m* **-n,-n** [ancient] German. **g~isch** *a* Germanic. **G~ist(in)** *m* **-en,-en** (*f* -,-nen) Germanist. **G~istik** *f* - German [language and literature]

gern[e] *adv* gladly; **g~ haben** like; (*lieben*) be fond of; **ich tanze/schwimme g~** I like dancing/swimming; **das kannst du g~ tun** you're welcome to do that; **willst du mit?—g~!** do you want to come?—I'd love to!

gerötet *a* red

Gerste *f* - barley. **G~nkorn** *nt* (*Med*) stye

Geruch *m* **-[e]s,-̈e** smell (**von/nach** of). **g~los** *a* odourless. **G~ssinn** *m* sense of smell

Gerücht *nt* **-[e]s,-e** rumour

geruhen *vi (haben)* deign (**zu** to)

gerührt *a* (*fig*) moved, touched

Gerümpel *nt* **-s** lumber, junk

Gerüst *nt* **-[e]s,-e** scaffolding; (*fig*) framework

gesalzen *a* salted; (*fam: hoch*) steep

gesammelt *a* collected; (*gefaßt*) composed

gesamt *a* entire, whole. **G~ausgabe** *f* complete edition. **G~betrag** *m* total amount. **G~eindruck** *m* overall impression. **G~heit** *f* - whole. **G~schule** *f* comprehensive school. **G~summe** *f* total

Gesandte(r) *m/f* envoy

Gesang *m* **-[e]s,-̈e** singing; (*Lied*) song; (*Kirchen-*) hymn. **G~buch** *nt* hymnbook. **G~verein** *m* choral society

Gesäß *nt* **-es** buttocks *pl*. **G~tasche** *f* hip pocket

Geschäft *nt* **-[e]s,-e** business; (*Laden*) shop, (*Amer*) store; (*Transaktion*) deal; (*fam: Büro*) office; **schmutzige G~e** shady dealings; **ein gutes G~ machen** do very well (**mit** out of); **sein G~ verstehen** know one's job. **g~ehalber** *adv* on business. **g~ig** *a* busy, *adv* -ily; ⟨*Treiben*⟩ bustling. **G~igkeit** *f* - activity. **g~lich** *a* business ... ● *adv* on business

Geschäfts|brief *m* business letter. **G~führer** *m* manager; (*Vereins-*) secretary. **G~mann** *m* (*pl* -leute) businessman. **G~reise** *f* business trip. **G~stelle** *f* office; (*Zweigstelle*) branch. **g~tüchtig** *a* **g~tüchtig sein** be a good businessman/-woman. **G~viertel** *nt* shopping area. **G~zeiten** *fpl* hours of business

geschehen† *vi (sein)* happen (*dat* to); **es ist ein Unglück g~** there has been an accident; **es ist um uns g~** we are done for; **das geschieht dir recht!** it serves you right! **gern g~!** you're welcome! **G~** *nt* **-s** events *pl*

gescheit *a* clever; **daraus werde ich nicht g~** I can't make head or tail of it

Geschenk *nt* -[e]s,-e present, gift. **G~korb** *m* gift hamper

Geschicht|e *f* -,-n history; (*Erzählung*) story; (*fam: Sache*) business. **g~lich** *a* historical, *adv* -ly

Geschick *nt* -[e]s fate; (*Talent*) skill; **G~ haben** be good (**zu** at). **G~lichkeit** *f* - skilfulness, skill. **g~t** *a* skilful, *adv* -ly; (*klug*) clever, *adv* -ly

geschieden *a* divorced. **G~e(r)** *m/f* divorcee

Geschirr *nt* -s,-e (*coll*) crockery; (*Porzellan*) china; (*Service*) service; (*Pferde-*) harness; **schmutziges G~** dirty dishes *pl.* **G~spülmaschine** *f* dishwasher. **G~tuch** *nt* tea-towel

Geschlecht *nt* -[e]s,-er sex; (*Gram*) gender; (*Familie*) family; (*Generation*) generation. **g~lich** *a* sexual, *adv* -ly. **G~skrankheit** *f* venereal disease. **G~steile** *ntpl* genitals. **G~sverkehr** *m* sexual intercourse. **G~swort** *nt* (*pl* -wörter) article

geschliffen *a* (*fig*) polished

geschlossen *a* closed ● *adv* unanimously; (*vereint*) in a body

Geschmack *m* -[e]s,ᵉe taste; (*Aroma*) flavour; (*G~ssinn*) sense of taste; **einen guten G~ haben** (*fig*) have good taste; **G~ finden an** (+ *dat*) acquire a taste for. **g~los** *a* tasteless, *adv* -ly; **g~los sein** (*fig*) be in bad taste. **G~ssache** *f* matter of taste. **g~voll** *a* (*fig*) tasteful, *adv* -ly

geschmeidig *a* supple; (*weich*) soft

Geschöpf *nt* -[e]s,-e creature

Geschoß *nt* -sses,-sse missile; (*Stockwerk*) storey, floor

geschraubt *a* (*fig*) stilted

Geschrei *nt* -s screaming; (*fig*) fuss

Geschütz *nt* -es,-e gun, cannon

geschützt *a* protected; (*Stelle*) sheltered

Geschwader *nt* -s,- squadron

Geschwätz *nt* -es talk. **g~ig** *a* garrulous

geschweift *a* curved

geschweige *conj* **g~ denn** let alone

geschwind *a* quick, *adv* -ly

Geschwindigkeit *f* -,-en speed; (*Phys*) velocity. **G~sbegrenzung, G~sbeschränkung** *f* speed limit

Geschwister *pl* brother[s] and sister[s]; siblings

geschwollen *a* swollen; (*fig*) pompous, *adv* -ly

Geschworene|(r) *m/f* juror; **die G~n** the jury *sg*

Geschwulst *f* -,ᵉe swelling; (*Tumor*) tumour

geschwungen *a* curved

Geschwür *nt* -s,-e ulcer

Geselle *m* -n,-n fellow; (*Handwerks-*) journeyman

gesellig *a* sociable; (*Zool*) gregarious; (*unterhaltsam*) convivial; **g~er Abend** social evening. **G~keit** *f* -,-en entertaining; **die G~keit lieben** love company

Gesellschaft *f* -,-en company; (*Veranstaltung*) party; **die G~** society; **jdm G~ leisten** keep s.o. company. **g~lich** *a* social, *adv* -ly. **G~sreise** *f* group tour. **G~sspiel** *nt* party game

Gesetz *nt* -es,-e law. **G~entwurf** *m* bill. **g~gebend** *a* legislative. **G~gebung** *f* - legislation. **g~lich** *a* legal, *adv* -ly. **g~los** *a* lawless. **g~mäßig** *a* lawful, *adv* -ly; (*gesetzlich*) legal, *adv* -ly

gesetzt *a* staid; (*Sport*) seeded ● *conj* **g~ den Fall** supposing

gesetzwidrig *a* illegal, *adv* -ly

gesichert *a* secure

Gesicht *nt* -[e]s,-er face; (*Aussehen*) appearance; **zu G~ bekommen** set eyes on. **G~sausdruck** *m* [facial] expression. **G~sfarbe** *f* complexion. **G~spunkt** *m* point of view. **G~szüge** *mpl* features

Gesindel *nt* -s riff-raff

gesinnt *a* **gut/übel g~** well/ill disposed (*dat* towards)

Gesinnung *f* -,-en mind; (*Einstellung*) attitude; **politische G~** political convictions *pl*

gesittet *a* well-mannered; (*zivilisiert*) civilized

gesondert *a* separate, *adv* -ly

Gespann *nt* -[e]s,-e team; (*Wagen*) horse and cart/carriage

gespannt *a* taut; (*fig*) tense, *adv* -ly; (*Beziehungen*) strained; (*neugierig*) eager, *adv* -ly; (*erwartungsvoll*) expectant, *adv* -ly; **g~ sein, ob** wonder whether; **auf etw/jdn g~ sein** look forward eagerly to sth/to seeing s.o.

Gespenst *nt* -[e]s,-er ghost. **g~isch** *a* ghostly; (*unheimlich*) eerie

Gespött *nt* -[e]s mockery; **zum G~ werden** become a laughing-stock

Gespräch *nt* -[e]s,-e conversation; (*Telefon-*) call; **ins G~ kommen** get talking; **im G~ sein** be under discussion. **g~ig** *a* talkative. **G~sgegenstand** *m*, **G~sthema** *nt* topic of conversation

gesprenkelt *a* speckled

Gespür *nt* -s feeling; (*Instinkt*) instinct

Gestalt *f* -,-en figure; (*Form*) shape, form; **G~ annehmen** (*fig*) take shape. **g~en** *vt* shape; (*organisieren*) arrange; (*schaffen*) create; (*entwerfen*) design; **sich g~en** turn out

geständ|ig *a* confessed; **g~ig sein** have confessed. **G~nis** *nt* -ses,-se confession

Gestank *m* -s stench, [bad] smell

gestatten *vt* allow, permit; **nicht gestattet** prohibited; **g~ Sie?** may I?

Geste /'gɛ-, 'ge:stə/ *f* -,-n gesture

Gesteck *nt* -[e]s,-e flower arrangement

gestehen† *vt/i* (*haben*) confess; confess to ⟨*Verbrechen*⟩; **offen gestanden** to tell the truth

Gestein *nt* -[e]s,-e rock

Gestell *nt* -[e]s,-e stand; (*Flaschen-*) rack; (*Rahmen*) frame

gestellt *a* **gut/schlecht g~** well/badly off; **auf sich** (*acc*) **selbst g~ sein** be thrown on one's own resources

gestelzt *a* (*fig*) stilted

gesteppt *a* quilted

gestern *adv* yesterday; **g~ nacht** last night

Gestik /'gɛstɪk/ *f* - gestures *pl*. **g~ulieren** *vi* (*haben*) gesticulate

gestrandet *a* stranded

gestreift *a* striped

gestrichelt *a* ⟨*Linie*⟩ dotted

gestrichen *a* **g~er Teelöffel** level teaspoon[ful]

gestrig /'gɛstrɪç/ *a* yesterday's; **am g~en Tag** yesterday

Gestrüpp *nt* -s,-e undergrowth

Gestüt *nt* -[e]s,-e stud [farm]

Gesuch *nt* -[e]s,-e request; (*Admin*) application. **g~t** *a* sought-after; (*gekünstelt*) contrived

gesund *a* healthy, *adv* -ily; **g~ sein** be in good health; ⟨*Sport, Getränk:*⟩ be good for one; **wieder g~ werden** get well again

Gesundheit *f* - health; **G~!** (*bei Niesen*) bless you! **g~lich** *a* health...; **g~licher Zustand** state of health ● *adv* **es geht ihm g~lich gut/schlecht** he is in good/poor health. **g~shalber** *adv* for health reasons. **g~sschädlich** *a* harmful. **G~szustand** *m* state of health

getäfelt *a* panelled

getigert *a* tabby

Getöse *nt* -s racket, din

getragen *a* solemn, *adv* -ly

Getränk *nt* -[e]s,-e drink. **G~ekarte** *f* wine-list

getrauen *vt* **sich** (*dat*) **etw g~** dare [to] do sth; **sich g~** dare

Getreide *nt* -s (*coll*) grain

getrennt *a* separate, *adv* -ly; **g~ leben** live apart. **g~schreiben†** *vt sep* write as two words

getreu *a* faithful, *adv* -ly ● *prep* (+ *dat*) true to; **der Wahrheit g~** truthfully. **g~lich** *adv* faithfully

Getriebe *nt* -s,- bustle; (*Techn*) gear; (*Auto*) transmission; (*Gehäuse*) gearbox

getrost *adv* with confidence

Getto *nt* -s,-s ghetto

Getue *nt* -s (*fam*) fuss

Getümmel *nt* -s tumult

getüpfelt *a* spotted

geübt *a* skilled; ⟨*Auge, Hand*⟩ practised

Gewächs *nt* -es,-e plant; (*Med*) growth

gewachsen *a* **jdm/etw g~ sein** be a match for s.o./be equal to sth

Gewächshaus *nt* greenhouse; (*Treibhaus*) hothouse

gewagt *a* daring

gewählt *a* refined

gewahr *a* **g~ werden** become aware (*acc/gen* of)

Gewähr *f* - guarantee

gewahren *vt* notice

gewähr|en *vt* grant; (*geben*) offer; **jdn g~en lassen** let s.o. have his way. **g~leisten** *vt* guarantee

Gewahrsam *m* -s safekeeping; (*Haft*) custody

Gewährsmann *m* (*pl* -männer & -leute) informant, source

Gewalt *f* -,-en power; (*Kraft*) force; (*Brutalität*) violence; **mit G~** by force; **G~ anwenden** use force; **sich in der G~ haben** be in control of oneself. **G~herrschaft** *f* tyranny. **g~ig** *a* powerful; (*fam: groß*) enormous, *adv* -ly; (*stark*) tremendous, *adv* -ly. **g~sam** *a* forcible, *adv* -bly; ⟨*Tod*⟩ violent. **g~tätig** *a* violent. **G~tätigkeit** *f* -,-en violence; (*Handlung*) act of violence

Gewand *nt* -[e]s,̈-er robe

gewandt *a* skilful, *adv* -ly; (*flink*) nimble, *adv* -bly. **G~heit** *f* - skill; nimbleness

Gewässer *nt* -s,- body of water; **G~** *pl* waters

Gewebe *nt* -s,- fabric; (*Anat*) tissue

Gewehr nt -s,-e rifle, gun

Geweih nt -[e]s,-e antlers pl

Gewerbe|e nt -s,- trade. **g~lich** a commercial, adv -ly. **g~smäßig** a professional, adv -ly

Gewerkschaft f -,-en trade union. **G~ler(in)** m -s,- (f -,-nen) trade unionist

Gewicht nt -[e]s,-e weight; (Bedeutung) importance. **G~heben** nt -s weight-lifting. **g~ig** a important

gewieft a (fam) crafty

gewillt a **g~ sein** be willing

Gewinde nt -s,- [screw] thread

Gewinn m -[e]s,-e profit; (fig) gain, benefit; (beim Spiel) winnings pl; (Preis) prize; (Los) winning ticket. **G~beteiligung** f profit-sharing. **g~bringend** a profitable, adv -bly. **g~en†** vt win; (erlangen) gain; (fördern) extract; **jdn für sich g~en** win s.o. over • vi (haben) win; **g~en an** (+ dat) gain in. **g~end** a engaging. **G~er(in)** m -s,- (f-,-nen) winner

Gewirr nt -s,-e tangle; (Straßen-) maze; **G~ von Stimmen** hubbub of voices

gewiß a (gewisser, gewissest) certain, adv -ly

Gewissen nt -s,- conscience. **g~haft** a conscientious, adv -ly. **g~los** a unscrupulous. **G~sbisse** mpl pangs of conscience

gewissermaßen adv to a certain extent; (sozusagen) as it were

Gewißheit f - certainty

Gewitt|er nt -s,- thunderstorm. **g~ern** vi (haben) **es g~ert** it is thundering. **g~rig** a thundery

gewogen a (fig) well-disposed (dat towards)

gewöhnen vt jdn/sich **g~ an** (+ acc) get s.o. used to/get used to; **[an]** jdn/etw **gewöhnt sein** be used to s.o./sth

Gewohnheit f -,-en habit. **g~smäßig** a habitual, adv -ly. **G~srecht** nt common law

gewöhnlich a ordinary, adv -ily; (üblich) usual, adv -ly; (ordinär) common

gewohnt a customary; (vertraut) familiar; (üblich) usual; **etw** (acc) **g~ sein** be used to sth

Gewöhnung f - getting used (an + acc to); (Süchtigkeit) addiction

Gewölb|e nt -s,- vault. **g~t** a curved; (Archit) vaulted

gewollt a forced

Gewühl nt -[e]s crush

gewunden a winding

gewürfelt a check[ed]

Gewürz nt -es,-e spice. **G~nelke** f clove

gezackt a serrated

gezähnt a serrated; (Säge) toothed

Gezeiten fpl tides

gezielt a specific; (Frage) pointed

geziemend a proper, adv -ly

geziert a affected, adv -ly

gezwungen a forced • adv **g~ lachen** give a forced laugh. **g~ermaßen** adv of necessity; **etw g~ermaßen tun** be forced to do sth

Gicht f - gout

Giebel m -s,- gable

Gier f - greed (**nach** for). **g~ig** a greedy, adv -ily

gieß|en† vt pour; water (Blumen, Garten); (Techn) cast • v impers **es g~t** it is pouring [with rain]. **G~erei** f -,-en foundry. **G~kanne** f watering-can

Gift nt -[e]s,-e poison; (Schlangen-) venom; (Biol, Med) toxin. **g~ig** a poisonous; (Schlange) venomous; (Med, Chem) toxic; (fig) spiteful, adv -ly. **G~müll** m toxic waste. **G~pilz** m poisonous fungus, toadstool. **G~zahn** m [poison] fang

gigantisch a gigantic

Gilde f -,-n guild

Gimpel m -s,- bullfinch; (fam: Tölpel) simpleton

Gin /dʒɪn/ m -s gin

Ginster m -s (Bot) broom

Gipfel m -s,- summit, top; (fig) peak. **G~konferenz** f summit conference. **g~n** vi (haben) culminate (**in** + dat in)

Gips m -es plaster. **G~abguß** m plaster cast. **G~er** m -s,- plasterer. **G~verband** m (Med) plaster cast

Giraffe f -,-n giraffe

Girlande f -,-n garland

Girokonto /ˈʒiːro-/ nt current account

Gischt m -[e]s & f - spray

Gitar|re f -,-n guitar. **G~rist(in)** m -en,-en (f -,-nen) guitarist

Gitter nt -s,- bars pl; (Rost) grating, grid; (Geländer, Zaun) railings pl; (Fenster-) grille; (Draht-) wire screen; **hinter G~n** (fam) behind bars. **G~netz** nt grid

Glanz m -es shine; (von Farbe, Papier) gloss; (Seiden-) sheen; (Politur) polish; (fig) brilliance; (Pracht) splendour

glänzen *vi (haben)* shine. **g~d** *a* shining; bright; ⟨*Papier, Haar*⟩ glossy; (*fig*) brilliant, *adv* -ly

glanz|los *a* dull. **G~stück** *nt* masterpiece; (*einer Sammlung*) showpiece. **g~voll** *a* (*fig*) brilliant, *adv* -ly; (*prachtvoll*) splendid, *adv* -ly. **G~zeit** *f* heyday

Glas *nt* -es,¨er glass; (*Brillen-*) lens; (*Fern-*) binoculars *pl*; (*Marmeladen-*) [glass] jar. **G~er** *m* -s,- glazier

gläsern *a* glass ...

Glashaus *nt* greenhouse

glasieren *vt* glaze; ice ⟨*Kuchen*⟩

glas|ig *a* glassy; (*durchsichtig*) transparent. **G~scheibe** *f* pane

Glasur *f* -,-en glaze; (*Culin*) icing

glatt *a* smooth; (*eben*) even; ⟨*Haar*⟩ straight; (*rutschig*) slippery; (*einfach*) straightforward; (*eindeutig*) downright; ⟨*Absage*⟩ flat ● *adv* smoothly; evenly; (*fam: völlig*) completely; (*gerade*) straight; (*leicht*) easily; ⟨*ablehnen*⟩ flatly; **g~ verlaufen** go off smoothly; **das ist g~ gelogen** it's a downright lie

Glätte *f* - smoothness; (*Rutschigkeit*) slipperiness

Glatteis *nt* [black] ice; **aufs G~ führen** (*fam*) take for a ride

glätten *vt* smooth; **sich g~** become smooth; ⟨*Wellen:*⟩ subside

glatt|gehen† *vi sep (sein)* (*fig*) go off smoothly. **g~rasiert** *a* cleanshaven. **g~streichen†** *vt sep* smooth out. **g~weg** *adv* (*fam*) outright

Glatz|e *f* -,-n bald patch; (*Voll-*) bald head; **eine G~e bekommen** go bald. **g~köpfig** *a* bald

Glaube *m* -ns belief (**an**+ *acc* in); (*Relig*) faith; **in gutem G~n** in good faith; **G~n schenken** (+ *dat*) believe. **g~n** *vt/i (haben)* believe (**an**+ *acc* in); (*vermuten*) think; **jdm g~n** believe s.o.; **nicht zu g~n** unbelievable, incredible. **G~nsbekenntnis** *nt* creed

glaubhaft *a* credible; (*überzeugend*) convincing, *adv* -ly

gläubig *a* religious; (*vertrauend*) trusting, *adv* -ly. **G~e(r)** *m/f* (*Relig*) believer; **die G~en** the faithful. **G~er** *m* -s,- (*Comm*) creditor

glaub|lich *a* **kaum g~lich** scarcely believable. **g~würdig** *a* credible; ⟨*Person*⟩ reliable. **G~würdigkeit** *f* - credibility; reliability

gleich *a* same; (*identisch*) identical; (*g~wertig*) equal; **2 mal 5 [ist] g~ 10** two times 5 equals 10; **das ist mir g~** it's all the same to me; **ganz g~, wo/ wer** no matter where/who ● *adv* equally; (*übereinstimmend*) identically, the same; (*sofort*) immediately; (*in Kürze*) in a minute; (*fast*) nearly; (*direkt*) right; **g~ alt/schwer sein** be the same age/weight. **g~altrig** *a* [of] the same age. **g~artig** *a* similar. **g~bedeutend** *a* synonymous. **g~berechtigt** *a* equal. **G~berechtigung** *f* equality. **g~bleibend** *a* constant

gleichen† *vi (haben)* **jdm/etw g~** be like *or* resemble s.o./sth; **sich g~** be alike

gleich|ermaßen *adv* equally. **g~falls** *adv* also, likewise; **danke g~falls** thank you, the same to you. **g~förmig** *a* uniform, *adv* -ly; (*eintönig*) monotonous, *adv* -ly. **G~förmigkeit** *f* - uniformity; monotony. **g~gesinnt** *a* like-minded. **G~gewicht** *nt* balance; (*Phys & fig*) equilibrium. **g~gültig** *a* indifferent, *adv* -ly; (*unwichtig*) unimportant. **G~gültigkeit** *f* indifference. **G~heit** *f* - equality; (*Ähnlichkeit*) similarity. **g~machen** *vt sep* make equal; **dem Erdboden g~machen** raze to the ground. **g~mäßig** *a* even, *adv* -ly, regular, *adv* -ly; (*beständig*) constant, *adv* -ly. **G~mäßigkeit** *f* - regularity. **G~mut** *m* equanimity. **g~mütig** *a* calm, *adv* -ly

Gleichnis *nt* -ses,-se parable

gleich|sam *adv* as it were. **G~schritt** *m* im G~schritt in step. **g~sehen†** *vi sep (haben)* **jdm g~sehen** look like s.o.; (*fam: typisch sein*) be just like s.o. **g~setzen** *vt sep* equate/(*g~stellen*) place on a par (*dat*/**mit** with). **g~stellen** *vt sep* place on a par (*dat* with). **G~strom** *m* direct current. **g~tun†** *vi sep* (*haben*) **es jdm g~tun** emulate s.o.

Gleichung *f* -,-en equation

gleich|viel *adv* no matter (**ob/wer** whether/who). **g~wertig** *a* of equal value. **g~zeitig** *a* simultaneous, *adv* -ly

Gleis *nt* -es,-e track; (*Bahnsteig*) platform; **G~ 5** platform 5

gleiten† *vi (sein)* glide; (*rutschen*) slide. **g~d** *a* sliding; **g~de Arbeitszeit** flexitime

Gleitzeit *f* flexitime

Gletscher m -s,- glacier. **G~spalte** f crevasse

Glied nt -[e]s,-er limb; (Teil) part; (Ketten-) link; (Mitglied) member; (Mil) rank. **g~ern** vt arrange; (einteilen) divide; **sich g~ern** be divided (**in** + acc into). **G~maßen** fpl limbs

glimmen† vi (haben) glimmer

glimpflich a lenient, adv -ly; **g~ davonkommen** get off lightly

glitschig a slippery

glitzern vi (haben) glitter

global a global, adv -ly

Globus m - & **-busses, -ben** & **-busse** globe

Glocke f -,-n bell. **G~nturm** m belltower, belfry

glorifizieren vt glorify

glorreich a glorious

Glossar nt -s,-e glossary

Glosse f -,-n comment

glotzen vi (haben) stare

Glück nt -[e]s [good] luck; (Zufriedenheit) happiness; **G~/kein G~ haben** be lucky/unlucky; **zum G~** luckily, fortunately; **auf gut G~** on the off chance; (wahllos) at random. **g~bringend** a lucky. **g~en** vi (sein) succeed; **es ist mir geglückt** I succeeded

gluckern vi (haben) gurgle

glücklich a lucky, fortunate; (zufrieden) happy; (sicher) safe ● adv happily; safely; (fam: endlich) finally. **g~erweise** adv luckily, fortunately

glückselig a blissfully happy. **G~keit** f bliss

glucksen vi (haben) gurgle

Glücksspiel nt game of chance; (Spielen) gambling

Glückwunsch m good wishes pl; (Gratulation) congratulations pl; **herzlichen G~!** congratulations! (zum Geburtstag) happy birthday! **G~karte** f greetings card

Glüh|birne f light-bulb. **g~en** vi (haben) glow. **g~end** a glowing; (rot-) red-hot; (Hitze) scorching; (leidenschaftlich) fervent, adv -ly. **G~faden** m filament. **G~wein** m mulled wine. **G~würmchen** nt -s,- glow-worm

Glukose f - glucose

Glut f - embers pl; (Röte) glow; (Hitze) heat; (fig) ardour

Glyzinie /-jə/ f -,-n wisteria

GmbH abbr (Gesellschaft mit beschränkter Haftung) ≈ plc

Gnade f - mercy; (Gunst) favour; (Relig) grace. **G~nfrist** f reprieve. **g~nlos** a merciless, adv -ly

gnädig a gracious, adv -ly; (mild) lenient, adv -ly; **g~e Frau** Madam

Gnom m -en,-en gnome

Gobelin /gobə'lɛ̃/ m -s,-s tapestry

Gold nt -[e]s gold. **g~en** a gold ...; (g~farben) golden; **g~ene Hochzeit** golden wedding. **G~fisch** m goldfish. **G~grube** f gold-mine. **g~ig** a sweet, lovely. **G~lack** m wallflower. **G~regen** m laburnum. **G~schmied** m goldsmith

Golf[1] m -[e]s,-e (Geog) gulf

Golf[2] nt -s golf. **G~platz** m golfcourse. **G~schläger** m golf-club. **G~spieler(in)** m(f) golfer

Gondel f -,-n gondola; (Kabine) cabin

Gong m -s,-s gong

gönnen vt jdm etw **g~** not begrudge s.o. sth; **jdm etw nicht g~** begrudge s.o. sth; **sie gönnte sich** (dat) **keine Ruhe** she allowed herself no rest

Gönner m -s,- patron. **g~haft** a patronizing, adv -ly

Gör nt -s,-en, **Göre** f -,-n (fam) kid

Gorilla m -s,-s gorilla

Gosse f -,-n gutter

Got|ik f - Gothic. **g~isch** a Gothic

Gott m -[e]s,-er God; (Myth) god

Götterspeise f jelly

Gottes|dienst m service. **g~lästerlich** a blasphemous, adv -ly. **G~lästerung** f blasphemy

Gottheit f -,-en deity

Göttin f -,-nen goddess

göttlich a divine, adv -ly

gott|los a ungodly; (atheistisch) godless. **g~verlassen** a God-forsaken

Götze m -n,-n, **G~nbild** nt idol

Gouver|nante /guvɐˈnantə/ f -,-n governess. **G~neur** /-ˈnøːɐ̯/ m -s,-e governor

Grab nt -[e]s,-er grave

graben† vi (haben) dig

Graben m -s,- ditch; (Mil) trench

Grab|mal nt tomb. **G~stein** m gravestone, tombstone

Grad m -[e]s,-e degree

Graf m -en,-en count

Grafik f -,-en graphics sg; (Kunst) graphic arts pl; (Druck) print

Gräfin f -,-nen countess

grafisch a graphic; **g~e Darstellung** diagram

Grafschaft *f* -,-en county

Gram *m* -s grief

grämen (sich) *vr* grieve

grämlich *a* morose, *adv* -ly

Gramm *nt* -s,-e gram

Gram|matik *f* -,-en grammar. **g~matikalisch, g~matisch** *a* grammatical, *adv* -ly

Granat *m* -[e]s,-e (*Miner*) garnet. **G~apfel** *m* pomegranate. **G~e** *f* -,-n shell; (*Hand-*) grenade

Granit *m* -s,-e granite

Graph|ik *f*, **g~isch** *a* = Grafik, grafisch

Gras *nt* -es,-̈er grass. **g~en** *vi* (*haben*) graze. **G~hüpfer** *m* -s,- grasshopper

grassieren *vi* (*haben*) be rife

gräßlich *a* dreadful, *adv* -ly

Grat *m* -[e]s,-e [mountain] ridge

Gräte *f* -,-n fishbone

Gratifikation /-'tsio:n/ *f* -,-en bonus

gratis *adv* free [of charge]. **G~probe** *f* free sample

Gratu|lant(in) *m* -en,-en (*f* -,-nen) well-wisher. **G~lation** /-'tsio:n/ *f* -,-en congratulations *pl*; (*Glückwünsche*) best wishes *pl*. **g~lieren** *vi* (*haben*) **jdm g~lieren** congratulate s.o. (**zu** on); (*zum Geburtstag*) wish s.o. happy birthday; **[ich] g~liere!** congratulations!

grau *a*, **G~** *nt* -s,- grey. **G~brot** *nt* mixed rye and wheat bread

grauen[1] *vi* (*haben*) **der Morgen** *od* **es graut** dawn is breaking

grauen[2] *v impers* **mir graut** [es] **davor** I dread it. **G~** *nt* -s dread. **g~haft, g~voll** *a* gruesome; (*gräßlich*) horrible, *adv* -bly

gräulich *a* greyish

Graupeln *fpl* soft hail *sg*

grausam *a* cruel, *adv* -ly. **G~keit** *f* -,-en cruelty

graus|en *v impers* **mir graust davor** I dread it. **G~en** *nt* -s horror, dread. **g~ig** *a* gruesome

gravieren *vt* engrave. **g~d** *a* (*fig*) serious

Grazie /'gra:tsiə/ *f* - grace

graziös *a* graceful, *adv* -ly

greifbar *a* tangible; **in g~er Nähe** within reach

greifen† *vt* take hold of; (*fangen*) catch • *vi* (*haben*) reach (**nach** for); **g~ zu** (*fig*) turn to; **um sich g~** (*fig*) spread. **G~** *nt* **G~spielen** play tag

Greis *m* -es,-e old man. **G~enalter** *nt* extreme old age. **g~enhaft** *a* old. **G~in** *f* -,-nen old woman

grell *a* glaring; (*Farbe*) garish; (*schrill*) shrill, *adv* -y

Gremium *nt* -s,-ien committee

Grenz|e *f* -,-n border; (*Staats-*) frontier; (*Grundstücks-*) boundary; (*fig*) limit. **g~en** *vi* (*haben*) border (**an** + *acc* on). **g~enlos** *a* boundless; (*maßlos*) infinite, *adv* -ly. **G~fall** *m* borderline case

Greuel *m* -s,- horror. **G~tat** *f* atrocity

greulich *a* horrible, *adv* -bly

Griech|e *m* -n,-n Greek. **G~enland** *nt* -s Greece. **G~in** *f* -,-nen Greek woman. **g~isch** *a* Greek. **G~isch** *nt* -[s] (*Lang*) Greek

griesgrämig *a* (*fam*) grumpy

Grieß *m* -es semolina

Griff *m* -[e]s,-e grasp, hold; (*Hand-*) movement of the hand; (*Tür-, Messer-*) handle; (*Schwert-*) hilt. **g~bereit** *a* handy

Grill *m* -s,-s grill; (*Garten-*) barbecue

Grille *f* -,-n (*Zool*) cricket; (*fig: Laune*) whim

grill|en *vt* grill; (*im Freien*) barbecue • *vi* (*haben*) have a barbecue. **G~fest** *nt* barbecue. **G~gericht** *nt* grill

Grimasse *f* -,-n grimace; **G~n schneiden** pull faces

grimmig *a* furious; (*Kälte*) bitter

grinsen *vi* (*haben*) grin. **G~** *nt* -s grin

Grippe *f* -,-n influenza, (*fam*) flu

grob *a* (**gröber, gröbst**) coarse, *adv* -ly; (*unsanft, ungefähr*) rough, *adv* -ly; (*unhöflich*) rude, *adv* -ly; (*schwer*) gross, *adv* -ly; (*Fehler*) bad; **g~e Arbeit** rough work; **g~ geschätzt** roughly. **G~ian** *m* -s,-e brute

gröblich *a* gross, *adv* -ly

grölen *vt/i* (*haben*) bawl

Groll *m* -[e]s resentment; **einen G~ gegen jdn hegen** bear s.o. a grudge. **g~en** *vi* (*haben*) be angry (*dat* with); (*Donner:*) rumble

Grönland *nt* -s Greenland

Gros[1] *nt* -ses,- (*Maß*) gross

Gros[2] /gro:/ *nt* - majority, bulk

Groschen *m* -s,- (*Aust*) groschen; (*fam*) ten-pfennig piece; **der G~ ist gefallen** (*fam*) the penny's dropped

groß *a* (**größer, größt**) big; (*Anzahl, Summe*) large; (*bedeutend, stark*) great; (*g~artig*) grand; (*Buchstabe*) capital; **g~e Ferien** summer holidays; **g~e Angst haben** be very frightened; **der größte Teil** the majority *or* bulk; **g~ werden** (*Person:*) grow up; **g~ in etw**

(dat) **sein** be good at sth; **g~ und klein** young and old; **im g~en und ganzen** on the whole ● *adv* ⟨*feiern*⟩ in style; *(fam: viel)* much; **jdn g~ ansehen** look at s.o. in amazement

groß|artig *a* magnificent, *adv* -ly. **G~aufnahme** *f* close-up. **G~britannien** *nt* -s Great Britain. **G~buchstabe** *m* capital letter. **G~e(r)** *m/f* **unser G~er** our eldest; **die G~en** the grown-ups; *(fig)* the great *pl*

Größe *f* -,-n size; *(Ausmaß)* extent; *(Körper-)* height; *(Bedeutsamkeit)* greatness; *(Math)* quantity; *(Person)* great figure

Groß|eltern *pl* grandparents. **g~enteils** *adv* largely

Größenwahnsinn *m* megalomania

Groß|handel *m* wholesale trade. **G~händler** *m* wholesaler. **g~herzig** *a* magnanimous, *adv* -ly. **G~macht** *f* superpower. **G~mut** *f* - magnanimity. **g~mütig** *a* magnanimous, *adv* -ly. **G~mutter** *f* grandmother. **G~onkel** *m* great-uncle. **G~reinemachen** *nt* -s spring-clean. **G~schreibung** *f* capitalization. **g~sprecherisch** *a* boastful. **g~spurig** *a* pompous, *adv* -ly; *(überheblich)* arrogant, *adv* -ly. **G~stadt** *f* [large] city. **g~städtisch** *a* city ... **G~tante** *f* great-aunt. **G~teil** *m* large proportion; *(Hauptteil)* bulk

größtenteils *adv* for the most part

groß|tun† **(sich)** *vr sep* brag. **G~vater** *m* grandfather. **g~ziehen†** *vt sep* bring up; rear ⟨*Tier*⟩. **g~zügig** *a* generous, *adv* -ly; *(weiträumig)* spacious. **G~zügigkeit** *f* - generosity

grotesk *a* grotesque, *adv* -ly

Grotte *f* -,-n grotto

Grübchen *nt* -s,- dimple

Grube *f* -,-n pit

grübeln *vi (haben)* brood

Gruft *f* -,̈e [burial] vault

grün *a* green; **im G~en** out in the country; **die G~en** the Greens. **G~** *nt* -s,- green; *(Laub, Zweige)* greenery

Grund *m* -[e]s,̈e ground; *(Boden)* bottom; *(Hinter-)* background; *(Ursache)* reason; **auf G~** (+ *gen*) on the strength of; **aus diesem G~e** for this reason; **von G~ auf** *(fig)* radically; **im G~e [genommen]** basically; **auf G~ laufen** *(Naut)* run aground. **G~begriffe** *mpl* basics. **G~besitz** *m* landed property. **G~besitzer** *m* landowner

gründ|en *vt* found, set up; start ⟨*Familie*⟩; *(fig)* base **(auf** + *acc* on); **sich g~en** be based **(auf** + *acc* on). **G~er(in)** *m* -s,- *(f* -,-*nen)* founder

Grund|farbe *f* primary colour. **G~form** *f (Gram)* infinitive. **G~gesetz** *nt (Pol)* constitution. **G~lage** *f* basis, foundation. **g~legend** *a* fundamental, *adv* -ly

gründlich *a* thorough, *adv* -ly. **G~keit** *f* - thoroughness

grund|los *a* bottomless; *(fig)* groundless ● *adv* without reason. **G~mauern** *fpl* foundations

Gründonnerstag *m* Maundy Thursday

Grund|regel *f* basic rule. **G~riß** *m* ground-plan; *(fig)* outline. **G~satz** *m* principle. **g~sätzlich** *a* fundamental, *adv* -ly; *(im allgemeinen)* in principle; *(prinzipiell)* on principle. **G~schule** *f* primary school. **G~stein** *m* foundation-stone. **G~stück** *nt* plot [of land]

Gründung *f* -,-en foundation

grün|en *vi (haben)* become green. **G~gürtel** *m* green belt. **G~span** *m* verdigris. **G~streifen** *m* grass verge; *(Mittel-)* central reservation, *(Amer)* median strip

grunzen *vi (haben)* grunt

Gruppe *f* -,-n group; *(Reise-)* party

gruppieren *vt* group; **sich g~** form a group/groups

Grusel|geschichte *f* horror story. **g~ig** *a* creepy

Gruß *m* -es,̈e greeting; *(Mil)* salute; **einen schönen G~ an X** give my regards to X; **viele/herzliche G~e** regards; **Mit freundlichen G~en** Yours sincerely/*(Comm)* faithfully

grüßen *vt/i (haben)* say hallo **(jdn** to s.o.); *(Mil)* salute; **g~ Sie X von mir** give my regards to X; **jdn g~ lassen** send one's regards to s.o.; **grüß Gott!** *(SGer, Aust)* good morning/afternoon/evening!

guck|en *vi (haben) (fam)* look. **G~loch** *nt* peep-hole

Guerilla /ge'rɪlja/ *f* - guerrilla warfare. **G~kämpfer** *m* guerrilla

Gulasch *nt* & *m* -[e]s goulash

gültig *a* valid, *adv* -ly. **G~keit** *f* - validity

Gummi *m* & *nt* -s,-[s] rubber; *(Harz)* gum. **G~band** *nt (pl* -bänder) elastic *or* rubber band; *(G~zug)* elastic

gummiert *a* gummed

Gummi|knüppel *m* truncheon. **G∼stiefel** *m* gumboot, wellington. **G∼zug** *m* elastic

Gunst *f* - favour; **zu jds G∼en** in s.o.'s favour

günstig *a* favourable, *adv* -bly; (*passend*) convenient, *adv* -ly

Günstling *m* -s, -e favourite

Gurgel *f* -, -n throat. **g∼n** *vi (haben)* gargle. **G∼wasser** *nt* gargle

Gurke *f* -, -n cucumber; (*Essig-*) gherkin

gurren *vi (haben)* coo

Gurt *m* -[e]s, -e strap; (*Gürtel*) belt; (*Auto*) safety-belt. **G∼band** *nt* (*pl* -bänder) waistband

Gürtel *m* -s, - belt. **G∼linie** *f* waistline. **G∼rose** *f* shingles *sg*

GUS *abbr* **(Gemeinschaft Unabhängiger Staaten)** CIS

Guß *m* -sses, ̈-sse (*Techn*) casting; (*Strom*) stream; (*Regen-*) downpour; (*Torten-*) icing. **G∼eisen** *nt* cast iron. **g∼eisern** *a* cast-iron

gut *a* (**besser, best**) good; (*Gewissen*) clear; (*gütig*) kind (**zu** to); **jdm gut sein** be fond of s.o.; **im g∼en** amicably; **zu g∼er Letzt** in the end; **schon gut** that's all right ● *adv* well; (*schmecken, riechen*) good; (*leicht*) easily; **es gut haben** be well off; (*Glück haben*) be lucky; **gut zu sehen** clearly visible; **gut drei Stunden** a good three hours; **du hast gut reden** it's easy for you to talk

Gut *nt* -[e]s, ̈-er possession, property; (*Land-*) estate; **Gut und Böse** good and evil; **Güter** (*Comm*) goods

Gutacht|en *nt* -s, - expert's report. **G∼er** *m* -s, - expert

gut|artig *a* good-natured; (*Med*) benign. **g∼aussehend** *a* good-looking. **g∼bezahlt** *a* well-paid. **G∼dünken** *nt* -s **nach eigenem G∼dünken** at one's own discretion

Gute|(s) *nt* **etwas/nichts G∼s** something/nothing good; **G∼s tun** do good; **das G∼ daran** the good thing about it all; **alles G∼!** all the best!

Güte *f* -, -n goodness, kindness; (*Qualität*) quality; **du meine G∼!** my goodness!

Güterzug *m* goods/(*Amer*) freight train

gut|gehen† *vi sep* (*sein*) go well; **es geht mir gut** I am well/(*geschäftlich*) doing well. **g∼gehend** *a* flourishing, thriving. **g∼gemeint** *a* well-meant. **g∼gläubig** *a* trusting. **g∼haben†**

vt sep **fünfzig Mark g∼haben** have fifty marks credit (**bei** with). **G∼haben** *nt* -s, - [credit] balance; (*Kredit*) credit. **g∼heißen†** *vt sep* approve of

gütig *a* kind, *adv* -ly

gütlich *a* amicable, *adv* -bly

gut|machen *vt sep* make up for; make good (*Schaden*). **g∼mütig** *a* good-natured, *adv* -ly. **G∼mütigkeit** *f* - good nature. **G∼schein** *m* credit note; (*Bon*) voucher; (*Geschenk-*) gift token. **g∼schreiben†** *vt sep* credit. **G∼schrift** *f* credit

Guts|haus *nt* manor house. **G∼hof** *m* manor

gut|situiert *a* well-to-do. **g∼tun†** *vi sep* (*haben*) **jdm/etw g∼tun** do s.o./sth good. **g∼willig** *a* willing, *adv* -ly

Gymnasium *nt* -s, -ien ≈ grammar school

Gymnast|ik *f* - [keep-fit] exercises *pl*; (*Turnen*) gymnastics *sg*. **g∼isch** *a* **g∼ische Übung** exercise

Gynäko|loge *m* -n, -n gynaecologist. **G∼logie** *f* - gynaecology. **g∼logisch** *a* gynaecological

H

H, h /ha:/ *nt* -, - (*Mus*) B, b

Haar *nt* -[e]s, -e hair; **sich** (*dat*) **die Haare** *od* **das H∼ waschen** wash one's hair; **um ein H∼** (*fam*) very nearly. **H∼bürste** *f* hairbrush. **h∼en** *vi* (*haben*) shed hairs; (*Tier:*) moult ● *vr* **sich h∼en** moult. **h∼ig** *a* hairy; (*fam*) tricky. **H∼klammer, H∼klemme** *f* hair-grip. **H∼nadel** *f* hairpin. **H∼nadelkurve** *f* hairpin bend. **H∼schleife** *f* bow. **H∼schnitt** *m* haircut. **H∼spange** *f* slide. **h∼sträubend** *a* hair-raising; (*empörend*) shocking. **H∼trockner** *m* -s, - hair-drier. **H∼waschmittel** *nt* shampoo

Habe *f* - possessions *pl*

haben† *vt aux* have; **Angst/Hunger/Durst h∼** be frightened/hungry/ thirsty; **ich hätte gern** I'd like; **sich h∼** (*fam*) make a fuss; **es gut/schlecht h∼** be well/badly off; **etw gegen jdn h∼** have sth against s.o.; **was hat er?** what's the matter with him? ● *v aux* have; **ich habe/hatte geschrieben** I have/had written; **er hätte ihr geholfen** he would have helped her

Habgier f greed. **h~ig** a greedy
Habicht m -[e]s,-e hawk
Hab|seligkeiten fpl belongings.
  H~sucht f = Habgier
Hachse f -,-n (Culin) knuckle
Hack|beil nt chopper. **H~braten** m
  meat loaf
Hacke[1] f -,-n hoe; (Spitz-) pick
Hacke[2] f -,-n, **Hacken** m -s,- heel
hack|en vt hoe; (schlagen, zer-
  kleinern) chop; ⟨Vogel:⟩ peck; **ge-
  hacktes Rindfleisch** minced/(Amer)
  ground beef. **H~fleisch** nt mince,
  (Amer) ground meat
Hafen m -s,- harbour; (See-) port.
  H~arbeiter m docker. **H~damm** m
  mole. **H~stadt** f port
Hafer m -s oats pl. **H~flocken** fpl
  [rolled] oats. **H~mehl** nt oatmeal
Haft f - (Jur) custody; (H~strafe) im-
  prisonment. **h~bar** a (Jur) liable.
  H~befehl m warrant [of arrest]
haften vi (haben) cling; (kleben)
  stick; (bürgen) vouch/(Jur) be liable
  (für for)
Häftling m -s,-e detainee
Haftpflicht f (Jur) liability. **H~ver-
  sicherung** f (Auto) third-party in-
  surance
Haftstrafe f imprisonment
Haftung f - (Jur) liability
Hagebutte f -,-n rose-hip
Hagel m -s hail. **H~korn** nt hailstone.
  h~n vi (haben) hail
hager a gaunt
Hahn m -[e]s,-e cock; (Techn) tap,
  (Amer) faucet
Hähnchen nt -s,- (Culin) chicken
Hai[fisch] m -[e]s,-e shark
Häkchen nt -s,- tick
häkel|n vt/i (haben) crochet. **H~
  nadel** f crochet-hook
Haken m -s,- hook; (Häkchen) tick;
  (fam: Schwierigkeit) snag. **h~** vt hook
  (an + acc to). **H~kreuz** nt swastika.
  H~nase f hooked nose
halb a half; **eine h~e Stunde** half an
  hour; **zum h~en Preis** at half price; **auf
  h~em Weg** half-way ● adv half; **h~
  drei** half past two; **fünf [Minuten] vor/
  nach h~ vier** twenty-five [minutes]
  past three/to four; **h~ und h~** half and
  half; (fast ganz) more or less. **H~blut**
  nt half-breed. **H~dunkel** nt semi-
  darkness. **H~e(r,s)** f/m/nt half [a
  litre]
halber prep (+ gen) for the sake of;
  Geschäfte h~ on business

Halb|finale nt semifinal. **H~heit** f
  -,-en (fig) half-measure
halbieren vt halve, divide in half;
  (Geom) bisect
Halb|insel f peninsula. **H~kreis** m
  semicircle. **H~kugel** f hemisphere.
  h~laut a low ● adv in an undertone. **h~mast** adv at half-mast.
  H~messer m -s,- radius. **H~mond**
  m half moon. **H~pension** f half-
  board. **h~rund** a semicircular.
  H~schuh m [flat] shoe. **h~stünd-
  lich** a & adv half-hourly. **h~tags** adv
  [for] half a day; **h~tags arbeiten** ≈
  work part-time. **H~ton** m semitone.
  h~wegs adv half-way; (ziemlich)
  more or less. **h~wüchsig** a ad-
  olescent. **H~zeit** f (Sport) half-time;
  (Spielzeit) half
Halde f -,-n dump, tip
Hälfte f -,-n half; **zur H~** half
Halfter[1] m & nt -s,- halter
Halfter[2] f -,-n & nt -s,- holster
Hall m -[e]s,-e sound
Halle f -,-n hall; (Hotel-) lobby; (Bahn-
  hofs-) station concourse
hallen vi (haben) resound; (wider-)
  echo
Hallen- pref indoor
hallo int hallo
Halluzination /-'tsjo:n/ f -,-en hallucination
Halm m -[e]s,-e stalk; (Gras-) blade
Hals m -es,-e neck; (Kehle) throat; **aus
  vollem H~e** at the top of one's voice;
  ⟨lachen⟩ out loud. **H~ausschnitt** m
  neckline. **H~band** nt (pl -bänder)
  collar. **H~kette** f necklace. **H~
  schmerzen** mpl sore throat sg. **h~
  starrig** a stubborn. **H~tuch** nt scarf
halt[1] adv (SGer) just; **es geht h~ nicht**
  it's just not possible
halt[2] int stop! (Mil) halt! (fam) wait a
  minute!
Halt m -[e]s,-e hold; (Stütze) support;
  (innerer) stability; (Anhalten) stop.
  h~bar a durable; (Tex) hard- wearing; (fig) tenable; **h~bar bis ...**
  (Comm) use by ...
halten† vt hold; make ⟨Rede⟩; give
  ⟨Vortrag⟩; (einhalten, bewahren)
  keep; [**sich** (dat)] **etw h~** keep ⟨Hund⟩;
  take ⟨Zeitung⟩; run ⟨Auto⟩; **warm h~**
  keep warm; **h~ für** regard as; **viel/
  nicht viel h~ von** think highly/little of;
  sich h~ hold on (an + dat to); (fig) hold
  out; ⟨Geschäft:⟩ keep going; (haltbar
  sein) keep; ⟨Wetter:⟩ hold; ⟨Blumen:⟩ last;

sich links h~ keep left; **sich gerade h~** hold oneself upright; **sich h~ an** (+*acc*) (*fig*) keep to ● *vi (haben)* hold; (*haltbar sein, bestehen bleiben*) keep; (*Freundschaft, Blumen:*) last; (*haltmachen*) stop; **h~ auf** (+*acc*) (*fig*) set great store by; **auf sich** (*acc*) **h~** take pride in oneself; **an sich** (*acc*) **h~** contain oneself; **zu jdm h~** be loyal to s.o.

Halter *m* -s,- holder

Halte|stelle *f* stop. **H~verbot** *nt* waiting restriction; **'H~verbot'** 'no waiting'

halt|los *a* (*fig*) unstable; (*unbegründet*) unfounded. **h~machen** *vi sep (haben)* stop

Haltung *f* -,-en (*Körper-*) posture; (*Verhalten*) manner; (*Einstellung*) attitude; (*Fassung*) composure; (*Halten*) keeping; **H~ annehmen** (*Mil*) stand to attention

Halunke *m* -n,-n scoundrel

Hamburger *m* -s,- hamburger

hämisch *a* malicious, *adv* -ly

Hammel *m* -s,- ram; (*Culin*) mutton. **H~fleisch** *nt* mutton

Hammer *m* -s,̈- hammer

hämmern *vt/i (haben)* hammer; (*Herz:*) pound

Hämorrhoiden /hɛmɔroˈiːdən/ *fpl* haemorrhoids

Hamster *m* -s,- hamster. **h~n** *vt/i* (*fam*) hoard

Hand *f* -,̈e hand; **jdm die H~ geben** shake hands with s.o.; **rechter/linker H~** on the right/left; **[aus] zweiter H~** second-hand; **unter der H~** unofficially; (*geheim*) secretly; **an H~ von** with the aid of; **H~ und Fuß haben** (*fig*) be sound. **H~arbeit** *f* manual work; (*handwerklich*) handicraft; (*Nadelarbeit*) needlework; (*Gegenstand*) hand-made article. **H~ball** *m* [German] handball. **H~besen** *m* brush. **H~bewegung** *f* gesture. **H~bremse** *f* handbrake. **H~buch** *nt* handbook, manual

Händedruck *m* handshake

Handel *m* -s trade, commerce; (*Unternehmen*) business; (*Geschäft*) deal; **H~ treiben** trade. **h~n** *vi (haben)* act; (*Handel treiben*) trade (**mit** in); **von etw** *od* **über etw** (*acc*) **h~n** deal with sth; **sich h~n um** be about, concern. **H~smarine** *f* merchant navy. **H~sschiff** *nt* merchant vessel. **H~sschule** *f* commercial college.

h~süblich *a* customary. **H~sware** *f* merchandise

Hand|feger *m* -s,- brush. **H~fertigkeit** *f* dexterity. **h~fest** *a* sturdy; (*fig*) solid. **H~fläche** *f* palm. **h~gearbeitet** *a* hand-made. **H~gelenk** *nt* wrist. **h~gemacht** *a* handmade. **H~gemenge** *nt* -s,- scuffle. **H~gepäck** *nt* hand-luggage. **h~geschrieben** *a* hand-written. **H~granate** *f* hand-grenade. **h~greiflich** *a* tangible; **h~greiflich werden** become violent. **H~griff** *m* handle; **mit einem H~griff** with a flick of the wrist

handhaben *vt insep (reg)* handle

Handikap /ˈhɛndikɛp/ *nt* -s,-s handicap

Hand|kuß *m* kiss on the hand. **H~lauf** *m* handrail

Händler *m* -s,- dealer, trader

handlich *a* handy

Handlung *f* -,-en act; (*Handeln*) action; (*Roman-*) plot; (*Geschäft*) shop. **H~sweise** *f* conduct

Hand|schellen *fpl* handcuffs. **H~schlag** *m* handshake. **H~schrift** *f* handwriting; (*Text*) manuscript. **H~schuh** *m* glove. **H~schuhfach** *nt* glove compartment. **H~stand** *m* handstand. **H~tasche** *f* handbag. **H~tuch** *nt* towel. **H~voll** *f* -,- handful

Handwerk *nt* craft, trade; **sein H~ verstehen** know one's job. **H~er** *m* -s,- craftsman; (*Arbeiter*) workman

Hanf *m* -[e]s hemp

Hang *m* -[e]s,̈e slope; (*fig*) inclination, tendency

Hänge|brücke *f* suspension bridge. **H~lampe** *f* [light] pendant. **H~matte** *f* hammock

hängen[1] *vt (reg)* hang

hängen[2]† *vi (haben)* hang; **h~ an** (+*dat*) (*fig*) be attached to. **h~bleiben†** *vi sep (sein)* stick (**an**+*dat* to); (*Kleid:*) catch (**an**+*dat* on). **h~lassen†** *vt sep* leave; **den Kopf h~lassen** be downcast

Hannover *nt* -s Hanover

hänseln *vt* tease

hantieren *vi (haben)* busy oneself

hapern *vi (haben)* **es hapert** there's a lack (**an**+*dat* of)

Happen *m* -s,- mouthful; **einen H~ essen** have a bite to eat

Harfe *f* -,-n harp

Harke f -,-n rake. **h~n** vt/i (haben) rake

harmlos a harmless; (arglos) innocent, adv -ly. **H~igkeit** f - harmlessness; innocence

Harmonie f -,-n harmony. **h~ren** vi (haben) harmonize; (gut auskommen) get on well

Harmonika f -,-s accordion; (Mund-) mouth-organ

harmonisch a harmonious, adv -ly

Harn m -[e]s urine. **H~blase** f bladder

Harpune f -,-n harpoon

hart (härter, härtest) a hard; (heftig) violent; (streng) harsh ● adv hard; (streng) harshly

Härte f -,-n hardness; (Strenge) harshness; (Not) hardship. **h~n** vt harden

Hart|faserplatte f hardboard. **h~gekocht** a hard-boiled. **h~herzig** a hard-hearted. **h~näckig** a stubborn, adv -ly; (ausdauernd) persistent, adv -ly. **H~näckigkeit** f - stubbornness; persistence

Harz nt -es,-e resin

Haschee nt -s,-s (Culin) hash

haschen vi (haben) **h~ nach** try to catch

Haschisch nt & m -[s] hashish

Hase m -n,-n hare; **falscher H~** meat loaf

Hasel f -,-n hazel. **H~maus** f dormouse. **H~nuß** f hazel-nut

Hasenfuß m (fam) coward

Haß m -sses hatred

hassen vt hate

häßlich a ugly; (unfreundlich) nasty, adv -ily. **H~keit** f - ugliness; nastiness

Hast f - haste. **h~en** vi (sein) hasten, hurry. **h~ig** a hasty, adv -ily, hurried, adv -ly

hast, hat, hatte, hätte s. haben

Haube f -,-n cap; (Trocken-) drier; (Kühler-) bonnet, (Amer) hood

Hauch m -[e]s breath; (Luft-) breeze; (Duft) whiff; (Spur) tinge. **h~dünn** a very thin; (Strümpfe) sheer. **h~en** vt/i (haben) breathe

Haue f -,-n pick; (fam: Prügel) beating. **h~n**† vt beat; (hämmern) knock; (meißeln) hew; **sich h~n** fight; **übers Ohr h~n** (fam) cheat ● vi (haben) bang (**auf**+acc on); **jdm ins Gesicht h~n** hit s.o. in the face

Haufen m -s,- heap, pile; (Leute) crowd

häufen vt heap or pile [up]; **sich h~** pile up; (zunehmen) increase

haufenweise adv in large numbers; **h~ Geld** pots of money

häufig a frequent, adv -ly. **H~keit** f - frequency

Haupt nt -[e]s, **Häupter** head. **H~bahnhof** m main station. **H~darsteller** m, **H~darstellerin** f male/female lead. **H~fach** nt main subject. **H~gericht** nt main course. **H~hahn** m mains tap; (Wasser-) stopcock

Häuptling m -s,-e chief

Haupt|mahlzeit f main meal. **H~mann** m (pl -leute) captain. **H~person** f most important person; (Theat) principal character. **H~post** f main post office. **H~quartier** nt headquarters pl. **H~rolle** f lead; (fig) leading role. **H~sache** f main thing; **in der H~sache** in the main. **h~sächlich** a main, adv -ly. **H~satz** m main clause. **H~schlüssel** m master key. **H~stadt** f capital. **H~straße** f main street. **H~verkehrsstraße** f main road. **H~verkehrszeit** f rush-hour. **H~wort** nt (pl -wörter) noun

Haus nt -es, **Häuser** house; (Gebäude) building; (Schnecken-) shell; **zu H~e** at home; **nach H~e** home. **H~angestellte(r)** m/f domestic servant. **H~arbeit** f housework; (Sch) homework. **H~arzt** m family doctor. **H~aufgaben** fpl homework sg. **H~besetzer** m -s,- squatter. **H~besuch** m house-call

hausen vi (haben) live; (wüten) wreak havoc

Haus|frau f housewife. **H~gehilfin** f domestic help. **h~gemacht** a home-made. **H~halt** m -[e]s,-e household; (Pol) budget. **h~halten**† vi sep (haben) **h~halten mit** manage carefully; conserve (Kraft). **H~hälterin** f -,-nen housekeeper. **H~haltsgeld** nt housekeeping [money]. **H~haltsplan** m budget. **H~herr** m head of the household; (Gastgeber) host. **h~hoch** a huge; (fam) big ● adv (fam) vastly; (verlieren) by a wide margin

hausier|en vi (haben) **h~en mit** hawk. **H~er** m -s,- hawker

Hauslehrer m [private] tutor. **H~in** f governess

häuslich a domestic; (Person) domesticated

Haus|meister m caretaker. **H~nummer** f house number.

H~**ordnung** f house rules pl.
H~**putz** m cleaning. H~**rat** m -[e]s
household effects pl. H~**schlüssel** m
front-door key. H~**schuh** m slipper.
H~**stand** m household. H~**suchung**
f [police] search. H~**suchungs-
befehl** m search-warrant. H~**tier** nt
domestic animal; (Hund, Katze) pet.
H~**tür** f front door. H~**wart** m
-[e]s,-e caretaker. H~**wirt** m landlord. H~**wirtin** f landlady

Haut f -, **Häute** skin; (Tier-) hide; **aus
der** H~ **fahren** (fam) fly off the handle.
H~**arzt** m dermatologist

häuten vt skin; **sich** h~ moult

haut|eng a skin-tight. H~**farbe** f
colour; (Teint) complexion

Haxe f -,-n = **Hachse**

Hbf. abbr s. **Hauptbahnhof**

Hebamme f -,-n midwife

Hebel m -s,- lever. H~**kraft**, H~-
wirkung f leverage

heben† vt lift; (hoch-, steigern) raise;
sich h~ rise; (Nebel:) lift; (sich verbessern) improve

hebräisch a Hebrew

hecheln vi (haben) pant

Hecht m -[e]s,-e pike

Heck nt -s,-s (Naut) stern; (Aviat) tail;
(Auto) rear

Hecke f -,-n hedge. H~**nschütze** m
sniper

Heck|fenster nt rear window.
H~**motor** m rear engine. H~**tür** f
hatchback

Heer nt -[e]s,-e army

Hefe f - yeast. H~**teig** m yeast dough.
H~**teilchen** nt Danish pastry

Heft[1] nt -[e]s,-e haft, handle

Heft[2] nt -[e]s,-e booklet; (Sch) exercise
book; (Zeitschrift) issue. h~**en** vt
(nähen) tack; (stecken) pin/(klammern) clip/(mit Heftmaschine) staple
(**an** + acc to). H~**er** m -s,- file

heftig a fierce, adv -ly, violent, adv
-ly; (Schlag, Regen) heavy, adv -ily;
(Schmerz, Gefühl) intense, adv -ly;
(Person) quick-tempered. H~**keit** f -
fierceness, violence; intensity

Heft|klammer f staple; (Büro-)
paper-clip. H~**maschine** f stapler.
H~**pflaster** nt sticking plaster.
H~**zwecke** f -,-n drawing-pin

hegen vt care for; (fig) cherish
(Hoffnung); harbour (Verdacht)

Hehl nt & m **kein[en]** H~ **machen aus**
make no secret of. H~**er** m -s,- receiver, fence

Heide[1] m -n,-n heathen

Heide[2] f -,-n heath; (Bot) heather.
H~**kraut** nt heather

Heidelbeere f bilberry, (Amer) blue-
berry

Heid|in f -,-nen heathen. h~**nisch** a
heathen

heikel a difficult, tricky; (delikat)
delicate; (dial) (Person) fussy

heil a undamaged, intact; (Person)
unhurt; (gesund) well; **mit** h~**er
Haut** (fam) unscathed

Heil nt -s salvation; **sein** H~ **versuchen**
try one's luck

Heiland m -s (Relig) Saviour

Heil|anstalt f sanatorium; (Nerven-)
mental hospital. H~**bad** nt spa.
h~**bar** a curable

Heilbutt m -[e]s,-e halibut

heilen vt cure; heal (Wunde) ● vi
(sein) heal

heilfroh a (fam) very relieved

Heilgymnastik f physiotherapy

heilig a holy; (geweiht) sacred; **der**
H~**e Abend** Christmas Eve; **die** h~**e
Anna** Saint Anne. H~**abend** m
Christmas Eve. H~**e(r)** m/f saint.
h~**en** vt keep, observe. H~**enschein**
m halo. h~**halten**† vt sep hold sacred; keep (Feiertag). H~**keit** f - sanctity, holiness. h~**sprechen**† vt sep
canonize. H~**tum** nt -s,-̈er shrine

heil|kräftig a medicinal. H~**kräu-
ter** ntpl medicinal herbs. h~**los** a
unholy. H~**mittel** nt remedy.
H~**praktiker** m -s,- practitioner of
alternative medicine. h~**sam** a (fig)
salutary. H~**sarmee** f Salvation
Army. H~**ung** f - cure

Heim nt -[e]s,-e home; (Studenten-)
hostel. h~ adv home

Heimat f -,-en home; (Land) native
land. H~**abend** m folk evening.
h~**los** a homeless. H~**stadt** f home
town

heim|begleiten vt sep see home.
h~**bringen**† vt sep bring home; (begleiten) see home. H~**computer** m
home computer. h~**fahren**† v sep
● vi (sein) go/drive home ● vt take/
drive home. H~**fahrt** f way home.
h~**gehen**† vi sep (sein) go home;
(sterben) die

heimisch a native, indigenous; (Pol)
domestic; h~ **sein/sich** h~ **fühlen** be/
feel at home

Heim|kehr f - return [home].
h~**kehren** vi sep (sein) return home.

h~kommen† *vi sep (sein)* come home

heimlich *a* secret, *adv* -ly. **H~keit** *f* -,-en secrecy; **H~keiten** secrets. **H~tuerei** *f* - secretiveness

Heim|reise *f* journey home. **h~reisen** *vi sep (sein)* go home. **H~spiel** *nt* home game. **h~suchen** *vt sep* afflict. **h~tückisch** *a* treacherous; ⟨*Krankheit*⟩ insidious. **h~wärts** *adv* home. **H~weg** *m* way home. **H~weh** *nt* -s homesickness; **H~weh haben** be homesick. **H~werker** *m* -s,- [home] handyman. **h~zahlen** *vt sep* jdm etw h~zahlen (*fig*) pay s.o. back for sth

Heirat *f* -,-en marriage. **h~en** *vt/i* (*haben*) marry. **H~santrag** *m* proposal; **jdm einen H~santrag machen** propose to s.o. **h~sfähig** *a* marriageable

heiser *a* hoarse, *adv* -ly. **H~keit** *f* - hoarseness

heiß *a* hot, *adv* -ly; ⟨*hitzig*⟩ heated; ⟨*leidenschaftlich*⟩ fervent, *adv* -ly; **mir ist h~** I am hot

heißen† *vi (haben)* be called; ⟨*bedeuten*⟩ mean; **ich heiße ...** my name is ...; **wie h~ Sie?** what is your name? **wie heißt ... auf englisch?** what's the English for ... ? **es heißt** it says; ⟨*man sagt*⟩ it is said; **das heißt** that is [to say]; **was soll das h~?** what does it mean? ⟨*empört*⟩ what is the meaning of this? ● *vt* call; **jdn etw tun h~** tell s.o. to do sth

heiß|geliebt *a* beloved. **h~hungrig** *a* ravenous. **H~wasserbereiter** *m* -s,- water heater

heiter *a* cheerful, *adv* -ly; ⟨*Wetter*⟩ bright; ⟨*amüsant*⟩ amusing; **aus h~em Himmel** (*fig*) out of the blue. **H~keit** *f* - cheerfulness; ⟨*Gelächter*⟩ mirth

Heiz|anlage *f* heating; ⟨*Auto*⟩ heater. **H~decke** *f* electric blanket. **h~en** *vt* heat; light ⟨*Ofen*⟩ ● *vi* (*haben*) put the heating on; ⟨*Ofen:*⟩ give out heat. **H~gerät** *nt* heater. **H~kessel** *m* boiler. **H~körper** *m* radiator. **H~lüfter** *m* -s,- fan heater. **H~material** *nt* fuel. **H~ofen** *m* heater. **H~ung** *f* -,-en heating; ⟨*Heizkörper*⟩ radiator

Hektar *nt & m* -s,- hectare

hektisch *a* hectic

Held *m* -en,-en hero. **h~enhaft** *a* heroic, *adv* -ally. **H~enmut** *m* heroism. **h~enmütig** *a* heroic, *adv* -ally.

H~entum *nt* -s heroism. **H~in** *f* -,-nen heroine

helf|en† *vi (haben)* help (**jdm** s.o.); ⟨*nützen*⟩ be effective; **sich** (*dat*) **nicht zu h~en wissen** not know what to do; **es hilft nichts** it's no use. **H~er(in)** *m* -s,- (*f* -,-nen) helper, as- sistant. **H~ershelfer** *m* accomplice

hell *a* light; ⟨*Licht ausstrahlend, klug*⟩ bright; ⟨*Stimme*⟩ clear; ⟨*fam: völlig*⟩ utter; **h~es Bier** ≈ lager ● *adv* brightly; **h~ begeistert** absolutely delighted. **h~hörig** *a* poorly soundproofed; **h~hörig werden** (*fig*) sit up and take notice

hellicht *a* **h~er Tag** broad daylight

Hell|igkeit *f* - brightness. **H~seher(in)** *m* -s,- (*f* -,-nen) clairvoyant. **h~wach** *a* wide awake

Helm *m* -[e]s,-e helmet

Hemd *nt* -[e]s,-en vest, ⟨*Amer*⟩ undershirt; ⟨*Ober-*⟩ shirt. **H~bluse** *f* shirt

Hemisphäre *f* -,-n hemisphere

hemm|en *vt* check; ⟨*verzögern*⟩ impede; (*fig*) inhibit. **H~ung** *f* -,-en (*fig*) inhibition; ⟨*Skrupel*⟩ scruple; **H~ungen haben** be inhibited. **h~ungslos** *a* unrestrained, *adv* -ly

Hendl *nt* -s,-[n] ⟨*Aust*⟩ chicken

Hengst *m* -[e]s,-e stallion. **H~fohlen** *nt* colt

Henkel *m* -s,- handle

henken *vt* hang

Henne *f* -,-n hen

her *adv* here; ⟨*zeitlich*⟩ ago; **her mit ...!** give me ...! **von oben/unten/Norden/weit her** from above/below/the north/far away; **vor/hinter jdm/etw her** in front of/behind s.o./sth; **von der Farbe/vom Thema her** as far as the colour/subject is concerned

herab *adv* down [here]; **von oben h~** from above; (*fig*) condescending, *adv* -ly. **h~blicken** *vi sep (haben)* = **h~sehen**

herablass|en† *vt sep* let down; **sich h~en** condescend (**zu** to). **h~end** *a* condescending, *adv* -ly. **H~ung** *f* - condescension

herab|sehen† *vi sep (haben)* look down (**auf** + *acc* on). **h~setzen** *vt sep* reduce, cut; (*fig*) belittle. **H~setzend** *a* disparaging, *adv* -ly. **h~würdigen** *vt sep* belittle, disparage

Heraldik *f* - heraldry

heran *adv* near; [**bis**] **h~ an** (+ *acc*) up to. **h~bilden** *vt sep* train.

h~gehen† *vi sep (sein)* h~gehen an (+ *acc*) go up to; get down to ⟨*Arbeit*⟩. h~kommen† *vi sep (sein)* approach; h~kommen an (+ *acc*) come up to; (*erreichen*) get at; (*fig*) measure up to. h~machen (sich) *vr sep* sich h~machen an (+ *acc*) approach; get down to ⟨*Arbeit*⟩. h~reichen *vi sep (haben)* h~reichen an (+ *acc*) reach; (*fig*) measure up to. h~wachsen† *vi sep (sein)* grow up. h~ziehen *v sep* ● *vt* pull up (an + *acc* to); (*züchten*) raise; (*h~bilden*) train; (*hinzuziehen*) call in ● *vi (sein)* approach

herauf *adv* up [here]; **die Treppe** h~ up the stairs. h~beschwören† *vt sep* evoke; (*verursachen*) cause. h~kommen† *vi sep (sein)* come up. h~setzen *vt sep* raise, increase

heraus *adv* out (aus of); h~ **damit** *od* **mit der Sprache!** out with it! h~bekommen† *vt sep* get out; (*ausfindig machen*) find out; (*lösen*) solve; **Geld** h~bekommen get change. h~bringen† *vt sep* bring out; (*fam*) get out. h~finden† *v sep* ● *vt* find out ● *vi (haben)* find one's way out. H~forderer *m* -s,- challenger. h~fordern *vt sep* provoke; challenge ⟨*Person*⟩. H~forderung *f* provocation; challenge. H~gabe *f* handing over; (*Admin*) issue; (*Veröffentlichung*) publication. H~geben† *vt sep* hand over; (*Admin*) issue; (*veröffentlichen*) publish; edit ⟨*Zeitschrift*⟩; **jdm Geld** h~geben give s.o. change ● *vi (haben)* give change (auf + *acc* for). H~geber *m* -s,- publisher; editor. h~gehen† *vi sep (sein)* ⟨*Fleck:*⟩ come out; **aus sich** h~gehen (*fig*) come out of one's shell. h~halten† (sich) *vr sep* (*fig*) keep out (aus of). h~holen *vt sep* get out. h~kommen† *vi sep (sein)* come out; (*aus Schwierigkeit, Takt*) get out; **auf eins** *od* **dasselbe** h~kommen (*fam*) come to the same thing. h~lassen† *vt sep* let out. h~machen *vt sep* get out; **sich gut** h~machen (*fig*) do well. h~nehmen† *vt sep* take out; **sich zuviel** h~nehmen (*fig*) take liberties. h~platzen *vi sep (haben)* (*fam*) burst out laughing. h~putzen (sich) *vr sep* doll oneself up. h~ragen *vi sep (haben)* jut out; (*fig*) stand out. h~reden (sich) *vr sep* make excuses. h~rücken *v sep* ● *vt* move out; (*hergeben*) hand over ● *vi (sein)*

h~rücken mit hand over; (*fig: sagen*) come out with. h~rutschen *vi sep (sein)* slip out. h~schlagen† *vt sep* knock out; (*fig*) gain. h~stellen *vt sep* put out; **sich** h~stellen turn out (als to be; daß that). h~suchen *vt sep* pick out. h~ziehen† *vt sep* pull out

herb *a* sharp; ⟨*Wein*⟩ dry; ⟨*Landschaft*⟩ austere; (*fig*) harsh

herbei *adv* here. h~führen *vt sep* (*fig*) bring about. h~lassen† (sich) *vr sep* condescend (zu to). h~schaffen *vt sep* get. h~sehnen *vt sep* long for

Herberg|e *f* -,-n [youth] hostel; (*Unterkunft*) lodging. H~svater *m* warden

herbestellen *vt sep* summon

herbitten† *vt sep* ask to come

herbringen† *vt sep* bring [here]

Herbst *m* -[e]s,-e autumn. h~lich *a* autumnal

Herd *m* -[e]s,-e stove, cooker; (*fig*) focus

Herde *f* -,-n herd; ⟨*Schaf-*⟩ flock

herein *adv* in [here]; h~! come in! h~bitten† *vt sep* ask in. h~brechen† *vi sep (sein)* burst in; (*fig*) set in; ⟨*Nacht:*⟩ fall; h~brechen über (+ *acc*) ⟨*fig*⟩ overtake. h~fallen† *vi sep (sein)* (*fam*) be taken in (auf + *acc* by). h~kommen† *vi sep (sein)* come in. h~lassen† *vt sep* let in. h~legen *vt sep* (*fam*) take for a ride. h~rufen† *vt sep* call in

Herfahrt *f* journey/drive here

herfallen† *vi sep (sein)* h~ **über** (+ *acc*) attack; fall upon ⟨*Essen*⟩

hergeben† *vt sep* hand over; (*fig*) give up; **sich** h~ **zu** (*fig*) be a party to

hergebracht *a* traditional

hergehen† *vi sep (sein)* h~ **vor/ neben/hinter** (+ *dat*) walk along in front of/beside/behind; **es ging lustig her** (*fam*) there was a lot of merriment

herhalten† *vt sep (haben)* hold out; h~ **müssen** be the one to suffer

herholen *vt sep* fetch; **weit hergeholt** (*fig*) far-fetched

Hering *m* -s,-e herring; (*Zeltpflock*) tent-peg

her|kommen† *vi sep (sein)* come here; **wo kommt das her?** where does it come from? h~kömmlich *a* traditional. H~kunft *f* - origin

herlaufen† *vi sep (sein)* h~ **vor/ neben/hinter** (+ *dat*) run-/(*gehen*) walk along in front of/beside/behind

herleiten vt sep derive

hermachen vt sep **viel/wenig h~** be impressive/unimpressive; (wichtig nehmen) make a lot of/little fuss (von of); **sich h~ über** (+ acc) fall upon; tackle ⟨Arbeit⟩

Hermelin¹ nt -s,-e (Zool) stoat

Hermelin² m -s,-e (Pelz) ermine

hermetisch a hermetic, adv -ally

Hernie /'hɛrniə/ f -,-n hernia

Heroin nt -s heroin

heroisch a heroic, adv -ally

Herr m -n,-en gentleman; (Gebieter) master (**über** + acc of); [Gott,] der H~ the Lord [God]; H~ Meier Mr Meier; **Sehr geehrte H~en** Dear Sirs. **H~chen** nt -s,- master. **h~enhaus** nt manor [house]. **h~enlos** a ownerless; ⟨Tier⟩ stray. **H~ensitz** m manor

Herrgott m der H~ the Lord; H~ [noch mal]! damn it!

herrichten vt sep prepare; **wieder h~** renovate

Herrin f -,-nen mistress

herrisch a imperious, adv -ly; ⟨Ton⟩ peremptory; (herrschsüchtig) over-bearing

herrlich a marvellous, adv -ly; (großartig) magnificent, adv -ly. **H~keit** f -,-en splendour

Herrschaft f -,-en rule; (Macht) power; (Kontrolle) control; **meine H~en!** ladies and gentlemen!

herrsch|en vi (haben) rule; (verbreitet sein) prevail; **es h~te Stille/ große Aufregung** there was silence/ great excitement. **H~er(in)** m -s,- (f -,-nen) ruler. **h~süchtig** a domineering

herrühren vi sep (haben) stem (von from)

hersein† vi sep (sein) come (von from); **h~ hinter** (+ dat) be after; **es ist schon lange/drei Tage her** it was a long time/three days ago

herstammen vi sep (haben) come (aus/von from)

herstell|en vt sep establish; (Comm) manufacture, make. **H~er** m -s,- manufacturer, maker. **H~ung** f -establishment; manufacture

herüber adv over [here]. **h~kommen†** vi sep come over [here]

herum adv **im Kreis h~** [round] in a circle; **falsch h~** the wrong way round; **um ... h~** round ...; (ungefähr) [round] about ... **h~albern** vi sep

(haben) fool around. **h~drehen** vt sep turn round/(wenden) over; turn ⟨Schlüssel⟩; **sich h~drehen** turn round/over. **h~gehen†** vi sep (sein) walk around; ⟨Zeit:⟩ pass; **h~gehen um** go round. **h~kommen†** vi sep (sein) get about; **h~kommen um** get round; come round ⟨Ecke⟩; **um etw [nicht] h~kommen** (fig) [not] get out of sth. **h~kriegen** vt sep jdn **h~kriegen** (fam) talk s.o. round. **h~liegen†** vi sep (sein) lie around. **h~lungern** vi sep (haben) loiter. **h~schnüffeln** vi sep (haben) (fam) nose about. **h~sitzen†** vi sep (haben) sit around; **h~sitzen um** sit round. **h~sprechen†** (sich) vr sep ⟨Gerücht:⟩ get about. **h~stehen†** vi sep (haben) stand around; **h~stehen um** stand round. **h~treiben†** (sich) vr sep hang around. **h~ziehen†** vi sep (sein) move around; (ziellos) wander about

herunter adv down [here]; **die Treppe h~** down the stairs. **h~fallen†** vi fall off. **h~gehen†** vi sep (sein) come down; (sinken) go/come down. **h~gekommen** a (fig) rundown; ⟨Gebäude⟩ dilapidated; ⟨Person⟩ down-at-heel. **h~kommen†** vi sep (sein) come down; (fig) go to rack and ruin; ⟨Firma, Person:⟩ go downhill; (gesundheitlich) get run down. **h~lassen†** vt sep let down, lower. **h~machen** vt sep (fam) reprimand; (herabsetzen) run down. **h~spielen** vt sep (fig) play down. **h~ziehen†** vt sep pull down

hervor adv out (aus of). **h~bringen†** vt sep produce; utter ⟨Wort⟩. **h~gehen†** vi sep (sein) come/(sich ergeben) emerge/(folgen) follow (aus from). **h~heben†** vt sep (fig) stress, emphasize. **h~quellen†** vi sep (sein) stream out; (h~treten) bulge. **h~ragen** vi sep (haben) jut out; (fig) stand out. **h~ragend** a (fig) outstanding. **h~rufen†** vt sep (fig) cause. **h~stehen†** vi sep (haben) protrude. **h~treten†** vi sep (sein) protrude, bulge; (fig) stand out. **h~tun†** (sich) vr sep (fig) distinguish oneself; (angeben) show off

Herweg m way here

Herz nt -ens,-en heart; (Kartenspiel) hearts pl; **sich** (dat) **ein H~ fassen** pluck up courage. **H~anfall** m heart attack

herzeigen vt sep show

herz|en vt hug. **H∼enslust** f nach
H∼enslust to one's heart's content.
h∼haft a hearty, adv -ily; (würzig)
savoury

herziehen† v sep ● vt hinter sich (dat)
h∼ pull along [behind one] ● vi (sein)
hinter jdn h∼ follow along behind s.o.;
über jdn h∼ (fam) run s.o. down

herz|ig a sweet, adorable. **H∼infarkt**
m heart attack. **H∼klopfen** nt -s pal-
pitations pl; ich hatte H∼klopfen my
heart was pounding

herzlich a cordial, adv -ly; (warm)
warm, adv -ly; (aufrichtig) sincere,
adv -ly; **h∼en Dank!** many thanks!
h∼e Grüße kind regards; **h∼ wenig**
precious little. **H∼keit** f - cordiality;
warmth; sincerity

herzlos a heartless

Herzog m -s, ⁻e duke. **H∼in** f -,-nen
duchess. **H∼tum** nt -s, ⁻er duchy

Herz|schlag m heartbeat; (Med)
heart failure. **h∼zerreißend** a
heart-breaking

Hessen nt -s Hesse

heterosexuell a heterosexual

Hetze f - rush; (Kampagne) virulent
campaign (gegen against). **h∼n** vt
chase; sich h∼n hurry ● vi (haben)
agitate; (sich beeilen) hurry ● vi (sein)
rush

Heu nt -s hay; **Geld wie Heu haben**
(fam) have pots of money

Heuchelei f - hypocrisy

heuch|eln vt feign ● vi (haben) pre-
tend. **H∼ler(in)** m -s,- (f -,-nen)
hypocrite. **h∼lerisch** a hypocritical,
adv -ly

heuer adv (Aust) this year

Heuer f -,-n (Naut) pay. **h∼n** vt hire;
sign on ⟨Matrosen⟩

heulen vi (haben) howl; (fam:
weinen) cry; ⟨Sirene:⟩ wail

Heurige(r) m (Aust) new wine

Heu|schnupfen m hay fever.
H∼schober m -s,- haystack. **H∼**
schrecke f -,-n grasshopper;
(Wander-) locust

heut|e adv today; (heutzutage) now-
adays; **h∼e früh** od **morgen** this
morning; **von h∼e auf morgen** from
one day to the next. **h∼ig** a today's
...; (gegenwärtig) present; **der**
h∼ige Tag today. **h∼zutage** adv nowadays

Hexe f -,-n witch. **h∼n** vi (haben)
work magic; **ich kann nicht h∼n**
(fam) I can't perform miracles.

H∼njagd f witch-hunt. **H∼nschuß**
m lumbago. **H∼rei** f - witchcraft

Hieb m -[e]s,-e blow; (Peitschen-) lash;
H∼e hiding sg

hier adv here; **h∼ und da** here and
there; (zeitlich) now and again

Hierarchie /hierar'çi:/ f -,-n hierarchy

hier|auf adv on this/these; (ant-
worten) to this; (zeitlich) after this.
h∼aus adv out of or from this/these.
h∼behalten† vt sep keep here.
h∼bleiben† vi sep (sein) stay here.
h∼durch adv through this/these;
(Ursache) as a result of this. **h∼für**
adv for this/these. **h∼her** adv here.
h∼hin adv here. **h∼in** adv in this/
these. **h∼lassen†** vt sep leave here.
h∼mit adv with this/these; (Comm)
herewith; (Admin) hereby. **h∼nach**
adv after this/these; (demgemäß) according to this/these **h∼sein†** vi sep
(sein) be here. **h∼über** adv over/
(höher) above this/these; (sprechen,
streiten) about this/these. **h∼unter**
adv under/(tiefer) below this/these;
(dazwischen) among these. **h∼von**
adv from this/these; (h∼über) about
this/these; (Menge) of this/these.
h∼zu adv to this/these; (h∼für) for
this/these. **h∼zulande** adv here

hiesig a local. **H∼e(r)** m/f local

Hilf|e f -,-n help, aid; **um H∼e rufen**
call for help; **jdm zu H∼e kommen**
come to s.o.'s aid. **h∼los** a helpless,
adv -ly. **H∼losigkeit** f - helplessness.
h∼reich a helpful

Hilfs|arbeiter m unskilled labourer.
h∼bedürftig a needy; **h∼bedürftig**
sein be in need of help. **h∼bereit** a
helpful, adv -ly. **H∼kraft** f helper.
H∼mittel nt aid. **H∼verb, H∼zeit-**
wort nt auxiliary verb

Himbeere f raspberry

Himmel m -s,- sky; (Relig & fig)
heaven; (Bett-) canopy; **am H∼** in the
sky; **unter freiem H∼** in the open
air. **H∼bett** nt four-poster [bed].
H∼fahrt f Ascension; **Mariä H∼**
fahrt Assumption. **h∼schreiend** a
scandalous. **H∼srichtung** f compass
point; **in alle H∼srichtungen** in all
directions. **h∼weit** a (fam) vast

himmlisch a heavenly

hin adv there; **hin und her** to and fro;
hin und zurück there and back; (Rail)
return; **hin und wieder** now and again;
an (+ dat) ... **hin** along; **auf** (+ acc) ...

hin in reply to ⟨*Brief, Anzeige*⟩; on ⟨*jds Rat*⟩; **zu** *od* **nach ... hin** towards; **vor sich hin reden** talk to oneself

hinab *adv* down [there]

hinauf *adv* up [there]; **die Treppe/ Straße h~** up the stairs/road. **h~gehen†** *vi sep (sein)* go up. **h~setzen** *vt sep* raise

hinaus *adv* out [there]; (*nach draußen*) outside; **zur Tür h~** out of the door; **auf Jahre h~** for years to come; **über etw** (*acc*) **h~** beyond sth; (*Menge*) [over and] above sth. **h~fliegen†** *v sep* • *vi (sein)* fly out; (*fam*) get the sack • *vt* fly out. **h~gehen†** *vi sep (sein)* go out; ⟨*Zimmer:*⟩ face (**nach Norden** north); **h~gehen über** (+*acc*) go beyond, exceed. **h~kommen†** *vi sep (sein)* get out; **h~kommen über** (+*acc*) get beyond. **h~laufen†** *vi sep (sein)* run out; **h~laufen auf** (+*acc*) (*fig*) amount to. **h~lehnen (sich)** *vr sep* lean out. **h~ragen** *vi sep (haben)* **h~ragen über** (+*acc*) project beyond; (*in der Höhe*) rise above; (*fig*) stand out above. **h~schicken** *vt sep* send out. **h~schieben†** *vt sep* push out; (*fig*) put off. **h~sehen†** *vi sep (haben)* look out. **h~sein†** *vi sep (haben)* **über etw** (*acc*) **h~sein** (*fig*) be past sth. **h~werfen†** *vt sep* throw out; (*fam: entlassen*) fire. **h~wollen†** *vt sep (haben)* want to go out; **h~wollen auf** (+*acc*) (*fig*) aim at; **hoch h~wollen** (*fig*) be ambitious. **h~ziehen†** *v sep* • *vt* pull out; (*in die Länge ziehen*) drag out; (*verzö- gern*) delay; **sich h~ziehen** drag on; be delayed • *vi (sein)* move out. **h~zögern** *vt sep* delay; **sich h~zögern** be delayed

Hinblick *m* **im H~ auf** (+*acc*) in view of; (*hinsichtlich*) regarding

hinbringen† *vt sep* take there; (*verbringen*) spend

hinder|lich *a* awkward; **jdm h~lich sein** hamper s.o. **h~n** *vt* hamper; (*verhindern*) prevent. **H~nis** *nt* **-ses,-se** obstacle. **H~nisrennen** *nt* steeplechase

hindeuten *vi sep (haben)* point (**auf** + *acc* to)

Hindu *m* **-s,-s** Hindu. **H~ismus** *m* - Hinduism

hindurch *adv* through it/them; **den Sommer h~** throughout the summer

hinein *adv* in [there]; (*nach drinnen*) inside; **h~ in** (+*acc*) into. **h~fallen†** *vi sep (sein)* fall in. **h~gehen†** *vi sep (sein)* go in; **h~gehen in** (+*acc*) go into. **h~laufen†** *vi sep (sein)* run in; **h~laufen in** (+*acc*) run into. **h~reden** *vi sep (haben)* **jdm h~reden** interrupt s.o.; (*sich einmischen*) interfere in s.o.'s affairs. **h~versetzen (sich)** *vr sep* **sich in jds Lage h~versetzen** put oneself in s.o.'s position. **h~ziehen†** *vt sep* pull in; **h~ziehen in** (+*acc*) pull into; **in etw** (*acc*) **h~gezogen werden** (*fig*) become involved in sth

hin|fahren† *v sep* • *vi (sein)* go/drive there • *vt* take/drive there. **H~fahrt** *f* journey/drive there; (*Rail*) outward journey. **h~fallen†** *vi sep (sein)* fall. **h~fällig** *a* (*gebrechlich*) frail; (*ungültig*) invalid. **h~fliegen†** *v sep* • *vi (sein)* fly there; (*fam*) fall • *vt* fly there. **H~flug** *m* flight there; (*Admin*) outward flight. **H~gabe** *f* - devotion; (*Eifer*) dedication

hingeb|en† *vt sep* give up; **sich h~en** (*fig*) devote oneself (**einer Aufgabe** to a task); abandon oneself (**dem Vergnügen** to pleasure). **H~ung** *f* - devotion. **h~ungsvoll** *a* devoted, *adv* -ly

hingegen *adv* on the other hand

hingehen† *vi sep (sein)* go/(**zu Fuß**) walk there; (*vergehen*) pass; **h~ zu** go up to; **wo gehst du hin?** where are you going? **etw h~ lassen** (*fig*) let sth pass

hingerissen *a* rapt, *adv* -ly; **h~ sein** be carried away (**von** by)

hin|halten† *vt sep* hold out; (*warten lassen*) keep waiting. **h~hocken (sich)** *vr sep* squat down. **h~kauern (sich)** *vr sep* crouch down

hinken *vi (haben/sein)* limp

hin|knien (sich) *vr sep* kneel down. **h~kommen†** *vi sep (sein)* get there; (*h~gehören*) belong, go; (*fam: auskommen*) manage (**mit** with); (*fam: stimmen*) be right. **h~länglich** *a* adequate, *adv* -ly. **h~laufen†** *vi sep (sein)* run/(*gehen*) walk there. **h~legen** *vt sep* lay or put down; **sich h~legen** lie down. **h~nehmen†** *vt sep* (*fig*) accept

hinreichen *v sep* • *vt* hand (**dat** to) • *vi (haben)* extend (**bis** to); (*ausreichen*) be adequate. **h~d** *a* adequate, *adv* -ly

Hinreise *f* journey there; (*Rail*) outward journey

hinreißen† *vt sep* (*fig*) carry away; **sich h~ lassen** get carried away. **h~d** *a* ravishing, *adv* -ly

hinricht|en *vt sep* execute. **H~ung** *f* execution

hinschicken *vt sep* send there

hinschleppen *vt sep* drag there; (*fig*) drag out; **sich h~** drag oneself along; (*fig*) drag on

hinschreiben† *vt sep* write there; (*aufschreiben*) write down

hinsehen† *vi sep* (*haben*) look

hinsein† *vi sep* (*sein*) (*fam*) be gone; (*kaputt, tot*) have had it; **[ganz] h~ von** be overwhelmed by; **es ist noch/ nicht mehr lange hin** it's a long time yet/not long to go

hinsetzen *vt sep* put down; **sich h~** sit down

Hinsicht *f* - **in dieser/gewisser H~** in this respect/in a certain sense; **in finanzieller H~** financially. **h~lich** *prep* (+ *gen*) regarding

hinstellen *vt sep* put *or* set down; park ⟨*Auto*⟩; (*fig*) make out (**als** to be); **sich h~** stand

hinstrecken *vt sep* hold out; **sich h~** extend

hintan|setzen, h~stellen *vt sep* ignore; (*vernachlässigen*) neglect

hinten *adv* at the back; **dort h~** back there; **nach/von h~** to the back/ from behind. **h~herum** *adv* round the back; (*fam*) by devious means; ⟨*erfahren*⟩ in a roundabout way

hinter *prep* (+ *dat/acc*) behind; (*nach*) after; **h~ jdm/etw herlaufen** run after s.o./sth; **h~ etw** (*dat*) **stecken** (*fig*) be behind sth; **h~ etw** (*acc*) **kommen** (*fig*) get to the bottom of sth; **etw h~ sich** (*acc*) **bringen** get sth over [and done] with. **H~bein** *nt* hind leg

Hinterbliebene *pl* (*Admin*) surviving dependants; **die H~n** the bereaved family *sg*

hinterbringen† *vt* tell (**jdm** s.o.)

hintere|(r,s) *a* back, rear; **h~s Ende** far end

hintereinander *adv* one behind/ (*zeitlich*) after the other; **dreimal h~** three times in succession/(*fam*) in a row

Hintergedanke *m* ulterior motive

hintergehen† *vt* deceive

Hinter|grund *m* background. **H~halt** *m* -[e]s,-e ambush; **aus dem H~halt überfallen** ambush. **h~hältig** *a* underhand

hinterher *adv* behind, after; (*zeitlich*) afterwards. **h~gehen†** *vi sep* (*sein*) follow (**jdm** s.o.). **h~kommen†** *vi sep* (*sein*) follow [behind]. **h~laufen†** *vi sep* (*sein*) run after (**jdm** s.o.)

Hinter|hof *m* back yard. **H~kopf** *m* back of the head

hinterlassen† *vt* leave [behind]; (*Jur*) leave, bequeath (*dat* to). **H~schaft** *f* -,-en (*Jur*) estate

hinterlegen *vt* deposit

Hinter|leib *m* (*Zool*) abdomen. **H~list** *f* deceit. **h~listig** *a* deceitful, *adv* -ly. **h~m** *prep* = **hinter dem**. **H~mann** *m* (*pl* -männer) person behind. **h~n** *prep* = **hinter den**. **H~n** *m* -s,- (*fam*) bottom, backside. **H~rad** *nt* rear *or* back wheel. **h~rücks** *adv* from behind. **h~s** *prep* = **hinter das**. **h~ ste(r,s)** *a* last; **h~ste Reihe** back row. **H~teil** *nt* (*fam*) behind

hintertreiben† *vt* (*fig*) block

Hinter|treppe *f* back stairs *pl*. **H~tür** *f* back door; (*fig*) loophole

hinterziehen† *vt* (*Admin*) evade

Hinterzimmer *nt* back room

hinüber *adv* over *or* across [there]. **h~gehen†** *vi sep* (*sein*) go over *or* across; **h~gehen über** (+ *acc*) cross

hinunter *adv* down [there]; **die Treppe/Straße h~** down the stairs/ road. **h~gehen†** *vi sep* (*sein*) go down. **h~schlucken** *vt sep* swallow

Hinweg *m* way there

hinweg *adv* away, off; **h~ über** (+ *acc*) over; **über eine Zeit h~** over a period. **h~gehen†** *vi sep* (*sein*) **h~gehen über** (+ *acc*) (*fig*) pass over. **h~kommen†** *vi sep* (*sein*) **h~kommen über** (+ *acc*) (*fig*) get over. **h~sehen†** *vi sep* (*haben*) **h~sehen über** (+ *acc*) see over; (*fig*) overlook. **h~setzen** (**sich**) *vr sep* **sich h~setzen über** (+ *acc*) ignore

Hinweis *m* -es,-e reference; (*Andeutung*) hint; (*Anzeichen*) indication; **unter H~ auf** (+ *acc*) with reference to. **h~en†** *v sep* ●*vi* (*haben*) point (**auf** + *acc* to) ●*vt* **jdn auf etw** (*acc*) **h~en** point sth out to s.o. **h~end** *a* (*Gram*) demonstrative

hin|wenden† *vt sep* turn; **sich h~wenden** turn (**zu** to). **h~werfen†**

vt sep throw down; drop ⟨*Bemerkung*⟩; (*schreiben*) jot down; (*zeichnen*) sketch; (*fam: aufgeben*) pack in

hinwieder *adv* on the other hand

hin|zeigen *vi sep* (*haben*) point (**auf** + *acc* to). **h~ziehen†** *vt sep* pull; (*fig: in die Länge ziehen*) drag out; (*verzögern*) delay; **sich h~ziehen** drag on; be delayed; **sich h~gezogen fühlen zu** (*fig*) feel drawn to

hinzu *adv* in addition. **h~fügen** *vt sep* add. **h~kommen†** *vi sep* (*sein*) be added; (*ankommen*) arrive [on the scene]; join (**zu jdm** s.o.). **h~rechnen** *vt sep* add. **h~ziehen†** *vt sep* call in

Hiobsbotschaft *f* bad news *sg*

Hirn *nt* **-s** brain; (*Culin*) brains *pl*. **H~gespinst** *nt* -[e]s,-e figment of the imagination. **H~hautentzündung** *f* meningitis. **h~verbrannt** *a* (*fam*) crazy

Hirsch *m* -[e]s,-e deer; (*männlich*) stag; (*Culin*) venison

Hirse *f* - millet

Hirt *m* -en,-en, **Hirte** *m* -n,-n shepherd

hissen *vt* hoist

Histor|iker *m* -s,- historian. **h~isch** *a* historical; (*bedeutend*) historic

Hit *m* -s,-s (*Mus*) hit

Hitz|e *f* - heat. **H~ewelle** *f* heat wave. **h~ig** *a* (*fig*) heated, *adv* -ly; (*Person*) hot-headed; (*jähzornig*) hot-tempered. **H~kopf** *m* hothead. **H~schlag** *m* heat-stroke

H-Milch /'haː-/ *f* long-life milk

Hobby *nt* -s,-s hobby

Hobel *m* -s,- (*Techn*) plane; (*Culin*) slicer. **h~n** *vt/i* (*haben*) plane. **H~späne** *mpl* shavings

hoch *a* (**höher, höchst**; *attrib* **hohe(r,s)**) high; ⟨*Baum, Mast*⟩ tall; (*Offizier*) high-ranking; ⟨*Alter*⟩ great; ⟨*Summe*⟩ large; ⟨*Strafe*⟩ heavy; **hohe Schuhe** ankle boots ● *adv* high; (*sehr*) highly; **die Treppe/den Berg h~** up the stairs/ hill; **sechs Mann h~** six of us/them. **H~** *nt* -s,-s cheer; (*Meteorol*) high

Hoch|achtung *f* high esteem. **H~achtungsvoll** *adv* Yours faithfully. **H~amt** *nt* High Mass. **H~arbeiten (sich)** *vr sep* work one's way up. **h~begabt** *attrib a* highly gifted. **H~betrieb** *m* great activity; **in den Geschäften herrscht H~betrieb** the shops are terribly busy. **H~burg** *f* (*fig*) stronghold. **H~deutsch** *nt*

High German. **H~druck** *m* high pressure. **H~ebene** *f* plateau. **h~fahren†** *vi sep* (*sein*) go up; (*auffahren*) start up; (*aufbrausen*) flare up. **h~fliegend** *a* (*fig*) ambitious. **h~gehen†** *vi sep* (*sein*) go up; (*explodieren*) blow up; (*aufbrausen*) flare up. **h~gestellt** *attrib a* high-ranking; ⟨*Zahl*⟩ superior. **h~gewachsen** *a* tall. **H~glanz** *m* high gloss. **h~gradig** *a* extreme, *adv* -ly. **h~hackig** *a* high-heeled. **h~halten†** *vt sep* hold up; (*fig*) uphold. **H~haus** *nt* high-rise building. **h~heben†** *vt sep* lift up; raise ⟨*Kopf, Hand*⟩. **h~herzig** *a* magnanimous, *adv* -ly. **h~kant** *adv* on end. **h~kommen†** *vi sep* (*sein*) come up; (*aufstehen*) get up; (*fig*) get on [in the world]. **H~konjunktur** *f* boom. **h~krempeln** *vt sep* roll up. **h~leben** *vi sep* (*haben*) **h~leben lassen** give three cheers for; **... lebe hoch!** three cheers for ...! **H~mut** *m* pride, arrogance. **h~mütig** *a* arrogant, *adv* -ly. **h~näsig** *a* (*fam*) snooty. **h~nehmen†** *vt sep* pick up; (*fam*) tease. **H~ofen** *m* blast-furnace. **h~ragen** *vi sep* rise [up]; ⟨*Turm:*⟩ soar. **H~ruf** *m* cheer. **H~saison** *f* high season. **H~schätzung** *f* high esteem. **h~schlagen†** *vt sep* turn up ⟨*Kragen*⟩. **h~schrecken†** *vi sep* (*sein*) start up. **H~schule** *f* university; (*Musik-, Kunst-*) academy. **h~sehen†** *vi sep* (*haben*) look up. **H~sommer** *m* midsummer. **H~spannung** *f* high/(*fig*) great tension. **h~spielen** *vt sep* (*fig*) magnify. **H~sprache** *f* standard language. **H~sprung** *m* high jump

höchst *adv* extremely, most

Hochstapler *m* -s,- confidence trickster

höchst|e(r,s) *a* highest; ⟨*Baum, Turm*⟩ tallest; (*oberste, größte*) top; **ist h~e Zeit** it is high time. **h~ens** *adv* at most; (*es sei denn*) except perhaps. **H~fall** *m* **im H~fall** at most. **H~geschwindigkeit** *f* top *or* maximum speed. **H~maß** *nt* maximum. **h~persönlich** *adv* in person. **H~preis** *m* top price. **H~temperatur** *f* maximum temperature. **h~wahrscheinlich** *adv* most probably

hoch|trabend *a* pompous, *adv* -ly. **h~treiben†** *vt sep* push up ⟨*Preis*⟩. **H~verrat** *m* high treason.

H~wasser nt high tide; (Über-schwemmung) floods pl. **H~würden** m -s Reverend; (Anrede) Father

Hochzeit f -,-en wedding; **H~ feiern** get married. **H~skleid** nt wedding dress. **H~sreise** f honeymoon [trip]. **H~stag** m wedding day/(Jahrestag) anniversary

hochziehen† vt sep pull up; (hissen) hoist; raise (Augenbrauen)

Hocke f - in der **H~ sitzen** squat; **in die H~ gehen** squat down. **h~n** vi (haben) squat ● vr **sich h~n** squat down

Hocker m -s,- stool

Höcker m -s,- bump; (Kamel-) hump

Hockey /'hɔki/ nt -s hockey

Hode f -,-n, **Hoden** m -s,- testicle

Hof m -[e]s,¨e [court]yard; (Bauern-) farm; (Königs-) court; (Schul-) play-ground; (Astr) halo

hoffen vt/i (haben) hope (**auf** + acc for). **h~tlich** adv I hope, let us hope; (als Antwort) **h~tlich/h~tlich nicht** let's hope so/not

Hoffnung f -,-en hope. **h~slos** a hopeless, adv -ly. **h~svoll** a hopeful, adv -ly

höflich a polite, adv -ly, courteous, adv -ly. **H~keit** f -,-en politeness, courtesy; (Äußerung) civility

hohe(r,s) a s. hoch

Höhe f -,-n height; (Aviat, Geog) alti-tude; (Niveau) level; (einer Summe) size; (An-) hill; **in die H~ gehen** rise, go up; **nicht auf der H~** (fam) under the weather; **das ist die H~!** (fam) that's the limit!

Hoheit f -,-en (Staats-) sovereignty; (Titel) Highness. **H~sgebiet** nt [sov-ereign] territory. **H~szeichen** nt national emblem

Höhe|nlinie f contour line. **H~nsonne** f sun-lamp. **H~nzug** m mountain range. **H~punkt** m (fig) climax, peak; (einer Vorstellung) highlight. **h~r** a & adv higher; **h~re Schule** secondary school

hohl a hollow; (leer) empty

Höhle f -,-n cave; (Tier-) den; (Hohlraum) cavity; (Augen-) socket

Hohl|maß nt measure of capacity. **H~raum** m cavity

Hohn m -s scorn, derision

höhn|en|en vt deride ● vi (haben) jeer. **h~isch** a scornful, adv -ly

holen vt fetch, get; (kaufen) buy; (nehmen) take (**aus** from); **h~ lassen**

send for; **[tief] Atem** od **Luft h~** take a [deep] breath; **sich** (dat) **etw h~** get sth; catch (Erkältung)

Holland nt -s Holland

Holländ|er m -s,- Dutchman; **die H~er** the Dutch pl. **H~erin** f -,-nen Dutchwoman. **h~isch** a Dutch

Höll|e f - hell. **h~isch** a infernal; (schrecklich) terrible, adv -bly

holpern vi (sein) jolt or bump along ● vi (haben) be bumpy

holp[e]rig a bumpy

Holunder m -s (Bot) elder

Holz nt -es,¨er wood; (Nutz-) timber. **H~blasinstrument** nt woodwind in-strument

hölzern a wooden

Holz|hammer m mallet. **h~ig** a woody. **H~kohle** f charcoal. **H~schnitt** m woodcut. **H~schuh** m [wooden] clog. **H~wolle** f wood shavings pl. **H~wurm** m woodworm

homogen a homogeneous

Homöopathie f - homoeopathy

homosexuell a homosexual. **H~e(r)** m/f homosexual

Honig m -s honey. **H~wabe** f honeycomb

Hono|rar nt -s,-e fee. **h~rieren** vt remunerate; (fig) reward

Hopfen m -s hops pl; (Bot) hop

hopsen vi (sein) jump

Hör|apparat m hearing-aid. **h~bar** a audible, adv -bly

horchen vi (haben) listen (**auf** + acc to); (heimlich) eavesdrop

Horde f -,-n horde; (Gestell) rack

hören vt hear; (an-) listen to ● vi (haben) hear; (horchen) listen; (ge-horchen) obey; **h~ auf** (+ acc) listen to. **H~sagen** nt vom **H~sagen** from hearsay

Hör|er m -s,- listener; (Teleph) receiver. **H~funk** m radio. **H~gerät** nt hear-ing-aid

Horizon|t m -[e]s horizon. **h~tal** a horizontal, adv -ly

Hormon nt -s,-e hormone

Horn nt -s,¨er horn. **H~haut** f hard skin; (Augen-) cornea

Hornisse f -,-n hornet

Horoskop nt -[e]s,-e horoscope

Hörrohr nt stethoscope

Horrorfilm m horror film

Hör|saal m (Univ) lecture hall. **h~spiel** nt radio play

Hort m -[e]s,-e (Schatz) hoard; (fig) refuge. **h~en** vt hoard

Hortensie /-jə/ f -,-n hydrangea

Hörweite f **in/außer H~** within/out of earshot

Hose f -,-n, **Hosen** pl trousers pl. **H~nrock** m culottes pl. **H~nschlitz** m fly, flies pl. **H~nträger** mpl braces, (Amer) suspenders

Hostess, Hosteß f -,-**tessen** hostess; (Aviat) air hostess

Hostie /'hɔstjə/ f -,-n (Relig) host

Hotel nt -s,-s hotel; **H~ garni** / gar'ni:/ bed-and-breakfast hotel. **H~ier** /-'lie:/ m -s,-s hotelier

hübsch a pretty, adv -ily; (nett) nice, adv -ly; (Summe) tidy

Hubschrauber m -s,- helicopter

huckepack adv jdn h~ **tragen** give s.o. a piggyback

Huf m -[e]s,-e hoof. **H~eisen** nt horse-shoe

Hüft|e f -,-n hip. **H~gürtel, H~halter** m -s,- girdle

Hügel m -s,- hill. **h~ig** a hilly

Huhn nt -s,-̈er chicken; (Henne) hen

Hühn|chen nt -s,- chicken. **H~erauge** nt corn. **H~erbrühe** f chicken broth. **H~erstall** m henhouse, chicken-coop

huldig|en vi (haben) pay homage (dat to). **H~ung** f - homage

Hülle f -,-n cover; (Verpackung) wrapping; (Platten-) sleeve; **in H~ und Fülle** in abundance. **h~n** vt wrap

Hülse f -,-n (Bot) pod; (Etui) case. **H~nfrüchte** fpl pulses

human a humane, adv -ly. **h~itär** a humanitarian. **H~ität** f - humanity

Hummel f -,-n bumble-bee

Hummer m -s,- lobster

Hum|or m -s humour; **H~or haben** have a sense of humour. **h~oristisch** a humorous. **h~orvoll** a humorous, adv -ly

humpeln vi (sein/haben) hobble

Humpen m -s,- tankard

Hund m -[e]s,-e dog; (Jagd-) hound. **H~ehalsband** nt dog-collar. **H~ehütte** f kennel. **H~eleine** f dog lead

hundert inv a one/a hundred. **H~** nt -s,-e hundred; **H~e von** hundreds of. **H~jahrfeier** f centenary, (Amer) centennial. **h~prozentig** a & adv one hundred per cent. **h~ste(r,s)** a hundredth. **H~stel** nt -s,- hundredth

Hündin f -,-nen bitch

Hüne m -n,-n giant

Hunger m -s hunger; **H~ haben** be hungry. **h~n** vi (haben) starve; **h~n**

nach (fig) hunger for. **H~snot** f famine

hungrig a hungry, adv -ily

Hupe f -,-n (Auto) horn. **h~n** vi (haben) sound one's horn

hüpf|en vi (sein) skip; (Vogel, Frosch:) hop; (Grashüpfer:) jump. **H~er** m -s,- skip, hop

Hürde f -,-n (Sport & fig) hurdle; (Schaf-) pen, fold

Hure f -,-n whore

hurra int hurray. **H~** nt -s,-s hurray; (Beifallsruf) cheer

Husche f -,-n [short] shower. **h~n** vi (sein) slip; (Eidechse:) dart; (Maus:) scurry; (Lächeln:) flit

hüsteln vi (haben) give a slight cough

husten vi (haben) cough. **H~** m -s cough. **H~saft** m cough mixture

Hut[1] m -[e]s,-̈e hat; (Pilz-) cap

Hut[2] f - **auf der H~ sein** be on one's guard (**vor** + dat against)

hüten vt watch over; tend (Tiere); (aufpassen) look after; **das Bett h~ müssen** be confined to bed; **sich h~** be on one's guard (**vor** + dat against); **sich h~, etw zu tun** take care not to do sth

Hütte f -,-n hut; (Hunde-) kennel; (Techn) iron and steel works. **H~nkäse** m cottage cheese. **H~nkunde** f metallurgy

Hyäne f -,-n hyena

Hybride f -,-n hybrid

Hydrant m -en,-en hydrant

hydraulisch a hydraulic, adv -ally

hydroelektrisch /hydro'e'lɛktrɪʃ/ a hydroelectric

Hygien|e /hy'gje:nə/ f - hygiene. **h~isch** a hygienic, adv -ally

hypermodern a ultra-modern

Hypno|se f - hypnosis. **h~tisch** a hypnotic. **H~tiseur** /-'zø:ɐ/ m -s,-e hypnotist. **h~tisieren** vt hypnotize

Hypochonder /hypo'xɔndɐ/ m -s,- hypochondriac

Hypothek f -,-en mortgage

Hypothe|se f -,-n hypothesis. **h~tisch** a hypothetical, adv -ly

Hys|terie f - hysteria. **h~terisch** a hysterical, adv -ly

I

ich pron I; **ich bin's** it's me. **Ich** nt -[s],-[s] self; (Psych) ego

IC-Zug /i'tse:-/ m inter-city train

ideal a ideal. **l∼** nt -s,-e ideal. **i∼i-sieren** vt idealize. **l∼ismus** m - idealism. **l∼ist(in)** m -en,-en (f -,-nen) idealist. **i∼istisch** a idealistic

Idee f -,-n idea; **fixe l∼** obsession; **eine l∼** (fam: wenig) a tiny bit

identifizieren vt identify.

identi|sch a identical. **l∼tät** f -,-en identity

Ideo|logie f -,-n ideology. **i∼logisch** a ideological

idiomatisch a idiomatic

Idiot m -en,-en idiot. **i∼isch** a idiotic, adv -ally

Idol nt -s,-e idol

idyllisch /i'dyliʃ/ a idyllic

Igel m -s,- hedgehog

ignorieren vt ignore

ihm pron (dat of **er, es**) [to] him; (Ding, Tier) [to] it; **Freunde von ihm** friends of his

ihn pron (acc of **er**) him; (Ding, Tier) it. **i∼en** pron (dat of **sie** pl) [to] them; **Freunde von i∼en** friends of theirs. **l∼en** pron (dat of **Sie**) [to] you; **Freunde von i∼en** friends of yours

ihr pron (2nd pers pl) you ● (dat of **sie** sg) [to] her; (Ding, Tier) [to] it; **Freunde von ihr** friends of hers ● poss pron her; (Ding, Tier) its; (pl) their. **Ihr** poss pron your. **i∼e(r,s)** poss pron hers; (pl) theirs. **l∼e(r,s)** poss pron yours. **i∼erseits** adv for her/(pl) their part. **l∼erseits** adv on your part. **i∼etwegen** adv for her/(Ding, Tier) its/(pl) their sake; (wegen) because of her/it/them, on her/its/their account. **l∼etwegen** adv for your sake; (wegen) because of you, on your account. **i∼etwillen** adv **um i∼etwillen** for her/(Ding, Tier) its/(pl) their sake. **l∼etwillen** adv **um l∼etwillen** for your sake. **i∼ige** poss pron **der/die/das i∼ige** hers; (pl) theirs. **l∼ige** poss pron **der/die/das l∼ige** yours. **i∼s** poss pron hers; (pl) theirs. **l∼s** poss pron yours

Ikone f -,-n icon

illegal a illegal, adv -ly

Illus|ion f -,-en illusion; **sich** (dat) **l∼ionen machen** delude oneself. **i∼o-risch** a illusory

Illustr|ation /-'tsjo:n/ f -,-en illustration. **i∼ieren** vt illustrate. **l∼ierte** f -n,-[n] [illustrated] magazine

Iltis m -ses,-se polecat

im prep = **in dem**; **im Mai** in May; **im Kino** at the cinema

Image /'imidʒ/ nt -[s],-s /-is/ [public] image

Imbiß m snack. **l∼halle, l∼stube** f snack-bar

Imit|ation /-'tsjo:n/ f -,-en imitation. **i∼ieren** vt imitate

Imker m -s,- bee-keeper

Immatrikul|ation /-'tsjo:n/ f - (Univ) enrolment. **i∼ieren** vt (Univ) enrol; **sich i∼ieren** enrol

immer adv always; **für i∼** for ever; (endgültig) for good; **i∼ noch** still; **i∼ mehr/weniger/wieder** more and more/less and less/again and again; **wer/was [auch] i∼** whoever/whatever. **i∼fort** adv = **i∼zu.** **i∼grün** a evergreen. **i∼hin** adv (wenigstens) at least; (trotzdem) all the same; (schließlich) after all. **i∼zu** adv all the time

Immobi|lien /-jən/ pl real estate sg. **l∼händler, l∼makler** m estate agent, (Amer) realtor

immun a immune (**gegen** to). **i∼isieren** vt immunize. **l∼ität** f - immunity

Imperativ m -s,-e imperative

Imperfekt nt -s,-e imperfect

Imperialismus m - imperialism

impf|en vt vaccinate, inoculate. **l∼stoff** m vaccine. **l∼ung** f -,-en vaccination, inoculation

Implantat nt -[e]s,-e implant

imponieren vi (haben) impress (**jdm** s.o.)

Impor|t m -[e]s,-e import. **l∼teur** /-'tø:ɐ/ m -s,-e importer. **i∼tieren** vt import

imposant a imposing

impoten|t a (Med) impotent. **l∼z** f - (Med) impotence

imprägnieren vt waterproof

Impressionismus m - impressionism

improvisieren vt/i (haben) improvise

Impuls m -es,-e impulse. **i∼iv** a impulsive, adv -ly

imstande pred a able (**zu** to); capable (**etw zu tun** of doing sth)

in prep (+ dat) in; (+ acc) into, in; (bei Bus, Zug) on; **in der Schule/Oper** at school/the opera; **in die Schule** to school ● a **in sein** be in

Inbegriff m embodiment. **i∼en** pred a included

Inbrunst f - fervour

inbrünstig a fervent, adv -ly

indem *conj* (*während*) while; (*dadurch*) by (+ -ing)

Inder(in) *m* -s,- (*f* -,-nen) Indian

indessen *conj* while ● *adv* (*unterdessen*) meanwhile; (*jedoch*) however

Indian *m* -s,-e (*Aust*) turkey

Indian|er(in) *m* -s,- (*f* -,-nen) (American) Indian. **i~isch** *a* Indian

Indien /'ɪndjən/ *nt* -s India

indigniert *a* indignant, *adv* -ly

Indikativ *m* -s,-e indicative

indirekt *a* indirect, *adv* -ly

indisch *a* Indian

indiskre|t *a* indiscreet. **I~tion** /-'tsjo:n/ *f* -,-en indiscretion

indiskutabel *a* out of the question

indisponiert *a* indisposed

Individu|alist *m* -en,-en individualist. **I~alität** *f* - individuality. **i~ell** *a* individual, *adv* -ly. **I~um** /-'vi:duʊm/ *nt* -s,-duen individual

Indizienbeweis /ɪn'di:tsjən-/ *m* circumstantial evidence

indoktrinieren *vt* indoctrinate

industri|alisiert *a* industrialized. **I~ie** *f* -,-n industry. **i~iell** *a* industrial. **I~ielle(r)** *m* industrialist

ineinander *adv* in/into one another

Infanterie *f* - infantry

Infektion /-'tsjo:n/ *f* -,-en infection. **I~skrankheit** *f* infectious disease

Infinitiv *m* -s,-e infinitive

infizieren *vt* infect; **sich i~** become/ ⟨*Person:*⟩ be infected

Inflation /-'tsjo:n/ *f* - inflation. **i~är** *a* inflationary

infolge *prep* (+ *gen*) as a result of. **i~dessen** *adv* consequently

Inform|atik *f* - information science. **I~ation** /-'tsjo:n/ *f* -,-en information; **I~ationen** information *sg*. **i~ieren** *vt* inform; **sich i~ieren** find out (**über** + *acc* about)

infrarot *a* infra-red

Ingenieur /ɪnʒe'njø:ɐ̯/ *m* -s,-e engineer

Ingwer *m* -s ginger

Inhaber(in) *m* -s,- (*f* -,-nen) holder; (*Besitzer*) proprietor; (*Scheck-*) bearer

inhaftieren *vt* take into custody

inhalieren *vt/i* (*haben*) inhale

Inhalt *m* -[e]s,-e contents *pl*; (*Bedeutung, Gehalt*) content; (*Geschichte*) story. **I~sangabe** *f* summary. **I~sverzeichnis** *nt* list/(*in Buch*) table of contents

Initiale /-'tsja:lə/ *f* -,-n initial

Initiative /iniˈtsjaˈti:və/ *f* -,-n initiative

Injektion /-'tsjo:n/ *f* -,-en injection. **injizieren** *vt* inject

inklusive *prep* (+ *gen*) including ● *adv* inclusive

inkognito *adv* incognito

inkonsequen|t *a* inconsistent, *adv* -ly. **I~z** *f* -,-en inconsistency

inkorrekt *a* incorrect, *adv* -ly

Inkubationszeit /-'tsjo:ns-/ *f* (*Med*) incubation period

Inland *nt* -[e]s home country; (*Binnenland*) interior. **I~sgespräch** *nt* inland call

inmitten *prep* (+ *gen*) in the middle of; (*unter*) amongst ● *adv* **i~ von** amongst, amidst

inne|haben† *vt sep* hold, have. **i~halten†** *vi sep* (*haben*) pause

innen *adv* inside; **nach i~** inwards. **I~architekt(in)** *m*(*f*) interior designer. **I~minister** *m* Minister of the Interior; (*in UK*) Home Secretary. **I~politik** *f* domestic policy. **I~stadt** *f* town centre

inner|e(r,s) *a* inner; (*Med, Pol*) internal. **I~e(s)** *nt* interior; (*Mitte*) centre; (*fig: Seele*) inner being. **I~eien** *fpl* (*Culin*) offal *sg*. **i~halb** *prep* (+ *gen*) inside; (*zeitlich & fig*) within; (*während*) during ● *adv* **i~halb von** within. **i~lich** *a* internal; (*seelisch*) inner; (*besinnlich*) intro- spective ● *adv* internally; (*im Inneren*) inwardly. **i~ste(r,s)** innermost; **im I~sten** (*fig*) deep down

innig *a* sincere, *adv* -ly; (*tief*) deep, *adv* -ly; (*eng*) intimate, *adv* -ly

Innung *f* -,-en guild

inoffiziell *a* unofficial, *adv* -ly

ins *prep* = **in das**; **ins Kino/Büro** to the cinema/office

Insasse *m* -n,-n inmate; (*im Auto*) occupant; (*Passagier*) passenger

insbesondere *adv* especially

Inschrift *f* inscription

Insekt *nt* -[e]s,-en insect. **I~envertilgungsmittel** *nt* insecticide

Insel *f* -,-n island

Inser|at *nt* -[e]s,-e [newspaper] advertisement. **I~ent** *m* -en,-en advertiser. **i~ieren** *vt/i* (*haben*) advertise

insgeheim *adv* secretly. **i~samt** *adv* [all] in all

Insignien /-jən/ *pl* insignia

insofern, insoweit *adv* /-'zo:-/ in
this respect; **i∼ als** in as much as
● *conj* /-zo'fɛrn, -'vaɪt/ **i∼ als** in so far
as

Insp|ektion /mspɛk'tsɪo:n/ *f* -,-en
inspection. **I∼ektor** *m* -en,-en
/-'to:rən/ inspector

Inspir|ation /mspira'tsɪo:n/ *f* -,-en
inspiration. **i∼ieren** *vt* inspire

inspizieren /-sp-/ *vt* inspect

Install|ateur /mstala'tø:ɐ̯/ *m* -s,-e
fitter; (*Klempner*) plumber. **i∼ieren** *vt*
install

instand *adv* **i∼ halten** maintain; (*pflegen*) look after; **i∼ setzen** restore; (*reparieren*) repair. **I∼haltung** *f* - maintenance, upkeep

inständig *a* urgent, *adv* -ly

Instandsetzung *f* - repair

Instant- /'mstənt-/ *pref* instant

Instanz /-st-/ *f* -,-en authority

Instinkt /-st-/ *m* -[e]s,-e instinct. **i∼iv**
a instinctive, *adv* -ly

Institu|t /-st-/ *nt* -[e]s,-e institute. **I∼
tion** /-'tsɪo:n/ *f* -,-en institution

Instrument /-st-/ *nt* -[e]s,-e instrument. **I∼almusik** *f* instrumental
music

Insulin *nt* -s insulin

inszenier|en *vt* (*Theat*) produce.
I∼ung *f* -,-en production

Integr|ation /-'tsɪo:n/ *f* - integration.
i∼ieren *vt* integrate; **sich i∼ieren** integrate. **I∼ität** *f* - integrity

Intellekt *m* -[e]s intellect. **i∼uell** *a* in-
tellectual

intelligen|t *a* intelligent, *adv* -ly.
I∼z *f* - intelligence; (*Leute*) intelligentsia

Intendant *m* -en,-en director

Intens|ität *f* - intensity. **i∼iv** *a*
intensive, *adv* -ly. **i∼ivieren** *vt* intensify. **I∼ivstation** *f* intensive-care
unit

inter|essant *a* interesting. **I∼esse**
nt -s,-n interest; **I∼esse haben** be
interested (**an** + *dat* in). **I∼es-
sengruppe** *f* pressure group.
I∼essent *m* -en,-en interested party;
(*Käufer*) prospective buyer. **I∼es-
sieren** *vt* interest; **sich i∼essieren** be
interested (**für** in)

intern *a* (*fig*) internal, *adv* -ly

Inter|nat *nt* -[e]s,-e boarding school.
i∼national *a* international, *adv* -ly.
i∼nieren *vt* intern. **I∼nierung** *f* -
internment. **I∼nist** *m* -en,-en specialist in internal diseases. **I∼pretation**

/-'tsɪo:n/ *f* -,-en interpretation. **i∼
pretieren** *vt* interpret. **I∼
punktion** /-'tsɪo:n/ *f* - punctuation.
I∼rogativpronomen *nt* interrogative pronoun. **I∼vall** *nt* -s,-e interval. **I∼vention** /-'tsɪo:n/ *f* -,-en
intervention

Interview /'mtɛvju:/ *nt* -s,-s interview. **i∼en** /-'vju:ən/ *vt* interview

intim *a* intimate, *adv* -ly. **I∼ität** *f* -,
-en intimacy

intoleran|t *a* intolerant. **I∼z** *f* -
intolerance

intransitiv *a* intransitive, *adv* -ly

intravenös *a* intravenous, *adv* -ly

Intrig|e *f* -,-n intrigue. **i∼ieren** *vi*
(*haben*) plot

introvertiert *a* introverted

Intui|tion /-'tsɪo:n/ *f* -,-en intuition.
i∼tiv *a* intuitive, *adv* -ly

Invalidenrente *f* disability pension

Invasion *f* -,-en invasion

Inven|tar *nt* -s,-e furnishings and
fittings *pl*; (*Techn*) equipment;
(*Bestand*) stock; (*Liste*) inventory. **I∼
tur** *f* -,-en stock-taking

investieren *vt* invest

inwendig *a* & *adv* inside

inwie|fern *adv* in what way. **i∼weit**
adv how far, to what extent

Inzest *m* -[e]s incest

inzwischen *adv* in the meantime

Irak (der) -[s] Iraq. **i∼isch** *a* Iraqi

Iran (der) -[s] Iran. **i∼isch** *a* Iranian

irdisch *a* earthly

Ire *m* -n,-n Irishman; **die I∼n** the Irish
pl

irgend *adv* **i∼ jemand/etwas** some-
one/something; (*fragend, verneint*)
anyone/anything; **wer/was/wann i∼**
whoever/whatever/whenever; **wenn
i∼ möglich** if at all possible. **i∼ein**
indef art some/any; **i∼ein anderer**
someone/anyone else. **i∼eine(r,s)**
pron any one; (*jemand*) someone/
anyone. **i∼wann** *pron* at some time
[or other]/at any time. **i∼was** *pron*
(*fam*) something [or other]/any-
thing. **i∼welche(r,s)** *pron* any.
i∼wer *pron* someone/anyone. **i∼
wie** *adv* somehow [or other]. **i∼wo**
adv somewhere/anywhere; **i∼wo
anders** somewhere else

Irin *f* -,-nen Irishwoman

Iris *f* -,- (*Anat, Bot*) iris

irisch *a* Irish

Irland *nt* -s Ireland

Ironie *f* - irony

ironisch *a* ironic, *adv* -ally
irr *a* = **irre**
irrational *a* irrational
irre *a* mad, crazy; (*fam: gewaltig*) incredible, *adv* -bly; **i~ werden** get confused. **l~(r)** *m/f* lunatic. **i~führen** *vt sep* (*fig*) mislead. **i~gehen†** *vi sep* (*sein*) lose one's way; (*sich täuschen*) be wrong
irrelevant *a* irrelevant
irre|machen *vt sep* confuse. **i~n** *vi/r* (*haben*) [**sich**] **i~n** be mistaken; **wenn ich mich nicht i~** if I am not mistaken ● *vi* (*sein*) wander. **l~nanstalt** *f*, **l~nhaus** *nt* lunatic asylum. **i~reden** *vi sep* (*haben*) ramble
Irr|garten *m* maze. **i~ig** *a* erroneous
irritieren *vt* irritate
Irr|sinn *m* madness, lunacy. **i~sinnig** *a* mad; (*fam: gewaltig*) incredible, *adv* -bly. **l~tum** *m* -s,-̈er mistake. **i~tümlich** *a* mistaken, *adv* -ly
Ischias *m* & *nt* - sciatica
Islam (der) -[s] Islam. **islamisch** *a* Islamic
Island *nt* -s Iceland
Isolier|band *nt* insulating tape. **i~en** *vt* isolate; (*Phys, Electr*) insulate; (*gegen Schall*) soundproof. **l~ung** *f* - isolation; insulation; soundproofing
Isra|el /ˈɪsraeːl/ *nt* -s Israel. **l~eli** *m* -[s],-s & *f* -,-[s] Israeli. **i~elisch** *a* Israeli
ist *s.* **sein**; **er ist** he is
Ital|ien /-jən/ *nt* -s Italy. **l~iener(in)** *m* -s,- (*f* -,-nen) Italian. **i~ienisch** *a* Italian. **l~ienisch** *nt* -[s] (*Lang*) Italian

J

ja *adv* yes; **ich glaube ja** I think so; **'ja nicht!** not on any account! **seid 'ja vorsichtig!** whatever you do, be careful! **da seid ihr ja!** there you are! **das ist es ja** that's just it; **das mag ja wahr sein** that may well be true
Jacht *f* -,-en yacht
Jacke *f* -,-n jacket; (*Strick-*) cardigan
Jackett /ʒaˈkɛt/ *nt* -s,-s jacket
Jade *m* -[s] & *f* - jade
Jagd *f* -,-en hunt; (*Schießen*) shoot; (*Jagen*) hunting; shooting; (*fig*) pursuit (**nach** *of*); **auf die J~ gehen** go hunting/shooting. **J~flugzeug** *nt* fighter

aircraft. **J~gewehr** *nt* sporting gun. **J~hund** *m* gun-dog; (*Hetzhund*) hound
jagen *vt* hunt; (*schießen*) shoot; (*verfolgen, wegjagen*) chase; (*treiben*) drive; **sich j~** chase each other; **in die Luft j~** blow up ● *vi* (*haben*) hunt, go hunting/shooting; (*fig*) chase (**nach** *after*) ● *vi* (*sein*) race, dash
Jäger *m* -s,- hunter
jäh *a* sudden, *adv* -ly; (*steil*) steep, *adv* -ly
Jahr *nt* -[e]s,-e year. **J~buch** *nt* yearbook. **j~elang** *adv* for years. **J~estag** *m* anniversary. **J~eszahl** *f* year. **J~eszeit** *f* season. **J~gang** *m* year; (*Wein*) vintage. **J~hundert** *nt* century. **J~hundertfeier** *f* centenary, (*Amer*) centennial
jährlich *a* annual, yearly ● *adv* annually, yearly
Jahr|markt *m* fair. **J~tausend** *nt* millennium. **J~zehnt** *nt* -[e]s,-e decade
Jähzorn *m* violent temper. **j~ig** *a* hot-tempered
Jalousie /ʒaluˈziː/ *f* -,-n venetian blind
Jammer *m* -s misery; (*Klagen*) lamenting; **es ist ein J~** it is a shame
jämmerlich *a* miserable, *adv* -bly; (*mitleiderregend*) pitiful, *adv* -ly
jammer|n *vi* (*haben*) lament ● *vt* **jdn j~n** arouse s.o.'s pity. **j~schade** *a* **j~schade sein** (*fam*) be a terrible shame
Jänner *m* -s,- (*Aust*) January
Januar *m* -s,-e January
Japan *nt* -s Japan. **J~aner(in)** *m* -s,- (*f* -,-nen) Japanese. **j~anisch** *a* Japanese. **J~anisch** *nt* -[s] (*Lang*) Japanese
Jargon /ʒarˈgõː/ *m* -s jargon
jäten *vt/i* (*haben*) weed
jauchzen *vi* (*haben*) (*liter*) exult
jaulen *vi* (*haben*) yelp
Jause *f* -,-n (*Aust*) snack
jawohl *adv* yes
Jawort *nt* **jdm sein J~ geben** accept s.o.'s proposal [of marriage]
Jazz /jats, dʒɛs/ *m* - jazz
je *adv* (*jemals*) ever; (*jeweils*) each; (*pro*) per; **je nach** according to; **seit eh und je** always; **besser denn je** better than ever ● *conj* **je mehr, desto** *od* **um so besser** the more the better ● *prep* (+ *acc*) per
Jeans /dʒiːns/ *pl* jeans

jed|e(r,s) *pron* every; (*j~er einzelne*) each; (*j~er beliebige*) any; (*substantivisch*) everyone; each one; anyone; **ohne j~en Grund** without any reason. **j~enfalls** *adv* in any case; (*wenigstens*) at least. **j~ermann** *pron* everyone. **j~erzeit** *adv* at any time. **j~esmal** *adv* every time; **j~esmal wenn** whenever
jedoch *adv & conj* however
jeher *adv* **von** *od* **seit j~** always
jemals *adv* ever
jemand *pron* someone, somebody; (*fragend, verneint*) anyone, anybody
jen|e(r,s) *pron* that; (*pl*) those; (*substantivisch*) that one; (*pl*) those. **j~seits** *prep* (+ *gen*) [on] the other side of
jetzig *a* present; (*Preis*) current
jetzt *adv* now. **J~zeit** *f* present
jeweil|ig *a* respective. **j~s** *adv* at a time
jiddisch *a*, **J~** *nt* -[s] Yiddish
Job /dʒɔp/ *m* -s,-s job. **j~ben** *vi* (*haben*) (*fam*) work
Joch *nt* -[e]s,-e yoke
Jockei, Jockey /'dʒɔki/ *m* -s,-s jockey
Jod *nt* -[e]s iodine
jodeln *vi* (*haben*) yodel
Joga *m & nt* -[s] yoga
jogg|en /'dʒɔgən/ *vi* (*haben/sein*) jog. **J~ing** *nt* -[s] jogging
Joghurt *m & nt* -[s] yoghurt
Johannisbeere *f* redcurrant; **schwarze J~** blackcurrant
johlen *vi* (*haben*) yell; (*empört*) jeer
Joker *m* -s,- (*Karte*) joker
Jolle *f* -,-n dinghy
Jongl|eur /ʒõ'gløːɐ̯/ *m* -s,-e juggler. **j~ieren** *vi* (*haben*) juggle
Joppe *f* -,-n [thick] jacket
Jordanien /-jən/ *nt* -s Jordan
Journal|ismus /ʒʊrna'lɪsmʊs/ *m* - journalism. **J~t(in)** *m* -en,-en (*f* -,-nen) journalist
Jubel *m* -s rejoicing, jubilation. **j~n** *vi* (*haben*) rejoice
Jubil|ar(in) *m* -s,-e (*f* -,-nen) person celebrating an anniversary. **J~äum** *nt* -s,-äen jubilee; (*Jahrestag*) anniversary
juck|en *vi* (*haben*) itch; **sich j~en** scratch; **es j~t mich** I have an itch; (*fam: möchte*) I'm itching (**zu** to). **J~reiz** *m* itch[ing]
Jude *m* -n,-n Jew. **J~ntum** *nt* -s Judaism; (*Juden*) Jewry

Jüd|in *f* -,-nen Jewess. **j~isch** *a* Jewish
Judo *nt* -[s] judo
Jugend *f* - youth; (*junge Leute*) young people *pl*. **J~herberge** *f* youth hostel. **J~klub** *m* youth club. **J~kriminalität** *f* juvenile delinquency. **j~lich** *a* youthful. **J~liche(r)** *m/f* young man/woman; (*Admin*) juvenile; **J~liche** *pl* young people. **J~stil** *m* art nouveau. **J~zeit** *f* youth
Jugoslaw|ien /-jən/ *nt* -s Yugoslavia. **j~isch** *a* Yugoslav
Juli *m* -[s],-s July
jung *a* (**jünger, jüngst**) young; (*Wein*) new ● *pron* **j~ und alt** young and old. **J~e** *m* -n,-n boy. **J~e(s)** *nt* young animal/bird; (*Katzen-*) kitten; (*Bären-, Löwen-*) cub; (*Hunde-, Seehund-*) pup; **die J~en** the young *pl*. **j~enhaft** *a* boyish
Jünger *m* -s,- disciple
Jungfer *f* -,-n **alte J~** old maid. **J~nfahrt** *f* maiden voyage
Jung|frau *f* virgin; (*Astr*) Virgo. **j~fräulich** *a* virginal. **J~geselle** *m* bachelor
Jüngling *m* -s,-e youth
jüngst|e(r,s) *a* youngest; (*neueste*) latest; **in j~er Zeit** recently
Juni *m* -[s],-s June
Junior *m* -s,-en /-'oːrən/ junior
Jura *pl* law *sg*
Jur|ist(in) *m* -en,-en (*f* -,-nen) lawyer. **j~isch** *a* legal, *adv* -ly
Jury /ʒy'riː/ *f* -,-s jury; (*Sport*) judges *pl*
justieren *vt* adjust
Justiz *f* - **die J~** justice. **J~irrtum** *m* miscarriage of justice. **J~minister** *m* Minister of Justice
Juwel *nt* -s,-en & (*fig*) -e jewel. **J~ier** *m* -s,-e jeweller
Jux *m* -es,-e (*fam*) joke; **aus Jux** for fun

K

Kabarett *nt* -s,-s & -e cabaret
kabbelig *a* choppy
Kabel *nt* -s,- cable. **K~fernsehen** *nt* cable television
Kabeljau *m* -s,-e & -s cod
Kabine *f* -,-n cabin; (*Umkleide-*) cubicle; (*Telefon-*) booth; (*einer K~nbahn*) car. **K~nbahn** *f* cable-car
Kabinett *nt* -s,-e (*Pol*) Cabinet
Kabriolett *nt* -s,-s convertible

Kachel *f* -,-n tile. **k~n** *vt* tile

Kadaver *m* -s,- carcass

Kadenz *f* -,-en (*Mus*) cadence; (*für Solisten*) cadenza

Kadett *m* -en,-en cadet

Käfer *m* -s,- beetle

Kaff *nt* -s,-s (*fam*) dump

Kaffee /'kafe:, ka'fe:/ *m* -s,-s coffee; (*Mahlzeit*) afternoon coffee. **K~grund** *m* = **K~satz. K~kanne** *f* coffee-pot. **K~maschine** *f* coffee-maker. **K~mühle** *f* coffee-grinder. **K~satz** *m* coffee-grounds *pl*

Käfig *m* -s,-e cage

kahl *a* bare; (*haarlos*) bald. **k~geschoren** *a* shaven. **k~köpfig** *a* bald-headed

Kahn *m* -s,¨e boat; (*Last-*) barge

Kai *m* -s,-s quay

Kaiser *m* -s,- emperor. **K~in** *f* -,-nen empress. **k~lich** *a* imperial. **K~reich** *nt* empire. **K~schnitt** *m* Caesarean [section]

Kajüte *f* -,-n (*Naut*) cabin

Kakao /ka'kau/ *m* -s cocoa

Kakerlak *m* -s & -en,-en cockroach

Kaktee /kak'te:ə/ *f* -,-n, **Kaktus** *m* -,-teen /-'te:ən/ cactus

Kalb *nt* -[e]s,¨er calf. **K~fleisch** *nt* veal

Kalender *m* -s,- calendar; (*Taschen-, Termin-*) diary

Kaliber *nt* -s,- calibre; (*Gewehr-*) bore

Kalium *nt* -s potassium

Kalk *m* -[e]s,-e lime; (*Kalzium*) calcium. **k~en** *vt* whitewash. **K~stein** *m* limestone

Kalkul|ation /-'tsio:n/ *f* -,-en calculation. **k~ieren** *vt/i* (*haben*) calculate

Kalorie *f* -,-n calorie

kalt *a* (**kälter, kältest**) cold; **es ist k~** it is cold; **mir ist k~** I am cold. **k~blütig** *a* cold-blooded, *adv* -ly; (*ruhig*) cool, *adv* -ly

Kälte *f* - cold; (*Gefühls-*) coldness; **10 Grad K~** 10 degrees below zero. **K~welle** *f* cold spell

kalt|herzig *a* cold-hearted. **k~schnäuzig** *a* (*fam*) cold, *adv* -ly

Kalzium *nt* -s calcium

Kamel *nt* -[e]s,-e camel; (*fam: Idiot*) fool

Kamera *f* -,-s camera

Kamerad|(in) *m* -en,-en (*f* -,-nen) companion; (*Freund*) mate; (*Mil, Pol*) comrade. **K~schaft** *f* - comradeship

Kameramann *m* (*pl* -männer & -leute*) cameraman

Kamille *f* - camomile

Kamin *m* -s,-e fireplace; (*SGer: Schornstein*) chimney. **K~feger** *m* -s,- (*SGer*) chimney-sweep

Kamm *m* -[e]s,¨e comb; (*Berg-*) ridge; (*Zool, Wellen-*) crest

kämmen *vt* comb; **jdn/sich k~** comb s.o.'s/one's hair

Kammer *f* -,-n small room; (*Techn, Biol, Pol*) chamber. **K~diener** *m* valet. **K~musik** *f* chamber music

Kammgarn *nt* (*Tex*) worsted

Kampagne /kam'panjə/ *f* -,-n (*Pol, Comm*) campaign

Kampf *m* -es,¨e fight; (*Schlacht*) battle; (*Wett-*) contest; (*fig*) struggle; **schwere K~e** heavy fighting *sg*; **den K~ ansagen** (+ *dat*) (*fig*) declare war on

kämpf|en *vi* (*haben*) fight; **sich k~en durch** fight one's way through. **K~er(in)** *m* -s,- (*f* -,-nen) fighter

kampf|los *adv* without a fight. **K~richter** *m* (*Sport*) judge

kampieren *vi* (*haben*) camp

Kanada *nt* -s Canada

Kanad|ier(in) /-iɐ, -iɐrın/ *m* -s,- (*f* -,-nen) Canadian. **k~isch** *a* Canadian

Kanal *m* -s,¨e canal; (*Abfluß-*) drain, sewer; (*Radio, TV*) channel; **der K~** the [English] Channel

Kanalis|ation /-'tsio:n/ *f* - sewerage system, drains *pl*. **k~ieren** *vt* canalize; (*fig: lenken*) channel

Kanarienvogel /-iən-/ *m* canary

Kanarisch *a* **K~e Inseln** Canaries

Kandi|dat(in) *m* -en,-en (*f* -,-nen) candidate. **k~dieren** *vi* (*haben*) stand (**für** for)

kandiert *a* candied

Känguruh *nt* -s,-s kangaroo

Kaninchen *nt* -s,- rabbit

Kanister *m* -s,- canister; (*Benzin-*) can

Kännchen *nt* -s,- [small] jug; (*Kaffee-*) pot

Kanne *f* -,-n jug; (*Kaffee-, Tee-*) pot; (*Öl-*) can; (*große Milch-*) churn; (*Gieß-*) watering-can

Kannibal|e *m* -n,-n cannibal. **K~ismus** *m* - cannibalism

Kanon *m* -s,-s canon; (*Lied*) round

Kanone *f* -,-n cannon, gun; (*fig: Könner*) ace

kanonisieren *vt* canonize

Kantate *f* -,-n cantata

Kante *f* -,-n edge; **auf die hohe K~ legen** (*fam*) put by

Kanten *m* -s,- crust [of bread]

Kanter *m* -s,- canter

kantig *a* angular

Kantine *f* -,-n canteen

Kanton *m* -s,-e (*Swiss*) canton

Kantor *m* -s,-en /-'to:rən/ choirmaster and organist

Kanu *nt* -s,-s canoe

Kanzel *f* -,-n pulpit; (*Aviat*) cockpit

Kanzleistil *m* officialese

Kanzler *m* -s,- chancellor

Kap *nt* -s,-s (*Geog*) cape

Kapazität *f* -,-en capacity; (*Experte*) authority

Kapelle *f* -,-n chapel; (*Mus*) band

Kaper *f* -,-n (*Culin*) caper

kapern *vt* (*Naut*) seize

kapieren *vt* (*fam*) understand, (*fam*) get

Kapital *nt* -s capital; **K~ schlagen aus** (*fig*) capitalize on. **K~ismus** *m* - capitalism. **K~ist** *m* -en,-en capitalist. **k~istisch** *a* capitalist

Kapitän *m* -s,-e captain

Kapitel *nt* -s,- chapter

Kapitul|ation /-'tsjo:n/ *f* - capitulation. **k~ieren** *vi* (*haben*) capitulate

Kaplan *m* -s,-e curate

Kappe *f* -,-n cap. **k~n** *vt* cut

Kapsel *f* -,-n capsule; (*Flaschen-*) top

kaputt *a* (*fam*) broken; (*zerrissen*) torn; (*defekt*) out of order; (*ruiniert*) ruined; (*erschöpft*) worn out. **k~gehen†** *vi sep* (*sein*) (*fam*) break; (*zerreißen*) tear; (*defekt werden*) pack up; ⟨*Ehe, Freundschaft:*⟩ break up. **k~lachen (sich)** *vr sep* (*fam*) be in stitches. **k~machen** *vt sep* (*fam*) break; (*zerreißen*) tear; (*defekt machen*) put out of order; (*erschöpfen*) wear out; **sich k~machen** wear oneself out

Kapuze *f* -,-n hood

Kapuzinerkresse *f* nasturtium

Karaffe *f* -,-n carafe; (*mit Stöpsel*) decanter

Karambolage /karambo'la:ʒə/ *f* -,-n collision

Karamel *m* -s caramel. **K~bonbon** *m* & *nt* ≈ toffee

Karat *nt* -[e]s,-e carat

Karawane *f* -,-n caravan

Kardinal *m* -s,-e cardinal. **K~zahl** *f* cardinal number

Karfiol *m* -s (*Aust*) cauliflower

Karfreitag *m* Good Friday

karg *a* (*kärger, kärgst*) meagre; (*frugal*) frugal; (*spärlich*) sparse; (*unfruchtbar*) barren; (*gering*) scant.

k~en *vi* (*haben*) be sparing (**mit** with)

kärglich *a* poor, meagre; (*gering*) scant

Karibik *f* - Caribbean

kariert *a* check[ed]; ⟨*Papier*⟩ squared; **schottisch k~** tartan

Karik|atur *f* -,-en caricature; (*Journ*) cartoon. **k~ieren** *vt* caricature

karitativ *a* charitable

Karneval *m* -s,-e & -s carnival

Karnickel *nt* -s,- (*dial*) rabbit

Kärnten *nt* -s Carinthia

Karo *nt* -s,- (*Raute*) diamond; (*Viereck*) square; (*Muster*) check; (*Kartenspiel*) diamonds *pl*. **K~muster** *nt* check

Karosserie *f* -,-n bodywork

Karotte *f* -,-n carrot

Karpfen *m* -s,- carp

Karre *f* -,-n = **Karren**

Karree *nt* -s,-s square; **ums K~** round the block

Karren *m* -s,- cart; (*Hand-*) barrow. **k~** *vt* cart

Karriere /ka'rjɛːrə/ *f* -,-n career; **K~ machen** get to the top

Karte *f* -,-n card; (*Eintritts-, Fahr-*) ticket; (*Speise-*) menu; (*Land-*) map

Kartei *f* -,-en card index. **K~karte** *f* index card

Karten|spiel *nt* card-game; (*Spielkarten*) pack/(*Amer*) deck of cards. **K~vorverkauf** *m* advance booking

Kartoffel *f* -,-n potato. **K~brei** *m*, **K~püree** *nt* mashed potatoes *pl*. **K~salat** *m* potato salad

Karton /kar'tɔŋ/ *m* -s,-s cardboard; (*Schachtel*) carton, cardboard box

Karussell *nt* -s,-s & -e roundabout

Karwoche *f* Holy Week

Käse *m* -s,- cheese. **K~kuchen** *m* cheesecake

Kaserne *f* -,-n barracks *pl*

Kasino *nt* -s,-s casino

Kasperle *nt* & *m* -s,- Punch. **K~theater** *nt* Punch and Judy show

Kasse *f* -,-n till; (*Registrier-*) cash register; (*Zahlstelle*) cash desk; (*im Supermarkt*) check-out; (*Theater-*) box-office; (*Geld*) pool [of money], (*fam*) kitty; (*Kranken-*) health insurance scheme; (*Spar-*) savings bank; **knapp/gut bei K~ sein** (*fam*) be short of cash/be flush. **K~npatient** *m* ≈ NHS patient. **K~nschlager** *m* box-office hit. **K~nwart** *m* -[e]s,-e treasurer. **K~nzettel** *m* receipt

Kasserolle f -,-n saucepan [with one handle]

Kassette f -,-n cassette; (*Film-, Farbband-*) cartridge; (*Schmuck-*) case; (*Geld-*) money-box. **K~nrecorder** /-'rəkordɐ/ m -s,- cassette recorder

kassier|en vi (haben) collect the money/(*im Bus*) the fares ● vt collect. **K~er(in)** m -s,- (f -,-nen) cashier

Kastagnetten /kastan'jɛtən/ pl castanets

Kastanie /kas'ta:njə/ f -,-n [horse] chestnut, (*fam*) conker. **k~nbraun** a chestnut

Kaste f -,-n caste

Kasten m -s,- box; (*Brot-*) bin; (*Flaschen-*) crate; (*Brief-*) letter-box; (*Aust: Schrank*) cupboard; (*Kleider-*) wardrobe

kastrieren vt castrate; neuter ⟨*Tier*⟩

Kasus m - /-u:s/ (*Gram*) case.

Katalog m -[e]s,-e catalogue. **k~isieren** vt catalogue

Katalysator m -s,-en /-'to:rən/ catalyst; (*Auto*) catalytic converter

Katapult nt -[e]s,-e catapult. **k~ieren** vt catapult

Katarrh m -s,-e catarrh

katastr|ophal a catastrophic. **K~ophe** f -,-n catastrophe

Katechismus m - catechism

Kateg|orie f -,-n category. **k~orisch** a categorical, adv-ly

Kater m -s,- tom-cat; (*fam: Katzenjammer*) hangover

Katheder nt -s,- [teacher's] desk

Kathedrale f -,-n cathedral

Kath|olik(in) m -en,-en (f -,-nen) Catholic. **k~olisch** a Catholic. **K~olizismus** m - Catholicism

Kätzchen nt -s,- kitten; (*Bot*) catkin

Katze f -,-n cat. **K~njammer** m (*fam*) hangover. **K~nsprung** m ein **K~nsprung** (*fam*) a stone's throw

Kauderwelsch nt -[s] gibberish

kauen vt/i (haben) chew; bite ⟨*Nägel*⟩

kauern vi (haben) crouch; **sich k~** crouch down

Kauf m -[e]s, Käufe purchase; **guter K~** bargain; **in K~ nehmen** (*fig*) put up with. **k~en** vt/i (haben) buy; **k~en bei** shop at

Käufer(in) m -s,- (f -,-nen) buyer; (*im Geschäft*) shopper

Kauf|haus nt department store. **K~kraft** f purchasing power. **K~laden** m shop

käuflich a saleable; (*bestechlich*) corruptible; **k~ sein** be for sale; **k~ erwerben** buy

Kauf|mann m (pl -leute) businessman; (*Händler*) dealer; (*dial*) grocer. **k~männisch** a commercial. **K~preis** m purchase price

Kaugummi m chewing-gum

Kaulquappe f -,-n tadpole

kaum adv hardly; **k~ glaublich** od **zu glauben** hard to believe

kauterisieren vt cauterize

Kaution /-'tsjo:n/ f -,-en surety; (*Jur*) bail; (*Miet-*) deposit

Kautschuk m -s rubber

Kauz m -es, Käuze owl; **komischer K~** (*fam*) odd fellow

Kavalier m -s,-e gentleman

Kavallerie f - cavalry

Kaviar m -s caviare

keck a bold; (*frech*) cheeky

Kegel m -s,- skittle; (*Geom*) cone; **mit Kind und K~** (*fam*) with all the family. **K~bahn** f skittle-alley. **k~förmig** a conical. **k~n** vi (haben) play skittles

Kehl|e f -,-n throat; **aus voller K~e** at the top of one's voice; **etw in die falsche K~e bekommen** (*fam*) take sth the wrong way. **K~kopf** m larynx. **K~kopfentzündung** f laryngitis

Kehr|e f -,-n [hairpin] bend. **k~en** vi (haben) (*fegen*) sweep ● vt sweep; (*wenden*) turn; **den Rücken k~en** turn one's back (*dat* on); **sich k~en** turn; **sich nicht k~en an** (+ *acc*) not care about. **K~icht** m -[e]s sweepings pl. **K~reim** m refrain. **K~seite** f (*fig*) drawback; **die K~seite der Medaille** the other side of the coin. **K~tmachen** vi sep (haben) turn back; (*sich umdrehen*) turn round. **K~twendung** f about-turn; (*fig*) U-turn

keifen vi (haben) scold

Keil m -[e]s,-e wedge

Keile f - (*fam*) hiding. **k~n (sich)** vr (*fam*) fight. **K~rei** f -,-en (*fam*) punch-up

Keil|kissen nt [wedge-shaped] bolster. **K~riemen** m fan belt

Keim m -[e]s,-e (*Bot*) sprout; (*Med*) germ; **im K~ ersticken** (*fig*) nip in the bud. **k~en** vi (haben) germinate; (*austreiben*) sprout. **k~frei** a sterile

kein pron no; not a; **auf k~en Fall** on no account; **k~e fünf Minuten** less than five minutes. **k~e(r,s)** pron no one, nobody; (*Ding*) none, not one. **k~esfalls** adv on no account.

k~eswegs *adv* by no means. k~mal *adv* not once. k~s *pron* none, not one

Keks *m* -[es], -[e] biscuit, (*Amer*) cookie

Kelch *m* -[e]s, -e goblet, cup; (*Relig*) chalice; (*Bot*) calyx

Kelle *f* -, -n ladle; (*Maurer-, Pflanz-*) trowel

Keller *m* -s, - cellar. K~ei *f* -, -en winery. K~geschoß *nt* cellar; (*bewohnbar*) basement. K~wohnung *f* basement flat

Kellner *m* -s, - waiter. K~in *f* -, -nen waitress

keltern *vt* press

keltisch *a* Celtic

Kenia *nt* -s Kenya

kenn|en† *vt* know. k~enlernen *vt sep* get to know; (*treffen*) meet; sich k~enlernen meet; (*näher*) get to know one another. K~er *m* -s, -, K~erin *f* -, -nen connoisseur; (*Experte*) expert. K~melodie *f* signature tune. k~tlich *a* recognizable; k~tlich machen mark. K~tnis *f* -, -se knowledge; zur K~tnis nehmen take note of; in K~tnis setzen inform (von of). K~wort *nt* (*pl* -wörter) reference; (*geheimes*) password. K~zeichen *nt* distinguishing mark *or* feature; (*Merkmal*) characteristic; (*Markierung*) mark, marking; (*Abzeichen*) badge; (*Auto*) registration. k~zeichnen *vt* distinguish; (*markieren*) mark. k~zeichnend *a* typical (für of). K~ziffer *f* reference number

kentern *vi* (*sein*) capsize

Keramik *f* -, -en pottery, ceramics *sg*; (*Gegenstand*) piece of pottery

Kerbe *f* -, -n notch

Kerbholz *nt* etwas auf dem K~ haben (*fam*) have a record

Kerker *m* -s, - dungeon; (*Gefängnis*) prison

Kerl *m* -s, -e & -s (*fam*) fellow, bloke

Kern *m* -s, -e pip; (*Kirsch-*) stone; (*Nuß-*) kernel; (*Techn*) core; (*Atom-, Zell- & fig*) nucleus; (*Stadt-*) centre; (*einer Sache*) heart. K~energie *f* nuclear energy. K~gehäuse *nt* core. k~gesund *a* perfectly healthy. k~ig *a* robust; (*Ausspruch*) pithy. k~los *a* seedless. K~physik *f* nuclear physics *sg*

Kerze *f* -, -n candle. k~ngerade *a* & *adv* straight. K~nhalter *m* -s, - candlestick

keß *a* (kesser, kessest) pert

Kessel *m* -s, - kettle; (*Heiz-*) boiler. K~stein *m* fur

Kette *f* -, -n chain; (*Hals-*) necklace. k~n *vt* chain (an + *acc* to). K~nladen *m* chain store. K~nraucher *m* chainsmoker. K~nreaktion *f* chain reaction

Ketze|r(in) *m* -s, - (*f* -, -nen) heretic. K~rei *f* - heresy

keuch|en *vi* (*haben*) pant. K~husten *m* whooping cough

Keule *f* -, -n club; (*Culin*) leg; (*Hühner-*) drumstick

keusch *a* chaste. K~heit *f* - chastity

Kfz *abbr* s. Kraftfahrzeug

Khaki *nt* - khaki. k~farben *a* khaki

kichern *vi* (*haben*) giggle

Kiefer¹ *f* -, -n pine[-tree]

Kiefer² *m* -s, - jaw

Kiel *m* -s, -e (*Naut*) keel. K~wasser *nt* wake

Kiemen *fpl* gills

Kies *m* -es gravel. K~el *m* -s, -, K~elstein *m* pebble. K~grube *f* gravel pit

Kilo *nt* -s, -[s] kilo. K~gramm *nt* kilogram. K~hertz *nt* kilohertz. K~meter *m* kilometre. K~meterstand *m* ≈ mileage. K~watt *nt* kilowatt

Kind *nt* -es, -er child; von K~ auf from childhood

Kinder|arzt *m*, K~ärztin *f* paediatrician. K~bett *nt* child's cot. K~ei *f* -, -en childish prank. K~garten *m* nursery school. K~gärtnerin *f* nursery-school teacher. K~geld *nt* child benefit. K~gottesdienst *m* Sunday school. K~lähmung *f* polio. k~leicht *a* very easy. k~los *a* childless. K~mädchen *nt* nanny. k~reich *a* k~reiche Familie large family. K~reim *m* nursery rhyme. K~spiel *nt* children's game; das ist ein/kein K~spiel that is dead easy/not easy. K~tagesstätte *f* day nursery. K~teller *m* children's menu. K~wagen *m* pram, (*Amer*) baby carriage. K~zimmer *nt* child's/children's room; (*für Baby*) nursery

Kind|heit *f* - childhood. k~isch *a* childish, puerile. k~lich *a* childlike

kinetisch *a* kinetic

Kinn *nt* -[e]s, -e chin. K~lade *f* jaw

Kino *nt* -s, -s cinema

Kiosk *m* -[e]s, -e kiosk

Kippe *f* -, -n (*Müll-*) dump; (*fam: Zigaretten-*) fag-end; auf der K~ stehen (*fam*) be in a precarious position; (*unsicher sein*) hang in the balance. **k~lig** *a* wobbly. **k~ln** *vi* (*haben*) wobble. **k~n** *vt* tilt; (*schütten*) tip (**in** + *acc* into) ● *vi* (*sein*) topple

Kirch|e *f* -,-n church. **K~enbank** *f* pew. **K~endiener** *m* verger. **K~enlied** *nt* hymn. **K~enschiff** *nt* nave. **K~hof** *m* churchyard. **k~lich** *a* church ... ● *adv* **k~lich getraut werden** be married in church. **K~turm** *m* church tower, steeple. **K~weih** *f* -,-en [village] fair

Kirmes *f* -,-sen = **Kirchweih**

Kirsch|e *f* -,-n cherry. **K~wasser** *nt* kirsch

Kissen *nt* -s,- cushion; (*Kopf-*) pillow

Kiste *f* -,-n crate; (*Zigarren-*) box

Kitsch *m* -es sentimental rubbish; (*Kunst*) kitsch. **k~ig** *a* slushy; (*Kunst*) kitschy

Kitt *m* -s [adhesive] cement; (*Fenster-*) putty

Kittel *m* -s,- overall, smock; (*Arzt-, Labor-*) white coat

kitten *vt* stick; (*fig*) cement

Kitz *nt* -es,-e (*Zool*) kid

Kitz|el *m* -s,- tickle; (*Nerven-*) thrill. **k~eln** *vt/i* (*haben*) tickle. **k~lig** *a* ticklish

Kladde *f* -,-n notebook

klaffen *vi* (*haben*) gape

kläffen *vi* (*haben*) yap

Klage *f* -,-n lament; (*Beschwerde*) complaint; (*Jur*) action. **k~n** *vi* (*haben*) lament; (*sich beklagen*) complain; (*Jur*) sue

Kläger(in) *m* -s,- (*f* -,-nen) (*Jur*) plaintiff

kläglich *a* pitiful, *adv* -ly; (*erbärmlich*) miserable, *adv* -bly

klamm *a* cold and damp; (*steif*) stiff. **K~** *f* -,-en (*Geog*) gorge

Klammer *f* -,-n (*Wäsche-*) peg; (*Büro-*) paper-clip; (*Heft-*) staple; (*Haar-*) grip; (*für Zähne*) brace; (*Techn*) clamp; (*Typ*) bracket. **k~n (sich)** *vr* cling (**an** + *acc* to)

Klang *m* -[e]s,-e sound; (*K~farbe*) tone. **k~voll** *a* resonant; (*Stimme*) sonorous

Klapp|bett *nt* folding bed. **K~e** *f* -,-n flap; (*fam: Mund*) trap. **k~en** *vt* fold; (*hoch-*) tip up ● *vi* (*haben*) (*fam*) work out. **K~entext** *m* blurb

Klapper *f* -,-n rattle. **k~n** *vi* (*haben*) rattle. **K~schlange** rattlesnake

klapp|rig *a* rickety; (*schwach*) decrepit. **K~stuhl** *m* folding chair. **K~tisch** *m* folding table

Klaps *m* -es,-e pat; (*strafend*) smack. **k~en** *vt* smack

klar *a* clear; **sich** (*dat*) **k~ od im k~en sein** realize ● *adv* clearly; (*fam: natürlich*) of course. **K~e(r)** *m* (*fam*) schnapps

klären *vt* clarify; **sich k~** clear; (*fig: sich lösen*) resolve itself

Klarheit *f* - clarity

Klarinette *f* -,-n clarinet

klar|machen *vt sep* make clear (*dat* to); **sich** (*dat*) **etw k~machen** understand sth. **K~sichtfolie** *f* transparent/(*haftend*) cling film. **k~stellen** *vt sep* clarify

Klärung *f* - clarification

klarwerden† *vi sep* (*sein*) (*fig*) become clear (*dat* to); **sich** (*dat*) **k~** make up one's mind; (*erkennen*) realize

Klasse *f* -,-n class; (*Sch*) class, form, (*Amer*) grade; (*Zimmer*) classroom; **erster/zweiter K~** first/second class. **k~** *inv a* (*fam*) super. **K~narbeit** *f* [written] test. **K~nbuch** *nt* ≈ register. **K~nkamerad(in)** *m*(*f*) class-mate. **K~nkampf** *m* class struggle. **K~nzimmer** *nt* classroom

klassifizier|en *vt* classify. **K~ung** *f* -,-en classification

Klass|ik *f* - classicism; (*Epoche*) classical period. **K~iker** *m* -s,- classical author/(*Mus*) composer. **k~isch** *a* classical; (*mustergültig, typisch*) classic

Klatsch *m* -[e]s gossip. **K~base** *f* (*fam*) gossip. **k~en** *vt* slap; **Beifall k~en** applaud ● *vi* (*haben*) make a slapping sound; (*im Wasser*) splash; (*tratschen*) gossip; (*applaudieren*) clap; **[in die Hände] k~en** clap one's hands ● *vi* (*haben/sein*) slap (**gegen** against). **K~maul** *nt* gossip. **k~naß** *a* (*fam*) soaking wet

klauben *vt* pick

Klaue *f* -,-n claw; (*fam: Schrift*) scrawl. **k~n** *vt/i* (*haben*) (*fam*) steal

Klausel *f* -,-n clause

Klaustrophobie *f* - claustrophobia

Klausur *f* -,-en (*Univ*) [examination] paper; (*Sch*) written test

Klaviatur *f* -,-en keyboard

Klavier *nt* -s,-e piano. **K~spieler(in)** *m*(*f*) pianist

kleb|en *vt* stick/(*mit Klebstoff*) glue (**an** + *acc* to) ● *vi* (*haben*) stick (**an**

+ *dat* to). **k~rig** *a* sticky. **K~stoff** *m* adhesive, glue. **K~streifen** *m* adhesive tape

kleckern *vi (haben) (fam)* = **klecksen**

Klecks *m* -es,-e stain; (*Tinten-*) blot; (*kleine Menge*) dab. **k~en** *vi (haben)* make a mess

Klee *m* -s clover. **K~blatt** *nt* clover leaf

Kleid *nt* -[e]s,-er dress; **K~er** dresses; (*Kleidung*) clothes. **k~en** *vt* dress; (*gut stehen*) suit; **sich k~en** dress. **K~erbügel** *m* coat-hanger. **K~erbürste** *f* clothes-brush. **K~erhaken** *m* coat-hook. **K~errock** *m* pinafore dress. **K~erschrank** *m* wardrobe, (*Amer*) clothes closet. **k~sam** *a* becoming. **K~ung** *f* - clothes *pl*, clothing. **K~ungsstück** *nt* garment

Kleie *f* - bran

klein *a* small, little; (*von kleinem Wuchs*) short; **von k~ auf** from childhood. **K~arbeit** *f* painstaking work. **K~bus** *m* minibus. **K~e(r,s)** *m/f/nt* little one. **K~geld** *nt* [small] change. **k~hacken** *vt sep* chop up small. **K~handel** *m* retail trade. **K~heit** *f* - smallness; (*Wuchs*) short stature. **K~holz** *nt* firewood. **K~igkeit** *f* -,-en trifle; (*Mahl*) snack. **K~kind** *nt* infant. **K~kram** *m (fam)* odds and ends *pl*; (*Angelegenheiten*) trivia *pl*. **k~laut** *a* subdued. **k~lich** *a* petty. **K~lichkeit** *f* - pettiness. **k~mütig** *a* faint-hearted

Kleinod *nt* -[e]s,-e jewel

klein|schneiden† *vt sep* cut into small pieces. **K~stadt** *f* small town. **k~städtisch** *a* provincial. **K~wagen** *m* small car

Kleister *m* -s paste. **k~n** *vt* paste

Klemme *f* -,-n [hair-]grip; **in der K~ sitzen** *(fam)* be in a fix. **k~n** *vt* jam; **sich** (*dat*) **den Finger k~n** get one's finger caught ● *vi (haben)* jam, stick

Klempner *m* -s,- plumber

Klerus (der) - the clergy

Klette *f* -,-n burr; **wie eine K~** (*fig*) like a limpet

kletter|n *vi (sein)* climb. **K~pflanze** *f* climber. **K~rose** *f* climbing rose

Klettverschluß *m* Velcro (P) fastening

klicken *vi (haben)* click

Klient(in) */*kli'ɛnt(ɪn)*/ m* -en,-en (*f* -,-nen) (*Jur*) client

Kliff *nt* -[e]s,-e cliff

Klima *nt* -s climate. **K~anlage** *f* airconditioning

klimat|isch *a* climatic. **k~isiert** *a* air-conditioned

klimpern *vi (haben)* jingle; **k~ auf** (+ *dat*) tinkle on ⟨*Klavier*⟩; strum ⟨*Gitarre*⟩

Klinge *f* -,-n blade

Klingel *f* -,-n bell. **k~n** *vi (haben)* ring; **es k~t** there's a ring at the door

klingen† *vi (haben)* sound

Klini|k *f* -,-en clinic. **k~sch** *a* clinical, *adv* -ly

Klinke *f* -,-n [door] handle

klipp *pred a* **k~ und klar** quite plain, *adv* -ly

Klipp *m* -s,-s = **Klips**

Klippe *f* -,-n [submerged] rock

Klips *m* -es,-e clip; (*Ohr-*) clip-on earring

klirren *vi (haben)* rattle; ⟨*Geschirr, Glas:*⟩ chink

Klischee *nt* -s,-s cliché

Klo *nt* -s,-s *(fam)* loo, (*Amer*) john

klobig *a* clumsy

klönen *vi (haben) (NGer fam)* chat

klopf|en *vi (haben)* knock; (*leicht*) tap; ⟨*Herz:*⟩ pound; **es k~te** there was a knock at the door ● *vt* beat; (*ein-*) knock

Klops *m* -es,-e meatball; (*Brat-*) rissole

Klosett *nt* -s,-s lavatory

Kloß *m* -es,-e dumpling; **ein K~ im Hals** (*fam*) a lump in one's throat

Kloster *nt* -s,- monastery; (*Nonnen-*) convent

klösterlich *a* monastic

Klotz *m* -es,-e block

Klub *m* -s,-s club

Kluft[1] *f* -,-e cleft; (*fig: Gegensatz*) gulf

Kluft[2] *f* -,-en outfit; (*Uniform*) uniform

klug *a* (klüger, klügst) intelligent, *adv* -ly; (*schlau*) clever, *adv* -ly; **k~ werden aus** not understand. **K~heit** *f* - cleverness

Klump|en *m* -s,- lump. **k~en** *vi (haben)* go lumpy. **k~ig** *a* lumpy

knabbern *vt/i (haben)* nibble

Knabe *m* -n,-n boy. **k~nhaft** *a* boyish

Knäckebrot *nt* crispbread

knack|en *vt/i (haben)* crack. **K~s** *m* -es,-e crack; **einen K~s haben** be cracked; (*fam: verrückt sein*) be crackers

Knall *m* -[e]s,-e bang. **K~bonbon** *m* cracker. **k~en** *vi (haben)* go bang; ⟨*Peitsche:*⟩ crack ● *vt* (*fam: werfen*) chuck; **jdm eine k~en** *(fam)* clout s.o.

k~ig a (fam) gaudy. **k~rot** a bright red

knapp a (gering) scant; (kurz) short; (mangelnd) scarce; (gerade ausreichend) bare; (eng) tight; **ein k~es Pfund** just under a pound. **k~halten†** vt sep (fam) keep short (mit of). **K~heit** f - scarcity

Knarre f -,-n rattle. **k~n** vi (haben) creak

Knast m -[e]s (fam) prison

knattern vi (haben) crackle; (Gewehr:) stutter

Knäuel m & nt -s,- ball

Knauf m -[e]s, **Knäufe** knob

knauser|ig a (fam) stingy. **k~n** vi (haben) (fam) be stingy

knautschen vt (fam) crumple ● vi (haben) crease

Knebel m -s,- gag. **k~n** vt gag

Knecht m -[e]s,-e farm-hand; (fig) slave. **k~en** vt (fig) enslave. **K~schaft** f - (fig) slavery

kneif|en† vt pinch ● vi (haben) pinch; (fam: sich drücken) chicken out. **K~zange** f pincers pl

Kneipe f -,-n (fam) pub, (Amer) bar

knet|en vt knead; (formen) mould. **K~masse** f Plasticine (P)

Knick m -[e]s,-e bend; (im Draht) kink; (Kniff) crease. **k~en** vt bend; (kniffen) fold; **geknickt sein** (fam) be dejected. **k~[e]rig** a (fam) stingy

Knicks m -es,-e curtsy. **k~en** vi (haben) curtsy

Knie nt -s,- /ˈkniːə/ knee. **K~bundhose** f knee-breeches pl. **K~kehle** f hollow of the knee

knien /ˈkniːən/ vi (haben) kneel ● vr sich **k~** kneel [down]

Knie|scheibe f kneecap. **K~strumpf** m knee-length sock

Kniff m -[e]s,-e pinch; (Falte) crease; (fam: Trick) trick. **k~en** vt fold. **k~[e]lig** a (fam) tricky

knipsen vt (lochen) punch; (Phot) photograph ● vi (haben) take a photograph/photographs

Knirps m -es,-e (fam) little chap; (P) (Schirm) telescopic umbrella

knirschen vi (haben) grate; (Schnee, Kies:) crunch; **mit den Zähnen k~** grind one's teeth

knistern vi (haben) crackle; (Papier:) rustle

Knitter|falte f crease. **k~frei** a crease-resistant. **k~n** vi (haben) crease

knobeln vi (haben) toss (**um** for); (fam: überlegen) puzzle

Knoblauch m -s garlic

Knöchel m -s,- ankle; (Finger-) knuckle

Knochen m -s,- bone. **K~mark** nt bone marrow. **k~trocken** a bone-dry

knochig a bony

Knödel m -s,- (SGer) dumpling

Knoll|e f -,-n tuber. **k~ig** a bulbous

Knopf m -[e]s,-̈e button; (Kragen-) stud; (Griff) knob

knöpfen vt button

Knopfloch nt buttonhole

Knorpel m -s gristle; (Anat) cartilage

knorrig a gnarled

Knospe f bud

Knötchen nt -s,- nodule

Knoten m -s,- knot; (Med) lump; (Haar-) bun, chignon. **k~** vt knot. **K~punkt** m junction

knotig a knotty; (Hände) gnarled

knuffen vt poke

knüll|en vt crumple ● vi (haben) crease. **K~er** m -s,- (fam) sensation

knüpfen vt knot; (verbinden) attach (**an**+ acc to)

Knüppel m -s,- club; (Gummi-) truncheon

knurr|en vi (haben) growl; (Magen:) rumble; (fam: schimpfen) grumble. **k~ig** a grumpy

knusprig a crunchy, crisp

knutschen vi (haben) (fam) smooch

k.o. /kaˈʔoː/ a **k.o. schlagen** knock out; **k.o. sein** (fam) be worn out. **K.o.** m -s,-s knock-out

Koalition /koaliˈtsjoːn/ f -,-en coalition

Kobold m -[e]s,-e goblin, imp

Koch m -[e]s,-̈e cook; (im Restaurant) chef. **K~buch** nt cookery book, (Amer) cookbook. **k~en** vt cook; (sieden) boil; make (Kaffee, Tee) ● vi (haben) cook; (sieden) boil; (fam) seethe (**vor**+ dat with). **K~en** nt -s cooking; (Sieden) boiling; **zum K~en bringen/kommen** bring/come to the boil. **k~end** a boiling ● adv **k~end heiß** boiling hot. **K~er** m -s,- cooker. **K~gelegenheit** f cooking facilities pl. **K~herd** m cooker, stove

Köchin f -,-nen [woman] cook

Koch|kunst f cookery. **K~löffel** m wooden spoon. **K~nische** f kitchenette. **K~platte** f hotplate. **K~topf** m saucepan

Kode /ko:t/ *m* -s,-s code
Köder *m* -s,- bait
Koexist|enz /'ko:?ɛksɪstɛnts/ *f* co-existence. **k~ieren** *vi (haben)* co-exist
Koffein /kɔfe'i:n/ *nt* -s caffeine. **k~frei** *a* decaffeinated
Koffer *m* -s,- suitcase. **K~kuli** *m* luggage trolley. **K~radio** *nt* portable radio. **K~raum** *m (Auto)* boot, *(Amer)* trunk
Kognak /'kɔnjak/ *m* -s,-s brandy
Kohl *m* -[e]s cabbage
Kohle *f* -,-n coal. **K~[n]hydrat** *nt* -[e]s,-e carbohydrate. **K~nbergwerk** *nt* coal-mine, colliery. **K~ndioxyd** *nt* carbon dioxide. **K~ngrube** *f* = **K~nbergwerk**. **K~nherd** *m* [kitchen] range. **K~nsäure** *f* carbon dioxide. **K~nstoff** *m* carbon. **K~papier** *nt* carbon paper
Kohl|kopf *m* cabbage. **K~rabi** *m* -[s],-[s] kohlrabi. **K~rübe** *f* swede
Koje *f* -,-n *(Naut)* bunk
Kokain /koka'i:n/ *nt* -s cocaine
kokett *a* flirtatious. **k~ieren** *vi (haben)* flirt
Kokon /ko'kõ:/ *m* -s,-s cocoon
Kokosnuß *f* coconut
Koks *m* -es coke
Kolben *m* -s,- *(Gewehr-)* butt; *(Mais-)* cob; *(Techn)* piston; *(Chem)* flask
Kolibri *m* -s,-s humming-bird
Kolik *f* -,-en colic
Kollabora|teur /-'tø:ɐ̯/ *m* -s,-e collaborator. **K~tion** /-'tsio:n/ *f* - collaboration
Kolleg *nt* -s,-s & -ien /-jən/ *(Univ)* course of lectures
Kolleg|e *m* -n,-n, **K~in** *f* -,-nen colleague. **K~ium** *nt* -s,-ien staff
Kollek|te *f* -,-n *(Relig)* collection. **K~tion** /-'tsio:n/ *f* -,-en collection. **k~tiv** *a* collective. **K~tivum** *nt* -s,-va collective noun
kolli|dieren *vi (sein)* collide. **K~sion** *f* -,-en collision
Köln *nt* -s Cologne. **K~ischwasser, K~isch Wasser** *nt* eau-de-Cologne
Kolonialwaren *fpl* groceries
Kolon|ie *f* -,-n colony. **k~isieren** *vt* colonize
Kolonne *f* -,-n column; *(Mil)* convoy
Koloß *m* -sses,-sse giant
kolossal *a* enormous, *adv* -ly
Kolumne *f* -,-n *(Journ)* column
Koma *nt* -s,-s coma

Kombi *m* -s,-s = **K~wagen**. **K~nation** /-'tsio:n/ *f* -,-en combination; *(Folgerung)* deduction; *(Kleidung)* co-ordinating outfit. **k~nieren** *vt* combine; *(fig)* reason; *(folgern)* deduce. **K~wagen** *m* estate car, *(Amer)* station-wagon
Kombüse *f* -,-n *(Naut)* galley
Komet *m* -en,-en comet. **k~enhaft** *a* *(fig)* meteoric
Komfort /kɔm'fo:ɐ̯/ *m* -s comfort; *(Luxus)* luxury. **k~abel** /-'ta:bəl/ *a* comfortable, *adv* -bly; *(luxuriös)* luxurious, *adv* -ly
Komik *f* - humour. **K~er** *m* -s,- comic, comedian
komisch *a* funny; *(Oper)* comic; *(sonderbar)* odd, funny ● *adv* funnily; oddly. **k~erweise** *adv* funnily enough
Komitee *nt* -s,-s committee
Komma *nt* -s,-s & -ta comma; *(Dezimal-)* decimal point; **drei K~ fünf** three point five
Komman|dant *m* -en,-en commanding officer. **K~deur** /-'dø:ɐ̯/ *m* -s,-e commander. **k~dieren** *vt* command; *(befehlen)* order; *(fam: herum-)* order about ● *vi (haben)* give the orders
Kommando *nt* -s,-s order; *(Befehlsgewalt)* command; *(Einheit)* detachment. **K~brücke** *f* bridge
kommen† *vi (sein)* come; *(eintreffen)* arrive; *(gelangen)* get *(nach* to); **k~ lassen** send for; **auf/hinter etw** *(acc)* **k~** think of/find out about sth; **um/zu etw k~** lose/acquire sth; **wieder zu sich k~** come round; **wie kommt das?** why is that? **K~** *nt* -s coming; **K~ und Gehen** coming and going. **k~d** *a* coming; **k~den Montag** next Monday
Kommen|tar *m* -s,-e commentary; *(Bemerkung)* comment. **K~tator** *m* -s,-en /-'to:rən/ commentator. **k~tieren** *vt* comment on
kommer|zialisieren *vt* commercialize. **k~ziell** *a* commercial, *adv* -ly
Kommili|tone *m* -n,-n, **K~tonin** *f* -,-nen fellow student
Kommiß *m* -sses *(fam)* army
Kommissar *m* -s,-e commissioner; *(Polizei-)* superintendent
Kommission *f* -,-en commission; *(Gremium)* committee
Kommode *f* -,-n chest of drawers
Kommunalwahlen *fpl* local elections

Kommunikation /-'tsjo:n/ *f* -,-en communication

Kommunion *f* -,-en [Holy] Communion

Kommuniqué /kɔmyni'ke:/ *nt* -s,-s communiqué

Kommun|ismus *m* - Communism. **K~ist(in)** *m* -en,-en (*f* -,-nen) Communist. **k~istisch** *a* Communist

kommunizieren *vi* (haben) receive [Holy] Communion

Komödie /ko'mø:djə/ *f* -,-n comedy

Kompagnon /'kɔmpanjõ:/ *m* -s,-s (Comm) partner

kompakt *a* compact. **K~schallplatte** *f* compact disc

Kompanie *f* -,-n (Mil) company

Komparativ *m* -s,-e comparative

Komparse *m* -n,-n (Theat) extra

Kompaß *m* -sses,-sse compass

kompatibel *a* compatible

kompeten|t *a* competent. **K~z** *f* -,-en competence

komplett *a* complete, *adv* -ly

Komplex *m* -es,-e complex. **k~** *a* complex

Komplikation /-'tsjo:n/ *f* -,-en complication

Kompliment *nt* -[e]s,-e compliment

Komplize *m* -n,-n accomplice

komplizier|en *vt* complicate. **k~t** *a* complicated

Komplott *nt* -[e]s,-e plot

kompo|nieren *vt/i* (haben) compose. **K~nist** *m* -en,-en composer. **K~sition** /-'tsjo:n/ *f* -,-en composition

Kompositum *nt* -s,-ta compound

Kompost *m* -[e]s compost

Kompott *nt* -[e]s,-e stewed fruit

Kompresse *f* -,-n compress

komprimieren *vt* compress

Kompromiß *m* -sses,-sse compromise; **einen K~ schließen** compromise. **k~los** *a* uncompromising

kompromittieren *vt* compromise

Konden|sation /-'tsjo:n/ *f* - condensation. **k~sieren** *vt* condense

Kondensmilch *f* evaporated/(gesüßt) condensed milk

Kondition /-'tsjo:n/ *f* - (Sport) fitness; **in K~** in form. **K~al** *m* -s,-e (Gram) conditional

Konditor *m* -s,-en /-'to:rən/ confectioner. **K~ei** *f* -,-en patisserie

Kondo|lenzbrief *m* letter of condolence. **k~lieren** *vi* (haben) express one's condolences

Kondom *nt* & *m* -s,-e condom

Konfekt *nt* -[e]s confectionery; (Pralinen) chocolates *pl*

Konfektion /-'tsjo:n/ *f* - ready-to-wear clothes *pl*

Konferenz *f* -,-en conference; (Besprechung) meeting

Konfession *f* -,-en [religious] denomination. **k~ell** *a* denominational. **k~slos** *a* non-denominational

Konfetti *nt* -s confetti

Konfirm|and(in) *m* -en,-en (*f* -,-nen) candidate for confirmation. **K~ation** /-'tsjo:n/ *f* -,-en (Relig) confirmation. **k~ieren** *vt* (Relig) confirm

Konfitüre *f* -,-n jam

Konflikt *m* -[e]s,-e conflict

Konföderation /-'tsjo:n/ *f* confederation

Konfront|ation /-'tsjo:n/ *f* -,-en confrontation. **k~ieren** *vt* confront

konfus *a* confused

Kongreß *m* -sses,-sse congress

König *m* -s,-e king. **K~in** *f* -,-nen queen. **k~lich** *a* royal, *adv* -ly; (hoheitsvoll) regal, *adv* -ly; (großzügig) handsome, *adv* -ly; (fam: groß) tremendous, *adv* -ly. **K~reich** *nt* kingdom

konisch *a* conical

Konjug|ation /-'tsjo:n/ *f* -,-en conjugation. **k~ieren** *vt* conjugate

Konjunktion /-'tsjo:n/ *f* -,-en (Gram) conjunction

Konjunktiv *m* -s,-e subjunctive

Konjunktur *f* - economic situation; (Hoch-) boom

konkav *a* concave

konkret *a* concrete

Konkurren|t(in) *m* -en,-en (*f* -,-nen) competitor, rival. **K~z** *f* - competition; **jdm K~z machen** compete with s.o. **k~zfähig** *a* (Comm) competitive. **K~zkampf** *m* competition, rivalry

konkurrieren *vi* (haben) compete

Konkurs *m* -es,-e bankruptcy; **K~ machen** go bankrupt

können† *vt/i* (haben) **etw k~** be able to do sth; (beherrschen) know sth; **k~ Sie Deutsch?** do you know any German? **das kann ich nicht** I can't do that; **er kann nicht mehr** he can't go on; **für etw nichts k~** not be to blame for sth ● *v aux* **lesen/schwimmen k~** be able to read/swim; **er kann/konnte es tun** he can/could do it; **das kann** *od* **könnte [gut] sein** that may [well] be. **K~** *nt* -s ability; (Wissen) knowledge

Könner(in) *m* -s,- (*f*-,-nen) expert
konsequen|t *a* consistent, *adv* -ly; (*logisch*) logical, *adv* -ly. **K~z** *f* -,-en consequence
konservativ *a* conservative
Konserv|en *fpl* tinned *or* canned food *sg*. **K~enbüchse, K~endose** *f* tin, can. **k~ieren** *vt* preserve; (*in Dosen*) tin, can. **K~ierungsmittel** *nt* preservative
Konsistenz *f* - consistency
konsolidieren *vt* consolidate
Konsonant *m* -en,-en consonant
konsterniert *a* dismayed
Konstitution /-'tsio:n/ *f* -,-en constitution. **k~ell** *a* constitutional
konstruieren *vt* construct; (*entwerfen*) design
Konstruk|tion /-'tsio:n/ *f* -,-en construction; (*Entwurf*) design. **k~tiv** *a* constructive
Konsul *m* -s,-n consul. **K~at** *nt* -[e]s,-e consulate
Konsult|ation /-'tsio:n/ *f* -,-en consultation. **k~ieren** *vt* consult
Konsum *m* -s consumption. **K~ent** *m* -en,-en consumer. **K~güter** *npl* consumer goods
Kontakt *m* -[e]s,-e contact. **K~linsen** *fpl* contact lenses. **K~person** *f* contact
kontern *vt/i* (*haben*) counter
Kontinent /'kɔn-, kɔnti'nɛnt/ *m* -s,-e continent
Kontingent *nt* -[e]s,-e (*Comm*) quota; (*Mil*) contingent
Kontinuität *f* - continuity
Konto *nt* -s,-s account. **K~auszug** *m* [bank] statement. **K~nummer** *f* account number. **K~stand** *m* [bank] balance
Kontrabaß *m* double-bass
Kontrast *m* -[e]s,-e contrast
Kontroll|abschnitt *m* counterfoil. **K~e** *f* -,-n control; (*Prüfung*) check. **K~eur** /-'lø:ɐ/ *m* -s,-e [ticket] inspector. **k~ieren** *vt* check; inspect (*Fahrkarten*); (*beherrschen*) control
Kontroverse *f* -,-n controversy
Kontur *f* -,-en contour
Konvention /-'tsio:n/ *f* -,-en convention. **k~ell** *a* conventional, *adv* -ly
Konversation /-'tsio:n/ *f* -,-en conversation. **K~slexikon** *nt* encyclopaedia
konvertieren *vi* (*haben*) (*Relig*) convert. **K~it** *m* -en,-en convert

konvex *a* convex
Konvoi /kɔn'vɔy/ *m* -s,-s convoy
Konzentration /-'tsio:n/ *f* -,-en concentration. **K~slager** *nt* concentration camp
konzentrieren *vt* concentrate; sich **k~** concentrate (**auf** + *acc* on)
Konzept *nt* -[e]s,-e [rough] draft; jdn aus dem **K~** bringen put s.o. off his stroke. **K~papier** *nt* rough paper
Konzern *m* -s,-e (*Comm*) group [of companies]
Konzert *nt* -[e]s,-e concert; (*Klavier-, Geigen-*) concerto. **K~meister** *m* leader, (*Amer*) concert-master
Konzession *f* -,-en licence; (*Zugeständnis*) concession
Konzil *nt* -s,-e (*Relig*) council
Kooperation /ko'ɔpera'tsio:n/ *f* cooperation
Koordin|ation /ko'ɔrdina'tsio:n/ *f* - co-ordination. **k~ieren** *vt* coordinate
Kopf *m* -[e]s,-e head; ein **K~** Kohl/ Salat a cabbage/lettuce; aus dem **K~** from memory; (*auswendig*) by heart; auf dem **K~** (*verkehrt*) upside down; **K~** an **K~** neck and neck; ⟨stehen⟩ shoulder to shoulder; sich (*dat*) den **K~** waschen wash one's hair; sich (*dat*) den **K~** zerbrechen rack one's brains. **K~ball** *m* header. **K~bedeckung** *f* head-covering
Köpf|chen *nt* -s,- little head; **K~chen** haben (*fam*) be clever. **k~en** *vt* behead; (*Fußball*) head
Kopf|ende *nt* head. **K~haut** *f* scalp. **K~hörer** *m* headphones *pl*. **K~kissen** *nt* pillow. **K~kissenbezug** *m* pillow-case. **k~los** *a* panic-stricken. **K~nicken** *nt* -s nod. **K~rechnen** *nt* mental arithmetic. **K~salat** *m* lettuce. **K~schmerzen** *mpl* headache *sg*. **K~schütteln** *nt* -s shake of the head. **K~sprung** *m* header, dive. **K~stand** *m* headstand. **K~steinpflaster** *nt* cobble-stones *pl*. **K~stütze** *f* head-rest. **K~tuch** *nt* headscarf. **k~über** *adv* head first; (*fig*) headlong. **K~wäsche** *f* shampoo. **K~weh** *nt* headache. **K~zerbrechen** *nt* -s sich (*dat*) **K~zerbrechen machen** rack one's brains; (*sich sorgen*) worry
Kopie *f* -,-n copy. **k~ren** *vt* copy
Koppel *f* -,-n enclosure; (*Pferde-*) paddock

Koppel[2] *nt* -s,- (*Mil*) belt. **k~n** *vt* couple

Koralle *f* -,-n coral

Korb *m* -[e]s,¨e basket; **jdm einen K~ geben** (*fig*) turn s.o. down. **K~ball** *m* [kind of] netball. **K~stuhl** *m* wicker chair

Kord *m* -s (*Tex*) corduroy

Kordel *f* -,-n cord

Korinthe *f* -,-n currant

Kork *m* -s cork. **K~en** *m* -s,- cork. **K~enzieher** *m* -s,- corkscrew

Korn[1] *nt* -[e]s,¨er grain; (*Samen-*) seed; (*coll: Getreide*) grain, corn; (*am Visier*) front sight

Korn[2] *m* -[e]s,- (*fam*) grain schnapps

Körn|chen *nt* -s,- granule. **k~ig** *a* granular

Körper *m* -s,- body; (*Geom*) solid. **K~bau** *m* build, physique. **k~behindert** *a* physically disabled. **k~lich** *a* physical, *adv* -ly; ⟨*Strafe*⟩ corporal. **K~pflege** *f* personal hygiene. **K~puder** *m* talcum powder. **K~schaft** *f* -,-en corporation, body. **K~strafe** *f* corporal punishment. **K~teil** *m* part of the body

Korps /koːɐ̯/ *nt* - /-[s],-s/ corps

korpulent *a* corpulent

korrekt *a* correct, *adv* -ly. **K~or** *m* -s,-en /-'toːrən/ proof-reader. **K~ur** *f* -,-en correction. **K~urabzug, K~urbogen** *m* proof

Korrespon|dent(in) *m* -en,-en (*f* -,-nen) correspondent. **K~denz** *f* -,-en correspondence. **k~dieren** *vi* (*haben*) correspond

Korridor *m* -s,-e corridor

korrigieren *vt* correct

Korrosion *f* - corrosion

korrumpieren *vt* corrupt

korrup|t *a* corrupt. **K~tion** /-'tsioːn/ *f* - corruption

Korsett *nt* -[e]s,-e corset

koscher *a* kosher

Kose|name *m* pet name. **K~wort** *nt* (*pl* **-wörter**) term of endearment

Kosmet|ik *f* - beauty culture. **K~ika** *ntpl* cosmetics. **K~ikerin** *f* -,-nen beautician. **k~isch** *a* cosmetic; ⟨*Chirurgie*⟩ plastic

kosm|isch *a* cosmic. **K~onaut(in)** *m* -en,-en (*f* -,-nen) cosmonaut. **k~opolitisch** *a* cosmopolitan

Kosmos *m* - cosmos

Kost *f* - food; (*Ernährung*) diet; (*Verpflegung*) board

kostbar *a* precious. **K~keit** *f* -,-en treasure

kosten[1] *vt/i* (*haben*) [**von**] etw **k~** taste sth

kosten[2] *vt* cost; (*brauchen*) take; **wieviel kostet es?** how much is it? **K~** *pl* expense *sg*, cost *sg*; (*Jur*) costs; **auf meine K~** at my expense. **K~[vor]anschlag** *m* estimate. **k~los** *a* free ● *adv* free [of charge]

Kosthappen *m* taste

köstlich *a* delicious; (*entzückend*) delightful. **K~keit** *f* -,-en (*fig*) gem; (*Culin*) delicacy

Kost|probe *f* taste; (*fig*) sample. **k~spielig** *a* expensive, costly

Kostüm *nt* -s,-e (*Theat*) costume; (*Verkleidung*) fancy dress; (*Schneider-*) suit. **K~fest** *nt* fancy-dress party. **k~iert** *a* **k~iert sein** be in fancy dress

Kot *m* -[e]s excrement; (*Schmutz*) dirt

Kotelett /kɔt'lɛt/ *nt* -s,-s chop, cutlet. **K~en** *pl* sideburns

Köter *m* -s,- (*pej*) dog

Kotflügel *m* (*Auto*) wing, (*Amer*) fender

kotzen *vi* (*haben*) (*sl*) throw up; **es ist zum K~** it makes you sick

Krabbe *f* -,-n crab; (*Garnele*) shrimp; (*rote*) prawn

krabbeln *vi* (*sein*) crawl

Krach *m* -[e]s,¨e din, racket; (*Knall*) crash; (*fam: Streit*) row; (*fam: Ruin*) crash. **k~en** *vi* (*haben*) crash; **es hat gekracht** there was a bang/(*fam: Unfall*) a crash ● (*sein*) break, crack; (*auftreffen*) crash (**gegen** into)

krächzen *vi* (*haben*) croak

Kraft *f* -,¨e strength; (*Gewalt*) force; (*Arbeits-*) worker; **in/außer K~** in/no longer in force; **in K~ treten** come into force. **k~** *prep* (+ *gen*) by virtue of. **K~ausdruck** *m* swear-word. **K~fahrer** *m* driver. **K~fahrzeug** *nt* motor vehicle. **K~fahrzeugbrief** *m* [vehicle] registration document

kräftig *a* strong; (*gut entwickelt*) sturdy; (*nahrhaft*) nutritious; (*heftig*) hard ● *adv* strongly; (*heftig*) hard. **k~en** *vt* strengthen

kraft|los *a* weak. **K~post** *f* post bus service. **K~probe** *f* trial of strength. **K~rad** *nt* motorcycle. **K~stoff** *m* (*Auto*) fuel. **k~voll** *a* strong, powerful. **K~wagen** *m* motor car. **K~werk** *nt* power station

Kragen *m* -s,- collar

Krähe *f* -,-n crow

krähen *vi (haben)* crow

krakeln *vt/i (haben)* scrawl

Kralle *f -,-n* claw. **k~n (sich)** *vr* clutch (**an jdn/etw** s.o./sth); ⟨*Katze:*⟩ dig its claws (**in** + *acc* into)

Kram *m -s (fam)* things *pl*, *(fam)* stuff; *(Angelegenheiten)* business; **wertloser K~** junk. **k~en** *vi (haben)* rummage about (**in** + *dat* in; **nach** for). **K~laden** *m* [small] general store

Krampf *m -[e]s,ˉe* cramp. **K~adern** *fpl* varicose veins. **k~haft** *a* convulsive, *adv* -ly; *(verbissen)* desperate, *adv* -ly

Kran *m -[e]s,ˉe (Techn)* crane

Kranich *m -s,-e (Zool)* crane

krank *a* (kränker, kränkst) sick; ⟨*Knie, Herz*⟩ bad; **k~ sein/werden/machen** be/fall/make ill; **sich k~ melden** report sick. **K~e(r)** *m/f* sick man/ woman, invalid; **die K~en** the sick *pl*

kränkeln *vi (haben)* be in poor health. **k~d** *a* ailing

kranken *vi (haben)* *(fig)* suffer (**an** + *dat* from)

kränken *vt* offend, hurt

Kranken|bett *nt* sick-bed. **K~geld** *nt* sickness benefit. **K~gymnast(in)** *m -en,-en (f -,-nen)* physiotherapist. **K~gymnastik** *f* physiotherapy. **K~haus** *nt* hospital. **K~kasse** *f* health insurance scheme/(*Amt*) office. **K~pflege** *f* nursing. **K~pfleger(in)** *m(f)* nurse. **K~saal** *m* [hospital] ward. **K~schein** *m* certificate of entitlement to medical treatment. **K~schwester** *f* nurse. **K~urlaub** *m* sick-leave. **K~versicherung** *f* health insurance. **K~wagen** *m* ambulance. **K~zimmer** *nt* sick-room

krank|haft *a* morbid; *(pathologisch)* pathological. **K~heit** *f -,-en* illness, disease

kränk|lich *a* sickly. **K~ung** *f -,-en* slight

Kranz *m -es,ˉe* wreath; *(Ring)* ring

Krapfen *m -s,-* doughnut

kraß *a* (krasser, krassest) glaring; *(offensichtlich)* blatant; *(stark)* gross; rank ⟨*Außenseiter*⟩

Krater *m -s,-* crater

krätz|bürstig *a (fam)* prickly. **k~en** *vt/i (haben)* scratch; **sich k~en** scratch oneself/⟨*Tier:*⟩ itself. **K~er** *m -s,-* scratch; *(Werkzeug)* scraper

Kraul *nt -s (Sport)* crawl. **k~en**[1] *vi (haben/sein) (Sport)* do the crawl

kraulen[2] *vt* tickle; **sich am Kopf k~** scratch one's head

kraus *a* wrinkled; ⟨*Haar*⟩ frizzy; *(verworren)* muddled; **k~ ziehen** wrinkle. **K~e** *f -,-n* frill, ruffle; *(Haar-)* frizziness

kräuseln *vt* wrinkle; frizz ⟨*Haar*⟩; gather ⟨*Stoff*⟩; ripple ⟨*Wasser*⟩; **sich k~** wrinkle; *(sich kringeln)* curl; ⟨*Haar:*⟩ go frizzy; ⟨*Wasser:*⟩ ripple

krausen *vt* wrinkle; frizz ⟨*Haar*⟩; gather ⟨*Stoff*⟩; **sich k~** wrinkle; ⟨*Haar:*⟩ go frizzy

Kraut *nt -[e]s, Kräuter* herb; *(SGer)* cabbage; *(Sauer-)* sauerkraut; **wie K~ und Rüben** *(fam)* higgledy- piggledy

Krawall *m -s,-e* riot; *(Lärm)* row

Krawatte *f -,-n* [neck]tie

kraxeln *vi (sein) (fam)* clamber

krea|tiv /krea'ti:f/ *a* creative. **K~tur** *f -,-en* creature

Krebs *m -es,-e* crayfish; *(Med)* cancer; *(Astr)* Cancer. **k~ig** *a* cancerous

Kredit *m -s,-e* credit; *(Darlehen)* loan; **auf K~** on credit. **K~karte** *f* credit card

Kreid|e *f -* chalk. **k~ebleich** *a* deathly pale. **k~ig** *a* chalky

kreieren /kre'i:rən/ *vt* create

Kreis *m -es,-e* circle; *(Admin)* district

kreischen *vt/i (haben)* screech; *(schreien)* shriek

Kreisel *m -s,-* [spinning] top; *(fam: Kreisverkehr)* roundabout

kreis|en *vi (haben)* circle; revolve (**um** around). **k~förmig** *a* circular. **K~lauf** *m* cycle; *(Med)* circulation. **k~rund** *a* circular. **K~säge** *f* circular saw. **K~verkehr** *m* [traffic] roundabout, *(Amer)* traffic circle

Krem *f -,-s* & *m -s,-e* cream

Krematorium *nt -s,-ien* crematorium

Krempe *f -,-n* [hat] brim

Krempel *m -s (fam)* junk

krempeln *vt* turn (**nach oben** up)

Kren *m -[e]s (Aust)* horseradish

krepieren *vi (sein)* explode; *(sl: sterben)* die

Krepp *m -s,-s* & *-e* crêpe

Kreppapier *nt* crêpe paper

Kresse *f -,-n* cress; *(Kapuziner-)* nasturtium

Kreta *nt -s* Crete

Kreuz *nt -es,-e* cross; *(Kreuzung)* intersection; *(Mus)* sharp; *(Kartenspiel)* clubs *pl*; *(Anat)* small of the back; **über K~** crosswise; **das K~ schlagen** cross oneself. **k~** *adv* **k~ und quer** in all directions. **k~en** *vt* cross; **sich k~en** cross; ⟨*Straßen:*⟩ intersect; ⟨*Meinungen:*⟩ clash ● *vi* (*haben/sein*) cruise; ⟨*Segelschiff:*⟩ tack. **K~er** *m* -s,- cruiser. **K~fahrt** *f* (*Naut*) cruise; (*K~zug*) crusade. **K~feuer** *nt* crossfire. **K~gang** *m* cloister

kreuzig|en *vt* crucify. **K~ung** *f* -,-en crucifixion

Kreuz|otter *f* adder, common viper. **K~ung** *f* -,-en intersection; (*Straßen-*) crossroads *sg*; (*Hybride*) cross. **K~verhör** *nt* cross-examination; **K~verhör nehmen** cross-examine. **K~weg** *m* crossroads *sg*; (*Relig*) Way of the Cross. **k~weise** *adv* crosswise. **K~worträtsel** *nt* crossword [puzzle]. **K~zug** *m* crusade

krjbbel|ig *a* (*fam*) edgy. **k~n** *vi* (*haben*) tingle; (*kitzeln*) tickle

krjech|en† *vi* (*sein*) crawl; (*fig*) grovel (**vor** + *dat* to). **k~erisch** *a* grovelling. **K~spur** *f* (*Auto*) crawler lane. **K~tier** *nt* reptile

Krjeg *m* -[e]s,-e war

krjegen *vt* (*fam*) get; **ein Kind k~** have a baby

Krjeger|denkmal *nt* war memorial. **k~isch** *a* warlike; (*militärisch*) military

krjegs|beschädigt *a* war-disabled. **K~dienstverweigerer** *m* -s,- conscientious objector. **K~gefangene(r)** *m* prisoner of war. **K~gefangenschaft** *f* captivity. **K~gericht** *nt* court martial. **K~list** *f* stratagem. **K~rat** *m* council of war. **K~recht** *nt* martial law. **K~schiff** *nt* warship. **K~verbrechen** *nt* war crime

Krjmi *m* -s,-s (*fam*) crime story/film. **K~nalität** *f* - crime; (*Vorkommen*) crime rate. **K~nalpolizei** *f* criminal investigation department. **K~nalroman** *m* crime novel. **k~nell** *a* criminal. **K~nelle(r)** *m* criminal

krjngeln (sich) *vr* curl [up]; (*vor Lachen*) fall about

Krjpo *f* - = Kriminalpolizei

Krjppe *f* -,-n manger; (*Weihnachts-*) crib; (*Kinder-*) crèche. **K~nspiel** *nt* Nativity play

Krjse *f* -,-n crisis

Kristall¹ *nt* -s (*Glas*) crystal; (*geschliffen*) cut glass

Kristall² *m* -s,-e crystal. **k~isjeren** *vi/r* (*haben*) [**sich**] **k~isieren** crystallize

Kritjerium *nt* -s,-ien criterion

Kritjk *f* -,-en criticism; (*Rezension*) review; **unter aller K~** (*fam*) abysmal

Kritj|ker *m* -s,- critic; (*Rezensent*) reviewer. **k~sch** *a* critical, *adv* -ly. **k~sjeren** *vt* criticize; review

krjtteln *vi* (*haben*) find fault (**an** + *acc* with)

krjtzeln *vt/i* (*haben*) scribble

Krokẹtte *f* -,-n (*Culin*) croquette

Krokodjl *nt* -s,-e crocodile

Krokus *m* -,-[se] crocus

Krone *f* -,-n crown; (*Baum-*) top

krönen *vt* crown

Kron|leuchter *m* chandelier. **K~prinz** *m* crown prince

Krönung *f* -,-en coronation; (*fig: Höhepunkt*) crowning event/(*Leistung*) achievement

Kropf *m* -[e]s,¨e (*Zool*) crop; (*Med*) goitre

Kröte *f* -,-n toad

Krücke *f* -,-n crutch; (*Stock-*) handle; **an K~n** on crutches

Krug *m* -[e]s,¨e jug; (*Bier-*) tankard

Krume *f* -,-n soft part [of loaf]; (*Krümel*) crumb; (*Acker-*) topsoil

Krümel *m* -s,- crumb. **k~ig** *a* crumbly. **k~n** *vt* crumble ● *vi* (*haben*) be crumbly; ⟨*Person:*⟩ drop crumbs

krumm *a* crooked; (*gebogen*) curved; (*verbogen*) bent. **k~beinig** *a* bow-legged

krümmen *vt* bend; crook ⟨*Finger*⟩; **sich k~** bend; (*sich winden*) writhe; (*vor Schmerzen/Lachen*) double up

krummnehmen† *vt sep* (*fam*) take amiss

Krümmung *f* -,-en bend; (*Kurve*) curve

Krüppel *m* -s,- cripple

Kruste *f* -,-n crust; (*Schorf*) scab

Kruzifix *nt* -es,-e crucifix

Krypta /'krypta/ *f* -,-ten crypt

Kub|a *nt* -s Cuba. **k~anisch** *a* Cuban

Kübel *m* -s,- tub; (*Eimer*) bucket; (*Techn*) skip

Kubik- *pref* cubic. **K~meter** *m* & *nt* cubic metre

Küche *f* -,-n kitchen; (*Kochkunst*) cooking; **kalte/warme K~** cold/hot food; **französische K~** French cuisine

Kuchen *m* -s,- cake

Küchen|herd *m* cooker, stove. **K~maschine** *f* food processor, mixer. **K~schabe** *f* -,-n cockroach. **K~zettel** *m* menu

Kuckuck *m* -s,-e cuckoo; **zum K∼!** (*fam*) hang it! **K∼suhr** *f* cuckoo clock

Kufe *f* -,-n [sledge] runner

Kugel *f* -,-n ball; (*Geom*) sphere; (*Gewehr-*) bullet; (*Sport*) shot. **k∼förmig** *a* spherical. **K∼lager** *nt* ball-bearing. **k∼n** *vt/i* (*haben*) roll; **sich k∼n** roll/ (*vor Lachen*) fall about. **k∼rund** *a* spherical; (*fam: dick*) tubby. **K∼schreiber** *m* -s,- ballpoint [pen]. **k∼sicher** *a* bullet-proof. **K∼stoßen** *nt* -s shot-putting

Kuh *f* -,ᵉe cow

kühl *a* cool, *adv* -ly; (*kalt*) chilly. **K∼box** *f* -,-en cool-box. **K∼e** *f* - coolness; chilliness. **k∼en** *vt* cool; refrigerate (*Lebensmittel*); chill (*Wein*). **K∼er** *m* -s,- ice-bucket; (*Auto*) radiator. **K∼erhaube** *f* bonnet, (*Amer*) hood. **K∼fach** *nt* frozen-food compartment. **K∼raum** *m* cold store. **K∼schrank** *m* refrigerator. **K∼truhe** *f* freezer. **K∼ung** *f* - cooling; (*Frische*) coolness. **K∼wasser** *nt* [radiator] water

Kuhmilch *f* cow's milk

kühn *a* bold, *adv* -ly; (*wagemutig*) daring. **K∼heit** *f* - boldness

Kuhstall *m* cowshed

Küken *nt* -s,- chick; (*Enten-*) duckling

Kukuruz *m* -[es] (*Aust*) maize

kulant *a* obliging

Kuli *m* -s,-s (*fam: Kugelschreiber*) ballpoint [pen], Biro (P)

kulinarisch *a* culinary

Kulissen *fpl* (*Theat*) scenery *sg*; (*seitlich*) wings; **hinter den K∼** (*fig*) behind the scenes

kullern *vt/i* (*sein*) (*fam*) roll

Kult *m* -[e]s,-e cult

kultivier|en *vt* cultivate. **k∼t** *a* cultured

Kultur *f* -,-en culture; **K∼en** plantations. **K∼beutel** *m* toilet-bag. **k∼ell** *a* cultural. **K∼film** *m* documentary film

Kultusminister *m* Minister of Education and Arts

Kümmel *m* -s caraway; (*Getränk*) kümmel

Kummer *m* -s sorrow, grief; (*Sorge*) worry; (*Ärger*) trouble

kümmer|lich *a* puny; (*dürftig*) meagre; (*armselig*) wretched. **k∼n** *vt* concern; **sich k∼n um** look after; (*sich befassen*) concern oneself with; (*beachten*) take notice of; **ich werde mich darum k∼n** I shall see to it; **k∼e dich um deine eigenen Angelegenheiten!** mind your own business!

kummervoll *a* sorrowful

Kumpel *m* -s,- (*fam*) mate

Kunde *m* -n,-n customer. **K∼ndienst** *m* [after-sales] service

Kund|gebung *f* -,-en (*Pol*) rally. **k∼ig** *a* knowledgeable; (*sach-*) expert

kündig|en *vt* cancel (*Vertrag*); give notice of withdrawal for (*Geld*); give notice to quit (*Wohnung*); **seine Stellung k∼en** give [in one's] notice ● *vi* (*haben*) give [in one's] notice; **jdm k∼en** give s.o. notice [of dismissal/ (*Vermieter:*) to quit]. **K∼ung** *f* -,-en cancellation; notice [of withdrawal/dismissal/to quit]; (*Entlassung*) dismissal. **K∼ungsfrist** *f* period of notice

Kund|in *f* -,-nen [woman] customer. **K∼machung** *f* -,-en (*Aust*) [public] notice. **K∼schaft** *f* - clientele, customers *pl*

künftig *a* future ● *adv* in future

Kunst *f* -,ᵉe art; (*Können*) skill. **K∼dünger** *m* artificial fertilizer. **K∼faser** *f* synthetic fibre. **k∼fertig** *a* skilful. **K∼fertigkeit** *f* skill. **K∼galerie** *f* art gallery. **k∼gerecht** *a* expert, *adv* -ly. **K∼geschichte** *f* history of art. **K∼gewerbe** *nt* arts and crafts *pl*. **K∼griff** *m* trick. **K∼händler** *m* art dealer

Künstler *m* -s,- artist; (*Könner*) master. **K∼in** *f* -,-nen [woman] artist. **k∼isch** *a* artistic, *adv* -ally. **K∼name** *m* pseudonym; (*Theat*) stage name

künstlich *a* artificial, *adv* -ly

kunst|los *a* simple. **K∼maler** *m* painter. **K∼stoff** *m* plastic. **K∼stopfen** *nt* invisible mending. **K∼stück** *nt* trick; (*große Leistung*) feat. **k∼voll** *a* artistic; (*geschickt*) skilful, *adv* -ly; (*kompliziert*) elaborate, *adv* -ly. **K∼werk** *nt* work of art

kunterbunt *a* multicoloured; (*gemischt*) mixed ● *adv* **k∼durcheinander** higgledy-piggledy

Kupfer *nt* -s copper. **k∼n** *a* copper

kupieren *vt* crop

Kupon /ku'põ:/ *m* -s,-s voucher; (*Zins-*) coupon; (*Stoff-*) length

Kuppe *f* -,-n [rounded] top; (*Finger-*) end, tip

Kuppel *f* -,-n dome

kupp|eln *vt* couple (**an**+ *acc* to) ● *vi* (*haben*) (*Auto*) operate the clutch. **K∼lung** *f* -,-en coupling; (*Auto*) clutch

Kur f -,-en course of treatment; (*im Kurort*) cure

Kür f -,-en (*Sport*) free exercise; (*Eislauf*) free programme

Kurbel f -,-n crank. **k~n** vt wind (**nach oben/unten** up/down). **K~welle** f crankshaft

Kürbis m -ses,-se pumpkin; (*Flaschen-*) marrow

Kurgast m health-resort visitor

Kurier m -s,-e courier

kurieren vt cure

kurios a curious, odd. **K~ität** f -,-en oddness; (*Objekt*) curiosity; (*Kunst*) curio

Kur|ort m health resort; (*Badeort*) spa. **K~pfuscher** m quack

Kurs m -es,-e course; (*Aktien-*) price. **K~buch** nt timetable

kursieren vi (haben) circulate

kursiv a italic ● adv in italics. **K~schrift** f italics pl

Kursus m -,**Kurse** course

Kurswagen m through carriage

Kurtaxe f visitors' tax

Kurve f -,-n curve; (*Straßen-*) bend

kurz a (**kürzer, kürzest**) short; (*knapp*) brief; (*rasch*) quick; (*schroff*) curt; **k~e Hosen** shorts; **vor k~em** a short time ago; **seit k~em** lately; **binnen k~em** shortly; **den kürzeren ziehen** get the worst of it ● adv briefly; quickly; curtly; **k~ vor/nach** a little way/(*zeitlich*) shortly before/after; **sich k~ fassen** be brief; **k~ und gut** in short; **über k~ oder lang** sooner or later; **zu k~ kommen** get less than one's fair share. **K~arbeit** f short-time working. **k~ärmelig** a short-sleeved. **k~atmig** a **k~atmig sein** be short of breath

Kürze f - shortness; (*Knappheit*) brevity; **in K~** shortly. **k~n** vt shorten; (*verringern*) cut

kurz|erhand adv without further ado. **k~fristig** a short-term ● adv at short notice. **K~geschichte** f short story. **k~lebig** a short-lived

kürzlich adv recently

Kurz|meldung f newsflash. **K~nachrichten** fpl news headlines. **K~schluß** m short circuit; (*fig*) brainstorm. **K~schrift** f shorthand. **k~sichtig** a short-sighted. **K~sichtigkeit** f - short-sightedness. **K~streckenrakete** f short-range missile. **k~um** adv in short

Kürzung f -,-en shortening; (*Verringerung*) cut (*gen* in)

Kurz|waren fpl haberdashery sg, (*Amer*) notions. **k~weilig** a amusing. **K~welle** f short wave

kuscheln (sich) vr snuggle (**an** + acc up to)

Kusine f -,-n [female] cousin

Kuß m -sses,-̈sse kiss

küssen vt/i (haben) kiss; **sich k~** kiss

Küste f -,-n coast. **K~nwache, K~nwacht** f coastguard

Küster m -s,- verger

Kustos m -,-oden /-'to:-/ curator

Kutsch|e f -,-n [horse-drawn] carriage/(*geschlossen*) coach. **K~er** m -s,- coachman, driver. **k~ieren** vt/i (haben) drive

Kutte f -,-n (*Relig*) habit

Kutter m -s,- (*Naut*) cutter

Kuvert /ku'veːɐ/ nt -s,-s envelope

KZ /kaː'tsɛt/ nt -[s],-[s] concentration camp

L

labil a unstable

Labo|r nt -s,-s & -e laboratory. **L~rant(in)** m -en,-en (f -,-nen) laboratory assistant. **L~ratorium** nt -s,-ien laboratory

Labyrinth nt -[e]s,-e maze, labyrinth

Lache f -,-n puddle; (*Blut-*) pool

lächeln vi (haben) smile. **L~** nt -s smile. **l~d** a smiling

lachen vi (haben) laugh. **L~** nt -s laugh; (*Gelächter*) laughter

lächerlich a ridiculous, adv -ly; **sich l~ machen** make a fool of oneself. **L~keit** f -,-en ridiculousness; (*Kleinigkeit*) triviality

lachhaft a laughable

Lachs m -es,-e salmon. **l~farben, l~rosa** a salmon-pink

Lack m -[e]s,-e varnish; (*Japan-*) lacquer; (*Auto*) paint. **l~en** vt varnish. **l~ieren** vt varnish; (*spritzen*) spray. **L~schuhe** mpl patent-leather shoes

Lade f -,-n drawer

laden† vt load; (*Electr*) charge; (*Jur: vor-*) summons

Laden m -s,-̈ shop, (*Amer*) store; (*Fenster-*) shutter. **L~dieb** m shoplifter. **L~diebstahl** m shop-lifting. **L~schluß** m [shop] closing-time. **L~tisch** m counter

Laderaum *m (Naut)* hold
lädieren *vt* damage
Ladung *f -,-en* load; *(Naut, Aviat)* cargo; *(elektrische, Spreng-)* charge; *(Jur: Vor-)* summons
Lage *f -,-n* position; *(Situation)* situation; *(Schicht)* layer; *(fam: Runde)* round; **nicht in der L~ sein** not be in a position **(zu** to)
Lager *nt -s,-* camp; *(L~haus)* warehouse; *(Vorrat)* stock; *(Techn)* bearing; *(Erz-, Ruhe-)* bed; *(eines Tieres)* lair; **[nicht] auf L~** [not] in stock. **L~haus** *nt* warehouse. **l~n** *vt* store; *(legen)* lay; **sich l~n** settle; *(sich legen)* lie down ● *vi (haben)* camp; *(liegen)* lie; ⟨*Waren*⟩ be stored. **L~raum** *m* storeroom. **L~stätte** *f (Geol)* deposit. **L~ung** *f* - storage
Lagune *f -,-n* lagoon
lahm *a* lame. **l~en** *vi (haben)* be lame
lähmen *vt* paralyse
lahmlegen *vt sep (fig)* paralyse
Lähmung *f -,-en* paralysis
Laib *m -[e]s,-e* loaf
Laich *m -[e]s (Zool)* spawn. **l~en** *vi (haben)* spawn
Laie *m -n,-n* layman; *(Theat)* amateur. **l~nhaft** *a* amateurish. **L~prediger** *m* lay preacher
Lake *f -,-n* brine
Laken *nt -s,-* sheet
lakonisch *a* laconic, *adv* -ally
Lakritze *f* - liquorice
lallen *vt/i (haben)* mumble; ⟨*Baby:*⟩ babble
Lametta *nt -s* tinsel
Lamm *nt -[e]s,¨er* lamb
Lampe *f -,-n* lamp; *(Decken-, Wand-)* light; *(Glüh-)* bulb. **L~nfieber** *nt* stage fright. **L~nschirm** *m* lampshade
Lampion /lam'pi̯oŋ/ *m -s,-s* Chinese lantern
lancieren /lã'si:rən/ *vt (Comm)* launch
Land *nt -[e]s,¨er* country; *(Fest-)* land; *(Bundes-)* state, Land; *(Aust)* province; **Stück L~** piece of land; **auf dem L~e** in the country; **an L~ gehen** *(Naut)* go ashore. **L~arbeiter** *m* agricultural worker. **L~ebahn** *f* runway. **l~einwärts** *adv* inland. **l~en** *vt/i (sein)* land; *(fam: gelangen)* end up
Ländereien *pl* estates
Länderspiel *nt* international
Landesteg *m* landing-stage
Landesverrat *m* treason

Land|karte *f* map. **l~läufig** *a* popular
ländlich *a* rural
Land|maschinen *fpl* agricultural machinery *sg*. **L~schaft** *f -,-en* scenery; *(Geog, Kunst)* landscape; *(Gegend)* country[side]. **l~schaftlich** *a* scenic; *(regional)* regional. **L~smann** *m (pl -leute)* fellow countryman, compatriot. **L~smännin** *f -,-nen* fellow countrywoman. **L~straße** *f* country road; *(Admin)* ≈ B road. **L~streicher** *m -s,-* tramp. **L~tag** *m* state/*(Aust)* provincial parliament
Landung *f -,-en* landing. **L~sbrücke** *f* landing-stage
Land|vermesser *m -s,-* surveyor. **L~weg** *m* country lane; **auf dem L~weg** overland. **L~wirt** *m* farmer. **L~wirtschaft** *f* agriculture; *(Hof)* farm. **l~wirtschaftlich** *a* agricultural
lang[1] *adv & prep* (+ *preceding acc or preceding* an + *dat*) along; **den** *od* **am Fluß l~** along the river
lang[2] *a* **(länger, längst)** long; *(groß)* tall; **seit l~em** for a long time ● *adv* **eine Stunde/Woche l~** for an hour/a week; **mein Leben l~** all my life. **l~ärmelig** *a* long-sleeved. **l~atmig** *a* long-winded. **l~e** *adv* a long time; ⟨*schlafen*⟩ late; **wie/zu l~e** how/too long; **schon l~e** [for] a long time; *(zurückliegend)* a long time ago; **l~e nicht** not for a long time; *(bei weitem nicht)* nowhere near
Länge *f -,-n* length; *(Geog)* longitude; **der L~ nach** lengthways; ⟨*liegen, fallen*⟩ full length
langen *vt* hand *(dat* to) ● *vi (haben)* reach **(an etw** *acc* sth; **nach** for); *(genügen)* be enough
Läng|engrad *m* degree of longitude. **L~enmaß** *nt* linear measure. **l~er** *a & adv* longer; *(längere Zeit)* [for] some time
Langeweile *f* - boredom; **L~ haben** be bored
lang|fristig *a* long-term; ⟨*Vorhersage*⟩ long-range. **l~jährig** *a* long-standing; ⟨*Erfahrung*⟩ long. **l~lebig** *a* long-lived
länglich *a* oblong. **l~rund** *a* oval
langmütig *a* long-suffering
längs *adv & prep* (+ *gen/dat*) along; *(der Länge nach)* lengthways
lang|sam *a* slow, *adv* -ly. **L~samkeit** *f* - slowness. **L~schläfer(in)** *m(f)*

(*fam*) late riser. **L~schrift** *f* longhand

längst *adv* [**schon**] I~ for a long time; (*zurückliegend*) a long time ago; I~ **nicht** nowhere near

Lang|strecken- *pref* long-distance; (*Mil, Aviat*) long-range. **I~weilen** *vt* bore; **sich I~weilen** be bored. **I~weilig** *a* boring, *adv* -ly. **L~welle** *f* long wave. **I~wierig** *a* lengthy

Lanze *f* -,-**n** lance

Lappalie /la'pa:liə/ *f* -,-**n** trifle

Lappen *m* -**s**,- cloth; (*Anat*) lobe

läppisch *a* silly

Lapsus *m* -,- slip

Lärche *f* -,-**n** larch

Lärm *m* -**s** noise. **I~en** *vi* (*haben*) make a noise. **I~end** *a* noisy

Larve /'larfə/ *f* -,-**n** larva; (*Maske*) mask

lasch *a* listless; (*schlaff*) limp; (*fade*) insipid

Lasche *f* -,-**n** tab; (*Verschluß-*) flap; (*Zunge*) tongue

Laser /'le:-, 'la:zɐ/ *m* -**s**,- laser

lassen† *vt* leave; (*zulassen*) let; **jdm etw I~** let s.o. keep sth; **sein Leben I~** lose one's life; **etw** [**sein** *od* **bleiben**] **I~** not do sth; (*aufhören*) stop [doing] sth; **laß das!** stop it! **jdn schlafen/ gewinnen I~** let s.o. sleep/win; **jdn warten I~** keep s.o. waiting; **etw machen/reparieren I~** have sth done/ repaired; **etw verschwinden I~** make sth disappear; **sich** [**leicht**] **biegen/ öffnen I~** bend/open [easily]; **sich gut waschen I~** wash well; **es läßt sich nicht leugnen** it is undeniable; **laßt uns gehen!** let's go!

lässig *a* casual, *adv* -ly. **L~keit** *f* - casualness

Lasso *nt* -**s**,-**s** lasso

Last *f* -,-**en** load; (*Gewicht*) weight; (*fig*) burden; **I~en** charges; (*Steuern*) taxes; **jdm zur L~ fallen** be a burden on s.o. **L~auto** *nt* lorry. **I~en** *vi* (*haben*) weigh heavily/(*liegen*) rest (**auf** + *dat* on). **L~enaufzug** *m* goods lift

Laster¹ *m* -**s**,- (*fam*) lorry, (*Amer*) truck

Laster² *nt* -**s**,- vice. **I~haft** *a* depraved; (*zügellos*) dissolute

läster|lich *a* blasphemous. **I~n** *vt* blaspheme ● *vi* (*haben*) make disparaging remarks (**über** + *acc* about). **L~ung** *f* -,-**en** blasphemy

lästig *a* troublesome; **I~ sein/ werden** be/become a nuisance

Last|kahn *m* barge. **L~[kraft]- wagen** *m* lorry, (*Amer*) truck. **L~- zug** *m* lorry with trailer[s]

Latein *nt* -[**s**] Latin. **L~amerika** *nt* Latin America. **I~isch** *a* Latin

latent *a* latent

Laterne *f* -,-**n** lantern; (*Straßen-*) street lamp. **L~npfahl** *m* lamp-post

latschen *vi* (*sein*) (*fam*) traipse; (*schlurfen*) shuffle

Latte *f* -,-**n** slat; (*Tor-, Hochsprung-*) bar

Latz *m* -**es**,ˆ**e** bib

Lätzchen *nt* -**s**,- [baby's] bib

Latzhose *f* dungarees *pl*

lau *a* lukewarm; (*mild*) mild

Laub *nt* -[**e**]**s** leaves *pl*; (*L~werk*) foliage. **L~baum** *m* deciduous tree

Laube *f* -,-**n** summer-house; (*gewachsen*) arbour. **L~ngang** *m* pergola; (*Archit*) arcades *pl*

Laub|säge *f* fretsaw. **L~wald** *m* deciduous forest

Lauch *m* -[**e**]**s** leeks *pl*

Lauer *f* **auf der L~ liegen** lie in wait. **I~n** *vi* (*haben*) lurk; **I~n auf** (+ *acc*) lie in wait for

Lauf *m* -[**e**]**s**, **Läufe** run; (*Laufen*) running; (*Verlauf*) course; (*Wett-*) race; (*Sport: Durchgang*) heat; (*Gewehr-*) barrel; **im L~[e]** (+ *gen*) in the course of. **L~bahn** *f* career. **I~en†** *vi* (*sein*) run; (*zu Fuß gehen*) walk; (*gelten*) be valid; **Ski/Schlittschuh I~en** ski/ skate. **I~end** *a* running; (*gegenwärtig*) current; (*regelmäßig*) regular; **I~ende Nummer** serial number; **auf dem I~enden sein/jdn auf dem I~enden halten** be/keep s.o. up to date ● *adv* continually. **I~enlassen†** *vt sep* (*fam*) let go

Läufer *m* -**s**,- (*Person, Teppich*) runner; (*Schach*) bishop

Lauf|gitter *nt* play-pen. **L~masche** *f* ladder. **L~rolle** *f* castor. **L~schritt** *m* **im L~schritt** at a run; (*Mil*) at the double. **L~stall** *m* play-pen. **L~- zettel** *m* circular

Lauge *f* -,-**n** soapy water

Laun|e *f* -,-**n** mood; (*Einfall*) whim; **guter L~e sein, gute L~e haben** be in a good mood. **L~enhaft** *a* capricious. **I~isch** *a* moody

Laus *f* -, **Läuse** louse; (*Blatt-*) greenfly. **L~bub** *m* (*fam*) rascal

lauschen *vi* (*haben*) listen; (*heimlich*) eavesdrop

lausig *a* (*fam*) lousy ● *adv* terribly

laut a loud, adv -ly; (geräuschvoll) noisy, adv -ily; l~ **lesen** read aloud; l~**er stellen** turn up ● prep (+gen/dat) according to. **L~** m -es,-e sound

Laute f -,-n (Mus) lute

lauten vi (haben) ⟨Text:⟩ run, read; **auf jds Namen** l~ be in s.o.'s name

läuten vt/i (haben) ring

lauter a pure; (ehrlich) honest; ⟨Wahrheit⟩ plain ● a inv sheer; (nichts als) nothing but. **L~keit** f - integrity

läutern vt purify

laut|hals adv at the top of one's voice; (lachen) out loud. **l~los** a silent, adv -ly; ⟨Stille⟩ hushed. **L~schrift** f phonetics pl. **L~sprecher** m loudspeaker. **l~stark** a vociferous, adv -ly. **L~stärke** f volume

lauwarm a lukewarm

Lava f -,-ven lava

Lavendel m -s lavender

lavieren vi (haben) manœuvre

Lawine f -,-n avalanche

lax a lax. **L~heit** f - laxity

Lazarett nt -[e]s,-e military hospital

leasen /'li:sən/ vt rent

Lebehoch nt cheer

leben vt/i (haben) live (**von** on); **leb wohl!** farewell! **L~** nt -s,- life; (Treiben) bustle; **am L~** alive. **l~d** a living

lebendig a live; (lebhaft) lively; (anschaulich) vivid, adv -ly; l~ **sein** be alive. **L~keit** f - liveliness; vividness

Lebens|abend m old age. **L~alter** nt age. **L~art** f manners pl. **l~fähig** a viable. **L~gefahr** f mortal danger; **in L~gefahr** in mortal danger; ⟨Patient⟩ critically ill. **l~gefährlich** a extremely dangerous; ⟨Verletzung⟩ critical ● adv critically. **L~größe** f **in L~größe** life-sized. **L~haltungskosten** pl cost of living sg. **l~lang** a lifelong. **l~länglich** a life ... ● adv for life. **L~lauf** m curriculum vitae. **L~mittel** ntpl food sg. **L~mittelgeschäft** nt food shop. **L~mittelhändler** m grocer. **l~notwendig** a vital. **L~retter** m rescuer; (beim Schwimmen) life-guard. **L~standard** m standard of living. **L~unterhalt** m livelihood; **seinen L~unterhalt verdienen** earn one's living. **L~versicherung** f life assurance. **L~wandel** m conduct. **l~wichtig** a vital. **L~zeichen** nt sign of life. **L~zeit** f **auf L~zeit** for life

Leber f -,-n liver. **L~fleck** m mole. **L~wurst** f liver sausage

Lebe|wesen nt living being. **L~wohl** nt -s,-s & -e farewell

leb|haft a lively; ⟨Farbe⟩ vivid. **L~haftigkeit** f - liveliness. **L~kuchen** m gingerbread. **l~los** a lifeless. **L~tag** m **mein/dein L~tag** all my/your life. **L~zeiten** fpl **zu jds L~zeiten** in s.o.'s lifetime

leck a leaking. **L~** nt -s,-s leak. **l~en**[1] vi (haben) leak

lecken[2] vt/i (haben) lick

lecker a tasty. **L~ bissen** m delicacy. **L~ei** f -,-en sweet

Leder nt -s,- leather. **l~n** a leather; (wie Leder) leathery

ledig a single. **l~lich** adv merely

Lee f & nt - **nach Lee** (Naut) to leeward

leer a empty; (unbesetzt) vacant; l~ **laufen** (Auto) idle. **L~e** f - emptiness; (leerer Raum) void. **l~en** vt empty; **sich l~en** empty. **L~lauf** m (Auto) neutral. **L~ung** f -,-en (Post) collection

legal a legal, adv -ly. **l~isieren** vt legalize. **L~ität** f - legality

Legas|thenie f - dyslexia. **L~theniker** m -s,- dyslexic

legen vt put; (hin-, ver-) lay; set ⟨Haare⟩; **Eier l~** lay eggs; **sich l~** lie down; ⟨Staub:⟩ settle; (nachlassen) subside

legendär a legendary

Legende f -,-en legend

leger /le'ʒe:ɐ̯/ a casual, adv -ly

legier|en vt alloy; (Culin) thicken. **L~ung** f -,-en alloy

Legion f -,-en legion

Legislative f - legislature

legitim a legitimate, adv -ly. **l~ieren (sich)** vr prove one's identity. **L~ität** f - legitimacy

Lehm m -s clay. **l~ig** a clayey

Lehn|e f -,-n (Rücken-) back; (Arm-) arm. **l~en** vt lean (**an** + acc against); **sich l~en** lean (**an** + acc against) ● vi (haben) be leaning (**an** + acc against). **L~sessel, L~stuhl** m armchair

Lehr|buch nt textbook. **L~e** f -,-n apprenticeship; (Anschauung) doctrine; (Theorie) theory; (Wissenschaft) science; (Ratschlag) advice; (Erfahrung) lesson; **jdm eine L~e erteilen** (fig) teach s.o. a lesson. **l~en** vt/i (haben) teach. **L~er** m -s,- teacher; (Fahr-, Ski-) instructor. **L~erin** f -, -nen teacher. **L~erzimmer** nt

staff-room. L~**fach** *nt (Sch)* subject.
L~**gang** *m* course. L~**kraft** *f*
teacher. L~**ling** *m* -s,-e apprentice;
(Auszubildender) trainee. L~**plan** *m*
syllabus. L~**reich** *a* instructive. L~
stelle *f* apprenticeship. L~**stuhl** *m*
(Univ) chair. L~**zeit** *f*
apprenticeship

Leib *m* -es,-er body; *(Bauch)* belly.
L~**eserziehung** *f (Sch)* physical
education. L~**eskraft** *f* aus L~**es-
kräften** as hard/*(schreien)* loud as one
can. L~**gericht** *nt* favourite dish. l~
haftig *a* der l~**haftige** Satan the
devil incarnate ● *adv* in the flesh. l~
lich *a* physical; *(blutsverwandt)* real,
natural. L~**speise** *f* = L~**gericht**.
L~**wache** *f (coll)* bodyguard. L~
wächter *m* bodyguard. L~**wäsche** *f*
underwear

Leiche *f* -,-n [dead] body; corpse.
L~**nbegängnis** *nt* -ses,-se funeral.
L~**nbestatter** *m* -s,- undertaker.
l~**nblaß** *a* deathly pale. L~**nhalle** *f*
mortuary. L~**nwagen** *m* hearse.
L~**nzug** *m* funeral procession, cortège

Leichnam *m* -s,-e [dead] body

leicht *a* light, *adv* -ly; *(Stoff, Anzug)*
lightweight; *(gering)* slight, *adv* -ly;
(mühelos) easy, *adv* -ily. L~**athletik** *f*
[track and field] athletics *sg.* l~
fallen† *vi sep (sein)* be easy *(dat* for).
l~**fertig** *a* thoughtless, *adv* -ly;
(vorschnell) rash, *adv* -ly; *(frivol)*
frivolous, *adv* -ly. L~**gewicht** *nt*
(Boxen) lightweight. l~**gläubig** *a*
gullible. l~**hin** *adv* casually. L~**igkeit** *f* - lightness; *(Mühelosigkeit)* ease;
(L~sein) easiness; **mit L~igkeit** with
ease. l~**lebig** *a* happy-go-lucky. l~
machen *vt sep* make easy *(dat* for); **es
sich** *(dat)* l~**machen** take the easy way
out. l~**nehmen†** *vt sep (fig)* take
lightly. L~**sinn** *m* carelessness; reck-
lessness; *(Frivolität)* frivolity. l~
sinnig *a* careless, *adv* -ly;
(unvorsichtig) reckless, *adv* -ly;
(frivol) frivolous, *adv* -ly

Leid *nt* -[e]s sorrow, grief; *(Böses)*
harm. l~ *a* jdn/etw l~ **sein/werden**
be/get tired of s.o./sth; **es tut mir** l~ I
am sorry; **er tut mir** l~ I feel sorry for
him

Leide|form *f* passive. l~**n†** *vt/i*
(haben) suffer **(an**+*dat* from); **jdn
[gut]** l~**n können** like s.o.; **jdn/etw
nicht** l~**n können** dislike s.o./sth.

L~**n** *nt* -s,- suffering; *(Med)* complaint;
(Krankheit) disease. l~**nd** *a* suffering;
l~**nd sein** be in poor health. L~**n-
schaft** *f* -,-en passion. l~**nschaftlich**
a passionate, *adv* -ly

leid|er *adv* unfortunately; l~**er ja/
nicht** I'm afraid so/not. l~**ig** *a*
wretched. l~**lich** *a* tolerable, *adv*
-bly. L~**tragende(r)** *m/f* person who
suffers; *(Trauernde)* mourner. L~
wesen *nt* **zu meinem** L~**wesen** to my
regret

Leier *f* -,-n **die alte** L~ *(fam)* the same
old story. L~**kasten** *m* barrel-organ.
l~**n** *vt/i (haben)* wind; *(herunter-)*
drone out

Leih|bibliothek, L~**bücherei** *f*
lending library. L~**e** *f* -,-n loan.
l~**en†** *vt* lend; **sich** *(dat)* **etw** l~**en**
borrow sth. L~**gabe** *f* loan. L~**ge-
bühr** *f* rental; *(für Bücher)* lending
charge. L~**haus** *nt* pawnshop. L~
wagen *m* hire-car. l~**weise** *adv* on
loan

Leim *m* -s glue. l~**en** *vt* glue

Leine *f* -,-n rope; *(Wäsche-)* line;
(Hunde-) lead, leash

Lein|en *nt* -s linen. l~**en** *a* linen. L~
tuch *nt* sheet. L~**wand** *f* linen;
(Kunst) canvas; *(Film-)* screen

leise *a* quiet, *adv* -ly; *(Stimme, Musik,
Berührung)* soft, *adv* -ly; *(schwach)*
faint, *adv* -ly; *(leicht)* light, *adv* -ly;
l~**r stellen** turn down

Leiste *f* -,-n strip; *(Holz-)* batten; *(Zier-)*
moulding; *(Anat)* groin

Leisten *m* -s,- [shoemaker's] last

leist|en *vt* achieve, accomplish; **sich**
(dat) **etw** l~**en** treat oneself to sth;
(fam: anstellen) get up to sth; **ich kann
es mir nicht** l~**en** I can't afford it.
L~**ung** *f* -,-en achievement; *(Sport,
Techn)* performance; *(Produktion)* output; *(Zahlung)* payment. l~**ungs-
fähig** *a* efficient. L~**ungsfähigkeit**
f efficiency

Leit|artikel *m* leader, editorial. L~
bild *nt (fig)* model. l~**en** *vt* run,
manage; *(an-/hinführen)* lead; *(Mus,
Techn, Phys)* conduct; *(lenken,
schicken)* direct. l~**end** *a* leading;
(Posten) executive

Leiter [1] *f* -,-n ladder

Leit|er [2] *m* -s,- director; *(Comm)* man-
ager; *(Führer)* leader; *(Sch)* head; *(Mus,
Phys)* conductor. L~**erin** *f* -,-nen
director; manageress; leader; head.
L~**faden** *m* manual. L~**kegel** *m*

[traffic] cone. L∼**planke** f crash barrier. L∼**spruch** m motto. L∼**ung** f -,-en (Führung) direction; (Comm) management; (Aufsicht) control; (Electr: Schnur) lead, flex; (Kabel) cable; (Telefon-) line; (Rohr-) pipe; (Haupt-) main. L∼**ungswasser** nt tap water

Lektion /-'tsjo:n/ f -,-en lesson

Lekt|or m -s,-en /-'to:rən/, L∼**orin** f -,-nen (Univ) assistant lecturer; (Verlags-) editor. L∼**üre** f -,-n reading matter; (Lesen) reading

Lende f -,-n loin

lenk|bar a steerable; (fügsam) tractable. l∼en vt guide; (steuern) steer; (Aust) drive; (regeln) control; **jds Aufmerksamkeit auf sich** (acc) l∼**en** attract s.o.'s attention. L∼**er** m -s,- driver; (L∼stange) handlebars pl. L∼**rad** nt steering-wheel. L∼**stange** f handlebars pl. L∼**ung** f - steering

Leopard m -en,-en leopard

Lepra f - leprosy

Lerche f -,-n lark

lernen vt/i (haben) learn; (für die Schule) study; **schwimmen l**∼ learn to swim

lesbar a readable; (leserlich) legible

Lesb|ierin /'lɛsbjərm/ f -,-nen lesbian. l∼**isch** a lesbian

Lese f -n harvest. L∼**buch** nt reader. l∼**n**† vt/i (haben) read; (Univ) lecture ● vt pick, gather. L∼**n** nt -s reading. L∼**r(in)** m -s,- (f -,-nen) reader. L∼**ratte** f (fam) bookworm. l∼**rlich** a legible, adv -bly. L∼**zeichen** nt bookmark

Lesung f -,-en reading

lethargisch a lethargic, adv -ally

Lettland nt -s Latvia

letzt|e(r,s) a last; (neueste) latest; **in** l∼**er Zeit** recently; l∼**en Endes** in the end. l∼**emal** adv **das** l∼**emal** the last time; **zum** l∼**enmal** for the last time. l∼**ens** adv recently; (zuletzt) lastly. l∼**ere(r,s)** a the latter; **der/die/das** l∼**ere** the latter

Leucht|e f -,-n light. l∼**en** vi (haben) shine. l∼**end** a shining. L∼**er** m -s,- candlestick. L∼**feuer** nt beacon. L∼**kugel**, L∼**rakete** f flare. L∼**reklame** f neon sign. L∼**[stoff]röhre** f fluorescent tube. L∼**turm** m lighthouse. L∼**zifferblatt** nt luminous dial

leugnen vt deny

Leukämie f - leukaemia

Leumund m -s reputation

Leute pl people; (Mil) men; (Arbeiter) workers

Leutnant m -s,-s second lieutenant

leutselig a affable, adv -bly

Levkoje /lɛf'ko:jə/ f -,-n stock

Lexikon nt -s,-ka encyclopaedia; (Wörterbuch) dictionary

Libanon (der) -s Lebanon

Libelle f -,-n dragonfly; (Techn) spirit-level; (Haarspange) slide

liberal a (Pol) Liberal

Libyen nt -s Libya

Licht nt -[e]s,-er light; (Kerze) candle; L∼ **machen** turn on the light; **hinters** L∼ **führen** (fam) dupe. l∼ a bright; (Med) lucid; (spärlich) sparse. L∼**bild** nt [passport] photograph; (Dia) slide. L∼**bildervortrag** m slide lecture. L∼**blick** m (fig) ray of hope. l∼**en** vt thin out; **den Anker** l∼**en** (Naut) weigh anchor; **sich** l∼**en** become less dense; (Haare;) thin. L∼**hupe** f headlight flasher; **die** L∼**hupe betätigen** flash one's headlights. L∼**maschine** f dynamo. L∼**schalter** m light-switch. L∼**ung** f -,-en clearing

Lid nt -[e]s,-er [eye]lid. L∼**schatten** m eye-shadow

lieb a dear; (nett) nice; (artig) good; **es ist mir** l∼ I'm glad (**daß** that); **es wäre mir** l∼**er** I should prefer it (**wenn** if). l∼**äugeln** vi (haben) l∼**äugeln mit** fancy; toy with (Gedanken)

Liebe f -,-n love. L∼**lei** f -,-en flirtation. l∼**n** vt love; (mögen) like; **sich** l∼**n** love each other; (körperlich) make love. l∼**nd** a loving ● adv **etw** l∼**nd gern tun** love to do sth. l∼**nswert** a lovable. l∼**nswürdig** a kind. l∼**nswürdigerweise** adv very kindly. L∼**nswürdigkeit** f -,-en kindness

lieber adv rather; (besser) better; l∼ **mögen** like better; **ich trinke** l∼ **Tee** I prefer tea

Liebes|brief m love letter. L∼**dienst** m favour. L∼**geschichte** f love story. L∼**kummer** m heartache; L∼**kummer haben** be depressed over an unhappy love-affair. L∼**paar** nt [pair of] lovers pl

lieb|evoll a loving, adv -ly; (zärtlich) affectionate, adv -ly. l∼**gewinnen**† vt sep grow fond of. l∼**haben**† vt sep be fond of; (lieben) love. L∼**haber** m

-s,- lover; (*Sammler*) collector. **L∼haberei** *f* **-,-en** hobby. **l∼kosen** *vt* caress. **L∼kosung** *f* **-,-en** caress. **l∼lich** *a* lovely; (*sanft*) gentle; (*süß*) sweet. **L∼ling** *m* **-s,-e** darling; (*Bevorzugte*) favourite. **L∼lings-** *pref* favourite. **l∼los** *a* loveless; (*Eltern*) uncaring; (*unfreundlich*) unkind ● *adv* unkindly; (*ohne Sorgfalt*) without care. **L∼schaft** *f* **-,-en** [love] affair. **l∼ste(r,s)** *a* dearest; (*bevorzugt*) favourite ● *adv* **am l∼sten** best [of all]; **jdn/etw am l∼sten mögen** like s.o./sth best [of all]; **ich hätte am l∼sten geweint** I felt like crying. **L∼ste(r)** *m/f* beloved; (*Schatz*) sweetheart

Lied *nt* **-[e]s,-er** song

liederlich *a* slovenly; (*unordentlich*) untidy; (*ausschweifend*) dissolute. **L∼keit** *f* **-** slovenliness; untidiness; dissoluteness

Lieferant *m* **-en,-en** supplier

liefer|bar *a* (*Comm*) available. **l∼n** *vt* supply; (*zustellen*) deliver; (*hervorbringen*) yield. **L∼ung** *f* **-,-en** delivery; (*Sendung*) consignment; (*per Schiff*) shipment. **L∼wagen** *m* delivery van

Liege *f* **-,-n** couch. **l∼n†** *vi* (*haben*) lie; (*gelegen sein*) be situated; **l∼n an** (+ *dat*) (*fig*) be due to; (*abhängen*) depend on; **jdm [nicht] l∼n** [not] suit s.o.; (*ansprechen*) [not] appeal to s.o.; **mir liegt viel/nicht daran** it is very/not important to me. **l∼nbleiben†** *vi sep* (*sein*) remain lying [there]; (*im Bett*) stay in bed; ⟨*Ding:*⟩ be left; ⟨*Schnee:*⟩ settle; ⟨*Arbeit:*⟩ remain undone; (*zurückgelassen werden*) be left behind; (*Panne haben*) break down. **l∼nlassen†** *vt sep* leave lying [there]; (*zurücklassen*) leave behind; (*nicht fortführen*) leave undone. **L∼sitz** *m* reclining seat. **L∼stuhl** *m* deck-chair. **L∼stütz** *m* **-es,-e** press-up, (*Amer*) push-up. **L∼wagen** *m* couchette car. **L∼wiese** *f* lawn for sunbathing

Lift *m* **-[e]s,-e** & **-s** lift, (*Amer*) elevator

Liga *f* **-,-gen** league

Likör *m* **-s,-e** liqueur

lila *inv a* mauve; (*dunkel*) purple

Lilie /'li:liə/ *f* **-,-n** lily

Liliputaner(in) *m* **-s,-** (*f* **-,-nen**) dwarf

Limo *f* **-,-[s]** (*fam*), **L∼nade** *f* **-,-n** fizzy drink, (*Amer*) soda; (*Zitronen-*) lemonade

Limousine /limu'zi:nə/ *f* **-,-n** saloon, (*Amer*) sedan; (*mit Trennscheibe*) limousine

lind *a* mild; (*sanft*) gentle

Linde *f* **-,-n** lime tree

linder|n *vt* relieve, ease. **L∼ung** *f* **-** relief

Line|al *nt* **-s,-e** ruler. **l∼ar** *a* linear

Linguistik *f* **-** linguistics *sg*

Linie /-iə/ *f* **-,-n** line; (*Zweig*) branch; (*Bus-*) route; **L∼ 4** number 4 [bus/tram]; **in erster L∼** primarily. **L∼nflug** *m* scheduled flight. **L∼nrichter** *m* linesman

lin[i]iert *a* lined, ruled

Link|e *f* **-n,-n** left side; (*Hand*) left hand; (*Boxen*) left; **die L∼e** (*Pol*) the left; **zu meiner L∼en** on my left. **l∼e(r, s)** *a* left; (*Pol*) left-wing; **l∼e Seite** left[-hand] side; (*von Stoff*) wrong side; **l∼e Masche** purl. **l∼isch** *a* awkward, *adv* -ly

links *adv* on the left; (*bei Stoff*) on the wrong side; (*verkehrt*) inside out; **von/nach l∼** from/to the left; **l∼ stricken** purl. **L∼händer(in)** *m* **-s,-** (*f* **-,-nen**) left-hander. **l∼händig** *a* & *adv* left-handed. **L∼verkehr** *m* driving on the left

Linoleum /-leʊm/ *nt* **-s** lino[leum]

Linse *f* **-,-n** lens; (*Bot*) lentil

Lippe *f* **-,-n** lip. **L∼nstift** *m* lipstick

Liquid|ation /-'tsio:n/ *f* **-,-en** liquidation. **l∼ieren** *vt* liquidate

lispeln *vt/i* (*haben*) lisp

List *f* **-,-en** trick, ruse; (*Listigkeit*) cunning

Liste *f* **-,-n** list

listig *a* cunning, crafty

Litanei *f* **-,-en** litany

Litauen *nt* **-s** Lithuania

Liter *m* & *nt* **-s,-** litre

liter|arisch *a* literary. **L∼atur** *f* **-** literature

Litfaßsäule *f* advertising pillar

Liturgie *f* **-,-n** liturgy

Litze *f* **-,-n** braid; (*Electr*) flex

live /laif/ *adv* (*Radio, TV*) live

Lizenz *f* **-,-en** licence

Lkw /εlka've:/ *m* **-[s],-s** = **Lastkraftwagen**

Lob *nt* **-[e]s** praise

Lobby /'lɔbi/ *f* **-** (*Pol*) lobby

loben *vt* praise. **l∼swert** *a* praiseworthy, laudable

löblich *a* praiseworthy

Lobrede *f* eulogy

Loch *nt* -[e]s, ¨er hole. **l~en** *vt* punch a hole/holes in; punch ⟨*Fahrkarte*⟩. **L~er** *m* -s,- punch

löcher|ig *a* full of holes. **l~n** *vt* (*fam*) pester

Locke *f* -,-n curl. **l~n**[1] *vt* curl; **sich l~n** curl

locken[2] *vt* lure, entice; (*reizen*) tempt. **l~d** *a* tempting

Lockenwickler *m* -s,- curler; (*Rolle*) roller

locker *a* loose, *adv* -ly; ⟨*Seil*⟩ slack; ⟨*Erde, Kuchen*⟩ light; (*zwanglos*) casual; (*zu frei*) lax; (*unmoralisch*) loose. **l~n** *vt* loosen; slacken ⟨*Seil, Zügel*⟩; break up ⟨*Boden*⟩; relax ⟨*Griff*⟩; **sich l~n** become loose; ⟨*Seil:*⟩ slacken; (*sich entspannen*) relax. **L~ungsübungen** *fpl* limbering-up exercises

lockig *a* curly

Lock|mittel *nt* bait. **L~ung** *f* -,-en lure; (*Versuchung*) temptation. **L~vogel** *m* decoy

Loden *m* -s (*Tex*) loden

lodern *vi* (*haben*) blaze

Löffel *m* -s,- spoon; (*L~voll*) spoonful. **l~n** *vt* spoon up

Logarithmus *m* -,-men logarithm

Logbuch *nt* (*Naut*) log-book

Loge /'lo:ʒə/ *f* -,-n lodge; (*Theat*) box

Logierbesuch /lo'ʒi:ɐ̯-/ *m* house guest/guests *pl*

Log|ik *f* - logic. **l~isch** *a* logical, *adv* -ly

Logo *nt* -s,-s logo

Lohn *m* -[e]s, ¨e wages *pl*, pay; (*fig*) reward. **L~empfänger** *m* wage-earner. **l~en** *vi/r* (*haben*) [sich] **l~en** be worth it *or* worth while ● *vt* be worth; **jdm etw l~en** reward s.o. for sth. **l~end** *a* worthwhile; (*befriedigend*) rewarding. **L~erhöhung** *f* [pay] rise; (*Amer*) raise. **L~steuer** *f* income tax

Lok *f* -,-s (*fam*) = **Lokomotive**

Lokal *nt* -s,-e restaurant; (*Trink-*) bar. **l~** *a* local. **l~isieren** *vt* locate; (*begrenzen*) localize

Lokomotiv|e *f* -,-n engine, locomotive. **L~führer** *m* engine driver

London *nt* -s London. **L~er** *a* London ... ● *m* -s,- Londoner

Lorbeer *m* -s,-en laurel; **echter L~** bay. **L~blatt** *nt* (*Culin*) bay-leaf

Lore *f* -,-n (*Rail*) truck

Los *nt* -es,-e lot; (*Lotterie-*) ticket; (*Schicksal*) fate; **das Große Los ziehen** hit the jackpot

los *pred a* **los sein** be loose; **jdn/etw los sein** be rid of s.o./sth; **was ist [mit ihm] los?** what's the matter [with him]? ● *adv* **los!** go on! **Achtung, fertig, los!** ready, steady, go!

lösbar *a* soluble

losbinden† *vt sep* untie

Lösch|blatt *nt* sheet of blotting-paper. **l~en**[1] *vt* put out, extinguish; quench ⟨*Durst*⟩; blot ⟨*Tinte*⟩; (*tilgen*) cancel; (*streichen*) delete; erase ⟨*Aufnahme*⟩

löschen[2] *vt* (*Naut*) unload

Lösch|fahrzeug *nt* fire-engine. **L~gerät** *nt* fire extinguisher. **L~papier** *nt* blotting-paper

lose *a* loose, *adv* -ly

Lösegeld *nt* ransom

losen *vi* (*haben*) draw lots (**um** for)

lösen *vt* undo; (*lockern*) loosen; (*entfernen*) detach; (*klären*) solve; (*auflösen*) dissolve; cancel ⟨*Vertrag*⟩; break off ⟨*Beziehung, Verlobung*⟩; (*kaufen*) buy; **sich l~** come off; (*sich trennen*) detach oneself/itself; (*lose werden*) come undone; (*sich entspannen*) relax; (*sich klären*) resolve itself; (*sich auflösen*) dissolve

los|fahren† *vi sep* (*sein*) start; ⟨*Auto:*⟩ drive off; **l~fahren auf** (+ *acc*) head for; (*fig: angreifen*) go for. **l~gehen**† *vi sep* (*sein*) set off; (*fam: anfangen*) start; (*fam: abgehen*) come off; ⟨*Bombe, Gewehr:*⟩ go off; **l~gehen auf** (+ *acc*) head for; (*fig: angreifen*) go for. **l~kommen**† *vi sep* (*sein*) get away (**von** from); **l~kommen auf** (+ *acc*) come towards. **l~lachen** *vi sep* (*haben*) burst out laughing. **l~lassen**† *vt sep* let go of; (*freilassen*) release

löslich *a* soluble

los|lösen *vt sep* detach; **sich l~lösen** become detached; (*fig*) break away (**von** from). **l~machen** *vt sep* detach; (*losbinden*) untie; **sich l~machen** free oneself/itself. **l~platzen** *vi sep* (*sein*) (*fam*) burst out laughing. **l~reißen**† *vt sep* tear off; **sich l~reißen** break free; (*fig*) tear oneself away. **l~sagen** (**sich**) *vr sep* renounce (**von etw** sth). **l~schicken** *vt sep* send off. **l~sprechen**† *vt sep* absolve (**von** from). **l~steuern** *vi sep* (*sein*) head (**auf** + *acc* for)

Losung *f* -,-en (*Pol*) slogan; (*Mil*) password

Lösung *f* -,-en solution. **L~smittel** *nt* solvent

los|werden† vt sep get rid of. **l~ziehen†** vi sep (sein) set off; **l~ziehen gegen** od **über** (+ acc) (beschimpfen) run down

Lot nt -[e]s,-e perpendicular; (Blei-) plumb[-bob]; **im Lot sein** (fig) be all right. **l~en** vt plumb

löt|en vt solder. **L~lampe** f blowlamp, (Amer) blowtorch. **L~metall** nt solder

lotrecht a perpendicular, adv -ly

Lotse m -n,-n (Naut) pilot. **l~n** vt (Naut) pilot; (fig) guide

Lotterie f -,-n lottery

Lotto nt -s,-s lotto; (Lotterie) lottery

Löw|e m -n,-n lion; (Astr) Leo. **L~enanteil** m (fig) lion's share. **L~enzahn** m (Bot) dandelion. **L~in** f -,-nen lioness

loyal /loa'ja:l/ a loyal. **L~ität** f - loyalty

Luchs m -es,-e lynx

Lücke f -,-n gap. **L~nbüßer** m -s,- stopgap. **l~nhaft** a incomplete; ⟨Wissen⟩ patchy. **l~nlos** a complete; ⟨Folge⟩ unbroken

Luder nt -s,- (sl) (Frau) bitch; **armes L~** poor wretch

Luft f -,"e air; **tief L~ holen** take a deep breath; **in die L~ gehen** explode. **L~angriff** m air raid. **L~aufnahme** f aerial photograph. **L~ballon** m balloon. **L~bild** nt aerial photograph. **L~blase** f air bubble

Lüftchen nt -s,- breeze

luft|dicht a airtight. **L~druck** m atmospheric pressure

lüften vt air; raise ⟨Hut⟩; reveal ⟨Geheimnis⟩

Luft|fahrt f aviation. **L~fahrtgesellschaft** f airline. **L~gewehr** nt airgun. **L~hauch** m breath of air. **l~ig** a airy; ⟨Kleid⟩ light. **L~kissenfahrzeug** nt hovercraft. **L~krieg** m aerial warfare. **L~kurort** m climatic health resort. **l~leer** a **l~leerer Raum** vacuum. **L~linie** f **100 km L~linie** 100 km as the crow flies. **L~loch** nt air-hole; (Aviat) air pocket. **L~matratze** f air-bed, inflatable mattress. **L~pirat** m [aircraft] hijacker. **L~post** f airmail. **L~pumpe** f air pump; (Fahrrad-) bicycle-pump. **L~röhre** f windpipe. **L~schiff** nt airship. **L~schlange** f [paper] streamer. **L~schlösser** ntpl castles in the air. **L~schutzbunker** m air-raid shelter

Lüftung f - ventilation

Luft|veränderung f change of air. **L~waffe** f air force. **L~weg** m **auf dem L~weg** by air. **L~zug** m draught

Lüg|e f -,-n lie. **l~en†** vt/i (haben) lie. **L~ner(in)** m -s,- (f -,-nen) liar. **l~nerisch** a untrue; ⟨Person⟩ untruthful

Luke f -,-n hatch; (Dach-) skylight

Lümmel m -s,- lout; (fam: Schelm) rascal. **l~n (sich)** vr loll

Lump m -en,-en scoundrel. **L~en** m -s,- rag; **in L~en** in rags. **l~en** vt **sich nicht l~en lassen** be generous. **L~engesindel, L~enpack** nt riff-raff. **L~ensammler** m rag-and-bone man. **l~ig** a mean, shabby; (gering) measly

Lunchpaket /'lan[t]ʃ-/ nt packed lunch

Lunge f -,-n lungs pl; (L~nflügel) lung. **L~nentzündung** f pneumonia

lungern vi (haben) loiter

Lunte f **L~ riechen** (fam) smell a rat

Lupe f -,-n magnifying glass

Lurch m -[e]s,-e amphibian

Lust f -,"e pleasure; (Verlangen) desire; (sinnliche Begierde) lust; **L~ haben** feel like (**auf etw** acc sth); **ich habe keine L~** I don't feel like it; (will nicht) I don't want to

Lüster m -s,- lustre; (Kronleuchter) chandelier

lüstern a greedy (**auf** + acc for); (sinnlich) lascivious; (geil) lecherous

lustig a jolly; (komisch) funny; **sich l~ machen über** (+ acc) make fun of

Lüstling m -s,-e lecher

lust|los a listless, adv -ly. **L~mörder** m sex killer. **L~spiel** nt comedy

lutherisch a Lutheran

lutsch|en vt/i (haben) suck. **L~er** m -s,- lollipop; (Schnuller) dummy, (Amer) pacifier

lütt a (NGer) little

Lüttich nt -s Liège

Luv f & nt - **nach Luv** (Naut) to windward

luxuriös a luxurious, adv -ly

Luxus m - luxury. **L~artikel** m luxury article. **L~ausgabe** f de luxe edition. **L~hotel** nt luxury hotel

Lymph|drüse /'lymf-/ f, **L~knoten** m lymph gland

lynchen /'lynçən/ vt lynch

Lyr|ik *f* - lyric poetry. **L~iker** *m* -s,- lyric poet. **l~isch** *a* lyrical; ⟨*Dichtung*⟩ lyric

M

Mach|art *f* style. **m~bar** *a* feasible. **m~en** *vt* make; get ⟨*Mahlzeit*⟩; take ⟨*Foto*⟩; (*ausführen, tun, in Ordnung bringen*) do; (*Math: ergeben*) be; (*kosten*) come to; **sich** (*dat*) **etw m~en lassen** have sth made; **was m~st du da?** what are you doing? **was m~t die Arbeit?** how is work? **das m~t 6 Mark [zusammen]** that's 6 marks [altogether]; **das m~t nichts** it doesn't matter; **sich** (*dat*) **wenig/nichts m~en aus** care little/nothing for • *vr* **sich m~en** do well; **sich an die Arbeit m~en** get down to work • *vi* (*haben*) **ins Bett m~en** (*fam*) wet the bed; **schnell m~en** hurry. **M~enschaften** *fpl* machinations

Macht *f* -,‑ẹe power; **mit aller M~** with all one's might. **M~haber** *m* -s,- ruler

mächtig *a* powerful; (*groß*) enormous • *adv* (*fam*) terribly

macht|los *a* powerless. **M~wort** *nt* **ein M~wort sprechen** put one's foot down

Mädchen *nt* -s,- girl; (*Dienst-*) maid. **m~haft** *a* girlish. **M~name** *m* girl's name; (*vor der Ehe*) maiden name

Made *f* -,-n maggot

Mädel *nt* -s,- girl

madig *a* maggoty; **jdn m~ machen** (*fam*) run s.o. down

Madonna *f* -,-nen madonna

Magazin *nt* -s,-e magazine; (*Lager*) warehouse; (*Raum*) store-room

Magd *f* -,‑ẹe maid

Magen *m* -s,‑: stomach. **M~schmerzen** *mpl* stomach-ache *sg*. **M~verstimmung** *f* stomach upset

mager *a* thin; ⟨*Fleisch*⟩ lean; ⟨*Boden*⟩ poor; (*dürftig*) meagre. **M~keit** *f* - thinness; leanness. **M~sucht** *f* anorexia

Magie *f* - magic

Mag|ier /'ma:giɐ/ *m* -s,- magician. **m~isch** *a* magic; (*geheimnisvoll*) magical

Magistrat *m* -s,-e city council

Magnesia *f* - magnesia

Magnet *m* -en & -[e]s,-e magnet. **m~isch** *a* magnetic. **m~isieren** *vt* magnetize. **M~ismus** *m* - magnetism

Mahagoni *nt* -s mahogany

Mäh|drescher *m* -s,- combine harvester. **m~en** *vt/i* (*haben*) mow

Mahl *nt* -[e]s,‑ẹer meal

mahlen† *vt* grind

Mahlzeit *f* meal; **M~!** enjoy your meal!

Mähne *f* -,-n mane

mahn|en *vt/i* (*haben*) remind (**wegen** about); (*ermahnen*) admonish; (*auffordern*) urge (**zu** to); **zur Vorsicht/Eile m~en** urge caution/haste. **M~ung** *f* -,-en reminder; admonition; (*Aufforderung*) ex‑ hortation

Mai *m* -[e]s,-e May; **der Erste Mai** May Day. **M~glöckchen** *nt* -s,- lily of the valley. **M~käfer** *m* cockchafer

Mailand *nt* -s Milan

Mais *m* -es maize, (*Amer*) corn; (*Culin*) sweet corn. **M~kolben** *m* corn-cob

Majestät *f* -,-en majesty. **m~isch** *a* majestic, *adv* -ally

Major *m* -s,-e major

Majoran *m* -s marjoram

Majorität *f* -,-en majority

makaber *a* macabre

Makel *m* -s,- blemish; (*Defekt*) flaw; (*fig*) stain. **m~los** *a* flawless; (*fig*) unblemished

mäkeln *vi* (*haben*) grumble

Makkaroni *pl* macaroni *sg*

Makler *m* -s,- (*Comm*) broker

Makrele *f* -,-n mackerel

Makrone *f* -,-n macaroon

mal *adv* (*Math*) times; (*bei Maßen*) by; (*fam: einmal*) once; (*eines Tages*) one day; **schon mal** once before; (*jemals*) ever; **nicht mal** not even; **hört/seht mal!** listen!/look!

Mal¹ *nt* -[e]s,-e time; **zum ersten Mal** for the first time; **mit einem Mal** all at once; **ein für alle Mal** once and for all

Mal² *nt* -[e]s,-e mark; (*auf der Haut*) mole; (*Mutter-*) birthmark

Mal|buch *nt* colouring book. **m~en** *vt/i* (*haben*) paint. **M~er** *m* -s,- painter. **M~erei** *f* -,-en painting. **M~erin** *f* -,-nen painter. **m~erisch** *a* picturesque

Malheur /ma'lø:ɐ/ *nt* -s,-e & -s (*fam*) mishap; (*Ärger*) trouble

Mallorca /ma'lɔrka, -'jɔrka/ *nt* -s Majorca

malnehmen† *vt sep* multiply (**mit** by)

Malz *nt* -es malt. **M~bier** *nt* malt beer

Mama /'mama, ma'ma:/ *f* -s,-s mummy

Mammut *nt* -s,-e & -s mammoth

mampfen *vt (fam)* munch

man *pron* one; you; *(die Leute)* people, they; **man sagt** they say, it is said

Manager /'mɛnɪdʒɐ/ *m* -s,- manager

manch *inv pron* **m~ ein(e)** many a; **m~ einer/eine** many a man/woman. **m~e(r,s)** *pron* many a; [so] **m~es** Mal many a time; **m~e Leute** some people ● *(substantivisch)* **m~er/m~e** many a man/woman; **m~e** *pl* some; *(Leute)* some people; *(viele)* many [people]; **m~es** some things; *(vieles)* many things. **m~erlei** *inv a* various ● *pron* various things

manchmal *adv* sometimes

Mandant(in) *m* -en,-en *(f* -,-nen) *(Jur)* client

Mandarine *f* -,-n mandarin

Mandat *nt* -[e]s,-e mandate; *(Jur)* brief; *(Pol)* seat

Mandel *f* -,-n almond; *(Anat)* tonsil. **M~entzündung** *f* tonsillitis

Manege /ma'ne:ʒə/ *f* -,-n ring; *(Reit-)* arena

Mangel¹ *m* -s,⸚ lack; *(Knappheit)* shortage; *(Med)* deficiency; *(Fehler)* defect; **M~ leiden** go short

Mangel² *f* -,-n mangle

mangel|haft *a* faulty, defective; *(Sch)* unsatisfactory. **m~n¹** *vi (haben)* **es m~t an** (+ *dat)* there is a lack/*(Knappheit)* shortage of

mangeln² *vt* put through the mangle

mangels *prep* (+ *gen)* for lack of

Mango *f* -,-s mango

Manie *f* -,-n mania; *(Sucht)* obsession

Manier *f* -,-en manner; **M~en** manners. **m~lich** *a* well-mannered ● *adv* properly

Manifest *nt* -[e]s,-e manifesto. **m~ieren (sich)** *vr* manifest itself

Maniküre *f* -,-n manicure; *(Person)* manicurist. **m~n** *vt* manicure

Manipul|ation /-'tsio:n/ *f* -,-en manipulation. **m~ieren** *vt* manipulate

Manko *nt* -s,-s disadvantage; *(Fehlbetrag)* deficit

Mann *m* -[e]s,⸚er man; *(Ehe-)* husband

Männchen *nt* -s,- little man; *(Zool)* male; **M~ machen** *(Hund:)* sit up

Mannequin /'manəkɛ̃/ *nt* -s,-s model

Männerchor *m* male voice choir

Mannes|alter *nt* manhood. **M~kraft** *f* virility

mannhaft *a* manful, *adv* -ly

mannigfaltig *a* manifold; *(verschieden)* diverse

männlich *a* male; *(Gram & fig)* masculine; *(mannhaft)* manly; ⟨*Frau*⟩ mannish. **M~keit** *f* - masculinity; *(fig)* manhood

Mannschaft *f* -,-en team; *(Naut)* crew. **M~sgeist** *m* team spirit

Manöv|er *nt* -s,- manoeuvre; *(Winkelzug)* trick. **m~rieren** *vt/i (haben)* manœuvre

Mansarde *f* -,-n attic room; *(Wohnung)* attic flat

Manschette *f* -,-n cuff; *(Blumentopf-)* paper frill. **M~nknopf** *m* cuff-link

Mantel *m* -s,⸚ coat; *(dick)* overcoat; *(Reifen-)* outer tyre

Manuskript *nt* -[e]s,-e manuscript

Mappe *f* -,-n folder; *(Akten-)* briefcase; *(Schul-)* bag

Marathon *m* -s,-s marathon

Märchen *nt* -s,- fairy-tale. **m~haft** *a* fairy-tale…; *(phantastisch)* fabulous

Margarine *f* - margarine

Marienkäfer /ma'ri:ən-/ *m* ladybird, *(Amer)* ladybug

Marihuana *nt* -s marijuana

Marille *f* -,-n *(Aust)* apricot

Marinade *f* -,-n marinade

Marine *f* marine; *(Kriegs-)* navy. **m~blau** *a* navy [blue]. **M~infanterist** *m* marine

marinieren *vt* marinade

Marionette *f* -,-n puppet, marionette

Mark¹ *f* -,- mark; **drei M~** three marks

Mark² *nt* -[e]s *(Knochen-)* marrow; *(Bot)* pith; *(Frucht-)* pulp; **bis ins M~ getroffen** *(fig)* cut to the quick

markant *a* striking

Marke *f* -,-n token; *(rund)* disc; *(Erkennungs-)* tag; *(Brief-)* stamp; *(Lebensmittel-)* coupon; *(Spiel-)* counter; *(Markierung)* mark; *(Fabrikat)* make; *(Tabak-)* brand. **M~nartikel** *m* branded article

markier|en *vt* mark; *(fam: vortäuschen)* fake. **M~ung** *f* -,-en marking

Markise *f* -,-n awning

Marktstück *nt* one-mark piece

Markt *m* -[e]s,⸚e market; *(M~platz)* market-place. **M~forschung** *f* market research. **M~platz** *m* market-place

Marmelade f -,-n jam; (Orangen-) marmalade

Marmor m -s marble

Marokko nt -s Morocco

Marone f -,-n [sweet] chestnut

Marotte f -,-n whim

Marsch[1] f -,-en marsh

Marsch[2] m -[e]s,ᵉe march. **m~** int (Mil) march! **m~ ins Bett!** off to bed!

Marschall m -s,ᵉe marshal

marschieren vi (sein) march

Marter f -,-n torture. **m~n** vt torture

Martinshorn nt [police] siren

Märtyrer(in) m -s,- (f -,-nen) martyr

Martyrium nt -s martyrdom

Mar|xismus m - Marxism. **m~ xistisch** a Marxist

März m -,-e March

Marzipan nt -s marzipan

Masche f -,-n stitch; (im Netz) mesh; (fam: Trick) dodge. **M~ndraht** m wire netting

Maschin|e f -,-n machine; (Flugzeug) plane; (Schreib-) typewriter. **m~e-geschrieben** a typewritten, typed. **m~ell** a machine ... ● adv by machine. **M~enbau** m mechanical engineering. **M~engewehr** nt machine-gun. **M~enpistole** f sub-machine-gun. **M~erie** f - machinery. **M~eschreiben** nt typing. **M~ist** m -en,-en machinist; (Naut) engineer

Masern pl measles sg

Maserung f -,-en [wood] grain

Maske f -,-n mask; (Theat) make-up. **M~rade** f -,-n disguise; (fig: Heuchelei) masquerade

maskieren vt mask; **sich m~** dress up (**als** as)

Maskottchen nt -s,- mascot

maskulin a masculine

Maskulinum nt -s,-na (Gram) masculine

Masochis|mus m /mazoˈxɪsmʊs/ - masochism. **M~t** m -en,-en masochist

Maß[1] nt -es,-e measure; (Abmessung) measurement; (Grad) degree; (Mäßigung) moderation; **in** od **mit Maß[en]** in moderation; **in hohem Maße** to a high degree

Maß[2] f -,- (SGer) litre [of beer]

Massage /maˈsaːʒə/ f -,-n massage

Massaker nt -s,- massacre

Maß|anzug m made-to-measure suit. **M~band** nt (pl -bänder) tape-measure

Masse f -,-n mass; (Culin) mixture; (Menschen-) crowd; **eine M~ Arbeit** (fam) masses of work. **M~nartikel** m mass-produced article. **m~nhaft** adv in huge quantities. **M~n-medien** pl mass media. **M~n-produktion** f mass production. **m~nweise** adv in huge numbers

Masseu|r /maˈsøːɐ̯/ m -s,-e masseur. **M~rin** f -,-nen, **M~se** /-ˈsøːzə/ f -,-n masseuse

maß|gebend a authoritative; (einflußreich) influential. **m~geblich** a decisive, adv -ly. **m~geschneidert** a made-to-measure. **m~halten**† vi sep (haben) exercise moderation

massieren[1] vt massage

massieren[2] (**sich**) vr mass

massig a massive

mäßig a moderate, adv -ly; (mittelmäßig) indifferent. **m~en** vt moderate; **sich m~en** moderate; (sich beherrschen) restrain oneself. **M~keit** f - moderation. **M~ung** f - moderation

massiv a solid; (stark) heavy

Maß|krug m beer mug. **m~los** a excessive; (grenzenlos) boundless; (äußerst) extreme, adv -ly. **M~nahme** f -,-n measure. **m~regeln** vt reprimand

Maßstab m scale; (Norm & fig) standard. **m~sgerecht**, **m~sgetreu** a scale ... ● adv to scale

maßvoll a moderate

Mast[1] m -[e]s,-en pole; (Überland-) pylon; (Naut) mast

Mast[2] f - fattening. **M~darm** m rectum

mästen vt fatten

Masturb|ation /-ˈtsjoːn/ f - masturbation. **m~ieren** vi (haben) masturbate

Material nt -s,-ien /-jən/ material; (coll) materials pl. **M~ismus** m - materialism. **m~istisch** a materialistic

Mater|ie /maˈteːrjə/ f -,-n matter; (Thema) subject. **m~iell** a material

Mathe f - (fam) maths sg

Mathe|matik f - mathematics sg. **M~matiker** m -s,- mathematician. **m~matisch** a mathematical

Matinee f -,-n (Theat) morning performance

Matratze f -,-n mattress

Mätresse f -,-n mistress

Matrose m -n,-n sailor

Matsch m -[e]s mud; (Schnee-) slush. **m~ig** a muddy; slushy; (weich) mushy

matt *a* weak; *(gedämpft)* dim; *(glanzlos)* dull; *(Politur, Farbe)* matt; **jdn m~ setzen** checkmate s.o. **M~** *nt* -s *(Schach)* mate

Matte *f* -,-n mat

Mattglas *nt* frosted glass

Matt|igkeit *f* - weakness; *(Müdigkeit)* weariness. **M~scheibe** *f (fam)* television screen

Matura *f* - *(Aust)* ≈ A levels *pl*

Mauer *f* -,-n wall. **m~n** *vt* build ● *vi (haben)* lay bricks. **M~werk** *nt* masonry

Maul *nt* -[e]s, Mäuler *(Zool)* mouth; **halt's M~!** *(fam)* shut up! **m~en** *vi (haben) (fam)* grumble. **M~korb** *m* muzzle. **M~tier** *nt* mule. **M~wurf** *m* mole. **M~wurfshaufen, M~ wurfshügel** *m* molehill

Maurer *m* -s,- bricklayer

Maus *f* -, Mäuse mouse. **M~efalle** *f* mousetrap

mausern (sich) *vr* moult; *(fam)* turn (**zu** into)

Maut *f* -,-en *(Aust)* toll. **M~straße** *f* toll road

maximal *a* maximum

Maximum *nt* -s,-ma maximum

Mayonnaise /majɔ'nɛ:zə/ *f* -,-n mayonnaise

Mäzen *m* -s,-e patron

Mechan|ik /me'ça:nɪk/ *f* - mechanics *sg*; *(Mechanismus)* mechanism. **M~iker** *m* -s,- mechanic. **m~isch** *a* mechanical, *adv* -ly. **m~isieren** *vt* mechanize. **M~ismus** *m* -,-men mechanism

meckern *vi (haben)* bleat; *(fam: nörgeln)* grumble

Medaill|e /me'daljə/ *f* -,-n medal. **M~on** /-'jõ:/ *nt* -s,-s medallion; *(Schmuck)* locket

Medikament *nt* -[e]s,-e medicine

Medit|ation /-'tsjo:n/ *f* -,-en meditation. **m~ieren** *vi (haben)* meditate

Medium *nt* -s,-ien medium; **die Medien** the media

Medizin *f* -,-en medicine. **M~er** *m* -s,- doctor; *(Student)* medical student. **m~isch** *a* medical; *(heilkräftig)* medicinal

Meer *nt* -[e]s,-e sea. **M~busen** *m* gulf. **M~enge** *f* strait. **M~esspiegel** *m* sea-level. **M~jungfrau** *f* mermaid. **M~rettich** *m* horseradish. **M~schweinchen** *nt* -s,- guinea-pig

Megaphon *nt* -s,-e megaphone

Mehl *nt* -[e]s flour. **m~ig** *a* floury. **M~schwitze** *f (Culin)* roux. **M~ speise** *f (Aust)* dessert; *(Kuchen)* pastry. **M~tau** *m (Bot)* mildew

mehr *pron & adv* more; **nicht m~** no more; *(zeitlich)* no longer; **nichts m~** no more; *(nichts weiter)* nothing else; **nie m~** never again. **m~deutig** *a* ambiguous. **m~en** *vt* increase; **sich m~en** increase. **m~ere** *pron* several. **m~eres** *pron* several things *pl*. **m~fach** *a* multiple; *(mehrmalig)* repeated ● *adv* several times. **M~fahrtenkarte** *f* book of tickets. **m~farbig** *a* [multi]coloured. **M~ heit** *f* -,-en majority. **m~malig** *a* repeated. **m~mals** *adv* several times. **m~sprachig** *a* multilingual. **m~stimmig** *a (Mus)* for several voices ● *adv* **m~stimmig singen** sing in harmony. **M~wertsteuer** *f* value-added tax, VAT. **M~zahl** *f* majority; *(Gram)* plural. **M~zweck-** *pref* multi-purpose

meiden† *vt* avoid, shun

Meierei *f* -,-en *(dial)* dairy

Meile *f* -,-n mile. **M~nstein** *m* milestone. **m~nweit** *adv* [for] miles

mein *poss pron* my. **m~e(r,s)** *poss pron* mine; **die M~en** *pl* my family *sg*

Meineid *m* perjury; **einen M~ leisten** perjure oneself

meinen *vt* mean; *(glauben)* think; *(sagen)* say; **es gut m~** mean well

mein|erseits *adv* for my part. **m~etwegen** *adv* for my sake; *(wegen mir)* because of me, on my account; *(fam: von mir aus)* as far as I'm concerned. **m~etwillen** *adv* **um m~etwillen** for my sake. **m~ige** *poss pron* **der/die/das m~ige** mine. **m~s** *poss pron* mine

Meinung *f* -,-en opinion; **jdm die M~ sagen** give s.o. a piece of one's mind. **M~sumfrage** *f* opinion poll

Meise *f* -,-n *(Zool)* tit

Meißel *m* -s,- chisel. **m~n** *vt/i (haben)* chisel

meist *adv* mostly; *(gewöhnlich)* usually. **m~e** *a* **der/die/das m~e** most; **die m~en Leute** most people; **die m~e Zeit** most of the time; **am m~en** [the] most ● *pron* **das m~e** most [of it]; **die m~en** most. **m~ens** *adv* mostly; *(gewöhnlich)* usually

Meister *m* -s,- master craftsman; *(Könner)* master; *(Sport)* champion.

m~**haft** *a* masterly ● *adv* in masterly fashion. **m~n** *vt* master. **M~schaft** *f* -,-en mastery; (*Sport*) championship. **M~stück, M~werk** *nt* masterpiece

Melanch|olie /melaŋko'li:/ *f* - melancholy. **m~olisch** *a* melancholy

meld|en *vt* report; (*anmelden*) register; (*ankündigen*) announce; **sich m~en** report (**bei** to); (*zum Militär*) enlist; (*freiwillig*) volunteer; (*Teleph*) answer; (*Sch*) put up one's hand; (*von sich hören lassen*) get in touch (**bei** with); **sich krank m~en** report sick. **M~ung** *f* -,-en report; (*Anmeldung*) registration

meliert *a* mottled; **grau m~es Haar** hair flecked with grey

melken† *vt* milk

Melod|ie *f* -,-n tune, melody. **m~iös** *a* melodious

melodisch *a* melodic; (*melodiös*) melodious, tuneful

melodramatisch *a* melodramatic, *adv* -ally

Melone *f* -,-n melon; [**schwarze**] **M~** (*fam*) bowler [hat]

Membran *f* -,-en membrane

Memoiren /me'moɑːrən/ *pl* memoirs

Menge *f* -,-n amount, quantity; (*Menschen*-) crowd; (*Math*) set; **eine M~ Geld** a lot of money. **m~n** *vt* mix

Mensa *f* -,-sen (*Univ*) refectory

Mensch *m* -en,-en human being; **der M~** man; **die M~en** people; **jeder/ kein M~** everybody/nobody. **M~enaffe** *m* ape. **M~enfeind** *m* misanthropist. **m~enfeindlich** *a* antisocial. **M~enfresser** *m* -s,- cannibal; (*Zool*) man-eater; (*fam*) ogre. **m~enfreundlich** *a* philanthropic. **M~enleben** *nt* human life; (*Lebenszeit*) lifetime. **m~enleer** *a* deserted. **M~enmenge** *f* crowd. **M~enraub** *m* kidnapping. **M~enrechte** *ntpl* human rights. **m~enscheu** *a* unsociable. **M~enskind** *int* (*fam*) good heavens! **M~enverstand** *m* **gesunder M~enverstand** common sense. **m~enwürdig** *a* humane, *adv* -ly. **M~heit** *f* - **die M~heit** mankind, humanity. **m~lich** *a* human; (*human*) humane, *adv* -ly. **M~lichkeit** *f* - humanity

Menstru|ation /-'tsio:n/ *f* - menstruation. **m~ieren** *vi* (*haben*) menstruate

Mentalität *f* -,-en mentality

Menü *nt* -s,-s menu; (*festes M~*) set meal

Menuett *nt* -[e]s,-e minuet

Meridian *m* -s,-e meridian

merk|bar *a* noticeable. **M~blatt** *nt* [explanatory] leaflet. **m~en** *vt* notice; **sich** (*dat*) **etw m~en** remember sth. **m~lich** *a* noticeable, *adv* -bly. **M~mal** *nt* feature

merkwürdig *a* odd, *adv* -ly, strange, *adv* -ly. **m~erweise** *adv* oddly enough

meß|bar *a* measurable. **M~becher** *m* (*Culin*) measure

Messe[1] *f* -,-n (*Relig*) mass; (*Comm*) [trade] fair

Messe[2] *f* -,-n (*Mil*) mess

messen† *vt/i* (*haben*) measure; (*ansehen*) look at; [**bei jdm**] **Fieber m~** take s.o.'s temperature; **sich m~** compete (**mit** with); **sich mit jdm m~/ nicht m~ können** be a/no match for s.o.

Messer *nt* -s,- knife

Messias *m* - Messiah

Messing *nt* -s brass

Messung *f* -,-en measurement

Metabolismus *m* - metabolism

Metall *nt* -s,-e metal. **m~en** *a* metal; (*metallisch*) metallic. **m~isch** *a* metallic

Metallurgie *f* - metallurgy

Metamorphose *f* -,-n metamorphosis

Metaph|er *f* -,-n metaphor. **m~orisch** *a* metaphorical, *adv* -ly

Meteor *m* -s,-e meteor. **M~ologe** *m* -n,-n meteorologist. **M~ologie** *f* - meteorology. **m~ologisch** *a* meteorological

Meter *m & nt* -s,- metre, (*Amer*) meter. **M~maß** *nt* tape-measure

Method|e *f* -,-n method. **m~isch** *a* methodical

metrisch *a* metric

Metropole *f* -,-n metropolis

metzeln *vt* (*fig*) massacre

Metzger *m* -s,- butcher. **M~ei** *f* -,-en butcher's shop

Meute *f* -,-n pack [of hounds]; (*fig: Menge*) mob

Meuterei *f* -,-en mutiny

meutern *vi* (*haben*) mutiny; (*fam: schimpfen*) grumble

Mexikan|er(in) *m* -s,- (*f* -,-nen*) Mexican. **m~isch** *a* Mexican

Mexiko *nt* -s Mexico

miauen *vi* (*haben*) mew, miaow

mich *pron* (*acc of* **ich**) me; (*refl*) myself

Mieder *nt* -s,- bodice; (*Korsett*) corset

Miene *f* -,-n expression; **M~ machen** make as if (**zu** to)

mies *a* (*fam*) lousy; **mir ist m~** I feel rotten

Miet|e *f* -,-n rent; (*Mietgebühr*) hire charge; **zur M~e wohnen** live in rented accommodation. **m~en** *vt* rent (*Haus, Zimmer*); hire (*Auto, Boot, Fernseher*). **M~er(in)** *m* -s,- (*f* -,-nen) tenant. **m~frei** *a & adv* rent-free. **M~shaus** *nt* block of rented flats. **M~vertrag** *m* lease. **M~wagen** *m* hire-car. **M~wohnung** *f* rented flat; (*zu vermieten*) flat to let

Mieze *f* -,-n (*fam*) puss[y]

Migräne *f* -,-n migraine

Mikrobe *f* -,-n microbe

Mikro|chip *m* microchip. **M~computer** *m* microcomputer. **M~film** *m* microfilm

Mikro|fon, M~phon *nt* -s,-e microphone. **M~prozessor** *m* -s,-en /-'so:rən/ microprocessor. **M~skop** *nt* -s,-e microscope. **m~skopisch** *a* microscopic

Mikrowelle *f* -,-n microwave. **M~ngerät** *nt*, **M~nherd** *m* microwave oven

Milbe *f* -,-n mite

Milch *f* - milk. **M~bar** *f* milk bar. **M~geschäft** *nt* dairy. **M~glas** *nt* opal glass. **m~ig** *a* milky. **M~kuh** *f* dairy cow. **M~mann** *m* (*pl* -männer) milkman. **M~mixgetränk** *nt* milk shake. **M~straße** *f* Milky Way

mild *a* mild; (*nachsichtig*) lenient; **m~e Gaben** alms. **M~e** *f* - mildness; leniency. **m~ern** *vt* make milder; (*mäßigen*) moderate; (*lindern*) alleviate, ease; **sich m~ern** become milder; (*sich mäßigen*) moderate; (*nachlassen*) abate; (*Schmerz:*) ease; **m~ernde Umstände** mitigating circumstances. **m~tätig** *a* charitable

Milieu /mi'ljø:/ *nt* -s,-s [social] environment

militant *a* militant

Militär *nt* -s army; (*Soldaten*) troops *pl*; **beim M~** in the army. **m~isch** *a* military

Miliz *f* -,-en militia

Milliarde /mɪ'ljardə/ *f* -,-n thousand million, billion

Milli|gramm *nt* milligram. **M~meter** *m & nt* millimetre. **M~meterpapier** *nt* graph paper

Million /mɪ'ljo:n/ *f* -,-en million. **M~är** *m* -s,-e millionaire. **M~ärin** *f* -,-nen millionairess

Milz *f* - (*Anat*) spleen

mim|en *vt* (*fam: vortäuschen*) act. **M~ik** *f* - [expressive] gestures and facial expressions *pl*

Mimose *f* -,-n mimosa

minder *a* lesser ● *adv* less; **mehr oder m~** more or less. **M~heit** *f* -,-en minority

minderjährig *a* (*Jur*) under-age; **m~ sein** be under age. **M~e(r)** *m/f* (*Jur*) minor. **M~keit** *f* - (*Jur*) minority

minder|n *vt* diminish; decrease (*Tempo*). **M~ung** *f* - decrease

minderwertig *a* inferior. **M~keit** *f* - inferiority. **M~keitskomplex** *m* inferiority complex

Mindest- *pref* minimum. **m~e** *a & pron* **der/die/das m~e** the least; **zum m~en** at least; **nicht im m~en** not in the least. **m~ens** *adv* at least. **M~lohn** *m* minimum wage. **M~maß** *nt* minimum

Mine *f* -,-n mine; (*Bleistift-*) lead; (*Kugelschreiber-*) refill. **M~nfeld** *nt* minefield. **M~nräumboot** *nt* minesweeper

Mineral *nt* -s,-e & -ien /-jən/ mineral. **m~isch** *a* mineral. **M~ogie** *f* - mineralogy. **M~wasser** *nt* mineral water

Miniatur *f* -,-en miniature

Minigolf *nt* miniature golf

minimal *a* minimal

Minimum *nt* -s,-ma minimum

Minirock *m* miniskirt

Mini|ster *m* -s,- minister. **m~steriell** *a* ministerial. **M~sterium** *nt* -s,-ien ministry

Minorität *f* -,-en minority

minus *conj, adv & prep* (+ *gen*) minus. **M~** *nt* - deficit; (*Nachteil*) disadvantage. **M~zeichen** *nt* minus [sign]

Minute *f* -,-n minute

mir *pron* (*dat of* **ich**) [to] me; (*refl*) myself; **mir nichts, dir nichts** without so much as a 'by your leave'

Misch|ehe *f* mixed marriage. **m~en** *vt* mix; blend (*Tee, Kaffee*); toss (*Salat*); shuffle (*Karten*); **sich m~en** mix; (*Person:*) mingle (**unter** + *acc* with); **sich m~en in** (+ *acc*) join in (*Gespräch*); meddle in (*Angelegenheit*) ● *vi* (*haben*) shuffle the cards. **M~ling** *m*

-s,-e half-caste; (*Hund*) cross. **M~
masch** *m* **-[e]s,-e** (*fam*) hotchpotch.
M~ung *f* **-,-en** mixture; blend
miserabel *a* abominable; (*erbärmlich*) wretched
mißachten *vt* disregard
Miß|achtung *f* disregard. **M~
behagen** *nt* [feeling of] unease. **M~
bildung** *f* deformity
mißbilligen *vt* disapprove of
Miß|billigung *f* disapproval.
M~brauch *m* abuse; **M~brauch
treiben mit** abuse
miß|brauchen *vt* abuse; (*verge-
waltigen*) rape. **m~deuten** *vt* mis-
interpret
missen *vt* do without; **ich möchte es
nicht m~** I should not like to be without it
Miß|erfolg *m* failure. **M~ernte** *f*
crop failure
Misse|tat *f* misdeed. **M~täter** *m*
(*fam*) culprit
mißfallen† *vi* (*haben*) displease (**jdm**
s.o.)
Miß|fallen *nt* **-s** displeasure; (*Miß-
billigung*) disapproval. **m~gebildet** *a*
deformed. **M~geburt** *f* freak; (*fig*)
monstrosity. **M~geschick** *nt* mishap; (*Unglück*) misfortune. **m~ge-
stimmt** *a* **m~gestimmt sein** be in a
bad mood
miß|glücken *vi* (*sein*) fail.
m~gönnen *vt* begrudge
Miß|griff *m* mistake. **M~gunst** *f* re-
sentment. **m~günstig** *a* resentful
mißhandeln *vt* ill-treat
Miß|handlung *f* ill-treatment.
M~helligkeit *f* **-,-en** disagreement
Mission *f* **-,-en** mission
Missionar(in) *m* **-s,-e** (*f* **-,-nen**)
missionary
Miß|klang *m* discord. **M~kredit** *m*
discredit; **in M~kredit bringen** discredit. **m~lich** *a* awkward. **m~
liebig** *a* unpopular
mißlingen† *vi* (*sein*) fail; **es mißlang
ihr** she failed. **M~** *nt* **-s** failure
Mißmut *m* ill humour. **m~ig** *a*
morose, *adv* -ly
mißraten† *vi* (*sein*) turn out badly
Miß|stand *m* abuse; (*Zustand*) un-
desirable state of affairs. **M~stim-
mung** *f* discord; (*Laune*) bad mood.
M~ton *m* discordant note
mißtrauen *vi* (*haben*) **jdm/etw m~**
mistrust s.o./sth; (*Argwohn hegen*) distrust s.o./sth

Miß|trau|en *nt* **-s** mistrust; (*Argwohn*)
distrust. **M~ensvotum** *nt* vote of no
confidence. **m~isch** *a* distrustful;
(*argwöhnisch*) suspicious
Miß|verhältnis *nt* disproportion.
M~verständnis *nt* misunder-
standing. **m~verstehen†** *vt* misunderstand. **M~wirtschaft** *f*
mismanagement
Mist *m* **-[e]s** manure; (*fam*) rubbish
Mistel *f* **-,-n** mistletoe
Misthaufen *m* dungheap
mit *prep* (+ *dat*) with; (*sprechen*) to;
(*mittels*) by; (*inklusive*) including;
(*bei*) at; **mit Bleistift** in pencil; **mit
lauter Stimme** in a loud voice; **mit drei
Jahren** at the age of three ● *adv* (*auch*)
as well; **mit anfassen** (*fig*) lend a hand;
es ist mit das ärmste Land der Welt it
is among the poorest countries in the
world
Mitarbeit *f* collaboration. **m~en**
vi sep collaborate (**an** + *dat* on).
M~er(in) *m(f)* collaborator; (*Kollege*) colleague; (*Betriebsangehörige*)
employee
Mitbestimmung *f* co-determina-
tion
mitbring|en† *vt sep* bring [along];
jdm Blumen m~en bring/(*hinbringen*) take s.o. flowers. **M~sel** *nt*
-s,- present (*brought back from holiday
etc*)
Mitbürger *m* fellow citizen
miteinander *adv* with each other
miterleben *vt sep* witness
Mitesser *m* (*Med*) blackhead
mitfahren† *vi sep* (*sein*) go/come
along; **mit jdm m~** go with s.o.;
(*mitgenommen werden*) be given a lift
by s.o.
mitfühlen *vi sep* (*haben*) sympathize. **m~d** *a* sympathetic;
(*mitleidig*) compassionate
mitgeben† *vt sep* **jdm etw m~** give
s.o. sth to take with him
Mitgefühl *nt* sympathy
mitgehen† *vi sep* (*sein*) **mit jdm m~**
go with s.o.; **etw m~ lassen** (*fam*)
pinch sth
mitgenommen *a* worn; **m~ sein** be
in a sorry state; (*erschöpft*) be exhausted
Mitgift *f* **-,-en** dowry
Mitglied *nt* member. **M~schaft** *f* -
membership
mithalten† *vi sep* (*haben*) join in; **mit
jdm nicht m~ können** not be able to
keep up with s.o.

Mithilfe f assistance

mitkommen† vi sep (sein) come [along] too; (fig: folgen können) keep up; (verstehen) follow

Mitlaut m consonant

Mitleid nt pity, compassion. **M~enschaft** f **in M~enschaft ziehen** affect. **m~erregend** a pitiful. **m~ig** a pitying; (mitfühlend) compassionate. **m~slos** a pitiless

mitmachen v sep ● vt take part in; (erleben) go through ● vi (haben) join in

Mitmensch m fellow man

mitnehmen† vt sep take along; (mitfahren lassen) give a lift to; (fig: schädigen) affect badly; (erschöpfen) exhaust; **'zum M~'** 'to take away', (Amer) 'to go'

mitnichten adv not at all

mitreden vi sep (haben) join in [the conversation]; (mit entscheiden) have a say (bei in)

mitreißen† vt sep sweep along; (fig: begeistern) carry away; **m~d** rousing

mitsamt prep (+ dat) together with

mitschneiden† vt sep record

mitschreiben† vt sep (haben) take down

Mitschuld f partial blame. **m~ig** a **m~ig sein** be partly to blame

Mitschüler(in) m(f) fellow pupil

mitspiel|en vi sep (haben) join in; (Theat) be in the cast; (beitragen) play a part; **jdm übel m~en** treat s.o. badly. **M~er** m fellow player; (Mitwirkender) participant

Mittag m midday, noon; (Mahlzeit) lunch; (Pause) lunch-break; **[zu] M~ essen** have lunch. **m~** adv **heute m~** at lunch-time today. **M~essen** nt lunch. **m~s** adv at noon; (als Mahlzeit) for lunch; **um 12 Uhr m~s** at noon. **M~spause** f lunch-hour; (Pause) lunch-break. **M~sschlaf** m after-lunch nap. **M~stisch** m lunch table; (Essen) lunch. **M~szeit** f lunch-time

Mittäter|(in) m(f) accomplice. **M~schaft** f - complicity

Mitte f -,-n middle; (Zentrum) centre; **die goldene M~** the golden mean; **M~ Mai** in mid-May; **in unserer M~** in our midst

mitteil|en vt sep **jdm etw m~en** tell s.o. sth; (amtlich) inform s.o. of sth. **m~sam** a communicative. **M~ung** f -,-en communication; (Nachricht) piece of news

Mittel nt -s,- means sg; (Heil-) remedy; (Medikament) medicine; (M~wert) mean; (Durchschnitt) average; **M~** pl (Geld-) funds, resources. **m~** pred a medium; (m~mäßig) middling. **M~alter** nt Middle Ages pl. **m~alterlich** a medieval. **m~bar** a indirect, adv -ly. **M~ding** nt (fig) cross. **m~europäisch** a Central European. **M~finger** m middle finger. **m~groß** a medium-sized; (Person) of medium height. **M~klasse** f middle range. **m~los** a destitute. **m~mäßig** a middling; **[nur] m~mäßig** mediocre. **M~meer** nt Mediterranean. **M~punkt** m centre; (fig) centre of attention

mittels prep (+ gen) by means of

Mittel|schule f = **Realschule. M~smann** m (pl -männer), **M~sperson** f intermediary, go- between. **M~stand** m middle class. **m~ste(r,s)** a middle. **M~streifen** m (Auto) central reservation, (Amer) median strip. **M~stürmer** m centre-forward. **M~weg** m (fig) middle course; **goldener M~weg** happy medium. **M~welle** f medium wave. **M~wort** nt (pl -wörter) participle

mitten adv **m~ in/auf** (dat/acc) in the middle of; **m~ unter** (dat/acc) amidst. **m~durch** adv [right] through the middle

Mitternacht f midnight

mittler|e(r,s) a middle; (Größe, Qualität) medium; (durchschnittlich) mean, average. **m~weile** adv meanwhile; (seitdem) by now

Mittwoch m -s,-e Wednesday. **m~s** adv on Wednesdays

mitunter adv now and again

mitwirk|en vi sep (haben) take part; (helfen) contribute. **M~ung** f participation

mix|en vt mix. **M~er** m -s,- (Culin) liquidizer, blender. **M~tur** f -,-en (Med) mixture

Möbel pl furniture sg. **M~stück** nt piece of furniture. **M~tischler** m cabinet-maker. **M~wagen** m removal van

mobil a mobile; (fam: munter) lively; (nach Krankheit) fit [and well]; **m~ machen** mobilize

Mobile nt -s,-s mobile

Mobiliar nt -s furniture

mobilisier|en vt mobilize. **M~ung** f - mobilization

Mobilmachung f - mobilization
möblier|en vt furnish; **m~tes Zimmer** furnished room
mochte, möchte s. **mögen**
Modalverb nt modal auxiliary
Mode f -,-n fashion; **M~ sein** be fashionable
Modell nt -s,-e model; **M~ stehen** pose (jdm for s.o.). **m~ieren** vt model
Modenschau f fashion show
Modera|tor m -s,-en /-'to:rən/, **M~torin** f -,-nen (TV) presenter
modern[1] vi (haben) decay
modern[2] a modern; (modisch) fashionable. **m~isieren** vt modernize
Mode|schmuck m costume jewellery. **M~schöpfer** m fashion designer
Modifi|kation /-'tsjo:n/ f -,-en modification. **m~zieren** vt modify
modisch a fashionable
Modistin f -,-nen milliner
modrig a musty
modulieren vt modulate
Mofa nt -s,-s moped
mogeln vi (haben) (fam) cheat
mögen† vt like; **lieber m~** prefer • v aux **ich möchte** I'd like; **möchtest du nach Hause?** do you want to go home? **ich mag nicht mehr** I've had enough; **ich hätte weinen m~** I could have cried; **ich mag mich irren** I may be wrong; **wer/was mag das sein?** whoever/whatever can it be? **wie mag es ihm ergangen sein?** I wonder how he got on; **[das] mag sein** that may well be; **mag kommen, was da will** come what may
möglich a possible; **alle m~en** all sorts of. **m~erweise** adv possibly. **M~keit** f -,-en possibility. **M~keitsform** f subjunctive. **m~st** adv if possible; **m~st viel/früh** as much/early as possible
Mohammedan|er(in) m -s,- (f -,-nen) Muslim. **m~isch** a Muslim
Mohn m -s poppy; (Culin) poppy-seed. **M~blume** f poppy
Möhre, Mohrrübe f -,-n carrot
mokieren (sich) vr make fun (**über** + acc of)
Mokka m -s mocha; (Geschmack) coffee
Molch m -[e]s,-e newt
Mole f -,-n (Naut) mole
Molekül nt -s,-e molecule
Molkerei f -,-en dairy
Moll nt - (Mus) minor

mollig a cosy; (warm) warm; (rundlich) plump
Moment m -s,-e moment; **im/jeden M~** at the/any moment; **M~ [mal]!** just a moment! **m~an** a momentary, adv -ily; (gegenwärtig) at the moment
Momentaufnahme f snapshot
Monarch m -en,-en monarch. **M~ie** f -,-n monarchy
Monat m -s,-e month. **m~elang** adv for months. **m~lich** a & adv monthly. **M~skarte** f monthly season ticket
Mönch m -[e]s,-e monk
Mond m -[e]s,-e moon
mondän a fashionable, adv -bly
Mond|finsternis f lunar eclipse. **m~hell** a moonlit. **M~sichel** f crescent moon. **M~schein** m moonlight
monieren vt criticize
Monitor m -s,-en /-'to:rən/ (Techn) monitor
Monogramm nt -s,-e monogram
Mono|log m -s,-e monologue. **M~pol** nt -s,-e monopoly. **m~polisieren** vt monopolize. **m~ton** a monotonous, adv -ly. **M~tonie** f - monotony
Monster nt -s,- monster
monstr|ös a monstrous. **M~osität** f -,-en monstrosity
Monstrum nt -s,-stren monster
Monsun m -s,-e monsoon
Montag m Monday
Montage /mɔn'ta:ʒə/ f -,-n fitting; (Zusammenbau) assembly; (Film-) editing; (Kunst) montage
montags adv on Mondays
Montanindustrie f coal and steel industry
Monteur /mɔn'tø:ɐ/ m -s,-e fitter. **M~anzug** m overalls pl
montieren vt fit; (zusammenbauen) assemble
Monument nt -[e]s,-e monument. **m~al** a monumental
Moor nt -[e]s,-e bog; (Heide-) moor
Moos nt -es,-e moss. **m~ig** a mossy
Mop m -s,-s mop
Moped nt -s,-s moped
Mops m -es,-̈e pug [dog]
Moral f - morals pl; (Selbstvertrauen) morale; (Lehre) moral. **m~isch** a moral, adv -ly. **m~isieren** vi (haben) moralize
Morast m -[e]s,-e morass; (Schlamm) mud

Mord *m* -[e]s,-e murder; (*Pol*) assassination. **M~anschlag** *m* murder/assassination attempt. **m~en** *vt/i* (*haben*) murder, kill

Mörder *m* -s,- murderer; (*Pol*) assassin. **M~in** *f* -,-nen murderess. **m~isch** *a* murderous; (*fam: schlimm*) dreadful

Mords- *pref* (*fam*) terrific. **m~mäßig** *a* (*fam*) frightful, *adv* -ly

morgen *adv* tomorrow; **m~ früh/nachmittag** tomorrow morning/afternoon; **heute/gestern/Montag m~** this/yesterday/Monday morning

Morgen *m* -s,- morning; (*Maß*) ≈ acre; **am M~** in the morning. **M~dämmerung** *f* dawn. **m~dlich** *a* morning ... **M~grauen** *nt* -s dawn; **im M~grauen** at dawn. **M~mantel**, **M~rock** *m* dressing-gown. **M~rot** *nt* red sky in the morning. **m~s** *a* in the morning

morgig *a* tomorrow's; **der m~e Tag** tomorrow

Morphium *nt* -s morphine

morsch *a* rotten

Morsealphabet *nt* Morse code

Mörtel *m* -s mortar

Mosaik /moza'i:k/ *nt* -s,-e[n] mosaic

Moschee *f* -,-n mosque

Mosel *f* - Moselle. **M~wein** *m* Moselle [wine]

Moskau *nt* -s Moscow

Moskito *m* -s,-s mosquito

Mos|lem *m* -s,-s Muslim. **m~lemisch** *a* Muslim

Most *m* -[e]s must; (*Apfel-*) ≈ cider

Mostrich *m* -s (*NGer*) mustard

Motel *nt* -s,-s motel

Motiv *nt* -s,-e motive; (*Kunst*) motif. **M~ation** /-'tsio:n/ *f* - motivation. **m~ieren** *vt* motivate

Motor /'mo:tɔr, mo'to:ɐ/ *m* -s,-en /-'to:rən/ engine; (*Elektro-*) motor. **M~boot** *nt* motor boat

motorisieren *vt* motorize

Motor|rad *nt* motor cycle. **M~radfahrer** *m* motor-cyclist. **M~roller** *m* motor scooter

Motte *f* -,-n moth. **M~nkugel** *f* mothball

Motto *nt* -s,-s motto

Möwe *f* -,-n gull

Mücke *f* -,-n gnat; (*kleine*) midge; (*Stech-*) mosquito

mucksen (sich) *vr* sich nicht m~ (*fam*) keep quiet

müd|e *a* tired; **nicht m~e werden/es m~e sein** not tire/be tired (**etw zu tun** of doing sth). **M~igkeit** *f* - tiredness

Muff *m* -s,-e muff

muffig *a* musty; (*fam: mürrisch*) grumpy

Mühe *f* -,-n effort; (*Aufwand*) trouble; **sich** (*dat*) **M~ geben** make an effort; (*sich bemühen*) try; **nicht der M~ wert** not worth while; **mit M~ und Not** with great difficulty; (*gerade noch*) only just. **m~los** *a* effortless, *adv* -ly

muhen *vi* (*haben*) moo

mühe|n (sich) *vr* struggle. **m~voll** *a* laborious; (*anstrengend*) arduous

Mühl|e *f* -,-n mill; (*Kaffee-*) grinder. **M~stein** *m* millstone

Müh|sal *f* -,-e (*liter*) toil; (*Mühe*) trouble. **m~sam** *a* laborious, *adv* -ly; (*beschwerlich*) difficult, *adv* with difficulty. **m~selig** *a* laborious, *adv* -ly

Mulde *f* -,-n hollow

Müll *m* -s refuse, (*Amer*) garbage. **M~abfuhr** *f* refuse collection

Mullbinde *f* gauze bandage

Mülleimer *m* waste bin; (*Mülltonne*) dustbin, (*Amer*) garbage can

Müller *m* -s,- miller

Müll|halde *f* [rubbish] dump. **M~schlucker** *m* refuse chute. **M~tonne** *f* dustbin, (*Amer*) garbage can. **M~wagen** *m* dust-cart, (*Amer*) garbage truck

mulmig *a* (*fam*) dodgy; ⟨*Gefühl*⟩ uneasy; **ihm war m~ zumute** he felt uneasy/(*übel*) queasy

multi|national *a* multinational. **M~plikation** /-'tsio:n/ *f* -,-en multiplication. **m~plizieren** *vt* multiply

Mumie /'mu:miə/ *f* -,-n mummy

mumifiziert *a* mummified

Mumm *m* -s (*fam*) energy

Mumps *m* - mumps

Mund *m* -[e]s,-̈er mouth; **halt den M~!** be quiet! (*sl*) shut up! **M~art** *f* dialect. **m~artlich** *a* dialect

Mündel *nt* & *m* -s,- (*Jur*) ward. **m~sicher** *a* gilt-edged

münden *vi* (*sein*) flow/⟨*Straße:*⟩ lead (**in** + *acc* into)

mund|faul *a* taciturn. **M~geruch** *m* bad breath. **M~harmonika** *f* mouth-organ

mündig *a* **m~ sein/werden** (*Jur*) be/come of age. **M~keit** *f* - (*Jur*) majority

mündlich *a* verbal, *adv* -ly; **m~e Prüfung** oral

Mund|stück *nt* mouthpiece; *(Zigaretten-)* tip. **m~tot** *a* **m~tot machen** *(fig)* gag

Mündung *f* -,-**en** *(Fluß-)* mouth; *(Gewehr-)* muzzle

Mund|voll *m* -,- mouthful. **M~wasser** *nt* mouthwash. **M~werk** *nt* **ein gutes M~werk haben** *(fam)* be very talkative. **M~winkel** *m* corner of the mouth

Munition /-'tsjo:n/ *f* - ammunition

munkeln *vt/i (haben)* talk (**von** of); **es wird gemunkelt** rumour has it (**daß** that)

Münster *nt* -s,- cathedral

munter *a* lively; *(heiter)* merry; **m~ sein** *(wach)* be wide awake/*(aufgestanden, gesund)* up and about; **gesund und m~** fit and well ● *adv* [**immer**] **m~** merrily

Münz|e *f* -,-**n** coin; *(M~stätte)* mint. **m~en** *vt* mint; **das war auf dich gemünzt** *(fam)* that was aimed at you. **M~fernsprecher** *m* coin-box telephone, payphone. **M~wäscherei** *f* launderette

mürbe *a* crumbly; ⟨*Obst*⟩ mellow; ⟨*Fleisch*⟩ tender; **jdn m~ machen** *(fig)* wear s.o. down. **M~teig** *m* short pastry

Murmel *f* -,-**n** marble

murmeln *vt/i (haben)* murmur; *(undeutlich)* mumble, mutter. **M~** *nt* -s murmur

Murmeltier *nt* marmot

murren *vt/i (haben)* grumble

mürrisch *a* surly

Mus *nt* -es purée

Muschel *f* -,-**n** mussel; *(Schale)* [sea] shell

Museum /mu'ze:om/ *nt* -s,-**seen** /-'ze:ən/ museum

Musik *f* - music. **M~alien** /-jən/ *pl* [printed] music *sg.* **m~alisch** *a* musical

Musikbox *f* juke-box

Musiker(in) *m* -s,- *(f* -,-**nen)** musician

Musik|instrument *nt* musical instrument. **M~kapelle** *f* band. **M~pavillon** *m* bandstand

musisch *a* artistic

musizieren *vi (haben)* make music

Muskat *m* -[e]s nutmeg

Muskel *m* -s,-**n** muscle. **M~kater** *m* stiff and aching muscles *pl*

Musku|latur *f* - muscles *pl*. **m~lös** *a* muscular

Müsli *nt* -s muesli

muß *s.* **müssen. Muß** *nt* - **ein Muß** a must

Muße *f* - leisure; **mit M~** at leisure

müssen† *v aux* etw tun **m~** have to/ *(fam)* have got to do sth; **ich muß jetzt gehen** I have to *or* must go now; **ich mußte lachen** I had to laugh; **ich muß es wissen** I need to know; **du müßtest es mal versuchen** you ought to *or* should try it; **muß das sein?** is that necessary?

müßig *a* idle; *(unnütz)* futile. **M~gang** *m* - idleness

mußte, müßte *s.* **müssen**

Muster *nt* -s,- pattern; *(Probe)* sample; *(Vorbild)* model. **M~beispiel** *nt* typical example; *(Vorbild)* perfect example. **M~betrieb** *m* model factory. **m~gültig, m~haft** *a* exemplary. **m~n** *vt* eye; *(inspizieren)* inspect. **M~schüler(in)** *m(f)* model pupil. **M~ung** *f* -,-**en** inspection; *(Mil)* medical; *(Muster)* pattern

Mut *m* -[e]s courage; **jdm Mut machen** encourage s.o.

Mutation /-'tsjo:n/ *f* -,-**en** *(Biol)* mutation

mut|ig *a* courageous, *adv* -ly. **m~los** *a* despondent; *(entmutigt)* disheartened

mutmaß|en *vt* presume; *(Vermutungen anstellen)* speculate. **m~lich** *a* probable, *adv* -bly; **der m~liche Täter** the suspect. **M~ung** *f* -,-**en** speculation, conjecture

Mutprobe *f* test of courage

Mutter[1] *f* -,-̈ mother; **werdende M~** mother-to-be

Mutter[2] *f* -,-**n** *(Techn)* nut

Muttergottes *f* -,- madonna

Mutter|land *nt* motherland. **M~leib** *m* womb

mütterlich *a* maternal; *(fürsorglich)* motherly. **m~erseits** *adv* on one's/ the mother's side

Mutter|mal *nt* birthmark; *(dunkel)* mole. **M~schaft** *f* - motherhood. **m~seelenallein** *a & adv* all alone. **M~sprache** *f* mother tongue. **M~tag** *m* Mother's Day

Mutti *f* -,-**s** *(fam)* mummy

Mutwill|e *m* wantonness. **m~ig** *a* wanton, *adv* -ly

Mütze *f* -,-**n** cap; **wollene M~** woolly hat

MwSt. *abbr* **(Mehrwertsteuer)** VAT

mysteriös *a* mysterious, *adv* -ly

Myst|ik /'mʏstɪk/ f - mysticism.
m~isch a mystical.
myth|isch a mythical. **M~ologie** f -
mythology. **M~os** m -,-**then** myth

N

na int well; **na gut** all right then; **na ja**
oh well; **na und?** so what?

Nabe f -,-**n** hub

Nabel m -s,- navel. **N~schnur** f umbilical cord

nach prep (+ dat) after; (Uhrzeit)
past; (Richtung) to; (greifen, rufen,
sich sehnen) for; (gemäß) according
to; **meiner Meinung n~** in my opinion; **n~ oben** upwards ● adv **n~ und
n~** gradually, bit by bit; **n~ wie vor**
still

nachäffen vt sep mimic

nachahm|en vt sep imitate. **N~ung**
f -,-**en** imitation

nacharbeiten vt sep make up for

nacharten vi sep (sein) **jdm n~** take
after s.o.

Nachbar|(in) m -n,-n (f -,-nen) neigh-
bour. **N~haus** nt house next door.
N~land nt neighbouring country.
n~lich a neighbourly; (Nachbar-)
neighbouring. **N~schaft** f - neighbourhood; **gute N~schaft** neigh-
bourliness

nachbestell|en vt sep reorder.
N~ung f repeat order

nachbild|en vt sep copy, reproduce.
N~ung f copy, reproduction

nachdatieren vt sep backdate

nachdem conj after; **je n~** it depends

nachdenk|en† vi sep (haben) think
(über + acc about). **N~en** nt -s reflection, thought. **n~lich** a thought-
ful, adv -ly

Nachdruck m (pl -e) reproduction;
(unveränderter) reprint; (Betonung)
emphasis

nachdrücklich a emphatic, adv -ally

nacheifern vi sep (haben) **jdm n~**
emulate s.o.

nacheilen vi sep (sein) (+ dat) hurry
after

nacheinander adv one after the
other

Nachfahre m -n,-n descendant

Nachfolg|e f succession. **n~en** vi
sep (sein) (+ dat) follow; (im Amt)
succeed. **N~er(in)** m -s,- (f -,-nen)
successor

nachforsch|en vi sep (haben) make
enquiries. **N~ung** f enquiry; **N~un-
gen anstellen** make enquiries

Nachfrage f (Comm) demand. **n~n**
vi sep (haben) enquire

nachfüllen vt sep refill (Behälter);
Wasser n~ fill up with water

nachgeben† v sep ● vi (haben) give
way; (sich fügen) give in, yield ● vt
jdm Suppe n~ give s.o. more soup

Nachgebühr f surcharge

nachgehen† vi sep (sein) (Uhr:) be
slow; **jdm/etw n~** follow s.o./sth;
follow up (Spur, Angelegenheit); pursue
(Angelegenheit, Tätigkeit); go about (Arbeit)

nachgeraten† vi sep (sein) **jdm n~**
take after s.o.

Nachgeschmack m after-taste

nachgiebig a indulgent; (gefällig)
compliant. **N~keit** f - indulgence;
compliance

nachgrübeln vi sep (haben) ponder
(über + acc on)

nachhallen vi sep (haben) reverberate

nachhaltig a lasting

nachhelfen† vi sep (haben) help

nachher adv later; (danach)
afterwards; **bis n~!** see you later!

Nachhilfeunterricht m coaching

nachhinein adv im n~ afterwards

nachhinken vi sep (sein) (fig) lag
behind

nachholen vt sep (später holen) fetch
later; (mehr holen) get more; (später
machen) do later; (aufholen) catch up
on; make up for (Zeit)

nachjagen vi sep (haben) (+ dat)
chase after

Nachkomme m -n,-n descendant.
n~n† vi sep (sein) follow [later],
come later; (Schritt halten) keep up;
etw (dat) **n~n** (fig) comply with (Bitte,
Wunsch); carry out (Versprechen,
Pflicht). **N~nschaft** f - descendants
pl, progeny

Nachkriegszeit f post-war period

Nachlaß m -lasses,-lässe discount;
(Jur) [deceased's] estate

nachlassen† v sep ● vi (haben)
decrease; (Regen, Hitze:) let up;
(Schmerz:) ease; (Sturm:) abate;
(Augen, Kräfte, Leistungen:) deteriorate; **er ließ nicht nach [mit Fragen]**
he persisted [with his questions] ● vt
etw vom Preis n~ take sth off the price

nachlässig *a* careless, *adv* -ly; (*leger*) casual, *adv* -ly; (*unordentlich*) sloppy, *adv* -ily. **N~keit** *f* - carelessness; sloppiness

nachlaufen† *vi sep (sein)* (+ *dat*) run after

nachlegen *vt sep* Holz/Kohlen n~ put more wood/coal on the fire

nachlesen† *vt sep* look up

nachlöse|n *vi sep (haben)* pay one's fare on the train/on arrival. **N~schalter** *m* excess-fare office

nachmachen *vt sep (später machen)* do later; (*imitieren*) imitate, copy; (*fälschen*) forge; **jdm etw n~** copy sth from s.o.; repeat (*Übung*) after s.o.

Nachmittag *m* afternoon. **n~** *adv* gestern/heute n~ yesterday/this afternoon. **n~s** *adv* in the afternoon

Nachnahme *f* etw per N~ schicken send sth cash on delivery *or* COD

Nachname *m* surname

Nachporto *nt* excess postage

nachprüfen *vt sep* check, verify

nachrechnen *vt sep* work out; (*prüfen*) check

Nachrede *f* üble N~ defamation

Nachricht *f* -,-en [piece of] news *sg*; N~en news *sg*; eine N~ hinterlassen leave a message; **jdm N~ geben** inform, notify s.o. **N~endienst** *m* (*Mil*) intelligence service. **N~ensendung** *f* news bulletin. **N~enwesen** *nt* communications *pl*

nachrücken *vi sep (sein)* move up

Nachruf *m* obituary

nachsagen *vt sep* repeat (**jdm** after s.o.); **jdm Schlechtes/Gutes n~** speak ill/well of s.o.; **man sagt ihm nach, daß er geizig ist** he is said to be stingy

Nachsaison *f* late season

Nachsatz *m* postscript

nachschicken *vt sep (später schicken)* send later; (*hinterher-*) send after (**jdm** s.o.); send on (*Post*) (**jdm** to s.o.)

nachschlag|en† *v sep* • *vt* look up • *vi (haben)* in einem Wörterbuch n~en consult a dictionary; **jdm n~en** take after s.o. **N~ewerk** *nt* reference book

Nachschlüssel *m* duplicate key

Nachschrift *f* transcript; (*Nachsatz*) postscript

Nachschub *m* (*Mil*) supplies *pl*

nachsehen† *v sep* • *vt* (*prüfen*) check; (*nachschlagen*) look up; (*hinwegsehen über*) overlook • *vi*

(*haben*) have a look; (*prüfen*) check; **im Wörterbuch n~** consult a dictionary; **jdm/etw n~** gaze after s.o./ sth. **N~** *nt* das N~ haben (*fam*) go empty-handed

nachsenden† *vt sep* forward (*Post*) (**jdm** to s.o.); **'bitte n~'** 'please forward'

Nachsicht *f* forbearance; (*Milde*) leniency; (*Nachgiebigkeit*) indulgence. **n~ig** *a* forbearing; lenient; indulgent

Nachsilbe *f* suffix

nachsitzen† *vi sep (haben)* n~ müssen be kept in [after school]; **jdn n~ lassen** give s.o. detention. **N~** *nt* -s (*Sch*) detention

Nachspeise *f* dessert, sweet

Nachspiel *nt* (*fig*) sequel

nachspionieren *vi sep (haben)* **jdm** n~ spy on s.o.

nachsprechen† *vt sep* repeat (**jdm** after s.o.)

nachspülen *vt sep* rinse

nächst /-çst/ *prep* (+ *dat*) next to. **n~beste(r,s)** *a* first [available]; (*zweitbeste*) next best. **n~e(r,s)** *a* next; (*nächstgelegene*) nearest; (*Verwandte*) closest; **n~e Woche** next week; **in n~er Nähe** close by; **am** n~en sein be nearest *or* closest • *pron* der/die/das n~e the next; **der n~e** bitte next please; **als n~es** next; **fürs** n~e for the time being. **N~e(r)** *m* fellow man

nachstehend *a* following • *adv* below

nachstellen *v sep* • *vt* readjust; put back (*Uhr*) • *vi (haben)* (+ *dat*) pursue

nächst|emal *adv* das n~emal [the] next time. **N~enliebe** *f* charity. **n~ens** *adv* shortly. **n~gelegen** *a* nearest. **n~liegend** *a* most obvious

nachstreben *vi sep (haben)* **jdm** n~ emulate s.o.

nachsuchen *vi sep (haben)* search; **n~ um** request

Nacht *f* -,¨e night; **über/bei N~** overnight/at night. **n~** *adv* Montag/ morgen n~ Monday/tomorrow night; **heute n~** tonight; (*letzte Nacht*) last night; **gestern n~** last night; (*vorletzte Nacht*) the night before last. **N~dienst** *m* night duty

Nachteil *m* disadvantage; **zum N~** to the detriment (*gen* of). **n~ig** *a* adverse, *adv* -ly

Nacht|essen nt (SGer) supper. **N~falter** m moth. **N~hemd** nt night-dress; (Männer-) night-shirt

Nachtigall f -,-en nightingale

Nachtisch m dessert

Nacht|klub m night-club. **N~leben** nt night-life

nächtlich a nocturnal, night ...

Nacht|lokal nt night-club. **N~mahl** nt (Aust) supper

Nachtrag m postscript; (Ergänzung) supplement. **n~en†** vt sep add; **jdm etw n~en** walk behind s.o. carrying sth; (fig) bear a grudge against s.o. for sth. **n~end** a vindictive; **n~end sein** bear grudges

nachträglich a subsequent, later; (verspätet) belated ● adv later; (nachher) afterwards; (verspätet) belatedly

nachtrauern vi sep (haben) (+ dat) mourn the loss of

Nacht|ruhe f night's rest; **angenehme N~ruhe!** sleep well! **n~s** adv at night; **2 Uhr n~s** 2 o'clock in the morning. **N~schicht** f night-shift. **N~tisch** m bedside table. **N~tischlampe** f bedside lamp. **N~topf** m chamber-pot. **N~wächter** m night-watchman. **N~zeit** f night-time

Nachuntersuchung f check-up

nachwachsen† vi sep (sein) grow again

Nachwahl f by-election

Nachweis m -es,-e proof. **n~bar** a demonstrable. **n~en†** vt sep prove; (aufzeigen) show; (vermitteln) give details of; **jdm nichts n~en können** have no proof against s.o. **n~lich** a demonstrable, adv -bly

Nachwelt f posterity

Nachwirkung f after-effect

Nachwort nt (pl -e) epilogue

Nachwuchs m new generation; (fam: Kinder) offspring. **N~spieler** m young player

nachzahlen vt/i sep (haben) pay extra; (später zahlen) pay later; **Steuern n~** pay tax arrears

nachzählen vt/i sep (haben) count again; (prüfen) check

Nachzahlung f extra/later payment; (Gehalts-) back-payment

nachzeichnen vt sep copy

Nachzügler m -s,- late-comer; (Zurückgebliebener) straggler

Nacken m -s,- nape or back of the neck

nackt a naked; (bloß, kahl) bare; (Wahrheit) plain. **N~baden** nt nude bathing. **N~heit** f - nakedness, nudity. **N~kultur** f nudism. **N~schnecke** f slug

Nadel f -,-n needle; (Häkel-) hook; (Schmuck-, Hut-) pin. **N~arbeit** f needlework. **N~baum** m conifer. **N~kissen** nt pincushion. **N~stich** m stitch; (fig) pinprick. **N~wald** m coniferous forest

Nagel m -s," nail. **N~bürste** f nail-brush. **N~feile** f nail-file. **N~haut** f cuticle. **N~lack** m nail varnish. **n~n** vt nail. **n~neu** a brand-new. **N~schere** f nail scissors pl

nagen vt/i (haben) gnaw (**an**+ dat at); **n~d** (fig) nagging

Nagetier nt rodent

nah a, adv & prep = nahe; **von nah und fern** from far and wide

Näharbeit f sewing; **eine N~** a piece of sewing

Nahaufnahme f close-up

nahe a (näher, nächst) nearby; (zeitlich) imminent; (eng) close; **der N~ Osten** the Middle East; **in n~r Zukunft** in the near future; **von n~m** [from] close to; **n~ sein** be close (dat to); **den Tränen n~** close to tears ● adv near, close; (verwandt) closely; **n~ an** (+ acc/dat) near [to], close to; **n~ daran sein, etw zu tun** nearly do sth; **jdm zu n~ treten** (fig) offend s.o. ● prep (+ dat) near [to], close to

Nähe f - nearness, proximity; **aus der N~** [from] close to; **in der N~** near or close by; **in der N~ der Kirche** near the church

nahebei adv near or close by

nahe|gehen† vi sep (sein) **jdm n~gehen** (fig) affect s.o. deeply. **n~kommen†** vi sep (sein) (fig) come close (dat to); (vertraut werden) get close (dat to). **n~legen** vt sep recommend (dat to); **jdm n~legen, etw zu tun** urge s.o. to do sth. **n~liegen†** vi sep (haben) (fig) be highly likely. **n~liegend** a obvious

nahen vi (sein) (liter) approach

nähen vt/i (haben) sew; (anfertigen) make; (Med) stitch [up]

näher a closer; (Weg) shorter; (Einzelheiten) further ● adv closer; (genauer) more closely; **sich n~ erkundigen** make further enquiries; **n~an** (+ acc/dat) nearer [to], closer to ● prep (+ dat) nearer [to], closer to.

N∼e[s] *nt* [further] details *pl.* n∼-
kommen† *vi sep (sein)* come closer,
approach; (*fig*) get closer (*dat* to).
n∼n (sich) *vr* approach
nahestehen† *vi sep (haben)* (*fig*) be
close (*dat* to)
nahezu *adv* almost
Nähgarn *nt* [sewing] cotton
Nahkampf *m* close combat
Näh|maschine *f* sewing machine.
N∼nadel *f* sewing-needle
nähren *vt* feed; (*fig*) nurture; **sich n∼
von** live on ● *vi (haben)* be nutritious
nahrhaft *a* nutritious
Nährstoff *m* nutrient
Nahrung *f* - food, nourishment.
N∼smittel *nt* food
Nährwert *m* nutritional value
Naht *f* -,∵e seam; (*Med*) suture. n∼los
a seamless
Nahverkehr *m* local service.
N∼szug *m* local train
Nähzeug *nt* sewing; (*Zubehör*) sewing kit
naiv /na'i:f/ *a* naïve, *adv* -ly. N∼ität
/-vi'tɛ:t/ *f* - naïvety
Name *m* -ns,-n name; **im N∼n** (+ *gen*)
in the name of; ⟨*handeln*⟩ on behalf of;
das Kind beim rechten N∼n nennen
(*fam*) call a spade a spade. n∼nlos *a*
nameless; (*unbekannt*) unknown,
anonymous. n∼ns *adv* by the name
of ● *prep* (+ *gen*) on behalf of. N∼ns-
tag *m* name-day. N∼nsvetter *m*
namesake. N∼nszug *m* signature.
n∼ntlich *adv* by name; (*besonders*)
especially
namhaft *a* noted; (*ansehnlich*) considerable; n∼ **machen** name
nämlich *adv* (*und zwar*) namely;
(*denn*) because
nanu *int* hallo
Napf *m* -[e]s,∵e bowl
Narbe *f* -,-n scar
Narkose *f* -,-n general anaesthetic.
N∼arzt *m* anaesthetist. N∼mittel
nt anaesthetic
Narkot|ikum *nt* -s,-ka narcotic;
(*Narkosemittel*) anaesthetic. n∼i-
sieren *vt* anaesthetize
Narr *m* -en,-en fool; **zum N∼en haben**
od **halten** make a fool of. n∼en *vt* fool.
n∼ensicher *a* foolproof. N∼heit *f*
-,-en folly
Närr|in /-ə(r)-/ *f* -,-nen fool. n∼isch *a* fool-
ish; (*fam: verrückt*) crazy (**auf** + *acc*
about)

Narzisse *f* -,-n narcissus; **gelbe N∼**
daffodil
nasal *a* nasal
nasch|en *vt/i* (*haben*) nibble (an
+ *dat* at); **wer hat vom Kuchen ge-
nascht?** who's been at the cake? n∼-
haft *a* sweet-toothed
Nase *f* -,-n nose; **an der N∼ herum-
führen** (*fam*) dupe
näseln *vi* (*haben*) speak through
one's nose; n∼d nasal
Nasen|bluten *nt* -s nosebleed. N∼-
loch *nt* nostril. N∼rücken *m* bridge
of the nose
Naseweis *m* -es,-e (*fam*) know-all
Nashorn *nt* rhinoceros
naß *a* (nasser, nassest) wet
Nässe *f* - wet; (*Naßsein*) wetness. n∼n
vt wet
naßkalt *a* cold and wet
Nation /na'tsjo:n/ *f* -,-en nation.
n∼al *a* national. N∼alhymne *f*
national anthem. N∼alismus *m* -
nationalism. N∼alität *f* -,-en
nationality. N∼alsozialismus *m*
National Socialism. N∼alspieler *m*
international
Natrium *nt* -s sodium
Natron *nt* -s doppeltkohlensaures
N∼ bicarbonate of soda
Natter *f* -,-n snake; (*Gift-*) viper
Natur *f* -,-en nature; **von N∼ aus** by
nature. N∼alien /-jən/ *pl* natural
produce *sg*. n∼alisieren *vt* natur-
alize. N∼alisierung *f* -,-en natura-
lization
Naturell *nt* -s,-e disposition
Natur|erscheinung *f* natural phe-
nomenon. n∼farben *a* natural-col-
oured. N∼forscher *m* naturalist. N∼-
kunde *f* natural history. N∼-
lehrpfad *m* nature trail
natürlich *a* natural ● *adv* naturally;
(*selbstverständlich*) of course. N∼-
keit *f* - naturalness
natur|rein *a* pure. N∼schutz *m*
nature conservation; **unter N∼-
schutz stehen** be protected. N∼-
schutzgebiet *nt* nature reserve.
N∼wissenschaft *f* [natural] science. N∼wissenschaftler *m* scientist. n∼wissenschaftlich *a*
scientific; (*Sch*) science . . .
nautisch *a* nautical
Navigation /-'tsjo:n/ *f* - navigation
Nazi *m* -s,-s Nazi
n.Chr. *abbr* (**nach Christus**) AD

Nebel m -s,- fog; (leicht) mist. **n~haft** a hazy. **N~horn** nt fog-horn. **n~ig** a = neblig

neben prep (+ dat/acc) next to, beside; (+ dat) (außer) apart from; **n~ mir** next to me. **n~an** adv next door

Neben|anschluß m (Teleph) extension. **N~ausgaben** fpl incidental expenses

nebenbei adv in addition; (beiläufig) casually; **n~ bemerkt** incidentally

Neben|bemerkung f passing remark. **N~beruf** m second job. **N~beschäftigung** f spare-time occupation. **N~buhler(in)** m -s,- (f-,-nen) rival

nebeneinander adv next to each other, side by side

Neben|eingang m side entrance. **N~fach** nt (Univ) subsidiary subject. **N~fluß** m tributary. **N~gleis** nt siding. **N~haus** nt house next door

nebenher adv in addition. **n~ gehen†** vi sep (sein) walk alongside

nebenhin adv casually

Neben|höhle f sinus. **N~kosten** pl additional costs. **N~mann** m (pl -männer) person next to one. **N~ produkt** nt by-product. **N~rolle** f supporting role; (kleine) minor role; **eine N~rolle spielen** (fig) be unimportant. **N~sache** f unimportant matter. **n~sächlich** a unimportant. **N~satz** m subordinate clause. **N~ straße** f minor road; (Seiten-) side street. **N~verdienst** m additional earnings pl. **N~wirkung** f side-effect. **N~zimmer** nt room next door

neblig a foggy; (leicht) misty

nebst prep (+ dat) [together] with

Necessaire /nesɛ'sɛ:ɐ̯/ nt -s,-s toilet bag; (Näh-, Nagel-) set

neck|en vt tease. **N~erei** f - teasing. **n~isch** a teasing; (keß) saucy

nee adv (fam) no

Neffe m -n,-n nephew

negativ a negative. **N~** nt -s,-e (Phot) negative

Neger m -s,- Negro

nehmen† vt take (dat from); **sich** (dat) **etw n~** take sth; help oneself to (Essen); **jdn zu sich n~** have s.o. to live with one

Neid m -[e]s envy, jealousy. **n~en** vt **jdm den Erfolg n~en** be jealous of s.o.'s success. **n~isch** a envious, jealous (auf + acc of); **auf jdn n~isch sein** envy s.o.

neig|en vt incline; (zur Seite) tilt; (beugen) bend; **sich n~en** incline; (Boden:) slope; (Person:) bend (über + acc over) ● vi (haben) **n~en zu** (fig) have a tendency towards; be prone to (Krankheit); incline towards (Ansicht); **dazu n~en, etw zu tun** tend to do sth. **N~ung** f -,-en inclination; (Gefälle) slope; (fig) tendency; (Hang) leaning; (Herzens-) affection

nein adv, **N~** nt -s no

Nektar m -s nectar

Nelke f -,- carnation; (Feder-) pink; (Culin) clove

nenn|en† vt call; (taufen) name; (angeben) give; (erwähnen) mention; **sich n~en** call oneself. **n~enswert** a significant. **N~ung** f -,-en mention; (Sport) entry. **N~wert** m face value

Neofaschismus m neofascism

Neon nt -s neon. **N~beleuchtung** f fluorescent lighting

neppen vt (fam) rip off

Nerv m -s,-en /-fən/ nerve; **die N~en verlieren** lose control of oneself. **n~en** vt **jdn n~en** (sl) get on s.o.'s nerves. **N~enarzt** m neurologist. **n~en-aufreibend** a nerve-racking. **N~enbündel** nt (fam) bundle of nerves. **N~enkitzel** m (fam) thrill. **N~ensystem** nt nervous system. **N~enzusammenbruch** m nervous breakdown

nervös a nervy, edgy; (Med) nervous; **n~ sein** be on edge

Nervosität f - nerviness, edginess

Nerz m -es,-e mink

Nessel f -,-n nettle

Nest nt -[e]s,-er nest; (fam: Ort) small place

nesteln vi (haben) fumble (an + dat with)

Nesthäkchen nt -s,- (fam) baby of the family

nett a nice, adv -ly; (freundlich) kind, adv -ly

netto adv net. **N~gewicht** nt net weight

Netz nt -es,-e net; (Einkaufs-) string bag; (Spinnen-) web; (auf Landkarte) grid; (System) network; (Electr) mains pl. **N~haut** f retina. **N~karte** f area season-ticket. **N~werk** nt network

neu a new; (modern) modern; **wie neu** as good as new; **das ist mir neu** it's news to me; **aufs n~e** [once] again; **von n~em** all over again ● *adv* newly; (*gerade erst*) only just; (*erneut*) again; **etw neu schreiben/streichen** rewrite/repaint sth. **N~ankömmling** *m* -s,-e newcomer. **N~anschaffung** *f* recent acquisition. **n~artig** *a* new [kind of]. **N~auflage** *f* new edition; (*unverändert*) reprint. **N~bau** *m* (*pl* -**ten**) new house/building

Neu|e(r) *m/f* new person, newcomer; (*Schüler*) new boy/girl. **N~e(s)** *nt* das **N~e** the new; **etwas N~es** something new; (*Neuigkeit*) a piece of news; **was gibt's N~es?** what's the news?

neuer|dings *adv* [just] recently. **n~lich** *a* renewed, new ● *adv* again. **N~ung** *f* -,-en innovation

neuest|e(r,s) *a* newest; (*letzte*) latest; **seit n~em** just recently. **N~e** *nt* das **N~e** the latest thing; (*Neuigkeit*) the latest news *sg*

neugeboren *a* newborn

Neugier, Neugierde *f* - curiosity; (*Wißbegierde*) inquisitiveness

neugierig *a* curious (**auf** + *acc* about), *adv* -ly; (*wißbegierig*) inquisitive, *adv* -ly

Neuheit *f* -,-en novelty; (*Neusein*) newness; **die letzte N~** the latest thing

Neuigkeit *f* -,-en piece of news; **N~en** news *sg*

Neujahr *nt* New Year's Day; **über N~** over the New Year

neulich *adv* the other day

Neu|ling *m* -s,-e novice. **n~modisch** *a* newfangled. **N~mond** *m* new moon

neun *inv a*, **N~** *f* -,-en nine. **N~malkluge(r)** *m* (*fam*) clever Dick. **n~te(r,s)** *a* ninth. **n~zehn** *inv a* nineteen. **n~zehnte(r,s)** *a* nineteenth. **n~zig** *inv a* ninety. **n~zigste(r,s)** *a* ninetieth

Neuralgie *f* -,-n neuralgia

neureich *a* nouveau riche

Neurologe *m* -n,-n neurologist

Neuro|se *f* -,-n neurosis. **n~tisch** *a* neurotic

Neuschnee *m* fresh snow

Neuseeland *nt* -s New Zealand

neuste(r,s) *a* = **neueste(r,s)**

neutral *a* neutral. **n~isieren** *vt* neutralize. **N~ität** *f* - neutrality

Neutrum *nt* -s,-tra neuter noun

neu|vermählt *a* **n~vermähltes Paar** newly-weds *pl*. **N~zeit** *f* modern times *pl*

nicht *adv* not; **ich kann n~** I cannot *or* can't; **er ist n~ gekommen** he hasn't come; **n~ mehr/besser als** no more/better than; **bitte n~!** please don't! **n~ berühren!** do not touch! **du kommst doch auch, ~ [wahr]?** you are coming too, aren't you? **du kennst ihn doch, n~?** you know him, don't you?

Nichtachtung *f* disregard; (*Geringschätzung*) disdain

Nichte *f* -,-n niece

nichtig *a* trivial; (*Jur*) [null and] void

Nichtraucher *m* non-smoker. **N~abteil** *nt* non-smoking compartment

nichts *pron* & *a* nothing; **n~ anderes/Besseres** nothing else/better; **n~ mehr** no more; **ich weiß n~** I know nothing *or* don't know anything. **N~** *nt* - nothingness; (*fig: Leere*) void; (*Person*) nonentity. **n~ahnend** *a* unsuspecting

Nichtschwimmer *m* non-swimmer

nichtsdesto|trotz *adv* all the same. **n~weniger** *adv* nevertheless

nichts|nutzig *a* good-for-nothing; (*fam: unartig*) naughty. **n~sagend** *a* meaningless; (*uninteressant*) nondescript. **N~tun** *nt* -s idleness

Nickel *nt* -s nickel

nicken *vi* (*haben*) nod. **N~** *nt* -s nod

Nickerchen *nt* -s,- (*fam*) nap; **ein N~ machen** have forty winks

nie *adv* never

nieder *a* low ● *adv* down. **n~brennen†** *vt/i sep* (*sein*) burn down. **N~deutsch** *nt* Low German. **N~gang** *m* (*fig*) decline. **n~gedrückt** *a* (*fig*) depressed. **n~gehen†** *vi sep* (*sein*) come down. **n~geschlagen** *a* dejected, despondent. **N~geschlagenheit** *f* - dejection, despondency. **N~kunft** *f* -,-̈e confinement. **N~lage** *f* defeat

Niederlande (die) *pl* the Netherlands

Niederländ|er *m* -s,- Dutchman; **die N~er** the Dutch *pl*. **N~erin** *f* -,-nen Dutchwoman. **n~isch** *a* Dutch

nieder|lassen† *vt sep* let down; **sich n~lassen** settle; (*sich setzen*) sit down. **N~lassung** *f* -,-en settlement; (*Zweigstelle*) branch. **n~legen** *vt sep* put *or* lay down; resign (*Amt*); **die Arbeit n~legen** go on strike; **sich n~legen** lie down. **n~machen, n~metzeln** *vt sep* massacre. **n~reißen†** *vt sep* tear down. **N~sachsen** *nt* Lower Saxony. **N~schlag** *m* precipitation; (*Regen*) rainfall; (*radioaktiver*) fall-out; (*Boxen*) knock-down. **n~schlagen**† *vt sep* knock down; lower ⟨*Augen*⟩; (*unterdrücken*) crush. **n~schmettern** *vt sep* (*fig*) shatter. **n~schreiben**† *vt sep* write down. **n~schreien**† *vt sep* shout down. **n~setzen** *vt sep* put *or* set down; **sich n~setzen** sit down. **n~strecken** *vt sep* fell; (*durch Schuß*) gun down

niederträchtig *a* base, vile

Niederung *f* -,-en low ground

nieder|walzen *vt* *sep* flatten. **n~werfen**† *vt sep* throw down; (*unterdrücken*) crush; **sich n~werfen** prostrate oneself

niedlich *a* pretty; (*goldig*) sweet; (*Amer*) cute

niedrig *a* low; (*fig: gemein*) base ● *adv* low

niemals *adv* never

niemand *pron* nobody, no one

Niere *f* -,-n kidney; **künstliche N~** kidney machine

niesel|n *vi* (*haben*) drizzle; **es n~t** it is drizzling. **N~regen** *m* drizzle

niesen *vi* (*haben*) sneeze. **N~** *nt* -s sneezing; (*Nieser*) sneeze

Niet *m* & *nt* -[e]s,-e, **Niete**[1] *f* -,-n rivet; (*an Jeans*) stud

Niete[2] *f* -,-n blank; (*fam*) failure

nieten *vt* rivet

Nikotin *nt* -s nicotine

Nil *m* -[s] Nile. **N~pferd** *nt* hippopotamus

nimmer *adv* (*SGer*) not any more; **nie und n~** never. **n~müde** *a* tireless. **n~satt** *a* insatiable. **N~wiedersehen** *nt* **auf N~wiedersehen** (*fam*) for good

nippen *vi* (*haben*) take a sip (**an** + *dat* of)

nirgend|s, n~wo *adv* nowhere

Nische *f* -,-n recess, niche

nisten *vi* (*haben*) nest

Nitrat *nt* -[e]s,-e nitrate

Niveau /ni'vo:/ *nt* -s,-s level; (*geistig, künstlerisch*) standard

nix *adv* (*fam*) nothing

Nixe *f* -,-n mermaid

nobel *a* noble; (*fam: luxuriös*) luxurious; (*fam: großzügig*) generous

noch *adv* still; (*zusätzlich*) as well; (*mit Komparativ*) even; **n~ nicht** not yet; **gerade n~** only just; **n~ immer** *od* **immer n~** still; **n~ letzte Woche** only last week; **es ist n~ viel Zeit** there's plenty of time yet; **wer/was/**

wo n~? who/what/where else? **n~ jemand/etwas** someone/something else; (*Frage*) anyone/anything else? **n~ einmal** again; **n~ ein Bier** another beer; **n~ größer** even bigger; **n~ so sehr/schön** however much/beautiful ● *conj* **weder ... n~** neither ... nor

nochmal|ig *a* further. **n~s** *adv* again

Nomad|e *m* -n,-n nomad. **n~isch** *a* nomadic

Nominativ *m* -s,-e nominative

nominell *a* nominal, *adv* -ly

nominier|en *vt* nominate. **N~ung** *f* -,-en nomination

nonchalant /nõʃa'lã:/ *a* nonchalant, *adv* -ly

Nonne *f* -,-n nun. **N~nkloster** *nt* convent

Nonstopflug *m* direct flight

Nord *m* -[e]s north. **N~amerika** *nt* North America. **n~deutsch** *a* North German

Norden *m* -s north; **nach N~** north

nordisch *a* Nordic

nördlich *a* northern; ⟨*Richtung*⟩ northerly ● *adv* & *prep* (+ *gen*) **n~ [von] der Stadt** [to the] north of the town

Nordosten *m* north-east

Nord|pol *m* North Pole. **N~see** *f* - North Sea. **n~wärts** *adv* northwards. **N~westen** *m* north-west

Nörgelei *f* -,-en grumbling

nörgeln *vi* (*haben*) grumble

Norm *f* -,-en norm; (*Techn*) standard; (*Soll*) quota

normal *a* normal, *adv* -ly. **n~erweise** *adv* normally. **n~isieren** *vt* normalize; **sich n~isieren** return to normal

normen, normieren *vt* standardize

Norwe|gen *nt* -s Norway. **N~ger(in)** *m* -s,- (*f* -,-nen) Norwegian. **n~gisch** *a* Norwegian

Nost|algie *f* - nostalgia. **n~algisch** *a* nostalgic

Not *f* -,-̈e need; (*Notwendigkeit*) necessity; (*Entbehrung*) hardship; (*seelisch*) trouble; **Not leiden** be in need, suffer hardship; **mit knapper Not** only just; **zur Not** if need be; (*äußerstenfalls*) at a pinch

Notar *m* -s,-e notary public

Not|arzt *m* emergency doctor. **N~ausgang** *m* emergency exit. **N~behelf** *m* -[e]s,-e makeshift. **N~bremse** *f* emergency brake. **N~dienst** *m* **N~dienst haben** be on call. **n~dürftig** a scant; (*behelfsmäßig*) makeshift

Note f -,-n note; (*Zensur*) mark; **ganze/ halbe N~** (*Mus*) semibreve/minim; (*Amer*) whole/half note; **N~n lesen** read music; **persönliche N~** personal touch. **N~nblatt** nt sheet of music. **N~nschlüssel** m clef. **N~nständer** m music-stand

Notfall m emergency; **im N~** in an emergency; (*notfalls*) if need be; **für den N~** just in case. **n~s** adv if need be

not|gedrungen adv of necessity. **N~groschen** m nest-egg

notieren vt note down; (*Comm*) quote; **sich** (*dat*) **etw n~** make a note of sth

nötig a necessary; **n~ haben** need; **das N~ste** the essentials pl ● adv urgently. **n~en** vt force; (*auffordern*) press; **laßt euch nicht n~en** help yourselves. **n~enfalls** adv if need be. **N~ung** f - coercion

Notiz f -,-en note; (*Zeitungs-*) item; **[keine] N~ nehmen** von take [no] notice of. **N~buch** nt notebook. **N~kalender** m diary

Not|lage f plight. **n~landen** vi (*sein*) make a forced landing. **N~landung** f forced landing. **n~leidend** a needy. **N~lösung** f stopgap. **N~lüge** f white lie

notorisch a notorious

Not|ruf m emergency call; (*Naut, Aviat*) distress call; (*Nummer*) emergency services number. **N~signal** nt distress signal. **N~stand** m state of emergency. **N~unterkunft** f emergency accommodation. **N~wehr** f - (*Jur*) self-defence

notwendig a necessary; (*unerläßlich*) essential ● adv urgently. **N~keit** f -,-en necessity

Notzucht f - (*Jur*) rape

Nougat /'nu:gat/ m & nt -s nougat

Novelle f -,-n novella; (*Pol*) amendment

November m -s,- November

Novität f -,-en novelty

Novize m -n,-n, **Novizin** f -,-nen (*Relig*) novice

Nu m **im Nu** (*fam*) in a flash

Nuance /'nyã:sə/ f -,-n nuance; (*Spur*) shade

nüchtern a sober; (*sachlich*) matter-of-fact; (*schmucklos*) bare; (*ohne Würze*) bland; **auf n~en Magen** on an empty stomach ● adv soberly

Nudel f -,-n piece of pasta; **N~n** pasta sg; (*Band-*) noodles. **N~holz** nt rolling-pin

Nudist m -en,-en nudist

nuklear a nuclear

null inv a zero, nought; (*Teleph*) 0; (*Sport*) nil; (*Tennis*) love; **n~ Fehler** no mistakes; **n~ und nichtig** (*Jur*) null and void. **N~** f -,-en nought, zero; (*fig: Person*) nonentity; **drei Grad unter N~** three degrees below zero. **N~punkt** m zero

numerieren vt number

numerisch a numerical

Nummer f -,-n number; (*Ausgabe*) issue; (*Darbietung*) item; (*Zirkus-*) act; (*Größe*) size. **N~nschild** nt number-/ (*Amer*) license-plate

nun adv now; (*na*) well; (*halt*) just; **von nun an** from now on; **nun gut!** very well then! **das Leben ist nun mal so** life's like that

nur adv only, just; **wo kann sie nur sein?** wherever can she be? **alles, was ich nur will** everything I could possibly want; **er soll es nur versuchen!** (*drohend*) just let him try! **könnte/ hätte ich nur . . .!** if only I could/had . . .! **nur Geduld!** just be patient!

Nürnberg nt -s Nuremberg

nuscheln vt/i (*haben*) mumble

Nuß f -, **Nüsse** nut. **N~baum** m walnut tree. **N~knacker** m -s,- nutcrackers pl. **N~schale** f nutshell

Nüstern fpl nostrils

Nut f -,-en, **Nute** f -,-n groove

Nutte f -,-n (*sl*) tart (*sl*)

nutz|bar a usable; **n~bar machen** utilize; cultivate (*Boden*). **n~bringend** a profitable, adv -bly

nütze a **zu etwas/nichts n~ sein** be useful/useless

nutzen vt use, utilize; (*aus-*) take advantage of ● vi (*haben*) = **nützen**. **N~** m -s benefit; (*Comm*) profit; **N~ ziehen aus** benefit from; **von N~ sein** be useful

nützen vi (*haben*) be useful or of use (*dat* to); (*Mittel:*) be effective; **nichts n~** be useless or no use; **was nützt mir das?** what good is that to me? ● vt = **nutzen**

Nutzholz nt timber

nützlich a useful; **sich n~ machen** make oneself useful. **N~keit** f - usefulness

nutz|los *a* useless; *(vergeblich)* vain. **N~losigkeit** *f* - uselessness. **N~nießer** *m* -s,- beneficiary. **N~ung** *f* - use, utilization

Nylon /'naɪlɔn/ *nt* -s nylon

Nymphe /'nʏmfə/ *f* -,-n nymph

O

o *int* **o ja/nein!** oh yes/no! **o weh!** oh dear!

Oase *f* -,-n oasis

ob *conj* whether; **ob reich, ob arm** rich or poor; **ob sie wohl krank ist?** I wonder whether she is ill; **und ob!** *(fam)* you bet!

Obacht *f* **O~ geben** pay attention; **O~ geben auf** (+ *acc*) look after; **O~!** look out!

Obdach *nt* -[e]s shelter. **o~los** *a* homeless. **O~lose(r)** *m/f* homeless person; **die O~losen** the homeless *pl*

Obduktion /-'tsi̯oːn/ *f* -,-en post-mortem

O-Beine *ntpl* *(fam)* bow-legs, bandy legs. **O-beinig** *a* bandy-legged

oben *adv* at the top; *(auf der Ober-seite)* on top; *(eine Treppe hoch)* upstairs; **da o~** up there; **o~ im Norden** up in the north; **siehe o~** see above; **o~ auf** (+ *acc/dat*) on top of; **nach o~** up[wards]; *(die Treppe hinauf)* upstairs; **von o~** from above/upstairs; **von o~ bis unten** from top to bottom/ ⟨Person⟩ to toe; **jdn von o~ bis unten mustern** look s.o. up and down. **o~an** *adv* at the top. **o~auf** *adv* on top; **o~auf sein** *(fig)* be cheerful. **o~drein** *adv* on top of that. **o~erwähnt, o~genannt** *a* above-mentioned. **o~hin** *adv* casually

Ober *m* -s,- waiter

Ober|arm *m* upper arm. **O~arzt** *m* ≈ senior registrar. **O~befehlshaber** *m* commander-in-chief. **O~begriff** *m* generic term. **O~deck** *nt* upper deck. **o~e(r,s)** *a* upper; *(höhere)* higher. **O~fläche** *f* surface. **o~flächlich** *a* superficial, *adv* -ly. **O~geschoß** *nt* upper storey. **o~halb** *adv & prep* (+ *gen*) above; **o~halb vom Dorf/des Dorfes** above the village. **O~hand** *f* **die O~hand gewinnen** gain the upper hand. **O~haupt** *nt* *(fig)* head. **O~haus** *nt* *(Pol)* upper house; *(in UK)* House of Lords. **O~hemd** *nt* [man's] shirt

Oberin *f* -,-nen matron; *(Relig)* mother superior

ober|irdisch *a* surface ... ● *adv* above ground. **O~kellner** *m* head waiter. **O~kiefer** *m* upper jaw. **O~körper** *m* upper part of the body. **O~leutnant** *m* lieutenant. **O~licht** *nt* overhead light; *(Fenster)* skylight; *(über Tür)* fanlight. **O~lippe** *f* upper lip

Obers *nt* - *(Aust)* cream

Ober|schenkel *m* thigh. **O~schicht** *f* upper class. **O~schule** *f* grammar school. **O~schwester** *f* *(Med)* sister. **O~seite** *f* upper/*(rechte Seite)* right side

Oberst *m* -en *& -s,-en* colonel

oberste(r,s) *a* top; *(höchste)* highest; *(Befehlshaber, Gerichtshof)* supreme; *(wichtigste)* first

Ober|stimme *f* treble. **O~stufe** *f* upper school. **O~teil** *nt* top. **O~weite** *f* chest/*(der Frau)* bust size

obgleich *conj* although

Obhut *f* - care; **in guter O~ sein** be well looked after

obig *a* above

Objekt *nt* -[e]s,-e object; *(Haus, Grundstück)* property; **O~ der Forschung** subject of research

Objektiv *nt* -s,-e lens. **o~** *a* objective, *adv* -ly. **O~ität** *f* - objectivity

Oblate *f* -,-n *(Relig)* wafer

obliga|t *a* *(fam)* inevitable. **O~tion** /-'tsi̯oːn/ *f* -,-en obligation; *(Comm)* bond. **o~torisch** *a* obligatory

Obmann *m* *(pl* **-männer**) [jury] foreman; *(Sport)* referee

Oboe /o'boːə/ *f* -,-n oboe

Obrigkeit *f* - authorities *pl*

obschon *conj* although

Observatorium *nt* -s,-ien observatory

obskur *a* obscure; *(zweifelhaft)* dubious

Obst *nt* -es *(coll)* fruit. **O~baum** *m* fruit-tree. **O~garten** *m* orchard. **O~händler** *m* fruiterer. **O~kuchen** *m* fruit flan. **O~salat** *m* fruit salad

obszön *a* obscene. **O~ität** *f* -,-en obscenity

O-Bus *m* trolley bus

obwohl *conj* although

Ochse *m* -n,-n ox. **o~n** *vi* *(haben)* *(fam)* swot. **O~nschwanzsuppe** *f* oxtail soup

öde a desolate; (*unfruchtbar*) barren; (*langweilig*) dull. **Öde** f - desolation; barrenness; dullness; (*Gegend*) waste
oder *conj* or; **du kennst ihn doch, o~?** you know him, don't you?
Ofen m -s,~̈ stove; (*Heiz-*) heater; (*Back-*) oven; (*Techn*) furnace
offen a open, *adv* -ly; (*Haar*) loose; (*Flamme*) naked; (*o~herzig*) frank, *adv* -ly; (*o~ gezeigt*) overt, *adv* -ly; (*unentschieden*) unsettled; **o~e Stelle** vacancy; **Tag der o~en Tür** open day; **Wein o~ verkaufen** sell wine by the glass; *adv* **o~ gesagt** *od* **gestanden** to be honest. **o~bar** a obvious ● *adv* apparently. **o~baren** *vt* reveal. **O~barung** f -,-en revelation. **o~bleiben†** *vi sep* (*sein*) remain open. **o~halten†** *vt sep* hold open (*Tür*); keep open (*Mund, Augen*). **O~heit** f - frankness, openness. **o~herzig** a frank, *adv* -ly. **O~herzigkeit** f - frankness. **o~kundig** a manifest, *adv* -ly. **o~lassen†** *vt sep* leave open; leave vacant (*Stelle*). **o~sichtlich** a obvious, *adv* -ly
offensiv a offensive. **O~e** f -,-n offensive
offenstehen† *vi sep* (*haben*) be open; (*Rechnung:*) be outstanding; **jdm o~** (*fig*) be open to s.o.
öffentlich a public, *adv* -ly. **Ö~keit** f - public; **an die Ö~keit gelangen** become public; **in aller Ö~keit** in public, publicly
Offerte f -,-n (*Comm*) offer
offiziell a official, *adv* -ly
Offizier m -s,-e (*Mil*) officer
öffn|en *vt/i* (*haben*) open; **sich ö~en** open. **Ö~er** m -s,- opener. **Ö~ung** f -,-en opening. **Ö~ungszeiten** *fpl* opening hours
oft *adv* often
öfter *adv* quite often. **ö~e(r,s)** a frequent; **des ö~en** frequently. **ö~s** *adv* (*fam*) quite often
oftmals *adv* often
oh *int* oh!
ohne *prep* (+ *acc*) without; **o~ mich!** count me out! **oben o~** topless; **nicht o~ sein** (*fam*) be not bad; (*nicht harmlos*) be quite nasty ● *conj* **o~ zu überlegen** without thinking; **o~ daß ich es merkte** without my noticing it. **o~dies** *adv* anyway. **o~gleichen** *pred* a unparalleled; **eine Frechheit o~gleichen** a piece of unprecedented insolence. **o~hin** *adv* anyway

Ohn|macht f -,-en faint; (*fig*) powerlessness; **in O~macht fallen** faint. **o~mächtig** a unconscious; (*fig*) powerless; **o~mächtig werden** faint
Ohr nt -[e]s,-en ear; **übers Ohr hauen** (*fam*) cheat
Öhr nt -[e]s,-e eye
ohren|betäubend a deafening. **O~schmalz** nt ear-wax. **O~schmerzen** *mpl* earache sg. **O~sessel** m wing-chair. **O~tropfen** *mpl* ear drops
Ohrfeige f slap in the face; **jdm eine O~ geben** slap s.o.'s face. **o~n** *vt* **jdn o~n** slap s.o.'s face
Ohr|läppchen nt -s,- ear-lobe. **O~ring** m ear-ring. **O~wurm** m earwig
oje *int* oh dear!
okay /o'ke:/ a & *adv* (*fam*) OK
okkult a occult
Öko|logie f - ecology. **ö~logisch** a ecological. **Ö~nomie** f - economy; (*Wissenschaft*) economics sg. **ö~nomisch** a economic; (*sparsam*) economical
Oktave f -,-n octave
Oktober m -s,- October
Okular nt -s,-e eyepiece
okulieren *vt* graft
ökumenisch a ecumenical
Öl nt -[e]s,-e oil; **in Öl malen** paint in oils. **Ölbaum** m olive-tree. **ölen** *vt* oil; **wie ein geölter Blitz** (*fam*) like greased lightning. **Ölfarbe** f oil-paint. **Ölfeld** nt oilfield. **Ölgemälde** nt oil-painting. **ölig** a oily
Oliv|e f -,-n olive. **O~enöl** nt olive oil. **o~grün** a olive[-green]
oll a (*fam*) old; (*fam: häßlich*) nasty
Ölmeßstab m dip-stick. **Ölsardinen** *fpl* sardines in oil. **Ölstand** m oil-level. **Öltanker** m oil-tanker. **Ölteppich** m oil-slick
Olympiade f -,-n Olympic Games *pl*, Olympics *pl*
Olymp|iasieger(in) /o'lʏmpia-/ m(f) Olympic champion. **o~isch** a Olympic; **O~ische Spiele** Olympic Games
Ölzeug nt oilskins *pl*
Oma f -,-s (*fam*) granny
Omelett nt -[e]s,-e & -s omelette
Omen nt -s,- omen
ominös a ominous
Omnibus m bus; (*Reise-*) coach
onanieren *vi* (*haben*) masturbate
Onkel m -s,- uncle

Opa *m* -s,-s (*fam*) grandad

Opal *m* -s,-e opal

Oper *f* -,-n opera

Operation /-'ts̮io:n/ *f* -,-en operation. **O∼ssaal** *m* operating-theatre

Operette *f* -,-n operetta

operieren *vt* operate on ⟨*Patient, Herz*⟩; **sich o∼ lassen** have an operation ● *vi (haben)* operate

Opern|glas *nt* opera-glasses *pl*. **O∼haus** *nt* opera-house. **O∼sänger(in)** *m(f)* opera-singer

Opfer *nt* -s,- sacrifice; (*eines Unglücks*) victim; **ein O∼ bringen** make a sacrifice; **jdm/etw zum O∼ fallen** fall victim to s.o./sth. **o∼n** *vt* sacrifice. **O∼ung** *f* -,-en sacrifice

Opium *nt* -s opium

opponieren *vi (haben)* **o∼ gegen** oppose

Opportunist *m* -en,-en opportunist. **o∼isch** *a* opportunist

Opposition /-'ts̮io:n/ *f* - opposition. **O∼spartei** *f* opposition party

Optik *f* - optics *sg*; (*fam: Objektiv*) lens. **O∼er** *m* -s,- optician

optimal *a* optimum

Optimis|mus *m* - optimism. **O∼t** *m* -en,-en optimist. **o∼tisch** *a* optimistic, *adv* -ally

Optimum *nt* -s,-ma optimum

Option /ɔp'ts̮io:n/ *f* -,-en option

optisch *a* optical; ⟨*Eindruck*⟩ visual

Orakel *nt* -s,- oracle

Orange /o'rãːʒə/ *f* -,-n orange. **o∼** *inv a* orange. **O∼ade** /orãʒaːdə/ *f* -,-n orangeade. **O∼nmarmelade** *f* [orange] marmalade. **O∼nsaft** *m* orange juice

Oratorium *nt* -s,-ien oratorio

Orchest|er /ɔr'kɛstɐ/ *nt* -s,- orchestra. **o∼rieren** *vt* orchestrate

Orchidee /ɔrçi'deːə/ *f* -,-n orchid

Orden *m* -s,- (*Ritter-, Kloster-*) order; (*Auszeichnung*) medal, decoration; **jdm einen O∼ verleihen** decorate s.o. **O∼stracht** *f* (*Relig*) habit

ordentlich *a* neat, tidy; (*anständig*) respectable; (*ordnungsgemäß, fam: richtig*) proper; ⟨*Mitglied, Versammlung*⟩ ordinary; (*fam: gut*) decent; (*fam: gehörig*) good ● *adv* neatly, tidily; respectably; properly; (*fam: gut, gehörig*) well; (*sehr*) very; (*regelrecht*) really

Order *f* -,-s & -n order

ordinär *a* common

Ordin|ation /-'ts̮io:n/ *f* -,-en (*Relig*) ordination; (*Aust*) surgery. **o∼ieren** *vt* (*Relig*) ordain

ordn|en *vt* put in order; (*aufräumen*) tidy; (*an-*) arrange; **sich zum Zug o∼en** form a procession. **O∼er** *m* -s,- steward; (*Akten-*) file

Ordnung *f* - order; **O∼ halten** keep order; **O∼ machen** tidy up; **in O∼ bringen** put in order; (*aufräumen*) tidy; (*reparieren*) mend; (*fig*) put right; **in O∼ sein** be in order; (*ordentlich sein*) be tidy; (*fig*) be all right; **ich bin mit dem Magen** *od* **mein Magen ist nicht ganz in O∼** I have a slight stomach upset; **[geht] in O∼!** OK! **o∼sgemäß** *a* proper, *adv* -ly. **O∼sstrafe** *f* (*Jur*) fine. **o∼swidrig** *a* improper, *adv* -ly

Ordonnanz *f* -,-en (*Mil*) orderly

Organ *nt* -s,-e organ; (*fam: Stimme*) voice

Organi|sation /-'ts̮io:n/ *f* -,-en organization. **O∼sator** *m* -s,-en /-'toːrən/ organizer

organisch *a* organic, *adv* -ally

organisieren *vt* organize; (*fam: beschaffen*) get [hold of]

Organismus *m* -,-men organism; (*System*) system

Organist *m* -en,-en organist

Organspenderkarte *f* donor card

Orgasmus *m* -,-men orgasm

Orgel *f* -,-n (*Mus*) organ. **O∼pfeife** *f* organ-pipe

Orgie /'ɔrgiə/ *f* -,-n orgy

Orien|t /'oːriɛnt/ *m* -s Orient. **o∼talisch** *a* Oriental

orientier|en /orjɛn'tiːrən/ *vt* inform (**über** + *acc* about); **sich o∼en** get one's bearings, orientate oneself; (*unterrichten*) inform oneself (**über** + *acc* about). **O∼ung** *f* - orientation; **die O∼ung verlieren** lose one's bearings

original *a* original. **O∼** *nt* -s,-e original; (*Person*) character. **O∼ität** *f* - originality. **O∼übertragung** *f* live transmission

originell *a* original; (*eigenartig*) unusual

Orkan *m* -s,-e hurricane

Ornament *nt* -[e]s,-e ornament

Ornat *m* -[e]s,-e robes *pl*

Ornithologie *f* - ornithology

Ort *m* -[e]s,-e place; (*Ortschaft*) [small] town; **am Ort** locally; **am Ort des Verbrechens** at the scene of the crime; **an Ort und Stelle** in the right place; (*sofort*) on the spot. **o∼en** *vt* locate

ortho|dox *a* orthodox. **O~graphie** *f* - spelling. **o~graphisch** *a* spelling . . . **O~päde** *m* -n,-n orthopaedic specialist. **o~pädisch** *a* orthopaedic

örtlich *a* local, *adv* -ly. **Ö~keit** *f* -,-en locality

Ortschaft *f* -,-en [small] town; (*Dorf*) village; **geschlossene O~** (*Auto*) built-up area

orts|fremd *a* **o~fremd sein** be a stranger. **O~gespräch** *nt* (*Teleph*) local call. **O~name** *m* place-name. **O~sinn** *m* sense of direction. **O~verkehr** *m* local traffic. **O~zeit** *f* local time

Öse *f* -,-n eyelet; (*Schlinge*) loop; **Haken und Öse** hook and eye

Ost *m* -[e]s east. **o~deutsch** *a* Eastern/(*Pol*) East German

Osten *m* -s east; **nach O~** east

ostentativ *a* pointed, *adv* -ly

Osteopath *m* -en,-en osteopath

Oster|ei /'o:stɐʔaj/ *nt* Easter egg. **O~fest** *nt* Easter. **O~glocke** *f* daffodil. **O~montag** *m* Easter Monday. **O~n** *nt* -,- Easter; **frohe O~n!** happy Easter!

Österreich *nt* -s Austria. **Ö~er** *m* -s,-, **Ö~erin** *f* -,-nen Austrian. **ö~isch** *a* Austrian

östlich *a* eastern; (*Richtung*) easterly ● *adv & prep* (+*gen*) **ö~ [von] der Stadt** [to the] east of the town

Ost|see *f* Baltic [Sea]. **o~wärts** *adv* eastwards

oszillieren *vi* (*haben*) oscillate

Otter[1] *m* -s,- otter

Otter[2] *f* -,-n adder

Ouverture /uvɛr'ty:rə/ *f* -,-n overture

oval *a* oval. **O~** *nt* -s,-e oval

Ovation /-'tsio:n/ *f* -,-en ovation

Ovulation /-'tsio:n/ *f* -,-en ovulation

Oxid, Oxyd *nt* -[e]s,-e oxide

Ozean *m* -s,-e ocean

Ozon *nt* -s ozone. **O~loch** *nt* hole in the ozone layer. **O~schicht** *f* ozone layer

P

paar *pron inv* **ein p~** a few; **alle p~ Tage** every few days. **P~** *nt* -[e]s,-e pair; (*Ehe-, Liebes-, Tanz-*) couple. **p~en** *vt* mate; (*verbinden*) combine; **sich p~en** mate. **P~ung** *f* -,-en mating. **p~weise** *adv* in pairs, in twos

Pacht *f* -,-en lease; (*P~summe*) rent. **p~en** *vt* lease

Pächter *m* -s,- lessee; (*eines Hofes*) tenant

Pachtvertrag *m* lease

Pack[1] *m* -[e]s,-e bundle

Pack[2] *nt* -[e]s (*sl*) rabble

Päckchen *nt* -s,- package, small packet

pack|en *vt/i* (*haben*) pack; (*ergreifen*) seize; (*fig: fesseln*) grip; **p~ dich!** (*sl*) beat it! **P~en** *m* -s,- bundle. **p~end** *a* (*fig*) gripping. **P~papier** *nt* [strong] wrapping paper. **P~ung** *f* -,-en packet; (*Med*) pack

Pädagog|e *m* -n,-n educationalist; (*Lehrer*) teacher. **P~ik** *f* - educational science. **p~isch** *a* educational

Paddel *nt* -s,- paddle. **P~boot** *nt* canoe. **p~n** *vt/i* (*haben/sein*) paddle. **P~sport** *m* canoeing

Page /'pa:ʒə/ *m* -n,-n page

Paillette /paj'jɛtə/ *f* -,-n sequin

Paket *nt* -[e]s,-e packet; (*Post-*) parcel

Pakist|an *nt* -s Pakistan. **P~aner(in)** *m* -s,- (*f* -,-nen) Pakistani. **p~anisch** *a* Pakistani

Pakt *m* -[e]s,-e pact

Palast *m* -[e]s,¨e palace

Paläst|ina *nt* -s Palestine. **P~i-nenser(in)** *m* -s,- (*f* -,-nen) Palestinian. **p~inensisch** *a* Palestinian

Palette *f* -,-n palette

Palm|e *f* -,-n palm[-tree]; **jdn auf die P~e bringen** (*fam*) drive s.o. up the wall. **P~sonntag** *m* Palm Sunday

Pampelmuse *f* -,-n grapefruit

Panier|mehl *nt* (*Culin*) breadcrumbs *pl*. **p~t** *a* (*Culin*) breaded

Panik *f* - panic; **in P~ geraten** panic

panisch *a* **p~e Angst** panic

Panne *f* -,-n breakdown; (*Reifen-*) flat tyre; (*Mißgeschick*) mishap. **P~dienst** *m* breakdown service

Panorama *nt* -s panorama

panschen *vt* adulterate ● *vi* (*haben*) splash about

Pantine *f* -,-n [wooden] clog

Pantoffel *m* -s,-n slipper; (*ohne Ferse*) mule. **P~held** *m* (*fam*) henpecked husband

Pantomime[1] *f* -,-n mime

Pantomime[2] *m* -n,-n mime artist

pantschen *vt/i* = panschen

Panzer *m* -s,- armour; (*Mil*) tank; (*Zool*) shell. **p~n** *vt* armour-plate. **P~schrank** *m* safe

Papa /'papa, pa'pa:/ *m* -s,-s daddy

Papagei *m* -s & -en,-en parrot

Papier *nt* -[e]s,-e paper. **P~korb** *m* waste-paper basket. **P~schlange** *f* streamer. **P~waren** *fpl* stationery *sg*

Pappe *f* - cardboard; *(dial: Kleister)* glue

Pappel *f* -,-n poplar

pappen *vt/i (haben) (fam)* stick

pappig *a (fam)* sticky

Papp|karton *m*, **P~schachtel** *f* cardboard box

Paprika *m* -s,-[s] [sweet] pepper; *(Gewürz)* paprika

Papst *m* -[e]s,¨e pope

päpstlich *a* papal

Parade *f* -,-n parade

Paradeiser *m* -s,- *(Aust)* tomato

Paradies *nt* -es,-e paradise. **p~isch** *a* heavenly

Paradox *nt* -es,-e paradox. **p~** *a* paradoxical

Paraffin *nt* -s paraffin

Paragraph *m* -en,-en section

parallel *a & adv* parallel. **P~e** *f* -,-n parallel

Paranuß *f* Brazil nut

Parasit *m* -en,-en parasite

parat *a* ready

Pärchen *nt* -s,- pair; *(Liebes-)* couple

Parcours /par'kuːɐ̯/ *m* -,- /-[s],-s/ *(Sport)* course

Pardon /par'dõː/ *int* sorry!

Parfüm *nt* -s,-e & -s perfume, scent. **p~iert** *a* perfumed, scented

parieren¹ *vt* parry

parieren² *vi (haben) (fam)* obey

Parität *f* - parity; *(in Ausschuß)* equal representation

Park *m* -s,-s park. **p~en** *vt/i (haben)* park. **P~en** *nt* -s parking; **'P~en verboten'** 'no parking'

Parkett *nt* -[e]s,-e parquet floor; *(Theat)* stalls *pl*

Park|haus *nt* multi-storey car park. **P~lücke** *f* parking space. **P~platz** *m* car park, *(Amer)* parking-lot; *(für ein Auto)* parking space; *(Autobahn-)* lay-by. **P~scheibe** *f* parking-disc. **P~schein** *m* car-park ticket. **P~uhr** *f* parking-meter. **P~verbot** *nt* parking ban; **'P~verbot'** 'no parking'

Parlament *nt* -[e]s,-e parliament. **p~arisch** *a* parliamentary

Parodie *f* -,-n parody. **p~ren** *vt* parody

Parole *f* -,-n slogan; *(Mil)* password

Part *m* -s,-s *(Theat, Mus)* part

Partei *f* -,-en *(Pol, Jur)* party; *(Miet-)* tenant; **für jdn P~ ergreifen** take s.o.'s part. **p~isch** *a* biased. **p~los** *a* independent

Parterre /par'tɛr/ *nt* -s,-s ground floor, *(Amer)* first floor; *(Theat)* rear stalls *pl*. **p~** *adv* on the ground floor

Partie *f* -,-n part; *(Tennis, Schach)* game; *(Golf)* round; *(Comm)* batch; **eine gute P~ machen** marry well

Partikel¹ *nt* -s,- particle

Partikel² *f* -,-n *(Gram)* particle

Partitur *f* -,-en *(Mus)* full score

Partizip *nt* -s,-ien /-ɪ̯ən/ participle; **erstes/zweites P~** present/past participle

Partner|(in) *m* -s,- *(f* -,-nen*)* partner. **P~schaft** *f* -,-en partnership. **P~stadt** *f* twin town

Party /'paːɐ̯ti/ *f* -,-s party

Parzelle *f* -,-n plot [of ground]

Paß *m* -sses,¨sse passport; *(Geog, Sport)* pass

passabel *a* passable

Passage /pa'saːʒə/ *f* -,-n passage; *(Einkaufs-)* shopping arcade

Passagier /pasa'ʒiːɐ̯/ *m* -s,-e passenger

Paßamt *nt* passport office

Passant(in) *m* -en,-en *(f* -,-nen*)* passer-by

Paßbild *nt* passport photograph

Passe *f* -,-n yoke

passen *vi (haben)* fit; *(geeignet sein)* be right *(für* for*)*; *(Sport)* pass the ball; *(aufgeben)* pass; **p~ zu** go [well] with; *(übereinstimmen)* match; **jdm p~** fit s.o.; *(gelegen sein)* suit s.o.; **seine Art paßt mir nicht** I don't like his manner; **[ich] passe** pass. **p~d** *a* suitable; *(angemessen)* appropriate; *(günstig)* convenient; *(übereinstimmend)* matching

passier|bar *a* passable. **p~en** *vt* pass; cross ⟨Grenze⟩; *(Culin)* rub through a sieve ● *vi (sein)* happen (**jdm** to s.o.); **es ist ein Unglück p~t** there has been an accident. **P~schein** *m* pass

Passion *f* -,-en passion. **p~iert** *a* very keen ⟨Jäger, Angler⟩

passiv *a* passive. **P~** *nt* -s,-e *(Gram)* passive

Paß|kontrolle *f* passport control. **P~straße** *f* pass

Paste *f* -,-n paste

Pastell *nt* -[e]s,-e pastel. **P~farbe** *f* pastel colour

Pastet|chen *nt* **-s,-** [individual] pie; (*Königin-*) vol-au-vent. **P~e** *f* **-,-n** pie; (*Gänseleber-*) pâté

pasteurisieren /pastøri'ziːrən/ *vt* pasteurize

Pastille *f* **-,-n** pastille

Pastinake *f* **-,-n** parsnip

Pastor *m* **-s,-en** /-'toːrən/ pastor

Pate *m* **-n,-n** godfather; (*fig*) sponsor; **P~n** godparents. **P~nkind** *nt* godchild. **P~nschaft** *f* - sponsorship. **P~nsohn** *m* godson

Patent *nt* **-[e]s,-e** patent; (*Offiziers-*) commission. **p~** *a* (*fam*) clever, *adv* -ly; (*Person*) resourceful. **p~ieren** *vt* patent

Patentochter *f* god-daughter

Pater *m* **-s,-** (*Relig*) Father

pathetisch *a* emotional ● *adv* with emotion

Patholog|e *m* **-n,-n** pathologist. **p~isch** *a* pathological, *adv* -ly

Pathos *nt* - emotion, feeling

Patience /pa'sjãːs/ *f* **-,-n** patience

Patient(in) /pa'tsjɛnt(ɪn)/ *m* **-en,-en** (*f* **-,-nen**) patient

Patin *f* **-,-nen** godmother

Patriot|(in) *m* **-en,-en** (*f* **-,-nen**) patriot. **p~isch** *a* patriotic. **P~ismus** *m* - patriotism

Patrone *f* **-,-nen** cartridge

Patrouill|e /pa'trʊljə/ *f* **-,-n** patrol. **p~ieren** /-'jiːrən/ *vi* (*haben/sein*) patrol

Patsch|e *f* in der **P~e sitzen** (*fam*) be in a jam. **p~en** *vi* (*haben/sein*) splash ● *vt* slap. **p~naß** *a* (*fam*) soaking wet

Patt *nt* **-s** stalemate

Patz|er *m* **-s,-** (*fam*) slip. **p~ig** *a* (*fam*) insolent

Pauk|e *f* **-,-n** kettledrum; **auf die P~e hauen** (*fam*) have a good time; (*prahlen*) boast. **p~en** *vt/i* (*haben*) (*fam*) swot. **P~er** *m* **-s,-** (*fam: Lehrer*) teacher

pausbäckig *a* chubby-cheeked

pauschal *a* all-inclusive; (*einheitlich*) flat-rate; (*fig*) sweeping (*Urteil*); **p~e Summe** lump sum ● *adv* in a lump sum; (*fig*) wholesale. **P~e** *f* **-,-n** lump sum. **P~reise** *f* package tour. **P~summe** *f* lump sum

Pause[1] *f* **-,-n** break; (*beim Sprechen*) pause; (*Theat*) interval; (*im Kino*) intermission; (*Mus*) rest; **P~ machen** have a break

Pause[2] *f* **-,-n** tracing. **p~n** *vt* trace

pausenlos *a* incessant, *adv* -ly

pausieren *vi* (*haben*) have a break; (*ausruhen*) rest

Pauspapier *nt* tracing-paper

Pavian *m* **-s,-e** baboon

Pavillon /'paviljõ/ *m* **-s,-s** pavilion

Pazifi|k *m* **-s** Pacific [Ocean]. **p~sch** *a* Pacific

Pazifist *m* **-en,-en** pacifist

Pech *nt* **-s** pitch; (*Unglück*) bad luck; **P~ haben** be unlucky. **p~schwarz** *a* pitch-black; (*Haare, Augen*) jet-black. **P~strähne** *f* run of bad luck. **P~vogel** *m* (*fam*) unlucky devil

Pedal *nt* **-s,-e** pedal

Pedant *m* **-en,-en** pedant. **p~isch** *a* pedantic, *adv* -ally

Pediküre *f* **-,-n** pedicure

Pegel *m* **-s,-** level; (*Gerät*) water-level indicator. **P~stand** *m* [water] level

peilen *vt* take a bearing on; **über den Daumen gepeilt** (*fam*) at a rough guess

Pein *f* - (*liter*) torment. **p~igen** *vt* torment

peinlich *a* embarrassing, awkward; (*genau*) scrupulous, *adv* -ly; **es war mir sehr p~** I was very embarrassed

Peitsche *f* **-,-n** whip. **p~n** *vt* whip; (*fig*) lash ● *vi* (*gegen*) lash (**an**+*acc* against). **P~nhieb** *m* lash

pekuniär *a* financial, *adv* -ly

Pelikan *m* **-s,-e** pelican

Pell|e *f* **-,-n** skin. **p~en** *vt* peel; shell (*Ei*); **sich p~en** peel. **P~kartoffeln** *fpl* potatoes boiled in their skins

Pelz *m* **-es,-e** fur. **P~mantel** *m* fur coat

Pendel *nt* **-s,-** pendulum. **p~n** *vi* (*haben*) swing ● *vi* (*sein*) commute. **P~verkehr** *m* shuttle-service; (*für Pendler*) commuter traffic

Pendler *m* **-s,-** commuter

penetrant *a* penetrating; (*fig*) obtrusive, *adv* -ly

penibel *a* fastidious, fussy; (*pedantisch*) pedantic

Penis *m* **-,-se** penis

Penne *f* **-,-n** (*fam*) school. **p~n** *vi* (*haben*) (*fam*) sleep. **P~r** *m* **-s,-** (*sl*) tramp

Pension /pã'zjoːn/ *f* **-,-en** pension; (*Hotel*) guest-house; **bei voller/halber P~** with full/half board. **P~är(in)** *m* **-s,-e** (*f* **-,-nen**) pensioner. **P~at** *nt* **-[e]s,-e** boarding-school. **p~ieren** *vt* retire. **p~iert** *a* retired. **P~ierung** *f* - retirement

Pensum *nt* -s [allotted] work

Peperoni *f* -,- chilli

per *prep* (+ *acc*) by; **per Luftpost** by airmail

perfekt *a* perfect, *adv* -ly; **p~ sein** ⟨*Vertrag:*⟩ be settled

Perfekt *nt* -s (*Gram*) perfect

Perfektion /-'tsjo:n/ *f* - perfection

perforiert *a* perforated

Pergament *nt* -[e]s,-e parchment. **P~papier** *nt* grease-proof paper

Period|e *f* -,-n period. **p~isch** *a* periodic, *adv* -ally

Perl|e *f* -,-n pearl; (*Glas-, Holz-*) bead; (*Sekt-*) bubble; (*fam: Hilfe*) treasure. **p~en** *vi* (*haben*) bubble. **P~mutt** *nt* -s, **P~mutter** *f* - & *nt* -s mother-of-pearl

perplex *a* (*fam*) perplexed

Perserkatze *f* Persian cat

Pers|ien /-jən/ *nt* -s Persia. **p~isch** *a* Persian

Person *f* -,-en person; (*Theat*) character; **ich für meine P~** [I] for my part; **für vier P~en** for four people

Personal *nt* -s personnel, staff. **P~ausweis** *m* identity card. **P~chef** *m* personnel manager. **P~ien** /-jən/ *pl* personal particulars. **P~mangel** *m* staff shortage. **P~pronomen** *nt* personal pronoun

Personen|kraftwagen *m* private car. **P~zug** *m* stopping train

personifizieren *vt* personify

persönlich *a* personal ● *adv* personally, in person. **P~keit** *f* -,-en personality

Perspektive *f* -,-n perspective; (*Zukunfts-*) prospect

Perücke *f* -,-n wig

pervers *a* [sexually] perverted. **P~ion** *f* -,-en perversion

Pessim|ismus *m* - pessimism. **P~t** *m* -en,-en pessimist. **p~tisch** *a* pessimistic, *adv* -ally

Pest *f* - plague

Petersilie /-jə/ *f* - parsley

Petroleum /-leʊm/ *nt* -s paraffin, (*Amer*) kerosene

Petze *f* -,-n (*fam*) sneak. **p~n** *vi* (*haben*) (*fam*) sneak

Pfad *m* -[e]s,-e path. **P~finder** *m* -s,- [Boy] Scout. **P~finderin** *f* -,-nen [Girl] Guide

Pfahl *m* -[e]s,-e stake, post

Pfalz (die) - the Palatinate

Pfand *nt* -[e]s,-er pledge; (*beim Spiel*) forfeit; (*Flaschen-*) deposit

pfänd|en *vt* (*Jur*) seize. **P~erspiel** *nt* game of forfeits

Pfand|haus *nt* pawnshop. **P~leiher** *m* -s,- pawnbroker

Pfändung *f* -,-en (*Jur*) seizure

Pfann|e *f* -,-n [frying-]pan. **P~kuchen** *m* pancake; **Berliner P~kuchen** doughnut

Pfarr|er *m* -s,- vicar, parson; (*katholischer*) priest. **P~haus** *nt* vicarage

Pfau *m* -s,-en peacock

Pfeffer *m* -s pepper. **P~kuchen** *m* gingerbread. **P~minzbonbon** *m* & *nt* [pepper]mint. **P~minze** *f* - (*Bot*) peppermint. **P~minztee** *m* peppermint tea. **p~n** *vt* pepper; (*fam: schmeißen*) chuck. **P~streuer** *m* -s,- pepper-pot

Pfeif|e *f* -,-n whistle; (*Tabak-, Orgel-*) pipe. **p~en†** *vt/i* (*haben*) whistle; (*als Signal*) blow the whistle; **ich p~e darauf!** (*fam*) I couldn't care less [about it]!

Pfeil *m* -[e]s,-e arrow

Pfeiler *m* -s,- pillar; (*Brücken-*) pier

Pfennig *m* -s,-e pfennig; **10 P~** 10 pfennigs

Pferch *m* -[e]s,-e [sheep] pen. **p~en** *vt* (*fam*) cram (**in** + *acc* into)

Pferd *nt* -es,-e horse; **zu P~e** on horseback; **das P~ beim Schwanz aufzäumen** put the cart before the horse. **P~erennen** *nt* horse-race; (*als Sport*) [horse-]racing. **P~eschwanz** *m* horse's tail; (*Frisur*) pony-tail. **P~estall** *m* stable. **P~estärke** *f* horsepower. **P~ewagen** *m* horse-drawn cart

Pfiff *m* -[e]s,-e whistle; **P~ haben** (*fam*) have style

Pfifferling *m* -s,-e chanterelle

pfiffig *a* smart

Pfingst|en *nt* -s Whitsun. **P~montag** *m* Whit Monday. **P~rose** *f* peony

Pfirsich *m* -s,-e peach. **p~farben** *a* peach[-coloured]

Pflanz|e *f* -,-n plant. **p~en** *vt* plant. **P~enfett** *nt* vegetable fat. **p~lich** *a* vegetable; ⟨*Mittel*⟩ herbal. **P~ung** *f* -,-en plantation

Pflaster *nt* -s,- pavement; (*Heft-*) plaster. **p~n** *vt* pave. **P~stein** *m* paving-stone

Pflaume *f* -,-n plum

Pflege *f* - care; (*Kranken-*) nursing; **in P~ nehmen** look after; (*Admin*) foster ⟨*Kind*⟩. **p~bedürftig** *a* in need of care. **P~eltern** *pl* foster-parents.

P~kind *nt* foster-child. **p~leicht** *a* easy-care. **P~mutter** *f* foster-mother. **p~n** *vt* look after, care for; nurse ⟨*Kranke*⟩; cultivate ⟨*Künste, Freundschaft*⟩. **P~r(in)** *m* -s,- (*f* -,-nen) nurse; (*Tier-*) keeper

Pflicht *f* -,-en duty; (*Sport*) compulsory exercise/routine. **p~bewußt** *a* conscientious, *adv* -ly. **p~eifrig** *a* zealous, *adv* -ly. **P~fach** *nt* (*Sch*) compulsory subject. **P~gefühl** *nt* sense of duty. **p~gemäß** *a* due ● *adv* duly

Pflock *m* -[e]s,ˑe peg

pflücken *vt* pick

Pflug *m* -[e]s,ˑe plough

pflügen *vt/i* (*haben*) plough

Pforte *f* -,-n gate

Pförtner *m* -s,- porter

Pfosten *m* -s,- post

Pfote *f* -,-n paw

Pfropfen *m* -s,- stopper; (*Korken*) cork. **p~** *vt* graft (**auf**+*acc* on [to]); (*fam: pressen*) cram (**in**+*acc* into)

pfui *int* ugh; **p~ schäm dich!** you should be ashamed of yourself!

Pfund *nt* -[e]s,-e & - pound

Pfusch|arbeit *f* (*fam*) shoddy work. **p~en** *vi* (*haben*) (*fam*) botch one's work. **P~er** *m* -s,- (*fam*) shoddy worker. **P~erei** *f* -,-en (*fam*) botch-up

Pfütze *f* -,-n puddle

Phänomen *nt* -s,-e phenomenon. **p~al** *a* phenomenal

Phantasie *f* -,-n imagination; **P~n** fantasies; (*Fieber-*) hallucinations. **p~los** *a* unimaginative. **p~ren** *vi* (*haben*) fantasize; (*im Fieber*) be delirious. **p~voll** *a* imaginative, *adv* -ly

phant|astisch *a* fantastic, *adv* -ally. **P~om** *nt* -s,-e phantom

pharma|zeutisch *a* pharmaceutical. **P~zie** *f* - pharmacy

Phase *f* -,-n phase

Philanthrop *m* -en,-en philanthropist. **p~isch** *a* philanthropic

Philolo|ge *m* -n,-n teacher/student of language and literature. **P~gie** *f* - [study of] language and literature

Philosoph *m* -en,-en philosopher. **P~ie** *f* -,-n philosophy. **p~ieren** *vi* (*haben*) philosophize

philosophisch *a* philosophical, *adv* -ly

phlegmatisch *a* phlegmatic

Phobie *f* -,-n phobia

Phonet|ik *f* - phonetics *sg*. **p~isch** *a* phonetic, *adv* -ally

Phonotypistin *f* -,-nen audio typist

Phosphor *m* -s phosphorus

Photo *nt*, **Photo-** *s*. Foto, Foto-

Phrase *f* -,-n empty phrase

Physik *f* - physics *sg*. **p~alisch** *a* physical

Physiker(in) *m* -s,- (*f* -,-nen) physicist

Physio|logie *f* - physiology. **P~therapie** *f* physiotherapy

physisch *a* physical, *adv* -ly

Pianist(in) *m* -en,-en (*f* -,-nen) pianist

Pickel *m* -s,- pimple, spot; (*Spitzhacke*) pick. **p~ig** *a* spotty

picken *vt/i* (*haben*) peck (**nach** at); (*fam: nehmen*) pick (**aus** out of); (*Aust fam: kleben*) stick

Picknick *nt* -s,-s picnic. **p~en** *vi* (*haben*) picnic

piep[s]|en *vi* (*haben*) ⟨*Vogel:*⟩ cheep; ⟨*Maus:*⟩ squeak; (*Techn*) bleep. **P~er** *m* -s,- bleeper

Pier *m* -s,-e [harbour] pier

Pietät /pie'tɛːt/ *f* - reverence. **p~los** *a* irreverent, *adv* -ly

Pigment *nt* -[e]s,-e pigment. **P~ierung** *f* - pigmentation

Pik *nt* -s,-s (*Karten*) spades *pl*

pikant *a* piquant; (*gewagt*) racy

piken *vt* (*fam*) prick

pikiert *a* offended, hurt

piksen *vt* (*fam*) prick

Pilger|(in) *m* -s,- (*f* -,-nen) pilgrim. **P~fahrt** *f* pilgrimage. **p~n** *vi* (*sein*) make a pilgrimage

Pille *f* -,-n pill

Pilot *m* -en,-en pilot

Pilz *m* -es,-e fungus; (*eßbarer*) mushroom; **wie P~e aus dem Boden schießen** (*fig*) mushroom

pingelig *a* (*fam*) fussy

Pinguin *m* -s,-e penguin

Pinie /-jə/ *f* -,-n stone-pine

pink *pred a* shocking pink

pinkeln *vi* (*haben*) (*fam*) pee

Pinsel *m* -s,- [paint]brush

Pinzette *f* -,-n tweezers *pl*

Pionier *m* -s,-e (*Mil*) sapper; (*fig*) pioneer. **P~arbeit** *f* pioneering work

Pirat *m* -en,-en pirate

pirschen *vi* (*haben*) **p~ auf** (+*acc*) stalk ● *vr* **sich p~** creep (**an**+*acc* up to)

pissen *vi* (*haben*) (*sl*) piss

Piste *f* -,-n (*Ski-*) run, piste; (*Renn-*) track; (*Aviat*) runway

Pistole f -,-n pistol
pitschnaß a (fam) soaking wet
pittoresk a picturesque
Pizza f -,-s pizza
Pkw /'pe:kave:/ m -s,-s (=**Personen-kraftwagen**) [private] car
placieren /-'tsi:rən/ vt = **plazieren**
Plackerei f - (fam) drudgery
plädieren vi (haben) plead (**für** for); **auf Freispruch p~** (Jur) ask for an acquittal
Plädoyer /plɛdoa'je:/ nt -s,-s (Jur) closing speech; (fig) plea
Plage f -,-n [hard] labour; (Mühe) trouble; (Belästigung) nuisance. **p~n** vt torment, plague; (bedrängen) pester; **sich p~n** struggle; (arbeiten) work hard
Plagi|at nt -[e]s,-e plagiarism. **p~ieren** vt plagiarize
Plakat nt -[e]s,-e poster
Plakette f -,-n badge
Plan m -[e]s,¨e plan
Plane f -,-n tarpaulin; (Boden-) ground-sheet
planen vt/i (haben) plan
Planet m -en,-en planet
planier|en vt level. **P~raupe** f bull-dozer
Planke f -,-n plank
plan|los a unsystematic, adv -ally. **p~mäßig** a systematic; (Ankunft) scheduled ● adv systematically; (nach Plan) according to plan; (ankommen) on schedule
Plansch|becken nt paddling pool. **p~en** vi (haben) splash about
Plantage /plan'ta:ʒə/ f -,-n plantation
Planung f - planning
Plapper|maul nt (fam) chatterbox. **p~n** vi (haben) chatter ● vt talk (Unsinn)
plärren vi (haben) bawl; (Radio:) blare
Plasma nt -s plasma
Plastik[1] f -,-en sculpture
Plast|ik[2] nt -s plastic. **p~isch** a three-dimensional; (formbar) plastic; (anschaulich) graphic, adv -ally; **p~ische Chirurgie** plastic surgery
Platane f -,-n plane [tree]
Plateau /pla'to:/ nt -s,-s plateau
Platin nt -s platinum
Platitüde f -,-n platitude
platonisch a platonic
platschen vi (sein) splash

plätschern vi (haben) splash; (Bach:) babble ● vi (sein) (Bach:) babble along
platt a & adv flat; **p~ sein** (fam) be flabbergasted. **P~** nt -[s] (Lang) Low German
Plättbrett nt ironing-board
Platte f -,-n slab; (Druck-) plate; (Metall-, Glas-) sheet; (Fliese) tile; (Koch-) hotplate; (Tisch-) top; (Auszieh-) leaf; (Schall-) record, disc; (zum Servieren) [flat] dish, platter; **kalte P~** assorted cold meats and cheeses pl
Plätt|eisen nt iron. **p~en** vt/i (haben) iron
Plattenspieler m record-player
Platt|form f -,-en platform. **P~füße** mpl flat feet. **P~heit** f -,-en platitude
Platz m -es,¨e place; (von Häusern umgeben) square; (Sitz-) seat; (Sport-) ground; (Fußball-) pitch; (Tennis-) court; (Golf-) course; (freier Raum) room, space; **P~ nehmen** take a seat; **P~ machen/lassen** make/leave room; **vom P~ stellen** (Sport) send off. **P~angst** f agoraphobia; (Klaustrophobie) claustrophobia. **P~anweiserin** f -,-nen usherette
Plätzchen nt -s,- spot; (Culin) biscuit
platzen vi (sein) burst; (auf-) split; (fam: scheitern) fall through; (Verlobung:) be off; **vor Neugier p~** be bursting with curiosity
Platz|karte f seat reservation ticket. **P~konzert** nt open-air concert. **P~mangel** m lack of space. **P~patrone** f blank. **P~regen** m downpour. **P~verweis** m (Sport) sending off. **P~wunde** f laceration
Plauderei f -,-en chat
plaudern vi (haben) chat
Plausch m -[e]s,-e (SGer) chat. **p~en** vi (haben) (SGer) chat
plausibel a plausible
plazieren vt place, put; **sich p~** (Sport) be placed
pleite a (fam) **p~ sein** be broke; (Firma:) be bankrupt; **p~ gehen** go bankrupt. **P~** f -,-n (fam) bankruptcy; (Mißerfolg) flop; **P~ machen** go bankrupt
plissiert a [finely] pleated
Plomb|e f -,-en seal; (Zahn-) filling. **p~ieren** vt seal; fill (Zahn)
plötzlich a sudden, adv -ly
plump a plump; (ungeschickt) clumsy, adv -ily
plumpsen vi (sein) (fam) fall

Plunder *m* -s *(fam)* junk, rubbish
plündern *vt/i (haben)* loot
Plunderstück *nt* Danish pastry
Plural *m* -s,-e plural
plus *adv, conj & prep* (+ *dat*) plus. **P~
nt** - surplus; *(Gewinn)* profit; *(Vorteil)*
advantage, plus. **P~punkt** *m (Sport)*
point; *(fig)* plus. **P~quamperfekt** *nt*
pluperfect. **P~zeichen** *nt* plus sign
Po *m* -s,-s *(fam)* bottom
Pöbel *m* -s mob, rabble. **p~haft** *a*
loutish
pochen *vi (haben)* knock; *(Herz:)*
pound; **p~ auf** (+ *acc*) *(fig)* insist on
pochieren /pɔˈʃiːrən/ *vt* poach
Pocken *pl* smallpox *sg*
Podest *nt* -[e]s,-e rostrum
Podium *nt* -s,-ien /-jən/ platform;
(Podest) rostrum
Poesie /poeˈziː/ *f* - poetry
poetisch *a* poetic
Pointe /ˈpo̯ɛːtə/ *f* -,-n point *(of a joke)*
Pokal *m* -s,-e goblet; *(Sport)* cup
pökeln *vt (Culin)* salt
Poker *nt* -s poker
Pol *m* -s,-e pole. **p~ar** *a* polar
polarisieren *vt* polarize
Polarstern *m* pole-star
Pole *m* -n,-n Pole. **P~n** *nt* -s Poland
Police /poˈliːsə/ *f* -,-n policy
Polier *m* -s,-e foreman
polieren *vt* polish
Polin *f* -,-nen Pole
Politesse *f* -,-n [woman] traffic war-
den
Politik *f* - politics *sg*; *(Vorgehen, Maß-
nahme)* policy
Politiker(in) *m* -s,- (*f* -,-nen) poli-
tician. **p~isch** *a* political, *adv* -ly
Politur *f* -,-en polish
Polizei *f* - police *pl*. **P~beamte(r)** *m*
police officer. **p~lich** *a* police ...
● *adv* by the police; *(sich anmelden)*
with the police. **P~streife** *f* police
patrol. **P~stunde** *f* closing time.
P~wache *f* police station
Polizist *m* -en,-en policeman. **P~in** *f*
-,-nen policewoman
Pollen *m* -s pollen
polnisch *a* Polish
Polohemd *nt* polo shirt
Polster *nt* -s,- pad; *(Kissen)* cushion;
(Möbel-) upholstery; *(fam: Rücklage)*
reserves *pl*. **P~er** *m* -s,- upholsterer.
P~möbel *pl* upholstered furniture
sg. **p~n** *vt* pad; upholster *(Möbel)*.
P~ung *f* - padding; upholstery

Polter|abend *m* wedding-eve party.
p~n *vi (haben)* thump, bang;
(schelten) bawl ● *vi (sein)* crash
down; *(gehen)* clump [along];
(fahren) rumble [along]
Polyäthylen *nt* -s polythene
Polyester *m* -s polyester
Polyp *m* -en,-en polyp; *(sl: Polizist)*
copper; **P~en** adenoids *pl*
Pomeranze *f* -,-n Seville orange
Pommes *pl (fam)* French fries
Pommes frites /pɔmˈfriːt/ *pl* chips;
(dünner) French fries
Pomp *m* -s pomp
Pompon /pɔ̃ˈpõ:/ *m* -s,-s pompon
pompös *a* ostentatious, *adv* -ly
Pony[1] *nt* -s,-s pony
Pony[2] *m* -s,-s fringe
Pop *m* -[s] pop. **P~musik** *f* pop music
Popo *m* -s,-s *(fam)* bottom
popul|är *a* popular. **P~arität** *f* - pop-
ularity
Pore *f* -,-n pore
Porno|graphie *f* - pornography. **p~
graphisch** *a* pornographic
porös *a* porous
Porree *m* -s leeks *pl*; **eine Stange P~**
a leek
Portal *nt* -s,-e portal
Portemonnaie /pɔrtmɔˈneː/ *nt* -s,-s
purse
Portier /pɔrˈtjeː/ *m* -s,-s doorman,
porter
Portion /-ˈtsi̯oːn/ *f* -,-en helping, por-
tion
Porto *nt* -s postage. **p~frei** *adv* post
free, post paid
Porträt /pɔrˈtrɛː/ *nt* -s,-s portrait.
p~tieren *vt* paint a portrait of
Portugal *nt* -s Portugal
Portugies|e *m* -n,-n, **P~in** *f* -,-nen
Portuguese. **p~isch** *a* Portuguese
Portwein *m* port
Porzellan *nt* -s china, porcelain
Posaune *f* -,-n trombone
Pose *f* -,-n pose
posieren *vi (haben)* pose
Position /-ˈtsi̯oːn/ *f* -,-en position
positiv *a* positive, *adv* -ly. **P~** *nt* -s,-e
(Phot) positive
Posse *f* -,-n *(Theat)* farce. **P~n** *m* -s,-
prank; **P~n** *pl* tomfoolery *sg*
Possessivpronomen *nt* possessive
pronoun
possierlich *a* cute
Post *f* - post office; *(Briefe)* mail, post;
mit der P~ by post
postalisch *a* postal

Post|amt *nt* post office. **P~anweisung** *f* postal money order. **P~bote** *m* postman

Posten *m* -s,- post; (*Wache*) sentry; (*Waren*-) batch; (*Rechnungs*-) item, entry; **P~ stehen** stand guard; **nicht auf dem P~** (*fam*) under the weather

Poster *nt & m* -s,- poster

Postfach *nt* post-office *or* PO box

postieren *vt* post, station; **sich p~** station oneself

Post|karte *f* postcard. **p~lagernd** *adv* poste restante. **P~leitzahl** *f* postcode, (*Amer*) Zip code. **P~scheckkonto** *nt* ≈ National Girobank account. **P~stempel** *m* postmark

postum *a* posthumous, *adv* -ly

post|wendend *adv* by return of post. **P~wertzeichen** *nt* [postage] stamp

Poten|tial /-'tsja:l/ *nt* -s,-e potential. **p~tiell** /-'tsjɛl/ *a* potential, *adv* -ly

Potenz *f* -,-en potency; (*Math & fig*) power

Pracht *f* - magnificence, splendour. **P~exemplar** *nt* magnificent specimen

prächtig *a* magnificent, *adv* -ly; (*prima*) splendid, *adv* -ly

prachtvoll *a* magnificent, *adv* -ly

Prädikat *nt* -[e]s,-e rating; (*Comm*) grade; (*Gram*) predicate. **p~iv** *a* (*Gram*) predicative, *adv* -ly. **P~swein** *m* high-quality wine

präge|n *vt* stamp (**auf** + *acc* on); emboss (*Leder, Papier*); mint (*Münze*); coin (*Wort, Ausdruck*); (*fig*) shape. **P~stempel** *m* die

pragmatisch *a* pragmatic, *adv* -ally

prägnant *a* succinct, *adv* -ly

prähistorisch *a* prehistoric

prahl|en *vi* (*haben*) boast, brag (**mit** about). **p~erisch** *a* boastful, *adv* -ly

Prakti|k *f* -,-en practice. **P~kant(in)** *m* -en,-en (*f* -,-nen) trainee

Prakti|kum *nt* -s,-ka practical training. **p~sch** *a* practical; (*nützlich*) handy; (*tatsächlich*) virtual; **p~scher Arzt** general practitioner ● *adv* practically; virtually; (*in der Praxis*) in practice; **p~sch arbeiten** do practical work. **p~zieren** *vt/i* (*haben*) practise; (*anwenden*) put into practice; (*fam: bekommen*) get

Praline *f* -,-n chocolate; **Schachtel P~n** box of chocolates

prall *a* bulging; (*dick*) plump; (*Sonne*) blazing ● *adv* **p~ gefüllt** full to bursting. **p~en** *vi* (*sein*) **p~ auf** (+ *acc*)/**gegen** collide with, hit; (*Sonne:*) blaze down on

Prämie /-jə/ *f* -,-n premium; (*Preis*) award

präm[i]ieren *vt* award a prize to

Pranger *m* -s,- pillory

Pranke *f* -,-n paw

Präpar|at *nt* -[e]s,-e preparation. **p~ieren** *vt* prepare; (*zerlegen*) dissect; (*ausstopfen*) stuff

Präposition /-'tsjo:n/ *f* -,-en preposition

Präsens *nt* - (*Gram*) present

präsentieren *vt* present; **sich p~** present itself/(*Person:*) oneself

Präsenz *f* - presence

Präservativ *nt* -s,-e condom

Präsident|(in) *m* -en,-en (*f* -,-nen) president. **P~schaft** *f* - presidency

Präsidium *nt* -s presidency; (*Gremium*) executive committee; (*Polizei*-) headquarters *pl*

prasseln *vi* (*haben*) (*Regen:*) beat down; (*Feuer:*) crackle ● *vi* (*sein*) **p~ auf** (+ *acc*)/**gegen** beat down on/beat against

prassen *vi* (*haben*) live extravagantly; (*schmausen*) feast

Präteritum *nt* -s imperfect

präventiv *a* preventive

Praxis *f* -,-xen practice; (*Erfahrung*) practical experience; (*Arzt*-) surgery; **in der P~** in practice

Präzedenzfall *m* precedent

präzis[e] *a* precise, *adv* -ly

Präzision *f* - precision

predig|en *vt/i* (*haben*) preach. **P~er** *m* -s,- preacher. **P~t** *f* -,-en sermon

Preis *m* -es,-e price; (*Belohnung*) prize; **um jeden/keinen P~** at any/not at any price. **P~ausschreiben** *nt* competition

Preiselbeere *f* (*Bot*) cowberry; (*Culin*) ≈ cranberry

preisen† *vt* praise; **sich glücklich p~** count oneself lucky

preisgeben† *vt sep* abandon (*dat* to); reveal (*Geheimnis*)

preis|gekrönt *a* award-winning. **P~gericht** *nt* jury. **p~günstig** *a* reasonably priced ● *adv* at a reasonable price. **P~lage** *f* price range. **p~lich** *a* price ... ● *adv* in price. **P~richter** *m* judge. **P~schild** *nt* price-tag. **P~träger(in)** *m(f)* prize-winner. **p~wert** *a* reasonable, *adv* -bly; (*billig*) inexpensive, *adv* -ly

prekär *a* difficult; (*heikel*) delicate

Prell|bock *m* buffers *pl.* **p~en** *vt* bounce; (*verletzen*) bruise; (*fam: betrügen*) cheat. **P~ung** *f* -,-en bruise

Premiere /prə'mjeːrə/ *f* -,-n première

Premierminister(in) /prə'mjeː-/ *m(f)* Prime Minister

Presse *f* -,-n press. **p~n** *vt* press; sich **p~n** press (**an** + *acc* against)

pressieren *vi* (*haben*) (*SGer*) be urgent

Preßluft *f* compressed air. **P~bohrer** *m* pneumatic drill

Prestige /prɛs'tiːʒə/ *nt* -s prestige

Preuß|en *nt* -s Prussia. **p~isch** *a* Prussian

prickeln *vi* (*haben*) tingle

Priester *m* -s,- priest

prima *inv* *a* first-class, first-rate; (*fam: toll*) fantastic, *adv* fantastically well

primär *a* primary, *adv* -ily

Primel *f* -,-n primula; (*Garten-*) polyanthus

primitiv *a* primitive

Prinz *m* -en,-en prince. **P~essin** *f* -,-nen princess

Prinzip *nt* -s,-ien /-jən/ principle; **im/ aus P~** in/on principle. **p~iell** *a* (*Frage*) of principle ● *adv* on principle; (*im Prinzip*) in principle

Priorität *f* -,-en priority

Prise *f* -,-n **P~ Salz** pinch of salt

Prisma *nt* -s,-men prism

privat *a* private, *adv* -ly; (*persönlich*) personal. **P~adresse** *f* home address. **p~isieren** *vt* privatize

Privat|leben *nt* private life. **P~lehrer** *m* private tutor. **P~lehrerin** *f* governess. **P~patient(in)** *m(f)* private patient

Privileg *nt* -[e]s,-ien /-jən/ privilege. **p~iert** *a* privileged

pro *prep* (+ *dat*) per. **Pro** *nt* - **das Pro und Kontra** the pros and cons *pl*

Probe *f* -,-n test, trial; (*Menge, Muster*) sample; (*Theat*) rehearsal; **auf die P~ stellen** put to the test. **P~fahrt** *f* test drive. **p~n** *vt/i* (*haben*) (*Theat*) rehearse. **p~weise** *adv* on a trial basis. **P~zeit** *f* probationary period

probieren *vt/i* (*haben*) try; (*kosten*) taste; (*proben*) rehearse

Problem *nt* -s,-e problem. **p~atisch** *a* problematic

problemlos *a* problem-free ● *adv* without any problems

Produkt *nt* -[e]s,-e product

Produk|tion /-'tsjoːn/ *f* -,-en production. **p~tiv** *a* productive. **P~tivität** *f* - productivity

Produ|zent *m* -en,-en producer. **p~zieren** *vt* produce; **sich p~zieren** (*fam*) show off

professionell *a* professional, *adv* -ly

Professor *m* -s,-en /-'soːrən/ professor

Profi *m* -s,-s (*Sport*) professional

Profil *nt* -s,-e profile; (*Reifen-*) tread; (*fig*) image. **p~iert** *a* (*fig*) distinguished

Profit *m* -[e]s,-e profit. **p~ieren** *vi* (*haben*) profit (**von** from)

Prognose *f* -,-n forecast; (*Med*) prognosis

Programm *nt* -s,-e programme; (*Computer-*) program; (*TV*) channel; (*Comm: Sortiment*) range. **p~ieren** *vt/i* (*haben*) (*Computer*) program. **P~ierer(in)** *m* -s,- (*f* -,-nen) [computer] programmer

progressiv *a* progressive

Projekt *nt* -[e]s,-e project

Projektor *m* -s,-en /-'toːrən/ projector

projizieren *vt* project

Proklam|ation /-'tsjoːn/ *f* -,-en proclamation. **p~ieren** *vt* proclaim

Prolet *m* -en,-en boor. **P~ariat** *nt* -[e]s proletariat. **P~arier** /-jɐ/ *m* -s,- proletarian

Prolog *m* -s,-e prologue

Promenade *f* -,-n promenade. **P~nmischung** *f* (*fam*) mongrel

Promille *pl* (*fam*) alcohol level *sg* in the blood; **zuviel P~ haben** (*fam*) be over the limit

prominen|t *a* prominent. **P~z** *f* - prominent figures *pl*

Promiskuität *f* - promiscuity

promovieren *vi* (*haben*) obtain one's doctorate

prompt *a* prompt, *adv* -ly; (*fam: natürlich*) of course

Pronomen *nt* -s,- pronoun

Propag|anda *f* - propaganda; (*Reklame*) publicity. **p~ieren** *vt* propagate

Propeller *m* -s,- propeller

Prophet *m* -en,-en prophet. **p~isch** *a* prophetic

prophezei|en vt prophesy. P~ung f -,-en prophecy

Proportion /-'tsio:n/ f -,-en proportion. p~al a proportional. p~iert a gut p~iert well proportioned

Prosa f - prose

prosaisch a prosaic, adv -ally

prosit int cheers!

Prospekt m -[e]s,-e brochure; (Comm) prospectus

prost int cheers!

Prostitu|ierte f -n,-n prostitute. P~tion /-'tsio:n/ f - prostitution

Protest m -[e]s,-e protest

Protestant|(in) m -en,-en (f -,-nen) (Relig) Protestant. p~isch a (Relig) Protestant

protestieren vi (haben) protest

Prothese f -,-n artificial limb; (Zahn-) denture

Protokoll nt -s,-e record; (Sitzungs-) minutes pl; (diplomatisches) protocol; (Strafzettel) ticket

Prototyp m -s,-en prototype

protz|en vi (haben) show off (mit etw sth). p~ig a ostentatious

Proviant m -s provisions pl

Provinz f -,-en province. p~iell a provincial

Provision f -,-en (Comm) commission

provisorisch a provisional, adv -ly, temporary, adv -ily

Provokation /-'tsio:n/ f -,-en provocation

provozieren vt provoke. p~d a provocative, adv -ly

Prozedur f -,-en [lengthy] business

Prozent nt -[e]s,-e & - per cent; 5 P~ 5 per cent. P~satz m percentage. p~ual a percentage . . .

Prozeß m -sses,-sse process; (Jur) lawsuit; (Kriminal-) trial

Prozession f -,-en procession

prüde a prudish

prüf|en vt test/(über-) check (auf + acc for); audit (Bücher); (Sch) examine; p~ender Blick searching look. P~er m -s,- inspector; (Buch-) auditor; (Sch) examiner. P~ling m -s,-e examination candidate. P~ung f -,-en examination; (Test) test; (Bücher-) audit; (fig) trial

Prügel m -s,- cudgel; P~ pl hiding sg, beating sg. P~ei f -,-en brawl, fight. p~n vt beat, thrash; sich p~n fight, brawl

Prunk m -[e]s magnificence, splendour. p~en vi (haben) show off (mit etw sth). p~voll a magnificent, adv -ly

prusten vi (haben) splutter; (schnauben) snort

Psalm m -s,-en psalm

Pseudonym nt -s,-e pseudonym

pst int shush!

Psychi|ater m -s,- psychiatrist. P~a-trie f - psychiatry. p~atrisch a psychiatric

psychisch a psychological, adv -ly; (Med) mental, adv -ly

Psycho|analyse f psychoanalysis. P~loge m -n,-n psychologist. P~logie f - psychology. p~logisch a psychological, adv -ly

Pubertät f - puberty

publik a p~ werden/machen become/make public

Publi|kum nt -s public; (Zuhörer) audience; (Zuschauer) spectators pl. p~zieren vt publish

Pudding m -s,-s blancmange; (im Wasserbad gekocht) pudding

Pudel m -s,- poodle

Puder m & (fam) nt -s,- powder; (Körper-) talcum [powder]. P~dose f [powder] compact. p~n vt powder. P~zucker m icing sugar

Puff[1] m -[e]s,-e push, poke

Puff[2] m & nt -s,-s (sl) brothel

puffen vt (fam) poke • vi (sein) puff along

Puffer m -s,- (Rail) buffer; (Culin) pancake. P~zone f buffer zone

Pull|i m -s,-s jumper. P~over m -s,- jumper; (Herren-) pullover

Puls m -es pulse. P~ader f artery. p~ieren vi (haben) pulsate

Pult nt -[e]s,-e desk; (Lese-) lectern

Pulver nt -s,- powder. p~ig a powdery. p~isieren vt pulverize

Pulver|kaffee m instant coffee. P~schnee m powder snow

pummelig a (fam) chubby

Pump m auf P~ (fam) on tick

Pumpe f -,-n pump. p~n vt/i (haben) pump; (fam: leihen) lend; [sich (dat)] etw p~n (fam: borgen) borrow sth

Pumps /pœmps/ pl court shoes

Punkt m -[e]s,-e dot; (Tex) spot; (Geom, Sport & fig) point; (Gram) full stop, period; P~ sechs Uhr at six o'clock sharp; nach P~en siegen win on points. p~iert a (Linie, Note) dotted

pünktlich a punctual, adv -ly. P~keit f - punctuality

Punsch m -[e]s,-e [hot] punch

Pupille f -,-n (Anat) pupil

Puppe *f* -,-n doll; (*Marionette*) puppet; (*Schaufenster-, Schneider-*) dummy; (*Zool*) chrysalis

pur *a* pure; (*fam: bloß*) sheer; **Whisky pur** neat whisky

Püree *nt* -s,-s purée; (*Kartoffel-*) mashed potatoes *pl*

puritanisch *a* puritanical

purpurrot *a* crimson

Purzel|baum *m* (*fam*) somersault. **p~n** *vi* (*sein*) (*fam*) tumble

pusseln *vi* (*haben*) (*fam*) potter

Puste *f* - (*fam*) breath; **aus der P~** out of breath. **p~n** *vt/i* (*haben*) (*fam*) blow

Pute *f* -,-n turkey; (*Henne*) turkey hen. **P~r** *m* -s,- turkey cock

Putsch *m* -[e]s,-e coup

Putz *m* -es plaster; (*Staat*) finery. **p~en** *vt* clean; (*Aust*) dry-clean; (*zieren*) adorn; **sich p~en** dress up; **sich** (*dat*) **die Zähne/Nase p~en** clean one's teeth/blow one's nose. **P~frau** *f* cleaner, charwoman. **p~ig** *a* (*fam*) amusing, cute; (*seltsam*) odd. **P~macherin** *f* -,-nen milliner

Puzzlespiel /'pazl-/ *nt* jigsaw

Pyramide *f* -,-n pyramid

Q

Quacksalber *m* -s,- quack

Quadrat *nt* -[e]s,-e square. **q~isch** *a* square. **Q~meter** *m* & *nt* square metre

quaken *vi* (*haben*) quack; (*Frosch:*) croak

quäken *vi* (*haben*) screech; (*Baby:*) whine

Quäker(in) *m* -s,- (*f -,-nen*) Quaker

Qual *f* -,-en torment; (*Schmerz*) agony

quälen *vt* torment; (*foltern*) torture; (*bedrängen*) pester; **sich q~** torment oneself; (*leiden*) suffer; (*sich mühen*) struggle. **q~d** *a* agonizing

Quälerei *f* -,-en torture; (*Qual*) agony

Quälgeist *m* (*fam*) pest

Qualifi|kation /-'tsio:n/ *f* -,-en qualification. **q~zieren** *vt* qualify; **sich q~zieren** qualify. **q~ziert** *a* qualified; (*fähig*) competent; (*Arbeit*) skilled

Qualität *f* -,-en quality

Qualle *f* -,-n jellyfish

Qualm *m* -s [thick] smoke. **q~en** *vi* (*haben*) smoke

qualvoll *a* agonizing

Quantität *f* -,-en quantity

Quantum *nt* -s,-ten quantity; (*Anteil*) share, quota

Quarantäne *f* - quarantine

Quark *m* -s quark, ≈ curd cheese; (*fam: Unsinn*) rubbish

Quartal *nt* -s,-e quarter

Quartett *nt* -[e]s,-e quartet

Quartier *nt* -s,-e accommodation; (*Mil*) quarters *pl*; **ein Q~ suchen** look for accommodation

Quarz *m* -es quartz

quasseln *vi* (*haben*) (*fam*) jabber

Quaste *f* -,-n tassel

Quatsch *m* -[e]s (*fam*) nonsense, rubbish; **Q~ machen** (*Unfug machen*) fool around; (*etw falsch machen*) do a silly thing. **q~en** (*fam*) *vi* (*haben*) talk; (*schwatzen*) natter; (*Wasser, Schlamm:*) squelch • *vt* talk. **q~naß** *a* (*fam*) soaking wet

Quecksilber *nt* mercury

Quelle *f* -,-n spring; (*Fluß- & fig*) source. **q~n†** *vi* (*sein*) well [up]/ (*fließen*) pour (*aus* from); (*aufquellen*) swell; (*hervortreten*) bulge

quengeln *vi* (*fam*) whine; (*Baby:*) grizzle

quer *adv* across, crosswise; (*schräg*) diagonally

Quere *f* - **der Q~ nach** across, crosswise; **jdm in die Q~ kommen** get in s.o.'s way

querfeldein *adv* across country

quer|gestreift *a* horizontally striped. **q~köpfig** *a* (*fam*) awkward. **Q~latte** *f* crossbar. **Q~schiff** *nt* transept. **Q~schnitt** *m* cross-section. **q~schnittsgelähmt** *a* paraplegic. **Q~straße** *f* side-street; **die erste Q~straße links** the first turning on the left. **Q~verweis** *m* cross-reference

quetsch|en *vt* squash; (*drücken*) squeeze; (*zerdrücken*) crush; (*Culin*) mash; **sich q~en in** (+ *acc*) squeeze into; **sich** (*dat*) **den Arm q~en** bruise one's arm. **Q~ung** *f* -,-en, **Q~wunde** *f* bruise

Queue /kø:/ *nt* -s,-s cue

quicklebendig *a* very lively

quieken *vi* (*haben*) squeal; (*Maus:*) squeak

quietschen *vi* (*haben*) squeal; (*Tür, Dielen:*) creak

Quintett *nt* -[e]s,-e quintet

Quirl *m* -[e]s,-e blender with a star-shaped head. **q~en** *vt* mix

quitt *a* **q~ sein** (*fam*) be quits
Quitte *f* -,-n quince
quittieren *vt* receipt ⟨*Rechnung*⟩; sign for ⟨*Geldsumme, Sendung*⟩; ⟨*reagieren auf*⟩ greet (**mit** with); **den Dienst q~** resign
Quittung *f* -,-en receipt
Quiz /kvɪs/ *nt* -,- quiz
Quote *f* -,-n proportion

R

Rabatt *m* -[e]s,-e discount
Rabatte *f* -,-n (*Hort*) border
Rabattmarke *f* trading stamp
Rabbiner *m* -s,- rabbi
Rabe *m* -n,-n raven. **r~nschwarz** *a* pitch-black
rabiat *a* violent, *adv* -ly; (*wütend*) furious, *adv* -ly
Rache *f* - revenge, vengeance
Rachen *m* -s,- pharynx; (*Maul*) jaws *pl*
rächen *vt* avenge; **sich r~** take revenge (**an**+*dat* on); ⟨*Fehler, Leichtsinn:*⟩ cost s.o. dear
Racker *m* -s,- (*fam*) rascal
Rad *nt* -[e]s,‥er wheel; (*Fahr-*) bicycle, (*fam*) bike
Radar *m & nt* -s radar
Radau *m* -s (*fam*) din, racket
radebrechen *vt/i* (*haben*) [Deutsch/ Englisch] **r~** speak broken German/ English
radeln *vi* (*sein*) (*fam*) cycle
Rädelsführer *m* ringleader
radfahren† *vi sep* (*sein*) cycle; **ich fahre gern Rad** I like cycling. **R~er(in)** *m(f)* -s,- (-*f*-,-nen) cyclist
radieren *vt/i* (*haben*) rub out; (*Kunst*) etch. **R~gummi** *m* eraser, rubber. **R~ung** *f* -,-en etching
Radieschen /-'diːsçən/ *nt* -s,- radish
radikal *a* radical, *adv* -ly; (*drastisch*) drastic, *adv* -ally. **R~e(r)** *m/f* (*Pol*) radical
Radio *nt* -s,-s radio
radioaktiv *a* radioactive. **R~ität** *f* - radioactivity
Radioapparat *m* radio [set]
Radius *m* -,-ien /-jən/ radius
Rad|kappe *f* hub-cap.
R~ler *m* -s,- cyclist; (*Getränk*) shandy. **R~weg** *m* cycle track
raffen *vt* grab; (*kräuseln*) gather; (*kürzen*) condense. **r~gierig** *a* avaricious

Raffin|ade *f* - refined sugar. **R~erie** *f* -,-n refinery. **R~esse** *f* -,-n refinement; (*Schlauheit*) cunning. **r~ieren** *vt* refine. **r~iert** *a* ingenious, *adv* -ly; (*durchtrieben*) crafty, *adv* -ily
Rage /'raːʒə/ *f* - (*fam*) fury
ragen *vi* (*haben*) rise [up]
Rahm *m* -s (*SGer*) cream
rahmen *vt* frame. **R~** *m* -s,- frame; (*fig*) framework; (*Grenze*) limits *pl*; (*einer Feier*) setting
Rain *m* -[e]s,-e grass verge
räkeln *v* = rekeln
Rakete *f* -,-n rocket; (*Mil*) missile
Rallye /'raːli/ *nt* -s,-s rally
rammen *vt* ram
Rampe *f* -,-n ramp; (*Theat*) front of the stage. **R~nlicht** *nt* im **R~nlicht stehen** (*fig*) be in the limelight
ramponieren *vt* (*fam*) damage; (*ruinieren*) ruin; **r~t** battered
Ramsch *m* -[e]s junk. **R~laden** *m* junk-shop
ran *adv* = heran
Rand *m* -[e]s,‥er edge; (*Teller-, Gläser-, Brillen-*) rim; (*Zier-*) border, edging; (*Buch-, Brief-*) margin; (*Stadt-*) outskirts *pl*; (*Ring*) ring; **am R~e des Ruins** on the brink of ruin; **am R~e erwähnen** mention in passing; **zu R~e kommen mit** (*fam*) cope with; **außer R~ und Band** (*fam: ausgelassen*) very boisterous
randalieren *vi* (*haben*) rampage
Rand|bemerkung *f* marginal note. **R~streifen** *m* (*Auto*) hard shoulder
Rang *m* -[e]s,‥e rank; (*Theat*) tier; **erster/zweiter R~** (*Theat*) dress/ upper circle; **ersten R~es** first-class
rangieren /raŋ'ʒiːrən/ *vt* shunt ● *vi* (*haben*) rank (**vor**+*dat* before); **an erster Stelle r~** come first
Rangordnung *f* order of importance; (*Hierarchie*) hierarchy
Ranke *f* -,-n tendril; (*Trieb*) shoot
ranken (sich) *vr* (*Bot*) trail; (*in die Höhe*) climb; **sich r~ um** twine around
Ranzen *m* -s,- (*Sch*) satchel
ranzig *a* rancid
Rappe *m* -n,-n black horse
rappeln *v* (*fam*) ● *vi* (*haben*) rattle ● *vr* **sich r~** pick oneself up; (*fig*) rally
Raps *m* -es (*Bot*) rape
rar *a* rare; **er macht sich rar** (*fam*) we don't see much of him. **R~ität** *f* -,-en rarity
rasant *a* fast; (*schnittig, schick*) stylish ● *adv* fast; stylishly

rasch a quick, adv -ly
rascheln vi (haben) rustle
Rasen m -s,- lawn
rasen vi (sein) tear [along]; ⟨Puls:⟩ race; ⟨Zeit:⟩ fly; **gegen eine Mauer r~** career into a wall ● vi (haben) rave; ⟨Sturm:⟩ rage; **vor Begeisterung r~** go wild with enthusiasm. **r~d** a furious; ⟨tobend⟩ raving; ⟨Sturm, Durst⟩ raging; ⟨Schmerz⟩ excruciating; ⟨Beifall⟩ tumultuous ● adv terribly [lotion]
Rasenmäher m lawn-mower
Raserei f - speeding; ⟨Toben⟩ frenzy
Rasier|apparat m razor. **r~en** vt shave; **sich r~en** shave. **R~klinge** f razor blade. **R~pinsel** m shaving-brush. **R~wasser** nt aftershave [lotion]
Raspel f -,-n rasp; (Culin) grater. **r~** vt grate
Rasse f -,-n race. **R~hund** m pedigree dog
Rassel f -,-n rattle. **r~n** vi (haben) rattle; ⟨Schlüssel:⟩ jangle; ⟨Kette:⟩ clank ● vi (sein) rattle [along]
Rassen|diskriminierung f racial discrimination. **R~trennung** f racial segregation
Rassepferd nt thoroughbred
rassisch a racial
Rassis|mus m - racism. **r~tisch** a racist
Rast f -,-en rest. **r~en** vi (haben) rest. **R~haus** nt motorway restaurant. **r~los** a restless, adv -ly; ⟨ununterbrochen⟩ ceaseless, adv -ly. **R~platz** m picnic area. **R~stätte** f motorway restaurant [and services]
Rasur f -,-en shave
Rat[1] m -[e]s [piece of] advice; **guter Rat** good advice; **zu Rat[e] ziehen** consult; **sich** (dat) **keinen Rat wissen** not know what to do
Rat[2] m -[e]s,-̈e ⟨Admin⟩ council; ⟨Person⟩ councillor
Rate f -,-n instalment
raten† vt guess; ⟨empfehlen⟩ advise ● vi (haben) guess; **jdm r~** advise s.o.
Ratenzahlung f payment by instalments
Rat|geber m -s,- adviser; ⟨Buch⟩ guide. **R~haus** nt town hall
ratifizier|en vt ratify. **R~ung** f -,-en ratification
Ration /ra'tsio:n/ f -,-en ration; **eiserne R~** iron rations pl. **r~al** a rational, adv -ly. **r~alisieren** vt/i

⟨haben⟩ rationalize. **r~ell** a efficient, adv -ly. **r~ieren** vt ration
rat|los a helpless, adv -ly; **r~los sein** not know what to do. **r~sam** pred a advisable; ⟨klug⟩ prudent. **R~schlag** m piece of advice; **R~schläge** advice sg
Rätsel nt -s,- riddle; ⟨Kreuzwort-⟩ puzzle; ⟨Geheimnis⟩ mystery. **r~haft** a puzzling, mysterious. **r~n** vi (haben) puzzle
Ratte f -,-n rat
rattern vi (haben) rattle ● vi (sein) rattle [along]
Raub m -[e]s robbery; ⟨Menschen-⟩ abduction; ⟨Beute⟩ loot, booty. **r~en** vt steal; abduct ⟨Menschen⟩; **jdm etw r~en** rob s.o. of sth
Räuber m -s,- robber
Raub|mord m robbery with murder. **R~tier** nt predator. **R~überfall** m robbery. **R~vogel** m bird of prey
Rauch m -[e]s smoke. **r~en** vt/i ⟨haben⟩ smoke. **R~en** nt -s smoking; **'R~en verboten'** 'no smoking'. **R~er** m -s,- smoker. **R~erabteil** nt smoking compartment
Räucher|lachs m smoked salmon. **r~n** vt (Culin) smoke
Rauch|fang m ⟨Aust⟩ chimney. **r~ig** a smoky. **R~verbot** nt smoking ban
räudig a mangy
rauf adv = herauf, hinauf
rauf|en vt pull; **sich** (dat) **die Haare r~en** ⟨fig⟩ tear one's hair ● vr/i ⟨haben⟩ [sich] r~en fight. **R~erei** f -,-en fight
rauh a rough, adv -ly; ⟨unfreundlich⟩ gruff, adv -ly; ⟨Klima, Wind⟩ harsh, raw; ⟨Landschaft⟩ rugged; ⟨heiser⟩ husky; ⟨Hals⟩ sore
Rauheit f - (s. rauh) roughness; gruffness; harshness; ruggedness
rauh|haarig a wire-haired. **R~reif** m hoar-frost
Raum m -[e]s, Räume room; ⟨Gebiet⟩ area; ⟨Welt-⟩ space
räumen vt clear; vacate ⟨Wohnung⟩; evacuate ⟨Gebäude, Gebiet, Mil Stellung⟩; ⟨bringen⟩ put (in/auf + acc into/on); ⟨holen⟩ get (aus out of); **beiseite r~** move/put to one side; **aus dem Weg r~** ⟨fam⟩ get rid of
Raum|fahrer m astronaut. **R~fahrt** f space travel. **R~fahrzeug** nt spacecraft. **R~flug** m space flight. **R~inhalt** m volume

räumlich a spatial. **R~keiten** fpl rooms

Raum|pflegerin f cleaner.

R~schiff nt spaceship

Räumung f - (s. **räumen**) clearing; vacating; evacuation. **R~sverkauf** m clearance/closing-down sale

raunen vt/i (haben) whisper

Raupe f -,-n caterpillar

raus adv = **heraus, hinaus**

Rausch m -[e]s, Räusche intoxication; (fig) exhilaration; **einen R~ haben** be drunk

rauschen vi (haben) ⟨Wasser, Wind:⟩ rush; ⟨Bäume, Blätter:⟩ rustle ● vi (sein) rush [along]; **aus dem Zimmer r~** sweep out of the room. **r~d** a rushing; rustling; ⟨Applaus⟩ tumultuous

Rauschgift nt [narcotic] drug; (coll) drugs pl. **R~süchtige(r)** m/f drug addict

räuspern (sich) vr clear one's throat

rausschmeiß|en† vt sep (fam) throw out; (entlassen) sack. **R~er** m -s,- (fam) bouncer

Raute f -,-n diamond

Razzia f -,-ien /-jən/ [police] raid

Reagenzglas nt test-tube

reagieren vi (haben) react (**auf** + acc to)

Reaktion /-'tsjo:n/ f -,-en reaction. **r~är** a reactionary

Reaktor m -s,-en /-'to:rən/ reactor

real a real; (gegenständlich) tangible; (realistisch) realistic, adv -ally. **r~i-sieren** vt realize

Realis|mus m - realism. **R~t** m -en,-en realist. **r~tisch** a realistic, adv -ally

Realität f -,-en reality

Realschule f ≈ secondary modern school

Rebe f -,-n vine

Rebell m -en,-en rebel. **r~ieren** vi (haben) rebel. **R~ion** f -,-en rebellion

rebellisch a rebellious

Rebhuhn nt partridge

Rebstock m vine

Rechen m -s,- rake. **r~** vt/i (haben) rake

Rechen|aufgabe f arithmetical problem; (Sch) sum. **R~fehler** m arithmetical error. **R~maschine** f calculator

Rechenschaft f - **R~ ablegen** give account (**über** + acc of); **jdn zur R~ ziehen** call s.o. to account

recherchieren /reʃɛr'ʃi:rən/ vt/i (haben) investigate; (Journ) research

rechnen vi (haben) do arithmetic; (schätzen) reckon; (zählen) count (**zu** among; **auf** + acc on); **r~ mit** reckon with; (erwarten) expect; **gut r~ können** be good at figures ● vt calculate, work out; do ⟨Aufgabe⟩; (dazu-) add (**zu** to); (fig) count (**zu** among). **R~** nt -s arithmetic

Rechner m -s,- calculator; (Computer) computer; **ein guter R~ sein** be good at figures

Rechnung f -,-en bill, (Amer) check; (Comm) invoice; (Berechnung) calculation; **R~ führen über** (+ acc) keep account of; **etw** ⟨dat⟩ **R~ tragen** (fig) take sth into account. **R~sjahr** nt financial year. **R~sprüfer** m auditor

Recht nt -[e]s, -e law; (Berechtigung) right (**auf** + acc to); **im R~ sein** be in the right; **mit** od **zu R~** rightly; **von R~s wegen** by right; (eigentlich) by rights

recht a right; (wirklich) real; **ich habe keine r~e Lust** I don't really feel like it; **es jdm r~ machen** please s.o.; **jdm r~ sein** be all right with s.o. ● **r~ haben/ behalten** be right; **r~ bekommen** be proved right; **jdm r~ geben** agree with s.o. ● adv correctly; (ziemlich) quite; (sehr) very; **r~ vielen Dank** many thanks

Recht|e f -n,-[n] right side; (Hand) right hand; (Boxen) right; **die R~e** (Pol) the right; **zu meiner R~en** on my right. **r~e(r,s)** a right; (Pol) right-wing; **r~e Masche** plain stitch. **R~e(r)** m/f der/die R~e the right man/woman; **du bist mir der/die R~e!** you're a fine one! **R~e(s)** nt das R~e the right thing; **etwas R~es lernen** learn something useful; **nach dem R~en sehen** see that everything is all right

Rechteck nt -[e]s,-e rectangle. **r~ig** a rectangular

rechtfertig|en vt justify; **sich r~en** justify oneself. **R~ung** f - justification

recht|haberisch a opinionated. **r~lich** a legal, adv -ly. **r~mäßig** a legitimate, adv -ly

rechts adv on the right; (bei Stoff) on the right side; **von/nach r~** from/to the right; **zwei r~, zwei links stricken** knit two, purl two. **R~anwalt** m, **R~anwältin** f lawyer

rechtschaffen *a* upright; (*ehrlich*) honest, *adv* -ly; **r~ müde** thoroughly tired

rechtschreib|en *vi* (*inf only*) spell correctly. **R~fehler** *m* spelling mistake. **R~ung** *f* - spelling

Rechts|händer(in) *m* -s,- (*f* -,-**nen**) right-hander. **r~händig** *a* & *adv* right-handed. **r~kräftig** *a* legal, *adv* -ly. **R~streit** *m* law suit. **R~verkehr** *m* driving on the right. **r~widrig** *a* illegal, *adv* -ly. **R~wissenschaft** *f* jurisprudence

recht|winklig *a* right-angled. **r~zeitig** *a* & *adv* in time

Reck *nt* -[e]s,-e horizontal bar

recken *vt* stretch; **sich r~** stretch; **den Hals r~** crane one's neck

Redakteur /redak'tø:ɐ̯/ *m* -s,-e editor; (*Radio, TV*) producer

Redaktion /-'tsjo:n/ *f* -,-en editing; (*Radio, TV*) production; (*Abteilung*) editorial/production department. **r~ell** *a* editorial

Rede *f* -,-n speech; **zur R~ stellen** demand an explanation from; **davon ist keine R~** there's no question of it; **nicht der R~ wert** not worth mentioning. **r~gewandt** *a* eloquent, *adv* -ly

reden *vi* (*haben*) talk (**von** about; **mit** to); (*eine Rede halten*) speak ● *vt* talk; speak (*Wahrheit*); **kein Wort r~** not say a word. **R~sart** *f* saying; (*Phrase*) phrase

Redewendung *f* idiom

redigieren *vt* edit

redlich *a* honest, *adv* -ly

Red|ner *m* -s,- speaker. **r~selig** *a* talkative

reduzieren *vt* reduce

Reeder *m* -s,- shipowner. **R~ei** *f* -,-en shipping company

reell *a* real; (*ehrlich*) honest, *adv* -ly; (*Preis, Angebot*) fair

Refer|at *nt* -[e]s,-e report; (*Abhandlung*) paper; (*Abteilung*) section. **R~ent(in)** *m* -en,-en (*f* -,-**nen**) speaker; (*Sachbearbeiter*) expert. **R~enz** *f* -,-en reference. **r~ieren** *vi* (*haben*) deliver a paper; (*berichten*) report (**über** + *acc* on)

reflektieren *vt/i* (*haben*) reflect (**über** + *acc* on)

Reflex *m* -es,-e reflex; (*Widerschein*) reflection. **R~ion** *f* -,-en reflection. **r~iv** *a* reflexive. **R~ivpronomen** *nt* reflexive pronoun

Reform *f* -,-en reform. **R~ation** /-'tsjo:n/ *f* - (*Relig*) Reformation

Reform|haus *nt* health-food shop. **r~ieren** *vt* reform

Refrain /rə'frɛ̃:/ *m* -s,-s refrain

Regal *nt* -s,-e [set of] shelves *pl*

Regatta *f* -,-ten regatta

rege *a* active; (*lebhaft*) lively; (*geistig*) alert; (*Handel*) brisk ● *adv* actively

Regel *f* -,-n rule; (*Monats-*) period; **in der R~** as a rule. **r~mäßig** *a* regular, *adv* -ly. **r~n** *vt* regulate; direct (*Verkehr*); (*erledigen*) settle. **r~recht** *a* real, proper ● *adv* really. **R~ung** *f* -,-en regulation; settlement. **r~widrig** *a* irregular, *adv* -ly

regen *vt* move; **sich r~** move; (*wach werden*) stir

Regen *m* -s,- rain. **R~bogen** *m* rainbow. **R~bogenhaut** *f* iris

Regener|ation /-'tsjo:n/ *f* - regeneration. **r~ieren** *vt* regenerate; **sich r~ieren** regenerate

Regen|mantel *m* raincoat. **R~schirm** *m* umbrella. **R~tag** *m* rainy day. **R~tropfen** *m* raindrop. **R~wetter** *nt* wet weather. **R~wurm** *m* earthworm

Regie /re'ʒi:/ *f* - direction; **R~ führen** direct

regier|en *vt/i* (*haben*) govern, rule; (*Monarch:*) reign [over]; (*Gram*) take. **r~end** *a* ruling; reigning. **R~ung** *f* -,-en government; (*Herrschaft*) rule; (*eines Monarchen*) reign

Regime /re'ʒi:m/ *nt* -s,- /-mə/ regime

Regiment[1] *nt* -[e]s,-er regiment

Regiment[2] *nt* -[e]s,-e rule

Region *f* -,-en region. **r~al** *a* regional, *adv* -ly

Regisseur /reʒɪ'sø:ɐ̯/ *m* -s,-e director

Register *nt* -s,- register; (*Inhaltsverzeichnis*) index; (*Orgel-*) stop

registrier|en *vt* register; (*Techn*) record. **R~kasse** *f* cash register

Regler *m* -s,- regulator

reglos *a* & *adv* motionless

regn|en *vi* (*haben*) rain; **es r~et** it is raining. **r~erisch** *a* rainy

regul|är *a* normal, *adv* -ly; (*rechtmäßig*) legitimate, *adv* -ly. **r~ieren** *vt* regulate

Regung *f* -,-en movement; (*Gefühls-*) emotion. **r~slos** *a* & *adv* motionless

Reh *nt* -[e]s,-e roe-deer; (*Culin*) venison

Rehabilit|ation /-'tsjo:n/ f - rehabilitation. **r~ieren** vt rehabilitate

Rehbock m roebuck

Reib|e f -,-n grater. **r~en†** vt rub; (Culin) grate; **blank r~en** polish ● vi (haben) rub. **R~ereien** fpl (fam) friction sg. **R~ung** f - friction. **r~ungslos** a (fig) smooth, adv -ly

reich a rich (**an**+ dat in), adv -ly; (r~haltig) abundant, adv -ly

Reich nt -[e]s,-e empire; (König-) kingdom; (Bereich) realm

Reich|e(r) m/f rich man/woman; **die R~en** the rich pl

reichen vt hand; (anbieten) offer ● vi (haben) be enough; (in der Länge) be long enough; **r~ bis zu** reach [up to]; (sich erstrecken) extend to; **mit dem Geld r~** have enough money; **mir reicht's!** I've had enough!

reich|haltig a extensive, large; (Mahlzeit) substantial. **r~lich** a ample; (Vorrat) abundant, plentiful; **eine r~liche Stunde** a good hour ● adv amply; abundantly; (fam: sehr) very. **R~tum** m -s,-tümer wealth (**an**+ dat of); **R~tümer** riches. **R~weite** f reach; (Techn, Mil) range

Reif m -[e]s [hoar-]frost

reif a ripe; (fig) mature; **r~ für** ready for. **R~e** f - ripeness; (fig) maturity. **r~en** vi (sein) ripen; (Wein, Käse & fig) mature

Reifen m -s,- hoop; (Arm-) bangle; (Auto-) tyre. **R~druck** m tyre pressure. **R~panne** f puncture, flat tyre

Reifeprüfung f ≈ A levels pl

reiflich a careful, adv -ly

Reihe f -,-n row; (Anzahl & Math) series; **der R~ nach** in turn; **außer der R~** out of turn; **wer ist an der od kommt an die R~?** whose turn is it? **r~n (sich)** vr sich r~n an (+ acc) follow. **R~nfolge** f order. **R~nhaus** nt terraced house. **r~nweise** adv in rows; (fam) in large numbers

Reiher m -s,- heron

Reim m -[e]s,-e rhyme. **r~en** vt rhyme; **sich r~en** rhyme

rein¹ a pure; (sauber) clean; (Unsinn, Dummheit) sheer; **ins r~e schreiben** make a fair copy of; **ins r~e bringen** (fig) sort out ● adv purely; (fam) absolutely

rein² adv = **herein, hinein**

Reineclaude /rɛ:nə'klo:də/ f -,-n greengage

Reinfall m (fam) let-down; (Mißerfolg) flop. **r~en†** vi sep (sein) fall in; (fam) be taken in (**auf**+ acc by)

Rein|gewinn m net profit. **R~heit** f - purity

reinig|en vt clean; (chemisch) dry-clean. **R~ung** f -,-en cleaning; (chemische) dry-cleaning; (Geschäft) dry cleaner's

Reinkarnation /reʔmkarna'tsjon:/ f -,-en reincarnation

reinlegen vt sep put in; (fam) dupe; (betrügen) take for a ride

reinlich a clean. **R~keit** f - cleanliness

Rein|machefrau f cleaner. **R~schrift** f fair copy. **r~seiden** a pure silk

Reis m -es rice

Reise f -,-n journey; (See-) voyage; (Urlaubs-, Geschäfts-) trip. **R~andenken** nt souvenir. **R~büro** nt travel agency. **R~bus** m coach. **R~führer** m tourist guide; (Buch) guide. **R~gesellschaft** f tourist group. **R~leiter(in)** m(f) courier. **r~n** vi (sein) travel. **R~nde(r)** m/f traveller. **R~paß** m passport. **R~scheck** m traveller's cheque. **R~unternehmer, R~veranstalter** m -s,- tour operator. **R~ziel** nt destination

Reisig nt -s brushwood

Reißaus m **R~ nehmen** (fam) run away

Reißbrett nt drawing-board

reißen† vt tear; (weg-) snatch; (töten) kill; **Witze r~** crack jokes; **aus dem Schlaf r~** awaken rudely; **an sich** (acc) **r~** snatch; seize (Macht); **mit sich r~** sweep away; **sich r~ um** (fam) fight for; (gern mögen) be keen on; **hin und her gerissen sein** (fig) be torn ● vi (sein) tear; (Seil, Faden:) break ● vi (haben) **r~ an** (+ dat) pull at. **r~d** a raging; (Tier) ferocious; (Schmerz) violent

Reißer m -s,- (fam) thriller; (Erfolg) big hit. **r~isch** a (fam) sensational

Reiß|nagel m = **R~zwecke**. **R~verschluß** m zip [fastener]. **R~wolf** m shredder. **R~zwecke** f -,-n drawing-pin, (Amer) thumbtack

reit|en† vt/i (sein) ride. **R~er(in)** m -s,- (f -,-nen) rider. **R~hose** f riding breeches pl. **R~pferd** nt saddle-horse. **R~schule** f riding-school. **R~weg** m bridle-path

Reiz m -es,-e stimulus; (Anziehungskraft) attraction, appeal;

(Charme) charm. **r~bar** *a* irritable.
R~barkeit *f* - irritability. **r~en** *vt*
provoke; *(Med)* irritate; *(interessieren, locken)* appeal to, attract; arouse
⟨*Neugier*⟩; *(beim Kartenspiel)* bid.
r~end *a* charming, *adv* -ly;
(entzückend) delightful. **R~ung** *f*
-,-en *(Med)* irritation. **r~voll** *a*
attractive

rekapitulieren *vt/i (haben)* recapitulate

rekeln (sich) *vr* stretch; *(lümmeln)*
sprawl

Reklamation /-'tsio:n/ *f* -,-en
(Comm) complaint

Reklam|e *f* -,-n advertising, publicity;
(Anzeige) advertisement; *(TV, Radio)*
commercial; **R~e machen** advertise
(für etw sth). **r~ieren** *vt* complain
about; *(fordern)* claim ● *vi (haben)*
complain

rekonstru|ieren *vt* reconstruct.
R~ktion /-'tsio:n/ *f* -,-en reconstruction

Rekonvaleszenz *f* - convalescence

Rekord *m* -[e]s,-e record

Rekrut *m* -en,-en recruit. **r~ieren** *vt*
recruit

Rek|tor *m* -s,-en /-'to:rən/ *(Sch)* head-
[master]; *(Univ)* vice-chancellor. **R~torin** *f* -,-nen head[mistress]; vice-
chancellor

Relais /rə'lɛː/ *nt* -,- /-s,-s/ *(Electr)* relay

relativ *a* relative, *adv* -ly. **R~pronomen** *nt* relative pronoun

relevan|t *a* relevant **(für** to). **R~z** *f* -
relevance

Relief /rə'ljɛf/ *nt* -s,-s relief

Religi|on *f* -,-en religion; *(Sch)*
religious education. **r~ös** *a* religious

Reling *f* -,-s *(Naut)* rail

Reliquie /re'li:kvjə/ *f* -,-n relic

Remouladensoße /remu'la:dən-/
f ≈ tartar sauce

rempeln *vt* jostle; *(stoßen)* push

Ren *nt* -s,-s reindeer

Reneklode *f* -,-n greengage

Renn|auto *nt* racing car. **R~bahn** *f*
race-track; *(Pferde-)* racecourse. **R~boot** *nt* speedboat. **r~en†** *vt/i (sein)*
run; **um die Wette r~en** have a race.
R~en *nt* -s,- race. **R~pferd** *nt* race-
horse. **R~sport** *m* racing. **R~wagen** *m* racing car

renommiert *a* renowned; ⟨*Hotel, Firma*⟩ of repute

renovier|en *vt* renovate; redecorate
⟨*Zimmer*⟩. **R~ung** *f* - renovation;
redecoration

rentabel *a* profitable, *adv* -bly

Rente *f* -,-n pension; **in R~ gehen**
(fam) retire. **R~nversicherung** *f*
pension scheme

Rentier *nt* reindeer

rentieren (sich) *vr* be profitable;
(sich lohnen) be worth while

Rentner(in) *m* -s,- *(f-,-nen)* [old-age]
pensioner

Reparatur *f* -,-en repair. **R~werkstatt** *f* repair workshop; *(Auto)*
garage

reparieren *vt* repair, mend

repatriieren *vt* repatriate

Repertoire /repɛr'toa:ɐ̯/ *nt* -s,-s
repertoire

Reportage /-'ta:ʒə/ *f* -,-n report

Reporter(in) *m* -s,- *(f-,-nen)* reporter

repräsent|ativ *a* representative **(für**
of); *(eindrucksvoll)* imposing; *(Prestige
verleihend)* prestigious. **r~ie ren** *vt*
represent ● *vi (haben)* perform
official/social duties

Repress|alie /-ljə/ *f* -,-n reprisal.
r~iv *a* repressive

Reprodu|ktion /-'tsio:n/ *f* -,-en re-
production. **r~zieren** *vt* reproduce

Reptil *nt* -s,-ien /-jən/ reptile

Republik *f* -,-en republic. **r~anisch** *a*
republican

requirieren *vt (Mil)* requisition

Requisiten *pl (Theat)* properties,
(fam) props

Reservat *nt* -[e]s,-e reservation

Reserve *f* -,-n reserve; *(Mil, Sport)*
reserves *pl.* **R~rad** *nt* spare wheel.
R~spieler *m* reserve. **R~tank** *m* reserve tank

reservier|en *vt* reserve; **r~en lassen**
book. **r~t** *a* reserved. **R~ung** *f* -,-en
reservation

Reservoir /rezɛr'voa:ɐ̯/ *nt* -s,-s
reservoir

Resid|enz *f* -,-en residence. **r~ieren**
vi (haben) reside

Resign|ation /-'tsio:n/ *f* - resigna-
tion. **r~ieren** *vi (haben) (fig)* give up.
r~iert *a* resigned, *adv* -ly

resolut *a* resolute, *adv* -ly

Resolution /-'tsio:n/ *f* -,-en resolution

Resonanz *f* -,-en resonance; *(fig: Widerhall)* response

Respekt /-sp-, -ʃp-/ *m* -[e]s respect
(vor + *dat* for). **r~abel** *a* respectable.
r~ieren *vt* respect

respekt|los *a* disrespectful, *adv* -ly.
r~voll *a* respectful, *adv* -ly

Ressort /rɛ'soːɐ̯/ *nt* -s,-s department
Rest *m* -[e]s,-e remainder; rest; **R~e**
remains; (*Essens-*) leftovers
Restaurant /rɛsto'rãː/ *nt* -s,-s
restaurant
Restaur|ation /rɛstaura'tsjoːn/ *f* -
restoration. **r~ieren** *vt* restore
Rest|betrag *m* balance. **r~lich** *a* re-
maining. **r~los** *a* utter, *adv* -ly
Resultat *nt* -[e]s,-e result
Retorte *f* -,-n (*Chem*) retort. **R~n-**
baby *nt* (*fam*) test-tube baby
rett|en *vt* save (**vor** + *dat* from); (*aus*
Gefahr befreien) rescue; **sich r~en** save
oneself; (*flüchten*) escape. **R~er** *m* -s,-
rescuer; (*fig*) saviour
Rettich *m* -s,-e white radish
Rettung *f* -,-en rescue; (*fig*) salvation;
jds letzte R~ s.o.'s last hope. **R~sboot**
nt lifeboat. **R~sdienst** *m* rescue service. **R~sgürtel** *m* lifebelt. **r~slos**
adv hopelessly. **R~sring** *m* lifebelt.
R~swagen *m* ambulance
retuschieren *vt* (*Phot*) retouch
Reu|e *f* - remorse; (*Relig*) repentance.
r~en *vt* fill with remorse; **es reut**
mich nicht I don't regret it. **r~ig** *a* pen-
itent. **r~mütig** *a* contrite, *adv* -ly
Revanch|e /re'vãːʃə/ *f* -,-n revenge;
R~e fordern (*Sport*) ask for a return
match. **r~ieren (sich)** *vr* take revenge; (*sich erkenntlich zeigen*)
reciprocate (**mit** with); **sich für eine**
Einladung r~ieren return an
invitation
Revers /re've:ɐ̯/ *nt* -,-/-[s],-s/ lapel
revidieren *vt* revise; (*prüfen*) check
Revier *nt* -s,-e district; (*Zool & fig*)
territory; (*Polizei-*) [police] station
Revision *f* -,-en revision; (*Prüfung*)
check; (*Bücher-*) audit; (*Jur*) appeal
Revolte *f* -,-n revolt
Revolution /-'tsjoːn/ *f* -,-en revo-
lution. **r~är** *a* revolutionary.
r~ieren *vt* revolutionize
Revolver *m* -s,- revolver
Revue /rə'vyː/ *f* -,-n revue
Rezen|sent *m* -en,-en reviewer. **r~-**
sieren *vt* review. **R~sion** *f* -,-en re-
view
Rezept *nt* -[e]s,-e prescription; (*Culin*)
recipe
Rezeption /-'tsjoːn/ *f* -,-en reception
Rezession *f* -,-en recession
rezitieren *vt* recite
R-Gespräch *nt* reverse-charge call,
(*Amer*) collect call
Rhabarber *m* -s rhubarb

Rhapsodie *f* -,-n rhapsody
Rhein *m* -s Rhine. **R~land** *nt* -s Rhine-
land. **R~wein** *m* hock
Rhetori|k *f* - rhetoric. **r~sch** *a* rhet-
orical
Rheum|a *nt* -s rheumatism. **r~atisch**
a rheumatic. **R~atismus** *m* - rheum-
atism
Rhinozeros *nt* -[ses],-se rhinoceros
rhyth|misch /'rʏt-/ *a* rhythmic[al],
adv -ally. **R~mus** *m* -,-men rhythm
Ribisel *f* -,-n (*Aust*) redcurrant
richten *vt* direct (**auf** + *acc* at); address
⟨*Frage, Briefe*⟩ (**an** + *acc* to); aim, train
⟨*Waffe*⟩ (**auf** + *acc* at); (*einstellen*) set;
(*vorbereiten*) prepare; (*reparieren*)
mend; (*hinrichten*) execute; (*SGer: or-*
dentlich machen) tidy; **in die Höhe r~**
raise [up]; **das Wort an jdn r~** address
s.o.; **sich r~** be directed (**auf** + *acc* at;
gegen against); ⟨*Blick:*⟩ turn (**auf** + *acc*
on); **sich r~ nach** comply with ⟨*Vor-*
schrift, jds Wünschen⟩; fit in with ⟨*jds*
Plänen⟩; (*befolgen*) go by; (*abhängen*)
depend on ● *vi* (*haben*) **r~ über** (+ *acc*)
judge
Richter *m* -s,- judge
Richtfest *nt* topping-out ceremony
richtig *a* right, correct; (*wirklich,*
echt) real; **das R~e** the right thing
● *adv* correctly; really; **die Uhr geht**
r~ the clock is right. **R~keit** *f* - cor-
rectness. **r~stellen** *vt sep* (*fig*) correct
Richtlinien *fpl* guidelines
Richtung *f* -,-en direction; (*fig*) trend
riechen† *vt/i* (*haben*) smell (**nach** of;
an etw *dat* sth)
Riegel *m* -s,- bolt; (*Seife*) bar
Riemen *m* -s,- strap; (*Ruder*) oar
Riese *m* -n,-n giant
rieseln *vi* (*sein*) trickle; ⟨*Schnee:*⟩ fall
lightly
Riesen|erfolg *m* huge success.
r~groß *a* huge, enormous
riesig *a* huge; (*gewaltig*) enormous
● *adv* (*fam*) terribly
Riff *nt* -[e]s,-e reef
rigoros *a* rigorous, *adv* -ly
Rille *f* -,-n groove
Rind *nt* -es,-er ox; (*Kuh*) cow; (*Stier*)
bull; (*R~fleisch*) beef; **R~er** cattle *pl*
Rinde *f* -,-n bark; (*Käse-*) rind; (*Brot-*)
crust
Rinderbraten *m* roast beef
Rind|fleisch *nt* beef. **R~vieh** *nt*
cattle *pl*; (*fam: Idiot*) idiot
Ring *m* -[e]s,-e ring

ringeln (sich) vr curl; ⟨Schlange:⟩ coil itself (**um** round)

ring|en† vi (haben) wrestle; (fig) struggle (**um/nach** for) ● vt wring ⟨Hände⟩. **R~en** nt -s wrestling. **R~er** m -s,- wrestler. **R~kampf** m wrestling match; (als Sport) wrestling. **R~richter** m referee

rings adv r~ **im Kreis** in a circle; r~ **um jdn/etw** all around s.o./sth. r~**herum,** r~**um** adv all around

Rinn|e f -,-n channel; (Dach-) gutter. **r~en†** vi (sein) run; (Sand:) trickle. **R~stein** m gutter

Rippe f -,-n rib. **R~nfellentzündung** f pleurisy. **R~nstoß** m dig in the ribs

Risiko nt -s,-s & -ken risk; **ein R~ eingehen** take a risk

risk|ant a risky. **r~ieren** vt risk

Riß m -sses,-sse tear; (Mauer-) crack; (fig) rift

rissig a cracked; ⟨Haut⟩ chapped

Rist m -[e]s,-e instep

Ritt m -[e]s,-e ride

Ritter m -s,- knight. **r~lich** a chivalrous, adv -ly. **R~lichkeit** f - chivalry

rittlings adv astride

Ritu|al nt -s,-e ritual. **r~ell** a ritual

Ritz m -es,-e scratch. **R~e** f -,-n crack; (Fels-) cleft; (zwischen Betten, Vorhängen) gap. **r~en** vt scratch

Rival|e m -n,-n, **R~in** f -,-nen rival. **r~isieren** vi (haben) compete (**mit** with). **r~isierend** a rival ... **R~ität** f -,-en rivalry

Robbe f -,-n seal. **R~n** vi (sein) crawl

Robe f -,-n gown; (Talar) robe

Roboter m -s,- robot

robust a robust

röcheln vi (haben) breathe stertorously

Rochen m -s,- (Zool) ray

Rock[1] m -[e]s,¨e skirt; (Jacke) jacket

Rock[2] m -[s] (Mus) rock

Rodel|bahn f toboggan run. **r~n** vi (sein/haben) toboggan. **R~schlitten** m toboggan

roden vt clear ⟨Land⟩; grub up ⟨Stumpf⟩

Rogen m -s,- [hard] roe

Roggen m -s rye

roh a rough; (ungekocht) raw; ⟨Holz⟩ bare; (brutal) brutal; **r~e Gewalt** brute force ● adv roughly; brutally. **R~bau** m -[e]s,-ten shell. **R~kost** f raw [vegetarian] food. **R~ling** m

-s,-e brute. **R~material** nt raw material. **R~öl** nt crude oil

Rohr nt -[e]s,-e pipe; (Geschütz-) barrel; (Bot) reed; (Zucker-, Bambus-) cane

Röhr|chen nt -s,- [drinking] straw; (Auto, fam) breathalyser (P). **R~e** f -,-n tube; (Radio-) valve; (Back-) oven

Rohstoff m raw material

Rokoko nt -s rococo

Rolladen m roller shutter

Rollbahn f taxiway; (Start-/ Landebahn) runway

Rolle f -,-n roll; (Garn-) reel; (Draht-) coil; (Techn) roller; (Seil-) pulley; (Wäsche-) mangle; (Lauf-) castor; (Schrift-) scroll; (Theat) part, role; **das spielt keine R~** (fig) that doesn't matter. **r~n** vt roll; (auf-) roll up; roll out ⟨Teig⟩; put through the mangle ⟨Wäsche⟩; **sich r~n** roll; (sich ein-) curl up ● vi (sein) roll; ⟨Flugzeug:⟩ taxi ● vi (haben) ⟨Donner:⟩ rumble. **R~r** m -s,- scooter

Roll|feld nt airfield. **R~kragen** m polo-neck. **R~mops** m rollmop[s] sg

Rollo nt -s,-s [roller] blind

Roll|schuh m roller-skate; **R~schuh laufen** roller-skate. **R~splitt** m -s loose chippings pl. **R~stuhl** m wheelchair. **R~treppe** f escalator

Rom nt -s Rome

Roman m -s,-e novel. **r~isch** a Romanesque; ⟨Sprache⟩ Romance. **R~schriftsteller(in)** m(f) novelist

Romant|ik f - romanticism. **r~isch** a romantic, adv -ally

Romanze f -,-n romance

Röm|er(in) m -s,- (f -,-nen) Roman. **r~isch** a Roman

Rommé /'rome:/ nt -s rummy

röntgen vt X-ray. **R~aufnahme** f, **R~bild** nt X-ray. **R~strahlen** mpl X-rays

rosa inv a, **R~** nt -[s],- pink

Rose f -,-n rose. **R~nkohl** m [Brussels] sprouts pl. **R~nkranz** m (Relig) rosary. **R~nmontag** m Monday before Shrove Tuesday

Rosette f -,-n rosette

rosig a rosy

Rosine f -,-n raisin

Rosmarin m -s rosemary

Roß nt Rosses, Rösser horse. **R~kastanie** f horse-chestnut

Rost[1] m -[e]s,-e grating; (Kamin-) grate; (Brat-) grill

Rost[2] m -[e]s rust. **r~en** vi (haben) rust

röst|en *vt* roast; toast ⟨*Brot*⟩. **R~er** *m*
   -s,- toaster
rostfrei *a* stainless
rostig *a* rusty
rot *a* (**röter, rötest**), **Rot** *nt* **-s,-** red; **rot**
   werden turn red; (*erröten*) go red,
   blush
Rotation /-'tsjo:n/ *f* **-,-en** rotation
Röte *f* - redness; (*Scham-*) blush
Röteln *pl* German measles *sg*
röten *vt* redden; **sich r~** turn red
rothaarig *a* red-haired
rotieren *vi* (*haben*) rotate
Rot|kehlchen *nt* **-s,-** robin. **R~kohl**
   m red cabbage
rötlich *a* reddish
Rot|licht *nt* red light. **R~wein** *m* red
   wine
Rou|lade /ru'la:də/ *f* **-,-n** beef olive.
   R~leau /-'lo:/ *nt* **-s,-s** [roller] blind
Route /'ru:tə/ *f* **-,-n** route
Routin|e /ru'ti:nə/ *f* **-,-n** routine;
   (*Erfahrung*) experience. **r~emäßig** *a*
   routine ... ● *adv* routinely. **r~iert** *a*
   experienced
Rowdy /'raudi/ *m* **-s,-s** hooligan
Rübe *f* **-,-n** beet; **rote R~** beetroot;
   gelbe R~ (*SGer*) carrot
rüber *adv* = **herüber, hinüber**
Rubin *m* **-s,-e** ruby
Rubrik *f* **-,-en** column; (*Kategorie*)
   category
Ruck *m* **-[e]s,-e** jerk
Rückantwort *f* reply
ruckartig *a* jerky, *adv* -ily
rück|bezüglich *a* (*Gram*) reflexive.
   R~blende *f* flashback. **R~blick** *m*
   (*fig*) review (**auf** + *acc* of). **r~-**
   blickend *adv* in retrospect. **r~da-**
   tieren *vt* (*inf & pp only*) backdate
rücken *vt/i* (*sein/haben*) move; **an**
   etw (*dat*) **r~** move sth
Rücken *m* **-s,-** back; (*Buch-*) spine;
   (*Berg-*) ridge. **R~lehne** *f* back.
   R~mark *nt* spinal cord.
   R~schwimmen *nt* backstroke. **R~-**
   wind *m* following wind; (*Aviat*) tail
   wind
rückerstatten *vt* (*inf & pp only*)
   refund
Rückfahr|karte *f* return ticket. **R~t**
   f return journey
Rück|fall *m* relapse. **r~fällig** *a* **r~-**
   fällig werden (*Jur*) re-offend. **R~flug**
   m return flight. **R~frage** *f* [further]
   query. **r~fragen** *vi* (*haben*) (*inf & pp*
   only) check (**bei** with). **R~gabe** *f*
   return. **R~gang** *m* decline; (*Preis-*)

drop, fall. `**r~gängig** *a* **r~gängig**
   machen cancel; break off ⟨*Verlobung*⟩.
   R~grat *nt* **-[e]s,-e** spine, backbone.
   R~halt *m* (*fig*) support. **R~hand** *f*
   backhand. **R~kehr** return. **R~-**
   lagen *fpl* reserves. **R~licht** *nt* rear-
   light. **r~lings** *adv* backwards; (*von*
   hinten) from behind. **R~reise** *f* return journey
Rucksack *m* rucksack
Rück|schau *f* review. **R~schlag** *m*
   (*Sport*) return; (*fig*) set-back. **R~-**
   schluß *m* conclusion. **R~schritt** *m*
   (*fig*) retrograde step. **r~schrittlich**
   a retrograde. **R~seite** *f* back; (*einer*
   Münze) reverse
Rücksicht *f* **-,-en** consideration; **R~**
   nehmen auf (+ *acc*) show consideration for; (*berücksichtigen*) take
   into consideration. **R~nahme** *f* - consideration. **r~slos** *a* inconsiderate,
   adv -ly; (*schonungslos*) ruthless, *adv*
   -ly. **r~svoll** *a* considerate, *adv* -ly
Rück|sitz *m* back seat; (*Sozius*) pil-
   lion. **R~spiegel** *m* rear-view mirror.
   R~spiel *nt* return match. **R~-**
   sprache *f* consultation; **R~sprache**
   nehmen mit consult. **R~stand** *m*
   (*Chem*) residue; (*Arbeits-*) backlog;
   R~stände arrears; **im R~stand sein**
   be behind. **r~ständig** *a* (*fig*) backward. **R~stau** *m* (*Auto*) tailback.
   R~strahler *m* **-s,-** reflector. **R~tritt**
   m resignation; (*Fahrrad*) back ped-
   alling. **r~vergüten** *vt* (*inf & pp only*)
   refund. **R~wanderer** *m* repatriate
rückwärt|ig *a* back ..., rear ... **r~s**
   adv backwards. **R~sgang** *m* reverse
   [gear]
Rückweg *m* way back
ruckweise *adv* jerkily
rück|wirkend *a* retrospective, *adv*
   -ly. **R~wirkung** *f* retrospective
   force; **mit R~wirkung vom** backdated
   to. **R~zahlung** *f* repayment. **R~zug**
   m retreat
Rüde *m* **-n,-n** [male] dog
Rudel *nt* **-s,-** herd; (*Wolfs-*) pack;
   (*Löwen-*) pride
Ruder *nt* **-s,-** oar; (*Steuer-*) rudder; **am**
   R~ (*Naut & fig*) at the helm. **R~boot**
   nt rowing boat. **R~er** *m* **-s,-** oarsman.
   r~n *vt/i* (*haben/sein*) row
Ruf *m* **-[e]s,-e** call; (*laut*) shout; (*Te-*
   lefon) telephone number; (*Ansehen*) reputation; **Künstler von Ruf** artist of
   repute. **r~en†** *vt/i* (*haben*) call (**nach**
   for); **r~en lassen** send for

Rüffel m -s,- (fam) telling-off. r~n vt (fam) tell off

Ruf|name m forename by which one is known. **R~nummer** f telephone number. **R~zeichen** nt dialling tone

Rüge f -,-n reprimand. **r~n** vt reprimand; (kritisieren) criticize

Ruhe f - rest; (Stille) quiet; (Frieden) peace; (innere) calm; (Gelassenheit) composure; **die R~ bewahren** keep calm; **in R~ lassen** leave in peace; **sich zur R~ setzen** retire; **R~ [da]!** quiet! **R~gehalt** nt [retirement] pension. **r~los** a restless, adv -ly. **r~n** vi (haben) rest (**auf** + dat on); ⟨Arbeit, Verkehr:⟩ have stopped; **hier ruht ...** here lies ... **R~pause** f rest, break. **R~stand** m retirement; **in den R~stand treten** retire; **im R~stand** retired. **R~störung** f disturbance of the peace. **R~tag** m day of rest; **'Montag R~tag'** 'closed on Mondays'

ruhig a quiet, adv -ly; (erholsam) restful; (friedlich) peaceful, adv -ly; (unbewegt, gelassen) calm, adv -ly; **r~ bleiben** remain calm; **sehen Sie sich r~ um** you're welcome to look round; **man kann r~ darüber sprechen** there's no harm in talking about it

Ruhm m -[e]s fame; (Ehre) glory

rühmen vt praise; **sich r~** boast (gen about)

ruhmreich a glorious

Ruhr f - (Med) dysentery

Rühr|ei nt scrambled eggs pl. **r~en** vt move; (Culin) stir; **sich r~en** move; **zu Tränen r~en** move to tears; **r~t euch!** (Mil) at ease! ● vi (haben) stir; **r~en an** (+ acc) touch; (fig) touch on; **r~en von** (fig) come from. **r~end** a touching, adv -ly

rühr|ig a active. **r~selig** a sentimental. **R~ung** f - emotion

Ruin m -s ruin. **R~e** f -,-n ruin; ruins pl (gen of). **r~ieren** vt ruin

rülpsen vi (haben) (fam) belch

Rum m -s rum

rum adv = herum

Rumän|ien /-jən/ nt -s Romania. **r~isch** a Romanian

Rummel m -s (fam) hustle and bustle; (Jahrmarkt) funfair. **R~platz** m fairground

rumoren vi (haben) make a noise; ⟨Magen:⟩ rumble

Rumpel|kammer f junk-room. **r~n** vi (haben/sein) rumble

Rumpf m -[e]s,ᵉe body, trunk; (Schiffs-) hull; (Aviat) fuselage

rümpfen vt **die Nase r~** turn up one's nose (**über** + acc at)

rund a round ● adv approximately; **r~ um** [a]round. **R~blick** m panoramic view. **R~brief** m circular [letter]

Runde f -,-n round; (Kreis) circle; (eines Polizisten) beat; (beim Rennen) lap; **eine R~ Bier** a round of beer. **r~n** vt round; **sich r~n** become round; ⟨Backen:⟩ fill out

Rund|fahrt f tour. **R~frage** f poll

Rundfunk m radio; **im R~** on the radio. **R~gerät** nt radio [set]

Rund|gang m round; (Spaziergang) walk (**durch** round). **r~heraus** adv straight out. **r~herum** adv all around. **r~lich** a rounded; (mollig) plump. **R~reise** f [circular] tour. **R~schreiben** nt circular. **r~um** adv all round. **R~ung** f -,-en curve. **r~weg** adv ⟨ablehnen⟩ flatly

runter adv = herunter, hinunter

Runzel f -,-n wrinkle. **r~n** vt **die Stirn r~n** frown

runzlig a wrinkled

Rüpel m -s,- (fam) lout. **r~haft** a (fam) loutish

rupfen vt pull out; pluck ⟨Geflügel⟩; (fam: schröpfen) fleece

ruppig a rude, adv -ly

Rüsche f -,-n frill

Ruß m -es soot

Russe m -n,-n Russian

Rüssel m -s,- (Zool) trunk

ruß|en vi (haben) smoke. **r~ig** a sooty

Russ|in f -,-nen Russian. **r~isch** a Russian. **R~isch** nt -[s] (Lang) Russian

Rußland nt -s Russia

rüsten vi (haben) prepare (**zu/für** for) ● vr **sich r~** get ready; **gerüstet sein** be ready

rüstig a sprightly

rustikal a rustic

Rüstung f -,-en armament; (Harnisch) armour. **R~skontrolle** f arms control

Rute f -,-n twig; (Angel-, Wünschel-) rod; (zur Züchtigung) birch; (Schwanz) tail

Rutsch m -[e]s,-e slide. **R~bahn** f slide. **R~e** f -,-n chute. **r~en** vt slide;

(*rücken*) move ● *vi* (*sein*) slide; (*aus-, ab-*) slip; (*Auto*) skid; (*rücken*) move [along]. **r~ig** *a* slippery

rütteln *vt* shake ● *vi* (*haben*) **r~ an** (*+ dat*) rattle

S

Saal *m* -[e]s, **Säle** hall; (*Theat*) auditorium; (*Kranken-*) ward

Saat *f* -,-en seed; (*Säen*) sowing; (*Gesätes*) crop. **S~gut** *nt* seed

sabbern *vi* (*haben*) (*fam*) slobber; ⟨*Baby:*⟩ dribble; (*reden*) jabber

Säbel *m* -s,- sabre

Sabo|tage /zabo'ta:ʒə/ *f* - sabotage. **S~teur** /-'tø:ɐ̯/ *m* -s,-e saboteur. **s~tieren** *vt* sabotage

Sach|bearbeiter *m* expert. **S~buch** *nt* non-fiction book. **s~dienlich** *a* relevant

Sache *f* -,-n matter, business; (*Ding*) thing; (*fig*) cause; **zur S~ kommen** come to the point

Sach|gebiet *nt* (*fig*) area, field. **s~gemäß** *a* proper, *adv* -ly. **S~kenntnis** *f* expertise. **s~kundig** *a* expert, *adv* -ly. **s~lich** *a* factual, *adv* -ly; (*nüchtern*) matter-of-fact, *adv* -ly; (*objektiv*) objective, *adv* -ly; (*schmucklos*) functional

sächlich *a* (*Gram*) neuter

Sachse *m* -n,-n Saxon. **S~n** *nt* -s Saxony

sächsisch *a* Saxon

sacht *a* gentle, *adv* -ly

Sach|verhalt *m* -[e]s facts *pl*. **s~verständig** *a* expert, *adv* -ly. **S~verständige(r)** *m/f* expert

Sack *m* -[e]s,¨e sack; **mit S~ und Pack** with all one's belongings

sacken *vi* (*sein*) sink; (*zusammen-*) go down; ⟨*Person:*⟩ slump

Sack|gasse *f* cul-de-sac; (*fig*) impasse. **S~leinen** *nt* sacking

Sadis|mus *m* - sadism. **S~t** *m* -en,-en sadist. **s~tisch** *a* sadistic, *adv* -ally

säen *vt/i* (*haben*) sow

Safe /ze:f/ *m* -s,-s safe

Saft *m* -[e]s,¨e juice; (*Bot*) sap. **s~ig** *a* juicy; ⟨*Wiese*⟩ lush; ⟨*Preis, Rechnung*⟩ hefty; ⟨*Witz*⟩ coarse. **s~los** *a* dry

Sage *f* -,-n legend

Säge *f* -,-n saw. **S~mehl** *nt* sawdust

sagen *vt* say; (*mitteilen*) tell; (*bedeuten*) mean; **das hat nichts zu s~** it doesn't mean anything

sägen *vt/i* (*haben*) saw

sagenhaft *a* legendary; (*fam: unglaublich*) fantastic, *adv* -ally

Säge|späne *mpl* wood shavings. **S~werk** *nt* sawmill

Sahn|e *f* - cream. **S~ebonbon** *m* & *nt* ≈ toffee. **s~ig** *a* creamy

Saison /zɛ'zõ:/ *f* -,-s season

Saite *f* -,-n (*Mus, Sport*) string. **S~ninstrument** *nt* stringed instrument

Sakko *m* & *nt* -s,-s sports jacket

Sakrament *nt* -[e]s,-e sacrament

Sakrileg *nt* -s,-e sacrilege

Sakrist|an *m* -s,-e verger. **S~ei** *f* -,-en vestry

Salat *m* -[e]s,-e salad; **ein Kopf S~** a lettuce. **S~soße** *f* salad-dressing

Salbe *f* -,-n ointment

Salbei *m* -s & *f* - sage

salben *vt* anoint

Saldo *m* -s,-dos & -den balance

Salon /za'lõ:/ *m* -s,-s salon; (*Naut*) saloon

salopp *a* casual, *adv* -ly; ⟨*Benehmen*⟩ informal, *adv* -ly; ⟨*Ausdruck*⟩ slangy

Salto *m* -s,-s somersault

Salut *m* -[e]s,-e salute. **s~ieren** *vi* (*haben*) salute

Salve *f* -,-n volley; (*Geschütz-*) salvo; (*von Gelächter*) burst

Salz *nt* -es,-e salt. **s~en†** *vt* salt. **S~faß** *nt* salt-cellar. **s~ig** *a* salty. **S~kartoffeln** *fpl* boiled potatoes. **S~säure** *f* hydrochloric acid

Samen *m* -s,- seed; (*Anat*) semen, sperm

sämig *a* (*Culin*) thick

Sämling *m* -s,-e seedling

Sammel|becken *nt* reservoir. **S~begriff** *m* collective term. **s~n** *vt/i* (*haben*) collect; (*suchen, versammeln*) gather; **sich s~n** collect; (*sich versammeln*) gather; (*sich fassen*) collect oneself. **S~name** *m* collective noun

Samm|ler(in) *m* -s,- (*f* -,-nen*) collector. **S~lung** *f* -,-en collection; (*innere*) composure

Samstag *m* -s,-e Saturday. **s~s** *adv* on Saturdays

samt *prep* (*+ dat*) together with ● *adv* **s~ und sonders** without exception

Samt *m* -[e]s velvet. **s~ig** *a* velvety

sämtlich *indef pron inv* all. **s~e(r,s)** *indef pron* all the; **s~e Werke** complete works; **meine s~en Bücher** all my books

Sanatorium *nt* -s,-ien sanatorium

Sand *m* -[e]s sand

Sandal|e *f* -,-n sandal. **S~ette** *f* -,-n high-heeled sandal

Sand|bank *f* sandbank. **S~burg** *f* sand-castle. **s~ig** *a* sandy. **S~kasten** *m* sand-pit. **S~kuchen** *m* Madeira cake. **S~papier** *nt* sandpaper. **S~stein** *m* sandstone

sanft *a* gentle, *adv* -ly. **s~mütig** *a* meek

Sänger(in) *m* -s,- (*f* -,-nen) singer

sanieren *vt* clean up; redevelop (*Gebiet*); (*modernisieren*) modernize; make profitable (*Industrie, Firma*); **sich s~** become profitable

sanitär *a* sanitary

Sanität|er *m* -s,- first-aid man; (*Fahrer*) ambulance man; (*Mil*) medical orderly. **S~swagen** *m* ambulance

Sanktion /zaŋk'tsio:n/ *f* -,-en sanction. **s~ieren** *vt* sanction

Saphir *m* -s,-e sapphire

Sardelle *f* -,-n anchovy

Sardine *f* -,-n sardine

Sarg *m* -[e]s,-e coffin

Sarkas|mus *m* - sarcasm. **s~tisch** *a* sarcastic, *adv* -ally

Sat|an *m* -s Satan; (*fam: Teufel*) devil. **s~anisch** *a* satanic

Satellit *m* -en,-en satellite. **S~enfernsehen** *nt* satellite television

Satin /za'tɛŋ/ *m* -s satin

Satir|e *f* -,-n satire. **s~isch** *a* satirical, *adv* -ly

satt *a* full; (*Farbe*) rich; **s~ sein** have had enough [to eat]; **sich s~ essen** eat as much as one wants; **s~ machen** feed; (*Speise:*) be filling; **etw s~ haben** (*fam*) be fed up with sth

Sattel *m* -s,¨ saddle. **s~n** *vt* saddle. **S~schlepper** *m* tractor unit. **S~zug** *m* articulated lorry

sättigen *vt* satisfy; (*Chem & fig*) saturate ● *vi* (*haben*) be filling. **s~d** *a* filling

Satz *m* -es,¨e sentence; (*Teil-*) clause; (*These*) proposition; (*Math*) theorem; (*Mus*) movement; (*Tennis, Zusammengehöriges*) set; (*Boden-*) sediment; (*Kaffee-*) grounds *pl*; (*Steuer-, Zins-*) rate; (*Druck-*) setting; (*Schrift-*) type;

(*Sprung*) leap, bound. **S~aussage** *f* predicate. **S~gegenstand** *m* subject. **S~zeichen** *nt* punctuation mark

Sau *f* -, Säue sow; (*sl: schmutziger Mensch*) dirty pig

sauber *a* clean; (*ordentlich*) neat, *adv* -ly; (*anständig*) decent, *adv* -ly; (*fam: nicht anständig*) fine. **s~halten†** *vt sep* keep clean. **S~keit** *f* - cleanliness; neatness; decency

säuberlich *a* neat, *adv* -ly

saubermachen *vt/i sep* (*haben*) clean

säuber|n *vt* clean; (*befreien*) rid/ (*Pol*) purge (**von** of). **S~ungsaktion** *f* (*Pol*) purge

Sauce /'zo:sə/ *f* -,-n sauce; (*Braten-*) gravy

Saudi-Arabien /-jən/ *nt* -s Saudi Arabia

sauer *a* sour; (*Chem*) acid; (*eingelegt*) pickled; (*schwer*) hard; **saurer Regen** acid rain; **s~ sein** (*fam*) be annoyed

Sauerei *f* -,-en = **Schweinerei**

Sauerkraut *nt* sauerkraut

säuerlich *a* slightly sour

Sauerstoff *m* oxygen

saufen† *vt/i* (*haben*) drink; (*sl*) booze

Säufer *m* -s,- (*sl*) boozer

saugen† *vt/i* (*haben*) suck; (*staub-*) vacuum, hoover; **sich voll Wasser s~** soak up water

säugen *vt* suckle

Sauger *m* -s,- [baby's] dummy, (*Amer*) pacifier; (*Flaschen-*) teat

Säugetier *nt* mammal

saugfähig *a* absorbent

Säugling *m* -s,-e infant

Säule *f* -,-n column

Saum *m* -[e]s, Säume hem; (*Rand*) edge

säumen[1] *vt* hem; (*fig*) line

säum|en[2] *vi* (*haben*) delay. **s~ig** *a* dilatory

Sauna *f* -,-nas & -nen sauna

Säure *f* -,-n acidity; (*Chem*) acid

säuseln *vi* (*haben*) rustle [softly]

sausen *vi* (*haben*) rush; (*Ohren:*) buzz ● *vi* (*sein*) rush [along]

Sauwetter *nt* (*sl*) lousy weather

Saxophon *nt* -s,-e saxophone

SB- /ɛs'be:-/ *pref* (= **Selbstbedienung**) self-service ...

S-Bahn *f* city and suburban railway

sch *int* shush! (*fort*) shoo!

Schabe *f* -,-n cockroach

schaben *vt/i* (*haben*) scrape

schäbig *a* shabby, *adv* -ily
Schablone *f* -,-n stencil; (*Muster*) pattern; (*fig*) stereotype
Schach *nt* -s chess; **S∼!** check! **in S∼ halten** (*fig*) keep in check. **S∼brett** *nt* chessboard
schachern *vi* (*haben*) haggle
Schachfigur *f* chess-man
schachmatt *a* **s∼ setzen** checkmate; **s∼!** checkmate!
Schachspiel *nt* game of chess
Schacht *m* -[e]s,¨e shaft
Schachtel *f* -,-n box; (*Zigaretten-*) packet
Schachzug *m* move
schade *a* **s∼ sein** be a pity *or* shame; **zu s∼ für** too good for; **[wie] s∼!** [what a] pity *or* shame!
Schädel *m* -s,- skull. **S∼bruch** *m* fractured skull
schaden *vi* (*haben*) (+ *dat*) damage; (*nachteilig sein*) hurt; **das schadet nichts** that doesn't matter. **S∼** *m* -s,¨- damage; (*Defekt*) defect; (*Nachteil*) disadvantage; **zu S∼ kommen** be hurt. **S∼ersatz** *m* damages *pl.* **S∼freude** *f* malicious glee. **s∼froh** *a* gloating
schadhaft *a* defective
schädig|en *vt* damage, harm. **S∼ung** *f* -,-en damage
schädlich *a* harmful
Schädling *m* -s,-e pest. **S∼sbekämpfungsmittel** *nt* pesticide
Schaf *nt* -[e]s,-e sheep; (*fam: Idiot*) idiot. **S∼bock** *m* ram
Schäfchen *nt* -s,- lamb
Schäfer *m* -s,- shepherd. **S∼hund** *m* sheepdog; **Deutscher S∼hund** German shepherd, alsatian
Schaffell *nt* sheepskin
schaffen¹† *vt* create; (*herstellen*) establish; make (*Platz*); **wie geschaffen für** made for
schaffen² *v* (*reg*) ● *vt* manage [to do]; pass (*Prüfung*); catch (*Zug*); (*bringen*) take; **jdm zu s∼ machen** trouble s.o.; **sich** (*dat*) **zu s∼ machen** busy oneself (**an**+ *dat* with) ● *vi* (*haben*) (*SGer: arbeiten*) work. **S∼** *nt* -s work
Schaffner *m* -s,- conductor; (*Zug-*) ticket-inspector
Schaffung *f* - creation
Schaft *m* -[e]s,¨e shaft; (*Gewehr-*) stock; (*Stiefel-*) leg. **S∼stiefel** *m* high boot
Schal *m* -s,-s scarf

schal *a* insipid; (*abgestanden*) flat; (*fig*) stale
Schale *f* -,-n skin; (*abgeschält*) peel; (*Eier-, Nuß-, Muschel-*) shell; (*Schüssel*) dish
schälen *vt* peel; **sich s∼** peel
schalkhaft *a* mischievous, *adv* -ly
Schall *m* -[e]s sound. **S∼dämpfer** *m* silencer. **s∼dicht** *a* soundproof. **s∼en** *vi* (*haben*) ring out; (*nachhallen*) resound; **s∼end lachen** roar with laughter. **S∼mauer** *f* sound barrier. **S∼platte** *f* record, disc
schalt|en *vt* switch ● *vi* (*haben*) switch/(*Ampel:*) turn (**auf**+ *acc* to); (*Auto*) change gear; (*fam: begreifen*) catch on. **S∼er** *m* -s,- switch; (*Post-, Bank-*) counter; (*Fahrkarten-*) ticket window. **S∼hebel** *m* switch; (*Auto*) gear-lever. **S∼jahr** *nt* leap year. **S∼kreis** *m* circuit. **S∼ung** *f* -,-en circuit; (*Auto*) gear change
Scham *f* - shame; (*Anat*) private parts *pl*; **falsche S∼** false modesty
schämen (sich) *vr* be ashamed; **schämt euch!** you should be ashamed of yourselves!
scham|haft *a* modest, *adv* -ly; (*schüchtern*) bashful, *adv* -ly. **s∼los** *a* shameless, *adv* -ly
Schampon *nt* -s shampoo. **s∼ieren** *vt* shampoo
Schande *f* - disgrace, shame; **S∼ machen** (+ *dat*) bring shame on
schänd|en *vt* dishonour; (*fig*) defile; (*Relig*) desecrate; (*sexuell*) violate. **s∼lich** *a* disgraceful, *adv* -ly. **S∼ung** *f* -,-en defilement; desecration; violation
Schanktisch *m* bar
Schanze *f* -,-n [ski-]jump
Schar *f* -,-en crowd; (*Vogel-*) flock; **in [hellen] S∼en** in droves
Scharade *f* -,-n charade
scharen *vt* **um sich s∼** gather round one; **sich s∼ um** flock round. **s∼weise** *adv* in droves
scharf *a* (**schärfer, schärfst**) sharp; (*stark*) strong; (*stark gewürzt*) hot; (*Geruch*) pungent; (*Frost, Wind, Augen, Verstand*) keen; (*streng*) harsh; (*Galopp, Ritt*) hard; (*Munition*) live; (*Hund*) fierce; **s∼ einstellen** (*Phot*) focus; **s∼ sein** (*Phot*) be in focus; **s∼ sein auf** (+ *acc*) (*fam*) be keen on ● *adv* sharply; (*hinsehen, nachdenken, bremsen, reiten*) hard; (*streng*) harshly; **s∼ schießen** fire live ammunition

Scharfblick m perspicacity
Schärfe f - (s. scharf) sharpness; strength; hotness; pungency; keenness; harshness. **s~n** vt sharpen
scharf|machen vt sep (fam) incite. **S~richter** m executioner. **S~schütze** m marksman. **s~sichtig** a perspicacious. **S~sinn** m astuteness. **s~sinnig** a astute, adv -ly
Scharlach m -s scarlet fever
Scharlatan m -s,-e charlatan
Scharnier nt -s,-e hinge
Schärpe f -,-n sash
scharren vi (haben) scrape; (Huhn:) scratch; (Pferd:) paw the ground • vt scrape
Schart|e f -,-n nick. **s~ig** a jagged
Schaschlik m & nt -s,-s kebab
Schatten m -s,- shadow; (schattige Stelle) shade; **im S~** in the shade. **s~haft** a shadowy. **S~riß** m silhouette. **S~seite** f shady side; (fig) disadvantage
schattier|en vt shade. **S~ung** f -,-en shading; (fig: Variante) shade
schattig a shady
Schatz m -es,-̈e treasure; (Freund, Freundin) sweetheart; (Anrede) darling
Schätzchen nt -s,- darling
schätzen vt estimate; (taxieren) value; (achten) esteem; (würdigen) appreciate; (fam: vermuten) reckon; **sich glücklich s~** consider oneself lucky
Schätzung f -,-en estimate; (Taxierung) valuation. **s~sweise** adv approximately
Schau f -,-en show; **zur S~ stellen** display. **S~bild** nt diagram
Schauder m -s shiver; (vor Abscheu) shudder. **s~haft** a dreadful, adv -ly. **s~n** vi (haben) shiver; (vor Abscheu) shudder; **mich s~te** I shivered/ shuddered
schauen vi (haben) (SGer, Aust) look; **s~, daß** make sure that
Schauer m -s,- shower; (Schauder) shiver. **S~geschichte** f horror story. **s~lich** a ghastly. **s~n** vi (haben) shiver; **mich s~te** I shivered
Schaufel f -,-n shovel; (Kehr-) dustpan. **s~n** vt shovel; (graben) dig
Schaufenster nt shop-window. **S~bummel** m window-shopping. **S~puppe** f dummy
Schaukasten m display case
Schaukel f -,-n swing. **s~n** vt rock • vi (haben) rock; (auf einer

Schaukel) swing; (schwanken) sway. **S~pferd** nt rocking-horse. **S~stuhl** m rocking-chair
schaulustig a curious
Schaum m -[e]s foam; (Seifen-) lather; (auf Bier) froth; (als Frisier-, Rasiermittel) mousse
schäumen vi (haben) foam, froth; (Seife:) lather
Schaum|gummi m foam rubber. **s~ig** a frothy; (Culin) cream. **S~krone** f white crest; (auf Bier) head. **S~speise** f mousse. **S~stoff** m [synthetic] foam. **S~wein** m sparkling wine
Schauplatz m scene
schaurig a dreadful, adv -ly; (unheimlich) eerie, adv eerily
Schauspiel nt play; (Anblick) spectacle. **S~er** m actor. **S~erin** f actress. **s~ern** vi (haben) act; (sich verstellen) play-act
Scheck m -s,-s cheque, (Amer) check. **S~buch, S~heft** nt cheque-book. **S~karte** f cheque card
Scheibe f -,-n disc; (Schieß-) target; (Glas-) pane; (Brot-, Wurst-) slice. **S~nwaschanlage** f windscreen washer. **S~nwischer** m -s,- windscreen-wiper
Scheich m -s,-e & -s sheikh
Scheide f -,-n sheath; (Anat) vagina
scheid|en† vt separate; (unterscheiden) distinguish; dissolve (Ehe); **sich s~en lassen** get divorced; sich **s~en** diverge; (Meinungen:) differ • vi (sein) leave; (voneinander) part. **S~ung** f -,-en divorce
Schein m -[e]s,-e light; (Anschein) appearance; (Bescheinigung) certificate; (Geld-) note; **etw nur zum S~ tun** only pretend to do sth. **s~bar** a apparent, adv -ly. **s~en†** vi (haben) shine; (den Anschein haben) seem, appear; **mir s~t** it seems to me
scheinheilig a hypocritical, adv -ly. **S~keit** f hypocrisy
Scheinwerfer m -s,- floodlight; (Such-) searchlight; (Auto) headlight; (Theat) spotlight
Scheiß-, scheiß- pref (vulg) bloody. **S~e** f - (vulg) shit. **s~en†** vi (haben) (vulg) shit
Scheit nt -[e]s,-e log
Scheitel m -s,- parting. **s~n** vt part (Haar)
scheitern vi (sein) fail

Schelle f -,-n bell. **s~n** vi (haben) ring

Schellfisch m haddock

Schelm m -s,-e rogue. **s~isch** a mischievous, adv -ly

Schelte f - scolding. **s~n**† vi (haben) grumble (**über** + acc about); **mit jdm s~n** scold s.o. ● vt scold; (bezeichnen) call

Schema nt -s,-mata model, pattern; (Skizze) diagram

Schemel m -s,- stool

Schenke f -,-n tavern

Schenkel m -s,- thigh; (Geom) side

schenken vt give [as a present]; **jdm Vertrauen/Glauben s~** trust/believe s.o.; **sich** (dat) **etw s~** give sth a miss

scheppern vi (haben) clank

Scherbe f -,-n [broken] piece

Schere f -,-n scissors pl; (Techn) shears pl; (Hummer-) claw. **s~n**¹† vt shear; crop ⟨Haar⟩; clip ⟨Hund⟩

scheren² vt (reg) (fam) bother; **sich nicht s~ um** not care about; **scher dich zum Teufel!** go to hell!

Scherenschnitt m silhouette

Scherereien fpl (fam) trouble sg

Scherz m -es,-e joke; **im/zum S~** as a joke. **s~en** vi (haben) joke. **S~frage** f riddle. **s~haft** a humorous

scheu a shy, adv -ly; ⟨Tier⟩ timid; **s~ werden** ⟨Pferd:⟩ shy; **s~ machen** startle. **S~** f - shyness; timidity; (Ehrfurcht) awe

scheuchen vt shoo

scheuen vt be afraid of; (meiden) shun; **keine Mühe/Kosten s~** spare no effort/expense; **sich s~** be afraid (**vor** + dat of); shrink (**etw zu tun** from doing sth) ● vi (haben) ⟨Pferd:⟩ shy

Scheuer|lappen m floor-cloth. **s~n** vt scrub; (mit Scheuerpulver) scour; (reiben) rub; **[wund] s~n** chafe ● vi (haben) rub, chafe. **S~tuch** nt floor-cloth

Scheuklappen fpl blinkers

Scheune f -,-n barn

Scheusal nt -s,-e monster

scheußlich a horrible, adv -bly

Schi m -s,-er ski; **S~ fahren** od **laufen** ski

Schicht f -,-en layer; (Geol) stratum; (Gesellschafts-) class; (Arbeits-) shift. **S~arbeit** f shift work. **s~en** vt stack [up]

schick a stylish, adv -ly; ⟨Frau⟩ chic; (fam: prima) great. **S~** m -[e]s style

schicken vt/i (haben) send; **s~ nach** send for; **sich s~ in** (+ acc) resign oneself to

schicklich a fitting, proper

Schicksal nt -s,-e fate. **s~haft** a fateful. **S~sschlag** m misfortune

Schieb|edach nt (Auto) sun-roof. **s~en**† vt push; (gleitend) slide; (fam: handeln mit) traffic in; **etw s~en auf** (+ acc) (fig) put sth down to; shift ⟨Schuld, Verantwortung⟩ on to ● vi (haben) push. **S~er** m -s,- slide; (Person) black marketeer. **S~etür** f sliding door. **S~ung** f -,-en (fam) illicit deal; (Betrug) rigging, fixing

Schieds|gericht nt panel of judges; (Jur) arbitration tribunal. **S~richter** m referee; (Tennis) umpire; (Jur) arbitrator

schief a crooked; (unsymmetrisch) lopsided; (geneigt) slanting, sloping; (nicht senkrecht) leaning; ⟨Winkel⟩ oblique; (fig) false; (mißtrauisch) suspicious ● adv not straight; **jdn s~ ansehen** look at s.o. askance

Schiefer m -s slate

schief|gehen† vi sep (sein) (fam) go wrong. **s~lachen (sich)** vr sep double up with laughter

schielen vi (haben) squint

Schienbein nt shin; (Knochen) shinbone

Schiene f -,-n rail; (Gleit-) runner; (Med) splint. **s~n** vt (Med) put in a splint

schier¹ adv almost

schier² a pure; ⟨Fleisch⟩ lean

Schießbude f shooting-gallery. **s~en**† vt shoot; fire ⟨Kugel⟩; score ⟨Tor⟩ ● vi (haben) shoot, fire (**auf** + acc at) ● vi (sein) shoot [along]; (strömen) gush; **in die Höhe s~en** shoot up. **S~erei** f -,-en shooting. **S~scheibe** f target. **S~stand** m shooting-range

Schifahr|en nt skiing. **S~er(in)** m(f) skier

Schiff nt -[e]s,-e ship; (Kirchen-) nave; (Seiten-) aisle

Schiffahrt f shipping

schiff|bar a navigable. **S~bau** m shipbuilding. **S~bruch** m shipwreck. **s~brüchig** a shipwrecked. **S~chen** nt -s,- small boat; (Tex) shuttle. **S~er** m -s,- skipper

Schikan|e f -,-n harassment; **mit allen S~en** (fam) with every refinement. **s~ieren** vt harass; (tyrannisieren) bully

Schi|laufen *nt* -s skiing. **S∼läu-fer(in)** *m(f)* -s,- (*f*-,-nen) skier

Schild¹ *m* -[e]s,-e shield; *etw im S∼e führen* (*fam*) be up to sth

Schild² *nt* -[e]s,-er sign; (*Namens-, Nummern-*) plate; (*Mützen-*) badge; (*Etikett*) label

Schilddrüse *f* thyroid [gland]

schilder|n *vt* describe. **S∼ung** *f* -,-en description

Schild|kröte *f* tortoise; (*See-*) turtle. **S∼patt** *nt* -[e]s tortoiseshell

Schilf *nt* -[e]s reeds *pl*

schillern *vi* (*haben*) shimmer

Schimmel *m* -s,- mould; (*Pferd*) white horse. **s∼ig** *a* mouldy. **s∼n** *vi* (*haben/sein*) go mouldy

Schimmer *m* -s gleam; (*Spur*) glimmer. **s∼n** *vi* (*haben*) gleam

Schimpanse *m* -n,-n chimpanzee

schimpf|en *vi* (*haben*) grumble (**mit** at; **über** + *acc* about); scold (**mit jdm** s.o.) ● *vt* call. **S∼name** *m* term of abuse. **S∼wort** *nt* (*pl* -wörter) swearword; (*Beleidigung*) insult

schind|en† *vt* work *or* drive hard; (*quälen*) ill-treat; **sich s∼en** slave [away]; **Eindruck s∼en** (*fam*) try to impress. **S∼er** *m* -s,- slave-driver. **S∼erei** *f* - slave-driving; (*Plackerei*) hard slog

Schinken *m* -s,- ham. **S∼speck** *m* bacon

Schippe *f* -,-n shovel. **s∼n** *vt* shovel

Schirm *m* -[e]s,-e umbrella; (*Sonnen-*) sunshade; (*Lampen-*) shade; (*Augen-*) visor; (*Mützen-*) peak; (*Ofen-, Bild-*) screen; (*fig: Schutz*) shield. **S∼herr** *m* patron. **S∼herrschaft** *f* patronage. **S∼mütze** *f* peaked cap

schizophren *a* schizophrenic. **S∼ie** *f* - schizophrenia

Schlacht *f* -,-en battle

schlachten *vt* slaughter, kill

Schlachter, Schlächter *m* -s,- (*NGer*) butcher

Schlacht|feld *nt* battlefield. **S∼haus** *nt*, **S∼hof** *m* abattoir. **S∼platte** *f* plate of assorted cooked meats and sausages. **S∼schiff** *nt* battleship

Schlacke *f* -,-n slag

Schlaf *m* -[e]s sleep; *im S∼* in one's sleep. **S∼anzug** *m* pyjamas *pl*, (*Amer*) pajamas *pl*. **S∼couch** *f* sofa bed

Schläfe *f* -,-n (*Anat*) temple

schlafen† *vi* (*haben*) sleep; (*fam: nicht aufpassen*) be asleep; **s∼ gehen**

go to bed; **er schläft noch** he is still asleep. **S∼zeit** *f* bedtime

Schläfer(in) *m* -s,- (*f*-,-nen) sleeper

schlaff *a* limp, *adv* -ly; (*Seil*) slack; (*Muskel*) flabby

Schlaf|lied *nt* lullaby. **s∼los** *a* sleepless. **S∼losigkeit** *f* - insomnia. **S∼mittel** *nt* sleeping drug

schläfrig *a* sleepy, *adv* -ily

Schlaf|saal *m* dormitory. **S∼sack** *m* sleeping-bag. **S∼tablette** *f* sleeping-pill. **s∼trunken** *a* [still] half asleep. **S∼wagen** *m* sleeping-car, sleeper. **s∼wandeln** *vi* (*haben/sein*) sleepwalk. **S∼zimmer** *nt* bedroom

Schlag *m* -[e]s,¨e blow; (*Faust-*) punch; (*Herz-, Puls-, Trommel-*) beat; (*einer Uhr*) chime; (*Glocken-, Gong- & Med*) stroke; (*elektrischer*) shock; (*Portion*) helping; (*Art*) type; (*Aust*) whipped cream; **S∼e bekommen** get a beating; **S∼ auf S∼** in rapid succession. **S∼ader** *f* artery. **S∼anfall** *m* stroke. **s∼artig** *a* sudden, *adv* -ly. **S∼baum** *m* barrier

schlagen† *vt* hit, strike; (*fällen*) fell; knock (*Loch, Nagel*) (**in** + *acc* into); (*prügeln, besiegen*) beat; (*Culin*) whisk (*Eiweiß*); whip (*Sahne*); (*legen*) throw; (*wickeln*) wrap; (*hinzufügen*) add (**zu** to); **sich s∼** fight; **sich geschlagen geben** admit defeat ● *vi* (*haben*) beat; (*Tür:*) bang; (*Uhr:*) strike; (*melodisch*) chime; **mit den Flügeln s∼** flap its wings; **um sich s∼** lash out; **es schlug sechs** the clock struck six ● *vi* (*sein*) **in etw** (*acc*) **s∼** (*Blitz, Kugel:*) strike sth; **s∼ an** (+ *acc*) knock against; **nach jdm s∼** (*fig*) take after s.o. **s∼d** *a* (*fig*) conclusive, *adv* -ly

Schlager *m* -s,- pop song; (*Erfolg*) hit

Schläger *m* -s,- racket; (*Tischtennis-*) bat; (*Golf-*) club; (*Hockey-*) stick; (*fam: Raufbold*) thug. **S∼ei** *f* -,-en fight, brawl

schlag|fertig *a* quick-witted. **S∼instrument** *nt* percussion instrument. **S∼loch** *nt* pot-hole. **S∼sahne** *f* whipped cream; (*ungeschlagen*) whipping cream. **S∼seite** *f* (*Naut*) list. **S∼stock** *m* truncheon. **S∼wort** *nt* (*pl* -worte) slogan. **S∼zeile** *f* headline. **S∼zeug** *nt* (*Mus*) percussion. **S∼zeuger** *m* -s,- percussionist; (*in Band*) drummer

schlaksig *a* gangling

Schlamassel *m* & *nt* -s (*fam*) mess

Schlamm *m* -[e]s mud. **s∼ig** *a* muddy

Schlamp|e f -,-n (fam) slut. **s~en**
vi (haben) (fam) be sloppy (**bei**
in). **S~erei** f -,-en sloppiness; (Unordnung) mess. **s~ig** a slovenly; ⟨Ar-
beit⟩ sloppy ● adv in a slovenly way;
sloppily

Schlange f -,-n snake; (Menschen-,
Auto-) queue; **S~ stehen** queue, (Amer)
stand in line

schlängeln (sich) vr wind; ⟨Person:⟩
weave (**durch** through)

Schlangen|biß m snakebite. **S~
linie** f wavy line

schlank a slim. **S~heit** f slimness.
S~heitskur f slimming diet

schlapp a tired; (schlaff) limp, adv
-ly. **S~e** f -,-n (fam) setback

schlau a clever, adv -ly; (gerissen)
crafty, adv -ily; **ich werde nicht s~
daraus** I can't make head or tail of it

Schlauch m -[e]s, Schläuche tube;
(Wasser-) hose[pipe]. **S~boot** nt rubber dinghy. **s~en** vt (fam) exhaust

Schlaufe f -,-n loop

schlecht a bad; (böse) wicked; (unzulänglich) poor; **s~ werden** go bad;
⟨Wetter:⟩ turn bad; **s~er werden** get
worse; **s~ aussehen** look bad/⟨Person:⟩
unwell; **mir ist s~** I feel sick ● adv
badly; poorly; (kaum) not really.
s~gehen† vi sep (sein) (+dat) **es
geht ihm s~** he's doing badly; (gesundheitlich) he's not well. **s~gelaunt**
attrib a bad-tempered. **s~hin** adv
quite simply. **S~igkeit** f - wicked-
ness. **s~machen** vt sep (fam) run
down

schlecken vt/i (haben) lick (**an etw
dat** sth); (auf-) lap up

Schlegel m -s,- mallet; (Trommel-)
stick; (SGer: Keule) leg; (Hühner-) drumstick

schleichen† vi (sein) creep; (langsam
gehen/fahren) crawl ● vr **sich s~**
creep. **s~d** a creeping; ⟨Krankheit⟩
insidious

Schleier m -s,- veil; (fig) haze. **s~haft**
a **es ist mir s~haft** (fam) it's a mystery
to me

Schleife f -,-n bow; (Fliege) bow-tie;
(Biegung) loop

schleifen¹ v (reg) ● vt drag; (zerstören)
raze to the ground ● vi (haben) trail,
drag

schleifen²† vt grind; (schärfen)
sharpen; cut ⟨Edelstein, Glas⟩;
(drillen) drill

Schleim m -[e]s slime; (Anat) mucus;
(Med) phlegm. **s~ig** a slimy

schlemm|en vi (haben) feast ● vt
feast on. **S~er** m -s,- gourmet

schlendern vi (sein) stroll

schlenkern vt/i (haben) swing; **s~
mit** swing; dangle ⟨Beine⟩

Schlepp|dampfer m tug. **S~e** f -,-n
train. **s~en** vt drag; (tragen) carry;
(ziehen) tow; **sich s~en** drag oneself;
(sich hinziehen) drag on; **sich s~en mit**
carry. **s~end** a slow, adv -ly. **S~er** m
-s,- tug; (Traktor) tractor. **S~kahn** m
barge. **S~lift** m T-bar lift. **S~tau** nt
tow-rope; **ins S~tau nehmen** take in
tow

Schleuder f -,-n catapult; (Wäsche-)
spin-drier. **s~n** vt hurl; spin ⟨Wäsche⟩;
extract ⟨Honig⟩ ● vi (sein) skid; **ins
S~n geraten** skid. **S~preise** mpl
knock-down prices. **S~sitz** m ejector
seat

schleunigst adv hurriedly; (sofort)
at once

Schleuse f -,-n lock; (Sperre) sluice
[-gate]. **s~n** vt steer

Schliche pl tricks; **jdm auf die S~
kommen** (fam) get on to s.o.

schlicht a plain, adv -ly; (einfach)
simple, adv -ply

schlicht|en vt settle ● vi (haben)
arbitrate. **S~ung** f - settlement;
(Jur) arbitration

Schlick m -[e]s silt

Schließe f -,-n clasp; (Schnalle) buckle

schließen† vt close; (ab-) lock; fasten
⟨Kleid, Verschluß⟩; (stillegen) close
down; (beenden, folgern) conclude;
enter into ⟨Vertrag⟩; **sich s~** close; **in
die Arme s~** embrace; **etw s~ an**
(+acc) connect sth to; **sich s~ an**
(+acc) follow ● vi (haben) close; (den
Betrieb einstellen) close down; (den
Schlüssel drehen) turn the key; (enden,
folgern) conclude; **s~ lassen auf**
(+acc) suggest

Schließ|fach nt locker. **s~lich** adv
finally, in the end; (immerhin) after
all. **S~ung** f -,-en closure

Schliff m -[e]s cut; (Schleifen) cutting;
(fig) polish; **der letzte S~** the finishing
touches pl

schlimm a bad, adv -ly; **s~er werden**
get worse; **nicht so s~!** it doesn't matter! **s~stenfalls** adv if the worst
comes to the worst

Schlinge f -,-n loop; (Henkers-) noose;
(Med) sling; (Falle) snare

Schlingel *m* -s, - *(fam)* rascal

schling|en† *vt* wind, wrap; tie 〈*Knoten*〉; **sich s~en um** coil around
● *vi (haben)* bolt one's food.
S~pflanze *f* climber

Schlips *m* -es, -e tie

Schlitten *m* -s, - sledge; *(Rodel-)* toboggan; *(Pferde-)* sleigh; **S~ fahren** toboggan

schlittern *vi (haben/sein)* slide

Schlittschuh *m* skate; **S~ laufen** skate. **S~läufer(in)** *m(f)* skater

Schlitz *m* -es, -e slit; *(für Münze)* slot; *(Jacken-)* vent; *(Hosen-)* flies *pl*. **s~en** *vt* slit

Schloß *nt* -sses, ¨sser lock; *(Vorhänge-)* padlock; *(Verschluß)* clasp; *(Gebäude)* castle; *(Palast)* palace

Schlosser *m* -s, - locksmith; *(Auto-)* mechanic; *(Maschinen-)* fitter

Schlot *m* -[e]s, -e chimney

schlottern *vi (haben)* shake, tremble; 〈*Kleider:*〉 hang loose

Schlucht *f* -, -en ravine, gorge

schluchz|en *vi (haben)* sob. **S~er** *m* -s, - sob

Schluck *m* -[e]s, -e mouthful; *(klein)* sip

Schluckauf *m* -s hiccups *pl*

schlucken *vt/i (haben)* swallow. **S~** *m* -s hiccups *pl*

schlud|ern *vi (haben)* be sloppy **(bei** in). **s~rig** *a* sloppy, *adv* -ily; 〈*Arbeit*〉 slipshod

Schlummer *m* -s slumber. **s~n** *vi (haben)* slumber

Schlund *m* -[e]s [back of the] throat; *(fig)* mouth

schlüpf|en *vi (sein)* slip; **[aus dem Ei] s~en** hatch. **S~er** *m* -s, - knickers *pl*. **s~rig** *a* slippery; *(anstößig)* smutty

schlurfen *vi (sein)* shuffle

schlürfen *vt/i (haben)* slurp

Schluß *m* -sses, ¨sse end; *(S~folgerung)* conclusion; **zum S~** finally; **S~ machen** stop **(mit etw** sth); finish **(mit jdm** with s.o.)

Schlüssel *m* -s, - key; *(Schrauben-)* spanner; *(Geheim-)* code; *(Mus)* clef.
S~bein *nt* collar-bone. **S~bund** *m & nt* bunch of keys. **S~loch** *nt* keyhole.
S~ring *m* key-ring

Schlußfolgerung *f* conclusion

schlüssig *a* conclusive, *adv* -ly; **sich** *(dat)* **s~ werden** make up one's mind

Schluß|licht *nt* rear-light. **S~verkauf** *m* [end of season] sale

Schmach *f* - disgrace

schmachten *vi (haben)* languish

schmächtig *a* slight

schmackhaft *a* tasty

schmal *a* narrow; *(dünn)* thin; *(schlank)* slender; *(karg)* meagre

schmälern *vt* diminish; *(herabsetzen)* belittle

Schmalz[1] *nt* -es lard; *(Ohren-)* wax

Schmalz[2] *m* -es *(fam)* schmaltz. **s~ig** *a (fam)* schmaltzy, slushy

schmarotz|en *vi (haben)* be parasitic **(auf**+ *acc* on); 〈*Person:*〉 sponge **(bei** on). **S~er** *m* -s, - parasite; *(Person)* sponger

Schmarren *m* -s, - *(Aust)* pancake [torn into strips]; *(fam: Unsinn)* rubbish

schmatzen *vi (haben)* eat noisily

schmausen *vi (haben)* feast

schmecken *vi (haben)* taste **(nach** of); **[gut] s~** taste good; **hat es dir geschmeckt?** did you enjoy it? ● *vt* taste

Schmeichelei *f* -, -en flattery; *(Kompliment)* compliment

schmeichel|haft *a* complimentary, flattering. **s~n** *vi (haben)* (+ *dat*) flatter

schmeißen† *vt/i (haben)* **s~ [mit]** *(fam)* chuck

Schmeißfliege *f* bluebottle

schmelz|en† *vt/i (sein)* melt; smelt 〈*Erze*〉. **S~wasser** *nt* melted snow

Schmerbauch *m (fam)* paunch

Schmerz *m* -es, -en pain; *(Kummer)* grief; **S~en haben** be in pain. **s~en** *vt* hurt; *(fig)* grieve ● *vi (haben)* hurt, be painful. **S~ensgeld** *nt* compensation for pain and suffering.
s~haft *a* painful. **s~lich** *a (fig)* painful; *(traurig)* sad, *adv* -ly. **s~los** *a* painless, *adv* -ly. **s~stillend** *a* pain-killing; **s~stillendes Mittel** analgesic, pain-killer. **S~tablette** *f* pain-killer

Schmetterball *m (Tennis)* smash

Schmetterling *m* -s, -e butterfly

schmettern *vt* hurl; *(Tennis)* smash; *(singen)* sing; *(spielen)* blare out ● *vi (haben)* sound; 〈*Trompeten:*〉 blare

Schmied *m* -[e]s, -e blacksmith

Schmiede *f* -, -n forge. **S~eisen** *nt* wrought iron. **s~n** *vt* forge; *(fig)* hatch; **Pläne s~n** make plans

schmieg|en *vt* press; **sich s~en an** (+ *acc*) nestle *or* snuggle up to; 〈*Kleid:*〉 cling to. **s~sam** *a* supple

Schmier|e *f* -, -n grease; *(Schmutz)* mess. **s~en** *vt* lubricate; *(streichen)* spread; *(schlecht schreiben)* scrawl;

(sl: bestechen) bribe ● vi (haben) smudge; (schreiben) scrawl. **S~fett** nt grease. **S~geld** nt (fam) bribe. **s~ig** a greasy; (schmutzig) grubby; (anstößig) smutty; (Person) slimy. **S~mittel** nt lubricant

Schminke f -,-n make-up. **S~n** vt make up; **sich s~n** put on make-up; **sich** (dat) **die Lippen s~n** put on lipstick

schmirgel|n vt sand down. **S~papier** nt emery-paper

schmökern vt/i (haben) (fam) read

schmollen vi (haben) sulk; (s~d den Mund verziehen) pout

schmor|en vt/i (haben) braise; (fam: schwitzen) roast. **S~topf** m casserole

Schmuck m -[e]s jewellery; (Verzierung) ornament, decoration

schmücken vt decorate, adorn; **sich s~** adorn oneself

schmucklos a plain. **S~stück** nt piece of jewellery; (fig) jewel

schmuddelig a grubby

Schmuggel m -s smuggling. **s~n** vt smuggle. **S~ware** f contraband

Schmuggler m -s,- smuggler

schmunzeln vi (haben) smile

schmusen vi (haben) cuddle

Schmutz m -es dirt; **in den S~ ziehen** (fig) denigrate. **s~en** vi (haben) get dirty. **S~fleck** m dirty mark. **s~ig** a dirty

Schnabel m -s,-̈ beak, bill; (eines Kruges) lip; (Tülle) spout

Schnake f -,-n mosquito; (Kohl-) daddy-long-legs

Schnalle f -,-n buckle. **s~n** vt strap; (zu-) buckle; **den Gürtel enger s~n** tighten one's belt

schnalzen vi (haben) **mit der Zunge/ den Fingern s~** click one's tongue/ snap one's fingers

schnapp|en vi (haben) **s~en nach** snap at; gasp for (Luft) ● vt snatch, grab; (fam: festnehmen) nab. **S~schloß** nt spring lock. **S~schuß** m snapshot

Schnaps m -es,-̈e schnapps

schnarchen vi (haben) snore

schnarren vi (haben) rattle; (Klingel:) buzz

schnattern vi (haben) cackle

schnauben vi (haben) snort ● vt sich (dat) **die Nase s~** blow one's nose

schnaufen vi (haben) puff, pant

Schnauze f -,-n muzzle; (eines Kruges) lip; (Tülle) spout

Schnecke f -,-n snail; (Nackt-) slug; (Spirale) scroll; (Gebäck) ≈ Chelsea bun. **S~nhaus** nt snail-shell

Schnee m -s snow; (Eier-) beaten egg-white. **S~ball** m snowball. **S~besen** m whisk. **S~brille** f snow-goggles pl. **S~fall** m snowfall. **S~flocke** f snowflake. **S~glöckchen** nt -s,- snowdrop. **S~kette** f snow chain. **S~mann** m (pl -männer) snow-man. **S~pflug** m snow-plough. **S~schläger** m whisk. **S~sturm** m snowstorm, blizzard. **S~wehe** f -,-n snow-drift

Schneid m -[e]s (SGer) courage

Schneide f -,-n [cutting] edge; (Klinge) blade

schneiden† vt cut; (in Scheiben) slice; (kreuzen) cross; (nicht beachten) cut dead; **Gesichter s~** pull faces; **sich s~** cut oneself; (über-) intersect; **sich** (dat/acc) **in den Finger s~** cut one's finger. **s~d** a cutting; (kalt) biting

Schneider m -s,- tailor. **S~in** f -,-nen dressmaker. **s~n** vt make (Anzug, Kostüm)

Schneidezahn m incisor

schneidig a dashing, adv -ly

schneien vi (haben) snow; **es schneit** it is snowing

Schneise f -,-n path; (Feuer-) firebreak

schnell a quick; (Auto, Tempo) fast ● adv quickly; (in s~em Tempo) fast; (bald) soon; **mach s~!** hurry up! **s~en** vi (sein) **in die Höhe s~en** shoot up. **S~igkeit** f - rapidity; (Tempo) speed. **S~imbiß** m snack-bar. **S~kochtopf** m pressure-cooker. **S~reinigung** f express cleaners. **s~stens** adv as quickly as possible. **S~zug** m express [train]

schnetzeln vt cut into thin strips

schneuzen (sich) vr blow one's nose

schnippen vt flick

schnippisch a pert, adv -ly

Schnipsel m & nt -s,- scrap

Schnitt m -[e]s,-e cut (Film-) cutting; (S~muster) [paper] pattern; **im S~** (durchschnittlich) on average

Schnitte f -,-n slice [of bread]; (belegt) open sandwich

schnittig a stylish; (stromlinienförmig) streamlined

Schnitt|käse m hard cheese. **S~lauch** m chives pl. **S~muster** nt [paper] pattern. **S~punkt** *m* [point of] intersection. **S~wunde** *f* cut

Schnitzel *nt* -s,- scrap; (*Culin*) escalope. **s~n** *vt* shred

schnitz|en *vt/i* (*haben*) carve. **S~er** *m* -s,- carver; (*fam: Fehler*) blunder. **S~erei** *f* -,-en carving

schnodderig *a* (*fam*) brash

schnöde *a* despicable, *adv* -bly; (*verächtlich*) contemptuous, *adv* -ly

Schnorchel *m* -s,- snorkel

Schnörkel *m* -s,- flourish; (*Kunst*) scroll. **s~ig** *a* ornate

schnorren *vt/i* (*haben*) (*fam*) scrounge

schnüffeln *vi* (*haben*) sniff (**an etw** *dat* sth); (*fam: spionieren*) snoop [around]

Schnuller *m* -s,- [baby's] dummy, (*Amer*) pacifier

schnupf|en *vt* sniff; **Tabak s~en** take snuff. **S~en** *m* -s,- [head] cold. **S~tabak** *m* snuff

schnuppern *vt/i* (*haben*) sniff (**an etw** *dat* sth)

Schnur *f* -,¨e string; (*Kordel*) cord; (*Besatz-*) braid; (*Electr*) flex; **eine S~** a piece of string

Schnür|chen *nt* -s,- **wie am S~chen** (*fam*) like clockwork. **s~en** *vt* tie; lace [up] ⟨*Schuhe*⟩

schnurgerade *a* & *adv* dead straight

Schnurr|bart *m* moustache. **s~en** *vi* (*haben*) hum; ⟨*Katze:*⟩ purr

Schnür|schuh *m* lace-up shoe. **S~senkel** *m* [shoe-]lace

schnurstracks *adv* straight

Schock *m* -[e]s,-s shock. **s~en** *vt* (*fam*) shock; **geschockt sein** be shocked. **s~ieren** *vt* shock; **s~ierend** shocking

Schöffe *m* -n,-n lay judge

Schokolade *f* - chocolate

Scholle *f* -,-n clod [of earth]; (*Eis-*) [ice-]floe; (*Fisch*) plaice

schon *adv* already; (*allein*) just; (*sogar*) even; (*ohnehin*) anyway; **s~ einmal** before; (*jemals*) ever; **s~ immer/oft/wieder** always/often/again; **hast du ihn s~ gesehen?** have you seen him yet? **s~ der Gedanke daran** the mere thought of it; **s~ deshalb** for that reason alone; **das ist s~ möglich** that's quite possible; **ja s~, aber** well yes, but; **nun geh/komm s~!** go/come on then!

schön *a* beautiful; ⟨*Wetter*⟩ fine; (*angenehm, nett*) nice; (*gut*) good; (*fam: beträchtlich*) pretty; **s~en Dank!**

thank you very much! **na s~** all right then ● *adv* beautifully; nicely; (*gut*) well; **s~ langsam** nice and slowly

schonen *vt* spare; (*gut behandeln*) look after; **sich s~** take things easy. **s~d** *a* gentle, *adv* -tly

Schönheit *f* -,-en beauty. **S~sfehler** *m* blemish. **S~skonkurrenz** *f*, **S~swettbewerb** *m* beauty contest

schönmachen *vt sep* smarten up; **sich s~** make oneself look nice

Schonung *f* -,-en gentle care; (*nach Krankheit*) rest; (*Baum-*) plantation. **s~slos** *a* ruthless, *adv* -ly

Schonzeit *f* close season

schöpf|en *vt* scoop [up]; ladle ⟨*Suppe*⟩; **Mut s~en** take heart; **frische Luft s~en** get some fresh air. **S~er** *m* -s,- creator; (*Kelle*) ladle. **s~erisch** *a* creative. **S~kelle** *f*, **S~löffel** *m* ladle. **S~ung** *f* -,-en creation

Schoppen *m* -s,- (*SGer*) ≈ pint

Schorf *m* -[e]s scab

Schornstein *m* chimney; (*Naut*) funnel. **S~feger** *m* -s,- chimney-sweep

Schoß *m* -es,¨e lap; (*Frack-*) tail

Schote *f* -,-n pod; (*Erbse*) pea

Schotte *m* -n,-n Scot, Scotsman

Schotter *m* -s gravel; (*für Gleise*) ballast

schott|isch *a* Scottish, Scots. **S~land** *nt* -s Scotland

schraffieren *vt* hatch

schräg *a* diagonal, *adv* -ly; (*geneigt*) sloping; **s~ halten** tilt. **S~e** *f* -,-n slope. **S~strich** *m* oblique stroke

Schramme *f* -,-n scratch. **s~n** *vt* scrape, scratch

Schrank *m* -[e]s,¨e cupboard; (*Kleider-*) wardrobe; (*Akten-, Glas-*) cabinet

Schranke *f* -,-n barrier

Schraube *f* -,-n screw; (*Schiffs-*) propeller. **s~n** *vt* screw; (*ab-*) unscrew; (*drehen*) turn; **sich in die Höhe s~n** spiral upwards. **S~nmutter** *f* nut. **S~nschlüssel** *m* spanner. **S~nzieher** *m* -s,- screwdriver

Schraubstock *m* vice

Schrebergarten *m* ≈ allotment

Schreck *m* -[e]s,-e fright; **jdm einen S~ einjagen** give s.o. a fright. **S~en** *m* -s,- fright; (*Entsetzen*) horror. **s~en** *vt* (*reg*) frighten; (*auf-*) startle ● *vi*† (*sein*) **in die Höhe s~en** start up

Schreck|gespenst *nt* spectre. **s~haft** *a* easily frightened; (*nervös*) jumpy. **s~lich** *a* terrible, *adv* -bly. **S~schuß** *m* warning shot

Schrei *m* -[e]s,-e cry, shout; (*gellend*) scream; **der letzte S~** (*fam*) the latest thing

Schreib|block *m* writing-pad. **s~en†** *vt/i* (*haben*) write; (*auf der Maschine*) type; **richtig/falsch s~en** spell right/wrong; **sich s~en** ⟨*Wort:*⟩ be spelt; (*korrespondieren*) correspond; **sich krank s~en lassen** get a doctor's certificate. **S~en** *nt* -s,- writing; (*Brief*) letter. **S~fehler** *m* spelling mistake. **S~heft** *nt* exercise book. **S~kraft** *f* clerical assistant; (*für Maschineschreiben*) typist. **S~maschine** *f* typewriter. **S~papier** *nt* writing-paper. **S~schrift** *f* script. **S~tisch** *m* desk. **S~ung** *f* -,-en spelling. **S~waren** *fpl* stationery *sg*. **S~weise** *f* spelling

schreien† *vt/i* (*haben*) cry; (*gellend*) scream; (*rufen, laut sprechen*) shout; **zum S~ sein** (*fam*) be a scream. **s~d** *a* (*fig*) glaring; (*grell*) garish

Schreiner *m* -s,- joiner

schreiten† *vi* (*sein*) walk

Schrift *f* -,-en writing; (*Druck-*) type; (*Abhandlung*) paper; **die Heilige S~** the Scriptures *pl*. **S~führer** *m* secretary. **s~lich** *a* written ● *adv* in writing. **S~sprache** *f* written language. **S~steller(in)** *m* -s,- (*f* -,-nen) writer. **S~stück** *nt* document. **S~zeichen** *nt* character

schrill *a* shrill, *adv* -y

Schritt *m* -[e]s,-e step; (*Entfernung*) pace; (*Gangart*) walk; (*der Hose*) crotch; **im S~** in step; (*langsam*) at walking pace; **S~ halten mit** (*fig*) keep pace with. **S~macher** *m* -s,- pace-maker. **s~weise** *adv* step by step

schroff *a* precipitous, *adv* -ly; (*abweisend*) brusque, *adv* -ly; (*unvermittelt*) abrupt, *adv* -ly; ⟨*Gegensatz*⟩ stark

schröpfen *vt* (*fam*) fleece

Schrot *m & nt* -[e]s coarse meal; (*Blei-*) small shot. **s~en** *vt* grind coarsely. **S~flinte** *f* shotgun

Schrott *m* -[e]s scrap[-metal]; **zu S~ fahren** (*fam*) write off. **S~platz** *m* scrap-yard. **s~reif** *a* ready for the scrap-heap

schrubb|en *vt/i* (*haben*) scrub. **S~er** *m* -s,- [long-handled] scrubbing-brush

Schrulle *f* -,-n whim; **alte S~e** (*fam*) old crone. **s~ig** *a* cranky

schrumpfen *vi* (*sein*) shrink; ⟨*Obst:*⟩ shrivel

schrump[e]lig *a* wrinkled

Schrunde *f* -,-n crack; (*Spalte*) crevasse

Schub *m* -[e]s,-̈e (*Phys*) thrust; (*S~fach*) drawer; (*Menge*) batch. **S~fach** *nt* drawer. **S~karre** *f*, **S~karren** *m* wheelbarrow. **S~lade** *f* drawer

Schubs *m* -es,-e push, shove. **s~en** *vt* push, shove

schüchtern *a* shy, *adv* -ly; (*zaghaft*) tentative, *adv* -ly. **S~heit** *f* - shyness

Schuft *m* -[e]s,-e (*pej*) swine. **s~en** *vi* (*haben*) (*fam*) slave away

Schuh *m* -[e]s,-e shoe. **S~anzieher** *m* -s,- shoehorn. **S~band** *nt* (*pl* -bänder*) shoe-lace. **S~creme** *f* shoe-polish. **S~löffel** *m* shoehorn. **S~macher** *m* -s,- shoemaker; (*zum Flicken*) [shoe] mender. **S~werk** *nt* shoes *pl*

Schul|abgänger *m* -s,- school-leaver. **S~arbeiten**, **S~aufgaben** *fpl* homework *sg*. **S~buch** *nt* school-book

Schuld *f* -,-en guilt; (*Verantwortung*) blame; (*Geld-*) debt; **S~en machen** get into debt; **S~ haben an** (+ *dat*) be to blame for ● **s~ haben** *od* **sein** be to blame (**an**+*dat* for); **jdm s~ geben** blame s.o. **s~en** *vt* owe

schuldig *a* guilty (*gen* of); (*gebührend*) due; **jdm etw s~ sein** owe s.o. sth. **S~keit** *f* - duty

schuld|los *a* innocent. **S~ner** *m* -s,- debtor. **S~spruch** *m* guilty verdict

Schule *f* -,-en school; **in der/die S~** at/ to school. **s~n** *vt* train

Schüler|(in) *m* -s,- (*f* -,-nen) pupil. **S~lotse** *m* pupil acting as crossing warden

schul|frei *a* **s~freier Tag** day without school; **wir haben morgen s~frei** there's no school tomorrow. **S~hof** *m* [school] playground. **S~jahr** *nt* school year; (*Klasse*) form. **S~junge** *m* schoolboy. **S~kind** *nt* schoolchild. **S~leiter(in)** *m*(*f*) head [teacher]. **S~mädchen** *nt* schoolgirl. **S~stunde** *f* lesson

Schulter *f* -,-n shoulder. **S~blatt** *nt* shoulder-blade. **s~n** *vt* shoulder. **S~tuch** *nt* shawl

Schulung *f* - training

schummeln *vi* (*haben*) (*fam*) cheat

Schund *m* -[e]s trash. **S~roman** *m* trashy novel

Schuppe f -,-n scale; **S~n** pl dandruff sg. **s~n (sich)** vr flake [off]

Schuppen m -s,- shed

Schur f - shearing

Schür|eisen nt poker. **s~en** vt poke; (fig) stir up

schürf|en vt mine; **sich** (dat) **das Knie s~en** graze one's knee ● vi (haben) **s~en nach** prospect for. **S~wunde** f abrasion, graze

Schürhaken m poker

Schurke m -n,-n villain

Schürze f -,-n apron. **s~n** vt (raffen) gather [up]; tie (Knoten); purse (Lippen). **S~njäger** m (fam) womanizer

Schuß m -sses,¨sse shot; (kleine Menge) dash

Schüssel f -,-n bowl; (TV) dish

schusselig a (fam) scatter-brained

Schuß|fahrt f (Ski) schuss. **S~waffe** f firearm

Schuster m -s,- = Schuhmacher

Schutt m -[e]s rubble. **S~ablade-platz** m rubbish dump

Schüttel|frost m shivering fit. **s~n** vt shake; **sich s~n** shake oneself/itself; (vor Ekel) shudder; **jdm die Hand s~n** shake s.o.'s hand

schütten vt pour; (kippen) tip; (ver-) spill ● vi (haben) **es schüttet** it is pouring [with rain]

Schutthaufen m pile of rubble

Schutz m -es protection; (Zuflucht) shelter; (Techn) guard; **S~ suchen** take refuge; **unter dem S~ der Dunkelheit** under cover of darkness. **S~anzug** m protective suit. **S~blech** nt mudguard. **S~brille** goggles pl

Schütze m -n,-n marksman; (Tor-) scorer; (Astr) Sagittarius; **guter S~** good shot

schützen vt protect/(Zuflucht gewähren) shelter (**vor** + dat from) ● vi (haben) give protection/shelter (**vor** + dat from). **s~d** a protective, adv -ly

Schützenfest nt fair with shooting competition

Schutz|engel m guardian angel. **S~heilige(r)** m/f patron saint

Schützling m -s,-e charge; (Protégé) protégé

schutz|los a defenceless, helpless. **S~mann** m (pl -männer & -leute) policeman. **S~umschlag** m dustjacket

Schwaben nt -s Swabia

schwäbisch a Swabian

schwach a (schwächer, schwächst) weak, adv -ly; (nicht gut; gering) poor, adv -ly; (leicht) faint, adv -ly

Schwäche f -,-n weakness. **s~n** vt weaken

Schwach|heit f - weakness. **S~kopf** m (fam) idiot

schwäch|lich a delicate. **S~ling** m -s,-e weakling

Schwachsinn m mental deficiency. **s~ig** a mentally deficient; (fam) idiotic

Schwächung f - weakening

schwafeln (fam) vi (haben) waffle ● vt talk

Schwager m -s,¨ brother-in-law

Schwägerin f -,-nen sister-in-law

Schwalbe f -,-n swallow

Schwall m -[e]s torrent

Schwamm m -[e]s,¨e sponge; (SGer: Pilz) fungus; (eßbar) mushroom. **s~ig** a spongy; (aufgedunsen) bloated

Schwan m -[e]s,¨e swan

schwanen vi (haben) (fam) **mir schwante, daß** I had a nasty feeling that

schwanger a pregnant

schwängern vt make pregnant

Schwangerschaft f -,-en pregnancy

Schwank m -[e]s,¨e (Theat) farce

schwank|en vi (haben) sway; (Boot:) rock; (sich ändern) fluctuate; (unentschieden sein) be undecided ● (sein) stagger. **S~ung** f -,-en fluctuation

Schwanz m -es,¨e tail

schwänzen vt (fam) skip; **die Schule s~** play truant

Schwarm m -[e]s,¨e swarm; (Fisch-) shoal; (fam: Liebe) idol

schwärmen vi (haben) swarm; **s~ für** (fam) adore; (verliebt sein) have a crush on; **s~ von** (fam) rave about

Schwarte f -,-n (Speck-) rind; (fam: Buch) tome

schwarz a (schwärzer, schwärzest) black; (fam: illegal) illegal, adv -ly; **s~er Markt** black market; **s~ gekleidet** dressed in black; **s~ auf weiß** in black and white; **ins S~e treffen** score a bull's-eye. **S~** nt -[e]s,- black. **S~arbeit** f moonlighting. **s~arbeiten** vi sep (haben) moonlight. **S~brot** nt black bread. **S~e(r)** m/f black

Schwärze f - blackness. **s~n** vt blacken

Schwarz|fahrer m fare-dodger. **S~handel** m black market (**mit** in).

S~händler *m* black marketeer.
S~markt *m* black market. s~
sehen† *vi sep (haben)* watch television without a licence; (*fig*)
be pessimistic. S~wald *m* Black Forest. s~weiß *a* black and white

Schwatz *m* -es (*fam*) chat

schwatzen, (*SGer*) schwätzen *vi*
(*haben*) chat; (*klatschen*) gossip;
(*Sch*) talk [in class] ● *vt* talk

schwatzhaft *a* garrulous

Schwebe *f* - in der S~ (*fig*) undecided. S~bahn *f* cable railway.
s~n *vi* (*haben*) float; (*fig*) be undecided; ⟨Verfahren:⟩ be pending; in
Gefahr s~n be in danger ● (*sein*) float

Schwed|e *m* -n,-n Swede. S~en *nt* -s
Sweden. S~in *f* -,-nen Swede. s~isch
a Swedish

Schwefel *m* -s sulphur. S~säure *f*
sulphuric acid

schweigen† *vi* (*haben*) be silent;
ganz zu s~ von to say nothing of, let
alone. S~ *nt* -s silence; zum S~
bringen silence. s~d *a* silent, *adv* -ly

schweigsam *a* silent; (*wortkarg*)
taciturn

Schwein *nt* -[e]s,-e pig; (*Culin*) pork;
(*sl*) (*schmutziger Mensch*) dirty pig;
(*Schuft*) swine; S~ haben (*fam*) be
lucky. S~ebraten *m* roast pork.
S~efleisch *nt* pork. S~ehund *m* (*sl*)
swine. S~erei *f* -,-en (*sl*) [dirty] mess;
(*Gemeinheit*) dirty trick. S~estall *m*
pigsty. s~isch *a* lewd. S~sleder *nt*
pigskin

Schweiß *m* -es sweat

schweiß|en *vt* weld. S~er *m* -s,-
welder

Schweiz (die) - Switzerland. S~er
a & m -s,-, S~erin *f* -,-nen Swiss.
s~erisch *a* Swiss

schwelen *vi* (*haben*) smoulder

schwelgen *vi* (*haben*) feast; s~ in
(+ *dat*) wallow in

Schwelle *f* -,-n threshold;
(*Eisenbahn-*) sleeper

schwell|en† *vi* (*sein*) swell. S~ung *f*
-,-en swelling

Schwemme *f* -,-n watering-place;
(*fig: Überangebot*) glut. s~n *vt* wash;
an Land s~n wash up

Schwenk *m* -[e]s swing. s~en *vt*
swing; (*schwingen*) wave; (*spülen*)
rinse; in Butter s~en toss in butter
● *vi* (*sein*) turn

schwer *a* heavy; (*schwierig*) difficult;
(*mühsam, streng*) hard; (*ernst*) serious; (*schlimm*) bad; 3 Pfund s~ sein

weigh 3 pounds ● *adv* heavily; with difficulty; (*mühsam, streng*) hard;
(*schlimm, sehr*) badly, seriously; s~
hören be hard of hearing; s~ arbeiten
work hard; s~ zu sagen difficult *or*
hard to say

Schwere *f* - heaviness; (*Gewicht*)
weight; (*Schwierigkeit*) difficulty;
(*Ernst*) gravity. S~losigkeit *f* -
weightlessness

schwer|fallen† *vi sep* (*sein*) be hard
(*dat* for). s~fällig *a* ponderous, *adv*
-ly; (*unbeholfen*) clumsy, *adv* -ily.
S~gewicht *nt* heavyweight. s~hö-
rig *a* s~hörig sein be hard of hearing.
S~kraft *f* (*Phys*) gravity. s~krank *a*
seriously ill. s~lich *adv* hardly.
s~machen *vt sep* make difficult
(*dat* for). s~mütig *a* melancholic.
s~nehmen† *vt sep* take seriously.
S~punkt *m* centre of gravity; (*fig*)
emphasis

Schwert *nt* -[e]s,-er sword. S~lilie *f*
iris

schwer|tun† (sich) *vr sep* have dif-
ficulty (mit with). S~verbrecher *m*
serious offender. s~verdaulich *a* indigestible. s~verletzt *a* seriously
injured. s~wiegend *a* weighty

Schwester *f* -,-n sister; (*Kranken-*)
nurse. s~lich *a* sisterly

Schwieger|eltern *pl* parents-in-
law. S~mutter *f* mother-in-law.
S~sohn *m* son-in-law. S~tochter *f*
daughter-in-law. S~vater *m* father-
in-law

Schwiele *f* -,-n callus

schwierig *a* difficult. S~keit *f* -,-en
difficulty

Schwimm|bad *nt* swimming-baths
pl. S~becken *nt* swimming-pool.
s~en† *vt/i* (*sein/haben*) swim; (*auf
dem Wasser treiben*) float. S~er *m* -s,-
swimmer; (*Techn*) float. S~weste *f*
life-jacket

Schwindel *m* -s dizziness, vertigo;
(*fam: Betrug*) fraud; (*Lüge*) lie. S~an-
fall *m* dizzy spell. s~frei *a* s~frei
sein have a good head for heights. s~n
vi (*haben*) (*lügen*) lie; mir *od* mich s~t
I feel dizzy

schwinden† *vi* (*sein*) dwindle;
(*vergehen*) fade; (*nachlassen*) fail

Schwindl|er *m* -s,- liar; (*Betrüger*)
fraud, con-man. s~ig *a* dizzy; mir ist
od wird s~ig I feel dizzy

schwing|en† *vi* (*haben*) swing;
(*Phys*) oscillate; (*vibrieren*) vibrate

● vt swing; wave 〈Fahne〉; 〈drohend〉 brandish. **S~tür** f swing-door. **S~ung** f -,-en oscillation; vibration

Schwips m -es,-e einen S~ haben (fam) be tipsy

schwirren vi (haben/sein) buzz; (surren) whirr

Schwitz|e f -,-n (Culin) roux. s~en vi (haben) sweat; **ich s~e** od **mich s~t** I am hot ● vt (Culin) sweat

schwören† vt/i (haben) swear (auf + acc by); **Rache s~** swear revenge

schwul a (fam: homosexuell) gay

schwül a close. **S~e** f - closeness

schwülstig a bombastic, adv -ally

Schwung m -[e]s,ˆe swing; 〈Bogen〉 sweep; 〈Schnelligkeit〉 momentum; 〈Kraft〉 vigour; 〈Feuer〉 verve; 〈fam: Anzahl〉 batch; **in S~ kommen** gather momentum; (fig) get going. **s~haft** a brisk, adv -ly. **s~los** a dull. **s~voll** a vigorous, adv -ly; 〈Bogen, Linie〉 sweeping; 〈mitreißend〉 spirited, lively

Schwur m -[e]s,ˆe vow; 〈Eid〉 oath. **S~gericht** nt jury [court]

sechs inv a, **S~** f -,-en six; 〈Sch〉 ≈ fail mark. **s~eckig** a hexagonal. **s~te(r,s)** a sixth

sech|zehn inv a sixteen. **s~ zehnte(r,s)** a sixteenth. **s~zig** inv a sixty. **s~zigste(r,s)** a sixtieth

sedieren vt sedate

See[1] m -s,-n /'ze:ən/ lake

See[2] f - sea; **an die/der See** to/at the seaside; **auf See** at sea. **S~bad** nt seaside resort. **S~fahrt** f [sea] voyage; 〈Schiffahrt〉 navigation. **S~gang** m schwerer S~gang rough sea. **S~ hund** m seal. **s~krank** a seasick

Seele f -,-n soul. **s~nruhig** a calm, adv -ly

seelisch a psychological, adv -ly; 〈geistig〉 mental, adv -ly

Seelsorger m -s,- pastor

See|luft f sea air. **S~macht** f maritime power. **S~mann** m (pl -leute) seaman, sailor. **S~not** f in S~not in distress. **S~räuber** m pirate. **S~ reise** f [sea] voyage. **S~rose** f waterlily. **S~sack** m kitbag. **S~stern** m starfish. **S~tang** m seaweed. **s~ tüchtig** a seaworthy. **S~weg** m sea route; **auf dem S~weg** by sea. **S~zunge** f sole

Segel nt -s,- sail. **S~boot** nt sailing-boat. **S~fliegen** nt gliding. **S~flieger** m glider pilot. **S~flugzeug** nt

glider. **s~n** vt/i (sein/haben) sail. **S~schiff** nt sailing-ship. **S~sport** m sailing. **S~tuch** nt canvas

Segen m -s blessing. **s~sreich** a beneficial; 〈gesegnet〉 blessed

Segler m -s,- yachtsman

Segment nt -[e]s,-e segment

segnen vt bless; **gesegnet mit** blessed with

sehen† vt see; watch 〈Fernsehsendung〉; **sich s~ lassen** show oneself ● vi (haben) see; 〈blicken〉 look (auf + acc at); 〈ragen〉 show (aus above); **gut/schlecht s~** have good/bad eyesight; **vom S~ kennen** know by sight; **s~ nach** keep an eye on; 〈betreuen〉 look after; 〈suchen〉 look for; **darauf s~, daß** see [to it] that. **s~swert, s~swürdig** a worth seeing. **S~swürdigkeit** f -,-en sight

Sehkraft f sight, vision

Sehne f -,-n tendon; 〈eines Bogens〉 string

sehnen (sich) vr long (nach for)

sehnig a sinewy; 〈zäh〉 stringy

sehn|lich[st] a 〈Wunsch〉 dearest ● adv longingly. **S~sucht** f - longing (nach for). **s~süchtig** a longing, adv -ly; 〈Wunsch〉 dearest

sehr adv very; 〈mit Verb〉 very much

seicht a shallow

seid s. sein[1]; **ihr s~** you are

Seide f -,-n silk

Seidel nt -s,- beer-mug

seiden a silk ... **S~papier** nt tissue paper. **S~raupe** f silkworm. **s~ weich** a silky-soft

seidig a silky

Seife f -,-n soap. **S~npulver** nt soap powder. **S~nschaum** m lather

seifig a soapy

seihen vt strain

Seil nt -[e]s,-e rope; 〈Draht-〉 cable. **S~bahn** f cable railway. **s~sprin gen**† vi (sein) (inf & pp only) skip. **S~tänzer(in)** m(f) tightrope walker

sein[1]† vi (sein) be; **er ist Lehrer** he is a teacher; **sei still!** be quiet! **mir ist kalt/ schlecht** I am cold/feel sick; **wie dem auch sei** be that as it may ● v aux have; **angekommen/gestorben s~** have arrived/died; **er war/wäre gefallen** he had/would have fallen; **es ist/war viel zu tun/nichts zu sehen** there is/was a lot to be done/nothing to be seen

sein[2] poss pron his; 〈Ding, Tier〉 its; 〈nach man〉 one's; **sein Glück versuchen** try one's luck. **s~e(r,s)** poss

pron his; *(nach man)* one's own; **das S~e tun** do one's share. **s~erseits** *adv* for his part. **s~erzeit** *adv* in those days. **s~etwegen** *adv* for his sake; *(wegen ihm)* because of him, on his account. **s~etwillen** *adv* **um s~etwillen** for his sake. **s~ige** *poss pron* **der/die/das s~ige** his

seinlassen† *vt sep* leave; *(aufhören mit)* stop

seins *poss pron* his; *(nach man)* one's own

seit *conj & prep* (+ *dat*) since; **s~ wann?** since when? **s~ einiger Zeit** for some time [past]; **ich wohne s~ zehn Jahren hier** I've lived here for ten years. **s~dem** *conj* since ● *adv* since then

Seite *f* -,-n side; *(Buch-)* page; **S~ an S~** side by side; **zur S~ legen/treten** put/step aside; **jds starke S~** s.o.'s strong point; **von S~n** (+ *gen*) on the part of; **auf der einen/anderen S~** *(fig)* on the one/other hand

seitens *prep* (+ *gen*) on the part of

Seiten|schiff *nt* [side] aisle. **S~sprung** *m* infidelity; **einen S~sprung machen** be unfaithful. **S~stechen** *nt* -s *(Med)* stitch. **S~straße** *f* side-street. **S~streifen** *m* verge; *(Autobahn-)* hard shoulder

seither *adv* since then

seit|lich *a* side ... ● *adv* at/on the side; **s~lich von** to one side of ● *prep* (+ *gen*) to one side of. **s~wärts** *adv* on/to one side; *(zur Seite)* sideways

Sekret *nt* -[e]s,-e secretion

Sekret|är *m* -s,-e secretary; *(Schrank)* bureau. **S~ariat** *nt* -[e]s,-e secretary's office. **S~ärin** *f* -,-nen secretary

Sekt *m* -[e]s [German] sparkling wine

Sekte *f* -,-n sect

Sektion /-'tsio:n/ *f* -,-en section; *(Sezierung)* autopsy

Sektor *m* -s,-en /-'to:rən/ sector

Sekundant *m* -en,-en *(Sport)* second

sekundär *a* secondary

Sekunde *f* -,-n second

selber *pron* *(fam)* = **selbst**

selbst *pron* oneself; **ich/du/er/sie s~** I myself/you yourself/he him- self/she herself; **wir/ihr/sie s~** we ourselves/ you yourselves/they themselves; **ich schneide mein Haar s~** I cut my own hair; **von s~** of one's own accord; *(automatisch)* automatically ● *adv* even. **S~achtung** *f* self-esteem, self-respect

selbständig *a* independent, *adv* -ly; self-employed *(Handwerker)*; **sich s~ machen** set up on one's own. **S~keit** *f* - independence

Selbstaufopferung *f* self-sacrifice

Selbstbedienung *f* self-service. **S~srestaurant** *nt* self-service restaurant, cafeteria

Selbst|befriedigung *f* masturbation. **S~beherrschung** *f* self-control. **S~bestimmung** *f* self-determination. **s~bewußt** *a* self-confident. **S~bewußtsein** *nt* self-confidence. **S~bildnis** *nt* self-portrait. **S~erhaltung** *f* self-preservation. **s~gefällig** *a* self-satisfied, smug, *adv* -ly. **s~gemacht** *a* home-made. **s~gerecht** *a* self-righteous. **S~gespräch** *nt* soliloquy; **S~gespräche führen** talk to oneself. **s~haftend** *a* self-adhesive. **s~herrlich** *a* autocratic, *adv* -ally. **S~hilfe** *f* self-help. **s~klebend** *a* self-adhesive. **S~kostenpreis** *m* cost price. **S~laut** *m* vowel. **s~los** *a* selfless, *adv* -ly. **S~mitleid** *nt* self-pity. **S~mord** *m* suicide. **S~mörder(in)** *m(f)* suicide. **s~mörderisch** *a* suicidal. **S~porträt** *nt* self-portrait. **s~sicher** *a* self-assured. **S~sicherheit** *f* self-assurance. **s~süchtig** *a* selfish, *adv* -ly. **S~tanken** *nt* self-service *(for petrol)*. **s~tätig** *a* automatic, *adv* -ally. **S~versorgung** *f* self-catering

selbstverständlich *a* natural, *adv* -ly; **etw für s~ halten** take sth for granted; **das ist s~** that goes without saying; **s~!** of course! **S~keit** *f* - matter of course; **das ist eine S~keit** that goes without saying

Selbst|verteidigung *f* self-defence. **S~vertrauen** *nt* self-confidence. **S~verwaltung** *f* self-government. **s~zufrieden** *a* complacent, *adv* -ly

selig *a* blissfully happy; *(Relig)* blessed; *(verstorben)* late. **S~keit** *f* - bliss

Sellerie *m* -s,-s & *f* -,- celeriac; *(Stangen-)* celery

selten *a* rare ● *adv* rarely, seldom; *(besonders)* exceptionally. **S~heit** *f* -,-en rarity

Selterswasser *nt* seltzer [water]

seltsam *a* odd, *adv* -ly, strange, *adv* -ly. **s~erweise** *adv* oddly/strangely enough

Semester *nt* -s,- *(Univ)* semester

Semikolon *nt* -s,-s semicolon

Seminar *nt* -s,-e seminar; (*Institut*) department; (*Priester-*) seminary

Semmel *f* -,-n [bread] roll. **S~brösel** *pl* breadcrumbs

Senat *m* -[e]s,-e senate. **S~or** *m* -s,-en /-'to:rən/ senator

senden[t] *vt* send

sende|n[2] *vt* (*reg*) broadcast; (*über Funk*) transmit, send. **S~r** *m* -s,- [broadcasting] station; (*Anlage*) transmitter. **S~reihe** *f* series

Sendung *f* -,-en consignment, shipment; (*Auftrag*) mission; (*Radio, TV*) programme

Senf *m* -s mustard

sengend *a* scorching

senil *a* senile. **S~ität** *f* - senility

Senior *m* -s,-en /-'o:rən/ senior; **S~en** senior citizens. **S~enheim** *nt* old people's home. **S~enteller** *m* senior citizen's menu

Senke *f* -,-n dip, hollow

Senkel *m* -s,- [shoe-]lace

senken *vt* lower; bring down (*Fieber, Preise*); bow (*Kopf*); **sich s~** come down, fall; (*absinken*) subside; (*abfallen*) slope down

senkrecht *a* vertical, *adv* -ly. **S~e** *f* -n,-n perpendicular

Sensation /-'tsi̯o:n/ *f* -,-en sensation. **s~ell** *a* sensational, *adv* -ly

Sense *f* -,-n scythe

sensib|el *a* sensitive, *adv* -ly. **S~ilität** *f* - sensitivity

sentimental *a* sentimental. **S~ität** *f* - sentimentality

separat *a* separate, *adv* -ly

September *m* -s,- September

Serenade *f* -,-n serenade

Serie /'ze:ri̯ə/ *f* -,-n series; (*Briefmarken*) set; (*Comm*) range. **S~nnummer** *f* serial number

seriös *a* respectable, *adv* -bly; (*zuverlässig*) reliable, *adv* -bly; (*ernstgemeint*) serious

Serpentine *f* -,-n winding road; (*Kehre*) hairpin bend

Serum *nt* -s, **Sera** serum

Service[1] /zɛr'vi:s/ *nt* -[s],- /-'vi:s[əs], -'vi:sə/ service, set

Service[2] /'zø:ɐvɪs/ *m & nt* -s /-vɪs[əs]/ (*Comm, Tennis*) service

servier|en *vt/i* (*haben*) serve. **S~erin** *f* -,-nen waitress. **S~wagen** *m* trolley

Serviette *f* -,-n napkin, serviette

Servus *int* (*Aust*) cheerio; (*Begrüßung*) hallo

Sessel *m* -s,- armchair. **S~bahn** *f*, **S~lift** *m* chair-lift

seßhaft *a* settled; **s~ werden** settle down

Set /zɛt/ *nt & m* -[s],-s set; (*Deckchen*) place-mat

setz|en *vt* put; (*abstellen*) set down; (*hin-*) sit down (*Kind*); move (*Spielstein*); (*pflanzen*) plant; (*schreiben, wetten*) put; **sich s~en** sit down; (*sinken*) settle ● *vi* (*sein*) leap ● *vi* (*haben*) **s~en auf** (+ *acc*) back. **S~ling** *m* -s,-e seedling

Seuche *f* -,-n epidemic

seufz|en *vi* (*haben*) sigh. **S~er** *m* -s,- sigh

Sex /zɛks/ *m* -[es] sex. **s~istisch** *a* sexist

Sexu|alität *f* - sexuality. **s~ell** *a* sexual, *adv* -ly

sexy /'zɛksi/ *inv a* sexy

sezieren *vt* dissect

Shampoo /ʃam'pu:/, **Shampoon** /ʃam'po:n/ *nt* -s shampoo

siamesisch *a* Siamese

sich *refl pron* oneself; (*mit er/sie/es*) himself/herself/itself; (*mit sie pl*) themselves; (*mit Sie*) yourself; (*pl*) yourselves; (*einander*) each other; **s~ kennen** know oneself/(*einander*) each other; **s~ waschen** have a wash; **s~** (*dat*) **die Zähne putzen/die Haare kämmen** clean one's teeth/comb one's hair; **s~** (*dat*) **das Bein brechen** break a leg; **s~ wundern/schämen** be surprised/ashamed; **s~ gut lesen/ verkaufen** read/sell well; **von s~ aus** of one's own accord

Sichel *f* -,-n sickle

sicher *a* safe; (*gesichert*) secure; (*gewiß*) certain; (*zuverlässig*) reliable; sure (*Urteil, Geschmack*); steady (*Hand*); (*selbstbewußt*) self-confident; **sich** (*dat*) **etw** (*gen*) **s~ sein** be sure of sth; **bist du s~?** are you sure? ● *adv* safely; securely; certainly; reliably; self-confidently; (*wahrscheinlich*) most probably; **er kommt s~** he is sure to come; **s~!** certainly! **s~gehen**[†] *vi sep* (*sein*) be sure

Sicherheit *f* - safety; (*Pol, Psych, Comm*) security; (*Gewißheit*) certainty; (*Zuverlässigkeit*) reliability; (*des Urteils, Geschmacks*) surety; (*Selbstbewußtsein*) self-confidence.

S∼**gurt** m safety-belt; (*Auto*) seat-belt. s∼**shalber** *adv* to be on the safe side. S∼**snadel** f safety-pin

sicherlich *adv* certainly; (*wahrscheinlich*) most probably

sicher|n vt secure; (*garantieren*) safeguard; (*schützen*) protect; put the safety-catch on ⟨Pistole⟩; **sich** (*dat*) **etw s∼n** secure sth. s∼**stellen** vt sep safeguard; (*beschlagnahmen*) seize. S∼**ung** f -,-en safeguard, protection; (*Gewehr*-) safety-catch; (*Electr*) fuse

Sicht f - view; (S∼*weite*) visibility; **in S∼ kommen** come into view; **auf lange S∼** in the long term. s∼**bar** a visible, *adv* -bly. s∼**en** vt sight; (*durchsehen*) sift through. s∼**lich** a obvious, *adv* -ly. S∼**vermerk** m visa. S∼**weite** f visibility; **in/außer S∼weite** within/out of sight

sickern vi (*sein*) seep

sie pron (*nom*) (*sg*) she; (*Ding, Tier*) it; (*pl*) they; (*acc*) (*sg*) her; (*Ding, Tier*) it; (*pl*) them

Sie pron you; **gehen/warten Sie!** go/wait!

Sieb nt -[e]s,-e sieve; (*Tee*-) strainer. s∼**en**[1] vt sieve, sift

sieben[2] *inv* a, S∼ f -,-en seven. S∼**sachen** fpl (*fam*) belongings. s∼**te(r,s)** a seventh

sieb|te(r,s) a seventh. s∼**zehn** *inv* a seventeen. s∼**zehnte(r,s)** a seventeenth. s∼**zig** *inv* a seventy. s∼**zigste(r,s)** a seventieth

siede|n† vt/i (*haben*) boil. S∼**punkt** m boiling point

Siedl|er m -s,- settler. S∼**ung** f -,-en [housing] estate; (*Niederlassung*) settlement

Sieg m -[e]s,-e victory

Siegel nt -s,- seal. S∼**ring** m signet-ring

sieg|en vi (*haben*) win. S∼**er(in)** m -s,- (f -,-nen) winner. s∼**reich** a victorious

siezen vt jdn s∼ call s.o. 'Sie'

Signal nt -s,-e signal. s∼**isieren** vt signal

signieren vt sign

Silbe f -,-n syllable. S∼**ntrennung** f word-division

Silber nt -s silver. S∼**hochzeit** f silver wedding. s∼**n** a silver. S∼**papier** nt silver paper

Silhouette /zɪˈlʊɛtə/ f -,-n silhouette

Silizium nt -s silicon

Silo m & nt -s,-s silo

Silvester nt -s New Year's Eve

simpel a simple, *adv* -ply; (*einfältig*) simple-minded

Simplex nt -,-e simplex

Sims m & nt -es,-e ledge; (*Kamin*-) mantelpiece

Simul|ant m -en,-en malingerer. s∼**ieren** vt feign; (*Techn*) simulate ● vi (*haben*) pretend; (*sich krank stellen*) malinger

simultan a simultaneous, *adv* -ly

sind s. **sein**[1]; **wir/sie s∼** we/they are

Sinfonie f -,-n symphony

singen† vt/i (*haben*) sing

Singular m -s,-e singular

Singvogel m songbird

sinken vi (*sein*) sink; (*nieder*-) drop; (*niedriger werden*) go down, fall; **den Mut s∼ lassen** lose courage

Sinn m -[e]s,-e sense; (*Denken*) mind; (*Zweck*) point; **im S∼ haben** have in mind; **in gewissem S∼e** in a sense; **es hat keinen S∼** it is pointless; **nicht bei S∼en sein** be out of one's mind. S∼**bild** nt symbol. s∼**en**† vi (*haben*) think; **auf Rache s∼en** plot one's revenge

sinnlich a sensory; (*sexuell*) sensual; ⟨Genüsse⟩ sensuous. S∼**keit** f - sensuality; sensuousness

sinn|los a senseless, *adv* -ly; (*zwecklos*) pointless, *adv* -ly. s∼**voll** a meaningful; (*vernünftig*) sensible, *adv* -bly

Sintflut f flood

Siphon /ˈziːfɔ̃/ m -s,-s siphon

Sipp|e f -,-n clan. S∼**schaft** f - clan; (*Pack*) crowd

Sirene f -,-n siren

Sirup m -s,-e syrup; (*schwarzer*) treacle

Sitte f -,-n custom; S∼**n** manners. s∼**nlos** a immoral

sittlich a moral, *adv* -ly. S∼**keit** f - morality. S∼**keitsverbrecher** m sex offender

sittsam a well-behaved; (*züchtig*) demure, *adv* -ly

Situ|ation /-ˈtsi̯oːn/ f -,-en situation. s∼**iert** a **gut/schlecht s∼iert** well/badly off

Sitz m -es,-e seat; (*Paßform*) fit

sitzen† vi (*haben*) sit; (*sich befinden*) be; (*passen*) fit; (*fam: treffen*) hit home; s∼ **bleiben** remain seated; **[im Gefängnis] s∼** (*fam*) be in jail. s∼**bleiben**† vi sep (*sein*) (*fam*) (*Sch*) stay or be kept down; (*nicht heiraten*) be left on the shelf; **s∼bleiben auf** (+ *dat*) be left with. **s∽d** *a* seated; ⟨*Tätigkeit*⟩ sedentary. **s∽lassen**† *vt sep* (*fam*) (*nicht heiraten*) jilt; (*im Stich lassen*) leave in the lurch; (*Sch*) keep down

Sitz|gelegenheit *f* seat. **S∽platz** *m* seat. **S∽ung** *f* -,-en session

Sizilien /-jən/ *nt* -s Sicily

Skala *f* -,-len scale; (*Reihe*) range

Skalpell *nt* -s,-e scalpel

skalpieren *vt* scalp

Skandal *m* -s,-e scandal. **s∽ös** *a* scandalous

skandieren *vt* scan ⟨*Verse*⟩; chant ⟨*Parolen*⟩

Skandinav|ien /-jən/ *nt* -s Scandinavia. **s∽isch** *a* Scandinavian

Skat *m* -s skat

Skelett *nt* -[e]s,-e skeleton

Skep|sis *f* - scepticism. **s∽tisch** *a* sceptical, *adv* -ly; (*mißtrauisch*) doubtful, *adv* -ly

Ski /ʃiː/ *m* -s,-er ski; **Ski fahren** *od* **laufen** ski. **S∽fahrer(in)**, **S∽läufer(in)** *m(f)* skier. **S∽sport** *m* skiing

Skizz|e *f* -,-n sketch. **s∽enhaft** *a* sketchy, *adv* -ily. **s∽ieren** *vt* sketch

Sklav|e *m* -n,-n slave. **S∽erei** *f* - slavery. **S∽in** *f* -,-nen slave. **s∽isch** *a* slavish, *adv* -ly

Skorpion *m* -s,-e scorpion; (*Astr*) Scorpio

Skrupel *m* -s,- scruple. **s∽los** *a* unscrupulous

Skulptur *f* -,-en sculpture

skurril *a* absurd, *adv* -ly

Slalom *m* -s,-s slalom

Slang /slɛn/ *m* -s slang

Slaw|e *m* -n,-n, **S∽in** *f* -,-nen Slav. **s∽isch** *a* Slav; (*Lang*) Slavonic

Slip *m* -s,-s briefs *pl*

Smaragd *m* -[e]s,-e emerald

Smoking *m* -s,-s dinner jacket, (*Amer*) tuxedo

Snob *m* -s,-s snob. **S∽ismus** *m* - snobbery. **s∽istisch** *a* snobbish

so *adv* so; (*so sehr*) so much; (*auf diese Weise*) like this/that; (*solch*) such; (*fam: sowieso*) anyway; (*fam: umsonst*) free; (*fam: ungefähr*) about; **nicht so schnell** not so fast; **so gut/ bald wie** as good/soon as; **so ein Mann** a man like that; **so ein Zufall!** what a coincidence! **so nicht** not like that; **mir ist so, als ob** I feel as if; **so oder so** in any case; **eine Stunde oder so** an hour or so; **so um zehn Mark** (*fam*) about ten marks; **[es ist] gut so** that's fine; **so, das ist geschafft** there, that's done; **so?**

really? **so kommt doch!** come on then! ● *conj* (*also*) so; (*dann*) then; **so daß** so that; **so gern ich auch käme** as much as I would like to come

sobald *conj* as soon as

Söckchen *nt* -s,- [ankle] sock

Socke *f* -,-n sock

Sockel *m* -s,- plinth, pedestal

Socken *m* -s,- sock

Soda *nt* -s soda. **S∽wasser** *nt* soda water

Sodbrennen *nt* -s heartburn

soeben *adv* just [now]

Sofa *nt* -s,-s settee, sofa

sofern *adv* provided [that]

sofort *adv* at once, immediately; (*auf der Stelle*) instantly. **s∽ig** *a* immediate

Software /ˈzɔftvɛːɐ̯/ *f* - software

sogar *adv* even

sogenannt *a* so-called

sogleich *adv* at once

Sohle *f* -,-n sole; (*Tal-*) bottom

Sohn *m* -[e]s,-̈e son

Sojabohne *f* soya bean

solange *conj* as long as

solch *inv pron* such; **s∽ ein(e)** such a; **s∽ einer/eine/eins** one/ (*Person*) someone like that. **s∽e(r,s)** *pron* such; **ein s∽er Mann/eine s∽e Frau** a man/ woman like that; **ich habe s∽e Angst** I am so afraid ● (*substantivisch*) **ein s∽er/eine s∽e/ein s∽es** one/ (*Person*) someone like that; **s∽e** (*pl*) those; (*Leute*) people like that

Sold *m* -[e]s (*Mil*) pay

Soldat *m* -en,-en soldier

Söldner *m* -s,- mercenary

solidarisch *a* **s∽e Handlung** act of solidarity; **sich s∽ erklären** declare one's solidarity

Solidarität *f* - solidarity

solide *a* solid, *adv* -ly; (*haltbar*) sturdy, *adv* -ily; (*sicher*) sound, *adv* -ly; (*anständig*) respectable, *adv* -bly

Solist(in) *m* -en,-en (*f* -,-nen) soloist

Soll *nt* -s (*Comm*) debit; (*Produktions-*) quota

sollen† *v aux* **er soll warten** he is to wait; (*möge*) let him wait; **was soll ich machen?** what shall I do? **du sollst nicht lügen** you shouldn't tell lies; **du sollst nicht töten** (*liter*) thou shalt not kill; **ihr sollt jetzt still sein!** will you be quiet now! **du solltest dich schämen** you ought to *or* should be ashamed of yourself; **es hat nicht sein s∽** it was not to be; **ich hätte es nicht tun s∽** I ought not to *or* should not have done it; **er soll sehr nett/reich sein** he is supposed to be very nice/rich; **sollte es regnen, so ...** if it should rain then ...; **das soll man nicht [tun]** you're not supposed to [do that]; **soll ich [mal versuchen]?** shall I [try]? **soll er doch!** let him! **was soll's!** so what!

Solo *nt* **-s, -los** & **-li** solo. **s~** *adv* solo

somit *adv* therefore, so

Sommer *m* **-s, -** summer. **S~ferien** *pl* summer holidays. **s~lich** *a* summery; (*Sommer-*) summer ... ● *adv* **s~lich warm** as warm as summer. **S~schlußverkauf** *m* summer sale. **S~sprossen** *fpl* freckles. **s~sprossig** *a* freckled

Sonate *f* **-, -n** sonata

Sonde *f* **-, -n** probe

Sonder|angebot *nt* special offer. **s~bar** *a* odd, *adv* -ly. **S~fahrt** *f* special excursion. **S~fall** *m* special case. **s~gleichen** *adv* **eine Gemeinheit/Grausamkeit s~gleichen** unparalleled meanness/cruelty. **s~lich** *a* particular, *adv* -ly; (*sonderbar*) odd, *adv* -ly. **S~ling** *m* **-s, -e** crank. **S~marke** *f* special stamp

sondern *conj* but; **nicht nur ... s~ auch** not only ... but also

Sonder|preis *m* special price. **S~schule** *f* special school. **S~zug** *m* special train

sondieren *vt* sound out

Sonett *nt* **-[e]s, -e** sonnet

Sonnabend *m* **-s, -e** Saturday. **s~s** *adv* on Saturdays

Sonne *f* **-, -n** sun. **s~n (sich)** *vr* sun oneself; (*fig*) bask (**in** + *dat* in)

Sonnen|aufgang *m* sunrise. **s~baden** *vi* (*haben*) sunbathe. **S~bank** *f* sun-bed. **S~blume** *f* sunflower. **S~brand** *m* sunburn. **S~brille** *f* sun-glasses *pl*. **S~energie** *f* solar energy. **S~finsternis** *f* solar eclipse. **S~milch** *f* sun-tan lotion. **S~öl** *nt* sun-tan oil. **S~schein** *m* sunshine. **S~schirm** *m* sunshade. **S~stich** *m* sunstroke. **S~uhr** *f* sundial. **S~untergang** *m* sunset. **S~wende** *f* solstice

sonnig *a* sunny

Sonntag *m* **-s, -e** Sunday. **s~s** *adv* on Sundays

sonst *adv* (*gewöhnlich*) usually; (*im übrigen*) apart from that; (*andernfalls*) otherwise, or [else]; **wer/was/wie/wo s~?** who/what/how/

where else? **s~ niemand/nichts** no one/nothing else; **s~ noch jemand/etwas?** anyone/anything else? **s~ noch Fragen?** any more questions? **s~ig** *a* other. **s~jemand** *pron* (*fam*) someone/(*fragend, verneint*) anyone else. **s~wer** *pron* = **s~jemand**. **s~wie** *adv* (*fam*) some/any other way. **s~wo** *adv* (*fam*) somewhere/anywhere else

sooft *conj* whenever

Sopran *m* **-s, -e** soprano

Sorge *f* **-, -n** worry (**um** about); (*Fürsorge*) care; **in S~ sein** be worried; **sich** (*dat*) **S~n machen** worry; **keine S~!** don't worry! **s~n** *vi* (*haben*) **s~n für** look after, care for; (*vorsorgen*) provide for; (*sich kümmern*) see to; **dafür s~n, daß** see [to it] *or* make sure that ● *vr* **sich s~n** worry. **s~nfrei** *a* carefree. **s~nvoll** *a* worried, *adv* -ly. **S~recht** *nt* (*Jur*) custody

Sorg|falt *f* - care. **s~fältig** *a* careful, *adv* -ly. **s~los** *a* careless, *adv* -ly; (*unbekümmert*) carefree. **s~sam** *a* careful, *adv* -ly

Sorte *f* **-, -n** kind, sort; (*Comm*) brand

sort|ieren *vt* sort [out]; (*Comm*) grade. **S~iment** *nt* **-[e]s, -e** range

sosehr *conj* however much

Soße *f* **-, -n** sauce; (*Braten-*) gravy; (*Salat-*) dressing

Souffl|eur /zuˈfløː̯ɐ̯/ *m* **-s, -e**, **S~euse** /-øːˈzə/ *f* **-, -n** prompter. **s~ieren** *vi* (*haben*) prompt

Souvenir /zuvəˈniːɐ̯/ *nt* **-s, -s** souvenir

souverän /zuvəˈrɛːn/ *a* sovereign; (*fig: überlegen*) expert, *adv* -ly. **S~ität** *f* - sovereignty

soviel *conj* however much; **s~ ich weiß** as far as I know ● *adv* as much (**wie** as); **s~ wie möglich** as much as possible

soweit *conj* as far as; (*insoweit*) [in] so far as ● *adv* on the whole; **s~ wie möglich** as far as possible; **s~ sein** be ready; **es ist s~** the time has come

sowenig *conj* however little ● *adv* no more (**wie** than); **s~ wie möglich** as little as possible

sowie *conj* as well as; (*sobald*) as soon as

sowieso *adv* anyway, in any case

sowjet|isch *a* Soviet. **S~union** *f* - Soviet Union

sowohl *adv* **s~ ... als** *od* **wie auch ... ... als well as ...; **s~ er als auch seine Frau** both he and his wife

sozial *a* social, *adv* -ly; ⟨*Einstellung, Beruf*⟩ caring. **S~arbeit** *f* social work. **S~arbeiter(in)** *m(f)* social worker. **S~demokrat** *m* social democrat. **S~hilfe** *f* social security

Sozialis|mus *m* - socialism. **S~t** *m* -en, -en socialist. **s~tisch** *a* socialist

Sozial|versicherung *f* National Insurance. **S~wohnung** *f* ≈ council flat

Soziol|oge *m* -n, -n sociologist. **S~ogie** *f* - sociology

Sozius *m* -, -se (*Comm*) partner; (*Beifahrersitz*) pillion

sozusagen *adv* so to speak

Spachtel *m* -s, - & *f* -, -n spatula

Spagat *m* -[e]s, -e (*Aust*) string; **S~ machen** do the splits *pl*

Spaghetti *pl* spaghetti *sg*

spähen *vi* (*haben*) peer

Spalier *nt* -s, -e trellis; **S~ stehen** line the route

Spalt *m* -[e]s, -e crack; (*im Vorhang*) chink

Spalt|e *f* -, -n crack, crevice; (*Gletscher-*) crevasse; (*Druck-*) column; (*Orangen-*) segment. **s~en†** *vt* split; **sich s~en** split. **S~ung** *f* -, -en splitting; (*Kluft*) split; (*Phys*) fission

Span *m* -[e]s, ⸚e [wood] chip; (*Hobel-*) shaving

Spange *f* -, -n clasp; (*Haar-*) slide; (*Zahn-*) brace; (*Arm-*) bangle

Span|ien /-jǝn/ *nt* -s Spain. **S~ier** *m* -s, -, **S~ierin** *f* -, -nen Spaniard. **s~isch** *a* Spanish. **S~isch** *nt* -[s] (*Lang*) Spanish

Spann *m* -[e]s instep

Spanne *f* -, -n span; (*Zeit-*) space; (*Comm*) margin

spann|en *vt* stretch; put up ⟨*Leine*⟩; (*straffen*) tighten; (*an-*) harness (**an** + *acc* to); **den Hahn s~en** cock the gun; **sich s~en** tighten ● *vi* (*haben*) be too tight. **s~end** *a* exciting. **S~er** *m* -s, - (*fam*) Peeping Tom. **S~ung** *f* -, -en tension; (*Erwartung*) suspense; (*Electr*) voltage

Spar|buch *nt* savings book. **S~büchse** *f* money-box. **s~en** *vt/i* (*haben*) save; (*sparsam sein*) economize (**mit/an** + *dat* on); **sich** (*dat*) **die Mühe s~en** save oneself the trouble. **S~er** *m* -s, - saver

Spargel *m* -s - asparagus

Spar|kasse *f* savings bank. **S~konto** *nt* deposit account

spärlich *a* sparse, *adv* -ly; (*dürftig*) meagre; (*knapp*) scanty, *adv* -ily

Sparren *m* -s, - rafter

sparsam *a* economical, *adv* -ly; ⟨*Person*⟩ thrifty. **S~keit** *f* - economy; thrift

Sparschwein *nt* piggy bank

spartanisch *a* Spartan

Sparte *f* -, -n branch; (*Zeitungs-*) section; (*Rubrik*) column

Spaß *m* -es, ⸚e fun; (*Scherz*) joke; **im/aus/zum S~** for fun; **S~ machen** be fun; ⟨*Person:*⟩ be joking; **es macht mir keinen S~** I don't enjoy it; **viel S~!** have a good time! **s~en** *vi* (*haben*) joke. **s~ig** *a* amusing, funny. **S~vogel** *m* joker

Spast|iker *m* -s, - spastic. **s~isch** *a* spastic

spät *a* & *adv* late; **wie s~ ist es?** what time is it? **zu s~** too late; **zu s~ kommen** be late. **s~abends** *adv* late at night

Spatel *m* -s, - & *f* -, -n spatula

Spaten *m* -s, - spade

später *a* later; (*zukünftig*) future ● *adv* later

spätestens *adv* at the latest

Spatz *m* -en, -en sparrow

Spätzle *pl* (*Culin*) noodles

spazieren *vi* (*sein*) stroll. **s~gehen†** *vi sep* (*sein*) go for a walk

Spazier|gang *m* walk; **einen S~gang machen** go for a walk. **S~gänger(in)** *m* -s, - (*f* -, -nen) walker. **S~stock** *m* walking-stick

Specht *m* -[e]s, -e woodpecker

Speck *m* -s bacon; (*fam: Fettpolster*) fat. **s~ig** *a* greasy

Spedi|teur /ʃpedi'tøː.ɐ/ *m* -s, -e haulage/(*für Umzüge*) removals contractor. **S~tion** /-'tsi̯oːn/ *f* -, -en carriage, haulage; (*Firma*) haulage/(*für Umzüge*) removals firm

Speer *m* -[e]s, -e spear; (*Sport*) javelin

Speiche *f* -, -n spoke

Speichel *m* -s saliva

Speicher *m* -s, - warehouse; (*dial: Dachboden*) attic; (*Computer*) memory. **s~n** *vt* store

speien† *vt* spit; (*erbrechen*) vomit

Speise *f* -, -n food; (*Gericht*) dish; (*Pudding*) blancmange. **S~eis** *nt* icecream. **S~kammer** *f* larder. **S~karte** *f* menu. **s~n** *vi* (*haben*) eat; **zu Abend s~n** have dinner ● *vt* feed. **S~röhre** *f* oesophagus. **S~saal** *m* dining-room. **S∼wagen** *m* dining-car

Spektakel *m* **-s** (*fam*) noise

spektakulär *a* spectacular

Spektrum *nt* **-s,-tra** spectrum

Spekul|ant *m* **-en,-en** speculator. **S∼ation** /-'tsjo:n/ *f* **-,-en** speculation. **s∼ieren** *vi* (*haben*) speculate; **s∼ieren auf** (+ *acc*) (*fam*) hope to get

Spelze *f* **-,-n** husk

spendabel *a* generous

Spende *f* **-,-n** donation. **s∼n** *vt* donate; give ⟨*Blut, Schatten*⟩; **Beifall s∼n** applaud. **S∼r** *m* **-s,-** donor; (*Behälter*) dispenser

spendieren *vt* pay for; **jdm etw/ein Bier s∼** treat s.o. to sth/stand s.o. a beer

Spengler *m* **-s,-** (*SGer*) plumber

Sperling *m* **-s,-e** sparrow

Sperre *f* **-,-n** barrier; (*Verbot*) ban; (*Comm*) embargo. **s∼n** *vt* close; (*ver-*) block; (*verbieten*) ban; cut off ⟨*Strom, Telefon*⟩; stop ⟨*Scheck, Kredit*⟩; **s∼n in** (+ *acc*) put in ⟨*Gefängnis, Käfig*⟩; **sich s∼n** balk (**gegen** at); **gesperrt gedruckt** (*Typ*) spaced

Sperr|holz *nt* plywood. **s∼ig** *a* bulky. **S∼müll** *m* bulky refuse. **S∼stunde** *f* closing time

Spesen *pl* expenses

spezial|isieren (sich) *vr* specialize (**auf** + *acc* in). **S∼ist** *m* **-en,-en** specialist. **S∼ität** *f* **-,-en** speciality

speziell *a* special, *adv* -ly

spezifisch *a* specific, *adv* -ally

Sphäre /'sfɛ:rə/ *f* **-,-n** sphere

spicken *vt* (*Culin*) lard; **gespickt mit** (*fig*) full of ● *vi* (*haben*) (*fam*) crib (**bei** from)

Spiegel *m* **-s,-** mirror; (*Wasser-, Alkohol-*) level. **S∼bild** *nt* reflection. **S∼ei** *nt* fried egg. **s∼n** *vt* reflect; **sich s∼n** be reflected ● *vi* (*haben*) reflect [the light]; (*glänzen*) gleam. **S∼ung** *f* **-,-en** reflection

Spiel *nt* **-[e]s,-e** game; (*Spielen*) playing; (*Glücks-*) gambling; (*Schau-*) play; (*Satz*) set; **ein S∼ Karten** a pack/ (*Amer*) deck of cards; **auf dem S∼ stehen** be at stake; **aufs S∼ setzen** risk. **S∼art** *f* variety. **S∼automat** *m* fruit machine. **S∼bank** *f* casino. **S∼dose** *f* musical box. **s∼en** *vt/i* (*haben*) play; (*im Glücksspiel*) gamble; (*vortäuschen*) act; ⟨*Roman:*⟩ be set (**in** + *dat* in); **s∼en mit** (*fig*) toy with. **s∼end** *a* (*mühelos*) effortless, *adv* -ly

Spieler|(in) *m* **-s,-** (*f* **-,-nen**) player; (*Glücks-*) gambler. **S∼ei** *f* **-,-en** amusement; (*Kleinigkeit*) trifle

Spiel|feld *nt* field, pitch. **S∼gefährte** *m*, **S∼gefährtin** *f* playmate. **S∼karte** *f* playing-card. **S∼marke** *f* chip. **S∼plan** *m* programme. **S∼platz** *m* playground. **S∼raum** *m* (*fig*) scope; (*Techn*) clearance. **S∼regeln** *fpl* rules [of the game]. **S∼sachen** *fpl* toys. **S∼verderber** *m* **-s,-** spoilsport. **S∼waren** *fpl* toys. **S∼warengeschäft** *nt* toyshop. **S∼zeug** *nt* toy; (*S∼sachen*) toys *pl*

Spieß *m* **-es,-e** spear; (*Brat-*) spit; (*für Schaschlik*) skewer; (*Fleisch-*) kebab; **den S∼ umkehren** turn the tables on s.o. **S∼bürger** *m* [petit] bourgeois. **s∼bürgerlich** *a* bourgeois. **s∼en** *vt* **etw auf etw** (*acc*) **s∼en** spear sth with sth. **S∼er** *m* **-s,-** [petit] bourgeois. **s∼ig** *a* bourgeois. **S∼ruten** *fpl* **S∼ruten laufen** run the gauntlet

Spike[s]reifen /'ʃpaɪk[s]-/ *m* studded tyre

Spinat *m* **-s** spinach

Spind *m* & *nt* **-[e]s,-e** locker

Spindel *f* **-,-n** spindle

Spinne *f* **-,-n** spider

spinn|en† *vt/i* (*haben*) spin; **er spinnt** (*fam*) he's crazy. **S∼ennetz** *nt* spider's web. **S∼[en]gewebe** *nt*, **S∼webe** *f* **-,-n** cobweb

Spion *m* **-s,-e** spy

Spionage /ʃpio'na:ʒə/ *f* **-** espionage, spying; **S∼ treiben** spy. **S∼abwehr** *f* counter-espionage

spionieren *vi* (*haben*) spy

Spionin *f* **-,-nen** [woman] spy

Spirale *f* **-,-n** spiral. **s∼ig** *a* spiral

Spiritis|mus *m* **-** spiritualism. **s∼tisch** *a* spiritualist

Spirituosen *pl* spirits

Spiritus *m* **-** alcohol; (*Brenn-*) methylated spirits *pl*. **S∼kocher** *m* spirit stove

Spital *nt* **-s,-̈er** (*Aust*) hospital

spitz *a* pointed; (*scharf*) sharp; (*schrill*) shrill; ⟨*Winkel*⟩ acute; **s∼e** **Bemerkung** dig. **S∼bube** *m* scoundrel; (*Schlingel*) rascal. **s∼bübisch** *a* mischievous, *adv* -ly

Spitze *f* **-,-n** point; (*oberer Teil*) top; (*vorderer Teil*) front; (*Pfeil-, Finger-, Nasen-*) tip; (*Schuh-, Strumpf-*) toe; (*Zigarren-, Zigaretten-*) holder; (*Höchstleistung*) maximum; (*Tex*) lace;

(fam: Anspielung) dig; **an der S~ liegen** be in the lead

Spitzel *m* **-s,-** informer

spitzen *vt* sharpen; purse *(Lippen)*; prick up *(Ohren)*; **sich s~ auf** *(+acc)* *(fam)* look forward to. **S~geschwindigkeit** *f* top speed

spitz|findig *a* over-subtle. **S~hacke** *f* pickaxe. **S~name** *m* nickname

Spleen */* ʃpliːn/ *m* **-s,-e** obsession; **einen S~ haben** be crazy. **s~ig** *a* eccentric

Splitter *m* **-s,-** splinter. **s~n** *vi (sein)* shatter. **s~[faser]nackt** *a (fam)* stark naked

sponsern *vt* sponsor

spontan *a* spontaneous, *adv* -ly

sporadisch *a* sporadic, *adv* -ally

Spore *f* **-,-n** *(Biol)* spore

Sporn *m* **-[e]s, Sporen** spur; **einem Pferd die Sporen geben** spur a horse

Sport *m* **-[e]s** sport; *(Hobby)* hobby. **S~art** *f* sport. **S~fest** *nt* sports day. **S~ler** *m* **-s,-** sportsman. **S~lerin** *f* **-,-nen** sportswoman. **s~lich** *a* sports ...; *(fair)* sporting, *adv* -ly; *(flott, schlank)* sporty. **S~platz** *m* sports ground. **S~verein** *m* sports club. **S~wagen** *m* sports car; *(Kinder-)* push-chair, *(Amer)* stroller

Spott *m* **-[e]s** mockery. **s~billig** *a & adv* dirt cheap

spötteln *vi (haben)* mock; **s~ über** *(+acc)* poke fun at

spotten *vi (haben)* mock; **s~ über** *(+acc)* make fun of; *(höhnend)* ridicule

spöttisch *a* mocking, *adv* -ly

Sprach|e *f* **-,-n** language; *(Sprechfähigkeit)* speech; **zur S~e bringen** bring up. **S~fehler** *m* speech defect. **S~labor** *nt* language laboratory. **s~lich** *a* linguistic, *adv* -ally. **s~los** *a* speechless

Spray /ʃpreː/ *nt & m* **-s,-s** spray. **S~dose** *f* aerosol [can]

Sprech|anlage *f* intercom. **S~chor** *m* chorus; **im S~chor rufen** chant

sprechen† *vi (haben)* speak/*(sich unterhalten)* talk **(über** + *acc*/**von** about/of); **deutsch/englisch s~** speak German/English ● *vt* speak; *(sagen, aufsagen)* say; pronounce *(Urteil)*; **schuldig s~** find guilty; **jdn s~** speak to s.o.; **Herr X ist nicht zu s~** Mr X is not available

Sprecher(in) *m* **-s,-** *(f* **-,-nen)** speaker; *(Radio, TV)* announcer; *(Wortführer)* spokesman, *f* spokeswoman

Sprechstunde *f* consulting hours *pl; (Med)* surgery. **S~nhilfe** *f (Med)* receptionist

Sprechzimmer *nt* consulting room

spreizen *vt* spread

Sprengel *m* **-s,-** parish

spreng|en *vt* blow up; blast *(Felsen)*; *(fig)* burst; *(begießen)* water; *(mit Sprenger)* sprinkle; dampen *(Wäsche)*. **S~er** *m* **-s,-** sprinkler. **S~kopf** *m* warhead. **S~körper** *m* explosive device. **S~stoff** *m* explosive

Spreu *f* - chaff

Sprich|wort *nt (pl* **-wörter)** proverb. **s~wörtlich** *a* proverbial

sprießen† *vi (sein)* sprout

Springbrunnen *m* fountain

spring|en† *vi (sein)* jump; *(Schwimmsport)* dive; *(Ball:)* bounce; *(spritzen)* spurt; *(zer-)* break; *(rissig werden)* crack; *(SGer: laufen)* run. **S~er** *m* **-s,-** jumper; *(Kunst-)* diver; *(Schach)* knight. **S~reiten** *nt* show-jumping. **S~seil** *nt* skipping-rope

Sprint *m* **-s,-s** sprint

Sprit *m* **-s** *(fam)* petrol

Spritz|e *f* **-,-n** syringe; *(Injektion)* injection; *(Feuer-)* hose. **s~en** *vt* spray; *(be-, ver-)* splash; *(Culin)* pipe; *(Med)* inject ● *vi (haben)* splash; *(Fett:)* spit ● *vi (sein)* splash; *(hervor-)* spurt; *(fam: laufen)* dash. **S~er** *m* **-s,-** splash; *(Schuß)* dash. **s~ig** *a* lively; *(Wein, Komödie)* sparkling. **S~tour** *f (fam)* spin

spröde *a* brittle; *(trocken)* dry; *(rissig)* chapped; *(Stimme)* harsh; *(abweisend)* aloof

Sproß *m* **-sses,-sse** shoot

Sprosse *f* **-,-n** rung. **S~nkohl** *m* *(Aust)* Brussels sprouts *pl*

Sprotte *f* **-,-n** sprat

Spruch *m* **-[e]s,-e** saying; *(Denk-)* motto; *(Zitat)* quotation. **S~band** *nt* *(pl* **-bänder)** banner

Sprudel *m* **-s,-** sparkling mineral water. **s~n** *vi (haben/sein)* bubble

Sprüh|dose *f* aerosol [can]. **s~en** *vt* spray ● *vi (sein) (Funken:)* fly; *(fig)* sparkle. **S~regen** *m* fine drizzle

Sprung *m* **-[e]s,-e** jump, leap; *(Schwimmsport)* dive; *(fam: Katzen-* stone's throw; *(Riß)* crack; **auf einen S~** *(fam)* for a moment. **S~brett** *nt* springboard. **s~haft** *a* erratic; *(plötzlich)* sudden, *adv* -ly. **S~schanze** *f* ski-jump. **S~seil** *nt* skipping-rope

Spucke f - spit. **s~n** vt/i (haben) spit; (sich übergeben) be sick

Spuk m -[e]s,-e [ghostly] apparition. **s~en** vi (haben) ⟨Geist:⟩ walk; **in diesem Haus s~t es** this house is haunted

Spülbecken nt sink

Spule f -,-n spool

Spüle f -,-n sink unit; (Becken) sink

spulen vt spool

spül|en vt rinse; (schwemmen) wash; **Geschirr s~en** wash up ● vi (haben) flush [the toilet]. **S~kasten** m cistern. **S~mittel** nt washing-up liquid. **S~tuch** nt dishcloth

Spur f -,-en track; (Fahr-) lane; (Fährte) trail; (Anzeichen) trace; (Hinweis) lead; **keine** od **nicht die S~** (fam) not in the least

spürbar a noticeable, adv -bly

spuren vi (haben) (fam) toe the line

spür|en vt feel; (seelisch) sense. **S~hund** m tracker dog

spurlos adv without trace

spurten vi (sein) put on a spurt; (fam: laufen) sprint

sputen (sich) vr hurry

Staat m -[e]s,-en state; (Land) country; (Putz) finery. **s~lich** a state ... ● adv by the state

Staatsangehörig|e(r) m/f national. **S~keit** f - nationality

Staats|anwalt m state prosecutor. **S~beamte(r)** m civil servant. **S~besuch** m state visit. **S~bürger(in)** m(f) national. **S~mann** m (pl -männer) statesman. **S~streich** m coup

Stab m -[e]s,ᵉe rod; (Gitter-) bar; (Sport) baton; (Mitarbeiter-) team; (Mil) staff

Stäbchen ntpl chopsticks

Stabhochsprung m pole-vault

stabil a stable; (gesund) robust; (solide) sturdy, adv -ily. **s~isieren** vt stabilize; **sich s~isieren** stabilize. **S~ität** f - stability

Stachel m -s,- spine; (Gift-) sting; (Spitze) spike. **S~beere** f gooseberry. **S~draht** m barbed wire. **s~ig** a prickly. **S~schwein** nt porcupine

Stadion nt -s,-ien stadium

Stadium nt -s,-ien stage

Stadt f -,ᵉe town; (Groß-) city

Städt|chen nt -s,- small town. **s~isch** a urban; (kommunal) municipal

Stadt|mauer f city wall. **S~mitte** f town centre. **S~plan** m street map.

S~teil m district. **S~zentrum** nt town centre

Staffel f -,-n team; (S~lauf) relay; (Mil) squadron

Staffelei f -,-en easel

Staffel|lauf m relay race. **s~n** vt stagger; (abstufen) grade

Stagn|ation /-'tsio:n/ f - stagnation. **s~ieren** vi (haben) stagnate

Stahl m -s steel. **S~beton** m reinforced concrete

Stall m -[e]s,ᵉe stable; (Kuh-) shed; (Schweine-) sty; (Hühner-) coop; (Kaninchen-) hutch

Stamm m -[e]s,ᵉe trunk; (Sippe) tribe; (Kern) core; (Wort-) stem. **S~baum** m family tree; (eines Tieres) pedigree

stammeln vt/i (haben) stammer

stammen vi (haben) come/(zeitlich) date (**von/aus** from); **das Zitat stammt von Goethe** the quotation is from Goethe

Stamm|gast m regular. **S~halter** m son and heir

stämmig a sturdy

Stamm|kundschaft f regulars pl. **S~lokal** nt favourite pub. **S~tisch** m table reserved for the regulars; (Treffen) meeting of the regulars

stampf|en vi (haben) stamp; ⟨Maschine:⟩ pound; **mit den Füßen s~en** stamp one's feet ● vi (sein) tramp ● vt pound; mash ⟨Kartoffeln⟩. **S~kartoffeln** fpl mashed potatoes

Stand m -[e]s,ᵉe standing position; (Zustand) state; (Spiel-) score; (Höhe) level; (gesellschaftlich) class; (Verkaufs-) stall; (Messe-) stand; (Taxi-) rank; **auf den neuesten S~ bringen** update

Standard m -s,-s standard. **s~isieren** vt standardize

Standarte f -,-n standard

Standbild nt statue

Ständchen nt -s,- serenade; **jdm ein S~ bringen** serenade s.o.

Ständer m -s,- stand; (Geschirr-, Platten-) rack; (Kerzen-) holder

Standes|amt nt registry office. **S~beamte(r)** m registrar. **S~unterschied** m class distinction

stand|haft a steadfast, adv -ly. **s~halten**† vi sep (haben) stand firm; **etw** (dat) **s~halten** stand up to sth

ständig a constant, adv -ly; (fest) permanent, adv -ly

Stand|licht nt sidelights pl. **S~ort** m position; (Firmen-) location; (Mil) garrison. **S~pauke** *f* (*fam*) dressing-down. **S~punkt** *m* point of view. **S~spur** *f* hard shoulder. **S~uhr** *f* grandfather clock

Stange *f* -,-n bar; (*Holz-*) pole; (*Gardinen-*) rail; (*Hühner-*) perch; (*Zimt-*) stick; **von der S~** (*fam*) off the peg. **S~nbohne** *f* runner bean. **S~nbrot** *nt* French bread

Stanniol *nt* -s tin foil. **S~papier** *nt* silver paper

stanzen *vt* stamp; (*aus-*) stamp out; punch ⟨*Loch*⟩

Stapel *m* -s,- stack, pile; **vom S~ laufen** be launched. **S~lauf** *m* launch[ing]. **s~n** *vt* stack *or* pile up; **sich s~n** pile up

stapfen *vi* (*sein*) tramp, trudge

Star¹ *m* -[e]s,-e starling

Star² *m* -[e]s (*Med*) [**grauer**] **S~** cataract; **grüner S~** glaucoma

Star³ *m* -s,-s (*Theat, Sport*) star

stark *a* (*stärker, stärkst*) strong; ⟨*Motor*⟩ powerful; ⟨*Verkehr, Regen*⟩ heavy; ⟨*Hitze, Kälte*⟩ severe; (*groß*) big; (*schlimm*) bad; (*dick*) thick; (*korpulent*) stout ● *adv* strongly; heavily; badly; (*sehr*) very much

Stärk|e *f* -,-n (*s. stark*) strength; power; thickness; stoutness; (*Größe*) size; (*Mais-, Wäsche-*) starch. **S~emehl** *nt* cornflour. **s~en** *vt* strengthen; starch ⟨*Wäsche*⟩; **sich s~en** fortify oneself. **S~ung** *f* -,-en strengthening; (*Erfrischung*) refreshment

starr *a* rigid, adv -ly; (*steif*) stiff, adv -ly; ⟨*Blick*⟩ fixed; (*unbeugsam*) inflexible, adv -bly

starren *vi* (*haben*) stare; **vor Schmutz s~** be filthy

starr|köpfig *a* stubborn. **S~sinn** *m* obstinacy. **s~sinnig** *a* obstinate, adv -ly

Start *m* -s,-s start; (*Aviat*) take-off. **S~bahn** *f* runway. **s~en** *vi* (*sein*) start; (*Aviat*) take off; (*aufbrechen*) set off; (*teilnehmen*) compete ● *vt* start; (*fig*) launch

Station -/-'tsjo:n/ *f* -,-en station; (*Haltestelle*) stop; (*Abschnitt*) stage; (*Med*) ward; **S~ machen** break one's journey; **bei freier S~** all found. **s~är** *adv* as an in-patient. **s~ieren** *vt* station

statisch *a* static

Statist(in) *m* -en,-en (*f* -,-nen) (*Theat*) extra

Statisti|k *f* -,-en statistics *sg*; (*Aufstellung*) statistics *pl*. **s~sch** *a* statistical, adv -ly

Stativ *nt* -s,-e (*Phot*) tripod

statt *prep* (+ *gen*) instead of; **s~ dessen** instead ● *conj* **s~ etw zu tun** instead of doing sth

Stätte *f* -,-n place

statt|finden† *vi sep* (*haben*) take place. **s~haft** *a* permitted

stattlich *a* imposing; (*beträchtlich*) considerable

Statue /'ʃta:tuə/ *f* -,-n statue

Statur *f* - build, stature

Status *m* - status. **S~symbol** *nt* status symbol

Statut *nt* -[e]s,-en statute

Stau *m* -[e]s,-e congestion; (*Auto*) [traffic] jam; (*Rück-*) tailback

Staub *m* -[e]s dust; **S~ wischen** dust; **S~ saugen** vacuum, hoover

Staubecken *nt* reservoir

staub|en *vi* (*haben*) raise dust; **es s~t** it's dusty. **s~ig** *a* dusty. **s~saugen** *vt/i* (*haben*) vacuum, hoover. **S~sauger** *m* vacuum cleaner, Hoover (P). **S~tuch** *nt* duster

Staudamm *m* dam

Staude *f* -,-n shrub

stauen *vt* dam up; **sich s~** accumulate; ⟨*Autos:*⟩ form a tailback

staunen *vi* (*haben*) be amazed *or* astonished. **S~** *nt* -s amazement, astonishment

Stau|see *m* reservoir. **S~ung** *f* -,-en congestion; (*Auto*) [traffic] jam

Steak /ʃte:k, ste:k/ *nt* -s,-s steak

stechen† *vt* stick (**in** + *acc* in); (*verletzen*) prick; (*mit Messer*) stab; ⟨*Insekt:*⟩ sting; ⟨*Mücke:*⟩ bite; (*gravieren*) engrave ● *vi* (*haben*) prick; ⟨*Insekt:*⟩ sting; ⟨*Mücke:*⟩ bite; (*mit Stechuhr*) clock in/out; **in See s~** put to sea. **s~d** *a* stabbing; ⟨*Geruch*⟩ pungent

Stech|ginster *m* gorse. **S~kahn** *m* punt. **S~mücke** *f* mosquito. **S~palme** *f* holly. **S~uhr** *f* time clock

Steck|brief *m* 'wanted' poster. **S~dose** *f* socket. **s~en** *vt* put; (*mit Nadel, Reißzwecke*) pin; (*pflanzen*) plant ● *vi* (*haben*) be; (*fest-*) be stuck; **hinter etw** (*dat*) **s~en** (*fig*) be behind sth

Stecken *m* -s,- (*SGer*) stick

stecken|bleiben† *vi sep* (*sein*) get stuck. **s~lassen**† *vt sep* leave. **S~pferd** *nt* hobby-horse

Steck|er *m* -s,- (*Electr*) plug. **S~ling** *m* -s,-e cutting. **S~nadel** *f* pin. **S~rübe** *f* swede

Steg *m* -[e]s,-e foot-bridge; (*Boots-*) landing-stage; (*Brillen-*) bridge. **S~reif** *m* **aus dem S~reif** extempore

stehen† *vi (haben)* stand; (*sich befinden*) be; (*still-*) be stationary; (*Maschine, Uhr:*) have stopped; **vor dem Ruin s~** face ruin; **zu jdm/etw s~** (*fig*) stand by s.o./sth; **gut s~** (*Getreide, Aktien:*) be doing well; (*Chancen:*) be good; **jdm [gut] s~** suit s.o.; **sich gut s~** be on good terms; **es steht 3 zu 1** the score is 3–1; **es steht schlecht um ihn** he is in a bad way. **S~** *nt* -s standing; **zum S~** **bringen/kommen** bring/come to a standstill. **s~bleiben†** *vi sep (sein)* stop; (*Motor:*) stall; (*Zeit:*) stand still; (*Gebäude:*) be left standing. **s~d** *a* standing; (*sich nicht bewegend*) stationary; (*Gewässer*) stagnant. **s~lassen†** *vt sep* leave; **sich (*dat*) einen Bart s~lassen** grow a beard

Steh|lampe *f* standard lamp. **S~leiter** *f* step-ladder

stehlen† *vt/i (haben)* steal; **sich s~** steal, creep

Steh|platz *m* standing place. **S~vermögen** *nt* stamina, staying-power

steif *a* stiff, *adv* -ly. **S~heit** *f* - stiffness

Steig|bügel *m* stirrup. **S~eisen** *nt* crampon

steigen† *vi (sein)* climb; (*hochgehen*) rise, go up; (*Schulden, Spannung:*) mount; **s~ auf** (+*acc*) climb on [to] (*Stuhl*); climb (*Berg, Leiter*); get on (*Pferd, Fahrrad*); **s~ in** (+*acc*) climb into; get in (*Auto*); get on (*Bus, Zug*); **s~ aus** climb out of; get out of (*Bett, Auto*); get off (*Bus, Zug*); **einen Drachen s~ lassen** fly a kite; **s~de Preise** rising prices

steiger|n *vt* increase; **sich s~n** increase; (*sich verbessern*) improve. **S~ung** *f* -,-en increase; improvement; (*Gram*) comparison

Steigung *f* -,-en gradient; (*Hang*) slope

steil *a* steep, *adv* -ly. **S~küste** *f* cliffs *pl*

Stein *m* -[e]s,-e stone; (*Ziegel-*) brick; (*Spiel-*) piece. **s~alt** *a* ancient. **S~bock** *m* ibex; (*Astr*) Capricorn. **S~bruch** *m* quarry. **S~garten** *m* rockery. **S~gut** *nt* earthenware. **s~hart** *a* rock-hard. **s~ig** *a* stony. **s~igen** *vt* stone. **S~kohle** *f* [hard]

coal. **s~reich** *a (fam)* very rich. **S~schlag** *m* rock fall

Stelle *f* -,-n place; (*Fleck*) spot; (*Abschnitt*) passage; (*Stellung*) job, post; (*Büro*) office; (*Behörde*) authority; **kahle S~** bare patch; **auf der S~** immediately; **an deiner S~** in your place

stellen *vt* put; (*aufrecht*) stand; set (*Wecker, Aufgabe*); ask (*Frage*); make (*Antrag, Forderung, Diagnose*); **zur Verfügung s~** provide; **lauter/leiser s~** turn up/down; **kalt/warm s~** chill/keep hot; **sich s~** [go and] stand; give oneself up (*der Polizei* to the police); **sich tot/schlafend s~** pretend to be dead/asleep; **gut gestellt sein** be well off

Stellen|anzeige *f* job advertisement. **S~vermittlung** *f* employment agency. **s~weise** *adv* in places

Stellung *f* -,-en position; (*Arbeit*) job; **S~ nehmen** make a statement (**zu** on). **s~slos** *a* jobless. **S~suche** *f* job-hunting

stellvertret|end *a* deputy ... ● *adv* as a deputy; **s~end für jdn** on s.o.'s behalf. **S~er** *m* deputy

Stellwerk *nt* signal-box

Stelzen *fpl* stilts. **s~** *vi (sein)* stalk

stemmen *vt* press; lift (*Gewicht*); **sich s~ gegen** brace oneself against

Stempel *m* -s,- stamp; (*Post-*) postmark; (*Präge-*) die; (*Feingehalts-*) hallmark. **s~n** *vt* stamp; hallmark (*Silber*); cancel (*Marke*)

Stengel *m* -s,- stalk, stem

Steno *f* - (*fam*) shorthand

Steno|gramm *nt* -[e]s,-e shorthand text. **S~graphie** *f* - shorthand. **s~graphieren** *vt* take down in shorthand ● *vi (haben)* do shorthand. **S~typistin** *f* -,-nen shorthand typist

Steppdecke *f* quilt

Steppe *f* -,-n steppe

Steptanz *m* tap-dance

sterben† *vi (sein)* die (**an**+*dat* of); **im S~ liegen** be dying

sterblich *a* mortal. **S~e(r)** *m/f* mortal. **S~keit** *f* - mortality

stereo *adv* in stereo. **S~anlage** *f* stereo [system]

stereotyp *a* stereotyped

steril *a* sterile. **s~isieren** *vt* sterilize. **S~ität** *f* - sterility

Stern *m* -[e]s,-e star. **S~bild** *nt* constellation. **S~chen** *nt* -s,- asterisk.

S~kunde *f* astronomy. **S~schnuppe** *f* -,-n shooting star. **S~warte** *f* -,-n observatory

stetig *a* steady, *adv* -ily

stets *adv* always

Steuer[1] *nt* -s,- steering-wheel; (*Naut*) helm; **am S~** at the wheel

Steuer[2] *f* -,-n tax

Steuer|bord *nt* -[e]s starboard [side]. **S~erklärung** *f* tax return. **s~frei** *a* & *adv* tax-free. **S~mann** *m* (*pl* -leute) helmsman; (*beim Rudern*) cox. **s~n** *vt* steer; (*Aviat*) pilot; (*Techn*) control • *vi* (*haben*) be at the wheel/ (*Naut*) helm • (*sein*) head (*nach* for). **s~pflichtig** *a* taxable. **S~rad** *nt* steering-wheel. **S~ruder** *nt* helm. **S~ung** *f* - steering; (*Techn*) controls *pl.* **S~zahler** *m* -s,- taxpayer

Stewardeß /'stju:ɐdɛs/ *f* -,-dessen air hostess, stewardess

Stich *m* -[e]s,-e prick; (*Messer-*) stab; (*S~wunde*) stab wound; (*Bienen-*) sting; (*Mücken-*) bite; (*Schmerz*) stabbing pain; (*Näh-*) stitch; (*Kupfer-*) engraving; (*Kartenspiel*) trick; **S~ ins Rötliche** tinge of red; **jdn im S~ lassen** leave s.o. in the lurch; (*Gedächtnis:*) fail s.o. **s~eln** *vi* (*haben*) make snide remarks

Stich|flamme *f* jet of flame. **s~haltig** *a* valid. **S~probe** *f* spot check. **S~wort** *nt* (*pl* -wörter) headword; (*pl* -worte) (*Theat*) cue; **S~worte** notes

stick|en *vt/i* (*haben*) embroider. **S~erei** *f* - embroidery

stickig *a* stuffy

Stickstoff *m* nitrogen

Stiefbruder *m* stepbrother

Stiefel *m* -s,- boot

Stief|kind *nt* stepchild. **S~mutter** *f* stepmother. **S~mütterchen** *nt* -s,- pansy. **S~schwester** *f* stepsister. **S~sohn** *m* stepson. **S~tochter** *f* stepdaughter. **S~vater** *m* stepfather

Stiege *f* -,-n stairs *pl*

Stiel *m* -[e]s,-e handle; (*Blumen-, Gläser-*) stem; (*Blatt-*) stalk

Stier *m* -[e]s,-e bull; (*Astr*) Taurus

stieren *vi* (*haben*) stare

Stier|kampf *m* bullfight

Stift[1] *m* -[e]s,-e pin; (*Nagel*) tack; (*Blei-*) pencil; (*Farb-*) crayon

Stift[2] *nt* -[e]s,-e [endowed] foundation. **s~en** *vt* endow; (*spenden*) donate; create (*Unheil, Verwirrung*); bring about (*Frieden*). **S~er** *m* -s,- founder;

(*Spender*) donor. **S~ung** *f* -,-en foundation; (*Spende*) donation

Stigma *nt* -s (*fig*) stigma

Stil *m* -[e]s,-e style; **in großem S~** in style. **s~isiert** *a* stylized. **s~istisch** *a* stylistic, *adv* -ally

still *a* quiet, *adv* -ly; (*reglos, ohne Kohlensäure*) still; (*heimlich*) secret, *adv* -ly; **der S~e Ozean** the Pacific; **im s~en** secretly; (*bei sich*) inwardly. **S~e** *f* - quiet; (*Schweigen*) silence

Stilleben *nt* still life

stilleg|en *vt sep* close down. **S~ung** *f* -,-en closure

stillen *vt* satisfy; quench (*Durst*); stop (*Schmerzen, Blutung*); breast-feed (*Kind*)

stillhalten† *vi sep* (*haben*) keep still

Stillschweigen *nt* silence. **s~d** *a* silent, *adv* -ly; (*fig*) tacit, *adv* -ly

stillsitzen† *vi sep* (*haben*) sit still. **S~stand** *m* standstill; **zum S~stand bringen** stop. **s~stehen**† *vi sep* (*haben*) stand still; (*anhalten*) stop; (*Verkehr:*) be at a standstill

Stil|möbel *pl* reproduction furniture *sg.* **s~voll** *a* stylish, *adv* -ly

Stimm|bänder *ntpl* vocal cords. **s~berechtigt** *a* entitled to vote. **S~bruch** *m* er **ist im S~bruch** his voice is breaking

Stimme *f* -,-n voice; (*Wahl-*) vote

stimmen *vi* (*haben*) be right; (*wählen*) vote; **stimmt das?** is that right/ (*wahr*) true? • *vt* tune; **jdn traurig/ fröhlich s~** make s.o. feel sad/happy

Stimm|enthaltung *f* abstention. **S~recht** *nt* right to vote

Stimmung *f* -,-en mood; (*Atmosphäre*) atmosphere. **s~svoll** *a* full of atmosphere

Stimmzettel *m* ballot-paper

stimulieren *vt* stimulate

stink|en† *vi* (*haben*) smell/(*stark*) stink (*nach* of). **S~tier** *nt* skunk

Stipendium *nt* -s,-ien scholarship; (*Beihilfe*) grant

Stirn *f* -,-en forehead; **die S~ bieten** (+ *dat*) (*fig*) defy. **S~runzeln** *nt* -s frown

stöbern *vi* (*haben*) rummage

stochern *vi* (*haben*) **s~ in** (+ *dat*) poke (*Feuer*); pick at (*Essen*); pick (*Zähne*)

Stock[1] *m* -[e]s,¨e stick; (*Ski-*) pole; (*Bienen-*) hive; (*Rosen-*) bush; (*Reb-*) vine

Stock[2] *m* -[e]s,- storey, floor. **S~bett** *nt* bunk-beds *pl.* **s~dunkel** *a* (*fam*) pitch-dark

stock|en vi (haben) stop; ⟨Verkehr:⟩ come to a standstill; ⟨Person:⟩ falter. **s~end** a hesitant, adv -ly. **s~taub** a (fam) stone-deaf. **S~ung** f -,-en hold-up

Stockwerk nt storey, floor

Stoff m -[e]s,-e substance; (Tex) fabric, material; (Thema) subject [matter]; (Gesprächs-) topic. **S~tier** nt soft toy. **S~wechsel** m metabolism

stöhnen vi (haben) groan, moan. **S~** nt -s groan, moan

stoisch a stoic, adv -ally

Stola f -,-len stole

Stollen m -s,- gallery; (Kuchen) stollen

stolpern vi (sein) stumble; **s~ über** (+ acc) trip over

stolz a proud (**auf** + acc of), adv -ly. **S~** m -es pride

stolzieren vi (sein) strut

stopfen vt stuff; (stecken) put; (ausbessern) darn ● vi (haben) be constipating; (fam: essen) guzzle

Stopp m -s,-s stop. **s~** int stop!

stoppel|ig a stubbly. **S~n** fpl stubble sg

stopp|en vt stop; (Sport) time ● vi (haben) stop. **S~schild** nt stop sign. **S~uhr** f stop-watch

Stöpsel m -s,- plug; (Flaschen-) stopper

Storch m -[e]s,-̈e stork

Store / ʃtoːɐ/ m -s,-s net curtain

stören vt disturb; disrupt ⟨Rede, Sitzung⟩; jam ⟨Sender⟩; (mißfallen) bother; **stört es Sie, wenn ich rauche?** do you mind if I smoke? ● vi (haben) be a nuisance; **entschuldigen Sie, daß ich störe** I'm sorry to bother you

stornieren vt cancel

störrisch a stubborn, adv -ly

Störung f -,-en (s. stören) disturbance; disruption; (Med) trouble; (Radio) interference; **technische S~** technical fault

Stoß m -es,-̈e push, knock; (mit Ellbogen) dig; (Hörner-) butt; (mit Waffe) thrust; (Schwimm-) stroke; (Ruck) jolt; (Erd-) shock; (Stapel) stack, pile. **S~dämpfer** m -s,- shock absorber

stoßen† vt push, knock; (mit Füßen) kick; (mit Kopf, Hörnern) butt; (an-) poke, nudge; (treiben) thrust; **sich s~** knock oneself; **sich** (dat) **den Kopf s~** hit one's head ● vi (haben) push; **s~ an** (+ acc) knock against; (angrenzen) adjoin ● vi (sein) **s~ gegen** knock against; bump into ⟨Tür⟩; **s~ auf** (+ acc) bump into; (entdecken) come

across; strike ⟨Öl⟩; (fig) meet with ⟨Ablehnung⟩

Stoß|stange f bumper. **S~verkehr** m rush-hour traffic. **S~zahn** m tusk. **S~zeit** f rush-hour

stottern vt/i (haben) stutter, stammer

Str. abbr (**Straße**) St

Straf|anstalt f prison. **S~arbeit** f (Sch) imposition. **s~bar** a punishable; **sich s~bar machen** commit an offence

Strafe f -,-n punishment; (Jur & fig) penalty; (Geld-) fine; (Freiheits-) sentence. **s~n** vt punish

straff a tight, taut. **s~en** vt tighten; **sich s~en** tighten

Strafgesetz nt criminal law

sträf|lich a criminal, adv -ly. **S~ling** m -s,-e prisoner

Straf|mandat nt (Auto) [parking/speeding] ticket. **S~porto** nt excess postage. **S~predigt** f (fam) lecture. **S~raum** m penalty area. **S~stoß** m penalty. **S~tat** f crime. **S~zettel** m (fam) = **S~mandat**

Strahl m -[e]s,-en ray; (einer Taschenlampe) beam; (Wasser-) jet. **s~en** vi (haben) shine; (funkeln) sparkle; (lächeln) beam. **S~enbehandlung** f radiotherapy. **s~end** a shining; sparkling; beaming; radiant ⟨Schönheit⟩. **S~entherapie** f radiotherapy. **S~ung** f - radiation

Strähn|e f -,-n strand. **s~ig** a straggly

stramm a tight, adv -ly; (kräftig) sturdy; (gerade) upright

Strampel|höschen nt -s,- rompers pl. **s~n** vi (haben) ⟨Baby:⟩ kick

Strand m -[e]s,-̈e beach. **s~en** vi (sein) run aground; (fig) fail. **S~korb** m wicker beach-chair. **S~promenade** f promenade

Strang m -[e]s,-̈e rope

Strapaz|e f -,-n strain. **s~ieren** vt be hard on; tax ⟨Nerven, Geduld⟩. **s~ierfähig** a hard-wearing. **s~iös** a exhausting

Straß m - & -sses paste

Straße f -,-n road; (in der Stadt auch) street; (Meeres-) strait; **auf der S~** in the road/street. **S~nbahn** f tram, (Amer) streetcar. **S~nkarte** f road-map. **S~nlaterne** f street lamp. **S~nsperre** f road-block

Strat|egie f -,-n strategy. **s~egisch** a strategic, adv -ally

sträuben *vt* ruffle up ⟨*Federn*⟩; **sich s∼** ⟨*Fell, Haar:*⟩ stand on end; (*fig*) resist

Strauch *m* -[e]s, **Sträucher** bush

straucheln *vi* (*sein*) stumble

Strauß[1] *m* -es, **Sträuße** bunch [of flowers]; (*Bukett*) bouquet

Strauß[2] *m* -es, -e ostrich

Strebe *f* -,-n brace, strut

streben *vi* (*haben*) strive (**nach** for) ● *vi* (*sein*) head (**nach/zu** for)

Streb|er *m* -s,- pushy person; (*Sch*) swot. **s∼sam** *a* industrious

Strecke *f* -,-n stretch, section; (*Entfernung*) distance; (*Rail*) line; (*Route*) route

strecken *vt* stretch; (*aus-*) stretch out; (*gerade machen*) straighten; (*Culin*) thin down; **sich s∼** stretch; (*sich aus-*) stretch out; **den Kopf aus dem Fenster s∼** put one's head out of the window

Streich *m* -[e]s,-e prank, trick; **jdm einen S∼ spielen** play a trick on s.o.

streicheln *vt* stroke

streichen† *vt* spread; (*weg-*) smooth; (*an-*) paint; (*aus-*) delete; (*kürzen*) cut ● *vi* (*haben*) **s∼ über** (+ *acc*) stroke

Streicher *m* -s,- string-player; **die S∼** the strings

Streichholz *nt* match. **S∼schachtel** *f* matchbox

Streich|instrument *nt* stringed instrument. **S∼käse** *m* cheese spread. **S∼orchester** *nt* string orchestra. **S∼ung** *f* -,-en deletion; (*Kürzung*) cut

Streife *f* -,-n patrol

streifen *vt* brush against; (*berühren*) touch; (*verletzen*) graze; (*fig*) touch on ⟨*Thema*⟩; (*ziehen*) slip (**über** + *acc* over); **mit dem Blick s∼** glance at ● *vi* (*sein*) roam

Streifen *m* -s,- stripe; (*Licht-*) streak; (*auf der Fahrbahn*) line; (*schmales Stück*) strip

Streif|enwagen *m* patrol car. **s∼ig** *a* streaky. **S∼schuß** *m* glancing shot; (*Wunde*) graze

Streik *m* -s,-s strike; **in den S∼ treten** go on strike. **S∼brecher** *m* strikebreaker, (*pej*) scab. **s∼en** *vi* (*haben*) strike; (*fam*) refuse; (*versagen*) pack up. **S∼ende(r)** *m* striker. **S∼posten** *m* picket

Streit *m* -[e]s,-e quarrel; (*Auseinandersetzung*) dispute. **s∼en**† *vr/i* (*haben*) [**sich**] **s∼en** quarrel. **s∼ig** *a* **jdm etw s∼ig machen** dispute s.o.'s

right to sth. **S∼igkeiten** *fpl* quarrels. **S∼kräfte** *fpl* armed forces. **s∼süchtig** *a* quarrelsome

streng *a* strict, *adv* -ly; ⟨*Blick, Ton*⟩ stern, *adv* -ly; ⟨*rauh, nüchtern*⟩ severe, *adv* -ly; ⟨*Geschmack*⟩ sharp. **S∼e** *f* - strictness; sternness; severity. **s∼genommen** *adv* strictly speaking. **s∼gläubig** *a* strict; (*orthodox*) orthodox. **s∼stens** *adv* strictly

Streß *m* -sses,-sse stress

streßig *a* (*fam*) stressful

streuen *vt* spread; (*ver-*) scatter; sprinkle ⟨*Zucker, Salz*⟩; **die Straßen s∼** grit the roads

streunen *vi* (*sein*) roam; **s∼der Hund** stray dog

Strich *m* -[e]s,-e line; (*Feder-, Pinsel-*) stroke; (*Morse-, Gedanken-*) dash; **gegen den S∼** the wrong way; (*fig*) against the grain. **S∼kode** *m* bar code. **S∼punkt** *m* semicolon

Strick *m* -[e]s,-e cord; (*Seil*) rope; (*fam: Schlingel*) rascal

strick|en *vt/i* (*haben*) knit. **S∼jacke** *f* cardigan. **S∼leiter** *f* rope-ladder. **S∼nadel** *f* knitting-needle. **S∼waren** *fpl* knitwear *sg*. **S∼zeug** *nt* knitting

striegeln *vt* groom

strikt *a* strict, *adv* -ly

strittig *a* contentious

Stroh *nt* -[e]s straw. **S∼blumen** *fpl* everlasting flowers. **S∼dach** *nt* thatched roof. **s∼gedeckt** *a* thatched. **S∼halm** *m* straw

Strolch *m* -[e]s,-e (*fam*) rascal

Strom *m* -[e]s,-e river; (*Menschen-, Auto-, Blut-*) stream; (*Tränen-*) flood; (*Schwall*) torrent; (*Electr*) current, power; **gegen den S∼** (*fig*) against the tide; **es regnet in Strömen** it is pouring with rain. **s∼abwärts** *adv* downstream. **s∼aufwärts** *adv* upstream

strömen *vi* (*sein*) flow; ⟨*Menschen, Blut:*⟩ stream, pour; **s∼der Regen** pouring rain

Strom|kreis *m* circuit. **s∼linienförmig** *a* streamlined. **S∼sperre** *f* power cut

Strömung *f* -,-en current

Strophe *f* -,-n verse

strotzen *vi* (*haben*) be full (**vor** + *dat* of); **vor Gesundheit s∼d** bursting with health

Strudel *m* -s,- whirlpool; (*SGer Culin*) strudel

Struktur *f* -,-en structure; *(Tex)* texture

Strumpf *m* -[e]s,ˑe stocking; *(Knie-)* sock. **S∼band** *nt* *(pl* -bänder*)* suspender, *(Amer)* garter. **S∼bandgürtel** *m* suspender-/*(Amer)* garter belt. **S∼halter** *m* = **S∼band. S∼hose** *f* tights *pl*, *(Amer)* pantyhose

Strunk *m* -[e]s,ˑe stalk; *(Baum-)* stump

struppig *a* shaggy

Stube *f* -,-n room. **s∼nrein** *a* housetrained

Stuck *m* -s stucco

Stück *nt* -[e]s,-e piece; *(Zucker-)* lump; *(Seife)* tablet; *(Theater-)* play; *(Gegenstand)* item; *(Exemplar)* specimen; **20 S∼ Vieh** 20 head of cattle; **ein S∼** *(Entfernung)* some way; **aus freien S∼en** voluntarily. **S∼chen** *nt* -s,- [little] bit. **s∼weise** *adv* bit by bit; *(einzeln)* singly

Student|(in) *m* -en,-en *(f* -,-nen*)* student. **s∼isch** *a* student...

Studie /-jə/ *f* -,-n study

studier|en *vt/i* *(haben)* study. **S∼zimmer** *nt* study

Studio *nt* -s,-s studio

Studium *nt* -s,-ien studies *pl*

Stufe *f* -,-n step; *(Treppen-)* stair; *(Raketen-)* stage; *(Niveau)* level. **s∼n** *vt* terrace; *(staffeln)* grade

Stuhl *m* -[e]s,ˑe chair; *(Med)* stools *pl*. **S∼gang** *m* bowel movement

stülpen *vt* put *(über + acc* over*)*

stumm *a* dumb; *(schweigsam)* silent, *adv* -ly

Stummel *m* -s,- stump; *(Zigaretten-)* butt; *(Bleistift-)* stub

Stümper *m* -s,- bungler. **s∼haft** *a* incompetent, *adv* -ly

stumpf *a* blunt; *(Winkel)* obtuse; *(glanzlos)* dull; *(fig)* apathetic, *adv* - ally. **S∼** *m* -[e]s,ˑe stump

Stumpfsinn *m* apathy; *(Langweiligkeit)* tedium. **s∼ig** *a* apathetic, *adv* -ally; *(langweilig)* tedious

Stunde *f* -,-n hour; *(Sch)* lesson

stunden *vt* jdm **eine Schuld s∼** give s.o. time to pay a debt

Stunden|kilometer *mpl* kilometres per hour. **s∼lang** *adv* for hours. **S∼lohn** *m* hourly rate. **S∼plan** *m* timetable. **s∼weise** *adv* by the hour

stündlich *a* & *adv* hourly

Stups *m* -es,-e nudge; *(Schubs)* push. **s∼en** *vt* nudge; *(schubsen)* push. **S∼nase** *f* snub nose

stur *a* pigheaded; *(phlegmatisch)* stolid, *adv* -ly; *(unbeirrbar)* dogged, *adv* -ly

Sturm *m* -[e]s,ˑe gale; *(schwer)* storm; *(Mil)* assault

stürm|en *vi* *(haben)* *(Wind:)* blow hard; **es s∼t** it's blowing a gale ● *vi* *(sein)* rush ● *vt* storm; *(bedrängen)* besiege. **S∼er** *m* -s,- forward. **s∼isch** *a* stormy; *(Überfahrt)* rough; *(fig)* tumultuous, *adv* -ly; *(ungestüm)* tempestuous, *adv* -ly

Sturz *m* -es,ˑe [heavy] fall; *(Preis-, Kurs-)* sharp drop; *(Pol)* overthrow

stürzen *vi* *(sein)* fall [heavily]; *(in die Tiefe)* plunge; *(Preise, Kurse:)* drop sharply; *(Regierung:)* fall; *(eilen)* rush ● *vt* throw; *(umkippen)* turn upside down; turn out *(Speise, Kuchen)*; *(Pol)* overthrow, topple; **sich s∼** throw oneself **(aus/in** + *acc* out of/ into); **sich s∼ auf** (+ *acc*) pounce on

Sturz|flug *m* *(Aviat)* dive. **S∼helm** *m* crash-helmet

Stute *f* -,-n mare

Stütze *f* -,-n support; *(Kopf-, Arm-)* rest

stutzen *vi* *(haben)* stop short ● *vt* trim; *(Hort)* cut back; *(kupieren)* crop

stützen *vt* support; *(auf-)* rest; **sich s∼ auf** (+ *acc*) lean on; *(beruhen)* be based on

Stutzer *m* -s,- dandy

stutzig *a* puzzled; *(mißtrauisch)* suspicious

Stützpunkt *m* *(Mil)* base

Subjekt *nt* -[e]s,-e subject. **s∼iv** *a* subjective, *adv* -ly

Subskription /-'tsjoːn/ *f* -,-en subscription

Substantiv *nt* -s,-e noun

Substanz *f* -,-en substance

subtil *a* subtle, *adv* -tly

subtra|hieren *vt* subtract. **S∼ktion** /-'tsjoːn/ *f* -,-en subtraction

Subvention /-'tsjoːn/ *f* -,-en subsidy. **s∼ieren** *vt* subsidize

subversiv *a* subversive

Such|e *f* - search; **auf der S∼e nach** looking for. **s∼en** *vt* look for; *(intensiv)* search for; seek *(Hilfe, Rat)*; **'Zimmer gesucht'** 'room wanted' ● *vi* *(haben)* look, search **(nach** for*)*. **S∼er** *m* -s,- *(Phot)* viewfinder

Sucht *f* -,ˑe addiction; *(fig)* mania

süchtig *a* addicted. **S∼e(r)** *m/f* addict

Süd *m* -[e]s south. **S∼afrika** *nt* South Africa. **S∼amerika** *nt* South America. **s∼deutsch** *a* South German

Süden *m* -s south; **nach S~** south
Süd|frucht *f* tropical fruit. **s~lich**
a southern; ⟨*Richtung*⟩ southerly
● *adv & prep* (+ *gen*) **s~lich [von] der
Stadt** [to the] south of the town. **S~
osten** *m* south-east. **S~pol** *m* South
Pole. **s~wärts** *adv* southwards.
S~westen *m* south-west
süffisant *a* smug, *adv* -ly
suggerieren *vt* suggest (*dat* to)
Suggest|ion /-'tio:n/ *f* -,-en sug-
gestion. **s~iv** *a* suggestive
Sühne *f* -,-n atonement; ⟨*Strafe*⟩ penalty. **s~n** *vt* atone for
Sultanine *f* -,-n sultana
Sülze *f* -,-n [meat] jelly;
⟨*Schweinskopf-*⟩ brawn
Summe *f* -,-n sum
summ|en *vi* (*haben*) hum; ⟨*Biene:*⟩
buzz ● *vt* hum. **S~er** *m* -s,- buzzer
summieren (sich) *vr* add up; ⟨*sich
häufen*⟩ increase
Sumpf *m* -[e]s,ᵉe marsh, swamp. **s~ig**
a marshy
Sünd|e *f* -,-n sin. **S~enbock** *m* scape-
goat. **S~er(in)** *m* -s,- (*f* -,-nen) sinner.
s~haft *a* sinful. **s~igen** *vi* (*haben*)
sin
super *inv* *a* (*fam*) great. **S~lativ** *m*
-s,-e superlative. **S~markt** *m* supermarket
Suppe *f* -,-n soup. **S~nlöffel** *m* soup-
spoon. **S~nteller** *m* soup-plate.
S~nwürfel *m* stock cube
Surf|brett /'sø:ɐf-/ *nt* surfboard.
S~en *nt* -s surfing
surren *vi* (*haben*) whirr
süß *a* sweet, *adv* -ly. **S~e** *f* - sweet-
ness. **s~en** *vt* sweeten. **S~igkeit** *f*
-,-en sweet. **s~lich** *a* sweetish; ⟨*fig*⟩
sugary. **S~speise** *f* sweet. **S~stoff**
m sweetener. **S~waren** *fpl* confectionery *sg*, sweets *pl*. **S~wasser-**
pref freshwater ...
Sylvester *nt* -s = **Silvester**
Symbol *nt* -s,-e symbol. **S~ik** *f* - sym-
bolism. **s~isch** *a* symbolic, *adv* -ally.
s~isieren *vt* symbolize
Sym|metrie *f* - symmetry. **s~
metrisch** *a* symmetrical, *adv* -ly
Sympathie *f* -,-n sympathy
sympath|isch *a* agreeable; ⟨*Person*⟩
likeable. **s~isieren** *vi* (*haben*) be
sympathetic (**mit** to)
Symphonie *f* -,-n = **Sinfonie**
Symptom *nt* -s,-e symptom. **s~a-
tisch** *a* symptomatic
Synagoge *f* -,-n synagogue

synchronisieren /zynkroni'zi:rən/
vt synchronize; dub ⟨*Film*⟩
Syndikat *nt* -[e]s,-e syndicate
Syndrom *nt* -s,-e syndrome
synonym *a* synonymous, *adv* -ly. **S~**
nt -s,-e synonym
Syntax /'zyntaks/ *f* - syntax
Synthe|se *f* -,-n synthesis. **S~tik** *nt*
-s synthetic material. **s~tisch** *a* synthetic, *adv* -ally
Syrien /-jən/ *nt* -s Syria
System *nt* -s,-e system. **s~atisch** *a*
systematic, *adv* -ally
Szene *f* -,-n scene. **S~rie** *f* scenery

T

Tabak *m* -s,-e tobacco
Tabelle *f* -,-n table; ⟨*Sport*⟩ league table
Tablett *nt* -[e]s,-s tray
Tablette *f* -,-n tablet
tabu *a* taboo. **T~** *nt* -s,-s taboo
Tacho *m* -s,-s, **Tachometer** *m & nt*
speedometer
Tadel *m* -s,- reprimand; ⟨*Kritik*⟩
censure; ⟨*Sch*⟩ black mark. **t~los** *a*
impeccable, *adv* -bly. **t~n** *vt* reprimand; censure. **t~nswert** *a* reprehensible
Tafel *f* -,-n ⟨*Tisch, Tabelle*⟩ table;
⟨*Platte*⟩ slab; ⟨*Anschlag-, Hinweis-*⟩
board; ⟨*Gedenk-*⟩ plaque; ⟨*Schiefer-*⟩
slate; ⟨*Wand-*⟩ blackboard; ⟨*Bild-*⟩ plate;
⟨*Schokolade*⟩ bar. **t~n** *vi* (*haben*) feast
Täfelung *f* - panelling
Tag *m* -[e]s,-e day; **Tag für Tag** day by
day; **am T~e** in the daytime; **eines
T~es** one day; **unter T~e** underground; **es wird Tag** it is getting light;
guten Tag! good morning/
afternoon! **t~aus** *adv* **t~aus, t~ein**
day in, day out
Tage|buch *nt* diary. **t~lang** *adv* for
days
tagen *vi* (*haben*) meet; ⟨*Gericht:*⟩ sit;
es tagt day is breaking
Tages|anbruch *m* daybreak. **T~aus-
flug** *m* day trip. **T~decke** *f* bedspread. **T~karte** *f* day ticket;
⟨*Speise-*⟩ menu of the day. **T~licht** *nt*
daylight. **T~mutter** *f* child-minder.
T~ordnung *f* agenda. **T~rück-
fahrkarte** *f* day return [ticket].
T~zeit *f* time of the day. **T~zeitung**
f daily [news]paper
täglich *a & adv* daily; **zweimal t~**
twice a day

tags *adv* by day; **t~ zuvor/darauf** the day before/after

tagsüber *adv* during the day

tag|täglich *a* daily ● *adv* every single day. **T~traum** *m* daydream. **T~undnachtgleiche** *f* -,-n equinox. **T~ung** *f* -,-en meeting; (*Konferenz*) conference

Taill|e /'taljə/ *f* -,-n waist. **t~iert** /ta'ji:ɐt/ *a* fitted

Takt *m* -[e]s,-e tact; (*Mus*) bar; (*Tempo*) time; (*Rhythmus*) rhythm; **im T~** in time [to the music]. **T~gefühl** *nt* tact

Takt|ik *f* - tactics *pl*. **t~isch** *a* tactical, *adv* -ly

takt|los *a* tactless, *adv* -ly. **T~losigkeit** *f* - tactlessness. **T~stock** *m* baton. **t~voll** *a* tactful, *adv* -ly

Tal *nt* -[e]s,-̈er valley

Talar *m* -s,-e robe; (*Univ*) gown

Talent *nt* -[e]s,-e talent. **t~iert** *a* talented

Talg *m* -s tallow; (*Culin*) suet

Talsperre *f* dam

Tampon /tam'põ:/ *m* -s,-s tampon

Tang *m* -s seaweed

Tangente *f* -,-n tangent; (*Straße*) by-pass

Tank *m* -s,-s tank. **t~en** *vt* fill up with (*Benzin*) ● *vi* (*haben*) fill up with petrol; (*Aviat*) refuel; **ich muß t~en** I need petrol. **T~er** *m* -s,- tanker. **T~stelle** *f* petrol-/(*Amer*) gas station. **T~wart** *m* -[e]s,-e petrol-pump attendant

Tanne *f* -,-n fir [tree]. **T~nbaum** *m* fir tree; (*Weihnachtsbaum*) Christmas tree. **T~nzapfen** *m* fir cone

Tante *f* -,-n aunt

Tantiemen /tan'tie:mən/ *pl* royalties

Tanz *m* -es,-̈e dance. **t~en** *vt/i* (*haben*) dance

Tänzer(in) *m* -s,- (*f* -,-nen) dancer

Tanz|lokal *nt* dance-hall. **T~musik** *f* dance music

Tapete *f* -,-n wallpaper. **T~nwechsel** *m* (*fam*) change of scene

tapezier|en *vt* paper. **T~er** *m* -s,- paperhanger, decorator

tapfer *a* brave, *adv* -ly. **T~keit** *f* - bravery

tappen *vi* (*sein*) walk hesitantly; (*greifen*) grope (**nach** for)

Tarif *m* -s,-e rate; (*Verzeichnis*) tariff

tarn|en *vt* disguise; (*Mil*) camouflage; **sich t~en** disguise/camouflage oneself. **T~ung** *f* - disguise; camouflage

Tasche *f* -,-n bag; (*Hosen-, Mantel-*) pocket. **T~nbuch** *nt* paperback. **T~ndieb** *m* pickpocket. **T~ngeld** *nt* pocket-money. **T~nlampe** *f* torch, (*Amer*) flashlight. **T~nmesser** *nt* penknife. **T~ntuch** *nt* handkerchief

Tasse *f* -,-n cup

Tastatur *f* -,-en keyboard

tast|bar *a* palpable. **T~e** *f* -,-n key; (*Druck-*) push-button. **t~en** *vi* (*haben*) feel, grope (**nach** for) ● *vt* key in (*Daten*); **sich t~en** feel one's way (**zu** to). **t~end** *a* tentative, *adv* -ly

Tat *f* -,-en action; (*Helden-*) deed; (*Straf-*) crime; **in der Tat** indeed; **auf frischer Tat ertappt** caught in the act. **t~enlos** *adv* passively

Täter(in) *m* -s,- (*f* -,-nen) culprit; (*Jur*) offender

tätig *a* active, *adv* -ly; **t~ sein** work. **T~keit** *f* -,-en activity; (*Funktionieren*) action; (*Arbeit*) work, job

Tatkraft *f* energy

tätlich *a* physical, *adv* -ly; **t~ werden** become violent. **T~keiten** *fpl* violence *sg*

Tatort *m* scene of the crime

tätowier|en *vt* tattoo. **T~ung** *f* -,-en tattooing; (*Bild*) tattoo

Tatsache *f* fact. **T~nbericht** *m* documentary

tatsächlich *a* actual, *adv* -ly

tätscheln *vt* pat

Tatze *f* -,-n paw

Tau¹ *m* -[e]s dew

Tau² *nt* -[e]s,-e rope

taub *a* deaf; (*gefühllos*) numb; (*Nuß*) empty; (*Gestein*) worthless

Taube *f* -,-n pigeon; (*Turtel- & fig*) dove. **T~nschlag** *m* pigeon-loft

Taub|heit *f* - deafness; (*Gefühllosigkeit*) numbness. **t~stumm** *a* deaf and dumb

tauch|en *vt* dip, plunge; (*unter-*) duck ● *vi* (*haben/sein*) dive/(*ein-*) plunge (**in** + *acc* into); (*auf-*) appear (**aus** out of). **T~er** *m* -s,- diver. **T~eranzug** *m* diving-suit. **T~sieder** *m* -s,- [small, portable] immersion heater

tauen *vi* (*sein*) melt, thaw ● *impers* **es taut** it is thawing

Tauf|becken *nt* font. **T~e** *f* -,-n christening, baptism. **t~en** *vt* christen, baptize. **T~pate** *m* godfather. **T~stein** *m* font

tauge|n *vi* (*haben*) **etwas/nichts t~n** be good/no good; **zu etw t~n/nicht**

t~n be good/no good for sth. **T~nichts** *m* -es,-e good-for-nothing

tauglich *a* suitable; (*Mil*) fit. **T~keit** *f* - suitability; fitness

Taumel *m* -s daze; **wie im T~** in a daze. **t~n** *vi* (*sein*) stagger

Tausch *m* -[e]s,-e exchange, (*fam*) swap. **t~en** *vt* exchange/(*handeln*) barter (**gegen** for); **die Plätze t~en** change places ● *vi* (*haben*) swap (**mit etw** sth; **mit jdm** with s.o.)

täuschen *vt* deceive, fool; betray ⟨*Vertrauen*⟩; **sich t~** delude oneself; (*sich irren*) be mistaken ● *vi* (*haben*) be deceptive. **t~d** *a* deceptive; (*Ähnlichkeit*) striking

Tausch|geschäft *nt* exchange. **T~handel** *m* barter; (*T~geschäft*) exchange

Täuschung *f* -,-en deception; (*Irrtum*) mistake; (*Illusion*) delusion

tausend *inv a* one/a thousand. **T~** *nt* -s,-e thousand. **T~füßler** *m* -s,- centipede. **t~ste(r,s)** *a* thousandth. **T~stel** *nt* -s,- thousandth

Tau|tropfen *m* dewdrop. **T~wetter** *nt* thaw. **T~ziehen** *nt* -s tug of war

Taxe *f* -,-n charge; (*Kur-*) tax; (*Taxi*) taxi

Taxi *nt* -s,-s taxi, cab

taxieren *vt* estimate/(*im Wert*) value (**auf** + *acc* at); (*fam: mustern*) size up

Taxi|fahrer *m* taxi driver. **T~stand** *m* taxi rank

Teakholz /'tiːk-/ *nt* teak

Team /tiːm/ *nt* -s,-s team

Techni|k *f* -,-en technology; (*Methode*) technique. **T~ker** *m* -s,- technician. **t~sch** *a* technical, *adv* -ly; (*technologisch*) technological, *adv* -ly; **T~sche Hochschule** Technical University

Techno|logie *f* -,-n technology. **t~logisch** *a* technological

Teckel *m* -s,- dachshund

Teddybär *m* teddy bear

Tee *m* -s,-s tea. **T~beutel** *m* tea-bag. **T~kanne** *f* teapot. **T~kessel** *m* kettle. **T~löffel** *m* teaspoon

Teer *m* -s tar. **t~en** *vt* tar

Tee|sieb *nt* tea-strainer. **T~tasse** *f* teacup. **T~wagen** *m* [tea] trolley

Teich *m* -[e]s,-e pond

Teig *m* -[e]s,-e pastry; (*Knet-*) dough; (*Rühr-*) mixture; (*Pfannkuchen-*) batter. **T~rolle** *f*, **T~roller** *m* rolling-pin. **T~waren** *fpl* pasta *sg*

Teil *m* -[e]s,-e part; (*Bestand-*) component; (*Jur*) party; **der vordere T~**

the front part; **zum T~** partly; **zum großen/größten T~** for the most part ● *m & nt* -[e]s (*Anteil*) share; **sein[en] T~** beitragen do one's share; **ich für mein[en] T~** for my part ● *nt* -[e]s,-e part; (*Ersatz-*) spare part; (*Anbau-*) unit

teil|bar *a* divisible. **T~chen** *nt* -s,- particle. **t~en** *vt* divide; (*auf-*) share out; (*gemeinsam haben*) share; (*Pol*) partition ⟨*Land*⟩; **sich** (*dat*) **etw [mit jdm] t~en** share sth [with s.o.]; **sich t~en** divide; (*sich gabeln*) fork; ⟨*Vorhang:*⟩ open; ⟨*Meinungen:*⟩ differ ● *vi* (*haben*) share

teilhab|en† *vi sep* (*haben*) share (**an etw** *dat* sth). **T~er** *m* -s,- (*Comm*) partner

Teilnahm|e *f* - participation; (*innere*) interest; (*Mitgefühl*) sympathy. **t~slos** *a* apathetic, *adv* -ally

teilnehm|en† *vi sep* (*haben*) **t~en an** (+*dat*) take part in; (*mitfühlen*) share [in]. **T~er(in)** *m* -s,- (*f* -,-nen) participant; (*an Wettbewerb*) competitor

teil|s *adv* partly. **T~ung** *f* -,-en division; (*Pol*) partition. **t~weise** *a* partial ● *adv* partially, partly; (*manchmal*) in some cases. **T~zahlung** *f* part-payment; (*Rate*) instalment. **T~zeitbeschäftigung** *f* part-time job

Teint /tɛ̃ː/ *m* -s,-s complexion

Telefax *nt* fax

Telefon *nt* -s,-e [tele]phone. **T~anruf** *m*, **T~at** *nt* -[e]s,-e [tele]phone call. **T~buch** *nt* [tele]phone book. **t~ieren** *vi* (*haben*) [tele]phone

telefon|isch *a* [tele]phone ... ● *adv* by [tele]phone. **T~ist(in)** *m* -en,-en (*f* -,-nen) telephonist. **T~karte** *f* phone card. **T~nummer** *f* [tele] phone number. **T~zelle** *f* [tele] phone box

Telegraf *m* -en,-en telegraph. **T~enmast** *m* telegraph pole. **t~ieren** *vi* (*haben*) send a telegram. **t~isch** *a* telegraphic ● *adv* by telegram

Telegramm *nt* -s,-e telegram

Telegraph *m* -en,-en = **Telegraf**

Teleobjektiv *nt* telephoto lens

Telepathie *f* - telepathy

Telephon *nt* -s,-e = **Telefon**

Teleskop *nt* -s,-e telescope. **t~isch** *a* telescopic

Telex *nt* -,-[e] telex. **t~en** *vt* telex

Teller *m* -s,- plate

Tempel *m* -s,- temple

Temperament nt -s,-e temperament; (Lebhaftigkeit) vivacity. t~los a dull. t~voll a vivacious; ⟨Pferd⟩ spirited

Temperatur f -,-en temperature

Tempo nt -s,-s speed; (Mus: pl -pi) tempo; T~ [T~]! hurry up!

Tend|enz f -,-en trend; (Neigung) tendency. t~ieren vi (haben) tend (zu towards)

Tennis nt - tennis. T~platz m tennis-court. T~schläger m tennis-racket

Tenor m -s,ⁿe (Mus) tenor

Teppich m -s,-e carpet. T~boden m fitted carpet

Termin m -s,-e date; (Arzt-) appointment; [letzter] T~ deadline. T~kalender m [appointments] diary

Terminologie f -,-n terminology

Terpentin nt -s turpentine

Terrain /tɛˈrɛ̃:/ nt -s,-s terrain

Terrasse f -,-n terrace

Terrier /ˈtɛrɪɐ/ m -s,- terrier

Terrine f -,-n tureen

Territorium nt -s,-ien territory

Terror m -s terror. t~isieren vt terrorize. T~ismus m - terrorism. T~ist m -en,-en terrorist

Terzett nt -[e]s,-e [vocal] trio

Tesafilm (P) m ≈ Sellotape (P)

Test m -[e]s,-s & -e test

Testament nt -[e]s,-e will; Altes/Neues T~ Old/New Testament. T~svollstrecker m -s,- executor

testen vt test

Tetanus m - tetanus

teuer a expensive, adv -ly; (lieb) dear; wie t~? how much? T~ung f -,-en rise in prices

Teufel m -s,- devil; zum T~! (sl) damn [it]! T~skreis m vicious circle

teuflisch a fiendish

Text m -[e]s,-e text; (Passage) passage; (Bild-) caption; (Lied-) lyrics pl, words pl; (Opern-) libretto. T~er m -s,- copywriter; (Schlager-) lyricist

Textil|ien /-jən/ pl textiles; (Textilwaren) textile goods. T~industrie f textile industry

Textverarbeitungssystem nt word processor

TH abbr = Technische Hochschule

Theater nt -s,- theatre; (fam: Getue) fuss, to-do; T~ spielen act; (fam) put on an act. T~kasse f box-office. T~stück nt play

theatralisch a theatrical, adv -ly

Theke f -,-n bar; (Ladentisch) counter

Thema nt -s,-men subject; (Mus) theme

Themse f - Thames

Theolo|ge m -n,-n theologian. T~gie f - theology

theor|etisch a theoretical, adv -ly. T~ie f -,-n theory

Therapeut|(in) m -en,-en (f -,-nen) therapist. t~isch a therapeutic

Therapie f -,-n therapy

Thermal|bad nt thermal bath; (Ort) thermal spa. T~quelle f thermal spring

Thermometer nt -s,- thermometer

Thermosflasche (P) f Thermos flask (P)

Thermostat m -[e]s,-e thermostat

These f -,-n thesis

Thrombose f -,-n thrombosis

Thron m -[e]s,-e throne. t~en vi (haben) sit [in state]. T~folge f succession. T~folger m -s,- heir to the throne

Thunfisch m tuna

Thymian m -s thyme

Tick m -s,-s (fam) quirk; einen T~ haben be crazy

ticken vi (haben) tick

tief a deep; (t~liegend, niedrig) low; (t~gründig) profound; t~er Teller soup-plate; im t~sten Winter in the depths of winter ● adv deep; low; (sehr) deeply, profoundly; ⟨schlafen⟩ soundly. T~ nt -s,-s (Meteorol) depression. T~bau m civil engineering. T~e f -,-n depth

Tief|ebene f [lowland] plain. T~garage f underground car park. t~gekühlt a [deep-]frozen. t~greifend a radical, adv -ly. t~gründig a (fig) profound

Tiefkühl|fach nt freezer compartment. T~kost f frozen food. T~truhe f deep-freeze

Tief|land nt lowlands pl. T~punkt m (fig) low. t~schürfend a (fig) profound. t~sinnig a (fig) profound; (trübsinnig) melancholy. T~stand m (fig) low

Tiefsttemperatur f minimum temperature

Tier nt -[e]s,-e animal. T~arzt m, T~ärztin f vet, veterinary surgeon. T~garten m zoo. t~isch a animal ...; (fig: roh) bestial. T~kreis m zodiac. T~kreiszeichen nt sign of the zodiac. T~kunde f zoology. T~quälerei f cruelty to animals

Tiger *m* -s, - tiger

tilgen *vt* pay off ⟨*Schuld*⟩; ⟨*streichen*⟩ delete; (*fig: auslöschen*) wipe out

Tinte *f* -,-n ink. **T∼nfisch** *m* squid

Tip *m* -s,-s (*fam*) tip

tipp|en *vt* (*fam*) type ● *vi* (*haben*) (*berühren*) touch (**auf/an etw** *acc* sth); (*fam: maschineschreiben*) type; **t∼en auf** (+*acc*) (*fam: wetten*) bet on. **T∼fehler** *m* (*fam*) typing error. **T∼schein** *m* pools/lottery coupon

tipptopp *a* (*fam*) immaculate, *adv* -ly

Tirol *nt* -s [the] Tyrol

Tisch *m* -[e]s,-e table; ⟨*Schreib-*⟩ desk; **nach T∼** after the meal. **T∼decke** *f* table-cloth. **T∼gebet** *nt* grace. **T∼ler** *m* -s,- joiner; (*Möbel-*) cabinet-maker. **T∼rede** *f* after-dinner speech. **T∼tennis** *nt* table tennis. **T∼tuch** *nt* table-cloth

Titel *m* -s,- title. **T∼rolle** *f* title-role

Toast /toːst/ *m* -[e]s,-e toast; ⟨*Scheibe*⟩ piece of toast; **einen T∼ ausbringen** propose a toast (**auf** + *acc* to). **T∼er** *m* -s,- toaster

tob|en *vi* (*haben*) rave; ⟨*Sturm:*⟩ rage; ⟨*Kinder:*⟩ play boisterously ● *vi* (*sein*) rush. **t∼süchtig** *a* raving mad

Tochter *f* -," daughter. **T∼gesellschaft** *f* subsidiary

Tod *m* -es dead. **t∼ernst** *a* deadly serious, *adv* -ly

Todes|angst *f* mortal fear. **T∼anzeige** *f* death announcement; (*Zeitungs-*) obituary. **T∼fall** *m* death. **T∼opfer** *nt* fatality, casualty. **T∼strafe** *f* death penalty. **T∼urteil** *nt* death sentence

Tod|feind *m* mortal enemy. **t∼krank** *a* dangerously ill

tödlich *a* fatal, *adv* -ly; ⟨*Gefahr*⟩ mortal, *adv* -ly; (*groß*) deadly; **t∼ gelangweilt** bored to death

tod|müde *a* dead tired. **t∼sicher** *a* (*fam*) dead certain ● *adv* for sure. **T∼sünde** *f* deadly sin. **t∼unglücklich** *a* desperately unhappy

Toilette /toaˈlɛtə/ *f* -,-n toilet. **T∼npapier** *nt* toilet paper

toler|ant *a* tolerant. **T∼anz** *f* - tolerance. **t∼ieren** *vt* tolerate

toll *a* crazy, mad; (*fam: prima*) fantastic; (*schlimm*) awful ● *adv* beautifully; (*sehr*) very; (*schlimm*) badly. **t∼en** *vi* (*haben/sein*) romp. **t∼kühn** *a* foolhardy. **T∼wut** *f* rabies. **t∼wütig** *a* rabid

tolpatschig *a* clumsy, *adv* -ily

Tölpel *m* -s,- fool

Tomate *f* -,-n tomato. **T∼nmark** *nt* tomato purée

Tombola *f* -,-s raffle

Ton¹ *m* -[e]s clay

Ton² *m* -[e]s,¨e tone; (*Klang*) sound; (*Note*) note; (*Betonung*) stress; (*Farb-*) shade; **der gute Ton** (*fig*) good form. **T∼abnehmer** *m* -s,- pick-up. **t∼angebend** *a* (*fig*) leading. **T∼art** *f* tone [of voice]; (*Mus*) key. **T∼band** *nt* (*pl* -**bänder**) tape. **T∼bandgerät** *nt* tape recorder

tönen *vi* (*haben*) sound ● *vt* tint

Ton|fall *m* tone [of voice]; (*Akzent*) intonation. **T∼leiter** *f* scale. **t∼los** *a* toneless, *adv* -ly

Tonne *f* -,-n barrel, cask; (*Müll-*) bin; (*Maß*) tonne, metric ton

Topf *m* -[e]s,¨e pot; (*Koch-*) pan

Topfen *m* -s (*Aust*) ≈ curd cheese

Töpfer|(in) *m* -s,- (*f* -,-nen) potter. **T∼ei** *f* -,-en pottery

Töpferwaren *fpl* pottery *sg*

Topf|lappen *m* oven-cloth. **T∼pflanze** *f* potted plant

Tor¹ *m* -en,-en fool

Tor² *nt* -[e]s,-e gate; (*Einfahrt*) gateway; (*Sport*) goal. **T∼bogen** *m* archway

Torf *m* -s peat

Torheit *f* -,-en folly

Torhüter *m* -s,- goalkeeper

töricht *a* foolish, *adv* -ly

torkeln *vi* (*sein/haben*) stagger

Tornister *m* -s,- knapsack; (*Sch*) satchel

torp|edieren *vt* torpedo. **T∼edo** *m* -s,-s torpedo

Torpfosten *m* goal-post

Torte *f* -,-n gâteau; (*Obst-*) flan

Tortur *f* -,-en torture

Torwart *m* -s,-e goalkeeper

tosen *vi* (*haben*) roar; ⟨*Sturm:*⟩ rage

tot *a* dead; **einen t∼en Punkt haben** (*fig*) be at a low ebb

total *a* total, *adv* -ly. **t∼itär** *a* totalitarian. **T∼schaden** *m* ≈ write-off

Tote(r) *m/f* dead man/woman; (*Todesopfer*) fatality; **die T∼n** the dead *pl*

töten *vt* kill

toten|blaß *a* deathly pale. **T∼gräber** *m* -s,- grave-digger. **T∼kopf** *m* skull. **T∼schein** *m* death certificate. **T∼stille** *f* deathly silence

tot|fahren† *vt sep* run over and kill. **t∼geboren** *a* stillborn. **t∼lachen (sich)** *vr sep* (*fam*) be in stitches

Toto *nt & m* **-s** football pools *pl.* **T~schein** *m* pools coupon

tot|schießen† *vt sep* shoot dead. **T~schlag** *m (Jur)* manslaughter. **t~schlagen†** *vt sep* kill. **t~schweigen†** *vt sep (fig)* hush up. **t~stellen (sich)** *vr sep* pretend to be dead

Tötung *f* -,-en killing; **fahrlässige T~** *(Jur)* manslaughter

Toup|et /tu'pe:/ *nt* -s,-s toupee. **t~ieren** *vt* back-comb

Tour /tu:ɐ̯/ *f* -,-en tour; *(Ausflug)* trip; *(Auto-)* drive; *(Rad-)* ride; *(Strecke)* distance; *(Techn)* revolution; *(fam: Weise)* way; **auf vollen T~en** at full speed; *(fam)* flat out

Touris|mus /tu'rɪsmʊs/ *m* - tourism. **T~t** *m* -en,-en tourist

Tournee /tor'ne:/ *f* -,-n tour

Trab *m* -[e]s trot

Trabant *m* -en,-en satellite

traben *vi (haben/sein)* trot

Tracht *f* -,-en [national] costume; **eine T~ Prügel** a good hiding

trachten *vi (haben)* strive **(nach** for); **jdm nach dem Leben t~** be out to kill s.o.

trächtig *a* pregnant

Tradition /-'tsio:n/ *f* -,-en tradition. **t~ell** *a* traditional, *adv* -ly

Trafik *f* -,-en *(Aust)* tobacconist's

Trag|bahre *f* stretcher. **t~bar** *a* portable; *(Kleidung)* wearable; *(erträglich)* bearable

träge *a* sluggish, *adv* -ly; *(faul)* lazy, *adv* -ily; *(Phys)* inert

tragen† *vt* carry; *(an-/aufhaben)* wear; *(fig)* bear ● *vi (haben)* carry; **gut t~** *(Baum:)* produce a good crop; **schwer t~** carry a heavy load; *(fig)* be deeply affected **(an** + *dat* by). **t~d** *a* *(Techn)* load-bearing; *(trächtig)* pregnant

Träger *m* -s,- porter; *(Inhaber)* bearer; *(eines Ordens)* holder; *(Bau-)* beam; *(Stahl-)* girder; *(Achsel-)* [shoulder] strap. **T~kleid** *nt* pinafore dress

Trag|etasche *f* carrier bag. **T~fläche** *f* *(Aviat)* wing; *(Naut)* hydrofoil. **T~flächenboot, T~flügelboot** *nt* hydrofoil

Trägheit *f* - sluggishness; *(Faulheit)* laziness; *(Phys)* inertia

Trag|ik *f* - tragedy. **t~isch** *a* tragic, *adv* -ally

Tragödie /-jə/ *f* -,-n tragedy

Tragweite *f* range; *(fig)* consequence

Train|er /'trɛ:nɐ/ *m* -s,- trainer; *(Tennis-)* coach. **t~ieren** *vt/i (haben)* train

Training /'trɛ:nɪŋ/ *nt* -s training. **T~sanzug** *m* tracksuit. **T~sschuhe** *mpl* trainers

Trakt *m* -[e]s,-e section; *(Flügel)* wing

traktieren *vi (haben)* **mit Schlägen/ Tritten t~** hit/kick

Traktor *m* -s,-en /-'to:rən/ tractor

trampeln *vi (haben)* stamp one's feet ● *vi (sein)* trample **(auf** + *acc* on) ● *vt* trample

trampen /'trɛmpən/ *vi (sein) (fam)* hitch-hike

Trance /'trã:sə/ *f* -,-n trance

Tranchier|messer /trã'ʃi:ɐ̯-/ *nt* carving-knife. **t~en** *vt* carve

Träne *f* -,-n tear. **t~n** *vi (haben)* water. **T~ngas** *nt* tear-gas

Tränke *f* -,-n watering-place; *(Trog)* drinking-trough. **t~n** *vt* water *(Pferd)*; *(nässen)* soak **(mit** with)

Trans|aktion *f* transaction. **T~fer** *m* -s,-s transfer. **T~formator** *m* -s,-en /-'to:rən/ transformer. **T~fusion** *f* -,-en [blood] transfusion

Transistor *m* -,-en /-'to:rən/ transistor

Transit /tran'zi:t/ *m* -s transit

transitiv *a* transitive, *adv* -ly

Transparent *nt* -[e]s,-e banner; *(Bild)* transparency

transpirieren *vi (haben)* perspire

Transplantation /-'tsio:n/ *f* -,-en transplant

Transport *m* -[e]s,-e transport; *(Güter-)* consignment. **t~ieren** *vt* transport. **T~mittel** *nt* means of transport

Trapez *nt* -es,-e trapeze; *(Geom)* trapezium

Tratsch *m* -[e]s *(fam)* gossip. **t~en** *vi (haben) (fam)* gossip

Tratte *f* -,-n *(Comm)* draft

Traube *f* -,-n bunch of grapes; *(Beere)* grape; *(fig)* cluster. **T~nzucker** *m* glucose

trauen *vi (haben)* (+ *dat)* trust; **ich traute kaum meinen Augen** I could hardly believe my eyes ● *vt* marry; **sich t~** dare **(etw zu tun** [to] do sth); venture **(in** + *acc/aus* into/out of)

Trauer *f* - mourning; *(Schmerz)* grief **(um** for); **T~ tragen** be [dressed] in mourning. **T~fall** *m* bereavement. **T~feier** *f* funeral service. **T~marsch** *m* funeral march. **t~n** *vi (haben)* grieve; **t~n um** mourn [for].

T~spiel *nt* tragedy. **T~weide** *f* weeping willow

traulich *a* cosy, *adv* -ily

Traum *m* -[e]s, **Träume** dream

Trau|ma *nt* -s,-men trauma. **t~matisch** *a* traumatic

träumen *vt/i (haben)* dream

traumhaft *a* dreamlike; *(schön)* fabulous, *adv* -ly

traurig *a* sad, *adv* -ly; *(erbärmlich)* sorry. **T~keit** *f* - sadness

Trau|ring *m* wedding-ring. **T~schein** *m* marriage certificate. **T~ung** *f* -,-en wedding [ceremony]

Treck *m* -s,-s trek

Trecker *m* -s,- tractor

Treff *nt* -s,-s *(Karten)* spades *pl*

treff|en† *vt* hit; *⟨Blitz:⟩* strike; *(fig: verletzen)* hurt; *(zusammenkommen mit)* meet; take *⟨Maßnahme⟩*; **sich t~en** meet **(mit jdm** s.o.); **sich gut t~en** be convenient; **es traf sich, daß** it so happened that; **es gut/schlecht t~en** be lucky/unlucky ● *vi (haben)* hit the target; **t~en auf** (+ *acc*) meet; *(fig)* meet with. **T~en** *nt* -s,- meeting. **t~end** *a* apt, *adv* -ly; *⟨Ähnlichkeit⟩* striking. **T~er** *m* -s,- hit; *(Los)* winner. **T~punkt** *m* meeting-place

treiben† *vt* drive; *(sich befassen mit)* do; carry on *⟨Gewerbe⟩*; indulge in *⟨Luxus⟩*; get up to *⟨Unfug⟩*; **Handel t~** trade; **Blüten/Blätter t~** come into flower/leaf; **zur Eile t~** hurry [up]; **was treibt ihr da?** *(fam)* what are you up to? ● *vi (sein)* drift; *(schwimmen)* float ● *vi (haben) (Bot)* sprout. **T~** *nt* -s activity; *(Getriebe)* bustle

Treib|haus *nt* hothouse. **T~hauseffekt** *m* greenhouse effect. **T~holz** *nt* driftwood. **T~riemen** *m* transmission belt. **T~sand** *m* quicksand. **T~stoff** *m* fuel

Trend *m* -s,-s trend

trenn|bar *a* separable. **t~en** *vt* separate/*(abmachen)* detach **(von** from); divide, split *(Wort)*; **sich t~en** separate; *(auseinandergehen)* part; **sich t~en von** leave; *(fortgeben)* part with. **T~ung** *f* -,-en separation; *(Silben-)* division. **T~ungsstrich** *m* hyphen. **T~wand** *f* partition

trepp|ab *adv* downstairs. **t~auf** *adv* upstairs

Treppe *f* -,-n stairs *pl*; *(Außen-)* steps *pl*; **eine T~** a flight of stairs/steps. **T~nflur** *m* landing. **T~ngeländer**

nt banisters *pl*. **T~nhaus** *nt* stairwell. **T~nstufe** *f* stair, step

Tresor *m* -s,-e safe

Tresse *f* -,-n braid

Treteimer *m* pedal bin

treten† *vi (sein/haben)* step; *(versehentlich)* tread; *(ausschlagen)* kick **(nach** at); **in Verbindung t~** get in touch ● *vt* tread; *(mit Füßen)* kick

treu *a* faithful, *adv* -ly; *(fest)* loyal, *adv* -ly. **T~e** *f* - faithfulness; loyalty; *(eheliche)* fidelity. **T~händer** *m* -s,- trustee. **t~herzig** *a* trusting, *adv* -ly; *(arglos)* innocent, *adv* -ly. **t~los** *a* disloyal, *adv* -ly; *(untreu)* unfaithful

Tribüne *f* -,-n platform; *(Zuschauer-)* stand

Tribut *m* -[e]s,-e tribute; *(Opfer)* toll

Trichter *m* -s,- funnel; *(Bomben-)* crater

Trick *m* -s,-s trick. **T~film** *m* cartoon. **t~reich** *a* clever

Trieb *m* -[e]s,-e drive, urge; *(Instinkt)* instinct; *(Bot)* shoot. **T~täter, T~verbrecher** *m* sex offender. **T~werk** *nt* *(Aviat)* engine; *(Uhr-)* mechanism

trief|en† *vi (haben)* drip; *(naß sein)* be dripping **(von/vor** + *dat* with). **t~naß** *a* dripping wet

triftig *a* valid

Trigonometrie *f* - trigonometry

Trikot[1] /tri'ko:/ *m* -s *(Tex)* jersey

Trikot[2] *nt* -s,-s *(Sport)* jersey; *(Fußball-)* shirt

Trimester *nt* -s,- term

Trimm-dich *nt* -s keep-fit

trimmen *vt* trim; *(fam)* train; tune *⟨Motor⟩*; **sich t~** keep fit

trink|bar *a* drinkable. **t~en†** *vt/i (haben)* drink. **T~er(in)** *m* -s,- *(f* -,-nen) alcoholic. **T~geld** *nt* tip. **T~halm** *m* [drinking-]straw. **T~spruch** *m* toast. **T~wasser** *nt* drinking-water

Trio *nt* -s,-s trio

trippeln *vi (sein)* trip along

trist *a* dreary

Tritt *m* -[e]s,-e step; *(Fuß-)* kick. **T~brett** *nt* step. **T~leiter** *f* stepladder

Triumph *m* -s,-e triumph. **t~ieren** *vi (haben)* rejoice; **t~ieren über** (+ *acc*) triumph over. **t~ierend** *a* triumphant, *adv* -ly

trocken *a* dry, *adv* drily. **T~haube** *f* drier. **T~heit** *f* -,-en dryness; *(Dürre)* drought. **t~legen** *vt sep* change *⟨Baby⟩*; drain *⟨Sumpf⟩*. **T~milch** *f* powdered milk

trockn|en *vt/i (sein)* dry. **T~er** *m* **-s,-** drier

Troddel *f* **-,-n** tassel

Trödel *m* **-s** *(fam)* junk. **T~laden** *m (fam)* junk-shop. **T~markt** *m (fam)* flea market. **t~n** *vi (haben)* dawdle

Trödler *m* **-s,-** *(fam)* slowcoach; *(Händler)* junk-dealer

Trog *m* **-[e]s,¨e** trough

Trommel *f* **-,-n** drum. **T~fell** *nt* eardrum. **t~n** *vi (haben)* drum

Trommler *m* **-s,-** drummer

Trompete *f* **-,-n** trumpet. **T~r** *m* **-s,-** trumpeter

Tropen *pl* tropics

Tropf *m* **-[e]s,-e** *(Med)* drip

tröpfeln *vt/i (sein/haben)* drip; **es tröpfelt** it's spitting with rain

tropfen *vt/i (sein/haben)* drip. **T~** *m* **-s,-** drop; *(fallend)* drip. **t~weise** *adv* drop by drop

tropf|naß *a* dripping wet. **T~stein** *m* stalagmite; *(hängend)* stalactite

Trophäe /tro'fɛ:ə/ *f* **-,-n** trophy

tropisch *a* tropical

Trost *m* **-[e]s** consolation, comfort

tröst|en *vt* console, comfort; **sich t~en** console oneself. **t~lich** *a* comforting

trost|los *a* desolate; *(elend)* wretched; *(reizlos)* dreary. **T~preis** *m* consolation prize. **t~reich** *a* comforting

Trott *m* **-s** amble; *(fig)* routine

Trottel *m* **-s,-** *(fam)* idiot

trotten *vi (sein)* traipse; *⟨Tier:⟩* amble

Trottoir /trɔ'toaːɐ̯/ *nt* **-s,-s** pavement, *(Amer)* sidewalk

trotz *prep (+ gen)* despite, in spite of. **T~** *m* **-es** defiance. **t~dem** *adv* nevertheless. **t~en** *vi (haben)* (+ *dat*) defy. **t~ig** *a* defiant, *adv* -ly; *⟨Kind⟩* stubborn

trübe *a* dull; *⟨Licht⟩* dim; *⟨Flüssigkeit⟩* cloudy; *(fig)* gloomy

Trubel *m* **-s** bustle

trüben *vt* dull; make cloudy *⟨Flüssigkeit⟩*; *(fig)* spoil; strain *⟨Verhältnis⟩*; **sich t~** *⟨Flüssigkeit:⟩* become cloudy; *⟨Himmel:⟩* cloud over; *⟨Augen:⟩* dim; *⟨Verhältnis, Erinnerung:⟩* deteriorate

Trüb|sal *f* - misery; **T~sal blasen** *(fam)* mope. **t~selig** *a* miserable; *(trübe)* gloomy, *adv* -ily. **T~sinn** *m* melancholy. **t~sinnig** *a* melancholy

Trugbild *nt* illusion

trüg|en† *vt* deceive ● *vi (haben)* be deceptive. **t~erisch** *a* false; *(täuschend)* deceptive

Trugschluß *m* fallacy

Truhe *f* **-,-n** chest

Trümmer *pl* rubble *sg*; *(T~teile)* wreckage *sg*; *(fig)* ruins. **T~haufen** *m* pile of rubble

Trumpf *m* **-[e]s,¨e** trump [card]; **T~ sein** be trumps. **t~en** *vi (haben)* play trumps

Trunk *m* **-[e]s** drink. **T~enbold** *m* **-[e]s,-e** drunkard. **T~enheit** *f* - drunkenness; **T~enheit am Steuer** drunken driving. **T~sucht** *f* alcoholism

Trupp *m* **-s,-s** group; *(Mil)* squad. **T~e** *f* **-,-n** *(Mil)* unit; *(Theat)* troupe; **T~en** troops

Truthahn *m* turkey

Tschech|e *m* **-n,-n**, **T~in** *f* **-,-nen** Czech. **t~isch** *a* Czech. **T~oslowakei (die)** - Czechoslovakia

tschüs *int* bye, cheerio

Tuba *f* **-,-ben** *(Mus)* tuba

Tube *f* **-,-n** tube

Tuberkulose *f* - tuberculosis

Tuch¹ *nt* **-[e]s,¨er** cloth; *(Hals-, Kopf-)* scarf; *(Schulter-)* shawl

Tuch² *nt* **-[e]s,-e** *(Stoff)* cloth

tüchtig *a* competent; *(reichlich, beträchtlich)* good; *(groß)* big ● *adv* competently; *(ausreichend)* well; *⟨regnen, schneien⟩* hard. **T~keit** *f* - competence

Tück|e *f* **-,-n** malice; **T~en haben** be temperamental; *(gefährlich sein)* be treacherous. **t~isch** *a* malicious, *adv* -ly; *(gefährlich)* treacherous

tüfteln *vi (haben)* *(fam)* fiddle **(an** + *dat* with); *(geistig)* puzzle **(an** + *dat* over)

Tugend *f* **-,en** virtue. **t~haft** *a* virtuous

Tülle *f* **-,-n** spout

Tulpe *f* **-,-n** tulip

tummeln (sich) *vr* romp [about]; *(sich beeilen)* hurry [up]

Tümmler *m* **-s,-** porpoise

Tumor *m* **-s,-en** /-'moːrən/ tumour

Tümpel *m* **-s,-** pond

Tumult *m* **-[e]s,-e** commotion; *(Aufruhr)* riot

tun† *vt* do; take *⟨Schritt, Blick⟩*; work *⟨Wunder⟩*; *(bringen)* put **(in** + *acc* into); **sich tun** happen; **jdm etwas tun** hurt s.o.; **viel zu tun haben** have a lot to do; **das tut man nicht** it isn't done; **das tut nichts** it doesn't matter ● *vi* *(haben)* act (**als ob** as if); **überrascht tun** pretend to be surprised; **er tut nur so** he's just pretending; **zu tun haben** have things/work to do; **[es] zu tun haben mit** have to deal with; **[es] mit dem Herzen zu tun haben** have heart trouble. **Tun** *nt* -s actions *pl*

Tünche *f* -,-n whitewash; *(fig)* veneer. **t~n** *vt* whitewash

Tunesien /-jən/ *nt* -s Tunisia

Tunke *f* -,-n sauce. **t~n** *vt/i (haben)* *(fam)* dip (**in** + *acc* into)

Tunnel *m* -s,- tunnel

tupf|en *vt* dab ● *vi (haben)* **t~en an/ auf** (+ *acc*) touch. **T~en** *m* -s,- spot. **T~er** *m* -s,- spot; *(Med)* swab

Tür *f* -,-en door

Turban *m* -s,-e turban

Turbine *f* -,-n turbine

turbulen|t *a* turbulent. **T~z** *f* -,-en turbulence

Türk|e *m* -n,-n Turk. **T~ei** (**die**) - Turkey. **T~in** *f* -,-nen Turk

türkis *inv a* turquoise. **T~** *m* -es,-e turquoise

türkisch *a* Turkish

Turm *m* -[e]s,ˆe tower; *(Schach)* rook, castle

Türm|chen *nt* -s,- turret. **t~en** *vt* pile [up]; **sich t~en** pile up ● *vi (sein) (fam)* escape

Turmspitze *f* spire

turn|en *vi (haben)* do gymnastics. **T~en** *nt* -s gymnastics *sg; (Sch)* physical education, *(fam)* gym. **T~er(in)** *m* -s,- *(f* -,-nen) gymnast. **T~halle** *f* gymnasium

Turnier *nt* -s,-e tournament; *(Reit-)* show

Turnschuhe *mpl* gym shoes

Türschwelle *f* doorstep, threshold

Tusch *m* -[e]s,-e fanfare

Tusche *f* -,-n [drawing] ink; *(Wasserfarbe)* watercolour

tuscheln *vt/i (haben)* whisper

Tüte *f* -,-n bag; *(Comm)* packet; *(Eis-)* cornet; **in die T~ blasen** *(fam)* be breathalysed

tuten *vi (haben)* hoot; *(Schiff:)* sound its hooter; *(Sirene:)* sound

TÜV *m* - ≈ MOT [test]

Typ *m* -s,-en type; *(fam: Kerl)* bloke. **T~e** *f* -,-en type; *(fam: Person)* character

Typhus *m* - typhoid

typisch *a* typical, *adv* -ly (**für** of)

Typographie *f* - typography

Typus *m* -, **Typen** type

Tyrann *m* -en,-en tyrant. **T~ei** *f* - tyranny. **t~isch** *a* tyrannical. **t~isieren** *vt* tyrannize

U

u.a. *abbr* (**unter anderem**) amongst other things

U-Bahn *f* underground, *(Amer)* subway

übel *a* bad; *(häßlich)* nasty, *adv* -ily; **mir ist/wird ü~** I feel sick. **Ü~** *nt* -s,- evil. **Ü~keit** *f* - nausea. **ü~nehmen†** *vt sep* take amiss; **jdm etw ü~nehmen** hold sth against s.o. **Ü~täter** *m* culprit

üben *vt/i (haben)* practise; **sich in etw** *(dat)* **ü~** practise sth

über *prep* (+ *dat/acc*) over; *(höher als)* above; *(betreffend)* about; *(Buch, Vortrag)* on; *(Scheck, Rechnung)* for; *(quer ü~)* across; **ü~ Köln fahren** go via Cologne; **ü~ Ostern** over Easter; **die Woche ü~** during the week; **heute ü~ eine Woche** a week today; **Fehler ü~ Fehler** mistake after mistake ● *adv* **ü~ und ü~** all over; **jdm ü~ sein** be better/*(stärker)* stronger than s.o. ● *a (fam)* **ü~ sein** be left over; **etw ü~ sein** be fed up with sth

überall *adv* everywhere

überanstrengen *vt insep* overtax; strain *(Augen)*; **sich ü~** overexert oneself

überarbeit|en *vt insep* revise; **sich ü~en** overwork. **Ü~ung** *f* - revision; overwork

überaus *adv* extremely

überbewerten *vt insep* overrate

überbieten† *vt insep* outbid; *(fig)* outdo; *(übertreffen)* surpass

Überblick *m* overall view; *(Abriß)* summary

überblicken *vt insep* overlook; *(abschätzen)* assess

überbringen† *vt insep* deliver

überbrücken *vt insep (fig)* bridge

überdauern *vt insep* survive

überdenken† *vt insep* think over

überdies *adv* moreover

überdimensional *a* oversized

Überdosis *f* overdose

Überdruß *m* -sses surfeit; **bis zum Ü~** ad nauseam

überdrüssig *a* **ü~ sein/werden** be/ grow tired *(gen* of)

übereignen *vt insep* transfer

übereilt *a* over-hasty, *adv* -ily
übereinander *adv* one on top of/
above the other; ⟨*sprechen*⟩ about
each other. **ü~schlagen†** *vt sep*
cross ⟨*Beine*⟩; fold ⟨*Arme*⟩
überein|kommen† *vi sep* ⟨*sein*⟩
agree. **Ü~kunft** *f* - agreement. **ü~
stimmen** *vi sep* ⟨*haben*⟩ agree; ⟨*Zahlen:*⟩ tally; ⟨*Ansichten:*⟩ coincide;
⟨*Farben:*⟩ match. **Ü~stimmung** *f*
agreement
überempfindlich *a* over-sensitive;
⟨*Med*⟩ hypersensitive
überfahren† *vt insep* run over
Überfahrt *f* crossing
Überfall *m* attack; ⟨*Bank-*⟩ raid
überfallen† *vt insep* attack; raid
⟨*Bank*⟩; ⟨*überkommen*⟩ come over; ⟨*fam:
besuchen*⟩ surprise
überfällig *a* overdue
überfliegen† *vt insep* fly over;
⟨*lesen*⟩ skim over
überflügeln *vt insep* outstrip
Überfluß *m* abundance; ⟨*Wohlstand*⟩
affluence
überflüssig *a* superfluous
überfluten *vt insep* flood
überfordern *vt insep* overtax
überführ|en *vt insep* transfer; ⟨*Jur*⟩
convict ⟨*gen* of⟩. **Ü~ung** *f* transfer;
⟨*Straße*⟩ flyover; ⟨*Fußgänger-*⟩ foot-
bridge
überfüllt *a* overcrowded
Übergabe *f* ⟨*s.* **übergeben**⟩ handing
over; transfer
Übergang *m* crossing; ⟨*Wechsel*⟩
transition. **Ü~sstadium** *nt* trans-
itional stage
übergeben† *vt insep* hand over;
⟨*übereignen*⟩ transfer; **sich ü~** be sick
übergehen'† *vi sep* ⟨*sein*⟩ pass
⟨**an**+*acc* to⟩; ⟨*überwechseln*⟩ go over
⟨**zu** to⟩; ⟨*werden zu*⟩ turn ⟨**in**+*acc*
into⟩; **zum Angriff ü~** start the attack
übergehen²† *vt insep* ⟨*fig*⟩ pass over;
⟨*nicht beachten*⟩ ignore; ⟨*auslassen*⟩
leave out
Übergewicht *nt* excess weight; ⟨*fig*⟩
predominance; **Ü~ haben** be over-
weight
übergießen† *vt insep* **mit Wasser ü~**
pour water over
überglücklich *a* overjoyed
über|greifen† *vi sep* ⟨*haben*⟩ spread
⟨**auf**+*acc* to⟩. **Ü~griff** *m* infringement

über|groß *a* outsize; ⟨*übertrieben*⟩
exaggerated. **Ü~größe** *f* outsize
überhaben† *vt sep* have on; ⟨*fam:
satthaben*⟩ be fed up with
überhandnehmen† *vi sep* ⟨*haben*⟩
increase alarmingly
überhängen *v sep* ● *vi†* ⟨*haben*⟩
overhang ● *vt* ⟨*reg*⟩ **sich** ⟨*dat*⟩ **etw ü~**
sling over one's shoulder ⟨*Gewehr*⟩; put
round one's shoulders ⟨*Jacke*⟩
überhäufen *vt insep* inundate ⟨**mit**
with⟩
überhaupt *adv* ⟨*im allgemeinen*⟩
altogether; ⟨*eigentlich*⟩ anyway;
⟨*überdies*⟩ besides; **ü~ nicht/nichts**
not/nothing at all
überheblich *a* arrogant, *adv* -ly.
Ü~keit *f* - arrogance
überhol|en *vt insep* overtake; ⟨*repa-
rieren*⟩ overhaul. **ü~t** *a* outdated.
Ü~ung *f* -,-en overhaul. **Ü~verbot**
nt '**Ü~verbot**' 'no overtaking'
überhören *vt insep* fail to hear;
⟨*nicht beachten*⟩ ignore
überirdisch *a* supernatural
überkochen *vi sep* ⟨*sein*⟩ boil over
überladen† *vt insep* overload ● *a*
over-ornate
überlassen† *vt insep* **jdm etw ü~**
leave sth to s.o.; ⟨*geben*⟩ let s.o. have sth;
sich seinem Schmerz ü~ abandon
oneself to one's grief; **sich** ⟨*dat*⟩
selbst ü~ sein be left to one's own de-
vices
überlasten *vt insep* overload; overtax ⟨*Person*⟩
Überlauf *m* overflow
überlaufen'† *vi sep* ⟨*sein*⟩ overflow;
⟨*Mil, Pol*⟩ defect
überlaufen²† *vt insep* **jdn ü~** ⟨*Gefühl:*⟩ come over s.o. ● *a* overrun;
⟨*Kursus*⟩ over-subscribed
Überläufer *m* defector
überleben *vt/i insep* ⟨*haben*⟩ survive. **Ü~de(r)** *m/f* survivor
überlegen' *vt sep* put over
überlegen² *v insep* ● *vt* [**sich** *dat*] **ü~**
think over, consider; **es sich** ⟨*dat*⟩ **anders ü~** change one's mind ● *vi*
⟨*haben*⟩ think, reflect; **ohne zu ü~**
without thinking
überlegen³ *a* superior; ⟨*herablassend*⟩
supercilious, *adv* -ly. **Ü~heit** *f* - su-
periority
Überlegung *f* -,-en reflection
überliefer|n *vt insep* hand down.
Ü~ung *f* tradition
überlisten *vt insep* outwit

überm *prep* = über dem

Über|macht *f* superiority. **ü~-mächtig** *a* superior; ⟨*Gefühl*⟩ over-powering

übermannen *vt insep* overcome

Über|maß *nt* excess. **ü~mäßig** *a* excessive, *adv* -ly

Übermensch *m* superman. **ü~lich** *a* superhuman

übermitteln *vt insep* convey; ⟨*senden*⟩ transmit

übermorgen *adv* the day after tomorrow

übermüdet *a* overtired

Über|mut *m* high spirits *pl*. **ü~-mütig** *a* high-spirited ● *adv* in high spirits

übern *prep* = über den

übernächst|e(r,s) *a* next ... but one; **ü~es Jahr** the year after next

übernacht|en *vi insep* (haben) stay overnight. **Ü~ung** *f* -,-en overnight stay; **Ü~ung und Frühstück** bed and breakfast

Übernahme *f* - taking over; ⟨*Comm*⟩ take-over

übernatürlich *a* supernatural

übernehmen† *vt insep* take over; ⟨*annehmen*⟩ take on; **sich ü~** overdo things; ⟨*finanziell*⟩ overreach oneself

überprüf|en *vt insep* check. **Ü~ung** *f* check

überqueren *vt insep* cross

überragen *vt insep* tower above; ⟨*fig*⟩ surpass. **ü~d** *a* outstanding

überrasch|en *vt insep* surprise. **ü~end** *a* surprising, *adv* -ly; ⟨*unerwartet*⟩ unexpected, *adv* -ly. **Ü~ung** *f* -,-en surprise

überreden *vt insep* persuade

überreichen *vt insep* present

überreizt *a* overwrought

überrennen† *vt insep* overrun

Überreste *mpl* remains

überrumpeln *vt insep* take by surprise

übers *prep* = über das

Überschall- *pref* supersonic

überschatten *vt insep* overshadow

überschätzen *vt insep* overestimate

Überschlag *m* rough estimate; ⟨*Sport*⟩ somersault

überschlagen¹† *vt sep* cross ⟨*Beine*⟩

überschlagen²† *vt insep* estimate roughly; ⟨*auslassen*⟩ skip; **sich ü~** somersault; ⟨*Ereignisse:*⟩ happen fast ● *a* tepid

überschnappen *vi sep* (sein) ⟨*fam*⟩ go crazy

überschneiden† (sich) *vr insep* intersect, cross; ⟨*zusammenfallen*⟩ overlap

überschreiben† *vt insep* entitle; ⟨*übertragen*⟩ transfer

überschreiten† *vt insep* cross; ⟨*fig*⟩ exceed

Überschrift *f* heading; ⟨*Zeitungs-*⟩ headline

Über|schuß *m* surplus. **ü~schüssig** *a* surplus

überschütten *vt insep* **ü~ mit** cover with; ⟨*fig*⟩ shower with

überschwemm|en *vt insep* flood; ⟨*fig*⟩ inundate. **Ü~ung** *f* -,-en flood

überschwenglich *a* effusive, *adv* -ly

Übersee in/nach Ü~ overseas; **aus/ von Ü~** from overseas. **Ü~dampfer** *m* ocean liner. **ü~isch** *a* overseas

übersehen† *vt insep* look out over; ⟨*abschätzen*⟩ assess; ⟨*nicht sehen*⟩ overlook, miss; ⟨*ignorieren*⟩ ignore

übersenden† *vt insep* send

übersetzen¹ *vi sep* (haben/sein) cross [over]

übersetz|en² *vt insep* translate. **Ü~er(in)** *m* -s,- ⟨*f* -,-nen⟩ translator. **Ü~ung** *f* -,-en translation

Übersicht *f* overall view; ⟨*Abriß*⟩ summary; ⟨*Tabelle*⟩ table. **ü~lich** *a* clear, *adv* -ly

übersiedel|n *vi sep* (sein), **über-siedeln** *vi insep* (sein) move ⟨nach to⟩. **Ü~lung** *f* move

übersinnlich *a* supernatural

überspannt *a* exaggerated; ⟨*ver-schroben*⟩ eccentric

überspielen *vt insep* ⟨*fig*⟩ cover up; **auf Band ü~** tape

überspitzt *a* exaggerated

überspringen† *vt insep* jump [over]; ⟨*auslassen*⟩ skip

überstehen¹† *vi sep* (haben) project, jut out

überstehen²† *vt insep* come through; get over ⟨*Krankheit*⟩; ⟨*überleben*⟩ survive

übersteigen† *vt insep* climb [over]; ⟨*fig*⟩ exceed

überstimmen *vt insep* outvote

überstreifen *vt sep* slip on

Überstunden *fpl* overtime *sg*; **ü~ machen** work overtime

überstürz|en *vt insep* rush; **sich**

ü~en ⟨*Ereignisse:*⟩ happen fast; ⟨*Worte:*⟩ tumble out. **ü~t a** hasty, *adv* -ily
übertölpeln *vt insep* dupe
übertönen *vt insep* drown [out]
übertrag|bar *a* transferable; ⟨*Med*⟩ infectious. **ü~en†** *vt insep* transfer; ⟨*übergeben*⟩ assign ⟨*dat* to⟩; ⟨*Techn, Med*⟩ transmit; ⟨*Radio, TV*⟩ broadcast; ⟨*übersetzen*⟩ translate; ⟨*anwenden*⟩ apply (**auf**+*acc* to) ● *a* transferred, figurative. **Ü~ung** *f* -,-en transfer; transmission; broadcast; translation; application
übertreffen† *vt insep* surpass; ⟨*übersteigen*⟩ exceed; **sich selbst ü~** excel oneself
übertreib|en† *vt insep* exaggerate; ⟨*zu weit treiben*⟩ overdo. **Ü~ung** *f* -,-en exaggeration
übertreten¹† *vi sep* (*sein*) step over the line; ⟨*Pol*⟩ go over/⟨*Relig*⟩ convert (**zu** to)
übertret|en²† *vt insep* infringe; break ⟨*Gesetz*⟩. **Ü~ung** *f* -,-en infringement; breach
übertrieben *a* exaggerated; ⟨*übermäßig*⟩ excessive, *adv* -ly
übervölkert *a* overpopulated
übervorteilen *vt insep* cheat
überwachen *vt insep* supervise; ⟨*kontrollieren*⟩ monitor; ⟨*bespitzeln*⟩ keep under surveillance
überwachsen *a* overgrown
überwältigen *vt insep* overpower; ⟨*fig*⟩ overwhelm. **ü~d** *a* overwhelming
überweis|en† *vt insep* transfer; refer ⟨*Patienten*⟩. **Ü~ung** *f* transfer; ⟨*ärztliche*⟩ referral
überwerfen¹† *vt sep* throw on ⟨*Mantel*⟩
überwerfen²† (**sich**) *vr insep* fall out (**mit** with)
überwiegen† *v insep* ● *vi* (*haben*) predominate ● *vt* outweigh. **ü~d** *a* predominant, *adv* -ly
überwind|en† *vt insep* overcome; **sich ü~en** force oneself. **Ü~ung** *f* effort
Überwurf *m* wrap; ⟨*Bett-*⟩ bedspread
Über|zahl *f* majority. **ü~zählig** *a* spare
überzeug|en *vt insep* convince; **sich [selbst] ü~en** satisfy oneself. **ü~end** *a* convincing, *adv* -ly. **Ü~ung** *f* -,-en conviction
überziehen¹† *vt sep* put on

überziehen²† *vt insep* cover; overdraw ⟨*Konto*⟩
Überzug *m* cover; ⟨*Schicht*⟩ coating
üblich *a* usual; ⟨*gebräuchlich*⟩ customary
U-Boot *nt* submarine
übrig *a* remaining; ⟨*andere*⟩ other; **alles ü~e** [all] the rest; **im ü~en** besides; ⟨*ansonsten*⟩ apart from that; **ü~ sein** be left [over]; **etw ü~ haben** have sth left [over]. **ü~bleiben†** *vi sep* ⟨*sein*⟩ be left [over]; **uns blieb nichts anderes ü~** we had no choice. **ü~ens** *adv* by the way. **ü~lassen†** *vt sep* leave [over]
Übung *f* -,-en exercise; ⟨*Üben*⟩ practice; **außer** *od* **aus der Ü~** out of practice

UdSSR *f* - USSR
Ufer *nt* -s,- shore; ⟨*Fluß-*⟩ bank
Uhr *f* -,-en clock; ⟨*Armband-*⟩ watch; ⟨*Zähler*⟩ meter; **um ein U~** at one o'clock; **wieviel U~ ist es?** what's the time? **U~armband** *nt* watch-strap. **U~macher** *m* -s,- watch and clockmaker. **U~werk** *nt* clock/watch mechanism. **U~zeiger** *m* [clock-/watch-]hand. **U~zeigersinn** *m* im/entgegen dem **U~zeigersinn** clockwise/anticlockwise. **U~zeit** *f* time
Uhu *m* -s,-s eagle owl
UKW *abbr* (**Ultrakurzwelle**) VHF
Ulk *m* -s fun; ⟨*Streich*⟩ trick. **u~en** *vi* (*haben*) joke. **u~ig** *a* funny; ⟨*seltsam*⟩ odd, *adv* -ly
Ulme *f* -,-n elm
Ultimatum *nt* -s,-ten ultimatum
Ultrakurzwelle *f* very high frequency
Ultraschall *m* ultrasound
ultraviolett *a* ultraviolet
um *prep* (+*acc*) [a]round; ⟨*Uhrzeit*⟩ at; ⟨*bitten, kämpfen*⟩ for; ⟨*streiten*⟩ over; ⟨*sich sorgen*⟩ about; ⟨*betrügen*⟩ out of; ⟨*bei Angabe einer Differenz*⟩ by; **um [... herum]** around, [round] about; **Tag um Tag** day after day; **einen Tag um den andern** every other day; **um seinetwillen** for his sake ● *adv* ⟨*ungefähr*⟩ around, about ● *conj* **um zu** to; ⟨*Absicht*⟩ [in order] to; **zu müde, um zu ... too** tired to ...; **um so besser** all the better
umändern *vt sep* alter
umarbeiten *vt sep* alter; ⟨*bearbeiten*⟩ revise

umarm|en vt insep embrace, hug.
U~ung f -, -en embrace, hug

Umbau m rebuilding; conversion (**zu**
into). **u~en** vt sep rebuild; convert
(**zu** into)

umbild|en vt sep change; (umge-
stalten) reorganize; reshuffle ⟨Ka-
binett⟩. **U~ung** f reorganization;
(Pol) reshuffle

umbinden† vt sep put on

umblättern v sep ● vt turn [over]
● vi (haben) turn the page

umblicken (sich) vr sep look round;
(zurück-) look back

umbringen† vt sep kill; **sich u~** kill
oneself

Umbruch m (fig) radical change

umbuchen v sep ● vt change;
(Comm) transfer ● vi (haben) change
one's booking

umdrehen v sep ● vt turn round/
(wenden) over; turn ⟨Schlüssel⟩;
(umkrempeln) turn inside out; **sich
u~** turn round; (im Liegen) turn over
● vi (haben/sein) turn back

Umdrehung f turn; (Motor-) revolution

umeinander adv around each other;
sich u~ sorgen worry about each
other

umfahren[1]† vt sep run over

umfahren[2]† vt insep go round; by-pass
⟨Ort⟩

umfallen† vi sep (sein) fall over;
(Person:) fall down

Umfang m girth; (Geom) circumference; (Größe) size; (Ausmaß) extent; (Mus) range

umfangen† vt insep embrace; (fig)
envelop

umfangreich a extensive; (dick) big

umfassen vt insep consist of, comprise; (umgeben) surround. **u~d** a
comprehensive

Umfrage f survey, poll

umfüllen vt sep transfer

umfunktionieren vt sep convert

Umgang m [social] contact;
(Umgehen) dealing (**mit** with); **U~
haben mit** associate with

umgänglich a sociable

Umgangs|formen fpl manners.
U~sprache f colloquial language.
u~sprachlich a colloquial, adv -ly

umgeb|en† vt/i insep (haben) sur-
round ● a **u~en von** surrounded by.
U~ung f -, -en surroundings pl

umgehen[1]† vi sep (sein) go round;
u~ mit treat, handle; (verkehren) associate with; **in dem Schloß geht ein
Gespenst um** the castle is haunted

umgehen[2]† vt insep avoid; (nicht
beachten) evade; ⟨Straße:⟩ bypass

umgehend a immediate, adv -ly

Umgehungsstraße f bypass

umgekehrt a inverse; ⟨Reihenfolge⟩
reverse; **es war u~** it was the other
way round ● adv conversely; **und u~**
and vice versa

umgraben† vt sep dig [over]

umhaben† vt sep have on

Umhang m cloak

umhauen† vt sep knock down;
(fällen) chop down

umher adv **weit u~** all around.
u~gehen† vi sep (sein) walk about

umhören (sich) vr sep ask around

Umkehr f - turning back. **u~en** v sep
● vi (sein) turn back ● vt turn round;
turn inside out ⟨Tasche⟩; (fig) reverse. **U~ung** f - reversal

umkippen v sep ● vt tip over; (versehentlich) knock over ● vi (sein) fall
over; ⟨Boot:⟩ capsize; (fam: ohnmächtig werden) faint

Umkleide|kabine f changing-
cubicle. **u~n (sich)** vr sep change.
U~raum m changing-room

umknicken v sep ● vt bend; (falten)
fold ● vi (sein) bend; (mit dem Fuß) go
over on one's ankle

umkommen† vi sep (sein) perish;
u~ lassen waste ⟨Lebensmittel⟩

Umkreis m surroundings pl; **im U~
von** within a radius of

umkreisen vt insep circle; (Astr)
revolve around; ⟨Satellit:⟩ orbit

umkrempeln vt sep turn up; (von
innen nach außen) turn inside out;
(ändern) change radically

Umlauf m circulation; (Astr) revolution. **U~bahn** f orbit

Umlaut m umlaut

umlegen vt sep lay or put down; flatten ⟨Getreide⟩; turn down ⟨Kragen⟩;
put on ⟨Schal⟩; throw ⟨Hebel⟩; (verlegen) transfer; (fam: niederschlagen) knock down; (töten) kill

umleit|en vt sep divert. **U~ung** f
diversion

umliegend a surrounding

umpflanzen vt sep transplant

umrahmen vt insep frame

umranden vt insep edge

umräumen vt sep rearrange

umrechn|en vt sep convert. **U~ung** f conversion

umreißen¹† vt sep tear down; knock down ⟨Person⟩

umreißen²† vt insep outline

umringen vt insep surround

Umriß m outline

umrühren vt/i sep (haben) stir

ums pron = um das; **u~ Leben kommen** lose one's life

Umsatz m (Comm) turnover

umschalten vt/i sep (haben) switch over; **auf Rot u~** ⟨Ampel:⟩ change to red

Umschau f **U~ halten nach** look out for. **u~en (sich)** vr sep look round/ ⟨zurück⟩ back

Umschlag m cover; ⟨Schutz-⟩ jacket; ⟨Brief-⟩ envelope; ⟨Med⟩ compress; ⟨Hosen-⟩ turn-up; ⟨Wechsel⟩ change. **u~en**† v sep ● vt turn up; turn over ⟨Seite⟩; ⟨fällen⟩ chop down ● vi (sein) topple over; ⟨Boot:⟩ capsize; ⟨Wetter:⟩ change; ⟨Wind:⟩ veer

umschließen† vt insep enclose

umschnallen vt sep buckle on

umschreiben¹† vt sep rewrite

umschreib|en²† vt insep define; ⟨anders ausdrücken⟩ paraphrase. **U~ung** f definition; paraphrase

umschulen vt sep retrain; ⟨Sch⟩ transfer to another school

Umschweife pl **keine U~ machen** come straight out with it; **ohne U~** straight out

Umschwung m ⟨fig⟩ change; ⟨Pol⟩ U-turn

umsehen† **(sich)** vr sep look round; ⟨zurück⟩ look back; **sich u~ nach** look for

umsein† vi sep (sein) (fam) be over; ⟨Zeit:⟩ be up

umseitig a & adv overleaf

umsetzen vt sep move; ⟨umpflanzen⟩ transplant; ⟨Comm⟩ sell

Umsicht f circumspection. **u~ig** a circumspect, adv -ly

umsied|eln v sep ● vt resettle ● vi (sein) move. **U~lung** f resettlement

umsonst adv in vain; ⟨grundlos⟩ without reason; ⟨gratis⟩ free

umspringen† vi sep (sein) change; ⟨Wind:⟩ veer; **übel u~ mit** treat badly

Umstand m circumstance; ⟨Tatsache⟩ fact; ⟨Aufwand⟩ fuss; ⟨Mühe⟩ trouble; **unter U~̃en** possibly; **U~̃e machen** make a fuss; **jdm U~̃e**

machen put s.o. to trouble; **in andern U~̃en** pregnant

umständlich a laborious, adv -ly; ⟨kompliziert⟩ involved; ⟨Person⟩ fussy

Umstands|kleid nt maternity dress. **U~wort** nt (pl -wörter) adverb

umstehen† vi insep surround

Umstehende pl bystanders

umsteigen† vi sep (sein) change

umstellen¹ vt insep surround

umstell|en² vt sep rearrange; transpose ⟨Wörter⟩; ⟨anders einstellen⟩ reset; ⟨Techn⟩ convert; ⟨ändern⟩ change; **sich u~en** adjust. **U~ung** f rearrangement; transposition; resetting; conversion; change; adjustment

umstimmen vt sep **jdn u~** change s.o.'s mind

umstoßen† vt sep knock over; ⟨fig⟩ overturn; upset ⟨Plan⟩

umstritten a controversial; ⟨ungeklärt⟩ disputed

umstülpen vt sep turn upside down; ⟨von innen nach außen⟩ turn inside out

Um|sturz m coup. **u~stürzen** v sep ● vt overturn; ⟨Pol⟩ overthrow ● vi (sein) fall over

umtaufen vt sep rename

Umtausch m exchange. **u~en** vt sep change; exchange ⟨gegen for⟩

umwälzend a revolutionary

umwandeln vt sep convert; ⟨fig⟩ transform

umwechseln vt sep change

Umweg m detour; **auf U~en** in a roundabout way

Umwelt f environment. **u~freundlich** a environmentally friendly. **U~schutz** m protection of the environment. **U~schützer** m environmentalist

umwenden† vt sep turn over; **sich u~** turn round

umwerfen† vt sep knock over; ⟨fig⟩ upset ⟨Plan⟩; ⟨fam⟩ bowl over ⟨Person⟩

umziehen† v sep ● vi (sein) move ● vt change; **sich u~** change

umzingeln vt insep surround

Umzug m move; ⟨Prozession⟩ procession

unabänderlich a irrevocable; ⟨Tatsache⟩ unalterable

unabhängig a independent, adv -ly; **u~ davon, ob** irrespective of whether. **U~keit** f - independence

unabkömmlich *pred a* busy
unablässig *a* incessant, *adv* -ly
unabsehbar *a* incalculable
unabsichtlich *a* unintentional,
 adv -ly
unachtsam *a* careless, *adv* -ly. **U∼keit** *f* - carelessness
unangebracht *a* inappropriate
unangemeldet *a* unexpected, *adv* -ly
unangemessen *a* inappropriate, *adv* -ly
unangenehm *a* unpleasant, *adv* -ly; (*peinlich*) embarrassing
Unannehmlichkeiten *fpl* trouble *sg*
unansehnlich *a* shabby; (*Person*) plain
unanständig *a* indecent, *adv* -ly
unantastbar *a* inviolable
unappetitlich *a* unappetizing
Unart *f* -,-en bad habit. **u∼ig** *a* naughty
unauffällig *a* inconspicuous, *adv* -ly, unobtrusive, *adv* -ly
unauffindbar *a* **u∼ sein** be nowhere to be found
unaufgefordert *adv* without being asked
unaufhaltsam *a* inexorable, *adv* -bly. **u∼hörlich** *a* incessant, *adv* -ly
unaufmerksam *a* inattentive
unaufrichtig *a* insincere
unausbleiblich *a* inevitable
unausgeglichen *a* unbalanced; (*Person*) unstable
unauslöschlich *a* (*fig*) indelible, *adv* -bly. **u∼sprechlich** *a* indescribable, *adv* -bly. **u∼stehlich** *a* insufferable
unbarmherzig *a* merciless, *adv* -ly
unbeabsichtigt *a* unintentional, *adv* -ly
unbedacht *a* rash, *adv* -ly
unbedenklich *a* harmless ● *adv* without hesitation
unbedeutend *a* insignificant; (*geringfügig*) slight, *adv* -ly
unbedingt *a* absolute, *adv* -ly; **nicht u∼** not necessarily
unbefangen *a* natural, *adv* -ly; (*unparteiisch*) impartial
unbefriedig|end *a* unsatisfactory. **u∼t** *a* dissatisfied
unbefugt *a* unauthorized ● *adv* without authorization
unbegreiflich *a* incomprehensible
unbegrenzt *a* unlimited ● *adv* indefinitely

unbegründet *a* unfounded
Unbehag|en *nt* unease; (*körperlich*) discomfort. **u∼lich** *a* uncomfortable, *adv* -bly
unbeholfen *a* awkward, *adv* -ly
unbekannt *a* unknown; (*nicht vertraut*) unfamiliar. **U∼e(r)** *m/f* stranger
unbekümmert *a* unconcerned; (*unbeschwert*) carefree
unbeliebt *a* unpopular. **U∼heit** *f* unpopularity
unbemannt *a* unmanned
unbemerkt *a & adv* unnoticed
unbenutzt *a* unused
unbequem *a* uncomfortable, *adv* -bly; (*lästig*) awkward
unberechenbar *a* unpredictable
unberechtigt *a* unjustified; (*unbefugt*) unauthorized
unberufen *int* touch wood!
unberührt *a* untouched; (*fig*) virgin; (*Landschaft*) unspoilt
unbescheiden *a* presumptuous
unbeschrankt *a* unguarded
unbeschränkt *a* unlimited ● *adv* without limit
unbeschreiblich *a* indescribable, *adv* -bly
unbeschwert *a* carefree
unbesiegbar *a* invincible
unbesiegt *a* undefeated
unbesonnen *a* rash, *adv* -ly
unbespielt *a* blank
unbeständig *a* inconsistent; (*Wetter*) unsettled
unbestechlich *a* incorruptible
unbestimmt *a* indefinite; (*Alter*) indeterminate; (*ungewiß*) uncertain; (*unklar*) vague ● *adv* vaguely
unbestreitbar *a* indisputable, *adv* -bly
unbestritten *a* undisputed ● *adv* indisputably
unbeteiligt *a* indifferent; **u∼ an** (+ *dat*) not involved in
unbetont *a* unstressed
unbewacht *a* unguarded
unbewaffnet *a* unarmed
unbeweglich *a & adv* motionless, still
unbewohnt *a* uninhabited
unbewußt *a* unconscious, *adv* -ly
unbezahlbar *a* priceless
unbezahlt *a* unpaid
unbrauchbar *a* useless
und *conj* and; **und so weiter** and so on; **nach und nach** bit by bit

Undank *m* ingratitude. **u~bar** *a* ungrateful; (*nicht lohnend*) thankless. **U~barkeit** *f* ingratitude

undefinierbar *a* indefinable

undenk|bar *a* unthinkable. **u~lich** *a* seit **u~lichen Zeiten** from time immemorial

undeutlich *a* indistinct, *adv* -ly; (*vage*) vague, *adv* -ly

undicht *a* leaking; **u~e Stelle** leak

Unding *nt* absurdity

undiplomatisch *a* undiplomatic, *adv* -ally

unduldsam *a* intolerant

undurch|dringlich *a* impenetrable; (*Miene*) inscrutable. **u~führbar** *a* impracticable

undurch|lässig *a* impermeable. **u~sichtig** *a* opaque; (*fig*) doubtful

uneben *a* uneven, *adv* -ly. **U~heit** *f* -,-**en** unevenness; (*Buckel*) bump

unecht *a* false; **u~er Schmuck/Pelz** imitation jewellery/fur

unehelich *a* illegitimate

unehr|enhaft *a* dishonourable, *adv* -bly. **u~lich** *a* dishonest, *adv* -ly. **U~lichkeit** *f* dishonesty

uneinig *a* (*fig*) divided; [sich (*dat*)] **u~ sein** disagree. **U~keit** *f* disagreement; (*Streit*) discord

uneins *a* **u~ sein** be at odds

unempfindlich *a* insensitive (**gegen** to); (*widerstandsfähig*) tough; (*Med*) immune

unendlich *a* infinite, *adv* -ly; (*endlos*) endless, *adv* -ly. **U~keit** *f* - infinity

unentbehrlich *a* indispensable

unentgeltlich *a* free; (*Arbeit*) unpaid ● *adv* free of charge; (*arbeiten*) without pay

unentschieden *a* undecided; (*Sport*) drawn; **u~ spielen** draw. **U~** *nt* -s,- draw

unentschlossen *a* indecisive; (*unentschieden*) undecided. **U~heit** *f* indecision

unentwegt *a* persistent, *adv* -ly; (*unaufhörlich*) incessant, *adv* -ly

unerbittlich *a* implacable, *adv* -bly; (*Schicksal*) inexorable

unerfahren *a* inexperienced. **U~heit** *f* - inexperience

unerfreulich *a* unpleasant, *adv* -ly

unergründlich *a* unfathomable

unerhört *a* enormous, *adv* -ly; (*empörend*) outrageous, *adv* -ly

unerklärlich *a* inexplicable

unerläßlich *a* essential

unerlaubt *a* unauthorized ● *adv* without permission

unermeßlich *a* immense, *adv* -ly

unermüdlich *a* tireless, *adv* -ly

unersättlich *a* insatiable

unerschöpflich *a* inexhaustible

unerschütterlich *a* unshakeable

unerschwinglich *a* prohibitive

unersetzlich *a* irreplaceable; (*Verlust*) irreparable

unerträglich *a* unbearable, *adv* -bly

unerwartet *a* unexpected, *adv* -ly

unerwünscht *a* unwanted; (*Besuch*) unwelcome

unfähig *a* incompetent; **u~, etw zu tun** incapable of doing sth; (*nicht in der Lage*) unable to do sth. **U~keit** *f* incompetence; inability (**zu** to)

unfair *a* unfair, *adv* -ly

Unfall *m* accident. **U~flucht** *f* failure to stop after an accident. **U~station** *f* casualty department

unfaßbar *a* incomprehensible; (*unglaublich*) unimaginable

unfehlbar *a* infallible. **U~keit** *f* - infallibility

unfolgsam *a* disobedient

unförmig *a* shapeless

unfreiwillig *a* involuntary, *adv* -ily; (*unbeabsichtigt*) unintentional, *adv* -ly

unfreundlich *a* unfriendly; (*unangenehm*) unpleasant, *adv* -ly. **U~keit** *f* unfriendliness; unpleasantness

Unfriede[n] *m* discord

unfruchtbar *a* infertile; (*fig*) unproductive. **U~keit** *f* infertility

Unfug *m* -s mischief; (*Unsinn*) nonsense

Ungar|(in) *m* -n,-n (*f* -,-**nen**) Hungarian. **u~isch** *a* Hungarian. **U~n** *nt* -s Hungary

ungastlich *a* inhospitable

ungeachtet *prep* (+ *gen*) in spite of.

ungebärdig *a* unruly. **ungebeugt** *a* (*Gram*) uninflected. **ungebraucht** *a* unused. **ungebührlich** *a* improper, *adv* -ly. **ungedeckt** *a* uncovered; (*Sport*) unmarked; (*Tisch*) unlaid

Ungeduld *f* impatience. **u~ig** *a* impatient, *adv* -ly

ungeeignet *a* unsuitable

ungefähr *a* approximate, *adv* -ly, rough, *adv* -ly

ungefährlich *a* harmless

ungehalten *a* angry, *adv* -ily

ungeheuer *a* enormous, *adv* -ly. **U~** *nt* **-s,** - monster

ungeheuerlich *a* outrageous

ungehobelt *a* uncouth

ungehörig *a* improper, *adv* -ly; (*frech*) impertinent, *adv* -ly

ungehorsam *a* disobedient. **U~** *m* disobedience

ungeklärt *a* unsolved; ⟨*Frage*⟩ unsettled; ⟨*Ursache*⟩ unknown

ungeladen *a* unloaded; ⟨*Gast*⟩ uninvited

ungelegen *a* inconvenient. **U~heiten** *fpl* trouble *sg*

ungelernt *a* unskilled. **ungemein** *a* tremendous, *adv* -ly

ungemütlich *a* uncomfortable, *adv* -bly; (*unangenehm*) unpleasant, *adv* -ly

ungenau *a* inaccurate, *adv* -ly; (*vage*) vague, *adv* -ly. **U~igkeit** *f* -,-**en** inaccuracy

ungeniert /'ʊnʒeniːɐt/ *a* uninhibited ● *adv* openly

ungenießbar *a* inedible; ⟨*Getränk*⟩ undrinkable. **ungenügend** *a* inadequate, *adv* -ly; ⟨*Sch*⟩ unsatisfactory. **ungepflegt** *a* neglected; ⟨*Person*⟩ unkempt. **ungerade** *a* ⟨*Zahl*⟩ odd

ungerecht *a* unjust, *adv* -ly. **U~igkeit** *f* -,-**en** injustice

ungern *adv* reluctantly

ungesalzen *a* unsalted

ungeschehen *a* **u~ machen** undo

Ungeschick|lichkeit *f* clumsiness. **u~t** *a* clumsy, *adv* -ily

ungeschminkt *a* without make-up; ⟨*Wahrheit*⟩ unvarnished. **ungeschrieben** *a* unwritten. **ungesehen** *a* & *adv* unseen. **ungesellig** *a* unsociable. **ungesetzlich** *a* illegal, *adv* -ly. **ungestört** *a* undisturbed. **ungestraft** *adv* with impunity. **ungestüm** *a* impetuous, *adv* -ly. **ungesund** *a* unhealthy. **ungesüßt** *a* unsweetened. **ungetrübt** *a* perfect

Ungetüm *nt* **-s,-e** monster

ungewiß *a* uncertain; **im ungewissen lassen** leave in the dark. **U~heit** *f* uncertainty

ungewöhnlich *a* unusual, *adv* -ly. **ungewohnt** *a* unaccustomed; (*nicht vertraut*) unfamiliar. **ungewollt** *a* unintentional, *adv* -ly; ⟨*Schwangerschaft*⟩ unwanted

Ungeziefer *nt* **-s** vermin

ungezogen *a* naughty, *adv* -ily

ungezwungen *a* informal, *adv* -ly; (*natürlich*) natural, *adv* -ly

ungläubig *a* incredulous

unglaublich *a* incredible, *adv* -bly, unbelievable, *adv* -bly

ungleich *a* unequal, *adv* -ly; (*verschieden*) different. **U~heit** *f* - inequality. **u~mäßig** *a* uneven, *adv* -ly

Unglück *nt* **-s,-e** misfortune; (*Pech*) bad luck; (*Mißgeschick*) mishap; (*Unfall*) accident; **U~ bringen** be unlucky. **u~lich** *a* unhappy, *adv* -ily; (*ungünstig*) unfortunate, *adv* -ly. **u~licherweise** *adv* unfortunately. **u~selig** *a* unfortunate. **U~sfall** *m* accident

ungültig *a* invalid; (*Jur*) void

ungünstig *a* unfavourable, *adv* -bly; (*unpassend*) inconvenient, *adv* -ly

ungut *a* ⟨*Gefühl*⟩ uneasy; **nichts für u~!** no offence!

unhandlich *a* unwieldy

Unheil *nt* **-s** disaster; **U~ anrichten** cause havoc

unheilbar *a* incurable, *adv* -bly

unheimlich *a* eerie; (*gruselig*) creepy; (*fam: groß*) terrific ● *adv* eerily; (*fam: sehr*) terribly

unhöflich *a* rude, *adv* -ly. **U~keit** *f* rudeness

unhörbar *a* inaudible, *adv* -bly

unhygienisch *a* unhygienic

Uni *f* -,-**s** (*fam*) university

uni /y'niː/ *inv a* plain

Uniform *f* -,-**en** uniform

uninteress|ant *a* uninteresting. **u~iert** *a* uninterested; (*unbeteiligt*) disinterested

Union *f* -,-**en** union

universal *a* universal

universell *a* universal, *adv* -ly

Universität *f* -,-**en** university

Universum *nt* **-s** universe

unkenntlich *a* unrecognizable. **U~nis** *f* ignorance

unklar *a* unclear; (*ungewiß*) uncertain; (*vage*) vague, *adv* -ly; **im u~en sein** be in the dark. **U~heit** *f* -,-**en** uncertainty

unklug *a* unwise, *adv* -ly

unkompliziert *a* uncomplicated

Unkosten *pl* expenses

Unkraut *nt* weed; (*coll*) weeds *pl*; **U~ jäten** weed. **U~vertilgungsmittel** *nt* weed-killer

unkultiviert *a* uncultured

unlängst *adv* recently

unlauter *a* dishonest; (*unfair*) unfair

unleserlich *a* illegible, *adv* -bly

unleugbar *a* undeniable, *adv* -bly

unlogisch *a* illogical, *adv* -ly

unlös|bar *a* (*fig*) insoluble. **u~lich** *a* (*Chem*) insoluble

unlustig *a* listless, *adv* -ly

unmäßig *a* excessive, *adv* -ly; (*äußerst*) extreme, *adv* -ly

Unmenge *f* enormous amount/(*Anzahl*) number

Unmensch *m* (*fam*) brute. **u~lich** *a* inhuman; (*entsetzlich*) appalling, *adv* -ly

unmerklich *a* imperceptible, *adv* -bly

unmißverständlich *a* unambiguous, *adv* -ly; (*offen*) unequivocal, *adv* -ly

unmittelbar *a* immediate, *adv* -ly; (*direkt*) direct, *adv* -ly

unmöbliert *a* unfurnished

unmodern *a* old-fashioned

unmöglich *a* impossible, *adv* -bly. **U~keit** *f* - impossibility

Unmoral *f* immorality. **u~isch** *a* immoral, *adv* -ly

unmündig *a* under-age

Unmut *m* displeasure

unnachahmlich *a* inimitable

unnachgiebig *a* intransigent

unnatürlich *a* unnatural, *adv* -ly

unnormal *a* abnormal, *adv* -ly

unnötig *a* unnecessary, *adv* -ily

unnütz *a* useless ● *adv* needlessly

unord|entlich *a* untidy, *adv* -ily; (*nachlässig*) sloppy, *adv* -ily. **U~nung** *f* disorder; (*Durcheinander*) muddle

unorganisiert *a* disorganized

unorthodox *a* unorthodox ● *adv* in an unorthodox manner

unparteiisch *a* impartial, *adv* -ly

unpassend *a* inappropriate, *adv* -ly; (*Moment*) inopportune

unpäßlich *a* indisposed

unpersönlich *a* impersonal

unpraktisch *a* impractical

unpünktlich *a* unpunctual ● *adv* late

unrasiert *a* unshaven

Unrast *f* restlessness

unrealistisch *a* unrealistic, *adv* -ally

unrecht *a* wrong, *adv* -ly ● *n* **u~ haben** be wrong; **jdm u~ tun** do s.o. an injustice; **jdm u~ geben** disagree with s.o. **U~** *nt* wrong; **zu U~** wrongly. **u~mäßig** *a* unlawful, *adv* -ly

unregelmäßig *a* irregular, *adv* -ly. **U~keit** *f* irregularity

unreif *a* unripe; (*fig*) immature

unrein *a* impure; (*Luft*) polluted; (*Haut*) bad; **ins u~e schreiben** make a rough draft of

unrentabel *a* unprofitable, *adv* -bly

unrichtig *a* incorrect

Unruh|e *f* -,-n restlessness; (*Erregung*) agitation; (*Besorgnis*) anxiety; **U~en** (*Pol*) unrest *sg*. **u~ig** *a* restless, *adv* -ly; (*Meer*) agitated; (*laut*) noisy, *adv* -ily; (*besorgt*) anxious, *adv* -ly

uns *pron* (*acc/dat of* **wir**) us; (*refl*) ourselves; (*einander*) each other; **ein Freund von uns** a friend of ours

unsagbar, unsäglich *a* indescribable, *adv* -bly

unsanft *a* rough, *adv* -ly

unsauber *a* dirty; (*nachlässig*) sloppy, *adv* -ily; (*unlauter*) dishonest, *adv* -ly

unschädlich *a* harmless

unscharf *a* blurred

unschätzbar *a* inestimable

unscheinbar *a* inconspicuous

unschicklich *a* improper, *adv* -ly

unschlagbar *a* unbeatable

unschlüssig *a* undecided

Unschuld *f* - innocence; (*Jungfräulichkeit*) virginity. **u~ig** *a* innocent, *adv* -ly

unselbständig *a* dependent ● *adv* **u~ denken** not think for oneself

unser *poss pron* our. **u~e(r,s)** *poss pron* ours. **u~erseits** *adv* for our part. **u~twegen** *adv* for our sake; (*wegen uns*) because of us, on our account. **u~twillen** *adv* **um u~twillen** for our sake

unsicher *a* unsafe; (*ungewiß*) uncertain; (*nicht zuverlässig*) unreliable; (*Schritte, Hand*) unsteady; (*Person*) insecure ● *adv* unsteadily. **U~heit** *f* uncertainty; unreliability; insecurity

unsichtbar *a* invisible

Unsinn *m* nonsense. **u~ig** *a* nonsensical, absurd

Unsitt|e *f* bad habit. **u~lich** *a* indecent, *adv* -ly

unsportlich *a* not sporty; (*unfair*) unsporting, *adv* -ly

uns|re(r,s) *poss pron* = **unsere(r,s)**. **u~rige** *poss pron* **der/die/das u~rige** ours

unsterblich *a* immortal. **U~keit** *f* immortality

unstet *a* restless, *adv* -ly; (*unbeständig*) unstable

Unstimmigkeit *f* -,-en inconsistency; (*Streit*) difference

Unsumme *f* vast sum

unsymmetrisch *a* not symmetrical

unsympathisch *a* unpleasant; **er ist mir u∼** I don't like him

untätig *a* idle, *adv* idly. **U∼keit** *f* - idleness

untauglich *a* unsuitable; (*Mil*) unfit

unteilbar *a* indivisible

unten *adv* at the bottom; (*auf der Unterseite*) underneath; (*eine Treppe tiefer*) downstairs; **hier/da u∼** down here/there; **nach u∼** down[wards]; (*die Treppe hinunter*) downstairs

unter *prep* (+ *dat/acc*) under; (*niedriger als*) below; (*inmitten, zwischen*) among; **u∼ anderem** among other things; **u∼ der Woche** during the week; **u∼ sich** by themselves; **u∼ uns gesagt** between ourselves

Unter|arm *m* forearm. **U∼bewußtsein** *nt* subconscious

unterbieten† *vt insep* undercut; beat (*Rekord*)

unterbinden† *vt insep* stop

unterbleiben† *vi insep* (*sein*) cease; **es hat zu u∼** it must stop

unterbrech|en† *vt insep* interrupt; break (*Reise*). **U∼ung** *f* -,-en interruption; break

unterbreiten *vt insep* present

unterbringen† *vt sep* put; (*beherbergen*) put up

unterdessen *adv* in the meantime

unterdrück|en *vt insep* suppress; oppress (*Volk*). **U∼ung** *f* - suppression; oppression

untere(r,s) *a* lower

untereinander *adv* one below the other; (*miteinander*) among ourselves/yourselves/themselves

unterernähr|t *a* undernourished. **U∼ung** *f* malnutrition

Unterfangen *nt* -s,- venture

Unterführung *f* underpass; (*Fußgänger-*) subway

Untergang *m* (*Astr*) setting; (*Naut*) sinking; (*Zugrundegehen*) disappearance; (*der Welt*) end

Untergebene(r) *m/f* subordinate

untergehen† *vi sep* (*sein*) (*Astr*) set; (*versinken*) go under; (*Schiff:*) go down, sink; (*zugrunde gehen*) disappear; (*Welt:*) come to an end

untergeordnet *a* subordinate

Untergeschoß *nt* basement

untergraben† *vt insep* (*fig*) undermine

Untergrund *m* foundation; (*Hintergrund*) background; (*Pol*) underground. **U∼bahn** *f* underground [railway], (*Amer*) subway

unterhaken *vt sep* **jdn u∼** take s.o.'s arm; **untergehakt** arm in arm

unterhalb *adv & prep* (+ *gen*) below

Unterhalt *m* maintenance

unterhalt|en† *vt insep* maintain; (*ernähren*) support; (*betreiben*) run; (*erheitern*) entertain; **sich u∼en** talk; (*sich vergnügen*) enjoy oneself. **u∼sam** *a* entertaining. **U∼ung** *f* -,-en maintenance; (*Gespräch*) conversation; (*Zeitvertreib*) entertainment

unterhandeln *vi insep* (*haben*) negotiate

Unter|haus *nt* (*Pol*) lower house; (*in UK*) House of Commons. **U∼hemd** *nt* vest. **U∼holz** *nt* undergrowth. **U∼hose** *f* underpants *pl*. **u∼irdisch** *a & adv* underground

unterjochen *vt insep* subjugate

Unterkiefer *m* lower jaw

unter|kommen† *vi sep* (*sein*) find accommodation; (*eine Stellung finden*) get a job. **u∼kriegen** *vt sep* (*fam*) get down

Unterkunft *f* -,-künfte accommodation

U|nterlage *f* pad; **U∼n** papers

Unterlaß *m* **ohne U∼** incessantly

unterlass|en† *vt insep* **etw u∼en** refrain from [doing] sth; **es u∼en, etw zu tun** fail *or* omit to do sth. **U∼ung** *f* -,-en omission

unterlaufen† *vi insep* (*sein*) occur; **mir ist ein Fehler u∼** I made a mistake

unterlegen[1] *vt sep* put underneath

unterlegen[2] *a* inferior; (*Sport*) losing; **zahlenmäßig u∼** outnumbered (*dat* by). **U∼e(r)** *m/f* loser

Unterleib *m* abdomen

unterliegen† *vi insep* (*sein*) lose (*dat* to); (*unterworfen sein*) be subject (*dat* to)

Unterlippe *f* lower lip

unterm *prep* = **unter dem**

Untermiete *f* **zur U∼ wohnen** be a lodger. **U∼r(in)** *m(f)* lodger

unterminieren *vt insep* undermine

untern *prep* = **unter den**

unternehm|en† *vt insep* undertake; take (*Schritte*); **etw/nichts u∼en** do sth/nothing. **U∼en** *nt* -s,- undertaking, enterprise; (*Betrieb*) concern.

u~end a enterprising. **U~er** m -s,- employer; (*Bau-*) contractor; (*Industrieller*) industrialist. **U~ung** f -,-en undertaking; (*Comm*) venture.

u~ungslustig a enterprising; (*abenteuerlustig*) adventurous

Unteroffizier m non-commissioned officer

unterordnen vt sep subordinate; **sich u~** accept a subordinate role

Unterredung f -,-en talk

Unterricht m -[e]s teaching; (*Privat-*) tuition; (*U~sstunden*) lessons pl; **U~ geben/nehmen** give/have lessons

unterrichten vt/i insep (haben) teach; (*informieren*) inform; **sich u~** inform oneself

Unterrock m slip

unters prep = **unter das**

untersagen vt insep forbid

Untersatz m mat; (*mit Füßen*) stand; (*Gläser-*) coaster

unterschätzen vt insep underestimate

unterscheid|en† vt/i insep (haben) distinguish; (*auseinanderhalten*) tell apart; **sich u~en** differ. **U~ung** f -,-en distinction

Unterschied m -[e]s,-e difference; (*Unterscheidung*) distinction; **im U~ zu ihm** unlike him. **u~lich** a different; (*wechselnd*) varying; **das ist u~lich** it varies. **u~slos** a equal, adv -ly

unterschlag|en† vt insep embezzle; (*verheimlichen*) suppress. **U~ung** f -,-en embezzlement; suppression

Unterschlupf m -[e]s shelter; (*Versteck*) hiding-place

unterschreiben† vt/i insep (haben) sign

Unter|schrift f signature; (*Bild-*) caption. **U~seeboot** nt submarine.

U~setzer m -s,- = **Untersatz**

untersetzt a stocky

Unterstand m shelter

unterste(r,s) a lowest, bottom

unterstehen¹† vi sep (haben) shelter

unterstehen²† v insep ● vi (haben) be answerable (dat to); (*unterliegen*) be subject (dat to) ● vr **sich u~** dare; **untersteh dich!** don't you dare!

unterstellen¹ vt sep put underneath; (*abstellen*) store; **sich u~** shelter

unterstellen² vt insep place under the control (dat of); (*annehmen*) assume; (*fälschlich zuschreiben*) impute (dat to)

unterstreichen† vt insep underline

unterstütz|en vt insep support; (*helfen*) aid. **U~ung** f -,-en support; (*finanziell*) aid; (*regelmäßiger Betrag*) allowance; (*Arbeitslosen-*) benefit

untersuch|en vt insep examine; (*Jur*) investigate; (*prüfen*) test; (*überprüfen*) check; (*durchsuchen*) search. **U~ung** f -,-en examination; investigation; test; check; search. **U~ungshaft** f detention on remand; **in U~ungshaft** on remand. **U~ungsrichter** m examining magistrate

Untertan m -s & -en,-en subject

Untertasse f saucer

untertauchen v sep ● vt duck ● vi (*sein*) go under; (*fig*) disappear

Unterteil nt bottom (part)

unterteilen vt insep subdivide; (*aufteilen*) divide

Untertitel m subtitle

Unterton m undertone

untervermieten vt/i insep (haben) sublet

unterwandern vt insep infiltrate

Unterwäsche f underwear

Unterwasser- pref underwater

unterwegs adv on the way; (*außer Haus*) out; (*verreist*) away

unterweisen† vt insep instruct

Unterwelt f underworld

unterwerfen† vt insep subjugate; **sich u~en** submit (dat to); **etw** (dat) **unterworfen sein** be subject to sth

unterwürfig a obsequious, adv -ly

unterzeichnen vt insep sign

unterziehen¹† vt sep put on underneath; (*Culin*) fold in

unterziehen²† vt insep **etw einer Untersuchung/Überprüfung u~** examine/check sth; **sich einer Operation/Prüfung u~** have an operation/take a test

Untier nt monster

untragbar a intolerable

untrennbar a inseparable

untreu a disloyal; (*in der Ehe*) unfaithful. **U~e** f disloyalty; infidelity

untröstlich a inconsolable

untrüglich a infallible

Untugend f bad habit

unüberlegt a rash, adv -ly

unüber|sehbar a obvious; (*groß*) immense. **u~troffen** a unsurpassed

unum|gänglich a absolutely necessary. **u~schränkt** a absolute. **u~wunden** adv frankly

ununterbrochen a incessant, adv -ly

unveränderlich *a* invariable; (*gleichbleibend*) unchanging

unverändert *a* unchanged

unverantwortlich *a* irresponsible, *adv* -bly

unverbesserlich *a* incorrigible

unverbindlich *a* non-committal; (*Comm*) not binding ● *adv* without obligation

unverblümt *a* blunt ● *adv* -ly

unverdaulich *a* indigestible

unver|einbar *a* incompatible. **u~geßlich** *a* unforgettable. **u~gleichlich** *a* incomparable

unver|hältnismäßig *adv* disproportionately. **u~heiratet** *a* unmarried. **u~hofft** *a* unexpected, *adv* -ly. **u~hohlen** *a* undisguised ● *adv* openly. **u~käuflich** *a* not for sale; ⟨*Muster*⟩ free

unverkennbar *a* unmistakable, *adv* -bly

unverletzt *a* unhurt

unvermeidlich *a* inevitable

unver|mindert *a* & *adv* undiminished. **u~mittelt** *a* abrupt, *adv* -ly. **u~mutet** *a* unexpected, *adv* -ly

Unver|nunft *f* folly. **u~nünftig** *a* foolish, *adv* -ly

unverschämt *a* insolent, *adv* -ly; (*fam: ungeheuer*) outrageous, *adv* -ly. **U~heit** *f* -,-en insolence

unver|sehens *adv* suddenly. **u~sehrt** *a* unhurt; (*unbeschädigt*) intact. **u~söhnlich** *a* irreconcilable; ⟨*Gegner*⟩ implacable

unverständ|lich *a* incomprehensible; (*undeutlich*) indistinct. **U~nis** *nt* lack of understanding

unverträglich *a* incompatible; ⟨*Person*⟩ quarrelsome; (*unbekömmlich*) indigestible

unverwandt *a* fixed, *adv* -ly

unver|wundbar *a* invulnerable. **u~wüstlich** *a* indestructible; ⟨*Person, Humor*⟩ irrepressible; ⟨*Gesundheit*⟩ robust. **u~zeihlich** *a* unforgivable

unverzüglich *a* immediate, *adv* -ly

unvollendet *a* unfinished

unvollkommen *a* imperfect; (*unvollständig*) incomplete. **U~heit** *f* -,-en imperfection

unvollständig *a* incomplete

unvor|bereitet *a* unprepared. **u~eingenommen** *a* unbiased. **u~hergesehen** *a* unforeseen

unvorsichtig *a* careless, *adv* -ly. **U~keit** *f* - carelessness

unvorstellbar *a* unimaginable, *adv* -bly

unvorteilhaft *a* unfavourable; (*nicht hübsch*) unattractive; ⟨*Kleid, Frisur*⟩ unflattering

unwahr *a* untrue. **U~heit** *f* -,-en untruth. **u~scheinlich** *a* unlikely; (*unglaublich*) improbable; (*fam: groß*) incredible, *adv* -bly

unweigerlich *a* inevitable, *adv* -bly

unweit *adv* & *prep* (+ *gen*) not far; **u~ vom Fluß/des Flusses** not far from the river

unwesentlich *a* unimportant ● *adv* slightly

Unwetter *nt* -s,- storm

unwichtig *a* unimportant

unwider|legbar *a* irrefutable. **u~ruflich** *a* irrevocable, *adv* -bly. **u~stehlich** *a* irresistible

Unwill|e *m* displeasure. **u~ig** *a* angry, *adv* -ily; (*widerwillig*) reluctant, *adv* -ly. **u~kürlich** *a* involuntary, *adv* -ily; (*instinktiv*) instinctive, *adv* -ly

unwirklich *a* unreal

unwirksam *a* ineffective

unwirsch *a* irritable, *adv* -bly

unwirtlich *a* inhospitable

unwirtschaftlich *a* uneconomic, *adv* -ally

unwissen|d *a* ignorant. **U~heit** *f* - ignorance

unwohl *a* unwell; (*unbehaglich*) uneasy. **U~sein** *nt* -s indisposition

unwürdig *a* unworthy (*gen* of); (*würdelos*) undignified

Unzahl *f* vast number. **unzählig** *a* innumerable, countless

unzerbrechlich *a* unbreakable

unzerstörbar *a* indestructible

unzertrennlich *a* inseparable

Unzucht *f* sexual offence; **gewerbsmäßige U~** prostitution

unzüchtig *a* indecent, *adv* -ly; ⟨*Schriften*⟩ obscene

unzufrieden *a* dissatisfied; (*innerlich*) discontented. **U~heit** *f* dissatisfaction; (*Pol*) discontent

unzulänglich *a* inadequate, *adv* -ly

unzulässig *a* inadmissible

unzumutbar *a* unreasonable

unzurechnungsfähig *a* insane. **U~keit** *f* insanity

unzusammenhängend *a* incoherent

unzutreffend *a* inapplicable; (*falsch*) incorrect

unzuverlässig *a* unreliable

unzweckmäßig *a* unsuitable, *adv* -bly

unzweideutig *a* unambiguous

unzweifelhaft *a* undoubted, *adv* -ly

üppig *a* luxuriant, *adv* -ly; (*überreichlich*) lavish, *adv* -ly; ⟨*Busen, Figur*⟩ voluptuous

uralt *a* ancient

Uran *nt* -s uranium

Uraufführung *f* first performance

urbar *a* u∼ **machen** cultivate

Ureinwohner *mpl* native inhabitants

Urenkel *m* great-grandson; (*pl*) great-grandchildren

Urgroß|mutter *f* great-grandmother. **U∼vater** *m* great-grandfather

Urheber *m* -s,- originator; (*Verfasser*) author. **U∼recht** *nt* copyright

Urin *m* -s,-e urine

Urkunde *f* -,-n certificate; (*Dokument*) document

Urlaub *m* -s holiday; (*Mil, Admin*) leave; **auf U∼** on holiday/leave; **U∼ haben** be on holiday/leave. **U∼er(in)** *m* -s,- (*f* -,-nen) holiday- maker. **U∼sort** *m* holiday resort

Urne *f* -,-n urn; (*Wahl-*) ballot-box

Ursache *f* cause; (*Grund*) reason; **keine U∼!** don't mention it!

Ursprung *m* origin

ursprünglich *a* original, *adv* -ly; (*anfänglich*) initial, *adv* -ly; (*natürlich*) natural

Urteil *nt* -s,-e judgement; (*Meinung*) opinion; (*U∼sspruch*) verdict; (*Strafe*) sentence. **u∼en** *vi* (*haben*) judge. **U∼svermögen** *nt* [power of] judgement

Urwald *m* primeval forest; (*tropischer*) jungle

urwüchsig *a* natural; (*derb*) earthy

Urzeit *f* primeval times *pl*; **seit U∼en** from time immemorial

USA *pl* USA *sg*

usw. *abbr* (**und so weiter**) etc.

Utensilien /-jən/ *ntpl* utensils

utopisch *a* Utopian

V

vage /'va:gə/ *a* vague, *adv* -ly

Vakuum /'va:kuɔm/ *nt* -s vacuum. **v∼verpackt** *a* vacuum-packed

Vanille /va'nɪljə/ *f* - vanilla

vari|abel /va'rja:bəl/ *a* variable. **V∼ante** *f* -,-n variant. **V∼ation** /-'tsjo:n/ *f* -,-en variation. **v∼ieren** *vt/i* (*haben*) vary

Vase /'va:zə/ *f* -,-n vase

Vater *m* -s,- father. **V∼land** *nt* fatherland

väterlich *a* paternal; (*fürsorglich*) fatherly. **v∼erseits** *adv* on one's/the father's side

Vater|schaft *f* - fatherhood; (*Jur*) paternity. **V∼unser** *nt* -s,- Lord's Prayer

Vati *m* -s,-s (*fam*) daddy

v. Chr. *abbr* (*vor Christus*) BC

Vegetar|ier(in) /vege'ta:rjɐ, -jərɪn/ *m*(*f*) -s,- (*f*-,-nen) vegetarian. **v∼isch** *a* vegetarian

Vegetation /vegeta'tsjo:n/ *f* -,-en vegetation

Veilchen *nt* -s,- violet

Vene /'ve:nə/ *f* -,-n vein

Venedig /ve'ne:dɪç/ *nt* -s Venice

Ventil /vɛn'ti:l/ *nt* -s,-e valve. **V∼ator** *m* -s,-en /-'to:rən/ fan

verabred|en *vt* arrange; **sich [mit jdm] v∼en** arrange to meet [s.o.]. **V∼ung** *f* -,-en arrangement; (*Treffen*) appointment

verabreichen *vt* administer

verabscheuen *vt* detest, loathe

verabschieden *vt* say goodbye to; (*aus dem Dienst*) retire; pass ⟨*Gesetz*⟩; **sich v∼** say goodbye

verachten *vt* despise. **v∼swert** *a* contemptible

verächtlich *a* contemptuous, *adv* -ly; (*unwürdig*) contemptible

Verachtung *f* - contempt

verallgemeiner|n *vt/i* (*haben*) generalize. **V∼ung** *f* -,-en generalization

veralte|n *vi* (*sein*) become obsolete. **v∼t** *a* obsolete

Veranda /ve'randa/ *f* -,-den veranda

veränder|lich *a* changeable; (*Math*) variable. **v∼n** *vt* change; **sich v∼n** change; (*beruflich*) change one's job. **V∼ung** *f* change

verängstigt *a* frightened, scared

verankern *vt* anchor

veranlag|t *a* **künstlerisch/musikalisch v∼t** sein have an artistic/a musical bent; **praktisch v∼t** practically minded. **V∼ung** *f* -,-en disposition; (*Neigung*) tendency; (*künstlerisch*) bent

veranlass|en *vt* (*reg*) arrange for; (*einleiten*) institute; **jdn v∼en** prompt s.o. (**zu** to). **V~ung** *f* - reason; **auf meine V~ung** at my suggestion; (*Befehl*) on my orders

veranschaulichen *vt* illustrate

veranschlagen *vt* (*reg*) estimate

veranstalt|en *vt* organize; hold, give ⟨*Party*⟩; make ⟨*Lärm*⟩. **V~er** *m* -**s**,- organizer. **V~ung** *f* -,-**en** event

verantwort|en *vt* take responsibility for; **sich v~en** answer (**für** for). **v~lich** *a* responsible; **v~lich machen** hold responsible. **V~ung** *f* - responsibility. **v~ungsbewußt** *a* responsible, *adv* -bly. **v~ungslos** *a* irresponsible, *adv* -bly. **v~ungsvoll** *a* responsible

verarbeiten *vt* use; (*Techn*) process; (*verdauen & fig*) digest; **v~ zu** make into

verärgern *vt* annoy

verarmt *a* impoverished

verästeln (sich) *vr* branch out

verausgaben (sich) *vr* spend all one's money; (*körperlich*) wear oneself out

veräußern *vt* sell

Verb /vɛrp/ *nt* -**s**,-**en** verb. **v~al** /vɛr'baːl/ *a* verbal, *adv* -ly

Verband *m* -**[e]s**,ˆe association; (*Mil*) unit; (*Med*) bandage; (*Wund-*) dressing. **V~szeug** *nt* first-aid kit

verbann|en *vt* exile; (*fig*) banish. **V~ung** *f* - exile

verbarrikadieren *vt* barricade

verbeißen† *vt* suppress; **ich konnte mir kaum das Lachen v~** I could hardly keep a straight face

verbergen† *vt* hide; **sich v~** hide

verbesser|n *vt* improve; (*berichtigen*) correct. **V~ung** *f* -,-**en** improvement; correction

verbeug|en (sich) *vr* bow. **V~ung** *f* bow

verbeulen *vt* dent

verbiegen† *vt* bend; **sich v~** bend

verbieten† *vt* forbid; (*Admin*) prohibit, ban

verbillig|en *vt* reduce [in price]. **v~t** *a* reduced

verbinden† *vt* connect (**mit** to); (*zusammenfügen*) join; (*verknüpfen*) combine; (*in Verbindung bringen*) associate; (*Med*) bandage; dress ⟨*Wunde*⟩; **sich v~** combine; (*sich zusammentun*) join together; **jdm die Augen v~** blindfold s.o.; **jdm verbunden sein** (*fig*) be obliged to s.o.

verbindlich *a* friendly; (*bindend*) binding. **V~keit** *f* -,-**en** friendliness; **V~keiten** obligations; (*Comm*) liabilities

Verbindung *f* connection; (*Verknüpfung*) combination; (*Kontakt*) contact; (*Vereinigung*) association; **chemische V~** chemical compound; **in V~ stehen/sich in V~ setzen** be/get in touch

verbissen *a* grim, *adv* -ly; (*zäh*) dogged, *adv* -ly

verbitten† *vt* **sich** (*dat*) **etw v~** not stand for sth

verbitter|n *vt* make bitter. **v~t** *a* bitter. **V~ung** *f* - bitterness

verblassen *vi* (*sein*) fade

Verbleib *m* -**s** whereabouts *pl*. **v~en†** *vi* (*sein*) remain

verbleichen† *vi* (*sein*) fade

verbleit *a* ⟨*Benzin*⟩ leaded

verblüff|en *vt* amaze, astound. **V~ung** *f* - amazement

verblühen *vi* (*sein*) wither, fade

verbluten *vi* (*sein*) bleed to death

verborgen[1] *a* hidden

verborgen[2] *vt* lend

Verbot *nt* -**[e]s**,-**e** ban. **v~en** *a* forbidden; (*Admin*) prohibited; **'Rauchen v~en'** 'no smoking'

Verbrauch *m* -**[e]s** consumption. **v~en** *vt* use; consume ⟨*Lebensmittel*⟩; (*erschöpfen*) use up, exhaust. **V~er** *m* -**s**,- consumer. **v~t** *a* worn; ⟨*Luft*⟩ stale

verbrechen† *vt* (*fam*) perpetrate. **V~** *nt* -**s**,- crime

Verbrecher *m* -**s**,- criminal. **v~isch** *a* criminal

verbreit|en *vt* spread; **sich v~en** spread. **v~ern** *vt* widen; **sich v~ern** widen. **v~et** *a* widespread. **V~ung** *f* - spread; (*Verbreiten*) spreading

verbrenn|en† *vt/i* (*sein*) burn; cremate ⟨*Leiche*⟩. **V~ung** *f* -,-**en** burning; cremation; (*Wunde*) burn

verbringen† *vt* spend

verbrühen *vt* scald

verbuchen *vt* enter; (*fig*) notch up ⟨*Erfolg*⟩

verbünd|en (sich) *vr* form an alliance. **V~ete(r)** *m/f* ally

verbürgen *vt* guarantee; **sich v~ für** vouch for

verbüßen *vt* serve ⟨*Strafe*⟩

Verdacht *m* -**[e]s** suspicion; **in** *or* **im V~ haben** suspect

verdächtig *a* suspicious, *adv* -ly.
v~en *vt* suspect (*gen* of). **V~te(r)** *m/f* suspect

verdamm|en *vt* condemn; (*Relig*) damn. **V~nis** *f* - damnation. **v~t** *a & adv (sl)* damned; **v~t!** damn!

verdampfen *vt/i* (*sein*) evaporate

verdanken *vt* owe (*dat* to)

verdau|en *vt* digest. **v~lich** *a* digestible. **V~ung** *f* - digestion

Verdeck *nt* -[e]s,-e hood; (*Oberdeck*) top deck. **v~en** *vt* cover; (*verbergen*) hide, conceal

verdenken† *vt* **das kann man ihm nicht v~** you can't blame him for it

verderb|en† *vi* (*sein*) spoil; (*Lebensmittel:*) go bad ● *vt* spoil; (*zerstören*) ruin; (*moralisch*) corrupt; **ich habe mir den Magen verdorben** I have an upset stomach. **V~en** *nt* -s ruin. **v~lich** *a* perishable; (*schädlich*) pernicious

verdeutlichen *vt* make clear

verdichten *vt* compress; **sich v~** (*Nebel:*) thicken

verdien|en *vt/i* (*haben*) earn; (*fig*) deserve. **V~er** *m* -s,- wage-earner

Verdienst¹ *m* -[e]s earnings *pl*
Verdienst² *nt* -[e]s,-e merit

verdient *a* well-deserved; (*Person*) of outstanding merit. **v~ermaßen** *adv* deservedly

verdoppeln *vt* double; (*fig*) redouble; **sich v~** double

verdorben *a* spoilt, ruined; (*Magen*) upset; (*moralisch*) corrupt; (*verkommen*) depraved

verdorren *vi* (*sein*) wither

verdrängen *vt* force out; (*fig*) displace; (*psychisch*) repress

verdreh|en *vt* twist; roll (*Augen*); (*fig*) distort. **v~t** *a* (*fam*) crazy

verdreifachen *vt* treble, triple

verdreschen† *vt* (*fam*) thrash

verdrießlich *a* morose, *adv* -ly

verdrücken *vt* crumple; (*fam: essen*) polish off; **sich v~** (*fam*) slip away

Verdruß *m* -sses annoyance

verdunk|eln *vt* darken; black out (*Zimmer*); **sich v~eln** darken. **V~[e]-lung** *f* - black-out

verdünnen *vt* dilute; **sich v~** taper off

verdunst|en *vi* (*sein*) evaporate. **V~ung** *f* - evaporation

verdursten *vi* (*sein*) die of thirst

verdutzt *a* baffled

veredeln *vt* refine; (*Hort*) graft

verehr|en *vt* revere; (*Relig*) worship; (*bewundern*) admire; (*schenken*) give. **V~er(in)** *m* -s,- (*f* -,-nen) admirer. **V~ung** *f* - veneration; worship; admiration

vereidigen *vt* swear in

Verein *m* -s,-e society; (*Sport-*) club

vereinbar *a* compatible. **v~en** *vt* arrange; **nicht zu v~en** incompatible. **V~ung** *f* -,-en agreement

vereinen *vt* unite; **sich v~** unite

vereinfachen *vt* simplify

vereinheitlichen *vt* standardize

vereinig|en *vt* unite; merge (*Firmen*); **sich v~en** unite; **V~te Staaten [von Amerika]** United States *sg* [of America]. **V~ung** *f* -,-en union; (*Organisation*) organization

vereinsamt *a* lonely

vereinzelt *a* isolated ● *adv* occasionally

vereist *a* frozen; (*Straße*) icy

vereiteln *vt* foil, thwart

vereitert *a* septic

verenden *vi* (*sein*) die

verengen *vt* restrict; **sich v~** narrow; (*Pupille:*) contract

vererb|en *vt* leave (*dat* to); (*Biol & fig*) pass on (*dat* to). **V~ung** *f* - heredity

verewigen *vt* immortalize; **sich v~** (*fam*) leave one's mark

verfahren† *vi* (*sein*) proceed; **v~ mit** deal with ● *vr* **sich v~** lose one's way ● *a* muddled. **V~** *nt* -s,- procedure; (*Techn*) process; (*Jur*) proceedings *pl*

Verfall *m* decay; (*eines Gebäudes*) dilapidation; (*körperlich & fig*) decline; (*Ablauf*) expiry. **v~en†** *vi* (*sein*) decay; (*Person, Sitten:*) decline; (*ablaufen*) expire; **v~en in** (+ *acc*) lapse into; **v~en auf** (+ *acc*) hit on (*Idee*); **jdm/etw v~en sein** be under the spell of s.o./sth; be addicted to (*Alkohol*)

verfälschen *vt* falsify; adulterate (*Wein, Lebensmittel*)

verfänglich *a* awkward

verfärben (sich) *vr* change colour; (*Stoff:*) discolour

verfass|en *vt* write; (*Jur*) draw up; (*entwerfen*) draft. **V~er** *m* -s,- author. **V~ung** *f* (*Pol*) constitution; (*Zustand*) state

verfaulen *vi* (*sein*) rot, decay

verfechten† *vt* advocate

verfehlen *vt* miss

verfeinde|n (sich) *vr* become enemies; **v~t sein** be enemies

verfeinern *vt* refine; (*verbessern*) improve

verfilmen *vt* film

verfilzt *a* matted

verfliegen† *vi* (*sein*) evaporate; ⟨*Zeit:*⟩ fly

verflixt *a* (*fam*) awkward; (*verdammt*) blessed; **v∼!** damn!

verfluch|en *vt* curse. **v∼t** *a* & *adv* (*fam*) damned; **v∼t!** damn!

verflüchtigen (sich) *vr* evaporate

verflüssigen *vt* liquefy

verfolg|en *vt* pursue; (*folgen*) follow; (*bedrängen*) pester; (*Pol*) persecute;   **strafrechtlich v∼en** prosecute. **V∼er** *m* **-s,-** pursuer. **V∼ung** *f* - pursuit; persecution

verfrachten *vt* ship

verfrüht *a* premature

verfügbar *a* available

verfüg|en *vt* order; (*Jur*) decree ● *vi* (*haben*) **v∼en über** (+ *acc*) have at one's disposal. **V∼ung** *f* -,-en order; (*Jur*) decree; **jdm zur V∼ung stehen/ stellen** be/place at s.o.'s disposal

verführ|en *vt* seduce; (*verlocken*) tempt. **V∼er** *m* seducer. **v∼erisch** *a* seductive; tempting. **V∼ung** *f* seduction; temptation

vergammelt *a* rotten; ⟨*Gebäude*⟩ decayed; ⟨*Person*⟩ scruffy

vergangen *a* past; (*letzte*) last. **V∼heit** *f* - past; (*Gram*) past tense

vergänglich *a* transitory

vergas|en *vt* gas. **V∼er** *m* **-s,-** carburettor

vergeb|en† *vt* award (**an** + *dat* to); (*weggeben*) give away; (*verzeihen*) forgive. **v∼ens** *adv* in vain. **v∼lich** *a* futile, vain ● *adv* in vain. **V∼ung** *f* - forgiveness

vergehen† *vi* (*sein*) pass; **v∼ vor** (+ *dat*) nearly die of; **sich v∼** violate (**gegen etw** sth); (*sexuell*) sexually assault (**an jdm** s.o.). **V∼** *nt* **-s,-** offence

vergelt|en† *vt* repay. **V∼ung** *f* - retaliation; (*Rache*) revenge. **V∼ungs- maßnahme** *f* reprisal

vergessen† *vt* forget; (*liegenlassen*) leave behind. **V∼heit** *f* - oblivion; **in V∼heit geraten** be forgotten

vergeßlich *a* forgetful. **V∼keit** *f* - forgetfulness

vergeuden *vt* waste, squander

vergewaltig|en *vt* rape. **V∼ung** *f* -,-en rape

vergewissern (sich) *vr* make sure (*gen* of)

vergießen† *vt* spill; shed ⟨*Tränen, Blut*⟩

vergift|en *vt* poison. **V∼ung** *f* -,-en poisoning

Vergißmeinnicht *nt* -[e]s,-[e] forget-me-not

vergittert *a* barred

verglasen *vt* glaze

Vergleich *m* -[e]s,-e comparison; (*Jur*) settlement. **v∼bar** *a* comparable. **v∼en†** *vt* compare (**mit** with/to). **v∼sweise** *adv* comparatively

vergnüg|en (sich) *vr* enjoy oneself. **V∼en** *nt* **-s,-** pleasure; (*Spaß*) fun; **viel V∼en!** have a good time! **v∼lich** *a* enjoyable. **v∼t** *a* cheerful, *adv* -ly; (*zufrieden*) happy, *adv* -ily; (*vergnüg- lich*) enjoyable. **V∼ungen** *fpl* entertainments

vergolden *vt* gild; (*plattieren*) gold-plate

vergönnen *vt* grant

vergöttern *vt* idolize

vergraben† *vt* bury

vergreifen (sich) *vr* **sich v∼ an** (+ *dat*) assault; (*stehlen*) steal

vergriffen *a* out of print

vergrößer|n *vt* enlarge; ⟨*Linse:*⟩ magnify; (*vermehren*) increase; (*erweitern*) extend; expand ⟨*Geschäft*⟩; **sich v∼n** grow bigger; ⟨*Firma:*⟩ expand; (*zunehmen*) increase. **V∼ung** *f* -,-en magnification; increase; expansion; (*Phot*) enlargement. **V∼ungsglas** *nt* magnifying glass

Vergünstigung *f* -,-en privilege

vergüt|en *vt* pay for; **jdm etw v∼en** reimburse s.o. for sth. **V∼ung** *f* -,-en remuneration; (*Erstattung*) reimbursement

verhaft|en *vt* arrest. **V∼ung** *f* -,-en arrest

verhalten† (sich) *vr* behave; (*handeln*) act; (*beschaffen sein*) be; **sich still v∼** keep quiet. **V∼** *nt* **-s** behaviour, conduct

Verhältnis *nt* -ses,-se relationship; (*Liebes-*) affair; (*Math*) ratio; **V∼se** circumstances; (*Bedingungen*) conditions; **über seine V∼se leben** live beyond one's means. **v∼mäßig** *adv* comparatively, relatively

verhand|eln *vt* discuss; (*Jur*) try ● *vi* (*haben*) negotiate; **v∼eln gegen** (*Jur*) try. **V∼lung** *f* (*Jur*) trial; **V∼lungen** negotiations

verhängen *vt* cover; (*fig*) impose

Verhängnis *nt* **-ses** fate, doom. **v~voll** *a* fatal, disastrous

verharmlosen *vt* play down

verharren *vi (haben)* remain

verhärten *vt/i (sein)* harden; **sich v~** harden

verhaßt *a* hated

verhätscheln *vt* spoil, pamper

verhauen† *vt (fam)* beat; make a mess of *(Prüfung)*

verheerend *a* devastating; *(fam)* terrible

verhehlen *vt* conceal

verheilen *vi (sein)* heal

verheimlichen *vt* keep secret

verheirat|en (sich) *vr* get married **(mit** to). **v~et** *a* married

verhelfen† *vi (haben)* **jdm zu etw v~** help s.o. get sth

verherrlichen *vt* glorify

verhexen *vt* bewitch; **es ist wie verhext** *(fam)* there is a jinx on it

verhinder|n *vt* prevent; **v~t sein** be unable to come. **V~ung** *f* - prevention

verhöhnen *vt* deride

Verhör *nt* **-s,-e** interrogation; **ins V~ nehmen** interrogate. **v~en** *vt* interrogate; **sich v~en** mishear

verhüllen *vt* cover; *(fig)* disguise. **v~d** *a* euphemistic, *adv* -ally

verhungern *vi (sein)* starve

verhüt|en *vt* prevent. **V~ung** *f* - prevention. **V~ungsmittel** *nt* contraceptive

verhutzelt *a* wizened

verirren (sich) *vr* get lost

verjagen *vt* chase away

verjüngen *vt* rejuvenate; **sich v~** taper

verkalkt *a (fam)* senile

verkalkulieren (sich) *vr* miscalculate

Verkauf *m* sale; **zum V~** for sale. **v~en** *vt* sell; **zu v~en** for sale

Verkäufer(in) *m(f)* seller; *(im Geschäft)* shop assistant

Verkehr *m* **-s** traffic; *(Kontakt)* contact; *(Geschlechts-)* intercourse; **aus dem V~ ziehen** take out of circulation. **v~en** *vi (haben)* operate; ⟨*Bus, Zug:*⟩ run; *(Umgang haben)* associate, mix **(mit** with); *(Gast sein)* visit **(bei jdm** s.o.); frequent **(in einem Lokal** a restaurant); **brieflich v~en** correspond • *vt* **ins Gegenteil v~en** turn round

Verkehrs|ampel *f* traffic lights *pl.* **V~büro** *nt* = **V~verein. V~funk** *m*

[radio] traffic information. **V~unfall** *m* road accident. **V~verein** *m* tourist office. **V~zeichen** *nt* traffic sign

verkehrt *a* wrong, *adv* -ly. **v~herum** *adv* the wrong way round; *(links)* inside out

verkennen† *vt* misjudge

verklagen *vt* sue **(auf** + *acc* for)

verkleid|en *vt* disguise; *(Techn)* line; **sich v~en** disguise oneself; *(für Kostümfest)* dress up. **V~ung** *f* -,-en disguise; *(Kostüm)* fancy dress; *(Techn)* lining

verkleiner|n *vt* reduce [in size]. **V~ung** *f* - reduction. **V~ungsform** *f* diminutive

verklemmt *a* jammed; *(psychisch)* inhibited

verkneifen† *vt* **sich** *(dat)* **etw v~** do without sth; *(verbeißen)* suppress sth

verknittern *vt/i (sein)* crumple

verknüpfen *vt* knot together; *(verbinden)* connect, link; *(zugleich tun)* combine

verkommen† *vi (sein)* be neglected; *(sittlich)* go to the bad; *(verfallen)* decay; ⟨*Haus:*⟩ fall into disrepair; ⟨*Gegend:*⟩ become run-down; ⟨*Lebensmittel:*⟩ go bad • *a* neglected; *(sittlich)* depraved; ⟨*Haus*⟩ dilapidated; ⟨*Gegend*⟩ run-down

verkörper|n *vt* embody, personify. **V~ung** *f* -,-en embodiment, personification

verkraften *vt* cope with

verkrampft *a (fig)* tense

verkriechen† (sich) *vr* hide

verkrümmt *a* crooked, bent

verkrüppelt *a* crippled; ⟨*Glied*⟩ deformed

verkühl|en (sich) *vr* catch a chill. **V~ung** *f* -,-en chill

verkümmer|n *vi (sein)* waste/ ⟨*Pflanze:*⟩ wither away. **v~t** *a* stunted

verkünd|en *vt* announce; pronounce ⟨*Urteil*⟩. **v~igen** *vt* announce; *(predigen)* preach

verkürzen *vt* shorten; *(verringern)* reduce; *(abbrechen)* cut short; while away ⟨*Zeit*⟩

verladen† *vt* load

Verlag *m* **-[e]s,-e** publishing firm

verlangen *vt* ask for; *(fordern)* demand; *(berechnen)* charge; **am Telefon verlangt werden** be wanted on the telephone. **V∼** *nt* **-s** desire; (*Bitte*) request; **auf V∼** on demand

verlänger|n *vt* extend; lengthen ⟨*Kleid*⟩; (*zeitlich*) prolong; renew ⟨*Paß, Vertrag*⟩; (*Culin*) thin down. **V∼ung** *f* **-,-en** extension; renewal. **V∼ungsschnur** *f* extension cable

verlangsamen *vt* slow down

Verlaß *m* **-sses auf ihn ist kein V∼** you cannot rely on him

verlassen† *vt* leave; (*im Stich lassen*) desert; **sich v∼ auf** (+ *acc*) rely or depend on ● *a* deserted. **V∼heit** *f* - desolation

verläßlich *a* reliable

Verlauf *m* course; **im V∼** (+ *gen*) in the course of. **v∼en†** *vi* (*sein*) run; (*ablaufen*) go; (*zerlaufen*) melt; **gut v∼en** go [off] well ● *vr* **sich v∼en** lose one's way; ⟨*Menge:*⟩ disperse; ⟨*Wasser:*⟩ drain away

verleben *vt* spend

verlegen *vt* move; (*verschieben*) postpone; (*vor-*) bring forward; (*verlieren*) mislay; (*versperren*) block; (*legen*) lay ⟨*Teppich, Rohre*⟩; (*veröffentlichen*) publish; **sich v∼ auf** (+ *acc*) take up ⟨*Beruf, Fach*⟩; resort to ⟨*Taktik, Bitten*⟩ ● *a* embarrassed; **nie v∼ um** never at a loss for. **V∼heit** *f* - embarrassment

Verleger *m* **-s,-** publisher

verleihen† *vt* lend; (*gegen Gebühr*) hire out; (*überreichen*) award, confer; (*fig*) give

verleiten *vt* induce/(*verlocken*) tempt (**zu** to)

verlernen *vt* forget

verlesen¹† *vt* read out; **ich habe mich v∼** I misread it

verlesen²† *vt* sort out

verletz|en *vt* injure; (*kränken*) hurt; (*verstoßen gegen*) infringe; violate ⟨*Grenze*⟩. **v∼end** *a* hurtful, wounding. **v∼lich** *a* vulnerable. **V∼te(r)** *m/f* injured person; (*bei Unfall*) casualty. **V∼ung** *f* **-,-en** injury; (*Verstoß*) infringement; violation

verleugnen *vt* deny; disown ⟨*Freund*⟩

verleumd|en *vt* slander; (*schriftlich*) libel. **v∼erisch** *a* slanderous; libellous. **V∼ung** *f* **-,-en** slander; (*schriftlich*) libel

verlieben (sich) *vr* fall in love (**in** + *acc* with); **verliebt sein** be in love (**in** + *acc* with)

verlier|en† *vt* lose; shed ⟨*Laub*⟩; **sich v∼en** disappear; ⟨*Weg:*⟩ peter out ● *vi* (*haben*) lose (**an etw** *dat* sth). **V∼er** *m* **-s,-** loser

verlob|en (sich) *vr* get engaged (**mit** to); **v∼t sein** be engaged. **V∼te** *f* fiancée. **V∼te(r)** *m* fiancé. **V∼ung** *f* **-,-en** engagement

verlock|en *vt* tempt; **v∼end** tempting. **V∼ung** *f* **-,-en** temptation

verlogen *a* lying

verloren *a* lost; **v∼e Eier** poached eggs. **v∼gehen†** *vi sep* (*sein*) get lost

verlos|en *vt* raffle. **V∼ung** *f* **-,-en** raffle; (*Ziehung*) draw

verlottert *a* run-down; ⟨*Person*⟩ scruffy; (*sittlich*) dissolute

Verlust *m* **-[e]s,-e** loss

vermachen *vt* leave, bequeath

Vermächtnis *nt* **-ses,-se** legacy

vermähl|en (sich) *vr* marry. **V∼ung** *f* **-,-en** marriage

vermehren *vt* increase; propagate ⟨*Pflanzen*⟩; **sich v∼** increase; (*sich fortpflanzen*) breed, multiply

vermeiden† *vt* avoid

vermeintlich *a* supposed, *adv* -ly

Vermerk *m* **-[e]s,-e** note. **v∼en** *vt* note [down]; **übel v∼en** take amiss

vermess|en† *vt* measure; survey ⟨*Gelände*⟩ ● *a* presumptuous. **V∼enheit** *f* - presumption. **V∼ung** *f* measurement; (*Land-*) survey

vermiet|en *vt* let, rent [out]; hire out ⟨*Boot, Auto*⟩; **zu v∼en** to let; ⟨*Boot:*⟩ for hire. **V∼er** *m* landlord. **V∼erin** *f* landlady

vermind|ern *vt* reduce, lessen. **V∼ung** *f* - reduction, decrease

vermischen *vt* mix; **sich v∼** mix

vermissen *vt* miss

vermißt *a* missing. **V∼e(r)** *m* missing person/(*Mil*) soldier

vermittel|n *vi* (*haben*) mediate ● *vt* arrange; (*beschaffen*) find; place ⟨*Arbeitskräfte*⟩; impart ⟨*Wissen*⟩; convey ⟨*Eindruck*⟩. **v∼s** *prep* (+ *gen*) by means of

Vermittl|er *m* **-s,-** agent; (*Schlichter*) mediator. **V∼ung** *f* **-,-en** arrangement; (*Agentur*) agency; (*Teleph*) exchange; (*Schlichtung*) mediation

vermögen† *vt* be able (**zu** to). **V∼** *nt* **-s,-** fortune. **v∼d** *a* wealthy

vermut|en *vt* suspect; (*glauben*) presume. **v∼lich** *a* probable ● *adv* presumably. **V∼ung** *f* **-,-en** supposition;

(*Verdacht*) suspicion; (*Mutmaßung*) conjecture

vernachlässig|en *vt* neglect. **V∼ung** *f* - neglect

vernehm|en† *vt* hear; (*verhören*) question; (*Jur*) examine. **V∼ung** *f* -,-en questioning

verneig|en (sich) *vr* bow. **V∼ung** *f* -,-en bow

vernein|en *vt* answer in the negative; (*ablehnen*) reject. **v∼end** *a* negative. **V∼ung** *f* -,-en negative answer; (*Gram*) negative

vernicht|en *vt* destroy; (*ausrotten*) exterminate. **v∼end** *a* devastating; (*Niederlage*) crushing. **V∼ung** *f* - destruction; extermination

Vernunft *f* - reason; **V∼ annehmen** see reason

vernünftig *a* reasonable, sensible; (*fam: ordentlich*) decent ● *adv* sensibly; (*fam*) properly

veröffentlich|en *vt* publish. **V∼ung** *f* -,-en publication

verordn|en *vt* prescribe (*dat* for). **V∼ung** *f* -,-en prescription; (*Verfügung*) decree

verpachten *vt* lease [out]

verpack|en *vt* pack; (*einwickeln*) wrap. **V∼ung** *f* packaging; wrapping

verpassen *vt* miss; (*fam: geben*) give

verpfänden *vt* pawn

verpflanzen *vt* transplant

verpfleg|en *vt* feed; **sich selbst v∼en** cater for oneself. **V∼ung** *f* - board; (*Essen*) food; **Unterkunft und V∼ung** board and lodging

verpflicht|en *vt* oblige; (*einstellen*) engage; (*Sport*) sign; **sich v∼en** undertake/(*versprechen*) promise (**zu** to); (*vertraglich*) sign a contract; **jdm v∼et sein** be indebted to s.o. **V∼ung** *f* -,-en obligation, commitment

verpfuschen *vt* make a mess of

verpönt *a* **v∼ sein** be frowned upon

verprügeln *vt* beat up, thrash

Verputz *m* -es plaster. **v∼en** *vt* plaster; (*fam: essen*) polish off

Verrat *m* -[e]s betrayal, treachery. **v∼en†** *vt* betray; give away (*Geheimnis*); (*fam: sagen*) tell; **sich v∼en** give oneself away

Verräter *m* -s,- traitor. **v∼isch** *a* treacherous; (*fig*) revealing

verräuchert *a* smoky

verrech|nen *vt* settle; clear (*Scheck*); **sich v∼nen** make a mistake; (*fig*) miscalculate. **V∼nungsscheck** *m* crossed cheque

verregnet *a* spoilt by rain; (*Tag*) rainy, wet

verreisen *vi* (*sein*) go away; **verreist sein** be away

verreißen† *vt* (*fam*) pan, slate

verrenken *vt* dislocate; **sich v∼** contort oneself

verricht|en *vt* perform, do; say (*Gebet*). **V∼ung** *f* -,-en task

verriegeln *vt* bolt

verringer|n *vt* reduce; **sich v∼n** decrease. **V∼ung** *f* - reduction; decrease

verrost|en *vi* (*sein*) rust. **v∼et** *a* rusty

verrücken *vt* move

verrückt *a* crazy, mad; **v∼ werden/machen** go/drive crazy. **V∼e(r)** *m/f* lunatic. **V∼heit** *f* -,-en madness; (*Torheit*) folly

Verruf *m* disrepute. **v∼en** *a* disreputable

verrühren *vt* mix

verrunzelt *a* wrinkled

verrutschen *vi* (*sein*) slip

Vers /fɛrs/ *m* -es,-e verse

versag|en *vi* (*haben*) fail ● *vt* **jdm/sich etw v∼en** deny s.o./oneself sth. **V∼en** *nt* -s,- failure. **V∼er** *m* -s,- failure

versalzen† *vt* put too much salt in/on; (*fig*) spoil

versamm|eln *vt* assemble; **sich v∼eln** assemble, meet. **V∼lung** *f* assembly, meeting

Versand *m* -[e]s dispatch. **V∼haus** *nt* mail-order firm

versäum|en *vt* miss; lose (*Zeit*); (*unterlassen*) neglect; **[es] v∼en, etw zu tun** fail *or* neglect to do sth. **V∼nis** *nt* -ses,-se omission

verschaffen *vt* get; **sich** (*dat*) **v∼** obtain; gain (*Respekt*)

verschämt *a* bashful, *adv* -ly

verschandeln *vt* spoil

verschärfen *vt* intensify; tighten (*Kontrolle*); increase (*Tempo*); aggravate (*Lage*); **sich v∼** intensify; increase; (*Lage:*) worsen

verschätzen (sich) *vr* **sich v∼ in** (+ *dat*) misjudge

verschenken *vt* give away

verscheuchen *vt* shoo/(*jagen*) chase away

verschicken *vt* send; *(Comm)* dispatch

verschieb|en† *vt* move; *(aufschieben)* put off, postpone; *(sl: handeln mit)* traffic in; **sich v~en** move, shift; *(verrutschen)* slip; *(zeitlich)* be postponed. **V~ung** *f* shift; postponement

verschieden *a* different; **v~e** *(pl)* different; *(mehrere)* various; **v~es** some things; *(dieses und jenes)* various things; **die v~sten Farben** a whole variety of colours; **das ist v~** it varies ● *adv* differently; **v~ groß/lang** of different sizes/lengths. **v~artig** *a* diverse. **V~heit** *f* - difference; *(Vielfalt)* diversity. **v~tlich** *adv* several times

verschimmel|n *vi (sein)* go mouldy. **v~t** *a* mouldy

verschlafen† *vi (haben)* oversleep ● *vt* sleep through *(Tag)*; *(versäumen)* miss *(Zug, Termin)*; **sich v~** oversleep ● *a* sleepy; **noch v~** still half asleep

Verschlag *m* -[e]s,¨e shed

verschlagen† *vt* lose *(Seite)*; **jdm die Sprache/den Atem v~** leave s.o. speechless/take s.o.'s breath away; **nach X v~ werden** end up in X ● *a* sly, *adv* -ly

verschlechter|n *vt* make worse; **sich v~n** get worse, deteriorate. **V~ung** *f* -,-en deterioration

verschleiern *vt* veil; *(fig)* hide

Verschleiß *m* -es wear and tear; *(Verbrauch)* consumption. **v~en†** *vt/i (sein)* wear out

verschleppen *vt* carry off; *(entführen)* abduct; spread *(Seuche)*; neglect *(Krankheit)*; *(hinausziehen)* delay

verschleudern *vt* sell at a loss; *(verschwenden)* squander

verschließen† *vt* close; *(abschließen)* lock; *(einschließen)* lock up

verschlimmer|n *vt* make worse; aggravate *(Lage)*; **sich v~n** get worse, deteriorate. **V~ung** *f* -,-en deterioration

verschlingen† *vt* intertwine; *(fressen)* devour; *(fig)* swallow

verschlissen *a* worn

verschlossen *a* reserved. **V~heit** *f* - reserve

verschlucken *vt* swallow; **sich v~** choke (**an** + *dat* on)

Verschluß *m* -sses,¨sse fastener, clasp; *(Fenster-, Koffer-)* catch; *(Flaschen-)* top;

(luftdicht) seal; *(Phot)* shutter; **unter V~** under lock and key

verschlüsselt *a* coded

verschmähen *vt* spurn

verschmelzen† *vt/i (sein)* fuse

verschmerzen *vt* get over

verschmutz|en *vt* soil; pollute *(Luft)* ● *vi (sein)* get dirty. **V~ung** *f* - pollution

verschnaufen *vi/r (haben)* [**sich**] **v~** get one's breath

verschneit *a* snow-covered

verschnörkelt *a* ornate

verschnüren *vt* tie up

verschollen *a* missing

verschonen *vt* spare

verschönern *vt* brighten up; *(verbessern)* improve

verschossen *a* faded

verschrammt *a* scratched

verschränken *vt* cross

verschreiben† *vt* prescribe; **sich v~** make a slip of the pen

verschrie[e]n *a* notorious

verschroben *a* eccentric

verschrotten *vt* scrap

verschulden *vt* be to blame for. **V~nt** -s fault

verschuldet *a* **v~ sein** be in debt

verschütten *vt* spill; *(begraben)* bury

verschweigen† *vt* conceal, hide

verschwend|en *vt* waste. **v~erisch** *a* extravagant, *adv* -ly; *(üppig)* lavish, *adv* -ly. **V~ung** *f* - extravagance; *(Vergeudung)* waste

verschwiegen *a* discreet; *(Ort)* secluded. **V~heit** *f* - discretion

verschwimmen† *vi (sein)* become blurred

verschwinden† *vi (sein)* disappear; [**mal**] **v~** *(fam)* spend a penny. **V~** *nt* -s disappearance

verschwommen *a* blurred

verschwör|en (sich) *vr* conspire. **V~ung** *f* -,-en conspiracy

versehen† *vt* perform; hold *(Posten)*; keep *(Haushalt)*; **v~ mit** provide with; **sich v~** make a mistake; **ehe man sich's versieht** before you know where you are. **V~** *nt* -s,- oversight; *(Fehler)* slip; **aus V~** by mistake. **v~tlich** *adv* by mistake

Versehrte(r) *m* disabled person

versenden† *vt* send [out]

versengen *vt* singe; *(stärker)* scorch

versenken *vt* sink; **sich v~ in** (+ *acc*) immerse oneself in

versẹssen *a* keen (**auf** + *acc* on)

versẹtz|en *vt* move; transfer ⟨*Person*⟩; (*Sch*) move up; (*verpfänden*) pawn; (*verkaufen*) sell; (*vermischen*) blend; (*antworten*) reply; **jdn v~en** (*fam: warten lassen*) stand s.o. up; **jdm einen Stoß/Schreck v~en** give s.o. a push/fright; **jdn in Angst/Erstaunen v~en** frighten/astonish s.o.; **sich in jds Lage v~en** put oneself in s.o.'s place. **V~ung** *f* -,-en move; transfer; (*Sch*) move to a higher class

versẹuch|en *vt* contaminate. **V~ung** *f* - contamination

versịcher|n *vt* insure; (*bekräftigen*) affirm; **jdm v~n** assure s.o. (**daß** that). **V~ung** *f* -,-en insurance; assurance

versịegeln *vt* seal

versịegen *vi* (*sein*) dry up

versiert /vɛrˈziːɐt/ *a* experienced

versịlbert *a* silver-plated

versịnken† *vi* (*sein*) sink; **in Gedanken versunken** lost in thought

Version /vɛrˈzjoːn/ *f* -,-en version

Versmaß /ˈfɛrs-/ *nt* metre

versöhn|en *vt* reconcile; **sich v~en** become reconciled. **v~lich** *a* conciliatory. **V~ung** *f* -,-en reconciliation

versọrg|en *vt* provide, supply (**mit** with); provide for (*Familie*); (*betreuen*) look after; keep (*Haushalt*). **V~ung** *f* - provision, supply; (*Betreuung*) care

verspät|en (sich) *vr* be late. **v~et** *a* late; (*Zug*) delayed; ⟨*Dank, Glückwunsch*⟩ belated ● *adv* late; belatedly. **V~ung** *f* - lateness; **V~ung haben** be late

verspẹrren *vt* block; bar (*Weg*)

verspiẹl|en *vt* gamble away; **sich v~en** play a wrong note. **v~t** *a* playful, *adv* -ly

verspọtten *vt* mock, ridicule

versprẹch|en† *vt* promise; **sich v~en** make a slip of the tongue; **sich** (*dat*) **viel v~en von** have high hopes of. **V~en** *nt* -s,- promise. **V~ungen** *fpl* promises

verspüren *vt* feel

verstaatlich|en *vt* nationalize. **V~ung** *f* - nationalization

Verstạnd *m* -[e]s mind; (*Vernunft*) reason; **den V~ verlieren** go out of one's mind. **v~esmäßig** *a* rational, *adv* -ly

verständig *a* sensible, *adv* -bly; (*klug*) intelligent, *adv* -ly. **v~en** *vt*

notify, inform; **sich v~en** communicate; (*sich verständlich machen*) make oneself understood; (*sich einigen*) reach agreement. **V~ung** *f* - notification; communication; (*Einigung*) agreement

verständlich *a* comprehensible, *adv* -bly; (*deutlich*) clear, *adv* -ly; (*begreiflich*) understandable; **sich v~ machen** make oneself understood. **v~erweise** *adv* understandably

Verständnis *nt* -ses understanding. **v~los** *a* uncomprehending, *adv* -ly. **v~voll** *a* understanding, *adv* -ly

verstärk|en *vt* strengthen, reinforce; (*steigern*) intensify, increase; amplify ⟨*Ton*⟩; **sich v~en** intensify. **V~er** *m* -s,- amplifier. **V~ung** *f* reinforcement; increase; amplification; (*Truppen*) reinforcements *pl*

verstaubt *a* dusty

verstauchen *vt* sprain

verstauen *vt* stow

Verstẹck *nt* -[e]s,-e hiding-place; **V~spielen** play hide-and-seek. **v~en** *vt* hide; **sich v~en** hide. **v~t** *a* hidden; (*heimlich*) secret; (*verstohlen*) furtive, *adv* -ly

verstẹhen† *vt* understand; (*können*) know; **falsch v~** misunderstand; **sich v~** understand one another; (*auskommen*) get on; **das versteht sich von selbst** that goes without saying

verstẹifen *vt* stiffen; **sich v~** stiffen; (*fig*) insist (**auf** + *acc* on)

verstẹiger|n *vt* auction. **V~ung** *f* auction

verstẹinert *a* fossilized

verstẹll|bar *a* adjustable. **v~en** *vt* adjust; (*versperren*) block; (*verändern*) disguise; **sich v~en** pretend. **V~ung** *f* - pretence

verstẹuern *vt* pay tax on

verstiẹgen *a* (*fig*) extravagant

verstịmm|t *a* disgruntled; ⟨*Magen*⟩ upset; (*Mus*) out of tune. **V~ung** *f* - ill humour; (*Magen*) upset

verstọckt *a* stubborn, *adv* -ly

verstọhlen *a* furtive, *adv* -ly

verstọpf|en *vt* plug; (*versperren*) block; **v~t** blocked; (*Person*) constipated. **V~ung** *f* -,-en blockage; (*Med*) constipation

verstọrben *a* late, deceased. **V~e(r)** *m/f* deceased

verstört *a* bewildered

Verstoß m infringement. **v~en†** vt disown ● vi (haben) **v~en gegen** contravene, infringe; offend against ⟨Anstand⟩

verstreichen† vt spread ● vi (sein) pass

verstreuen vt scatter

verstümmeln vt mutilate; garble ⟨Text⟩

verstummen vi (sein) fall silent; ⟨Gespräch, Lärm:⟩ cease

Versuch m -[e]s,-e attempt; (Experiment) experiment. **v~en** vt/i (haben) try; **sich v~en in** (+ dat) try one's hand at; **v~t sein** be tempted (**zu** to). **V~skaninchen** nt (fig) guineapig. **v~sweise** adv as an experiment. **V~ung** f -,-en temptation

versündigen (sich) vr sin (**an** + dat against)

vertagen vt adjourn; (aufschieben) postpone; **sich v~** adjourn

vertauschen vt exchange; (verwechseln) mix up

verteidig|en vt defend. **V~er** m -s,- defender; (Jur) defence counsel. **V~ung** f -,-en defence

verteil|en vt distribute; (zuteilen) allocate; (ausgeben) hand out; (verstreichen) spread; **sich v~en** spread out. **V~ung** f - distribution; allocation

vertief|en vt deepen; **v~t sein in** (+ acc) be engrossed in. **V~ung** f -,-en hollow, depression

vertikal /vɛrtiˈkaːl/ a vertical, adv -ly

vertilgen vt exterminate; kill [off] ⟨Unkraut⟩; (fam: essen) demolish

vertippen (sich) vr make a typing mistake

vertonen vt set to music

Vertrag m -[e]s,-̈e contract; (Pol) treaty

vertragen† vt tolerate, stand; take ⟨Kritik, Spaß⟩; **sich v~** get on; (passen) go (**mit** with); **sich wieder v~** make it up ● a worn

verträglich a contractual

verträglich a good-natured; (bekömmlich) digestible

vertrauen vi (haben) trust (**jdm/etw** s.o./sth; **auf** + acc in). **V~** nt -s trust, confidence (**zu** in); **im V~** in confidence. **V~smann** m (pl -leute) representative; (Sprecher) spokesman. **v~svoll** a trusting, adv -ly. **v~swürdig** a trustworthy

vertraulich a confidential, adv -ly; (intim) familiar, adv -ly

vertraut a intimate; (bekannt) familiar; **sich v~ machen mit** familiarize oneself with. **V~heit** f - intimacy; familiarity

vertreib|en† vt drive away; drive out ⟨Feind⟩; (Comm) sell; **sich** (dat) **die Zeit v~en** pass the time. **V~ung** f -,-en expulsion

vertret|en† vt represent; (einspringen für) stand in or deputize for; (verfechten) support; hold ⟨Meinung⟩; **sich** (dat) **den Fuß v~en** twist one's ankle; **sich** (dat) **die Beine v~en** stretch one's legs. **V~er** m -s,- representative; deputy; (Arzt-) locum; (Verfechter) supporter, advocate. **V~ung** f -,-en representation; (Person) deputy; (eines Arztes) locum; (Handels-) agency

Vertrieb m -[e]s (Comm) sale. **V~ene(r)** m/f displaced person

vertrocknen vi (sein) dry up

vertrösten vt jdn auf später v~ put s.o. off until later

vertun† vt waste; **sich v~** (fam) make a mistake

vertuschen vt hush up

verübeln vt jdm etw v~ hold sth against s.o.

verüben vt commit

verunglimpfen vt denigrate

verunglücken vi (sein) be involved in an accident; (fam: mißglücken) go wrong; **tödlich v~** be killed in an accident

verunreinigen vt pollute; (verseuchen) contaminate; (verschmutzen) soil

verunstalten vt disfigure

veruntreu|en vt embezzle. **V~ung** f - embezzlement

verursachen vt cause

verurteil|en vt condemn; (Jur) convict (**wegen** of); sentence (**zum Tode** to death). **V~ung** f - condemnation; (Jur) conviction

vervielfachen vt multiply

vervielfältigen vt duplicate

vervollkommnen vt perfect

vervollständigen vt complete

verwachsen a deformed

verwählen (sich) vr misdial

verwahren vt keep; (verstauen) put away; **sich v~** (fig) protest

verwahrlost a neglected; ⟨Haus⟩ dilapidated; (sittlich) depraved

Verwahrung f - keeping; **in V∼ neh-men** take into safe keeping

verwaist a orphaned

verwalt|en vt administer; (leiten) manage; govern ⟨Land⟩. **V∼er** m -s,- administrator; manager. **V∼ung** f -,-en administration; management; government

verwand|eln vt transform, change (**in** + acc into); **sich v∼eln** change, turn (**in** + acc into). **V∼lung** f transformation

verwandt a related (**mit** to). **V∼e(r)** m/f relative. **V∼schaft** f - relationship; (Menschen) relatives pl

verwarn|en vt warn, caution. **V∼ung** f warning, caution

verwaschen a washed out, faded

verwechs|eln vt mix up, confuse; (halten für) mistake (**mit** for). **V∼lung** f -,-en mix-up

verwegen a audacious, adv -ly

Verwehung f -,-en [snow-]drift

verweichlicht a (fig) soft

verweiger|n vt/i (haben) refuse (**jdm etw** s.o sth); **den Gehorsam v∼n** refuse to obey. **V∼ung** f refusal

verweilen vi (haben) stay

Verweis m -es,-e reference (**auf** + acc to); (Tadel) reprimand. **v∼en†** vt refer (**auf/an** + acc to); (tadeln) reprimand; **von der Schule v∼en** expel

verwelken vi (sein) wilt

verwend|en† vt use; spend ⟨Zeit, Mühe⟩. **V∼ung** f use

verwerf|en† vt reject; **sich v∼en** warp. **v∼lich** a reprehensible

verwert|en vt utilize, use; (Comm) exploit. **V∼ung** f - utilization; exploitation

verwesen vi (sein) decompose

verwick|eln vt involve (**in** + acc in); **sich v∼eln** get tangled up; **in etw** (acc) **v∼elt sein** (fig) be involved or mixed up in sth. **v∼elt** a complicated

verwildert a wild; ⟨Garten⟩ overgrown; ⟨Aussehen⟩ unkempt

verwinden† vt (fig) get over

verwirken vt forfeit

verwirklichen vt realize; **sich v∼be** realized

verwirr|en vt tangle up; (fig) confuse; **sich v∼en** get tangled; (fig) become confused. **v∼t** a confused. **V∼ung** f - confusion

verwischen vt smudge

verwittert a weathered; ⟨Gesicht⟩ weather-beaten

verwitwet a widowed

verwöhn|en vt spoil. **v∼t** a spoilt; (anspruchsvoll) discriminating

verworren a confused

verwund|bar a vulnerable. **v∼en** vt wound

verwunder|lich a surprising. **v∼n** vt surprise; **sich v∼n** be surprised. **V∼ung** f - surprise

Verwund|ete(r) m wounded soldier; **die V∼eten** the wounded pl. **V∼ung** f -,-en wound

verwünsch|en vt curse. **v∼t** a confounded

verwüst|en vt devastate, ravage. **V∼ung** f -,-en devastation

verzagen vi (haben) lose heart

verzählen (sich) vr miscount

verzärteln vt mollycoddle

verzaubern vt bewitch; (fig) enchant; **v∼ in** (+ acc) turn into

Verzehr m -s consumption. **v∼en** vt eat; (aufbrauchen) use up; **sich v∼en** (fig) pine away

verzeich|nen vt list; (registrieren) register. **V∼nis** nt -ses,-se list; (Inhalts-) index

verzeih|en† vt forgive; **v∼en Sie!** excuse me! **V∼ung** f - forgiveness; **um V∼ung bitten** apologize; **V∼ung!** sorry! (bei Frage) excuse me!

verzerren vt distort; contort ⟨Gesicht⟩; pull ⟨Muskel⟩

Verzicht m -[e]s renunciation (**auf** + acc of). **v∼en** vi (haben) do without; **v∼en auf** (+ acc) give up; renounce ⟨Recht, Erbe⟩

verziehen† vt pull out of shape; (verwöhnen) spoil; **sich v∼** lose shape; ⟨Holz:⟩ warp; ⟨Gesicht:⟩ twist; (verschwinden) disappear; ⟨Nebel:⟩ disperse; ⟨Gewitter:⟩ pass; **das Gesicht v∼** pull a face ● vi (sein) move [away]

verzier|en vt decorate. **V∼ung** f -,-en decoration

verzinsen vt pay interest on

verzöger|n vt delay; (verlangsamen) slow down; **sich v∼n** be delayed. **V∼ung** f -,-en delay

verzollen vt pay duty on; **haben Sie etwas zu v∼?** have you anything to declare?

verzück|t a ecstatic, adv -ally. **V∼ung** f - rapture, ecstasy

Verzug m delay; **in V∼** in arrears

verzweif|eln vi (sein) despair. **v∼elt** a desperate, adv -ly; **v∼elt sein** be in despair; *(ratlos)* be desperate. **V~lung** *f* - despair; *(Ratlosigkeit)* desperation

verzweigen (sich) *vr* branch [out]

verzwickt *a (fam)* tricky

Veto /'ve:to/ *nt* -s,-s veto

Vetter *m* -s,-n cousin. **V~nwirtschaft** *f* nepotism

vgl. *abbr* **(vergleiche)** cf.

Viadukt /via'dʊkt/ *nt* -[e]s,-e viaduct

vibrieren /vi'bri:rən/ *vi (haben)* vibrate

Video /'vi:deo/ *nt* -s,-s video. **V~kassette** *f* video cassette. **V~recorder** /-rəkɔrdɐ/ *m* -s,- video recorder

Vieh *nt* -[e]s livestock; *(Rinder)* cattle *pl*; *(fam: Tier)* creature. **v~isch** *a* brutal, *adv* -ly

viel *pron* a great deal/ *(fam)* a lot of; *(pl)* many, *(fam)* a lot of; *(substantivisch)* **v~[es]** much, *(fam)* a lot; **nicht/zu v~** not/too much; **v~e** *pl* many; **das v~e Geld/Lesen** all that money/reading ● *adv* much, *(fam)* a lot; **v~ mehr/weniger** much more/less; **v~ zu groß/klein** much or far too big/small

viel|deutig *a* ambiguous. **v~erlei** *inv a* many kinds of ● *pron* many things. **v~fach** *a* multiple ● *adv* many times; *(fam: oft)* frequently. **V~falt** *f* - diversity, [great] variety. **v~fältig** *a* diverse, varied

vielleicht *adv* perhaps, maybe; *(fam: wirklich)* really

vielmals *adv* very much; **danke v~!** thank you very much!

viel|mehr *adv* rather; *(im Gegenteil)* on the contrary. **v~sagend** *a* meaningful, *adv* -ly

vielseitig *a* varied; *(Person)* versatile ● *adv* **v~ begabt** versatile. **V~keit** *f* - versatility

vielversprechend *a* promising

vier *inv a*, **V~** *f* -,-en four; *(Sch)* / fair. **V~eck** *nt* -[e]s,-e oblong, rectangle; *(Quadrat)* square. **v~eckig** *a* oblong, rectangular; square. **v~fach** *a* quadruple. **V~linge** *mpl* quadruplets

Viertel /'fɪrtəl/ *nt* -s,- quarter; *(Wein)* quarter litre; **v~ vor/nach sechs** [a] quarter to/past six; **V~ neun** [a] quarter past eight; **drei V~ neun** [a] quarter to nine. **V~finale** *nt* quarter-final. **V~jahr** *nt* three months *pl*; *(Comm)* quarter. **v~jährlich** *a & adv* quarterly. **v~n** *vt* quarter. **V~note** *f* crotchet, *(Amer)* quarter note. **V~stunde** *f* quarter of an hour

vier|zehn /'fɪr-/ *inv a* fourteen. **v~zehnte(r,s)** *a* fourteenth. **v~zig** *inv a* forty. **v~zigste(r,s)** *a* fortieth

Villa /'vɪla/ *f* -,-len villa

violett /vio'lɛt/ *a* violet

Vio|line /vio'li:nə/ *f* -,-n violin. **V~linschlüssel** *m* treble clef. **V~loncello** /-lɔn'tʃɛlo/ *nt* cello

Virtuose /vɪr'tuo:zə/ *m* -n,-n virtuoso

Virus /'vi:rʊs/ *nt* -,-ren virus

Visier /vi'zi:ɐ/ *nt* -s,-e visor

Vision /vi'zjo:n/ *f* -,-en vision

Visite /vi'zi:tə/ *f* -,-n round; **V~ machen** do one's round

visuell /vi'zuɛl/ *a* visual, *adv* -ly

Visum /'vi:zʊm/ *nt* -s,-sa visa

vital /vi'ta:l/ *a* vital; *(Person)* energetic. **V~ität** *f* - vitality

Vitamin /vita'mi:n/ *nt* -s,-e vitamin

Vitrine /vi'tri:nə/ *f* -,-n display cabinet/ *(im Museum)* case

Vizepräsident /'fi:tsə-/ *m* vice president

Vogel *m* -s,- bird; **einen V~ haben** *(fam)* have a screw loose. **V~scheuche** *f* -,-n scarecrow

Vokab|eln /vo'ka:bəln/ *fpl* vocabulary *sg.* **V~ular** *nt* -s,-e vocabulary

Vokal /vo'ka:l/ *m* -s,-e vowel

Volant /vo'lã:/ *m* -s,-s flounce; *(Auto)* steering-wheel

Volk *nt* -[e]s,-er people *sg*; *(Bevölkerung)* people *pl*; *(Bienen-)* colony

Völker|kunde *f* ethnology. **V~mord** *m* genocide. **V~recht** *nt* international law

Volks|abstimmung *f* plebiscite. **V~fest** *nt* public festival. **V~hochschule** *f* adult education classes *pl*/ *(Gebäude)* centre. **V~lied** *nt* folksong. **V~tanz** *m* folk-dance. **v~tümlich** *a* popular. **V~wirt** *m* economist. **V~wirtschaft** *f* economics *sg.* **V~zählung** *f* [national] census

voll *a* full *(von od mit* of); *(Haar)* thick; *(Erfolg, Ernst)* complete; *(Wahrheit)* whole; **v~ machen** fill up; **die Uhr schlug v~** *(fam)* the clock struck the hour ● *adv (ganz)* completely; *(arbeiten)* full-time; *(auszahlen)* in full; **v~ und ganz** completely

vollauf *adv* fully, completely

Voll|beschäftigung *f* full employment. **V~blut** *nt* thoroughbred

vollbringen† *vt insep* accomplish; work *(Wunder)*

vollende|n *vt insep* complete. **v~t** *a* perfect, *adv* -ly; **v~te Gegenwart/ Vergangenheit** perfect/pluperfect
vollends *adv* completely
Vollendung *f* completion; (*Vollkommenheit*) perfection
voller *inv a* full of; **v~ Angst/Freude** filled with fear/joy; **v~ Flecken** covered with stains
Völlerei *f* - gluttony
Volleyball /'voli-/ *m* volleyball
vollführen *vt insep* perform
vollfüllen *vt sep* fill up
Vollgas *nt* **V~ geben** put one's foot down; **mit V~** flat out
völlig *a* complete, *adv* -ly
volljährig *a* **v~ sein** (*Jur*) be of age. **V~keit** *f* - (*Jur*) majority
Vollkaskoversicherung *f* fully comprehensive insurance
vollkommen *a* perfect, *adv* -ly; (*völlig*) complete, *adv* -ly. **V~heit** *f* - perfection
Voll|kornbrot *nt* wholemeal bread. **V~macht** *f* -,-en authority; (*Jur*) power of attorney. **V~mond** *m* full moon. **V~pension** *f* full board. **v~schlank** *a* with a fuller figure
vollständig *a* complete, *adv* -ly
vollstrecken *vt insep* execute; carry out ⟨*Urteil*⟩
volltanken *vi sep* (*haben*) (*Auto*) fill up [with petrol]
Volltreffer *m* direct hit
vollzählig *a* complete; **sind wir v~?** are we all here?
vollziehen† *vt insep* carry out; perform ⟨*Handlung*⟩; consummate ⟨*Ehe*⟩; **sich v~** take place
Volt /volt/ *nt* -[s],- volt
Volumen /vo'lu:mən/ *nt* -s,- volume
vom *prep* = **von dem; vom Rauchen** from smoking
von *prep* (+ *dat*) of; (*über*) about; (*Ausgangspunkt, Ursache*) from; (*beim Passiv*) by; **Musik von Mozart** music by Mozart; **einer von euch** one of you; **von hier/heute an** from here/ today; **von mir aus** I don't mind
voneinander *adv* from each other; ⟨*abhängig*⟩ on each other
vonstatten *adv* **v~ gehen** take place; **gut v~ gehen** go [off] well
vor *prep* (+ *dat/acc*) in front of; (*zeitlich, Reihenfolge*) before; (+ *dat*) (*bei Uhrzeit*) to; ⟨*warnen, sich fürchten/ schämen*⟩ of; ⟨*schützen, davonlaufen*⟩ from; ⟨*Respekt haben*⟩ for; **vor Angst/**

Kälte zittern tremble with fear/cold; **vor drei Tagen/Jahren** three days/ years ago; **vor sich** (*acc*) **hin murmeln** mumble to oneself; **vor allen Dingen** above all ● *adv* forward; **vor und zurück** backwards and forwards
Vor|abend *m* eve. **V~ahnung** *f* premonition
voran *adv* at the front; (*voraus*) ahead; (*vorwärts*) forward. **v~gehen†** *vi sep* (*sein*) lead the way; (*Fortschritte machen*) make progress; **jdm/etw v~gehen** precede s.o./sth. **v~kommen†** *vi sep* (*sein*) make progress; (*fig*) get on
Vor|anschlag *m* estimate. **V~anzeige** *f* advance notice. **V~arbeit** *f* preliminary work. **V~arbeiter** *m* foreman
voraus *adv* ahead (*dat* of); (*vorn*) at the front; (*vorwärts*) forward ● **im voraus** in advance. **v~bezahlen** *vt sep* pay in advance. **v~gehen†** *vi sep* (*sein*) go on ahead; **jdm/etw v~gehen** precede s.o./sth. **V~sage** *f* -,-n prediction. **v~sagen** *vt sep* predict. **v~sehen†** *vt sep* foresee
voraussetz|en *vt sep* take for granted; (*erfordern*) require; **vorausgesetzt, daß** provided that. **V~ung** *f* -,-en assumption; (*Erfordernis*) prerequisite; **unter der V~ung, daß** on condition that
Voraussicht *f* foresight; **aller V~ nach** in all probability. **v~lich** *a* anticipated, *expected* ● *adv* probably
Vorbehalt *m* -[e]s,-e reservation. **v~en†** *vt sep* **sich** (*dat*) **v~en** reserve ⟨*Recht*⟩; **jdm v~en sein/bleiben** be left to s.o. **v~los** unreserved, *adv* -ly
vorbei *adv* past (**an jdm/etw** s.o./ sth); (*zu Ende*) over. **v~fahren†** *vi sep* (*sein*) drive/go past. **v~gehen†** *vi sep* (*sein*) go past; (*verfehlen*) miss; (*vergehen*) pass; (*fam: besuchen*) drop in (**bei** on). **v~kommen†** *vi sep* (*sein*) pass/(*v~können*) get past (**an jdm/etw** s.o./sth); (*fam: besuchen*) drop in (**bei** on)
vorbereit|en *vt sep* prepare; prepare for ⟨*Reise*⟩; **sich v~en** prepare [oneself] (**auf** + *acc* for). **V~ung** *f* -,-en preparation
vorbestellen *vt sep* order/(*im Theater, Hotel*) book in advance
vorbestraft *a* **v~ sein** have a [criminal] record

vorbeug|en *v sep* ● *vt* bend forward; **sich v~en** bend *or* lean forward ● *vi* (*haben*) prevent (**etw** *dat* sth); **v~end** preventive. **V~ung** *f* - prevention

Vorbild *nt* model. **v~lich** *a* exemplary, model ● *adv* in an exemplary manner

vorbringen† *vt sep* put forward; offer ⟨*Entschuldigung*⟩

vordatieren *vt sep* post-date

Vorder|bein *nt* foreleg. **v~e(r,s)** *a* front. **V~grund** *m* foreground. **V~mann** *m* (*pl* -**männer**) person in front; **auf V~mann bringen** (*fam*) lick into shape; (*aufräumen*) tidy up. **V~rad** *nt* front wheel. **V~seite** *f* front; (*einer Münze*) obverse. **v~ste(r,s)** *a* front, first. **V~teil** *nt* front

vor|drängeln (sich) *vr sep* (*fam*) jump the queue. **v~drängen (sich)** *vr sep* push forward. **v~dringen†** *vi sep* (*sein*) advance

vor|ehelich *a* pre-marital. **v~eilig** *a* rash, *adv* -ly

voreingenommen *a* biased, prejudiced. **V~heit** *f* - bias

vorenthalten† *vt sep* withhold

vorerst *adv* for the time being

Vorfahr *m* -en,-en ancestor

vorfahren† *vi sep* (*sein*) drive up; (*vorwärts*-) move forward; (*voraus*-) drive on ahead

Vorfahrt *f* right of way; **'V~ beachten'** 'give way'. **V~sstraße** *f* ≈ major road

Vorfall *m* incident. **v~en†** *vi sep* (*sein*) happen

vorfinden† *vt sep* find

Vorfreude *f* [happy] anticipation

vorführ|en *vt sep* present, show; (*demonstrieren*) demonstrate; (*aufführen*) perform. **V~ung** *f* presentation; demonstration; performance

Vor|gabe *f* (*Sport*) handicap. **V~gang** *m* occurrence; (*Techn*) process. **V~gänger(in)** *m* -s,- (*f* -,-nen) predecessor. **V~garten** *m* front garden

vorgeben† *vt sep* pretend

vor|gefaßt *a* preconceived. **v~gefertigt** *a* prefabricated

vorgehen† *vi sep* (*sein*) go forward; (*voraus*-) go on ahead; ⟨*Uhr:*⟩ be fast; (*wichtig sein*) take precedence; (*verfahren*) act, proceed; (*geschehen*) happen, go on. **V~** *nt* -s action

vor|geschichtlich *a* prehistoric. **V~geschmack** *m* foretaste. **V~gesetzte(r)** *m/f* superior. **v~gestern** *adv* the day before yesterday

vorhaben† *vt sep* propose, intend (**zu** to); **etw v~** have sth planned; **nichts v~** have no plans. **V~** *nt* -s,- plan; (*Projekt*) project

vorhalt|en† *v sep* ● *vt* hold up; **jdm etw v~en** reproach s.o. for sth ● *vi* (*haben*) last. **V~ungen** *fpl* **jdm V~ungen machen** reproach s.o. (**wegen** for)

Vorhand *f* (*Sport*) forehand

vorhanden *a* existing; **v~ sein** exist; (*verfügbar sein*) be available. **V~sein** *nt* -s existence

Vorhang *m* curtain

Vorhängeschloß *nt* padlock

vorher *adv* before[hand]

vorhergehend *a* previous

vorherig *a* prior; (*vorhergehend*) previous

Vorherrsch|aft *f* supremacy. **v~en** *vi sep* (*haben*) predominate. **v~end** *a* predominant

Vorher|sage *f* -,-n prediction; (*Wetter*-) forecast. **v~sagen** *vt sep* predict; forecast ⟨*Wetter*⟩. **v~sehen†** *vt sep* foresee

vorhin *adv* just now

vorige(r,s) *a* last, previous

Vor|kämpfer *m* (*fig*) champion. **V~kehrungen** *fpl* precautions. **V~kenntnisse** *fpl* previous knowledge *sg*

vorkommen† *vi sep* (*sein*) happen; (*vorhanden sein*) occur; (*nach vorn kommen*) come forward; (*hervorkommen*) come out; (*zu sehen sein*) show; **jdm bekannt/verdächtig v~** seem familiar/suspicious to s.o.; **sich** (*dat*) **dumm/alt v~** feel stupid/old. **V~** *nt* -s,- occurrence; (*Geol*) deposit

Vorkriegszeit *f* pre-war period

vorlad|en† *vt sep* (*Jur*) summons. **V~ung** *f* summons

Vorlage *f* model; (*Muster*) pattern; (*Gesetzes*-) bill

vorlassen† *vt sep* admit; **jdn v~** (*fam*) let s.o. pass; (*den Vortritt lassen*) let s.o. go first

Vor|lauf *m* (*Sport*) heat. **V~läufer** *m* forerunner. **v~läufig** *a* provisional, *adv* -ly; (*zunächst*) for the time being. **v~laut** *a* forward. **V~leben** *nt* past

vorleg|en *vt sep* put on ⟨*Kette*⟩; (*unterbreiten*) present; (*vorzeigen*)

show; **jdm Fleisch v~en** serve s.o. with meat. **V~er** m -s,- mat; (*Bett-*) rug
vorles|en† vt sep read [out]; **jdm v~en** read to s.o. **V~ung** f lecture
vorletzt|e(r,s) a last ... but one; (*Silbe*) penultimate; **v~es Jahr** the year before last
Vorliebe f preference
vorliebnehmen† vt sep make do (**mit** with)
vorliegen† vi sep (*haben*) be present/(*verfügbar*) available; (*bestehen*) exist, be; **es muß ein Irrtum v~** there must be some mistake. **v~d** a present; (*Frage*) at issue
vorlügen† vt sep lie (*dat* to)
vorm prep = **vor dem**
vormachen vt sep put up; put on (*Kette*); push (*Riegel*); (*zeigen*) demonstrate; **jdm etwas v~** (*fam: täuschen*) kid s.o.
Vormacht f supremacy
vormals adv formerly
Vormarsch m (*Mil & fig*) advance
vormerken vt sep make a note of; (*reservieren*) reserve
Vormittag m morning. **v~** adv **gestern/heute v~** yesterday/this morning. **v~s** adv in the morning
Vormund m -[e]s,-munde & -münder guardian
vorn adv at the front; **nach v~** to the front; **von v~** from the front/(*vom Anfang*) beginning; **von v~ anfangen** start afresh
Vorname m first name
vorne adv = **vorn**
vornehm a distinguished; (*elegant*) smart, adv -ly
vornehmen† vt sep carry out; **sich** (*dat*) **v~, etw zu tun** plan/(*beschließen*) resolve to do sth
vorn|herein adv **von v~herein** from the start. **v~über** adv forward
Vor|ort m suburb. **V~rang** m priority, precedence (**vor** + *dat* over). **V~rat** m -[e]s,-e supply, stock (**an** + *dat* of). **v~rätig** a available; **v~rätig haben** have in stock. **V~ratskammer** f larder. **V~raum** m anteroom. **V~recht** nt privilege. **V~richtung** f device
vorrücken vt/i sep (*sein*) move forward; (*Mil*) advance
Vorrunde f qualifying round
vors prep = **vor das**
vorsagen vt/i sep (*haben*) recite; **jdm** [**die Antwort**] **v~** tell s.o. the answer

Vor|satz m resolution. **v~sätzlich** a deliberate, adv -ly; (*Jur*) premeditated
Vorschau f preview; (*Film-*) trailer
Vorschein m **zum V~ kommen** appear
vorschießen† vt sep advance (*Geld*)
Vorschlag m suggestion, proposal. **v~en†** vt sep suggest, propose
vorschnell a rash, adv -ly
vorschreiben† vt sep lay down; dictate (*dat* to); **vorgeschriebene Dosis** prescribed dose
Vorschrift f regulation; (*Anweisung*) instruction; **jdm V~en machen** tell s.o. what to do; **Dienst nach V~** work to rule. **v~smäßig** a correct, adv -ly
Vorschule f nursery school
Vorschuß m advance
vorschützen vt sep plead [as an excuse]; feign (*Krankheit*)
vorseh|en† v sep ● vt intend (**für/als** for/as); (*planen*) plan; **sich v~en** be careful (**vor** + *dat* of) ● vi (*haben*) peep out. **V~ung** f - providence
vorsetzen vt sep move forward; **jdm etw v~** serve s.o. sth
Vorsicht f - care; (*bei Gefahr*) caution; **V~!** careful! (*auf Schild*) 'caution'. **v~ig** a careful, adv -ly; cautious, adv -ly. **v~shalber** adv to be on the safe side. **V~smaßnahme** f precaution
Vorsilbe f prefix
Vorsitz m chairmanship; **den V~ führen** be in the chair. **v~en†** vi sep (*haben*) preside (*dat* over). **V~ende(r)** m/f chairman
Vorsorge f **V~ treffen** take precautions; make provisions (**für** for). **v~n** vi sep (*haben*) provide (**für** for). **V~untersuchung** f check-up
vorsorglich adv as a precaution
Vorspeise f starter
Vorspiel nt prelude. **v~en** v sep ● vt perform/(*Mus*) play (*dat* for) ● vi (*haben*) audition
vorsprechen† v sep ● vt recite; (*zum Nachsagen*) say (*dat* to) ● vi (*haben*) (*Theat*) audition; **bei jdm v~** call on s.o.
vorspringen† vi sep (*sein*) jut out; **v~des Kinn** prominent chin
Vor|sprung m projection; (*Fels-*) ledge; (*Vorteil*) lead (**vor** + *dat* over). **V~stadt** f suburb. **v~städtisch** a suburban. **V~stand** m board [of

directors]; (*Vereins-*) committee; (*Partei-*) executive

vorsteh|en† *vi sep* (*haben*) project, protrude; **einer Abteilung v~en** be in charge of a department; **v~end** protruding; (*Augen*) bulging. **V~er** *m* -s,- head; (*Gemeinde-*) chairman

vorstell|bar *a* imaginable, conceivable. **v~en** *vt sep* put forward (*Bein, Uhr*); (*darstellen*) represent; (*bekanntmachen*) introduce; **sich v~en** introduce oneself; (*als Bewerber*) go for an interview; **sich** (*dat*) **etw v~en** imagine sth. **V~ung** *f* introduction; (*bei Bewerbung*) interview; (*Aufführung*) performance; (*Idee*) idea; (*Phantasie*) imagination. **V~ungsgespräch** *nt* interview. **V~ungskraft** *f* imagination

Vorstoß *m* advance

Vorstrafe *f* previous conviction

Vortag *m* day before

vortäuschen *vt sep* feign, fake

Vorteil *m* advantage. **v~haft** *a* advantageous, *adv* -ly; (*Kleidung, Farbe*) flattering

Vortrag *m* -[e]s,-̈e talk; (*wissenschaftlich*) lecture; (*Klavier-, Gedicht-*) recital. **v~en†** *vt sep* perform; (*aufsagen*) recite; (*singen*) sing; (*darlegen*) present (*dat* to); express (*Wunsch*)

vortrefflich *a* excellent, *adv* -ly

vortreten† *vi sep* (*sein*) step forward; (*hervor-*) protrude

Vortritt *m* precedence; **jdm den V~ lassen** let s.o. go first

vorüber *adv* **v~ sein** be over; **an etw** (*dat*) **v~** past sth. **v~gehen†** *vi sep* (*sein*) walk past; (*vergehen*) pass. **v~gehend** *a* temporary, *adv* -ily

Vor|urteil *nt* prejudice. **V~verkauf** *m* advance booking

vorverlegen *vt sep* bring forward

Vor|wahl[nummer] *f* dialling code. **V~wand** *m* -[e]s,-̈e pretext; (*Ausrede*) excuse

vorwärts *adv* forward[s]. **v~kommen†** *vi sep* (*sein*) make progress; (*fig*) get on

vorweg *adv* beforehand; (*vorn*) in front; (*voraus*) ahead. **v~nehmen†** *vt sep* anticipate

vorweisen† *vt sep* show

vorwerfen† *vt sep* throw (*dat* to); **jdm etw v~** reproach s.o. with sth; (*beschuldigen*) accuse s.o. of sth

vorwiegend *adv* predominantly

Vorwort *nt* (*pl* -worte) preface

Vorwurf *m* reproach; **jdm Vorwürfe machen** reproach s.o. **v~svoll** *a* reproachful, *adv* -ly

Vorzeichen *nt* sign; (*fig*) omen

vorzeigen *vt sep* show

vorzeitig *a* premature, *adv* -ly

vorziehen† *vt sep* pull forward; draw (*Vorhang*); (*vorverlegen*) bring forward; (*lieber mögen*) prefer; (*bevorzugen*) favour

Vor|zimmer *nt* ante-room; (*Büro*) outer office. **V~zug** *m* preference; (*gute Eigenschaft*) merit, virtue; (*Vorteil*) advantage

vorzüglich *a* excellent, *adv* -ly

vorzugsweise *adv* preferably

vulgär /vʊlˈgɛːɐ̯/ *a* vulgar ● *adv* in a vulgar way

Vulkan /vʊlˈkaːn/ *m* -s,-e volcano

W

Waage *f* -,-n scales *pl*; (*Astr*) Libra. **w~recht** *a* horizontal, *adv* -ly

Wabe *f* -,-n honeycomb

wach *a* awake; (*aufgeweckt*) alert; **w~ werden** wake up

Wach|e *f* -,-n guard; (*Posten*) sentry; (*Dienst*) guard duty; (*Naut*) watch; (*Polizei-*) station; **W~e halten** keep watch; **W~e stehen** stand guard. **w~en** *vi* (*haben*) be awake; **w~en über** (+ *acc*) watch over. **W~hund** *m* guard-dog

Wacholder *m* -s juniper

Wachposten *m* sentry

Wachs *nt* -es wax

wachsam *a* vigilant, *adv* -ly. **W~keit** *f* -vigilance

wachsen†[1] *vi* (*sein*) grow

wachs|en[2] *vt* (*reg*) wax. **W~figur** *f* waxwork. **W~tuch** *nt* oilcloth

Wachstum *nt* -s growth

Wächter *m* -s,- guard; (*Park-*) keeper; (*Parkplatz-*) attendant

Wacht|meister *m* [police] constable. **W~posten** *m* sentry

Wachturm *m* watch-tower

wackel|ig *a* wobbly; (*Stuhl*) rickety; (*Person*) shaky. **W~kontakt** *m* loose connection. **w~n** *vi* (*haben*) wobble; (*zittern*) shake ● *vi* (*sein*) totter

wacklig *a* = wackelig

Wade *f* -,-n (*Anat*) calf

Waffe *f* -,-n weapon; **W~n** arms

Waffel *f* -,-n waffle; (*Eis-*) wafer

Waffen|ruhe f cease-fire. **W~schein** m firearms licence. **W~stillstand** m armistice

Wagemut m daring. **w~ig** a daring, adv -ly

wagen vt risk; **es w~, etw zu tun** dare [to] do sth; **sich w~** (gehen) venture

Wagen m -s,- cart; (Eisenbahn-) carriage, coach; (Güter-) wagon; (Kinder-) pram; (Auto) car. **W~heber** m -s,- jack

Waggon /va'gõ:/ m -s,-s wagon

waghalsig a daring, adv -ly

Wagnis nt -ses,-se risk

Wahl f -,-en choice; (Pol, Admin) election; (geheime) ballot; **zweite W~** (Comm) seconds pl

wähl|en vt/i (haben) choose; (Pol, Admin) elect; (stimmen) vote; (Teleph) dial. **W~er(in)** m -s,- (f -,-nen) voter. **w~erisch** a choosy, fussy

Wahl|fach nt optional subject. **w~frei** a optional. **W~kampf** m election campaign. **W~kreis** m constituency. **W~lokal** nt polling-station. **w~los** a indiscriminate, adv -ly. **W~recht** nt [right to] vote

Wählscheibe f (Teleph) dial

Wahl|spruch m motto. **W~urne** f ballot-box

Wahn m -[e]s delusion; (Manie) mania

wähnen vt believe

Wahnsinn m madness. **w~ig** a mad, insane; (fam: unsinnig) crazy; (fam: groß) terrible; **w~ig werden** go mad ● adv (fam) terribly. **W~ige(r)** m/f maniac

wahr a true; (echt) real; **w~ werden** come true; **du kommst doch, nicht w~?** you are coming, aren't you?

wahren vt keep; (verteidigen) safeguard; **den Schein w~** keep up appearances

währen vi (haben) last

während prep (+ gen) during ● conj while; (wohingegen) whereas. **w~dessen** adv in the meantime

wahrhaben vt **etw nicht w~ wollen** refuse to admit sth

wahrhaftig adv really, truly

Wahrheit f -,-en truth. **w~sgemäß** a truthful, adv -ly

wahrnehm|bar a perceptible. **w~en†** vt sep notice; (nutzen) take advantage of; exploit (Vorteil); look after (Interessen). **W~ung** f -,-en perception

wahrsag|en v sep ● vt predict ● vi (haben) **jdm w~en** tell s.o.'s fortune. **W~erin** f -,-nen fortune-teller

wahrscheinlich a probable, adv -bly. **W~keit** f - probability

Währung f -,-en currency

Wahrzeichen nt symbol

Waise f -,-n orphan. **W~nhaus** nt orphanage. **W~nkind** nt orphan

Wal m -[e]s,-e whale

Wald m -[e]s,¨er wood; (groß) forest. **w~ig** a wooded

Walis|er m -s,- Welshman. **w~isch** a Welsh

Wall m -[e]s,¨e mound; (Mil) rampart

Wallfahr|er(in) m(f) pilgrim. **W~t** f pilgrimage

Walnuß f walnut

Walze f -,-n roller. **w~n** vt roll

wälzen vt roll; pore over (Bücher); mull over (Probleme); **sich w~** roll [about]; (schlaflos) toss and turn

Walzer m -s,- waltz

Wand f -,¨e wall; (Trenn-) partition; (Seite) side; (Fels-) face

Wandel m -s change. **w~bar** a changeable. **w~n** vi (sein) stroll ● vr **sich w~n** change

Wander|er m -s,-, **W~in** f -,-nen hiker, rambler. **w~n** vi (sein) hike, ramble; (ziehen) travel; (gemächlich gehen) wander; (ziellos) roam. **W~schaft** f - travels pl. **W~ung** f -,-en hike, ramble; (länger) walking tour. **W~weg** m footpath

Wandgemälde nt mural

Wandlung f -,-en change, transformation

Wand|malerei f mural. **W~tafel** f blackboard. **W~teppich** m tapestry

Wange f -,-n cheek

wank|elmütig a fickle. **w~en** vi (haben) sway; (Person:) stagger; (fig) waver ● vi (sein) stagger

wann adv when

Wanne f -,-n tub

Wanze f -,-n bug

Wappen nt -s,- coat of arms. **W~kunde** f heraldry

war, wäre s. sein[1]

Ware f -,-n article; (Comm) commodity; (coll) merchandise; **W~n** goods. **W~nhaus** nt department store. **W~nprobe** f sample. **W~nzeichen** nt trademark

warm a (wärmer, wärmst) warm; (Mahlzeit) hot; **w~ machen** heat ● adv warmly; **w~ essen** have a hot meal

Wärm|e f - warmth; (*Phys*) heat; **10 Grad W~e** 10 degrees above zero. **w~en** vt warm; heat ⟨*Essen, Wasser*⟩. **W~flasche** f hot-water bottle

warmherzig a warm-hearted

Warn|blinkanlage f hazard [warning] lights pl. **w~en** vt/i (haben) warn (**vor** + dat of). **W~ung** f -,-en warning

Warteliste f waiting list

warten vi (haben) wait (**auf** + acc for; **auf sich** (acc) **w~ lassen** take one's/ its time ● vt service

Wärter(in) m -s,- (f -,-nen) keeper; (*Museums-*) attendant; (*Gefängnis-*) warder, (*Amer*) guard; (*Kranken-*) orderly

Warte|raum, W~saal m waiting-room. **W~zimmer** nt (*Med*) waiting-room

Wartung f - (*Techn*) service

warum adv why

Warze f -,-n wart

was pron what; **was für [ein]?** what kind of [a]? **was für ein Pech!** what bad luck! **das gefällt dir, was?** you like that, don't you? ● rel pron that; **alles, was ich brauche** all [that] I need ● indef pron (*fam*: etwas) something; (*fragend, verneint*) anything; **was zu essen** something to eat; **so was Ärgerliches!** what a nuisance! ● adv (*fam*)(*warum*) why; (*wie*) how

wasch|bar a washable. **W~becken** nt wash-basin. **W~beutel** m sponge-bag

Wäsche f - washing; (*Unter-*) underwear; **in der W~** in the wash

waschecht a colour-fast; (*fam*) genuine

Wäsche|klammer f clothes-peg. **W~leine** f clothes-line

waschen† vt wash; **sich w~** have a wash; **sich** (dat) **die Hände w~** wash one's hands; **W~ und Legen** shampoo and set ● vi (haben) do the washing

Wäscherei f -,-en laundry

Wäsche|schleuder f spin-drier. **W~trockner** m tumble-drier

Wasch|küche f laundry-room. **W~lappen** m face-flannel, (*Amer*) washcloth; (*fam: Feigling*) sissy. **W~maschine** f washing machine. **W~mittel** nt detergent. **W~pulver** nt washing-powder. **W~raum** m wash-room. **W~salon** m launderette. **W~zettel** m blurb

Wasser nt -s water; (*Haar-*) lotion; **ins W~ fallen** (*fam*) fall through; **mir lief das W~ im Mund zusammen** my mouth was watering. **W~ball** m beach-ball; (*Spiel*) water polo. **w~dicht** a watertight; ⟨*Kleidung*⟩ waterproof. **W~fall** m waterfall. **W~farbe** f watercolour. **W~hahn** m tap, (*Amer*) faucet. **W~kasten** m cistern. **W~kraft** f water-power. **W~kraftwerk** nt hydroelectric power-station. **W~leitung** f water-main; **aus der W~leitung** from the tap. **W~mann** m (*Astr*) Aquarius

wässern vt soak; (*begießen*) water ● vi (haben) water

Wasser|scheide f watershed. **W~ski** nt -s water-skiing. **W~stoff** m hydrogen. **W~straße** f waterway. **W~waage** f spirit-level. **W~werfer** m -s,- water-cannon. **W~zeichen** nt watermark

wäßrig a watery

waten vi (sein) wade

watschein vi (sein) waddle

Watt¹ nt -[e]s mud-flats pl

Watt² nt -s,- (*Phys*) watt

Watt|e f - cotton wool. **w~iert** a padded; (*gesteppt*) quilted

WC /ve'tse:/ nt -s,-s WC

web|en vt/i (haben) weave. **W~er** m -s,- weaver. **W~stuhl** m loom

Wechsel m -s,- change; (*Tausch*) exchange; (*Comm*) bill of exchange. **W~geld** nt change. **w~haft** a changeable. **W~jahre** npl menopause sg. **W~kurs** m exchange rate. **w~n** vt change; (*tauschen*) exchange ● vi (haben) change; (*ab-*) alternate; (*verschieden sein*) vary. **w~nd** a changing; (*verschieden*) varying. **w~seitig** a mutual, adv -ly. **W~strom** m alternating current. **W~stube** f bureau de change. **w~weise** adv alternately. **W~wirkung** f interaction

weck|en vt wake [up]; (*fig*) awaken ● vi (haben) ⟨*Wecker:*⟩ go off. **W~er** m -s,- alarm [clock]

wedeln vi (haben) wave; **mit dem Schwanz w~** wag its tail

weder conj **w~ ... noch** neither ... nor

Weg m -[e]s,-e way; (*Fuß-*) path; (*Fahr-*) track; (*Gang*) errand; **auf dem Weg** on the way (**nach** to); **sich auf den Weg machen** set off; **im Weg sein** be in the way

weg *adv* away, off; *(verschwunden)* gone; **weg sein** be away; *(gegangen/verschwunden)* have gone; *(fam: schlafen)* be asleep; **Hände weg!** hands off! **w~bleiben†** *vi sep (sein)* stay away. **w~bringen†** *vt sep* take away. **wegen** *prep (+ gen)* because of; *(um ... willen)* for the sake of; *(bezüglich)* about

weg|fahren† *vi sep (sein)* go away; *(abfahren)* leave. **w~fallen†** *vi sep (sein)* be dropped/*(ausgelassen)* omitted; *(entfallen)* no longer apply; *(aufhören)* cease. **w~geben†** *vt sep* give away; send to the laundry ⟨Wäsche⟩. **w~gehen†** *vi sep (sein)* leave, go away; *(ausgehen)* go out; *⟨Fleck:⟩* come out. **w~jagen** *vt sep* chase away. **w~kommen†** *vi sep (sein)* get away; *(verlorengehen)* disappear. **w~lassen†** *vt sep* let go; *(auslassen)* omit. **w~laufen†** *vi sep (sein)* run away. **w~machen** *vt sep* remove. **w~nehmen†** *vt sep* take away. **w~räumen** *vt sep* put away; *(entfernen)* clear away. **w~schicken** *vt sep* send away; *(abschicken)* send off. **w~tun†** *vt sep* put away; *(wegwerfen)* throw away

Wegweiser *m* -s,- signpost

weg|werfen† *vt sep* throw away. **w~ziehen†** *v sep* • *vt* pull away • *vi (sein)* move away

weh *a* sore; **weh tun** hurt; ⟨Kopf, Rücken:⟩ ache; **jdm weh tun** hurt s.o. • *int* **oh weh!** oh dear!

wehe *int* alas; **w~ [dir/euch]!** *(drohend)* don't you dare!

wehen *vi (haben)* blow; *(flattern)* flutter • *vt* blow

Wehen *fpl* contractions; **in den W~ liegen** be in labour

weh|leidig *a* soft; *(weinerlich)* whining. **W~mut** *f* - wistfulness. **w~mütig** *a* wistful, *adv* -ly

Wehr¹ *nt* -[e]s,-e weir

Wehr² *f* **sich zur W~ setzen** resist. **W~dienst** *m* military service. **W~dienstverweigerer** *m* -s,- conscientious objector

wehren (sich) *vr* resist; *(gegen Anschuldigung)* protest; *(sich sträuben)* refuse

wehr|los *a* defenceless. **W~macht** *f* armed forces *pl*. **W~pflicht** *f* conscription

Weib *nt* -[e]s,-er woman; *(Ehe-)* wife. **W~chen** *nt* -s,- *(Zool)* female.

W~erheld *m* womanizer. **w~isch** *a* effeminate. **w~lich** *a* feminine; *(Biol)* female. **W~lichkeit** *f* - femininity

weich *a* soft, *adv* -ly; *(gar)* done; ⟨Ei⟩ soft-boiled; ⟨Mensch⟩ soft-hearted; **w~ werden** *(fig)* relent

Weiche *f* -,-n *(Rail)* points *pl*

weichen¹ *vi (sein) (reg)* soak

weichen²† *vi (sein)* give way *(dat* to); **nicht von jds Seite w~** not leave s.o.'s side

Weich|heit *f* - softness. **w~herzig** *a* soft-hearted. **w~lich** *a* soft; ⟨Charakter⟩ weak. **W~spüler** *m* -s,- *(Tex)* conditioner. **W~tier** *nt* mollusc

Weide¹ *f* -,-n *(Bot)* willow

Weide² *f* -,-n pasture. **w~n** *vt/i (haben)* graze; **sich w~n an** *(+ dat)* enjoy; *(schadenfroh)* gloat over

weiger|n (sich) *vr* refuse. **W~ung** *f* -,-en refusal

Weihe *f* -,-n consecration; *(Priester-)* ordination. **w~n** *vt* consecrate; *(zum Priester)* ordain; dedicate ⟨Kirche⟩ *(dat* to)

Weiher *m* -s,- pond

Weihnacht|en *nt* -s & *pl* Christmas. **w~lich** *a* Christmassy. **W~sbaum** *m* Christmas tree. **W~sfest** *nt* Christmas. **W~slied** *nt* Christmas carol. **W~smann** *m (pl* -männer) Father Christmas. **W~stag** *m* **erster/zweiter W~stag** Christmas Day/Boxing Day

Weih|rauch *m* incense. **W~wasser** *nt* holy water

weil *conj* because; *(da)* since

Weile *f* - while

Wein *m* -[e]s,-e wine; *(Bot)* vines *pl*; *(Trauben)* grapes *pl*. **W~bau** *m* wine-growing. **W~beere** *f* grape. **W~berg** *m* vineyard. **W~brand** *m* -[e]s brandy

wein|en *vt/i (haben)* cry, weep. **w~erlich** *a* tearful, *adv* -ly

Wein|glas *nt* wineglass. **W~karte** *f* wine-list. **W~keller** *m* wine-cellar. **W~lese** *f* grape harvest. **W~liste** *f* wine-list. **W~probe** *f* wine-tasting. **W~rebe** *f*, **W~stock** *m* vine. **W~stube** *f* wine-bar. **W~traube** *f* bunch of grapes; *(W~beere)* grape

weise *a* wise, *adv* -ly

Weise *f* -,-n way; *(Melodie)* tune; **auf diese W~** in this way

weisen† *vt* show; **von sich w~** *(fig)* reject • *vi (haben)* point (**auf** + *acc* at)

Weisheit *f* -,-en wisdom. **W~szahn** *m* wisdom tooth

weiß *a*, **W~** *nt* -,- white

weissag|en *vt/i insep (haben)* prophesy. **W~ung** *f* -,-en prophecy

Weiß|brot *nt* white bread. **W~e(r)** *m/f* white man/woman. **w~en** *vt* whitewash. **W~wein** *m* white wine

Weisung *f* -,-en instruction; *(Befehl)* order

weit *a* wide; *(ausgedehnt)* extensive; *(lang)* long ● *adv* widely; *(offen, öffnen)* wide; *(lang)* far; **von w~em** from a distance; **bei w~em** by far; **w~ und breit** far and wide; **ist es noch w~?** is it much further? **ich bin so w~** I'm ready; **zu w~ gehen** *(fig)* go too far. **w~aus** *adv* far. **W~blick** *m (fig)* far-sightedness. **w~blickend** *a (fig)* far-sighted

Weite *f* -,-n expanse; *(Entfernung)* distance; *(Größe)* width. **w~n** *vt* widen; stretch *(Schuhe)*; **sich w~n** widen; stretch; *(Pupille)* dilate

weiter *a* further ● *adv* further; *(außerdem)* in addition; *(anschließend)* then; **etw w~ tun** go on doing sth; **w~ nichts/niemand** nothing/no one else; **und so w~** and so on. **w~arbeiten** *vi sep (haben)* go on working

weiter|e(r,s) *a* further; **im w~en Sinne** in a wider sense; **ohne w~es** just like that; *(leicht)* easily; **bis auf w~es** until further notice; *(vorläufig)* for the time being

weiter|erzählen *vt sep* go on with; *(w~sagen)* repeat. **w~fahren†** *vi sep (sein)* go on. **w~geben†** *vt sep* pass on. **w~gehen†** *vi sep (sein)* go on. **w~hin** *adv (immer noch)* still; *(in Zukunft)* in future; *(außerdem)* furthermore; **etw w~hin tun** go on doing sth. **w~kommen†** *vi sep (sein)* get on. **w~machen** *vi sep (haben)* carry on. **w~sagen** *vt sep* pass on; *(verraten)* repeat

weit|gehend *a* extensive ● *adv* to a large extent. **w~hin** *adv* a long way; *(fig)* widely. **w~läufig** *a* spacious; *(entfernt)* distant, *adv* -ly; *(ausführlich)* lengthy, *adv* at length. **w~reichend** *a* far-reaching. **w~schweifig** *a* long-winded. **w~sichtig** *a* long-sighted; *(fig)* far-sighted. **w~sprung** *m* long jump. **w~verbreitet** *a* widespread

Weizen *m* -s wheat

welch *inv pron* what; **w~ ein(e)** what a. **w~e(r,s)** *pron* which; **um w~e Zeit?** at what time? ● *rel pron* which; *(Person)* who ● *indef pron* some; *(fragend)* any; **was für w~e?** what sort of?

welk *a* wilted; *(Laub)* dead. **w~en** *vi (haben)* wilt; *(fig)* fade

Wellblech *nt* corrugated iron

Well|e *f* -,-n wave; *(Techn)* shaft. **W~enlänge** *f* wavelength. **W~enlinie** *f* wavy line. **W~enreiten** *nt* surfing. **W~ensittich** *m* -s,-e budgerigar. **w~ig** *a* wavy

Welt *f* -,-en world; **auf der W~** in the world; **auf die** *od* **zur W~ kommen** be born. **W~all** *nt* universe. **w~berühmt** *a* world-famous. **w~fremd** *a* unworldly. **w~gewandt** *a* sophisticated. **W~kugel** *f* globe. **w~lich** *a* worldly; *(nicht geistlich)* secular

Weltmeister|(in) *m(f)* world champion. **W~schaft** *f* world championship

Weltraum *m* space. **W~fahrer** *m* astronaut

Welt|rekord *m* world record. **w~weit** *a & adv* world-wide

wem *pron (dat of wer)* to whom

wen *pron (acc of wer)* whom

Wende *f* -,-n change. **W~kreis** *m* *(Geog)* tropic

Wendeltreppe *f* spiral staircase

wenden[1] *vt (reg)* turn; **sich zum Guten w~** take a turn for the better ● *vi (haben)* turn [round]

wenden[2]† *(& reg) vt* turn; **sich w~** turn; **sich an jdn w~** turn/*(schriftlich)* write to s.o.

Wend|epunkt *m (fig)* turning-point. **w~ig** *a* nimble; *(Auto)* manœuvrable. **W~ung** *f* -,-en turn; *(Biegung)* bend; *(Veränderung)* change

wenig *pron* little; *(pl)* few; **w~e** *pl* few ● *adv* little; *(kaum)* not much. **w~er** *pron* less; *(pl)* fewer; **immer w~er** less and less ● *adv & conj* less. **w~ste(r,s)** least; **am w~sten** least *[of all]*. **w~stens** *adv* at least

wenn *conj* if; *(sobald)* when; **immer w~** whenever; **w~ nicht** *od* **außer w~** unless; **w~ auch** even though

wer *pron* who; *(fam: jemand)* someone; *(fragend)* anyone; **ist da wer?** is anyone there?

Werbe|agentur *f* advertising agency. **w~n†** *vt* recruit; attract

⟨Kunden, Besucher⟩ ● vi (haben) w~n für advertise; canvass for ⟨Partei⟩; w~n um try to attract ⟨Besucher⟩; court ⟨Frau, Gunst⟩. **W~spot** /-sp-/ m -s,-s commercial
Werbung f - advertising
werden† vi (sein) become; ⟨müde, alt, länger⟩ get, grow; ⟨blind, wahnsinnig⟩ go; **blaß w~** turn pale; **krank w~** fall ill; **es wird warm/dunkel** it is getting warm/dark; **mir wurde schlecht/schwindlig** I felt sick/dizzy; **er will Lehrer w~** he wants to be a teacher; **was ist aus ihm geworden?** what has become of him? ● v aux (Zukunft) shall; **wir w~ sehen** we shall see; **es wird bald regnen** it's going to rain soon; **würden Sie so nett sein?** would you be so kind? ● (Passiv; pp **worden**) be; **geliebt/geboren w~** be loved/born; **es wurde gemunkelt** it was rumoured
werfen† vt throw; cast ⟨Blick, Schatten⟩; **sich w~** ⟨Holz:⟩ warp ● vi (haben) **w~ mit** throw
Werft f -,-en shipyard
Werk nt -[e]s,-e work; ⟨Fabrik⟩ works sg, factory; ⟨Trieb-⟩ mechanism. **W~en** nt -s ⟨Sch⟩ handicraft. **W~statt** f -,-ẹn workshop; ⟨Auto-⟩ garage; ⟨Künstler-⟩ studio. **W~tag** m weekday. **w~tags** adv on weekdays. **w~tätig** a working. **W~unterricht** m ⟨Sch⟩ handicraft
Werkzeug nt tool; ⟨coll⟩ tools pl. **W~maschine** f machine tool
Wermut m -s vermouth
wert a **viel/50 Mark w~** worth a lot/50 marks; **nichts w~ sein** be worthless; **jds/etw** (gen) **w~ sein** be worthy of s.o./sth. **W~** m -[e]s,-e value; (Nenn-) denomination; **im W~ von** worth; **W~ legen auf** (+ acc) set great store by. **w~en** vt rate
Wert|gegenstand m object of value; **W~gegenstände** valuables. **w~los** a worthless. **W~minderung** f depreciation. **W~papier** nt (Comm) security. **W~sachen** fpl valuables. **w~voll** a valuable
Wesen nt -s,- nature; (Lebe-) being; (Mensch) creature
wesentlich a essential; (grundlegend) fundamental; (erheblich) considerable; **im w~en** essentially ● adv considerably, much
weshalb adv why
Wespe f -,-n wasp

wessen pron (gen of **wer**) whose
westdeutsch a West German
Weste f -,-n waistcoat, (Amer) vest
Westen m -s west; **nach W~** west
Western m -[s],- western
Westfalen nt -s Westphalia
Westindien nt West Indies pl
west|lich a western; ⟨Richtung⟩ westerly ● adv & prep (+ gen) **w~lich [von] der Stadt** [to the] west of the town. **w~wärts** adv westwards
weswegen adv why
wett a **w~ sein** be quits
Wett|bewerb m -s,-e competition. **W~büro** nt betting shop
Wette f -,-n bet; **um die W~ laufen** race (**mit jdm** s.o.)
wetteifern vi (haben) compete
wetten vt/i (haben) bet (**auf** + acc on); **mit jdm w~** have a bet with s.o.
Wetter nt -s,- weather; (Un-) storm. **W~bericht** m weather report. **W~hahn** m weathercock. **W~lage** f weather conditions pl. **W~vorhersage** f weather forecast. **W~warte** f -,-n meteorological station
Wett|kampf m contest. **W~kämpfer(in)** m(f) competitor. **W~lauf** m race. **w~machen** vt sep make up for. **W~rennen** nt race. **W~streit** m contest
wetzen vt sharpen ● vi (sein) (fam) dash
Whisky m -s whisky
wichsen vt polish
wichtig a important; **w~ nehmen** take seriously. **W~keit** f - importance. **w~tuerisch** a self-important
Wicke f -,-n sweet pea
Wickel m -s,- compress
wick|eln vt wind; (ein-) wrap; (bandagieren) bandage; **ein Kind frisch w~eln** change a baby. **W~ler** m -s,- curler
Widder m -s,- ram; (Astr) Aries
wider prep (+ acc) against; (entgegen) contrary to; **w~ Willen** against one's will
widerfahren† vi insep (sein) **jdm w~** happen to s.o.
widerhallen vi insep (haben) echo
widerlegen vt insep refute
wider|lich a repulsive; (unangenehm) nasty, adv -ily. **w~rechtlich** a unlawful, adv -ly. **W~rede** f contradiction; **keine W~rede!** don't argue!

widerrufen† *vt/i insep (haben)* retract; revoke ⟨*Befehl*⟩

Widersacher *m* -s,- adversary

widersetzen (sich) *vr insep* resist (**jdm/etw** s.o./sth)

wider|sinnig *a* absurd. **w~spenstig** *a* unruly; (*störrisch*) stubborn

widerspiegeln *vt sep* reflect; **sich w~** be reflected

widersprechen† *vi insep (haben)* contradict (**jdm/etw** s.o./sth)

Wider|spruch *m* contradiction; (*Protest*) protest. **w~sprüchlich** *a* contradictory. **w~spruchslos** *adv* without protest

Widerstand *m* resistance; **W~ leisten** resist. **w~sfähig** *a* resistant; (*Bot*) hardy

widerstehen† *vi insep (haben)* resist (**jdm/etw** s.o./sth); (*anwidern*) be repugnant (**jdm** to s.o.)

widerstreben *vi insep (haben)* es **widerstrebt mir** I am reluctant (**zu** to). **W~** *nt* -s reluctance. **w~d** *a* reluctant, *adv* -ly

widerwärtig *a* disagreeable, unpleasant; (*ungünstig*) adverse

Widerwill|e *m* aversion, repugnance. **w~ig** *a* reluctant, *adv* -ly

widm|en *vt* dedicate (*dat* to); (*verwenden*) devote (*dat* to); **sich w~en** (+*dat*) devote oneself to. **W~ung** *f* -,-en dedication

widrig *a* adverse, unfavourable

wie *adv* how; **wie viele?** how many? **wie ist Ihr Name?** what is your name? **wie ist das Wetter?** what is the weather like? ● *conj* as; (*gleich wie*) like; (*sowie*) as well as; (*als*) when, as; **genau wie du** just like you; **so gut/ reich wie** as good/rich as; **nichts wie** nothing but; **größer wie ich** (*fam*) bigger than me

wieder *adv* again; **er ist w~ da** he is back

Wiederaufbau *m* reconstruction. **w~en** *vt sep* reconstruct

wieder|aufnehmen† *vt sep* resume. **W~aufrüstung** *f* rearmament

wieder|bekommen† *vt sep* get back. **w~beleben** *vt sep* revive. **W~belebung** *f* - resuscitation. **w~bringen**† *vt sep* bring back. **w~erkennen**† *vt sep* recognize. **W~gabe** *f* (*s.* **w~geben**) return; portrayal; rendering; reproduction. **w~geben**† *vt sep* give back, return;

(*darstellen*) portray; (*ausdrücken, übersetzen*) render; (*zitieren*) quote; (*Techn*) reproduce. **W~geburt** *f* reincarnation

wiedergutmach|en *vt sep* (*fig*) make up for; redress ⟨*Unrecht*⟩; (*bezahlen*) pay for. **W~ung** *f* - reparation; (*Entschädigung*) compensation

wiederher|stellen *vt sep* reestablish; restore ⟨*Gebäude*⟩; restore to health ⟨*Kranke*⟩; be fully recovered. **W~stellung** *f* reestablishment; restoration; (*Genesung*) recovery

wiederholen[1] *vt sep* get back

wiederhol|en[2] *vt insep* repeat; (*Sch*) revise; **sich w~en** recur; ⟨*Person:*⟩ repeat oneself. **w~t** *a* repeated, *adv* -ly. **W~ung** *f* -,-en repetition; (*Sch*) revision

Wieder|hören *nt* **auf W~hören!** goodbye! **W~käuer** *m* -s,- ruminant. **W~kehr** *f* - return; (*W~holung*) recurrence. **w~kehren** *vi sep (sein)* return; (*sich wiederholen*) recur. **w~kommen**† *vi sep (sein)* come back

wiedersehen† *vt sep* see again. **W~** *nt* -s,- reunion; **auf W~!** goodbye!

wiederum *adv* again; (*andererseits*) on the other hand

wiedervereinig|en *vt sep* reunify ⟨*Land*⟩. **W~ung** *f* reunification

wieder|verheiraten (sich) *vr sep* remarry. **w~verwenden**† *vt sep* reuse. **w~verwerten** *vt sep* recycle. **w~wählen** *vt sep* re-elect

Wiege *f* -,-n cradle

wiegen[1]† *vt/i (haben)* weigh

wiegen[2] *vt (reg)* rock; **sich w~** sway; (*schaukeln*) rock. **W~lied** *nt* lullaby

wiehern *vi (haben)* neigh

Wien *nt* -s Vienna. **W~er** *a* Viennese; **W~er Schnitzel** Wiener schnitzel ● *m* -s,- Viennese ● *f* -,- ≈ frankfurter. **w~erisch** *a* Viennese

Wiese *f* -,-n meadow

Wiesel *nt* -s,- weasel

wieso *adv* why

wieviel *pron* how much/(*pl*) many; **um w~ Uhr?** at what time? **w~te(r,s)** *a* which; **der W~te ist heute?** what is the date today?

wieweit *adv* how far

wild *a* wild, *adv* -ly; ⟨*Stamm*⟩ savage; **w~er Streik** wildcat strike; **w~ wachsen** grow wild. **W~** *nt* -[e]s

game; (*Rot-*) deer; (*Culin*) venison. **W~dieb** *m* poacher. **W~e(r)** *m/f* savage
Wilder|er *m* -s,- poacher. **w~n** *vt/i* (*haben*) poach
wildfremd *a* totally strange; **w~e Leute** total strangers
Wild|heger, W~hüter *m* -s,- gamekeeper. **W~leder** *nt* suede. **w~ledern** *a* suede. **W~nis** *f* - wilderness. **W~schwein** *nt* wild boar. **W~westfilm** *m* western
Wille *m* -ns will; **Letzter W~** will; seinen **W~n durchsetzen** get one's [own] way; **mit W~n** intentionally
willen *prep* (+ *gen*) **um ... w~** for the sake of ...
Willens|kraft *f* will-power. **w~stark** *a* strong-willed
willig *a* willing, *adv* -ly
willkommen *a* welcome; **w~ heißen** welcome. **W~** *nt* -s welcome
willkürlich *a* arbitrary, *adv* -ily
wimmeln *vi* (*haben*) swarm
wimmern *vi* (*haben*) whimper
Wimpel *m* -s,- pennant
Wimper *f* -,-n [eye]lash; **nicht mit der W~ zucken** (*fam*) not bat an eyelid. **W~ntusche** *f* mascara
Wind *m* -[e]s,-e wind
Winde *f* -,-n (*Techn*) winch
Windel *f* -,-n nappy, (*Amer*) diaper
winden† *vt* wind; make (*Kranz*); **in die Höhe w~** winch up; **sich w~** wind (**um** round); (*sich krümmen*) writhe
Wind|hund *m* greyhound. **w~ig** *a* windy. **W~mühle** *f* windmill. **W~pocken** *fpl* chickenpox *sg.* **W~schutzscheibe** *f* windscreen, (*Amer*) windshield. **w~still** *a* calm. **W~stille** *f* calm. **W~stoß** *m* gust of wind. **W~surfen** *nt* windsurfing
Windung *f* -,-en bend; (*Spirale*) spiral
Wink *m* -[e]s,-e sign; (*Hinweis*) hint
Winkel *m* -s,- angle; (*Ecke*) corner. **W~messer** *m* -s,- protractor
winken *vi* (*haben*) wave; **jdm w~/wave/(herbei~)** beckon to s.o.
winseln *vi* (*haben*) whine
Winter *m* -s,- winter. **w~lich** *a* wintry; (*Winter-*) winter ... **W~schlaf** *m* hibernation; **W~schlaf halten** hibernate. **W~sport** *m* winter sports *pl*
Winzer *m* -s,- winegrower
winzig *a* tiny, minute
Wipfel *m* -s,- [tree-]top
Wippe *f* -,-n see-saw. **w~n** *vi* (*haben*) bounce; (*auf Wippe*) play on the see-saw

wir *pron* we; **wir sind es** it's us
Wirbel *m* -s,- eddy; (*Drehung*) whirl; (*Trommel-*) roll; (*Anat*) vertebra; (*Haar-*) crown; (*Aufsehen*) fuss. **w~n** *vt/i* (*sein/haben*) whirl. **W~säule** *f* spine. **W~sturm** *m* cyclone. **W~tier** *nt* vertebrate. **W~wind** *m* whirlwind
wird *s.* werden
wirken *vi* (*haben*) have an effect (**auf** + *acc* on); (*zur Geltung kommen*) be effective; (*tätig sein*) work; (*scheinen*) seem ● *vt* (*Tex*) knit; **Wunder w~** work miracles
wirklich *a* real, *adv* -ly. **W~keit** *f* -,-en reality
wirksam *a* effective, *adv* -ly. **W~keit** *f* - effectiveness
Wirkung *f* -,-en effect. **w~slos** *a* ineffective, *adv* -ly. **w~svoll** *a* effective, *adv* -ly
wirr *a* tangled; (*Haar*) tousled; (*verwirrt, verworren*) confused. **W~warr** *m* -s tangle; (*fig*) confusion; (*von Stimmen*) hubbub
Wirt *m* -[e]s,-e landlord. **W~in** *f* -,-nen landlady
Wirtschaft *f* -,-en economy; (*Gast-*) restaurant; (*Kneipe*) pub. **w~en** *vi* (*haben*) manage one's finances; (*sich betätigen*) busy oneself; **sie kann nicht w~en** she's a bad manager. **W~erin** *f* -,-nen housekeeper. **w~lich** *a* economic, *adv* -ally; (*sparsam*) economical, *adv* -ly. **W~sgeld** *nt* housekeeping [money]. **W~sprüfer** *m* auditor
Wirtshaus *nt* inn; (*Kneipe*) pub
Wisch *m* -[e]s,-e (*fam*) piece of paper
wischen *vt/i* (*haben*) wipe; wash (*Fußboden*) ● *vi* (*sein*) slip; (*Maus:*) scurry. **W~lappen** *m* cloth; (*Aufwisch-*) floor-cloth
wispern *vt/i* (*haben*) whisper
wissen† *vt/i* (*haben*) know; **weißt du noch?** do you remember? **nichts w~ wollen von** not want anything to do with. **W~** *nt* -s knowledge; **meines W~s** to my knowledge
Wissenschaft *f* -,-en science. **W~ler** *m* -s,- academic; (*Natur-*) scientist. **w~lich** *a* academic, *adv* -ally; scientific, *adv* -ally
wissen|swert *a* worth knowing. **w~tlich** *a* deliberate ● *adv* knowingly
wittern *vt* scent; (*ahnen*) sense. **W~ung** *f* - scent; (*Wetter*) weather

Witwe *f* -,-n widow. **W~r** *m* -s,- widower

Witz *m* -es,-e joke; (*Geist*) wit. **W~bold** *m* -[e]s,-e joker. **w~ig** *a* funny; (*geistreich*) witty

wo *adv* where; (*als*) when; (*irgendwo*) somewhere; **wo immer** wherever ● *conj* seeing that; (*obwohl*) although; (*wenn*) if

woanders *adv* somewhere else

wobei *adv* how; (*relativ*) during the course of which

Woche *f* -,-n week. **W~nende** *nt* weekend. **W~nkarte** *f* weekly ticket. **W~nlang** *adv* for weeks. **W~ntag** *m* day of the week; (*Werktag*) weekday. **w~ntags** *adv* on weekdays

wöchentlich *a & adv* weekly

Wodka *m* -s vodka

wodurch *adv* how; (*relativ*) through/ (*Ursache*) by which; (*Folge*) as a result of which

wofür *adv* what … for; (*relativ*) for which

Woge *f* -,-n wave

wogegen *adv* what … against; (*relativ*) against which ● *conj* whereas

woher *adv* where from; **woher weißt du das?** how do you know that? **wohin** *adv* where [to]; **wohin gehst du?** where are you going? **wohingegen** *conj* whereas

wohl *adv* well; (*vermutlich*) probably; (*etwa*) about; (*zwar*) perhaps; **w~ kaum** hardly; **w~ oder übel** willy-nilly; **sich w~ fühlen** feel well/ (*behaglich*) comfortable; **der ist w~ verrückt!** he must be mad! **W~** *nt* -[e]s welfare, well-being; **auf jds W~ trinken** drink s.o.'s health; **zum W~** (+*gen*) for the good of; **zum W~!** cheers!

wohlauf *a* **w~ sein** be well

Wohl|befinden *nt* well-being. **W~behagen** *nt* feeling of well-being. **w~behalten** *a* safe, *adv* -ly. **W~ergehen** *nt* -s welfare. **w~erzogen** *a* well brought-up

Wohlfahrt *f* - welfare. **W~sstaat** *m* Welfare State

Wohl|gefallen *nt* -s pleasure. **W~geruch** *m* fragrance. **W~gesinnt** *a* well disposed (*dat* towards). **w~habend** *a* prosperous, well-to-do. **w~ig** *a* comfortable, *adv* -bly. **w~klingend** *a* melodious. **w~riechend** *a* fragrant. **w~schmeckend** *a* tasty

Wohlstand *m* prosperity. **W~sgesellschaft** *f* affluent society

Wohltat *f* [act of] kindness; (*Annehmlichkeit*) treat; (*Genuß*) bliss

Wohltät|er *m* benefactor. **w~ig** *a* charitable

wohl|tuend *a* agreeable, *adv* -bly. **w~tun†** *vi sep* (*haben*) **jdm w~tun** do s.o. good. **w~verdient** *a* well-deserved. **w~weislich** *adv* deliberately

Wohlwollen *nt* -s goodwill; (*Gunst*) favour. **w~d** *a* benevolent, *adv* -ly

Wohn|anhänger *m* = **Wohnwagen**. **W~block** *m* block of flats. **w~en** *vi* (*haben*) live; (*vorübergehend*) stay. **W~gegend** *f* residential area. **w~haft** *a* resident. **W~haus** *nt* [dwelling-]house. **W~heim** *nt* hostel; (*Alten-*) home. **w~lich** *a* comfortable, *adv* -bly. **W~mobil** *nt* -s,-e camper. **W~ort** *m* place of residence. **W~raum** *m* living space; (*Zimmer*) living-room. **W~sitz** *m* place of residence

Wohnung *f* -,-en flat, (*Amer*) apartment; (*Unterkunft*) accommodation. **W~snot** *f* housing shortage

Wohn|wagen *m* caravan, (*Amer*) trailer. **W~zimmer** *nt* living-room

wölben *vt* curve; arch (*Rücken*). **W~ung** *f* -,-en curve; (*Archit*) vault

Wolf *m* -[e]s,ˈe wolf; (*Fleisch-*) mincer; (*Reiß-*) shredder

Wolke *f* -,-n cloud. **W~nbruch** *m* cloudburst. **W~nkratzer** *m* skyscraper. **w~nlos** *a* cloudless. **w~ig** *a* cloudy

Woll|decke *f* blanket. **W~e** *f* -,-n wool

wollen† *vt/i* (*haben*) & *v aux* want; **etw tun w~** want to do sth; (*beabsichtigen*) be going to do sth; **ich will nach Hause** I want to go home; **wir wollten gerade gehen** we were just going; **ich wollte, ich könnte dir helfen** I wish I could help you; **der Motor will nicht anspringen** the engine won't start

wollen *a* woollen. **w~ig** *a* woolly. **W~sachen** *fpl* woollens

wollüstig *a* sensual, *adv* -ly

womit *adv* what … with; (*relativ*) with which. **womöglich** *adv* possibly. **wonach** *adv* what … after/(*suchen*) for/(*riechen*) of; (*relativ*) after/for/of which

Wonn|e *f* -,-n bliss; (*Freude*) joy.
w~ig *a* sweet

woran *adv* what ... on/⟨*denken, sterben*⟩ of; (*relativ*) on/of which; **woran hast du ihn erkannt?** how did you recognize him? **worauf** *adv* what ... on/⟨*warten*⟩ for; (*relativ*) on/for which; (*woraufhin*) whereupon.

woraufhin *adv* whereupon. **woraus** *adv* what ... from; (*relativ*) from which. **worin** *adv* what ... in; (*relativ*) in which

Wort *nt* -[e]s,-̈er & -e word; **jdm ins W~ fallen** interrupt s.o.; **ein paar W~e sagen** say a few words. **w~brüchig** *a* **w~brüchig werden** break one's word

Wörterbuch *nt* dictionary

Wort|führer *m* spokesman. **w~getreu** *a* & *adv* word-for-word. **w~gewandt** *a* eloquent, *adv* -ly. **w~karg** *a* taciturn. **W~laut** *m* wording

wörtlich *a* literal, *adv* -ly; (*wortgetreu*) word-for-word

wort|los *a* silent ● *adv* without a word. **W~schatz** *m* vocabulary. **W~spiel** *nt* pun, play on words. **W~wechsel** *m* exchange of words; (*Streit*) argument. **w~wörtlich** *a* & *adv* = wörtlich

worüber *adv* what ... over/⟨*lachen, sprechen*⟩ about; (*relativ*) over/ about which. **worum** *adv* what ... round/⟨*bitten, kämpfen*⟩ for; (*relativ*) round/for which; **worum geht es?** what is it about? **worunter** *adv* what ... under/⟨*wozwischen*⟩ among; (*relativ*) under/among which. **wovon** *adv* what ... from/ ⟨*sprechen*⟩ about; (*relativ*) from/about which. **wovor** *adv* what ... in front of; ⟨*sich fürchten*⟩ what ... of; (*relativ*) in front of which; of which. **wozu** *adv* what ... to/⟨*brauchen, benutzen*⟩ for; (*relativ*) to/for which; **wozu?** what for?

Wrack *nt* -s,-s wreck

wringen† *vt* wring

wucher|n *vi* (*haben/sein*) grow profusely. **W~preis** *m* extortionate price. **W~ung** *f* -,-en growth

Wuchs *m* -es growth; (*Gestalt*) stature

Wucht *f* - force. **w~en** *vt* heave. **w~ig** *a* massive

wühlen *vi* (*haben*) rummage; (*in der Erde*) burrow ● *vt* dig

Wulst *m* -[e]s,-̈e bulge; (*Fett-*) roll. **w~ig** *a* bulging; ⟨*Lippen*⟩ thick

wund *a* sore; **w~ reiben** chafe. **W~brand** *m* gangrene

Wunde *f* -,-n wound

Wunder *nt* -s,- wonder, marvel; (*übernatürliches*) miracle; **kein W~!** no wonder! **w~bar** *a* miraculous; (*herrlich*) wonderful, *adv* -ly, marvellous, *adv* -ly. **W~kind** *nt* infant prodigy. **w~lich** *a* odd, *adv* -ly. **w~n** *vt* surprise; **sich w~n** be surprised (**über** + *acc* at). **w~schön** *a* beautiful, *adv* -ly. **w~voll** *a* wonderful, *adv* -ly

Wundstarrkrampf *m* tetanus

Wunsch *m* -[e]s,-̈e wish; (*Verlangen*) desire; (*Bitte*) request

wünschen *vt* want; **sich** (*dat*) **etw w~** want sth; (*bitten um*) ask for sth; **jdm Glück/gute Nacht w~** wish s.o. luck/good night; **ich wünschte, ich könnte** ... I wish I could . . .; **Sie w~?** can I help you? **w~swert** *a* desirable

Wunsch|konzert *nt* musical request programme. **W~traum** *m* (*fig*) dream

wurde, würde *s.* werden

Würde *f* -,-n dignity; (*Ehrenrang*) honour. **w~los** *a* undignified. **W~nträger** *m* dignitary. **w~voll** *a* dignified ● *adv* with dignity

würdig *a* dignified; (*wert*) worthy. **w~en** *vt* recognize; (*schätzen*) appreciate; **keines Blickes w~en** not deign to look at

Wurf *m* -[e]s,-̈e throw; (*Junge*) litter

Würfel *m* -s,- cube; (*Spiel-*) dice; (*Zucker-*) lump. **w~n** *vi* (*haben*) throw the dice; **w~n um** play dice for ● *vt* throw; (*in Würfel schneiden*) dice. **W~zucker** *m* cube sugar

würgen *vt* choke ● *vi* (*haben*) retch; **choke** (**an** + *dat* on)

Wurm *m* -[e]s,-̈er worm; (*Made*) maggot. **w~en** *vi* (*haben*) **jdn w~en** (*fam*) rankle [with s.o.]. **w~stichig** *a* worm-eaten

Wurst *f* -,-̈e sausage; **das ist mir W~** (*fam*) I couldn't care less

Würstchen *nt* -s,- small sausage; **Frankfurter W~** frankfurter

Würze *f* -,-n spice; (*Aroma*) aroma

Wurzel *f* -,-n root; **W~n schlagen** take root. **w~n** *vi* (*haben*) root

würz|en *vt* season. **w~ig** *a* tasty; (*aromatisch*) aromatic; (*pikant*) spicy

wüst *a* chaotic; *(wirr)* tangled; *(öde)* desolate; *(wild)* wild, *adv* -ly; *(schlimm)* terrible, *adv* -bly

Wüste *f* -,-n desert

Wut *f* - rage, fury. **W~anfall** *m* fit of rage

wüten *vi (haben)* rage. **w~d** *a* furious, *adv* -ly; **w~d machen** infuriate

X

x /ɪks/ *inv a (Math)* x; *(fam)* umpteen. **X-Beine** *ntpl* knock-knees. **x-beinig** *a* knock-kneed. **x-beliebig** *a (fam)* any; **eine x-beliebige Zahl** any number [you like]. **x-mal** *adv (fam)* umpteen times

Y

Yoga /ˈjoːga/ *m & nt* -[s] yoga

Z

Zack|e *f* -,-n point; *(Berg-)* peak; *(Gabel-)* prong. **z~ig** *a* jagged; *(gezackt)* serrated; *(fam: schneidig)* smart, *adv* -ly

zaghaft *a* timid, *adv* -ly; *(zögernd)* tentative, *adv* -ly

zäh *a* tough; *(hartnäckig)* tenacious, *adv* -ly; *(zähflüssig)* viscous; *(schleppend)* sluggish, *adv* -ly. **z~flüssig** *a* viscous; *(Verkehr)* slow-moving. **Z~igkeit** *f* - toughness; tenacity

Zahl *f* -,-en number; *(Ziffer, Betrag)* figure

zahl|bar *a* payable. **z~en** *vt/i (haben)* pay; *(bezahlen)* pay for; **bitte z~en!** the bill please!

zählen *vi (haben)* count; **z~ zu** *(fig)* be one/*(pl)* some of; **z~ auf** (+*acc*) count on ● *vt* count; **z~ zu** add to; *(fig)* count among; **die Stadt zählt 5000 Einwohner** the town has 5000 inhabitants

zahlenmäßig *a* numerical, *adv* -ly

Zähler *m* -s,- meter

Zahl|grenze *f* fare-stage. **Z~karte** *f* paying-in slip. **z~los** *a* countless. **z~reich** *a* numerous; ⟨*Anzahl, Gruppe*⟩ large ● *adv* in large numbers. **Z~ung** *f* -,-en payment; **in Z~ung nehmen** take in part-exchange

Zählung *f* -,-en count

zahlungsunfähig *a* insolvent

Zahlwort *nt (pl* **-wörter)** numeral

zahm *a* tame

zähmen *vt* tame; *(fig)* restrain

Zahn *m* -[e]s,ˑe tooth; *(am Zahnrad)* cog. **Z~arzt** *m*, **Z~ärztin** *f* dentist. **Z~belag** *m* plaque. **Z~bürste** *f* toothbrush. **z~en** *vi (haben)* be teething. **Z~fleisch** *nt* gums *pl.* **z~los** *a* toothless. **Z~pasta** *f* -,-en toothpaste. **Z~rad** *nt* cog-wheel. **Z~schmelz** *m* enamel. **Z~schmerzen** *mpl* toothache *sg.* **Z~spange** *f* brace. **Z~stein** *m* tartar. **Z~stocher** *m* -s,- toothpick

Zange *f* -,-en pliers *pl; (Kneif-)* pincers *pl; (Kohlen-, Zucker-)* tongs *pl; (Geburts-)* forceps *pl*

Zank *m* -[e]s squabble. **z~en** *vr* sich **z~en** squabble ● *vi (haben)* scold (**mit jdm** s.o.)

zänkisch *a* quarrelsome

Zäpfchen *nt* -s,- *(Anat)* uvula; *(Med)* suppository

Zapfen *m* -s,- *(Bot)* cone; *(Stöpsel)* bung; *(Eis-)* icicle. **z~** *vt* tap, draw. **Z~streich** *m (Mil)* tattoo

Zapf|hahn *m* tap. **Z~säule** *f* petrol-pump

zappel|ig *a* fidgety; *(nervös)* jittery. **z~n** *vi (haben)* wriggle; ⟨*Kind:*⟩ fidget

zart *a* delicate, *adv* -ly; *(weich, zärtlich)* tender, *adv* -ly; *(sanft)* gentle, *adv* -ly. **Z~gefühl** *nt* tact. **Z~heit** *f* - delicacy; tenderness; gentleness

zärtlich *a* tender, *adv* -ly; *(liebevoll)* loving, *adv* -ly. **Z~keit** *f* -,-en tenderness; *(Liebkosung)* caress

Zauber *m* -s magic; *(Bann)* spell. **Z~er** *m* -s,- magician. **z~haft** *a* enchanting. **Z~künstler** *m* con- juror. **Z~kunststück** *nt* = **Z~trick. Z~n** *vi (haben)* do magic; *(Zaubertricks ausführen)* do conjuring tricks ● *vt* produce as if by magic. **Z~stab** *m* magic wand. **Z~trick** *m* conjuring trick

zaudern *vi (haben)* delay; *(zögern)* hesitate

Zaum *m* -[e]s, Zäume bridle; **im Z~ halten** *(fig)* restrain

Zaun *m* -[e]s, Zäune fence. **Z~könig** *m* wren

z.B. *abbr* **(zum Beispiel)** e.g.

Zebra *nt* -s,-s zebra. **Z~streifen** *m* zebra-crossing

Zeche *f* -,-en bill; *(Bergwerk)* pit

zechen *vi (haben) (fam)* drink
Zeder *f* -,-n cedar
Zeh *m* -[e]s,-en toe. **Z~e** *f* -,-n toe;
(*Knoblauch-*) clove. **Z~ennagel** *m* toenail
zehn *inv a*, **Z~** *f* -,-en ten. **z~te(r,s)** *a*
tenth. **Z~tel** *nt* -s,- tenth
Zeichen *nt* -s,- sign; (*Signal*) signal.
Z~setzung *f* - punctuation. **Z~trick-
film** *m* cartoon [film]
zeichn|en *vt/i (haben)* draw; (*kenn-*)
mark; (*unter-*) sign. **Z~er** *m* -s,-
draughtsman. **Z~ung** *f* -,-en drawing;
(*auf Fell*) markings *pl*
Zeige|finger *m* index finger. **z~n** *vt*
show; **sich z~n** appear; (*sich herausstellen*) become clear; **das wird sich
z~n** we shall see ● *vi (haben)* point
(**auf** + *acc* to). **Z~r** *m* -s,- pointer;
(*Uhr-*) hand
Zeile *f* -,-n line; (*Reihe*) row
zeit *prep* (+ *gen*) **z~ meines/seines
Lebens** all my/his life
Zeit *f* -,-en time; **sich** (*dat*) **Z~ lassen**
take one's time; **es hat Z~** there's no
hurry; **mit der Z~** in time; **in nächster Z~** in the near future; **die erste
Z~** at first; **von Z~ zu Z~** from time
to time; **zur Z~** at present; (*rechtzeitig*)
in time; **[ach] du liebe Z~!** (*fam*)
good heavens!
Zeit|alter *nt* age, era. **Z~arbeit** *f*
temporary work. **Z~bombe** *f* time
bomb. **z~gemäß** *a* modern, up-to-
date. **Z~genosse** *m*, **Z~genossin** *f*
contemporary. **z~genössisch** *a* contemporary. **z~ig** *a & adv* early.
Z~lang *f* **eine Z~lang** for a time *or*
while. **z~lebens** *adv* all one's life
zeitlich *a* (*Dauer*) in time; (*Folge*)
chronological ● *adv* **z~ begrenzt**
for a limited time
zeit|los *a* timeless. **Z~lupe** *f* slow
motion. **Z~punkt** *m* time. **z~rau-
bend** *a* time-consuming. **Z~raum** *m*
period. **Z~schrift** *f* magazine, periodical
Zeitung *f* -,-en newspaper. **Z~spa-
pier** *nt* newspaper
Zeit|verschwendung *f* waste of
time. **Z~vertreib** *m* pastime; **zum
Z~vertreib** to pass the time. **z~wei-
lig** *a* temporary ● *adv* temporarily;
(*hin und wieder*) at times. **z~weise**
adv at times. **Z~wort** *nt* (*pl* -**wörter**)
verb. **Z~zünder** *m* time fuse
Zelle *f* -,-n cell; (*Telefon-*) box

Zelt *nt* -[e]s,-e tent; (*Fest-*) marquee.
z~en *vi (haben)* camp. **Z~en** *nt* -s
camping. **Z~plane** *f* tarpaulin.
Z~platz *m* campsite
Zement *m* -[e]s cement. **z~ieren** *vt*
cement
zen|sieren *vt* (*Sch*) mark; censor
(*Presse, Film*). **Z~sur** *f* -,-en (*Sch*)
mark, (*Amer*) grade; (*Presse-*) cen-
sorship
Zentimeter *m & nt* centimetre.
Z~maß *nt* tape-measure
Zentner *m* -s,- [metric] hun-
dredweight (*50 kg*)
zentral *a* central, *adv* -ly. **Z~e** *f* -,-n
central office; (*Partei-*) headquarters *pl*;
(*Teleph*) exchange. **Z~heizung** *f* central heating. **z~isieren** *vt* centralize
Zentrum *nt* -s,-tren centre
zerbrech|en† *vt/i (sein)* break; **sich**
(*dat*) **den Kopf z~en** rack one's brains.
z~lich *a* fragile
zerdrücken *vt* crush; mash (*Kartoffeln*)
Zeremonie *f* -,-n ceremony
Zeremoniell *nt* -s,-e ceremonial. **z~**
a ceremonial, *adv* -ly
Zerfall *m* disintegration; (*Verfall*)
decay. **z~en†** *vi (sein)* disintegrate;
(*verfallen*) decay; **in drei Teile z~en**
be divided into three parts
zerfetzen *vt* tear to pieces
zerfließen† *vi (sein)* melt; (*Tinte:*)
run
zergehen† *vi (sein)* melt; (*sich auflösen*) dissolve
zergliedern *vt* dissect
zerkleinern *vt* chop/(*schneiden*) cut
up; (*mahlen*) grind
zerknirscht *a* contrite
zerknüllen *vt* crumple [up]
zerkratzen *vt* scratch
zerlassen† *vt* melt
zerlegen *vt* take to pieces, dismantle;
(*zerschneiden*) cut up; (*tranchieren*)
carve
zerlumpt *a* ragged
zermalmen *vt* crush
zermürb|en *vt* (*fig*) wear down.
Z~ungskrieg *m* war of attrition
zerplatzen *vi (sein)* burst
zerquetschen *vt* squash, crush;
mash (*Kartoffeln*)
Zerrbild *nt* caricature
zerreißen† *vt* tear; (*in Stücke*) tear
up; break (*Faden, Seil*) ● *vi (sein)*
tear; break

zerren vt drag; pull ⟨Muskel⟩ ● vi
(haben) pull (an + dat at)

zerrinnen† vi (sein) melt

zerrissen a torn

zerrütten vt ruin, wreck; shatter
⟨Nerven⟩; **zerrüttete Ehe** broken marriage

zerschlagen† vt smash; smash up
⟨Möbel⟩; **sich z~** (fig) fall through;
⟨Hoffnung:⟩ be dashed ● a (erschöpft)
worn out

zerschmettern vt/i (sein) smash

zerschneiden† vt cut; (in Stücke) cut
up

zersetzen vt corrode; undermine
⟨Moral⟩; **sich z~** decompose

zersplittern vi (sein) splinter; ⟨Glas:⟩
shatter ● vt shatter

zerspringen† vi (sein) shatter; (ber-
sten) burst

Zerstäuber m -s,- atomizer

zerstör|en vt destroy; (zunichte
machen) wreck. **Z~er** m -s,- de-
stroyer. **Z~ung** f destruction

zerstreu|en vt scatter; disperse
⟨Menge⟩; dispel ⟨Zweifel⟩; **sich z~en**
disperse; (sich unterhalten) amuse oneself. **z~t** a absent-minded, adv -ly.
Z~ung f -,-en (Unterhaltung) en-
tertainment

zerstückeln vt cut up into pieces

zerteilen vt divide up

Zertifikat nt -[e]s,-e certificate

zertreten† vt stamp on; (zerdrücken)
crush

zertrümmern vt smash [up]; wreck
⟨Gebäude, Stadt⟩

zerzaus|en vt tousle. **z~t** a dish-
evelled; ⟨Haar⟩ tousled

Zettel m -s,- piece of paper; (Notiz)
note; (Bekanntmachung) notice; (Re-
klame-) leaflet

Zeug nt -s (fam) stuff; (Sachen) things
pl; (Ausrüstung) gear; **dummes Z~**
nonsense; **das Z~ haben zu** have the
makings of

Zeuge m -n,-n witness. **z~n** vi
(haben) testify; **z~n von** (fig) show
● vt father. **Z~naussage** f testimony.
Z~nstand m witness box/ (Amer)
stand

Zeugin f -,-nen witness

Zeugnis nt -ses,-se certificate; (Sch)
report; (Referenz) reference; (fig: Beweis) evidence

Zickzack m -[e]s,-e zigzag

Ziege f -,-n goat

Ziegel m -s,- brick; (Dach-) tile.
Z~stein m brick

ziehen† vt pull; (sanfter; zücken;
zeichnen) draw; (heraus-) pull out;
extract ⟨Zahn⟩; raise ⟨Hut⟩; put on
⟨Bremse⟩; move ⟨Schachfigur⟩; put up
⟨Leine, Zaun⟩; (dehnen) stretch; make
⟨Grimasse, Scheitel⟩; (züchten) breed;
grow ⟨Rosen, Gemüse⟩; **nach sich z~**
(fig) entail ● vr **sich z~** (sich erstrecken) run; (sich verziehen) warp ● vi
(haben) pull (an + dat on/at); ⟨Tee,
Ofen:⟩ draw; (Culin) simmer; **es zieht**
there is a draught; **solche Filme z~
nicht mehr** films like that are no longer popular ● vi (sein) (um-) move (**nach**
to); ⟨Menge:⟩ march; ⟨Vögel:⟩ migrate;
⟨Wolken, Nebel:⟩ drift. **Z~** nt -s ache

Ziehharmonika f accordion

Ziehung f -,-en draw

Ziel nt -[e]s,-e destination; (Sport) finish; (Z~scheibe & Mil) target; (Zweck)
aim, goal. **z~bewußt** a purposeful,
adv -ly. **z~en** vi (haben) aim
(**auf** + acc at). **z~end** a (Gram) transitive. **z~los** a aimless, adv -ly.
Z~scheibe f target; (fig) butt.
z~strebig a single-minded, adv -ly

ziemen (sich) vr be seemly

ziemlich a (fam) fair ● adv rather,
fairly; (fast) pretty well

Zier|de f -,-n ornament. **z~en** vt
adorn; **sich z~en** make a fuss; (sich
bitten lassen) need coaxing

zierlich a dainty, adv -ily; (fein) delicate, adv -ly; ⟨Frau⟩ petite

Ziffer f -,-n figure, digit; (Zahlzeichen)
numeral. **Z~blatt** nt dial

zig inv a (fam) umpteen

Zigarette f -,-n cigarette

Zigarre f -,-n cigar

Zigeuner(in) m -s,- (f -,-nen) gypsy

Zimmer nt -s,- room. **Z~mädchen** nt
chambermaid. **Z~mann** m (pl
-leute) carpenter. **z~n** vt make ● vi
(haben) do carpentry. **Z~nachweis**
m accommodation bureau. **Z~-
pflanze** f house plant

zimperlich a squeamish; (wehleidig)
soft; (prüde) prudish

Zimt m -[e]s cinnamon

Zink nt -s zinc

Zinke f -,-n prong; (Kamm-) tooth

Zinn m -s tin; (Gefäße) pewter

Zins|en mpl interest sg; **Z~en tragen**
earn interest. **Z~eszins** m -es,-en
compound interest. **Z~fuß, Z~satz** m
interest rate

Zipfel *m* -s,- corner; (*Spitze*) point; (*Wurst*-) [tail-]end

zirka *adv* about

Zirkel *m* -s,- [pair of] compasses *pl*; (*Gruppe*) circle

Zirkul|ation /-'tsi̯o:n/ *f* - circulation. **z~ieren** *vi* (*sein*) circulate

Zirkus *m* -,-se circus

zirpen *vi* (*haben*) chirp

zischen *vi* (*haben*) hiss; (*Fett:*) sizzle ● *vt* hiss

Zit|at *nt* -[e]s,-e quotation. **z~ieren** *vt/i* (*haben*) quote; (*rufen*) summon

Zitr|onat *nt* -[e]s candied lemon-peel. **Z~one** *f* -,-n lemon. **Z~onen-limonade** *f* lemonade

zittern *vi* (*haben*) tremble; (*vor Kälte*) shiver; (*beben*) shake

zittrig *a* shaky, *adv* -ily

Zitze *f* -,-n teat

zivil *a* civilian; (*Ehe, Recht, Luftfahrt*) civil; (*mäßig*) reasonable. **Z~** *nt* -s civilian clothes *pl*. **Z~courage** /-kura: ʒə/ *f* - courage of one's convictions. **Z~dienst** *m* community service

Zivili|sation /-'tsi̯o:n/ *f* -,-en civilization. **z~sieren** *vt* civilize. **z~siert** *a* civilized ● *adv* in a civilized manner

Zivilist *m* -en,-en civilian

zögern *vi* (*haben*) hesitate. **Z~** *nt* -s hesitation. **z~d** *a* hesitant, *adv* -ly

Zoll¹ *m* -[e]s,- inch

Zoll² *m* -[e]s,-̈e [customs] duty; (*Behörde*) customs *pl*. **Z~abfertigung** *f* customs clearance. **Z~beamte(r)** *m* customs officer. **z~frei** *a* & *adv* duty-free. **Z~kontrolle** *f* customs check

Zone *f* -,-n zone

Zoo *m* -s,-s zoo

Zoo|loge /tsoo'lo:gə/ *m* -n,-n zoologist. **Z~logie** *f* - zoology. **z~lo-gisch** *a* zoological

Zopf *m* -[e]s,-̈e plait

Zorn *m* -[e]s anger. **z~ig** *a* angry, *adv* -ily

zotig *a* smutty, dirty

zottig *a* shaggy

z.T. *abbr* (**zum Teil**) partly

zu *prep* (+ *dat*) to; (*dazu*) with; (*zeitlich, preislich*) at; (*Zweck*) for; (*über*) about; **zu . . . hin** towards; **zu Hause** at home; **zu Fuß/Pferde** on foot/horseback; **zu beiden Seiten** on both sides; **zu Ostern** at Easter; **zu diesem Zweck** for this purpose; **zu meinem Erstaunen/Entsetzen** to my surprise/

horror; **zu Dutzenden** by the dozen; **eine Marke zu 60 Pfennig** a 60-pfennig stamp; **das Stück zu zwei Mark** at two marks each; **wir waren zu dritt/viert** there were three/four of us; **es steht 5 zu 3** the score is 5-3; **zu etw werden** turn into sth ● *adv* (*allzu*) too; (*Richtung*) towards; (*geschlossen*) closed; (*an Schalter, Hahn*) off; **zu groß/weit** too big/far; **nach dem Fluß zu** towards the river; **Augen zu!** close your eyes! **Tür zu!** shut the door! **nur zu!** go on! **macht zu!** (*fam*) hurry up! ● *conj* to; **etwas zu essen** something to eat; **nicht zu glauben** unbelievable; **zu erörternde Probleme** problems to be discussed

zuallererst *adv* first of all. **z~letzt** *adv* last of all

Zubehör *nt* -s accessories *pl*

zubereit|en *vt sep* prepare. **Z~ung** *f* - preparation; (*in Rezept*) method

zubilligen *vt sep* grant

zubinden† *vt sep* tie [up]

zubring|en† *vt sep* spend. **Z~er** *m* -s,- access road; (*Bus*) shuttle

Zucchini /tsu'ki:ni/ *pl* courgettes

Zucht *f* -,-en breeding; (*Pflanzen*-) cultivation; (*Art, Rasse*) breed; (*von Pflanzen*) strain; (*Z~farm*) farm; (*Pferde*-) stud; (*Disziplin*) discipline

züchten *vt* breed; cultivate, grow (*Rosen, Gemüse*). **Z~er** *m* -s,- breeder; grower

Zuchthaus *nt* prison

züchtigen *vt* chastise

Züchtung *f* -,-en breeding; (*Pflanzen*-) cultivation; (*Art, Rasse*) breed; (*von Pflanzen*) strain

zucken *vi* (*haben*) twitch; (*sich z~d bewegen*) jerk; (*Blitz:*) flash; (*Flamme:*) flicker ● *vt* **die Achseln z~** shrug one's shoulders

zücken *vt* draw (*Messer*)

Zucker *m* -s sugar. **Z~dose** *f* sugar basin. **Z~guß** *m* icing. **z~krank** *a* diabetic. **Z~krankheit** *f* diabetes. **z~n** *vt* sugar. **Z~rohr** *nt* sugar cane. **Z~rübe** *f* sugar beet. **z~süß** *a* sweet; (*fig*) sugary. **Z~watte** *f* candyfloss. **Z~zange** *f* sugar tongs *pl*

zuckrig *a* sugary

zudecken *vt sep* cover up; (*im Bett*) tuck up; cover (*Topf*)

zudem *adv* moreover

zudrehen *vt sep* turn off; **jdm den Rücken z~** turn one's back on s.o.

zudringlich *a* pushing, (*fam*) pushy

zudrücken *vt sep* press *or* push shut; close ⟨*Augen*⟩

zueinander *adv* to one another; **z~ passen** go together. **z~halten†** *vi sep* (*haben*) (*fig*) stick together

zuerkennen† *vt sep* award (*dat* to)

zuerst *adv* first; (*anfangs*) at first; **mit dem Kopf z~** head first

zufahr|en† *vi sep* (*sein*) **z~en auf** (+ *acc*) drive towards. **Z~t** *f* access; (*Einfahrt*) drive

Zufall *m* chance; (*Zusammentreffen*) coincidence; **durch Z~** by chance/ coincidence. **z~en†** *vi sep* (*sein*) close, shut; **jdm z~en** ⟨*Aufgabe:*⟩ fall/ ⟨*Erbe:*⟩ go to s.o.

zufällig *a* chance, accidental ● *adv* by chance; **ich war z~ da** I happened to be there

Zuflucht *f* refuge; (*Schutz*) shelter. **Z~sort** *m* refuge

zufolge *prep* (+ *dat*) according to

zufrieden *a* contented, *adv* -ly; (*befriedigt*) satisfied. **z~geben† (sich)** *vr sep* be satisfied. **Z~heit** *f* - contentment; satisfaction. **z~lassen†** *vt sep* leave in peace. **z~stellen** *vt sep* satisfy. **z~stellend** *a* satisfactory, *adv* -ily

zufrieren† *vi sep* (*sein*) freeze over

zufügen *vt sep* inflict (*dat* on); do ⟨*Unrecht*⟩ (*dat* to)

Zufuhr *f* - supply

zuführen *vt sep* ● *vt* supply ● *vi* (*haben*) **z~ auf** (+ *acc*) lead to

Zug *m* -[e]s, ⸚e train; (*Kolonne*) column; (*Um-*) procession; (*Mil*) platoon; (*Vogelschar*) flock; (*Ziehen, Zugkraft*) pull; (*Wandern, Ziehen*) migration; (*Schluck, Luft-*) draught; (*Atem-*) breath; (*beim Rauchen*) puff; (*Schach-*) move; (*beim Schwimmen, Rudern*) stroke; (*Gesichts-*) feature; (*Wesens-*) trait; **etw in vollen Zügen genießen** enjoy sth to the full; **in einem Zug[e]** at one go

Zugabe *f* (*Geschenk*) [free] gift; (*Mus*) encore

Zugang *m* access

zugänglich *a* accessible; ⟨*Mensch:*⟩ approachable; (*fig*) amenable (*dat*/ **für** to)

Zugbrücke *f* drawbridge

zugeben† *vt sep* add; (*gestehen*) admit; (*erlauben*) allow. **zugegebenermaßen** *adv* admittedly

zugegen *a* **z~ sein** be present

zugehen† *vi sep* (*sein*) close; **jdm z~** be sent to s.o.; **z~ auf** (+ *acc*) go towards; **dem Ende z~** draw to a close; ⟨*Vorräte:*⟩ run low; **auf der Party ging es lebhaft zu** the party was pretty lively

Zugehörigkeit *f* - membership

Zügel *m* -s, - rein

zugelassen *a* registered

zügel|los *a* unrestrained, *adv* -ly; (*sittenlos*) licentious. **z~n** *vt* rein in; (*fig*) curb

Zuge|ständnis *nt* concession. **z~stehen†** *vt sep* grant

zugetan *a* fond (*dat* of)

zugig *a* draughty

zügig *a* quick, *adv* -ly

Zug|kraft *f* pull; (*fig*) attraction. **z~kräftig** *a* effective; (*anreizend*) popular; ⟨*Titel*⟩ catchy

zugleich *adv* at the same time

Zug|luft *f* draught. **Z~pferd** *nt* draught-horse; (*fam*) draw

zugreifen† *vi sep* (*haben*) grab it/ them; (*bei Tisch*) help oneself; (*bei Angebot*) jump at it; (*helfen*) lend a hand

zugrunde *adv* **z~ richten** destroy; **z~ gehen** be destroyed; ⟨*Ehe:*⟩ founder; (*sterben*) die; **z~ liegen** form the basis (*dat* of)

zugucken *vi sep* (*haben*) = **zusehen**

zugunsten *prep* (+ *gen*) in favour of; ⟨*Sammlung*⟩ in aid of

zugute *adv* **jdm/etw z~ kommen** benefit s.o./sth; **jdm seine Jugend z~ halten** make allowances for s.o.'s youth

Zugvogel *m* migratory bird

zuhalten† *v sep* ● *vt* keep closed; (*bedecken*) cover; **sich** (*dat*) **die Nase z~** hold one's nose ● *vi* (*haben*) **z~ auf** (+ *acc*) head for

Zuhälter *m* -s, - pimp

Zuhause *nt* -s, - home

zuhör|en *vi sep* (*haben*) listen (*dat* to). **Z~er(in)** *m*(*f*) listener

zujubeln *vi sep* (*haben*) **jdm z~** cheer s.o.

zukehren *vt sep* turn (*dat* to)

zukleben *vt sep* seal

zuknallen *vt/i sep* (*sein*) slam

zuknöpfen *vt sep* button up

zukommen† *vi sep* (*sein*) **z~ auf** (+ *acc*) come towards; (*sich nähern*) approach; **z~ lassen** send (**jdm** s.o.); devote ⟨*Pflege*⟩ (*dat* to); **jdm z~** be s.o.'s right

Zukunft *f* - future. **zukünftig** *a* future ● *adv* in future

zulächeln *vi sep* (*haben*) smile (*dat* at)

Zulage *f* -,-n extra allowance

zulangen *vi sep (haben)* help oneself; **tüchtig z~** tuck in

zulassen† *vt sep* allow, permit; *(teilnehmen lassen)* admit; *(Admin)* license, register; *(geschlossen lassen)* leave closed; leave unopened *(Brief)*

zulässig *a* permissible

Zulassung *f* -,-en admission; registration; *(Lizenz)* licence

zulaufen† *vi sep (sein)* z~ **auf** (+ *acc*) run towards; **spitz z~** taper to a point

zulegen *vt sep* add; **sich** *(dat)* **etw z~** get sth; grow *(Bart)*

zuleide *adv* jdm etwas z~ tun hurt s.o.

zuletzt *adv* last; *(schließlich)* in the end; **nicht z~** not least

zuliebe *adv* jdm/etw z~ for the sake of s.o./sth

zum *prep* = zu dem; zum Spaß for fun; etw zum Lesen sth to read

zumachen *v sep* • *vt* close, shut; do up *(Jacke)*; seal *(Umschlag)*; turn off *(Hahn)*; *(stillegen)* close down • *vi (haben)* close, shut; *(stillgelegt werden)* close down

zumal *adv* especially • *conj* especially since

zumeist *adv* for the most part

zumindest *adv* at least

zumutbar *a* reasonable

zumute *adv* mir ist traurig/elend z~ I feel sad/wretched; **mir ist nicht danach z~** I don't feel like it

zumut|en *vt sep* jdm etw z~en ask or expect sth of s.o.; **sich** *(dat)* **zuviel z~en** overdo things. **Z~ung** *f* - imposition; **eine Z~ung sein** be unreasonable

zunächst *adv* first [of all]; *(anfangs)* at first; *(vorläufig)* for the moment • *prep* (+ *dat*) nearest to

Zunahme *f* -,-n increase

Zuname *m* surname

zünd|en *vt/i (haben)* ignite; **z~ende Rede** rousing speech. **Z~er** *m* -s,- detonator, fuse. **Z~holz** *nt* match. **Z~kerze** *f* sparking-plug. **Z~schlüssel** *m* ignition key. **Z~schnur** *f* fuse. **Z~ung** *f* -,-en ignition

zunehmen† *vi sep (haben)* increase (an + *dat* in); *(Mond:)* wax; *(an Gewicht)* put on weight. **z~d** *a* increasing, *adv* -ly

Zuneigung *f* - affection

Zunft *f* -,"e guild

zünftig *a* proper, *adv* -ly

Zunge *f* -,-n tongue. **Z~nbrecher** *m* tongue-twister

zunichte *a* z~ machen wreck; z~ werden come to nothing

zunicken *vi sep (haben)* nod (dat to)

zunutze *a* sich *(dat)* etw z~ machen make use of sth; *(ausnutzen)* take advantage of sth

zuoberst *adv* right at the top

zuordnen *vt sep* assign (dat to)

zupfen *vt/i (haben)* pluck (an + *dat* at); pull out *(Unkraut)*

zur *prep* = zu der; zur Schule/Arbeit to school/work; zur Zeit at present

zurechnungsfähig *a* of sound mind

zurecht|finden† *(sich)* *vr sep* find one's way. **z~kommen†** *vi sep (sein)* cope (mit with); *(rechtzeitig kommen)* be in time. **z~legen** *vt sep* put out ready; **sich** *(dat)* **eine Ausrede z~legen** have an excuse all ready. **z~machen** *vt sep* get ready; **sich z~machen** get ready. **z~weisen†** *vt sep* reprimand. **Z~weisung** *f* reprimand

zureden *vi sep (haben)* jdm z~ try to persuade s.o.

zurichten *vt sep* prepare; *(beschädigen)* damage; *(verletzen)* injure

zuriegeln *vt sep* bolt

zurück *adv* back; **Berlin, hin und z~** return to Berlin. **z~behalten†** *vt sep* keep back; be left with *(Narbe)*. **z~bekommen†** *vt sep* get back; **20 Pfennig z~bekommen** get 20 pfennigs change. **z~bleiben†** *vi sep (sein)* stay behind; *(nicht mithalten)* lag behind. **z~blicken** *vi sep (haben)* look back. **z~bringen†** *vt sep* bring back; *(wieder hinbringen)* take back. **z~erobern** *vt sep* recapture; *(fig)* regain. **z~erstatten** *vt sep* refund. **z~fahren†** *v sep* • *vt* drive back • *vi (sein)* return, go back; *(im Auto)* drive back; *(zurückweichen)* recoil. **z~finden†** *vi sep (haben)* find one's way back. **z~führen** *v sep* • *vt* take back; *(fig)* attribute (auf + *acc* to) • *vi (haben)* lead back. **z~geben†** *vt sep* give back, return. **z~geblieben** *a* retarded. **z~gehen†** *vi sep (sein)* go back, return; *(abnehmen)* go down; **z~gehen auf** (+ *acc*) *(fig)* go back to

zurückgezogen *a* secluded. **Z~heit** *f* - seclusion

zurückhalt|en† *vt sep* hold back; *(abhalten)* stop; **sich z~en** restrain oneself. **z~end** *a* reserved. **Z~ung** *f* - reserve

zurück|kehren *vi sep (sein)* return. **z~kommen†** *vi sep (sein)* come back, return; *(ankommen)* get back; **z~kommen auf** (*+acc*) *(fig)* come back to. **z~lassen†** *vt sep* leave behind; *(z~kehren lassen)* allow back. **z~legen** *vt sep* put back; *(reservieren)* keep; *(sparen)* put by; cover *〈Strecke〉*. **z~lehnen (sich)** *vr sep* lean back. **z~liegen†** *vi sep (haben)* be in the past; *(Sport)* be behind; **das liegt lange zurück** that was long ago. **z~melden (sich)** *vr sep* report back. **z~nehmen†** *vt sep* take back. **z~rufen†** *vt/i sep (haben)* call back. **z~scheuen** *vi sep (sein)* shrink (**vor**+*dat* from). **z~schicken** *vt sep* send back. **z~schlagen†** *v sep ● vi (haben)* hit back ● *vt* hit back; *(abwehren)* beat back; *(umschlagen)* turn back. **z~schneiden†** *vt sep* cut back. **z~schrecken†** *vi sep (sein)* shrink back, recoil; *(fig)* shrink (**vor**+*dat* from). **z~setzen** *v sep ● vt* put back; *(Auto)* reverse, back; *(herabsetzen)* reduce; *(fig)* neglect ● *vi (haben)* reverse, back. **z~stellen** *vt sep* put back; *(reservieren)* keep; *(fig)* put aside; *(aufschieben)* postpone. **z~stoßen†** *v sep ● vt* push back ● *vi (sein)* reverse, back. **z~treten†** *vi sep (sein)* step back; *(vom Amt)* resign; *(verzichten)* withdraw. **z~weichen†** *vi sep (sein)* draw back; *(z~schrecken)* shrink back. **z~weisen†** *vt sep* turn away; *(fig)* reject. **z~werfen†** *vt* throw back; *(reflektieren)* reflect. **z~zahlen** *vt sep* pay back. **z~ziehen†** *vt sep* draw back; *(fig)* withdraw; **sich z~ziehen** withdraw; *(vom Beruf)* retire; *(Mil)* retreat

Zuruf *m* shout. **z~en†** *vt sep* shout *(dat* to)

Zusage *f* -,-n acceptance; *(Versprechen)* promise. **z~n** *v sep ● vt* promise ● *vi (haben)* accept; **jdm z~n** appeal to s.o.

zusammen *adv* together; *(insgesamt)* altogether. **Z~arbeit** *f* co-operation. **z~arbeiten** *vi sep (haben)* co-operate. **z~bauen** *vt sep* assemble. **z~beißen†** *vt sep* **die Zähne z~beißen** clench/*(fig)* grit one's teeth. **z~bleiben†** *vi sep (sein)* stay together. **z~brechen†** *vi sep (sein)* collapse. **z~bringen†** *vt sep* bring together; *(beschaffen)* raise.

Z~bruch *m* collapse; *(Nerven-* & *fig)* breakdown. **z~fahren†** *vi sep (sein)* collide; *(z~zucken)* start. **z~fallen†** *vi sep (sein)* collapse; *(zeitlich)* coincide. **z~falten** *vt sep* fold up. **z~fassen** *vt sep* summarize, sum up. **Z~fassung** *f* summary. **z~fügen** *vt sep* fit together. **z~führen** *vt sep* bring together. **z~gehören** *vi sep (haben)* belong together; *(z~passen)* go together. **z~gesetzt** *a (Gram)* compound. **z~halten†** *v sep ● vt* hold together; *(beisammenhalten)* keep together ● *vi (haben) (fig)* stick together. **Z~hang** *m* connection; *(Kontext)* context. **z~hängen†** *vi sep (haben)* be connected. **z~hanglos** *a* incoherent, *adv* -ly. **z~klappen** *v sep ● vt* fold up ● *vi (sein)* collapse. **z~kommen†** *vi sep (sein)* meet; *(sich sammeln)* accumulate. **Z~kunft** *f* -,-̈e meeting. **z~laufen†** *vi sep (sein)* gather; *〈Flüssigkeit:〉* collect; *〈Linien:〉* converge. **z~leben** *vi sep (haben)* live together. **z~legen** *v sep ● vt* put together; *(z~falten)* fold up; *(vereinigen)* amalgamate; pool *〈Geld〉* ● *vi (haben)* club together. **z~nehmen†** *vt sep* gather up; summon up *〈Mut〉*; collect *〈Gedanken〉*; **sich z~nehmen** pull oneself together. **z~passen** *vi sep (haben)* go together, match; *〈Personen:〉* be well matched. **Z~prall** *m* collision. **z~prallen** *vi sep (sein)* collide. **z~rechnen** *vt sep* add up. **z~reißen† (sich)** *vr sep (fam)* pull oneself together. **z~rollen** *vt sep* roll up; **sich z~rollen** curl up. **z~schlagen†** *vt sep* smash up; *(prügeln)* beat up. **z~schließen† (sich)** *vr sep* join together; *〈Firmen:〉* merge. **Z~schluß** *m* union; *(Comm)* merger. **z~schreiben†** *vt sep* write as one word

zusammensein† *vi sep (sein)* be together. **Z~** *nt* -s get-together

zusammensetz|en *vt sep* put together; *(Techn)* assemble; **sich z~en** sit [down] together; *(bestehen)* be made up (**aus** from). **Z~ung** *f* -,-en composition; *(Techn)* assembly; *(Wort)* compound

zusammen|stellen *vt sep* put together; *(gestalten)* compile. **Z~stoß** *m* collision; *(fig)* clash. **z~stoßen†** *vi sep (sein)* collide. **z~treffen†** *vi sep (sein)* meet; *(zeitlich)* coincide. **Z~treffen** *nt* meeting; coincidence.

z~zählen *vt sep* add up. z~ziehen†
v sep ● *vt* draw together; (*addieren*)
add up; (*konzentrieren*) mass; sich
z~ziehen contract; (*Gewitter:*) gather
● *vi (sein)* move in together; move in
(mit with). z~zucken *vi sep (sein)*
start; (*vor Schmerz*) wince

Zusatz *m* addition; (*Jur*) rider;
(*Lebensmittel-*) additive. Z~gerät *nt*
attachment. zusätzlich *a* additional
● *adv* in addition

zuschanden *adv* z~ machen ruin,
wreck; z~ fahren wreck

zuschau|en *vi sep (haben)* watch.
Z~er(in) *m* -s,- (*f* -,-nen) spectator;
(*TV*) viewer. Z~erraum *m* audi-
torium

zuschicken *vt sep* send (*dat* to)

Zuschlag *m* surcharge; (*D-Zug-*) supplement. z~en† *v sep* ● *vt* shut; (*heftig*) slam; (*bei Auktion*) knock down
(jdm to s.o.) ● *vi (haben)* hit out;
(*Feind:*) strike ● *vi (sein)* slam shut.
z~pflichtig *a* for which a supplement is payable

zuschließen† *v sep* ● *vt* lock ● *vi
(haben)* lock up

zuschneiden† *vt sep* cut out; cut to
size (*Holz*)

zuschreiben† *vt sep* attribute (*dat*
to); jdm die Schuld z~ blame s.o.

Zuschrift *f* letter; (*auf Annonce*)
reply

zuschulden *adv* sich (*dat*) etwas z~
kommen lassen do wrong

Zuschuß *m* contribution; (*staatlich*)
subsidy

zusehen† *vi sep (haben)* watch; z~,
daß see [to it] that

zusehends *adv* visibly

zusein† *vi sep (sein)* be closed

zusenden† *vt sep* send (*dat* to)

zusetzen *v sep* ● *vt* add; (*einbüßen*)
lose ● *vi (haben)* jdm z~ pester s.o.;
(*Hitze:*) take it out of s.o.

zusicher|n *vt sep* promise. Z~ung *f*
promise

Zuspätkommende(r) *m/f* late-
comer

zuspielen *vt sep* (*Sport*) pass

zuspitzen (sich) *vr sep* (*fig*) become
critical

zusprechen† *v sep* ● *vt* award (jdm
s.o.); jdm Trost/Mut z~ comfort/en-
courage s.o. ● *vi (haben)* dem Essen z~
eat heartily

Zustand *m* condition, state

zustande *adv* z~ bringen/kommen
bring/come about

zuständig *a* competent; (*verantwortlich*) responsible. Z~keit *f* -
competence; responsibility

zustehen† *vi sep (haben)* jdm z~ be
s.o.'s right; (*Urlaub:*) be due to s.o.; es
steht ihm nicht zu he is not entitled to
it; (*gebührt*) it is not for him (zu to)

zusteigen† *vi sep (sein)* get on; noch
jemand zugestiegen? tickets please;
(*im Bus*) any more fares please?

zustell|en *vt sep* block; (*bringen*) de-
liver. Z~ung *f* delivery

zusteuern *v sep* ● *vi (sein)* head
(auf + *acc* for) ● *vt* contribute

zustimm|en *vi sep (haben)* agree;
(*billigen*) approve (*dat* of). Z~ung *f*
consent; approval

zustoßen† *vi sep (sein)* happen (*dat*
to)

Zustrom *m* influx

zutage *adv* z~ treten *od* kommen/
bringen come/bring to light

Zutat *f* (*Culin*) ingredient

zuteil|en *vt sep* allocate; assign (*Auf-
gabe*). Z~ung *f* allocation

zutiefst *adv* deeply

zutragen† *vt sep* carry/(*fig*) report
(*dat* to); sich z~ happen

zutrau|en *vt sep* jdm etw z~ believe
s.o. capable of sth. Z~en *nt* -s confidence. z~lich *a* trusting, *adv* -ly;
(*Tier*) friendly

zutreffen† *vi sep (haben)* be correct;
z~ auf (+ *acc*) apply to. z~d *a* applicable (auf + *acc* to); (*richtig*) correct,
adv -ly

zutrinken† *vi sep (haben)* jdm z~
drink to s.o.

Zutritt *m* admittance

zuunterst *adv* right at the bottom

zuverlässig *a* reliable, *adv* -bly.
Z~keit *f* - reliability

Zuversicht *f* - confidence. z~lich *a*
confident, *adv* -ly

zuviel *pron* & *adv* too much; (*pl*) too
many

zuvor *adv* before; (*erst*) first

zuvorkommen† *vi sep (sein)* (+ *dat*)
anticipate; jdm z~ beat s.o. to it. z~d
a obliging, *adv* -ly

Zuwachs *m* -es increase

zuwege *adv* z~ bringen achieve

zuweilen *adv* now and then

zuweisen† *vt sep* assign; (*zuteilen*)
allocate

zuwend|en† *vt sep* turn (*dat* to); **sich z~en** (+ *dat*) turn to; (*fig*) devote oneself to. **Z~ung** *f* donation; (*Fürsorge*) care

zuwenig *pron & adv* too little; (*pl*) too few

zuwerfen† *vt sep* slam ⟨*Tür*⟩; **jdm etw z~** throw s.o. sth; give s.o. ⟨*Blick, Lächeln*⟩

zuwider *adv* **jdm z~ sein** be repugnant to s.o. ● *prep* (+ *dat*) contrary to. **z~handeln** *vi sep* (*haben*) contravene (**etw** *dat* sth)

zuzahlen *vt sep* pay extra

zuziehen† *v sep* ● *vt* pull tight; draw ⟨*Vorhänge*⟩; (*hinzu-*) call in; **sich** (*dat*) **etw z~** contract ⟨*Krankheit*⟩; sustain ⟨*Verletzung*⟩; incur ⟨*Zorn*⟩ ● *vi* (*sein*) move into the area

zuzüglich *prep* (+ *gen*) plus

Zwang *m* -[e]s,¨e compulsion; (*Gewalt*) force; (*Verpflichtung*) obligation

zwängen *vt* squeeze

zwanglos *a* informal, *adv* -ly; ⟨*Benehmen*⟩ free and easy. **Z~igkeit** *f* - informality

Zwangs|jacke *f* straitjacket. **Z~lage** *f* predicament. **z~läufig** *a* inevitable, *adv* -bly

zwanzig *inv a* twenty. **z~ste(r,s)** *a* twentieth

zwar *adv* admittedly; **und z~** to be precise

Zweck *m* -[e]s,-e purpose; (*Sinn*) point; **es hat keinen Z~** there is no point. **z~dienlich** *a* appropriate; (*Information*) relevant. **z~los** *a* pointless. **z~mäßig** *a* suitable, *adv* -bly; (*praktisch*) functional, *adv* -ly. **z~s** *prep* (+ *gen*) for the purpose of

zwei *inv a*, **Z~** *f* -,-en two; (*Sch*) ≈ B. **Z~bettzimmer** *nt* twinbedded room

zweideutig *a* ambiguous, *adv* -ly; (*schlüpfrig*) suggestive, *adv* -ly. **Z~keit** *f* -,-en ambiguity

zweierlei *inv a* two kinds of ● *pron* two things. **z~fach** *a* double

Zweifel *m* -s,- doubt. **z~haft** *a* doubtful; (*fragwürdig*) dubious. **z~los** *adv* undoubtedly. **z~n** *vi* (*haben*) doubt (**an etw** *dat* sth)

Zweig *m* -[e]s,-e branch. **Z~geschäft** *nt* branch. **Z~stelle** *f* branch [office]

Zwei|kampf *m* duel. **z~mal** *adv* twice. **z~reihig** *a* double-breasted. **z~sprachig** *a* bilingual

zweit *adv* **zu z~** in twos; **wir waren zu z~** there were two of us. **z~beste(r,s)** *a* second-best. **z~e(r,s)** *a* second

zwei|teilig *a* two-piece; ⟨*Film, Programm*⟩ two-part. **z~tens** *adv* secondly

zweitklassig *a* second-class

Zwerchfell *nt* diaphragm

Zwerg *m* -[e]s,-e dwarf

Zwetsch[g]e *f* -,-n quetsche

Zwickel *m* -s,- gusset

zwicken *vt/i* (*haben*) pinch

Zwieback *m* -[e]s,¨e rusk

Zwiebel *f* -,-n onion; (*Blumen-*) bulb

Zwielicht *nt* half-light; (*Dämmerlicht*) twilight. **z~ig** *a* shady

Zwie|spalt *m* conflict. **z~spältig** *a* conflicting. **Z~tracht** *f* - discord

Zwilling *m* -s,-e twin; **Z~e** (*Astr*) Gemini

zwingen† *vt* force; **sich z~** force oneself. **z~d** *a* compelling

Zwinger *m* -s,- run; (*Zucht-*) kennels *pl*

zwinkern *vi* (*haben*) blink; (*als Zeichen*) wink

Zwirn *m* -[e]s button thread

zwischen *prep* (+ *dat/acc*) between; (*unter*) among[st]. **Z~bemerkung** *f* interjection. **Z~ding** *nt* (*fam*) cross. **z~durch** *adv* in between; (*in der Z~zeit*) in the meantime; (*ab und zu*) now and again. **Z~fall** *m* incident. **Z~händler** *m* middleman. **Z~landung** *f* stop-over. **Z~raum** *m* gap, space. **Z~ruf** *m* interjection. **Z~stecker** *m* adaptor. **Z~wand** *f* partition. **Z~zeit** *f* **in der Z~zeit** in the meantime

Zwist *m* -[e]s,-e discord; (*Streit*) feud. **Z~igkeiten** *fpl* quarrels

zwitschern *vi* (*haben*) chirp

zwo *inv a* two

zwölf *inv a* twelve. **z~te(r,s)** *a* twelfth

zwote(r,s) *a* second

Zyklus *m* -,-klen cycle

Zylind|er *m* -s,- cylinder; (*Hut*) top hat. **z~risch** *a* cylindrical

Zyn|iker *m* -s,- cynic. **z~isch** *a* cynical, *adv* -ly. **Z~ismus** *m* - cynicism

Zypern *nt* -s Cyprus

Zypresse *f* -,-n cypress

Zyste /'tsystə/ *f* -,-n cyst

z.Zt. *abbr* (**zur Zeit**) at present

ENGLISH–GERMAN
ENGLISCH–DEUTSCH

A

a /ə, *betont* eɪ/ (*vor einem Vokal* **an**) *indef art* ein(e); (*each*) pro; **not a** kein(e)

aback /ə'bæk/ *adv* **be taken ~** verblüfft sein

abandon /ə'bændən/ *vt* verlassen; (*give up*) aufgeben ● *n* Hingabe *f*. **~ed** *a* verlassen; ⟨*behaviour*⟩ hemmungslos

abase /ə'beɪs/ *vt* demütigen

abashed /ə'bæʃt/ *a* beschämt, verlegen

abate /ə'beɪt/ *vi* nachlassen

abattoir /'æbətwɑ:(r)/ *n* Schlachthof *m*

abb|ey /'æbɪ/ *n* Abtei *f*. **~ot** *n* Abt *m*

abbreviat|e /ə'bri:vɪeɪt/ *vt* abkürzen. **~ion** /-'eɪʃn/ *n* Abkürzung *f*

abdicat|e /'æbdɪkeɪt/ *vi* abdanken. **~ion** /-'keɪʃn/ *n* Abdankung *f*

abdom|en /'æbdəmən/ *n* Unterleib *m*. **~inal** /-'dɒmɪnl/ *a* Unterleibs-

abduct /əb'dʌkt/ *vt* entführen. **~ion** /-ʌkʃn/ *n* Entführung *f*. **~or** *n* Entführer *m*

aberration /æbə'reɪʃn/ *n* Abweichung *f*; (*mental*) Verwirrung *f*

abet /ə'bet/ *vt* (*pt/pp* **abetted**) **aid and ~** (*Jur*) Beihilfe leisten (+ *dat*)

abeyance /ə'beɪəns/ *n* **in ~** [zeitweilig] außer Kraft; **fall into ~** außer Kraft kommen

abhor /əb'hɔ:(r)/ *vt* (*pt/pp* **abhorred**) verabscheuen. **~rence** /-'hɒrəns/ *n* Abscheu *f*. **~rent** /-'hɒrənt/ *a* abscheulich

abid|e /ə'baɪd/ *vt* (*pt/pp* **abided**) (*tolerate*) aushalten; ausstehen ⟨*person*⟩ ● *vi* **~e by** sich halten an (+ *acc*). **~ing** *a* bleibend

ability /ə'bɪlətɪ/ *n* Fähigkeit *f*; (*talent*) Begabung *f*

abject /'æbdʒekt/ *a* erbärmlich; (*humble*) demütig

ablaze /ə'bleɪz/ *a* in Flammen; **be ~** in Flammen stehen

able /'eɪbl/ *a* (**-r, -st**) fähig; **be ~ to do sth** etw tun können. **~-'bodied** *a* körperlich gesund; (*Mil*) tauglich

ably /'eɪblɪ/ *adv* gekonnt

abnormal /æb'nɔ:ml/ *a* anormal; (*Med*) abnorm. **~ity** /-'mælətɪ/ *n* Abnormität *f*. **~ly** *adv* ungewöhnlich

aboard /ə'bɔ:d/ *adv & prep* an Bord (+ *gen*)

abode /ə'bəʊd/ *n* Wohnsitz *m*

abol|ish /ə'bɒlɪʃ/ *vt* abschaffen. **~ition** /æbə'lɪʃn/ *n* Abschaffung *f*

abominable /ə'bɒmɪnəbl/ *a*, **-bly** *adv* abscheulich

abominate /ə'bɒmɪneɪt/ *vt* verabscheuen

aborigines /æbə'rɪdʒəni:z/ *npl* Ureinwohner *pl*

abort /ə'bɔ:t/ *vt* abtreiben. **~ion** /-ɔ:ʃn/ *n* Abtreibung *f*; **have an ~ion** eine Abtreibung vornehmen lassen. **~ive** /-tɪv/ *a* ⟨*attempt*⟩ vergeblich

abound /ə'baʊnd/ *vi* reichlich vorhanden sein; **~ in** reich sein an (+ *dat*)

about /ə'baʊt/ *adv* umher, herum; (*approximately*) ungefähr; **be ~** (*in circulation*) umgehen; (*in existence*) vorhanden sein; **be up and ~** auf den Beinen sein; **be ~ to do sth** im Begriff sein, etw zu tun; **there are a lot ~** es gibt viele; **there was no one ~** es war kein Mensch da; **run/play ~** herumlaufen/-spielen ● *prep* um (+ *acc*) [... herum]; (*concerning*) über (+ *acc*); **what is it ~?** worum geht es? ⟨*book*:⟩ wovon handelt es? **I know nothing ~ it** ich weiß nichts davon; **talk/know ~** reden/wissen von

about: **~-'face** *n*, **-'turn** *n* Kehrtwendung *f*

above /ə'bʌv/ *adv* oben ● *prep* über (+ *dat*/*acc*). **~ all** vor allem

above: **~-'board** *a* legal. **~mentioned** *a* obenerwähnt

abrasion /ə'breɪʒn/ *n* Schürfwunde *f*

abrasive /ə'breɪsɪv/ *a* Scheuer-; ⟨*remark*⟩ verletzend ● *n* Scheuermittel *nt*; (*Techn*) Schleifmittel *nt*

abreast /ə'brest/ *adv* nebeneinander; **keep ~ of** Schritt halten mit

abridge /ə'brɪdʒ/ *vt* kürzen

abroad /ə'brɔːd/ *adv* im Ausland; **go ~ ins** Ausland fahren

abrupt /ə'brʌpt/ *a*, **-ly** *adv* abrupt; (*sudden*) plötzlich; (*curt*) schroff

abscess /'æbsɪs/ *n* Abszeß *m*

abscond /əb'skɒnd/ *vi* entfliehen

absence /'æbsəns/ *n* Abwesenheit *f*

absent¹ /'æbsənt/ *a*, **-ly** *adv* abwesend; **be ~** fehlen

absent² /æb'sent/ *vt* **~ oneself** fernbleiben

absentee /æbsən'tiː/ *n* Abwesende(r) *m/f*

absent-minded /æbsənt'maɪndɪd/ *a*, **-ly** *adv* geistesabwesend; (*forgetful*) zerstreut

absolute /'æbsəluːt/ *a*, **-ly** *adv* absolut

absolution /æbsə'luːʃn/ *n* Absolution *f*

absolve /əb'zɒlv/ *vt* lossprechen

absorb /əb'sɔːb/ *vt* absorbieren, aufsaugen; **~ed in** vertieft in (+*acc*). **~ent** /-ənt/ *a* saugfähig

absorption /əb'sɔːpʃn/ *n* Absorption *f*

abstain /əb'steɪn/ *vi* sich enthalten (**from** *gen*); **~ from voting** sich der Stimme enthalten

abstemious /əb'stiːmɪəs/ *a* enthaltsam

abstention /əb'stenʃn/ *n* (*Pol*) [Stimm]enthaltung *f*

abstinence /'æbstɪnəns/ *n* Enthaltsamkeit *f*

abstract /'æbstrækt/ *a* abstrakt ● *n* (*summary*) Abriß *m*

absurd /əb'sɜːd/ *a*, **-ly** *adv* absurd. **~ity** *n* Absurdität *f*

abundan|ce /ə'bʌndəns/ *n* Fülle *f* (**of** an + *acc*). **~t** *a* reichlich

abuse¹ /ə'bjuːz/ *vt* mißbrauchen; (*insult*) beschimpfen

abus|e² /ə'bjuːs/ *n* Mißbrauch *m*; (*insults*) Beschimpfungen *pl*. **~ive** /-ɪv/ ausfallend

abut /ə'bʌt/ *vi* (*pt/pp* **abutted**) angrenzen (**on to** an + *acc*)

abysmal /ə'bɪzml/ *a* (*fam*) katastrophal

abyss /ə'bɪs/ *n* Abgrund *m*

academic /ækə'demɪk/ *a*, **-ally** *adv* akademisch ● *n* Akademiker(in) *m(f)*

academy /ə'kædəmɪ/ *n* Akademie *f*

accede /ək'siːd/ *vi* **~ to** zustimmen (+*dat*); besteigen ⟨*throne*⟩

accelerat|e /ək'seləreɪt/ *vt* beschleunigen ● *vi* die Geschwindigkeit erhöhen. **~ion** /-'reɪʃn/ *n* Beschleunigung *f*. **~or** *n* (*Auto*) Gaspedal *nt*

accent¹ /'æksənt/ *n* Akzent *m*

accent² /æk'sent/ *vt* betonen

accentuate /ək'sentjʊeɪt/ *vt* betonen

accept /ək'sept/ *vt* annehmen; (*fig*) akzeptieren ● *vi* zusagen. **~able** /-əbl/ *a* annehmbar. **~ance** *n* Annahme *f*; (*of invitation*) Zusage *f*

access /'ækses/ *n* Zugang *m*; (*road*) Zufahrt *f*. **~ible** /ək'sesəbl/ *a* zugänglich

accession /ək'seʃn/ *n* (*to throne*) Thronbesteigung *f*

accessor|y /ək'sesərɪ/ *n* (*Jur*) Mitschuldige(r) *m/f*; **~ies** *pl* (*fashion*) Accessoires *pl*; (*Techn*) Zubehör *nt*

accident /'æksɪdənt/ *n* Unfall *m*; (*chance*) Zufall *m*; **by ~** zufällig; (*unintentionally*) versehentlich. **~al** /-'dentl/ *a*, **-ly** *adv* zufällig; (*unintentional*) versehentlich

acclaim /ə'kleɪm/ *n* Beifall *m* ● *vt* feiern (**as als**)

acclimate /'æklɪmeɪt/ *vt* (*Amer*) = **acclimatize**

acclimatize /ə'klaɪmətaɪz/ *vt* **become ~d** sich akklimatisieren

accolade /'ækəleɪd/ *n* Auszeichnung *f*

accommodat|e /ə'kɒmədeɪt/ *vt* unterbringen; (*oblige*) entgegenkommen (+*dat*). **~ing** *a* entgegenkommend. **~ion** /-'deɪʃn/ *n* (*rooms*) Unterkunft *f*

accompan|iment /ə'kʌmpənɪmənt/ *n* Begleitung *f*. **~ist** *n* (*Mus*) Begleiter(in) *m(f)*

accompany /ə'kʌmpənɪ/ *vt* (*pt/pp* **-ied**) begleiten

accomplice /ə'kʌmplɪs/ *n* Komplize/-zin *m/f*

accomplish /ə'kʌmplɪʃ/ *vt* erfüllen ⟨*task*⟩; (*achieve*) erreichen. **~ed** *a* fähig. **~ment** *n* Fertigkeit *f*; (*achievement*) Leistung *f*

accord /ə'kɔːd/ *n* (*treaty*) Abkommen *nt*; **of one ~** einmütig; **of one's own ~** aus eigenem Antrieb ● *vt* gewähren. **~ance** *n* **in ~ance with** entsprechend (+*dat*)

according /ə'kɔːdɪŋ/ *adv* **~ to** nach (+*dat*). **~ly** *adv* entsprechend

accordion /əˈkɔːdɪən/ n Akkordeon nt

accost /əˈkɒst/ vt ansprechen

account /əˈkaʊnt/ n Konto nt; (bill) Rechnung f; (description) Darstellung f; (report) Bericht m; ~s pl (Comm) Bücher pl; on ~ of wegen (+gen); on no ~ auf keinen Fall; on this ~ deshalb; on my ~ meinetwegen; of no ~ ohne Bedeutung; take into ~ in Betracht ziehen, berücksichtigen ● vi ~ for Rechenschaft ablegen für; (explain) erklären

accountant /əˈkaʊntənt/ n Buchhalter(in) m(f); (chartered) Wirtschaftsprüfer m; (for tax) Steuerberater m

accoutrements /əˈkuːtrəmənts/ npl Ausrüstung f

accredited /əˈkredɪtɪd/ a akkreditiert

accrue /əˈkruː/ vi sich ansammeln

accumulat|e /əˈkjuːmjʊleɪt/ vt ansammeln, anhäufen ● vi sich ansammeln, sich anhäufen. ~ion /-ˈleɪʃn/ n Ansammlung f, Anhäufung f. ~or n (Electr) Akkumulator m

accura|cy /ˈækjʊrəsɪ/ n Genauigkeit f. ~te /-rət/ a, -ly adv genau

accusation /ækjuːˈzeɪʃn/ n Anklage f

accusative /əˈkjuːzətɪv/ a & n ~ [case] (Gram) Akkusativ m

accuse /əˈkjuːz/ vt (Jur) anklagen (of gen); ~ s.o. of doing sth jdn beschuldigen, etw getan zu haben. ~d n the ~d der/die Angeklagte

accustom /əˈkʌstəm/ vt gewöhnen (to an + dat); grow or get ~ed to sich gewöhnen an (+ acc). ~ed a gewohnt

ace /eɪs/ n (Cards, Sport) As nt

ache /eɪk/ n Schmerzen pl ● vi weh tun, schmerzen

achieve /əˈtʃiːv/ vt leisten; (gain) erzielen; (reach) erreichen. ~ment n (feat) Leistung f

acid /ˈæsɪd/ a sauer; (fig) beißend ● n Säure f. ~ity /əˈsɪdətɪ/ n Säure f. ~ 'rain n saurer Regen m

acknowledge /əkˈnɒlɪdʒ/ vt anerkennen; (admit) zugeben; erwidern (greeting); ~ receipt of den Empfang bestätigen (+gen). ~ment n Anerkennung f; (of letter) Empfangsbestätigung f

acne /ˈæknɪ/ n Akne f

acorn /ˈeɪkɔːn/ n Eichel f

acoustic /əˈkuːstɪk/ a, -ally adv akustisch. ~s npl Akustik f

acquaint /əˈkweɪnt/ vt ~ s.o. with jdn bekannt machen mit; be ~ed with kennen; vertraut sein mit (fact). ~ance n Bekanntschaft f; (person) Bekannte(r) m/f; make s.o.'s ~ance jdn kennenlernen

acquiesce /ækwɪˈes/ vi einwilligen (to in + acc). ~nce n Einwilligung f

acquire /əˈkwaɪə(r)/ vt erwerben

acquisit|ion /ækwɪˈzɪʃn/ n Erwerb m; (thing) Erwerbung f. ~ive /əˈkwɪzətɪv/ a habgierig

acquit /əˈkwɪt/ vt (pt/pp acquitted) freisprechen; ~ oneself well seiner Aufgabe gerecht werden. ~tal n Freispruch m

acre /ˈeɪkə(r)/ n I Morgen m

acrid /ˈækrɪd/ a scharf

acrimon|ious /ækrɪˈməʊnɪəs/ a bitter. ~y /ˈækrɪmənɪ/ n Bitterkeit f

acrobat /ˈækrəbæt/ n Akrobat(in) m(f). ~ic /-ˈbætɪk/ a akrobatisch

across /əˈkrɒs/ adv hinüber/herüber; (wide) breit; (not lengthwise) quer; (in crossword) waagerecht; **come ~ sth** auf etw (acc) stoßen; **go ~** hinübergehen; **bring ~** herüberbringen ● prep über (+ acc); (crosswise) quer über (+ acc/dat); (on the other side of) auf der anderen Seite (+ gen)

act /ækt/ n Tat f; (action) Handlung f; (law) Gesetz nt; (Theat) Akt m; (item) Nummer f; put on an ~ (fam) sich verstellen ● vi handeln; (behave) sich verhalten; (Theat) spielen; (pretend) sich verstellen; ~ as fungieren als ● vt spielen (role). ~ing a (deputy) stellvertretend ● n (Theat) Schauspielerei f. ~ing profession n Schauspielerberuf m

action /ˈækʃn/ n Handlung f; (deed) Tat f; (Mil) Einsatz m; (Jur) Klage f; (effect) Wirkung f; (Techn) Mechanismus m; out of ~ (machine:) außer Betrieb; take ~ handeln; killed in ~ gefallen. ~ 'replay n (TV) Wiederholung f

activate /ˈæktɪveɪt/ vt betätigen; (Chem, Phys) aktivieren

activ|e /ˈæktɪv/ a, -ly adv aktiv; on ~e service im Einsatz. ~ity /-ˈtɪvətɪ/ n Aktivität f

act|or /ˈæktə(r)/ n Schauspieler m. ~ress n Schauspielerin f

actual /'æktʃʊəl/ *a*, **-ly** *adv* eigentlich; *(real)* tatsächlich. **~ity** /-'ælətɪ/ *n* Wirklichkeit *f*

acumen /'ækjʊmən/ *n* Scharfsinn *m*

acupuncture /'ækjʊ-/ *n* Akupunktur *f*

acute /ə'kjuːt/ *a* scharf; *(angle)* spitz; *(illness)* akut. **~ly** *adv* sehr

ad /æd/ *n (fam)* = **advertisement**

AD *abbr* (**Anno Domini**) n.Chr.

adamant /'ædəmənt/ *a* **be ~ that** darauf bestehen, daß

adapt /ə'dæpt/ *vt* anpassen; bearbeiten *(play)* ● *vi* sich anpassen. **~ability** /-ə'bɪlətɪ/ *n* Anpassungsfähigkeit *f*. **~able** /-əbl/ *a* anpassungsfähig

adaptation /ædæp'teɪʃn/ *n* (*Theat*) Bearbeitung *f*

adapter, adaptor /ə'dæptə(r)/ *n* (*Techn*) Adapter *m*; (*Electr*) (*two-way*) Doppelstecker *m*

add /æd/ *vt* hinzufügen; (*Math*) addieren ● *vi* zusammenzählen, addieren; **~ to** hinzufügen zu; (*fig: increase*) steigern; (*compound*) verschlimmern. **~ up** *vt* zusammenzählen *(figures)* ● *vi* zusammenzählen, addieren; **~ up to** machen; **it doesn't ~ up** *(fig)* da stimmt etwas nicht

adder /'ædə(r)/ *n* Kreuzotter *f*

addict /'ædɪkt/ *n* Süchtige(r) *m/f*

addict|ed /ə'dɪktɪd/ *a* süchtig; **~ed to drugs** drogensüchtig. **~ion** /-ɪkʃn/ *n* Sucht *f*. **~ive** /-ɪv/ *a* **be ~ive** zur Süchtigkeit führen

addition /ə'dɪʃn/ *n* Hinzufügung *f*; (*Math*) Addition *f*; (*thing added*) Ergänzung *f*; **in ~** zusätzlich. **~al** *a*, **-ly** *adv* zusätzlich

additive /'ædɪtɪv/ *n* Zusatz *m*

address /ə'dres/ *n* Adresse *f*, Anschrift *f*; (*speech*) Ansprache *f*; **form of ~** Anrede *f* ● *vt* adressieren (**to** an + *acc*); *(speak to)* anreden *(person)*; sprechen vor (+ *dat*) *(meeting)*. **~ee** /ædre'siː/ *n* Empfänger *m*

adenoids /'ædənɔɪdz/ *npl* [Rachen]polypen *pl*

adept /'ædept/ *a* geschickt (**at** in + *dat*)

adequate /'ædɪkwət/ *a*, **-ly** *adv* ausreichend

adhere /əd'hɪə(r)/ *vi* kleben/(*fig*) festhalten (**to an** + *dat*). **~nce** *n* Festhalten *nt*

adhesive /əd'hiːsɪv/ *a* klebend ● *n* Klebstoff *m*

adjacent /ə'dʒeɪsnt/ *a* angrenzend

adjective /'ædʒɪktɪv/ *n* Adjektiv *nt*

adjoin /ə'dʒɔɪn/ *vt* angrenzen an (+ *acc*). **~ing** *a* angrenzend

adjourn /ə'dʒɜːn/ *vt* vertagen (**until** auf + *acc*) ● *vi* sich vertagen. **~ment** *n* Vertagung *f*

adjudicate /ə'dʒuːdɪkeɪt/ *vi* entscheiden; (*in competition*) Preisrichter sein

adjust /ə'dʒʌst/ *vt* einstellen; (*alter*) verstellen ● *vi* sich anpassen (**to** *dat*). **~able** /-əbl/ *a* verstellbar. **~ment** *n* Einstellung *f*; Anpassung *f*

ad lib /æd'lɪb/ *adv* aus dem Stegreif ● *vi* (*pt/pp* **ad libbed**) *(fam)* improvisieren

administer /əd'mɪnɪstə(r)/ *vt* verwalten; verabreichen *(medicine)*

administrat|ion /ədmɪn'streɪʃn/ *n* Verwaltung *f*; (*Pol*) Regierung *f*. **~or** /əd'mɪnɪstreɪtə(r)/ *n* Verwaltungsbeamte(r) *m/*-beamtin *f*

admirable /'ædmərəbl/ *a* bewundernswert

admiral /'ædmərəl/ *n* Admiral *m*

admiration /ædmə'reɪʃn/ *n* Bewunderung *f*

admire /əd'maɪə(r)/ *vt* bewundern. **~r** *n* Verehrer(in) *m(f)*

admissible /əd'mɪsəbl/ *a* zulässig

admission /əd'mɪʃn/ *n* Eingeständnis *nt*; (*entry*) Eintritt *m*

admit /əd'mɪt/ *vt* (*pt/pp* **admitted**) (*let in*) hereinlassen; (*acknowledge*) zugeben; **~ to sth** etw zugeben. **~tance** *n* Eintritt *m*. **~tedly** *adv* zugegebenermaßen

admoni|sh /əd'mɒnɪʃ/ *vt* ermahnen. **~tion** /ædmə'nɪʃn/ *n* Ermahnung *f*

ado /ə'duː/ *n* **without more ~** ohne weiteres

adolescen|ce /ædə'lesns/ *n* Jugend *f*, Pubertät *f*. **~t** *a* Jugend-; *(boy, girl)* halbwüchsig ● *n* Jugendliche(r) *m/f*

adopt /ə'dɒpt/ *vt* adoptieren; ergreifen *(measure)*; (*Pol*) annehmen *(candidate)*. **~ion** /-ɒpʃn/ *n* Adoption *f*. **~ive** /-ɪv/ *a* Adoptiv-

ador|able /ə'dɔːrəbl/ *a* bezaubernd. **~ation** /ædə'reɪʃn/ *n* Anbetung *f*

adore /ə'dɔː(r)/ *vt (worship)* anbeten; *(fam: like)* lieben

adorn /ə'dɔːn/ *vt* schmücken. **~ment** *n* Schmuck *m*

adrenalin /əˈdrenəlɪn/ n Adrenalin nt

Adriatic /eɪdrɪˈætɪk/ a & n ~ [Sea] Adria f

adrift /əˈdrɪft/ a be ~ treiben; **come** ~ sich losreißen

adroit /əˈdrɔɪt/ a, **-ly** adv gewandt, geschickt

adulation /ædjuˈleɪʃn/ n Schwärmerei f

adult /ˈædʌlt/ n Erwachsene(r) m/f

adulterate /əˈdʌltəreɪt/ vt verfälschen; panschen ⟨wine⟩

adultery /əˈdʌltərɪ/ n Ehebruch m

advance /ədˈvɑːns/ n Fortschritt m; (Mil) Vorrücken nt; (payment) Vorschuß m; **in** ~ im voraus ● vi vorankommen; (Mil) vorrücken; (make progress) Fortschritte machen ● vt fördern ⟨cause⟩; vorbringen ⟨idea⟩; vorschießen ⟨money⟩. ~ **booking** n Kartenvorverkauf m. ~**d** a fortgeschritten; (progressive) fortschrittlich. ~**ment** n Förderung f; (promotion) Beförderung f

advantage /ədˈvɑːntɪdʒ/ n Vorteil m; **take** ~ of ausnutzen. ~**ous** /ædvənˈteɪdʒəs/ a vorteilhaft

advent /ˈædvent/ n Ankunft f; **A~** (season) Advent m

adventur|e /ədˈventʃə(r)/ n Abenteuer nt. ~**er** n Abenteurer m. ~**ous** /-rəs/ a abenteuerlich; ⟨person⟩ abenteuerlustig

adverb /ˈædvɜːb/ n Adverb nt

adversary /ˈædvəsərɪ/ n Widersacher m

advers|e /ˈædvɜːs/ a ungünstig. ~**ity** /ədˈvɜːsətɪ/ n Not f

advert /ˈædvɜːt/ n (fam) = **advertisement**

advertise /ˈædvətaɪz/ vt Reklame machen für; (by small ad) inserieren ● vi Reklame machen; inserieren; ~ **for** per Anzeige suchen

advertisement /ədˈvɜːtɪsmənt/ n Anzeige f; (publicity) Reklame f; (small ad) Inserat nt

advertis|er /ˈædvətaɪzə(r)/ n Inserent m. ~**ing** n Werbung f ● attrib Werbe-

advice /ədˈvaɪs/ n Rat m. ~ **note** n Benachrichtigung f

advisable /ədˈvaɪzəbl/ a ratsam

advis|e /ədˈvaɪz/ vt raten (**s.o.** jdm); (counsel) beraten; (inform) benachrichtigen; ~**e s.o. against sth** jdm

von etw abraten ● vi raten. ~**er** n Berater(in) m(f). ~**ory** a beratend

advocate[1] /ˈædvəkət/ n [Rechts]anwalt m/-anwältin f; (supporter) Befürworter m

advocate[2] /ˈædvəkeɪt/ vt befürworten

aerial /ˈeərɪəl/ a Luft- ● n Antenne f

aerobics /eəˈrəʊbɪks/ n Aerobic nt

aero|drome /ˈeərədrəʊm/ n Flugplatz m. ~**plane** n Flugzeug nt

aerosol /ˈeərəsɒl/ n Spraydose f

aesthetic /iːsˈθetɪk/ a ästhetisch

afar /əˈfɑː(r)/ adv **from** ~ aus der Ferne

affable /ˈæfəbl/ a, **-bly** adv freundlich

affair /əˈfeə(r)/ n Angelegenheit f, Sache f; (scandal) Affäre f; **[love-]** ~ [Liebes]verhältnis nt

affect /əˈfekt/ vt sich auswirken auf (+ acc); (concern) betreffen; (move) rühren; (pretend) vortäuschen. ~**ation** /æfekˈteɪʃn/ n Affektiertheit f. ~**ed** a affektiert

affection /əˈfekʃn/ n Liebe f. ~**ate** /-ət/ a, **-ly** adv liebevoll

affiliated /əˈfɪlɪeɪtɪd/ a angeschlossen (**to** dat)

affinity /əˈfɪnətɪ/ n Ähnlichkeit f; (attraction) gegenseitige Anziehung f

affirm /əˈfɜːm/ vt behaupten; (Jur) eidesstattlich erklären

affirmative /əˈfɜːmətɪv/ a bejahend ● n Bejahung f

affix /əˈfɪks/ vt anbringen (**to** dat); (stick) aufkleben (**to** auf + acc); setzen ⟨signature⟩ (**to** unter + acc)

afflict /əˈflɪkt/ vt **be** ~**ed with** behaftet sein mit. ~**ion** /-ɪkʃn/ n Leiden nt

affluen|ce /ˈæfluəns/ n Reichtum m. ~**t** a wohlhabend. ~**t society** n Wohlstandsgesellschaft f

afford /əˈfɔːd/ vt (provide) gewähren; **be able to** ~ **sth** sich (dat) etw leisten können. ~**able** /-əbl/ a erschwinglich

affray /əˈfreɪ/ n Schlägerei f

affront /əˈfrʌnt/ n Beleidigung f ● vt beleidigen

afield /əˈfiːld/ adv **further** ~ weiter weg

afloat /əˈfləʊt/ a **be** ~ ⟨ship:⟩ flott sein; **keep** ~ ⟨person:⟩ sich über Wasser halten

afoot /əˈfʊt/ a im Gange

aforesaid /ə'fɔ:sed/ *a* (*Jur*) obenerwähnt

afraid /ə'freɪd/ *a* **be ~** Angst haben (**of** vor + *dat*); **I'm ~ not** leider nicht; **I'm ~ so** [ja] leider; **I'm ~ I can't help you** ich kann Ihnen leider nicht helfen

afresh /ə'freʃ/ *adv* von vorne

Africa /'æfrɪkə/ *n* Afrika *nt*. **~n** *a* afrikanisch ● *n* Afrikaner(in) *m(f)*

after /'ɑ:ftə(r)/ *adv* danach ● *prep* nach (+ *dat*); **~ that** danach; **~ all** schließlich; **the day ~ tomorrow** übermorgen; **be ~** aussein auf (+ *acc*) ● *conj* nachdem

after: ~-effect *n* Nachwirkung *f*. **~math** /-mɑ:θ/ *n* Auswirkungen *pl*. **~'noon** *n* Nachmittag *m*; **good ~noon!** guten Tag! **~sales service** *n* Kundendienst *m*. **~shave** *n* Rasierwasser *nt*. **~thought** *n* nachträglicher Einfall *m*. **~wards** *adv* nachher

again /ə'geɪn/ *adv* wieder; (*once more*) noch einmal; (*besides*) außerdem; **~ and ~** immer wieder

against /ə'geɪnst/ *prep* gegen (+ *acc*)

age /eɪdʒ/ *n* Alter *nt*; (*era*) Zeitalter *nt*; **~s** (*fam*) ewig; **under ~** minderjährig; **of ~** volljährig; **two years of ~** zwei Jahre alt ● *v* (*pres p* **ageing**) ● *vt* älter machen ● *vi* altern; (*mature*) reifen

aged¹ /eɪdʒd/ *a* **~ two** zwei Jahre alt

aged² /'eɪdʒɪd/ *a* betagt ● *n* **the ~** *pl* die Alten

ageless /'eɪdʒlɪs/ *a* ewig jung

agency /'eɪdʒənsɪ/ *n* Agentur *f*; (*office*) Büro *nt*; **have the ~ for** die Vertretung haben für

agenda /ə'dʒendə/ *n* Tagesordnung *f*; **on the ~** auf dem Programm

agent /'eɪdʒənt/ *n* Agent(in) *m(f)*; (*Comm*) Vertreter(in) *m(f)*; (*substance*) Mittel *nt*

aggravat|e /'ægrəveɪt/ *vt* verschlimmern; (*fam: annoy*) ärgern. **~ion** /-'veɪʃn/ *n* (*fam*) Ärger *m*

aggregate /'ægrɪgət/ *a* gesamt ● *n* Gesamtzahl *f*; (*sum*) Gesamtsumme *f*

aggress|ion /ə'greʃn/ *n* Aggression *f*. **~ive** /-sɪv/ *a*, **-ly** *adv* aggressiv. **~iveness** *n* Aggressivität *f*. **~or** *n* Angreifer(in) *m(f)*

aggrieved /ə'gri:vd/ *a* verletzt

aggro /'ægrəʊ/ *n* (*fam*) Ärger *m*

aghast /ə'gɑ:st/ *a* entsetzt

agil|e /'ædʒaɪl/ *a* flink, behende; ⟨*mind*⟩ wendig. **~ity** /ə'dʒɪlətɪ/ *n* Flinkheit *f*, Behendigkeit *f*

agitat|e /'ædʒɪteɪt/ *vt* bewegen; (*shake*) schütteln ● *vi* (*fig*) **~ for** agitieren für. **~ed** *a*, **-ly** *adv* erregt. **~ion** /-'teɪʃn/ *n* Erregung *f*; (*Pol*) Agitation *f*. **~or** *n* Agitator *m*

agnostic /æg'nɒstɪk/ *n* Agnostiker *m*

ago /ə'gəʊ/ *adv* vor (+ *dat*); **a month ~** vor einem Monat; **a long time ~** vor langer Zeit; **how long ~ is it?** wie lange ist es her?

agog /ə'gɒg/ *a* gespannt

agoniz|e /'ægənaɪz/ *vi* [innerlich] ringen. **~ing** *a* qualvoll

agony /'ægənɪ/ *n* Qual *f*; **be in ~** furchtbare Schmerzen haben

agree /ə'gri:/ *vt* vereinbaren; (*admit*) zugeben; **~ to do sth** sich bereit erklären, etw zu tun ● *vi* (*people, figures*.) übereinstimmen; (*reach agreement*) sich einigen; (*get on*) gut miteinander auskommen; (*consent*) einwilligen (**to** in + *acc*); **~ with s.o.** der Meinung bin ich auch; **~ with s.o.** jdm zustimmen; (*food*:) jdm bekommen; **~ with sth** (*approve of*) mit etw einverstanden sein

agreeable /ə'gri:əbl/ *a* angenehm; **be ~** einverstanden sein (**to** mit)

agreed /ə'gri:d/ *a* vereinbart

agreement /ə'gri:mənt/ *n* Übereinstimmung *f*; (*consent*) Einwilligung *f*; (*contract*) Abkommen *nt*; **reach ~** sich einigen

agricultur|al /ægrɪ'kʌltʃərəl/ *a* landwirtschaftlich. **~e** /'ægrɪkʌltʃə(r)/ *n* Landwirtschaft *f*

aground /ə'graʊnd/ *a* gestrandet; **run ~** ⟨*ship*:⟩ stranden

ahead /ə'hed/ *adv* voraus; **~ of** vor + dat; **be ~ of s.o./sth** vor jdm/etw sein; (*fig*) voraus sein; **draw ~** nach vorne ziehen; **go on ~** vorgehen; **get ~** vorankommen; **go ~!** (*fam*) bitte! **look/plan ~** vorausblicken/ -planen

aid /eɪd/ *n* Hilfe *f*; (*financial*) Unterstützung *f*; **~ in ~ of** zugunsten (+ *gen*) ● *vt* helfen (+ *dat*)

aide /eɪd/ *n* Berater *m*

Aids /eɪdz/ *n* Aids *nt*

ail|ing /'eɪlɪŋ/ *a* kränkelnd. **~ment** *n* Leiden *nt*

aim /eɪm/ *n* Ziel *nt*; **take ~** zielen ● *vt* richten (**at** auf + *acc*) ● *vi* zielen (**at** auf

+ *acc*); ~ **to do sth** beabsichtigen, etw zu tun. ~**less** *a*, **-ly** *adv* ziellos

air /eə(r)/ *n* Luft *f*; (*tune*) Melodie *f*; (*expression*) Miene *f*; (*appearance*) Anschein *m*; **be on the** ~ (*programme:*) gesendet werden; (*person:*) senden, auf Sendung sein; **put on** ~**s** vornehm tun; **by** ~ auf dem Luftweg; (*airmail*) mit Luftpost ● *vt* lüften; vorbringen (*views*)

air: ~**-bed** *n* Luftmatratze *f*. ~**-conditioned** *a* klimatisiert. ~**-conditioning** *n* Klimaanlage *f*. ~**craft** *n* Flugzeug *nt*. ~ **fare** *n* Flugpreis *m*. ~**field** *n* Flugplatz *m*. ~ **force** *n* Luftwaffe *f*. ~ **freshener** *n* Raumspray *nt*. ~**gun** *n* Luftgewehr *nt*. ~ **hostess** *n* Stewardeß *f*. ~ **letter** *n* Aerogramm *nt*. ~**line** *n* Fluggesellschaft *f*. ~**lock** *n* Luftblase *f*. ~**mail** *n* Luftpost *f*. ~**man** *n* Flieger *m*. ~**plane** *n* (*Amer*) Flugzeug *nt*. ~ **pocket** *n* Luftloch *nt*. ~**port** *n* Flughafen *m*. ~ **raid** *n* Luftangriff *m*. ~**-raid shelter** *n* Luftschutzbunker *m*. ~**ship** *n* Luftschiff *nt*. ~ **ticket** *n* Flugschein *m*. ~**tight** *a* luftdicht. ~ **traffic** *n* Luftverkehr *m*. ~**-traffic controller** *n* Fluglotse *m*. ~**worthy** *a* flugtüchtig

airy /'eərɪ/ *a* (**-ier, -iest**) luftig; (*manner*) nonchalant

aisle /aɪl/ *n* Gang *m*

ajar /ə'dʒɑ:(r)/ *a* angelehnt

akin /ə'kɪn/ *a* ~ **to** verwandt mit; (*similar*) ähnlich (**to** *dat*)

alabaster /'æləbɑ:stə(r)/ *n* Alabaster *m*

alacrity /ə'lækrətɪ/ *n* Bereitfertigkeit *f*

alarm /ə'lɑ:m/ *n* Alarm *m*; (*device*) Alarmanlage *f*; (*clock*) Wecker *m*; (*fear*) Unruhe *f* ● *vt* erschrecken; alarmieren. ~ **clock** *n* Wecker *m*

alas /ə'læs/ *int* ach!

album /'ælbəm/ *n* Album *nt*

alcohol /'ælkəhɒl/ *n* Alkohol *m*. ~**ic** /-'hɒlɪk/ *a* alkoholisch ● *n* Alkoholiker(in) *m(f)*. ~**ism** *n* Alkoholismus *m*

alcove /'ælkəʊv/ *n* Nische *f*

alert /ə'lɜ:t/ *a* aufmerksam ● *n* Alarm *m*; **on the** ~ auf der Hut ● *vt* alarmieren

algae /'ældʒi:/ *npl* Algen *pl*

algebra /'ældʒɪbrə/ *n* Algebra *f*

Algeria /æl'dʒɪərɪə/ *n* Algerien *nt*

alias /'eɪlɪəs/ *n* Deckname *m* ● *adv* alias

alibi /'ælɪbaɪ/ *n* Alibi *nt*

alien /'eɪlɪən/ *a* fremd ● *n* Ausländer(in) *m(f)*

alienat|e /'eɪlɪəneɪt/ *vt* entfremden. ~**ion** /-'neɪʃn/ *n* Entfremdung *f*

alight[1] /ə'laɪt/ *vi* aussteigen (**from** aus); (*bird:*) sich niederlassen

alight[2] *a* **be** ~ brennen; **set** ~ anzünden

align /ə'laɪn/ *vt* ausrichten. ~**ment** *n* Ausrichtung *f*; **out of** ~**ment** nicht richtig ausgerichtet

alike /ə'laɪk/ *a & adv* ähnlich; (*same*) gleich; **look** ~ sich (*dat*) ähnlich sehen

alimony /'ælɪmənɪ/ *n* Unterhalt *m*

alive /ə'laɪv/ *a* lebendig; **be** ~ leben; **be** ~ **with** wimmeln von

alkali /'ælkəlaɪ/ *n* Base *f*, Alkali *nt*

all /ɔ:l/ *a* alle *pl*; (*whole*) ganz; ~ **[the] children** alle Kinder; ~ **our children** alle unsere Kinder; ~ **the others** alle anderen; ~ **day** den ganzen Tag; ~ **the wine** der ganze Wein; **for** ~ **that** (*nevertheless*) trotzdem; **in** ~ **innocence** in aller Unschuld ● *pron* alle *pl*; (*everything*) alles; ~ **of you/them** Sie/ sie alle; ~ **of the town** die ganze Stadt; **not at** ~ gar nicht; **in** ~ insgesamt; ~ **in** ~ alles in allem; **most of** ~ am meisten; **once and for** ~ ein für allemal ● *adv* ganz; ~ **but** fast; ~ **at once** auf einmal; ~ **too soon** viel zu früh; ~ **the same** (*nevertheless*) trotzdem; ~ **the better** um so besser; **be** ~ **in** (*fam*) völlig erledigt sein; **four** ~ (*Sport*) vier zu vier

allay /ə'leɪ/ *vt* zerstreuen

allegation /ælɪ'geɪʃn/ *n* Behauptung *f*

allege /ə'ledʒ/ *vt* behaupten. ~**d** *a*, **-ly** /-ɪdlɪ/ *adv* angeblich

allegiance /ə'li:dʒəns/ *n* Treue *f*

allegor|ical /ælɪ'gɒrɪkl/ *a* allegorisch. ~**y** /'ælɪgərɪ/ *n* Allegorie *f*

allerg|ic /ə'lɜ:dʒɪk/ *a* allergisch (**to** gegen). ~**y** /'ælədʒɪ/ *n* Allergie *f*

alleviate /ə'li:vɪeɪt/ *vt* lindern

alley /'ælɪ/ *n* Gasse *f*; (*for bowling*) Bahn *f*

alliance /ə'laɪəns/ *n* Verbindung *f*; (*Pol*) Bündnis *nt*

allied /'ælaɪd/ *a* alliiert; (*fig: related*) verwandt (**to** mit)

alligator /'ælɪgeɪtə(r)/ *n* Alligator *m*

allocat|e /'æləkeɪt/ *vt* zuteilen; (*share out*) verteilen. ~**ion** /-'keɪʃn/ *n* Zuteilung *f*

allot /ə'lɒt/ vt (pt/pp **allotted**) zuteilen (**s.o.** jdm). **~ment** n ≈ Schrebergarten m

allow /ə'laʊ/ vt erlauben; (give) geben; (grant) gewähren; (reckon) rechnen; (agree, admit) zugeben; **~ for** berücksichtigen; **~ s.o. to do sth** jdm erlauben, etw zu tun; **be ~ed to do sth** etw tun dürfen

allowance /ə'laʊəns/ n [finanzielle] Unterstützung f; **~ for petrol** Benzingeld nt; **make ~s for** berücksichtigen

alloy /'ælɔɪ/ n Legierung f

allude /ə'lu:d/ vi anspielen (**to** auf + acc)

allure /ə'lʊə(r)/ n Reiz m

allusion /ə'lu:ʒn/ n Anspielung f

ally[1] /'ælaɪ/ n Verbündete(r) m/f; **the Allies** pl die Alliierten

ally[2] /ə'laɪ/ vt (pt/pp -**ied**) verbinden; **~ oneself with** sich verbünden mit

almighty /ɔ:l'maɪtɪ/ a allmächtig; (fam: big) Riesen- ● n **the A~** der Allmächtige

almond /'ɑ:mənd/ n (Bot) Mandel f

almost /'ɔ:lməʊst/ adv fast, beinahe

alms /ɑ:mz/ npl (liter) Almosen pl

alone /ə'ləʊn/ a & adv allein; **leave me ~** laß mich in Ruhe; **leave that ~!** laß die Finger davon! **let ~** ganz zu schweigen von

along /ə'lɒŋ/ prep entlang (+ acc); **~ the river** den Fluß entlang ● adv **~ with** zusammen mit; **all ~** die ganze Zeit; **come ~** komm doch; **I'll bring it ~** ich bringe es mit; **move ~** weitergehen

along'side adv daneben ● prep neben (+ dat)

aloof /ə'lu:f/ a distanziert

aloud /ə'laʊd/ adv laut

alphabet /'ælfəbet/ n Alphabet nt. **~ical** /-'betɪkl/ a, **-ly** adv alphabetisch

alpine /'ælpaɪn/ a alpin; **A~** Alpen-**Alps** /ælps/ npl Alpen pl

already /ɔ:l'redɪ/ adv schon

Alsace /æl'sæs/ n Elsaß nt

Alsatian /æl'seɪʃn/ n (dog) [deutscher] Schäferhund m

also /'ɔ:lsəʊ/ adv auch

altar /'ɔ:ltə(r)/ n Altar m

alter /'ɔ:ltə(r)/ vt ändern ● vi sich verändern. **~ation** /-'reɪʃn/ n Änderung f

alternate[1] /'ɔ:ltəneɪt/ vi [sich] abwechseln ● vt abwechseln

alternate[2] /ɔ:l'tɜ:nət/ a, **-ly** adv abwechselnd; (Amer: alternative) andere(r,s); **on ~ days** jeden zweiten Tag

'alternating current n Wechselstrom m

alternative /ɔ:l'tɜ:nətɪv/ a andere(r, s) ● n Alternative f. **~ly** adv oder aber

although /ɔ:l'ðəʊ/ conj obgleich, obwohl

altitude /'æltɪtju:d/ n Höhe f

altogether /ɔ:ltə'geðə(r)/ adv insgesamt; (on the whole) alles in allem

altruistic /æltru:'ɪstɪk/ altruistisch

aluminium /æljʊ'mɪnɪəm/ n, (Amer) **aluminum** /ə'lu:mɪnəm/ n Aluminium nt

always /'ɔ:lweɪz/ adv immer

am /æm/ see **be**

a.m. abbr (ante meridiem) vormittags

amalgamate /ə'mælgəmeɪt/ vt vereinigen; (Chem) amalgamieren ● vi sich vereinigen; (Chem) sich amalgamieren

amass /ə'mæs/ vt anhäufen

amateur /'æmətə(r)/ n Amateur m ● attrib Amateur-; (Theat) Laien-. **~ish** a laienhaft

amaze /ə'meɪz/ vt erstaunen. **~d** a erstaunt. **~ment** n Erstaunen nt

amazing /ə'meɪzɪŋ/ a, **-ly** adv erstaunlich

ambassador /æm'bæsədə(r)/ n Botschafter m

amber /'æmbə(r)/ n Bernstein m ● a (colour) gelb

ambidextrous /æmbɪ'dekstrəs/ a **be ~** mit beiden Händen gleich geschickt sein

ambience /'æmbɪəns/ n Atmosphäre f

ambigu|ity /æmbɪ'gju:ətɪ/ n Zweideutigkeit f. **~ous** /-'bɪgjʊəs/ a, **-ly** adv zweideutig

ambiti|on /æm'bɪʃn/ n Ehrgeiz m; (aim) Ambition f. **~ous** /-ʃəs/ a ehrgeizig

ambivalent /æm'bɪvələnt/ a zwiespältig; **be/feel ~** im Zwiespalt sein

amble /'æmbl/ vi schlendern

ambulance /'æmbjʊləns/ n Krankenwagen m. **~ man** n Sanitäter m

ambush /'æmbʊʃ/ n Hinterhalt m ● vt aus dem Hinterhalt überfallen

amen /ɑ:'men/ int amen

amenable /ə'mi:nəbl/ a **~ to** zugänglich (**to** dat)

amend /ə'mend/ *vt* ändern. ~ment
n Änderung *f*. ~s *npl* make ~s for
sth etw wiedergutmachen

amenities /ə'mi:nətɪz/ *npl* Einrichtungen *pl*

America /ə'merɪkə/ *n* Amerika *nt*.
~n *a* amerikanisch ●*n* Ameri-
kaner(in) *m(f)*. ~nism *n* Ameri-
kanismus *m*

amiable /'eɪmɪəbl/ *a* nett

amicable /'æmɪkəbl/ *a*, -bly *adv*
freundschaftlich; ⟨agreement⟩ gütlich

amid[st] /ə'mɪd[st]/ *prep* inmitten
(+ *gen*)

amiss /ə'mɪs/ *a* be ~ nicht stimmen
● *adv* not come ~ nicht unangebracht
sein; take sth ~ etw übelnehmen

ammonia /ə'məʊnɪə/ *n* Ammoniak
nt

ammunition /æmjʊ'nɪʃn/ *n* Munition *f*

amnesia /æm'ni:zɪə/ *n* Amnesie *f*

amnesty /'æmnəstɪ/ *n* Amnestie *f*

among[st] /ə'mʌŋ[st]/ *prep* unter
(+ *dat/acc*); ~ yourselves untereinander

amoral /eɪ'mɒrəl/ *a* amoralisch

amorous /'æmərəs/ *a* zärtlich

amount /ə'maʊnt/ *n* Menge *f*; ⟨sum
of money⟩ Betrag *m*; ⟨total⟩ Gesamtsumme *f* ● *vi* ~ to sich belaufen
auf (+ *acc*); ⟨fig⟩ hinauslaufen auf
(+ *acc*)

amp /æmp/ *n* Ampere *nt*

amphibi|an /æm'fɪbɪən/ *n* Am-
phibie *f*. ~ous /-ɪəs/ *a* amphibisch

amphitheatre /'æmfɪ-/ *n* Amphitheater *nt*

ample /'æmpl/ *a* (-r, -st), -ly *adv*
reichlich; ⟨large⟩ füllig

amplif|ier /'æmplɪfaɪə(r)/ *n* Ver-
stärker *m*. ~y /-faɪ/ *vt* (pt/pp -ied)
weiter ausführen; verstärken ⟨sound⟩

amputat|e /'æmpjʊteɪt/ *vt* ampu-
tieren. ~ion /-'teɪʃn/ *n* Amputation
f

amuse /ə'mju:z/ *vt* amüsieren, be-
lustigen; ⟨entertain⟩ unterhalten.
~ment *n* Belustigung *f*; Unterhaltung *f*. ~ment arcade *n* Spiel-
halle *f*

amusing /ə'mju:zɪŋ/ *a* amüsant

an /ən, *betont* æn/ *see* a

anaem|ia /ə'ni:mɪə/ *n* Blutarmut *f*,
Anämie *f*. ~ic *a* blutarm

anaesthesia /ænəs'θi:zɪə/ *n* Betäubung *f*

anaesthetic /ænəs'θetɪk/ *n* Narkosemittel *nt*, Betäubungsmittel *nt*;
under [an] ~ in Narkose; give s.o. an
~ jdm eine Narkose geben

anaesthet|ist /ə'ni:sθətɪst/ *n* Nar-
kosearzt *m*. ~ize /-taɪz/ *vt* betäuben

analog[ue] /'ænəlɒg/ *n* Analog-

analogy /ə'nælədʒɪ/ *n* Analogie *f*

analyse /'ænəlaɪz/ *vt* analysieren

analysis /ə'næləsɪs/ *n* Analyse *f*

analyst /'ænəlɪst/ *n* Chemiker(in)
m(f); ⟨Psych⟩ Analytiker *m*

analytical /ænə'lɪtɪkl/ *a* analytisch

anarch|ist /'ænəkɪst/ *n* Anarchist *m*.
~y *n* Anarchie *f*

anathema /ə'næθəmə/ *n* Greuel *m*

anatom|ical /ænə'tɒmɪkl/ *a*, -ly *adv*
anatomisch. ~y /ə'nætəmɪ/ *n* Ana-
tomie *f*

ancest|or /'ænsestə(r)/ *n* Vorfahr *m*.
~ry *n* Abstammung *f*

anchor /'æŋkə(r)/ *n* Anker *m* ● *vi*
ankern ● *vt* verankern

anchovy /'æntʃəvɪ/ *n* Sardelle *f*

ancient /'eɪnʃənt/ *a* alt

ancillary /æn'sɪlərɪ/ *a* Hilfs-

and /ənd, *betont* ænd/ *conj* und; ~ so
on und so weiter; six hundred ~ two
sechshundertzwei; more ~ more immer mehr; nice ~ warm schön warm;
try ~ come versuche zu kommen

anecdote /'ænɪkdəʊt/ *n* Anekdote *f*

anew /ə'nju:/ *adv* von neuem

angel /'eɪndʒl/ *n* Engel *m*. ~ic
/æn'dʒelɪk/ *a* engelhaft

anger /'æŋgə(r)/ *n* Zorn *m* ● *vt* zornig machen

angle¹ /'æŋgl/ *n* Winkel *m*; ⟨fig⟩
Standpunkt *m*; at an ~ schräg

angle² *vi* angeln; ~ for ⟨fig⟩ fischen
nach. ~r *n* Angler *m*

Anglican /'æŋglɪkən/ *a* anglikanisch ● *n* Anglikaner(in) *m(f)*

Anglo-Saxon /æŋgləʊ'sæksn/ *a* angelsächsisch ● *n* Angelsächsisch *nt*

angry /'æŋgrɪ/ *a* (-ier, -iest), -ily *adv*
zornig; be ~ with böse sein auf (+ *acc*)

anguish /'æŋgwɪʃ/ *n* Qual *f*

angular /'æŋgjʊlə(r)/ *a* eckig;
⟨features⟩ kantig

animal /'ænɪml/ *n* Tier *nt* ● *a* tierisch

animate¹ /'ænɪmət/ *a* lebendig

animat|e² /'ænɪmeɪt/ *vt* beleben.
~ed *a* lebhaft. ~ion /-'meɪʃn/ *n*
Lebhaftigkeit *f*

animosity /ænɪ'mɒsətɪ/ *n* Feind-
seligkeit *f*

aniseed /'ænɪsi:d/ *n* Anis *m*

ankle /'æŋkl/ n [Fuß]knöchel m

annex /ə'neks/ vt annektieren

annex[e] /'æneks/ n Nebengebäude nt; (extension) Anbau m

annihilat|e /ə'naɪəleɪt/ vt vernichten. **~ion** /-'leɪʃn/ n Vernichtung f

anniversary /ænɪ'vɜːsərɪ/ n Jahrestag m

annotate /'ænəteɪt/ vt kommentieren

announce /ə'naʊns/ vt bekanntgeben; (over loudspeaker) durchsagen; (at reception) ankündigen; (Radio, TV) ansagen; (in newspaper) anzeigen. **~ment** n Bekanntgabe f, Bekanntmachung f; Durchsage f; Ansage f; Anzeige f. **~r** n Ansager(in) m(f)

annoy /ə'nɔɪ/ vt ärgern; (pester) belästigen; **get ~ed** sich ärgern. **~ance** n Ärger m. **~ing** a ärgerlich

annual /'ænjʊəl/ a, -ly adv jährlich ● n (Bot) einjährige Pflanze f, (book) Jahresalbum nt

annuity /ə'njuːətɪ/ n [Leib]rente f

annul /ə'nʌl/ vt (pt/pp annulled) annullieren

anoint /ə'nɔɪnt/ vt salben

anomaly /ə'nɒmɪ/ n Anomalie f

anonymous /ə'nɒnɪməs/ a, -ly adv anonym

anorak /'ænəræk/ n Anorak m

anorexia /ænə'reksɪə/ n Magersucht f

another /ə'nʌðə(r)/ a & pron ein anderer/eine andere/ein anderes; (additional) noch ein(e); **~ [one]** noch einer/eine/eins; **~ day** an einem anderen Tag; **in ~ way** auf andere Weise; **~ time** ein andermal; **one ~** einander

answer /'ɑːnsə(r)/ n Antwort f; (solution) Lösung f ● vt antworten (s.o. jdm); beantworten (question, letter); **~ the door/telephone** an die Tür/ans Telefon gehen ● vi antworten; (Teleph) sich melden; **~ back** eine freche Antwort geben; **~ for** verantwortlich sein für. **~able** /-əbl/ a verantwortlich. **~ing machine** n (Teleph) Anrufbeantworter m

ant /ænt/ n Ameise f

antagonis|m /æn'tægənɪzm/ n Antagonismus m. **~tic** /-'nɪstɪk/ a feindselig

antagonize /æn'tægənaɪz/ vt gegen sich aufbringen

Antarctic /ænt'ɑːktɪk/ n Antarktis f

antelope /'æntɪləʊp/ n Antilope f

antenatal /æntɪ'neɪtl/ a **~ care** Schwangerschaftsfürsorge f

antenna /æn'tenə/ n Fühler m; (Amer: aerial) Antenne f

ante-room /'æntɪ-/ n Vorraum m

anthem /'ænθəm/ n Hymne f

anthology /æn'θɒlədʒɪ/ n Anthologie f

anthropology /ænθrə'pɒlədʒɪ/ n Anthropologie f

anti-'aircraft /æntɪ-/ a Flugabwehr-

antibiotic /æntɪbaɪ'ɒtɪk/ n Antibiotikum nt

'antibody n Antikörper m

anticipat|e /æn'tɪsɪpeɪt/ vt vorhersehen; (forestall) zuvorkommen (+ dat); (expect) erwarten. **~ion** /-'peɪʃn/ n Erwartung f

anti'climax n Enttäuschung f

anti'clockwise a & adv gegen den Uhrzeigersinn

antics /'æntɪks/ npl Mätzchen pl

anti'cyclone n Hochdruckgebiet nt

antidote /'æntɪdəʊt/ n Gegengift nt

'antifreeze n Frostschutzmittel nt

antipathy /æn'tɪpəθɪ/ n Abneigung f, Antipathie f

antiquarian /æntɪ'kweərɪən/ a antiquarisch. **~ bookshop** n Antiquariat nt

antiquated /'æntɪkweɪtɪd/ a veraltet

antique /æn'tiːk/ a antik ● n Antiquität f. **~ dealer** n Antiquitätenhändler m

antiquity /æn'tɪkwətɪ/ n Altertum nt

anti-Semitic /æntɪsɪ'mɪtɪk/ a antisemitisch

anti'septic a antiseptisch ● n Antiseptikum nt

anti'social a asozial; (fam) ungesellig

antithesis /æn'tɪθəsɪs/ n Gegensatz m

antlers /'æntləz/ npl Geweih nt

anus /'eɪnəs/ n After m

anvil /'ænvɪl/ n Amboß m

anxiety /æŋ'zaɪətɪ/ n Sorge f

anxious /'æŋkʃəs/ a, -ly adv ängstlich; (worried) besorgt; **be ~ to do sth** etw gerne machen wollen

any /'enɪ/ a irgendein(e); pl irgendwelche; (every) jede(r,s); pl alle; (after negative) kein(e); pl keine; **~ colour/**

number you like eine beliebige Farbe/ Zahl; **have you ~ wine/apples?** haben Sie Wein/Äpfel? **for ~ reason** aus irgendeinem Grund ● *pron* [irgend] einer/eine/eins; *pl* [irgend]welche; (*some*) welche(r,s); *pl* welche; (*all*) alle *pl*; (*negative*) keiner/keine/keins; *pl* keine; **I don't want ~ of it** ich will nichts davon; **there aren't ~** es gibt eine; **I need wine/apples/ money—have we ~?** ich brauche Wein/Äpfel/Geld—haben wir welchen/welche/welches? ● *adv* noch; **~ quicker/slower** noch schneller/lang- samer; **is it ~ better?** geht es et- was besser? **would you like ~ more?** möchten Sie noch [etwas]? **I can't eat ~ more** ich kann nichts mehr essen; **I can't go ~ further** ich kann nicht mehr weiter

'anybody *pron* [irgend] jemand; (*after negative*) niemand; **~ can do that** das kann jeder

'anyhow *adv* jedenfalls; (*never- theless*) trotzdem; (*badly*) irgendwie

'anyone *pron* = **anybody**

'anything *pron* [irgend] etwas; (*after negative*) nichts; (*everything*) alles

'anyway *adv* jedenfalls; (*in any case*) sowieso

'anywhere *adv* irgendwo; (*after negative*) nirgendwo; ⟨*be, live*⟩ überall; **I'd go ~** ich würde über- allhin gehen

apart /ə'pɑːt/ *adv* auseinander; **live ~** getrennt leben; **~ from** abgesehen von

apartment /ə'pɑːtmənt/ *n* Zimmer *nt*; (*Amer: flat*) Wohnung *f*

apathy /'æpəθɪ/ *n* Apathie *f*

ape /eɪp/ *n* [Menschen]affe *m* ● *vt* nachäffen

aperitif /ə'perətiːf/ *n* Aperitif *m*

aperture /'æpətʃə(r)/ *n* Öffnung *f*; (*Phot*) Blende *f*

apex /'eɪpeks/ *n* Spitze *f*; (*fig*) Gipfel *m*

apiece /ə'piːs/ *adv* pro Person; (*thing*) pro Stück

apologetic /əpɒlə'dʒetɪk/ *a*, **-ally** *adv* entschuldigend; **be ~** sich ent- schuldigen

apologize /ə'pɒlədʒaɪz/ *vi* sich ent- schuldigen (**to** bei)

apology /ə'pɒlədʒɪ/ *n* Entschuldi- gung *f*

apostle /ə'pɒsl/ *n* Apostel *m*

apostrophe /ə'pɒstrəfɪ/ *n* Apo- stroph *m*

appal /ə'pɔːl/ *vt* (*pt/pp* **appalled**) entsetzen. **~ling** *a* entsetzlich

apparatus /æpə'reɪtəs/ *n* Apparatur *f*; (*Sport*) Geräte *pl*; (*single piece*) Ge- rät *nt*

apparel /ə'pærəl/ *n* Kleidung *f*

apparent /ə'pærənt/ *a* offenbar; (*seeming*) scheinbar. **~ly** *adv* offen- bar, anscheinend

apparition /æpə'rɪʃn/ *n* Er- scheinung *f*

appeal /ə'piːl/ *n* Appell *m*, Aufruf *m*; (*request*) Bitte *f*; (*attraction*) Reiz *m*; (*Jur*) Berufung *f* ● *vi* appellieren (**to** an + *acc*); (*ask*) bitten (**for** um); (*be attractive*) zusagen (**to** *dat*); (*Jur*) Be- rufung einlegen. **~ing** *a* ansprechend

appear /ə'pɪə(r)/ *vi* erscheinen; (*seem*) scheinen; (*Theat*) auftreten. **~ance** *n* Erscheinen *nt*; (*look*) Aus- sehen *nt*; **to all ~ances** allem An- schein nach

appease /ə'piːz/ *vt* beschwichtigen

append /ə'pend/ *vt* nachtragen; setzen ⟨*signature*⟩ (**to** unter + *acc*). **~age** /-ɪdʒ/ *n* Anhängsel *nt*

appendicitis /əpendɪ'saɪtɪs/ *n* Blind- darmentzündung *f*

appendix /ə'pendɪks/ *n* (*pl* **-ices** /-ɪsiːz/) (*of book*) Anhang *m* ● (*pl* **-es**) (*Anat*) Blinddarm *m*

appertain /æpə'teɪn/ *vi* **~ to** be- treffen

appetite /'æpɪtaɪt/ *n* Appetit *m*

appetizing /'æpɪtaɪzɪŋ/ *a* appe- titlich

applau|d /ə'plɔːd/ *vt/i* Beifall klat- schen (+ *dat*). **~se** *n* Beifall *m*

apple /'æpl/ *n* Apfel *m*

appliance /ə'plaɪəns/ *n* Gerät *nt*

applicable /'æplɪkəbl/ *a* anwendbar (**to** auf + *acc*); (*on form*) **not ~** nicht zutreffend

applicant /'æplɪkənt/ *n* Bewer- ber(in) *m(f)*

application /æplɪ'keɪʃn/ *n* Anwen- dung *f*; (*request*) Antrag *m*; (*for job*) Bewerbung *f*; (*diligence*) Fleiß *m*

applied /ə'plaɪd/ *a* angewandt

apply /ə'plaɪ/ *vt* (*pt/pp* **-ied**) auf- tragen ⟨*paint*⟩; anwenden ⟨*force, rule*⟩ ● *vi* zutreffen (**to** auf + *acc*); **~ for** be- antragen; sich bewerben um ⟨*job*⟩

appoint /ə'pɔɪnt/ *vt* ernennen; (*fix*) festlegen; **well ~ed** gut ausgestattet. **~ment** *n* Ernennung *f*; (*meeting*)

Verabredung *f*; (*at doctor's, hairdresser's*) Termin *m*; (*job*) Posten *m*; **make an ~ment** sich anmelden

apposite /'æpəzɪt/ *a* treffend

appraise /ə'preɪz/ *vt* abschätzen

appreciable /ə'priːʃəbl/ *a* merklich; (*considerable*) beträchtlich

appreciat|e /ə'priːʃɪeɪt/ *vt* zu schätzen wissen; (*be grateful for*) dankbar sein für; (*enjoy*) schätzen; (*understand*) verstehen ● *vi* (*increase in value*) im Wert steigen. **~ion** /-'eɪʃn/ *n* (*gratitude*) Dankbarkeit *f*; **in ~ion** als Dank (**of** für). **~ive** /-ətɪv/ *a* dankbar

apprehend /æprɪ'hend/ *vt* festnehmen

apprehens|ion /æprɪ'henʃn/ *n* Festnahme *f*; (*fear*) Angst *f*. **~ive** /-sɪv/ *a* ängstlich

apprentice /ə'prentɪs/ *n* Lehrling *m*. **~ship** *n* Lehre *f*

approach /ə'prəʊtʃ/ *n* Näherkommen *nt*; (*of time*) Nahen *nt*; (*access*) Zugang *m*; (*road*) Zufahrt *f* ● *vi* sich nähern; (*time:*) nahen ● *vt* sich nähern (+ *dat*); (*with request*) herantreten an (+ *acc*); (*set about*) sich heranmachen an (+ *acc*). **~able** /-əbl/ *a* zugänglich

approbation /æprə'beɪʃn/ *n* Billigung *f*

appropriate[1] /ə'prəʊprɪət/ *a* angebracht, angemessen

appropriate[2] /ə'prəʊprɪeɪt/ *vt* sich (*dat*) aneignen

approval /ə'pruːvl/ *n* Billigung *f*; **on ~** zur Ansicht

approv|e /ə'pruːv/ *vt* billigen ● *vi* **~e of sth/s.o.** mit etw/jdm einverstanden sein. **~ing** *a*, **-ly** *adv* anerkennend

approximate[1] /ə'prɒksɪmeɪt/ *vi* **~ to** nahekommen (+ *dat*)

approximate[2] /ə'prɒksɪmət/ *a* ungefähr. **~ly** *adv* ungefähr, etwa

approximation /əprɒksɪ'meɪʃn/ *n* Schätzung *f*

apricot /'eɪprɪkɒt/ *n* Aprikose *f*

April /'eɪprəl/ *n* April *m*; **make an ~ fool of** in den April schicken

apron /'eɪprən/ *n* Schürze *f*

apropos /'æprəpəʊ/ *adv* **~ [of]** betreffs (+ *gen*)

apt /æpt/ *a*, **-ly** *adv* passend; (*pupil*) begabt; **be ~ to do sth** dazu neigen, etw zu tun

aptitude /'æptɪtjuːd/ *n* Begabung *f*

aqualung /'ækwəlʌŋ/ *n* Tauchgerät *nt*

aquarium /ə'kweərɪəm/ *n* Aquarium *nt*

Aquarius /ə'kweərɪəs/ *n* (*Astr*) Wassermann *m*

aquatic /ə'kwætɪk/ *a* Wasser-

Arab /'ærəb/ *a* arabisch ● *n* Araber(in) *m(f)*. **~ian** /ə'reɪbɪən/ *a* arabisch

Arabic /'ærəbɪk/ *a* arabisch

arable /'ærəbl/ *a* **~ land** Ackerland *nt*

arbitrary /'ɑːbɪtrərɪ/ *a*, **-ily** *adv* willkürlich

arbitrat|e /'ɑːbɪtreɪt/ *vi* schlichten. **~ion** /-'treɪʃn/ *n* Schlichtung *f*

arc /ɑːk/ *n* Bogen *m*

arcade /ɑː'keɪd/ *n* Laubengang *m*; (*shops*) Einkaufspassage *f*

arch /ɑːtʃ/ *n* Bogen *m*; (*of foot*) Gewölbe *nt* ● *vt* **~ its back** (*cat:*) einen Buckel machen

archaeological /ɑːkɪə'lɒdʒɪkl/ *a* archäologisch

archaeolog|ist /ɑːkɪ'ɒlədʒɪst/ *n* Archäologe *m*/-login *f*. **~y** *n* Archäologie *f*

archaic /ɑː'keɪɪk/ *a* veraltet

arch'bishop /ɑːtʃ-/ *n* Erzbischof *m*

arch-'enemy *n* Erzfeind *m*

archer /'ɑːtʃə(r)/ *n* Bogenschütze *m*. **~y** *n* Bogenschießen *nt*

architect /'ɑːkɪtekt/ *n* Architekt(in) *m(f)*. **~ural** /ɑː'kɪtektʃərəl/ *a*, **-ly** *adv* architektonisch

architecture /'ɑːkɪtektʃə(r)/ *n* Architektur *f*

archives /'ɑːkaɪvz/ *npl* Archiv *nt*

archway /'ɑːtʃweɪ/ *n* Torbogen *m*

Arctic /'ɑːktɪk/ *a* arktisch ● *n* **the ~** die Arktis

ardent /'ɑːdənt/ *a*, **-ly** *adv* leidenschaftlich

ardour /'ɑːdə(r)/ *n* Leidenschaft *f*

arduous /'ɑːdjʊəs/ *a* mühsam

are /ɑː(r)/ *see* be

area /'eərɪə/ *n* (*surface*) Fläche *f*; (*Geom*) Flächeninhalt *m*; (*region*) Gegend *f*; (*fig*) Gebiet *nt*. **~ code** *n* Vorwahlnummer *f*

arena /ə'riːnə/ *n* Arena *f*

aren't /ɑːnt/ = **are not**. *See* be

Argentina /ɑːdʒən'tiːnə/ *n* Argentinien *nt*

Argentin|e /'ɑːdʒəntaɪn/, **~ian** /-'tɪnɪən/ *a* argentinisch

argue /'ɑːgjuː/ *vi* streiten (**about** über + *acc*); (*two people:*) sich streiten;

(debate) diskutieren; **don't ~!** keine
Widerrede! ● *vt (debate)* diskutieren;
(reason) ~ **that** argumentieren, daß
argument /ˈɑːgjʊmənt/ *n* Streit *m*,
Auseinandersetzung *f*; *(reasoning)*
Argument *nt*; **have an ~** sich streiten.
~ative /-ˈmentətɪv/ *a* streitlustig
aria /ˈɑːrɪə/ *n* Arie *f*
arid /ˈærɪd/ *a* dürr
Aries /ˈeəriːz/ *n (Astr)* Widder *m*
arise /əˈraɪz/ *vi (pt* **arose**, *pp* **arisen)**
sich ergeben **(from** aus)
aristocracy /ærɪˈstɒkrəsɪ/ *n* Aristo-
kratie *f*
aristocrat /ˈærɪstəkræt/ *n* Aristo-
krat(in) *m(f)*. **~ic** /-ˈkrætɪk/ *a*
aristokratisch
arithmetic /əˈrɪθmətɪk/ *n* Rechnen
nt
ark /ɑːk/ *n* **Noah's A~** die Arche Noah
arm /ɑːm/ *n* Arm *m*; *(of chair)* Arm-
lehne *f*; **~s** *pl (weapons)* Waffen *pl*;
(Heraldry) Wappen *nt*; **up in ~s** *(fam)*
empört ● *vt* bewaffnen
armament /ˈɑːməmənt/ *n* Bewaff-
nung*f*; **~s** *pl* Waffen *pl*
'armchair *n* Sessel *m*
armed /ɑːmd/ *a* bewaffnet; **~ forces**
Streitkräfte *pl*
armistice /ˈɑːmɪstɪs/ *n* Waffenstillstand *m*
armour /ˈɑːmə(r)/ *n* Rüstung *f*. **~ed**
a Panzer-
'armpit *n* Achselhöhle *f*
army /ˈɑːmɪ/ *n* Heer *nt*; *(specific)*
Armee*f*; **join the ~** zum Militär gehen
aroma /əˈrəʊmə/ *n* Aroma *nt*, Duft
m. **~tic** /ærəˈmætɪk/ *a* aromatisch
arose /əˈrəʊz/ *see* **arise**
around /əˈraʊnd/ *adv* **[all]** ~ rings
herum; **he's not ~** er ist nicht da; **look/
turn ~** sich umsehen/umdrehen;
travel ~ herumreisen ● *prep* um
(+ acc) ... herum; *(approximately)*
gegen
arouse /əˈraʊz/ *vt* aufwecken; *(excite)* erregen
arrange /əˈreɪndʒ/ *vt* arrangieren;
anordnen *(furniture, books)*; *(settle)*
abmachen; **I have ~d to go there** ich
habe abgemacht, daß ich dahingehe.
~ment *n* Anordnung *f*; *(agreement)*
Vereinbarung *f*; *(of flowers)* Gesteck
nt; **make ~ments** Vorkehrungen
treffen
arrears /əˈrɪəz/ *npl* Rückstände *pl*; **in
~** im Rückstand

arrest /əˈrest/ *n* Verhaftung *f*; **under
~** verhaftet ● *vt* verhaften
arrival /əˈraɪvl/ *n* Ankunft *f*; **new ~s**
pl Neuankömmlinge *pl*
arrive /əˈraɪv/ *vi* ankommen; **~ at**
(fig) gelangen zu
arrogan|ce /ˈærəgəns/ *n* Arroganz*f*.
~t *a*, **-ly** *adv* arrogant
arrow /ˈærəʊ/ *n* Pfeil *m*
arse /ɑːs/ *n (vulg)* Arsch *m*
arsenic /ˈɑːsənɪk/ *n* Arsen *nt*
arson /ˈɑːsn/ *n* Brandstiftung *f*.
~ist /-sənɪst/ *n* Brandstifter *m*
art /ɑːt/ *n* Kunst *f*; **work of ~** Kunst-
werk *nt*; **~s and crafts** *pl* Kunstge-
werbe *nt*; **A~s** *pl (Univ)*
Geisteswissenschaften *pl*
artery /ˈɑːtərɪ/ *n* Schlagader *f*, Arterie*f*
artful /ˈɑːtfl/ *a* gerissen
'art gallery *n* Kunstgalerie *f*
arthritis /ɑːˈθraɪtɪs/ *n* Arthritis *f*
artichoke /ˈɑːtɪtʃəʊk/ *n* Artischocke
f
article /ˈɑːtɪkl/ *n* Artikel *m*; *(object)*
Gegenstand *m*; **~ of clothing** Kleidungsstück *nt*
articulate[1] /ɑːˈtɪkjʊlət/ *a* deutlich;
be ~ sich gut ausdrücken können
articulate[2] /ɑːˈtɪkjʊleɪt/ *vt* aussprechen. **~d lorry** *n* Sattelzug *m*
artifice /ˈɑːtɪfɪs/ *n* Arglist *f*
artificial /ɑːtɪˈfɪʃl/ *a*, **-ly** *adv* künstlich
artillery /ɑːˈtɪlərɪ/ *n* Artillerie*f*
artist /ˈɑːtɪst/ *n* Künstler(in) *m(f)*
artiste /ɑːˈtiːst/ *n (Theat)* Artist(in)
m(f)
artistic /ɑːˈtɪstɪk/ *a*, **-ally** *adv* künstlerisch
artless /ˈɑːtlɪs/ *a* unschuldig
as /æz/ *conj (because)* da; *(when)* als;
(while) während ● *prep* als; **as a
child/foreigner** als Kind/Ausländer
● *adv* **as well** auch; **as soon as** sobald;
as much as soviel wie; **as quick as you**
so schnell wie du; **as you know** wie Sie
wissen; **as far as I'm concerned** was
mich betrifft
asbestos /æzˈbestɒs/ *n* Asbest *m*
ascend /əˈsend/ *vi* [auf]steigen ● *vt*
besteigen *(throne)*
Ascension /əˈsenʃn/ *n (Relig)*
[Christi] Himmelfahrt *f*
ascent /əˈsent/ *n* Aufstieg *m*
ascertain /æsəˈteɪn/ *vt* ermitteln
ascribe /əˈskraɪb/ *vt* zuschreiben **(to**
dat)

ash¹ /æʃ/ n (tree) Esche f
ash² n Asche f
ashamed /əˈʃeɪmd/ a beschämt; **be ~ sich schämen** (**of** über + acc)
ashore /əˈʃɔː(r)/ adv an Land
ash: ~tray n Aschenbecher m. **A~ 'Wednesday** n Aschermittwoch m
Asia /ˈeɪʃə/ n Asien nt. ~n a asiatisch ● n Asiat(in) m(f). ~tic /eɪʃɪˈætɪk/ a asiatisch
aside /əˈsaɪd/ adv beiseite; ~ **from** (Amer) außer (+ dat)
ask /ɑːsk/ vt/i fragen; stellen (question); (invite) einladen; ~ **for** bitten um; verlangen (s.o.); ~ **after** sich erkundigen nach; ~ **s.o. in** jdn hereinbitten; ~ **s.o. to do sth** jdn bitten, etw zu tun
askance /əˈskɑːns/ adv **look ~ at** schief ansehen
askew /əˈskjuː/ a & adv schief
asleep /əˈsliːp/ a **be ~** schlafen; **fall ~** einschlafen
asparagus /əˈspærəgəs/ n Spargel m
aspect /ˈæspekt/ n Aspekt m
aspersions /əˈspɜːʃnz/ npl **cast ~ on** schlechtmachen
asphalt /ˈæsfælt/ n Asphalt m
asphyxia /əsˈfɪksɪə/ n Erstickung f. ~te /æˈsfɪksɪeɪt/ vt/i ersticken. ~tion /-ˈeɪʃn/ n Erstickung f
aspirations /æspəˈreɪʃnz/ npl Streben nt
aspire /əˈspaɪə(r)/ vi ~ **to** streben nach
ass /æs/ n Esel m
assail /əˈseɪl/ vt bestürmen. ~ant n Angreifer(in) m(f)
assassin /əˈsæsɪn/ n Mörder(in) m(f). ~ate vt ermorden. ~ation /-ˈneɪʃn/ n [politischer] Mord m
assault /əˈsɔːlt/ n (Mil) Angriff m; (Jur) Körperverletzung f ● vt [tätlich] angreifen
assemble /əˈsembl/ vi sich versammeln ● vt versammeln; (Techn) montieren
assembly /əˈsemblɪ/ n Versammlung f; (Sch) Andacht f; (Techn) Montage f. ~ **line** n Fließband nt
assent /əˈsent/ n Zustimmung f ● vi zustimmen (**to** dat)
assert /əˈsɜːt/ vt behaupten; ~ **oneself** sich durchsetzen. ~ion /-ɜːʃn/ n Behauptung f. ~ive /-tɪv/ a **be ~ive** sich durchsetzen können
assess /əˈses/ vt bewerten; (fig & for tax purposes) einschätzen; schätzen

(value). ~ment n Einschätzung f; (of tax) Steuerbescheid m
asset /ˈæset/ n Vorteil m; ~s pl (money) Vermögen nt; (Comm) Aktiva pl
assiduous /əˈsɪdjʊəs/ a, **-ly** adv fleißig
assign /əˈsaɪn/ vt zuweisen (**to** dat). ~ment n (task) Aufgabe f
assimilate /əˈsɪmɪleɪt/ vt aufnehmen; (integrate) assimilieren
assist /əˈsɪst/ vt/i helfen (+ dat). ~ance n Hilfe f. ~ant a Hilfs- ● n Assistent(in) m(f); (in shop) Verkäufer(in) m(f)
associat|e¹ /əˈsəʊʃɪeɪt/ vt verbinden; (Psych) assoziieren ● vi ~ **with** verkehren mit. ~ion /-ˈeɪʃn/ n Verband m. **A~ion 'football** n Fußball m
associate² /əˈsəʊʃɪət/ a assoziiert ● n Kollege m/-gin f
assort|ed /əˈsɔːtɪd/ a gemischt. ~ment n Mischung f
assum|e /əˈsjuːm/ vt annehmen; übernehmen (office); ~ing **that** angenommen, daß
assumption /əˈsʌmpʃn/ n Annahme f; **on the ~** in der Annahme (**that** daß)
assurance /əˈʃʊərəns/ n Versicherung f; (confidence) Selbstsicherheit f
assure /əˈʃʊə(r)/ vt versichern (**s.o.** jdm); **I ~ you [of that]** das versichere ich Ihnen. ~d a sicher
asterisk /ˈæstərɪsk/ n Sternchen nt
astern /əˈstɜːn/ adv achtern
asthma /ˈæsmə/ n Asthma nt. ~tic /æsˈmætɪk/ a asthmatisch
astonish /əˈstɒnɪʃ/ vt erstaunen. ~ing a erstaunlich. ~ment n Erstaunen nt
astound /əˈstaʊnd/ vt in Erstaunen setzen
astray /əˈstreɪ/ adv **go ~** verlorengehen; (person.) sich verlaufen; (fig) vom rechten Weg abkommen; **lead ~** verleiten
astride /əˈstraɪd/ adv rittlings ● prep rittlings auf (+ dat/acc)
astringent /əˈstrɪndʒənt/ a adstringierend; (fig) beißend
astrolog|er /əˈstrɒlədʒə(r)/ n Astrologe m/-gin f. ~y n Astrologie f
astronaut /ˈæstrənɔːt/ n Astronaut(in) m(f)
astronom|er /əˈstrɒnəmə(r)/ n Astronom m. ~ical /æstrəˈnɒmɪkl/ a astronomisch. ~y n Astronomie f

astute /ə'stjuː:t/ *a* scharfsinnig.
~ness *n* Scharfsinn *m*

asylum /ə'saɪləm/ *n* Asyl *nt*; **[lunatic]**
~ Irrenanstalt *f*

at /ət, *betont* æt/ *prep* an (+ *dat/acc*);
(*with town*) in; (*price*) zu; (*speed*) mit;
at the station am Bahnhof; **at the
beginning/end** am Anfang/Ende; **at
home** zu Hause; **at John's** bei John; **at
work/the hairdresser's** bei der Ar-
beit/beim Friseur; **at school/the office** in der Schule/im Büro; **at a party/
wedding** auf einer Party/Hochzeit; **at
one o'clock** um ein Uhr; **at Christmas/
Easter** zu Weihnachten/Ostern; **at the
age of** im Alter von; **not at all** gar
nicht; **at times** manchmal; **two at a
time** zwei auf einmal; **good/bad at
languages** gut/schlecht in Sprachen

ate /et/ *see* **eat**

atheist /'eɪθɪɪst/ *n* Atheist(in) *m(f)*

athlet|e /'æθliː:t/ *n* Athlet(in) *m(f)*.
~ic /-'letɪk/ *a* sportlich. ~ics
/-'letɪks/ *n* Leichtathletik *f*

Atlantic /ət'læntɪk/ *a & n* **the ~
[Ocean]** der Atlantik

atlas /'ætləs/ *n* Atlas *m*

atmospher|e /'ætməsfɪə(r)/ *n* Atmo-
sphäre *f*. ~ic /-'ferɪk/ *a* atmo-
sphärisch

atom /'ætəm/ *n* Atom *nt*. ~ **bomb** *f*
Atombombe *f*

atomic /ə'tɒmɪk/ *a* Atom-

atone /ə'təʊn/ *vi* büßen (**for** für).
~ment *n* Buße *f*

atrocious /ə'trəʊʃəs/ *a* abscheulich

atrocity /ə'trɒsətɪ/ *n* Greueltat *f*

attach /ə'tætʃ/ *vt* befestigen (**to** an
+ *dat*); beimessen ⟨*importance*⟩ (**to**
dat); **be ~ed to** ⟨*fig*⟩ hängen an (+ *dat*)

attaché /ə'tæʃeɪ/ *n* Attaché *m*. ~
case *n* Aktenkoffer *m*

attachment /ə'tætʃmənt/ *n* Bindung *f*; ⟨*tool*⟩ Zubehörteil *nt*;
⟨*additional*⟩ Zusatzgerät *nt*

attack /ə'tæk/ *n* Angriff *m*; ⟨*Med*⟩
Anfall *m* ● *vt/i* angreifen. ~er *n* Angreifer *m*

attain /ə'teɪn/ *vt* erreichen; ⟨*get*⟩ erlangen. ~able /-əbl/ *a* erreichbar

attempt /ə'tempt/ *n* Versuch *m* ● *vt*
versuchen

attend /ə'tend/ *vt* anwesend sein bei;
(*go regularly to*) besuchen; (*take part
in*) teilnehmen an (+ *dat*); (*accompany*) begleiten; ⟨*doctor:*⟩ behandeln ● *vi* anwesend sein; (*pay

attention*) aufpassen; ~ **to** sich kümmern um; (*in shop*) bedienen. ~ance *f*
Anwesenheit *f*; (*number*) Besu-
cherzahl *f*. ~ant *n* Wärter(in) *m(f)*;
(*in car park*) Wächter *m*

attention /ə'tenʃn/ *n* Aufmerksamkeit *f*; ~! ⟨*Mil*⟩ still-
gestanden! **pay** ~ aufpassen; **pay** ~ **to**
beachten, achten auf (+ *acc*); **need** ~
reparaturbedürftig sein; **for the** ~ **of**
zu Händen von

attentive /ə'tentɪv/ *a*, **-ly** *adv* aufmerksam

attest /ə'test/ *vt/i* ~ **[to]** bezeugen

attic /'ætɪk/ *n* Dachboden *m*

attire /ə'taɪə(r)/ *n* Kleidung *f* ● *vt*
kleiden

attitude /'ætɪtjuː:d/ *n* Haltung *f*

attorney /ə'tɜːnɪ/ *n* (*Amer: lawyer*)
Rechtsanwalt *m*; **power of** ~ Vollmacht *f*

attract /ə'trækt/ *vt* anziehen; erregen ⟨*attention*⟩; ~ **s.o.'s attention**
jds Aufmerksamkeit auf sich (*acc*)
lenken. ~ion /-ækʃn/ *n* Anziehungskraft *f*; ⟨*charm*⟩ Reiz *m*; ⟨*thing*⟩ Attraktion *f*. ~ive /-tɪv/ *a*, **-ly** *adv*
attraktiv

attribute[1] /'ætrɪbjuː:t/ *n* Attribut *nt*

attribut|e[2] /ə'trɪbjuː:t/ *vt* zu-
schreiben (**to** *dat*). ~ive /-tɪv/ *a*, **-ly**
adv attributiv

attrition /ə'trɪʃn/ *n* **war of** ~ Zer-
mürbungskrieg *m*

aubergine /'əʊbəʒiː:n/ *n* Aubergine *f*

auburn /'ɔːbən/ *a* kastanienbraun

auction /'ɔːkʃn/ *n* Auktion *f*, Ver-
steigerung *f* ● *vt* versteigern. ~eer
/-ʃə'nɪə(r)/ *n* Auktionator *m*

audaci|ous /ɔː'deɪʃəs/ *a*, **-ly** *adv*
verwegen. ~ty /-'dæsətɪ/ *n*
Verwegenheit *f*; (*impudence*) Drei-
stigkeit *f*

audible /'ɔːdəbl/ *a*, **-bly** *adv* hörbar

audience /'ɔːdɪəns/ *n* Publikum *nt*;
(*Theat, TV*) Zuschauer *pl*; (*Radio*)
Zuhörer *pl*; (*meeting*) Audienz *f*

audio /'ɔːdɪəʊ/: ~ **typist** *n* Phonotypistin *f*. ~'**visual** *a* audiovisuell

audit /'ɔːdɪt/ *n* Bücherrevision *f* ● *vt*
(*Comm*) prüfen

audition /ɔː'dɪʃn/ *n* (*Theat*) Vor-
sprechen *nt*; (*Mus*) Vorspielen *nt*;
(*for singer*) Vorsingen *nt* ● *vi* vor-
sprechen; vorspielen; vorsingen

auditor /'ɔːdɪtə(r)/ *n* Buchprüfer *m*

auditorium /ɔːdɪ'tɔːrɪəm/ *n* Zu-
schauerraum *m*

augment /ɔːg'ment/ vt vergrößern

augur /'ɔːgə(r)/ vi ~ **well/ill** etwas/ nichts Gutes verheißen

august /ɔː'gʌst/ a hoheitsvoll

August /'ɔːgəst/ n August m

aunt /ɑːnt/ n Tante f

au pair /əu'peə(r)/ n ~ **[girl]** Au-pair-Mädchen nt

aura /'ɔːrə/ n Fluidum nt

auspices /'ɔːspɪsɪz/ npl (protection) Schirmherrschaft f

auspicious /ɔː'spɪʃəs/ a günstig; ⟨occasion⟩ freudig

auster|e /ɔː'stɪə(r)/ a streng; (simple) nüchtern. ~**ity** /-'terətɪ/ n Strenge f; (hardship) Entbehrung f

Australia /ɒ'streɪlɪə/ n Australien nt. ~**n** a australisch ● n Australier(in) m(f)

Austria /'ɒstrɪə/ n Österreich nt. ~**n** a österreichisch ● n Österreicher(in) m(f)

authentic /ɔː'θentɪk/ a echt, authentisch. ~**ate** vt beglaubigen. ~**ity** /-'tɪsətɪ/ n Echtheit f

author /'ɔːθə(r)/ n Schriftsteller m, Autor m; (of document) Verfasser m

authoritarian /ɔːθɒrɪ'teərɪən/ a autoritär

authoritative /ɔː'θɒrɪtətɪv/ a maßgebend; **be** ~ Autorität haben

authority /ɔː'θɒrətɪ/ n Autorität f; (public) Behörde f; **in** ~ verantwortlich

authorization /ɔːθəraɪ'zeɪʃn/ n Ermächtigung f

authorize /'ɔːθəraɪz/ vt ermächtigen ⟨s.o.⟩; genehmigen ⟨sth⟩

autobi'ography /ɔːtə-/ n Autobiographie f

autocratic /ɔːtə'krætɪk/ a autokratisch

autograph /'ɔːtə-/ n Autogramm nt

automatic /ɔːtə'mætɪk/ a, **-ally** adv automatisch ● n (car) Fahrzeug nt mit Automatikgetriebe; (washing machine) Waschautomat m

automation /ɔːtə'meɪʃn/ n Automation f

automobile /'ɔːtəməbiːl/ n Auto nt

autonom|ous /ɔː'tɒnəməs/ a autonom. ~**y** n Autonomie f

autopsy /'ɔːtɒpsɪ/ n Autopsie f

autumn /'ɔːtəm/ n Herbst m. ~**al** /-'tʌmnl/ a herbstlich

auxiliary /ɔːg'zɪlɪərɪ/ a Hilfs- ● n Helfer(in) m(f), Hilfskraft f

avail /ə'veɪl/ n **to no** ~ vergeblich ● vi ~ **oneself of** Gebrauch machen von

available /ə'veɪləbl/ a verfügbar; (obtainable) erhältlich

avalanche /'ævəlɑːnʃ/ n Lawine f

avaric|e /'ævərɪs/ n Habsucht f. ~**ious** /-'rɪʃəs/ a habgierig, habsüchtig

avenge /ə'vendʒ/ vt rächen

avenue /'ævənjuː/ n Allee f

average /'ævərɪdʒ/ a Durchschnitts-, durchschnittlich ● n Durchschnitt m; **on** ~ im Durchschnitt, durchschnittlich ● vt durchschnittlich schaffen ● vi ~ **out at** im Durchschnitt ergeben

avers|e /ə'vɜːs/ a **not be** ~**e to** sth etw (dat) nicht abgeneigt sein. ~**ion** /-ɜːʃn/ n Abneigung f (**to** gegen)

avert /ə'vɜːt/ vt abwenden

aviary /'eɪvɪərɪ/ n Vogelhaus nt

aviation /eɪvɪ'eɪʃn/ n Luftfahrt f

avid /'ævɪd/ a gierig (**for** nach); (keen) eifrig

avocado /ævə'kɑːdəu/ n Avocado f

avoid /ə'vɔɪd/ vt vermeiden; ~ **s.o.** jdm aus dem Weg gehen. ~**able** /-əbl/ a vermeidbar. ~**ance** n Vermeidung f

await /ə'weɪt/ vt warten auf (+ acc)

awake /ə'weɪk/ a wach; **wide** ~ hellwach ● vi (pt awoke, pp awoken) erwachen

awaken /ə'weɪkn/ vt wecken ● vi erwachen. ~**ing** n Erwachen nt

award /ə'wɔːd/ n Auszeichnung f; (prize) Preis m ● vt zuerkennen (**to** s.o. dat); verleihen ⟨prize⟩

aware /ə'weə(r)/ a **become** ~ gewahr werden (**of** gen); **be** ~ **that** wissen, daß. ~**ness** n Bewußtsein nt

awash /ə'wɒʃ/ a **be** ~ unter Wasser stehen

away /ə'weɪ/ adv weg, fort; (absent) abwesend; **be** ~ nicht da sein; **far** ~ weit weg; **four kilometres** ~ vier Kilometer entfernt; **play** ~ (Sport) auswärts spielen; **go/stay** ~ weggehen/-bleiben. ~ **game** n Auswärtsspiel nt

awe /ɔː/ n Ehrfurcht f

awful /'ɔːfl/ a, **-ly** adv furchtbar

awhile /ə'waɪl/ adv eine Weile

awkward /'ɔːkwəd/ a schwierig; (clumsy) ungeschickt; (embarrassing) peinlich; (inconvenient) ungünstig. ~**ly** adv ungeschickt; (embarrassedly) verlegen

awning /'ɔːnɪŋ/ n Markise f

awoke(n) /əˈwəʊk(ən)/ *see* **awake**

awry /əˈraɪ/ *adv* schief

axe /æks/ *n* Axt *f* ● *vt* (*pres p* **axing**) streichen; (*dismiss*) entlassen

axis /ˈæksɪs/ *n* (*pl* **axes** /-siːz/) Achse *f*

axle /ˈæksl/ *n* (*Techn*) Achse *f*

ay[e] /aɪ/ *adv* ja ● *n* Jastimme *f*

B

B /biː/ *n* (*Mus*) H *nt*

BA *abbr of* **Bachelor of Arts**

babble /ˈbæbl/ *vi* plappern; ⟨*stream:*⟩ plätschern

baboon /bəˈbuːn/ *n* Pavian *m*

baby /ˈbeɪbɪ/ *n* Baby *nt*; (*Amer, fam*) Schätzchen *nt*

baby: ∼ **carriage** *n* (*Amer*) Kinderwagen *m*. ∼**ish** *a* kindisch. ∼**-minder** *n* Tagesmutter *f*. ∼**-sit** *vi* babysitten. ∼**-sitter** *n* Babysitter *m*

bachelor /ˈbætʃələ(r)/ *n* Junggeselle *m*; **B∼ of Arts/Science** Bakkalaureus Artium/Scientium

bacillus /bəˈsɪləs/ *n* (*pl* **-lli**) Bazillus *m*

back /bæk/ *n* Rücken *m*; (*reverse*) Rückseite *f*; (*of chair*) Rückenlehne *f*; (*Sport*) Verteidiger *m*; **at/**(*Auto*) **in the** ∼ hinten; **on the** ∼ auf der Rückseite; ∼ **to front** verkehrt; **at the** ∼ **of beyond** am Ende der Welt ● *a* Hinter- ● *adv* zurück; ∼ **here/there** hier/da hinten; ∼ **at home** zu Hause; **go/pay** ∼ zurückgehen/-zahlen ● *vt* (*support*) unterstützen; (*with money*) finanzieren; (*Auto*) zurücksetzen; (*Betting*) [Geld] setzen auf (+ *acc*); (*cover the back of*) mit einer Verstärkung versehen ● *vi* (*Auto*) zurücksetzen. ∼ **down** *vi* klein beigeben. ∼ **in** *vi* rückwärts hineinfahren. ∼ **out** *vi* rückwärts hinaus-/herausfahren; (*fig*) aussteigen (**of** aus). ∼ **up** *vt* unterstützen; (*confirm*) bestätigen ● *vi* (*Auto*) zurücksetzen

back: ∼**ache** *n* Rückenschmerzen *pl*. ∼**biting** *n* gehässiges Gerede *nt*. ∼**bone** *n* Rückgrat *nt*. ∼**chat** *n* Widerrede *f*. ∼**-comb** *vt* toupieren. ∼**date** *vt* rückdatieren; ∼**dated to** rückwirkend von. ∼ ˈ**door** *n* Hintertür *f*

backer /ˈbækə(r)/ *n* Geldgeber *m*

back: ∼ˈ**fire** *vi* (*Auto*) fehlzünden; (*fig*) fehlschlagen. ∼**ground** *n* Hintergrund *m*; **family** ∼**ground** Familienverhältnisse *pl*. ∼**hand** *n* (*Sport*) Rückhand *f*. ∼ˈ**handed** *a* ⟨*compliment*⟩ zweifelhaft. ∼ˈ**hander** *n* (*Sport*) Rückhandschlag *m*; (*fam: bribe*) Schmiergeld *nt*

backing /ˈbækɪŋ/ *n* (*support*) Unterstützung *f*; (*material*) Verstärkung *f*

back: ∼**lash** *n* (*fig*) Gegenschlag *m*. ∼**log** *n* Rückstand *m* (**of** an + *dat*). ∼ˈ**seat** *n* Rücksitz *m*. ∼**side** *n* (*fam*) Hintern *m*. ∼**stage** *adv* hinter der Bühne. ∼**stroke** *n* Rückenschwimmen *nt*. ∼**-up** *n* Unterstützung *f*; (*Amer: traffic jam*) Stau *m*

backward /ˈbækwəd/ *a* zurückgeblieben; ⟨*country*⟩ rückständig ● *adv* rückwärts. ∼**s** *adv* rückwärts; ∼**s and forwards** hin und her

back: ∼**water** *n* (*fig*) unberührtes Fleckchen *nt*. ∼ ˈ**yard** *n* Hinterhof *m*; **not in my** ∼ **yard** (*fam*) nicht vor meiner Haustür

bacon /ˈbeɪkn/ *n* [Schinken]speck *m*

bacteria /bækˈtɪərɪə/ *npl* Bakterien *pl*

bad /bæd/ *a* (**worse, worst**) schlecht; (*serious*) schwer, schlimm; (*naughty*) unartig; ∼ **language** gemeine Ausdrucksweise *f*; **feel** ∼ sich schlecht fühlen; (*feel guilty*) ein schlechtes Gewissen haben; **go** ∼ schlecht werden

bade /bæd/ *see* **bid**²

badge /bædʒ/ *n* Abzeichen *nt*

badger /ˈbædʒə(r)/ *n* Dachs *m* ● *vt* plagen

badly /ˈbædlɪ/ *adv* schlecht; (*seriously*) schwer; ∼ **off** schlecht gestellt; ∼ **behaved** unerzogen; **want** ∼ sich (*dat*) sehnsüchtig wünschen; **need** ∼ dringend brauchen

bad-ˈmannered *a* mit schlechten Manieren

badminton /ˈbædmɪntən/ *n* Federball *m*

bad-ˈtempered *a* schlecht gelaunt

baffle /ˈbæfl/ *vt* verblüffen

bag /bæg/ *n* Tasche *f*; (*of paper*) Tüte *f*; (*pouch*) Beutel *m*; ∼**s of** (*fam*) jede Menge ● *vt* (*fam: reserve*) in Beschlag nehmen

baggage /ˈbægɪdʒ/ *n* [Reise]gepäck *nt*

baggy /ˈbægɪ/ *a* ⟨*clothes*⟩ ausgebeult

ˈbagpipes *npl* Dudelsack *m*

bail /beɪl/ *n* Kaution *f*; **on** ~ gegen Kaution ● *vt* ~ **s.o. out** jdn gegen Kaution freibekommen; (*fig*) jdm aus der Patsche helfen. ~ **out** *vt* (*Naut*) ausschöpfen ● *vi* (*Aviat*) abspringen

bailiff /'beɪlɪf/ *n* Gerichtsvollzieher *m*; (*of estate*) Gutsverwalter *m*

bait /beɪt/ *n* Köder *m* ● *vt* mit einem Köder versehen; (*fig: torment*) reizen

bake /beɪk/ *vt/i* backen

baker /'beɪkə(r)/ *n* Bäcker *m*; ~**'s [shop]** Bäckerei *f*. ~**y** *n* Bäckerei *f*

baking /'beɪkɪŋ/ *n* Backen *nt*. ~**-powder** *n* Backpulver *nt*. ~**-tin** *n* Backform *f*

balance /'bæləns/ *n* (*equilibrium*) Gleichgewicht *nt*, Balance *f*; (*scales*) Waage *f*; (*Comm*) Saldo *m*; (*outstanding sum*) Restbetrag *m*; **[bank]** ~ Kontostand *m*; **in the** ~ (*fig*) in der Schwebe ● *vt* balancieren; (*equalize*) ausgleichen; (*Comm*) abschließen ⟨*books*⟩ ● *vi* balancieren; (*fig & Comm*) sich ausgleichen. ~**d** *a* ausgewogen. ~ **sheet** *n* Bilanz *f*

balcony /'bælkənɪ/ *n* Balkon *m*

bald /bɔːld/ *a* (**-er, -est**) kahl; ⟨*person*⟩ kahlköpfig; **go** ~ eine Glatze bekommen

balderdash /'bɔːldədæʃ/ *n* Unsinn *m*

bald|ing /'bɔːldɪŋ/ *a* **be** ~**ing** eine Glatze bekommen. ~**ly** *adv* unverblümt. ~**ness** *n* Kahlköpfigkeit *f*

bale /beɪl/ *n* Ballen *m*

baleful /'beɪlfl/ *a*, ~**ly** *adv* böse

balk /bɔːlk/ *vt* vereiteln ● *vi* ~ **at** zurückschrecken vor (+ *dat*)

Balkans /'bɔːlknz/ *npl* Balkan *m*

ball¹ /bɔːl/ *n* Ball *m*; (*Billiards, Croquet*) Kugel *f*; (*of yarn*) Knäuel *m* & *nt*; **on the** ~ (*fam*) auf Draht

ball² *n* (*dance*) Ball *m*

ballad /'bæləd/ *n* Ballade *f*

ballast /'bæləst/ *n* Ballast *m*

ball-'bearing *n* Kugellager *nt*

ballerina /bælə'riːnə/ *n* Ballerina *f*

ballet /'bæleɪ/ *m* Ballett *nt*. ~ **dancer** *n* Ballettänzer(in) *m*(*f*)

ballistic /bə'lɪstɪk/ *a* ballistisch. ~**s** *n* Ballistik *f*

balloon /bə'luːn/ *n* Luftballon *m*; (*Aviat*) Ballon *m*

ballot /'bælət/ *n* [geheime] Wahl *f*; (*on issue*) [geheime] Abstimmung *f*. ~**-box** *n* Wahlurne *f*. ~**-paper** *n* Stimmzettel *m*

ball: ~**-point** **['pen]** *n* Kugelschreiber *m*. ~**room** *n* Ballsaal *m*

balm /bɑːm/ *n* Balsam *m*

balmy /'bɑːmɪ/ *a* (**-ier, -iest**) *a* sanft; (*fam: crazy*) verrückt

Baltic /'bɔːltɪk/ *a & n* **the** ~ **[Sea]** die Ostsee

balustrade /bælə'streɪd/ *n* Balustrade *f*

bamboo /bæm'buː/ *n* Bambus *m*

bamboozle /bæm'buːzl/ *vt* (*fam*) übers Ohr hauen

ban /bæn/ *n* Verbot *nt* ● *vt* (*pt/pp* **banned**) verbieten

banal /bə'nɑːl/ *a* banal. ~**ity** /-'ælətɪ/ *n* Banalität *f*

banana /bə'nɑːnə/ *n* Banane *f*

band /bænd/ *n* Band *nt*; (*stripe*) Streifen *m*; (*group*) Schar *f*; (*Mus*) Kapelle *f* ● *vi* ~ **together** sich zusammenschließen

bandage /'bændɪdʒ/ *n* Verband *m*; (*for support*) Bandage *f* ● *vt* verbinden; bandagieren ⟨*limb*⟩

b. & b. *abbr of* **bed and breakfast**

bandit /'bændɪt/ *n* Bandit *m*

band: ~**stand** *n* Musikpavillon *m*. ~**wagon** *n* **jump on the** ~**wagon** (*fig*) sich einer erfolgreichen Sache anschließen

bandy¹ /'bændɪ/ *vt* (*pt/pp* **-ied**) wechseln ⟨*words*⟩

bandy² *a* (**-ier, -iest**) **be** ~ O-Beine haben. ~**-legged** *a* O-beinig

bang /bæŋ/ *n* (*noise*) Knall *m*; (*blow*) Schlag *m* ● *adv* **go** ~ knallen ● *int* bums! peng! ● *vt* knallen; (*shut noisily*) zuknallen; (*strike*) schlagen auf (+ *acc*); ~ **one's head** sich (*dat*) den Kopf stoßen (**on** an + *acc*) ● *vi* schlagen; ⟨*door:*⟩ zuknallen

banger /'bæŋə(r)/ *n* (*firework*) Knallfrosch *m*; (*fam: sausage*) Wurst *f*; **old** ~ (*fam: car*) Klapperkiste *f*

bangle /'bæŋgl/ *n* Armreifen *m*

banish /'bænɪʃ/ *vt* verbannen

banisters /'bænɪstəz/ *npl* [Treppen]geländer *nt*

banjo /'bændʒəʊ/ *n* Banjo *nt*

bank¹ /bæŋk/ *n* (*of river*) Ufer *nt*; (*slope*) Hang *m* ● *vi* (*Aviat*) in die Kurve gehen

bank² *n* Bank *f* ● *vt* einzahlen; ~ **with** ein Konto haben bei. ~ **on** *vt* sich verlassen auf (+ *acc*)

'bank account *n* Bankkonto *nt*

banker /'bæŋkə(r)/ *n* Bankier *m*

bank: ~ 'holiday n gesetzlicher Feiertag m. ~ing n Bankwesen nt. ~note n Banknote f

bankrupt /'bæŋkrʌpt/ a bankrott; **go** ~ **bankrott machen** ● n Bankrotteur m ● vt bankrott machen. ~cy n Bankrott m

banner /'bænə(r)/ n Banner nt; (carried by demonstrators) Transparent nt, Spruchband nt

banns /bænz/ npl (Relig) Aufgebot nt

banquet /'bæŋkwɪt/ n Bankett nt

banter /'bæntə(r)/ n Spötteleif

bap /bæp/ n weiches Brötchen nt

baptism /'bæptɪzm/ n Taufe f

Baptist /'bæptɪst/ n Baptist(in) m(f)

baptize /bæp'taɪz/ vt taufen

bar /bɑː(r)/ n Stange f; (of cage) [Gitter]stab m; (of gold) Barren m; (of chocolate) Tafel f; (of soap) Stück nt; (long) Riegel m; (café) Bar f; (counter) Theke f; (Mus) Takt m; (fig: obstacle) Hindernis nt; **parallel** ~s (Sport) Barren m; **be called to the** ~ (Jur) als plädierender Anwalt zugelassen werden; **behind** ~s (fam) hinter Gittern ● vt (pt/pp **barred**) versperren ⟨way, door⟩; ausschließen ⟨person⟩ ● prep außer; ~ **none** ohne Ausnahme

barbarian /bɑː'beərɪən/ n Barbar m

barbar|ic /bɑː'bærɪk/ a barbarisch. ~ity n Barbarei f. ~ous /'bɑːbərəs/ a barbarisch

barbecue /'bɑːbɪkjuː/ n Grill m; (party) Grillfest nt ● vt [im Freien] grillen

barbed /'bɑːbd/ a ~ **wire** Stacheldraht m

barber /'bɑːbə(r)/ n [Herren]friseur m

barbiturate /bɑː'bɪtjʊrət/ n Barbiturat nt

'bar code n Strichkode m

bare /beə(r)/ a (-r, -st) nackt, bloß; ⟨tree⟩ kahl; (empty) leer; (mere) bloß ● vt entblößen; fletschen ⟨teeth⟩

bare: ~**back** adv ohne Sattel. ~**faced** a schamlos. ~**foot** adv barfuß. ~**headed** a mit unbedecktem Kopf

barely /'beəlɪ/ adv kaum

bargain /'bɑːgɪn/ n (agreement) Geschäft nt; (good buy) Gelegenheitskauf m; **into the** ~ noch dazu; **make a** ~ sich einigen ● vi handeln; (haggle) feilschen; ~ **for** (expect) rechnen mit

barge /bɑːdʒ/ n Lastkahn m; (towed) Schleppkahn m ● vi ~ **in** (fam) hereinplatzen

baritone /'bærɪtəʊn/ n Bariton m

bark¹ /bɑːk/ n (of tree) Rinde f

bark² n Bellen nt ● vi bellen

barley /'bɑːlɪ/ n Gerste f

bar: ~**maid** n Schankmädchen nt. ~**man** Barmann m

barmy /'bɑːmɪ/ a (fam) verrückt

barn /bɑːn/ n Scheune f

barometer /bə'rɒmɪtə(r)/ n Barometer nt

baron /'bærn/ n Baron m. ~**ess** n Baronin f

baroque /bə'rɒk/ a barock ● n Barock nt/m

barracks /'bærəks/ npl Kaserne f

barrage /'bærɑːʒ/ n (in river) Wehr nt; (Mil) Sperrfeuer nt; (fig) Hagel m

barrel /'bærl/ n Faß nt; (of gun) Lauf m; (of cannon) Rohr nt. ~-**organ** n Drehorgel f

barren /'bærn/ a unfruchtbar; ⟨landscape⟩ öde

barricade /bærɪ'keɪd/ n Barrikade f ● vt verbarrikadieren

barrier /'bærɪə(r)/ n Barriere f; (across road) Schranke f; (Rail) Sperre f; (fig) Hindernis nt

barring /'bɑːrɪŋ/ prep ~ **accidents** wenn alles gutgeht

barrister /'bærɪstə(r)/ n [plädierender] Rechtsanwalt m

barrow /'bærəʊ/ n Karre f, Karren m. ~ **boy** n Straßenhändler m

barter /'bɑːtə(r)/ vt tauschen (for gegen)

base /beɪs/ n Fuß m; (fig) Basis f; (Mil) Stützpunkt m ● a gemein; ⟨metal⟩ unedel ● vt stützen (on auf + acc); **be** ~**d on** basieren auf (+ dat)

base: ~**ball** n Baseball m. ~**less** a unbegründet. ~**ment** n Kellergeschoß nt. ~**ment flat** n Kellerwohnung f

bash /bæʃ/ n Schlag m; **have a** ~! (fam) probier es mal! ● vt hauen; (dent) einbeulen; ~**ed** in verbeult

bashful /'bæʃfl/ a, -ly adv schüchtern

basic /'beɪsɪk/ a Grund-; (fundamental) grundlegend; (essential) wesentlich; (unadorned) einfach; **the** ~s das Wesentliche. ~**ally** adv grundsätzlich

basil /'bæzɪl/ n Basilikum nt

basilica /bə'zɪlɪkə/ n Basilika f

basin /'beɪsn/ n Becken nt; (for washing) Waschbecken nt; (for food) Schüssel f

basis /'beɪsɪs/ n (pl -ses /-siːz/) Basis f

bask /ba:sk/ *vi* sich sonnen

basket /'ba:skɪt/ *n* Korb *m*. **~ball** *n* Basketball *m*

Basle /ba:l/ *n* Basel *nt*

bass /beɪs/ *a* Baß-; **~ voice** Baßstimme *f* ● *n* Baß *m*; (*person*) Bassist *m*

bassoon /bə'su:n/ *n* Fagott *nt*

bastard /'ba:stəd/ *n* (*sl*) Schuft *m*

baste[1] /beɪst/ *vt* (*sew*) heften

baste[2] *vt* (*Culin*) begießen

bastion /'bæstɪən/ *n* Bastion *f*

bat[1] /bæt/ *n* Schläger *m*; **off one's own ~** (*fam*) auf eigene Faust ● *vt* (*pt/pp* **batted**) schlagen; **not ~ an eyelid** (*fig*) nicht mit der Wimper zucken

bat[2] *n* (*Zool*) Fledermaus *f*

batch /bætʃ/ *n* (*of people*) Gruppe *f*; (*of papers*) Stoß *m*; (*of goods*) Sendung *f*; (*of bread*) Schub *m*

bated /'beɪtɪd/ *a* **with ~ breath** mit angehaltenem Atem

bath /ba:θ/ *n* (*pl* **~s** /ba:ðz/) Bad *nt*; (*tub*) Badewanne *f*; **~s** *pl* Badeanstalt *f*; **have a ~** baden ● *vt/i* baden

bathe /beɪð/ *n* Bad *nt* ● *vt/i* baden. **~r** *n* Badende(r) *m/f*

bathing /'beɪðɪŋ/ *n* Baden *nt*. **~-cap** *n* Bademütze *f*. **~-costume** *n* Badeanzug *m*

bath: **~-mat** *n* Bademattef. **~robe** *n* (*Amer*) Bademantel *m*. **~-room** *n* Badezimmer *nt*. **~-towel** *n* Badetuch *nt*

baton /'bætn/ *n* (*Mus*) Taktstock *m*; (*Mil*) Stab *m*

battalion /bə'tælɪən/ *n* Bataillon *nt*

batten /'bætn/ *n* Latte *f*

batter /'bætə(r)/ *n* (*Culin*) flüssiger Teig *m* ● *vt* schlagen. **~ed** *a* (*car*) verbeult; (*wife*) mißhandelt

battery /'bætərɪ/ *n* Batterie *f*

battle /'bætl/ *n* Schlacht *f*; (*fig*) Kampf *m* ● *vi* (*fig*) kämpfen (**for** um)

battle: **~axe** *n* (*fam*) Drachen *m*. **~field** *n* Schlachtfeld *nt*. **~ship** *n* Schlachtschiff *nt*

batty /'bætɪ/ *a* (*fam*) verrückt

Bavaria /bə'veərɪə/ *n* Bayern *nt*. **~n** *a* bayrisch ● *n* Bayer(in) *m(f)*

bawdy /'bɔ:dɪ/ *a* (**-ier, -iest**) derb

bawl /bɔ:l/ *vt/i* brüllen

bay[1] /beɪ/ *n* (*Geog*) Bucht *f*; (*Archit*) Erker *m*

bay[2] *n* **keep at ~** fernhalten

bay[3] *n* (*horse*) Braune(r) *m*

bay[4] *n* (*Bot*) [echter] Lorbeer *m*. **~-leaf** *n* Lorbeerblatt *nt*

bayonet /'beɪənet/ *n* Bajonett *nt*

bay 'window *n* Erkerfenster *nt*

bazaar /bə'za:(r)/ *n* Basar *m*

BC *abbr* (**before Christ**) v. Chr.

be /bi:/ *vi* (*pres* **am, are, is,** *pl* **are;** *pt* **was,** *pl* **were;** *pp* **been**) sein; (*lie*) liegen; (*stand*) stehen; (*cost*) kosten; **he is a teacher** er ist Lehrer; **be quiet!** sei still! **I am cold/hot** mir ist kalt/heiß; **how are you?** wie geht es Ihnen? **I am well** mir geht es gut; **there is/are** es gibt; **what do you want to be?** was willst du werden? **I have been to Vienna** ich bin in Wien gewesen; **has the postman been?** war der Briefträger schon da? **it's hot, isn't it?** es ist heiß, nicht [wahr]? **you are coming too, aren't you?** du kommst mit, nicht [wahr]? **it's yours, is it?** das gehört also Ihnen? **yes he is/I am** ja; (*negating previous statement*) doch; **three and three are six** drei und drei macht sechs ● *v aux* **~ reading/going** lesen/gehen; **I am coming/staying** ich komme/ bleibe; **what is he doing?** was macht er? **I am being lazy** ich faulenze; **I was thinking of you** ich dachte an dich; **you were going to ...** du wolltest ...; **I am to stay** ich soll bleiben; **you are not to ...** du darfst nicht ...; **you are to do that immediately** das mußt du sofort machen ● *passive* werden; **be attacked/deceived** überfallen/betrogen werden

beach /bi:tʃ/ *n* Strand *m*. **~wear** *n* Strandkleidung *f*

beacon /'bi:kn/ *n* Leuchtfeuer *nt*; (*Naut, Aviat*) Bake *f*

bead /bi:d/ *n* Perle *f*

beak /bi:k/ *n* Schnabel *m*

beaker /'bi:kə(r)/ *n* Becher *m*

beam /bi:m/ *n* Balken *m*; (*of light*) Strahl *m* ● *vi* strahlen. **~ing** *a* [freude]strahlend

bean /bi:n/ *n* Bohne *f*; **spill the ~s** (*fam*) alles ausplaudern

bear[1] /beə(r)/ *n* Bär *m*

bear[2] *vt/i* (*pt* **bore,** *pp* **borne**) tragen; (*endure*) ertragen; gebären (*child*); **~ right** sich rechts halten. **~able** /-əbl/ *a* erträglich

beard /bɪəd/ *n* Bart *m*. **~ed** *a* bärtig

bearer /'beərə(r)/ *n* Träger *m*; (*of news, cheque*) Überbringer *m*; (*of passport*) Inhaber(in) *m(f)*

bearing /'beərɪŋ/ *n* Haltung *f*; (*Techn*) Lager *nt*; **have a ~ on** von Belang sein für; **get one's ~s** sich orientieren; **lose one's** ∼s die Orientierung verlieren

beast /biːst/ n Tier nt; (fam: person) Biest nt

beastly /'biːstlɪ/ a (-ier, -iest) (fam) scheußlich; ⟨person⟩ gemein

beat /biːt/ n Schlag m; (of policeman) Runde f; (rhythm) Takt m ● vt/i (pt beat, pp beaten) schlagen; (thrash) verprügeln; klopfen ⟨carpet⟩; (hammer) hämmern (on an + acc); ∼ a retreat (Mil) sich zurückziehen; ∼ it! (fam) hau ab! it ∼s me (fam) das begreife ich nicht. ∼ up vt zusammenschlagen

beat|en /biːtn/ a off the ∼en track abseits. ∼ing n Prügel pl

beautician /bjuː'tɪʃn/ n Kosmetikerin f

beauti|ful /'bjuːtɪfl/ a, -ly adv schön. ∼fy /-faɪ/ vt (pt/pp -ied) verschönern

beauty /'bjuːtɪ/ n Schönheit f. ∼ parlour n Kosmetiksalon m. ∼ spot n Schönheitsfleck m; (place) landschaftlich besonders reizvolle Stelle f

beaver /'biːvə(r)/ n Biber m

became /bɪ'keɪm/ see become

because /bɪ'kɒz/ conj weil ● adv ∼ of wegen (+ gen)

beckon /'bekn/ vt/i ∼ [to] herbeiwinken

becom|e /bɪ'kʌm/ vt/i (pt became, pp become) werden. ∼ing a ⟨clothes⟩ kleidsam

bed /bed/ n Bett nt; (layer) Schicht f; (of flowers) Beet nt; in ∼ im Bett; go to ∼ ins od zu Bett gehen; ∼ and breakfast Zimmer mit Frühstück. ∼clothes npl. ∼ding n Bettzeug nt

bedlam /'bedləm/ n Chaos nt

'bedpan n Bettpfanne f

bedraggled /bɪ'drægld/ a naß und verschmutzt

bed: ∼ridden a bettlägerig. ∼room n Schlafzimmer nt

'bedside n at his ∼ an seinem Bett. ∼ 'lamp n Nachttischlampe f. ∼ 'rug n Bettvorleger m. ∼ 'table n Nachttisch m

bed: ∼'sitter n, ∼'sitting-room n Wohnschlafzimmer nt. ∼spread n Tagesdecke f. ∼time n at ∼time vor dem Schlafengehen

bee /biː/ n Biene f

beech /biːtʃ/ n Buche f

beef /biːf/ n Rindfleisch nt. ∼burger n Hamburger m

bee: ∼hive n Bienenstock m. ∼-keeper n Imker(in) m(f). ∼-keeping n Bienenzucht f. ∼-line n make a ∼-line for (fam) zusteuern auf (+ acc)

been /biːn/ see be

beer /bɪə(r)/ n Bier nt

beet /biːt/ n (Amer: beetroot) rote Bete f; [sugar] ∼ Zuckerrübe f

beetle /'biːtl/ n Käfer m

'beetroot n rote Bete f

before /bɪ'fɔː(r)/ prep vor (+ dat/acc); the day ∼ yesterday vorgestern; ∼ long bald ● adv vorher; (already) schon; never ∼ noch nie; ∼ that davor ● conj (time) ehe, bevor. ∼hand adv vorher, im voraus

befriend /bɪ'frend/ vt sich anfreunden mit

beg /beg/ v (pt/pp begged) ● vi betteln ● vt (entreat) anflehen; (ask) bitten (for um)

began /bɪ'gæn/ see begin

beggar /'begə(r)/ n Bettler(in) m(f); (fam) Kerl m

begin /bɪ'gɪn/ vt/i (pt began, pp begun, pres p beginning) anfangen, beginnen; to ∼ with anfangs. ∼ner n Anfänger(in) m(f). ∼ning n Anfang m, Beginn m

begonia /bɪ'gəʊnɪə/ n Begonie f

begrudge /bɪ'grʌdʒ/ vt mißgönnen

beguile /bɪ'gaɪl/ vt betören

begun /bɪ'gʌn/ see begin

behalf /bɪ'hɑːf/ n on ∼ of im Namen von; on my ∼ meinetwegen

behave /bɪ'heɪv/ vi sich verhalten; ∼ oneself sich benehmen

behaviour /bɪ'heɪvjə(r)/ n Verhalten nt; good/bad ∼ gutes/schlechtes Benehmen nt; ∼ pattern Verhaltensweise f

behead /bɪ'hed/ vt enthaupten

beheld /bɪ'held/ see behold

behind /bɪ'haɪnd/ prep hinter (+ dat/acc); be ∼ sth hinter etw (dat) stecken ● adv hinten; (late) im Rückstand; a long way ∼ weit zurück; in the car ∼ im Wagen dahinter ● n (fam) Hintern m. ∼hand adv im Rückstand

behold /bɪ'həʊld/ vt (pt/pp beheld) (liter) sehen

beholden /bɪ'həʊldn/ a verbunden (to dat)

beige /beɪʒ/ a beige

being /'biːɪŋ/ n Dasein nt; living ∼ Lebewesen nt; come into ∼ entstehen

belated /bɪ'leɪtɪd/ a, -ly adv verspätet

belch /beltʃ/ vi rülpsen ● vt ~ out ausstoßen ⟨smoke⟩

belfry /'belfrɪ/ n Glockenstube f; ⟨tower⟩ Glockenturm m

Belgian /'beldʒən/ a belgisch ● n Belgier(in) m(f)

Belgium /'beldʒəm/ n Belgien nt

belief /bɪ'li:f/ n Glaube m

believable /bɪ'li:vəbl/ a glaubhaft

believe /bɪ'li:v/ vt/i glauben (s.o. jdm; in an + acc). ~r n ⟨Relig⟩ Gläubige(r) m/f

belittle /bɪ'lɪtl/ vt herabsetzen

bell /bel/ n Glocke f; ⟨on door⟩ Klingel f

belligerent /bɪ'lɪdʒərənt/ a kriegführend; ⟨aggressive⟩ streitlustig

bellow /'beləʊ/ vt/i brüllen

bellows /'beləʊz/ npl Blasebalg m

belly /'belɪ/ n Bauch m

belong /bɪ'lɒŋ/ vi gehören (to dat); ⟨be member⟩ angehören (to dat). ~ings npl Sachen pl

beloved /bɪ'lʌvɪd/ a geliebt ● n Geliebte(r) m/f

below /bɪ'ləʊ/ prep unter (+ dat/acc) ● adv unten; ⟨Naut⟩ unter Deck

belt /belt/ n Gürtel m; ⟨area⟩ Zone f; ⟨Techn⟩ [Treib]riemen m ● vi ⟨fam: rush⟩ rasen ● vt ⟨fam: hit⟩ hauen

bemused /bɪ'mju:zd/ a verwirrt

bench /bentʃ/ n Bank f; ⟨work-⟩ Werkbank f; **the B~** ⟨Jur⟩ ≈ die Richter pl

bend /bend/ n Biegung f; ⟨in road⟩ Kurve f; **round the ~** ⟨fam⟩ verrückt ● v ⟨pt/pp bent⟩ ● vt biegen; beugen ⟨arm, leg⟩ ● vi sich bücken; ⟨thing:⟩ sich biegen; ⟨road:⟩ eine Biegung machen. ~ **down** vi sich bücken. ~ **over** vi sich vornüberbeugen

beneath /bɪ'ni:θ/ prep unter (+ dat/ acc); ~ **him** ⟨fig⟩ unter seiner Würde; ~ **contempt** unter aller Würde ● adv darunter

benediction /benɪ'dɪkʃn/ n ⟨Relig⟩ Segen m

benefactor /'benɪfæktə(r)/ n Wohltäter(in) m(f)

beneficial /benɪ'fɪʃl/ a nützlich

beneficiary /benɪ'fɪʃərɪ/ n Begünstigte(r) m/f

benefit /'benɪfɪt/ n Vorteil m; ⟨allowance⟩ Unterstützung f; ⟨insurance⟩ Leistung f; **sickness ~** Krankengeld nt ● v ⟨pt/pp -fited, pres p -fiting⟩ ● vt nützen (+ dat) ● vi profitieren (from von)

benevolen|ce /bɪ'nevələns/ n Wohlwollen nt. ~t a, -ly adv wohlwollend

benign /bɪ'naɪn/ a, -ly adv gütig; ⟨Med⟩ gutartig

bent /bent/ see bend ● a ⟨person⟩ gebeugt; ⟨distorted⟩ verbogen; ⟨fam: dishonest⟩ korrupt; **be ~ on doing sth** darauf erpicht sein, etw zu tun ● n Hang m, Neigung f (for zu); **artistic ~** künstlerische ~

be|queath /bɪ'kwi:ð/ vt vermachen (to dat). ~**quest** /-'kwest/ n Vermächtnis nt

bereave|d /bɪ'ri:vd/ n **the ~d** pl die Hinterbliebenen. ~**ment** n Trauerfall m; ⟨state⟩ Trauer f

bereft /bɪ'reft/ a ~ **of** beraubt (+ gen)

beret /'bereɪ/ n Baskenmütze f

Berne /bɜ:n/ n Bern nt

berry /'berɪ/ n Beere f

berserk /bə'sɜːk/ a **go ~** wild werden

berth /bɜːθ/ n ⟨on ship⟩ [Schlaf]koje f; ⟨ship's anchorage⟩ Liegeplatz m; **give a wide ~ to** ⟨fam⟩ einen großen Bogen machen um ● vi anlegen

beseech /bɪ'si:tʃ/ vt ⟨pt/pp beseeched or besought⟩ anflehen

beside /bɪ'saɪd/ prep neben (+ dat/ acc); ~ **oneself** außer sich ⟨dat⟩

besides /bɪ'saɪdz/ prep außer (+ dat) ● adv außerdem

besiege /bɪ'si:dʒ/ vt belagern

besought /bɪ'sɔːt/ see beseech

bespoke /bɪ'spəʊk/ a ⟨suit⟩ maßgeschneidert

best /best/ a & n beste(r,s); **the ~** der/die/das Beste; **at ~** bestenfalls; **all the ~!** alles Gute! **do one's ~** sein Bestes tun; **the ~ part of a year** fast ein Jahr; **to the ~ of my knowledge** soviel ich weiß; **make the ~ of it** das Beste daraus machen ● adv am besten; **as ~ I could** so gut ich konnte. ~ '**man** n ≈ Trauzeuge m

bestow /bɪ'stəʊ/ vt schenken (on dat)

best'seller n Bestseller m

bet /bet/ n Wette f ● v ⟨pt/pp bet or betted⟩ ● vt ~ **s.o. £5** mit jdm um £5 wetten ● vi wetten; ~ **on** [Geld] setzen auf (+ acc)

betray /bɪ'treɪ/ vt verraten. ~**al** n Verrat m

better /'betə(r)/ a besser; **get ~** sich bessern; ⟨after illness⟩ sich erholen ● adv besser; ~ **off** besser dran; ~ **not** lieber nicht; **all the ~** um so besser; **the sooner the ~** je eher, desto besser;

think ~ **of sth** sich eines Besseren besinnen; **you'd** ~ **stay** du bleibst am besten hier ● *vt* verbessern; (*do better than*) übertreffen; ~ **oneself** sich verbessern

'betting shop *n* Wettbüro *nt*

between /brˈtwiːn/ *prep* zwischen (+ *dat/acc*); ~ **you and me** unter uns; ~ **us** (*together*) zusammen ● *adv* **[in]** ~ dazwischen

beverage /ˈbevərɪdʒ/ *n* Getränk *nt*

bevy /ˈbevɪ/ *n* Schar *f*

beware /brˈweə(r)/ *vi* sich in acht nehmen (**of** vor + *dat*); ~ **of the dog!** Vorsicht, bissiger Hund!

bewilder /brˈwɪldə(r)/ *vt* verwirren. ~**ment** *n* Verwirrung *f*

bewitch /brˈwɪtʃ/ *vt* verzaubern; (*fig*) bezaubern

beyond /brˈjɒnd/ *prep* über (+ *acc*) ... hinaus; (*further*) weiter als; ~ **reach** außer Reichweite; ~ **doubt** ohne jeden Zweifel; **it's** ~ **me** (*fam*) das geht über meinen Horizont ● *adv* darüber hinaus

bias /ˈbaɪəs/ *n* Voreingenommenheit *f*; (*preference*) Vorliebe *f*; (*Jur*) Befangenheit *f*; **cut on the** ~ schräg geschnitten ● *vt* (*pt/pp* **biased**) (*influence*) beeinflussen. ~**ed** *a* voreingenommen; (*Jur*) befangen

bib /bɪb/ *n* Lätzchen *nt*

Bible /ˈbaɪbl/ *n* Bibel *f*

biblical /ˈbɪblɪkl/ *a* biblisch

bibliography /bɪblɪˈɒɡrəfɪ/ *n* Bibliographie *f*

bicarbonate /baɪˈkɑːbəneɪt/ *n* ~ **of soda** doppeltkohlensaures Natron *nt*

bicker /ˈbɪkə(r)/ *vi* sich zanken

bicycle /ˈbaɪsɪkl/ *n* Fahrrad *nt* ● *vi* mit dem Rad fahren

bid[1] /bɪd/ *n* Gebot *nt*; (*attempt*) Versuch *m* ● *vt/i* (*pt/pp* **bid**, *pres p* **bidding**) bieten (**for** auf + *acc*); (*Cards*) reizen

bid[2] *vt* (*pt* **bade** *or* **bid**, *pp* **bidden** *or* **bid**, *pres p* **bidding**) (*liter*) heißen; ~ **s.o. welcome** jdn willkommen heißen

bidder /ˈbɪdə(r)/ *n* Bieter(in) *m(f)*

bide /baɪd/ *vt* ~ **one's time** den richtigen Moment abwarten

biennial /baɪˈenɪəl/ *a* zweijährlich; (*lasting two years*) zweijährig

bier /bɪə(r)/ *n* [Toten]bahre *f*

bifocals /baɪˈfəʊklz/ *npl* [**pair of**] ~ Bifokalbrille *f*

big /bɪɡ/ *a* (**bigger, biggest**) groß ● *adv* **talk** ~ (*fam*) angeben

bigam|ist /ˈbɪɡəmɪst/ *n* Bigamist *m*. ~**y** *n* Bigamie *f*

big-'headed *a* (*fam*) eingebildet

bigot /ˈbɪɡət/ *n* Eiferer *m*. ~**ed** *a* engstirnig

'bigwig *n* (*fam*) hohes Tier *nt*

bike /baɪk/ *n* (*fam*) [Fahr]rad *nt*

bikini /brˈkiːnɪ/ *n* Bikini *m*

bilberry /ˈbɪlbərɪ/ *n* Heidelbeere *f*

bile /baɪl/ *n* Galle *f*

bilingual /baɪˈlɪŋɡwəl/ *a* zweisprachig

bilious /ˈbɪljəs/ *a* (*Med*) ~ **attack** verdorbener Magen *m*

bill[1] /bɪl/ *n* Rechnung *f*; (*poster*) Plakat *nt*; (*Pol*) Gesetzentwurf *m*; (*Amer: note*) Banknote *f*; ~ **of exchange** Wechsel *m* ● *vt* eine Rechnung schicken (+ *dat*)

bill[2] *n* (*beak*) Schnabel *m*

billet /ˈbɪlɪt/ *n* (*Mil*) Quartier *nt* ● *vt* (*pt/pp* **billeted**) einquartieren (**on** bei)

'billfold *n* (*Amer*) Brieftasche *f*

billiards /ˈbɪljədz/ *n* Billard *nt*

billion /ˈbɪljən/ *n* (*thousand million*) Milliarde *f*; (*million million*) Billion *f*

billy-goat /ˈbɪlɪ-/ *n* Ziegenbock *m*

bin /bɪn/ *n* Mülleimer *m*; (*for bread*) Kasten *m*

bind /baɪnd/ *vt* (*pt/pp* **bound**) binden (**to** an + *acc*); (*bandage*) verbinden; (*Jur*) verpflichten; (*cover the edge of*) einfassen. ~**ing** *a* verbindlich ● *n* Einband *m*; (*braid*) Borte *f*; (*on ski*) Bindung *f*

binge /bɪndʒ/ *n* (*fam*) **go on the** ~ eine Sauftour machen

binoculars /brˈnɒkjʊləz/ *npl* [**pair of**] ~ Fernglas *nt*

bio|'chemistry /baɪəʊ-/ *n* Biochemie *f*. ~**degradable** /-dɪ-ˈɡreɪdəbl/ *a* biologisch abbaubar

biograph|er /baɪˈɒɡrəfə(r)/ *n* Biograph(in) *m(f)*. ~**y** *n* Biographie *f*

biological /baɪəˈlɒdʒɪkl/ *a* biologisch

biolog|ist /baɪˈɒlədʒɪst/ *n* Biologe *m*. ~**y** *n* Biologie *f*

birch /bɜːtʃ/ *n* Birke *f*; (*whip*) Rute *f*

bird /bɜːd/ *n* Vogel *m*; (*fam: girl*) Mädchen *nt*; **kill two** ~**s with one stone** zwei Fliegen mit einer Klappe schlagen

Biro (P) /ˈbaɪrəʊ/ *n* Kugelschreiber *m*

birth /bɜːθ/ *n* Geburt *f*

birth-: ~ **certificate** *n* Geburtsurkunde *f*. ~**-control** *n* Geburtenregelung *f*. ~**day** *n* Geburtstag *m*.

~**mark** n Muttermal nt. ~**-rate** n Geburtenziffer f. ~**right** n Geburtsrecht nt

biscuit /'bɪskɪt/ n Keks m

bisect /baɪ'sekt/ vt halbieren

bishop /'bɪʃəp/ n Bischof m; (Chess) Läufer m

bit[1] /bɪt/ n Stückchen nt; (for horse) Gebiß nt; (Techn) Bohreinsatz m; **a** ~ ein bißchen; ~ **by** ~ nach und nach; **a** ~ **of bread** ein bißchen Brot; **do one's** ~ sein Teil tun

bit[2] see **bite**

bitch /bɪtʃ/ n Hündin f; (sl) Luder nt. ~**y** a gehässig

bit|e /baɪt/ n Biß m; [**insect**] ~ Stich m; (mouthful) Bissen m ● vt/i (pt **bit**, pp **bitten**) beißen; (insect:) stechen; kauen ⟨one's nails⟩. ~**ing** a beißend

bitter /'bɪtə(r)/ a, **-ly** adv bitter; **cry** ~**ly** bitterlich weinen; ~**ly cold** bitterkalt ● n bitteres Bier nt. ~**ness** n Bitterkeit f

bitty /'bɪtɪ/ a zusammengestoppelt

bizarre /bɪ'zɑː(r)/ a bizarr

blab /blæb/ vi (pt/pp **blabbed**) alles ausplaudern

black /blæk/ a (**-er, -est**) schwarz; **be** ~ **and blue** grün und blau sein ● n Schwarz nt; (person) Schwarze(r) m/f ● vt schwärzen; boykottieren ⟨goods⟩. ~ **out** vt verdunkeln ● vi (lose consciousness) das Bewußtsein verlieren

black: ~**berry** n Brombeere f. ~**bird** n Amsel f. ~**board** n (Sch) [Wand]tafel f. ~**currant** n schwarze Johannisbeere f

blacken vt/i schwärzen

black: ~ '**eye** n blaues Auge nt. **B**~ '**Forest** n Schwarzwald m. ~ '**ice** n Glatteis nt. ~**leg** n Streikbrecher m. ~**list** vt auf die schwarze Liste setzen. ~**mail** n Erpressung f ● vt erpressen. ~**mailer** n Erpresser(in) m(f). ~ '**market** n schwarzer Markt m. ~**out** n Verdunkelung f; **have a** ~**out** (Med) das Bewußtsein verlieren. ~ '**pudding** n Blutwurst f. ~**smith** n [Huf]schmied m

bladder /'blædə(r)/ n (Anat) Blase f

blade /bleɪd/ n Klinge f; (of grass) Halm m

blame /bleɪm/ n Schuld f ● vt die Schuld geben (+ dat); **no one is to** ~ keiner ist schuld daran. ~**less** a schuldlos

blanch /blɑːntʃ/ vi blaß werden ● vt (Culin) blanchieren

blancmange /blə'mɒnʒ/ n Pudding m

bland /blænd/ a (**-er, -est**) mild

blank /blæŋk/ a leer; ⟨look⟩ ausdruckslos ● n Lücke f; (cartridge) Platzpatrone f. ~ '**cheque** n Blankoscheck m

blanket /'blæŋkɪt/ n Decke f; **wet** ~ (fam) Spielverderber(in) m(f)

blank 'verse n Blankvers m

blare /bleə(r)/ vt/i schmettern

blasé /'blɑːzeɪ/ a blasiert

blaspheme /blæs'fiːm/ vi lästern

blasphem|ous /'blæsfəməs/ a [gottes]lästerlich. ~**y** n [Gottes]lästerung f

blast /blɑːst/ n (gust) Luftstoß m; (sound) Stoß m ● vt sprengen ● int (sl) verdammt. ~**ed** a (sl) verdammt

blast: ~**-furnace** n Hochofen m. ~**-off** n (of missile) Start m

blatant /'bleɪtənt/ a offensichtlich

blaze /bleɪz/ n Feuer nt ● vi brennen

blazer /'bleɪzə(r)/ n Blazer m

bleach /bliːtʃ/ n Bleichmittel nt ● vt/i bleichen

bleak /bliːk/ a (**-er, -est**) öde; (fig) trostlos

bleary-eyed /'blɪərɪ-/ a mit trüben/ (on waking up) verschlafenen Augen

bleat /bliːt/ vi blöken; (goat:) meckern

bleed /bliːd/ v (pt/pp **bled**) ● vi bluten ● vt entlüften ⟨radiator⟩

bleep /bliːp/ n Piepton m ● vi piepsen ● vt mit dem Piepser rufen. ~**er** n Piepser m

blemish /'blemɪʃ/ n Makel m

blend /blend/ n Mischung f ● vt mischen ● vi sich vermischen. ~**er** n (Culin) Mixer m

bless /bles/ vt segnen. ~**ed** /'blesɪd/ a heilig; (sl) verflixt. ~**ing** n Segen m

blew /bluː/ see **blow**[2]

blight /blaɪt/ n (Bot) Brand m ● vt (spoil) vereiteln

blind /blaɪnd/ a blind; ⟨corner⟩ unübersichtlich; ~ **man/woman** Blinde(r) m/f ● n [**roller**] ~ Rouleau nt ● vt blenden

blind: ~ '**alley** n Sackgasse f. ~**fold** a & adv mit verbundenen Augen ● n Augenbinde f ● vt die Augen verbinden (+ dat). ~**ly** adv blindlings. ~**ness** n Blindheit f

blink /blɪŋk/ *vi* blinzeln; ⟨*light:*⟩ blinken

blinkers /'blɪŋkəz/ *npl* Scheuklappen *pl*

bliss /blɪs/ *n* Glückseligkeit *f*. **~ful** *a* glücklich

blister /'blɪstə(r)/ *n* (*Med*) Blase *f* ● *vi* ⟨*paint:*⟩ Blasen werfen

blitz /blɪts/ *n* Luftangriff *m*; (*fam*) Großaktion *f*

blizzard /'blɪzəd/ *n* Schneesturm *m*

bloated /'bləʊtɪd/ *a* aufgedunsen

blob /blɒb/ *n* Klecks *m*

bloc /blɒk/ *n* (*Pol*) Block *m*

block /blɒk/ *n* Block *m*; (*of wood*) Klotz *m*; (*of flats*) [Wohn]block *m* ● *vt* blockieren. **~ up** *vt* zustopfen

blockade /blɒ'keɪd/ *n* Blockade *f* ● *vt* blockieren

blockage /'blɒkɪdʒ/ *n* Verstopfung *f*

block: ~head *n* (*fam*) Dummkopf *m*. **~ 'letters** *npl* Blockschrift *f*

bloke /bləʊk/ *n* (*fam*) Kerl *m*

blonde /blɒnd/ *a* blond ● *n* Blondine *f*

blood /blʌd/ *n* Blut *nt*

blood: ~ count *n* Blutbild *nt*. **~-curdling** *a* markerschütternd. **~ donor** *n* Blutspender *m*. **~ group** *n* Blutgruppe *f*. **~hound** *n* Bluthund *m*. **~-poisoning** *n* Blutvergiftung *f*. **~ pressure** *n* Blutdruck *m*. **~ relative** *n* Blutsverwandte(r) *m/f*. **~shed** *n* Blutvergießen *nt*. **~shot** *a* blutunterlaufen. **~ sports** *npl* Jagdsport *m*. **~-stained** *a* blutbefleckt. **~stream** *n* Blutbahn *f*. **~ test** *n* Blutprobe *f*. **~thirsty** *a* blutdürstig. **~ transfusion** *n* Blutübertragung *f*. **~-vessel** *n* Blutgefäß *nt*

bloody /'blʌdɪ/ *a* (**-ier, -iest**) blutig; (*sl*) verdammt. **~-'minded** *a* (*sl*) stur

bloom /bluːm/ *n* Blüte *f* ● *vi* blühen

bloom|er /'bluːmə(r)/ *n* (*fam*) Schnitzer *m*. **~ing** *a* (*fam*) verdammt

blossom /'blɒsəm/ *n* Blüte *f* ● *vi* blühen. **~ out** *vi* (*fig*) aufblühen

blot /blɒt/ *n* [Tinten]klecks *m*; (*fig*) Fleck *m* ● *vt* (*pt/pp* **blotted**) löschen. **~ out** *vt* (*fig*) auslöschen

blotch /blɒtʃ/ *n* Fleck *m*. **~y** *a* fleckig

'blotting-paper *n* Löschpapier *nt*

blouse /blaʊz/ *n* Bluse *f*

blow[1] /bləʊ/ *n* Schlag *m*

blow[2] *v* (*pt* **blew**, *pp* **blown**) ● *vt* blasen; (*fam: squander*) verpulvern; **~ one's nose** sich (*dat*) die Nase putzen ● *vi* blasen; ⟨*fuse:*⟩ durchbrennen. **~ away** *vt* wegblasen ● *vi* wegfliegen. **~ down** *vt* umwehen ● *vi* umfallen. **~ out** *vt* (*extinguish*) ausblasen. **~ over** *vi* umfallen; (*fig: die down*) vorübergehen. **~ up** *vt* (*inflate*) aufblasen; (*enlarge*) vergrößern; (*shatter by explosion*) sprengen ● *vi* explodieren

blow: ~-dry *vt* fönen. **~fly** *n* Schmeißfliege *f*. **~lamp** *n* Lötlampe *f*

blown /bləʊn/ *see* **blow**[2]

'blowtorch *n* (*Amer*) Lötlampe *f*

blowy /'bləʊɪ/ *a* windig

bludgeon /'blʌdʒn/ *vt* (*fig*) zwingen

blue /bluː/ *a* (**-r, -st**) blau; **feel ~** deprimiert sein ● *n* Blau *nt*; **have the ~s** deprimiert sein; **out of the ~** aus heiterem Himmel

blue: ~bell *n* Sternhyazinthe *f*. **~berry** *n* Heidelbeere *f*. **~bottle** *n* Schmeißfliege *f*. **~ film** *n* Pornofilm *m*. **~print** *n* (*fig*) Entwurf *m*

bluff /blʌf/ *n* Bluff *m* ● *vi* bluffen

blunder /'blʌndə(r)/ *n* Schnitzer *m* ● *vi* einen Schnitzer machen

blunt /blʌnt/ *a* stumpf; ⟨*person*⟩ geradeheraus. **~ly** *adv* unverblümt, geradeheraus

blur /blɜː(r)/ *n* **it's all a ~** alles ist verschwommen ● *vt* (*pt/pp* **blurred**) verschwommen machen; **~red** verschwommen

blurb /blɜːb/ *n* Klappentext *m*

blurt /blɜːt/ *vt* **~ out** herausplatzen mit

blush /blʌʃ/ *n* Erröten *nt* ● *vi* erröten

bluster /'blʌstə(r)/ *n* Großtuerei *f*. **~y** *a* windig

boar /bɔː(r)/ *n* Eber *m*

board /bɔːd/ *n* Brett *nt*; (*for notices*) schwarzes Brett *nt*; (*committee*) Ausschuß *m*; (*of directors*) Vorstand *m*; **on ~** an Bord; **full ~** Vollpension *f*; **~ and lodging** Unterkunft und Verpflegung *pl*; **go by the ~** (*fam*) unter den Tisch fallen ● *vt* einsteigen in (+ *acc*); (*Naut, Aviat*) besteigen ● *vi* an Bord gehen; **~ with** in Pension wohnen bei. **~ up** *vt* mit Brettern verschlagen

boarder /'bɔːdə(r)/ *n* Pensionsgast *m*; (*Sch*) Internatsschüler(in) *m(f)*

board: ~-**game** n Brettspiel nt.
~**ing-house** n Pension f.
~**ing-school** n Internat nt

boast /bəʊst/ vt sich rühmen (+ gen)
● vi prahlen (**about** mit). ~**ful** a, -**ly**
adv prahlerisch

boat /bəʊt/ n Boot nt; (ship) Schiff m.
~**er** n (hat) flacher Strohhut m

bob /bɒb/ n Bubikopf m ● vi (pt/pp
bobbed) (curtsy) knicksen; ~ **up and
down** sich auf und ab bewegen

bobbin /'bɒbɪn/ n Spule f

'**bob-sleigh** n Bob m

bode /bəʊd/ vi ~ **well/ill** etwas/
nichts Gutes verheißen

bodice /'bɒdɪs/ n Mieder nt

bodily /'bɒdɪlɪ/ a körperlich ● adv
(forcibly) mit Gewalt

body /'bɒdɪ/ n Körper m; (corpse)
Leiche f; (corporation) Körperschaft
f; **the main** ~ der Hauptanteil.
~**guard** n Leibwächter m. ~**work** n
(Auto) Karosserie f

bog /bɒg/ n Sumpf m ● vt (pt/pp
bogged) **get** ~**ged down** steckenbleiben

boggle /'bɒgl/ vi **the mind** ~**s** es ist
kaum vorstellbar

bogus /'bəʊgəs/ a falsch

boil[1] /bɔɪl/ n Furunkel m

boil[2] n **bring/come to the** ~ zum Kochen bringen/kommen ● vt/i kochen;
~**ed potatoes** Salzkartoffeln pl. ~
down vi (fig) hinauslaufen (**to** auf
+ acc). ~ **over** vi überkochen. ~ **up**
vt aufkochen

boiler /'bɔɪlə(r)/ n Heizkessel m.
~**suit** n Overall m

'**boiling point** n Siedepunkt m

boisterous /'bɔɪstərəs/ a übermütig

bold /bəʊld/ a (-er, -est), -**ly** adv kühn;
(Typ) fett. ~**ness** n Kühnheit f

bollard /'bɒlɑːd/ n Poller m

bolster /'bəʊlstə(r)/ n Nackenrolle f
● vt ~ **up** Mut machen (+ dat)

bolt /bəʊlt/ n Riegel m; (Techn)
Bolzen m; **nuts and** ~**s** Schrauben und
Muttern pl ● vt schrauben (**to**
an + acc); verriegeln (door);
hinunterschlingen (food) ● vi abhauen;
(horse:) durchgehen ● adv ~ **upright**
adv kerzengerade

bomb /bɒm/ n Bombe f ● vt bombardieren

bombard /bɒm'bɑːd/ vt beschießen;
(fig) bombardieren

bombastic /bɒm'bæstɪk/ a bombastisch

bomb|er /'bɒmə(r)/ n (Aviat)
Bomber m; (person) Bomben-
leger(in) m(f). ~**shell** n **be a** ~**shell**
(fig) wie eine Bombe einschlagen

bond /bɒnd/ n (fig) Band nt; (Comm)
Obligation f; **be in** ~ unter Zollver-
schluß stehen

bondage /'bɒndɪdʒ/ n (fig) Sklave-
rei f

bone /bəʊn/ n Knochen m; (of fish)
Gräte f ● vt von den Knochen lösen
(meat); entgräten (fish). ~-'**dry** a
knochentrocken

bonfire /'bɒn-/ n Gartenfeuer nt;
(celebratory) Freudenfeuer nt

bonnet /'bɒnɪt/ n Haube f

bonus /'bəʊnəs/ n Prämie f;
(gratuity) Gratifikation f; (fig) Plus
nt

bony /'bəʊnɪ/ a (-ier, -iest) knochig;
(fish) grätig

boo /buː/ int buh! ● vt ausbuhen ● vi
buhen

boob /buːb/ n (fam: mistake)
Schnitzer m ● vi (fam) einen
Schnitzer machen

book /bʊk/ n Buch nt; (of tickets) Heft
nt; **keep the** ~**s** (Comm) die Bücher
führen ● vt/i buchen; (reserve) [vor]
bestellen; (for offence) aufschreiben.
~**able** /-əbl/ a im Vorverkauf erhältlich

book: ~**case** n Bücherregal nt.
~-**ends** npl Buchstützen pl. ~**ing-
office** n Fahrkartenschalter m.
~**keeping** n Buchführung f. ~**let** n
Broschüre f. ~**maker** n Buchmacher
m. ~**mark** n Lesezeichen nt. ~**seller**
n Buchhändler(in) m(f). ~**shop** n
Buchhandlung f. ~-**stall** n Bücher-
stand m. ~**worm** n Bücherwurm m

boom /buːm/ n (Comm) Hoch-
konjunktur f; (upturn) Aufschwung
m ● vi dröhnen; (fig) blühen

boon /buːn/ n Segen m

boor /bʊə(r)/ n Flegel m. ~**ish** a
flegelhaft

boost /buːst/ n Auftrieb m ● vt Auftrieb geben (+ dat). ~**er** n (Med)
Nachimpfung f

boot /buːt/ n Stiefel m; (Auto) Kofferraum m

booth /buːð/ n Bude f; (cubicle) Kabine f

booty /'buːtɪ/ n Beute f

booze /buːz/ n (fam) Alkohol m ● vi
(fam) saufen

border /'bɔːdə(r)/ n Rand m; (frontier) Grenze f; (in garden) Rabatte f • vi ~ on grenzen an (+acc). ~line n Grenzlinie f. ~line case n Grenzfall m

bore[1] /bɔː(r)/ see **bear**[2]

bore[2] /bɔːs/ n (fam) Chef m • vi bohren

bor|e[3] n (of gun) Kaliber nt; (person) langweiliger Mensch m; (thing) langweilige Sache f • vt langweilen; be ~ed sich langweilen. ~edom n Langeweile f. ~ing a langweilig

born /bɔːn/ pp be ~ geboren werden • a geboren

borne /bɔːn/ see **bear**[2]

borough /'bʌrə/ n Stadtgemeinde f

borrow /'bɒrəʊ/ vt [sich (dat)] borgen od leihen (**from** von)

bosom /'bʊzm/ n Busen m

boss /bɒs/ n (fam) Chef m • vt herumkommandieren. ~y a herrschsüchtig

botanical /bə'tænɪkl/ a botanisch

botan|ist /'bɒtənɪst/ n Botaniker(in) m(f). ~y n Botanik f

botch /bɒtʃ/ vt verpfuschen

both /bəʊθ/ a & pron beide; ~ [of] the children beide Kinder; ~ of them beide [von ihnen] • adv ~ men and women sowohl Männer als auch Frauen

bother /'bɒðə(r)/ n Mühe f; (minor trouble) Ärger m • int (fam) verflixt! • vt belästigen; (disturb) stören • vi sich kümmern (**about** um); **don't** ~ nicht nötig

bottle /'bɒtl/ n Flasche f • vt auf Flaschen abfüllen; (preserve) einmachen. ~ **up** vt (fig) in sich (dat) aufstauen

bottle: ~-**neck** n (fig) Engpaß m. ~-**opener** n Flaschenöffner m

bottom /'bɒtəm/ a unterste(r,s) • n (of container) Boden m; (of river) Grund m; (of page, hill) Fuß m; (buttocks) Hintern m; **at the** ~ unten; **get to the** ~ **of sth** (fig) hinter etw (acc) kommen. ~**less** a bodenlos

bough /baʊ/ n Ast m

bought /bɔːt/ see **buy**

boulder /'bəʊldə(r)/ n Felsblock m

bounce /baʊns/ vi [auf]springen; (cheque:) (fam) nicht gedeckt sein • vt aufspringen lassen (ball)

bouncer /'baʊnsə(r)/ n (fam) Rausschmeißer m

bouncing /'baʊnsɪŋ/ a ~ **baby** strammer Säugling m

bound[1] /baʊnd/ n Sprung m • vi springen

bound[2] see **bind** • a ~ **for** (ship) mit Kurs auf (+acc); **be** ~ **to do sth** etw bestimmt machen; (obliged) verpflichtet sein, etw zu machen

boundary /'baʊndərɪ/ n Grenze f

'boundless a grenzenlos

bounds /baʊndz/ npl (fig) Grenzen pl; **out of** ~ verboten

bouquet /bʊ'keɪ/ n [Blumen]strauß m; (of wine) Bukett nt

bourgeois /'bʊəʒwaː/ a (pej) spießbürgerlich

bout /baʊt/ n (Med) Anfall m; (Sport) Kampf m

bow[1] /bəʊ/ n (weapon & Mus) Bogen m; (knot) Schleife f

bow[2] /baʊ/ n Verbeugung f • vi sich verbeugen • vt neigen (head)

bow[3] /baʊ/ n (Naut) Bug m

bowel /'baʊəl/ n Darm m; ~ **movement** Stuhlgang m. ~**s** pl Eingeweide pl; (digestion) Verdauung f

bowl[1] /bəʊl/ n Schüssel f; (shallow) Schale f; (of pipe) Kopf m; (of spoon) Schöpfteil m

bowl[2] n (ball) Kugel f • vt/i werfen. ~ **over** vt umwerfen

bow-legged /bəʊ'legd/ a O-beinig

bowler[1] /'bəʊlə(r)/ n (Sport) Werfer m

bowler[2] n ~ [**hat**] Melone f

bowling /'bəʊlɪŋ/ n Kegeln nt. ~-**alley** n Kegelbahn f

bowls /bəʊlz/ n Bowlsspiel nt

bow-'tie /bəʊ-/ n Fliege f

box[1] /bɒks/ n Schachtel f; (wooden) Kiste f; (cardboard) Karton m; (Theat) Loge f

box[2] vt/i (Sport) boxen; ~ **s.o.'s ears** jdn ohrfeigen

box|er /'bɒksə(r)/ n Boxer m. ~**ing** n Boxen nt. **B**~**ing Day** n zweiter Weihnachtstag m

box: ~-**office** n (Theat) Kasse f. ~-**room** n Abstellraum m

boy /bɔɪ/ n Junge m

boycott /'bɔɪkɒt/ n Boykott m • vt boykottieren

boy: ~**friend** n Freund m. ~**ish** a jungenhaft

bra /braː/ n BH m

brace /breɪs/ n Strebe f, Stütze f; (dental) Zahnspange f; ~**s** npl Hosenträger mpl • vt ~ **oneself** sich stemmen (**against** gegen); (fig) sich gefaßt machen (**for** auf +acc)

bracelet /'breɪslɪt/ n Armband nt

bracing /'breɪsɪŋ/ a stärkend

bracken /'brækn/ n Farnkraut nt

bracket /'brækɪt/ n Konsole f; (group) Gruppe f; (Typ) **round/ square** ~s runde/eckige Klammern ● vt einklammern

brag /bræg/ vi (pt/pp **bragged**) prahlen (**about** mit)

braid /breɪd/ n Borte f

braille /breɪl/ n Blindenschrift f

brain /breɪn/ n Gehirn nt; ~s (fig) Intelligenz f

brain: ~**child** n geistiges Produkt nt. ~**less** a dumm. ~**wash** vt einer Gehirnwäsche unterziehen. ~**wave** n Geistesblitz m

brainy /'breɪnɪ/ a (-ier, -iest) klug

braise /breɪz/ vt schmoren

brake /breɪk/ n Bremse f ● vt/i bremsen. ~-**light** n Bremslicht nt

bramble /'bræmbl/ n Brombeer- strauch m

bran /bræn/ n Kleie f

branch /brɑːntʃ/ n Ast m; (fig) Zweig m; (Comm) Zweigstelle f; (shop) Filiale f ● vi sich gabeln. ~ **off** vi abzweigen. ~ **out** vi ~ **out into** sich verlegen auf (+ acc)

brand /brænd/ n Marke f; (on animal) Brandzeichen nt ● vt mit dem Brandeisen zeichnen (animal); (fig) brandmarken als

brandish /'brændɪʃ/ vt schwingen

brand-'new a nagelneu

brandy /'brændɪ/ n Weinbrand m

brash /bræʃ/ a naßforsch

brass /brɑːs/ n Messing nt; (Mus) Blech nt; **get down to** ~ **tacks** (fam) zur Sache kommen; **top** ~ (fam) hohe Tiere pl. ~ **band** n Blaskapelle f

brassiere /'bræzɪə(r)/ n Büsten- halter m

brassy /'brɑːsɪ/ a (-ier, -iest) (fam) or- dinär

brat /bræt/ n (pej) Balg nt

bravado /brə'vɑːdəʊ/ n Forschheit f

brave /breɪv/ a (-r, -st), -ly adv tapfer ● vt die Stirn bieten (+ dat). ~**ry** /-ərɪ/ n Tapferkeit f

bravo /brɑː'vəʊ/ int bravo!

brawl /brɔːl/ n Schlägerei f ● vi sich schlagen

brawn /brɔːn/ n (Culin) Sülze f

brawny /'brɔːnɪ/ a muskulös

bray /breɪ/ vi iahen

brazen /'breɪzn/ a unverschämt

brazier /'breɪzɪə(r)/ n Kohlenbecken nt

Brazil /brə'zɪl/ n Brasilien nt. ~**ian** a brasilianisch. ~**nut** n Paranuß f

breach /briːtʃ/ n Bruch m; (Mil & fig) Bresche f; ~ **of contract** Vertragsbruch m ● vt durchbrechen; brechen (contract)

bread /bred/ n Brot nt; **slice of** ~ **and butter** Butterbrot nt

bread: ~**crumbs** npl Brotkrümel pl; (Culin) Paniermehl nt. ~**line** n **be on the** ~**line** gerade genug zum Leben haben

breadth /bredθ/ n Breite f

'bread-winner n Brotverdiener m

break /breɪk/ n Bruch m; (interval) Pause f; (interruption) Unter- brechung f; (fam: chance) Chance f ● v (pt **broke**, pp **broken**) ● vt brechen; (smash) zerbrechen; (damage) kaputt- machen; (fam); (interrupt) unter- brechen; ~ **one's arm** sich (dat) den Arm brechen ● vi brechen; (day:) an- brechen; (storm:) losbrechen; (thing:) kaputtgehen (fam); (rope, thread:) reißen; (news:) bekanntwerden; **his voice** is ~**ing** er ist im Stimmbruch. ~ **away** vi sich losreißen/(fig) sich absetzen (**from** von). ~ **down** vi zu- sammenbrechen; (Techn) Panne haben; (negotiations:) scheitern ● vt aufbrechen (door); aufgliedern (figures). ~ **in** vi einbrechen. ~ **off** vt/i abbrechen; lösen (engagement). ~ **out** vi ausbrechen. ~ **up** vt zer- brechen ● vi (crowd:) sich zerstreuen; (marriage, couple:) auseinandergehen; (Sch) Ferien bekommen

break|able /'breɪkəbl/ a zerbrech- lich. ~**age** /-ɪdʒ/ n Bruch m. ~**down** n (Techn) Panne f; (Med) Zu- sammenbruch m; (of figures) Auf- gliederung f. ~**er** n (wave) Brecher m

breakfast /'brekfəst/ n Frühstück nt

break: ~**through** n Durchbruch m. ~**water** n Buhne f

breast /brest/ n Brust f. ~**bone** n Brustbein nt. ~**feed** vt stillen. ~**stroke** n Brustschwimmen nt

breath /breθ/ n Atem m; **out of** ~ außer Atem; **under one's** ~ vor sich (acc) hin

breathalyse /'breθəlaɪz/ vt ins Röhrchen blasen lassen. ~**r** (P) n Röhrchen nt. ~**r test** n Alcotest (P) m

breathe /briːð/ vt/i atmen. ~ **in** vt/i einatmen. ~ **out** vt/i ausatmen

breath|er /'briːðə(r)/ n Atempause f.
~**ing** n Atmen nt
breath /'breθ-/: ~**less** a atemlos.
~**taking** a atemberaubend. ~ **test**
n Alcotest (P) m
bred /bred/ see **breed**
breeches /'britʃɪz/ npl Kniehose f;
(for riding) Reithose f
breed /briːd/ n Rasse f ● v (pt/pp
bred) ● vt züchten; (give rise to)
erzeugen ● vi sich vermehren. ~**er** n
Züchter m. ~**ing** n Zucht f; (fig)
[gute] Lebensart f
breez|e /briːz/ n Lüftchen nt; (Naut)
Brise f. ~**y** a [leicht] windig
brevity /'brevətɪ/ n Kürze f
brew /bruː/ n Gebräu nt ● vt brauen;
kochen (tea) ● vi (fig) sich zu-
sammenbrauen. ~**er** n Brauer m.
~**ery** n Brauerei f
bribe /braɪb/ n (money) Be-
stechungsgeld nt ● vt bestechen.
~**ry** /-ərɪ/ n Bestechung f
brick /brɪk/ n Ziegelstein m, Back-
stein m ● vt ~ **up** zumauern
'**bricklayer** n Maurer m
bridal /'braɪdl/ a Braut-
bride /braɪd/ n Braut f. ~**groom** n
Bräutigam m. ~**smaid** n Brautjung-
fer f
bridge[1] /brɪdʒ/ n Brücke f; (of nose)
Nasenrücken m; (of spectacles) Steg m
● vt (fig) überbrücken
bridge[2] n (Cards) Bridge nt
bridle /'braɪdl/ n Zaum m. ~**-path** n
Reitweg m
brief[1] /briːf/ a (-er, -est) kurz; **be** ~
⟨person:⟩ sich kurz fassen
brief[2] n Instruktionen pl; (Jur: case)
Mandat nt ● vt Instruktionen geben
(+ dat); (Jur) beauftragen. ~**case** n
Aktentasche f
brief|ing /'briːfɪŋ/ n Informa-
tionsgespräch nt. ~**ly** adv kurz.
~**ness** n Kürze f
briefs /briːfs/ npl Slip m
brigad|e /brɪ'geɪd/ n Brigade f.
~**ier** /-ə'dɪə(r)/ n Brigadegeneral m
bright /braɪt/ a (-er, -est), -**ly** adv hell;
⟨day⟩ heiter; ~ **red** hellrot
bright|en /'braɪtn/ v ~**en [up]** ● vt
aufheitern ● vi sich aufheitern. ~**ness**
n Helligkeit f
brilliance /'brɪljəns/ n Glanz m; (of
person) Genialität f
brilliant /'brɪljənt/ a, -**ly** adv glänzend; ⟨person⟩ genial

brim /brɪm/ n Rand m; (of hat)
Krempe f ● vi (pt/pp **brimmed**) ~
over überfließen
brine /braɪn/ n Salzwasser nt; (Culin)
[Salz]lake f
bring /brɪŋ/ vt (pt/pp **brought**)
bringen; ~ **them with you** bring sie
mit. ~ **about** vt verursachen. ~
along vt mitbringen. ~ **back** vt zurückbringen. ~ **down** vt herunter-
bringen; senken ⟨price⟩. ~ **off** vt
vollbringen. ~ **on** vt (cause) verursachen. ~ **out** vt herausbringen. ~
round vt vorbeibringen; (persuade)
überreden; wieder zum Bewußtsein
bringen ⟨unconscious person⟩. ~ **up**
vt heraufbringen; (vomit) erbrechen;
aufziehen ⟨children⟩; erwähnen
⟨question⟩
brink /brɪŋk/ n Rand m
brisk /brɪsk/ a (-er, -est), -**ly** adv
lebhaft; (quick) schnell
brist|le /'brɪsl/ n Borste f. ~**ly** a bor-
stig
Brit|ain /'brɪtn/ n Großbritannien
nt. ~**ish** a britisch; **the** ~**ish** die
Briten pl. ~**on** n Brite m/Britin f
Brittany /'brɪtənɪ/ n die Bretagne
brittle /'brɪtl/ a brüchig, spröde
broach /brəʊtʃ/ vt anzapfen; an-
schneiden ⟨subject⟩
broad /brɔːd/ a (-er, -est) breit; ⟨hint⟩
deutlich; **in** ~ **daylight** am hellichten
Tag. ~ **beans** npl dicke Bohnen pl
'**broadcast** n Sendung f ● vt/i (pt/
pp -**cast**) senden. ~**er** n Rundfunk-
und Fernsehpersönlichkeit f. ~**ing**
n Funk und Fernsehen pl
broaden /'brɔːdn/ vt verbreitern;
(fig) erweitern ● vi sich verbreitern
broadly /'brɔːdlɪ/ adv breit; ~
speaking allgemein gesagt
broad'minded a tolerant
brocade /brə'keɪd/ n Brokat m
broccoli /'brɒkəlɪ/ n inv Brokkoli pl
brochure /'brəʊʃə(r)/ n Broschüre f
brogue /brəʊg/ n (shoe) Wander-
schuh m; **Irish** ~ irischer Akzent m
broke /brəʊk/ see **break** ● a (fam)
pleite
broken /'brəʊkn/ see **break** ● a zer-
brochen, (fam) kaputt; ~ **English** ge-
brochenes Englisch nt. ~**-hearted** a
untröstlich
broker /'brəʊkə(r)/ n Makler m
brolly /'brɒlɪ/ n (fam) Schirm m
bronchitis /brɒn'kaɪtɪs/ n Bronchitis f

bronze /brɒnz/ n Bronze f

brooch /brəʊtʃ/ n Brosche f

brood /bruːd/ n Brut f ● vi brüten; (fig) grübeln

brook¹ /brʊk/ n Bach m

brook² vt dulden

broom /bruːm/ n Besen m; (Bot) Ginster m. ~**stick** n Besenstiel m

broth /brɒθ/ n Brühe f

brothel /'brɒθl/ n Bordell nt

brother /'brʌðə(r)/ n Bruder m

brother: ~**-in-law** n (pl -s-in-law) Schwager m. ~**ly** a brüderlich

brought /brɔːt/ see bring

brow /braʊ/ n Augenbraue f; (forehead) Stirn f; (of hill) [Berg]-kuppe f

'browbeat vt (pt -beat, pp -beaten) einschüchtern

brown /braʊn/ a (-er, -est) braun; ~ 'paper Packpapier nt ● n Braun nt ● vt bräunen ● vi braun werden

Brownie /'braʊnɪ/ n Wichtel m

browse /braʊz/ vi (read) schmö-kern; (in shop) sich umsehen

bruise /bruːz/ n blauer Fleck m ● vt beschädigen ⟨fruit⟩; ~ one's arm sich (dat) den Arm quetschen

brunch /brʌntʃ/ n Brunch m

brunette /bruː'net/ n Brünette f

Brunswick /'brʌnzwɪk/ n Braun-schweig nt

brunt /brʌnt/ n the ~ of die volle Wucht (+ gen)

brush /brʌʃ/ n Bürste f; (with handle) Handfeger m; (for paint, pastry) Pinsel m; (bushes) Unterholz nt; (fig: conflict) Zusammenstoß m ● vt bürsten; putzen ⟨teeth⟩; ~ against streifen [gegen]; ~ aside (fig) abtun. ~ off vt abbürsten; (reject) zurückweisen. ~ up vt/i (fig) ~up [on] auffrischen

brusque /brʊsk/ a, -ly adv brüsk

Brussels /'brʌslz/ n Brüssel nt. ~ sprouts npl Rosenkohl m

brutal /'bruːtl/ a, -ly adv brutal. ~ity /-'tælətɪ/ n Brutalität f

brute /bruːt/ n Unmensch m. ~ force n rohe Gewalt f

B.Sc. abbr of **Bachelor of Science**

bubble /'bʌbl/ n [Luft]blase f ● vi sprudeln

buck¹ /bʌk/ n (deer & Gym) Bock m; (rabbit) Rammler m ● vi ⟨horse:⟩ bocken. ~ up vi (fam) sich aufhei-tern; (hurry) sich beeilen

buck² n (Amer, fam) Dollar m

buck³ n pass the ~ die Verantwortung abschieben

bucket /'bʌkɪt/ n Eimer m

buckle /'bʌkl/ n Schnalle f ● vt zuschnallen ● vi sich verbiegen

bud /bʌd/ n Knospe f ● vi (pt/pp budded) knospen

Buddhis|m /'bʊdɪzm/ n Buddhismus m. ~**t** a buddhistisch ● n Bud-dhist(in) m(f)

buddy /'bʌdɪ/ n (fam) Freund m

budge /bʌdʒ/ vt bewegen ● vi sich [von der Stelle] rühren

budgerigar /'bʌdʒərɪgɑː(r)/ n Wellensittich m

budget /'bʌdʒɪt/ n Budget nt; (Pol) Haushaltsplan m; (money available) Etat m ● vi (pt/pp budgeted) ~ for sth etw einkalkulieren

buff /bʌf/ a (colour) sandfarben ● n Sandfarbe f; (Amer, fam) Fan m ● vt polieren

buffalo /'bʌfələʊ/ n (inv or pl -es) Büffel m

buffer /'bʌfə(r)/ n (Rail) Puffer m; old ~ (fam) alter Knacker m; ~ zone Pufferzone f

buffet¹ /'bʊfeɪ/ n Büfett nt; (on station) Imbißstube f

buffet² /'bʌfɪt/ vt (pt/pp buffeted) hin und her werfen

buffoon /bə'fuːn/ n Narr m

bug /bʌg/ n Wanze f; (fam: virus) Ba-zillus m; (fam: device) Abhörgerät nt, (fam) Wanze f ● vt (pt/pp bugged) (fam) verwanzen ⟨room⟩; abhören ⟨tele-phone⟩; (Amer: annoy) ärgern

buggy /'bʌgɪ/ n [Kinder]sportwagen m

bugle /'bjuːgl/ n Signalhorn m

build /bɪld/ n (of person) Körperbau m ● vt/i (pt/pp built) bauen. ~ on vt anbauen (to an + acc). ~ up vt auf-bauen ● vi zunehmen; ⟨traffic:⟩ sich stauen

builder /'bɪldə(r)/ n Bauunter-nehmer m

building /'bɪldɪŋ/ n Gebäude nt. ~ site n Baustelle f. ~ society n Bau-sparkasse f

built /bɪlt/ see build. ~**-in** a ein-gebaut. ~**-in 'cupboard** n Ein-bauschrank m. ~**-up area** n bebautes Gebiet nt; (Auto) ge-schlossene Ortschaft f

bulb /bʌlb/ n [Blumen]zwiebel f; (Electr) [Glüh]birne f

bulbous /'bʌlbəs/ a bauchig

Bulgaria /bʌl'geərɪə/ n Bulgarien nt
bulg|e /bʌldʒ/ n Ausbauchung f ● vi
sich ausbauchen. ~**ing** a prall; ⟨eyes⟩
hervorquellend; ~**ing with** prall gefüllt mit
bulk /bʌlk/ n Masse f; (greater part)
Hauptteil m; **in** ~ en gros; (loose) lose.
~**y** a sperrig; (large) massig
bull /bʊl/ n Bulle m, Stier m
'**bulldog** n Bulldogge f
bulldozer /'bʊldəʊzə(r)/ n Planier-
raupe f
bullet /'bʊlɪt/ n Kugel f
bulletin /'bʊlɪtɪn/ n Bulletin nt
'**bullet-proof** a kugelsicher
'**bullfight** n Stierkampf m. ~**er** n
Stierkämpfer m
'**bullfinch** n Dompfaff m
bullion /'bʊlɪən/ n **gold** ~ Barrengold
nt
bullock /'bʊlək/ n Ochse m
bull: ~**ring** n Stierkampfarena f.
~'**s-eye** n **score a** ~'**s-eye** ins
Schwarze treffen
bully /'bʊlɪ/ n Tyrann m ● vt tyrannisieren
bum[1] /bʌm/ n (sl) Hintern m
bum[2] n (Amer, fam) Landstreicher m
bumble-bee /'bʌmbl-/ n Hummel f
bump /bʌmp/ n Bums m; (swelling)
Beule f; (in road) holperige Stelle f
● vt stoßen; ~ **into** stoßen gegen;
(meet) zufällig treffen. ~ **off** vt (fam)
um die Ecke bringen
bumper /'bʌmpə(r)/ a Rekord- ● n
(Auto) Stoßstange f
bumpkin /'bʌmpkɪn/ n **country** ~
Tölpel m
bumptious /'bʌmpʃəs/ a aufgeblasen
bumpy /'bʌmpɪ/ a holperig
bun /bʌn/ n Milchbrötchen nt; (hair)
[Haar]knoten m
bunch /bʌntʃ/ n (of flowers) Strauß
m; (of radishes, keys) Bund m; (of
people) Gruppe f; ~ **of grapes** [ganze]
Weintraube f
bundle /'bʌndl/ n Bündel nt ● vt ~
[**up**] bündeln
bung /bʌŋ/ vt (fam) (throw)
schmeißen. ~ **up** vt (fam) verstopfen
bungalow /'bʌŋɡələʊ/ n Bungalow
m
bungle /'bʌŋɡl/ vt verpfuschen
bunion /'bʌnjən/ n (Med) Ballen m
bunk /bʌŋk/ n [Schlaf]koje f.
~-**beds** npl Etagenbett nt
bunker /'bʌŋkə(r)/ n Bunker m

bunkum /'bʌŋkəm/ n Quatsch m
bunny /'bʌnɪ/ n (fam) Kaninchen nt
buoy /bɔɪ/ n Boje f. ~ **up** vt (fig)
stärken
buoyan|cy /'bɔɪənsɪ/ n Auftrieb m.
~**t** a **be** ~**t** schwimmen; ⟨water:⟩ gut
tragen
burden /'bɜːdn/ n Last f ● vt belasten. ~**some** /-səm/ a lästig
bureau /'bjʊərəʊ/ n (pl -**x** /-əʊz/ or
~**s**) (desk) Sekretär m; (office) Büro nt
bureaucracy /bjʊə'rɒkrəsɪ/ n Bürokratie f
bureaucrat /'bjʊərəkræt/ n Büro-
krat m. ~**ic** /-'krætɪk/ a büro-
kratisch
burger /'bɜːɡə(r)/ n Hamburger m
burglar /'bɜːɡlə(r)/ n Einbrecher m.
~ **alarm** n Alarmanlage f
burglar|ize /'bɜːɡləraɪz/ vt (Amer)
einbrechen in (+ acc). ~**y** n Einbruch m
burgle /'bɜːɡl/ vt einbrechen in
(+ acc); **they have been** ~**d** bei ihnen
ist eingebrochen worden
Burgundy /'bɜːɡəndɪ/ n Burgund nt;
b~ (wine) Burgunder m
burial /'berɪəl/ n Begräbnis nt
burlesque /bɜː'lesk/ n Burleske f
burly /'bɜːlɪ/ a (-ier, -iest) stämmig
Burm|a /'bɜːmə/ n Birma nt. ~**ese**
/-'miːz/ a birmanisch
burn /bɜːn/ n Verbrennung f; (on
skin) Brandwunde f; (on material)
Brandstelle f ● v (pt/pp **burnt** or
burned) ● vt verbrennen ● vi brennen;
⟨food:⟩ anbrennen. ~ **down** vt/i
niederbrennen
burnish /'bɜːnɪʃ/ vt polieren
burnt /bɜːnt/ see **burn**
burp /bɜːp/ vi (fam) aufstoßen
burrow /'bʌrəʊ/ n Bau m ● vi
wühlen
bursar /'bɜːsə(r)/ n Rechnungs-
führer m. ~**y** n Stipendium nt
burst /bɜːst/ n Bruch m; (surge) Ausbruch m ● v (pt/pp **burst**) ● vt platzen
machen ● vi platzen; ⟨bud:⟩ aufgehen;
~ **into tears** in Tränen ausbrechen
bury /'berɪ/ vt (pt/pp -**ied**) begraben;
(hide) vergraben
bus /bʌs/ n [Auto]bus m ● vt/i (pt/pp
bussed) mit dem Bus fahren
bush /bʊʃ/ n Strauch m; (land)
Busch m. ~**y** a (-ier, -iest) buschig
busily /'bɪzɪlɪ/ adv eifrig
business /'bɪznɪs/ n Angelegenheit f;
(Comm) Geschäft nt; **on** ~ ge-
schäftlich; **he has no** ~ **to** er hat kein

Recht, zu; **mind one's own** ~ sich um seine eigenen Angelegenheiten kümmern; **that's none of your** ~ das geht Sie nichts an. **~-like** *a* geschäftsmäßig. **~man** *n* Geschäftsmann *m*

busker /'bʌskə(r)/ *n* Straßenmusikant *m*

'**bus-stop** *n* Bushaltestelle *f*

bust[1] /bʌst/ *n* Büste *f*. ~ **size** *n* Oberweite *f*

bust[2] *a* (*fam*) kaputt; **go** ~ pleite machen ● *v* (*pt/pp* **busted** *or* **bust**) (*fam*) ● *vt* kaputtmachen ● *vi* kaputtgehen

bustl|e /'bʌsl/ *n* Betrieb *m*, Getriebe *nt* ● *vi* ~**e about** geschäftig hin und her laufen. ~**ing** *a* belebt

'**bust-up** *n* (*fam*) Streit *m*, Krach *m*

busy /'bɪzɪ/ *a* (**-ier, -iest**) beschäftigt; (*day*) voll; (*street*) belebt; (*with traffic*) stark befahren; (*Amer Teleph*) besetzt; **be** ~ zu tun haben ● *vt* ~ **oneself** sich beschäftigen (**with** mit)

'**busybody** *n* Wichtigtuer(in) *m(f)*

but /bʌt, *unbetont* bət/ *conj* aber; (*after negative*) sondern ● *prep* außer (+ *dat*); ~ **for** (*without*) ohne (+ *acc*); **the last** ~ **one** der/die/das vorletzte; **the next** ~ **one** der/die/ das übernächste ● *adv* nur

butcher /'bʊtʃə(r)/ *n* Fleischer *m*, Metzger *m*; ~'**s** [**shop**] Fleischerei *f*, Metzgerei *f* ● *vt* [ab]schlachten

butler /'bʌtlə(r)/ *n* Butler *m*

butt /bʌt/ *n* (*of gun*) [Gewehr]kolben *m*; (*fig: target*) Zielscheibe *f*; (*of cigarette*) Stummel *m*; (*for water*) Regentonne *f* ● *vt* mit dem Kopf stoßen ● *vi* ~ **in** unterbrechen

butter /'bʌtə(r)/ *n* Butter *f* ● *vt* mit Butter bestreichen. ~ **up** *vt* (*fam*) schmeicheln (+ *dat*)

butter: ~**cup** *a* Butterblume *f*, Hahnenfuß *m*. ~**fly** *n* Schmetterling *m*

buttocks /'bʌtəks/ *npl* Gesäß *nt*

button /'bʌtn/ *n* Knopf *m* ● *vt* ~ [**up**] zuknöpfen ● *vi* geknöpft werden. ~**hole** *n* Knopfloch *nt*

buttress /'bʌtrɪs/ *n* Strebepfeiler *m*; **flying** ~ Strebebogen *m*

buxom /'bʌksəm/ *a* drall

buy /baɪ/ *n* Kauf *m* ● *vt* (*pt/pp* **bought**) kaufen. ~**er** *n* Käufer(in) *m(f)*

buzz /bʌz/ *n* Summen *nt* ● *vi* summen. ~ **off** *vi* (*fam*) abhauen

buzzard /'bʌzəd/ *n* Bussard *m*

buzzer /'bʌzə(r)/ *n* Summer *m*

by /baɪ/ *prep* (*close to*) bei (+ *dat*); (*next to*) neben (+ *dat/acc*); (*past*) an (+ *dat*) ... vorbei; (*to the extent of*) um (+ *acc*); (*at the latest*) bis; (*by means of*) durch; **by Mozart/Dickens** von Mozart/Dickens; ~ **oneself** allein; ~ **the sea** am Meer; ~ **car/bus** mit dem Auto/Bus; ~ **sea** mit dem Schiff; ~ **day/night** bei Tag/Nacht; ~ **the hour** pro Stunde; ~ **the metre** meterweise; **six metres** ~ **four** sechs mal vier Meter; **win** ~ **a length** mit einer Länge Vorsprung gewinnen; **miss the train** ~ **a minute** den Zug um eine Minute verpassen ● *adv* ~ **and** ~ mit der Zeit; ~ **and large** im großen und ganzen; **put** ~ beiseite legen; **go/pass** ~ vorbeigehen

bye /baɪ/ *int* (*fam*) tschüs

by: ~-**election** *n* Nachwahl *f*. ~**gone** *a* vergangen. ~-**law** *n* Verordnung *f*. ~**pass** *n* Umgehungsstraße *f*; (*Med*) Bypass *m* ● *vt* umfahren. ~-**product** *n* Nebenprodukt *nt*. ~-**road** *n* Nebenstraße *f*. ~**stander** *n* Zuschauer(in) *m(f)*

Byzantine /'bɪ'zæntaɪn/ *a* byzantinisch

C

cab /kæb/ *n* Taxi *nt*; (*of lorry, train*) Führerhaus *nt*

cabaret /'kæbəreɪ/ *n* Kabarett *nt*

cabbage /'kæbɪdʒ/ *n* Kohl *m*

cabin /'kæbɪn/ *n* Kabine *f*; (*hut*) Hütte *f*

cabinet /'kæbɪnɪt/ *n* Schrank *m*; [**display**] ~ Vitrine *f*; (*TV, Radio*) Gehäuse *nt*; **C**~ (*Pol*) Kabinett *nt*. ~-**maker** *n* Möbeltischler *m*

cable /'keɪbl/ *n* Kabel *nt*; (*rope*) Tau *nt*. ~ '**railway** *n* Seilbahn *f*. ~ '**television** *n* Kabelfernsehen *nt*

cache /kæʃ/ *n* Versteck *nt*; ~ **of arms** Waffenlager *nt*

cackle /'kækl/ *vi* gackern

cactus /'kæktəs/ *n* (*pl* -**ti** /-taɪ/ *or* -**tuses**) Kaktus *m*

caddie /'kædɪ/ *n* Caddie *m*

caddy /'kædɪ/ *n* [**tea-**]~ Teedose *f*

cadet /kə'det/ *n* Kadett *m*

cadge /kædʒ/ *vt/i* (*fam*) schnorren

Caesarean /sɪ'zeərɪən/ *a & n* ~ [**section**] Kaiserschnitt *m*

café /'kæfeɪ/ *n* Café *nt*

cafeteria /kæfə'tɪərɪə/ *n* Selbstbedienungsrestaurant *nt*

caffeine /'kæfiːn/ *n* Koffein *nt*

cage /keɪdʒ/ *n* Käfig *m*

cagey /'keɪdʒɪ/ *a* (*fam*) **be** ~ mit der Sprache nicht herauswollen

cajole /kə'dʒəʊl/ *vt* gut zureden (+ *dat*)

cake /keɪk/ *n* Kuchen *m*; (*of soap*) Stück *nt*. ~**d** a verkrustet (**with** mit)

calamity /kə'læmətɪ/ *n* Katastrophe *f*

calcium /'kælsɪəm/ *n* Kalzium *nt*

calculat|e /'kælkjʊlət/ *vt* berechnen; (*estimate*) kalkulieren. ~**ing** *a* (*fig*) berechnend. ~**ion** /-'leɪʃn/ *n* Rechnung *f*, Kalkulation *f*. ~**or** *n* Rechner *m*

calendar /'kælɪndə(r)/ *n* Kalender *m*

calf[1] /kɑːf/ *n* (*pl* **calves**) Kalb *nt*

calf[2] *n* (*pl* **calves**) (*Anat*) Wade *f*

calibre /'kælɪbə(r)/ *n* Kaliber *nt*

calico /'kælɪkəʊ/ *n* Kattun *m*

call /kɔːl/ *n* Ruf *m*; (*Teleph*) Anruf *m*; (*visit*) Besuch *m*; **be on** ~ (*doctor:*) Bereitschaftsdienst haben ● *vt* rufen; (*Teleph*) anrufen; (*wake*) wecken; ausrufen (*strike*); (*name*) nennen; **be** ~**ed** heißen ● *vi* rufen; ~ [**in** *or* **round**] vorbeikommen. ~ **back** *vt* zurückrufen ● *vi* noch einmal vorbeikommen. ~ **for** *vt* rufen nach; (*demand*) verlangen; (*fetch*) abholen. ~ **off** *vt* zurückrufen (*dog*); (*cancel*) absagen. ~ **on** *vt* bitten (**for** um); (*appeal to*) appellieren an (+ *acc*); (*visit*) besuchen. ~ **out** *vt* rufen; aufrufen (*names*) ● *vi* rufen. ~ **up** *vt* (*Mil*) einberufen; (*Teleph*) anrufen

call: ~**box** *n* Telefonzelle *f*. ~**er** *n* Besucher *m*; (*Teleph*) Anrufer *m*. ~**ing** *n* Berufung *f*

callous /'kæləs/ *a* gefühllos

'call-up *n* (*Mil*) Einberufung *f*

calm /kɑːm/ *a* (**-er, -est**), **-ly** *adv* ruhig ● *n* Ruhe *f* ● *vt* ~ [**down**] beruhigen ● *vi* ~ **down** sich beruhigen. ~**ness** *n* Ruhe *f*; (*of sea*) Stille *f*

calorie /'kælərɪ/ *n* Kalorie *f*

calves /kɑːvz/ *npl see* **calf**[1] & [2]

camber /'kæmbə(r)/ *n* Wölbung *f*

came /keɪm/ *see* **come**

camel /'kæml/ *n* Kamel *nt*

camera /'kæmərə/ *n* Kamera *f*. ~**man** *n* Kameramann *m*

camouflage /'kæməflɑːʒ/ *n* Tarnung *f* ● *vt* tarnen

camp /kæmp/ *n* Lager *nt* ● *vi* campen; (*Mil*) kampieren

campaign /kæm'peɪn/ *n* Feldzug *m*; (*Comm, Pol*) Kampagne *f* ● *vi* kämpfen; (*Pol*) im Wahlkampf arbeiten

camp: ~**-bed** *n* Feldbett *nt*. ~**er** *n* Camper *m*; (*Auto*) Wohnmobil *nt*. ~**ing** *n* Camping *nt*. ~**site** *n* Campingplatz *m*

campus /'kæmpəs/ *n* (*pl* **-puses**) (*Univ*) Campus *m*

can[1] /kæn/ *n* (*for petrol*) Kanister *m*; (*tin*) Dose *f*, Büchse *f*; **a** ~ **of beer** eine Dose Bier ● *vt* in Dosen *od* Büchsen konservieren

can[2] /kæn, *unbetont* kən/ *v aux* (*pres* **can**; *pt* **could**) können; **I cannot/can't go** ich kann nicht gehen; **he could not go** er konnte nicht gehen; **if I could go** wenn ich gehen könnte

Canad|a /'kænədə/ *n* Kanada *nt*. ~**ian** /kə'neɪdɪən/ *a* kanadisch ● *n* Kanadier(in) *m(f)*

canal /kə'næl/ *n* Kanal *m*

Canaries /kə'neərɪz/ *npl* Kanarische Inseln *pl*

canary /kə'neərɪ/ *n* Kanarienvogel *m*

cancel /'kænsl/ *vt/i* (*pt/pp* **cancelled**) absagen; entwerten (*stamp*); (*annul*) rückgängig machen; (*Comm*) stornieren; abbestellen (*newspaper*); **be** ~**led** ausfallen. ~**lation** /-ə'leɪʃn/ *n* Absage *f*

cancer /'kænsə(r)/ *n*, & (*Astr*) **C**~ Krebs *m*. ~**ous** /-rəs/ *a* krebsig

candelabra /kændɪ'lɑːbrə/ *n* Armleuchter *m*

candid /'kændɪd/ *a*, **-ly** *adv* offen

candidate /'kændɪdət/ *n* Kandidat(in) *m(f)*

candied /'kændɪd/ *a* kandiert

candle /'kændl/ *n* Kerze *f*. ~**stick** *n* Kerzenständer *m*, Leuchter *m*

candour /'kændə(r)/ *n* Offenheit *f*

candy /'kændɪ/ *n* (*Amer*) Süßigkeiten *pl*; [**piece of**] ~ Bonbon *m*. ~**floss** /-flɒs/ *n* Zuckerwatte *f*

cane /keɪn/ *n* Rohr *nt*; (*stick*) Stock *m* ● *vt* mit dem Stock züchtigen

canine /'keɪnaɪn/ *a* Hunde-. ~ **tooth** *n* Eckzahn *m*

canister /'kænɪstə(r)/ *n* Blechdose *f*

cannabis /'kænəbɪs/ *n* Haschisch *nt*

canned /kænd/ *a* Dosen-, Büchsen-; ~ **music** (*fam*) Musik *f* aus der Konserve

cannibal /'kænɪbl/ n Kannibale m.
~**ism** n Kannibalismus m

cannon /'kænən/ n inv Kanone f.
~**-ball** n Kanonenkugel f

cannot /'kænɒt/ see **can²**

canny /'kænɪ/ a schlau

canoe /kə'nu:/ n Paddelboot nt;
(Sport) Kanu nt ● vi paddeln; (Sport)
Kanu fahren

canon /'kænən/ n Kanon m; (person)
Kanonikus m. ~**ize** /-aɪz/ vt kanonisieren

'**can-opener** n Dosenöffner m,
Büchsenöffner m

canopy /'kænəpɪ/ n Baldachin m

cant /kænt/ n Heuchelei f

can't /kɑ:nt/ = **cannot**. See **can²**

cantankerous /kæn'tæŋkərəs/ a
zänkisch

canteen /kæn'ti:n/ n Kantine f; ~ of
cutlery Besteckkasten m

canter /'kæntə(r)/ n Kanter m ● vi
kantern

canvas /'kænvəs/ n Segeltuch nt;
(Art) Leinwand f; (painting) Gemälde nt

canvass /'kænvəs/ vi um Stimmen
werben

canyon /'kænjən/ n Cañon m

cap /kæp/ n Kappe f, Mütze f;
(nurse's) Haube f; (top, lid) Verschluß
m ● vt (pt/pp **capped**) (fig) übertreffen

capability /keɪpə'bɪlətɪ/ n Fähigkeit
f

capable /'keɪpəbl/ a, **-bly** adv fähig;
be ~ **of doing sth** fähig sein, etw zu
tun

capacity /kə'pæsətɪ/ n Fassungs-
vermögen nt; (ability) Fähigkeit f; **in
my** ~ **as** in meiner Eigenschaft als

cape¹ /keɪp/ n (cloak) Cape nt

cape² n (Geog) Kap nt

caper¹ /'keɪpə(r)/ vi herumspringen

caper² n (Culin) Kaper f

capital /'kæpɪtl/ a (letter) groß ● n
(town) Hauptstadt f; (money) Kapital
nt; (letter) Großbuchstabe m

capital|ism /'kæpɪtəlɪzm/ n Kapi-
talismus m. ~**ist** /-ɪst/ a kapitali-
stisch ● n Kapitalist m. ~**ize** /-aɪz/ vt
~**ize on** (fig) Kapital schlagen aus. ~
'**letter** n Großbuchstabe m. ~ '**punishment** n Todesstrafe f

capitulat|e /kə'pɪtjʊleɪt/ vi kapi-
tulieren. ~**ion** /-'leɪʃn/ n Kapitulation f

capricious /kə'prɪʃəs/ a launisch

Capricorn /'kæprɪkɔːn/ n (Astr)
Steinbock m

capsize /kæp'saɪz/ vi kentern ● vt
zum Kentern bringen

capsule /'kæpsjʊl/ n Kapsel f

captain /'kæptɪn/ n Kapitän m; (Mil)
Hauptmann m ● vt anführen (team)

caption /'kæpʃn/ n Überschrift f; (of
illustration) Bildtext m

captivate /'kæptɪveɪt/ vt bezaubern

captiv|e /'kæptɪv/ a **hold/take** ~**e**
gefangenhalten/-nehmen ● n Gefan-
gene(r) m/f. ~**ity** /-'tɪvətɪ/ n Ge-
fangenschaft f

capture /'kæptʃə(r)/ n Gefan-
gennahme f ● vt gefangennehmen;
[ein]fangen (animal); (Mil) einnehmen (town)

car /kɑ:(r)/ n Auto nt, Wagen m; **by** ~
mit dem Auto od Wagen

carafe /kə'ræf/ n Karaffe f

caramel /'kærəmel/ n Karamel m

carat /'kærət/ n Karat nt

caravan /'kærəvæn/ n Wohnwagen
m; (procession) Karawane f

carbohydrate /kɑ:bə'haɪdreɪt/ n
Kohlenhydrat nt

carbon /'kɑ:bən/ n Kohlenstoff m;
(paper) Kohlepapier nt; (copy)
Durchschlag m

carbon: ~ **copy** n Durchschlag m. ~
di'oxide n Kohlendioxyd nt; (in
drink) Kohlensäure f. ~ **paper** n
Kohlepapier nt

carburettor /kɑ:bjʊ'retə(r)/ n Ver-
gaser m

carcass /'kɑ:kəs/ n Kadaver m

card /kɑ:d/ n Karte f

'**cardboard** n Pappe f, Karton m. ~
'**box** n Pappschachtel f; (large)
[Papp]karton m

'**card-game** n Kartenspiel nt

cardiac /'kɑ:dɪæk/ a Herz-

cardigan /'kɑ:dɪɡən/ n Strickjacke f

cardinal /'kɑ:dɪnl/ a Kardinal-; ~
number Kardinalzahl f ● n (Relig)
Kardinal m

card 'index n Kartei f

care /keə(r)/ n Sorgfalt f; (caution)
Vorsicht f; (protection) Obhut f;
(looking after) Pflege f; (worry) Sorge
f; ~ **of** (on letter abbr **c/o**) bei; **take** ~
vorsichtig sein; **take into** ~ in Pflege
nehmen; **take** ~ **of** sich kümmern um
● vi ~ **about** sich kümmern um; ~ **for**
(like) mögen; (look after) betreuen; **I
don't** ~ das ist mir gleich

career /kə'rɪə(r)/ *n* Laufbahn *f*;
(*profession*) Beruf *m* ● *vi* rasen

care: ~**free** *a* sorglos. ~**ful** *a*, **-ly** *adv*
sorgfältig; (*cautious*) vorsichtig. ~**less**
a, **-ly** *adv* nachlässig. ~**lessness** *n*
Nachlässigkeit *f*

caress /kə'res/ *n* Liebkosung *f* ● *vt*
liebkosen

'**caretaker** *n* Hausmeister *m*

'**car ferry** *n* Autofähre *f*

cargo /'kɑːgəʊ/ *n* (*pl* **-es**) Ladung *f*

Caribbean /kærɪ'biːən/ *n* **the** ~ die
Karibik

caricature /'kærɪkətjʊə(r)/ *n* Karikatur *f* ● *vt* karikieren

caring /'keərɪŋ/ *a* (*parent*) liebevoll;
(*profession, attitude*) sozial

carnage /'kɑːnɪdʒ/ *n* Gemetzel *nt*

carnal /'kɑːnl/ *a* fleischlich

carnation /kɑː'neɪʃn/ *n* Nelke *f*

carnival /'kɑːnɪvl/ *n* Karneval *m*

carnivorous /kɑː'nɪvərəs/ *a* fleisch-
fressend

carol /'kærl/ *n* [**Christmas**] ~ Weih-
nachtslied *nt*

carp[1] /kɑːp/ *n inv* Karpfen *m*

carp[2] *vi* nörgeln; ~ **at** herumnörgeln an
(+ *dat*)

'**car park** *n* Parkplatz *m*; (*multi-
storey*) Parkhaus *nt*; (*underground*)
Tiefgarage *f*

carpent|er /'kɑːpɪntə(r)/ *n* Zim-
mermann *m*; (*joiner*) Tischler *m*.
~**ry** *n* Tischlerei *f*

carpet /'kɑːpɪt/ *n* Teppich *m* ● *vt* mit
Teppich auslegen

carriage /'kærɪdʒ/ *n* Kutsche *f*;
(*Rail*) Wagen *m*; (*of goods*) Beförderung *f*; (*cost*) Frachtkosten *pl*;
(*bearing*) Haltung *f*. ~**way** *n*
Fahrbahn *f*

carrier /'kærɪə(r)/ *n* Träger(in) *m(f)*;
(*Comm*) Spediteur *m*; ~[**-bag**] Tra-
getasche *f*

carrot /'kærət/ *n* Möhre *f*, Karotte *f*

carry /'kærɪ/ *vt/i* (*pt/pp* **-ied**) tragen;
be carried away (*fam*) hingerissen
sein. ~ **off** *vt* wegtragen; gewinnen
(*prize*). ~ **on** *vi* weitermachen; ~ **on
at** (*fam*) herumnörgeln an (+ *dat*); ~
on with (*fam*) eine Affäre haben mit
● *vt* führen; (*continue*) fortführen. ~
out *vt* hinaus-/heraustragen; (*perform*) ausführen

'**carry-cot** *n* Babytragetasche *f*

cart /kɑːt/ *n* Karren *m*; **put the** ~ **before the horse** das Pferd beim

cartilage /'kɑːtɪlɪdʒ/ *n* (*Anat*) Knorpel *m*

carton /'kɑːtn/ *n* [Papp]karton *m*;
(*for drink*) Tüte *f*; (*of cream, yoghurt*)
Becher *m*

cartoon /kɑː'tuːn/ *n* Karikatur *f*;
(*joke*) Witzzeichnung *f*; (*strip*) Comic Strips *pl*; (*film*) Zeichentrick-
film *m*; (*Art*) Karton *m*. ~**ist** *n* Kari-
katurist *m*

cartridge /'kɑːtrɪdʒ/ *n* Patrone *f*;
(*for film, typewriter ribbon*) Kassette
f; (*of record player*) Tonabnehmer *m*

carve /kɑːv/ *vt* schnitzen; (*in stone*)
hauen; (*Culin*) aufschneiden

carving /'kɑːvɪŋ/ *n* Schnitzerei *f*.
~**-knife** *n* Tranchiermesser *nt*

'**car wash** *n* Autowäsche *f*; (*place*)
Autowaschanlage *f*

case[1] /keɪs/ *n* Fall *m*; **in any** ~ auf
jeden Fall; **just in** ~ für alle Fälle; **in** ~
he comes falls er kommt

case[2] *n* Kasten *m*; (*crate*) Kiste *f*; (*for
spectacles*) Etui *nt*; (*suitcase*) Koffer *m*;
(*for display*) Vitrine *f*

cash /kæʃ/ *n* Bargeld *nt*; **pay [in]** ~
[in] bar bezahlen; ~ **on delivery** per
Nachnahme ● *vt* einlösen ⟨*cheque*⟩. ~
desk *n* Kasse *f*

cashier /kæ'ʃɪə(r)/ *n* Kassierer(in)
m(f)

'**cash register** *n* Registrierkasse *f*

casino /kə'siːnəʊ/ *n* Kasino *nt*

cask /kɑːsk/ *n* Faß *nt*

casket /'kɑːskɪt/ *n* Kasten *m*; (*Amer:
coffin*) Sarg *m*

casserole /'kæsərəʊl/ *n* Schmortopf
m; (*stew*) Eintopf *m*

cassette /kə'set/ *n* Kassette *f*. ~ **recorder** *n* Kassettenrecorder *m*

cast /kɑːst/ *n* (*throw*) Wurf *m*;
(*mould*) Form *f*; (*model*) Abguß *m*;
(*Theat*) Besetzung *f*; [**plaster**] ~
(*Med*) Gipsverband *m* ● *vt* (*pt/pp* **cast**)
(*throw*) werfen; (*shed*) abwerfen; abgeben ⟨*vote*⟩; gießen ⟨*metal*⟩; (*Theat*)
besetzen ⟨*role*⟩; ~ **a glance at** einen
Blick werfen auf (+ *acc*). ~ **off** *vi*
(*Naut*) ablegen ● *vt* (*Knitting*) ab-
ketten. ~ **on** *vt* (*Knitting*)
anschlagen

castanets /kæstə'nets/ *npl* Kastagnetten *pl*

castaway /'kɑːstəweɪ/ *n* Schiff-
brüchige(r) *m/f*

caste /kɑːst/ *n* Kaste *f*

cast 'iron n Gußeisen nt
cast-'iron a gußeisern
castle /'kɑ:sl/ n Schloß nt; (fortified)
Burg f; (Chess) Turm m
'cast-offs npl abgelegte Kleidung f
castor /'kɑ:stə(r)/ n (wheel) [Lauf]-
rolle f
'castor sugar n Streuzucker m
castrat|e /kæ'streɪt/ vt kastrieren.
~ion /-eɪʃn/ n Kastration f
casual /'kæʒʊəl/ a, -ly adv (chance)
zufällig; (offhand) lässig; (informal)
zwanglos; (not permanent) Gelegen-
heits-; ~ **wear** Freizeitbekleidung f
casualty /'kæʒʊəltɪ/ n [Todes]opfer
nt; (injured person) Verletzte(r) m/f;
~ [**department**] Unfallstation f
cat /kæt/ n Katze f
catalogue /'kætəlɒg/ n Katalog m
● vt katalogisieren
catalyst /'kætəlɪst/ n (Chem & fig)
Katalysator m
catalytic /kætə'lɪtɪk/ a ~ **converter**
(Auto) Katalysator m
catapult /'kætəpʌlt/ n Katapult nt
● vt katapultieren
cataract /'kætərækt/ n (Med) grauer
Star m
catarrh /kə'tɑ:(r)/ n Katarrh m
catastroph|e /kə'tæstrəfɪ/ n Kata-
strophe f. ~ic /kætə'strɒfɪk/ a
katastrophal
catch /kætʃ/ n (of fish) Fang m;
(fastener) Verschluß m; (on door)
Klinke f; (fam: snag) Haken m (fam)
● v (pt/pp caught) ● vt fangen; (be in
time for) erreichen; (travel by) fahren
mit; bekommen (illness); ~ **a cold** sich
erkälten; ~ **sight of** erblicken; ~ **s.o.**
stealing jdn beim Stehlen erwischen;
~ **one's finger in the door** sich (dat)
den Finger in der Tür [ein]klemmen
● vi (burn) anbrennen; (get stuck) klemmen. ~ **on** vi (fam) (understand)
kapieren; (become popular) sich
durchsetzen. ~ **up** vt einholen ● vi
aufholen; ~ **up** with einholen (s.o.);
nachholen (work)
catching /'kætʃɪŋ/ a ansteckend
catch: ~-**phrase** n, ~**word** n
Schlagwort nt
catchy /'kætʃɪ/ a (-ier, -iest) ein-
prägsam
catechism /'kætɪkɪzm/ n Katechismus m
categor|ical /kætɪ'gɒrɪkl/ a, -ly adv
kategorisch. ~**y** /'kætɪgərɪ/ n
Kategorie f

cater /'keɪtə(r)/ vi ~ **for** beköstigen;
⟨firm:⟩ das Essen liefern für ⟨party⟩;
(fig) eingestellt sein auf (+ acc). ~**ing**
n (trade) Gaststättengewerbe nt
caterpillar /'kætəpɪlə(r)/ n Raupe f
cathedral /kə'θi:drl/ n Dom m,
Kathedrale f
Catholic /'kæθəlɪk/ a katholisch ● n
Katholik(in) m(f). **C**~**ism** /kə-
'θɒlɪsɪzm/ n Katholizismus m
catkin /'kætkɪn/ n (Bot) Kätzchen nt
cattle /'kætl/ npl Vieh nt
catty /'kætɪ/ a (-ier, -iest) boshaft
caught /kɔ:t/ see **catch**
cauldron /'kɔ:ldrən/ n [großer] Kessel m
cauliflower /'kɒlɪ-/ n Blumenkohl m
cause /kɔ:z/ n Ursache f; (reason)
Grund m; **good** ~ gute Sache f ● vt
verursachen; ~ **s.o. to do sth** jdn veranlassen, etw zu tun
'causeway n [Insel]damm m
caustic /'kɔ:stɪk/ a ätzend; (fig)
beißend
cauterize /'kɔ:təraɪz/ vt kauterisieren
caution /'kɔ:ʃn/ n Vorsicht f; (warning) Verwarnung f ● vt (Jur) ver-
warnen
cautious /'kɔ:ʃəs/ a, -ly adv vorsichtig
cavalry /'kævəlrɪ/ n Kavallerie f
cave /keɪv/ n Höhle f ● vi ~ **in** einstürzen
cavern /'kævən/ n Höhle f
caviare /'kævɪɑ:(r)/ n Kaviar m
caving /'keɪvɪŋ/ n Höhlenforschung
f
cavity /'kævətɪ/ n Hohlraum m; (in
tooth) Loch nt
cavort /kə'vɔ:t/ vi tollen
cease /si:s/ n **without** ~ unaufhörlich
● vt/i aufhören. ~-**fire** n Waffenruhe
f. ~**less** a, -ly adv unaufhörlich
cedar /'si:də(r)/ n Zeder f
cede /si:d/ vt abtreten (**to** an + acc)
ceiling /'si:lɪŋ/ n [Zimmer]decke f;
(fig) oberste Grenze f
celebrat|e /'selɪbreɪt/ vt/i feiern.
~**ed** a berühmt (**for** wegen). ~**ion**
/-'breɪʃn/ n Feier f
celebrity /sɪ'lebrətɪ/ n Berühmtheit
f
celery /'selərɪ/ n [Stangen]sellerie m
& f
celiba|cy /'selɪbəsɪ/ n Zölibat nt. ~**te**
a **be** ~**te** im Zölibat leben
cell /sel/ n Zelle f

cellar /'selə(r)/ n Keller m
cellist /'tʃelɪst/ n Cellist(in) m(f)
cello /'tʃeləʊ/ n Cello nt
Celsius /'selsɪəs/ a Celsius
Celt /kelt/ n Kelte m/Keltin f. ~ic a
keltisch
cement /sɪ'ment/ n Zement m; (adhesive) Kitt m ● vt zementieren;
(stick) kitten
cemetery /'semətrɪ/ n Friedhof m
censor /'sensə(r)/ n Zensor m ● vt
zensieren. ~ship n Zensur f
censure /'senʃə(r)/ n Tadel m ● vt
tadeln
census /'sensəs/ n Volkszählung f
cent /sent/ n (coin) Cent m
centenary /sen'tiːnərɪ/ n, (Amer)
centennial /sen'tenɪəl/ n Hundert-
jahrfeier f
center /'sentə(r)/ n (Amer) = centre
centi|grade /'sentɪ-/ a Celsius-; 5° ~
5° Celsius. ~metre m Zenti-
meter m & nt. ~pede /-piːd/ n
Tausendfüßler m
central /'sentrəl/ a, -ly adv zentral. ~
'heating n Zentralheizung f. ~
ize vt zentralisieren. ~ reser'vation n (Auto) Mittelstreifen m
centre /'sentə(r)/ n Zentrum nt;
(middle) Mitte f ● v (pt/pp centred)
● vt zentrieren; ~ on (fig) sich drehen
um. ~-'forward n Mittelstürmer m
centrifugal /sentrɪ'fjuːgl/ a ~ force
Fliehkraft f
century /'sentʃərɪ/ n Jahrhundert nt
ceramic /sɪ'ræmɪk/ a Keramik-. ~s
n Keramik f
cereal /'sɪərɪəl/ n Getreide nt; (breakfast food) Frühstücksflocken pl
cerebral /'serɪbrl/ a Gehirn-
ceremon|ial /serɪ'məʊnɪəl/ a, -ly
adv zeremoniell, feierlich ● n Zeremoniell nt. ~ious /-ɪəs/ a, -ly adv
formell
ceremony /'serɪmənɪ/ n Zeremonie
f, Feier f; without ~ ohne weitere
Umstände
certain /'sɜːtn/ a sicher; (not named)
gewiß; for ~ mit Bestimmtheit; make
~ (check) sich vergewissern (that daß);
(ensure) dafür sorgen (that daß); he is
~ to win er wird ganz bestimmt
siegen. ~ly adv bestimmt, sicher;
~ly not! auf keinen Fall! ~ty n
Sicherheit f, Gewißheit f; it's a ~ty es
ist sicher
certificate /sə'tɪfɪkət/ n Bescheinigung f; (Jur) Urkunde f; (Sch)
Zeugnis nt

certify /'sɜːtɪfaɪ/ vt (pt/pp -ied) be-
scheinigen; (declare insane) für geisteskrank erklären
cessation /se'seɪʃn/ n Ende nt
cesspool /'ses-/ n Senkgrube f
cf abbr (compare) vgl
chafe /tʃeɪf/ vt wund reiben
chaff /tʃɑːf/ n Spreu f
chaffinch /'tʃæfɪntʃ/ n Buchfink m
chain /tʃeɪn/ n Kette f ● vt ketten (to
an + acc). ~ up vt anketten
chain: ~ re'action n Kettenreaktion
f. ~-smoker n Kettenraucher m. ~
store n Kettenladen m
chair /tʃeə(r)/ n Stuhl m; (Univ)
Lehrstuhl m ● vt den Vorsitz führen
bei. ~-lift n Sessellift m. ~man n
Vorsitzende(r) m/f
chalet /'ʃæleɪ/ n Chalet nt
chalice /'tʃælɪs/ n (Relig) Kelch m
chalk /tʃɔːk/ n Kreide f. ~y a kreidig
challeng|e /'tʃælɪndʒ/ n Heraus-
forderung f; (Mil) Anruf m ● vt
herausfordern; (Mil) anrufen; (fig)
anfechten (statement). ~er n
Herausforderer m. ~ing a heraus-
fordernd; (demanding) anspruchsvoll
chamber /'tʃeɪmbə(r)/ n Kammer f;
~s pl (Jur) [Anwalts]büro nt; C~ of
Commerce Handelskammer f
chamber: ~maid n Zimmer-
mädchen nt. ~ music n Kammer-
musik f. ~-pot n Nachttopf m
chamois¹ /'ʃæmwɑː/ n inv (animal)
Gemse f
chamois² /'ʃæmɪ/ n ~[-leather]
Ledertuch nt
champagne /ʃæm'peɪn/ n Champagner m
champion /'tʃæmpɪən/ n (Sport)
Meister(in) m(f); (of cause) Ver-
fechter m ● vt sich einsetzen für.
~ship n (Sport) Meisterschaft f
chance /tʃɑːns/ n Zufall m; (prospect)
Chancen pl; (likelihood) Aussicht f;
(opportunity) Gelegenheit f; by ~
zufällig; take a ~ ein Risiko eingehen;
give s.o. a ~ jdm eine Chance geben
● attrib zufällig ● vt ~ it es riskieren
chancellor /'tʃɑːnsələ(r)/ n Kanzler
m; (Univ) Rektor m; C~ of the
Exchequer Schatzkanzler m
chancy /'tʃɑːnsɪ/ a riskant
chandelier /ʃændə'lɪə(r)/ n Kronleuchter m
change /tʃeɪndʒ/ n Veränderung f;
(alteration) Änderung f; (money)

Wechselgeld *nt*; **for a ~** zur Abwechslung ● *vt* wechseln; (*alter*) ändern; (*exchange*) umtauschen (**for** gegen); (*transform*) verwandeln; trocken legen ⟨*baby*⟩; **~ one's clothes** sich umziehen; **~ trains** umsteigen ● *vi* sich verändern; (**~** *clothes*) sich umziehen; (**~** *trains*) umsteigen; **all ~!** alles aussteigen!

changeable /'tʃeɪndʒəbl/ *a* wechselhaft

'**changing-room** *n* Umkleideraum *m*

channel /'tʃænl/ *n* Rinne *f*; (*Radio, TV*) Kanal *m*; (*fig*) Weg *m*; **the [English] C~** der Ärmelkanal; **the C~ Islands** die Kanalinseln ● *vt* (*pt/pp* **channelled**) leiten; (*fig*) lenken

chant /tʃɑːnt/ *n* liturgischer Gesang *m* ● *vt* singen; ⟨*demonstrators:*⟩ skandieren

chao|s /'keɪɒs/ *n* Chaos *nt*. **~tic** /-'ɒtɪk/ *a* chaotisch

chap /tʃæp/ *n* (*fam*) Kerl *m*

chapel /'tʃæpl/ *n* Kapelle *f*

chaperon /'ʃæpərəʊn/ *n* Anstandsdame *f* ● *vt* begleiten

chaplain /'tʃæplɪn/ *n* Geistliche(r) *m*

chapped /tʃæpt/ *a* ⟨*skin*⟩ aufgesprungen

chapter /'tʃæptə(r)/ *n* Kapitel *nt*

char[1] /tʃɑː(r)/ *n* (*fam*) Putzfrau *f*

char[2] *vt* (*pt/pp* **charred**) (*burn*) verkohlen

character /'kærɪktə(r)/ *n* Charakter *m*; (*in novel, play*) Gestalt *f*; (*Typ*) Schriftzeichen *nt*; **out of ~** uncharakteristisch; **quite a ~** (*fam*) ein Original

characteristic /kærɪktə'rɪstɪk/ *a*, **-ally** *adv* charakteristisch (**of** für) ● *n* Merkmal *nt*

characterize /'kærɪktəraɪz/ *vt* charakterisieren

charade /ʃə'rɑːd/ *n* Scharade *f*

charcoal /'tʃɑː-/ *n* Holzkohle *f*

charge /tʃɑːdʒ/ *n* (*price*) Gebühr *f*; (*Electr*) Ladung *f*; (*attack*) Angriff *m*; (*Jur*) Anklage *f*; **free of ~** kostenlos; **be in ~** verantwortlich sein (**of** für); **take ~** die Aufsicht übernehmen (**of** über + *acc*) ● *vt* berechnen (*fee*); (*Electr*) laden; (*attack*) angreifen; (*Jur*) anklagen (**with** *gen*); **~ s.o. for sth** jdm etw berechnen ● *vi* (*attack*) angreifen

chariot /'tʃærɪət/ *n* Wagen *m*

charisma /kə'rɪzmə/ *n* Charisma *nt*. **~tic** /kærɪz'mætɪk/ *a* charismatisch

charitable /'tʃærɪtəbl/ *a* wohltätig; ⟨*kind*⟩ wohlwollend

charity /'tʃærətɪ/ *n* Nächstenliebe *f*; (*organization*) wohltätige Einrichtung *f*; **for ~** für Wohltätigkeitszwecke; **live on ~** von Almosen leben

charlatan /'ʃɑːlətən/ *n* Scharlatan *m*

charm /tʃɑːm/ *n* Reiz *m*; (*of person*) Charme *f*; (*object*) Amulett *nt* ● *vt* bezaubern. **~ing** *a*, **-ly** *adv* reizend; ⟨*person, smile*⟩ charmant

chart /tʃɑːt/ *n* Karte *f*; (*table*) Tabelle *f*

charter /'tʃɑːtə(r)/ *n* **~** [**flight**] Charterflug *m* ● *vt* chartern; **~ed accountant** Wirtschaftsprüfer(in) *m(f)*

charwoman /'tʃɑː-/ *n* Putzfrau *f*

chase /tʃeɪs/ *n* Verfolgungsjagd *f* ● *vt* jagen, verfolgen. **~ away** *or* **off** *vt* wegjagen

chasm /'kæzm/ *n* Kluft *f*

chassis /'ʃæsɪ/ *n* (*pl* **chassis** /-sɪz/) Chassis *nt*

chaste /tʃeɪst/ *a* keusch

chastise /tʃæ'staɪz/ *vt* züchtigen

chastity /'tʃæstətɪ/ *n* Keuschheit *f*

chat /tʃæt/ *n* Plauderei *f*; **have a ~ with** plaudern mit ● *vi* (*pt/pp* **chatted**) plaudern. **~ show** *n* Talk-Show *f*

chatter /'tʃætə(r)/ *n* Geschwätz *nt* ● *vi* schwatzen; ⟨*child:*⟩ plappern; ⟨*teeth:*⟩ klappern. **~box** *n* (*fam*) Plappermaul *nt*

chatty /'tʃætɪ/ *a* (**-ier**, **-iest**) geschwätzig

chauffeur /'ʃəʊfə(r)/ *n* Chauffeur *m*

chauvin|ism /'ʃəʊvɪnɪzm/ *n* Chauvinismus *m*. **~ist** *n* Chauvinist *m*; **male ~ist** (*fam*) Chauvi *m*

cheap /tʃiːp/ *a* & *adv* (**-er**, **-est**), **-ly** *adv* billig. **~en** *vt* entwürdigen; **~en oneself** sich erniedrigen

cheat /tʃiːt/ *n* Betrüger(in) *m(f)*; (*at games*) Mogler *m* ● *vt* betrügen ● *vi* (*at games*) mogeln (*fam*)

check[1] /tʃek/ *a* (*squared*) kariert ● *n* Karo *nt*

check[2] *n* Überprüfung *f*; (*inspection*) Kontrolle *f*; (*Chess*) Schach *nt*; (*Amer: bill*) Rechnung *f*; (*Amer: cheque*) Scheck *m*; (*Amer: tick*) Haken *m*; **keep a ~ on** kontrollieren ● *vt* [über]prüfen; (*inspect*) kontrollieren; (*restrain*) hemmen; (*stop*) aufhalten ● *vi* [**go and**] **~** nachsehen. **~ in** *vi* sich anmelden; (*Aviat*) einchecken ● *vt* abfertigen; einchecken. **~ out** *vi* sich abmelden.

~ **up** *vi* prüfen, kontrollieren; ~ **up on** überprüfen

check|ed /tʃekt/ *a* kariert. ~**ers** *n* (*Amer*) Damespiel *nt*

check: ~**mate** *int* schachmatt! ~**-out** *n* Kasse *f*. ~**room** *n* (*Amer*) Garderobe *f*. ~**-up** *n* (*Med*) [Kontroll]untersuchung *f*

cheek /tʃiːk/ *n* Backe *f*; (*impudence*) Frechheit *f*. ~**y** *a*, **-ily** *adv* frech

cheep /tʃiːp/ *vi* piepen

cheer /tʃɪə(r)/ *n* Beifallsruf *m*; **three** ~**s** ein dreifaches Hoch (**for** auf + *acc*); ~**s!** prost! (*goodbye*) tschüs! ● *vt* zujubeln (+ *dat*) ● *vi* jubeln. ~ **up** *vt* aufmuntern; aufheitern ● *vi* munterer werden. ~**ful** *a*, **-ly** *adv* fröhlich. ~**fulness** *n* Fröhlichkeit *f*

cheerio /tʃɪərɪˈəʊ/ *int* (*fam*) tschüs!

'**cheerless** *a* trostlos

cheese /tʃiːz/ *n* Käse *m*. ~**cake** *n* Käsekuchen *m*

cheetah /'tʃiːtə/ *n* Gepard *m*

chef /ʃef/ *n* Koch *m*

chemical /'kemɪkl/ *a*, **-ly** *adv* chemisch ● *n* Chemikalie *f*

chemist /'kemɪst/ *n* (*pharmacist*) Apotheker(in) *m*(*f*); (*scientist*) Chemiker(in) *m*(*f*); ~'**s [shop]** Drogerie *f*; (*dispensing*) Apotheke *f*. ~**ry** *n* Chemie *f*

cheque /tʃek/ *n* Scheck *m*. ~**-book** *n* Scheckbuch *nt*. ~ **card** *n* Scheckkarte *f*

cherish /'tʃerɪʃ/ *vt* lieben; (*fig*) hegen

cherry /'tʃerɪ/ *n* Kirsche *f* ● *attrib* Kirsch-

cherub /'tʃerəb/ *n* Engelchen *nt*

chess /tʃes/ *n* Schach *nt*

chess: ~**board** *n* Schachbrett *nt*. ~**-man** *n* Schachfigur *f*

chest /tʃest/ *n* Brust *f*; (*box*) Truhe *f*

chestnut /'tʃesnʌt/ *n* Eßkastanie *f*, Marone *f*; (*horse-*) [Roß]kastanie *f*

chest of 'drawers *n* Kommode *f*

chew /tʃuː/ *vt* kauen. ~**ing-gum** *n* Kaugummi *m*

chic /ʃiːk/ *a* schick

chick /tʃɪk/ *n* Küken *nt*

chicken /'tʃɪkɪn/ *n* Huhn *nt* ● *attrib* Hühner- ● *a* (*fam*) feige ● *vi* ~ **out** (*fam*) kneifen. ~**pox** *n* Windpocken *pl*

chicory /'tʃɪkərɪ/ *n* Chicorée *f*; (*in coffee*) Zichorie *f*

chief /tʃiːf/ *a* Haupt- ● *n* Chef *m*; (*of tribe*) Häuptling *m*. ~**ly** *adv* hauptsächlich

chilblain /'tʃɪlbleɪn/ *n* Frostbeule *f*

child /tʃaɪld/ *n* (*pl* ~**ren**) Kind *nt*

child: ~**birth** *n* Geburt *f*. ~**hood** *n* Kindheit *f*. ~**ish** *a* kindisch. ~**less** *a* kinderlos. ~**like** *a* kindlich. ~**-minder** *n* Tagesmutter *f*

children /'tʃɪldrən/ *npl see* **child**

Chile /'tʃɪlɪ/ *n* Chile *nt*

chill /tʃɪl/ *n* Kälte *f*; (*illness*) Erkältung *f* ● *vt* kühlen

chilli /'tʃɪlɪ/ *n* (*pl* -**es**) Chili *m*

chilly /'tʃɪlɪ/ *a* kühl; **I felt** ~ mich fröstelte [es]

chime /tʃaɪm/ *vi* läuten; ⟨*clock:*⟩ schlagen

chimney /'tʃɪmnɪ/ *n* Schornstein *m*. ~**-pot** *n* Schornsteinaufsatz *m*. ~**-sweep** *n* Schornsteinfeger *m*

chimpanzee /tʃɪmpæn'ziː/ *n* Schimpanse *m*

chin /tʃɪn/ *n* Kinn *nt*

china /'tʃaɪnə/ *n* Porzellan *nt*

Chin|a *n* China *nt*. ~**ese** /-'niːz/ *a* chinesisch ● *n* (*Lang*) Chinesisch *nt*; **the** ~**ese** *pl* die Chinesen. ~**ese 'lantern** *n* Lampion *m*

chink[1] /tʃɪŋk/ *n* (*slit*) Ritze *f*

chink[2] *n* Geklirr *nt* ● *vi* klirren; ⟨*coins:*⟩ klimpern

chip /tʃɪp/ *n* (*fragment*) Span *m*; (*in china, paintwork*) angeschlagene Stelle *f*; (*Computing, Gambling*) Chip *m*; ~**s** *pl* (*Culin*) Pommes frites *pl*; (*Amer: crisps*) Chips *pl* ● *vt* (*pt/pp* **chipped**) (*damage*) anschlagen. ~**ped** *a* angeschlagen

chiropod|ist /kɪ'rɒpədɪst/ *n* Fußpfleger(in) *m*(*f*). ~**y** *n* Fußpflege *f*

chirp /tʃɜːp/ *vi* zwitschern; ⟨*cricket:*⟩ zirpen. ~**y** *a* (*fam*) munter

chisel /'tʃɪzl/ *n* Meißel *m* ● *vt/i* (*pt/pp* **chiselled**) meißeln

chit /tʃɪt/ *n* Zettel *m*

chival|rous /'ʃɪvlrəs/ *a*, **-ly** *adv* ritterlich. ~**ry** *n* Ritterlichkeit *f*

chives /tʃaɪvz/ *npl* Schnittlauch *m*

chlorine /'klɔːriːn/ *n* Chlor *nt*

chloroform /'klɒrəfɔːm/ *n* Chloroform *nt*

chocolate /'tʃɒkələt/ *n* Schokolade *f*; (*sweet*) Praline *f*

choice /tʃɔɪs/ *n* Wahl *f*; (*variety*) Auswahl *f* ● *a* auserlesen

choir /'kwaɪə(r)/ *n* Chor *m*. ~**boy** *n* Chorknabe *m*

choke /tʃəʊk/ *n* (*Auto*) Choke *m* ● *vt* würgen; (*to death*) erwürgen ● *vi* sich verschlucken; ~ **on** [fast] ersticken an (+ *dat*)

cholera /'kɒlərə/ *n* Cholera *f*

cholesterol /kə'lestərɒl/ *n* Cholesterin *nt*

choose /tʃuːz/ *vt/i* (*pt* **chose**, *pp* **chosen**) wählen; (*select*) sich (*dat*) aussuchen; ~ **to do/go** [freiwillig] tun/gehen; **as you** ~ wie Sie wollen

choos[e]y /'tʃuːzɪ/ *a* (*fam*) wählerisch

chop /tʃɒp/ *n* (*blow*) Hieb *m*; (*Culin*) Kotelett *nt* ● *vt* (*pt/pp* **chopped**) hacken. ~ **down** *vt* abhacken; fällen ⟨*tree*⟩. ~ **off** *vt* abhacken

chop|per /'tʃɒpə(r)/ *n* Beil *nt*; (*fam*) Hubschrauber *m*. ~**py** *a* kabbelig

'chopsticks *npl* Eßstäbchen *pl*

choral /'kɔːrəl/ *a* Chor-; ~ **society** Gesangverein *m*

chord /kɔːd/ *n* (*Mus*) Akkord *m*

chore /tʃɔː(r)/ *n* lästige Pflicht *f*; **[household]** ~s Hausarbeit *f*

choreography /kɒrɪ'ɒɡrəfɪ/ *n* Choreographie *f*

chortle /'tʃɔːtl/ *vi* [vor Lachen] glucksen

chorus /'kɔːrəs/ *n* Chor *m*; (*of song*) Refrain *m*

chose, chosen /tʃəʊz, 'tʃəʊzn/ *see* **choose**

Christ /kraɪst/ *n* Christus *m*

christen /'krɪsn/ *vt* taufen. ~**ing** *n* Taufe *f*

Christian /'krɪstʃən/ *a* christlich ● *n* Christ(in) *m*(*f*). ~**ity** /-stɪ'ænətɪ/ *n* Christentum *nt*. ~ **name** *n* Vorname *m*

Christmas /'krɪsməs/ *n* Weihnachten *nt*. ~ **card** *n* Weihnachtskarte *f*. ~ **'Day** *n* erster Weihnachtstag *m*. ~ **'Eve** *n* Heiligabend *m*. ~ **tree** *n* Weihnachtsbaum *m*

chrome /krəʊm/ *n*, **chromium** /'krəʊmɪəm/ *n* Chrom *nt*

chromosome /'krəʊməsəʊm/ *n* Chromosom *nt*

chronic /'krɒnɪk/ *a* chronisch

chronicle /'krɒnɪkl/ *n* Chronik *f*

chronological /krɒnə'lɒdʒɪkl/ *a*, **-ly** *adv* chronologisch

chrysalis /'krɪsəlɪs/ *n* Puppe *f*

chrysanthemum /krɪ'sænθəməm/ *n* Chrysantheme *f*

chubby /'tʃʌbɪ/ *a* (**-ier, -iest**) mollig

chuck /tʃʌk/ *vt* (*fam*) schmeißen. ~ **out** *vt* (*fam*) rausschmeißen

chuckle /'tʃʌkl/ *vi* in sich (*acc*) hineinlachen

chum /tʃʌm/ *n* Freund(in) *m*(*f*)

chunk /tʃʌŋk/ *n* Stück *nt*

church /tʃɜːtʃ/ *n* Kirche *f*. ~**yard** *n* Friedhof *m*

churlish /'tʃɜːlɪʃ/ *a* unhöflich

churn /tʃɜːn/ *n* Butterfaß *nt*; (*for milk*) Milchkanne *f* ● *vt* ~ **out** am laufenden Band produzieren

chute /ʃuːt/ *n* Rutsche *f*; (*for rubbish*) Müllschlucker *m*

CID *abbr* (**Criminal Investigation Department**) Kripo *f*

cider /'saɪdə(r)/ *n* Apfelwein *m*

cigar /sɪ'ɡɑː(r)/ *n* Zigarre *f*

cigarette /sɪɡə'ret/ *n* Zigarette *f*

cine-camera /'sɪnɪ-/ *n* Filmkamera *f*

cinema /'sɪnɪmə/ *n* Kino *nt*

cinnamon /'sɪnəmən/ *n* Zimt *m*

cipher /'saɪfə(r)/ *n* (*code*) Chiffre *f*; (*numeral*) Ziffer *f*; (*fig*) Null *f*

circle /'sɜːkl/ *n* Kreis *m*; (*Theat*) Rang *m* ● *vt* umkreisen ● *vi* kreisen

circuit /'sɜːkɪt/ *n* Runde *f*; (*racetrack*) Rennbahn *f*; (*Electr*) Stromkreis *m*. ~**ous** /sə'kjuːɪtəs/ *a* ~ **route** Um- weg *m*

circular /'sɜːkjʊlə(r)/ *a* kreisförmig ● *n* Rundschreiben *nt*. ~ **'saw** *n* Kreissäge *f*. ~ **'tour** *n* Rundfahrt *f*

circulat|e /'sɜːkjʊleɪt/ *vt* in Umlauf setzen ● *vi* zirkulieren. ~**ion** /-'leɪʃn/ *n* Kreislauf *m*; (*of newspaper*) Auflage *f*

circumcis|e /'sɜːkəmsaɪz/ *vt* beschneiden. ~**ion** /-'sɪʒn/ *n* Beschneidung *f*

circumference /sə'kʌmfərəns/ *n* Umfang *m*

circumspect /'sɜːkəmspekt/ *a*, **-ly** *adv* umsichtig

circumstance /'sɜːkəmstəns/ *n* Umstand *m*; ~**s** *pl* Umstände *pl*; (*financial*) Verhältnisse *pl*

circus /'sɜːkəs/ *n* Zirkus *m*

CIS *abbr* (**Commonwealth of Independent States**) GUS *f*

cistern /'sɪstən/ *n* (*tank*) Wasserbehälter *m*; (*of WC*) Spülkasten *m*

cite /saɪt/ *vt* zitieren

citizen /'sɪtɪzn/ *n* Bürger(in) *m*(*f*). ~**ship** *n* Staatsangehörigkeit *f*

citrus /'sɪtrəs/ *n* ~ **[fruit]** Zitrusfrucht *f*

city /'sɪtɪ/ *n* [Groß]stadt *f*

civic /'sɪvɪk/ *a* Bürger-
civil /'sɪvl/ *a* bürgerlich; ⟨*aviation, defence*⟩ zivil; (*polite*) höflich. ~ **engi'neering** *n* Hoch- und Tiefbau *m*
civilian /sɪ'vɪljən/ *a* Zivil-; **in** ~ **clothes** in Zivil ● *n* Zivilist *m*
civility /sɪ'vɪlətɪ/ *n* Höflichkeit *f*
civiliz|ation /sɪvəlaɪ'zeɪʃn/ *n* Zivilisation *f*. ~**e** /'sɪvəlaɪz/ *vt* zivilisieren
civil: ~ '**servant** *n* Beamte(r) *m*/ Beamtin *f*. **C**~ '**Service** *n* Staatsdienst *m*
clad /klæd/ *a* gekleidet (**in** in + *acc*)
claim /kleɪm/ *n* Anspruch *m*; (*application*) Antrag *m*; (*demand*) Forderung *f*; (*assertion*) Behauptung *f* ● *vt* beanspruchen; (*apply for*) beantragen; (*demand*) fordern; (*assert*) behaupten; (*collect*) abholen. ~**ant** *n* Antragsteller *m*
clairvoyant /kleə'vɔɪənt/ *n* Hellseher(in) *m*(*f*)
clam /klæm/ *n* Klaffmuschel *f*
clamber /'klæmbə(r)/ *vi* klettern
clammy /'klæmɪ/ *a* (**-ier, -iest**) feucht
clamour /'klæmə(r)/ *n* Geschrei *nt* ● *vi* ~ **for** schreien nach
clamp /klæmp/ *n* Klammer *f* ● *vt* [ein]spannen ● *vi* (*fam*) ~ **down** durchgreifen; ~ **down on** vorgehen gegen
clan /klæn/ *n* Clan *m*
clandestine /klæn'destɪn/ *a* geheim
clang /klæŋ/ *n* Schmettern *nt*. ~**er** *n* (*fam*) Schnitzer *m*
clank /klæŋk/ *vi* klirren
clap /klæp/ *n* **give s.o. a** ~ jdm Beifall klatschen; ~ **of thunder** Donnerschlag *m* ● *vt/i* (*pt/pp* **clapped**) Beifall klatschen (+ *dat*); ~ **one's hands** [in die Hände] klatschen
claret /'klærət/ *n* roter Bordeaux *m*
clari|fication /klærɪfɪ'keɪʃn/ *n* Klärung *f*. ~**fy** /'klærɪfaɪ/ *vt/i* (*pt/pp* **-ied**) klären
clarinet /klærɪ'net/ *n* Klarinette *f*
clarity /'klærətɪ/ *n* Klarheit *f*
clash /klæʃ/ *n* Geklirr *nt*; (*fig*) Konflikt *m* ● *vi* klirren; ⟨*colours:*⟩ sich beißen; ⟨*events:*⟩ ungünstig zusammenfallen
clasp /klɑːsp/ *n* Verschluß *m* ● *vt* ergreifen; (*hold*) halten
class /klɑːs/ *n* Klasse *f*; **first/second** ~ erster/zweiter Klasse ● *vt* einordnen
classic /'klæsɪk/ *a* klassisch ● *n* Klassiker *m*; ~**s** *pl* (*Univ*) Altphilologie *f*. ~**al** *a* klassisch

classi|fication /klæsɪfɪ'keɪʃn/ *n* Klassifikation *f*. ~**fy** /'klæsɪfaɪ/ *vt* (*pt/pp* **-ied**) klassifizieren
'**classroom** *n* Klassenzimmer *nt*
classy /'klɑːsɪ/ *a* (**-ier, -iest**) (*fam*) schick
clatter /'klætə(r)/ *n* Geklapper *nt* ● *vi* klappern
clause /klɔːz/ *n* Klausel *f*; (*Gram*) Satzteil *m*
claustrophobia /klɔːstrə'fəʊbɪə/ *n* Klaustrophobie *f*, (*fam*) Platzangst *f*
claw /klɔː/ *n* Kralle *f*; (*of bird of prey* & *Techn*) Klaue *f*; (*of crab, lobster*) Schere *f* ● *vt* kratzen
clay /kleɪ/ *n* Lehm *m*; (*pottery*) Ton *m*
clean /kliːn/ *a* (**-er, -est**) sauber ● *adv* glatt ● *vt* saubermachen; putzen ⟨*shoes, windows*⟩; ~ **one's teeth** sich (*dat*) die Zähne putzen; **have sth** ~**ed** etw reinigen lassen. ~ **up** *vt* saubermachen
cleaner /'kliːnə(r)/ *n* Putzfrau *f*; (*substance*) Reinigungsmittel *nt*; [**dry**] ~'**s** chemische Reinigung *f*
cleanliness /'klenlɪnɪs/ *n* Sauberkeit *f*
cleanse /klenz/ *vt* reinigen. ~**r** *n* Reinigungsmittel *nt*
clean-shaven *a* glattrasiert
cleansing cream /'klenz-/ *n* Reinigungscreme *f*
clear /klɪə(r)/ *a* (**-er, -est**), **-ly** *adv* klar; (*obvious*) eindeutig; (*distinct*) deutlich; ⟨*conscience*⟩ rein; (*without obstacles*) frei; **make sth** ~ etw klarmachen (**to** *dat*) ● *adv* **stand** ~ zurücktreten; **keep** ~ **of** aus dem Wege gehen (+ *dat*) ● *vt* räumen; abräumen ⟨*table*⟩; (*acquit*) freisprechen; (*authorize*) genehmigen; (*jump over*) überspringen; ~ **one's throat** sich räuspern ● *vi* ⟨*fog:*⟩ sich auflösen. ~ **away** *vt* wegräumen. ~ **off** *vi* (*fam*) abhauen. ~ **out** *vt* ausräumen ● *vi* (*fam*) abhauen. ~ **up** *vt* (*tidy*) aufräumen; (*solve*) aufklären ● *vi* ⟨*weather:*⟩ sich aufklären
clearance /'klɪərəns/ *n* Räumung *f*; (*authorization*) Genehmigung *f*; (*customs*) [Zoll]abfertigung *f*; (*Techn*) Spielraum *m*. ~ **sale** *n* Räumungsverkauf *m*
clear|ing /'klɪərɪŋ/ *n* Lichtung *f*. ~**way** *n* (*Auto*) Straße *f* mit Halteverbot
cleavage /'kliːvɪdʒ/ *n* Spaltung *f*; (*woman's*) Dekolleté *nt*
clef /klef/ *n* Notenschlüssel *m*

cleft /kleft/ n Spalte f

clemen|cy /'klemənsɪ/ n Milde f. ∼t a mild

clench /klentʃ/ vt ∼ one's fist die Faust ballen; ∼ one's teeth die Zähne zusammenbeißen

clergy /'klɜːdʒɪ/ npl Geistlichkeit f. ∼man n Geistliche(r) m

cleric /'klerɪk/ n Geistliche(r) m. ∼al a Schreib-; (Relig) geistlich

clerk /klɑːk, Amer: klɜːk/ n Büroangestellte(r) m/f; (Amer: shop assistant) Verkäufer(in) m(f)

clever /'klevə(r)/ a (-er, -est), -ly adv klug; (skilful) geschickt

cliché /'kliːʃeɪ/ n Klischee nt

click /klɪk/ vi klicken

client /'klaɪənt/ n Kunde m/Kundin f; (Jur) Klient(in) m(f)

clientele /kliːɒn'tel/ n Kundschaft f

cliff /klɪf/ n Kliff nt

climat|e /'klaɪmət/ n Klima nt. ∼ic /-'mætɪk/ a klimatisch

climax /'klaɪmæks/ n Höhepunkt m

climb /klaɪm/ n Aufstieg m ● vt besteigen (mountain); steigen auf (+ acc) (ladder, tree) ● vi klettern; (rise) steigen (road:) ansteigen. ∼ down vi hinunter-/herunterklettern; (from ladder, tree) heruntersteigen; (fam) nachgeben.

climber /'klaɪmə(r)/ n Bergsteiger m; (plant) Kletterpflanze f

clinch /klɪntʃ/ vt perfekt machen (deal) ● vi (boxing) clinchen

cling /klɪŋ/ vi (pt/pp clung) sich klammern (to an + acc); (stick) haften (to an + dat). ∼ film n Sichtfolie f mit Hafteffekt

clinic /'klɪnɪk/ n Klinik f. ∼al a, -ly adv klinisch

clink /klɪŋk/ n Klirren nt; (fam: prison) Knast m ● vi klirren

clip[1] /klɪp/ n Klammer f; (jewellery) Klipp m ● vt (pt/pp clipped) anklammern (to an + acc)

clip[2] n (extract) Ausschnitt m ● vt schneiden; knipsen (ticket). ∼board n Klemmbrett nt. ∼pers npl Schere f. ∼ping n (extract) Ausschnitt m

clique /kliːk/ n Clique f

cloak /kləʊk/ n Umhang m. ∼room n Garderobe f; (toilet) Toilette f

clobber /'klɒbə(r)/ n (fam) Zeug nt ● vt (fam: hit, defeat) schlagen

clock /klɒk/ n Uhr f; (fam: speedometer) Tacho m ● vi ∼ in/out stechen

clock: ∼ tower n Uhrenturm m. ∼wise a & adv im Uhrzeigersinn. ∼work n Uhrwerk nt; (of toy) Aufziehmechanismus m; like ∼work (fam) wie am Schnürchen

clod /klɒd/ n Klumpen m

clog /klɒg/ n Holzschuh m ● vt/i (pt/pp clogged) ∼ [up] verstopfen

cloister /'klɔɪstə(r)/ n Kreuzgang m

close[1] /kləʊs/ a (-r, -st) nah[e] (to dat); (friend) eng; (weather) schwül; have a ∼ shave (fam) mit knapper Not davonkommen ● adv nahe; ∼ by nicht weit weg ● n (street) Sackgasse f

close[2] /kləʊz/ n Ende nt; draw to a ∼ sich dem Ende nähern ● vt zumachen, schließen; (bring to an end) beenden; sperren (road) ● vi sich schließen; (shop:) schließen, zumachen; (end) enden. ∼ down vt schließen; stillegen (factory) ● vi schließen; (factory:) stillgelegt werden

closed 'shop /kləʊzd-/ n ≈ Gewerkschaftszwang m

closely /'kləʊslɪ/ adv eng, nah[e]; (with attention) genau

close season /'kləʊs-/ n Schonzeit f

closet /'klɒzɪt/ n (Amer) Schrank m

close-up /'kləʊs-/ n Nahaufnahme f

closure /'kləʊʒə(r)/ n Schließung f; (of factory) Stillegung f; (of road) Sperrung f

clot /klɒt/ n [Blut]gerinnsel nt; (fam: idiot) Trottel m ● vi (pt/pp clotted) (blood:) gerinnen

cloth /klɒθ/ n Tuch nt

clothe /kləʊð/ vt kleiden

clothes /kləʊðz/ npl Kleider pl. ∼-brush n Kleiderbürste f. ∼-line n Wäscheleine f

clothing /'kləʊðɪŋ/ n Kleidung f

cloud /klaʊd/ n Wolke f ● vi ∼ over sich bewölken. ∼burst n Wolkenbruch m

cloudy /'klaʊdɪ/ a (-ier, -iest) wolkig, bewölkt; (liquid) trübe

clout /klaʊt/ n (fam) Schlag m; (influence) Einfluß m ● vt (fam) hauen

clove /kləʊv/ n [Gewürz]nelke f; ∼ of garlic Knoblauchzehe f

clover /'kləʊvə(r)/ n Klee m. ∼ leaf n Kleeblatt nt

clown /klaʊn/ n Clown m ● vi ∼ [about] herumalbern

club /klʌb/ n Klub m; (weapon) Keule f; (Sport) Schläger m; ∼s pl (Cards) Kreuz nt, Treff nt ● v (pt/pp clubbed)

● *vt* knüppeln ● *vi* ~ **together** zusammenlegen

cluck /klʌk/ *vi* glucken

clue /klu:/ *n* Anhaltspunkt *m*; (*in crossword*) Frage *f*; **I haven't a** ~ (*fam*) ich habe keine Ahnung

clump /klʌmp/ *n* Gruppe *f*

clumsiness /'klʌmzɪnɪs/ *n* Ungeschicklichkeit *f*

clumsy /'klʌmzɪ/ *a* (**-ier, -iest**), **-ily** *adv* ungeschickt; (*unwieldy*) unförmig

clung /klʌŋ/ *see* cling

cluster /'klʌstə(r)/ *n* Gruppe *f*; (*of flowers*) Büschel *nt* ● *vi* sich scharen (**round** um)

clutch /klʌtʃ/ *n* Griff *m*; (*Auto*) Kupplung *f*; **be in s.o.'s** ~**es** (*fam*) in jds Klauen sein ● *vt* festhalten; (*grab*) ergreifen ● *vi* ~ **at** greifen nach

clutter /'klʌtə(r)/ *n* Kram *m* ● *vt* ~ **[up]** vollstopfen

c/o *abbr* (**care of**) bei

coach /kəʊtʃ/ *n* [Reise]bus *m*; (*Rail*) Wagen *m*; (*horse-drawn*) Kutsche *f*; (*Sport*) Trainer *m* ● *vt* Nachhilfestunden geben (+ *dat*); (*Sport*) trainieren

coagulate /kəʊ'ægjʊleɪt/ *vi* gerinnen

coal /kəʊl/ *n* Kohle *f*

coalition /kəʊə'lɪʃn/ *n* Koalition *f*

'coal-mine *n* Kohlenbergwerk *nt*

coarse /kɔ:s/ *a* (**-r, -st**), **-ly** *adv* grob

coast /kəʊst/ *n* Küste *f* ● *vi* (*free-wheel*) im Freilauf fahren; (*Auto*) im Leerlauf fahren. ~**al** *a* Küsten-. ~**er** *n* (*mat*) Untersatz *m*

coast: ~**guard** *n* Küstenwache *f*. ~**line** *n* Küste *f*

coat /kəʊt/ *n* Mantel *m*; (*of animal*) Fell *nt*; (*of paint*) Anstrich *m*; ~ **of arms** Wappen *nt* ● *vt* überziehen; (*with paint*) [an]streichen. ~- **hanger** *n* Kleiderbügel *m*. ~**-hook** *n* Kleiderhaken *m*

coating /'kəʊtɪŋ/ *n* Überzug *m*, Schicht *f*; (*of paint*) Anstrich *m*

coax /kəʊks/ *vt* gut zureden (+ *dat*)

cob /kɒb/ *n* (*of corn*) [Mais]kolben *m*

cobble¹ /'kɒbl/ *n* Kopfstein *m*; ~**s** *pl* Kopfsteinpflaster *nt*

cobble² *vt* flicken. ~**r** *m* Schuster *m*

'cobblestones *npl* = **cobbles**

cobweb /'kɒb-/ *n* Spinnengewebe *nt*

cocaine /kə'keɪn/ *n* Kokain *nt*

cock /kɒk/ *n* Hahn *m*; (*any male bird*) Männchen *nt* ● *vt* ⟨*animal:*⟩ ~ **its ears** die Ohren spitzen; ~ **the gun** den Hahn

spannen. ~**-and-'bull story** *n* (*fam*) Lügengeschichte *f*

cockerel /'kɒkərəl/ *n* [junger] Hahn *m*

cock-'eyed *a* (*fam*) schief; (*absurd*) verrückt

cockle /'kɒkl/ *n* Herzmuschel *f*

cockney /'kɒknɪ/ *n* (*dialect*) Cockney *nt*; (*person*) Cockney *m*

cock: ~**pit** *n* (*Aviat*) Cockpit *nt*. ~**roach** /-rəʊtʃ/ *n* Küchenschabe *f*. ~**tail** *n* Cocktail *m*. ~**-up** *n* (*sl*) **make a** ~**-up** Mist bauen (**of** bei)

cocky /'kɒkɪ/ *a* (**-ier, -iest**) (*fam*) eingebildet

cocoa /'kəʊkəʊ/ *n* Kakao *m*

coconut /'kəʊkənʌt/ *n* Kokosnuß *f*

cocoon /kə'ku:n/ *n* Kokon *m*

cod /kɒd/ *n inv* Kabeljau *m*

COD *abbr* (**cash on delivery**) per Nachnahme

coddle /'kɒdl/ *vt* verhätscheln

code /kəʊd/ *n* Kode *m*; (*Computing*) Code *m*; (*set of rules*) Kodex *m*. ~**d** *a* verschlüsselt

coedu'cational /kəʊ-/ *a* gemischt. ~ **school** *n* Koedukationsschule *f*

coerc|e /kəʊ'ɜ:s/ *vt* zwingen. ~**ion** /-'ɜ:ʃn/ *n* Zwang *m*

coe'xist *vi* koexistieren. ~**ence** *n* Koexistenz *f*

coffee /'kɒfɪ/ *n* Kaffee *m*

coffee: ~**-grinder** *n* Kaffeemühle *f*. ~**-pot** *n* Kaffeekanne *f*. ~**-table** *n* Couchtisch *m*

coffin /'kɒfɪn/ *n* Sarg *m*

cog /kɒg/ *n* (*Techn*) Zahn *m*

cogent /'kəʊdʒənt/ *a* überzeugend

cog-wheel *n* Zahnrad *nt*

cohabit /kəʊ'hæbɪt/ *vi* (*Jur*) zusammenleben

coherent /kəʊ'hɪərənt/ *a* zusammenhängend; (*comprehensible*) verständlich

coil /kɔɪl/ *n* Rolle *f*; (*Electr*) Spule *f*; (*one ring*) Windung *f* ● *vt* ~ **[up]** zusammenrollen

coin /kɔɪn/ *n* Münze *f* ● *vt* prägen

coincide /kəʊɪn'saɪd/ *vi* zusammenfallen; (*agree*) übereinstimmen

coinciden|ce /kəʊ'ɪnsɪdəns/ *n* Zufall *m*. ~**tal** /-'dentl/ *a*, **-ly** *adv* zufällig

coke /kəʊk/ *n* Koks *m*

Coke (P) *n* (*drink*) Cola *f*

colander /'kʌləndə(r)/ *n* (*Culin*) Durchschlag *m*

cold /kəʊld/ *a* (**-er, -est**) kalt; **I am** *or* **feel** ~ mir ist kalt ● *n* Kälte *f*; (*Med*) Erkältung *f*

cold: ~-'**blooded** *a* kaltblütig. ~-'**hearted** *a* kaltherzig. ~**ly** *adv* (*fig*) kalt, kühl. ~**ness** *n* Kälte *f*

coleslaw /'kəʊlslɔ:/ *n* Krautsalat *m*

colic /'kɒlɪk/ *n* Kolik *f*

collaborat|e /kə'læbəreɪt/ *vi* zusammenarbeiten (**with** mit); ~**e on sth** mitarbeiten bei etw. ~**ion** /-'reɪʃn/ *n* Zusammenarbeit *f*, Mitarbeit *f*; (*with enemy*) Kollaboration *f*. ~**or** *n* Mitarbeiter(in) *m(f)*; Kollaborateur *m*

collaps|e /kə'læps/ *n* Zusammenbruch *m*; Einsturz *m* ● *vi* zusammenbrechen; ⟨*roof, building:*⟩ einstürzen. ~**ible** *a* zusammenklappbar

collar /'kɒlə(r)/ *n* Kragen *m*; (*for animal*) Halsband *nt*. ~-**bone** *n* Schlüsselbein *nt*

colleague /'kɒli:g/ *n* Kollege *m*/ Kollegin *f*

collect /kə'lekt/ *vt* sammeln; (*fetch*) abholen; einsammeln ⟨*tickets*⟩; einziehen ⟨*taxes*⟩ ● *vi* sich [an]sammeln ● *adv* **call** ~ (*Amer*) ein R-Gespräch führen. ~**ed** /-ɪd/ *a* gesammelt; (*calm*) gefaßt

collection /kə'lekʃn/ *n* Sammlung *f*; (*in church*) Kollekte *f*; (*of post*) Leerung *f*; (*designer's*) Kollektion *f*

collective /kə'lektɪv/ *a* gemeinsam; (*Pol*) kollektiv. ~ '**noun** *n* Kollektivum *nt*

collector /kə'lektə(r)/ *n* Sammler(in) *m(f)*

college /'kɒlɪdʒ/ *n* College *nt*

collide /kə'laɪd/ *vi* zusammenstoßen

colliery /'kɒlɪərɪ/ *n* Kohlengrube *f*

collision /kə'lɪʒn/ *n* Zusammenstoß *m*

colloquial /kə'ləʊkwɪəl/ *a*, -**ly** *adv* umgangssprachlich. ~**ism** *n* umgangssprachlicher Ausdruck *m*

Cologne /kə'ləʊn/ *n* Köln *nt*

colon /'kəʊlən/ *n* Doppelpunkt *m*; (*Anat*) Dickdarm *m*

colonel /'kɜ:nl/ *n* Oberst *m*

colonial /kə'ləʊnɪəl/ *a* Kolonial-

colon|ize /'kɒlənaɪz/ *vt* kolonisieren. ~**y** *n* Kolonie *f*

colossal /kə'lɒsl/ *a* riesig

colour /'kʌlə(r)/ *n* Farbe *f*; (*complexion*) Gesichtsfarbe *f*; (*race*) Hautfarbe *f*; ~**s** *pl* (*flag*) Fahne *f*, **off** ~ (*fam*) nicht ganz auf der Höhe ● *vt* färben; ~ [**in**] ausmalen ● *vi* (*blush*) erröten

colour: ~ **bar** *n* Rassenschranke *f*. ~-**blind** *a* farbenblind. ~**ed** *a* farbig ● *n* (*person*) Farbige(r) *m/f*. ~-**fast** *a* farbecht. ~ **film** *n* Farbfilm *m*. ~**ful** *a* farbenfroh. ~**less** *a* farblos. ~ **photo[graph]** *n* Farbaufnahme *f*. ~ **television** *n* Farbfernsehen *nt*

colt /kəʊlt/ *n* junger Hengst *m*

column /'kɒləm/ *n* Säule *f*; (*of soldiers, figures*) Kolonne *f*; (*Typ*) Spalte *f*; (*Journ*) Kolumne *f*. ~**ist** /-nɪst/ *n* Kolumnist *m*

coma /'kəʊmə/ *n* Koma *nt*

comb /kəʊm/ *n* Kamm *m* ● *vt* kämmen; (*search*) absuchen; ~ **one's hair** sich (*dat*) [die Haare] kämmen

combat /'kɒmbæt/ *n* Kampf *m* ● *vt* (*pt/pp* **combated**) bekämpfen

combination /kɒmbɪ'neɪʃn/ *n* Verbindung *f*; (*for lock*) Kombination *f*

combine[1] /kəm'baɪn/ *vt* verbinden ● *vi* sich verbinden; ⟨*people:*⟩ sich zusammenschließen

combine[2] /'kɒmbaɪn/ *n* (*Comm*) Konzern *m*. ~ [**harvester**] *n* Mähdrescher *m*

combustion /kəm'bʌstʃn/ *n* Verbrennung *f*

come /kʌm/ *vi* (*pt* **came**, *pp* **come**) kommen; (*reach*) reichen (**to an** + *acc*); **that** ~**s to £10** das macht £10; ~ **into money** zu Geld kommen; ~ **true** wahr werden; ~ **in two sizes** in zwei Größen erhältlich sein; **the years to** ~ die kommenden Jahre; **how** ~? (*fam*) wie das? ~ **about** *vi* geschehen. ~ **across** *vi* herüberkommen; (*fam*) klar werden ● *vt* stoßen auf (+ *acc*). ~ **apart** *vi* sich auseinandernehmen lassen; (*accidentally*) auseinandergehen. ~ **away** *vi* weggehen; ⟨*thing:*⟩ abgehen. ~ **back** *vi* zurückkommen. ~ **by** *vi* vorbeikommen ● *vt* (*obtain*) bekommen. ~ **in** *vi* hereinkommen. ~ **off** *vi* abgehen; (*take place*) stattfinden; (*succeed*) klappen (*fam*). ~ **out** *vi* herauskommen; ⟨*book:*⟩ erscheinen; ⟨*stain:*⟩ herausgehen. ~ **round** *vi* vorbeikommen; (*after fainting*) [wieder] zu sich kommen; (*change one's mind*) sich umstimmen lassen. ~ **to** *vi* [wieder] zu sich kommen. ~ **up** *vi* heraufkommen; ⟨*plant:*⟩ aufgehen; (*reach*) reichen (**to** bis); ~ **up with** sich (*dat*) einfallen lassen

'**come-back** *n* Comeback *nt*

comedian /kə'miːdɪən/ n Komiker m

'**come-down** n Rückschritt m

comedy /'kɒmədɪ/ n Komödie f

comet /'kɒmɪt/ n Komet m

come-uppance /kʌm'ʌpəns/ n **get one's ~** (fam) sein Fett abkriegen

comfort /'kʌmfət/ n Bequemlichkeit f; (consolation) Trost m ● vt trösten

comfortable /'kʌmfətəbl/ a, **-bly** adv bequem

'**comfort station** n (Amer) öffentliche Toilette f

comfy /'kʌmfɪ/ a (fam) bequem

comic /'kɒmɪk/ a komisch ● n Komiker m; (periodical) Comic-Heft nt. **~al** a, **-ly** adv komisch. **~ strip** n Comic Strips pl

coming /'kʌmɪŋ/ a kommend ● n Kommen nt; **~s and goings** Kommen und Gehen nt

comma /'kɒmə/ n Komma nt

command /kə'mɑːnd/ n Befehl m; (Mil) Kommando nt; (mastery) Beherrschung f ● vt befehlen (+ dat); kommandieren ⟨army⟩

commandeer /kɒmən'dɪə(r)/ vt beschlagnahmen

command|er /kə'mɑːndə(r)/ n Befehlshaber m; (of unit) Kommandeur m; (of ship) Kommandant m. **~ing** a ⟨view⟩ beherrschend. **~ing officer** n Befehlshaber m. **~ment** n Gebot nt

commemorat|e /kə'meməreɪt/ vt gedenken (+ gen). **~ion** /-'reɪʃn/ n Gedenken nt. **~ive** /-ətɪv/ a Gedenk-

commence /kə'mens/ vt/i anfangen, beginnen. **~ment** n Anfang m, Beginn m

commend /kə'mend/ vt loben; (recommend) empfehlen (**to** dat). **~able** /-əbl/ a lobenswert. **~ation** /kɒmen'deɪʃn/ n Lob nt

commensurate /kə'menʃərət/ a angemessen; **be ~ with** entsprechen (+ dat)

comment /'kɒment/ n Bemerkung f; **no ~!** kein Kommentar! ● vi sich äußern (**on** zu); **~ on** ⟨Journ⟩ kommentieren

commentary /'kɒməntrɪ/ n Kommentar m; **[running] ~** ⟨Radio, TV⟩ Reportage f

commentator /'kɒmənteɪtə(r)/ n Kommentator m; (Sport) Reporter m

commerce /'kɒmɜːs/ n Handel m

commercial /kə'mɜːʃl/ a, **-ly** adv kommerziell ● n ⟨Radio, TV⟩ Werbespot m. **~ize** vt kommerzialisieren

commiserate /kə'mɪzəreɪt/ vi sein Mitleid ausdrücken (**with** dat)

commission /kə'mɪʃn/ n (order for work) Auftrag m; (body of people) Kommission f; (payment) Provision f; (Mil) [Offiziers]patent nt; **out of ~** außer Betrieb ● vt beauftragen ⟨s.o.⟩; in Auftrag geben ⟨thing⟩; (Mil) zum Offizier ernennen

commissionaire /kəmɪʃə'neə(r)/ n Portier m

commissioner /kə'mɪʃənə(r)/ n Kommissar m; **~ for oaths** Notar m

commit /kə'mɪt/ vt (pt/pp committed) begehen; (entrust) anvertrauen (**to** dat); (consign) einweisen (**to** in + acc); **~ oneself** sich festlegen; (involve oneself) sich engagieren; **~ sth to memory** sich (dat) etw einprägen. **~ment** n Verpflichtung f; (involvement) Engagement nt. **~ted** a engagiert

committee /kə'mɪtɪ/ n Ausschuß m, Komitee nt

commodity /kə'mɒdətɪ/ n Ware f

common /'kɒmən/ a (-er, -est) gemeinsam; (frequent) häufig; (ordinary) gewöhnlich; (vulgar) ordinär ● n Gemeindeland nt; **have in ~** gemeinsam haben; **House of C~s** Unterhaus nt. **~er** n Bürgerliche(r) m/f

common: ~ law n Gewohnheitsrecht nt. **~ly** adv allgemein. **C~ 'Market** n Gemeinsamer Markt m. **~place** a häufig. **~-room** n Aufenthaltsraum m. **~ 'sense** n gesunder Menschenverstand m

commotion /kə'məʊʃn/ n Tumult m

communal /'kɒmjʊnl/ a gemeinschaftlich

communicable /kə'mjuːnɪkəbl/ a ⟨disease⟩ übertragbar

communicate /kə'mjuːnɪkeɪt/ vt mitteilen (**to** dat); übertragen ⟨disease⟩ ● vi sich verständigen; (be in touch) Verbindung haben

communication /kəmjuːnɪ'keɪʃn/ n Verständigung f; (contact) Verbindung f; (of disease) Übertragung f; (message) Mitteilung f; **~s** pl (technology) Nachrichtenwesen nt. **~ cord** n Notbremse f

communicative /kə'mjuːnɪkətɪv/ a mitteilsam

Communion /kə'mjuːnɪən/ n [Holy] ~ das [heilige] Abendmahl; (Roman Catholic) die [heilige] Kommunion

communiqué /kə'mjuːnɪkeɪ/ n Kommuniqué nt

Communis|m /'kɒmjʊnɪzm/ n Kommunismus m. ~t /-ɪst/ a kommunistisch ● n Kommunist(in) m(f)

community /kə'mjuːnətɪ/ n Gemeinschaft f; local ~ Gemeinde f. ~ centre n Gemeinschaftszentrum nt

commute /kə'mjuːt/ vi pendeln ● vt (Jur) umwandeln. ~r n Pendler(in) m(f)

compact[1] /kəm'pækt/ a kompakt

compact[2] /'kɒmpækt/ n Puderdose f. ~ disc n CD f

companion /kəm'pænjən/ n Begleiter(in) m(f). ~ship n Gesellschaft f

company /'kʌmpənɪ/ n Gesellschaft f; (firm) Firma f; (Mil) Kompanie f; (fam: guests) Besuch m. ~ car n Firmenwagen m

comparable /'kɒmpərəbl/ a vergleichbar

comparative /kəm'pærətɪv/ a vergleichend; (relative) relativ ● n (Gram) Komparativ m. ~ly adv verhältnismäßig

compare /kəm'peə(r)/ vt vergleichen (with/to mit) ● vi sich vergleichen lassen

comparison /kəm'pærɪsn/ n Vergleich m

compartment /kəm'pɑːtmənt/ n Fach nt; (Rail) Abteil nt

compass /'kʌmpəs/ n Kompaß m. ~es npl pair of ~es Zirkel m

compassion /kəm'pæʃn/ n Mitleid nt. ~ate /-ʃənət/ a mitfühlend

compatible /kəm'pætəbl/ a vereinbar; (drugs) verträglich; (Techn) kompatibel; be ~ (people:) [gut] zueinander passen

compatriot /kəm'pætrɪət/ n Landsmann m/-männin f

compel /kəm'pel/ vt (pt/pp compelled) zwingen

compensat|e /'kɒmpənseɪt/ vt entschädigen ● vi ~e for (fig) ausgleichen. ~ion /-'seɪʃn/ n Entschädigung f; (fig) Ausgleich m

compère /'kɒmpeə(r)/ n Conférencier m

compete /kəm'piːt/ vi konkurrieren; (take part) teilnehmen (in an + dat)

competen|ce /'kɒmpɪtəns/ n Tüchtigkeit f; (ability) Fähigkeit f; (Jur) Kompetenz f. ~t a tüchtig; fähig; (Jur) kompetent

competition /kɒmpə'tɪʃn/ n Konkurrenz f; (contest) Wettbewerb m; (in newspaper) Preisausschreiben nt

competitive /kəm'petətɪv/ a (Comm) konkurrenzfähig

competitor /kəm'petɪtə(r)/ n Teilnehmer m; (Comm) Konkurrent m

compile /kəm'paɪl/ vt zusammenstellen; verfassen (dictionary)

complacen|cy /kəm'pleɪsənsɪ/ n Selbstzufriedenheit f. ~t a, -ly adv selbstzufrieden

complain /kəm'pleɪn/ vi klagen (about/of über + acc); (formally) sich beschweren. ~t n Klage f; (formal) Beschwerde f; (Med) Leiden nt

complement[1] /'kɒmplɪmənt/ n Ergänzung f; full ~ volle Anzahl f

complement[2] /'kɒmplɪment/ vt ergänzen; ~ each other sich ergänzen. ~ary /-'mentərɪ/ a sich ergänzend; be ~ary sich ergänzen

complete /kəm'pliːt/ a vollständig; (finished) fertig; (utter) völlig ● vt vervollständigen; (finish) abschließen; (fill in) ausfüllen. ~ly adv völlig

completion /kəm'pliːʃn/ n Vervollständigung f; (end) Abschluß m

complex /'kɒmpleks/ a komplex ● n Komplex m

complexion /kəm'plekʃn/ n Teint m; (colour) Gesichtsfarbe f; (fig) Aspekt m

complexity /kəm'pleksətɪ/ n Komplexität f

compliance /kəm'plaɪəns/ n Einverständnis nt; in ~ with gemäß (+ dat)

complicat|e /'kɒmplɪkeɪt/ vt komplizieren. ~ed a kompliziert. ~ion /-'keɪʃn/ n Komplikation f

complicity /kəm'plɪsətɪ/ n Mittäterschaft f

compliment /'kɒmplɪmənt/ n Kompliment nt; ~s pl Grüße pl ● vt ein Kompliment machen (+ dat). ~ary /-'mentərɪ/ a schmeichelhaft; (given free) Frei-

comply /kəm'plaɪ/ vi (pt/pp -ied) ~ with nachkommen (+ dat)

component /kəm'pəʊnənt/ a & n ~ [part] Bestandteil m, Teil nt

compose /kəm'pəʊz/ *vt* verfassen; (*Mus*) komponieren; ~ **oneself** sich fassen; **be** ~**d of** sich zusammensetzen aus. ~**d** *a* (*calm*) gefaßt. ~**r** *n* Komponist *m*

composition /kɒmpə'zɪʃn/ *n* Komposition *f*; (*essay*) Aufsatz *m*

compost /'kɒmpɒst/ *n* Kompost *m*

composure /kəm'pəʊzə(r)/ *n* Fassung *f*

compound[1] /kəm'paʊnd/ *vt* (*make worse*) verschlimmern

compound[2] /'kɒmpaʊnd/ *a* zusammengesetzt; (*fracture*) kompliziert ● *n* (*Chem*) Verbindung *f*; (*Gram*) Kompositum *nt*; (*enclosure*) Einfriedigung *f*. ~ '**interest** *n* Zinseszins *m*

comprehen|d /kɒmprɪ'hend/ *vt* begreifen, verstehen; (*include*) umfassen. ~**sible** *a*, -**bly** *adv* verständlich. ~**sion** /-'henʃn/ *n* Verständnis *nt*

comprehensive /kɒmprɪ'hensɪv/ *a* & *n* umfassend; ~ [**school**] Gesamtschule *f*. ~ **insurance** *n* (*Auto*) Vollkaskoversicherung *f*

compress[1] /'kɒmpres/ *n* Kompresse *f*

compress[2] /kəm'pres/ *vt* zusammenpressen; ~**ed air** Druckluft *f*

comprise /kəm'praɪz/ *vt* umfassen, bestehen aus

compromise /'kɒmprəmaɪz/ *n* Kompromiß *m* ● *vt* kompromittieren (*person*) ● *vi* einen Kompromiß schließen

compuls|ion /kəm'pʌlʃn/ *n* Zwang *m*. ~**ive** /-sɪv/ *a* zwanghaft; ~**ive eating** Eßzwang *m*. ~**ory** /-sərɪ/ *a* obligatorisch; ~**ory subject** Pflichtfach *nt*

compunction /kəm'pʌŋkʃn/ *n* Gewissensbisse *pl*

comput|er /kəm'pju:tə(r)/ *n* Computer *m*. ~**erize** *vt* computerisieren (*data*); auf Computer umstellen (*firm*). ~**ing** *n* Computertechnik *f*

comrade /'kɒmreɪd/ *n* Kamerad *m*; (*Pol*) Genosse *m*/Genossin *f*. ~**ship** *n* Kameradschaft *f*

con[1] /kɒn/ *see* pro

con[2] *n* (*fam*) Schwindel *m* ● *vt* (*pt/pp* conned) (*fam*) beschwindeln

concave /'kɒŋkeɪv/ *a* konkav

conceal /kən'si:l/ *vt* verstecken; (*keep secret*) verheimlichen

concede /kən'si:d/ *vt* zugeben; (*give up*) aufgeben

conceit /kən'si:t/ *n* Einbildung *f*. ~**ed** *a* eingebildet

conceivable /kən'si:vəbl/ *a* denkbar

conceive /kən'si:v/ *vt* (*Biol*) empfangen; (*fig*) sich (*dat*) ausdenken ● *vi* schwanger werden. ~ **of** (*fig*) sich (*dat*) vorstellen

concentrat|e /'kɒnsəntreɪt/ *vt* konzentrieren ● *vi* sich konzentrieren. ~**ion** /-'treɪʃn/ *n* Konzentration *f*. ~**ion camp** *n* Konzentrationslager *nt*

concept /'kɒnsept/ *n* Begriff *m*. ~**ion** /kən'sepʃn/ *n* Empfängnis *f*; (*idea*) Vorstellung *f*

concern /kən'sɜːn/ *n* Angelegenheit *f*; (*worry*) Sorge *f*; (*Comm*) Unternehmen *nt* ● *vt* (*be about, affect*) betreffen; (*worry*) kümmern; **be** ~**ed about** besorgt sein um; ~ **oneself with** sich beschäftigen mit; **as far as I am** ~**ed** was mich angeht *od* betrifft. ~**ing** *prep* bezüglich (+ *gen*)

concert /'kɒnsət/ *n* Konzert *nt*; **in** ~ im Chor. ~**ed** /kən'sɜːtɪd/ *a* gemeinsam

concertina /kɒnsə'tiːnə/ *n* Konzertina *f*

'**concert-master** *n* (*Amer*) Konzertmeister *m*

concerto /kən'tʃeətəʊ/ *n* Konzert *nt*

concession /kən'seʃn/ *n* Zugeständnis *nt*; (*Comm*) Konzession *f*; (*reduction*) Ermäßigung *f*. ~**ary** *a* (*reduced*) ermäßigt

conciliation /kənsɪlɪ'eɪʃn/ *n* Schlichtung *f*

concise /kən'saɪs/ *a*, -**ly** *adv* kurz

conclude /kən'kluːd/ *vt/i* schließen

conclusion /kən'kluːʒn/ *n* Schluß *m*; **in** ~ abschließend, zum Schluß

conclusive /kən'kluːsɪv/ *a* schlüssig

concoct /kən'kɒkt/ *vt* zusammenstellen; (*fig*) fabrizieren. ~**ion** /-ɒkʃn/ *n* Zusammenstellung *f*; (*drink*) Gebräu *nt*

concourse /'kɒŋkɔːs/ *n* Halle *f*

concrete /'kɒnkriːt/ *a* konkret ● *n* Beton *m* ● *vt* betonieren

concur /kən'kɜː(r)/ *vi* (*pt/pp* concurred) übereinstimmen

concurrently /kən'kʌrəntlɪ/ *adv* gleichzeitig

concussion /kən'kʌʃn/ *n* Gehirnerschütterung *f*

condemn /kən'dem/ vt verurteilen; (declare unfit) für untauglich erklären. ∼**ation** /kɒndem'neɪʃn/ n Verurteilung f

condensation /kɒnden'seɪʃn/ n Kondensation f

condense /kən'dens/ vt zusammenfassen; (Phys) kondensieren ● vi sich kondensieren. ∼**d milk** n Kondensmilch f

condescend /kɒndɪ'send/ vi sich herablassen (**to** zu). ∼**ing** a, -**ly** adv herablassend

condiment /'kɒndɪmənt/ n Gewürz nt

condition /kən'dɪʃn/ n Bedingung f; (state) Zustand m; ∼**s** pl Verhältnisse pl: **on** ∼ **that** unter der Bedingung, daß ● vt (Psych) konditionieren. ∼**al** a bedingt; **be** ∼**al on** abhängen von ● n (Gram) Konditional m. ∼**er** n Haarkur f; (for fabrics) Weichspüler m

condolences /kən'dəʊlənsɪz/ npl Beileid nt

condom /'kɒndəm/ n Kondom nt

condominium /kɒndə'mɪnɪəm/ n (Amer) l Eigentumswohnung f

condone /kən'dəʊn/ vt hinwegsehen über (+ acc)

conducive /kən'djuːsɪv/ a förderlich (**to** dat)

conduct[1] /'kɒndʌkt/ n Verhalten nt; (Sch) Betragen nt

conduct[2] /kən'dʌkt/ vt führen; (Phys) leiten; (Mus) dirigieren. ∼**or** n Dirigent m; (of bus) Schaffner m; (Phys) Leiter m. ∼**ress** n Schaffnerin f

cone /kəʊn/ n Kegel m; (Bot) Zapfen m; (for ice-cream) [Eis]tüte f; (Auto) Leitkegel m

confectioner /kən'fekʃənə(r)/ n Konditor m. ∼**y** n Süßwaren pl

confederation /kənfedə'reɪʃn/ n Bund m; (Pol) Konföderation f

confer /kən'fɜː(r)/ v (pt/pp conferred) ● vt verleihen (**on** dat) ● vi sich beraten

conference /'kɒnfərəns/ n Konferenz f

confess /kən'fes/ vt/i gestehen; (Relig) beichten. ∼**ion** /-eʃn/ n Geständnis nt; (Relig) Beichte f. ∼**ional** /-eʃənəl/ n Beichtstuhl m. ∼**or** n Beichtvater m

confetti /kən'fetɪ/ n Konfetti nt

confide /kən'faɪd/ vt anvertrauen ● vi ∼ **in s.o.** sich jdm anvertrauen

confidence /'kɒnfɪdəns/ n (trust) Vertrauen nt; (self-assurance) Selbstvertrauen nt; (secret) Geheimnis nt; **in** ∼ im Vertrauen. ∼ **trick** n Schwindel m

confident /'kɒnfɪdənt/ a, -**ly** adv zuversichtlich; (self-assured) selbstsicher

confidential /kɒnfɪ'denʃl/ a, -**ly** adv vertraulich

confine /kən'faɪn/ vt beschränken; (keep shut up) einsperren; ∼ **oneself to** sich beschränken auf (+ acc); **be** ∼**d to bed** das Bett hüten müssen. ∼**d** a (narrow) eng. ∼**ment** n Haft f

confines /'kɒnfaɪnz/ npl Grenzen pl

confirm /kən'fɜːm/ vt bestätigen; (Relig) konfirmieren; (Roman Catholic) firmen. ∼**ation** /kɒnfə'meɪʃn/ n Bestätigung f; Konfirmation f; Firmung f. ∼**ed** a ∼**ed bachelor** eingefleischter Junggeselle m

confiscat|e /'kɒnfɪskeɪt/ vt beschlagnahmen. ∼**ion** /-'keɪʃn/ n Beschlagnahme f

conflict[1] /'kɒnflɪkt/ n Konflikt m

conflict[2] /kən'flɪkt/ vi im Widerspruch stehen (**with** zu). ∼**ing** a widersprüchlich

conform /kən'fɔːm/ vi (person:) sich anpassen; (thing:) entsprechen (**to** dat). ∼**ist** n Konformist m

confounded /kən'faʊndɪd/ a (fam) verflixt

confront /kən'frʌnt/ vt konfrontieren. ∼**ation** /kɒnfrən'teɪʃn/ n Konfrontation f

confus|e /kən'fjuːz/ vt verwirren; (mistake for) verwechseln (**with** mit). ∼**ing** a verwirrend. ∼**ion** /-juːʒn/ n Verwirrung f; (muddle) Durcheinander nt

congeal /kən'dʒiːl/ vi fest werden; (blood:) gerinnen

congenial /kən'dʒiːnɪəl/ a angenehm

congenital /kən'dʒenɪtl/ a angeboren

congest|ed /kən'dʒestɪd/ a verstopft; (with people) überfüllt. ∼**ion** /-estʃn/ n Verstopfung f; Überfüllung f

congratulat|e /kən'grætjʊleɪt/ vt gratulieren (+ dat) (**on** zu). ∼**ions** /-'leɪnz/ npl Glückwünsche pl; ∼**ions!** [ich] gratuliere!

congregat|e /'kɒŋgrɪgeɪt/ vi sich versammeln. **~ion** /-'geɪʃn/ n (Relig) Gemeinde f

congress /'kɒŋgres/ n Kongreß m. **~man** n Kongreßabgeordnete(r) m

conical /'kɒnɪkl/ a kegelförmig

conifer /'kɒnɪfə(r)/ n Nadelbaum m

conjecture /kən'dʒektʃə(r)/ n Mutmaßung f ● vt/i mutmaßen

conjugal /'kɒndʒʊgl/ a ehelich

conjugat|e /'kɒndʒʊgeɪt/ vt konjugieren. **~ion** /-'geɪʃn/ n Konjugation f

conjunction /kən'dʒʌŋkʃn/ n Konjunktion f; **in ~ with** zusammen mit

conjunctivitis /kəndʒʌŋktɪ'vaɪtɪs/ n Bindehautentzündung f

conjur|e /'kʌndʒə(r)/ vi zaubern ● vt **~e up** heraufbeschwören. **~or** n Zauberkünstler m

conk /kɒŋk/ vi **~ out** (fam) 〈machine:〉 kaputtgehen; 〈person:〉 zusammenklappen

conker /'kɒŋkə(r)/ n (fam) [Roß]kastanie f

'con-man n (fam) Schwindler m

connect /kə'nekt/ vt verbinden (**to** mit); (Electr) anschließen (**to** an + acc) ● vi verbunden sein; 〈train:〉 Anschluß haben (**with** an + acc); **be ~ed with** zu tun haben mit; (be related to) verwandt sein mit

connection /kə'nekʃn/ n Verbindung f; (Rail, Electr) Anschluß m; **in ~ with** in Zusammenhang mit. **~s** npl Beziehungen pl

conniv|ance /kə'naɪvəns/ n stillschweigende Duldung f. **~e** vi **~e at** stillschweigend dulden

connoisseur /kɒnə'sɜ:(r)/ n Kenner m

connotation /kɒnə'teɪʃn/ n Assoziation f

conquer /'kɒŋkə(r)/ vt erobern; (fig) besiegen. **~or** n Eroberer m

conquest /'kɒŋkwest/ n Eroberung f

conscience /'kɒnʃəns/ n Gewissen nt

conscientious /kɒnʃɪ'enʃəs/ a, **-ly** adv gewissenhaft. **~ ob'jector** n Kriegsdienstverweigerer m

conscious /'kɒnʃəs/ a, **-ly** adv bewußt; **[fully] ~** bei [vollem] Bewußtsein; **be/become ~ of sth** sich (dat) etw (gen) bewußt sein/werden. **~ness** n Bewußtsein nt

conscript[1] /'kɒnskrɪpt/ n Einberufene(r) m

conscript[2] /kən'skrɪpt/ vt einberufen. **~ion** /-ɪpʃn/ n allgemeine Wehrpflicht f

consecrat|e /'kɒnsɪkreɪt/ vt weihen; einweihen 〈church〉. **~ion** /-'kreɪʃn/ n Weihe f; Einweihung f

consecutive /kən'sekjʊtɪv/ a aufeinanderfolgend. **~ly** adv fortlaufend

consensus /kən'sensəs/ n Übereinstimmung f

consent /kən'sent/ n Einwilligung f, Zustimmung f ● vi einwilligen (**to** in + acc), zustimmen (**to** dat)

consequen|ce /'kɒnsɪkwəns/ n Folge f; (importance) Bedeutung f. **~t** a daraus folgend. **~tly** adv folglich

conservation /kɒnsə'veɪʃn/ n Erhaltung f, Bewahrung f. **~ist** n Umweltschützer m

conservative /kən'sɜ:vətɪv/ a konservativ; 〈estimate〉 vorsichtig. **C~** (Pol) a konservativ ● n Konservative(r) m/f

conservatory /kən'sɜ:vətrɪ/ n Wintergarten m

conserve /kən'sɜ:v/ vt erhalten, bewahren; sparen 〈energy〉

consider /kən'sɪdə(r)/ vt erwägen; (think over) sich (dat) überlegen; (take into account) berücksichtigen; (regard as) betrachten als; **~ doing sth** erwägen, etw zu tun. **~able** /-əbl/ a, **-bly** adv erheblich

consider|ate /kən'sɪdərət/ a, **-ly** adv rücksichtsvoll. **~ation** /-'reɪʃn/ n Erwägung f; (thoughtfulness) Rücksicht f; (payment) Entgelt nt; **take into ~ation** berücksichtigen. **~ing** prep wenn man bedenkt (**that** daß); **~ing the circumstances** unter den Umständen

consign /kən'saɪn/ vt übergeben (**to** dat). **~ment** n Lieferung f

consist /kən'sɪst/ vi **~ of** bestehen aus

consisten|cy /kən'sɪstənsɪ/ n Konsequenz f; (density) Konsistenz f. **~t** a konsequent; (unchanging) gleichbleibend; **be ~t with** entsprechen (+ dat). **~tly** adv konsequent; (constantly) ständig

consolation /kɒnsə'leɪʃn/ n Trost m. **~ prize** n Trostpreis m

console /kən'səʊl/ vt trösten

consolidate /kən'sɒlɪdeɪt/ vt konsolidieren

consonant /'kɒnsənənt/ n Konsonant m

consort /'kɒnsɔ:t/ n Gemahl(in) m(f)

conspicuous /kən'spɪkjʊəs/ a auffällig

conspiracy /kən'spɪrəsɪ/ n Verschwörung f

conspire /kən'spaɪə(r)/ vi sich verschwören

constable /'kʌnstəbl/ n Polizist m

constant /'kɒnstənt/ a, **-ly** adv beständig; (continuous) ständig

constellation /kɒnstə'leɪʃn/ n Sternbild nt

consternation /kɒnstə'neɪʃn/ n Bestürzung f

constipat|ed /'kɒnstɪpeɪtɪd/ a verstopft. **~ion** /-'peɪʃn/ n Verstopfung f

constituency /kən'stɪtjʊənsɪ/ n Wahlkreis m

constituent /kən'stɪtjʊənt/ n Bestandteil m; (Pol) Wähler(in) m(f)

constitut|e /'kɒnstɪtju:t/ vt bilden. **~ion** /-'tju:ʃn/ n (Pol) Verfassung f; (of person) Konstitution f. **~ional** /-'tju:ʃənl/ a Verfassungs- ● n Verdauungsspaziergang m

constrain /kən'streɪn/ vt zwingen. **~t** n Zwang m; (restriction) Beschränkung f; (strained manner) Gezwungenheit f

constrict /kən'strɪkt/ vt einengen

construct /kən'strʌkt/ vt bauen. **~ion** /-ʌkʃn/ n Bau m; (Gram) Konstruktion f; (interpretation) Deutung f; **under ~ion** im Bau. **~ive** /-ɪv/ a konstruktiv

construe /kən'stru:/ vt deuten

consul /'kɒnsl/ n Konsul m. **~ate** /'kɒnsjʊlət/ n Konsulat nt

consult /kən'sʌlt/ vt [um Rat] fragen; konsultieren (doctor); nachschlagen in (+ dat) (book). **~ant** n Berater m; (Med) Chefarzt m. **~ation** /kɒnsl'teɪʃn/ n Beratung f; (Med) Konsultation f

consume /kən'sju:m/ vt verzehren; (use) verbrauchen. **~r** n Verbraucher m. **~r goods** npl Konsumgüter pl

consummat|e /'kɒnsəmeɪt/ vt vollziehen. **~ion** /-'meɪʃn/ n Vollzug m

consumption /kən'sʌmpʃn/ n Konsum m; (use) Verbrauch m

contact /'kɒntækt/ n Kontakt m; (person) Kontaktperson f ● vt sich in

Verbindung setzen mit. **~ 'lenses** npl Kontaktlinsen pl

contagious /kən'teɪdʒəs/ a direkt übertragbar

contain /kən'teɪn/ vt enthalten; (control) beherrschen. **~er** n Behälter m; (Comm) Container m

contaminat|e /kən'tæmɪneɪt/ vt verseuchen. **~ion** /-'neɪʃn/ n Verseuchung f

contemplat|e /'kɒntəmpleɪt/ vt betrachten; (meditate) nachdenken über (+ acc); **~e doing sth** daran denken, etw zu tun. **~ion** /-'pleɪʃn/ n Betrachtung f; Nachdenken nt

contemporary /kən'tempərərɪ/ a zeitgenössisch ● n Zeitgenosse m/ -genossin f

contempt /kən'tempt/ n Verachtung f; **beneath ~** verabscheuungswürdig; **~ of court** Mißachtung f des Gerichts. **~ible** /-əbl/ a verachtenswert. **~uous** /-tjʊəs/ a, **-ly** adv verächtlich

contend /kən'tend/ vi kämpfen (**with** mit) ● vt (assert) behaupten. **~er** n Bewerber(in) m(f); (Sport) Wettkämpfer(in) m(f)

content[1] /'kɒntent/ n & **contents** pl Inhalt m

content[2] /kən'tent/ a zufrieden ● n **to one's heart's ~** nach Herzenslust ● vt **~ oneself** sich begnügen (**with** mit). **~ed** a, **-ly** adv zufrieden

contention /kən'tenʃn/ n (assertion) Behauptung f

contentment /kən'tentmənt/ n Zufriedenheit f

contest[1] /'kɒntest/ n Kampf m; (competition) Wettbewerb m

contest[2] /kən'test/ vt (dispute) bestreiten; (Jur) anfechten; (Pol) kandidieren in (+ dat). **~ant** n Teilnehmer m

context /'kɒntekst/ n Zusammenhang m

continent /'kɒntɪnənt/ n Kontinent m

continental /kɒntɪ'nentl/ a Kontinental-. **~ breakfast** n kleines Frühstück nt. **~ quilt** n Daunendecke f

contingen|cy /kən'tɪndʒənsɪ/ n Eventualität f. **~t** a **be ~t upon** abhängen von ● n (Mil) Kontingent nt

continual /kən'tɪnjʊəl/ a, **-ly** adv dauernd

continuation /kəntɪnjʊ'eɪʃn/ n
Fortsetzung f

continue /kən'tɪnju:/ vt fortsetzen; ~
doing or **to do sth** fortfahren, etw zu
tun; **to be ~d** Fortsetzung folgt ● vi
weitergehen; (doing sth) weitermachen; (speaking) fortfahren;
⟨weather:⟩ anhalten

continuity /kɒntɪ'nju:ətɪ/ n Kontinuität f

continuous /kən'tɪnjʊəs/ a, **-ly** adv
anhaltend, ununterbrochen

contort /kən'tɔ:t/ vt verzerren.
~**ion** /-ɔ:ʃn/ n Verzerrung f

contour /'kɒntʊə(r)/ n Kontur f;
(line) Höhenlinie f

contraband /'kɒntrəbænd/ n
Schmuggelware f

contracep|tion /kɒntrə'sepʃn/ n
Empfängnisverhütung f. ~**tive**
/-tɪv/ a empfängnisverhütend ● n
Empfängnisverhütungsmittel nt

contract[1] /'kɒntrækt/ n Vertrag m

contract[2] /kən'trækt/ vi sich zusammenziehen ● vt zusammenziehen; (get) zuziehen (illness).
~**ion** /-ækʃn/ n Zusammenziehung
f; (abbreviation) Abkürzung f; (in
childbirth) Wehe f. ~**or** n Un-
ternehmer m

contradict /kɒntrə'dɪkt/ vt widersprechen (+ dat). ~**ion** /-ɪkʃn/ n
Widerspruch m. ~**ory** a widersprüchlich

contra-flow /'kɒntrə-/ n Umleitung
f [auf die entgegengesetzte Fahr-
bahn]

contralto /kən'træltəʊ/ n Alt m;
(singer) Altistin f

contraption /kən'træpʃn/ n (fam)
Apparat m

contrary[1] /'kɒntrərɪ/ a & adv entgegengesetzt; ~ **to** entgegen (+ dat)
● n Gegenteil nt; **on the** ~ im Gegenteil

contrary[2] /kən'treərɪ/ a widerspenstig

contrast[1] /'kɒntrɑ:st/ n Kontrast m

contrast[2] /kən'trɑ:st/ vt gegen-
überstellen (**with** dat) ● vi einen Kontrast bilden (**with** zu). ~**ing** a
gegensätzlich; ⟨colour⟩ Kontrast-

contraven|e /kɒntrə'vi:n/ vt ver-
stoßen gegen. ~**tion** /-'venʃn/ n
Verstoß m (**of** gegen)

contribut|e /kən'trɪbju:t/ vt/i bei-
tragen; beisteuern ⟨money⟩; (donate)
spenden. ~**ion** /kɒntrɪ'bju:ʃn/ n Beitrag m; (donation) Spende f. ~**or** n
Beitragende(r) m/f

contrite /kən'traɪt/ a reuig

contrivance /kən'traɪvəns/ n Vor-
richtung f

contrive /kən'traɪv/ vt verfertigen;
~ **to do sth** es fertigbringen, etw zu tun

control /kən'trəʊl/ n Kontrolle f;
(mastery) Beherrschung f; (Techn)
Regler m; ~**s** pl (of car, plane) Steuerung f; **get out of** ~ außer Kontrolle
geraten ● vt (pt/pp **controlled**) kontrollieren; (restrain) unter Kontrolle
halten; ~ **oneself** sich beherrschen

controvers|ial /kɒntrə'vɜ:ʃl/ a um-
stritten. ~**y** /'kɒntrəvɜ:sɪ/ n Kontroverse f

conundrum /kə'nʌndrəm/ n Rätsel
nt

conurbation /kɒnɜ:'beɪʃn/ n Bal-
lungsgebiet nt

convalesce /kɒnvə'les/ vi sich erholen. ~**nce** n Erholung f

convalescent /kɒnvə'lesnt/ a **be**
~ noch erholungsbedürftig sein. ~
home n Erholungsheim nt

convector /kən'vektə(r)/ n ~
[**heater**] Konvektor m

convene /kən'vi:n/ vt einberufen
● vi sich versammeln

convenience /kən'vi:nɪəns/ n Bequemlichkeit f; [**public**] ~ öffentliche
Toilette f; **with all modern** ~**s** mit allem Komfort

convenient /kən'vi:nɪənt/ a, **-ly** adv
günstig; **be** ~ **for s.o.** jdm gelegen sein
od jdm passen; **if it is** ~ [**for you**] wenn
es Ihnen paßt

convent /'kɒnvənt/ n [Nonnen]klo-
ster nt

convention /kən'venʃn/ n (custom)
Brauch m, Sitte f; (agreement) Konvention f; (assembly) Tagung f. ~**al**
a, **-ly** adv konventionell

converge /kən'vɜ:dʒ/ vi zusammenlaufen

conversant /kən'vɜ:sənt/ a ~ **with**
vertraut mit

conversation /kɒnvə'seɪʃn/ n Gespräch nt; (Sch) Konversation f

converse[1] /kən'vɜ:s/ vi sich unterhalten

converse[2] /'kɒnvɜ:s/ n Gegenteil nt.
~**ly** adv umgekehrt

conversion /kən'vɜ:ʃn/ n Umbau m;
(Relig) Bekehrung f; (calculation)
Umrechnung f

convert[1] /'kɒnvɜ:t/ n Bekehrte(r) m/
f, Konvertit m

convert[2] /kən'vɜːt/ vt bekehren (person); (change) umwandeln (into in + acc); umbauen (building); (calculate) umrechnen; (Techn) umstellen. ~ible /-əbl/ a verwandelbar ● n (Auto) Kabriolett nt

convex /'kɒnveks/ a konvex

convey /kən'veɪ/ vt befördern; vermitteln (idea, message). ~ance n Beförderung f; (vehicle) Beförderungsmittel nt. ~or belt n Förderband nt

convict[1] /'kɒnvɪkt/ n Sträfling m

convict[2] /kən'vɪkt/ vt verurteilen (of wegen). ~ion /-ɪkʃn/ n Verurteilung f; (belief) Überzeugung f; previous ~ion Vorstrafe f

convinc|e /kən'vɪns/ vt überzeugen. ~ing a, -ly adv überzeugend

convivial /kən'vɪvɪəl/ a gesellig

convoluted /'kɒnvəluːtɪd/ a verschlungen; (fig) verwickelt

convoy /'kɒnvɔɪ/ n Konvoi m

convuls|e /kən'vʌls/ vt be ~ed sich krümmen (with vor + dat). ~ion /-ʌlʃn/ n Krampf m

coo /kuː/ vi gurren

cook /kʊk/ n Koch m/Köchin f ● vt/i kochen; is it ~ed? ist es gar? ~ the books (fam) die Bilanz frisieren. ~book n (Amer) Kochbuch nt

cooker /'kʊkə(r)/ n [Koch]herd m; (apple) Kochapfel m. ~y n Kochen nt. ~y book n Kochbuch nt

cookie /'kʊkɪ/ n (Amer) Keks m

cool /kuːl/ a (-er, -est), -ly adv kühl ● n Kühle f ● vt kühlen ● vi abkühlen. ~-box n Kühlbox f. ~ness n Kühle f

coop /kuːp/ n [Hühner]stall m ● vt ~ up einsperren

co-operat|e /kəʊ'ɒpəreɪt/ vi zusammenarbeiten. ~ion /-'reɪʃn/ n Kooperation f

co-operative /kəʊ'ɒpərətɪv/ a hilfsbereit ● n Genossenschaft f

co-opt /kəʊ'ɒpt/ vt hinzuwählen

co-ordinat|e /kəʊ'ɔːdɪneɪt/ vt koordinieren. ~ion /-'neɪʃn/ n Koordination f

cop /kɒp/ n (fam) Polizist m

cope /kəʊp/ vi (fam) zurechtkommen; ~ with fertig werden mit

copious /'kəʊpɪəs/ a reichlich

copper[1] /'kɒpə(r)/ n Kupfer nt; ~s pl Kleingeld nt ● a kupfern

copper[2] n (fam) Polizist m

copper 'beech n Blutbuche f

coppice /'kɒpɪs/ n, **copse** /kɒps/ n Gehölz nt

copulate /'kɒpjʊleɪt/ vi sich begatten

copy /'kɒpɪ/ n Kopie f; (book) Exemplar nt ● vt (pt/pp -ied) kopieren; (imitate) nachahmen; (Sch) abschreiben

copy: ~right n Copyright nt. ~writer n Texter m

coral /'kɒrl/ n Koralle f

cord /kɔːd/ n Schnur f; (fabric) Cordsamt m; ~s pl Cordhose f

cordial /'kɔːdɪəl/ a, -ly adv herzlich ● n Fruchtsirup m

cordon /'kɔːdn/ n Kordon m ● vt ~ off absperren

corduroy /'kɔːdərɔɪ/ n Cordsamt m

core /kɔː(r)/ n Kern m; (of apple, pear) Kerngehäuse nt

cork /kɔːk/ n Kork m; (for bottle) Korken m. ~screw n Korkenzieher m

corn[1] /kɔːn/ n Korn nt; (Amer: maize) Mais m

corn[2] n (Med) Hühnerauge nt

cornea /'kɔːnɪə/ n Hornhaut f

corned beef /kɔːnd'biːf/ n Corned beef nt

corner /'kɔːnə(r)/ n Ecke f; (bend) Kurve f; (football) Eckball m ● vt (fig) in die Enge treiben; (Comm) monopolisieren (market). ~stone n Eckstein m

cornet /'kɔːnɪt/ n (Mus) Kornett nt; (for ice-cream) [Eis]tüte f

corn: ~flour n, (Amer) ~starch n Stärkemehl nt

corny /'kɔːnɪ/ a (fam) abgedroschen

coronary /'kɒrənərɪ/ a & n ~ [thrombosis] Koronarthrombose f

coronation /kɒrə'neɪʃn/ n Krönung f

coroner /'kɒrənə(r)/ n Beamte(r) m, der verdächtige Todesfälle untersucht

coronet /'kɒrənet/ n Adelskrone f

corporal[1] /'kɔːpərəl/ n (Mil) Stabsunteroffizier m

corporal[2] a körperlich; ~ punishment körperliche Züchtigung f

corporate /'kɔːpərət/ a gemeinschaftlich

corporation /kɔːpə'reɪʃn/ n Körperschaft f; (of town) Stadtverwaltung f

corps /kɔː(r)/ n (pl corps /kɔːz/) Korps nt

corpse /kɔːps/ n Leiche f

corpulent /'kɔːpjʊlənt/ a korpulent

corpuscle /'kɔ:pʌsl/ n Blutkörperchen nt

correct /kə'rekt/ a, -ly adv richtig; (proper) korrekt ● vt verbessern; (Sch, Typ) korrigieren. ∼ion /-ekʃn/ n Verbesserung f; (Typ) Korrektur f

correlation /kɒrə'leɪʃn/ n Wechselbeziehung f

correspond /kɒrɪ'spɒnd/ vi entsprechen (to dat); ⟨two things:⟩ sich entsprechen; (write) korrespondieren. ∼ence n Briefwechsel m; (Comm) Korrespondenz f. ∼ent n Korrespondent(in) m(f). ∼ing a, -ly adv entsprechend

corridor /'kɒrɪdɔ:(r)/ n Gang m; (Pol, Aviat) Korridor m

corroborate /kə'rɒbəreɪt/ vt bestätigen

corro|de /kə'rəʊd/ vt zerfressen ● vi rosten. ∼sion /-'rəʊʒn/ n Korrosion f

corrugated /'kɒrəgeɪtɪd/ a gewellt. ∼ iron n Wellblech nt

corrupt /kə'rʌpt/ a korrupt ● vt korrumpieren; (spoil) verderben. ∼ion /-ʌpʃn/ n Korruption f

corset /'kɔ:sɪt/ n & -s pl Korsett nt

Corsica /'kɔ:sɪkə/ n Korsika nt

cortège /kɔ:'teɪʒ/ n [funeral] ∼ Leichenzug m

cosh /kɒʃ/ n Totschläger m

cosmetic /kɒz'metɪk/ a kosmetisch ● n ∼s pl Kosmetika pl

cosmic /'kɒzmɪk/ a kosmisch

cosmonaut /'kɒzmənɔ:t/ n Kosmonaut(in) m(f)

cosmopolitan /kɒzmə'pɒlɪtən/ a kosmopolitisch

cosmos /'kɒzmɒs/ n Kosmos m

cosset /'kɒsɪt/ vt verhätscheln

cost /kɒst/ n Kosten pl; ∼s pl (Jur) Kosten; at all ∼ um jeden Preis; I learnt to my ∼ es ist mich teuer zu stehen gekommen ● vt (pt/pp cost) kosten; it ∼ me £20 es hat mich £20 gekostet ● vt (pt/pp costed) ∼ [out] die Kosten kalkulieren für

costly /'kɒstlɪ/ a (-ier, -iest) teuer

cost: ∼ of 'living n Lebenshaltungskosten pl. ∼ price n Selbstkostenpreis m

costume /'kɒstju:m/ n Kostüm nt; (national) Tracht f. ∼ jewellery n Modeschmuck m

cosy /'kəʊzɪ/ a (-ier, -iest) gemütlich ● n (tea-, egg-) Wärmer m

cot /kɒt/ n Kinderbett nt; (Amer: camp-bed) Feldbett nt

cottage /'kɒtɪdʒ/ n Häuschen nt. ∼ 'cheese n Hüttenkäse m

cotton /'kɒtn/ n Baumwolle f; (thread) Nähgarn nt ● a baumwollen ● vi ∼ on (fam) kapieren

cotton 'wool n Watte f

couch /kaʊtʃ/ n Liege f

couchette /ku:'ʃet/ n (Rail) Liegeplatz m

cough /kɒf/ n Husten m ● vi husten. ∼ up vt/i husten; (fam: pay) blechen

'cough mixture n Hustensaft m

could /kʊd, unbetont kəd/ see can²

council /'kaʊnsl/ n Rat m; (Admin) Stadtverwaltung f; (rural) Gemeindeverwaltung f. ∼ house n ≈ Sozialwohnung f

councillor /'kaʊnsələ(r)/ n Stadtverordnete(r) m/f

'council tax n Gemeindesteuer f

counsel /'kaʊnsl/ n Rat m; (Jur) Anwalt m ● vt (pt/pp counselled) beraten. ∼lor n Berater(in) m(f)

count¹ /kaʊnt/ n Graf m

count² n Zählung f; keep ∼ zählen ● vt/i zählen. ∼ on vt rechnen auf (+ acc)

countenance /'kaʊntənəns/ n Gesicht nt ● vt dulden

counter¹ /'kaʊntə(r)/ n (in shop) Ladentisch m; (in bank) Schalter m; (in café) Theke f; (Games) Spielmarke f

counter² adv ∼ to gegen (+ acc) ● a Gegen- ● vt/i kontern

counter'act vt entgegenwirken (+ dat)

'counter-attack n Gegenangriff m

counter-'espionage n Spionageabwehr f

'counterfeit /-fɪt/ a gefälscht ● n Fälschung f ● vt fälschen

'counterfoil n Kontrollabschnitt m

'counterpart n Gegenstück nt

counter-pro'ductive a be ∼ das Gegenteil bewirken

'countersign vt gegenzeichnen

countess /'kaʊntɪs/ n Gräfin f

countless /'kaʊntlɪs/ a unzählig

countrified /'kʌntrɪfaɪd/ a ländlich

country /'kʌntrɪ/ n Land nt; (native land) Heimat f; (countryside) Landschaft f; in the ∼ auf dem Lande. ∼man n [fellow] ∼man Landsmann m. ∼side n Landschaft f

county /'kaʊntɪ/ n Grafschaft f

coup /ku:/ n (Pol) Staatsstreich m

couple /'kʌpl/ n Paar nt; a ~ **of** (two) zwei ● vt verbinden; (Rail) koppeln

coupon /'ku:pɒn/ n Kupon m; (voucher) Gutschein m; (entry form) Schein m

courage /'kʌrɪdʒ/ n Mut m. ~**ous** / kə'reɪdʒəs/ a, -**ly** adv mutig

courgettes /kʊə'ʒets/ npl Zucchini pl

courier /'kʊrɪə(r)/ n Bote m; (diplomatic) Kurier m; (for tourists) Reiseleiter(in) m(f)

course /kɔ:s/ n (Naut, Sch) Kurs m; (Culin) Gang m; (for golf) Platz m; ~ **of treatment** (Med) Kur f; **of** ~ natürlich, selbstverständlich; **in the** ~ **of** im Lauf[e] (+ gen)

court /kɔ:t/ n Hof m; (Sport) Platz m; (Jur) Gericht nt ● vt werben um; herausfordern (danger)

courteous /'kɜ:tɪəs/ a, -**ly** adv höflich

courtesy /'kɜ:təsɪ/ n Höflichkeit f

court: ~ '**martial** n (pl ~**s martial**) Militärgericht nt. ~ **shoes** npl Pumps pl. ~**yard** n Hof m

cousin /'kʌzn/ n Vetter m, Cousin m; (female) Kusine f

cove /kəʊv/ n kleine Bucht f

cover /'kʌvə(r)/ n Decke f; (of cushion) Bezug m; (of umbrella) Hülle f; (of typewriter) Haube f; (of book, lid) Deckel m; (of magazine) Umschlag m; (protection) Deckung f, Schutz m; **take** ~ Deckung nehmen; **under separate** ~ mit getrennter Post ● vt bedecken; beziehen (cushion); decken (costs, needs); zurücklegen (distance); (Journ) berichten über (+ acc); (insure) versichern. ~ **up** vt zudecken; (fig) vertuschen

coverage /'kʌvərɪdʒ/ n (Journ) Berichterstattung f (**of** über + acc)

cover: ~ **charge** n Gedeck nt. ~**ing** n Decke f; (for floor) Belag m. ~-**up** n Vertuschung f

covet /'kʌvɪt/ vt begehren

cow /kaʊ/ n Kuh f

coward /'kaʊəd/ n Feigling m. ~**ice** /-ɪs/ n Feigheit f. ~**ly** a feige

'**cowboy** n Cowboy m; (fam) unsolider Handwerker m

cower /'kaʊə(r)/ vi sich [ängstlich] ducken

'**cowshed** n Kuhstall m

cox /kɒks/ n, **coxswain** /'kɒksn/ n Steuermann m

coy /kɔɪ/ a (-**er**, -**est**) gespielt schüchtern

crab /kræb/ n Krabbe f. ~-**apple** n Holzapfel m

crack /kræk/ n Riß m; (in china, glass) Sprung m; (noise) Knall m; (fam: joke) Witz m; (fam: attempt) Versuch m ● a (fam) erstklassig ● vt knacken (nut, code); einen Sprung machen in (+ acc) (china, glass); (fam) reißen (joke); (fam) lösen (problem) ● vi (china, glass:) springen; (whip:) knallen. ~ **down** vi (fam) durchgreifen

cracked /krækt/ a gesprungen; (rib) angebrochen; (fam: crazy) verrückt

cracker /'krækə(r)/ n (biscuit) Kräcker m; (firework) Knallkörper m; [**Christmas**] ~ Knallbonbon m. ~**s** a **be** ~**s** (fam) einen Knacks haben

crackle /'krækl/ vi knistern

cradle /'kreɪdl/ n Wiege f

craft[1] /krɑ:ft/ n inv (boat) [Wasser]fahrzeug nt

craft[2] n Handwerk nt; (technique) Fertigkeit f. ~**sman** n Handwerker m

crafty /'krɑ:ftɪ/ a (-**ier**, -**iest**), -**ily** adv gerissen

crag /kræg/ n Felszacken m. ~**gy** a felsig; (face) kantig

cram /kræm/ v (pt/pp **crammed**) ● vt hineinstopfen (**into** in + acc); vollstopfen (**with** mit) ● vi (for exams) pauken

cramp /kræmp/ n Krampf m. ~**ed** a eng

crampon /'kræmpən/ n Steigeisen nt

cranberry /'krænbərɪ/ n (Culin) Preiselbeere f

crane /kreɪn/ n Kran m; (bird) Kranich m ● vt ~ **one's neck** den Hals recken

crank[1] /kræŋk/ n (fam) Exzentriker m

crank[2] n (Techn) Kurbel f. ~**shaft** n Kurbelwelle f

cranky /'kræŋkɪ/ a exzentrisch; (Amer: irritable) reizbar

cranny /'krænɪ/ n Ritze f

crash /kræʃ/ n (noise) Krach m; (Auto) Zusammenstoß m; (Aviat) Absturz m ● vi krachen (**into** gegen); (cars:) zusammenstoßen; (plane:) abstürzen ● vt einen Unfall haben mit (car)

crash: ~ **course** n Schnellkurs m. ~-**helmet** n Sturzhelm m. ~-**landing** n Bruchlandung f

crate /kreɪt/ n Kiste f

crater /'kreɪtə(r)/ n Krater m

cravat /krə'væt/ n Halstuch nt

crav|e /kreɪv/ vi ~e for sich sehnen nach. ~ing n Gelüst nt

crawl /krɔ:l/ n (Swimming) Kraul nt; **do the** ~ kraulen; **at a** ~ im Kriechtempo ● vi kriechen; ⟨baby:⟩ krabbeln; ~ **with** wimmeln von. ~**er lane** n (Auto) Kriechspur f

crayon /'kreɪən/ n Wachsstift m; (pencil) Buntstift m

craze /kreɪz/ n Mode f

crazy /'kreɪzɪ/ a (-ier, -iest) verrückt; **be** ~ **about** verrückt sein nach

creak /kri:k/ n Knarren nt ● vi knarren

cream /kri:m/ n Sahne f; (Cosmetic, Med, Culin) Creme f ● a (colour) cremefarben ● vt (Culin) cremig rühren. ~ '**cheese** n ≈ Quark m. ~**y** a sahnig; (smooth) cremig

crease /kri:s/ n Falte f; (unwanted) Knitterfalte f ● vt falten; (accidentally) zerknittern ● vi knittern. ~**-resistant** a knitterfrei

creat|e /kri:'eɪt/ vt schaffen. ~**ion** /-'eɪʃn/ n Schöpfung f. ~**ive** /-tɪv/ a schöpferisch. ~**or** n Schöpfer m

creature /'kri:tʃə(r)/ n Geschöpf nt

crèche /kreʃ/ n Kinderkrippe f

credentials /krɪ'denʃlz/ npl Beglaubigungsschreiben nt

credibility /kredə'bɪlətɪ/ n Glaubwürdigkeit f

credible /'kredəbl/ a glaubwürdig

credit /'kredɪt/ n Kredit m; (honour) Ehre f ● vt glauben; ~ **s.o. with sth** (Comm) jdm etw gutschreiben; (fig) jdm etw zuschreiben. ~**able** /-əbl/ a lobenswert

credit: ~ **card** n Kreditkarte f. ~**or** n Gläubiger m

creed /kri:d/ n Glaubensbekenntnis nt

creek /kri:k/ n enge Bucht f; (Amer: stream) Bach m

creep /kri:p/ vi (pt/pp **crept**) schleichen ● n (fam) fieser Kerl m; **it gives me the** ~**s** es ist mir unheimlich. ~**er** n Kletterpflanze f. ~**y** a gruselig

cremat|e /krɪ'meɪt/ vt einäschern. ~**ion** /-'eɪʃn/ n Einäscherung f

crematorium /kremə'tɔ:rɪəm/ n Krematorium nt

crêpe /kreɪp/ n Krepp m. ~ **paper** n Kreppapier nt

crept /krept/ see **creep**

crescent /'kresənt/ n Halbmond m

cress /kres/ n Kresse f

crest /krest/ n Kamm m; (coat of arms) Wappen nt

Crete /kri:t/ n Kreta nt

crevasse /krɪ'væs/ n [Gletscher]-spalte f

crevice /'krevɪs/ n Spalte f

crew /kru:/ n Besatzung f; (gang) Bande f. ~ **cut** n Bürstenschnitt m

crib[1] /krɪb/ n Krippe f

crib[2] vt/i (pt/pp **cribbed**) (fam) abschreiben

crick /krɪk/ n ~ **in the neck** steifes Genick nt

cricket[1] /'krɪkɪt/ n (insect) Grille f

cricket[2] n Kricket nt. ~**er** n Kricketspieler m

crime /kraɪm/ n Verbrechen nt; (rate) Kriminalität f

criminal /'krɪmɪnl/ a kriminell, verbrecherisch; ⟨law, court⟩ Straf- ● n Verbrecher m

crimson /'krɪmzn/ a purpurrot

cringe /krɪndʒ/ vi sich [ängstlich] ducken

crinkle /'krɪŋkl/ vt/i knittern

cripple /'krɪpl/ n Krüppel m ● vt zum Krüppel machen; (fig) lahmlegen. ~**d** a verkrüppelt

crisis /'kraɪsɪs/ n (pl **-ses** /-si:z/) Krise f

crisp /krɪsp/ a (-er, -est) knusprig. ~**bread** n Knäckebrot nt. ~**s** npl Chips pl

criss-cross /'krɪs-/ a schräg gekreuzt

criterion /kraɪ'tɪərɪən/ n (pl **-ria** /-rɪə/) Kriterium nt

critic /'krɪtɪk/ n Kritiker m. ~**al** a kritisch. ~**ally** adv kritisch; ~**ally ill** schwer krank

criticism /'krɪtɪsɪzm/ n Kritik f

criticize /'krɪtɪsaɪz/ vt kritisieren

croak /krəʊk/ vi krächzen; ⟨frog:⟩ quaken

crochet /'krəʊʃeɪ/ n Häkelarbeit f ● vt/i häkeln. ~**-hook** n Häkelnadel f

crock /krɒk/ n (fam) **old** ~ (person) Wrack m; (car) Klapperkiste f

crockery /'krɒkərɪ/ n Geschirr nt

crocodile /'krɒkədaɪl/ n Krokodil nt

crocus /'krəʊkəs/ n (pl **-es**) Krokus m

crony /'krəʊnɪ/ n Kumpel m

crook /krʊk/ n (stick) Stab m; (fam: criminal) Schwindler m, Gauner m

crooked /'krʊkɪd/ a schief; (bent) krumm; (fam: dishonest) unehrlich

crop /krɒp/ n Feldfrucht f; (harvest) Ernte f; (of bird) Kropf m ● v (pt/pp **cropped**) ● vt stutzen ● vi ~ **up** (fam) zur Sprache kommen; (occur) dazwischenkommen

croquet /'krəʊkeɪ/ n Krocket nt

croquette /krəʊ'ket/ n Krokette f

cross /krɒs/ a, **-ly** adv (annoyed) böse (with auf + acc); **talk at ~ purposes** aneinander vorbeireden ● n Kreuz nt; (Bot, Zool) Kreuzung f; **on the ~** schräg ● vt kreuzen (cheque, animals); überqueren (road); ~ **oneself** sich bekreuzigen; ~ **one's arms** die Arme verschränken; ~ **one's legs** die Beine übereinanderschlagen; **keep one's fingers ~ed for s.o.** jdm die Daumen drücken; **it ~ed my mind** es fiel mir ein ● vi (go across) hinübergehen/-fahren; (lines:) sich kreuzen. ~ **out** vt durchstreichen

cross: **~bar** n Querlatte f; (on bicycle) Stange f. **~-'country** n (Sport) Crosslauf m. **~-ex'amine** vt ins Kreuzverhör nehmen. **~-exami'nation** n Kreuzverhör nt. **~-'eyed** a schielend; **be ~-eyed** schielen. **~fire** n Kreuzfeuer nt. **~ing** n Übergang m; (sea journey) Überfahrt f. **~-'reference** n Querverweis m. **~roads** n [Straßen]kreuzung f. **~-'section** n Querschnitt m. **~-stitch** n Kreuzstich m. **~wise** adv quer. **~word** n **~word [puzzle]** Kreuzworträtsel nt

crotchet /'krɒtʃɪt/ n Viertelnote f

crotchety /'krɒtʃɪtɪ/ a griesgrämig

crouch /kraʊtʃ/ vi kauern

crow /krəʊ/ n Krähe f; **as the ~ flies** Luftlinie ● vi krähen. **~bar** n Brechstange f

crowd /kraʊd/ n [Menschen]menge f ● vi sich drängen. **~ed** /'kraʊdɪd/ a [gedrängt] voll

crown /kraʊn/ n Krone f ● vt krönen; überkronen (tooth)

crucial /'kru:ʃl/ a höchst wichtig; (decisive) entscheidend (**to** für)

crucifix /'kru:sɪfɪks/ n Kruzifix nt

cruci'f|ixion /'kru:sɪ'fɪkʃn/ n Kreuzigung f. **~y** /'kru:sɪfaɪ/ vt (pt/pp -ied) kreuzigen

crude /kru:d/ a (-r, -st) (raw) roh

cruel /kru:əl/ a (**crueller, cruellest**), **-ly** adv grausam (**to** gegen). **~ty** n Grausamkeit f; **~ty to animals** Tierquälerei f

cruis|e /kru:z/ n Kreuzfahrt f ● vi kreuzen; (car:) fahren. **~er** n (Mil) Kreuzer m; (motor boat) Kajütboot nt. **~ing speed** n Reisegeschwindigkeit f

crumb /krʌm/ n Krümel m

crumb|le /'krʌmbl/ vt/i krümeln; (collapse) einstürzen. **~ly** a krümelig

crumple /'krʌmpl/ vt zerknittern ● vi knittern

crunch /krʌntʃ/ n (fam) **when it comes to the ~** wenn es [wirklich] drauf ankommt ● vt mampfen ● vi knirschen

crusade /kru:'seɪd/ n Kreuzzug m; (fig) Kampagne f. **~r** n Kreuzfahrer m; (fig) Kämpfer m

crush /krʌʃ/ n (crowd) Gedränge nt ● vt zerquetschen; zerknittern (clothes); (fig: subdue) niederschlagen

crust /krʌst/ n Kruste f

crutch /krʌtʃ/ n Krücke f

crux /krʌks/ n (fig) springender Punkt m

cry /kraɪ/ n Ruf m; (shout) Schrei m; **a far ~ from** (fig) weit entfernt von ● vi (pt/pp **cried**) (weep) weinen; (baby:) schreien; (call) rufen

crypt /krɪpt/ n Krypta f. **~ic** a rätselhaft

crystal /'krɪstl/ n Kristall m; (glass) Kristall nt. **~lize** vi [sich] kristallisieren

cub /kʌb/ n (Zool) Junge(s) nt; **C~** [Scout] Wölfling m

Cuba /'kju:bə/ n Kuba nt

cubby-hole /'kʌbɪ-/ n Fach nt

cub|e /kju:b/ n Würfel m. **~ic** a Kubik-

cubicle /'kju:bɪkl/ n Kabine f

cuckoo /'kʊku:/ n Kuckuck m. **~ clock** n Kuckucksuhr f

cucumber /'kju:kʌmbə(r)/ n Gurke f

cuddl|e /'kʌdl/ vt herzen ● vi **~e up to** sich kuscheln an (+ acc). **~y** a kuschelig. **~y 'toy** n Plüschtier nt

cudgel /'kʌdʒl/ n Knüppel m

cue[1] /kju:/ n Stichwort nt

cue[2] n (Billiards) Queue nt

cuff /kʌf/ n Manschette f; (Amer: turn-up) [Hosen]aufschlag m; (blow) Klaps m; **off the ~** (fam) aus dem Stegreif ● vt einen Klaps geben (+ dat). **~-link** n Manschettenknopf m

cul-de-sac /'kʌldəsæk/ n Sackgasse f

culinary /'kʌlɪnərɪ/ a kulinarisch
cull /kʌl/ vt pflücken ⟨flowers⟩; (kill)
ausmerzen
culminat|e /'kʌlmɪneɪt/ vi gipfeln
(in in +dat). ~ion /-'neɪʃn/ n Gip-
felpunkt m
culottes /kju:'lɒts/ npl Hosenrock m
culprit /'kʌlprɪt/ n Täter m
cult /kʌlt/ n Kult m
cultivate /'kʌltɪveɪt/ vt anbauen
⟨crop⟩; bebauen ⟨land⟩
cultural /'kʌltʃərəl/ a kulturell
culture /'kʌltʃə(r)/ n Kultur f. ~d a
kultiviert
cumbersome /'kʌmbəsəm/ a hin-
derlich; (unwieldy) unhandlich
cumulative /'kju:mjʊlətɪv/ a kumu-
lativ
cunning /'kʌnɪŋ/ a listig ● n List f
cup /kʌp/ n Tasse f; (prize) Pokal m
cupboard /'kʌbəd/ n Schrank m
Cup 'Final n Pokalendspiel nt
Cupid /'kju:pɪd/ n Amor m
curable /'kjʊərəbl/ a heilbar
curate /'kjʊərət/ n Vikar m; (Roman
Catholic) Kaplan m
curator /kjʊə'reɪtə(r)/ n Kustos m
curb /kɜ:b/ vt zügeln
curdle /'kɜ:dl/ vi gerinnen
cure /kjʊə(r)/ n [Heil]mittel nt ● vt
heilen; (salt) pökeln; (smoke) räuchern; gerben ⟨skin⟩
curfew /'kɜ:fju:/ n Ausgangssperre f
curio /'kjʊərɪəʊ/ n Kuriosität f
curiosity /kjʊərɪ'ɒsɪtɪ/ n Neugier f;
(object) Kuriosität f
curious /'kjʊərɪəs/ a, -ly adv neugierig; (strange) merkwürdig, seltsam
curl /kɜ:l/ n Locke f ● vt locken ● vi
sich locken. ~ up vi sich zusammenrollen
curler /'kɜ:lə(r)/ n Lockenwickler m
curly /'kɜ:lɪ/ a (-ier, -iest) lockig
currant /'kʌrənt/ n (dried) Korinthe
f
currency /'kʌrənsɪ/ n Geläufigkeit f;
(money) Währung f; foreign ~
Devisen pl
current /'kʌrənt/ a augenblicklich,
gegenwärtig; (in general use) geläufig, gebräuchlich ● n Strömung f;
(Electr) Strom m. ~ affairs or
events npl Aktuelle(s) nt. ~ly adv
zur Zeit
curriculum /kə'rɪkjʊləm/ n Lehrplan m. ~ vitae /-'vi:taɪ/ n Lebens-
lauf m

curry /'kʌrɪ/ n Curry nt & m; (meal)
Currygericht nt ● vt (pt/pp -ied) ~
favour sich einschmeicheln (with bei)
curse /kɜ:s/ n Fluch m ● vt ver-
fluchen ● vi fluchen
cursory /'kɜ:sərɪ/ a flüchtig
curt /kɜ:t/ a, -ly adv barsch
curtail /kɜ:'teɪl/ vt abkürzen
curtain /'kɜ:tn/ n Vorhang m
curtsy /'kɜ:tsɪ/ n Knicks m ● vi (pt/
pp -ied) knicksen
curve /kɜ:v/ n Kurve f ● vi einen
Bogen machen; ~ to the right/left
nach rechts/links biegen. ~d a gebogen
cushion /'kʊʃn/ n Kissen nt ● vt
dämpfen; (protect) beschützen
cushy /'kʊʃɪ/ a (-ier, -iest) (fam)
bequem
custard /'kʌstəd/ n Vanillesoße f
custodian /kʌ'stəʊdɪən/ n Hüter m
custody /'kʌstədɪ/ n Obhut f; (of
child) Sorgerecht nt; (imprisonment)
Haft f
custom /'kʌstəm/ n Brauch m;
(habit) Gewohnheit f; (Comm) Kundschaft f. ~ary a üblich; (habitual) gewohnt. ~er n Kunde m/Kundin f
customs /'kʌstəmz/ npl Zoll m. ~
officer n Zollbeamte(r) m
cut /kʌt/ n Schnitt m; (Med) Schnitt-
wunde f; (reduction) Kürzung f; (in
price) Senkung f; ~ [of meat]
[Fleisch]stück m ● vt/i (pt/pp cut, pres
p cutting) schneiden; (mow) mähen;
abheben ⟨cards⟩; (reduce) kürzen;
senken ⟨price⟩; ~ one's finger sich in
den Finger schneiden; ~ s.o.'s hair jdm
die Haare schneiden; ~ short abkürzen. ~ back vt zurückschneiden;
(fig) einschränken, kürzen. ~ down
vt fällen; (fig) einschränken. ~ off vt
abschneiden; (disconnect) abstellen;
be ~ off (Teleph) unterbrochen
werden. ~ out vt ausschneiden; (delete) streichen; be ~ out for (fam)
geeignet sein zu. ~ up vt zerschneiden; (slice) aufschneiden
'cut-back n Kürzung f, Einschränkung f
cute /kju:t/ a (-r, -st) (fam) niedlich
cut 'glass n Kristall nt
cuticle /'kju:tɪkl/ n Nagelhaut f
cutlery /'kʌtlərɪ/ n Besteck nt
cutlet /'kʌtlɪt/ n Kotelett nt
'cut-price a verbilligt
cutting /'kʌtɪŋ/ a ⟨remark⟩ bissig ● n
(from newspaper) Ausschnitt m; (of
plant) Ableger m

CV *abbr of* **curriculum vitae**

cyclamen /'sɪkləmən/ *n* Alpenveilchen *nt*

cycl|e /'saɪkl/ *n* Zyklus *m*; (*bicycle*) [Fahr]rad *nt* ● *vi* mit dem Rad fahren. **~ing** *n* Radfahren *nt*. **~ist** *n* Radfahrer(in) *m*(*f*)

cyclone /'saɪkləʊn/ *n* Wirbelsturm *m*

cylind|er /'sɪlɪndə(r)/ *n* Zylinder *m*. **~rical** /-'lɪndrɪkl/ *a* zylindrisch

cymbals /'sɪmblz/ *npl* (*Mus*) Becken *nt*

cynic /'sɪnɪk/ *n* Zyniker *m*. **~al** *a*, **-ly** *adv* zynisch. **~ism** /-sɪzm/ *n* Zynismus *m*

cypress /'saɪprəs/ *n* Zypresse *f*

Cyprus /'saɪprəs/ *n* Zypern *nt*

cyst /sɪst/ *n* Zyste *f*. **~itis** /-'taɪtɪs/ *n* Blasenentzündung *f*

Czech /tʃek/ *a* tschechisch ● *n* Tscheche *m*/Tschechin *f*

Czechoslovak /tʃekə'sləʊvæk/ *a* tschechoslowakisch. **~ia** /-'vækɪə/ *n* die Tschechoslowakei. **~ian** /-'vækɪən/ *a* tschechoslowakisch

D

dab /dæb/ *n* Tupfer *m*; (*of butter*) Klecks *m*; **a ~ of** ein bißchen ● *vt* (*pt/pp* **dabbed**) abtupfen; betupfen (**with** mit)

dabble /'dæbl/ *vi* **~ in sth** (*fig*) sich nebenbei mit etw befassen

dachshund /'dækshʊnd/ *n* Dackel *m*

dad[dy] /'dæd[i]/ *n* (*fam*) Vati *m*

daddy-'long-legs *n* [Kohl]schnake *f*; (*Amer: spider*) Weberknecht *m*

daffodil /'dæfədɪl/ *n* Osterglocke *f*, gelbe Narzisse *f*

daft /dɑːft/ *a* (**-er, -est**) dumm

dagger /'dægə(r)/ *n* Dolch *m*; (*Typ*) Kreuz *nt*; **be at ~s drawn** (*fam*) auf Kriegsfuß stehen

dahlia /'deɪlɪə/ *n* Dahlie *f*

daily /'deɪlɪ/ *a & adv* täglich ● *n* (*newspaper*) Tageszeitung *f*; (*fam: cleaner*) Putzfrau *f*

dainty /'deɪntɪ/ *a* (**-ier, -iest**) zierlich

dairy /'deərɪ/ *n* Molkerei *f*; (*shop*) Milchgeschäft *nt*. **~ cow** *n* Milchkuh *f*. **~ products** *pl* Milchprodukte *pl*

dais /'deɪs/ *n* Podium *nt*

daisy /'deɪzɪ/ *n* Gänseblümchen *nt*

dale /deɪl/ *n* (*liter*) Tal *nt*

dally /'dælɪ/ *vi* (*pt/pp* **-ied**) trödeln

dam /dæm/ *n* [Stau]damm *m* ● *vt* (*pt/pp* **dammed**) eindämmen

damag|e /'dæmɪdʒ/ *n* Schaden *m* (**to** an + *dat*); **~es** *pl* (*Jur*) Schadenersatz *m* ● *vt* beschädigen; (*fig*) beeinträchtigen. **~ing** *a* schädlich

damask /'dæməsk/ *n* Damast *m*

dame /deɪm/ *n* (*liter*) Dame *f*; (*Amer sl*) Weib *nt*

damn /dæm/ *a*, *int & adv* (*fam*) verdammt ● *n* **I don't care** *or* **give a ~** (*fam*) ich schere mich einen Dreck darum ● *vt* verdammen. **~ation** /-'neɪʃn/ *n* Verdammnis *f* ● *int* (*fam*) verdammt!

damp /dæmp/ *a* (**-er, -est**) feucht ● *n* Feuchtigkeit *f* ● *vt* = **dampen**

damp|en *vt* anfeuchten; (*fig*) dämpfen. **~ness** *n* Feuchtigkeit *f*

dance /dɑːns/ *n* Tanz *m*; (*function*) Tanzveranstaltung *f* ● *vt/i* tanzen. **~-hall** *n* Tanzlokal *nt*. **~ music** *n* Tanzmusik *f*

dancer /'dɑːnsə(r)/ *n* Tänzer(in) *m*(*f*)

dandelion /'dændɪlaɪən/ *n* Löwenzahn *m*

dandruff /'dændrʌf/ *n* Schuppen *pl*

Dane /deɪn/ *n* Däne *m*/Dänin *f*; **Great ~** [deutsche] Dogge *f*

danger /'deɪndʒə(r)/ *n* Gefahr *f*; **in/out of ~** in/außer Gefahr. **~ous** /-rəs/ *a*, **-ly** *adv* gefährlich; **~ously ill** schwer erkrankt

dangle /'dæŋgl/ *vi* baumeln ● *vt* baumeln lassen

Danish /'deɪnɪʃ/ *a* dänisch. **~ 'pastry** *n* Hefeteilchen *nt*, Plunderstück *nt*

dank /dæŋk/ *a* (**-er, -est**) naßkalt

Danube /'dænjuːb/ *n* Donau *f*

dare /deə(r)/ *n* Mutprobe *f* ● *vt/i* (*challenge*) herausfordern (**to** zu); **~ [to] do sth** [es] wagen, etw zu tun; **I ~ say!** das mag wohl sein! **~devil** *n* Draufgänger *m*

daring /'deərɪŋ/ *a* verwegen ● *n* Verwegenheit *f*

dark /dɑːk/ *a* (**-er, -est**) dunkel; **~ blue/brown** dunkelblau/-braun; **~ horse** (*fig*) stilles Wasser *nt*; **keep sth ~** (*fig*) etw geheimhalten ● *n* Dunkelheit *f*; **after ~** nach Einbruch der Dunkelheit; **in the ~** im Dunkeln; **keep in the ~** (*fig*) im dunkeln lassen

dark|en /'dɑːkn/ *vt* verdunkeln ● *vi* dunkler werden. **~ness** *n* Dunkelheit *f*

'dark-room n Dunkelkammer f
darling /'dɑːlɪŋ/ a allerliebst ● n
Liebling m
darn /dɑːn/ vt stopfen. **~ing-needle**
n Stopfnadel f
dart /dɑːt/ n Pfeil m; (Sewing) Ab-
näher m; **~s** sg (game) [Wurf]-pfeil m
● vi flitzen
dash /dæʃ/ n (Typ) Gedankenstrich
m; (in Morse) Strich m; **a ~ of milk**
ein Schuß Milch; **make a ~** losstürzen
(**for** auf +acc) ● vi rennen ● vt
schleudern. **~ off** vi losstürzen ● vt
(write quickly) hinwerfen
'dashboard n Armaturenbrett nt
dashing /'dæʃɪŋ/ a schneidig
data /'deɪtə/ npl & sg Daten pl. **~**
processing n Datenverarbeitung f
date¹ /deɪt/ n (fruit) Dattel f
date² n Datum nt; (fam) Verabredung
f; **to ~** bis heute; **out of ~** überholt;
(expired) ungültig; **be up to ~** auf dem
laufenden sein ● vt/i datieren; (Amer,
fam: go out with) ausgehen mit; **~ back**
to zurückgehen auf (+acc)
dated /'deɪtɪd/ a altmodisch
'date-line n Datumsgrenze f
dative /'deɪtɪv/ a & n (Gram) **~**
[case] Dativ m
daub /dɔːb/ vt beschmieren (**with**
mit); schmieren (paint)
daughter /'dɔːtə(r)/ n Tochter f.
~-in-law n (pl **~s-in-law**)
Schwiegertochter f
daunt /dɔːnt/ vt entmutigen; **noth-**
ing ~ed unverzagt. **~less** a furchtlos
dawdle /'dɔːdl/ vi trödeln
dawn /dɔːn/ n Morgendämmerung f;
at ~ bei Tagesanbruch ● vi anbrechen;
it ~ed on me (fig) es ging mir auf
day /deɪ/ n Tag m; **~ by ~** Tag für
Tag; **~ after ~** Tag um Tag; **these ~s**
heutzutage; **in those ~s** zu der Zeit; **it's**
had its ~ (fam) es hat ausgedient
day: **~break** n **at ~break** bei Tagesanbruch m. **~-dream** n Tagtraum m
● vi [mit offenen Augen] träumen.
~light n Tageslicht nt. **~ re'turn** n
(ticket) Tagesrückfahrkarte f. **~**
time n in the **~time** am Tage
daze /deɪz/ n **in a ~** wie benommen.
~d a benommen
dazzle /'dæzl/ vt blenden
deacon /'diːkn/ n Diakon m
dead /ded/ a tot; (flower) verwelkt;
(numb) taub; **~ body** Leiche f; **be ~**
on time auf die Minute pünktlich kommen; **~ centre** genau in der Mitte

● adv **~ tired** todmüde; **~ slow** sehr
langsam; **stop ~** stehenbleiben ● n the
~ pl die Toten; **in the ~ of night** mitten in der Nacht
deaden /'dedn/ vt dämpfen (sound);
betäuben (pain)
dead: **~'end** n Sackgasse f. **~ 'heat**
n totes Rennen nt. **~line** n [letzter]
Termin m. **~lock** n reach **~lock** (fig)
sich festfahren
deadly /'dedlɪ/ a (-ier, -iest) tödlich;
(fam: dreary) sterbenslangweilig; **~**
sins pl Todsünden pl
deaf /def/ a (-er, -est) taub; **~ and**
dumb taubstumm. **~-aid** n Hörgerät
nt
deaf|en /'defn/ vt betäuben;
(permanently) taub machen. **~ening**
a ohrenbetäubend. **~ness** n Taub-
heit f
deal /diːl/ n (transaction) Geschäft
nt; **whose ~?** (Cards) wer gibt? **a good**
or great ~ eine Menge; **get a raw ~**
(fam) sehr schlecht abschneiden ● v
(pt/pp **dealt** /delt/) ● vt (Cards) geben;
~ out austeilen; **~ s.o. a blow** jdm
einen Schlag versetzen ● vi **~ in** handeln mit; **~ with** zu tun haben mit;
(handle) sich befassen mit; (cope with)
fertig werden mit; (be about) handeln
von; **that's been dealt with** das ist
schon erledigt
deal|er /'diːlə(r)/ n Händler m;
(Cards) Kartengeber m. **~ings** npl
have ~ings with zu tun haben mit
dean /diːn/ n Dekan m
dear /dɪə(r)/ a (-er, -est) lieb; (expensive) teuer; (in letter) liebe(r,s)/(formal)
sehr geehrte(r,s) ● n Liebe(r) m/f ● int
oh ~! oje! **~ly** adv (love) sehr; (pay)
teuer
dearth /dɜːθ/ n Mangel m (**of** an
+dat)
death /deθ/ n Tod m; **three ~s** drei
Todesfälle. **~ certificate** n Sterbe-
urkunde f. **~ duty** n Erbschafts-
steuer f
deathly a **~ silence** Totenstille f ● adv
~ pale totenblaß
death: **~ penalty** n Todesstrafe f.
~'s head n Totenkopf m. **~-trap** n
Todesfalle f
debar /dɪ'bɑː(r)/ vt (pt/pp **debarred**)
ausschließen
debase /dɪ'beɪs/ vt erniedrigen
debatable /dɪ'beɪtəbl/ a strittig
debate /dɪ'beɪt/ n Debatte f ● vt/i
debattieren

debauchery /dɪˈbɔːtʃərɪ/ n Aus-
schweifung f

debility /dɪˈbɪlətɪ/ n Entkräftung f

debit /ˈdebɪt/ n Schuldbetrag m; ~
[side] Soll nt ● vt (pt/pp debited)
(Comm) belasten; abbuchen ⟨sum⟩

debris /ˈdebriː/ n Trümmer pl

debt /det/ n Schuld f; in ~ verschuldet. ~or n Schuldner m

début /ˈdeɪbuː/ n Debüt nt

decade /ˈdekeɪd/ n Jahrzehnt nt

decaden|ce /ˈdekədəns/ n Dekadenz
f. ~t a dekadent

decaffeinated /diːˈkæfɪneɪtɪd/ a kof-
feinfrei

decant /dɪˈkænt/ vt umfüllen. ~er n
Karaffe f

decapitate /dɪˈkæpɪteɪt/ vt köpfen

decay /dɪˈkeɪ/ n Verfall m; (rot)
Verwesung f; (of tooth) Zahnfäule f
● vi verfallen; (rot) verwesen;
⟨tooth:⟩ schlecht werden

decease /dɪˈsiːs/ n Ableben nt. ~d a
verstorben ● n the ~d der/die Ver-
storbene

deceit /dɪˈsiːt/ n Täuschung f. ~ful
a, -ly adv unaufrichtig

deceive /dɪˈsiːv/ vt täuschen; (be unfaithful to) betrügen

December /dɪˈsembə(r)/ n Dezember m

decency /ˈdiːsənsɪ/ n Anstand m

decent /ˈdiːsənt/ a, -ly adv anständig

decentralize /diːˈsentrəlaɪz/ vt de-
zentralisieren

decept|ion /dɪˈsepʃn/ n Täuschung
f; (fraud) Betrug m. ~ive /-tɪv/ a, -ly
adv täuschend

decibel /ˈdesɪbel/ n Dezibel nt

decide /dɪˈsaɪd/ vt entscheiden ● vi
sich entscheiden (on für)

decided /dɪˈsaɪdɪd/ a, -ly adv entschieden

deciduous /dɪˈsɪdjʊəs/ a ~ tree
Laubbaum m

decimal /ˈdesɪml/ a Dezimal- ● n De-
zimalzahl f. ~ 'point n Komma nt. ~
system n Dezimalsystem nt

decimate /ˈdesɪmeɪt/ vt dezimieren

decipher /dɪˈsaɪfə(r)/ vt entziffern

decision /dɪˈsɪʒn/ n Entscheidung f;
(firmness) Entschlossenheit f

decisive /dɪˈsaɪsɪv/ a ausschlag-
gebend; (firm) entschlossen

deck[1] /dek/ vt schmücken

deck[2] n (Naut) Deck nt; on ~ an Deck;
top ~ (of bus) Oberdeck nt; ~ of cards

(Amer) [Karten]spiel nt. ~-chair n
Liegestuhl m

declaration /dekləˈreɪʃn/ n Erklärung f

declare /dɪˈkleə(r)/ vt erklären; angeben ⟨goods⟩; **anything to** ~? etwas
zu verzollen?

declension /dɪˈklenʃn/ n Dekli-
nation f

decline /dɪˈklaɪn/ n Rückgang m; (in
health) Verfall m ● vt ablehnen;
(Gram) deklinieren ● vi ablehnen;
(fall) sinken; (decrease) nachlassen

decode /diːˈkəʊd/ vt entschlüsseln

decompos|e /diːkəmˈpəʊz/ vi sich
zersetzen

décor /ˈdeɪkɔː(r)/ n Ausstattung f

decorat|e /ˈdekəreɪt/ vt (adorn)
schmücken; verzieren ⟨cake⟩; (paint)
streichen; (wallpaper) tapezieren;
(award medal to) einen Orden verleihen (+ dat). ~ion /-ˈreɪʃn/ n Verzierung f; (medal) Orden m; ~ions pl
Schmuck m. ~ive /-rətɪv/ a dekorativ. ~or n painter and ~or
Maler und Tapezierer m

decorous /ˈdekərəs/ a, -ly adv
schamhaft

decorum /dɪˈkɔːrəm/ n Anstand m

decoy[1] /ˈdiːkɔɪ/ n Lockvogel m

decoy[2] /dɪˈkɔɪ/ vt locken

decrease[1] /ˈdiːkriːs/ n Verringerung
f; (in number) Rückgang m; **be on the**
~ zurückgehen

decrease[2] /dɪˈkriːs/ vt verringern;
herabsetzen ⟨price⟩ ● vi sich verringern; ⟨price:⟩ sinken

decree /dɪˈkriː/ n Erlaß m ● vt (pt/pp
decreed) verordnen

decrepit /dɪˈkrepɪt/ a altersschwach

dedicat|e /ˈdedɪkeɪt/ vt widmen;
(Relig) weihen. ~ed a hingebungs-
voll; ⟨person⟩ aufopfernd. ~ion
/-ˈkeɪʃn/ n Hingabe f; (in book) Wid-
mung f

deduce /dɪˈdjuːs/ vt folgern (from
aus)

deduct /dɪˈdʌkt/ vt abziehen

deduction /dɪˈdʌkʃn/ n Abzug m;
(conclusion) Folgerung f

deed /diːd/ n Tat f; (Jur) Urkunde f

deem /diːm/ vt halten für

deep /diːp/ a (-er, -est), -ly adv tief;
go off the ~ **end** (fam) auf die Palme
gehen ● adv tief

deepen /ˈdiːpn/ vt vertiefen ● vi
tiefer werden; (fig) sich vertiefen

deep-'freeze *n* Gefriertruhe *f*; (*upright*) Gefrierschrank *m*

deer /dɪə(r)/ *n inv* Hirsch *m*; (*roe*) Reh *nt*

deface /dɪ'feɪs/ *vt* beschädigen

defamat|ion /defə'meɪʃn/ *n* Verleumdung *f*. **~ory** /dɪ'fæmətərɪ/ *a* verleumderisch

default /dɪ'fɔːlt/ *n* (*Jur*) Nichtzahlung *f*; (*failure to appear*) Nichterscheinen *nt*; **win by ~** (*Sport*) kampflos gewinnen ● *vi* nicht zahlen; nicht erscheinen

defeat /dɪ'fiːt/ *n* Niederlage *f*; (*defeating*) Besiegung *f*; (*rejection*) Ablehnung *f* ● *vt* besiegen; ablehnen; (*frustrate*) vereiteln

defect[1] /dɪ'fekt/ *vi* (*Pol*) überlaufen

defect[2] /'diːfekt/ *n* Fehler *m*; (*Techn*) Defekt *m*. **~ive** /dɪ'fektɪv/ *a* fehlerhaft; (*Techn*) defekt

defence /dɪ'fens/ *n* Verteidigung *f*. **~less** *a* wehrlos

defend /dɪ'fend/ *vt* verteidigen; (*justify*) rechtfertigen. **~ant** *n* (*Jur*) Beklagte(r) *m/f*; (*in criminal court*) Angeklagte(r) *m/f*

defensive /dɪ'fensɪv/ *a* defensiv ● *n* Defensive *f*

defer /dɪ'fɜː(r)/ *vt* (*pt/pp* **deferred**) (*postpone*) aufschieben; **~ to s.o.** sich jdm fügen

deferen|ce /'defərəns/ *n* Ehrerbietung *f*. **~tial** /-'renʃl/ *a*, **-ly** *adv* ehrerbietig

defian|ce /dɪ'faɪəns/ *n* Trotz *m*; **in ~ce of** zum Trotz (+ *dat*). **~t** *a*, **-ly** *adv* aufsässig

deficien|cy /dɪ'fɪʃənsɪ/ *n* Mangel *m*. **~t** *a* mangelhaft; **he is ~t in ...** ihm mangelt es an ... (*dat*)

deficit /'defɪsɪt/ *n* Defizit *nt*

defile /dɪ'faɪl/ *vt* (*fig*) schänden

define /dɪ'faɪn/ *vt* bestimmen; definieren (*word*)

definite /'defnɪt/ *a*, **-ly** *adv* bestimmt; (*certain*) sicher

definition /defɪ'nɪʃn/ *n* Definition *f*; (*Phot*, *TV*) Schärfe *f*

definitive /dɪ'fɪnətɪv/ *a* endgültig; (*authoritative*) maßgeblich

deflat|e /dɪ'fleɪt/ *vt* die Luft auslassen aus. **~ion** /-eɪʃn/ *n* (*Comm*) Deflation *f*

deflect /dɪ'flekt/ *vt* ablenken

deform|ed /dɪ'fɔːmd/ *a* mißgebildet. **~ity** *n* Mißbildung *f*

defraud /dɪ'frɔːd/ *vt* betrügen (**of** um)

defray /dɪ'freɪ/ *vt* bestreiten

defrost /diː'frɒst/ *vt* entfrosten; abtauen (*fridge*); auftauen (*food*)

deft /deft/ *a* (**-er**, **-est**), **-ly** *adv* geschickt. **~ness** *n* Geschicklichkeit *f*

defunct /dɪ'fʌŋkt/ *a* aufgelöst; (*law*) außer Kraft gesetzt

defuse /diː'fjuːz/ *vt* entschärfen

defy /dɪ'faɪ/ *vt* (*pt/pp* **-ied**) trotzen (+ *dat*); widerstehen (+ *dat*) (*attempt*)

degenerate[1] /dɪ'dʒenəreɪt/ *vi* degenerieren; **~ into** (*fig*) ausarten in (+ *acc*)

degenerate[2] /dɪ'dʒenərət/ *a* degeneriert

degrading /dɪ'greɪdɪŋ/ *a* entwürdigend

degree /dɪ'griː/ *n* Grad *m*; (*Univ*) akademischer Grad *m*; **20 ~s** 20 Grad

dehydrate /diː'haɪdreɪt/ *vt* Wasser entziehen (+ *dat*). **~d** /-ɪd/ *a* ausgetrocknet

de-ice /diː'aɪs/ *vt* enteisen

deign /deɪn/ *vi* **~ to do sth** sich herablassen, etw zu tun

deity /'diːɪtɪ/ *n* Gottheit *f*

dejected /dɪ'dʒektɪd/ *a*, **-ly** *adv* niedergeschlagen

delay /dɪ'leɪ/ *n* Verzögerung *f*; (*of train*, *aircraft*) Verspätung *f*; **without ~** unverzüglich ● *vt* aufhalten; (*postpone*) aufschieben; **be ~ed** (*person*.) aufgehalten werden; (*train*, *aircraft*.) Verspätung haben ● *vi* zögern

delegate[1] /'delɪgət/ *n* Delegierte(r) *m/f*

delegat|e[2] /'delɪgeɪt/ *vt* delegieren. **~ion** /-'geɪʃn/ *n* Delegation *f*

delet|e /dɪ'liːt/ *vt* streichen. **~ion** /-iːʃn/ *n* Streichung *f*

deliberate[1] /dɪ'lɪbərət/ *a*, **-ly** *adv* absichtlich; (*slow*) bedächtig

deliberat|e[2] /dɪ'lɪbəreɪt/ *vt/i* überlegen. **~ion** /-'reɪʃn/ *n* Überlegung *f*; **with ~ion** mit Bedacht

delicacy /'delɪkəsɪ/ *n* Feinheit *f*; Zartheit *f*; (*food*) Delikatesse *f*

delicate /'delɪkət/ *a* fein; (*fabric*, *health*) zart; (*situation*) heikel; (*mechanism*) empfindlich

delicatessen /delɪkə'tesn/ *n* Delikatessengeschäft *nt*

delicious /dɪ'lɪʃəs/ *a* köstlich

delight /dɪ'laɪt/ *n* Freude *f* ● *vt* entzücken ● *vi* **~ in** sich erfreuen an

(+ *dat*). **~ed** *a* hocherfreut; **be ~ed**
sich sehr freuen. **~ful** *a* reizend

delinquen|cy /dɪˈlɪŋkwənsɪ/ *n* Kri-
minalität *f*. **~t** *a* straffällig ● *n* Straf-
fällige(r) *m/f*

deli|rious /dɪˈlɪrɪəs/ *a* **be ~rious** im
Delirium sein. **~rium** /-rɪəm/ *n* Delirium *nt*

deliver /dɪˈlɪvə(r)/ *vt* liefern; zustellen ⟨*post, newspaper*⟩; halten
⟨*speech*⟩; überbringen ⟨*message*⟩; versetzen ⟨*blow*⟩; ⟨*set free*⟩ befreien; **~ a**
baby ein Kind zur Welt bringen.
~ance *n* Erlösung *f*. **~y** *n* Lieferung
f; ⟨*of post*⟩ Zustellung *f*; (*Med*)
Entbindung *f*; **cash on ~y** per
Nachnahme

delta /ˈdeltə/ *n* Delta *nt*

delude /dɪˈluːd/ *vt* täuschen; **~ one-**
self sich ⟨*dat*⟩ Illusionen machen

deluge /ˈdeljuːdʒ/ *n* Flut *f*; ⟨*heavy*
rain⟩ schwerer Guß *m* ● *vt* überschwemmen

delusion /dɪˈluːʒn/ *n* Täuschung *f*

de luxe /dəˈlʌks/ *a* Luxus-

delve /delv/ *vi* hineingreifen (**into**
in + *acc*); (*fig*) eingehen (**into** auf + *acc*)

demand /dɪˈmɑːnd/ *n* Forderung *f*;
(*Comm*) Nachfrage *f*; **in ~** gefragt; **on**
~ auf Verlangen ● *vt* verlangen, fordern (**of/from** von). **~ing** *a* anspruchsvoll

demarcation /diːmɑːˈkeɪʃn/ *n*
Abgrenzung *f*

demean /dɪˈmiːn/ *vt* **~ oneself** sich
erniedrigen

demeanour /dɪˈmiːnə(r)/ *n* Verhalten *nt*

demented /dɪˈmentɪd/ *a* verrückt

demise /dɪˈmaɪz/ *n* Tod *m*

demister /diːˈmɪstə(r)/ *n* (*Auto*) De-
froster *m*

demo /ˈdeməʊ/ *n* (*pl* **~s**) (*fam*)
Demonstration *f*

demobilize /diːˈməʊbɪlaɪz/ *vt* (*Mil*)
entlassen

democracy /dɪˈmɒkrəsɪ/ *n* Demo-
kratie *f*

democrat /ˈdeməkræt/ *n* Demokrat
m. **~ic** /-ˈkrætɪk/ *a*, **-ally** *adv* de-
mokratisch

demo|lish /dɪˈmɒlɪʃ/ *vt* abbre-
chen; (*destroy*) zerstören. **~lition**
/deməˈlɪʃn/ *n* Abbruch *m*

demon /ˈdiːmən/ *n* Dämon *m*

demonstrat|e /ˈdemənstreɪt/ *vt*
beweisen; vorführen ⟨*appliance*⟩
● *vi* (*Pol*) demonstrieren. **~ion**

/-ˈstreɪʃn/ *n* Vorführung *f*; (*Pol*) Demonstration *f*

demonstrative /dɪˈmɒnstrətɪv/ *a*
(*Gram*) demonstrativ; **be ~** seine
Gefühle zeigen

demonstrator /ˈdemənstreɪtə(r)/ *n*
Vorführer *m*; (*Pol*) Demonstrant *m*

demoralize /dɪˈmɒrəlaɪz/ *vt* demoralisieren

demote /dɪˈməʊt/ *vt* degradieren

demure /dɪˈmjʊə(r)/ *a*, **-ly** *adv* sittsam

den /den/ *n* Höhle *f*; (*room*) Bude *f*

denial /dɪˈnaɪəl/ *n* Leugnen *nt*;
official ~ Dementi *nt*

denigrate /ˈdenɪɡreɪt/ *vt* herabsetzen

denim /ˈdenɪm/ *n* Jeansstoff *m*; **~s**
pl Jeans *pl*

Denmark /ˈdenmɑːk/ *n* Dänemark *nt*

denomination /dɪnɒmɪˈneɪʃn/ *n*
(*Relig*) Konfession *f*; (*money*)
Nennwert *m*

denote /dɪˈnəʊt/ *vt* bezeichnen

denounce /dɪˈnaʊns/ *vt* denunzieren; (*condemn*) verurteilen

dens|e /dens/ *a* (**-r, -st**), **-ly** *adv* dicht;
(*fam: stupid*) blöd[e]. **~ity** *n* Dichte *f*

dent /dent/ *n* Delle *f*, Beule *f* ● *vt* einbeulen; **~ed** /-ɪd/ verbeult

dental /ˈdentl/ *a* Zahn-; ⟨*treatment*⟩
zahnärztlich. **~ floss** /flɒs/ *n* Zahn-
seide *f*. **~ surgeon** *n* Zahnarzt *m*

dentist /ˈdentɪst/ *n* Zahnarzt *m* /
-ärztin *f*. **~ry** *n* Zahnmedizin *f*

denture /ˈdentʃə(r)/ *n* Zahnprothese
f; **~s** *pl* künstliches Gebiß *nt*

denude /dɪˈnjuːd/ *vt* entblößen

denunciation /dɪnʌnsɪˈeɪʃn/ *n* De-
nunziation *f*; (*condemnation*) Verurteilung *f*

deny /dɪˈnaɪ/ *vt* (*pt/pp* **-ied**) leugnen;
(*officially*) dementieren; **~ s.o. sth**
jdm etw verweigern

deodorant /diːˈəʊdərənt/ *n* Deodorant *nt*

depart /dɪˈpɑːt/ *vi* abfahren; (*Aviat*)
abfliegen; (*go away*) weggehen/
-fahren; (*deviate*) abweichen (**from**
von)

department /dɪˈpɑːtmənt/ *n* Abteilung *f*; (*Pol*) Ministerium *nt*. **~**
store *n* Kaufhaus *nt*

departure /dɪˈpɑːtʃə(r)/ *n* Abfahrt *f*;
(*Aviat*) Abflug *m*; (*from rule*) Abweichung *f*; **new ~** Neuerung *f*

depend /dɪˈpend/ *vi* abhängen (**on**
von); (*rely*) sich verlassen (**on** auf

+ *acc*); **it all ~s** das kommt darauf an.
~able /-əbl/ *a* zuverlässig. **~ant** *n*
Abhängige(r) *m/f.* **~ence** *n* Abhängigkeit *f.* **~ent** *a* abhängig (**on** von)

depict /dɪ'pɪkt/ *vt* darstellen

depilatory /dɪ'pɪlətərɪ/ *n* Enthaarungsmittel *nt*

deplete /dɪ'pliːt/ *vt* verringern

deplor|able /dɪ'plɔːrəbl/ *a* bedauerlich. **~e** *vt* bedauern

deploy /dɪ'plɔɪ/ *vt* (*Mil*) einsetzen
● *vi* sich aufstellen

depopulate /diː'pɒpjʊleɪt/ *vt* entvölkern

deport /dɪ'pɔːt/ *vt* deportieren, ausweisen. **~ation** /diːpɔː'teɪʃn/ *n* Ausweisung *f*

deportment /dɪ'pɔːtmənt/ *n* Haltung *f*

depose /dɪ'pəʊz/ *vt* absetzen

deposit /dɪ'pɒzɪt/ *n* Anzahlung *f*; (*against damage*) Kaution *f*; (*on bottle*) Pfand *nt*; (*sediment*) Bodensatz *m*; (*Geol*) Ablagerung *f* ● *vt* (*pt/pp* **deposited**) legen; (*for safety*) deponieren; (*Geol*) ablagern. **~ account** *n* Sparkonto *nt*

depot /'depəʊ/ *n* Depot *nt*; (*Amer: railway station*) Bahnhof *m*

deprav|e /dɪ'preɪv/ *vt* verderben. **~ed** *a* verkommen. **~ity** /-'prævɪtɪ/ *n* Verderbtheit *f*

deprecate /'deprəkeɪt/ *vt* mißbilligen

depreciat|e /dɪ'priːʃɪeɪt/ *vi* an Wert verlieren. **~ion** /-'eɪʃn/ *n* Wertminderung *f*; (*Comm*) Abschreibung *f*

depress /dɪ'pres/ *vt* deprimieren; (*press down*) herunterdrücken. **~ed** *a* deprimiert; **~ed area** Notstandsgebiet *nt*. **~ing** *a* deprimierend. **~ion** /-eʃn/ *n* Vertiefung *f*; (*Med*) Depression *f*; (*Meteorol*) Tief *nt*

deprivation /deprɪ'veɪʃn/ *n* Entbehrung *f*

deprive /dɪ'praɪv/ *vt* entziehen; **~ s.o. of sth** jdm etw entziehen. **~d** *a* benachteiligt

depth /depθ/ *n* Tiefe *f*; **in ~** gründlich; **in the ~s of winter** im tiefsten Winter

deputation /depjʊ'teɪʃn/ *n* Abordnung *f*

deputize /'depjʊtaɪz/ *vi* **~ for** vertreten

deputy /'depjʊtɪ/ *n* Stellvertreter *m*
● *attrib* stellvertretend

derail /dɪ'reɪl/ *vt* **be ~ed** entgleisen.
~ment *n* Entgleisung *f*

deranged /dɪ'reɪndʒd/ *a* geistesgestört

derelict /'derəlɪkt/ *a* verfallen; (*abandoned*) verlassen

deri|de /dɪ'raɪd/ *vt* verhöhnen.
~sion /-'rɪʒn/ *n* Hohn *m*

derisive /dɪ'raɪsɪv/ *a*, **-ly** *adv* höhnisch

derisory /dɪ'raɪsərɪ/ *a* höhnisch; (*offer*) lächerlich

derivation /derɪ'veɪʃn/ *n* Ableitung *f*

derivative /dɪ'rɪvətɪv/ *a* abgeleitet
● *n* Ableitung *f*

derive /dɪ'raɪv/ *vt/i* (*obtain*) gewinnen (**from** aus); **be ~d from** (*word*) hergeleitet sein aus

dermatologist /dɜːmə'tɒlədʒɪst/ *n* Hautarzt *m* /-ärztin *f*

derogatory /dɪ'rɒɡətrɪ/ *a* abfällig

derrick /'derɪk/ *n* Bohrturm *m*

derv /dɜːv/ *n* Diesel[kraftstoff] *m*

descend /dɪ'send/ *vt/i* hinunter-/heruntergehen; (*vehicle, lift:*) hinunter-/herunterfahren; **be ~ed from** abstammen von. **~ant** *n* Nachkomme *m*

descent /dɪ'sent/ *n* Abstieg *m*; (*lineage*) Abstammung *f*

describe /dɪ'skraɪb/ *vt* beschreiben

descrip|tion /dɪ'skrɪpʃn/ *n* Beschreibung *f*; (*sort*) Art *f.* **~tive** /-tɪv/ *a* beschreibend; (*vivid*) anschaulich

desecrat|e /'desɪkreɪt/ *vt* entweihen. **~ion** /-'kreɪʃn/ *n* Entweihung *f*

desert[1] /'dezət/ *n* Wüste *f* ● *a* Wüsten-; **~ island** verlassene Insel *f*

desert[2] /dɪ'zɜːt/ *vt* verlassen ● *vi* > desertieren. **~ed** *a* verlassen. **~er** *n* (*Mil*) Deserteur *m.* **~ion** /-ɜːʃn/ *n* Fahnenflucht *f*

deserts /dɪ'zɜːts/ *npl* **get one's ~** seinen verdienten Lohn bekommen

deserv|e /dɪ'zɜːv/ *vt* verdienen.
~edly /-ɪdlɪ/ *adv* verdientermaßen.
~ing *a* verdienstvoll; **~ing cause** guter Zweck *m*

design /dɪ'zaɪn/ *n* Entwurf *m*; (*pattern*) Muster *nt*; (*construction*) Konstruktion *f*; (*aim*) Absicht *f* ● *vt* entwerfen; (*construct*) konstruieren; **be ~ed for** bestimmt sein für

designat|e /'dezɪgneɪt/ *vt* bezeichnen; (*appoint*) ernennen. **~ion** /-'neɪʃn/ *n* Bezeichnung *f*

designer /dɪ'zaɪnə(r)/ *n* Designer *m*; (*Techn*) Konstrukteur *m*; (*Theat*) Bühnenbildner *m*

desirable /dɪ'zaɪrəbl/ *a* wünschenswert; (*sexually*) begehrenswert

desire /dɪ'zaɪə(r)/ *n* Wunsch *m*; (*longing*) Verlangen *nt* (**for** nach); (*sexual*) Begierde *f* ● *vt* [sich (*dat*)] wünschen; (*sexually*) be- gehren

desk /desk/ *n* Schreibtisch *m*; (*Sch*) Pult *nt*; (*Comm*) Kasse *f*; (*in hotel*) Rezeption *f*

desolat|e /'desələt/ *a* trostlos. **~ion** /-'leɪʃn/ *n* Trostlosigkeit *f*

despair /dɪ'speə(r)/ *n* Verzweiflung *f*; **in ~** verzweifelt ● *vi* verzweifeln

desperat|e /'despərət/ *a*, **-ly** *adv* verzweifelt; (*urgent*) dringend; **be ~e** (*criminal:*) zum Äußersten entschlossen sein; **be ~e for** dringend brauchen. **~ion** /-'reɪʃn/ *n* Verzweiflung *f*; **in ~ion** aus Verzweiflung

despicable /dɪ'spɪkəbl/ *a* verachtenswert

despise /dɪ'spaɪz/ *vt* verachten

despite /dɪ'spaɪt/ *prep* trotz (+ *gen*)

despondent /dɪ'spɒndənt/ *a* niedergeschlagen

despot /'despɒt/ *n* Despot *m*

dessert /dɪ'zɜːt/ *n* Dessert *nt*, Nachtisch *m*. **~ spoon** *n* Dessertlöffel *m*

destination /destɪ'neɪʃn/ *n* [Reise] ziel *nt*; (*of goods*) Bestimmungsort *m*

destine /'destɪn/ *vt* bestimmen

destiny /'destɪnɪ/ *n* Schicksal *nt*

destitute /'destɪtjuːt/ *a* völlig mittellos

destroy /dɪ'strɔɪ/ *vt* zerstören; (*totally*) vernichten. **~er** *n* (*Naut*) Zerstörer *m*

destruc|tion /dɪ'strʌkʃn/ *n* Zerstörung *f*; Vernichtung *f*. **-tive** /-tɪv/ *a* zerstörerisch; (*fig*) destruktiv

detach /dɪ'tætʃ/ *vt* abnehmen; (*tear off*) abtrennen. **~able** /-əbl/ *a* abnehmbar. **~ed** *a* (*fig*) distanziert; **~ed house** Einzelhaus *nt*

detachment /dɪ'tætʃmənt/ *n* Distanz *f*; (*objectivity*) Abstand *m*; (*Mil*) Sonderkommando *nt*

detail /'diːteɪl/ *n* Einzelheit *f*, Detail *nt*; **in ~** ausführlich ● *vt* einzeln aufführen; (*Mil*) abkommandieren. **~ed** *a* ausführlich

detain /dɪ'teɪn/ *vt* aufhalten; ⟨*police:*⟩ in Haft behalten; (*take into custody*) in Haft nehmen. **~ee** /diːteɪ'niː/ *n* Häftling *m*

detect /dɪ'tekt/ *vt* entdecken; (*perceive*) wahrnehmen. **~ion** /-ekʃn/ *n* Entdeckung *f*

detective /dɪ'tektɪv/ *n* Detektiv *m*. **~ story** *n* Detektivroman *m*

detector /dɪ'tektə(r)/ *n* Suchgerät *nt*; (*for metal*) Metalldetektor *m*

detention /dɪ'tenʃn/ *n* Haft *f*; (*Sch*) Nachsitzen *nt*

deter /dɪ'tɜː(r)/ *vt* (*pt/pp* **deterred**) abschrecken; (*prevent*) abhalten

detergent /dɪ'tɜːdʒənt/ *n* Waschmittel *nt*

deteriorat|e /dɪ'tɪərɪəreɪt/ *vi* sich verschlechtern. **~ion** /-'reɪʃn/ *n* Verschlechterung *f*

determination /dɪtɜːmɪ'neɪʃn/ *n* Entschlossenheit *f*

determine /dɪ'tɜːmɪn/ *vt* bestimmen; **~ to** (*resolve*) sich entschließen zu. **~d** *a* entschlossen

deterrent /dɪ'terənt/ *n* Abschreckungsmittel *nt*

detest /dɪ'test/ *vt* verabscheuen. **~able** /-əbl/ *a* abscheulich

detonat|e /'detəneɪt/ *vt* zünden ● *vi* explodieren. **~or** *n* Zünder *m*

detour /'diːtʊə(r)/ *n* Umweg *m*; (*for traffic*) Umleitung *f*

detract /dɪ'trækt/ *vi* **~ from** beeinträchtigen

detriment /'detrɪmənt/ *n* **to the ~** zum Schaden (**of** *gen*). **~al** /-'mentl/ *a* schädlich (**to** *dat*)

deuce /djuːs/ *n* (*Tennis*) Einstand *m*

devaluation /diːvæljʊ'eɪʃn/ *n* Abwertung *f*

de'value *vt* abwerten ⟨*currency*⟩

devastat|e /'devəsteɪt/ *vt* verwüsten. **~ed** /-ɪd/ *a* (*fam*) erschüttert. **~ing** *a* verheerend. **~ion** /-'steɪʃn/ *n* Verwüstung *f*

develop /dɪ'veləp/ *vt* entwickeln; bekommen ⟨*illness*⟩; erschließen ⟨*area*⟩ ● *vi* sich entwickeln (**into** zu). **~er** *n* [property] **~er** Bodenspekulant *m*

de'veloping country *n* Entwicklungsland *nt*

development /dɪ'veləpmənt/ *n* Entwicklung *f*

deviant /'diːvɪənt/ *a* abweichend
deviat|e /'diːvɪeɪt/ *vi* abweichen.
~**ion** /-'eɪʃn/ *n* Abweichung *f*
device /dɪ'vaɪs/ *n* Gerät *nt*; (*fig*) Mittel *nt*; **leave s.o. to his own** ~**s** jdn
sich (*dat*) selbst überlassen
devil /'devl/ *n* Teufel *m*. ~**ish** *a*
teuflisch
devious /'diːvɪəs/ *a* verschlagen; ~
route Umweg *m*
devise /dɪ'vaɪz/ *vt* sich (*dat*) ausdenken
devoid /dɪ'vɔɪd/ *a* ~ **of** ohne
devolution /diːvə'luːʃn/ *n* Dezentralisierung *f*; (*of power*)
Übertragung *f*
devot|e /dɪ'vəʊt/ *vt* widmen (**to** *dat*).
~**ed** *a*, **-ly** *adv* ergeben; ⟨*care*⟩ liebevoll;
be ~**ed to** s.o. sehr an jdm hängen.
~**ee** /devə'tiː/ *n* Anhänger(in) *m(f)*
devotion /dɪ'vəʊʃn/ *n* Hingabe *f*; ~**s**
pl (*Relig*) Andacht *f*
devour /dɪ'vaʊə(r)/ *vt* verschlingen
devout /dɪ'vaʊt/ *a* fromm
dew /djuː/ *n* Tau *m*
dexterity /dek'sterətɪ/ *n* Geschicklichkeit *f*
diabet|es /daɪə'biːtiːz/ *n* Zuckerkrankheit *f*. ~**ic** /-'betɪk/ *a* zuckerkrank ● *n* Zuckerkranke(r) *m/f*,
Diabetiker(in) *m(f)*
diabolical /daɪə'bɒlɪkl/ *a* teuflisch
diagnose /'daɪəgnəʊz/ *vt* diagnostizieren
diagnosis /daɪəg'nəʊsɪs/ *n* (*pl*
-oses /-siːz/) Diagnose *f*
diagonal /daɪ'ægənl/ *a*, **-ly** *adv* diagonal ● *n* Diagonale *f*
diagram /'daɪəgræm/ *n* Diagramm
nt
dial /'daɪəl/ *n* (*of clock*) Zifferblatt *nt*;
(*Techn*) Skala *f*; (*Teleph*) Wählscheibe *f* ● *vt/i* (*pt/pp* **dialled**)
(*Teleph*) wählen; ~ **direct** durchwählen
dialect /'daɪəlekt/ *n* Dialekt *m*
dialling: ~ **code** *n* Vorwahlnummer
f. ~ **tone** *n* Amtszeichen *nt*
dialogue /'daɪəlɒg/ *n* Dialog *m*
'**dial tone** *n* (*Amer, Teleph*) Amtszeichen *nt*
diameter /daɪ'æmɪtə(r)/ *n* Durchmesser *m*
diametrically /daɪə'metrɪkəlɪ/ *adv*
~ **opposed** genau entgegengesetzt (**to**
dat)
diamond /'daɪəmənd/ *n* Diamant *m*;
(*cut*) Brillant *m*; (*shape*) Raute *f*; ~**s**
pl (*Cards*) Karo *nt*

diaper /'daɪəpə(r)/ *n* (*Amer*) Windel *f*
diaphragm /'daɪəfræm/ *n* (*Anat*)
Zwerchfell *nt*; (*Phot*) Blende *f*
diarrhoea /daɪə'riːə/ *n* Durchfall *m*
diary /'daɪərɪ/ *n* Tagebuch *nt*; (*for
appointments*) [Termin]kalender *m*
dice /daɪs/ *n inv* Würfel *m* ● *vt* (*Culin*) in Würfel schneiden
dicey /'daɪsɪ/ *a* (*fam*) riskant
dictat|e /dɪk'teɪt/ *vt/i* diktieren.
~**ion** /-eɪʃn/ *n* Diktat *nt*
dictator /dɪk'teɪtə(r)/ *n* Diktator *m*.
~**ial** /-tə'tɔːrɪəl/ *a* diktatorisch.
~**ship** *n* Diktatur *f*
diction /'dɪkʃn/ *n* Aussprache *f*
dictionary /'dɪkʃənrɪ/ *n* Wörterbuch
nt
did /dɪd/ *see* **do**
didactic /dɪ'dæktɪk/ *a* didaktisch
diddle /'dɪdl/ *vt* (*fam*) übers Ohr
hauen
didn't /'dɪdnt/ = **did not**
die[1] /daɪ/ *n* (*Techn*) Prägestempel *m*;
(*metal mould*) Gußform *f*
die[2] *vi* (*pres p* **dying**) sterben (**of** an
+ *dat*); ⟨*plant, animal:*⟩ eingehen;
⟨*flower:*⟩ verwelken; **be dying to do
sth** (*fam*) darauf brennen, etw zu tun;
be dying for sth (*fam*) sich nach etw
sehnen. ~ **down** *vi* nachlassen;
⟨*fire:*⟩ herunterbrennen. ~ **out** *vi*
aussterben
diesel /'diːzl/ *n* Diesel *m*. ~ **engine** *n*
Dieselmotor *m*
diet /'daɪət/ *n* Kost *f*; (*restricted*) Diät
f; (*for slimming*) Schlankheitskur *f*;
be on a ~ diät leben; **eine
Schlankheitskur machen** ● *vi* diät
leben; eine Schlankheitskur machen
dietician /daɪə'tɪʃn/ *n* Diätassistent(in) *m(f)*
differ /'dɪfə(r)/ *vi* sich unterscheiden; (*disagree*) verschiedener
Meinung sein
differen|ce /'dɪfrəns/ *n* Unterschied
m; (*disagreement*) Meinungsverschiedenheit *f*. ~**t** *a* andere(r,s);
(*various*) verschiedene; **be** ~**t** anders
sein (**from** als)
differential /dɪfə'renʃl/ *a* Differential- ● *n* Unterschied *m*; (*Techn*) Differential *nt*
differentiate /dɪfə'renʃɪeɪt/ *vt/i*
unterscheiden (**between** zwischen
+ *dat*)
differently /'dɪfrəntlɪ/ *adv* anders
difficult /'dɪfɪkəlt/ *a* schwierig,
schwer. ~**y** *n* Schwierigkeit *f*

diffiden|ce /'dıfıdəns/ n Zaghaftigkeit f. ~t a zaghaft

diffuse¹ /dı'fjuːs/ a ausgebreitet; (wordy) langatmig

diffuse² /dı'fjuːz/ vt (Phys) streuen

dig /dıg/ n (poke) Stoß m; (remark) spitze Bemerkung f; (Archaeol) Ausgrabung f; ~s pl (fam) möbliertes Zimmer nt ● vt/i (pt/pp dug, pres p **digging**) graben; umgraben ⟨garden⟩; ~ s.o. in the ribs jdm einen Rippenstoß geben. ~ **out** vt ausgraben. ~ **up** vt ausgraben; umgraben ⟨garden⟩; aufreißen ⟨street⟩

digest¹ /'daıdʒest/ n Kurzfassung f

digest² /dı'dʒest/ vt verdauen. ~**ible** a verdaulich. ~**ion** /-estʃn/ n Verdauung f

digger /'dıgə(r)/ n (Techn) Bagger m

digit /'dıdʒıt/ n Ziffer f; (finger) Finger m; (toe) Zehe f

digital /'dıdʒıtl/ a Digital-; ~ **clock** Digitaluhr f

dignified /'dıgnıfaıd/ a würdevoll

dignitary /'dıgnıtərı/ n Würdenträger m

dignity /'dıgnıtı/ n Würde f

digress /daı'gres/ vi abschweifen. ~**ion** /-eʃn/ n Abschweifung f

dike /daık/ n Deich m; (ditch) Graben m

dilapidated /dı'læpıdeıtıd/ a baufällig

dilate /daı'leıt/ vt erweitern ● vi sich erweitern

dilatory /'dılətərı/ a langsam

dilemma /dı'lemə/ n Dilemma nt

dilettante /dılı'tæntı/ n Dilettant(in) m(f)

diligen|ce /'dılıdʒəns/ n Fleiß m. ~t a, -ly adv fleißig

dill /dıl/ n Dill m

dilly-dally /'dılıdælı/ vi (pt/pp -ied) (fam) trödeln

dilute /daı'luːt/ vt verdünnen

dim /dım/ a (dimmer, dimmest), -ly adv (weak) schwach; (dark) trüb[e]; (indistinct) undeutlich; (fam: stupid) dumm, (fam) doof ● v (pt/pp dimmed) ● vt dämpfen ● vi schwächer werden

dime /daım/ n (Amer) Zehncentstück nt

dimension /daı'menʃn/ n Dimension f; ~s pl Maße pl

diminish /dı'mınıʃ/ vt verringern ● vi sich verringern

diminutive /dı'mınjʊtıv/ a winzig ● n Verkleinerungsform f

dimple /'dımpl/ n Grübchen nt

din /dın/ n Krach m, Getöse nt

dine /daın/ vi speisen. ~**r** n Speisende(r) m/f; (Amer: restaurant) Eßlokal nt

dinghy /'dıŋgı/ n Dinghi nt; (inflatable) Schlauchboot nt

dingy /'dındʒı/ a (-ier, -iest) trübe

dining /'daınıŋ/: ~-**car** n Speisewagen m. ~-**room** n Eßzimmer nt. ~-**table** n Eßtisch m

dinner /'dınə(r)/ n Abendessen nt; (at midday) Mittagessen nt; (formal) Essen nt. ~-**jacket** n Smoking m

dinosaur /'daınəsɔː(r)/ n Dinosaurier m

dint /dınt/ n **by** ~ **of** durch (+ acc)

diocese /'daısıs/ n Diözese f

dip /dıp/ n (in ground) Senke f; (Culin) Dip m; **go for a** ~ kurz schwimmen gehen ● v (pt/pp dipped) vt [ein]tauchen; ~ **one's headlights** (Auto) [die Scheinwerfer] abblenden ● vi sich senken

diphtheria /dıf'θıərıə/ n Diphtherie f

diphthong /'dıfθɒŋ/ n Diphthong m

diploma /dı'pləʊmə/ n Diplom nt

diplomacy /dı'pləʊməsı/ n Diplomatie f

diplomat /'dıpləmæt/ n Diplomat m. ~**ic** /-'mætık/ a, -ally adv diplomatisch

'dip-stick n (Auto) Ölmeßstab m

dire /'daıə(r)/ a (-r, -st) bitter; ⟨situation, consequences⟩ furchtbar

direct /dı'rekt/ a & adv direkt ● vt (aim) richten (at auf / (fig) an + acc); (control) leiten; (order) anweisen; ~ s.o. (show the way) jdm den Weg sagen; ~ **a film/play** bei einem Film/ Theaterstück Regie führen. ~ '**current** n Gleichstrom m

direction /dı'rekʃn/ n Richtung f; (control) Leitung f; (of play, film) Regie f; ~s pl Anweisungen pl; ~s **for use** Gebrauchsanweisung f

directly /dı'rektlı/ adv direkt; (at once) sofort ● conj (fam) sobald

director /dı'rektə(r)/ n (Comm) Direktor m; (of play, film) Regisseur m

directory /dı'rektərı/ n Verzeichnis nt; (Teleph) Telefonbuch nt

dirt /dɜːt/ n Schmutz m; (soil) Erde f; ~ **cheap** (fam) spottbillig

dirty /'dɜːtı/ a (-ier, -iest) schmutzig ● vt schmutzig machen

dis|a'bility /dɪs-/ n Behinderung f. **~abled** /dɪ'seɪbld/ a [kör-per]behindert

disad'van|tage n Nachteil m; **at a ~tage** im Nachteil. **~taged** a benachteiligt. **~'tageous** a nachteilig

disaf'fected a unzufrieden; (disloyal) illoyal

disa'gree vi nicht übereinstimmen (**with** mit); **I ~** ich bin anderer Meinung; **we ~** wir sind verschiedener Meinung; **oysters ~ with me** Austern bekommen mir nicht

disa'greeable a unangenehm

disa'greement n Meinungsverschiedenheit f

disap'pear vi verschwinden. **~ance** n Verschwinden nt

disap'point vt enttäuschen. **~ment** n Enttäuschung f

disap'proval n Mißbilligung f

disap'prove vi dagegen sein; **~ of** mißbilligen

dis'arm vt entwaffnen ● vi (Mil) abrüsten. **~ament** n Abrüstung f. **~ing** a entwaffnend

disar'ray n Unordnung f

disast|er /dɪ'zɑːstə(r)/ n Katastrophe f; (accident) Unglück nt. **~rous** /-rəs/ a katastrophal

dis'band vt auflösen ● vi sich auflösen

disbe'lief n Ungläubigkeit f; **in ~** ungläubig

disc /dɪsk/ n Scheibe f; (record) [Schall]platte f; (CD) CD f

discard /dɪ'skɑːd/ vt ablegen; (throw away) wegwerfen

discern /dɪ'sɜːn/ vt wahrnehmen. **~ible** a wahrnehmbar. **~ing** a anspruchsvoll

'discharge[1] n Ausstoßen nt; (Naut, Electr) Entladung f; (dismissal) Entlassung f; (Jur) Freispruch m; (Med) Ausfluß m

dis'charge[2] vt ausstoßen; (Naut, Electr) entladen; (dismiss) entlassen; (Jur) freisprechen ⟨accused⟩; **~ a duty** sich einer Pflicht entledigen

disciple /dɪ'saɪpl/ n Jünger m; (fig) Schüler m

disciplinary /'dɪsɪplɪnəri/ a disziplinarisch

discipline /'dɪsɪplɪn/ n Disziplin f ● vt Disziplin beibringen (+ dat); (punish) bestrafen

'disc jockey n Diskjockey m

dis'claim vt abstreiten. **~er** n Verzichterklärung f

dis'clos|e vt enthüllen. **~ure** n Enthüllung f

disco /'dɪskəʊ/ n (fam) Disko f

dis'colour vt verfärben ● vi sich verfärben

dis'comfort n Beschwerden pl; (fig) Unbehagen nt

disconcert /dɪskən'sɜːt/ vt aus der Fassung bringen

discon'nect vt trennen; (Electr) ausschalten; (cut supply) abstellen

disconsolate /dɪs'kɒnsələt/ a untröstlich

discon'tent n Unzufriedenheit f. **~ed** a unzufrieden

discon'tinue vt einstellen; (Comm) nicht mehr herstellen

'discord n Zwietracht f; (Mus & fig) Mißklang m. **~ant** /dɪ'skɔːdənt/ a **~ant note** Mißklang m

discothèque /'dɪskətek/ n Diskothek f

'discount[1] n Rabatt m

dis'count[2] vt außer acht lassen

dis'courage vt entmutigen; (dissuade) abraten (+ dat)

'discourse n Rede f

dis'courteous a, -ly adv unhöflich

discover /dɪ'skʌvə(r)/ vt entdecken. **~y** n Entdeckung f

dis'credit n Mißkredit m ● vt in Mißkredit bringen

discreet /dɪ'skriːt/ a, -ly adv diskret

discrepancy /dɪ'skrepənsi/ n Diskrepanz f

discretion /dɪ'skreʃn/ n Diskretion f; (judgement) Ermessen nt

discriminat|e /dɪ'skrɪmɪneɪt/ vi unterscheiden (**between** zwischen + dat); **~e against** diskriminieren. **~ing** a anspruchsvoll. **~ion** /-'neɪʃn/ n Diskriminierung f; (quality) Urteilskraft f

discus /'dɪskəs/ n Diskus m

discuss /dɪ'skʌs/ vt besprechen; (examine critically) diskutieren. **~ion** /-ʌʃn/ n Besprechung f; Diskussion f

disdain /dɪs'deɪn/ n Verachtung f ● vt verachten. **~ful** a verächtlich

disease /dɪ'ziːz/ n Krankheit f. **~d** a krank

disem'bark vi an Land gehen

disen'chant vt ernüchtern. **~ment** n Ernüchterung f

disen'gage vt losmachen; **~ the clutch** (Auto) auskuppeln

disen'tangle *vt* entwirren

dis'favour *n* Ungnade *f*; (*disapproval*) Mißfallen *nt*

dis'figure *vt* entstellen

dis'gorge *vt* ausspeien

dis'grace *n* Schande *f*; **in ~** in Ungnade ● *vt* Schande machen (+*dat*). **~ful** *a* schändlich

disgruntled /dɪsˈgrʌntld/ *a* verstimmt

disguise /dɪsˈgaɪz/ *n* Verkleidung *f*; **in ~** verkleidet ● *vt* verkleiden; verstellen ⟨*voice*⟩; ⟨*conceal*⟩ verhehlen

disgust /dɪsˈgʌst/ *n* Ekel *m*; **in ~** empört ● *vt* anekeln; (*appal*) empören. **~ing** *a* eklig; (*appalling*) abscheulich

dish /dɪʃ/ *n* Schüssel *f*; (*shallow*) Schale *f*; (*small*) Schälchen *nt*; (*food*) Gericht *nt*. **~ out** *vt* austeilen. **~ up** *vt* auftragen

'dishcloth *n* Spültuch *nt*

dis'hearten *vt* entmutigen. **~ing** *a* entmutigend

dishevelled /dɪˈʃevld/ *a* zerzaust

dis'honest *a*, **-ly** *adv* unehrlich. **~y** *n* Unehrlichkeit *f*

dis'honour *n* Schande *f* ● *vt* entehren; nicht honorieren ⟨*cheque*⟩. **~able** *a*, **-bly** *adv* unehrenhaft

'dishwasher *n* Geschirrspülmaschine *f*

disil'lusion *vt* ernüchtern. **~ment** *n* Ernüchterung *f*

disin'fect *vt* desinfizieren. **~ant** *n* Desinfektionsmittel *nt*

disin'herit *vt* enterben

dis'integrate *vi* zerfallen

dis'interested *a* unvoreingenommen; (*uninterested*) uninteressiert

dis'jointed *a* unzusammenhängend

disk /dɪsk/ *n* = **disc**

dis'like *n* Abneigung *f* ● *vt* nicht mögen

dislocate /ˈdɪsləkeɪt/ *vt* ausrenken; **~ one's shoulder** sich (*dat*) den Arm auskugeln

dis'lodge *vt* entfernen

dis'loyal *a*, **-ly** *adv* illoyal. **~ty** *n* Illoyalität *f*

dismal /ˈdɪzməl/ *a* trüb[e]; ⟨*person*⟩ trübselig; (*fam: poor*) kläglich

dismantle /dɪsˈmæntl/ *vt* auseinandernehmen; (*take down*) abbauen

dis'may *n* Bestürzung *f*. **~ed** *a* bestürzt

dis'miss *vt* entlassen; (*reject*) zurückweisen. **~al** *n* Entlassung *f*; Zurückweisung *f*

dis'mount *vi* absteigen

diso'bedien|ce *n* Ungehorsam *m*. **~t** *a* ungehorsam

diso'bey *vt/i* nicht gehorchen (+*dat*); nicht befolgen ⟨*rule*⟩

dis'order *n* Unordnung *f*; (*Med*) Störung *f*. **~ly** *a* unordentlich; **~ly conduct** ungebührliches Benehmen *nt*

dis'organized *a* unorganisiert

dis'orientate *vt* verwirren; **be ~d** die Orientierung verloren haben

dis'own *vt* verleugnen

disparaging /dɪˈspærɪdʒɪŋ/ *a*, **-ly** *adv* abschätzig

disparity /dɪˈspærətɪ/ *n* Ungleichheit *f*

dispassionate /dɪsˈpæʃənət/ *a*, **-ly** *adv* gelassen; (*impartial*) unparteiisch

dispatch /dɪˈspætʃ/ *n* (*Comm*) Versand *m*; (*Mil*) Nachricht *f*; (*report*) Bericht *m*; **with ~** prompt ● *vt* [ab]senden; (*deal with*) erledigen; (*kill*) töten. **~-rider** *n* Meldefahrer *m*

dispel /dɪˈspel/ *vt* (*pt/pp* **dispelled**) vertreiben

dispensable /dɪˈspensəbl/ *a* entbehrlich

dispensary /dɪˈspensərɪ/ *n* Apotheke *f*

dispense /dɪˈspens/ *vt* austeilen; **~ with** verzichten auf (+*acc*). **~r** *n* Apotheker(in) *m(f)*; (*device*) Automat *m*

dispers|al /dɪˈspɜːsl/ *n* Zerstreuung *f*. **~e** /dɪˈspɜːs/ *vt* zerstreuen ● *vi* sich zerstreuen

dispirited /dɪˈspɪrɪtɪd/ *a* entmutigt

dis'place *vt* verschieben; **~d person** Vertriebene(r) *m/f*

display /dɪˈspleɪ/ *n* Ausstellung *f*; (*Comm*) Auslage *f*; (*performance*) Vorführung *f* ● *vt* zeigen; ausstellen ⟨*goods*⟩

dis'please *vt* mißfallen (+*dat*)

dis'pleasure *n* Mißfallen *nt*

disposable /dɪˈspəʊzəbl/ *a* Wegwerf-; ⟨*income*⟩ verfügbar

disposal /dɪˈspəʊzl/ *n* Beseitigung *f*; **be at s.o.'s ~** jdm zur Verfügung stehen

dispose /dɪˈspəʊz/ *vi* **~ of** beseitigen; (*deal with*) erledigen; **be well ~d** wohlgesinnt sein (**to** *dat*)

disposition /dɪspəˈzɪʃn/ *n* Veranlagung *f*; (*nature*) Wesensart *f*

disproportionate /dɪsprə'pɔːʃənət/
a, **-ly** *adv* unverhältnismäßig

dis'prove *vt* widerlegen

dispute /dɪ'spjuːt/ *n* Disput *m*;
(quarrel) Streit *m* ● *vt* bestreiten

disqualifi'cation *n* Dis-
qualifikation *f*

dis'qualify *vt* disqualifizieren; ∼
s.o. from driving jdm den Führerschein entziehen

disquieting /dɪs'kwaɪətɪŋ/ *a* beunruhigend

disre'gard *n* Nichtbeachtung *f* ● *vt*
nicht beachten, ignorieren

disre'pair *n* fall into ∼ verfallen

dis'reputable *a* verrufen

disre'pute *n* Verruf *m*

disre'spect *n* Respektlosigkeit *f*.
∼**ful** *a*, **-ly** *adv* respektlos

disrupt /dɪs'rʌpt/ *vt* stören. ∼**ion**
/-ʌpʃn/ *n* Störung *f*. ∼**ive** /-tɪv/ *a*
störend

dissatis'faction *n* Unzufriedenheit
f

dis'satisfied *a* unzufrieden

dissect /dɪ'sekt/ *vt* zergliedern;
(Med) sezieren. ∼**ion** /-ekʃn/ *n*
Zergliederung *f*; *(Med)* Sektion *f*

disseminat|e /dɪ'semɪneɪt/ *vt* ver-
breiten. ∼**ion** /-'neɪʃn/ *n* Verbreitung *f*

dissent /dɪ'sent/ *n* Nicht-
übereinstimmung *f* ● *vi* nicht übereinstimmen

dissertation /dɪsə'teɪʃn/ *n* Dissertation *f*

dis'service *n* schlechter Dienst *m*

dissident /'dɪsɪdənt/ *n* Dissident *m*

dis'similar *a* unähnlich (**to** *dat*)

dissociate /dɪ'səʊʃɪeɪt/ *vt* trennen;
∼ **oneself** sich distanzieren (**from**
von)

dissolute /'dɪsəluːt/ *a* zügellos; ⟨*life*⟩
ausschweifend

dissolution /dɪsə'luːʃn/ *n* Auflösung
f

dissolve /dɪ'zɒlv/ *vt* auflösen ● *vi*
sich auflösen

dissuade /dɪ'sweɪd/ *vt* abbringen
(**from** von)

distance /'dɪstəns/ *n* Entfernung *f*;
long/short ∼ lange/kurze Strecke *f*; **in
the/from a** ∼ in/aus der Ferne

distant /'dɪstənt/ *a* fern; *(aloof)*
kühl; ⟨*relative*⟩ entfernt

dis'taste *n* Abneigung *f*. ∼**ful** *a* unangenehm

distend /dɪ'stend/ *vi* sich [auf]
blähen

distil /dɪ'stɪl/ *vt* *(pt/pp* **distilled**) brennen; *(Chem)* destillieren. ∼**lation**
/-'leɪʃn/ *n* Destillation *f*. ∼**lery**
/-ərɪ/ *n* Brennerei *f*

distinct /dɪ'stɪŋkt/ *a* deutlich;
(different) verschieden. ∼**ion**
/-ɪŋkʃn/ *n* Unterschied *m*; *(Sch)* Auszeichnung *f*. ∼**ive** /-tɪv/ *a* kenn-
zeichnend; *(unmistakable)* un-
verwechselbar. ∼**ly** *adv* deutlich

distinguish /dɪ'stɪŋgwɪʃ/ *vt/i* unterscheiden; *(make out)* erkennen; ∼
oneself sich auszeichnen. ∼**ed** *a* angesehen; ⟨*appearance*⟩ distinguiert

distort /dɪ'stɔːt/ *vt* verzerren; *(fig)*
verdrehen. ∼**ion** /-ɔːʃn/ *n* Verzerrung *f*; *(fig)* Verdrehung *f*

distract /dɪ'strækt/ *vt* ablenken.
∼**ed** /-ɪd/ *a* [völlig] aufgelöst. ∼**ion**
/-ækʃn/ *n* Ablenkung *f*; *(despair)*
Verzweiflung *f*

distraught /dɪ'strɔːt/ *a* [völlig] aufgelöst

distress /dɪ'stres/ *n* Kummer *m*;
(pain) Schmerz *m*; *(poverty, danger)*
Not *f* ● *vt* Kummer/Schmerz bereiten (+ *dat*); *(sadden)* bekümmern;
(shock) erschüttern. ∼**ing** *a*
schmerzlich; *(shocking)* er-
schütternd. ∼ **signal** *n* Notsignal *nt*

distribut|e /dɪ'strɪbjuːt/ *vt* ver-
teilen; *(Comm)* vertreiben. ∼**ion**
/-'bjuːʃn/ *n* Verteilung *f*; Vertrieb *m*.
∼**or** *n* Verteiler *m*

district /'dɪstrɪkt/ *n* Gegend *f*; *(Admin)* Bezirk *m*. ∼ **nurse** *n* Gemeinde-
schwester *f*

dis'trust *n* Mißtrauen *nt* ● *vt* mißtrauen (+ *dat*). ∼**ful** *a* mißtrauisch

disturb /dɪ'stɜːb/ *vt* stören; *(perturb)*
beunruhigen; *(touch)* anrühren.
∼**ance** *n* Unruhe *f*; *(interruption)*
Störung *f*. ∼**ed** *a* beunruhigt; **[men-
tally]** ∼**ed** geistig gestört. ∼**ing** *a* beunruhigend

dis'used *a* stillgelegt; *(empty)* leer

ditch /dɪtʃ/ *n* Graben *m* ● *vt* *(fam:
abandon)* fallenlassen ⟨*plan*⟩; weg-
schmeißen ⟨*thing*⟩

dither /'dɪðə(r)/ *vi* zaudern

ditto /'dɪtəʊ/ *n* dito; *(fam)* ebenfalls

divan /dɪ'væn/ *n* Polsterbett *nt*

dive /daɪv/ *n* [Kopf]sprung *m*;
(Aviat) Sturzflug *m*; *(fam: place)* Spe-
lunke *f* ● *vi* einen Kopfsprung
machen; *(when in water)* tauchen;

(*Aviat*) einen Sturzflug machen; (*fam:rush*) stürzen

diver /'daɪvə(r)/ *n* Taucher *m*; (*Sport*) [Kunst]springer *m*

diver|ge /daɪ'vɜ:dʒ/ *vi* auseinandergehen. **~gent** /-ənt/ *a* abweichend

diverse /daɪ'vɜ:s/ *a* verschieden

diversify /daɪ'vɜ:sɪfaɪ/ *vt/i* (*pt/pp* -ied) variieren; (*Comm*) diversifizieren

diversion /daɪ'vɜ:ʃn/ *n* Umleitung *f*; (*distraction*) Ablenkung *f*

diversity /daɪ'vɜ:sətɪ/ *n* Vielfalt *f*

divert /daɪ'vɜ:t/ *vt* umleiten; ablenken ⟨*attention*⟩; (*entertain*) unterhalten

divest /daɪ'vest/ *vt* sich entledigen (*of* + *gen*); (*fig*) entkleiden

divide /dɪ'vaɪd/ *vt* teilen; (*separate*) trennen; (*Math*) dividieren (**by** durch) ● *vi* sich teilen

dividend /'dɪvɪdend/ *n* Dividende *f*

divine /dɪ'vaɪn/ *a* göttlich

diving /'daɪvɪŋ/ *n* (*Sport*) Kunstspringen *nt*. **~-board** *n* Sprungbrett *nt*. **~-suit** *n* Taucheranzug *m*

divinity /dɪ'vɪnətɪ/ *n* Göttlichkeit *f*; (*subject*) Theologie *f*

divisible /dɪ'vɪzɪbl/ *a* teilbar (**by** durch)

division /dɪ'vɪʒn/ *n* Teilung *f*; (*separation*) Trennung *f*; (*Math*, *Mil*) Division *f*; (*Parl*) Hammelsprung *m*; (*line*) Trennlinie *f*; (*group*) Abteilung *f*

divorce /dɪ'vɔ:s/ *n* Scheidung *f* ● *vt* sich scheiden lassen von. **~d** *a* geschieden; **get ~d** sich scheiden lassen

divorcee /dɪvɔ:'si:/ *n* Geschiedene(r) *m/f*

divulge /daɪ'vʌldʒ/ *vt* preisgeben

DIY *abbr* of **do-it-yourself**

dizziness /'dɪzɪnɪs/ *n* Schwindel *m*

dizzy /'dɪzɪ/ *a* (**-ier, -iest**) schwindlig; **I feel~** mir ist schwindlig

do /du:/ *n* (*pl* **dos** *or* **do's**) (*fam*) Veranstaltung *f* ● *v* (*3 sg pres tense* **does**; *pt* **did**; *pp* **done**) ● *vt/i* tun, machen; (*be suitable*) passen; (*be enough*) reichen, genügen; (*cook*) kochen; (*clean*) putzen; (*Sch: study*) durchnehmen; (*fam: cheat*) beschwindeln (**out of** um); **do without** auskommen ohne; **do away with** abschaffen; **be done** (*Culin*) gar sein; **well done** gut gemacht! (*Culin*) gut durchgebraten; **done in** (*fam*) kaputt, fertig; **done for** (*fam*) verloren, erledigt; **do the flowers** die Blumen arrangieren; **do the potatoes** die

Kartoffeln schälen; **do the washing up** abwaschen, spülen; **do one's hair** sich frisieren; **do well/badly** gut/schlecht abschneiden; **how is he doing?** wie geht es ihm? **this won't do** das geht nicht; **are you doing anything today?** haben Sie heute etwas vor? **I could do with a spanner** ich könnte einen Schraubenschlüssel gebrauchen ● *aux* **do you speak German?** sprechen Sie deutsch? **yes, I do** ja; (*emphatic*) doch; **no, I don't** nein; **I don't smoke** ich rauche nicht; **don't you/doesn't he?** nicht [wahr]? **so do I** ich auch; **do come in** kommen Sie doch herein; **how do you do?** guten Tag. **do in** *vt* (*fam*) um die Ecke bringen. **do up** *vt* (*fasten*) zumachen; (*renovate*) renovieren; (*wrap*) einpacken

docile /'dəʊsaɪl/ *a* fügsam

dock[1] /dɒk/ *n* (*Jur*) Anklagebank *f*

dock[2] *n* Dock *nt* ● *vi* anlegen, docken ● *vt* docken. **~er** *n* Hafenarbeiter *m*. **~yard** *n* Werft *f*

doctor /'dɒktə(r)/ *n* Arzt *m*/Ärztin *f*; (*Univ*) Doktor *m* ● *vt* kastrieren; (*spay*) sterilisieren. **~ate** /-ət/ *n* Doktorwürde *f*

doctrine /'dɒktrɪn/ *n* Lehre *f*, Doktrin *f*

document /'dɒkjʊmənt/ *n* Dokument *nt*. **~ary** /-'mentərɪ/ *a* Dokumentar- ● *n* Dokumentarbericht *m*; (*film*) Dokumentarfilm *m*

doddery /'dɒdərɪ/ *a* (*fam*) tatterig

dodge /dɒdʒ/ *n* (*fam*) Trick *m*, Kniff *m* ● *vt/i* ausweichen (+ *dat*); **~ out of the way** zur Seite springen

dodgems /'dɒdʒəmz/ *npl* Autoskooter *pl*

dodgy /'dɒdʒɪ/ *a* (**-ier, -iest**) (*fam*) (*awkward*) knifflig; (*dubious*) zweifelhaft

doe /dəʊ/ *n* Ricke *f*; (*rabbit*) [Kaninchen]weibchen *nt*

does /dʌz/ *see* **do**

doesn't /'dʌznt/ = **does not**

dog /dɒg/ *n* Hund *m* ● *vt* (*pt/pp* **dogged**) verfolgen

dog: **~-biscuit** *n* Hundekuchen *m*. **~-collar** *n* Hundehalsband *nt*; (*Relig, fam*) Kragen *m* eines Geistlichen. **~-eared** *a* **be ~-eared** Eselsohren haben

dogged /'dɒgɪd/ *a*, **-ly** *adv* beharrlich

dogma /'dɒgmə/ *n* Dogma *nt*. **~tic** /-'mætɪk/ *a* dogmatisch

'dogsbody *n* (*fam*) Mädchen *nt* für alles

doily /'dɔɪlɪ/ *n* Deckchen *nt*

do-it-yourself /duːɪtjə'self/ *n* Heimwerken *nt*. ~ **shop** *n* Heimwerkerladen *m*

doldrums /'dɒldrəmz/ *npl* **be in the** ~ niedergeschlagen sein; ⟨*business:*⟩ darniederliegen

dole /dəʊl/ *n* (*fam*) Stempelgeld *nt*; **be on the** ~ arbeitslos sein ● *vt* ~ **out** austeilen

doleful /'dəʊlfl/ *a*, **-ly** *adv* trauervoll

doll /dɒl/ *n* Puppe *f* ● *vt* (*fam*) ~ **oneself up** sich herausputzen

dollar /'dɒlə(r)/ *n* Dollar *m*

dollop /'dɒləp/ *n* (*fam*) Klecks *m*

dolphin /'dɒlfɪn/ *n* Delphin *m*

domain /də'meɪn/ *n* Gebiet *nt*

dome /dəʊm/ *n* Kuppel *m*

domestic /də'mestɪk/ *a* häuslich; (*Pol*) Innen-; (*Comm*) Binnen-. ~ **animal** *n* Haustier *nt*

domesticated /də'mestɪkeɪtɪd/ *a* häuslich; ⟨*animal*⟩ zahm

domestic: ~ **flight** *n* Inlandflug *m*. ~ **'servant** Hausangestellte(r) *m/f*

dominant /'dɒmɪnənt/ *a* vorherrschend

dominat|e /'dɒmɪneɪt/ *vt* beherrschen ● *vi* dominieren; ~**e over** beherrschen. ~**ion** /-'neɪʃn/ *n* Vorherrschaft *f*

domineer /dɒmɪ'nɪə(r)/ *vi* ~ **over** tyrannisieren. ~**ing** *a* herrschsüchtig

dominion /də'mɪnjən/ *n* Herrschaft *f*

domino /'dɒmɪnəʊ/ *n* (*pl* **-es**) Dominostein *m*; ~**es** *sg* (*game*) Domino *nt*

don[1] /dɒn/ *vt* (*pt/pp* **donned**) (*liter*) anziehen

don[2] *n* [Universitäts]dozent *m*

donat|e /dəʊ'neɪt/ *vt* spenden. ~**ion** /-eɪʃn/ *n* Spende *f*

done /dʌn/ *see* **do**

donkey /'dɒŋkɪ/ *n* Esel *m*; ~**'s years** (*fam*) eine Ewigkeit. ~**-work** *n* Routinearbeit *f*

donor /'dəʊnə(r)/ *n* Spender(in) *m*(*f*)

don't /dəʊnt/ = **do not**

doodle /'duːdl/ *vi* kritzeln

doom /duːm/ *n* Schicksal *nt*; (*ruin*) Verhängnis *nt* ● *vt* **be** ~**ed to failure** zum Scheitern verurteilt sein

door /dɔː(r)/ *n* Tür *f*; **out of** ~**s** im Freien

door: ~**man** *n* Portier *m*. ~**mat** *n* [Fuß]abtreter *m*. ~**step** *n* Türschwelle *f*; **on the** ~**step** vor der Tür. ~**way** *n* Türöffnung *f*

dope /dəʊp/ *n* (*fam*) Drogen *pl*; (*fam: information*) Informationen *pl*; (*fam: idiot*) Trottel *m* ● *vt* betäuben; (*Sport*) dopen

dopey /'dəʊpɪ/ *a* (*fam*) benommen; (*stupid*) blöd[e]

dormant /'dɔːmənt/ *a* ruhend

dormer /'dɔːmə(r)/ *n* ~ **[window]** Mansardenfenster *nt*

dormitory /'dɔːmɪtərɪ/ *n* Schlafsaal *m*

dormouse /'dɔː-/ *n* Haselmaus *f*

dosage /'dəʊsɪdʒ/ *n* Dosierung *f*

dose /dəʊs/ *n* Dosis *f*

doss /dɒs/ *vi* (*sl*) pennen. ~**er** *n* Penner *m*. ~**-house** *n* Penne *f*

dot /dɒt/ *n* Punkt *m*; **on the** ~ pünktlich

dote /dəʊt/ *vi* ~ **on** vernarrt sein in (+ *acc*)

dotted /'dɒtɪd/ *a* ~ **line** punktierte Linie *f*; **be** ~ **with** bestreut sein mit

dotty /'dɒtɪ/ *a* (**-ier, -iest**) (*fam*) verdreht

double /'dʌbl/ *a* & *adv* doppelt; ⟨*bed, chin*⟩ Doppel-; ⟨*flower*⟩ gefüllt ● *n* das Doppelte; (*person*) Doppelgänger *m*; ~**s** *pl* (*Tennis*) Doppel *nt*; **at the** ~ im Laufschritt ● *vt* verdoppeln; (*fold*) falten ● *vi* sich verdoppeln. ~ **back** *vi* zurückgehen. ~ **up** *vi* sich krümmen (**with** vor + *dat*)

double: ~**-'bass** *n* Kontrabaß *m*. ~**-breasted** *a* zweireihig. ~**-'cross** *vt* im Doppelspiel treiben mit. ~**-'decker** *n* Doppeldecker *m*. ~**-'Dutch** *n* (*fam*) Kauderwelsch *nt*. ~ **'glazing** *n* Doppelverglasung *f*. ~ **'room** *n* Doppelzimmer *nt*

doubly /'dʌblɪ/ *adv* doppelt

doubt /daʊt/ *n* Zweifel *m* ● *vt* bezweifeln. ~**ful** *a*, **-ly** *adv* zweifelhaft; (*disbelieving*) skeptisch. ~**less** *adv* zweifellos

dough /dəʊ/ *n* [fester] Teig *m*; (*fam: money*) Pinke *f*. ~**nut** *n* Berliner [Pfannkuchen] *m*, Krapfen *m*

douse /daʊs/ *vt* übergießen; ausgießen ⟨*flames*⟩

dove /dʌv/ *n* Taube *f*. ~**tail** *n* (*Techn*) Schwalbenschwanz *m*

dowdy /'daʊdɪ/ *a* (**-ier, -iest**) unschick

down[1] /daʊn/ *n* (*feathers*) Daunen *pl*

down[2] *adv* unten; (*with movement*)
nach unten; **go ~** hinuntergehen;
come ~ herunterkommen; **~ there** da
unten; **£50 ~** £50 Anzahlung; **~!** (*to
dog*) Platz! **~ with . . .!** nieder mit . . .!
● *prep* **~ the road/stairs** die Straße/
Treppe hinunter; **~ the river** den Fluß
abwärts; **be ~ the pub** (*fam*) in der
Kneipe sein ● *vt* (*fam*) (*drink*) run-
terkippen; **~ tools** die Arbeit nie-
derlegen

down: ~-and-'out *n* Penner *m*.
~cast *a* niedergeschlagen. **~fall** *n*
Sturz *m*; (*ruin*) Ruin *m*. **~'grade** *vt*
niedriger einstufen. **~-'hearted** *a*
entmutigt. **~'hill** *adv* bergab. **~
payment** *n* Anzahlung *f*. **~pour** *n*
Platzregen *m*. **~right** *a & adv* ausgesprochen. **~'stairs** *adv* unten; (*go*)
nach unten ● *a* /'--/ im Erdgeschoß.
~'stream *adv* stromabwärts.
~-to-'earth *a* sachlich. **~town** *adv*
(*Amer*) im Stadtzentrum. **~trodden**
a unterdrückt. **~ward** *a* nach unten;
(*slope*) abfallend ● *adv & ~wards* abwärts, nach unten

downy /'daʊnɪ/ *a* (**-ier, -iest**) flaumig
dowry /'daʊrɪ/ *n* Mitgift *f*
doze /dəʊz/ *n* Nickerchen *nt* ● *vi*
dösen. **~ off** *vi* einnicken
dozen /'dʌzn/ *n* Dutzend *nt*
Dr *abbr of* **doctor**
draft[1] /drɑːft/ *n* Entwurf *m*; (*Comm*)
Tratte *f*; (*Amer Mil*) Einberufung *f*
● *vt* entwerfen; (*Amer Mil*) einberufen
draft[2] *n* (*Amer*) = **draught**
drag /dræg/ *n* (*fam*) Klotz *m* am
Bein; **in ~** (*fam*) (*man*) als Frau gekleidet ● *vt* (*pt/pp* **dragged**)
schleppen; absuchen (*river*). **~ on** *vi*
sich in die Länge ziehen
dragon /'drægən/ *n* Drache *m*. **~-fly**
n Libelle *f*
'**drag show** *n* Transvestitenshow *f*
drain /dreɪn/ *n* Abfluß *m*;
(*underground*) Kanal *m*; **the ~s** die
Kanalisation ● *vt* entwässern (*land*);
ablassen (*liquid*); das Wasser ablassen
aus (*tank*); abgießen (*vegetables*); austrinken (*glass*) ● *vi* **~ [away]** ablaufen;
leave sth to ~ etw abtropfen lassen
drain|age /'dreɪnɪdʒ/ *n* Kanalisation
f; (*of land*) Dränage *f*. **~ing board** *n*
Abtropfbrett *nt*. **~-pipe** *n* Abfluß-
rohr *nt*
drake /dreɪk/ *n* Enterich *m*

drama /'drɑːmə/ *n* Drama *nt*; (*quality*) Dramatik *f*
dramatic /drə'mætɪk/ *a*, **-ally** *adv*
dramatisch
dramat|ist /'dræmətɪst/ *n* Drama-
tiker *m*. **~ize** *vt* für die Bühne bearbeiten; (*fig*) dramatisieren
drank /dræŋk/ *see* **drink**
drape /dreɪp/ *n* (*Amer*) Vorhang *m*
● *vt* drapieren
drastic /'dræstɪk/ *a*, **-ally** *adv* drastisch
draught /drɑːft/ *n* [Luft]zug *m*; **~s** *sg*
(*game*) Damespiel *nt*; **there is a ~** es
zieht
draught: ~ beer *n* Bier *nt* vom Faß.
~sman *n* technischer Zeichner *m*
draughty /'drɑːftɪ/ *a* zugig; **it's ~** es
zieht
draw /drɔː/ *n* Attraktion *f*; (*Sport*)
Unentschieden *nt*; (*in lottery*) Zie-
hung *f* ● *v* (*pt* **drew**, *pp* **drawn**) ● *vt*
ziehen; (*attract*) anziehen; zeichnen
(*picture*); abheben (*money*); holen
(*water*); **~ the curtains** die Vorhänge
zuziehen/(*back*) aufziehen; **~ lots**
losen (**for** um) ● *vi* (*tea:*) ziehen; (*Sport*)
unentschieden spielen. **~ back** *vt*
zurückziehen ● *vi* (*recoil*) zurückweichen. **~ in** *vt* einziehen ● *vi*
einfahren; (*days:*) kürzer werden. **~
out** *vt* herausziehen; abheben
(*money*) ● *vi* ausfahren; (*days:*)
länger werden. **~ up** *vt* aufsetzen
(*document*); herrücken (*chair*); **~
oneself up** sich aufrichten ● *vi* [an]-
halten
draw: ~back *n* Nachteil *m*. **~bridge**
n Zugbrücke *f*
drawer /drɔː(r)/ *n* Schublade *f*
drawing /'drɔːɪŋ/ *n* Zeichnung *f*
drawing: ~-board *n* Reißbrett *nt*.
~-pin *n* Reißzwecke *f*. **~-room** *n*
Wohnzimmer *nt*
drawl /drɔːl/ *n* schleppende Aussprache *f*
drawn /drɔːn/ *see* **draw**
dread /dred/ *n* Furcht *f* (**of** vor + *dat*)
● *vt* fürchten
dreadful *a*, **-ly** *adv* fürchterlich
dream /driːm/ *n* Traum *m* ● *attrib*
Traum- ● *vt/i* (*pt/pp* **dreamt**
/dremt/ *or* **dreamed**) träumen
(**about/of** von)
dreary /'drɪərɪ/ *a* (**-ier, -iest**) trüb[e];
(*boring*) langweilig
dredge /dredʒ/ *vt/i* baggern. **~r** *n*
[Naß]bagger *m*

dregs /dregz/ npl Bodensatz m

drench /drentʃ/ vt durchnässen

dress /dres/ n Kleid nt; (clothing) Kleidung f ● vt anziehen; (decorate) schmücken; (Culin) anmachen; (Med) verbinden; ~ **oneself, get** ~**ed** sich anziehen ● vi sich anziehen. ~ **up** vi sich schön anziehen; (in disguise) sich verkleiden (**as** als)

dress: ~ **circle** n (Theat) erster Rang m. ~**er** n (furniture) Anrichte f; (Amer: dressing-table) Frisiertisch m

dressing n (Culin) Soße f; (Med) Verband m

dressing: ~ '**down** n (fam) Standpauke f. ~**-gown** n Morgenmantel m. ~**-room** n Ankleidezimmer nt; (Theat) [Künstler]garderobe f. ~**-table** n Frisiertisch m

dress: ~**maker** n Schneiderin f. ~**making** n Damenschneiderei f. ~ **rehearsal** n Generalprobe f

dressy /'dresɪ/ a (**-ier, -iest**) schick

drew /druː/ see **draw**

dribble /'drɪbl/ vi sabbern; (Sport) dribbeln

dried /draɪd/ a getrocknet; ~ **fruit** Dörrobst nt

drier /'draɪə(r)/ n Trockner m

drift /drɪft/ n Abtrift f; (of snow) Schneewehe f; (meaning) Sinn m ● vi treiben; (off course) abtreiben; (snow:) Wehen bilden; (fig) (person:) sich treiben lassen; ~ **apart** (persons:) sich auseinanderleben. ~**wood** n Treibholz nt

drill /drɪl/ n Bohrer m; (Mil) Drill m ● vt/i bohren (**for** nach); (Mil) drillen

drily /'draɪlɪ/ adv trocken

drink /drɪŋk/ n Getränk nt; (alcoholic) Drink m; (alcohol) Alkohol m; **have a** ~ etwas trinken ● vt/i (pt **drank**, pp **drunk**) trinken. ~ **up** vt/i austrinken

drink|able /'drɪŋkəbl/ a trinkbar. ~**er** n Trinker m

'**drinking-water** n Trinkwasser nt

drip /drɪp/ n Tropfen nt; (drop) Tropfen m; (Med) Tropf m; (fam: person) Niete f ● vi (pt/pp **dripped**) tropfen. ~**'dry** a bügelfrei. ~**ping** n Schmalz nt

drive /draɪv/ n [Auto]fahrt f; (entrance) Einfahrt f; (energy) Elan m; (Psych) Trieb m; (Pol) Aktion f; (Sport) Treibschlag m; (Techn) Antrieb m ● v (pt **drove**, pp **driven**) ● vt treiben; fahren (car); (Sport: hit)

schlagen; (Techn) antreiben; ~ **s.o. mad** (fam) jdn verrückt machen; **what are you driving at?** (fam) worauf willst du hinaus? ● vi fahren. ~ **away** vt vertreiben ● vi abfahren. ~ **in** vt hinein-/hereinfahren. ~ **off** vt vertreiben ● vi abfahren. ~ **on** vi weiterfahren. ~ **up** vi vorfahren

'**drive-in** a ~ **cinema** Autokino nt

drivel /'drɪvl/ n (fam) Quatsch m

driven /'drɪvn/ see **drive**

driver /'draɪvə(r)/ n Fahrer(in) m(f); (of train) Lokführer m

driving /'draɪvɪŋ/ a (rain) peitschend; (force) treibend

driving: ~ **lesson** n Fahrstunde f. ~ **licence** n Führerschein m. ~ **school** n Fahrschule f. ~ **test** Fahrprüfung f; **take one's** ~ **test** den Führerschein machen

drizzle /'drɪzl/ n Nieselregen m ● vi nieseln

drone /drəʊn/ n Drohne f; (sound) Brummen nt

droop /druːp/ vi herabhängen; (flowers:) die Köpfe hängen lassen

drop /drɒp/ n Tropfen m; (fall) Fall m; (in price, temperature) Rückgang m ● v (pt/pp **dropped**) ● vt fallen lassen; abwerfen (bomb); (omit) auslassen; (give up) aufgeben ● vi fallen; (fall lower) sinken; (wind:) nachlassen. ~ **in** vi vorbeikommen. ~ **off** vt absetzen (person) ● vi abfallen; (fall asleep) einschlafen. ~ **out** vi herausfallen; (give up) aufgeben

'**drop-out** n Aussteiger m

droppings /'drɒpɪŋz/ npl Kot m

drought /draʊt/ n Dürre f

drove /drəʊv/ see **drive**

droves /drəʊvz/ npl **in** ~ in Scharen

drown /draʊn/ vi ertrinken ● vt ertränken; übertönen (noise); **be** ~**ed** ertrinken

drowsy /'draʊzɪ/ a schläfrig

drudgery /'drʌdʒərɪ/ n Plackerei f

drug /drʌg/ n Droge f ● vt (pt/pp **drugged**) betäuben

drug: ~ **addict** n Drogenabhängige(r) m/f. ~**gist** n (Amer) Apotheker m. ~**store** n (Amer) Drogerie f; (dispensing) Apotheke f

drum /drʌm/ n Trommel f; (for oil) Tonne f ● v (pt/pp **drummed**) ● vi trommeln ● vt ~ **sth into s.o.** (fam) jdm etw einbleuen. ~**mer** n Trommler m; (in pop-group)

Schlagzeuger *m.* ~**stick** *n* Trommelschlegel *m*; (*Culin*) Keule *f*

drunk /drʌŋk/ *see* **drink** ● *a* betrunken; **get** ~ sich betrinken ● *n* Betrunkene(r) *m*

drunk|ard /'drʌŋkəd/ *n* Trinker *m.* ~**en** *a* betrunken; ~**en driving** Trunkenheit *f* am Steuer

dry /draɪ/ *a* (**drier, driest**) trocken ● *vt/i* trocknen; ~ **one's eyes** sich *dat* die Tränen abwischen. ~ **up** *vi* austrocknen; (*fig*) versiegen ● *vt* austrocknen; abtrocknen ⟨*dishes*⟩

dry: ~-'**clean** *vt* chemisch reinigen. ~-'**cleaner's** *n* (*shop*) chemische Reinigung *f.* ~**ness** *n* Trockenheit *f*

dual /'dju:əl/ *a* doppelt

dual: ~ '**carriageway** *n* ≈ Schnellstraße *f.* ~-'**purpose** *a* zweifach verwendbar

dub /dʌb/ *vt* (*pt/pp* **dubbed**) synchronisieren ⟨*film*⟩; kopieren ⟨*tape*⟩; ⟨*name*⟩ nennen

dubious /'dju:bɪəs/ *a* zweifelhaft; **be** ~ **about** Zweifel haben über (+ *acc*)

duchess /'dʌtʃɪs/ *n* Herzogin *f*

duck /dʌk/ *n* Ente *f* ● *vt* (*in water*) untertauchen; ~ **one's head** den Kopf einziehen ● *vi* sich ducken. ~**ling** *n* Entchen *nt*; (*Culin*) Ente *f*

duct /dʌkt/ *n* Rohr *nt*; (*Anat*) Gang *m*

dud /dʌd/ *a* (*fam*) nutzlos; ⟨*coin*⟩ falsch; ⟨*cheque*⟩ ungedeckt; ⟨*forged*⟩ gefälscht ● *n* (*fam*) ⟨*banknote*⟩ Blüte *f*; (*Mil: shell*) Blindgänger *m*

due /dju:/ *a* angemessen; **be** ~ fällig sein; ⟨*baby:*⟩ erwartet werden; ⟨*train:*⟩ planmäßig ankommen; ~ **to** (*owing to*) wegen (+ *gen*); **be** ~ **to** zurückzuführen sein auf (+ *acc*); **in** ~ **course** im Laufe der Zeit; ⟨*write*⟩ zu gegebener Zeit ● *adv* ~ **west** genau westlich

duel /'dju:əl/ *n* Duell *nt*

dues /dju:z/ *npl* Gebühren *pl*

duet /dju:'et/ *n* Duo *nt*; (*vocal*) Duett *nt*

dug /dʌg/ *see* **dig**

duke /dju:k/ *n* Herzog *m*

dull /dʌl/ *a* (**-er, -est**) (*overcast, not bright*) trüb[e]; (*not shiny*) matt; ⟨*sound*⟩ dumpf; ⟨*boring*⟩ langweilig; ⟨*stupid*⟩ schwerfällig ● *vt* betäuben; abstumpfen ⟨*mind*⟩

duly /'dju:lɪ/ *adv* ordnungsgemäß

dumb /dʌm/ *a* (**-er, -est**) stumm; (*fam: stupid*) dumm. ~**founded** *a* sprachlos

dummy /'dʌmɪ/ *n* (*tailor's*) [Schneider]puppe *f*; (*for baby*) Schnuller *m*; (*Comm*) Attrappe *f*

dump /dʌmp/ *n* Abfallhaufen *m*; (*for refuse*) Müllhalde *f*, Deponie *f*; (*fam: town*) Kaff *nt*; **be down in the** ~**s** (*fam*) deprimiert sein ● *vt* abladen; (*fam: put down*) hinwerfen (**on** auf + *acc*)

dumpling /'dʌmplɪŋ/ *n* Kloß *m*, Knödel *m*

dunce /dʌns/ *n* Dummkopf *m*

dune /dju:n/ *n* Düne *f*

dung /dʌŋ/ *n* Mist *m*

dungarees /dʌŋgə'ri:z/ *npl* Latzhose *f*

dungeon /'dʌndʒən/ *n* Verlies *nt*

dunk /dʌŋk/ *vt* eintunken

duo /'dju:əʊ/ *n* Paar *nt*; (*Mus*) Duo *nt*

dupe /dju:p/ *n* Betrogene(r) *m/f* ● *vt* betrügen

duplicate[1] /'dju:plɪkət/ *a* Zweit- ● *n* Doppel *nt*; (*document*) Duplikat *nt*; **in** ~ in doppelter Ausfertigung *f*

duplicat|e[2] /'dju:plɪkeɪt/ *vt* kopieren; (*do twice*) zweimal machen. ~**or** *n* Vervielfältigungsapparat *m*

durable /'djʊərəbl/ *a* haltbar

duration /djʊə'reɪʃn/ *n* Dauer *f*

duress /djʊə'res/ *n* Zwang *m*

during /'djʊərɪŋ/ *prep* während (+ *gen*)

dusk /dʌsk/ *n* [Abend]dämmerung *f*

dust /dʌst/ *n* Staub *m* ● *vt* abstauben; (*sprinkle*) bestäuben (**with** mit) ● *vi* Staub wischen

dust: ~**bin** *n* Mülltonne *f.* ~-**cart** *n* Müllwagen *m.* ~**er** *n* Staubtuch *nt.* ~-**jacket** *n* Schutzumschlag *m.* ~**man** *n* Müllmann *m.* ~**pan** *n* Kehrschaufel *f*

dusty /'dʌstɪ/ *a* (**-ier, -iest**) staubig

Dutch /dʌtʃ/ *a* holländisch; **go** ~ (*fam*) getrennte Kasse machen ● *n* (*Lang*) Holländisch *nt*; **the** ~ *pl* die Holländer. ~**man** *n* Holländer *m*

dutiable /'dju:tɪəbl/ *a* zollpflichtig

dutiful /'dju:tɪfl/ *a*, **-ly** *adv* pflichtbewußt; (*obedient*) gehorsam

duty /'dju:tɪ/ *n* Pflicht *f*; (*task*) Aufgabe *f*; (*tax*) Zoll *m*; **be on** ~ Dienst haben. ~-**free** *a* zollfrei

duvet /'du:veɪ/ *n* Steppdecke *f*

dwarf /dwɔ:f/ *n* (*pl* **-s** or **dwarves**) Zwerg *m*

dwell /dwel/ *vi* (*pt/pp* **dwelt**) (*liter*) wohnen; ~ **on** (*fig*) verweilen bei. ~**ing** *n* Wohnung *f*

dwindle /'dwɪndl/ vi abnehmen, schwinden

dye /daɪ/ n Farbstoff m ● vt (pres p **dyeing**) färben

dying /'daɪɪŋ/ see **die**²

dynamic /daɪ'næmɪk/ a dynamisch. **~s** n Dynamik f

dynamite /'daɪnəmaɪt/ n Dynamit nt

dynamo /'daɪnəməʊ/ n Dynamo m

dynasty /'dɪnəstɪ/ n Dynastie f

dysentery /'dɪsəntrɪ/ n Ruhr f

dyslex|ia /dɪs'leksɪə/ n Legasthenie f. **~ic** a legasthenisch; **be ~ic** Legastheniker sein

E

each /iːtʃ/ a & pron jede(r,s); (per) je; **~ other** einander; **£1~** £1 pro Person; (for thing) pro Stück

eager /'iːgə(r)/ a, **-ly** adv eifrig; **be ~ to do sth** etw gerne machen wollen. **~ness** n Eifer m

eagle /'iːgl/ n Adler m

ear¹ /ɪə(r)/ n (of corn) Ähre f

ear² n Ohr nt. **~ache** n Ohrenschmerzen pl. **~-drum** n Trommelfell nt

earl /ɜːl/ n Graf m

early /'ɜːlɪ/ a & adv (**-ier, -iest**) früh; ⟨reply⟩ baldig; **be ~** früh dran sein; **~ in the morning** früh am Morgen

'earmark vt **~ for** bestimmen für

earn /ɜːn/ vt verdienen

earnest /'ɜːnɪst/ a, **-ly** adv ernsthaft ● n **in ~** im Ernst

earnings /'ɜːnɪŋz/ npl Verdienst m

ear: ~phones npl Kopfhörer pl. **~-ring** n Ohrring m; (clip-on) Ohrklips m. **~shot** n **within/out of ~shot** in/außer Hörweite

earth /ɜːθ/ n Erde f; (of fox) Bau m; **where/what on ~?** wo/was in aller Welt? ● vt (Electr) erden

earthenware /'ɜːθn-/ n Tonwaren pl

earthly /'ɜːθlɪ/ a irdisch; **be no ~ use** (fam) völlig nutzlos sein

'earthquake n Erdbeben nt

earthy /'ɜːθɪ/ a erdig; (coarse) derb

earwig /'ɪəwɪg/ n Ohrwurm m

ease /iːz/ n Leichtigkeit f; **at ~!** (Mil) rührt euch! **be/feel ill at ~** ein ungutes Gefühl haben ● vt erleichtern; lindern ⟨pain⟩ ● vi ⟨pain:⟩ nachlassen; ⟨situation:⟩ sich entspannen

easel /'iːzl/ n Staffelei f

easily /'iːzɪlɪ/ adv leicht, mit Leichtigkeit

east /iːst/ n Osten m; **to the ~ of** östlich von ● a Ost-, ost- ● adv nach Osten

Easter /'iːstə(r)/ n Ostern nt ● attrib Oster-. **~ egg** n Osterei nt

east|erly /'iːstəlɪ/ a östlich. **~ern** a östlich. **~ward[s]** /-wəd[z]/ adv nach Osten

easy /'iːzɪ/ a (**-ier, -iest**) leicht; **take it ~** (fam) sich schonen; **take it ~!** beruhige dich! **go ~ with** (fam) sparsam umgehen mit

easy: ~ chair n Sessel m. **~'going** a gelassen; **too ~going** lässig

eat /iːt/ vt/i (pt **ate**, pp **eaten**) essen; ⟨animal:⟩ fressen. **~ up** vt aufessen

eat|able /'iːtəbl/ a genießbar. **~er** (apple) Eßapfel m

eau-de-Cologne /əʊdəkə'ləʊn/ n Kölnisch Wasser nt

eaves /iːvz/ npl Dachüberhang m. **~drop** vi (pt/pp **~dropped**) [heimlich] lauschen; **~drop on** belauschen

ebb /eb/ n (tide) Ebbe f; **at a low ~** (fig) auf einem Tiefstand ● vi zurückgehen; (fig) verebben

ebony /'ebənɪ/ n Ebenholz nt

ebullient /ɪ'bʌlɪənt/ a überschwenglich

EC abbr (**European Community**) EG f

eccentric /ɪk'sentrɪk/ a exzentrisch ● n Exzentriker m

ecclesiastical /ɪkliːzɪ'æstɪkl/ a kirchlich

echo /'ekəʊ/ n (pl **-es**) Echo nt, Widerhall m ● v (pt/pp **echoed**, pres p **echoing**) ● vt zurückwerfen; (imitate) nachsagen ● vi widerhallen (**with** von)

eclipse /ɪ'klɪps/ n (Astr) Finsternis f ● vt (fig) in den Schatten stellen

ecolog|ical /iːkə'lɒdʒɪkl/ a ökologisch. **~y** /iː'kɒlədʒɪ/ n Ökologie f

economic /iːkə'nɒmɪk/ a wirtschaftlich. **~al** a sparsam. **~ally** adv wirtschaftlich; (thriftily) sparsam. **~s** n Volkswirtschaft f

economist /ɪ'kɒnəmɪst/ n Volkswirt m; (Univ) Wirtschaftswissenschaftler m

economize /ɪ'kɒnəmaɪz/ vi sparen (**on** an + dat)

economy /ɪ'kɒnəmɪ/ n Wirtschaft f; (thrift) Sparsamkeit f

ecstasy /'ekstəsɪ/ n Ekstase f

ecstatic /ɪk'stætɪk/ a, **-ally** adv ekstatisch

ecu /'eɪkjuː/ n Ecu m

ecumenical /iːkjʊˈmenɪkl/ *a* ökumenisch

eczema /ˈeksɪmə/ *n* Ekzem *nt*

eddy /ˈedɪ/ *n* Wirbel *m*

edge /edʒ/ *n* Rand *m*; (*of table, lawn*) Kante *f*; (*of knife*) Schneide *f*; **on ~** (*fam*) nervös; **have the ~ on** (*fam*) etwas besser sein als ● *vt* einfassen. **~ forward** *vi* sich nach vorn schieben

edging /ˈedʒɪŋ/ *n* Einfassung *f*

edgy /ˈedʒɪ/ *a* (*fam*) nervös

edible /ˈedɪbl/ *a* eßbar

edict /ˈiːdɪkt/ *n* Erlaß *m*

edifice /ˈedɪfɪs/ *n* [großes] Gebäude *nt*

edify /ˈedɪfaɪ/ *vt* (*pt/pp* -**ied**) erbauen. **~ing** *a* erbaulich

edit /ˈedɪt/ *vt* (*pt/pp* **edited**) redigieren; herausgeben ⟨*anthology, dictionary*⟩; schneiden ⟨*film, tape*⟩

edition /ɪˈdɪʃn/ *n* Ausgabe *f*; (*impression*) Auflage *f*

editor /ˈedɪtə(r)/ *n* Redakteur *m*; (*of anthology, dictionary*) Herausgeber *m*; (*of newspaper*) Chefredakteur *m*; (*of film*) Cutter(in) *m(f)*

editorial /edɪˈtɔːrɪəl/ *a* redaktionell, Redaktions- ● *n* (*Journ*) Leitartikel *m*

educate /ˈedjʊkeɪt/ *vt* erziehen; **be ~d at X** auf die X-Schule gehen. **~d** *a* gebildet

education /edjʊˈkeɪʃn/ *n* Erziehung *f*; (*culture*) Bildung *f*. **~al** *a* pädagogisch; (*visit*) kulturell

eel /iːl/ *n* Aal *m*

eerie /ˈɪərɪ/ *a* (-**ier**, -**iest**) unheimlich

effect /ɪˈfekt/ *n* Wirkung *f*, Effekt *m*; **in ~** in Wirklichkeit; **take ~** in Kraft treten ● *vt* bewirken

effective /ɪˈfektɪv/ *a*, -**ly** *adv* wirksam, effektiv; (*striking*) wirkungsvoll, effektvoll; (*actual*) tatsächlich. **~ness** *n* Wirksamkeit *f*

effeminate /ɪˈfemɪnət/ *a* unmännlich

effervescent /efəˈvesnt/ *a* sprudelnd

efficiency /ɪˈfɪʃənsɪ/ *n* Tüchtigkeit *f*; (*of machine, organization*) Leistungsfähigkeit *f*

efficient /ɪˈfɪʃənt/ *a* tüchtig; (*machine, organization*) leistungsfähig; (*method*) rationell. **~ly** *adv* gut; (*function*) rationell

effigy /ˈefɪdʒɪ/ *n* Bildnis *nt*

effort /ˈefət/ *n* Anstrengung *f*; **make an ~** sich (*dat*) Mühe geben. **~less** *a*, -**ly** *adv* mühelos

effrontery /ɪˈfrʌntərɪ/ *n* Unverschämtheit *f*

effusive /ɪˈfjuːsɪv/ *a*, -**ly** *adv* überschwenglich

e.g. *abbr* (**exempli gratia**) z.B.

egalitarian /ɪgælɪˈteərɪən/ *a* egalitär

egg[1] /eg/ *vt* **~ on** (*fam*) anstacheln

egg[2] *n* Ei *nt*. **~-cup** *n* Eierbecher *m*. **~shell** *n* Eierschale *f*. **~-timer** *n* Eieruhr *f*

ego /ˈiːgəʊ/ *n* Ich *nt*. **~centric** /-ˈsentrɪk/ *a* egozentrisch. **~ism** *n* Egoismus *m*. **~ist** *n* Egoist *m*. **~tism** *n* Ichbezogenheit *f*. **~tist** *n* ichbezogener Mensch *m*

Egypt /ˈiːdʒɪpt/ *n* Ägypten *nt*. **~ian** /ɪˈdʒɪpʃn/ *a* ägyptisch ● *n* Ägypter(in) *m(f)*

eiderdown /ˈaɪdə-/ *n* (*quilt*) Daunendecke *f*

eight /eɪt/ *a* acht ● *n* Acht *f*; (*boat*) Achter *m*. **~teen** *a* achtzehn. **~teenth** *a* achtzehnte(r,s)

eighth /eɪtθ/ *a* achte(r,s) ● *n* Achtel *nt*

eightieth /ˈeɪtɪɪθ/ *a* achtzigste(r,s)

eighty /ˈeɪtɪ/ *a* achtzig

either /ˈaɪðə(r)/ *a & pron* **~** [**of them**] einer von [den] beiden; (*both*) beide; **on ~ side** auf beiden Seiten ● *adv* **I don't ~** ich auch nicht ● *conj* **~... or** entweder... oder

eject /ɪˈdʒekt/ *vt* hinauswerfen

eke /iːk/ *vt* **~ out** strecken; (*increase*) ergänzen; **~ out a living** sich kümmerlich durchschlagen

elaborate[1] /ɪˈlæbərət/ *a*, -**ly** *adv* kunstvoll; (*fig*) kompliziert

elaborate[2] /ɪˈlæbəreɪt/ *vi* ausführlicher sein; **~ on** näher ausführen

elapse /ɪˈlæps/ *vi* vergehen

elastic /ɪˈlæstɪk/ *a* elastisch ● *n* Gummiband *nt*. **~ 'band** *n* Gummiband *nt*

elasticity /ɪlæsˈtɪsətɪ/ *n* Elastizität *f*

elated /ɪˈleɪtɪd/ *a* überglücklich

elbow /ˈelbəʊ/ *n* Ellbogen *m*

elder[1] /ˈeldə(r)/ *n* Holunder *m*

elder[2] *a* ältere(r,s) ● *n* the **~er** der/die Ältere. **~erly** *a* alt. **~est** *a* älteste(r, s) ● *n* the **~est** der/die Älteste

elect /ɪˈlekt/ *a* the **president ~** der designierte Präsident ● *vt* wählen; **~ to do sth** sich dafür entscheiden, etw zu tun. **~ion** /-ekʃn/ *n* Wahl *f*

elector /ɪ'lektə(r)/ n Wähler(in) m(f). ∼al a Wahl-; ∼al roll Wählerverzeichnis nt. ∼ate /-rət/ n Wählerschaft f

electric /ɪ'lektrɪk/ a, -ally adv elektrisch

electrical /ɪ'lektrɪkl/ a elektrisch; ∼ engineering Elektrotechnik f

electric: ∼ 'blanket n Heizdecke f. ∼ 'fire n elektrischer Heizofen m

electrician /ɪlek'trɪʃn/ n Elektriker m

electricity /ɪlek'trɪsətɪ/ n Elektrizität f; (supply) Strom m

electrify /ɪ'lektrɪfaɪ/ vt (pt/pp -ied) elektrifizieren. ∼ing a (fig) elektrisierend

electrocute /ɪ'lektrəkju:t/ vt durch einen elektrischen Schlag töten; (execute) auf dem elektrischen Stuhl hinrichten

electrode /ɪ'lektrəʊd/ n Elektrode f

electron /ɪ'lektrɒn/ n Elektron nt

electronic /ɪlek'trɒnɪk/ a elektronisch. ∼s n Elektronik f

elegance /'elɪgəns/ n Eleganz f

elegant /'elɪgənt/ a, -ly adv elegant

elegy /'elɪdʒɪ/ n Elegie f

element /'elɪmənt/ n Element nt. ∼ary /-'mentərɪ/ a elementar

elephant /'elɪfənt/ n Elefant m

elevat|e /'elɪveɪt/ vt heben; (fig) erheben. ∼ion /-'veɪʃn/ n Erhebung f

elevator /'elɪveɪtə(r)/ n (Amer) Aufzug m, Fahrstuhl m

eleven /ɪ'levn/ a elf ● n Elf f. ∼th a elfte(r,s); at the ∼th hour (fam) in letzter Minute

elf /elf/ n (pl elves) Elfe f

elicit /ɪ'lɪsɪt/ vt herausbekommen

eligible /'elɪdʒəbl/ a berechtigt; ∼ young man gute Partie f

eliminate /ɪ'lɪmɪneɪt/ vt ausschalten; (excrete) ausscheiden

élite /eɪ'li:t/ n Elite f

ellip|se /ɪ'lɪps/ n Ellipse f. ∼tical a elliptisch

elm /elm/ n Ulme f

elocution /elə'kju:ʃn/ n Sprecherziehung f

elongate /'i:lɒŋgeɪt/ vt verlängern

elope /ɪ'ləʊp/ vi durchbrennen (fam)

eloquen|ce /'eləkwəns/ n Beredsamkeit f. ∼t a, -ly adv beredt

else /els/ adv sonst; who ∼? wer sonst? nothing ∼ sonst nichts; or ∼

oder; (otherwise) sonst; **someone/somewhere** ∼ jemand/irgendwo anders; **anyone** ∼ jeder andere; (as question) sonst noch jemand? **anything** ∼ alles andere; (as question) sonst noch etwas? ∼**where** adv woanders

elucidate /ɪ'lu:sɪdeɪt/ vt erläutern

elude /ɪ'lu:d/ vt entkommen (+ dat); (avoid) ausweichen (+ dat)

elusive /ɪ'lu:sɪv/ a be ∼ schwer zu fassen sein

emaciated /ɪ'meɪsɪeɪtɪd/ a abgezehrt

emanate /'eməneɪt/ vi ausgehen (from von)

emancipat|ed /ɪ'mænsɪpeɪtɪd/ a emanzipiert. ∼ion /-'peɪʃn/ n Emanzipation f; (of slaves) Freilassung f

embalm /ɪm'bɑ:m/ vt einbalsamieren

embankment /ɪm'bæŋkmənt/ n Böschung f; (of railway) Bahndamm m

embargo /em'bɑ:gəʊ/ n (pl -es) Embargo nt

embark /ɪm'bɑ:k/ vi sich einschiffen; ∼ on anfangen mit. ∼ation /embɑ:'keɪʃn/ n Einschiffung f

embarrass /ɪm'bærəs/ vt in Verlegenheit bringen. ∼ed a verlegen. ∼ing a peinlich. ∼ment n Verlegenheit f

embassy /'embəsɪ/ n Botschaft f

embedded /ɪm'bedɪd/ a be deeply ∼ in tief stecken in (+ dat)

embellish /ɪm'belɪʃ/ vt verzieren; (fig) ausschmücken

embers /'embəz/ npl Glut f

embezzle /ɪm'bezl/ vt unterschlagen. ∼ment n Unterschlagung f

embitter /ɪm'bɪtə(r)/ vt verbittern

emblem /'embləm/ n Emblem nt

embodiment /ɪm'bɒdɪmənt/ n Verkörperung f

embody /ɪm'bɒdɪ/ vt (pt/pp -ied) verkörpern; (include) enthalten

emboss /ɪm'bɒs/ vt prägen

embrace /ɪm'breɪs/ n Umarmung f ● vt umarmen; (fig) umfassen ● vi sich umarmen

embroider /ɪm'brɔɪdə(r)/ vt besticken; sticken (design); (fig) ausschmücken ● vi sticken. ∼y n Stickerei f

embroil /ɪm'brɔɪl/ vt become ∼ed in sth in etw (acc) verwickelt werden

embryo /'embrɪəʊ/ n Embryo m

emerald /'emərəld/ n Smaragd m

emer|ge /ɪˈmɜːdʒ/ vi auftauchen (**from** aus); (become known) sich herausstellen; (come into being) entstehen. **~gence** /-əns/ n Auftauchen nt; Entstehung f

emergency /ɪˈmɜːdʒənsɪ/ n Notfall m; **in an ~** im Notfall. **~ exit** n Notausgang m

emery-paper /ˈeməri-/ n Schmirgelpapier nt

emigrant /ˈemɪɡrənt/ n Auswanderer m

emigrat|e /ˈemɪɡreɪt/ vi auswandern. **~ion** /-ˈɡreɪʃn/ n Auswanderung f

eminent /ˈemɪnənt/ a, **-ly** adv eminent

emission /ɪˈmɪʃn/ n Ausstrahlung f; (of pollutant) Emission f

emit /ɪˈmɪt/ vt (pt/pp emitted) ausstrahlen ⟨light, heat⟩; ausstoßen ⟨smoke, fumes, cry⟩

emotion /ɪˈməʊʃn/ n Gefühl nt. **~al** a emotional; **become ~al** sich erregen

emotive /ɪˈməʊtɪv/ a emotional

empath|ize /ˈempəθaɪz/ vi **~ize with s.o.** sich in jdn einfühlen. **~y** n Einfühlungsvermögen nt

emperor /ˈempərə(r)/ n Kaiser m

emphasis /ˈemfəsɪs/ n Betonung f

emphasize /ˈemfəsaɪz/ vt betonen

emphatic /ɪmˈfætɪk/ a, **-ally** adv nachdrücklich

empire /ˈempaɪə(r)/ n Reich nt

empirical /emˈpɪrɪkl/ a empirisch

employ /ɪmˈplɔɪ/ vt beschäftigen; (appoint) einstellen; (fig) anwenden. **~ee** /emplɔɪˈiː/ n Beschäftigte(r) m/f; (in contrast to employer) Arbeitnehmer m. **~er** n Arbeitgeber m. **~ment** n Beschäftigung f; (work) Arbeit f. **~ment agency** n Stellenvermittlung f

empower /ɪmˈpaʊə(r)/ vt ermächtigen

empress /ˈemprɪs/ n Kaiserin f

empties /ˈemptɪz/ npl leere Flaschen pl

emptiness /ˈemptɪnɪs/ n Leere f

empty /ˈemptɪ/ a leer ● vt leeren; ausleeren ⟨container⟩ ● vi sich leeren

emulate /ˈemjʊleɪt/ vt nacheifern (+ dat)

emulsion /ɪˈmʌlʃn/ n Emulsion f

enable /ɪˈneɪbl/ vt **~ s.o. to** es jdm möglich machen, zu

enact /ɪˈnækt/ vt (Theat) aufführen

enamel /ɪˈnæml/ n Email nt; (on teeth) Zahnschmelz m; (paint) Lack m ● vt (pt/pp enamelled) emaillieren

enamoured /ɪˈnæməd/ a **be ~ of** sehr angetan sein von

enchant /ɪnˈtʃɑːnt/ vt bezaubern. **~ing** a bezaubernd. **~ment** n Zauber m

encircle /ɪnˈsɜːkl/ vt einkreisen

enclave /ˈenkleɪv/ n Enklave f

enclos|e /ɪnˈkləʊz/ vt einschließen; (in letter) beilegen (**with** dat). **~ure** /-ʒə(r)/ n (at zoo) Gehege nt; (in letter) Anlage f

encompass /ɪnˈkʌmpəs/ vt umfassen

encore /ˈɒŋkɔː(r)/ n Zugabe f ● int bravo!

encounter /ɪnˈkaʊntə(r)/ n Begegnung f; (battle) Zusammenstoß m ● vt begegnen (+ dat); (fig) stoßen auf (+ acc)

encourag|e /ɪnˈkʌrɪdʒ/ vt ermutigen; (promote) fördern. **~ement** n Ermutigung f. **~ing** a ermutigend

encroach /ɪnˈkrəʊtʃ/ vi **~ on** eindringen in (+ acc) ⟨land⟩; beanspruchen ⟨time⟩

encumb|er /ɪnˈkʌmbə(r)/ vt belasten (**with** mit). **~rance** /-rəns/ n Belastung f

encyclopaed|ia /ɪnsaɪklə'piːdɪə/ n Enzyklopädie f, Lexikon nt. **~ic** a enzyklopädisch

end /end/ n Ende nt; (purpose) Zweck m; **in the ~** schließlich; **at the ~ of May** Ende Mai; **on ~** hochkant; **for days on ~** tagelang; **make ~s meet** (fam) [gerade] auskommen; **no ~ of** (fam) unheimlich viel(e) ● vt beenden ● vi enden; **~ up in** (fam: arrive at) landen in (+ dat)

endanger /ɪnˈdeɪndʒə(r)/ vt gefährden

endear|ing /ɪnˈdɪərɪŋ/ a liebenswert. **~ment** n **term of ~ment** Kosewort nt

endeavour /ɪnˈdevə(r)/ n Bemühung f ● vi sich bemühen (**to** zu)

ending /ˈendɪŋ/ n Schluß m, Ende nt; (Gram) Endung f

endive /ˈendaɪv/ n Endivie f

endless /ˈendlɪs/ a, **-ly** adv endlos

endorse /enˈdɔːs/ vt (Comm) indossieren; (confirm) bestätigen. **~ment** n (Comm) Indossament nt; (fig) Bestätigung f; (on driving licence) Strafvermerk m

endow /ɪn'dau/ vt stiften; **be ~ed with** (*fig*) haben. **~ment** n Stiftung f

endur|able /ɪn'djuərəbl/ a erträglich. **~ance** /-rəns/ n Durchhaltevermögen nt; **beyond ~ance** unerträglich

endur|e /ɪn'djuə(r)/ vt ertragen ● vi [lange] bestehen. **~ing** a dauernd

enemy /'enəmɪ/ n Feind m ● attrib feindlich

energetic /enə'dʒetɪk/ a tatkräftig; **be ~** voller Energie sein

energy /'enədʒɪ/ n Energie f

enforce /ɪn'fɔːs/ vt durchsetzen. **~d** a unfreiwillig

engage /ɪn'geɪdʒ/ vt einstellen ⟨staff⟩; (*Theat*) engagieren; (*Auto*) einlegen ⟨gear⟩ ● vi sich beteiligen (**in** an + dat); (*Techn*) ineinandergreifen. **~d** a besetzt; ⟨person⟩ beschäftigt; (*to be married*) verlobt; **get ~d** sich verloben (**to** mit). **~ment** n Verlobung f; (*appointment*) Verabredung f; (*Mil*) Gefecht nt

engaging /ɪn'geɪdʒɪŋ/ a einnehmend

engender /ɪn'dʒendə(r)/ vt (*fig*) erzeugen

engine /'endʒɪn/ n Motor m; (*Naut*) Maschine f; (*Rail*) Lokomotive f; (*of jet-plane*) Triebwerk nt. **~-driver** n Lokomotivführer m

engineer /endʒɪ'nɪə(r)/ n Ingenieur m; (*service, installation*) Techniker m; (*Naut*) Maschinist m; (*Amer*) Lokomotivführer m ● vt (*fig*) organisieren. **~ing** n [**mechanical**] **~ing** Maschinenbau m

England /'ɪŋglənd/ n England nt

English /'ɪŋglɪʃ/ a englisch; **the ~ Channel** der Ärmelkanal ● n (*Lang*) Englisch nt; **in ~** auf englisch; **into ~** ins Englische; **the ~** pl die Engländer. **~man** n Engländer m. **~woman** n Engländerin f

engrav|e /ɪn'greɪv/ vt eingravieren. **~ing** n Stich m

engross /ɪn'grəus/ vt **be ~ed in** vertieft sein in (+ acc)

engulf /ɪn'gʌlf/ vt verschlingen

enhance /ɪn'hɑːns/ vt verschönern; (*fig*) steigern

enigma /ɪ'nɪgmə/ n Rätsel nt. **~tic** /enɪg'mætɪk/ a rätselhaft

enjoy /ɪn'dʒɔɪ/ vt genießen; **~ one-self** sich amüsieren; **~ cooking/paint-ing** gern kochen/malen; **I ~ed it** it es hat mir gut gefallen/⟨food:⟩ geschmeckt. **~able** /-əbl/ a angenehm, nett. **~ment** n Vergnügen nt

enlarge /ɪn'lɑːdʒ/ vt vergrößern ● vi **~ upon** sich näher auslassen über (+ acc). **~ment** n Vergrößerung f

enlighten /ɪn'laɪtn/ vt aufklären. **~ment** n Aufklärung f

enlist /ɪn'lɪst/ vt (*Mil*) einziehen; **~ s.o.'s help** jdn zur Hilfe heranziehen ● vi (*Mil*) sich melden

enliven /ɪn'laɪvn/ vt beleben

enmity /'enmɪtɪ/ n Feindschaft f

enormity /ɪ'nɔːmətɪ/ n Ungeheuerlichkeit f

enormous /ɪ'nɔːməs/ a, **-ly** adv riesig

enough /ɪ'nʌf/ a, adv & n genug; **be ~** reichen; **funnily ~** komischerweise; **I've had ~!** (*fam*) jetzt reicht's mir aber!

enquir|e /ɪn'kwaɪə(r)/ vi sich erkundigen (**about** nach) ● vt sich erkundigen nach. **~y** n Erkundigung f; (*investigation*) Untersuchung f

enrage /ɪn'reɪdʒ/ vt wütend machen

enrich /ɪn'rɪtʃ/ vt bereichern; (*improve*) anreichern

enrol /ɪn'rəul/ v (*pt/pp* **-rolled**) ● vt einschreiben ● vi sich einschreiben. **~ment** n Einschreibung f

ensemble /ɒn'sɒmbl/ n (*clothing & Mus*) Ensemble nt

ensign /'ensaɪn/ n Flagge f

enslave /ɪn'sleɪv/ vt versklaven

ensue /ɪn'sjuː/ vi folgen; (*result*) sich ergeben (**from** aus)

ensure /ɪn'ʃuə(r)/ vt sicherstellen; **~ that** dafür sorgen, daß

entail /ɪn'teɪl/ vt erforderlich machen; **what does it ~?** was ist damit verbunden?

entangle /ɪn'tæŋgl/ vt **get ~d** sich verfangen (**in** in + dat); (*fig*) sich verstricken (**in** in + acc)

enter /'entə(r)/ vt eintreten/ ⟨vehicle:⟩ einfahren in (+ acc); einreisen in (+ acc) ⟨country⟩; (*register*) eintragen; sich anmelden zu ⟨competition⟩ ● vi eintreten; ⟨vehicle:⟩ einfahren; (*Theat*) auftreten; (*register as competitor*) sich anmelden; (*take part*) sich beteiligen (**in** an + dat)

enterpris|e /'entəpraɪz/ n Unternehmen nt; (*quality*) Unternehmungsgeist m. **~ing** a unternehmend

entertain /entə'teɪn/ vt unterhalten; (*invite*) einladen; (*to meal*) bewirten

⟨guest⟩; ⟨fig⟩ in Erwägung ziehen ● vi unterhalten; ⟨have guests⟩ Gäste haben. ~er n Unterhalter m. ~ment n Unterhaltung f

enthral /ɪn'θrɔ:l/ vt (pt/pp enthralled) be ~led gefesselt sein ⟨by von⟩

enthuse /ɪn'θju:z/ vi ~ over schwärmen von

enthusias|m /ɪn'θju:zɪæzm/ n Begeisterung f. ~t n Enthusiast m. ~tic /-'æstɪk/ a, -ally adv begeistert

entice /ɪn'taɪs/ vt locken. ~ment n Anreiz m

entire /ɪn'taɪə(r)/ a ganz. ~ly adv ganz, völlig. ~ty /-rətɪ/ n in its ~ty in seiner Gesamtheit

entitle /ɪn'taɪtl/ vt berechtigen; ~d... mit dem Titel...; be ~d to sth das Recht auf etw ⟨acc⟩ haben. ~ment n Berechtigung f; ⟨claim⟩ Anspruch m (to auf + acc)

entity /'entətɪ/ n Wesen nt

entomology /entə'mɒlədʒɪ/ n Entomologie f

entourage /'ɒntʊrɑ:ʒ/ n Gefolge nt

entrails /'entreɪlz/ npl Eingeweide pl

entrance[1] /ɪn'trɑ:ns/ vt bezaubern

entrance[2] /'entrəns/ n Eintritt m; ⟨Theat⟩ Auftritt m; ⟨way in⟩ Eingang m; ⟨for vehicle⟩ Einfahrt f. ~ examination n Aufnahmeprüfung f. ~ fee n Eintrittsgebühr f

entrant /'entrənt/ n Teilnehmer(in) m(f)

entreat /ɪn'tri:t/ vt anflehen (for um)

entrench /ɪn'trentʃ/ vt be ~ed in verwurzelt sein in (+ dat)

entrust /ɪn'trʌst/ vt ~ s.o. with sth, ~ sth to s.o. jdm etw anvertrauen

entry /'entrɪ/ n Eintritt m; ⟨into country⟩ Einreise f; ⟨on list⟩ Eintrag m; no ~ Zutritt/⟨Auto⟩ Einfahrt verboten. ~form n Anmeldeformular nt. ~ visa n Einreisevisum nt

enumerate /ɪ'nju:məreɪt/ vt aufzählen

enunciate /ɪ'nʌnsɪeɪt/ vt [deutlich] aussprechen; ⟨state⟩ vorbringen

envelop /ɪn'veləp/ vt (pt/pp enveloped) einhüllen

envelope /'envələʊp/ n [Brief]umschlag m

enviable /'envɪəbl/ a beneidenswert

envious /'envɪəs/ a, -ly adv neidisch (of auf + acc)

environment /ɪn'vaɪərənmənt/ n Umwelt f

environmental /ɪnvaɪərən'mentl/ a Umwelt-. ~ist n Umweltschützer m. ~ly adv ~ly friendly umweltfreundlich

envisage /ɪn'vɪzɪdʒ/ vt sich ⟨dat⟩ vorstellen

envoy /'envɔɪ/ n Gesandte(r) m

envy /'envɪ/ n Neid m ● vt (pt/pp -ied) ~ s.o. sth jdn um etw beneiden

enzyme /'enzaɪm/ n Enzym nt

epic /'epɪk/ a episch ● n Epos nt

epidemic /epɪ'demɪk/ n Epidemie f

epilep|sy /'epɪlepsɪ/ n Epilepsie f. ~tic /-'leptɪk/ a epileptisch ● n Epileptiker(in) m(f)

epilogue /'epɪlɒg/ n Epilog m

episode /'epɪsəʊd/ n Episode f; ⟨instalment⟩ Folge f

epistle /ɪ'pɪsl/ n ⟨liter⟩ Brief m

epitaph /'epɪtɑ:f/ n Epitaph nt

epithet /'epɪθet/ n Beiname m

epitom|e /ɪ'pɪtəmɪ/ n Inbegriff m. ~ize vt verkörpern

epoch /'i:pɒk/ n Epoche f. ~-making a epochemachend

equal /'i:kwl/ a gleich (to dat); be ~ to a task einer Aufgabe gewachsen sein ● n Gleichgestellte(r) m/f ● vt (pt/pp equalled) gleichen (+ dat). ⟨fig⟩ gleichkommen (+ dat). ~ity /ɪ'kwɒlətɪ/ n Gleichheit f

equalize /'i:kwəlaɪz/ vt/i ausgleichen. ~r n ⟨Sport⟩ Ausgleich[streffer] m

equally /'i:kwəlɪ/ adv gleich; ⟨divide⟩ gleichmäßig; ⟨just as⟩ genauso

equanimity /ekwə'nɪmətɪ/ n Gleichmut f

equat|e /ɪ'kweɪt/ vt gleichsetzen (with mit). ~ion /-eɪʒn/ n ⟨Math⟩ Gleichung f

equator /ɪ'kweɪtə(r)/ n Äquator m. ~ial /ekwə'tɔ:rɪəl/ a Äquator-

equestrian /ɪ'kwestrɪən/ a Reit-

equilibrium /i:kwɪ'lɪbrɪəm/ n Gleichgewicht nt

equinox /'i:kwɪnɒks/ n Tagundnachtgleiche f

equip /ɪ'kwɪp/ vt (pt/pp equipped) ausrüsten; ⟨furnish⟩ ausstatten. ~ment n Ausrüstung f; Ausstattung f

equitable /'ekwɪtəbl/ a gerecht

equity /'ekwətɪ/ n Gerechtigkeit f

equivalent /ɪ'kwɪvələnt/ a gleichwertig; ⟨corresponding⟩ entsprechend ● n Äquivalent nt; ⟨value⟩

Gegenwert *m*; (*counterpart*) Gegenstück *nt*

equivocal /ɪˈkwɪvəkl/ *a* zweideutig

era /ˈɪərə/ *n* Ära *f*, Zeitalter *nt*

eradicate /ɪˈrædɪkeɪt/ *vt* ausrotten

erase /ɪˈreɪz/ *vt* ausradieren; (*from tape*) löschen; (*fig*) auslöschen. **~r** *n* Radiergummi *m*

erect /ɪˈrekt/ *a* aufrecht ● *vt* errichten. **~ion** /-ekʃn/ *n* Errichtung *f*; (*building*) Bau *m*; (*Biol*) Erektion *f*

ermine /ˈɜːmɪn/ *n* Hermelin *m*

ero|de /ɪˈrəʊd/ *vt* (*water:*) auswaschen; (*acid:*) angreifen. **~sion** /-əʊʒn/ *n* Erosion *f*

erotic /ɪˈrɒtɪk/ *a* erotisch. **~ism** /-tɪsɪzm/ *n* Erotik *f*

err /ɜː(r)/ *vi* sich irren; (*sin*) sündigen

errand /ˈerənd/ *n* Botengang *m*

erratic /ɪˈrætɪk/ *a* unregelmäßig; (*person*) unberechenbar

erroneous /ɪˈrəʊnɪəs/ *a* falsch; (*belief, assumption*) irrig. **~ly** *adv* fälschlich; irrigerweise

error /ˈerə(r)/ *n* Irrtum *m*; (*mistake*) Fehler *m*; **in ~** irrtümlicherweise

erudit|e /ˈerʊdaɪt/ *a* gelehrt. **~ion** /-ˈdɪʃn/ *n* Gelehrsamkeit *f*

erupt /ɪˈrʌpt/ *vi* ausbrechen. **~ion** /-ʌpʃn/ *n* Ausbruch *m*

escalat|e /ˈeskəleɪt/ *vt/i* eskalieren. **~ion** /-ˈleɪʃn/ *n* Eskalation *f*. **~or** *n* Rolltreppe *f*

escapade /ˈeskəpeɪd/ *n* Eskapade *f*

escape /ɪˈskeɪp/ *n* Flucht *f*; (*from prison*) Ausbruch *m*; **have a narrow ~** gerade noch davonkommen ● *vi* flüchten; (*prisoner:*) ausbrechen; entkommen (**from** aus; **from s.o.** jdm); (*gas:*) entweichen ● *vt* ~ **notice** unbemerkt bleiben; **the name ~s me** der Name entfällt mir

escapism /ɪˈskeɪpɪzm/ *n* Flucht *f* vor der Wirklichkeit, Eskapismus *m*

escort[1] /ˈeskɔːt/ *n* (*of person*) Begleiter *m*; (*Mil*) Eskorte *f*; **under ~** unter Bewachung

escort[2] /ɪˈskɔːt/ *vt* begleiten; (*Mil*) eskortieren

Eskimo /ˈeskɪməʊ/ *n* Eskimo *m*

esoteric /esəˈterɪk/ *a* esoterisch

especial /ɪˈspeʃl/ *a* besondere(r,s). **~ly** *adv* besonders

espionage /ˈespɪɒnɑːʒ/ *n* Spionage *f*

essay /ˈeseɪ/ *n* Aufsatz *m*

essence /ˈesns/ *n* Wesen *nt*; (*Chem, Culin*) Essenz *f*; **in ~** im wesentlichen

essential /ɪˈsenʃl/ *a* wesentlich; (*indispensable*) unentbehrlich ● *n* **the ~s** das Wesentliche; (*items*) das Nötigste. **~ly** *adv* im wesentlichen

establish /ɪˈstæblɪʃ/ *vt* gründen; (*form*) bilden; (*prove*) beweisen. **~ment** *n* (*firm*) Unternehmen *nt*

estate /ɪˈsteɪt/ *n* Gut *nt*; (*possessions*) Besitz *m*; (*after death*) Nachlaß *m*; (*housing*) [Wohn]siedlung *f*. **~ agent** *n* Immobilienmakler *m*. **~ car** *n* Kombi[wagen] *m*

esteem /ɪˈstiːm/ *n* Achtung *f* ● *vt* hochschätzen

estimate[1] /ˈestɪmət/ *n* Schätzung *f*; (*Comm*) [Kosten]voranschlag *m*; **at a rough ~** grob geschätzt

estimat|e[2] /ˈestɪmeɪt/ *vt* schätzen. **~ion** /-ˈmeɪʃn/ *n* Einschätzung *f*; (*esteem*) Achtung *f*; **in my ~ion** meiner Meinung nach

estuary /ˈestjʊərɪ/ *n* Mündung *f*

etc. /et'setərə/ *abbr* (**et cetera**) und so weiter, usw.

etching /ˈetʃɪŋ/ *n* Radierung *f*

eternal /ɪˈtɜːnl/ *a*, **-ly** *adv* ewig

eternity /ɪˈtɜːnətɪ/ *n* Ewigkeit *f*

ether /ˈiːθə(r)/ *n* Äther *m*

ethic /ˈeθɪk/ *n* Ethik *f*. **~al** *a* ethisch; (*morally correct*) moralisch einwandfrei. **~s** *n* Ethik *f*

Ethiopia /iːθɪˈəʊpɪə/ *n* Äthiopien *nt*

ethnic /ˈeθnɪk/ *a* ethnisch

etiquette /ˈetɪket/ *n* Etikette *f*

etymology /etɪˈmɒlədʒɪ/ *n* Etymologie *f*

eucalyptus /juːkəˈlɪptəs/ *n* Eukalyptus *m*

eulogy /ˈjuːlədʒɪ/ *n* Lobrede *f*

euphemis|m /ˈjuːfəmɪzm/ *n* Euphemismus *m*. **~tic** /-ˈmɪstɪk/ *a*, **-ally** *adv* verhüllend

euphoria /juːˈfɔːrɪə/ *n* Euphorie *f*

Euro-: /ˈjʊərəʊ-/ *pref* **~cheque** *n* Euroscheck *m*. **~passport** *n* Europaß *m*

Europe /ˈjʊərəp/ *n* Europa *nt*

European /jʊərəˈpɪən/ *a* europäisch; **~ Community** Europäische Gemeinschaft *f* ● *n* Europäer(in) *m(f)*

evacuat|e /ɪˈvækjʊeɪt/ *vt* evakuieren; räumen (*building, area*). **~ion** /-ˈeɪʃn/ *n* Evakuierung *f*; Räumung *f*

evade /ɪˈveɪd/ *vt* sich entziehen (+ *dat*); hinterziehen (*taxes*); **~ the issue** ausweichen

evaluate /ɪˈvæljʊeɪt/ *vt* einschätzen

evange|lical /iːvænˈdʒelɪkl/ *a* evangelisch. **~list** /ɪˈvændʒəlɪst/ *n* Evangelist *m*

evaporat|e /ɪˈvæpəreɪt/ *vi* verdunsten; **~ed milk** Kondensmilch *f*, Dosenmilch *f*. **~ion** /-ˈreɪʃn/ *n* Verdampfung *f*

evasion /ɪˈveɪʒn/ *n* Ausweichen *nt;* **~ of taxes** Steuerhinterziehung *f*

evasive /ɪˈveɪsɪv/ *a*, **-ly** *adv* ausweichend; **be ~** ausweichen

eve /iːv/ *n* (*liter*) Vorabend *m*

even /ˈiːvn/ *a* (*level*) eben; (*same, equal*) gleich; (*regular*) gleichmäßig; ⟨*number*⟩ gerade; **get ~ with** (*fam*) es jdm heimzahlen ● *adv* sogar, selbst; **~ so** trotzdem; **not ~** nicht einmal ● *vt* **~ the score** ausgleichen. **~ up** *vt* ausgleichen ● *vi* sich ausgleichen

evening /ˈiːvnɪŋ/ *n* Abend *m*; **this ~** heute abend; **in the ~** abends, am Abend. **~ class** *n* Abendkurs *m*

evenly /ˈiːvnlɪ/ *adv* gleichmäßig

event /ɪˈvent/ *n* Ereignis *nt*; (*function*) Veranstaltung *f*; (*Sport*) Wettbewerb *m*; **in the ~ of** im Falle (+*gen*); **in the ~** wie es sich ergab. **~ful** *a* ereignisreich

eventual /ɪˈventjʊəl/ *a* **his ~ success** der Erfolg, der ihm schließlich zuteil wurde. **~ity** /-ˈælətɪ/ *n* Eventualität *f*, Fall *m*. **~ly** *adv* schließlich

ever /ˈevə(r)/ *adv* je[mals]; **not ~** nie; **for ~** für immer; **hardly ~** fast nie; **since** seitdem; **~ so** (*fam*) sehr, furchtbar (*fam*)

'evergreen *n* immergrüner Strauch *m*/(*tree*) Baum *m*

ever'lasting *a* ewig

every /ˈevrɪ/ *a* jede(r,s); **~ one** jede(r,s) einzelne; **~ other day** jeden zweiten Tag

every: **~body** *pron* jeder[mann]; alle *pl*. **~day** *a* alltäglich. **~one** *pron* jeder[mann]; alle *pl*. **~thing** *pron* alles. **~where** *adv* überall

evict /ɪˈvɪkt/ *vt* [aus der Wohnung] hinausweisen. **~ion** /-ɪkʃn/ *n* Ausweisung *f*

eviden|ce /ˈevɪdəns/ *n* Beweise *pl*; (*Jur*) Beweismaterial *nt*; (*testimony*) Aussage *f*; **give ~ce** aussagen. **~t** *a*, **-ly** *adv* offensichtlich

evil /ˈiːvl/ *a* böse ● *n* Böse *nt*

evocative /ɪˈvɒkətɪv/ *a* **be ~ of** heraufbeschwören

evoke /ɪˈvəʊk/ *vt* heraufbeschwören

evolution /iːvəˈluːʃn/ *n* Evolution *f*

evolve /ɪˈvɒlv/ *vt* entwickeln ● *vi* sich entwickeln

ewe /juː/ *n* Schaf *nt*

exacerbate /ekˈsæsəbeɪt/ *vt* verschlimmern; verschärfen ⟨*situation*⟩

exact /ɪɡˈzækt/ *a*, **-ly** *adv* genau; **not ~ly** nicht gerade. ● *vt* erzwingen. **~ing** *a* anspruchsvoll. **~itude** /-ɪtjuːd/ *n*, **~ness** *n* Genauigkeit *f*

exaggerat|e /ɪɡˈzædʒəreɪt/ *vt/i* übertreiben. **~ion** /-ˈreɪʃn/ *n* Übertreibung *f*

exalt /ɪɡˈzɔːlt/ *vt* erheben; (*praise*) preisen

exam /ɪɡˈzæm/ *n* (*fam*) Prüfung *f*

examination /ɪɡzæmɪˈneɪʃn/ *n* Untersuchung *f*; (*Sch*) Prüfung *f*

examine /ɪɡˈzæmɪn/ *vt* untersuchen; (*Sch*) prüfen; (*Jur*) verhören. **~r** *n* (*Sch*) Prüfer *m*

example /ɪɡˈzɑːmpl/ *n* Beispiel *nt* (**of** für); **for ~** zum Beispiel; **make an ~of** ein Exempel statuieren an (+*dat*)

exasperat|e /ɪɡˈzæspəreɪt/ *vt* zur Verzweiflung treiben. **~ion** /-ˈreɪʃn/ *n* Verzweiflung *f*

excavat|e /ˈekskəveɪt/ *vt* ausschachten; (*Archaeol*) ausgraben. **~ion** /-ˈveɪʃn/ *n* Ausgrabung *f*

exceed /ɪkˈsiːd/ *vt* übersteigen. **~ingly** *adv* äußerst

excel /ɪkˈsel/ *v* (*pt/pp* **excelled**) *vi* sich auszeichnen ● *vt* **~ oneself** sich selbst übertreffen

excellen|ce /ˈeksələns/ *n* Vorzüglichkeit *f*. **E~cy** *n* (*title*) Exzellenz *f*. **~t** *a*, **-ly** *adv* ausgezeichnet, vorzüglich

except /ɪkˈsept/ *prep* außer (+*dat*); **~ for** abgesehen von ● *vt* ausnehmen. **~ing** *prep* außer (+*dat*)

exception /ɪkˈsepʃn/ *n* Ausnahme *f*; **take ~ to** Anstoß nehmen an (+*dat*). **~al** *a*, **-ly** *adv* außergewöhnlich

excerpt /ˈeksɜːpt/ *n* Auszug *m*

excess /ɪkˈses/ *n* Übermaß *nt* (**of** an +*dat*); (*surplus*) Überschuß *m*; **~es** *pl* Exzesse *pl*; **in ~ of** über (+*dat*)

excess 'fare /ˈekses-/ *n* Nachlösegebühr *f*

excessive /ɪkˈsesɪv/ *a*, **-ly** *adv* übermäßig

exchange /ɪksˈtʃeɪndʒ/ *n* Austausch *m*; (*Teleph*) Fernsprechamt *nt*; (*Comm*) [Geld]wechsel *m*; **[stock] ~** Börse *f*; **in ~** dafür ● *vt* austauschen (**for** gegen); tauschen ⟨*places, greetings, money*⟩. ~ **rate** *n* Wechselkurs *m*

exchequer /ɪks'tʃekə(r)/ *n* (*Pol*) Staatskasse *f*

excise[1] /'eksaɪz/ *n* ~ **duty** Verbrauchssteuer *f*

excise[2] /ek'saɪz/ *vt* herausschneiden

excitable /ɪk'saɪtəbl/ *a* [leicht] erregbar

excit|e /ɪk'saɪt/ *vt* aufregen; (*cause*) erregen. ~**ed** *a*, **-ly** *adv* aufgeregt; **get** ~**ed** sich aufregen. ~**ement** *n* Aufregung *f*; Erregung *f*. ~**ing** *a* aufregend; (*story*) spannend

exclaim /ɪk'skleɪm/ *vt/i* ausrufen

exclamation /eksklə'meɪʃn/ *n* Ausruf *m*. ~ **mark** *n*, (*Amer*) ~ **point** *n* Ausrufezeichen *nt*

exclu|de /ɪk'sklu:d/ *vt* ausschließen. ~**ding** *prep* ausschließlich (+ *gen*). ~**sion** /-ʒn/ *n* Ausschluß *m*

exclusive /ɪk'sklu:sɪv/ *a*, **-ly** *adv* ausschließlich; (*select*) exklusiv; ~ **of** ausschließlich (+ *gen*)

excommunicate /ekskə'mju:nɪkeɪt/ *vt* exkommunizieren

excrement /'ekskrɪmənt/ *n* Kot *m*

excrete /ɪk'skri:t/ *vt* ausscheiden

excruciating /ɪk'skru:ʃɪeɪtɪŋ/ *a* gräßlich

excursion /ɪk'skɜ:ʃn/ *n* Ausflug *m*

excusable /ɪk'skju:zəbl/ *a* entschuldbar

excuse[1] /ɪk'skju:s/ *n* Entschuldigung *f*; (*pretext*) Ausrede *f*

excuse[2] /ɪk'skju:z/ *vt* entschuldigen; ~ **from** freistellen von; ~ **me!** Entschuldigung!

ex-di'rectory *a* **be** ~ nicht im Telefonbuch stehen

execute /'eksɪkju:t/ *vt* ausführen; (*put to death*) hinrichten

execution /eksɪ'kju:ʃn/ *n* (*see* execute) Ausführung *f*; Hinrichtung *f*. ~**er** *n* Scharfrichter *m*

executive /ɪg'zekjʊtɪv/ *a* leitend ● *n* leitende(r) Angestellte(r) *m/f*; (*Pol*) Exekutive *f*

executor /ɪg'zekjʊtə(r)/ *n* (*Jur*) Testamentsvollstrecker *m*

exemplary /ɪg'zemplərɪ/ *a* beispielhaft; (*as a warning*) exemplarisch

exemplify /ɪg'zemplɪfaɪ/ *vt* (*pt/pp* **-ied**) veranschaulichen

exempt /ɪg'zempt/ *a* befreit ● *vt* befreien (**from** von). ~**ion** /-empʃn/ *n* Befreiung *f*

exercise /'eksəsaɪz/ *n* Übung *f*; **physical** ~ körperliche Bewegung *f*; **take** ~ sich bewegen ● *vt* (*use*) ausüben; bewegen ⟨*horse*⟩; spazierenführen ⟨*dog*⟩ ● *vi* sich bewegen. ~ **book** *n* [Schul]heft *nt*

exert /ɪg'zɜ:t/ *vt* ausüben; ~ **oneself** sich anstrengen. ~**ion** /-ɜ:ʃn/ *n* Anstrengung *f*

exhale /eks'heɪl/ *vt/i* ausatmen

exhaust /ɪg'zɔ:st/ *n* (*Auto*) Auspuff *m*; (*pipe*) Auspuffrohr *nt*; (*fumes*) Abgase *pl* ● *vt* erschöpfen. ~**ed** *a* erschöpft. ~**ing** *a* anstrengend. ~**ion** /-ɔ:stʃn/ *n* Erschöpfung *f*. ~**ive** /-ɪv/ *a* (*fig*) erschöpfend

exhibit /ɪg'zɪbɪt/ *n* Ausstellungsstück *nt*; (*Jur*) Beweisstück *nt* ● *vt* ausstellen; (*fig*) zeigen

exhibition /eksɪ'bɪʃn/ *n* Ausstellung *f*; (*Univ*) Stipendium *nt*. ~**ist** *n* Exhibitionist(in) *m(f)*

exhibitor /ɪg'zɪbɪtə(r)/ *n* Aussteller *m*

exhilarat|ed /ɪg'zɪləreɪtɪd/ *a* beschwingt. ~**ing** *a* berauschend. ~**ion** /-'reɪʃn/ *n* Hochgefühl *nt*

exhort /ɪg'zɔ:t/ *vt* ermahnen

exhume /ɪg'zju:m/ *vt* exhumieren

exile /'eksaɪl/ *n* Exil *nt*; (*person*) im Exil Lebende(r) *m/f* ● *vt* ins Exil schicken

exist /ɪg'zɪst/ *vi* bestehen, existieren. ~**ence** /-əns/ *n* Existenz *f*; **be in** ~**ence** existieren

exit /'eksɪt/ *n* Ausgang *m*; (*Auto*) Ausfahrt *f*; (*Theat*) Abgang *m* ● *vi* (*Theat*) abgehen. ~ **visa** *n* Ausreisevisum *nt*

exonerate /ɪg'zɒnəreɪt/ *vt* entlasten

exorbitant /ɪg'zɔ:bɪtənt/ *a* übermäßig hoch

exorcize /'eksɔ:saɪz/ *vt* austreiben

exotic /ɪg'zɒtɪk/ *a* exotisch

expand /ɪk'spænd/ *vt* ausdehnen; (*explain better*) weiter ausführen ● *vi* sich ausdehnen; (*Comm*) expandieren; ~ **on** (*fig*) weiter ausführen

expans|e /ɪk'spæns/ *n* Weite *f*. ~**ion** /-ænʃn/ *n* Ausdehnung *f*; (*Techn, Pol, Comm*) Expansion *f*. ~**ive** /-ɪv/ *a* mitteilsam

expatriate /eks'pætrɪət/ *n* **be an** ~ im Ausland leben

expect /ɪk'spekt/ *vt* erwarten; (*suppose*) annehmen; **I** ~ **so** wahrscheinlich; **we** ~ **to arrive on Monday**

wir rechnen damit, daß wir am Montag ankommen

expectan|cy /ɪk'spektənsɪ/ n Erwartung f. ~t a, -ly adv erwartungsvoll; ~t **mother** werdende Mutter f

expectation /ekspek'teɪʃn/ n Erwartung f; ~ **of life** Lebenserwartung f

expedient /ɪk'spiːdɪənt/ a zweckdienlich

expedite /'ekspɪdaɪt/ vt beschleunigen

expedition /ekspɪ'dɪʃn/ n Expedition f. ~**ary** a (Mil) Expeditions-

expel /ɪk'spel/ vt (pt/pp expelled) ausweisen (from aus); (from school) von der Schule verweisen

expend /ɪk'spend/ vt aufwenden. ~**able** /-əbl/ a entbehrlich

expenditure /ɪk'spendɪtʃə(r)/ n Ausgaben pl

expense /ɪk'spens/ n Kosten pl; **business** ~s pl Spesen pl; **at my** ~ auf meine Kosten; **at the** ~ **of** (fig) auf Kosten (+ gen)

expensive /ɪk'spensɪv/ a, -ly adv teuer

experience /ɪk'spɪərɪəns/ n Erfahrung f; (event) Erlebnis nt ● vt erleben. ~**d** a erfahren

experiment /ɪk'sperɪmənt/ n Versuch m, Experiment nt ● /-ment/ vi experimentieren. ~**al** /-'mentl/ a experimentell

expert /'ekspɜːt/ a, -ly adv fachmännisch ● n Fachmann m, Experte m

expertise /ekspɜː'tiːz/ n Sachkenntnis f; (skill) Geschick nt

expire /ɪk'spaɪə(r)/ vi ablaufen

expiry /ɪk'spaɪərɪ/ n Ablauf m. ~ **date** n Verfallsdatum nt

explain /ɪk'spleɪn/ vt erklären

explana|tion /eksplə'neɪʃn/ n Erklärung f. ~**tory** /ɪk'splænətərɪ/ a erklärend

expletive /ɪk'spliːtɪv/ n Kraftausdruck m

explicit /ɪk'splɪsɪt/ a, -ly adv deutlich

explode /ɪk'spləʊd/ vi explodieren ● vt zur Explosion bringen

exploit[1] /'eksplɔɪt/ n [Helden]tat f

exploit[2] /ɪk'splɔɪt/ vt ausbeuten. ~**ation** /eksplɔɪ'teɪʃn/ n Ausbeutung f

explora|tion /eksplə'reɪʃn/ n Erforschung f. ~**tory** /ɪk'splɒrətərɪ/ a Probe-

explore /ɪk'splɔː(r)/ vt erforschen. ~**r** n Forschungsreisende(r) m

explos|ion /ɪk'spləʊʒn/ n Explosion f. ~**ive** /-sɪv/ a explosiv ● n Sprengstoff m

exponent /ɪk'spəʊnənt/ n Vertreter m

export[1] /'ekspɔːt/ n Export m, Ausfuhr f

export[2] /ɪk'spɔːt/ vt exportieren, ausführen. ~**er** n Exporteur m

expos|e /ɪk'spəʊz/ vt freilegen; (to danger) aussetzen (**to** dat); (reveal) aufdecken; (Phot) belichten. ~**ure** /-ʒə(r)/ n Aussetzung f; (Med) Unterkühlung f; (Phot) Belichtung f; **24** ~**ures** 24 Aufnahmen

expound /ɪk'spaʊnd/ vt erläutern

express /ɪk'spres/ a ausdrücklich; (purpose) fest ● adv (send) per Eilpost ● n (train) Schnellzug m ● vt ausdrücken; ~ **oneself** sich ausdrücken. ~**ion** /-ʃn/ n Ausdruck m. ~**ive** /-ɪv/ a ausdrucksvoll. ~**ly** adv ausdrücklich

expulsion /ɪk'spʌlʃn/ n Ausweisung f; (Sch) Verweisung f von der Schule

expurgate /'ekspɜːgeɪt/ vt zensieren

exquisite /ek'skwɪzɪt/ a erlesen

ex-'serviceman n Veteran m

extempore /ɪk'stempərɪ/ adv (speak) aus dem Stegreif

extend /ɪk'stend/ vt verlängern; (stretch out) ausstrecken; (enlarge) vergrößern ● vi sich ausdehnen; (table:) sich ausziehen lassen

extension /ɪk'stenʃn/ n Verlängerung f; (to house) Anbau m; (Teleph) Nebenanschluß m; ~ **7** Apparat 7

extensive /ɪk'stensɪv/ a weit; (fig) umfassend. ~**ly** adv viel

extent /ɪk'stent/ n Ausdehnung f; (scope) Ausmaß nt, Umfang m; **to a certain** ~ in gewissem Maße

extenuating /ɪk'stenjʊeɪtɪŋ/ a mildernd

exterior /ɪk'stɪərɪə(r)/ a äußere(r,s) ● n the ~ das Äußere

exterminat|e /ɪk'stɜːmɪneɪt/ vt ausrotten. ~**ion** /-'neɪʃn/ n Ausrottung f

external /ɪk'stɜːnl/ a äußere(r,s); **for** ~ **use only** (Med) nur äußerlich. ~**ly** adv äußerlich

extinct /ɪk'stɪŋkt/ a ausgestorben; (volcano) erloschen. ~**ion** /-ɪŋkʃn/ n Aussterben nt

extinguish /ɪk'stɪŋgwɪʃ/ vt löschen. ~**er** n Feuerlöscher m

extol /ɪk'stəʊl/ vt (pt/pp **extolled**) preisen

extort /ɪk'stɔːt/ vt erpressen. **~ion** /-ɔːʃn/ n Erpressung f

extortionate /ɪk'stɔːʃənət/ a übermäßig hoch

extra /'ekstrə/ a zusätzlich ● adv extra; (especially) besonders; **~ strong** extrastark ● n (Theat) Statist(in) m(f); **~s** pl Nebenkosten pl; (Auto) Extras pl

extract[1] /'ekstrækt/ n Auszug m; (Culin) Extrakt m

extract[2] /ɪk'strækt/ vt herausziehen; ziehen (tooth); (fig) erzwingen. **~or [fan]** n Entlüfter m

extradit|e /'ekstrədaɪt/ vt (Jur) ausliefern. **~ion** /-'dɪʃn/ n (Jur) Auslieferung f

extra'marital a außerehelich

extraordinary /ɪk'strɔːdnəri/ a, **-ily** adv außerordentlich; (strange) seltsam

extravagan|ce /ɪk'strævəgəns/ n Verschwendung f; **an ~ce** ein Luxus m. **~t** a verschwenderisch; (exaggerated) extravagant

extrem|e /ɪk'striːm/ a äußerste(r,s); (fig) extrem ● n Extrem nt; **in the ~e** im höchsten Grade. **~ely** adv äußerst. **~ist** n Extremist m

extremit|y /ɪk'streməti/ n (distress) Not f; **the ~ies** pl die Extremitäten pl

extricate /'ekstrɪkeɪt/ vt befreien

extrovert /'ekstrəvɜːt/ n extravertierter Mensch m

exuberant /ɪg'zjuːbərənt/ a überglücklich

exude /ɪg'zjuːd/ vt absondern; (fig) ausstrahlen

exult /ɪg'zʌlt/ vi frohlocken

eye /aɪ/ n Auge nt; (of needle) Öhr nt; (for hook) Öse f; **keep an ~ on** aufpassen auf (+ acc); **see ~ to ~** einer Meinung sein ● vt (pt/pp **eyed**, pres p **ey[e]ing**) ansehen

eye: ~ball n Augapfel m. **~brow** n Augenbraue f. **~lash** n Wimper f. **~let** /-lɪt/ n Öse f. **~lid** n Augenlid nt. **~-shadow** n Lidschatten m. **~sight** n Sehkraft f. **~sore** n (fam) Schandfleck m. **~-tooth** n Eckzahn m. **~witness** n Augenzeuge m

F

fable /'feɪbl/ n Fabel f

fabric /'fæbrɪk/ n Stoff m; (fig) Gefüge nt

fabrication /fæbrɪ'keɪʃn/ n Erfindung f

fabulous /'fæbjʊləs/ a (fam) phantastisch

façade /fə'sɑːd/ n Fassade f

face /feɪs/ n Gesicht nt; (grimace) Grimasse f; (surface) Fläche f; (of clock) Zifferblatt nt; **pull ~s** Gesichter schneiden; **in the ~ of** angesichts (+ gen); **on the ~ of it** allem Anschein nach ● vt/i gegenüberstehen (+ dat); **~ north** (house:) nach Norden liegen; **~ me!** sieh mich an! **~ the fact that** sich damit abfinden, daß; **~ up to s.o.** jdm die Stirn bieten

face: ~-flannel n Waschlappen m. **~less** a anonym. **~-lift** n Gesichtsstraffung f

facet /'fæsɪt/ n Facette f; (fig) Aspekt m

facetious /fə'siːʃəs/ a, **-ly** adv spöttisch

'face value n Nennwert m

facial /'feɪʃl/ a Gesichts-

facile /'fæsaɪl/ a oberflächlich

facilitate /fə'sɪlɪteɪt/ vt erleichtern

facilit|y /fə'sɪləti/ n Leichtigkeit f; (skill) Gewandtheit f; **~ies** pl Einrichtungen pl

facing /'feɪsɪŋ/ n Besatz m

facsimile /fæk'sɪməli/ n Faksimile nt

fact /fækt/ n Tatsache f; **in ~** tatsächlich; (actually) eigentlich

faction /'fækʃn/ n Gruppe f

factor /'fæktə(r)/ n Faktor m

factory /'fæktəri/ n Fabrik f

factual /'fæktʃʊəl/ a, **-ly** adv sachlich

faculty /'fækəlti/ n Fähigkeit f; (Univ) Fakultät f

fad /fæd/ n Fimmel m

fade /feɪd/ vi verblassen; (material:) verbleichen; (sound:) abklingen; (flower:) verwelken. **~ in/out** vt (Radio, TV) ein-/ausblenden

fag /fæg/ n (chore) Plage f; (fam: cigarette) Zigarette f; (Amer sl) Homosexuelle(r) m

fagged /fægd/ a **~ out** (fam) völlig erledigt

Fahrenheit /'færənhaɪt/ a Fahrenheit

fail /feɪl/ n **without ~** unbedingt ● vi (attempt:) scheitern; (grow weak) nachlassen; (break down) versagen; (in exam) durchfallen; **~ to do sth** etw nicht tun; **he ~ed to break the record** es gelang ihm nicht, den Rekord zu brechen ● *vt* nicht bestehen ⟨*exam*⟩; durchfallen lassen ⟨*candidate*⟩; ⟨*disappoint*⟩ enttäuschen; **words ~ me** ich weiß nicht, was ich sagen soll

failing /'feɪlɪŋ/ *n* Fehler *m* ● *prep ~* **that** andernfalls

failure /'feɪljə(r)/ *n* Mißerfolg *m*; ⟨*breakdown*⟩ Versagen *nt*; ⟨*person*⟩ Versager *m*

faint /feɪnt/ *a* (**-er, -est**), **-ly** *adv* schwach; **I feel ~** mir ist schwach ● *n* Ohnmacht *f* ● *vi* ohnmächtig werden

faint:~-'hearted *a* zaghaft. **~ness** *n* Schwäche *f*

fair[1] /feə(r)/ *n* Jahrmarkt *m*; ⟨*Comm*⟩ Messe *f*

fair[2] *a* (**-er, -est**) ⟨*hair*⟩ blond; ⟨*skin*⟩ hell; ⟨*weather*⟩ heiter; ⟨*just*⟩ gerecht, fair; ⟨*quite good*⟩ ziemlich gut; ⟨*Sch*⟩ genügend; **a ~ amount** ziemlich viel ● *adv* **play ~** fair sein. **~ly** *adv* gerecht; ⟨*rather*⟩ ziemlich. **~ness** *n* Blondheit *f*; Helle *f*; Gerechtigkeit *f*; ⟨*Sport*⟩ Fairneß *f*

fairy /'feərɪ/ *n* Elfe *f*; **good/wicked ~** gute/böse Fee *f*. **~ story, ~-tale** *n* Märchen *nt*

faith /feɪθ/ *n* Glaube *m*; ⟨*trust*⟩ Vertrauen *nt* (**in** zu); **in good ~** in gutem Glauben

faithful /'feɪθfl/ *a*, **-ly** *adv* treu; ⟨*exact*⟩ genau; **Yours ~ly** Hochachtungsvoll. **~ness** *n* Treue *f*; Genauigkeit *f*

'faith-healer *n* Gesundbeter *m* *m(f)*

fake /feɪk/ *a* falsch ● *n* Fälschung *f*; ⟨*person*⟩ Schwindler *m* ● *vt* fälschen; ⟨*pretend*⟩ vortäuschen

falcon /'fɔːlkən/ *n* Falke *m*

fall /fɔːl/ *n* Fall *m*; ⟨*heavy*⟩ Sturz *m*; ⟨*in prices*⟩ Fallen *nt*; ⟨*Amer: autumn*⟩ Herbst *m*; **have a ~** fallen ● *vi* (*pt* **fell**, *pp* **fallen**) fallen; ⟨*heavily*⟩ stürzen; ⟨*night:*⟩ anbrechen; **~ in love** sich verlieben; **~ back on** zurückgreifen auf (+ *acc*); **~ for s.o.** ⟨*fam*⟩ sich in jdn verlieben; **~ for sth** ⟨*fam*⟩ auf etw ⟨*acc*⟩ hereinfallen. **~ about** *vi* ⟨*with laughter*⟩ sich [vor Lachen] kringeln. **~ down** *vi* umfallen; ⟨*thing:*⟩ herunterfallen; ⟨*building:*⟩ einstürzen. **~ in** *vi* hineinfallen; ⟨*collapse*⟩ einfallen; ⟨*Mil*⟩ antreten; **~ in with** sich anschließen (+ *dat*). **~ off** *vi* herunterfallen; ⟨*diminish*⟩ abnehmen. **~**

out *vi* her- ausfallen; ⟨*hair:*⟩ ausfallen; ⟨*quarrel*⟩ sich überwerfen. **~ over** *vi* hinfallen. **~ through** *vi* durchfallen; ⟨*plan:*⟩ ins Wasser fallen

fallacy /'fæləsɪ/ *n* Irrtum *m*

fallible /'fæləbl/ *a* fehlbar

'fall-out *n* [radioaktiver] Niederschlag *m*

fallow /'fæləʊ/ *a* **lie ~** brachliegen

false /fɔːls/ *a* falsch; ⟨*artificial*⟩ künstlich; **~ start** ⟨*Sport*⟩ Fehlstart *m*. **~hood** *n* Unwahrheit *f*. **~ly** *adv* falsch. **~ness** *n* Falschheit *f*

false 'teeth *npl* [künstliches] Gebiß *nt*

falsify /'fɔːlsɪfaɪ/ *vt* (*pt/pp* **-ied**) fälschen; ⟨*misrepresent*⟩ verfälschen

falter /'fɔːltə(r)/ *vi* zögern; ⟨*stumble*⟩ straucheln

fame /feɪm/ *n* Ruhm *m*. **~d** *a* berühmt

familiar /fə'mɪljə(r)/ *a* vertraut; ⟨*known*⟩ bekannt; **too ~** familiär. **~ity** /-lɪ'ærətɪ/ *n* Vertrautheit *f*. **~ize** *vt* vertraut machen (**with** mit)

family /'fæməlɪ/ *n* Familie *f*

family: ~ al'lowance *n* Kindergeld *nt*. **~ 'doctor** *n* Hausarzt *m*. **~ 'life** *n* Familienleben *nt*. **~ 'planning** *n* Familienplanung *f*. **~ 'tree** *n* Stammbaum *m*

famine /'fæmɪn/ *n* Hungersnot *f*

famished /'fæmɪʃt/ *a* sehr hungrig

famous /'feɪməs/ *a* berühmt

fan[1] /fæn/ *n* Fächer *m*; ⟨*Techn*⟩ Ventilator *m* ● *v* (*pt/pp* **fanned**) ● *vt* fächeln; **~ oneself** sich fächeln ● *vi ~* **out** sich fächerförmig ausbreiten

fan[2] *n* ⟨*admirer*⟩ Fan *m*

fanatic /fə'nætɪk/ *n* Fanatiker *m*. **~al** *a*, **-ly** *adv* fanatisch. **~ism** /-sɪzm/ *n* Fanatismus *m*

'fan belt *n* Keilriemen *m*

fanciful /'fænsɪfl/ *a* phantastisch; ⟨*imaginative*⟩ phantasiereich

fancy /'fænsɪ/ *n* Phantasie *f*; **have a ~ to** Lust haben, zu; **I have taken a real ~ to him** er hat es mir angetan ● *a* ausgefallen; **~ cakes and biscuits** Feingebäck *nt* ● *vt* ⟨*believe*⟩ meinen; ⟨*imagine*⟩ sich ⟨*dat*⟩ einbilden; ⟨*fam: want*⟩ Lust haben auf (+ *acc*); **~ that!** stell dir vor! ⟨*really*⟩ tatsächlich! **~ 'dress** *n* Kostüm *nt*

fanfare /'fænfeə(r)/ *n* Fanfare *f*

fang /fæŋ/ *n* Fangzahn *m*; ⟨*of snake*⟩ Giftzahn *m*

fan: ~ **heater** n Heizlüfter m. ~**light** n Oberlicht nt

fantas|ize /'fæntəsaız/ vi phantasieren. ~**tic** /-'tæstık/ a phantastisch. ~**y** n Phantasie f; (Mus) Fantasie f

far /fɑ:(r)/ adv weit; (much) viel; **by** ~ bei weitem; ~ **away** weit weg; **as** ~ **as I know** soviel ich weiß; **as** ~ **as the church** bis zur Kirche ● a **at the** ~ **end** am anderen Ende; **the F**~ **East** der Ferne Osten

farc|e /fɑ:s/ n Farce f. ~**ical** a lächerlich

fare /feə(r)/ n Fahrpreis m; (money) Fahrgeld nt; (food) Kost f; **air** ~ Flugpreis m. ~-**dodger** /-dɒdʒə(r)/ n Schwarzfahrer m

farewell /feə'wel/ int (liter) lebe wohl! ● n Lebewohl nt; ~ **dinner** Abschiedsessen nt

far-'fetched a weit hergeholt; **be** ~ an den Haaren herbeigezogen sein

farm /fɑ:m/ n Bauernhof m ● vi Landwirtschaft betreiben ● vt bewirtschaften (land). ~**er** n Landwirt m

farm: ~**house** n Bauernhaus nt. ~**ing** n Landwirtschaft f. ~**yard** n Hof m

far: ~-'**reaching** a weitreichend. ~-'**sighted** a (fig) umsichtig; (Amer: long-sighted) weitsichtig

fart /fɑ:t/ n (vulg) Furz m ● vi (vulg) furzen

farther /'fɑ:ðə(r)/ adv weiter; ~ **off** weiter entfernt ● a **at the** ~ **end** am anderen Ende

fascinat|e /'fæsıneıt/ vt faszinieren. ~**ing** a faszinierend. ~**ion** /-'neıʃn/ n Faszination f

fascis|m /'fæʃızm/ n Faschismus m. ~**t** n Faschist m ● a faschistisch

fashion /'fæʃn/ n Mode f; (manner) Art f ● vt machen; (mould) formen. ~**able** /-əbl/ a, **-bly** adv modisch; **be** ~**able** Mode sein

fast[1] /fɑ:st/ a & adv (-**er**, -**est**) schnell; (firm) fest; (colour) waschecht; **be** ~ (clock:) vorgehen; **be** ~ **asleep** fest schlafen

fast[2] n Fasten nt ● vi fasten

'fastback n (Auto) Fließheck nt

fasten /'fɑ:sn/ vt zumachen; (fix) befestigen (**to** an + dat); ~ **one's seat-belt** sich anschnallen. ~**er** n, ~**ing** n Verschluß m

fastidious /fə'stıdıəs/ a wählerisch; (particular) penibel

fat /fæt/ a (**fatter, fattest**) dick; (meat) fett ● n Fett nt

fatal /'feıtl/ a tödlich; (error) verhängnisvoll. ~**ism** /-təlızm/ n Fatalismus m. ~**ist** /-təlıst/ n Fatalist m. ~**ity** /fə'tælətı/ n Todesopfer nt. ~**ly** adv tödlich

fate /feıt/ n Schicksal nt. ~**ful** a verhängnisvoll

'fat-head n (fam) Dummkopf m

father /'fɑ:ðə(r)/ n Vater m; **F**~ **Christmas** der Weihnachtsmann ● vt zeugen

father: ~**hood** n Vaterschaft f. ~-**in-law** n (pl ~**s-in-law**) Schwiegervater m. ~**ly** a väterlich

fathom /'fæðəm/ n (Naut) Faden m ● vt verstehen; ~ **out** ergründen

fatigue /fə'ti:g/ n Ermüdung f ● vt ermüden

fatten /'fætn/ vt mästen (animal). ~**ing** a **cream is** ~**ing** Sahne macht dick

fatty /'fætı/ a fett; (foods) fetthaltig

fatuous /'fætjʊəs/ a, **-ly** adv albern

faucet /'fɔ:sıt/ n (Amer) Wasserhahn m

fault /fɔ:lt/ n Fehler m; (Techn) Defekt m; (Geol) Verwerfung f; **at** ~ im Unrecht; **find** ~ **with** etwas auszusetzen haben an (+ dat); **it's your** ~ du bist schuld ● vt etwas auszusetzen haben an (+ dat). ~**less** a, **-ly** adv fehlerfrei

faulty /'fɔ:ltı/ a fehlerhaft

fauna /'fɔ:nə/ n Fauna f

favour /'feıvə(r)/ n Gunst f; **I am in** ~ ich bin dafür; **do s.o. a** ~ jdm einen Gefallen tun ● vt begünstigen; (prefer) bevorzugen. ~**able** /-əbl/ a, **-bly** adv günstig; (reply) positiv

favourit|e /'feıvərıt/ a Lieblings- ● n Liebling m; (Sport) Favorit(in) m(f). ~**ism** n Bevorzugung f

fawn[1] /fɔ:n/ a rehbraun ● n Hirschkalb nt

fawn[2] vi sich einschmeicheln (**on** bei)

fax /fæks/ n Fax nt ● vt faxen (s.o. jdm). ~ **machine** n Faxgerät nt

fear /fıə(r)/ n Furcht f, Angst f (**of** vor + dat); **no** ~! (fam) keine Angst! ● vt/i fürchten

fear|ful /'fıəfl/ a besorgt; (awful) furchtbar. ~**less** a, **-ly** adv furchtlos. ~**some** /-səm/ a furchterregend

feas|ibility /fiːzə'bɪlətɪ/ n Durchführbarkeit f. ~**ible** a durchführbar; (possible) möglich

feast /fiːst/ n Festmahl nt; (Relig) Fest nt ● vi ~ [on] schmausen

feat /fiːt/ n Leistung f

feather /'feðə(r)/ n Feder f

feature /'fiːtʃə(r)/ n Gesichtszug m; (quality) Merkmal nt; (Journ) Feature nt ● vt darstellen; ⟨film:⟩ in der Hauptrolle zeigen. ~ **film** n Hauptfilm m

February /'februərɪ/ n Februar m

feckless /'feklɪs/ a verantwortungslos

fed /fed/ see feed ● a be ~ up (fam) die Nase voll haben (with von)

federal /'fedərəl/ a Bundes-

federation /fedə'reɪʃn/ n Föderation f

fee /fiː/ n Gebühr f; (professional) Honorar nt

feeble /'fiːbl/ a (-r, -st), -bly adv schwach

feed /fiːd/ n Futter nt; (for baby) Essen nt ● v (pt/pp fed) ● vt füttern; (support) ernähren; (into machine) eingeben; speisen ⟨computer⟩ ● vi sich ernähren (on von)

'feedback n Feedback nt

feel /fiːl/ v (pt/pp felt) ● vt fühlen; (experience) empfinden; (think) meinen ● vi sich fühlen; ~ **soft/hard** sich weich/hart anfühlen; **I ~ hot/ill** mir ist heiß/schlecht; **I don't ~ like it** ich habe keine Lust dazu. ~**er** n Fühler m. ~**ing** n Gefühl nt; **no hard ~ings** nichts für ungut

feet /fiːt/ see foot

feign /feɪn/ vt vortäuschen

feint /feɪnt/ n Finte f

feline /'fiːlaɪn/ a Katzen-; (catlike) katzenartig

fell[1] /fel/ vt fällen

fell[2] see fall

fellow /'feləʊ/ n (of society) Mitglied nt; (fam: man) Kerl m

fellow: ~-'**countryman** n Landsmann m. ~ **men** pl Mitmenschen pl. ~**ship** n Kameradschaft f; (group) Gesellschaft f

felony /'felənɪ/ n Verbrechen nt

felt[1] /felt/ see feel

felt[2] n Filz m. ~[-**tipped**] '**pen** n Filzstift m

female /'fiːmeɪl/ a weiblich ● nt Weibchen nt; (pej: woman) Weib nt

femin|ine /'femɪnɪn/ a weiblich ● n (Gram) Femininum nt. ~**inity** /-'nɪnətɪ/ n Weiblichkeit f. ~**ist** a feministisch ● n Feminist(in) m(f)

fenc|e /fens/ n Zaun m; (fam: person) Hehler m ● vi (Sport) fechten ● vt ~**e in** einzäunen. ~**er** n Fechter m. ~**ing** n Zaun m; (Sport) Fechten nt

fend /fend/ vi ~ **for oneself** sich allein durchschlagen. ~ **off** vt abwehren

fender /'fendə(r)/ n Kaminvorsetzer m; (Naut) Fender m; (Amer: wing) Kotflügel m

fennel /'fenl/ n Fenchel m

ferment[1] /'fɜːment/ n Erregung f

ferment[2] /fə'ment/ vi gären ● vt gären lassen. ~**ation** /fɜːmen'teɪʃn/ n Gärung f

fern /fɜːn/ n Farn m

feroc|ious /fə'rəʊʃəs/ a wild. ~**ity** /-'rɒsətɪ/ n Wildheit f

ferret /'ferɪt/ n Frettchen nt

ferry /'ferɪ/ n Fähre f ● vt ~ [**across**] übersetzen

fertil|e /'fɜːtaɪl/ a fruchtbar. ~**ity** /fɜː'tɪlətɪ/ n Fruchtbarkeit f

fertilize /'fɜːtəlaɪz/ vt befruchten; düngen ⟨land⟩. ~**r** n Dünger m

fervent /'fɜːvənt/ a leidenschaftlich

fervour /'fɜːvə(r)/ n Leidenschaft f

fester /'festə(r)/ vi eitern

festival /'festɪvl/ n Fest nt; (Mus, Theat) Festspiele pl

festiv|e /'festɪv/ a festlich; ~**e season** Festzeit f. ~**ities** /fe'stɪvətɪz/ npl Feierlichkeiten pl

festoon /fe'stuːn/ vt behängen (with mit)

fetch /fetʃ/ vt holen; (collect) abholen; (be sold for) einbringen

fetching /'fetʃɪŋ/ a anziehend

fête /feɪt/ n Fest nt ● vt feiern

fetish /'fetɪʃ/ n Fetisch m

fetter /'fetə(r)/ vt fesseln

fettle /'fetl/ n **in fine** ~ in bester Form

feud /fjuːd/ n Fehde f

feudal /'fjuːdl/ a Feudal-

fever /'fiːvə(r)/ n Fieber nt. ~**ish** a fiebrig; (fig) fieberhaft

few /fjuː/ a (-er, -est) wenige; **every ~ days** alle paar Tage ● n a ~ ein paar; **quite a** ~ ziemlich viele

fiancé /fɪ'ɒnseɪ/ n Verlobte(r) m. **fiancée** n Verlobte f

fiasco /fɪ'æskəʊ/ n Fiasko nt

fib /fɪb/ n kleine Lüge; **tell a** ~ schwindeln

fibre /'faɪbə(r)/ n Faser f

fickle /'fɪkl/ *a* unbeständig

fiction /'fɪkʃn/ *n* Erfindung *f*; **[works of]** ∼ Erzählungsliteratur *f.* ∼**al** *a* erfunden

fictitious /fɪk'tɪʃəs/ *a* [frei] erfunden

fiddle /'fɪdl/ *n* (*fam*) Geige *f*; (*cheating*) Schwindel *m* ● *vi* herumspielen (**with** mit) ● *vt* (*fam*) frisieren (*accounts*); (*arrange*) arrangieren

fiddly /'fɪdlɪ/ *a* knifflig

fidelity /fɪ'delətɪ/ *n* Treue *f*

fidget /'fɪdʒɪt/ *vi* zappeln. ∼**y** *a* zappelig

field /fiːld/ *n* Feld *nt*; (*meadow*) Wiese *f*; (*subject*) Gebiet *nt*

field: ∼ **events** *npl* Sprung- und Wurfdisziplinen *pl.* ∼**-glasses** *npl* Feldstecher *m*. **F**∼ **'Marshal** *n* Feldmarschall *m*. ∼**work** *n* Feldforschung *f*

fiend /fiːnd/ *n* Teufel *m*. ∼**ish** *a* teuflisch

fierce /fɪəs/ *a* (**-r, -st**), **-ly** *adv* wild; (*fig*) heftig. ∼**ness** *n* Wildheit *f*; (*fig*) Heftigkeit *f*

fiery /'faɪərɪ/ *a* (**-ier, -iest**) feurig

fifteen /fɪf'tiːn/ *a* fünfzehn ● *n* Fünfzehn *f*. ∼**th** *a* fünfzehnte(r,s)

fifth /fɪfθ/ *a* fünfte(r,s)

fiftieth /'fɪftɪɪθ/ *a* fünfzigste(r,s)

fifty /'fɪftɪ/ *a* fünfzig

fig /fɪg/ *n* Feige *f*

fight /faɪt/ *n* Kampf *m*; (*brawl*) Schlägerei *f*; (*between children, dogs*) Rauferei *f* ● *v* (*pt/pp* **fought**) ● *vt* kämpfen gegen; (*fig*) bekämpfen ● *vi* kämpfen; (*brawl*) sich schlagen; (*children, dogs:*) sich raufen. ∼**er** *n* Kämpfer *m*; (*Aviat*) Jagdflugzeug *nt*. ∼**ing** *n* Kampf *m*

figment /'fɪgmənt/ *n* ∼ **of the imagination** Hirngespinst *nt*

figurative /'fɪgjərətɪv/ *a*, **-ly** *adv* bildlich, übertragen

figure /'fɪgə(r)/ *n* (*digit*) Ziffer *f*; (*number*) Zahl *f*; (*sum*) Summe *f*; (*carving, sculpture, woman's*) Figur *f*; (*form*) Gestalt *f*; (*illustration*) Abbildung *f*; ∼ **of speech** Redefigur *f*; **good at** ∼**s** gut im Rechnen ● *vi* (*appear*) erscheinen ● *vt* (*Amer: think*) glauben. ∼ **out** *vt* ausrechnen

figure: ∼**-head** *n* Galionsfigur *f*; (*fig*) Repräsentationsfigur *f*. ∼ **skating** *n* Eiskunstlauf *m*

filament /'fɪləmənt/ *n* Faden *m*; (*Electr*) Glühfaden *m*

filch /fɪltʃ/ *vt* (*fam*) klauen

file[1] /faɪl/ *n* Akte *f*; (*for documents*) [Akten]ordner *m* ● *vt* ablegen (*documents*); (*Jur*) einreichen

file[2] *n* (*line*) Reihe *f*; **in single** ∼ im Gänsemarsch

file[3] *n* (*Techn*) Feile *f* ● *vt* feilen

filigree /'fɪlɪgriː/ *n* Filigran *nt*

filings /'faɪlɪŋz/ *npl* Feilspäne *pl*

fill /fɪl/ *n* **eat one's** ∼ sich satt essen ● *vt* füllen; plombieren (*tooth*) ● *vi* sich füllen. ∼ **in** *vt* auffüllen; ausfüllen (*form*). ∼ **out** *vt* ausfüllen (*form*). ∼ **up** *vi* sich füllen ● *vt* vollfüllen; (*Auto*) volltanken; ausfüllen (*form*)

fillet /'fɪlɪt/ *n* Filet *nt* ● *vt* (*pt/pp* **filleted**) entgräten

filling /'fɪlɪŋ/ *n* Füllung *f*; (*of tooth*) Plombe *f*. ∼ **station** *n* Tankstelle *f*

filly /'fɪlɪ/ *n* junge Stute *f*

film /fɪlm/ *n* Film *m*; (*Culin*) **[cling]** ∼ Klarsichtfolie *f* ● *vt/i* filmen; verfilmen (*book*). ∼ **star** *n* Filmstar *m*

filter /'fɪltə(r)/ *n* Filter *m* ● *vt* filtern. ∼ **through** *vi* durchsickern. ∼ **tip** *n* Filter *m*; (*cigarette*) Filterzigarette *f*

filth /fɪlθ/ *n* Dreck *m*. ∼**y** *a* (**-ier, -iest**) dreckig

fin /fɪn/ *n* Flosse *f*

final /'faɪnl/ *a* letzte(r,s); (*conclusive*) endgültig; ∼ **result** Endresultat *nt* ● *n* (*Sport*) Finale *nt*, Endspiel *nt*; ∼**s** *pl* (*Univ*) Abschlußprüfung *f*

finale /fɪ'nɑːlɪ/ *n* Finale *nt*

final|ist /'faɪnəlɪst/ *n* Finalist(in) *m(f)*. ∼**ity** /-'nælətɪ/ *n* Endgültigkeit *f*

final|ize /'faɪnəlaɪz/ *vt* endgültig festlegen. ∼**ly** *adv* schließlich

finance /faɪ'næns/ *n* Finanz *f* ● *vt* finanzieren

financial /faɪ'nænʃl/ *a*, **-ly** *adv* finanziell

finch /fɪntʃ/ *n* Fink *m*

find /faɪnd/ *n* Fund *m* ● *vt* (*pt/pp* **found**) finden; (*establish*) feststellen; **go and** ∼ holen; **try to** ∼ suchen; ∼ **guilty** (*Jur*) schuldig sprechen. ∼ **out** *vt* herausfinden; (*learn*) erfahren ● *vi* (*enquire*) sich erkundigen

findings /'faɪndɪŋz/ *npl* Ergebnisse *pl*

fine[1] /faɪn/ *n* Geldstrafe *f* ● *vt* zu einer Geldstrafe verurteilen

fine[2] *a* (**-r, -st**), **-ly** *adv* fein; (*weather*) schön; **he's** ∼ es geht ihm gut ● *adv* gut; **cut it** ∼ (*fam*) sich (*dat*) wenig Zeit lassen. ∼ **arts** *npl* schöne Künste *pl*

finery /'faɪnərɪ/ n Putz m, Staat m

finesse /fɪ'nes/ n Gewandtheit f

finger /'fɪŋgə(r)/ n Finger m ● vt anfassen

finger ~-**mark** n Fingerabdruck m. ~-**nail** n Fingernagel m. ~**print** n Fingerabdruck m. ~**tip** n Fingerspitze f; **have sth at one's** ~**tips** etw im kleinen Finger haben

finicky /'fɪnɪkɪ/ a knifflig; (choosy) wählerisch

finish /'fɪnɪʃ/ n Schluß m; (Sport) Finish nt; (line) Ziel nt; (of product) Ausführung f ● vt beenden; (use up) aufbrauchen; ~ **one's drink** austrinken; ~ **reading** zu Ende lesen ● vi fertig werden; (performance:) zu Ende sein; (runner:) durchs Ziel gehen

finite /'faɪnaɪt/ a begrenzt

Finland /'fɪnlənd/ n Finnland nt

Finn /fɪn/ n Finne m/Finnin f. ~**ish** a finnisch

fiord /fjɔ:d/ n Fjord m

fir /fɜ:(r)/ n Tanne f

fire /'faɪə(r)/ n Feuer nt; (forest, house) Brand m; **be on** ~ brennen; **catch** ~ Feuer fangen; **set** ~ **to** anzünden; (arsonist:) in Brand stecken; **under** ~ unter Beschuß ● vt brennen (pottery); abfeuern (shot); schießen mit (gun); (fam: dismiss) feuern ● vi schießen (**at** auf + acc); (engine:) anspringen

fire: ~ **alarm** n Feueralarm m; (apparatus) Feuermelder m. ~**arm** n Schußwaffe f. ~ **brigade** n Feuerwehr f. ~-**engine** n Löschfahrzeug nt. ~-**escape** n Feuertreppe f. ~ **extinguisher** n Feuerlöscher m. ~**man** n Feuerwehrmann m. ~**place** n Kamin m. ~**side** n **by** or **at the** ~**side** am Kamin. ~ **station** n Feuerwache f. ~**wood** n Brennholz nt. ~**work** n Feuerwerkskörper m; ~**works** pl (display) Feuerwerk nt

'**firing squad** n Erschießungskommando nt

firm[1] /fɜ:m/ n Firma f

firm[2] a (-er, -est), -**ly** adv fest; (resolute) entschlossen; (strict) streng

first /fɜ:st/ a & n erste(r,s); **at** ~ zuerst; **who's** ~? wer ist der erste? **at** ~ **sight** auf den ersten Blick; **for the** ~ **time** zum ersten Mal; **from the** ~ von Anfang an ● adv zuerst; (firstly) erstens

first: ~ '**aid** n Erste Hilfe. ~-'**aid kit** n Verbandkasten m. ~-**class** a erstklassig; (Rail) erster Klasse ● /·'·/ adv (travel) erster Klasse. ~ **e'dition** n Erstausgabe f. ~ '**floor** n erster Stock; (Amer: ground floor) Erdgeschoß nt. ~**ly** adv erstens. ~ **name** n Vorname m. ~-**rate** a erstklassig

fish /fɪʃ/ n Fisch m ● vt/i fischen; (with rod) angeln. ~ **out** vt herausfischen

fish: ~**bone** n Gräte f. ~**erman** n Fischer m. ~-**farm** n Fischzucht f. ~ '**finger** n Fischstäbchen n

fishing /'fɪʃɪŋ/ n Fischerei f. ~ **boat** n Fischerboot nt. ~-**rod** n Angel[rute] f

fish: ~**monger** /-mʌŋgə(r)/ n Fischhändler m. ~-**slice** n Fischheber m. ~**y** a Fisch-; (fam: suspicious) verdächtig

fission /'fɪʃn/ n (Phys) Spaltung f

fist /fɪst/ n Faust f

fit[1] /fɪt/ n (attack) Anfall m

fit[2] a (**fitter, fittest**) (suitable) geeignet; (healthy) gesund; (Sport) fit; ~ **to eat** eßbar; **keep** ~ sich fit halten; **see** ~ es für angebracht halten (**to** zu)

fit[3] n (of clothes) Sitz m; **be a good** ~ gut passen ● v (pt/pp **fitted**) ● vi (be the right size) passen ● vt anbringen (**to** an + dat); (install) einbauen; (clothes:) passen (+ dat); ~ **with** versehen mit. ~ **in** vi hineinpassen; (adapt) sich einfügen (**with** in + acc) ● vt (accommodate) unterbringen

fit|ful /'fɪtfl/ a, -**ly** adv (sleep) unruhig. ~**ment** n Einrichtungsgegenstand m; (attachment) Zusatzgerät nt. ~**ness** n Eignung f; [**physical**] ~**ness** Gesundheit f; (Sport) Fitneß f. ~**ted** a eingebaut; (garment) tailliert

fitted: ~ '**carpet** n Teppichboden m. ~ '**cupboard** n Einbauschrank m. ~ '**kitchen** n Einbauküche f. ~ '**sheet** n Spannlaken nt

fitter /'fɪtə(r)/ n Monteur m

fitting /'fɪtɪŋ/ a passend ● n (of clothes) Anprobe f; (of shoes) Weite f; (Techn) Zubehörteil nt; ~**s** pl Zubehör nt. ~ **room** n Anprobekabine f

five /faɪv/ a fünf ● n Fünf f. ~**r** n Fünfpfundschein m

fix /fɪks/ n (sl: drugs) Fix m; **be in a** ~ (fam) in der Klemme sitzen ● vt befestigen (**to** an + dat); (arrange) festlegen; (repair) reparieren; (Phot) fixieren; ~ **a meal** (*Amer*) Essen machen

fixation /fɪkˈseɪʃn/ *n* Fixierung *f*

fixed /ˈfɪkst/ *a* fest

fixture /ˈfɪkstʃə(r)/ *n* (*Sport*) Veranstaltung *f*; ~**s and fittings** zu einer Wohnung gehörende Einrichtungen *pl*

fizz /fɪz/ *vi* sprudeln

fizzle /ˈfɪzl/ *vi* ~ **out** verpuffen

fizzy /ˈfɪzɪ/ *a* sprudelnd. ~ **drink** *n* Brause[limonade] *f*

flabbergasted /ˈflæbəɡɑːstɪd/ *a* **be** ~ platt sein (*fam*)

flabby /ˈflæbɪ/ *a* schlaff

flag¹ /flæɡ/ *n* Fahne *f*; (*Naut*) Flagge *f* ● *vt* (*pt/pp* **flagged**) ~ **down** anhalten ⟨*taxi*⟩

flag² *vi* (*pt/pp* **flagged**) ermüden

flagon /ˈflæɡən/ *n* Krug *m*

'flag-pole *n* Fahnenstange *f*

flagrant /ˈfleɪɡrənt/ *a* flagrant

'flagstone *n* [Pflaster]platte *f*

flair /fleə(r)/ *n* Begabung *f*

flake /fleɪk/ *n* Flocke *f* ● *vi* ~ **[off]** abblättern

flaky /ˈfleɪkɪ/ *a* blättrig. ~ **pastry** *n* Blätterteig *m*

flamboyant /flæmˈbɔɪənt/ *a* extravagant

flame /fleɪm/ *n* Flamme *f*

flammable /ˈflæməbl/ *a* feuergefährlich

flan /flæn/ *n* [**fruit**] ~ Obsttorte *f*

flank /flæŋk/ *n* Flanke *f* ● *vt* flankieren

flannel /ˈflænl/ *n* Flanell *m*; (*for washing*) Waschlappen *m*

flannelette /flænəˈlet/ *n* (*Tex*) Biber *m*

flap /flæp/ *n* Klappe *f*; **in a** ~ (*fam*) aufgeregt ● *v* (*pt/pp* **flapped**) *vi* flattern; (*fam*) sich aufregen ● *vt* ~ **its wings** mit den Flügeln schlagen

flare /fleə(r)/ *n* Leuchtsignal *nt.* ● *vi* ~ **up** auflodern; (*fam: get angry*) aufbrausen. ~**d** *a* ⟨*garment*⟩ ausgestellt

flash /flæʃ/ *n* Blitz *m*; **in a** ~ (*fam*) im Nu ● *vi* blitzen; (*repeatedly*) blinken; ~ **past** vorbeirasen ● *vt* aufleuchten lassen; ~ **one's headlights** die Lichthupe betätigen

flash: ~**back** *n* Rückblende *f*. ~**bulb** *n* (*Phot*) Blitzbirne *f*. ~**er** *n* (*Auto*) Blinker *m*. ~**light** *n* (*Phot*) Blitzlicht *nt*; (*Amer: torch*) Taschenlampe *f*. ~**y** *a* auffällig

flask /flɑːsk/ *n* Flasche *f*; (*Chem*) Kolben *m*; (*vacuum* ~) Thermosflasche (P) *f*

flat /flæt/ *a* (**flatter, flattest**) flach; ⟨*surface*⟩ eben; ⟨*refusal*⟩ glatt; ⟨*beer*⟩ schal; ⟨*battery*⟩ verbraucht/(*Auto*) leer; ⟨*tyre*⟩ platt; (*Mus*) **A** ~ As *nt*; **B** ~ B *nt* ● *n* Wohnung *f*; (*Mus*) Erniedrigungszeichen *nt*; (*fam: puncture*) Reifenpanne *f*

flat: ~ **'feet** *npl* Plattfüße *pl*. ~**-fish** *n* Plattfisch *m*. ~**ly** *adv* ⟨*refuse*⟩ glatt. ~ **rate** *n* Einheitspreis *m*

flatten /ˈflætn/ *vt* platt drücken

flatter /ˈflætə(r)/ *vt* schmeicheln (+ *dat*). ~**y** *n* Schmeichelei *f*

flat 'tyre *n* Reifenpanne *f*

flatulence /ˈflætjʊləns/ *n* Blähungen *pl*

flaunt /flɔːnt/ *vt* prunken mit

flautist /ˈflɔːtɪst/ *n* Flötist(in) *m(f)*

flavour /ˈfleɪvə(r)/ *n* Geschmack *m* ● *vt* abschmecken. ~**ing** *n* Aroma *nt*

flaw /flɔː/ *n* Fehler *m*. ~**less** *a* tadellos; ⟨*complexion*⟩ makellos

flax /flæks/ *n* Flachs *m*. ~**en** *a* flachsblond

flea /fliː/ *n* Floh *m*. ~ **market** *n* Flohmarkt *m*

fleck /flek/ *n* Tupfen *m*

fled /fled/ *see* **flee**

flee /fliː/ *v* (*pt/pp* **fled**) ● *vi* fliehen (**from** vor + *dat*) ● *vt* flüchten aus

fleece /fliːs/ *n* Vlies *nt* ● *vt* (*fam*) schröpfen. ~**y** *a* flauschig

fleet /fliːt/ *n* Flotte *f*; (*of cars*) Wagenpark *m*

fleeting /ˈfliːtɪŋ/ *a* flüchtig

Flemish /ˈflemɪʃ/ *a* flämisch

flesh /fleʃ/ *n* Fleisch *nt*; **in the** ~ (*fam*) in Person. ~**y** *a* fleischig

flew /fluː/ *see* **fly²**

flex¹ /fleks/ *vt* anspannen ⟨*muscle*⟩

flex² *n* (*Electr*) Schnur *f*

flexib|ility /fleksəˈbɪlətɪ/ *n* Biegsamkeit *f*; (*fig*) Flexibilität *f*. ~**le** *a* biegsam; (*fig*) flexibel

'flexitime /ˈfleksɪ-/ *n* Gleitzeit *f*

flick /flɪk/ *vt* schnippen. ~ **through** *vi* schnell durchblättern

flicker /ˈflɪkə(r)/ *vi* flackern

flier /ˈflaɪə(r)/ *n* = **flyer**

flight¹ /flaɪt/ *n* (*fleeing*) Flucht *f*; **take** ~ die Flucht ergreifen

flight² *n* (*flying*) Flug *m*; ~ **of stairs** Treppe *f*

flight: ~ **path** *n* Flugschneise *f*. ~ **recorder** *n* Flugschreiber *m*

flighty /ˈflaɪtɪ/ *a* (**-ier, -iest**) flatterhaft

flimsy /'flɪmzɪ/ a (-ier, -iest) dünn; ⟨excuse⟩ fadenscheinig

flinch /flɪntʃ/ vi zurückzucken

fling /flɪŋ/ n **have a ∼** (fam) sich austoben ● vt (pt/pp **flung**) schleudern

flint /flɪnt/ n Feuerstein m

flip /flɪp/ vt/i schnippen; **∼ through** durchblättern

flippant /'flɪpənt/ a, **-ly** adv leichtfertig

flipper /'flɪpə(r)/ n Flosse f

flirt /flɜːt/ n kokette Frau f ● vi flirten

flirtat|ion /flɜː'teɪʃn/ n Flirt m. **∼i-ous** /-ʃəs/ a kokett

flit /flɪt/ vi (pt/pp **flitted**) flattern

float /fləʊt/ n Schwimmer m; (in procession) Festwagen m; (money) Wechselgeld nt ● vi ⟨thing:⟩ schwimmen; ⟨person:⟩ sich treiben lassen; (in air) schweben; (Comm) floaten

flock /flɒk/ n Herde f; (of birds) Schwarm m ● vi strömen

flog /flɒg/ vt (pt/pp **flogged**) auspeitschen; (fam: sell) verkloppen

flood /flʌd/ n Überschwemmung f; (fig) Flut f; **be in ∼** ⟨river:⟩ Hochwasser führen ● vt überschwemmen ● vi ⟨river:⟩ über die Ufer treten

'floodlight n Flutlicht nt ● vt (pt/pp **floodlit**) anstrahlen

floor /flɔː(r)/ n Fußboden m; (storey) Stock m ● vt (baffle) verblüffen

floor: ∼board n Dielenbrett nt. **∼-cloth** n Scheuertuch nt. **∼-polish** n Bohnerwachs nt. **∼ show** n Kabarettvorstellung f

flop /flɒp/ n (fam) (failure) Reinfall m; (Theat) Durchfall m ● vi (pt/pp **flopped**) (fam) (fail) durchfallen; **∼ down** sich plumpsen lassen

floppy /'flɒpɪ/ a schlapp. **∼ 'disc** n Diskette f

flora /'flɔːrə/ n Flora f

floral /'flɔːrl/ a Blumen-

florid /'flɒrɪd/ a ⟨complexion⟩ gerötet; ⟨style⟩ blumig

florist /'flɒrɪst/ n Blumenhändler(in) m(f)

flounce /flaʊns/ n Volant m ● vi **∼ out** hinausstolzieren

flounder¹ /'flaʊndə(r)/ vi zappeln

flounder² n (fish) Flunder f

flour /'flaʊə(r)/ n Mehl nt

flourish /'flʌrɪʃ/ n große Geste f; (scroll) Schnörkel m ● vi gedeihen; (fig) blühen ● vt schwenken

floury /'flaʊərɪ/ a mehlig

flout /flaʊt/ vt mißachten

flow /fləʊ/ n Fluß m; (of traffic, blood) Strom m ● vi fließen

flower /'flaʊə(r)/ n Blume f ● vi blühen

flower: ∼-bed n Blumenbeet nt. **∼ed** a geblümt. **∼pot** n Blumentopf m. **∼y** a blumig

flown /fləʊn/ see **fly²**

flu /fluː/ n (fam) Grippe f

fluctuat|e /'flʌktjʊeɪt/ vi schwanken. **∼ion** /-'eɪʃn/ n Schwankung f

fluent /'fluːənt/ a, **-ly** adv fließend

fluff /flʌf/ n Fusseln pl; (down) Flaum m. **∼y** a (-ier, -iest) flauschig

fluid /'fluːɪd/ a flüssig; (fig) veränderlich ● n Flüssigkeit f

fluke /fluːk/ n [glücklicher] Zufall m

flung /flʌŋ/ see **fling**

flunk /flʌŋk/ vt/i (Amer, fam) durchfallen (in + dat)

fluorescent /flʊə'resnt/ a fluoreszierend; **∼ lighting** Neonbeleuchtung f

fluoride /'flʊəraɪd/ n Fluor nt

flurry /'flʌrɪ/ n (snow) Gestöber nt; (fig) Aufregung f

flush /flʌʃ/ n (blush) Erröten nt ● vi rot werden ● vt spülen ● a in einer Ebene (**with** mit); (fam: affluent) gut bei Kasse

flustered /'flʌstəd/ a nervös

flute /fluːt/ n Flöte f

flutter /'flʌtə(r)/ n Flattern nt ● vi flattern

flux /flʌks/ n **in a state of ∼** im Fluß

fly¹ /flaɪ/ n (pl **flies**) Fliege f

fly² v (pt **flew**, pp **flown**) ● vi fliegen; ⟨flag:⟩ wehen; (rush) sausen ● vt fliegen; führen ⟨flag⟩

fly³ n & **flies** pl (on trousers) Hosenschlitz m

flyer /'flaɪə(r)/ n Flieger(in) m(f); (Amer: leaflet) Flugblatt nt

flying: ∼ 'buttress n Strebebogen m. **∼ 'saucer** n fliegende Untertasse f. **∼ 'visit** n Stippvisite f

fly: ∼leaf n Vorsatzblatt nt. **∼over** n Überführung f

foal /fəʊl/ n Fohlen nt

foam /fəʊm/ n Schaum m; (synthetic) Schaumstoff m ● vi schäumen. **∼ 'rubber** n Schaumgummi m

fob /fɒb/ vt (pt/pp **fobbed**) **∼ sth off** etw andrehen (**on s.o.** jdm); **∼ s.o. off** jdn abspeisen (**with** mit)

focal /'fəʊkl/ n Brenn-

focus /'fəʊkəs/ n Brennpunkt m; **in ∼** scharf eingestellt ● v (pt/pp **focused**

or **focussed**) ● *vt* einstellen (**on** auf + *acc*); (*fig*) konzentrieren (**on** auf + *acc*) ● *vi* (*fig*) sich konzentrieren (**on** auf + *acc*)

fodder /'fɒdə(r)/ *n* Futter *nt*

foe /fəʊ/ *n* Feind *m*

foetus /'fi:təs/ *n* (*pl* **-tuses**) Fötus *m*

fog /fɒg/ *n* Nebel *m*

foggy /'fɒgɪ/ *a* (**foggier, foggiest**) neblig

'fog-horn *n* Nebelhorn *nt*

fogy /'fəʊgɪ/ *n* **old** ~ alter Knacker *m*

foible /'fɔɪbl/ *n* Eigenart *f*

foil[1] /fɔɪl/ *n* Folie *f*; (*Culin*) Alufolie *f*

foil[2] *vt* (*thwart*) vereiteln

foil[3] *n* (*Fencing*) Florett *nt*

foist /fɔɪst/ *vt* andrehen (**on s.o.** jdm)

fold[1] /fəʊld/ *n* (*for sheep*) Pferch *m*

fold[2] *n* Falte *f*; (*in paper*) Kniff *m* ● *vt* falten; ~ **one's arms** die Arme verschränken ● *vi* sich falten lassen; (*fail*) eingehen. ~ **up** *vt* zusammenfalten; zusammenklappen ⟨*chair*⟩ ● *vi* sich zusammenfalten/ -klappen lassen; (*fam*) ⟨*business*:⟩ eingehen

fold|er /'fəʊldə(r)/ *n* Mappe *f*. ~**ing** *a* Klapp-

foliage /'fəʊlɪɪdʒ/ *n* Blätter *pl*; (*of tree*) Laub *nt*

folk /fəʊk/ *npl* Leute *pl*

folk: ~**-dance** *n* Volkstanz *m*. ~**lore** *n* Folklore *f*. ~**song** *n* Volkslied *nt*

follow /'fɒləʊ/ *vt/i* folgen (+ *dat*); (*pursue*) verfolgen; (*in vehicle*) nachfahren (+ *dat*); ~ **suit** (*fig*) dasselbe tun. ~ **up** *vt* nachgehen (+ *dat*)

follow|er /'fɒləʊə(r)/ *n* Anhänger(in) *m*(*f*). ~**ing** *a* folgend ● *n* Folgende(s) *nt*; (*supporters*) Anhängerschaft *f* ● *prep* im Anschluß an (+ *acc*)

folly /'fɒlɪ/ *n* Torheit *f*

fond /fɒnd/ *a* (**-er, -est**), **-ly** *adv* liebevoll; **be** ~ **of** gern haben; gern essen ⟨*food*⟩

fondle /'fɒndl/ *vt* liebkosen

fondness /'fɒndnɪs/ *n* Liebe *f* (**for** zu)

font /fɒnt/ *n* Taufstein *m*

food /fu:d/ *n* Essen *nt*; (*groceries*) Lebensmittel *pl*

food: ~ **mixer** *n* Küchenmaschine *f*. ~ **poisoning** *n* Lebensmittelvergiftung *f*. ~ **processor** *n* Küchenmaschine *f*. ~ **value** *n* Nährwert *m*

fool[1] /fu:l/ *n* (*Culin*) Fruchtcreme *f*

fool[2] *n* Narr *m*; **you are a** ~ du bist dumm; **make a** ~ **of oneself** sich

lächerlich machen ● *vt* hereinlegen ● *vi* ~ **around** herumalbern

'fool|hardy *a* tollkühn. ~**ish** *a*, **-ly** *adv* dumm. ~**ishness** *n* Dummheit *f*. ~**proof** *a* narrensicher

foot /fʊt/ *n* (*pl* **feet**) Fuß *m*; (*measure*) Fuß *m* (30,48 *cm*); (*of bed*) Fußende *nt*; **on** ~ zu Fuß; **on one's feet** auf den Beinen; **put one's** ~ **in it** (*fam*) ins Fettnäpfchen treten

foot: ~**-and-'mouth disease** *n* Maul- und Klauenseuche *f*. ~**ball** *n* Fußball *m*. ~**baller** *n* Fußballspieler *m*. ~**ball pools** *npl* Fußballtoto *nt*. ~**brake** *n* Fußbremse *f*. ~**bridge** *n* Fußgängerbrücke *f*. ~**hills** *npl* Vorgebirge *nt*. ~**hold** *n* Halt *m*. ~**ing** *n* Halt *m*; (*fig*) Basis *f*. ~**lights** *npl* Rampenlicht *nt*. ~**man** *n* Lakai *m*. ~**note** *n* Fußnote *f*. ~**path** *n* Fußweg *m*. ~**print** *n* Fußabdruck *m*. ~**step** *n* Schritt *m*; **follow in s.o.'s** ~**steps** (*fig*) in jds Fußstapfen treten. ~**stool** *n* Fußbank *f*. ~**wear** *n* Schuhwerk *nt*

for /fə(r), *betont* fɔ:(r)/ *prep* für (+ *acc*); ⟨*send, long*⟩ nach; ⟨*ask, fight*⟩ um; **what** ~? wozu? ~ **supper** zum Abendessen; ~ **nothing** umsonst; ~ **all that** trotz allem; ~ **this reason** aus diesem Grund; ~ **a month** einen Monat; **I have lived here** ~ **ten years** ich wohne seit zehn Jahren hier ● *conj* denn

forage /'fɒrɪdʒ/ *n* Futter *nt* ● *vi* ~ **for** suchen nach

forbade /fə'bæd/ *see* **forbid**

forbear|ance /fɔ:'beərəns/ *n* Nachsicht *f*. ~**ing** *a* nachsichtig

forbid /fə'bɪd/ *vt* (*pt* **forbade**, *pp* **forbidden**) verbieten (**s.o.** jdm). ~**ding** *a* bedrohlich; (*stern*) streng

force /fɔ:s/ *n* Kraft *f*; (*of blow*) Wucht *f*; (*violence*) Gewalt *f*; **in** ~ gültig; (*in large numbers*) in großer Zahl; **come into** ~ in Kraft treten; **the** ~**s** *pl* die Streitkräfte *pl* ● *vt* zwingen; (*break open*) aufbrechen; ~ **sth on s.o.** jdm etw aufdrängen

forced /fɔ:st/ *a* gezwungen; ~ **landing** Notlandung *f*

force: ~**-'feed** *vt* (*pt/pp* **-fed**) zwangsernähren. ~**ful** *a*, **-ly** *adv* energisch

forceps /'fɔ:seps/ *n inv* Zange *f*

forcibl|e /'fɔ:səbl/ *a* gewaltsam. ~**y** *adv* mit Gewalt

ford /fɔːd/ n Furt f ● vt durchwaten; (in vehicle) durchfahren
fore /fɔː(r)/ a vordere(r,s) ● n to the ~ im Vordergrund
fore: ~arm n Unterarm m. ~boding /-ˈbəʊdɪŋ/ n Vorahnung f. ~cast n Voraussage f; (for weather) Vorhersage f ● vt (pt/pp ~cast) voraussagen, vorhersagen. ~court n Vorhof m. ~fathers npl Vorfahren pl. ~finger n Zeigefinger m. ~front n be in the ~front führend sein. ~gone a be a ~gone conclusion von vornherein feststehen. ~ground n Vordergrund m. ~head /ˈfɒrɪd/ n Stirn f. ~hand n Vorhand f
foreign /ˈfɒrən/ a ausländisch; (country) fremd; he is ~ er ist Ausländer. ~ currency n Devisen pl. ~er n Ausländer(in) m(f). ~ language n Fremdsprache f
Foreign: ~ Office n ≈ Außenministerium nt. ~ 'Secretary n ≈ Außenminister m
fore: ~leg n Vorderbein nt. ~man n Vorarbeiter m. ~most a führend ● adv first and ~most zuallererst. ~name n Vorname m
forensic /fəˈrensɪk/ a ~ medicine Gerichtsmedizin f
'forerunner n Vorläufer m
fore'see vt (pt -saw, pp -seen) voraussehen, vorhersehen. ~able /-əbl/ a in the ~able future in absehbarer Zeit
'foresight n Weitblick m
forest /ˈfɒrɪst/ n Wald m. ~er n Förster m
fore'stall vt zuvorkommen (+ dat)
forestry /ˈfɒrɪstrɪ/ n Forstwirtschaft f
'foretaste n Vorgeschmack m
fore'tell vt (pt/pp -told) vorhersagen
forever /fəˈrevə(r)/ adv für immer
fore'warn vt vorher warnen
foreword /ˈfɔːwɜːd/ n Vorwort nt
forfeit /ˈfɔːfɪt/ n (in game) Pfand nt ● vt verwirken
forgave /fəˈɡeɪv/ see **forgive**
forge[1] /fɔːdʒ/ vi ~ ahead (fig) Fortschritte machen
forge[2] n Schmiede f ● vt schmieden; (counterfeit) fälschen. ~r n Fälscher m. ~ry n Fälschung f
forget /fəˈɡet/ vt/i (pt -got, pp -gotten) vergessen; verlernen (language, skill). ~ful a vergeßlich. ~fulness n Vergeßlichkeit f. ~-me-not n Vergißmeinnicht nt

forgive /fəˈɡɪv/ vt (pt -gave, pp -given) ~ s.o. for sth jdm etw vergeben od verzeihen. ~ness n Vergebung f, Verzeihung f
forgo /fɔːˈɡəʊ/ vt (pt -went, pp -gone) verzichten auf (+ acc)
forgot(ten) /fəˈɡɒt(n)/ see **forget**
fork /fɔːk/ n Gabel f; (in road) Gabelung f ● vi (road:) sich gabeln; ~ right rechts abzweigen. ~ out vt (fam) blechen
fork-lift 'truck n Gabelstapler m
forlorn /fəˈlɔːn/ a verlassen; (hope) schwach
form /fɔːm/ n Form f; (document) Formular nt; (bench) Bank f; (Sch) Klasse f ● vt formen (into zu); (create) bilden ● vi sich bilden; (idea:) Gestalt annehmen
formal /ˈfɔːml/ a, -ly adv formell, förmlich. ~ity /-ˈmælətɪ/ n Förmlichkeit f; (requirement) Formalität f
format /ˈfɔːmæt/ n Format nt
formation /fɔːˈmeɪʃn/ n Formation f
formative /ˈfɔːmətɪv/ a ~ years Entwicklungsjahre pl
former /ˈfɔːmə(r)/ a ehemalig; the ~ der/die/das erstere. ~ly adv früher
formidable /ˈfɔːmɪdəbl/ a gewaltig
formula /ˈfɔːmjʊlə/ n (pl -ae /-liː/ or -s) Formel f
formulate /ˈfɔːmjʊleɪt/ vt formulieren
forsake /fəˈseɪk/ vt (pt -sook /-sʊk/, pp -saken) verlassen
fort /fɔːt/ n (Mil) Fort nt
forte /ˈfɔːteɪ/ n Stärke f
forth /fɔːθ/ adv back and ~ hin und her; and so ~ und so weiter
forth: ~'coming a bevorstehend; (fam: communicative) mitteilsam. ~right a direkt. ~'with adv umgehend
fortieth /ˈfɔːtɪɪθ/ a vierzigste(r,s)
fortification /fɔːtɪfɪˈkeɪʃn/ n Befestigung f
fortify /ˈfɔːtɪfaɪ/ vt (pt/pp -ied) befestigen; (fig) stärken
fortitude /ˈfɔːtɪtjuːd/ n Standhaftigkeit f
fortnight /ˈfɔːt-/ n vierzehn Tage pl. ~ly a vierzehntäglich ● adv alle vierzehn Tage
fortress /ˈfɔːtrɪs/ n Festung f
fortuitous /fɔːˈtjuːɪtəs/ a, -ly adv zufällig
fortunate /ˈfɔːtʃʊnət/ a glücklich; be ~ Glück haben. ~ly adv glücklicherweise

fortune /ˈfɔːtʃuːn/ n Glück nt; (money) Vermögen nt. ∼**-teller** n Wahrsagerin f

forty /ˈfɔːtɪ/ a vierzig; **have** ∼ **winks** (fam) ein Nickerchen machen ● n Vierzig f

forum /ˈfɔːrəm/ n Forum nt

forward /ˈfɔːwəd/ adv vorwärts; (to the front) nach vorn ● a Vorwärts-; (presumptuous) anmaßend ● n (Sport) Stürmer m ● vt nachsenden (letter). ∼**s** adv vorwärts

fossil /ˈfɒsl/ n Fossil nt. ∼**ized** a versteinert

foster /ˈfɒstə(r)/ vt fördern; in Pflege nehmen (child). ∼**-child** n Pflegekind nt. ∼**-mother** n Pflegemutter f

fought /fɔːt/ see **fight**

foul /faʊl/ a (-er, -est) widerlich; (language) unflätig; ∼ **play** (Jur) Mord m ● n (Sport) Foul nt ● vt verschmutzen; (obstruct) blockieren; (Sport) foulen. ∼**-smelling** a übelriechend

found¹ /faʊnd/ see **find**

found² vt gründen

foundation /faʊnˈdeɪʃn/ n (basis) Grundlage f; (charitable) Stiftung f; ∼**s** pl Fundament nt. ∼**-stone** n Grundstein m

founder¹ /ˈfaʊndə(r)/ n Gründer(in) m(f)

founder² vi (ship:) sinken; (fig) scheitern

foundry /ˈfaʊndrɪ/ n Gießerei f

fountain /ˈfaʊntɪn/ n Brunnen m. ∼**-pen** n Füllfederhalter m

four /fɔː(r)/ a vier ● n Vier f

four: ∼**-'poster** n Himmelbett nt. ∼**some** /ˈfɔːsəm/ n in a ∼**some** zu viert. ∼**teen** a vierzehn ● n Vierzehn f. ∼**teenth** a vierzehnte(r,s)

fourth /fɔːθ/ a vierte(r,s)

fowl /faʊl/ n Geflügel nt

fox /fɒks/ n Fuchs m ● vt (puzzle) verblüffen

foyer /ˈfɔɪeɪ/ n Foyer nt; (in hotel) Empfangshalle f

fraction /ˈfrækʃn/ n Bruchteil m; (Math) Bruch m

fracture /ˈfræktʃə(r)/ n Bruch m ● vt/i brechen

fragile /ˈfrædʒaɪl/ a zerbrechlich

fragment /ˈfrægmənt/ n Bruchstück nt, Fragment nt. ∼**ary** a bruchstückhaft

fragran|ce /ˈfreɪgrəns/ n Duft m. ∼**t** a duftend

frail /freɪl/ a (-er, -est) gebrechlich

frame /freɪm/ n Rahmen m; (of spectacles) Gestell nt; (Anat) Körperbau m; ∼ **of mind** Gemütsverfassung f ● vt einrahmen; (fig) formulieren; (sl) ein Verbrechen anhängen (+ dat). ∼**work** n Gerüst nt; (fig) Gerippe nt

franc /fræŋk/ n (French, Belgian) Franc m; (Swiss) Franken m

France /frɑːns/ n Frankreich nt

franchise /ˈfræntʃaɪz/ n (Pol) Wahlrecht nt; (Comm) Franchise nt

frank¹ /fræŋk/ vt frankieren

frank² a, **-ly** adv offen

frankfurter /ˈfræŋkfɜːtə(r)/ n Frankfurter f

frantic /ˈfræntɪk/ a, **-ally** adv verzweifelt; **be** ∼ außer sich (dat) sein (**with** vor)

fraternal /frəˈtɜːnl/ a brüderlich

fraud /frɔːd/ n Betrug m; (person) Betrüger(in) m(f). ∼**ulent** /-jʊlənt/ a betrügerisch

fraught /frɔːt/ a ∼ **with danger** gefahrvoll

fray¹ /freɪ/ n Kampf m

fray² vi ausfransen

freak /friːk/ n Mißbildung f; (person) Mißgeburt f; (phenomenon) Ausnahmeerscheinung f ● a anormal. ∼**ish** a anormal

freckle /ˈfrekl/ n Sommersprosse f. ∼**d** a sommersprossig

free /friː/ a (**freer, freest**) frei; (ticket, copy, time) Frei-; (lavish) freigebig; ∼ **[of charge]** kostenlos; **set** ∼ freilassen; (rescue) befreien; **you are** ∼ **to...** es steht Ihnen frei, zu... ● vt (pt/pp **freed**) freilassen; (rescue) befreien; (disentangle) freibekommen

free: ∼**dom** n Freiheit f. ∼**hand** adv aus freier Hand. ∼**hold** n [freier] Grundbesitz m. ∼ **'kick** n Freistoß m. ∼**lance** a & adv freiberuflich. ∼**ly** adv frei; (voluntarily) freiwillig; (generously) großzügig. **F∼mason** n Freimaurer m. **F∼masonry** n Freimaurerei f. ∼**-range** a ∼**-range eggs** Landeier pl. ∼ **'sample** n Gratisprobe f. ∼**style** n Freistil m. ∼**way** n (Amer) Autobahn f. ∼**-'wheel** vi im Freilauf fahren

freez|e /friːz/ vt (pt **froze**, pp **frozen**) einfrieren; stoppen (wages) ● vi gefrieren; **it's** ∼**ing** es friert

freez|er /ˈfriːzə(r)/ n Gefriertruhe f; (upright) Gefrierschrank m. ∼**ing** a eiskalt ● n **below** ∼**ing** unter Null

freight /freɪt/ n Fracht f. ~**er** n
Frachter m. ~ **train** n (Amer) Güterzug m

French /frentʃ/ a französisch • n
(Lang) Französisch nt; **the** ~ pl die
Franzosen

French: ~ '**beans** npl grüne Bohnen
pl. ~ '**bread** n Stangenbrot nt. ~
'**fries** npl Pommes frites pl. ~**man** n
Franzose m. ~ '**window** n Ter-
rassentür f. ~**woman** n Französin f

frenzied /'frenzɪd/ a rasend

frenzy /'frenzɪ/ n Raserei f

frequency /'friːkwənsɪ/ n Häu-
figkeit f; (Phys) Frequenz f

frequent[1] /'friːkwənt/ a, **-ly** adv häufig

frequent[2] /frɪ'kwent/ vt regelmäßig
besuchen

fresco /'freskəʊ/ n Fresko nt

fresh /freʃ/ a (-er, -est), **-ly** adv frisch;
(new) neu; (Amer: cheeky) frech

freshen /'freʃn/ vi (wind:) auffrischen. ~ **up** vt auffrischen • vi sich
frisch machen

freshness /'freʃnɪs/ n Frische f

'**freshwater** a Süßwasser-

fret /fret/ vi (pt/pp fretted) sich
grämen. ~**ful** a weinerlich

'**fretsaw** n Laubsäge f

friar /'fraɪə(r)/ n Mönch m

friction /'frɪkʃn/ n Reibung f; (fig)
Reibereien pl

Friday /'fraɪdeɪ/ n Freitag m

fridge /frɪdʒ/ n Kühlschrank m

fried /fraɪd/ see **fry**[2] • a gebraten; ~
egg Spiegelei nt

friend /frend/ n Freund(in) m(f).
~**liness** n Freundlichkeit f. ~**ly** a
(-ier, -iest) freundlich; ~**ly with** befreundet mit. ~**ship** n Freundschaft f

frieze /friːz/ n Fries m

fright /fraɪt/ n Schreck m

frighten /'fraɪtn/ vt angst machen
(+ dat); (startle) erschrecken; **be**
~**ed** Angst haben (**of** vor + dat). ~**ing**
a angsterregend

frightful /'fraɪtfl/ a, **-ly** adv schrecklich

frigid /'frɪdʒɪd/ a frostig; (Psych) fri-
gide. ~**ity** /-'dʒɪdətɪ/ n Frostigkeit f;
Frigidität f

frill /frɪl/ n Rüsche f; (paper) Manschette f. ~**y** a rüschenbesetzt

fringe /frɪndʒ/ n Fransen pl; (of hair)
Pony m; (fig: edge) Rand m. ~ **be-
nefits** npl zusätzliche Leistungen pl

frisk /frɪsk/ vi herumspringen • vt
(search) durchsuchen, (fam) filzen

frisky /'frɪskɪ/ a (-ier, -iest) lebhaft

fritter /'frɪtə(r)/ vt ~ [**away**] ver-
plempern (fam)

frivol|ity /frɪ'vɒlətɪ/ n Frivolität f.
~**ous** /'frɪvələs/ a, **-ly** adv frivol,
leichtfertig

frizzy /'frɪzɪ/ a kraus

fro /frəʊ/ see **to**

frock /frɒk/ n Kleid nt

frog /frɒg/ n Frosch m. ~**man** n
Froschmann m. ~**-spawn** n Frosch-
laich m

frolic /'frɒlɪk/ vi (pt/pp **frolicked**)
herumtollen

from /frɒm/ prep von (+ dat); (out
of) aus (+ dat); (according to) nach
(+ dat); ~ **Monday** ab Montag; ~ **that
day** seit dem Tag

front /frʌnt/ n Vorderseite f; (fig)
Fassade f; (of garment) Vorderteil nt;
(sea-) Strandpromenade f; (Mil, Pol,
Meteorol) Front f; **in** ~ **of** vor; **in** or **at
the** ~ vorne; **to the** ~ nach vorne • a
vordere(r,s) ⟨page, row⟩ erste(r,s);
⟨tooth, wheel⟩ Vorder-

frontal /'frʌntl/ a Frontal-

front: ~ '**door** n Haustür f. ~ '**garden** n Vorgarten m

frontier /'frʌntɪə(r)/ n Grenze f

front-wheel '**drive** n Vorder-
radantrieb m

frost /frɒst/ n Frost m; (hoar-) Rau-
reif m; **ten degrees of** ~ zehn Grad
Kälte. ~**bite** n Erfrierung f. ~**bitten**
a erfroren

frost|ed /'frɒstɪd/ a ~**ed glass** Matt-
glas nt. ~**ing** n (Amer Culin)
Zuckerguß m. ~**y** a, **-ily** adv frostig

froth /frɒθ/ n Schaum m • vi schäumen. ~**y** a schaumig

frown /fraʊn/ n Stirnrunzeln nt • vi
die Stirn runzeln; ~ **on** mißbilligen

froze /frəʊz/ see **freeze**

frozen /'frəʊzn/ see **freeze** • a gefroren; (Culin) tiefgekühlt; **I'm** ~ (fam)
mir ist eiskalt. ~ **food** n Tiefkühlkost
f

frugal /'fruːgl/ a, **-ly** adv sparsam;
⟨meal⟩ frugal

fruit /fruːt/ n Frucht f; (collectively)
Obst nt. ~ **cake** n englischer [Tee]-
kuchen m

fruit|erer /'fruːtərə(r)/ n Obst-
händler m. ~**ful** a fruchtbar

fruition /fruː'ɪʃn/ n **come to** ~ sich
verwirklichen

fruit: ~ **juice** n Obstsaft m. ~**less** a, **-ly** adv fruchtlos. ~ **machine** n Spielautomat m. ~ **'salad** n Obstsalat m

fruity /'fruːtɪ/ a fruchtig

frumpy /'frʌmpɪ/ a unmodisch

frustrat|e /frʌ'streɪt/ vt vereiteln; (Psych) frustrieren. ~**ing** a frustrierend. ~**ion** /-eɪʃn/ n Frustration f

fry[1] /fraɪ/ n inv **small** ~ (fig) kleine Fische pl

fry[2] vt/i (pt/pp **fried**) [in der Pfanne] braten. ~**ing-pan** n Bratpfanne f

fuck /fʌk/ vt/i (vulg) ficken. ~**ing** a (vulg) Scheiß-

fuddy-duddy /'fʌdɪdʌdɪ/ n (fam) verknöcherter Kerl m

fudge /fʌdʒ/ n weiche Karamellen pl

fuel /'fjuːəl/ n Brennstoff m; (for car) Kraftstoff m; (for aircraft) Treibstoff m

fugitive /'fjuːdʒətɪv/ n Flüchtling m

fugue /fjuːg/ n (Mus) Fuge f

fulfil /fʊl'fɪl/ vt (pt/pp **-filled**) erfüllen. ~**ment** n Erfüllung f

full /fʊl/ a & adv (**-er, -est**) voll; (detailed) ausführlich; ⟨skirt⟩ weit; ~ **of** voll von (+ dat), voller (+ gen); **at** ~ **speed** in voller Fahrt ● n **in** ~ vollständig

full: ~ **'moon** n Vollmond m. ~**-scale** a ⟨model⟩ in Originalgröße; ⟨rescue, alert⟩ großangelegt. ~ **'stop** n Punkt m. ~**-time** a ganztägig ● adv ganztags

fully /'fʊlɪ/ adv völlig; (in detail) ausführlich

fulsome /'fʊlsəm/ a übertrieben

fumble /'fʌmbl/ vi herumfummeln (**with** an + dat)

fume /fjuːm/ vi vor Wut schäumen

fumes /fjuːmz/ npl Dämpfe pl; (from car) Abgase pl

fumigate /'fjuːmɪgeɪt/ vt ausräuchern

fun /fʌn/ n Spaß m; **for** ~ aus od zum Spaß; **make** ~ **of** sich lustig machen über (+ acc); **have** ~! viel Spaß!

function /'fʌŋkʃn/ n Funktion f; (event) Veranstaltung f ● vi funktionieren; (serve) dienen (**as** als). ~**al** a zweckmäßig

fund /fʌnd/ n Fonds m; (fig) Vorrat m; ~**s** pl Geldmittel pl ● vt finanzieren

fundamental /fʌndə'mentl/ a grundlegend; (essential) wesentlich

funeral /'fjuːnərl/ n Beerdigung f; (cremation) Feuerbestattung f

funeral: ~ **directors** pl, (Amer) ~ **home** n Bestattungsinstitut nt. ~ **march** n Trauermarsch m. ~ **parlour** n (Amer) Bestattungsinstitut nt. ~ **service** n Trauergottesdienst m

'funfair n Jahrmarkt m, Kirmes f

fungus /'fʌŋgəs/ n (pl **-gi** /-gaɪ/) Pilz m

funicular /fjuː'nɪkjʊlə(r)/ n Seilbahn f

funnel /'fʌnl/ n Trichter m; (on ship, train) Schornstein m

funnily /'fʌnɪlɪ/ adv komisch; ~ **enough** komischerweise

funny /'fʌnɪ/ a (**-ier, -iest**) komisch. ~**-bone** n (fam) Musikantenknochen m

fur /fɜː(r)/ n Fell nt; (for clothing) Pelz m; (in kettle) Kesselstein m. ~ **'coat** n Pelzmantel m

furious /'fjʊərɪəs/ a, **-ly** adv wütend (**with** auf + acc)

furnace /'fɜːnɪs/ n (Techn) Ofen m

furnish /'fɜːnɪʃ/ vt einrichten; (supply) liefern. ~**ed** a ~**ed room** möbliertes Zimmer nt. ~**ings** npl Einrichtungsgegenstände pl

furniture /'fɜːnɪtʃə(r)/ n Möbel pl

furred /fɜːd/ a ⟨tongue⟩ belegt

furrow /'fʌrəʊ/ n Furche f

furry /'fɜːrɪ/ a ⟨animal⟩ Pelz-; ⟨toy⟩ Plüsch-

further /'fɜːðə(r)/ a weitere(r,s); **at the** ~ **end** am anderen Ende; **until** ~ **notice** bis auf weiteres ● adv weiter; ~ **off** weiter entfernt ● vt fördern

further: ~ **edu'cation** n Weiterbildung f. ~**'more** adv überdies

furthest /'fɜːðɪst/ a am weitesten entfernt ● adv am weitesten

furtive /'fɜːtɪv/ a, **-ly** adv verstohlen

fury /'fjʊərɪ/ n Wut f

fuse[1] /fjuːz/ n (of bomb) Zünder m; (cord) Zündschnur f

fuse[2] n (Electr) Sicherung f ● vt/i verschmelzen; **the lights have** ~**d** die Sicherung [für das Licht] ist durchgebrannt. ~**-box** n Sicherungskasten m

fuselage /'fjuːzəlɑːʒ/ n (Aviat) Rumpf m

fusion /'fjuːʒn/ n Verschmelzung f, Fusion f

fuss /fʌs/ n Getue nt; **make a** ~ **of** verwöhnen; (caress) liebkosen ● vi Umstände machen

fussy /'fʌsɪ/ a (**-ier, -iest**) wählerisch; (particular) penibel

fusty /'fʌstɪ/ *a* moderig
futil|e /'fju:taɪl/ *a* zwecklos. **~ity**
/-'tɪlətɪ/ *n* Zwecklosigkeit *f*
future /'fju:tʃə(r)/ *a* zukünftig ● *n*
Zukunft *f*; (*Gram*) [erstes] Futur *nt*;
~ perfect zweites Futur *nt*; **in ~** in
Zukunft
futuristic /fju:tʃə'rɪstɪk/ *a* futuri-
stisch
fuzz /fʌz/ *n* **the ~** (*sl*) die Bullen *pl*
fuzzy /'fʌzɪ/ *a* (**-ier, -iest**) ⟨*hair*⟩ kraus;
(*blurred*) verschwommen

G

gab /gæb/ *n* (*fam*) **have the gift of
the ~** gut reden können
gabble /'gæbl/ *vi* schnell reden
gable /'geɪbl/ *n* Giebel *m*
gad /gæd/ *vi* (*pt/pp* **gadded**) **~ about**
dauernd ausgehen
gadget /'gædʒɪt/ *n* [kleines] Gerät *nt*
Gaelic /'geɪlɪk/ *n* Gälisch *nt*
gaffe /gæf/ *n* Fauxpas *m*
gag /gæg/ *n* Knebel *m*; (*joke*) Witz *m*;
(*Theat*) Gag *m* ● *vt* (*pt/pp* **gagged**)
knebeln
gaiety /'geɪətɪ/ *n* Fröhlichkeit *f*
gaily /'geɪlɪ/ *adv* fröhlich
gain /geɪn/ *n* Gewinn *m*; (*increase*)
Zunahme *f* ● *vt* gewinnen; (*obtain*) erlangen; **~ weight** zunehmen ● *vi*
⟨*clock:*⟩ vorgehen. **~ful** *a* **~ful employment** Erwerbstätigkeit *f*
gait /geɪt/ *n* Gang *m*
gala /'gɑ:lə/ *n* Fest *nt*; **swimming ~**
Schwimmfest *nt* ● *attrib* Gala-
galaxy /'gæləksɪ/ *n* Galaxie *f*; **the
G~** die Milchstraße
gale /geɪl/ *n* Sturm *m*
gall /gɔ:l/ *n* Galle *f*; (*impudence*)
Frechheit *f*
gallant /'gælənt/ *a*, **-ly** *adv* tapfer;
(*chivalrous*) galant. **~ry** *n* Tapferkeit *f*
'gall-bladder *n* Gallenblase *f*
gallery /'gælərɪ/ *n* Galerie *f*
galley /'gælɪ/ *n* (*ship's kitchen*) Kombüse *f*; **~ [proof]** [Druck]fahne *f*
gallivant /'gælɪvænt/ *vi* (*fam*) ausgehen
gallon /'gælən/ *n* Gallone *f* (= 4,5 *l*;
Amer = 3,785 *l*)
gallop /'gæləp/ *n* Galopp *m* ● *vi*
galoppieren
gallows /'gæləʊz/ *n* Galgen *m*
'gallstone *n* Gallenstein *m*

galore /gə'lɔ:(r)/ *adv* in Hülle und
Fülle
galvanize /'gælvənaɪz/ *vt* galvanisieren
gambit /'gæmbɪt/ *n* Eröffnungs-
manöver *nt*
gamble /'gæmbl/ *n* (*risk*) Risiko *nt*
● *vi* [um Geld] spielen; **~ on** (*rely*)
sich verlassen auf (+ *acc*). **~r** *n* Spie-
ler(in) *m(f)*
game /geɪm/ *n* Spiel *nt*; (*animals,
birds*) Wild *nt*; **~s** (*Sch*) Sport *m* ● *a*
(*brave*) tapfer; (*willing*) bereit (**for** zu).
~keeper *n* Wildhüter *m*
gammon /'gæmən/ *n* [geräucherter]
Schinken *m*
gamut /'gæmət/ *n* Skala *f*
gander /'gændə(r)/ *n* Gänserich *m*
gang /gæŋ/ *n* Bande *f*; (*of workmen*)
Kolonne *f* ● *vi* **~ up** sich zusam-
menrotten (**on** gegen)
gangling /'gæŋglɪŋ/ *a* schlaksig
gangrene /'gæŋgri:n/ *n* Wundbrand
m
gangster /'gæŋstə(r)/ *n* Gangster *m*
gangway /'gæŋweɪ/ *n* Gang *m*;
(*Naut, Aviat*) Gangway *f*
gaol /dʒeɪl/ *n* Gefängnis *nt* ● *vt* ins
Gefängnis sperren. **~er** *n* Ge-
fängniswärter *m*
gap /gæp/ *n* Lücke *f*; (*interval*) Pause
f; (*difference*) Unterschied *m*
gap|e /geɪp/ *vi* gaffen; **~e at** an-
starren. **~ing** *a* klaffend
garage /'gærɑ:ʒ/ *n* Garage *f*; (*for
repairs*) Werkstatt *f*; (*for petrol*)
Tankstelle *f*
garb /gɑ:b/ *n* Kleidung *f*
garbage /'gɑ:bɪdʒ/ *n* Müll *m*. **~ can**
n (*Amer*) Mülleimer *m*
garbled /'gɑ:bld/ *a* verworren
garden /'gɑ:dn/ *n* Garten *m*; [**public**]
~s *pl* [öffentliche] Anlagen *pl* ● *vi* im
Garten arbeiten. **~er** *n* Gärtner(in)
m(f). **~ing** *n* Gartenarbeit *f*
gargle /'gɑ:gl/ *n* (*liquid*) Gurgel-
wasser *nt* ● *vi* gurgeln
gargoyle /'gɑ:gɔɪl/ *n* Wasserspeier
m
garish /'geərɪʃ/ *a* grell
garland /'gɑ:lənd/ *n* Girlande *f*
garlic /'gɑ:lɪk/ *n* Knoblauch *m*
garment /'gɑ:mənt/ *n* Kleidungsstück *nt*
garnet /'gɑ:nɪt/ *n* Granat *m*
garnish /'gɑ:nɪʃ/ *n* Garnierung *f* ● *vt*
garnieren
garret /'gærɪt/ *n* Dachstube *f*

garrison /'gærɪsn/ n Garnison f

garrulous /'gærʊləs/ a geschwätzig

garter /'gɑːtə(r)/ n Strumpfband nt; (Amer: suspender) Strumpfhalter m

gas /gæs/ n Gas nt; (Amer fam: petrol) Benzin nt ● v (pt/pp gassed) ● vt vergasen ● vi (fam) schwatzen. **cooker** n Gasherd m. ~ **'fire** n Gasofen m

gash /gæʃ/ n Schnitt m; (wound) klaffende Wunde f ● vt ~ one's arm sich (dat) den Arm aufschlitzen

gasket /'gæskɪt/ n (Techn) Dichtung f

gas: ~ **mask** n Gasmaske f. ~**-meter** n Gaszähler m

gasoline /'gæsəliːn/ n (Amer) Benzin nt

gasp /gɑːsp/ vi keuchen; (in surprise) hörbar die Luft einziehen

'gas station n (Amer) Tankstelle f

gastric /'gæstrɪk/ a Magen-. ~ **'flu** n Darmgrippe f. ~ **'ulcer** n Magengeschwür nt

gastronomy /gæ'strɒnəmɪ/ n Gastronomie f

gate /geɪt/ n Tor nt; (to field) Gatter nt; (barrier) Schranke f; (at airport) Flugsteig m

gâteau /'gætəʊ/ n Torte f

gate: ~**crasher** n ungeladener Gast m. ~**way** n Tor nt

gather /'gæðə(r)/ vt sammeln; (pick) pflücken; (conclude) folgern (from aus); (Sewing) kräuseln; ~ **speed** schneller werden ● vi sich versammeln; ⟨storm.⟩ sich zusammenziehen. ~**ing** n **family** ~**ing** Familientreffen nt

gaudy /'gɔːdɪ/ a (-ier, -iest) knallig

gauge /geɪdʒ/ n Stärke f; (Rail) Spurweite f; (device) Meßinstrument nt ● vt messen; (estimate) schätzen

gaunt /gɔːnt/ a hager

gauntlet /'gɔːntlɪt/ n **run the** ~ Spießruten laufen

gauze /gɔːz/ n Gaze f

gave /geɪv/ see **give**

gawky /'gɔːkɪ/ a (-ier, -iest) schlaksig

gawp /gɔːp/ vi (fam) glotzen; ~ **at** anglotzen

gay /geɪ/ a (-er, -est) fröhlich; (fam) homosexuell, (fam) schwul

gaze /geɪz/ n [langer] Blick m ● vi sehen; ~ **at** ansehen

gazelle /gə'zel/ n Gazelle f

GB abbr of **Great Britain**

gear /gɪə(r)/ n Ausrüstung f; (Techn) Getriebe nt; (Auto) Gang m; **in** ~ mit eingelegtem Gang; **change** ~ schalten ● vt anpassen (**to** dat)

gear: ~**box** n (Auto) Getriebe nt. ~**-lever** n, (Amer) ~**-shift** n Schalthebel m

geese /giːs/ see **goose**

geezer /'giːzə(r)/ n (sl) Typ m

gel /dʒel/ n Gel nt

gelatine /'dʒelətɪn/ n Gelatine f

gelignite /'dʒelɪgnaɪt/ n Gelatinedynamit nt

gem /dʒem/ n Juwel nt

Gemini /'dʒemɪnaɪ/ n (Astr) Zwillinge pl

gender /'dʒendə(r)/ n (Gram) Geschlecht nt

gene /dʒiːn/ n Gen nt

genealogy /dʒiːnɪ'ælədʒɪ/ n Genealogie f

general /'dʒenrəl/ a allgemein ● n General m; **in** ~ im allgemeinen. **e'lection** n allgemeine Wahlen pl

generaliz|ation /dʒenrəlaɪ'zeɪʃn/ n Verallgemeinerung f. ~**e** /'dʒenrəlaɪz/ vi verallgemeinern

generally /'dʒenrəlɪ/ adv im allgemeinen

general prac'titioner n praktischer Arzt m

generate /'dʒenəreɪt/ vt erzeugen

generation /dʒenə'reɪʃn/ n Generation f

generator /'dʒenəreɪtə(r)/ n Generator m

generic /dʒɪ'nerɪk/ a ~ **term** Oberbegriff m

generosity /dʒenə'rɒsɪtɪ/ n Großzügigkeit f

generous /'dʒenərəs/ a, **-ly** adv großzügig

genetic /dʒɪ'netɪk/ a genetisch. ~ **engineering** n Gentechnologie f. ~**s** n Genetik f

Geneva /dʒɪ'niːvə/ n Genf nt

genial /'dʒiːnɪəl/ a, **-ly** adv freundlich

genitals /'dʒenɪtlz/ pl [äußere] Geschlechtsteile pl

genitive /'dʒenɪtɪv/ a & n ~ **[case]** Genitiv m

genius /'dʒiːnɪəs/ n (pl **-uses**) Genie nt; (quality) Genialität f

genocide /'dʒenəsaɪd/ n Völkermord m

genre /'ʒɑːrə/ n Gattung f, Genre nt

gent /dʒent/ n (fam) Herr m; **the** ~**s** sg die Herrentoilette f

genteel /dʒen'tiːl/ a vornehm

gentle /'dʒentl/ a (**-r, -st**) sanft

gentleman /'dʒentlmən/ n Herr m; (*well-mannered*) Gentleman m

gent|leness /'dʒentlnɪs/ n Sanftheit f. **~ly** adv sanft

genuine /'dʒenjʊɪn/ a echt; (*sincere*) aufrichtig. **~ly** adv (*honestly*) ehrlich

genus /'dʒiːnəs/ n (*Biol*) Gattung f

geograph|ical /dʒɪə'græfɪkl/ a, **-ly** adv geographisch. **~y** /dʒɪ'ɒgrəfɪ/ n Geographie f, Erdkunde f

geological /dʒɪə'lɒdʒɪkl/ a, **-ly** adv geologisch

geolog|ist /dʒɪ'ɒlədʒɪst/ n Geologe m/ -gin f. **~y** n Geologie f

geometr|ic(al) /dʒɪə'metrɪk(l)/ a geometrisch. **~y** /dʒɪ'ɒmətrɪ/ n Geometrie f

geranium /dʒə'reɪnɪəm/ n Geranie f

geriatric /dʒerɪ'ætrɪk/ a geriatrischer ● n geriatrischer Patient m. **~s** n Geriatrie f

germ /dʒɜːm/ n Keim m; **~s** pl (*fam*) Bazillen pl

German /'dʒɜːmən/ a deutsch ● n (*person*) Deutsche(r) m/f; (*Lang*) Deutsch nt; **in ~** auf deutsch; **into ~** ins Deutsche

Germanic /dʒə'mænɪk/ a germanisch

German: ~ 'measles n Röteln pl. **~ 'shepherd [dog]** n [deutscher] Schäferhund m

Germany /'dʒɜːmənɪ/ n Deutschland nt

germinate /'dʒɜːmɪneɪt/ vi keimen

gesticulate /dʒe'stɪkjʊleɪt/ vi gestikulieren

gesture /'dʒestʃə(r)/ n Geste f

get /get/ v (pt/pp got, pp Amer also gotten, pres p getting) ● vt bekommen, (*fam*) kriegen; (*procure*) besorgen; (*buy*) kaufen; (*fetch*) holen; (*take*) bringen; (*on telephone*) erreichen; (*fam: understand*) kapieren; machen (*meal*); **~ s.o. to do sth** jdn dazu bringen, etw zu tun ● vi (*become*) werden; **~ to** kommen zu/nach (*town*); (*reach*) erreichen; **~ dressed** sich anziehen; **~ married** heiraten. **~ at** vt herankommen an (+ *acc*); **what are you ~ting at?** worauf willst du hinaus? **~ away** vi (*leave*) wegkommen; (*escape*) entkommen. **~ back** vi zurückkommen ● vt (*recover*) zurückbekommen; **~ one's**

own back sich revanchieren. **~ by** vi vorbeikommen; (*manage*) sein Auskommen haben. **~ down** vi heruntersteigen; **~ down to** sich [heran]machen an (+ *acc*) ● vt (*depress*) deprimieren. **~ in** vi einsteigen ● vt (*fetch*) hereinholen. **~ off** vi (*dismount*) absteigen; (*from bus*) aussteigen; (*leave*) wegkommen; (*Jur*) freigesprochen werden ● vt (*remove*) abbekommen. **~ on** vi (*mount*) aufsteigen; (*to bus*) einsteigen; (*be on good terms*) gut auskommen (**with** mit); (*make progress*) Fortschritte machen; **how are you ~ting on?** wie geht's? **~ out** vi herauskommen; (*of car*) aussteigen; **~ out of** (*avoid doing*) sich drücken um ● vt herausholen; herausbekommen (*cork, stain*). **~ over** vi hinübersteigen ● vt (*fig*) hinwegkommen über (+ *acc*). **~ round** vi herumkommen; (*avoid*) umgehen; **I never ~ round to it** ich komme nie dazu ● vt herumkriegen. **~ through** vi durchkommen. **~ up** vi aufstehen

get: ~away n Flucht f. **~-up** n Aufmachung f

geyser /'giːzə(r)/ n Durchlauferhitzer m; (*Geol*) Geysir m

ghastly /'gɑːstlɪ/ a (**-ier, -iest**) gräßlich; (*pale*) blaß

gherkin /'gɜːkɪn/ n Essiggurke f

ghetto /'getəʊ/ n Getto nt

ghost /gəʊst/ n Geist m, Gespenst nt. **~ly** a geisterhaft

ghoulish /'guːlɪʃ/ a makaber

giant /'dʒaɪənt/ n Riese m ● a riesig

gibberish /'dʒɪbərɪʃ/ n Kauderwelsch nt

gibe /dʒaɪb/ n spöttische Bemerkung f ● vi spotten (**at** über + *acc*)

giblets /'dʒɪblɪts/ npl Geflügelklein nt

giddiness /'gɪdɪnɪs/ n Schwindel m

giddy /'gɪdɪ/ a (**-ier, -iest**) schwindlig; **I feel ~** mir ist schwindlig

gift /gɪft/ n Geschenk nt; (*to charity*) Gabe f; (*talent*) Begabung f. **~ed** /-ɪd/ a begabt. **~-wrap** vt als Geschenk einpacken

gig /gɪg/ n (*fam, Mus*) Gig m

gigantic /dʒaɪ'gæntɪk/ a riesig, riesengroß

giggle /'gɪgl/ n Kichern nt ● vi kichern

gild /gɪld/ vt vergolden

gills /gɪlz/ npl Kiemen pl

gilt 375 glut

gilt /gɪlt/ a vergoldet ● n Vergoldung f. ~-edged a (Comm) mündelsicher
gimmick /'gɪmɪk/ n Trick m
gin /dʒɪn/ n Gin m
ginger /'dʒɪndʒə(r)/ a rotblond; ⟨cat⟩ rot ● n Ingwer m. ~bread n Pfefferkuchen m
gingerly /'dʒɪndʒəlɪ/ adv vorsichtig
gipsy /'dʒɪpsɪ/ n = gypsy
giraffe /dʒɪ'rɑ:f/ n Giraffe f
girder /'gɜ:də(r)/ n (Techn) Träger m
girdle /'gɜ:dl/ n Bindegürtel m; ⟨corset⟩ Hüfthalter m
girl /gɜ:l/ n Mädchen nt; ⟨young woman⟩ junge Frau f. ~friend n Freundin f. ~ish a, -ly adv mädchenhaft
giro /'dʒaɪərəʊ/ n Giro nt; ⟨cheque⟩ Postscheck m
girth /gɜ:θ/ n Umfang m; ⟨for horse⟩ Bauchgurt m
gist /dʒɪst/ n the ~ das Wesentliche
give /gɪv/ n Elastizität f ● v (pt gave, pp given) ● vt geben/⟨as present⟩ schenken (to dat); ⟨donate⟩ spenden; ⟨lecture⟩ halten; ⟨one's name⟩ angeben ● vi geben; ⟨yield⟩ nachgeben. ~ away vt verschenken; ⟨betray⟩ verraten; ⟨distribute⟩ verteilen; ~ away the bride ≈ Brautführer sein. ~ back vt zurückgeben. ~ in vt einreichen ● vi ⟨yield⟩ nachgeben. ~ off vt abgeben. ~ up vt/i aufgeben; ~ oneself up sich stellen. ~ way vi nachgeben; ⟨Auto⟩ die Vorfahrt beachten
given /'gɪvn/ see give ● a ~ name Vorname m
glacier /'glæsɪə(r)/ n Gletscher m
glad /glæd/ a froh (of über + acc). ~den /'glædn/ vt erfreuen
glade /gleɪd/ n Lichtung f
gladly /'glædlɪ/ adv gern[e]
glamorous /'glæmərəs/ a glanzvoll; ⟨film star⟩ glamourös
glamour /'glæmə(r)/ n [betörender] Glanz m
glance /glɑ:ns/ n [flüchtiger] Blick m ● vi ~ at einen Blick werfen auf (+ acc). ~ up vi aufblicken
gland /glænd/ n Drüse f
glandular /'glændjʊlə(r)/ a Drüsen-
glare /gleə(r)/ n grelles Licht nt; ⟨look⟩ ärgerlicher Blick m ● vi ~ at böse ansehen
glaring /'gleərɪŋ/ a grell; ⟨mistake⟩ kraß
glass /glɑ:s/ n Glas nt; ⟨mirror⟩ Spiegel m; ~es pl ⟨spectacles⟩ Brille f. ~y a glasig

glaze /gleɪz/ n Glasur f ● vt verglasen; ⟨Culin, Pottery⟩ glasieren
glazier /'gleɪzɪə(r)/ n Glaser m
gleam /gli:m/ n Schein m ● vi glänzen
glean /gli:n/ vi Ähren lesen ● vt ⟨learn⟩ erfahren
glee /gli:/ n Frohlocken nt. ~ful a, -ly adv frohlockend
glen /glen/ n [enges] Tal nt
glib /glɪb/ a, -ly adv (pej) gewandt
glid|e /glaɪd/ vi gleiten; ⟨through the air⟩ schweben. ~er n Segelflugzeug nt. ~ing n Segelfliegen nt
glimmer /'glɪmə(r)/ n Glimmen nt ● vi glimmen
glimpse /glɪmps/ n catch a ~ of flüchtig sehen ● vt flüchtig sehen
glint /glɪnt/ n Blitzen nt ● vi blitzen
glisten /'glɪsn/ vi glitzern
glitter /'glɪtə(r)/ vi glitzern
gloat /gləʊt/ vi schadenfroh sein; ~ over sich weiden an (+ dat)
global /'gləʊbl/ a, -ly adv global
globe /gləʊb/ n Kugel f; ⟨map⟩ Globus m
gloom /glu:m/ n Düsterkeit f; ⟨fig⟩ Pessimismus m
gloomy /'glu:mɪ/ a (-ier, -iest), -ily adv düster; ⟨fig⟩ pessimistisch
glorif|y /'glɔ:rɪfaɪ/ vt (pt/pp -ied) verherrlichen; a ~ied waitress eine bessere Kellnerin f
glorious /'glɔ:rɪəs/ a herrlich; ⟨deed, hero⟩ glorreich
glory /'glɔ:rɪ/ n Ruhm m; ⟨splendour⟩ Pracht f ● vi ~ in genießen
gloss /glɒs/ n Glanz m ● a Glanz- ● vi ~ over beschönigen
glossary /'glɒsərɪ/ n Glossar nt
glossy /'glɒsɪ/ a (-ier, -iest) glänzend
glove /glʌv/ n Handschuh m. ~ compartment n ⟨Auto⟩ Handschuhfach nt
glow /gləʊ/ n Glut f; ⟨of candle⟩ Schein m ● vi glühen; ⟨candle:⟩ scheinen. ~ing a glühend; ⟨account⟩ begeistert
'glow-worm n Glühwürmchen nt
glucose /'glu:kəʊs/ n Traubenzucker m, Glukose f
glue /glu:/ n Klebstoff m ● vt (pres p gluing) kleben (to an + acc)
glum /glʌm/ a (glummer, glummest), -ly adv niedergeschlagen
glut /glʌt/ n Überfluß m (of an + dat); ~ of fruit Obstschwemme f

glutton /'glʌtn/ n Vielfraß m.
~**ous** /-əs/ a gefräßig. ~**y** n Ge-
fräßigkeit f

gnarled /nɑːld/ a knorrig; ⟨hands⟩
knotig

gnash /næʃ/ vt ~ **one's teeth** mit den
Zähnen knirschen

gnat /næt/ n Mücke f

gnaw /nɔː/ vt/i nagen (**at** an + dat)

gnome /nəʊm/ n Gnom m

go /gəʊ/ n (pl **goes**) Energie f;
⟨attempt⟩ Versuch m; **on the go** auf
Trab; **at one go** auf einmal; **it's your
go** du bist dran; **make a go of it** Erfolg
haben ● vi (pt **went**, pp **gone**) gehen;
⟨in vehicle⟩ fahren; ⟨leave⟩ weggehen;
⟨on journey⟩ abfahren; ⟨time:⟩ vergehen;
⟨vanish⟩ verschwinden; ⟨fail⟩ versagen; ⟨become⟩ werden; ⟨belong⟩
kommen; **go swimming/shopping**
schwimmen/einkaufen gehen; **where
are you going?** wo gehst du hin? **it's
all gone** es ist nichts mehr übrig; **I am
not going to** ich werde es nicht tun; **'to
go'** (Amer) 'zum Mitnehmen'. **go
away** vi weggehen/-fahren. **go back**
vi zurückgehen/-fahren. **go by** vi
vorbeigehen/-fahren; ⟨time:⟩ vergehen. **go down** vi hinuntergehen/
-fahren; ⟨sun, ship:⟩ untergehen;
⟨prices:⟩ fallen; ⟨temperature, swelling:⟩ zurückgehen. **go for** vt holen;
⟨fam: attack⟩ losgehen auf (+ acc).
go in vi hineingehen/-fahren; **go in
for** teilnehmen an (+ dat) ⟨com-
petition⟩; ⟨take up⟩ sich verlegen auf
(+ acc). **go off** vi weggehen/-fahren;
⟨alarm:⟩ klingeln; ⟨gun, bomb:⟩ losgehen; ⟨go bad⟩ schlecht werden; **go
off well** gut verlaufen. **go on** vi
weitergehen/-fahren; ⟨continue⟩
weitermachen; ⟨talking:⟩ fortfahren;
⟨happen⟩ vorgehen; **go on at** (fam)
herumnörgeln an (+ dat). **go out** vi
ausgehen; ⟨leave⟩ hinausgehen/
-fahren. **go over** vi hinübergehen/
-fahren ● vt ⟨check⟩ durchgehen.
go round vi herumgehen/-fahren;
⟨visit⟩ vorbeigehen; ⟨turn⟩ sich drehen; ⟨be enough⟩ reichen. **go through**
vi durchgehen/-fahren ● vt ⟨suffer⟩
durchmachen; ⟨check⟩ durchgehen.
go under vi untergehen; ⟨fail⟩
scheitern. **go up** vi hinaufgehen/
-fahren; ⟨lift:⟩ hochfahren; ⟨prices:⟩
steigen. **go without** vt verzichten
auf (+ acc) ● vi darauf verzichten

goad /gəʊd/ vt anstacheln (**into** zu);
⟨taunt⟩ reizen

'go-ahead a fortschrittlich; ⟨enter-
prising⟩ unternehmend ● n ⟨fig⟩
grünes Licht nt

goal /gəʊl/ n Ziel nt; ⟨Sport⟩ Tor nt.
~**keeper** n Torwart m. ~**-post** n
Torpfosten m

goat /gəʊt/ n Ziege f

gobble /'gɒbl/ vt hinunterschlingen

'go-between n Vermittler(in) m(f)

goblet /'gɒblɪt/ n Pokal m; ⟨glass⟩
Kelchglas nt

goblin /'gɒblɪn/ n Kobold m

God, god /gɒd/ n Gott m

god: ~**child** n Patenkind nt. ~
daughter n Patentochter f. ~**dess** n
Göttin f. ~**father** n Pate m. **G**~**-for-
saken** a gottverlassen. ~**mother** n
Patin f. ~**parents** npl Paten pl.
~**send** n Segen m. ~**son** n Paten-
sohn m

goggle /'gɒgl/ vi ⟨fam⟩ ~ **at** anglotzen. ~**s** npl Schutzbrille f

going /'gəʊɪŋ/ a ⟨price, rate⟩ gängig;
⟨concern⟩ gutgehend ● n **it is hard** ~
es ist schwierig; **while the** ~ **is good**
solange es noch geht. ~**s-'on** npl
[seltsame] Vorgänge pl

gold /gəʊld/ n Gold nt ● a golden

golden /'gəʊldn/ a golden. ~ **'handshake** n hohe Abfindungssumme f.
~ **'wedding** n goldene Hochzeit f

gold: ~**fish** n inv Goldfisch m.
~**-mine** n Goldgrube f. ~**-plated** a
vergoldet. ~**smith** n Goldschmied m

golf /gɒlf/ n Golf nt

golf: ~**-club** n Golfklub m;
⟨implement⟩ Golfschläger m. ~
course n Golfplatz m. ~**er** m Golf-
spieler(in) m(f)

gondola /'gɒndələ/ n Gondel f. ~
lier /-'lɪə(r)/ n Gondoliere m

gone /gɒn/ see **go**

gong /gɒŋ/ n Gong m

good /gʊd/ a (**better, best**) gut; ⟨well-
behaved⟩ brav, artig; ~ **at** gut in
(+ dat); **a** ~ **deal** ziemlich viel; **as** ~ **as**
so gut wie; ⟨almost⟩ fast; ~ **morning/
evening** guten Morgen/Abend; ~
afternoon guten Tag; ~ **night** gute
Nacht ● n **the** ~ das Gute; **for** ~ für
immer; **do** ~ Gutes tun; **do s.o.** ~ jdm
guttun; **it's no** ~ es ist nutzlos; ⟨hope-
less⟩ da ist nichts zu machen; **be up to
no** ~ nichts Gutes im Schilde führen

goodbye /gʊd'baɪ/ int auf Wiedersehen; ⟨Teleph, Radio⟩ auf Wieder-
hören

good: ~-**for-nothing** *a* nichtsnutzig ● *n* Taugenichts *m.* **G~ 'Friday** *n* Karfreitag *m.* ~-'**looking** *a* gutaussehend. ~-'**natured** *a* gutmütig

goodness /'gʊdnɪs/ *n* Güte *f*; **my ~!** du meine Güte! **thank ~!** Gott sei Dank!

goods /gʊdz/ *npl* Waren *pl.* ~ **train** *n* Güterzug *m*

good'will *n* Wohlwollen *nt*; (*Comm*) Goodwill *m*

goody /'gʊdɪ/ *n* (*fam*) Gute(r) *m/f.* ~-**goody** *n* Musterkind *nt*

gooey /'gu:ɪ/ *a* (*fam*) klebrig

goof /gu:f/ *vi* (*fam*) einen Schnitzer machen

goose /gu:s/ *n* (*pl* **geese**) Gans *f*

gooseberry /'gʊzbərɪ/ *n* Stachelbeere *f*

goose /gu:s/: ~-**flesh** *n,* ~**pimples** *npl* Gänsehaut *f*

gore[1] /gɔ:(r)/ *n* Blut *nt*

gore[2] *vt* mit den Hörnern aufspießen

gorge /gɔ:dʒ/ *n* (*Geog*) Schlucht *f* ● *vt* ~ **oneself** sich vollessen

gorgeous /'gɔ:dʒəs/ *a* prachtvoll; (*fam*) herrlich

gorilla /gə'rɪlə/ *n* Gorilla *m*

gormless /'gɔ:mlɪs/ *a* (*fam*) doof

gorse /gɔ:s/ *n inv* Stechginster *m*

gory /'gɔ:rɪ/ *a* (-**ier, -iest**) blutig; ⟨*story*⟩ blutrünstig

gosh /gʊʃ/ *int* (*fam*) Mensch!

go-'slow *n* Bummelstreik *m*

gospel /'gʊspl/ *n* Evangelium *nt*

gossip /'gʊsɪp/ *n* Klatsch *m*; (*person*) Klatschbase *f* ● *vi* klatschen. ~**y** *a* geschwätzig

got /gʊt/ *see* **get; have** ~ haben; **have ~ to** müssen; **have** ~ **to do sth** etw tun müssen

Gothic /'gʊθɪk/ *a* gotisch

gotten /'gʊtn/ *see* **get**

gouge /gaʊdʒ/ *vt* ~ **out** aushöhlen

goulash /'gu:læʃ/ *n* Gulasch *nt*

gourmet /'gʊəmeɪ/ *n* Feinschmecker *m*

gout /gaʊt/ *n* Gicht *f*

govern /'gʌvn/ *vt/i* regieren; (*determine*) bestimmen. ~**ess** *n* Gouvernante *f*

government /'gʌvnmənt/ *n* Regierung *f.* ~**al** /-'mentl/ *a* Regierungs-

governor /'gʌvənə(r)/ *n* Gouverneur *m*; (*on board*) Vorstandsmitglied *nt*; (*of prison*) Direktor *m*; (*fam: boss*) Chef *m*

gown /gaʊn/ *n* [elegantes] Kleid *nt*; (*Univ, Jur*) Talar *m*

GP *abbr of* **general practitioner**

grab /græb/ *vt* (*pt/pp* **grabbed**) ergreifen; ~ [**hold of**] packen

grace /greɪs/ *n* Anmut *f*; (*before meal*) Tischgebet *nt*; (*Relig*) Gnade *f*; **with good** ~ mit Anstand; **say ~** [vor dem Essen] beten; **three days'** ~ drei Tage Frist. ~**ful** *a,* -**ly** *adv* anmutig

gracious /'greɪʃəs/ *a* gnädig; (*elegant*) vornehm

grade /greɪd/ *n* Stufe *f*; (*Comm*) Güteklasse *f*; (*Sch*) Note *f*; (*Amer, Sch: class*) Klasse *f*; (*Amer*) = **gradient** ● *vt* einstufen; (*Comm*) sortieren. ~ **crossing** *n* (*Amer*) Bahnübergang *m*

gradient /'greɪdɪənt/ *n* Steigung *f*; (*downward*) Gefälle *nt*

gradual /'grædʒʊəl/ *a,* -**ly** *adv* allmählich

graduate[1] /'grædʒʊət/ *n* Akademiker(in) *m(f)*

graduate[2] /'grædʒʊeɪt/ *vi* (*Univ*) sein Examen machen. ~**d** *a* abgestuft; ⟨*container*⟩ mit Maßeinteilung

graffiti /grə'fi:ti:/ *npl* Graffiti *pl*

graft /grɑ:ft/ *n* (*Bot*) Pfropfreis *nt*; (*Med*) Transplantat *nt*; (*fam: hard work*) Plackerei *f* ● *vt* (*Bot*) aufpfropfen; (*Med*) übertragen

grain /greɪn/ *n* (*sand, salt, rice*) Korn *nt*; (*cereals*) Getreide *nt*; (*in wood*) Maserung *f*; **against the** ~ (*fig*) gegen den Strich

gram /græm/ *n* Gramm *nt*

grammar /'græmə(r)/ *n* Grammatik *f.* ~ **school** *n* ≈ Gymnasium *nt*

grammatical /grə'mætɪkl/ *a,* -**ly** *adv* grammatisch

granary /'grænərɪ/ *n* Getreidespeicher *m*

grand /grænd/ *a* (-**er, -est**) großartig

grandad /'grændæd/ *n* (*fam*) Opa *m*

'**grandchild** *n* Enkelkind *nt*

'**granddaughter** *n* Enkelin *f*

grandeur /'grændʒə(r)/ *n* Pracht *f*

'**grandfather** *n* Großvater *m.* ~ **clock** *n* Standuhr *f*

grandiose /'grændɪəʊs/ *a* grandios

grand: ~**mother** *n* Großmutter *f.* ~**parents** *npl* Großeltern *pl.* ~ **pi'ano** *n* Flügel *m.* ~**son** *n* Enkel *m.* ~**stand** *n* Tribüne *f*

granite /'grænɪt/ *n* Granit *m*

granny /'grænɪ/ *n* (*fam*) Oma *f*

grant /grɑ:nt/ *n* Subvention *f*; (*Univ*) Studienbeihilfe *f* ● *vt* gewähren;

(*admit*) zugeben; **take sth for ~ed**
etw als selbstverständlich hinnehmen

granular /'grænjʊlə(r)/ *a* körnig

granulated /'grænjʊleɪtɪd/ *a* ~
sugar Kristallzucker *m*

granule /'grænju:l/ *n* Körnchen *nt*

grape /greɪp/ *n* [Wein]traube *f*;
bunch of ~s [ganze] Weintraube *f*

grapefruit /'greɪp-/ *n inv* Grapefruit
f, Pampelmuse *f*

graph /grɑ:f/ *n* Kurvendiagramm *nt*

graphic /'græfɪk/ *a*, **-ally** *adv* grafisch; (*vivid*) anschaulich. **~s** *n* (*design*) grafische Gestaltung *f*

'graph paper *n* Millimeterpapier *nt*

grapple /'græpl/ *vi* ringen

grasp /grɑ:sp/ *n* Griff *m* ● *vt* ergreifen; (*understand*) begreifen.
~ing *a* habgierig

grass /grɑ:s/ *n* Gras *nt*; (*lawn*) Rasen
m; **at the ~ roots** an der Basis. **~-
hopper** *n* Heuschrecke *f*. **~land** *n*
Weideland *nt*

grassy /'grɑ:sɪ/ *a* grasig

grate[1] /greɪt/ *n* Feuerrost *m*; (*hearth*)
Kamin *m*

grate[2] *vt* (*Culin*) reiben; **~ one's teeth**
mit den Zähnen knirschen

grateful /'greɪtfl/ *a*, **-ly** *adv* dankbar
(**to** *dat*)

grater /'greɪtə(r)/ *n* (*Culin*) Reibe *f*

gratify /'grætɪfaɪ/ *vt* (*pt/pp* **-ied**) be-
friedigen. **~ing** *a* erfreulich

grating /'greɪtɪŋ/ *n* Gitter *nt*

gratis /'grɑ:tɪs/ *adv* gratis

gratitude /'grætɪtju:d/ *n* Dank-
barkeit *f*

gratuitous /grə'tju:ɪtəs/ *a* (*uncalled
for*) überflüssig

gratuity /grə'tju:ətɪ/ *n* (*tip*) Trinkgeld *nt*

grave[1] /greɪv/ *a* (**-r, -st**), **-ly** *adv* ernst;
~ly ill schwer krank

grave[2] *n* Grab *nt*. **~-digger** *n* Toten-
gräber *m*

gravel /'grævl/ *n* Kies *m*

grave: ~stone *n* Grabstein *m*.
~yard *n* Friedhof *m*

gravitate /'grævɪteɪt/ *vi* gravitieren

gravity /'grævətɪ/ *n* Ernst *m*; (*force*)
Schwerkraft *f*

gravy /'greɪvɪ/ *n* [Braten]soße *f*

gray /greɪ/ *a* (*Amer*) = **grey**

graze[1] /greɪz/ *vi* ⟨*animal:*⟩ weiden

graze[2] *n* Schürfwunde *f* ● *vt* ⟨*car*⟩ streifen; ⟨*knee*⟩ aufschürfen

grease /gri:s/ *n* Fett *nt*; (*lubricant*)
Schmierfett *m* ● *vt* einfetten; (*lubricate*) schmieren. **~-proof 'paper**
n Pergamentpapier *nt*

greasy /'gri:sɪ/ *a* (**-ier, -iest**) fettig

great /greɪt/ *a* (**-er, -est**) groß; (*fam:
marvellous*) großartig

great: ~-'aunt *n* Großtante *f*. **G~
'Britain** *n* Großbritannien *nt*.
~-'grandchildren *npl* Urenkel *pl*.
~-'grandfather *n* Urgroßvater *m*.
~-'grandmother *n* Urgroßmutter *f*

great|ly /'greɪtlɪ/ *adv* sehr. **~ness** *n*
Größe *f*

great-'uncle *n* Großonkel *m*

Greece /gri:s/ *n* Griechenland *nt*

greed /gri:d/ *n* [Hab]gier *f*

greedy /'gri:dɪ/ *a* (**-ier, -iest**), **-ily** *adv*
gierig; **don't be ~** sei nicht so unbescheiden

Greek /gri:k/ *a* griechisch ● *n* Grie-
che *m*/Griechin *f*; (*Lang*) Griechisch
nt

green /gri:n/ *a* (**-er, -est**) grün; (*fig*)
unerfahren ● *n* Grün *nt*; (*grass*) Wiese
f; **~s** *pl* Kohl *m*; **the G~s** *pl* (*Pol*) die
Grünen *pl*

greenery /'gri:nərɪ/ *n* Grün *nt*

'greenfly *n* Blattlaus *f*

greengage /'gri:ngeɪdʒ/ *n* Reneklode *f*

green: ~grocer *n* Obst- und
Gemüsehändler *m*. **~house** *n*
Gewächshaus *nt*. **~house effect** *n*
Treibhauseffekt *m*

Greenland /'gri:nlənd/ *n* Grönland
nt

greet /gri:t/ *vt* grüßen; (*welcome*) begrüßen. **~ing** *n* Gruß *m*; (*welcome*)
Begrüßung *f*. **~ings card** *n* Glück-
wunschkarte *f*

gregarious /grɪ'geərɪəs/ *a* gesellig

grenade /grɪ'neɪd/ *n* Granate *f*

grew /gru:/ *see* **grow**

grey /greɪ/ *a* (**-er, -est**) grau ● *n* Grau
nt ● *vi* grau werden. **~hound** *n* Wind-
hund *m*

grid /grɪd/ *n* Gitter *nt*; (*on map*) Git-
ternetz *nt*; (*Electr*) Überland-
leitungsnetz *nt*

grief /gri:f/ *n* Trauer *f*; **come to ~**
scheitern

grievance /'gri:vəns/ *n* Beschwerde
f

grieve /gri:v/ *vt* betrüben ● *vi*
trauern (**for** um)

grievous /'gri:vəs/ *a*, **-ly** *adv* schwer

grill /grɪl/ n Gitter nt; (Culin) Grill m; **mixed** ~ Gemischtes nt vom Grill ● vt/ i grillen; (interrogate) [streng] verhören

grille /grɪl/ n Gitter nt

grim /grɪm/ a (grimmer, grimmest), **-ly** adv ernst; (determination) verbissen

grimace /grɪˈmeɪs/ n Grimasse f ● vi Grimassen schneiden

grime /graɪm/ n Schmutz m

grimy /ˈgraɪmɪ/ a (-ier, -iest) schmutzig

grin /grɪn/ n Grinsen nt ● vi (pt/pp grinned) grinsen

grind /graɪnd/ n (fam: hard work) Plackerei f ● vt (pt/pp ground) mahlen; (smooth, sharpen) schleifen; (Amer: mince) durchdrehen; ~ one's teeth mit den Zähnen knirschen

grip /grɪp/ n Griff m; (bag) Reisetasche f ● vt (pt/pp gripped) ergreifen; (hold) festhalten; fesseln (interest)

gripe /graɪp/ vi (sl: grumble) meckern

gripping /ˈgrɪpɪŋ/ a fesselnd

grisly /ˈgrɪzlɪ/ a (-ier, -iest) grausig

gristle /ˈgrɪsl/ n Knorpel m

grit /grɪt/ n [grober] Sand m; (for roads) Streugut nt; (courage) Mut m ● vt (pt/pp gritted) streuen (road); ~ one's teeth die Zähne zusammenbeißen

grizzle /ˈgrɪzl/ vi quengeln

groan /grəʊn/ n Stöhnen nt ● vi stöhnen

grocer /ˈgrəʊsə(r)/ n Lebensmittelhändler m; ~'s [shop] Lebensmittelgeschäft nt. ~ies npl Lebensmittel pl

groggy /ˈgrɒgɪ/ a schwach; (unsteady) wackelig [auf den Beinen]

groin /grɔɪn/ n (Anat) Leiste f

groom /gruːm/ n Bräutigam m; (for horse) Pferdepfleger(in) m(f) ● vt striegeln (horse)

groove /gruːv/ n Rille f

grope /grəʊp/ vi tasten (for nach)

gross /grəʊs/ a (-er, -est) fett; (coarse) derb; (glaring) grob; (Comm) brutto; (salary, weight) Brutto- ● n inv Gros nt. ~ly adv (very) sehr

grotesque /grəʊˈtesk/ a, **-ly** adv grotesk

grotto /ˈgrɒtəʊ/ n (pl -es) Grotte f

grotty /ˈgrɒtɪ/ a (fam) mies

ground[1] /graʊnd/ see **grind**

ground[2] n Boden m; (terrain) Gelände nt; (reason) Grund m; (Amer, Electr) Erde f; ~s pl (park) Anlagen pl; (of coffee) Satz m ● vi (ship:) auflaufen ● vt aus dem Verkehr ziehen (aircraft); (Amer, Electr) erden

ground: ~ **floor** n Erdgeschoß nt. ~ing n Grundlage f. ~less a grundlos. ~ 'meat n Hackfleisch nt. ~sheet n Bodenplane f. ~work n Vorarbeiten pl

group /gruːp/ n Gruppe f ● vt gruppieren ● vi sich gruppieren

grouse[1] /graʊs/ n inv schottisches Moorschneehuhn nt

grouse[2] vi (fam) meckern

grovel /ˈgrɒvl/ vi (pt/pp grovelled) kriechen. ~ling a kriecherisch

grow /grəʊ/ v (pt grew, pp grown) ● vi wachsen; (become) werden; (increase) zunehmen ● vt anbauen; ~ one's hair sich (dat) die Haare wachsen lassen. ~ up vi aufwachsen; (town:) entstehen

growl /graʊl/ n Knurren nt ● vi knurren

grown /grəʊn/ see **grow**. ~-up a erwachsen ● n Erwachsene(r) m/f

growth /grəʊθ/ n Wachstum nt; (increase) Zunahme f; (Med) Gewächs nt

grub /grʌb/ n (larva) Made f; (fam: food) Essen nt

grubby /ˈgrʌbɪ/ a (-ier, -iest) schmuddelig

grudge /grʌdʒ/ n Groll m; **bear s.o. a** ~e einen Groll gegen jdn hegen ● vt ~e s.o. sth jdm etw mißgönnen. ~ing a, **-ly** adv widerwillig

gruelling /ˈgruːəlɪŋ/ a strapaziös

gruesome /ˈgruːsəm/ a grausig

gruff /grʌf/ a, **-ly** adv barsch

grumble /ˈgrʌmbl/ vi schimpfen (at mit)

grumpy /ˈgrʌmpɪ/ a (-ier, -iest) griesgrämig

grunt /grʌnt/ n Grunzen nt ● vi grunzen

guarant|ee /gærənˈtiː/ n Garantie f; (document) Garantieschein m ● vt garantieren; garantieren für (quality, success); **be** ~eed (product:) Garantie haben. ~or n Bürge m

guard /gɑːd/ n Wache f; (security) Wächter m; (on train) ≈ Zugführer m; (Techn) Schutz m; **be on** ~ Wache stehen; **on one's** ~ auf der Hut ● vt bewachen; (protect) schützen ● vi ~ **against** sich hüten vor (+ dat). ~-**dog** n Wachhund m

guarded /'gɑːdɪd/ *a* vorsichtig
guardian /'gɑːdɪən/ *n* Vormund *m*
guerrilla /gə'rɪlə/ *n* Guerillakämpfer *m*. **~ warfare** *n* Partisanenkrieg *m*
guess /ges/ *n* Vermutung *f* ● *vt* erraten ● *vi* raten; (*Amer: believe*) glauben. **~work** *n* Vermutung *f*
guest /gest/ *n* Gast *m*. **~-house** *n* Pension *f*
guffaw /gʌ'fɔː/ *n* derbes Lachen *nt* ● *vi* derb lachen
guidance /'gaɪdəns/ *n* Führung *f*, Leitung *f*; (*advice*) Beratung *f*
guide /gaɪd/ *n* Führer(in) *m(f)*; (*book*) Führer *m*; **[Girl] G~** Pfadfinderin *f* ● *vt* führen, leiten. **~book** *n* Führer *m*
guided /'gaɪdɪd/ *a* **~ missile** Fernlenkgeschoß *nt*; **~ tour** Führung *f*
guide: **~-dog** *n* Blindenhund *m*. **~lines** *npl* Richtlinien *pl*
guild /gɪld/ *n* Gilde *f*, Zunft *f*
guile /gaɪl/ *n* Arglist *f*
guillotine /'gɪləti:n/ *n* Guillotine *f*; (*for paper*) Papierschneidemaschine *f*
guilt /gɪlt/ *n* Schuld *f*. **~ily** *adv* schuldbewußt
guilty /'gɪltɪ/ *a* (**-ier, -iest**) *a* schuldig (**of** *gen*); (*look*) schuldbewußt; (*conscience*) schlecht
guinea-pig /'gɪnɪ-/ *n* Meerschweinchen *nt*; (*person*) Versuchskaninchen *nt*
guise /gaɪz/ *n* **in the ~ of** in Gestalt (+ *gen*)
guitar /gɪ'tɑː(r)/ *n* Gitarre *f*. **~ist** *n* Gitarrist(in) *m(f)*
gulf /gʌlf/ *n* (*Geog*) Golf *m*; (*fig*) Kluft *f*
gull /gʌl/ *n* Möwe *f*
gullet /'gʌlɪt/ *n* Speiseröhre *f*; (*throat*) Kehle *f*
gullible /'gʌlɪbl/ *a* leichtgläubig
gully /'gʌlɪ/ *n* Schlucht *f*; (*drain*) Rinne *f*
gulp /gʌlp/ *n* Schluck *m* ● *vi* schlucken ● *vt* **~ down** hinunterschlucken
gum[1] /gʌm/ *n* & **-s** *pl* (*Anat*) Zahnfleisch *nt*
gum[2] *n* Gummi[harz] *nt*; (*glue*) Klebstoff *m*; (*chewing-gum*) Kaugummi *m* ● *vt* (*pt/pp* **gummed**) kleben (**to** an + *acc*). **~boot** *n* Gummistiefel *m*
gummed /gʌmd/ *see* **gum**[2] ● *a* ⟨*label*⟩ gummiert

gumption /'gʌmpʃn/ *n* (*fam*) Grips *m*
gun /gʌn/ *n* Schußwaffe *f*; (*pistol*) Pistole *f*; (*rifle*) Gewehr *nt*; (*cannon*) Geschütz *nt* ● *vt* (*pt/pp* **gunned**) **~ down** niederschießen
gun: **~fire** *n* Geschützfeuer *nt*. **~man** bewaffneter Bandit *m*
gunner /'gʌnə(r)/ *n* Artillerist *m*
gun: **~powder** *n* Schießpulver *nt*. **~shot** *n* Schuß *m*
gurgle /'gɜːgl/ *vi* gluckern; (*of baby*) glucksen
gush /gʌʃ/ *vi* strömen; (*enthuse*) schwärmen (**over** von). **~ out** *vi* herausströmen
gusset /'gʌsɪt/ *n* Zwickel *m*
gust /gʌst/ *n* (*of wind*) Windstoß *m*; (*Naut*) Bö *f*
gusto /'gʌstəʊ/ *n* **with ~** mit Schwung
gusty /'gʌstɪ/ *a* böig
gut /gʌt/ *n* Darm *m*; **~s** *pl* Eingeweide *pl*; (*fam: courage*) Schneid *m* ● *vt* (*pt/pp* **gutted**) (*Culin*) ausnehmen; **~ted by fire** ausgebrannt
gutter /'gʌtə(r)/ *n* Rinnstein *m*; (*fig*) Gosse *f*; (*on roof*) Dachrinne *f*
guttural /'gʌtərl/ *a* guttural
guy /gaɪ/ *n* (*fam*) Kerl *m*
guzzle /'gʌzl/ *vt/i* schlingen; (*drink*) schlürfen
gym /dʒɪm/ *n* (*fam*) Turnhalle *f*; (*gymnastics*) Turnen *nt*
gymnasium /dʒɪm'neɪzɪəm/ *n* Turnhalle *f*
gymnast /'dʒɪmnæst/ *n* Turner(in) *m(f)*. **~ics** /-'næstɪks/ *n* Turnen *nt*
gym: **~ shoes** *pl* Turnschuhe *pl*. **~-slip** *n* (*Sch*) Trägerkleid *nt*
gynaecolog|ist /gaɪnɪ'kɒlədʒɪst/ *n* Frauenarzt *m*/-ärztin *f*. **~y** *n* Gynäkologie *f*
gypsy /'dʒɪpsɪ/ *n* Zigeuner(in) *m(f)*
gyrate /dʒaɪə'reɪt/ *vi* sich drehen

H

haberdashery /'hæbədæʃərɪ/ *n* Kurzwaren *pl*; (*Amer*) Herrenmoden *pl*
habit /'hæbɪt/ *n* Gewohnheit *f*; (*Relig: costume*) Ordenstracht *f*; **be in the ~** die Angewohnheit haben (**of** zu)
habitable /'hæbɪtəbl/ *a* bewohnbar
habitat /'hæbɪtæt/ *n* Habitat *nt*

habitation /ˌhæbɪˈteɪʃn/ *n* **unfit for human** ~ für Wohnzwecke ungeeignet
habitual /həˈbɪtjʊəl/ *a* gewohnt; (*inveterate*) gewohnheitsmäßig. ~**ly** *adv* gewohnheitsmäßig; (*constantly*) ständig
hack[1] /hæk/ *n* (*writer*) Schreiberling *m*; (*hired horse*) Mietpferd *nt*
hack[2] *vt* hacken; ~ **to pieces** zerhacken
hackneyed /ˈhæknɪd/ *a* abgedroschen
'hacksaw *n* Metallsäge *f*
had /hæd/ *see* **have**
haddock /ˈhædək/ *n inv* Schellfisch *m*
haemorrhage /ˈhemərɪdʒ/ *n* Blutung *f*
haemorrhoids /ˈhemərɔɪdz/ *npl* Hämorrhoiden *pl*
hag /hæg/ *n* **old** ~ alte Hexe *f*
haggard /ˈhægəd/ *a* abgehärmt
haggle /ˈhægl/ *vi* feilschen (**over** um)
hail[1] /heɪl/ *vt* begrüßen; herbeirufen ⟨taxi⟩ ● *vi* ~ **from** kommen aus
hail[2] *n* Hagel *m* ● *vi* hageln. ~**stone** *n* Hagelkorn *nt*
hair /heə(r)/ *n* Haar *nt*; **wash one's** ~ sich (*dat*) die Haare waschen
hair: ~**brush** *n* Haarbürste *f*. ~**cut** *n* Haarschnitt *m*; **have a** ~**cut** sich (*dat*) die Haare schneiden lassen. ~**do** *n* (*fam*) Frisur *f*. ~**dresser** *n* Friseur *m*/Friseuse *f*. ~**drier** *n* Haartrockner *m*; (*hand-held*) Fön (P) *m*. ~**grip** *n* [Haar]klemme *f*. ~**pin** *n* Haarnadel *f*. ~**pin 'bend** *n* Haarnadelkurve *f*. ~**raising** *a* haarsträubend. ~**style** *n* Frisur *f*
hairy /ˈheərɪ/ *a* (-**ier**, -**iest**) behaart; (*excessively*) haarig; (*fam: frightening*) brenzlig
hake /heɪk/ *n inv* Seehecht *m*
hale /heɪl/ *a* ~ **and hearty** gesund und munter
half /hɑːf/ *n* (*pl* **halves**) Hälfte *f*; **cut in** ~ halbieren; **one and a** ~ eineinhalb, anderthalb; **a dozen** ein halbes Dutzend; ~ **an hour** eine halbe Stunde ● *a* & *adv* halb; ~ **past two** halb drei; **[at]** ~ **price** zum halben Preis
half: ~**-board** *n* Halbpension *f*. ~**-caste** *n* Mischling *m*. ~**-'hearted** *a* lustlos. ~**'hourly** *a* & *adv* halbstündlich. ~**-'mast** *n* **at** ~**-mast** auf halbmast. ~**-measure** *n* Halbheit *f*. ~**'term** *n* schulfreie Tage nach dem halben Trimester. ~**-'timbered** *a* Fachwerk-.

~**-'time** *n* (*Sport*) Halbzeit *f*. ~**-'way** *a* **the** ~**-way mark/stage** die Hälfte ● *adv* auf halbem Weg; **get** ~**-way** den halben Weg zurücklegen; (*fig*) bis zur Hälfte kommen. ~**-wit** *n* Idiot *m*
halibut /ˈhælɪbət/ *n inv* Heilbutt *m*
hall /hɔːl/ *n* Halle *f*; (*room*) Saal *m*; (*Sch*) Aula *f*; (*entrance*) Flur *m*; (*mansion*) Gutshaus *nt*; ~ **of residence** (*Univ*) Studentenheim *nt*
'hallmark *n* [Feingehalts]stempel *m*; (*fig*) Kennzeichen *nt* (**of** für) ● *vt* stempeln
hallo /həˈləʊ/ *int* [guten] Tag! (*fam*) hallo!
Hallowe'en /hæləʊˈiːn/ *n* der Tag vor Allerheiligen
hallucination /həluːsɪˈneɪʃn/ *n* Halluzination *f*
halo /ˈheɪləʊ/ *n* (*pl* -**es**) Heiligenschein *m*; (*Astr*) Hof *m*
halt /hɔːlt/ *n* Halt *m*; **come to a** ~ stehenbleiben; (*traffic:*) zum Stillstand kommen ● *vi* haltmachen; ~! halt! ~**ing** *a*, *adv* -**ly** zögernd
halve /hɑːv/ *vt* halbieren; (*reduce*) um die Hälfte reduzieren
ham /hæm/ *n* Schinken *m*
hamburger /ˈhæmbɜːgə(r)/ *n* Hamburger *m*
hamlet /ˈhæmlɪt/ *n* Weiler *m*
hammer /ˈhæmə(r)/ *n* Hammer *m* ● *vt/i* hämmern (**at** an + *acc*)
hammock /ˈhæmək/ *n* Hängematte *f*
hamper[1] /ˈhæmpə(r)/ *n* Picknickkorb *m*; **[gift]** ~ Geschenkkorb *m*
hamper[2] *vt* behindern
hamster /ˈhæmstə(r)/ *n* Hamster *m*
hand /hænd/ *n* Hand *f*; (*of clock*) Zeiger *m*; (*writing*) Handschrift *f*; (*worker*) Arbeiter(in) *m*(*f*); (*Cards*) Blatt *nt*; **all** ~**s** (*Naut*) alle Mann; **at** ~ in der Nähe; **on the one/other** ~ einer-/andererseits; **out of** ~ außer Kontrolle; (*summarily*) kurzerhand; **in** ~ unter Kontrolle; (*available*) verfügbar; **give s.o. a** ~ jdm behilflich sein ● *vt* reichen (**to** *dat*). ~ **in** *vt* abgeben. ~ **out** *vt* austeilen. ~ **over** *vt* überreichen
hand: ~**bag** *n* Handtasche *f*. ~**book** *n* Handbuch *nt*. ~**brake** *n* Handbremse *f*. ~**cuffs** *npl* Handschellen *pl*. ~**ful** *n* Handvoll *f*; **be [quite] a** ~**ful** (*fam*) nicht leicht zu haben sein
handicap /ˈhændɪkæp/ *n* Behinderung *f*; (*Sport & fig*) Handikap *nt*.

~ped *a* mentally/physically ~ped geistig/körperlich behindert

handi|craft /'hændɪkrɑ:ft/ *n* Basteln *nt*; (*Sch*) Werken *nt*. ~work *n* Werk *nt*

handkerchief /'hæŋkətʃɪf/ *n* (*pl* ~s & -chieves) Taschentuch *nt*

handle /'hændl/ *n* Griff *m*; (*of door*) Klinke *f*; (*of cup*) Henkel *m*; (*of broom*) Stiel *m*; **fly off the** ~ (*fam*) aus der Haut fahren ● *vt* handhaben; (*treat*) umgehen mit; (*touch*) anfassen. ~bars *npl* Lenkstange *f*

hand: ~luggage *n* Handgepäck *nt*. ~made *a* handgemacht. ~out *n* Prospekt *m*; (*money*) Unterstützung *f*. ~rail *n* Handlauf *m*. ~shake *n* Händedruck *m*

handsome /'hænsəm/ *a* gutaussehend; (*generous*) großzügig; (*large*) beträchtlich

hand: ~stand *n* Handstand *m*. ~writing *n* Handschrift *f*. ~-written *a* handgeschrieben

handy /'hændɪ/ *a* (-ier, -iest) handlich; (*person*) geschickt; **have/keep** ~ griffbereit haben/halten. ~man *n* [home] ~man Heimwerker *m*

hang /hæŋ/ *vt/i* (*pt/pp* hung) hängen; (*wallpaper*) tapezieren ● *vt* (*pt/pp* hanged) hängen (*criminal*); ~ oneself sich erhängen ● *n* get the ~ of it (*fam*) den Dreh herauskriegen. ~ about *vi* sich herumdrücken. ~ on *vi* sich festhalten (**to** an + *dat*); (*fam: wait*) warten. ~ out *vi* heraushängen; (*fam: live*) wohnen ● *vt* draußen aufhängen (*washing*). ~ up *vt/i* aufhängen

hangar /'hæŋə(r)/ *n* Flugzeughalle *f*

hanger /'hæŋə(r)/ *n* [Kleider]bügel *m*

hang: ~-glider *n* Drachenflieger *m*. ~-gliding *n* Drachenfliegen *nt*. ~man *n* Henker *m*. ~over *n* (*fam*) Kater *m* (*fam*). ~-up *n* (*fam*) Komplex *m*

hanker /'hæŋkə(r)/ *vi* ~ after sth sich (*dat*) etw wünschen

hanky /'hæŋkɪ/ *n* (*fam*) Taschentuch *nt*

hanky-panky /'hæŋkɪ'pæŋkɪ/ *n* (*fam*) Mauscheleien *pl*

haphazard /hæp'hæzəd/ *a*, **-ly** *adv* planlos

happen /'hæpn/ *vi* geschehen, passieren; **as it** ~s zufälligerweise; **I** ~ed to be there ich war zufällig da; **what**

~ped **to him?** was ist mit ihm los? (*become of*) was ist aus ihm geworden? ~ing *n* Ereignis *nt*

happi|ly /'hæpɪlɪ/ *adv* glücklich; (*fortunately*) glücklicherweise. ~ness *n* Glück *nt*

happy /'hæpɪ/ *a* (-ier, -iest) glücklich. ~-go-'lucky *a* sorglos

harass /'hærəs/ *vt* schikanieren. ~ed *a* abgehetzt. ~ment *n* Schikane *f*; (*sexual*) Belästigung *f*

harbour /'hɑ:bə(r)/ *n* Hafen *m* ● *vt* Unterschlupf gewähren (+ *dat*); hegen (*grudge*)

hard /hɑ:d/ *a* (-er, -est) hart; (*difficult*) schwer; ~ **of hearing** schwerhörig ● *adv* hart; (*work*) schwer; (*pull*) kräftig; (*rain, snow*) stark; **think** ~! denk mal nach! **be** ~ **up** (*fam*) knapp bei Kasse sein; **be** ~ **done by** (*fam*) ungerecht behandelt werden

hard: ~back *n* gebundene Ausgabe *f*. ~board *n* Hartfaserplatte *f*. ~-boiled *a* hartgekocht

harden /'hɑ:dn/ *vi* hart werden

hard-'hearted *a* hartherzig

hard|ly /'hɑ:dlɪ/ *adv* kaum; ~ly ever kaum [jemals]. ~ness *n* Härte *f*. ~ship *n* Not *f*

hard: ~ 'shoulder *n* (*Auto*) Randstreifen *m*. ~ware *n* Haushaltswaren *pl*; (*Computing*) Hardware *f*. ~-'wearing *a* strapazierfähig. ~-'working *a* fleißig

hardy /'hɑ:dɪ/ *a* (-ier, -iest) abgehärtet; (*plant*) winterhart

hare /heə(r)/ *n* Hase *m*. ~'lip *n* Hasenscharte *f*

hark /hɑ:k/ *vi* ~! hört! ~ back *vi* ~ back to (*fig*) zurückkommen auf (+ *acc*)

harm /hɑ:m/ *n* Schaden *m*; out of ~'s way in Sicherheit; **it won't do any** ~ es kann nichts schaden ● *vt* ~ s.o. jdm etwas antun. ~ful *a* schädlich. ~less *a* harmlos

harmonica /hɑ:'mɒnɪkə/ *n* Mundharmonika *f*

harmonious /hɑ:'məʊnɪəs/ *a*, **-ly** *adv* harmonisch

harmon|ize /'hɑ:mənaɪz/ *vi* (*fig*) harmonieren. ~y *n* Harmonie *f*

harness /'hɑ:nɪs/ *n* Geschirr *nt*; (*of parachute*) Gurtwerk *nt* ● *vt* anschirren (*horse*); (*use*) nutzbar machen

harp /hɑ:p/ *n* Harfe *f* ● *vi* ~ on [about] (*fam*) herumreiten auf (+ *dat*). ~ist *n* Harfenist(in) *m*(*f*)

harpoon /hɑːˈpuːn/ n Harpune f

harpsichord /ˈhɑːpsɪkɔːd/ n Cembalo nt

harrow /ˈhærəʊ/ n Egge f. ~ing a grauenhaft

harsh /hɑːʃ/ a (-er, -est), -ly adv hart; ⟨voice⟩ rauh; ⟨light⟩ grell. ~ness n Härte f; Rauheit f

harvest /ˈhɑːvɪst/ n Ernte f ● vt ernten

has /hæz/ see **have**

hash /hæʃ/ n (Culin) Haschee nt; **make a ~ of** ⟨fam⟩ verpfuschen

hashish /ˈhæʃɪʃ/ n Haschisch nt

hassle /ˈhæsl/ n ⟨fam⟩ Ärger m ● vt schikanieren

hassock /ˈhæsək/ n Kniekissen nt

haste /heɪst/ n Eile f; **make ~ sich** beeilen

hasten /ˈheɪsn/ vi sich beeilen (to zu); ⟨go quickly⟩ eilen ● vt beschleunigen

hasty /ˈheɪstɪ/ a (-ier, -iest), -ily adv hastig; ⟨decision⟩ voreilig

hat /hæt/ n Hut m; ⟨knitted⟩ Mütze f

hatch[1] /hætʃ/ n (for food) Durchreiche f; (Naut) Luke f

hatch[2] vi ~ [out] ausschlüpfen ● vt ausbrüten

'**hatchback** n (Auto) Modell nt mit Hecktür

hatchet /ˈhætʃɪt/ n Beil nt

hate /heɪt/ n Haß m ● vt hassen. ~ful a abscheulich

hatred /ˈheɪtrɪd/ n Haß m

haughty /ˈhɔːtɪ/ a (-ier, -iest), -ily adv hochmütig

haul /hɔːl/ n (fish) Fang m; (loot) Beute f ● vt/i ziehen (on an + dat). ~age /-ɪdʒ/ n Transport m. ~ier /-ɪə(r)/ n Spediteur m

haunt /hɔːnt/ n Lieblingsaufenthalt m ● vt umgehen in (+ dat); **this house is ~ed** in diesem Haus spukt es

have /hæv/ vt (3 sg pres tense **has**; pt/pp **had**) haben; bekommen ⟨baby⟩; holen ⟨doctor⟩; ~ **a meal/drink** etwas essen/trinken; ~ **lunch** zu Mittag essen; ~ **a walk** spazierengehen; ~ **a dream** träumen; ~ **a rest** sich ausruhen; ~ **a swim** schwimmen; ~ **sth done** etw machen lassen; ~ **sth made** sich ⟨dat⟩ etw machen lassen; ~ **to do sth** etw tun müssen; ~ **it out with** zur Rede stellen; **so I ~!** tatsächlich! **he has [got] two houses** er hat zwei Häuser; **you have got the money, haven't you?** du hast das Geld, nicht [wahr]?

● v aux haben; (with verbs of motion & some others) sein; **I ~ seen him** ich habe ihn gesehen; **he has never been there** er ist nie da gewesen. ~ **on** vt (be wearing) anhaben; (dupe) anführen

haven /ˈheɪvn/ n (fig) Zuflucht f

haversack /ˈhævə-/ n Rucksack m

havoc /ˈhævək/ n Verwüstung f; **play ~ with** (fig) völlig durcheinanderbringen

haw /hɔː/ see **hum**

hawk[1] /hɔːk/ n Falke m

hawk[2] vt hausieren mit. ~er n Hausierer m

hawthorn /ˈhɔː-/ n Hagedorn m

hay /heɪ/ n Heu nt. ~ **fever** n Heuschnupfen m. ~stack n Heuschober m

'**haywire** a ⟨fam⟩ **go ~** verrückt spielen; ⟨plans:⟩ über den Haufen geworfen werden

hazard /ˈhæzəd/ n Gefahr f; (risk) Risiko nt ● vt riskieren. ~ous /-əs/ a gefährlich; (risky) riskant. ~ **[warning] lights** npl (Auto) Warnblinkanlage f

haze /heɪz/ n Dunst m

hazel /ˈheɪzl/ n Haselbusch m. ~-**nut** n Haselnuß f

hazy /ˈheɪzɪ/ a (-ier, -iest) dunstig; (fig) unklar

he /hiː/ pron er

head /hed/ n Kopf m; (chief) Oberhaupt nt; (of firm) Chef(in) m(f); (of school) Schulleiter(in) m(f); (on beer) Schaumkrone f; (of bed) Kopfende nt; **20 ~ of cattle** 20 Stück Vieh; ~ **first** kopfüber ● vt anführen; (Sport) köpfen ⟨ball⟩ ● vi ~ **for** zusteuern auf (+ acc). ~ache n Kopfschmerzen pl. ~-dress n Kopfschmuck m

head|er /ˈhedə(r)/ n Kopfball m; (dive) Kopfsprung m. ~ing n Überschrift f

head: ~lamp n (Auto) Scheinwerfer m. ~land n Landspitze f. ~light n (Auto) Scheinwerfer m. ~line n Schlagzeile f. ~long adv kopfüber. ~'master n Schulleiter m. ~'mistress n Schulleiterin f. ~-on a & adv frontal. ~phones npl Kopfhörer m. ~quarters npl Hauptquartier nt; (Pol) Zentrale f. ~-rest n Kopfstütze f. ~room n lichte Höhe f. ~scarf n Kopftuch nt. ~strong a eigenwillig. ~ 'waiter n Oberkellner m. ~way n **make ~way**

Fortschritte machen. ～ **wind** n Gegenwind m. ～**word** n Stichwort nt

heady /'hedɪ/ a berauschend

heal /hiːl/ vt/i heilen

health /helθ/ n Gesundheit f

health: ～ **farm** n Schönheitsfarm f. ～ **foods** npl Reformkost f. ～**-food shop** n Reformhaus nt. ～ **insurance** n Krankenversicherung f

healthy /'helθɪ/ a (-ier, -iest), -ily adv gesund

heap /hiːp/ n Haufen m; ～s (fam) jede Menge ● vt ～ [up] häufen; ～ed **teaspoon** gehäufter Teelöffel

hear /hɪə(r)/ vt/i (pt/pp **heard**) hören; ～, ～! hört, hört! **he would not** ～ **of it** er ließ es nicht zu

hearing /'hɪərɪŋ/ n Gehör nt; (Jur) Verhandlung f. ～**-aid** n Hörgerät nt

'**hearsay** n from ～ vom Hörensagen

hearse /hɜːs/ n Leichenwagen m

heart /hɑːt/ n Herz nt; (courage) Mut m; ～s pl (Cards) Herz nt; **by** ～ auswendig

heart: ～**ache** n Kummer m. ～ **attack** n Herzanfall m. ～**beat** n Herzschlag m. ～**-break** n Leid nt. ～**-breaking** a herzzerreißend. ～**-broken** a untröstlich. ～**burn** n Sodbrennen nt. ～**en** vt (fig) steigern ～**felt** a herzlich[st]

hearth /hɑːθ/ n Herd m; (fireplace) Kamin m. ～**rug** n Kaminvorleger m

heart|ily /'hɑːtɪlɪ/ adv herzlich; (eat) viel. ～**less** a, -ly adv herzlos. ～**y** a herzlich; (meal) groß; (person) burschikos

heat /hiːt/ n Hitze f; (Sport) Vorlauf m ● vt heiß machen; heizen (room). ～**ed** a geheizt; (swimming pool) beheizt; (discussion) hitzig. ～**er** n Heizgerät nt; (Auto) Heizanlage f

heath /hiːθ/ n Heide f

heathen /'hiːðn/ a heidnisch ● n Heide m/Heidin f

heather /'heðə(r)/ n Heidekraut nt

heating /'hiːtɪŋ/ n Heizung f

heat: ～**stroke** n Hitzschlag m. ～**wave** n Hitzewelle f

heave /hiːv/ vt/i ziehen; (lift) heben; (fam: throw) schmeißen; ～ **a sigh** einen Seufzer ausstoßen

heaven /'hevn/ n Himmel m. ～**ly** a himmlisch

heavy /'hevɪ/ a (-ier, -iest), -ily adv schwer; (traffic, rain) stark; (sleep) tief. ～**weight** n Schwergewicht nt

Hebrew /'hiːbruː/ a hebräisch

heckle /'hekl/ vt [durch Zwischenrufe] unterbrechen. ～**r** n Zwischenrufer m

hectic /'hektɪk/ a hektisch

hedge /hedʒ/ n Hecke f ● vi (fig) ausweichen. ～**hog** n Igel m

heed /hiːd/ n **pay** ～ **to** Beachtung schenken (+ dat) ● vt beachten. ～**less** a ungeachtet (of gen)

heel[1] /hiːl/ n Ferse f; (of shoe) Absatz m; **down at** ～ heruntergekommen; **take to one's** ～**s** (fam) Fersengeld geben

heel[2] vi ～ **over** (Naut) sich auf die Seite legen

hefty /'heftɪ/ a (-ier, -iest) kräftig; (heavy) schwer

heifer /'hefə(r)/ n Färse f

height /haɪt/ n Höhe f; (of person) Größe f. ～**en** vt (fig) steigern

heir /eə(r)/ n Erbe m. ～**ess** n Erbin f. ～**loom** n Erbstück nt

held /held/ see **hold**[2]

helicopter /'helɪkɒptə(r)/ n Hubschrauber m

hell /hel/ n Hölle f; **go to** ～! (sl) geh zum Teufel! ● int verdammt!

hello /hə'ləʊ/ int [guten] Tag! (fam) hallo!

helm /helm/ n [Steuer]ruder nt; **at the** ～ (fig) am Ruder

helmet /'helmɪt/ n Helm m

help /help/ n Hilfe f; (employees) Hilfskräfte pl; **that's no** ～ das nützt nichts ● vt/i helfen (s.o. jdm); ～ **oneself to sth** sich (dat) etw nehmen; ～ **yourself** (at table) greif zu; **I could not** ～ **laughing** ich mußte lachen; **it cannot be** ～**ed** es läßt sich nicht ändern; **I can't** ～ **it** ich kann nichts dafür

help|er /'helpə(r)/ n Helfer(in) m(f). ～**ful** a, -ly adv hilfsbereit; (advice) nützlich. ～**ing** n Portion f. ～**less** a, -ly adv hilflos

helter-skelter /heltə'skeltə(r)/ adv holterdiepolter ● n Rutschbahn f

hem /hem/ n Saum m ● vt (pt/pp **hemmed**) säumen; ～ **in** umzingeln

hemisphere /'hemɪ-/ n Hemisphäre f

'**hem-line** n Rocklänge f

hemp /hemp/ n Hanf m

hen /hen/ n Henne f; (any female bird) Weibchen nt

hence /hens/ adv daher; **five years** ～ in fünf Jahren. ～'**forth** adv von nun an

henchman /'hentʃmən/ n (pej) Gefolgsmann m

'henpecked *a* ~ **husband** Pantoffelheld *m*

her /hɜː(r)/ *a* ihr ● *pron* (*acc*) sie; (*dat*) ihr; **I know** ~ ich kenne sie; **give** ~ **the money** gib ihr das Geld

herald /'herəld/ *vt* verkünden. **~ry** *n* Wappenkunde *f*

herb /hɜːb/ *n* Kraut *nt*

herbaceous /hɜː'beɪʃəs/ *a* krautartig; ~ **border** Staudenrabatte *f*

herd /hɜːd/ *n* Herde *f* ● *vt* (*tend*) hüten; (*drive*) treiben. ~ **together** *vi* sich zusammendrängen ● *vt* zusammentreiben

here /hɪə(r)/ *adv* hier; (*to this place*) hierher; **in** ~ hier drinnen; **come/ bring** ~ herkommen/herbringen. **~'after** *adv* im folgenden. **~'by** *adv* hiermit

hereditary /hə'redɪtərɪ/ *a* erblich. **~y** *n* Vererbung *f*

here|sy /'herəsɪ/ *n* Ketzerei *f*. **~tic** *n* Ketzer(in) *m(f)*

here'with *adv* (*Comm*) beiliegend

heritage /'herɪtɪdʒ/ *n* Erbe *nt*

hermetic /hɜː'metɪk/ *a*, **-ally** *adv* hermetisch

hermit /'hɜːmɪt/ *n* Einsiedler *m*

hernia /'hɜːnɪə/ *n* Bruch *m*, Hernie *f*

hero /'hɪərəʊ/ *n* (*pl* **-es**) Held *m*

heroic /hɪ'rəʊɪk/ *a*, **-ally** *adv* heldenhaft

heroin /'herəʊɪn/ *n* Heroin *nt*

hero|ine /'herəʊɪn/ *n* Heldin *f*. **~ism** *n* Heldentum *nt*

heron /'hern/ *n* Reiher *m*

herring /'herɪŋ/ *n* Hering *m*; **red** ~ (*fam*) falsche Spur *f*. **~bone** *n* (*pattern*) Fischgrätenmuster *nt*

hers /hɜːz/ *poss pron* ihre(r), ihrs; **a friend of** ~ ein Freund von ihr; **that is** ~ das gehört ihr

her'self *pron* selbst; (*refl*) sich; **by** ~ allein

hesitant /'hezɪtənt/ *a*, **-ly** *adv* zögernd

hesitat|e /'hezɪteɪt/ *vi* zögern. **~ion** /-'teɪʃn/ *n* Zögern *nt*; **without** ~**ion** ohne zu zögern

het /het/ *a* ~ **up** (*fam*) aufgeregt

hetero'sexual /hetərəʊ-/ *a* heterosexuell

hew /hjuː/ *vt* (*pt* **hewed**, *pp* **hewed** *or* **hewn**) hauen

hexagonal /hek'sægənl/ *a* sechseckig

heyday /'heɪ-/ *n* Glanzzeit *f*

hi /haɪ/ *int* he! (*hallo*) Tag!

hiatus /haɪ'eɪtəs/ *n* (*pl* **-tuses**) Lücke *f*

hibernat|e /'haɪbəneɪt/ *vi* Winterschlaf halten. **~ion** /-'neɪʃn/ *n* Winterschlaf *m*

hiccup /'hɪkʌp/ *n* Hick *m*; (*fam: hitch*) Panne *f*; **have the** ~**s** den Schluckauf haben ● *vi* hick machen

hid /hɪd/, **hidden** *see* hide[2]

hide[1] /haɪd/ *n* (*Comm*) Haut *f*; (*leather*) Leder *nt*

hide[2] *v* (*pt* **hid**, *pp* **hidden**) ● *vt* verstecken; (*keep secret*) verheimlichen ● *vi* sich verstecken. **~-and-'seek** *n* play ~**-and-seek** Versteck spielen

hideous /'hɪdɪəs/ *a*, **-ly** *adv* häßlich; (*horrible*) gräßlich

'hide-out *n* Versteck *nt*

hiding[1] /'haɪdɪŋ/ *n* (*fam*) **give s.o. a** ~ jdn verdreschen

hiding[2] *n* **go into** ~ untertauchen

hierarchy /'haɪərɑːkɪ/ *n* Hierarchie *f*

hieroglyphics /haɪərə'glɪfɪks/ *npl* Hieroglyphen *pl*

higgledy-piggledy /hɪgldɪ'pɪgldɪ/ *adv* kunterbunt durcheinander

high /haɪ/ *a* (**-er**, **-est**) hoch; *attrib* hohe(r,s); (*meat*) angegangen; (*wind*) stark; (*on drugs*) high; **it's** ~ **time** es ist höchste Zeit ● *adv* hoch; ~ **and low** überall ● *n* Hoch *nt*; (*temperature*) Höchsttemperatur *f*

high: ~**-brow** *a* intellektuell. ~ **chair** *n* Kinderhochstuhl *m*. ~**-'handed** *a* selbstherrlich. ~**-'heeled** *a* hochhackig. ~ **jump** *n* Hochsprung *m*

highlight *n* (*fig*) Höhepunkt *m*; ~**s** *pl* (*in hair*) helle Strähnen *pl* ● *vt* (*emphasize*) hervorheben

highly /'haɪlɪ/ *adv* hoch; **speak** ~ **of** loben; **think** ~ **of** sehr schätzen. ~**-'strung** *a* nervös

Highness /'haɪnɪs/ *n* Hoheit *f*

high: ~**-rise** *a* ~**-rise flats** *pl* Wohnturm *m*. ~ **season** *n* Hochsaison *f*. ~ **street** *n* Hauptstraße *f*. ~ '**tide** *n* Hochwasser *nt*. ~**way** *n* public ~**way** öffentliche Straße *f*

hijack /'haɪdʒæk/ *vt* entführen. ~**er** *n* Entführer *m*

hike /haɪk/ *n* Wanderung *f* ● *vi* wandern. ~**r** *n* Wanderer *m*

hilarious /hɪ'leərɪəs/ *a* sehr komisch

hill /hɪl/ *n* Berg *m*; (*mound*) Hügel *m*; (*slope*) Hang *m*

hill: ~**-billy** *n* (*Amer*) Hinterwäldler *m*. ~**side** *n* Hang *m*. ~**y** *a* hügelig

hilt /hɪlt/ *n* Griff *m*; **to the** ~ (*fam*) voll und ganz

him /hɪm/ *pron* (*acc*) ihn; (*dat*) ihm; **I know** ~ ich kenne ihn; **give** ~ **the money** gib ihm das Geld. ~'**self** *pron* selbst; (*refl*) sich; **by** ~**self** allein

hind /haɪnd/ *a* Hinter-

hind|er /'hɪndə(r)/ *vt* hindern. ~**rance** /-rəns/ *n* Hindernis *nt*

hindsight /'haɪnd-/ *n* **with** ~ rückblickend

Hindu /'hɪnduː/ *n* Hindu *m* • *a* Hindu. ~**ism** *n* Hinduismus *m*

hinge /hɪndʒ/ *n* Scharnier *nt*; (*on door*) Angel *f* • *vi* ~ **on** (*fig*) ankommen auf (+ *acc*)

hint /hɪnt/ *n* Wink *m*, Andeutung *f*; (*advice*) Hinweis *m*; (*trace*) Spur *f* • *vi* ~ **at** anspielen auf (+ *acc*)

hip /hɪp/ *n* Hüfte *f*

hippie /'hɪpɪ/ *n* Hippie *m*

hip 'pocket *n* Gesäßtasche *f*

hippopotamus /hɪpə'pɒtəməs/ *n* (*pl* -**muses** *or* -**mi** /-maɪ/) Nilpferd *nt*

hire /'haɪə(r)/ *vt* mieten ⟨*car*⟩; ⟨*suit*⟩; einstellen ⟨*person*⟩; ~ [**out**] vermieten; verleihen • *n* Mieten *nt*; Leihen *nt*. ~-**car** *n* Leihwagen *m*

his /hɪz/ *a* sein • *poss pron* seine(r), seins; **a friend of** ~ ein Freund von ihm; **that is** ~ das gehört ihm

hiss /hɪs/ *n* Zischen *nt* • *vt/i* zischen

historian /hɪ'stɔːrɪən/ *n* Historiker(in) *m*(*f*)

historic /hɪ'stɒrɪk/ *a* historisch. ~**al** *a*, -**ly** *adv* geschichtlich, historisch

history /'hɪstərɪ/ *n* Geschichte *f*

hit /hɪt/ *n* (*blow*) Schlag *m*; (*fam: success*) Erfolg *m*; **direct** ~ Volltreffer *m* • *vt/i* (*pt/pp* **hit**, *pres p* **hitting**) schlagen; (*knock against, collide with, affect*) treffen; ~ **the target** das Ziel treffen; ~ **on** (*fig*) kommen auf (+ *acc*); ~ **it off** gut auskommen (**with** mit); ~ **one's head on sth** sich (*dat*) den Kopf an etw (*dat*) stoßen

hitch /hɪtʃ/ *n* Problem *nt*; **technical** ~ Panne *f* • *vt* festmachen (**to** an + *dat*); ~ **up** hochziehen; ~ **a lift** per Anhalter fahren, (*fam*) trampen. ~-**hike** *vi* per Anhalter fahren, (*fam*) trampen. ~-**hiker** *n* Anhalter(in) *m*(*f*)

hither /'hɪðə(r)/ *adv* hierher; ~ **and thither** hin und her. ~'**to** *adv* bisher

hive /haɪv/ *n* Bienenstock *m*. ~ **off** *vt* (*Comm*) abspalten

hoard /hɔːd/ *n* Hort *m* • *vt* horten, hamstern

hoarding /'hɔːdɪŋ/ *n* Bauzaun *m*; (*with advertisements*) Reklamewand *f*

hoar-frost /'hɔː-/ *n* Rauhreif *m*

hoarse /hɔːs/ *a* (-**r**, -**st**), -**ly** *adv* heiser. ~**ness** *n* Heiserkeit *f*

hoax /həʊks/ *n* übler Scherz *m*; (*false alarm*) blinder Alarm *m*

hob /hɒb/ *n* Kochmulde *f*

hobble /'hɒbl/ *vi* humpeln

hobby /'hɒbɪ/ *n* Hobby *nt*. ~**horse** *n* (*fig*) Lieblingsthema *nt*

hobnailed /'hɒb-/ *a* ~ **boots** *pl* genagelte Schuhe *pl*

hock /hɒk/ *n* [weißer] Rheinwein *m*

hockey /'hɒkɪ/ *n* Hockey *nt*

hoe /həʊ/ *n* Hacke *f* • *vt* (*pres p* **hoeing**) hacken

hog /hɒg/ *n* [Mast]schwein *nt* • *vt* (*pt/pp* **hogged**) (*fam*) mit Beschlag belegen

hoist /hɔɪst/ *n* Lastenaufzug *m* • *vt* hochziehen; hissen ⟨*flag*⟩

hold[1] /həʊld/ *n* (*Naut*) Laderaum *m*

hold[2] *n* Halt *m*; (*Sport*) Griff *m*; (*fig: influence*) Einfluß *m*; **get** ~ **of** fassen; (*fam: contact*) erreichen • *v* (*pt/pp* **held**) • *vt* halten; ⟨*container:*⟩ fassen; (*believe*) meinen; (*possess*) haben; anhalten ⟨*breath*⟩; ~ **one's tongue** den Mund halten • *vi* ⟨*rope:*⟩ halten; ⟨*weather:*⟩ sich halten; **not** ~ **with** (*fam*) nicht einverstanden sein mit. ~ **back** *vt* zurückhalten • *vi* zögern. ~ **on** *vi* (*wait*) warten; (*on telephone*) am Apparat bleiben; ~ **on to** (*keep*) behalten; (*cling to*) sich festhalten an (+ *dat*). ~ **out** *vt* hinhalten • *vi* (*resist*) aushalten. ~ **up** *vt* hochhalten; (*delay*) aufhalten; (*rob*) überfallen

'**hold|all** *n* Reisetasche *f*. ~**er** *n* Inhaber(in) *m*(*f*); (*container*) Halter *m*. ~-**up** *n* Verzögerung *f*; (*attack*) Überfall *m*

hole /həʊl/ *n* Loch *nt*

holiday /'hɒlədeɪ/ *n* Urlaub *m*; (*Sch*) Ferien *pl*; (*public*) Feiertag *m*; (*day off*) freier Tag *m*; **go on** ~ in Urlaub fahren. ~-**maker** *n* Urlauber(in) *m*(*f*)

holiness /'həʊlɪnɪs/ *n* Heiligkeit *f*

Holland /'hɒlənd/ *n* Holland *nt*

hollow /'hɒləʊ/ *a* hohl; ⟨*promise*⟩ leer • *n* Vertiefung *f*; (*in ground*) Mulde *f*. ~ **out** *vt* aushöhlen

holly /'hɒlɪ/ *n* Stechpalme *f*

'**hollyhock** *n* Stockrose *f*

hologram /'hɒləɡræm/ n Hologramm nt

holster /'həʊlstə(r)/ n Pistolentasche f

holy /'həʊlɪ/ a (-ier, -iest) heilig. **H~ Ghost** or **Spirit** n Heiliger Geist m. **~ water** n Weihwasser nt. **H~ Week** n Karwoche f

homage /'hɒmɪdʒ/ n Huldigung f; **pay ~ to** huldigen (+ dat)

home /həʊm/ n Zuhause nt; (house) Haus nt; (institution) Heim nt; (native land) Heimat f • adv **at ~** zu Hause; **come/go ~** nach Hause kommen/gehen

home: ~ ad'dress n Heimatanschrift f. **~ com'puter** n Heimcomputer m. **~ game** n Heimspiel nt. **~help** n Haushaltshilfe f. **~land** n Heimatland nt. **~less** a obdachlos

homely /'həʊmlɪ/ a (-ier, -iest) a gemütlich; (Amer: ugly) unscheinbar

home: ~-'made a selbstgemacht. **H~ Office** n Innenministerium nt. **H~ 'Secretary** n Innenminister m. **~sick** a **be ~sick** Heimweh haben (**for** nach). **~sickness** n Heimweh nt. **~ 'town** n Heimatstadt f. **~work** n (Sch) Hausaufgaben pl

homicide /'hɒmɪsaɪd/ n Totschlag m; (murder) Mord m

homoeopath|ic /həʊmɪə'pæθɪk/ a homöopathisch. **~y** /-'ɒpəθɪ/ n Homöopathie f

homogeneous /hɒmə'dʒiːnɪəs/ a homogen

homo'sexual a homosexuell • n Homosexuelle(r) m/f

honest /'ɒnɪst/ a, **-ly** adv ehrlich. **~y** n Ehrlichkeit f

honey /'hʌnɪ/ n Honig m; (fam: darling) Schatz m

honey: ~comb n Honigwabe f. **~moon** n Flitterwochen pl; (journey) Hochzeitsreise f. **~suckle** n Geißblatt nt

honk /hɒŋk/ vi hupen

honorary /'ɒnərərɪ/ a ehrenamtlich; (member, doctorate) Ehren-

honour /'ɒnə(r)/ n Ehre f • vt ehren; honorieren (cheque). **~able** /-əbl/ a, **-bly** adv ehrenhaft

hood /hʊd/ n Kapuze f; (of pram) [Klapp]verdeck nt; (over cooker) Abzugshaube f; (Auto, Amer) Kühlerhaube f

hoodlum /'huːdləm/ n Rowdy m

'hoodwink vt (fam) reinlegen

hoof /huːf/ n (pl ~s or **hooves**) Huf m

hook /hʊk/ n Haken m; **by ~ or by crook** mit allen Mitteln • vt festhaken (**to** an + acc)

hook|ed /hʊkt/ a **~ed nose** Hakennase f; **~ed on** (fam) abhängig von; (keen on) besessen von. **~er** n (Amer, sl) Nutte f

hookey /'hʊkɪ/ n **play ~** (Amer, fam) schwänzen

hooligan /'huːlɪɡən/ n Rowdy m. **~ism** n Rowdytum nt

hoop /huːp/ n Reifen m

hooray /hʊ'reɪ/ int & n = **hurrah**

hoot /huːt/ n Ruf m; **~s of laughter** schallendes Gelächter nt • vi (owl:) rufen; (car:) hupen; (jeer) johlen. **~er** n (of factory) Sirene f; (Auto) Hupe f

hoover /'huːvə(r)/ n **H~** (P) Staubsauger m • vt/i [staub]saugen

hop¹ /hɒp/ n, & **~s** pl Hopfen m

hop² n Hüpfer m; **catch s.o. on the ~** (fam) jdm ungelegen kommen • vi (pt/pp **hopped**) hüpfen; **~ it!** (fam) hau ab! **~ in** vi (fam) einsteigen. **~ out** vi (fam) aussteigen

hope /həʊp/ n Hoffnung f; (prospect) Aussicht f (**of** auf + acc) • vt/i hoffen (**for** auf + acc); **I ~ so** hoffentlich

hope|ful /'həʊpfl/ a hoffnungsvoll; **be ~ful that** hoffen, daß. **~fully** adv hoffnungsvoll; (it is hoped) hoffentlich. **~less** a, **-ly** adv hoffnungslos; (useless) nutzlos; (incompetent) untauglich

horde /hɔːd/ n Horde f

horizon /hə'raɪzn/ n Horizont m; **on the ~** am Horizont

horizontal /hɒrɪ'zɒntl/ a, **-ly** adv horizontal. **~'bar** n Reck nt

horn /hɔːn/ n Horn nt; (Auto) Hupe f

hornet /'hɔːnɪt/ n Hornisse f

horny /'hɔːnɪ/ a schwielig

horoscope /'hɒrəskəʊp/ n Horoskop nt

horrible /'hɒrɪbl/ a, **-bly** adv schrecklich

horrid /'hɒrɪd/ a gräßlich

horrific /hə'rɪfɪk/ a entsetzlich

horrify /'hɒrɪfaɪ/ vt (pt/pp **-ied**) entsetzen

horror /'hɒrə(r)/ n Entsetzen nt. **~ film** n Horrorfilm m

hors-d'œuvre /ɔː'dɜːvr/ n Vorspeise f

horse /hɔːs/ n Pferd nt

horse: ~**back** n on ~**back** zu Pferde.
~**'chestnut** n [Roß]kastanie f.
~**man** n Reiter m. ~**play** n Toben nt.
~**power** n Pferdestärke f. ~**racing**
n Pferderennen nt. ~**radish** n Meer-
rettich m. ~**shoe** n Hufeisen nt

horti'cultural /hɔ:tɪ-/ a Garten-
'**horticulture** n Gartenbau m

hose /həʊz/ n (pipe) Schlauch m ● vt
~ **down** abspritzen

hosiery /'həʊʒərɪ/ n Strumpfwaren pl

hospice /'hɒspɪs/ n Heim nt; (for the
terminally ill) Sterbeklinik f

hospitable /hɒ'spɪtəbl/ a, **-bly** adv
gastfreundlich

hospital /'hɒspɪtl/ n Krankenhaus
nt

hospitality /hɒspɪ'tælətɪ/ n Gast-
freundschaft f

host[1] /həʊst/ n **a ~ of** eine Menge von

host[2] n Gastgeber m

host[3] n (Relig) Hostie f

hostage /'hɒstɪdʒ/ n Geisel f

hostel /'hɒstl/ n [Wohn]heim nt

hostess /'həʊstɪs/ n Gastgeberin f

hostile /'hɒstaɪl/ a feindlich; (unfriendly) feindselig

hostilit|y /hɒ'stɪlətɪ/ n Feindschaft
f; ~**ies** pl Feindseligkeiten pl

hot /hɒt/ a (**hotter, hottest**) heiß;
(meal) warm; (spicy) scharf; **I am** or **feel**
~ mir ist heiß

'**hotbed** n (fig) Brutstätte f

hotchpotch /'hɒtʃpɒtʃ/ n Misch-
masch m

hotel /həʊ'tel/ n Hotel nt. ~**ier**
/-ɪə(r)/ n Hotelier m

hot: ~**head** n Hitzkopf m.
~'**headed** a hitzköpfig. ~**house** n
Treibhaus nt. ~**ly** adv (fig) heiß, heftig. ~**plate** n Tellerwärmer m; (of
cooker) Kochplatte f. ~ **tap** n Warm-
wasserhahn m. ~**tempered** a jäh-
zornig. ~'**water bottle** n
Wärmflasche f

hound /haʊnd/ n Jagdhund m ● vt
(fig) verfolgen

hour /'aʊə(r)/ n Stunde f. ~**ly** a & adv
stündlich; ~**ly pay** or **rate** Stun-
denlohn m

house[1] /haʊs/ n Haus nt; **at my** ~ bei
mir

house[2] /haʊz/ vt unterbringen

house /haʊs/: ~**boat** n Hausboot nt.
~**breaking** n Einbruch m. ~**hold** n
Haushalt m. ~**holder** n Haus-
inhaber(in) m(f). ~**keeper** n

Haushälterin f. ~**keeping** n Haus-
wirtschaft f; (money) Haushaltsgeld
nt. ~**plant** n Zimmerpflanze f.
~**trained** a stubenrein.
~**warming** n **have a** ~**warming
party** Einstand feiern. ~**wife** n Haus-
frau f. ~**work** n Hausarbeit f

housing /'haʊzɪŋ/ n Wohnungen pl;
(Techn) Gehäuse nt. ~ **estate** n
Wohnsiedlung f

hovel /'hɒvl/ n elende Hütte f

hover /'hɒvə(r)/ vi schweben; (be
undecided) schwanken; (linger)
herumstehen. ~**craft** n Luftkissen-
fahrzeug nt

how /haʊ/ adv wie; ~ **do you do?**
guten Tag! ~ **many** wie viele; ~ **much**
wieviel; **and** ~! und ob!

how'ever adv (in question) wie;
(nevertheless) jedoch, aber; ~ **small**
wie klein es auch sein mag

howl /haʊl/ n Heulen nt ● vi heulen;
(baby:) brüllen. ~**er** n (fam) Schnitzer m

hub /hʌb/ n Nabe f; (fig) Mittelpunkt
m

hubbub /'hʌbʌb/ n Stimmengewirr
nt

'**hub-cap** n Radkappe f

huddle /'hʌdl/ vi ~ **together** sich
zusammendrängen

hue[1] /hju:/ n Farbe f

hue[2] n ~ **and cry** Aufruhr m

huff /hʌf/ n **in a** ~ beleidigt

hug /hʌg/ n Umarmung f ● vt (pt/pp
hugged) umarmen

huge /hju:dʒ/ a, **-ly** adv riesig

hulking /'hʌlkɪŋ/ a (fam) unge-
schlacht

hull /hʌl/ n (Naut) Rumpf m

hullo /hə'ləʊ/ int = **hallo**

hum /hʌm/ n Summen nt; Brummen
nt ● vt/i (pt/pp **hummed**) summen;
(motor:) brummen; ~ **and haw** nicht
mit der Sprache herauswollen

human /'hju:mən/ a menschlich ● n
Mensch m. ~ **being** n Mensch m

humane /hju:'meɪn/ a, **-ly** adv
human

humanitarian /hju:mænɪ'teərɪən/ a
humanitär

humanit|y /hju:'mænətɪ/ n Mensch-
heit f; ~**ies** pl (Univ) Geisteswissenschaften pl

humble /'hʌmbl/ a (**-r, -st**), **-bly** adv
demütig ● vt demütigen

'**humdrum** a eintönig

humid /'hju:mɪd/ *a* feucht. **~ity**
/-'mɪdətɪ/ *n* Feuchtigkeit *f*

humiliat|e /hju:'mɪlɪeɪt/ *vt* de-
mütigen. **~ion** /-'eɪʃn/ *n* Demütigung *f*

humility /hju:'mɪlətɪ/ *n* Demut *f*

'**humming-bird** *n* Kolibri *m*

humorous /'hju:mərəs/ *a*, **-ly** *adv*
humorvoll; ⟨*story*⟩ humoristisch

humour /'hju:mə(r)/ *n* Humor *m*;
(*mood*) Laune *f*; **have a sense of ~**
Humor haben ● *vt* ~ **s.o.** jdm seinen
Willen lassen

hump /hʌmp/ *n* Buckel *m*; (*of camel*)
Höcker *m* ● *vt* schleppen

hunch /hʌntʃ/ *n* (*idea*) Ahnung *f*

'**hunch|back** *n* Bucklige(r) *m/f*.
~ed *a* ⟍**ed up** gebeugt

hundred /'hʌndrəd/ *a* **one/a ~** [ein]-
hundert ● *n* Hundert *nt*; (*written
figure*) Hundert *f*. **~th** *a* hundert-
ste(r,s) ● *n* Hundertstel *nt*. **~weight**
n ≈ Zentner *m*

hung /hʌŋ/ *see* hang

Hungarian /hʌŋ'geərɪən/ *a* unga-
risch ● *n* Ungar(in) *m(f)*

Hungary /'hʌŋgərɪ/ *n* Ungarn *nt*

hunger /'hʌŋgə(r)/ *n* Hunger *m*.
~-strike *n* Hungerstreik *m*

hungry /'hʌŋgrɪ/ *a* (**-ier, -iest**), **-ily**
adv hungrig; **be ~** Hunger haben

hunk /hʌŋk/ *n* [großes] Stück *nt*

hunt /hʌnt/ *n* Jagd *f*; (*for criminal*)
Fahndung *f* ● *vt/i* jagen; fahnden
nach ⟨*criminal*⟩; **~ for** suchen. **~er** *n*
Jäger *m*; (*horse*) Jagdpferd *nt*. **~ing**
n Jagd *f*

hurdle /'hɜ:dl/ *n* (*Sport & fig*) Hürde
f. **~r** *n* Hürdenläufer(in) *m(f)*

hurl /hɜ:l/ *vt* schleudern

hurrah /hʊ'rɑ:/, **hurray** /hʊ'reɪ/ *int*
hurra! ● *n* Hurra *nt*

hurricane /'hʌrɪkən/ *n* Orkan *m*

hurried /'hʌrɪd/ *a*, **-ly** *adv* eilig;
(*superficial*) flüchtig

hurry /'hʌrɪ/ *n* Eile *f*; **be in a ~** es eilig
haben ● *vi* (*pt/pp* **-ied**) sich beeilen; (*go
quickly*) eilen. **~ up** *vi* sich beeilen
● *vt* antreiben

hurt /hɜ:t/ *n* Schmerz *m* ● *vt/i* (*pt/pp*
hurt) weh tun (+ *dat*); (*injure*) verletzen; (*offend*) kränken. **~ful** *a* verletzend

hurtle /'hɜ:tl/ *vi* ~ **along** rasen

husband /'hʌzbənd/ *n* [Ehe]mann *m*

hush /hʌʃ/ *n* Stille *f* ● *vt* ~ **up** vertuschen. **~ed** *a* gedämpft. **~-'hush**
a (*fam*) streng geheim

husk /hʌsk/ *n* Spelze *f*

husky /'hʌskɪ/ *a* (**-ier, -iest**) heiser;
(*burly*) stämmig

hustle /'hʌsl/ *vt* drängen ● *n* Gedränge *nt*; ~ **and bustle** geschäftiges
Treiben *nt*

hut /hʌt/ *n* Hütte *f*

hutch /hʌtʃ/ *n* [Kaninchen]stall *m*

hybrid /'haɪbrɪd/ *a* hybrid ● *n*
Hybride *f*

hydrangea /haɪ'dreɪndʒə/ *n* Hortensie *f*

hydrant /'haɪdrənt/ *n* [**fire**] ~
Hydrant *m*

hydraulic /haɪ'drɔ:lɪk/ *a*, **-ally** *adv*
hydraulisch

hydrochloric /haɪdrə'klɔ:rɪk/ *a* ~
acid Salzsäure *f*

hydroe'lectric /haɪdrəʊ-/ *a* hydroelektrisch. ~ **power station** *n*
Wasserkraftwerk *nt*

hydrofoil /'haɪdrə-/ *n* Tragflügel-
boot *nt*

hydrogen /'haɪdrədʒən/ *n* Wasser-
stoff *m*

hyena /haɪ'i:nə/ *n* Hyäne *f*

hygien|e /'haɪdʒi:n/ *n* Hygiene *f*.
~ic /haɪ'dʒi:nɪk/ *a*, **-ally** *adv* hygienisch

hymn /hɪm/ *n* Kirchenlied *nt*.
~-book *n* Gesangbuch *nt*

hyphen /'haɪfn/ *n* Bindestrich *m*.
~ate *vt* mit Bindestrich schreiben

hypno|sis /hɪp'nəʊsɪs/ *n* Hypnose *f*.
~tic /-'nɒtɪk/ *a* hypnotisch

hypno|tism /'hɪpnətɪzm/ *n* Hyp-
notik *f*. **~tist** /-tɪst/ *n* Hypnotiseur
m. **~tize** *vt* hypnotisieren

hypochondriac /haɪpə'kɒndrɪæk/ *a*
hypochondrisch ● *n* Hypochonder *m*

hypocrisy /hɪ'pɒkrəsɪ/ *n* Heuchelei *f*

hypocrit|e /'hɪpəkrɪt/ *n* Heuch-
ler(in) *m(f)*. **~ical** /-'krɪtɪkl/ *a*, **-ly**
adv heuchlerisch

hypodermic /haɪpə'dɜ:mɪk/ *a & n* ~
[**syringe**] Injektionsspritze *f*

hypothe|sis /haɪ'pɒθəsɪs/ *n* Hypo-
these *f*. **~tical** /-ə'θetɪkl/ *a*, **-ly** *adv*
hypothetisch

hyster|ia /hɪ'stɪərɪə/ *n* Hysterie *f*.
~ical /-'sterɪkl/ *a*, **-ly** *adv* hysterisch.
~ics /hɪ'sterɪks/ *npl* hysterischer
Anfall *m*

I

I /aɪ/ *pron* ich

ice /aɪs/ *n* Eis *nt* ● *vt* mit Zuckerguß
überziehen ⟨*cake*⟩

ice: ~ **age** *n* Eiszeit *f.* ~**-axe** *n* Eispickel *m.* ~**berg** /-bɜːg/ *n* Eisberg *m.* ~**box** *n* (*Amer*) Kühlschrank *m.* ~**-'cream** *n* [Speise]eis *nt.* ~**-'cream parlour** *n* Eisdiele *f.* ~**-cube** *n* Eiswürfel *m*

Iceland /'aɪslənd/ *n* Island *nt*

ice: ~ **'lolly** *n* Eis *nt* am Stiel. ~ **rink** *n* Eisbahn *f*

icicle /'aɪsɪkl/ *n* Eiszapfen *m*

icing /'aɪsɪŋ/ *n* Zuckerguß *m.* ~ **sugar** *n* Puderzucker *m*

icon /'aɪkɒn/ *n* Ikone *f*

icy /'aɪsɪ/ *a* (**-ier, -iest**), **-ily** *adv* eisig; ⟨*road*⟩ vereist

idea /aɪ'dɪə/ *n* Idee *f;* (*conception*) Vorstellung *f.* **I have no** ~! ich habe keine Ahnung!

ideal /aɪ'dɪəl/ *a* ideal ● *n* Ideal *nt.* ~**ism** *n* Idealismus *m.* ~**ist** *n* Idealist(in) *m(f).* ~**istic** /-'lɪstɪk/ *a* idealistisch. ~**ize** *vt* idealisieren. ~**ly** *adv* ideal; (*in ideal circumstances*) idealerweise

identical /aɪ'dentɪkl/ *a* identisch; ⟨*twins*⟩ eineiig

identi|fication /aɪdentɪfɪ'keɪʃn/ *n* Identifizierung *f;* (*proof of identity*) Ausweispapiere *pl.* ~**fy** /aɪ'dentɪfaɪ/ *vt* (*pt/pp* **-ied**) identifizieren

identity /aɪ'dentətɪ/ *n* Identität *f.* ~ **card** *n* [Personal]ausweis *m*

ideolog|ical /aɪdɪə'lɒdʒɪkl/ *a* ideologisch. ~**y** /aɪdɪ'ɒlədʒɪ/ *n* Ideologie *f*

idiom /'ɪdɪəm/ *n* [feste] Redewendung *f.* ~**atic** /-'mætɪk/ *a,* **-ally** *adv* idiomatisch

idiosyncrasy /ɪdɪə'sɪŋkrəsɪ/ *n* Eigenart *f*

idiot /'ɪdɪət/ *n* Idiot *m.* ~**ic** /-'ɒtɪk/ *a* idiotisch

idle /'aɪdl/ *a* (**-r, -st**), **-ly** *adv* untätig; (*lazy*) faul; (*empty*) leer; ⟨*machine*⟩ nicht in Betrieb ● *vi* faulenzen; ⟨*engine:*⟩ leer laufen. ~**ness** *n* Untätigkeit *f;* Faulheit *f*

idol /'aɪdl/ *n* Idol *nt.* ~**ize** /'aɪdəlaɪz/ *vt* vergöttern

idyllic /ɪ'dɪlɪk/ *a* idyllisch

i.e. *abbr* (**id est**) d.h.

if /ɪf/ *conj* wenn; (*whether*) ob; **as if** als ob

ignite /ɪg'naɪt/ *vt* entzünden ● *vi* sich entzünden

ignition /ɪg'nɪʃn/ *n* (*Auto*) Zündung *f.* ~ **key** *n* Zündschlüssel *m*

ignoramus /ɪgnə'reɪməs/ *n* Ignorant *m*

ignoran|ce /'ɪgnərəns/ *n* Unwissenheit *f.* ~**t** *a* unwissend; (*rude*) ungehobelt

ignore /ɪg'nɔː(r)/ *vt* ignorieren

ilk /ɪlk/ *n* (*fam*) **of that** ~ von der Sorte

ill /ɪl/ *a* krank; (*bad*) schlecht; **feel** ~ **at ease** sich unbehaglich fühlen ● *adv* schlecht ● *n* Schlechte(s) *nt;* (*evil*) Übel *nt.* ~**-advised** *a* unklug. ~**-bred** *a* schlecht erzogen

illegal /ɪ'liːgl/ *a,* **-ly** *adv* illegal

illegible /ɪ'ledʒəbl/ *a,* **-bly** *adv* unleserlich

illegitima|cy /ɪlɪ'dʒɪtɪməsɪ/ *n* Unehelichkeit *f.* ~**te** /-mət/ *a* unehelich; ⟨*claim*⟩ unberechtigt

illicit /ɪ'lɪsɪt/ *a,* **-ly** *adv* illegal

illitera|cy /ɪ'lɪtərəsɪ/ *n* Analphabetentum *nt.* ~**te** /-rət/ *a* **be** ~**te** nicht lesen und schreiben können ● *n* Analphabet(in) *m(f)*

illness /'ɪlnɪs/ *n* Krankheit *f*

illogical /ɪ'lɒdʒɪkl/ *a,* **-ly** *adv* unlogisch

ill-treat /ɪl'triːt/ *vt* mißhandeln. ~**ment** *n* Mißhandlung *f*

illuminat|e /ɪ'luːmɪneɪt/ *vt* beleuchten. ~**ing** *a* aufschlußreich. ~**ion** /-'neɪʃn/ *n* Beleuchtung *f*

illusion /ɪ'luːʒn/ *n* Illusion *f;* **be under the** ~ **that** sich (*dat*) einbilden, daß

illusory /ɪ'luːsərɪ/ *a* illusorisch

illustrat|e /'ɪləstreɪt/ *vt* illustrieren. ~**ion** /-'streɪʃn/ *n* Illustration *f*

illustrious /ɪ'lʌstrɪəs/ *a* berühmt

image /'ɪmɪdʒ/ *n* Bild *nt;* (*statue*) Standbild *nt;* (*figure*) Figur *f;* (*exact likeness*) Ebenbild *nt;* [**public**] ~ Image *nt*

imagin|able /ɪ'mædʒɪnəbl/ *a* vorstellbar. ~**ary** /-ərɪ/ *a* eingebildet

imaginat|ion /ɪmædʒɪ'neɪʃn/ *n* Phantasie *f;* (*fancy*) Einbildung *f.* ~**ive** /ɪ'mædʒɪnətɪv/ *a,* **-ly** *adv* phantasievoll; (*full of ideas*) einfallsreich

imagine /ɪ'mædʒɪn/ *vt* sich (*dat*) vorstellen; (*wrongly*) sich (*dat*) einbilden

im'balance *n* Unausgeglichenheit *f*

imbecile /'ɪmbəsiːl/ *n* Schwachsinnige(r) *m/f;* (*pej*) Idiot *m*

imbibe /ɪm'baɪb/ vt trinken; (fig) aufnehmen

imbue /ɪm'bjuː/ vt be ~d with erfüllt sein von

imitat|e /'ɪmɪteɪt/ vt nachahmen, imitieren. ~ion /-'teɪʃn/ n Nachahmung f, Imitation f

immaculate /ɪ'mækjʊlət/ a, -ly adv tadellos; (Relig) unbefleckt

imma'terial a (unimportant) unwichtig, unwesentlich

imma'ture a unreif

immediate /ɪ'miːdɪət/ a sofortig; (nearest) nächste(r,s). ~ly adv sofort; ~ly next to unmittelbar neben ● conj sobald

immemorial /ɪmə'mɔːrɪəl/ a from time ~ seit Urzeiten

immense /ɪ'mens/ a, -ly adv riesig; (fam) enorm; (extreme) äußerst

immers|e /ɪ'mɜːs/ vt untertauchen; be ~ed in (fig) vertieft sein in (+ acc). ~ion /-ɜːʃn/ n Untertauchen nt. ~ion heater n Heißwasserbereiter m

immigrant /'ɪmɪɡrənt/ n Einwanderer m

immigrat|e /'ɪmɪɡreɪt/ vi einwandern. ~ion /-'ɡreɪʃn/ n Einwanderung f

imminent /'ɪmɪnənt/ a be ~ unmittelbar bevorstehen

immobil|e /ɪ'məʊbaɪl/ a unbeweglich. ~ize /-bəlaɪz/ vt (fig) lähmen; (Med) ruhigstellen

immoderate /ɪ'mɒdərət/ a übermäßig

immodest /ɪ'mɒdɪst/ a unbescheiden

immoral /ɪ'mɒrəl/ a, -ly adv unmoralisch. ~ity /ɪmə'rælətɪ/ n Unmoral f

immortal /ɪ'mɔːtl/ a unsterblich. ~ity /-'tælətɪ/ n Unsterblichkeit f. ~ize vt verewigen

immovable /ɪ'muːvəbl/ a unbeweglich; (fig) fest

immune /ɪ'mjuːn/ a immun (to/from gegen). ~ system n Abwehrsystem nt

immunity /ɪ'mjuːnətɪ/ n Immunität f

immunize /'ɪmjʊnaɪz/ vt immunisieren

imp /ɪmp/ n Kobold m

impact /'ɪmpækt/ n Aufprall m; (collision) Zusammenprall m; (of bomb) Einschlag m; (fig) Auswirkung f

impair /ɪm'peə(r)/ vt beeinträchtigen

impale /ɪm'peɪl/ vt aufspießen

impart /ɪm'pɑːt/ vt übermitteln (to dat); vermitteln (knowledge)

im'parti|al a unparteiisch. ~'ality n Unparteilichkeit f

im'passable a unpassierbar

impasse /æm'pɑːs/ n (fig) Sackgasse f

impassioned /ɪm'pæʃnd/ a leidenschaftlich

im'passive a, -ly adv unbeweglich

im'patien|ce n Ungeduld f. ~t a, -ly adv ungeduldig

impeach /ɪm'piːtʃ/ vt anklagen

impeccable /ɪm'pekəbl/ a, -bly adv tadellos

impede /ɪm'piːd/ vt behindern

impediment /ɪm'pedɪmənt/ n Hindernis nt; (in speech) Sprachfehler m

impel /ɪm'pel/ vt (pt/pp impelled) treiben; feel ~led sich genötigt fühlen (to zu)

impending /ɪm'pendɪŋ/ a bevorstehend

impenetrable /ɪm'penɪtrəbl/ a undurchdringlich

imperative /ɪm'perətɪv/ a be ~ dringend notwendig sein ● n (Gram) Imperativ m, Befehlsform f

imper'ceptible a nicht wahrnehmbar

im'perfect a unvollkommen; (faulty) fehlerhaft ● n (Gram) Imperfekt nt. ~ion /-'fekʃn/ n Unvollkommenheit f; (fault) Fehler m

imperial /ɪm'pɪərɪəl/ a kaiserlich. ~ism n Imperialismus m

imperil /ɪm'perəl/ vt (pt/pp imperilled) gefährden

imperious /ɪm'pɪərɪəs/ a, -ly adv herrisch

im'personal a unpersönlich

impersonat|e /ɪm'pɜːsəneɪt/ vt sich ausgeben als; (Theat) nachahmen, imitieren. ~or n Imitator m

impertinen|ce /ɪm'pɜːtɪnəns/ n Frechheit f. ~t a frech

imperturbable /ɪmpə'tɜːbəbl/ a unerschütterlich

impervious /ɪm'pɜːvɪəs/ a ~ to (fig) unempfänglich für

impetuous /ɪm'petjʊəs/ a, -ly adv ungestüm

impetus /'ɪmpɪtəs/ n Schwung m

impish /'ɪmpɪʃ/ a schelmisch

implacable /ɪm'plækəbl/ *a* unerbittlich

im'plant[1] *vt* einpflanzen

'implant[2] *n* Implantat *nt*

implement[1] /'ɪmplɪmənt/ *n* Gerät *nt*

implement[2] /'ɪmplɪment/ *vt* ausführen

implicat|e /'ɪmplɪkeɪt/ *vt* verwickeln. **~ion** /-'keɪʃn/ *n* Verwicklung *f*; **~ions** *pl* Auswirkungen *pl*; **by ~ion** implizit

implicit /ɪm'plɪsɪt/ *a*, **-ly** *adv* unausgesprochen; (*absolute*) unbedingt

implore /ɪm'plɔː(r)/ *vt* anflehen

imply /ɪm'plaɪ/ *vt* (*pt/pp* **-ied**) andeuten; **what are you ~ing?** was wollen Sie damit sagen?

impo'lite *a*, **-ly** *adv* unhöflich

import[1] /'ɪmpɔːt/ *n* Import *m*, Einfuhr *f*; (*importance*) Wichtigkeit *f*; (*meaning*) Bedeutung *f*

import[2] /ɪm'pɔːt/ *vt* importieren, einführen

importan|ce /ɪm'pɔːtns/ *n* Wichtigkeit *f*. **~t** *a* wichtig

importer /ɪm'pɔːtə(r)/ *n* Importeur *m*

impos|e /ɪm'pəʊz/ *vt* auferlegen (**on** *dat*) ● *vi* sich aufdrängen (**on** *dat*). **~ing** *a* eindrucksvoll. **~ition** /ɪmpə'zɪʃn/ *n* **be an ~ition** eine Zumutung sein

impossi'bility *n* Unmöglichkeit *f*

im'possible *a*, **-bly** *adv* unmöglich

impostor /ɪm'pɒstə(r)/ *n* Betrüger(in) *m(f)*

impoten|ce /'ɪmpətəns/ *n* Machtlosigkeit *f*; (*Med*) Impotenz *f*. **~t** *a* machtlos; (*Med*) impotent

impound /ɪm'paʊnd/ *vt* beschlagnahmen

impoverished /ɪm'pɒvərɪʃt/ *a* verarmt

im'practicable *a* undurchführbar

im'practical *a* unpraktisch

impre'cise *a* ungenau

impregnable /ɪm'pregnəbl/ *a* uneinnehmbar

impregnate /'ɪmpregneɪt/ *vt* tränken; (*Biol*) befruchten

im'press *vt* beeindrucken; **~ sth [up]on s.o.** jdm etw einprägen

impression /ɪm'preʃn/ *n* Eindruck *m*; (*imitation*) Nachahmung *f*; (*imprint*) Abdruck *m*; (*edition*) Auflage *f*. **~ism** *n* Impressionismus *m*

impressive /ɪm'presɪv/ *a* eindrucksvoll

'imprint[1] *n* Abdruck *m*

im'print[2] *vt* prägen; (*fig*) einprägen (**on** *dat*)

im'prison *vt* gefangenhalten; (*put in prison*) ins Gefängnis sperren

im'probable *a* unwahrscheinlich

impromptu /ɪm'prɒmptjuː/ *a* improvisiert ● *adv* aus dem Stegreif

im'proper *a*, **-ly** *adv* inkorrekt; (*indecent*) unanständig

impro'priety *n* Unkorrektheit *f*

improve /ɪm'pruːv/ *vt* verbessern; verschönern ⟨*appearance*⟩ ● *vi* sich bessern; **~ [up]on** übertreffen. **~ment** /-mənt/ *n* Verbesserung *f*; (*in health*) Besserung *f*

improvise /'ɪmprəvaɪz/ *vt/i* improvisieren

im'prudent *a* unklug

impuden|ce /'ɪmpjʊdəns/ *n* Frechheit *f*. **~t** *a*, **-ly** *adv* frech

impuls|e /'ɪmpʌls/ *n* Impuls *m*; **on [an] ~e** impulsiv. **~ive** /-'pʌlsɪv/ *a*, **-ly** *adv* impulsiv

impunity /ɪm'pjuːnətɪ/ *n* **with ~** ungestraft

im'pur|e *a* unrein. **~ity** *n* Unreinheit *f*; **~ities** *pl* Verunreinigungen *pl*

impute /ɪm'pjuːt/ *vt* zuschreiben (**to** *dat*)

in /ɪn/ *prep* in (+ *dat*/(*into*) + *acc*); **sit in the garden** im Garten sitzen; **go in the garden** in den Garten gehen; **in May** im Mai; **in the summer/winter** im Sommer/Winter; **in 1992** [im Jahre] 1992; **in this heat** bei dieser Hitze; **in the rain/sun** im Regen/in der Sonne; **in the evening** am Abend; **in the sky** am Himmel; **in the world** auf der Welt; **in the street** auf der Straße; **deaf in one ear** auf einem Ohr taub; **in the army** beim Militär; **in English/German** auf englisch/deutsch; **in ink/pencil** mit Tinte/ Bleistift; **in a soft/loud voice** mit leiser/lauter Stimme; **in doing this, he …** indem er das tut/ tat, … er ● *adv* (*at home*) zu Hause; (*indoors*) drinnen; **he's not in yet** er ist noch nicht da; **all in** alles inbegriffen; (*fam: exhausted*) kaputt; **day in, day out** tagaus, tagein; **keep in with s.o.** sich mit jdm gut stellen; **have it in for s.o.** (*fam*) es auf jdn abgesehen haben; **let oneself in for sth** sich auf etw (*acc*) einlassen; **send/go in** hineinschicken/ -gehen; **come/bring in** hereinkommen/-bringen ● *a* (*fam: in*

fashion) in ● *n* **the ins and outs** alle
Einzelheiten *pl*
ina'bility *n* Unfähigkeit *f*
inac'cessible *a* unzugänglich
in'accura|cy *n* Ungenauigkeit *f*.
~**te** *a*, ~**ly** *adv* ungenau
in'ac|tive *a* untätig. ~'**tivity** *n* Un-
tätigkeit *f*
in'adequate *a*, ~**ly** *adv* unzulänglich;
feel ~ sich der Situation nicht gewachsen fühlen
inad'missible *a* unzulässig
inadvertently /ɪnəd'vɜːtəntlɪ/ *adv*
versehentlich
inad'visable *a* nicht ratsam
inane /ɪ'neɪn/ *a*, ~**ly** *adv* albern
in'animate *a* unbelebt
in'applicable *a* nicht zutreffend
inap'propriate *a* unangebracht
inar'ticulate *a* undeutlich; **be** ~
sich nicht gut ausdrücken können
inat'tentive *a* unaufmerksam
in'audible *a*, **-bly** *adv* unhörbar
inaugural /ɪ'nɔːɡjʊrl/ *a* Antritts-
inaugurat|e /ɪ'nɔːɡjʊreɪt/ *vt* [feier-
lich] in sein Amt einführen. ~**ion**
/-'reɪʃn/ *n* Amtseinführung *f*
inau'spicious *a* ungünstig
inborn /'ɪnbɔːn/ *a* angeboren
inbred /ɪn'bred/ *a* angeboren
incalculable /ɪn'kælkjʊləbl/ *a* nicht
berechenbar; (*fig*) unabsehbar
in'capable *a* unfähig; **be** ~ **of doing
sth** nicht fähig sein, etw zu tun
incapacitate /ɪnkə'pæsɪteɪt/ *vt* unfähig machen
incarcerate /ɪn'kɑːsəreɪt/ *vt* ein-
kerkern
incarnat|e /ɪn'kɑːnət/ *a* **the devil** ~**e**
der leibhaftige Satan. ~**ion** /-'neɪʃn/ *n*
Inkarnation *f*
incendiary /ɪn'sendɪərɪ/ *a & n* ~
[bomb] Brandbombe *f*
incense[1] /'ɪnsens/ *n* Weihrauch *m*
incense[2] /ɪn'sens/ *vt* wütend machen
incentive /ɪn'sentɪv/ *n* Anreiz *m*
inception /ɪn'sepʃn/ *n* Beginn *m*
incessant /ɪn'sesnt/ *a*, ~**ly** *adv* unaufhörlich
incest /'ɪnsest/ *n* Inzest *m*, Blut-
schande *f*
inch /ɪntʃ/ *n* Zoll *m* ● *vi* ~ **forward**
sich ganz langsam vorwärtsschieben
inciden|ce /'ɪnsɪdəns/ *n* Vorkommen
nt. ~**t** *n* Zwischenfall *m*
incidental /ɪnsɪ'dentl/ *a* neben-
sächlich; (*remark*) beiläufig; (*expenses*) Neben-. ~**ly** *adv* übrigens

incinerat|e /ɪn'sɪnəreɪt/ *vt* verbren-
nen. ~**or** *n* Verbrennungsofen *m*
incipient /ɪn'sɪpɪənt/ *a* angehend
incision /ɪn'sɪʒn/ *n* Einschnitt *m*
incisive /ɪn'saɪsɪv/ *a* scharfsinnig
incisor /ɪn'saɪzə(r)/ *n* Schneidezahn
m
incite /ɪn'saɪt/ *vt* aufhetzen. ~**ment**
n Aufhetzung *f*
inci'vility *n* Unhöflichkeit *f*
in'clement *a* rauh
inclination /ɪnklɪ'neɪʃn/ *n* Neigung *f*
incline[1] /ɪn'klaɪn/ *vt* neigen; **be** ~**d to
do sth** dazu neigen, etw zu tun ● *vi* sich
neigen
incline[2] /'ɪnklaɪn/ *n* Neigung *f*
inclu|de /ɪn'kluːd/ *vt* einschließen;
(*contain*) enthalten; (*incorporate*)
aufnehmen (**in** in + *acc*). ~**ding** *prep*
einschließlich (+ *gen*). ~**sion** /-uː-
ʒn/ *n* Aufnahme *f*
inclusive /ɪn'kluːsɪv/ *a* Inklusiv-; ~
of einschließlich (+ *gen*) ● *adv* inklusive
incognito /ɪnkɒɡ'niːtəʊ/ *adv* inkognito
inco'herent *a*, ~**ly** *adv* zusam-
menhanglos; (*incomprehensible*) un-
verständlich
income /'ɪnkəm/ *n* Einkommen *nt*.
~ **tax** *n* Einkommensteuer *f*
'incoming *a* ankommend; (*mail,
call*) eingehend. ~ **tide** *n* steigende
Flut *f*
in'comparable *a* unvergleichlich
incom'patible *a* unvereinbar; **be** ~
(*people:*) nicht zueinander passen
in'competen|ce *n* Unfähigkeit *f*.
~**t** *a* unfähig
incom'plete *a* unvollständig
incompre'hensible *a* unverständ-
lich
incon'ceivable *a* undenkbar
incon'clusive *a* nicht schlüssig
incongruous /ɪn'kɒŋɡrʊəs/ *a* unpassend
inconsequential /ɪnkɒnsɪ'kwenʃl/
a unbedeutend
incon'siderate *a* rücksichtslos
incon'sistent *a*, ~**ly** *adv* widersprüchlich; (*illogical*) inkonsequent;
be ~ nicht übereinstimmen
inconsolable /ɪnkən'səʊləbl/ *a* untröstlich
incon'spicuous *a* unauffällig
incontinen|ce /ɪn'kɒntɪnəns/ *n* In-
kontinenz *f*. ~**t** *a* inkontinent

incon'venien|ce n Unannehmlichkeit f; (drawback) Nachteil m; **put s.o. to ∼ce** jdm Umstände machen. **∼t** a, **-ly** adv ungünstig; **be ∼t for s.o.** jdm nicht passen

incorporate /ın'kɔːpəreıt/ vt aufnehmen; (contain) enthalten

incor'rect a, **-ly** adv inkorrekt

incorrigible /ın'kʊrıdʒəbl/ a unverbesserlich

incorruptible /ınkə'rʌptəbl/ a unbestechlich

increase[1] /'ınkriːs/ n Zunahme f; (rise) Erhöhung f; **be on the ∼** zunehmen

increas|e[2] /ın'kriːs/ vt vergrößern; (raise) erhöhen ● vi zunehmen; (rise) sich erhöhen. **∼ing** a, **-ly** adv zunehmend

in'credible a, **-bly** adv unglaublich

incredulous /ın'kredjʊləs/ a ungläubig

increment /'ınkrımənt/ n Gehaltszulage f

incriminate /ın'krımıneıt/ vt (Jur) belasten

incubat|e /'ınkjʊbeıt/ vt ausbrüten. **∼ion** /-'beıʃn/ n Ausbrüten nt. **∼ion period** n (Med) Inkubationszeit f. **∼or** n (for baby) Brutkasten m

inculcate /'ınkʌlkeıt/ vt einprägen (in dat)

incumbent /ın'kʌmbənt/ a **be ∼ on s.o.** jds Pflicht sein

incur /ın'kɜː(r)/ vt (pt/pp incurred) sich (dat) zuziehen; machen ⟨debts⟩

in'curable a, **-bly** adv unheilbar

incursion /ın'kɜːʃn/ n Einfall m

indebted /ın'detıd/ a verpflichtet (to dat)

in'decent a, **-ly** adv unanständig

inde'cision n Unentschlossenheit f

inde'cisive a ergebnislos; ⟨person⟩ unentschlossen

indeed /ın'diːd/ adv in der Tat, tatsächlich; **yes ∼!** allerdings! **∼ I am/ do** och doch! **very much ∼** sehr; **thank you very much ∼** vielen herzlichen Dank

indefatigable /ındı'fætıgəbl/ a unermüdlich

in'definite a unbestimmt. **∼ly** adv unbegrenzt; ⟨postpone⟩ auf unbestimmte Zeit

indelible /ın'delıbl/ a, **-bly** adv nicht zu entfernen; (fig) unauslöschlich

indemni|fy /ın'demnıfaı/ vt (pt/pp -ied) versichern; (compensate) entschädigen. **∼ty** f Versicherung f; Entschädigung f

indent /ın'dent/ vt (Typ) einrücken. **∼ation** /-'teıʃn/ n Einrückung f; (notch) Kerbe f

inde'penden|ce n Unabhängigkeit f; (self-reliance) Selbständigkeit f. **∼t** a, **-ly** adv unabhängig; selbständig

indescribable /ındı'skraıbəbl/ a, **-bly** adv unbeschreiblich

indestructible /ındı'strʌktəbl/ a unzerstörbar

indeterminate /ındı'tɜːmınət/ a unbestimmt

index /'ındeks/ n Register nt

index: ∼ card n Karteikarte f. **∼ finger** n Zeigefinger m. **∼-linked** a ⟨pension⟩ dynamisch

India /'ındıə/ n Indien nt. **∼n** a indisch; (American) indianisch ● n Inder(in) m(f); (American) Indianer(in) m(f)

Indian: ∼ 'ink n Tusche f. **∼ 'summer** n Nachsommer m

indicat|e /'ındıkeıt/ vt zeigen; (point at) zeigen auf (+ acc); (hint) andeuten; (register) anzeigen ● vi (Auto) blinken. **∼ion** /-'keıʃn/ n Anzeichen nt

indicative /ın'dıkətıv/ a **be ∼ of** schließen lassen auf (+ acc) ● n (Gram) Indikativ m

indicator /'ındıkeıtə(r)/ n (Auto) Blinker m

indict /ın'daıt/ vt anklagen. **∼ment** n Anklage f

in'differen|ce n Gleichgültigkeit f. **∼t** a, **-ly** adv gleichgültig; (not good) mittelmäßig

indigenous /ın'dıdʒınəs/ a einheimisch

indi'gest|ible a unverdaulich; (difficult to digest) schwerverdaulich. **∼ion** n Magenverstimmung f

indigna|nt /ın'dıgnənt/ a, **-ly** adv entrüstet, empört. **∼tion** /-'neıʃn/ n Entrüstung f, Empörung f

in'dignity n Demütigung f

indi'rect a, **-ly** adv indirekt

indi'screet a indiskret

indis'cretion n Indiskretion f

indiscriminate /ındı'skrımınət/ a, **-ly** adv wahllos

indi'spensable a unentbehrlich

indisposed /ındı'spəʊzd/ a indisponiert

indisputable /ɪndɪ'spjuːtəbl/ *a*, **-bly** *adv* unbestreitbar

indi'stinct *a*, **-ly** *adv* undeutlich

indistinguishable /ɪndɪ'stɪŋgwɪʃəbl/ *a* **be** ~ nicht zu unterscheiden sein; *(not visible)* nicht erkennbar sein

individual /ɪndɪ'vɪdjʊəl/ *a*, **-ly** *adv* individuell; *(single)* einzeln ● *n* Individuum *nt.* ~**ity** /-'ælətɪ/ *n* Individualität *f*

indi'visible *a* unteilbar

indoctrinate /ɪn'dɒktrɪneɪt/ *vt* indoktrinieren

indolen|ce /'ɪndələns/ *n* Faulheit *f*. ~**t** *a* faul

indomitable /ɪn'dɒmɪtəbl/ *a* unbeugsam

indoor /'ɪndɔː(r)/ *a* Innen-; *(clothes)* Haus-; *(plant)* Zimmer-; *(Sport)* Hallen-. ~**s** /-'dɔːz/ *adv* im Haus, drinnen; **go** ~**s** ins Haus gehen

induce /ɪn'djuːs/ *vt* dazu bewegen (**to** zu); *(produce)* herbeiführen. ~**ment** *n* *(incentive)* Anreiz *m*

indulge /ɪn'dʌldʒ/ *vt* frönen (+ *dat)*; verwöhnen *(child)* ● *vi* ~ **in** frönen (+ *dat).* ~**nce** /-əns/ *n* Nachgiebigkeit *f*; *(leniency)* Nachsicht *f*. ~**nt** *a* [zu] nachgiebig; nachsichtig

industrial /ɪn'dʌstrɪəl/ *a* Industrie-; **take** ~ **action** streiken. ~**ist** *n* Industrielle(r) *m*. ~**ized** *a* industrialisiert

industr|ious /ɪn'dʌstrɪəs/ *a*, **-ly** *adv* fleißig. ~**y** /'ɪndəstrɪ/ *n* Industrie *f*; *(zeal)* Fleiß *m*

inebriated /ɪ'niːbrɪeɪtɪd/ *a* betrunken

in'edible *a* nicht eßbar

inef'fective *a*, **-ly** *adv* unwirksam; *(person)* untauglich

inef'fectual /ɪnɪ'fektʃʊəl/ *a* unwirksam; *(person)* untauglich

inef'ficient *a* unfähig; *(organization)* nicht leistungsfähig; *(method)* nicht rationell

in'eligible *a* nicht berechtigt

inept /ɪ'nept/ *a* ungeschickt

ine'quality *n* Ungleichheit *f*

inert /ɪ'nɜːt/ *a* unbeweglich; *(Phys)* träge. ~**ia** /ɪ'nɜːʃə/ *n* Trägheit *f*

inescapable /ɪnɪ'skeɪpəbl/ *a* unvermeidlich

inestimable /ɪn'estɪməbl/ *a* unschätzbar

inevitab|le /ɪn'evɪtəbl/ *a* unvermeidlich. ~**ly** *adv* zwangsläufig

ine'xact *a* ungenau

inex'cusable *a* unverzeihlich

inexhaustible /ɪnɪg'zɔːstəbl/ *a* unerschöpflich

inexorable /ɪn'eksərəbl/ *a* unerbittlich

inex'pensive *a*, **-ly** *adv* preiswert

inex'perience *n* Unerfahrenheit *f*. ~**d** *a* unerfahren

inexplicable /ɪnɪk'splɪkəbl/ *a* unerklärlich

in'fallible *a* unfehlbar

infam|ous /'ɪnfəməs/ *a* niederträchtig; *(notorious)* berüchtigt. ~**y** *n* Niederträchtigkeit *f*

infan|cy /'ɪnfənsɪ/ *n* frühe Kindheit *f*; *(fig)* Anfangsstadium *nt.* ~**t** *n* Kleinkind *nt.* ~**tile** *a* kindisch

infantry /'ɪnfəntrɪ/ *n* Infanterie *f*

infatuated /ɪn'fætʃʊeɪtɪd/ *a* vernarrt (**with** in + *acc)*

infect /ɪn'fekt/ *vt* anstecken, infizieren; **become** ~**ed** *(wound:)* sich infizieren. ~**ion** /-'fekʃn/ *n* Infektion *f*. ~**ious** /-'fekʃəs/ *a* ansteckend

infer /ɪn'fɜː(r)/ *vt* *(pt/pp* **inferred***)* folgern (**from** aus); *(imply)* andeuten. ~**ence** /'ɪnfərəns/ *n* Folgerung *f*

inferior /ɪn'fɪərɪə(r)/ *a* minderwertig; *(in rank)* untergeordnet ● *n* Untergebene(r) *m/f*

inferiority /ɪnfɪərɪ'ɒrətɪ/ *n* Minderwertigkeit *f*. ~ **complex** *n* Minderwertigkeitskomplex *m*

infern|al /ɪn'fɜːnl/ *a* höllisch. ~**o** *n* flammendes Inferno *nt*

in'fer'tile *a* unfruchtbar. ~**'tility** *n* Unfruchtbarkeit *f*

infest /ɪn'fest/ *vt* **be** ~**ed with** befallen sein von; *(place)* verseucht sein mit

infi'delity *n* Untreue *f*

infighting /'ɪnfaɪtɪŋ/ *n* *(fig)* interne Machtkämpfe *pl*

infiltrate /'ɪnfɪltreɪt/ *vt* infiltrieren; *(Pol)* unterwandern

infinite /'ɪnfɪnət/ *a*, **-ly** *adv* unendlich

infinitesimal /ɪnfɪnɪ'tesɪml/ *a* unendlich klein

infinitive /ɪn'fɪnətɪv/ *n* *(Gram)* Infinitiv *m*

infinity /ɪn'fɪnətɪ/ *n* Unendlichkeit *f*

infirm /ɪn'fɜːm/ *a* gebrechlich. ~**ary** *n* Krankenhaus *nt.* ~**ity** *n* Gebrechlichkeit *f*

inflame /ɪn'fleɪm/ *vt* entzünden; **become** ~**d** sich entzünden. ~**d** *a* entzündet

in'flammable *a* feuergefährlich

inflammation /ɪnfləˈmeɪʃn/ *n* Entzündung *f*

inflammatory /ɪnˈflæmətrɪ/ *a* aufrührerisch

inflatable /ɪnˈfleɪtəbl/ *a* aufblasbar

inflat|e /ɪnˈfleɪt/ *vt* aufblasen; (*with pump*) aufpumpen. **~ion** /-eɪʃn/ *n* Inflation *f*. **~ionary** /-eɪʃənərɪ/ *a* inflationär

in'flexible *a* starr; (*person*) unbeugsam

inflexion /ɪnˈflekʃn/ *n* Tonfall *m*; (*Gram*) Flexion *f*

inflict /ɪnˈflɪkt/ *vt* zufügen (**on** *dat*); versetzen (*blow*) (**on** *dat*)

influen|ce /ˈɪnflʊəns/ *n* Einfluß *m* ● *vt* beeinflussen. **~tial** /-ˈenʃl/ *a* einflußreich

influenza /ɪnflʊˈenzə/ *n* Grippe *f*

influx /ˈɪnflʌks/ *n* Zustrom *m*

inform /ɪnˈfɔːm/ *vt* benachrichtigen; (*officially*) informieren; **~ s.o. of sth** jdm etw mitteilen; **keep s.o. ~ed** jdn auf dem laufenden halten ● *vi* **~ against** denunzieren

in'for|mal *a*, **-ly** *adv* zwanglos; (*unofficial*) inoffiziell. **~'mality** *n* Zwanglosigkeit *f*

informant /ɪnˈfɔːmənt/ *n* Gewährsmann *m*

informat|ion /ɪnfəˈmeɪʃn/ *n* Auskunft *f*; **a piece of ~ion** eine Auskunft. **~ive** /-ˈfɔːmətɪv/ *a* aufschlußreich; (*instructive*) lehrreich

informer /ɪnˈfɔːmə(r)/ *n* Spitzel *m*; (*Pol*) Denunziant *m*

infra-'red /ɪnfrə-/ *a* infrarot

in'frequent *a*, **-ly** *adv* selten

infringe /ɪnˈfrɪndʒ/ *vt/i* **~ [on]** verstoßen gegen. **~ment** *n* Verstoß *m*

infuriat|e /ɪnˈfjʊərɪeɪt/ *vt* wütend machen. **~ing** *a* ärgerlich; **he is ~ing** er kann einen zur Raserei bringen

infusion /ɪnˈfjuːʒn/ *n* Aufguß *m*

ingenious /ɪnˈdʒiːnɪəs/ *a* erfinderisch; (*thing*) raffiniert

ingenuity /ɪndʒɪˈnjuːətɪ/ *n* Geschicklichkeit *f*

ingenuous /ɪnˈdʒenjʊəs/ *a* unschuldig

ingot /ˈɪŋgət/ *n* Barren *m*

ingrained /ɪnˈgreɪnd/ *a* eingefleischt; **be ~** (*dirt:*) tief sitzen

ingratiate /ɪnˈgreɪʃɪeɪt/ *vt* **~ oneself** sich einschmeicheln (**with** bei)

in'gratitude *n* Undankbarkeit *f*

ingredient /ɪnˈgriːdɪənt/ *n* (*Culin*) Zutat *f*

ingrowing /ˈɪngrəʊɪŋ/ *a* (*nail*) eingewachsen

inhabit /ɪnˈhæbɪt/ *vt* bewohnen. **~ant** *n* Einwohner(in) *m(f)*

inhale /ɪnˈheɪl/ *vt/i* einatmen; (*Med & when smoking*) inhalieren

inherent /ɪnˈhɪərənt/ *a* natürlich

inherit /ɪnˈherɪt/ *vt* erben. **~ance** /-əns/ *n* Erbschaft *f*, Erbe *nt*

inhibit /ɪnˈhɪbɪt/ *vt* hemmen. **~ed** *a* gehemmt. **~ion** /-ˈbɪʃn/ *n* Hemmung *f*

inho'spitable *a* ungastlich

in'human *a* unmenschlich

inimitable /ɪˈnɪmɪtəbl/ *a* unnachahmlich

iniquitous /ɪˈnɪkwɪtəs/ *a* schändlich; (*unjust*) ungerecht

initial /ɪˈnɪʃl/ *a* anfänglich, Anfangs- ● *n* Anfangsbuchstabe *m*; **my ~s** meine Initialen ● *vt* (*pt/pp* **initialled**) abzeichnen; (*Pol*) paraphieren. **~ly** *adv* anfangs, am Anfang

initiat|e /ɪˈnɪʃɪeɪt/ *vt* einführen. **~ion** /-ˈeɪʃn/ *n* Einführung *f*

initiative /ɪˈnɪʃətɪv/ *n* Initiative *f*

inject /ɪnˈdʒekt/ *vt* einspritzen, injizieren. **~ion** /-ekʃn/ *n* Spritze *f*, Injektion *f*

injunction /ɪnˈdʒʌŋkʃn/ *n* gerichtliche Verfügung *f*

injur|e /ˈɪndʒə(r)/ *vt* verletzen. **~y** *n* Verletzung *f*

in'justice *n* Ungerechtigkeit *f*; **do s.o. an ~** jdm unrecht tun

ink /ɪŋk/ *n* Tinte *f*

inkling /ˈɪŋklɪŋ/ *n* Ahnung *f*

inlaid /ɪnˈleɪd/ *a* eingelegt

inland /ˈɪnlənd/ *a* Binnen- ● *adv* landeinwärts. **I~ Revenue** *n* ≈ Finanzamt *nt*

in-laws /ˈɪnlɔːz/ *npl* (*fam*) Schwiegereltern *pl*

inlay /ˈɪnleɪ/ *n* Einlegearbeit *f*

inlet /ˈɪnlet/ *n* schmale Bucht *f*; (*Techn*) Zuleitung *f*

inmate /ˈɪnmeɪt/ *n* Insasse *m*

inn /ɪn/ *n* Gasthaus *nt*

innards /ˈɪnədz/ *npl* (*fam*) Eingeweide *pl*

innate /ɪˈneɪt/ *a* angeboren

inner /ˈɪnə(r)/ *a* innere(r,s). **~most** *a* innerste(r,s)

'innkeeper *n* Gastwirt *m*

innocen|ce /'ɪnəsəns/ *n* Unschuld *f.* ~t *a* unschuldig. ~tly *adv* in aller Unschuld

innocuous /ɪ'nɒkjʊəs/ *a* harmlos

innovat|e /'ɪnəveɪt/ *vi* neu einführen. ~ion /-'veɪʃn/ *n* Neuerung *f.* ~or *n* Neuerer *m*

innuendo /ɪnjuː'endəʊ/ *n* (*pl* -es) [versteckte] Anspielung *f*

innumerable /ɪ'njuːmərəbl/ *a* unzählig

inoculat|e /ɪ'nɒkjʊleɪt/ *vt* impfen. ~ion /-'leɪʃn/ *n* Impfung *f*

inof'fensive *a* harmlos

in'operable *a* nicht operierbar

in'opportune *a* unpassend

inordinate /ɪ'nɔːdɪnət/ *a*, **-ly** *adv* übermäßig

inor'ganic *a* anorganisch

'in-patient *n* [stationär behandelter] Krankenhauspatient *m*

input /'ɪnpʊt/ *n* Input *m* & *nt*

inquest /'ɪnkwest/ *n* gerichtliche Untersuchung *f*

inquir|e /ɪn'kwaɪə(r)/ *vi* sich erkundigen (**about** nach); ~e **into** untersuchen ● *vt* sich erkundigen nach. ~y *n* Erkundigung *f*; (*investigation*) Untersuchung *f*

inquisitive /ɪn'kwɪzətɪv/ *a*, **-ly** *adv* neugierig

inroad /'ɪnrəʊd/ *n* Einfall *m*; **make** ~**s into sth** etw angreifen

in'sane *a* geisteskrank; (*fig*) wahnsinnig

in'sanitary *a* unhygienisch

in'sanity *n* Geisteskrankheit *f*

insatiable /ɪn'seɪʃəbl/ *a* unersättlich

inscri|be /ɪn'skraɪb/ *vt* eingravieren. ~ption /-'skrɪpʃn/ *n* Inschrift *f*

inscrutable /ɪn'skruːtəbl/ *a* unergründlich; (*expression*) undurchdringlich

insect /'ɪnsekt/ *n* Insekt *nt.* ~icide /-'sektɪsaɪd/ *n* Insektenvertilgungsmittel *nt*

inse'cur|e *a* nicht sicher; (*fig*) unsicher. ~ity *n* Unsicherheit *f*

insemination /ɪnsemɪ'neɪʃn/ *n* Besamung *f*; (*Med*) Befruchtung *f*

in'sensible *a* (*unconscious*) bewußtlos

in'sensitive *a* gefühllos; ~ **to** unempfindlich gegen

in'separable *a* untrennbar; (*people*) unzertrennlich

insert[1] /'ɪnsɜːt/ *n* Einsatz *m*

insert[2] /ɪn'sɜːt/ *vt* einfügen, einsetzen; einstecken ⟨*key*⟩; einwerfen ⟨*coin*⟩. ~ion /-ɜːʃn/ *n* (*insert*) Einsatz *m*; (*in text*) Einfügung *f*

inside /ɪn'saɪd/ *n* Innenseite *f*; (*of house*) Innere(s) *nt* ● *attrib* Innen- ● *adv* innen; (*indoors*) drinnen; **go** ~ hineingehen; **come** ~ hereinkommen; ~ **out** links [herum]; **know sth** ~ **out** etw in- und auswendig kennen ● *prep* ~ **[of]** in (+ *dat*/(*into*) + *acc*)

insidious /ɪn'sɪdɪəs/ *a*, **-ly** *adv* heimtückisch

insight /'ɪnsaɪt/ *n* Einblick *m* (**into** in + *acc*); (*understanding*) Einsicht *f*

insignia /ɪn'sɪgnɪə/ *npl* Insignien *pl*

insig'nificant *a* unbedeutend

insin'cere *a* unaufrichtig

insinuat|e /ɪn'sɪnjʊeɪt/ *vt* andeuten. ~ion /-'eɪʃn/ *n* Andeutung *f*

insipid /ɪn'sɪpɪd/ *a* fade

insist /ɪn'sɪst/ *vi* darauf bestehen; ~ **on** bestehen auf (+ *dat*) ● *vt* ~ **that** darauf bestehen, daß. ~ence *n* Bestehen *nt.* ~ent *a*, **-ly** *adv* beharrlich; **be** ~ent darauf bestehen

'insole *n* Einlegesohle *f*

insolen|ce /'ɪnsələns/ *n* Unverschämtheit *f.* ~t *a*, **-ly** *adv* unverschämt

in'soluble *a* unlöslich; (*fig*) unlösbar

in'solvent *a* zahlungsunfähig

insomnia /ɪn'sɒmnɪə/ *n* Schlaflosigkeit *f*

inspect /ɪn'spekt/ *vt* inspizieren; (*test*) prüfen; kontrollieren ⟨*ticket*⟩. ~ion /-ekʃn/ *n* Inspektion *f.* ~or *n* Inspektor *m*; (*of tickets*) Kontrolleur *m*

inspiration /ɪnspə'reɪʃn/ *n* Inspiration *f*

inspire /ɪn'spaɪə(r)/ *vt* inspirieren; ~ **sth in s.o.** jdm etw einflößen

insta'bility *n* Unbeständigkeit *f*; (*of person*) Labilität *f*

install /ɪn'stɔːl/ *vt* installieren; [in ein Amt] einführen ⟨*person*⟩. ~ation /-stə'leɪʃn/ *n* Installation *f*; Amtseinführung *f*

instalment /ɪn'stɔːlmənt/ *n* (*Comm*) Rate *f*; (*of serial*) Fortsetzung *f*; (*Radio, TV*) Folge *f*

instance /'ɪnstəns/ *n* Fall *m*; (*example*) Beispiel *nt*; **in the first** ~ zunächst; **for** ~ zum Beispiel

instant /'mstənt/ a sofortig; (Culin)
Instant- ● n Augenblick m, Moment
m. **~aneous** /-'teiniəs/ a unverzüglich, unmittelbar; **death was
~aneous** der Tod trat sofort ein
instant 'coffee n Pulverkaffee m
instantly /'mstəntli/ adv sofort
instead /m'sted/ adv statt dessen; ~
of statt (+ gen), anstelle von; ~ **of me**
an meiner Stelle; ~ **of going** anstatt zu
gehen
'**instep** n Spann m, Rist m
instigat|e /'mstigeit/ vt anstiften;
einleiten (proceedings). **~ion**
/-'geiʃn/ n Anstiftung f; **at his ~ion**
auf seine Veranlassung. **~or** n An-
stifter(in) m(f)
instil /m'stil/ vt (pt/pp instilled) einprägen (**into s.o.** jdm)
instinct /'mstiŋkt/ n Instinkt m.
~ive /m'stiŋktiv/ a, **-ly** adv instinktiv
institut|e /'mstitju:t/ n Institut nt
● vt einführen; einleiten (search).
~ion /-'tju:ʃn/ n Institution f;
(home) Anstalt f
instruct /m'strʌkt/ vt unterrichten;
(order) anweisen. **~ion** /-ʌkʃn/ n
Unterricht m; Anweisung f; **~ions** pl
for use Gebrauchsanweisung f. **~ive** /
-iv/ a lehrreich. **~or** n Lehrer(in)
m(f); (Mil) Ausbilder m
instrument /'mstrəmənt/ n Instrument nt. **~al** /-'mentl/ a In-
strumental-; **be ~al in** eine
entscheidende Rolle spielen bei
insu'bordi|nate a ungehorsam.
~nation /-'neiʃn/ n Ungehorsam m;
(Mil) Insubordination f
in'sufferable a unerträglich
insuf'ficient a, **-ly** adv nicht genügend
insular /'msjʊlə(r)/ a (fig) engstirnig
insulat|e /'msjʊleit/ vt isolieren.
~ing tape n Isolierband nt. **~ion**
/-'leiʃn/ n Isolierung f
insulin /'msjʊlin/ n Insulin nt
insult[1] /'msʌlt/ n Beleidigung f
insult[2] /m'sʌlt/ vt beleidigen
insuperable /m'su:pərəbl/ a un-
überwindlich
insur|ance /m'ʃʊərəns/ n Versiche-
rung f. **~e** vt versichern
insurrection /msə'rekʃn/ n Aufstand m
intact /m'tækt/ a unbeschädigt;
(complete) vollständig
'**intake** n Aufnahme f

in'tangible a nicht greifbar
integral /'mtigrl/ a wesentlich
integrat|e /'mtigreit/ vt integrieren
● vi sich integrieren. **~ion**
/-'greiʃn/ n Integration f
integrity /m'tegrəti/ n Integrität f
intellect /'mtəlekt/ n Intellekt m.
~ual /-'lektjʊəl/ a intellektuell
intelligen|ce /m'telidʒəns/ n Intel-
ligenz f; (Mil) Nachrichtendienst m;
(information) Meldungen pl. **~t** a, **-ly**
adv intelligent
intelligentsia /mtelı'dʒentsıə/ n
Intelligenz f
intelligible /m'telidʒəbl/ a verständlich
intend /m'tend/ vt beabsichtigen; **be
~ed for** bestimmt sein für
intense /m'tens/ a intensiv; (pain)
stark. **~ly** adv äußerst; (study)
intensiv
intensi|fication /mtensifr'keiʃn/ n
Intensivierung f. **~fy** /-'tensifai/ v
(pt/pp -ied) ● vt intensivieren ● vi
zunehmen
intensity /m'tensəti/ n Intensität f
intensive /m'tensiv/ a, **-ly** adv intensiv; **be in ~ care** auf der In-
tensivstation sein
intent /m'tent/ a, **-ly** adv aufmerksam; **~ on** (absorbed in) vertieft
in (+ acc); **be ~ on doing sth** fest entschlossen sein, etw zu tun ● n Absicht
f; **to all ~s and purposes** im Grunde
intention /m'tenʃn/ n Absicht f. **~al**
a, **-ly** adv absichtlich
inter /m'tɜ:(r)/ vt (pt/pp interred) be-
statten
inter'action n Wechselwirkung f
intercede /mtə'si:d/ vi Fürsprache
einlegen (**on behalf of** für)
intercept /mtə'sept/ vt abfangen
'**interchange**[1] n Austausch m; (Auto)
Autobahnkreuz nt
inter'change[2] vt austauschen.
~able a austauschbar
intercom /'mtəkɒm/ n [Gegen]-
sprechanlage f
'**intercourse** n Verkehr m; (sexual)
Geschlechtsverkehr m
interest /'mtrəst/ n Interesse nt;
(Comm) Zinsen pl; **have an ~** (Comm)
beteiligt sein (**in an** + dat) ● vt interessieren; **be ~ed** sich interessieren
(**in** für). **~ing** a interessant. **~ rate** n
Zinssatz m
interfere /mtə'fiə(r)/ vi sich einmischen. **~nce** /-əns/ n Einmischung
f; (Radio, TV) Störung f

interim /'ɪntərɪm/ *a* Zwischen-; (*temporary*) vorläufig ● *n* **in the ~** in der Zwischenzeit

interior /ɪn'tɪərɪə(r)/ *a* innere(r,s), Innen- ● *n* Innere(s) *nt*

interject /ɪntə'dʒekt/ *vt* einwerfen. **~ion** /-ekʃn/ *n* Interjektion *f*; (*remark*) Einwurf *m*

inter'lock *vi* ineinandergreifen

interloper /'ɪntələʊpə(r)/ *n* Eindringling *m*

interlude /'ɪntəluːd/ *n* Pause *f*; (*performance*) Zwischenspiel *nt*

inter'marry *vi* untereinander heiraten; ⟨*different groups:*⟩ Mischehen schließen

intermediary /ɪntə'miːdɪərɪ/ *n* Vermittler(in) *m(f)*

intermediate /ɪntə'miːdɪət/ *a* Zwischen-

interminable /ɪn'tɜːmɪnəbl/ *a* endlos [lang]

intermission /ɪntə'mɪʃn/ *n* Pause *f*

intermittent /ɪntə'mɪtənt/ *a* in Abständen auftretend

intern /ɪn'tɜːn/ *vt* internieren

internal /ɪn'tɜːnl/ *a* innere(r,s); ⟨*matter, dispute*⟩ intern. **~ly** *adv* innerlich; ⟨*deal with*⟩ intern

inter'national *a*, **-ly** *adv* international ● *n* Länderspiel *nt*; (*player*) Nationalspieler(in) *m(f)*

internist /ɪn'tɜːnɪst/ *n* (*Amer*) Internist *m*

internment /ɪn'tɜːnmənt/ *n* Internierung *f*

'interplay *n* Wechselspiel *nt*

interpolate /ɪn'tɜːpəleɪt/ *vt* einwerfen

interpret /ɪn'tɜːprɪt/ *vt* interpretieren; auslegen ⟨*text*⟩; deuten ⟨*dream*⟩; (*translate*) dolmetschen ● *vi* dolmetschen. **~ation** /-'teɪʃn/ *n* Interpretation *f*. **~er** *n* Dolmetscher(in) *m(f)*

interre'lated *a* verwandt; ⟨*facts*⟩ zusammenhängend

interrogate /ɪn'terəgeɪt/ *vt* verhören. **~ion** /-'geɪʃn/ *n* Verhör *nt*

interrogative /ɪntə'rɒgətɪv/ *a & n* **~ [pronoun]** Interrogativpronomen *nt*

interrupt /ɪntə'rʌpt/ *vt/i* unterbrechen; **don't ~!** red nicht dazwischen! **~ion** /-ʌpʃn/ *n* Unterbrechung *f*

intersect /ɪntə'sekt/ *vi* sich kreuzen; (*Geom*) sich schneiden. **~ion** /-ekʃn/ *n* Kreuzung *f*

interspersed /ɪntə'spɜːst/ *a* **~ with** durchsetzt mit

inter'twine *vi* sich ineinanderschlingen

interval /'ɪntəvl/ *n* Abstand *m*; (*Theat*) Pause *f*; (*Mus*) Intervall *nt*; **at hourly ~s** alle Stunde; **bright ~s** *pl* Aufheiterungen *pl*

intervene /ɪntə'viːn/ *vi* eingreifen; (*occur*) dazwischenkommen. **~tion** /-'venʃn/ *n* Eingreifen *nt*; (*Mil, Pol*) Intervention *f*

interview /'ɪntəvjuː/ *n* (*Journ*) Interview *nt*; (*for job*) Vorstellungsgespräch *nt*; **go for an ~** sich vorstellen ● *vt* interviewen; ein Vorstellungsgespräch führen mit. **~er** *n* Interviewer(in) *m(f)*

intestine /ɪn'testɪn/ *n* Darm *m*

intimacy /'ɪntɪməsɪ/ *n* Vertrautheit *f*; (*sexual*) Intimität *f*

intimate¹ /'ɪntɪmət/ *a*, **-ly** *adv* vertraut; ⟨*friend*⟩ eng; (*sexually*) intim

intimate² /'ɪntɪmeɪt/ *vt* zu verstehen geben; (*imply*) andeuten

intimidate /ɪn'tɪmɪdeɪt/ *vt* einschüchtern. **~ion** /-'deɪʃn/ *n* Einschüchterung *f*

into /'ɪntə, *vor einem Vokal* 'ɪntʊ/ *prep* in (+ *acc*); **go ~ the house** ins Haus [hinein]gehen; **be ~** (*fam*) sich auskennen mit; **7 ~ 21** 21 [geteilt] durch 7

in'tolerable *a* unerträglich

in'toleran|ce *n* Intoleranz *f*. **~t** *a* intolerant

intonation /ɪntə'neɪʃn/ *n* Tonfall *m*

intoxicat|ed /ɪn'tɒksɪkeɪtɪd/ *a* betrunken; (*fig*) berauscht. **~ion** /-'keɪʃn/ *n* Rausch *m*

intractable /ɪn'træktəbl/ *a* widerspenstig; ⟨*problem*⟩ hartnäckig

intransigent /ɪn'trænsɪdʒənt/ *a* unnachgiebig

in'transitive *a*, **-ly** *adv* intransitiv

intravenous /ɪntrə'viːnəs/ *a*, **-ly** *adv* intravenös

intrepid /ɪn'trepɪd/ *a* kühn, unerschrocken

intricate /'ɪntrɪkət/ *a* kompliziert

intrigue /ɪn'triːg/ *n* Intrige *f* ● *vt* faszinieren ● *vi* intrigieren. **~ing** *a* faszinierend

intrinsic /ɪn'trɪnsɪk/ *a* **~ value** Eigenwert *m*

introduce /ɪntrə'djuːs/ *vt* vorstellen; (*bring in, insert*) einführen

introduct|ion /mtrə'dʌkʃn/ *n* Einführung *f*; (*to person*) Vorstellung *f*; (*to book*) Einleitung *f*. **~ory** /-təri/ *a* einleitend

introspective /mtrə'spektɪv/ *a* in sich (*acc*) gerichtet

introvert /'mtrəvɜːt/ *n* introvertierter Mensch *m*

intru|de /m'truːd/ *vi* stören. **~der** *n* Eindringling *m*. **~sion** /-uːʒn/ *n* Störung *f*

intuit|ion /mtjuː'ɪʃn/ *n* Intuition *f*. **~ive** /-'tjuːɪtɪv/ *a*, **-ly** *adv* intuitiv

inundate /'mʌndeɪt/ *vt* überschwemmen

invade /m'veɪd/ *vt* einfallen in (+ *acc*). **~r** *n* Angreifer *m*

invalid[1] /'mvəlɪd/ *n* Kranke(r) *m/f*

invalid[2] /m'vælɪd/ *a* ungültig. **~ate** *vt* ungültig machen

invaluable *a* unschätzbar; ⟨*person*⟩ unersetzlich

invariab|le *a* unveränderlich. **~ly** *adv* immer

invasion /m'veɪʒn/ *n* Invasion *f*

invective /m'vektɪv/ *n* Beschimpfungen *pl*

invent /m'vent/ *vt* erfinden. **~ion** /-enʃn/ *n* Erfindung *f*. **~ive** /-tɪv/ *a* erfinderisch. **~or** *n* Erfinder *m*

inventory /'mvəntri/ *n* Bestandsliste *f*; **make an ~** ein Inventar aufstellen

inverse /m'vɜːs/ *a*, **-ly** *adv* umgekehrt ● *n* Gegenteil *nt*

invert /m'vɜːt/ *vt* umkehren. **~ed commas** *npl* Anführungszeichen *pl*

invest /m'vest/ *vt* investieren, anlegen; **~ in** (*fam: buy*) sich (*dat*) zulegen

investigat|e /m'vestɪgeɪt/ *vt* untersuchen. **~ion** /-'geɪʃn/ *n* Untersuchung *f*

invest|ment /m'vestmənt/ *n* Anlage *f*; **be a good ~ment** (*fig*) sich bezahlt machen. **~or** *n* Kapitalanleger *m*

inveterate /m'vetərət/ *a* Gewohnheits-; ⟨*liar*⟩ unverbesserlich

invidious /m'vɪdɪəs/ *a* unerfreulich; (*unfair*) ungerecht

invigilate /m'vɪdʒɪleɪt/ *vi* (*Sch*) Aufsicht führen

invigorate /m'vɪgəreɪt/ *vt* beleben

invincible /m'vmsəbl/ *a* unbesiegbar

inviolable /m'vaɪələbl/ *a* unantastbar

in'visible *a* unsichtbar. **~ mending** *n* Kunststopfen *nt*

invitation /mvɪ'teɪʃn/ *n* Einladung *f*

invit|e /m'vaɪt/ *vt* einladen. **~ing** *a* einladend

invoice /'mvɔɪs/ *n* Rechnung *f* ● *vt* **~ s.o.** jdm eine Rechnung schicken

invoke /m'vəʊk/ *vt* anrufen

in'voluntary *a*, **-ily** *adv* unwillkürlich

involve /m'vɒlv/ *vt* beteiligen; (*affect*) betreffen; (*implicate*) verwickeln; (*entail*) mit sich bringen; (*mean*) bedeuten; **be ~d in** beteiligt sein an (+ *dat*); (*implicated*) verwickelt sein in (+ *acc*); **get ~d with s.o.** sich mit jdm einlassen. **~d** *a* kompliziert

in'vulnerable *a* unverwundbar; ⟨*position*⟩ unangreifbar

inward /'mwəd/ *a* innere(r,s). **~ly** *adv* innerlich. **~s** *adv* nach innen

iodine /'aɪədiːn/ *n* Jod *nt*

iota /aɪ'əʊtə/ *n* Jota *nt*; (*fam*) Funke *m*

IOU *abbr* (**I owe you**) Schuldschein *m*

Iran /ɪ'rɑːn/ *n* der Iran

Iraq /ɪ'rɑːk/ *n* der Irak

irascible /ɪ'ræsəbl/ *a* aufbrausend

irate /aɪ'reɪt/ *a* wütend

Ireland /'aɪələnd/ *n* Irland *nt*

iris /'aɪərɪs/ *n* (*Anat*) Regenbogenhaut *f*, Iris *f*; (*Bot*) Schwertlilie *f*

Irish /'aɪərɪʃ/ *a* irisch ● **the ~** *pl* die Iren. **~man** *n* Ire *m*. **~woman** *n* Irin *f*

irk /ɜːk/ *vt* ärgern. **~some** /-səm/ *a* lästig

iron /'aɪən/ *a* Eisen-; (*fig*) eisern ● *n* Eisen *nt*; (*appliance*) Bügeleisen *nt* ● *vt/i* bügeln. **~ out** *vt* ausbügeln

ironic[al] /aɪ'rɒnɪk[l]/ *a* ironisch

ironing /'aɪənɪŋ/ *n* Bügeln *nt*; (*articles*) Bügelwäsche *f*; **do the ~** bügeln. **~-board** *n* Bügelbrett *nt*

ironmonger /'-mʌŋgə(r)/ *n* **~'s [shop]** Haushaltswarengeschäft *nt*

irony /'aɪərənɪ/ *n* Ironie *f*

irradiate /ɪ'reɪdɪeɪt/ *vt* bestrahlen

irrational /ɪ'ræʃənl/ *a* irrational

irreconcilable /ɪ'rekənsaɪləbl/ *a* unversöhnlich

irrefutable /ɪrɪ'fjuːtəbl/ *a* unwiderlegbar

irregular /ɪ'regjələ(r)/ *a*, **-ly** *adv* unregelmäßig; (*against rules*) regelwidrig. **~ity** /-'lærətɪ/ *n* Unregelmäßigkeit *f*; Regelwidrigkeit *f*

irrelevant /ɪ'reləvənt/ a irrelevant
irreparable /ɪ'repərəbl/ a unersetzlich; **be** ∼ nicht wiedergut-
zumachen sein
irreplaceable /ɪrɪ'pleɪsəbl/ a unersetzlich
irrepressible /ɪrɪ'presəbl/ a
unverwüstlich; **be** ∼ ⟨person:⟩ nicht
unterzukriegen sein
irresistible /ɪrɪ'zɪstəbl/ a unwider-
stehlich
irresolute /ɪ'rezəluː:t/ a unentschlossen
irrespective /ɪrɪ'spektɪv/ a ∼ **of**
ungeachtet (+ gen)
irresponsible /ɪrɪ'spɒnsəbl/ a, **-bly**
adv unverantwortlich; ⟨person⟩ verantwortungslos
irreverent /ɪ'revərənt/ a, **-ly** adv
respektlos
irreversible /ɪrɪ'vɜːsəbl/ a unwiderruflich; (Med) irreversibel
irrevocable /ɪ'revəkəbl/ a, **-bly** adv
unwiderruflich
irrigat|e /'ɪrɪgeɪt/ vt bewässern.
∼**ion** /-'geɪʃn/ n Bewässerung f
irritability /ɪrɪtə'bɪləti/ n Gereizt-
heit f
irritable /'ɪrɪtəbl/ a reizbar
irritant /'ɪrɪtənt/ n Reizstoff m
irritat|e /'ɪrɪteɪt/ vt irritieren; (Med)
reizen. ∼**ion** /-'teɪʃn/ n Ärger m;
(Med) Reizung f
is /ɪz/ see **be**
Islam /'ɪzlɑː:m/ n der Islam. ∼**ic**
/-'læmɪk/ a islamisch
island /'aɪlənd/ n Insel f. ∼**er** n
Inselbewohner(in) m(f)
isle /aɪl/ n Insel f
isolat|e /'aɪsəleɪt/ vt isolieren. ∼**ed**
a (remote) abgelegen; (single)
einzeln. ∼**ion** /-'leɪʃn/ n Isoliertheit
f; (Med) Isolierung f
Israel /'ɪzreɪl/ n Israel nt. ∼**i** /ɪz'reɪlɪ/
a israelisch ● n Israeli m/f
issue /'ɪʃuː/ n Frage f; (outcome) Ergebnis nt; (of magazine, stamps) Ausgabe f; (offspring) Nachkommen pl;
what is at ∼? worum geht es? **take** ∼
with s.o. jdm widersprechen ● vt ausgeben; ausstellen ⟨passport⟩; erteilen
⟨order⟩; herausgeben ⟨book⟩; **be** ∼**d**
with sth etw erhalten ● vi ∼ **from**
herausströmen aus
isthmus /'ɪsməs/ n (pl **-muses**) Land-
enge f
it /ɪt/ pron es; (m) er; (f) sie; (as direct
object) es; (m) ihn; (f) sie; (as indirect

object) ihm; (f) ihr; **it is raining** es
regnet; **it's me** ich bin's; **who is it?** wer
ist da? **of/from it** davon; **with it** damit;
out of it daraus
Italian /ɪ'tæljən/ a italienisch ● n
Italiener(in) m(f); (Lang) Italienisch nt
italic /ɪ'tælɪk/ a kursiv. ∼**s** npl Kur-
sivschrift f; **in** ∼**s** kursiv
Italy /'ɪtəli/ n Italien nt
itch /ɪtʃ/ n Juckreiz m; **I have an** ∼ es
juckt mich ● vi jucken; **I'm** ∼**ing** (fam)
es juckt mich (**to** zu). ∼**y** a **be** ∼**y**
jucken
item /'aɪtəm/ n Gegenstand m;
(Comm) Artikel m; (on agenda)
Punkt m; (on invoice) Posten m; (act)
Nummer f; ∼ **[of news]** Nachricht f.
∼**ize** vt einzeln aufführen; spezi-
fizieren ⟨bill⟩
itinerant /aɪ'tɪnərənt/ a Wander-
itinerary /aɪ'tɪnərərɪ/ n [Reise]route
f
its /ɪts/ poss pron sein; (f) ihr
it's = **it is, it has**
itself /ɪt'self/ pron selbst; (refl) sich;
by ∼ von selbst; (alone) allein
ivory /'aɪvərɪ/ n Elfenbein nt ● attrib
Elfenbein-
ivy /'aɪvɪ/ n Efeu m

J

jab /dʒæb/ n Stoß m; (fam: injection)
Spritze f ● vt (pt/pp jabbed) stoßen
jabber /'dʒæbə(r)/ vi plappern
jack /dʒæk/ n (Auto) Wagenheber m;
(Cards) Bube m ● vt ∼ **up** (Auto) aufbocken
jackdaw /'dʒækdɔː/ n Dohle f
jacket /'dʒækɪt/ n Jacke f; (of book)
Schutzumschlag m. ∼ **po'tato** n in
der Schale gebackene Kartoffel f
'jackpot n **hit the** ∼ das Große Los
ziehen
jade /dʒeɪd/ n Jade m
jaded /'dʒeɪdɪd/ a abgespannt
jagged /'dʒægɪd/ a zackig
jail /dʒeɪl/ = **gaol**
jalopy /dʒə'lɒpɪ/ n (fam) Klapperkiste f
jam¹ /dʒæm/ n Marmelade f
jam² n Gedränge nt; (Auto) Stau m;
(fam: difficulty) Klemme f ● v (pt/pp
jammed) ● vt klemmen (**in in** + acc);
stören ⟨broadcast⟩ ● vi klemmen
Jamaica /dʒə'meɪkə/ n Jamaika nt

jangle /'dʒæŋgl/ vi klimpern ● vt
klimpern mit

janitor /'dʒænɪtə(r)/ n Hausmeister
m

January /'dʒænjʊərɪ/ n Januar m

Japan /dʒə'pæn/ n Japan nt. **~ese**
/dʒæpə'ni:z/ a japanisch ● n Japa-
ner(in) m(f); (Lang) Japanisch nt

jar¹ /dʒɑ:(r)/ n Glas nt; (earthenware)
Topf m

jar² v (pt/pp jarred) vi stören ● vt
erschüttern

jargon /'dʒɑ:gən/ n Jargon m

jaundice /'dʒɔ:ndɪs/ n Gelbsucht f.
~d a (fig) zynisch

jaunt /dʒɔ:nt/ n Ausflug m

jaunty /'dʒɔ:ntɪ/ a (-ier, -iest), -ily
adv keck

javelin /'dʒævlɪn/ n Speer m

jaw /dʒɔ:/ n Kiefer m; ~s pl Rachen m
● vi (fam) quatschen

jay /dʒeɪ/ n Eichelhäher m.
~-walker n achtloser Fußgänger m

jazz /dʒæz/ n Jazz m. **~y** a knallig

jealous /'dʒeləs/ a, -ly adv eifer-
süchtig (of auf + acc). **~y** n Eifer-
sucht f

jeans /dʒi:nz/ npl Jeans pl

jeer /dʒɪə(r)/ n Johlen nt ● vi johlen;
~at verhöhnen

jell /dʒel/ vi gelieren

jelly /'dʒelɪ/ n Gelee nt; (dessert) Götterspeise f. **~fish** n Qualle f

jemmy /'dʒemɪ/ n Brecheisen nt

jeopar|dize /'dʒepədaɪz/ vt gefähr-
den. **~dy** /-dɪ/ n in ~dy gefährdet

jerk /dʒɜ:k/ n Ruck m ● vt stoßen;
(pull) reißen ● vi rucken; ⟨limb,
muscle:⟩ zucken. **~ily** adv ruckweise. **~y** a ruckartig

jersey /'dʒɜ:zɪ/ n Pullover m; (Sport)
Trikot nt; (fabric) Jersey m

jest /dʒest/ n Scherz m; in ~ im Spaß
● vi scherzen

jet¹ /dʒet/ n (Miner) Jett m

jet² n (of water) [Wasser]strahl m;
(nozzle) Düse f; (plane) Düsenflugzeug
nt

jet: ~-'black a pechschwarz. ~ lag n
Jet-lag nt. **~-pro'pelled** a mit
Düsenantrieb

jettison /'dʒetɪsn/ vt über Bord werfen

jetty /'dʒetɪ/ n Landesteg m; (breakwater) Buhne f

Jew /dʒu:/ n Jude m/Jüdin f

jewel /'dʒu:əl/ n Edelstein m; (fig)
Juwel nt. **~ler** n Juwelier m; **~ler's**

[shop] Juweliergeschäft nt. **~lery** n
Schmuck m

Jew|ess /'dʒu:ɪs/ n Jüdin f. **~ish** a
jüdisch

jib /dʒɪb/ vi (pt/pp jibbed) (fig) sich
sträuben (at gegen)

jiffy /'dʒɪfɪ/ n (fam) in a ~ in einem
Augenblick

jigsaw /'dʒɪgsɔ:/ n ~ [puzzle] Puzzlespiel nt

jilt /dʒɪlt/ vt sitzenlassen

jingle /'dʒɪŋgl/ n (rhyme) Verschen
nt ● vi klimpern ● vt klimpern mit

jinx /dʒɪŋks/ n (fam) it's got a ~ on it
es ist verhext

jitter|s /'dʒɪtəz/ npl (fam) have the
~s nervös sein. **~y** a (fam) nervös

job /dʒɒb/ n Aufgabe f; (post) Stelle f,
(fam) Job m; be a ~ (fam) nicht leicht
sein; it's a good ~ that es ist [nur] gut,
daß. **~centre** n Arbeitsvermitt-
lungsstelle f. **~less** a arbeitslos

jockey /'dʒɒkɪ/ n Jockei m

jocular /'dʒɒkjʊlə(r)/ a, -ly adv
spaßhaft

jog /dʒɒg/ n Stoß m; at a ~ im Dauer-
lauf ● v (pt/pp jogged) ● vt anstoßen;
~ s.o.'s memory jds Gedächtnis
nachhelfen ● vi (Sport) joggen. **~ging**
n Jogging nt

john /dʒɒn/ n (Amer, fam) Klo nt

join /dʒɔɪn/ n Nahtstelle f ● vt verbinden (to mit); sich anschließen
(+ dat) ⟨person⟩; (become member of)
beitreten (+ dat); eintreten in (+ acc)
⟨firm⟩ ● vi ⟨roads:⟩ sich treffen. ~ in vi
mitmachen. ~ up vi (Mil) Soldat
werden ● vt zusammenfügen

joiner /'dʒɔɪnə(r)/ n Tischler m

joint /dʒɔɪnt/ a, -ly adv gemeinsam
● n Gelenk nt; (in wood, brickwork)
Fuge f; (Culin) Braten m; (fam: bar)
Lokal nt

joist /dʒɔɪst/ n Dielenbalken m

jok|e /dʒəʊk/ n Scherz m; (funny
story) Witz m; (trick) Streich m ● vi
scherzen. **~er** n Witzbold m; (Cards)
Joker m. **~ing** n ~ing apart Spaß beiseite. **~ingly** adv im Spaß

jollity /'dʒɒlɪtɪ/ n Lustigkeit f

jolly /'dʒɒlɪ/ a (-ier, -iest) lustig ● adv
(fam) sehr

jolt /dʒəʊlt/ n Ruck m ● vt einen
Ruck versetzen (+ dat) ● vi holpern

Jordan /'dʒɔ:dn/ n Jordanien nt

jostle /'dʒɒsl/ vt anrempeln ● vi
drängeln

jot /dʒɒt/ *n* Jota *nt* ● *vt* (*pt/pp* **jotted**) ~ [**down**] sich (*dat*) notieren. ~**ter** *n* Notizblock *m*

journal /'dʒɜːnl/ *n* Zeitschrift *f*; (*diary*) Tagebuch *nt*. ~**ese** /-ə'liːz/ *n* Zeitungsjargon *m*. ~**ism** *n* Journalismus *m*. ~**ist** *n* Journalist(in) *m(f)*

journey /'dʒɜːnɪ/ *n* Reise *f*

jovial /'dʒəʊvɪəl/ *a* lustig

joy /dʒɔɪ/ *n* Freude *f*. ~**ful** *a*, **-ly** *adv* freudig, froh. ~**ride** *n* (*fam*) Spritztour *f* [im gestohlenen Auto]

jubil|ant /'dʒuːbɪlənt/ *a* überglücklich. ~**ation** /-'leɪʃn/ *n* Jubel *m*

jubilee /'dʒuːbɪliː/ *n* Jubiläum *nt*

Judaism /'dʒuːdeɪɪzm/ *n* Judentum *nt*

judder /'dʒʌdə(r)/ *vi* rucken

judge /dʒʌdʒ/ *n* Richter *m*; (*of competition*) Preisrichter *m* ● *vt* beurteilen; (*estimate*) [ein]schätzen ● *vi* urteilen (**by** nach). ~**ment** *n* Beurteilung *f*; (*Jur*) Urteil *nt*; (*fig*) Urteilsvermögen *nt*

judic|ial /dʒuː'dɪʃl/ *a* gerichtlich. ~**iary** /-ʃərɪ/ *n* Richterstand *m*. ~**ious** /-ʃəs/ *a* klug

judo /'dʒuːdəʊ/ *n* Judo *nt*

jug /dʒʌg/ *n* Kanne *f*; (*small*) Kännchen *nt*; (*for water, wine*) Krug *m*

juggernaut /'dʒʌgənɔːt/ *n* (*fam*) Riesenlaster *m*

juggle /'dʒʌgl/ *vi* jonglieren. ~**r** *n* Jongleur *m*

juice /dʒuːs/ *n* Saft *m*. ~ **extractor** *n* Entsafter *m*

juicy /'dʒuːsɪ/ *a* (**-ier, -iest**) saftig; (*fam*) ⟨*story*⟩ pikant

juke-box /'dʒuːk-/ *n* Musikbox *f*

July /dʒʊ'laɪ/ *n* Juli *m*

jumble /'dʒʌmbl/ *n* Durcheinander *nt* ● *vt* ~ [**up**] durcheinanderbringen. ~ **sale** *n* [Wohltätigkeits]basar *m*

jumbo /'dʒʌmbəʊ/ *n* ~ [**jet**] Jumbo-[-Jet] *m*

jump /dʒʌmp/ *n* Sprung *m*; (*in prices*) Anstieg *m*; (*in horse racing*) Hindernis *nt* ● *vi* springen; (*start*) zusammenzucken; **make s.o.** ~ jdn erschrecken; ~ **at** (*fig*) sofort zugreifen bei (*offer*); ~ **to conclusions** voreilige Schlüsse ziehen ● *vt* überspringen; ~ **the gun** (*fig*) vorschnell handeln. ~ **up** *vi* aufspringen

jumper /'dʒʌmpə(r)/ *n* Pullover *m*, Pulli *m*

jumpy /'dʒʌmpɪ/ *a* nervös

junction /'dʒʌŋkʃn/ *n* Kreuzung *f*; (*Rail*) Knotenpunkt *m*

juncture /'dʒʌŋktʃə(r)/ *n* **at this** ~ zu diesem Zeitpunkt

June /dʒuːn/ *n* Juni *m*

jungle /'dʒʌŋgl/ *n* Dschungel *m*

junior /'dʒuːnɪə(r)/ *a* jünger; (*in rank*) untergeordnet; (*Sport*) Junioren- ● *n* Junior *m*. ~ **school** *n* Grundschule *f*

juniper /'dʒuːnɪpə(r)/ *n* Wacholder *m*

junk /dʒʌŋk/ *n* Gerümpel *nt*, Trödel *m*

junkie /'dʒʌŋkɪ/ *n* (*sl*) Fixer *m*

junk-shop *n* Trödelladen *m*

juris|diction /dʒʊərɪs'dɪkʃn/ *n* Gerichtsbarkeit *f*. ~'**prudence** *n* Rechtswissenschaft *f*

juror /'dʒʊərə(r)/ *n* Geschworene(r) *m/f*

jury /'dʒʊərɪ/ *n* **the** ~ die Geschworenen *pl*; (*for competition*) die Jury

just /dʒʌst/ *a* gerecht ● *adv* gerade; (*only*) nur; (*simply*) einfach; (*exactly*) genau; ~ **as tall** ebenso groß; ~ **listen!** hör doch mal! **I'm** ~ **going** ich gehe schon; ~ **put it down** stell es nur hin

justice /'dʒʌstɪs/ *n* Gerechtigkeit *f*; **do** ~ **to** gerecht werden (+ *dat*); **J~ of the Peace** ≈ Friedensrichter *m*

justifiab|le /dʒʌstɪfaɪəbl/ *a* berechtigt. ~**ly** *adv* berechtigterweise

justi|fication /dʒʌstɪfɪ'keɪʃn/ *n* Rechtfertigung *f*. ~**fy** /'dʒʌstɪfaɪ/ *vt* (*pt/pp* **-ied**) rechtfertigen

justly /'dʒʌstlɪ/ *adv* zu Recht

jut /dʒʌt/ *vi* (*pt/pp* **jutted**) ~ **out** vorstehen

juvenile /'dʒuːvənaɪl/ *a* jugendlich; (*childish*) kindisch ● *n* Jugendliche(r) *m/f*. ~ **delinquency** *n* Jugendkriminalität *f*

juxtapose /dʒʌkstə'pəʊz/ *vt* nebeneinanderstellen

K

kangaroo /kæŋgə'ruː/ *n* Känguruh *nt*

karate /kə'rɑːtɪ/ *n* Karate *nt*

kebab /kɪ'bæb/ *n* (*Culin*) Spießchen *nt*

keel /kiːl/ *n* Kiel *m* ● *vi* ~ **over** umkippen; (*Naut*) kentern

keen /ki:n/ *a* (**-er, -est**) (*sharp*) scharf; (*intense*) groß; (*eager*) eifrig, begeistert; ~ **on** (*fam*) erpicht auf (+ *acc*); ~ **on s.o.** von jdm sehr angetan; **be ~ to do sth** etw gerne machen wollen. ~**ly** *adv* tief. ~**ness** *n* Eifer *m*, Begeisterung *f*

keep /ki:p/ *n* (*maintenance*) Unterhalt *m*; (*of castle*) Bergfried *m*; **for** ~**s** für immer ● *v* (*pt/pp* **kept**) ● *vt* behalten; (*store*) aufbewahren; (*not throw away*) aufheben; (*support*) unterhalten; (*detain*) aufhalten; freihalten (*seat*); halten (*promise, animals*); führen, haben (*shop*); einhalten (*law, rules*); ~ **sth hot** etw warm halten; ~ **s.o. from doing sth** jdn davon abhalten, etw zu tun; ~ **s.o. waiting** jdn warten lassen; ~ **sth to oneself** etw nicht weitersagen; **where do you ~ the sugar?** wo hast du den Zucker? ● *vi* (*remain*) bleiben; (*food:*) sich halten; ~ **left/right** sich links/rechts halten; ~ **doing sth** etw dauernd machen; ~ **on doing sth** etw weitermachen; ~ **in with** sich gut stellen mit. ~ **up** *vi* Schritt halten ● *vt* (*continue*) weitermachen

keep|er /ki:pə(r)/ *n* Wärter(in) *m*(*f*). ~**ing** *n* Obhut *f*; **be in** ~**ing with** passen zu. ~**sake** *n* Andenken *nt*

keg /keg/ *n* kleines Faß *nt*

kennel /kenl/ *n* Hundehütte *f*; ~**s** *pl* (*boarding*) Hundepension *f*; (*breeding*) Zwinger *m*

Kenya /kenjə/ *n* Kenia *nt*

kept /kept/ *see* **keep**

kerb /kɜ:b/ *n* Bordstein *m*

kernel /kɜ:nl/ *n* Kern *m*

kerosene /kerəsi:n/ *n* (*Amer*) Petroleum *nt*

ketchup /ketʃʌp/ *n* Ketchup *m*

kettle /ketl/ *n* [Wasser]kessel *m*; **put the ~ on** Wasser aufsetzen; **a pretty ~ of fish** (*fam*) eine schöne Bescherung *f*

key /ki:/ *n* Schlüssel *m*; (*Mus*) Tonart *f*; (*of piano, typewriter*) Taste *f* ● *vt* ~ **in** *vt* eintasten

key: ~**board** *n* Tastatur *f*; (*Mus*) Klaviatur *f*. ~**boarder** *n* Taster(in) *m*(*f*). ~**hole** *n* Schlüsselloch *nt*. ~**ring** *n* Schlüsselring *m*

khaki /ka:kɪ/ *a* khakifarben ● *n* Khaki *nt*

kick /kɪk/ *n* [Fuß]tritt *m*; **for** ~**s** (*fam*) zum Spaß ● *vt* treten; ~ **the bucket** (*fam*) abkratzen ● *vi* (*animal:*) ausschlagen. ~-**off** *n* (*Sport*) Anstoß *m*

kid /kɪd/ *n* Kitz *nt*; (*fam: child*) Kind *nt* ● *vt* (*pt/pp* **kidded**) (*fam*) ~ **s.o.** jdm etwas vormachen. ~ **gloves** *npl* Glacéhandschuhe *pl*

kidnap /kɪdnæp/ *vt* (*pt/pp* -**napped**) entführen. ~**per** *n* Entführer *m*. ~**ping** *n* Entführung *f*

kidney /kɪdnɪ/ *n* Niere *f*. ~ **machine** *n* künstliche Niere *f*

kill /kɪl/ *vt* töten; (*fam*) totschlagen (*time*); ~ **two birds with one stone** zwei Fliegen mit einer Klappe schlagen. ~**er** *n* Mörder(in) *m*(*f*). ~**ing** *n* Tötung *f*; (*murder*) Mord *m*

'killjoy *n* Spielverderber *m*

kiln /kɪln/ *n* Brennofen *m*

kilo /ki:ləʊ/ *n* Kilo *nt*

kilo /kɪlə/: ~**gram** *n* Kilogramm *nt*. ~**hertz** /-hɜːts/ *n* Kilohertz *nt*. ~**metre** *n* Kilometer *m*. ~**watt** *n* Kilowatt *nt*

kilt /kɪlt/ *n* Schottenrock *m*

kin /kɪn/ *n* Verwandtschaft *f*; **next of** ~ nächster Verwandter *m*/nächste Verwandte *f*

kind[1] /kaɪnd/ *n* Art *f*; (*brand, type*) Sorte *f*; **what ~ of car?** was für ein Auto? ~ **of** (*fam*) irgendwie

kind[2] *a* (**-er, -est**) nett; ~ **to animals** gut zu Tieren; ~ **regards** herzliche Grüße

kindergarten /kɪndəga:tn/ *n* Vorschule *f*

kindle /kɪndl/ *vt* anzünden

kind|ly /kaɪndlɪ/ *a* (**-ier, -iest**) nett ● *adv* netterweise; (*if you please*) gefälligst. ~**ness** *n* Güte *f*; (*favour*) Gefallen *m*

kindred /kɪndrɪd/ *a* ~ **spirit** Gleichgesinnte(r) *m*/*f*

kinetic /kɪˈnetɪk/ *a* kinetisch

king /kɪŋ/ *n* König *m*; (*Draughts*) Dame *f*. ~**dom** *n* Königreich *nt*; (*fig & Relig*) Reich *nt*

king: ~**fisher** *n* Eisvogel *m*. ~-**sized** *a* extragroß

kink /kɪŋk/ *n* Knick *m*. ~**y** *a* (*fam*) pervers

kiosk /ki:ɒsk/ *n* Kiosk *m*

kip /kɪp/ *n* **have a** ~ (*fam*) pennen ● *vi* (*pt/pp* **kipped**) (*fam*) pennen

kipper /kɪpə(r)/ *n* Räucherhering *m*

kiss /kɪs/ *n* Kuß *m* ● *vt/i* küssen

kit /kɪt/ *n* Ausrüstung *f*; (*tools*) Werkzeug *nt*; (*construction* ~) Bausatz *m* ● *vt* (*pt/pp* **kitted**) ~ **out** ausrüsten. ~**bag** *n* Seesack *m*

kitchen /'kɪtʃɪn/ n Küche f • attrib Küchen-. **~ette** /kɪtʃɪ'net/ n Kochnische f
kitchen: ~ **'garden** n Gemüsegarten m. ~ **'sink** n Spülbecken nt
kite /kaɪt/ n Drachen m
kith /kɪθ/ n **with ~ and kin** mit der ganzen Verwandtschaft
kitten /'kɪtn/ n Kätzchen nt
kitty /'kɪtɪ/ n (money) [gemeinsame] Kasse f
kleptomaniac /kleptə'meɪnɪæk/ n Kleptomane m/-manin f
knack /næk/ n Trick m, Dreh m
knapsack /'næp-/ n Tornister m
knead /niːd/ vt kneten
knee /niː/ n Knie nt. **~cap** n Kniescheibe f
kneel /niːl/ vi (pt/pp knelt) knien; ~ **[down]** sich [nieder]knien
knelt /nelt/ see **kneel**
knew /njuː/ see **know**
knickers /'nɪkəz/ npl Schlüpfer m
knick-knacks /'nɪknæks/ npl Nippsachen pl
knife /naɪf/ n (pl knives) Messer nt • vt einen Messerstich versetzen (+ dat); (to death) erstechen
knight /naɪt/ n Ritter m; (Chess) Springer m • vt adeln
knit /nɪt/ vt/i (pt/pp knitted) stricken; ~ **one, purl one** eine rechts, eine links; ~ **one's brow** die Stirn runzeln. **~ting** n Stricken nt; (work) Strickzeug nt. **~ting-needle** n Stricknadel f. **~wear** n Strickwaren pl
knives /naɪvz/ npl see **knife**
knob /nɒb/ n Knopf m; (on door) Knauf m; (small lump) Beule f; (small piece) Stückchen nt. **~bly** a knorrig; (bony) knochig
knock /nɒk/ n Klopfen nt; (blow) Schlag m; **there was a ~ at the door** es klopfte • vt anstoßen; (at door) klopfen an (+ acc); (fam: criticize) heruntermachen; ~ **a hole in sth** ein Loch in etw (acc) schlagen; ~ **one's head** sich (dat) den Kopf stoßen (**on** an + dat) • vi klopfen. ~ **about** vt schlagen • vi (fam) herumkommen. ~ **down** vt herunterwerfen; (with fist) niederschlagen; (in car) anfahren; (demolish) abreißen; (fam: reduce) herabsetzen. ~ **off** vt herunterwerfen; (fam: steal) klauen; (fam: complete quickly) hinhauen • vi

(fam: cease work) Feierabend machen. ~ **out** vt ausschlagen; (make unconscious) bewußtlos schlagen; (Boxing) k.o. schlagen. ~ **over** vt umwerfen; (in car) anfahren
knock: **~-down** a **~-down prices** Schleuderpreise pl. **~er** n Türklopfer m. **~-kneed** /-'niːd/ a X-beinig. **~-out** n (Boxing) K.o. m
knot /nɒt/ n Knoten m • vt (pt/pp knotted) knoten
knotty /'nɒtɪ/ a (-ier, -iest) (fam) verwickelt
know /nəʊ/ vt/i (pt knew, pp known) wissen; kennen (person); können (language); **get to ~** kennenlernen • n **in the ~** (fam) im Bild
know: **~-all** n (fam) Alleswisser m. **~-how** n (fam) [Sach]kenntnis f. **~ing** a wissend. **~ingly** adv wissend; (intentionally) wissentlich
knowledge /'nɒlɪdʒ/ n Kenntnis f (of von/gen); (general) Wissen nt; (specialized) Kenntnisse pl. **~able** /-əbl/ a **be ~able** viel wissen
known /nəʊn/ see **know** • a bekannt
knuckle /'nʌkl/ n [Finger]knöchel m; (Culin) Hachse f • vi ~ **under** sich fügen; ~ **down** sich dahinterklemmen
kosher /'kəʊʃə(r)/ a koscher
kowtow /kaʊ'taʊ/ vi Kotau machen (**to** vor + dat)
kudos /'kjuːdɒs/ n (fam) Prestige nt

L

lab /læb/ n (fam) Labor nt
label /'leɪbl/ n Etikett nt • vt (pt/pp labelled) etikettieren
laboratory /lə'bɒrətrɪ/ n Labor nt
laborious /lə'bɔːrɪəs/ a, **-ly** adv mühsam
labour /'leɪbə(r)/ n Arbeit f; (workers) Arbeitskräfte pl; (Med) Wehen pl; **L~** (Pol) die Labourpartei • attrib Labour- • vi arbeiten • vt (fig) sich lange auslassen über (+ acc). **~er** n Arbeiter m
'labour-saving a arbeitssparend
laburnum /lə'bɜːnəm/ n Goldregen m
labyrinth /'læbərɪnθ/ n Labyrinth nt
lace /leɪs/ n Spitze f; (of shoe) Schnürsenkel m • vt schnüren; **~d with rum** mit einem Schuß Rum
lacerate /'læsəreɪt/ vt zerreißen

lack /læk/ n Mangel m (**of** an + dat)
● vt I ~ **the time** mir fehlt die Zeit ● vi
be ~**ing** fehlen

lackadaisical /lækə'deızıkl/ a lustlos

laconic /lə'kɒnık/ a, **-ally** adv
lakonisch

lacquer /'lækə(r)/ n Lack m; (for
hair) [Haar]spray m

lad /læd/ n Junge m

ladder /'lædə(r)/ n Leiter f; (in
fabric) Laufmasche f

laden /'leıdn/ a beladen

ladle /'leıdl/ n [Schöpf]kelle f ● vt
schöpfen

lady /'leıdı/ n Dame f; (title) Lady f

lady: ~**bird** n, (Amer) ~**bug** n
Marienkäfer m. ~**like** a damenhaft

lag¹ /læg/ vi (pt/pp lagged) ~ **behind**
zurückbleiben; (fig) nachhinken

lag² vt (pt/pp lagged) umwickeln
⟨pipes⟩

lager /'lɑ:gə(r)/ n Lagerbier nt

lagoon /lə'gu:n/ n Lagune f

laid /leıd/ see **lay**³

lain /leın/ see **lie**²

lair /leə(r)/ n Lager nt

laity /'leıətı/ n Laienstand m

lake /leık/ n See m

lamb /læm/ n Lamm nt

lame /leım/ a (**-r, -st**) lahm

lament /lə'ment/ n Klage f; (song)
Klagelied nt ● vt beklagen ● vi
klagen. ~**able** /'læməntəbl/ a be-
klagenswert

laminated /'læmıneıtıd/ a laminiert

lamp /læmp/ n Lampe f; (in street)
Laterne f. ~**post** n Laternenpfahl m.
~**shade** n Lampenschirm m

lance /lɑ:ns/ n Lanze f ● vt (Med)
aufschneiden. ~**-'corporal** n Ge-
freite(r) m

land /lænd/ n Land nt; **plot of** ~
Grundstück nt ● vt/i landen; ~ **s.o.**
with sth (fam) jdm etw aufhalsen

landing /'lændıŋ/ n Landung f; (top
of stairs) Treppenflur m. ~**-stage** n
Landesteg m

land: ~**lady** n Wirtin f. ~**-locked** a
~**-locked country** Binnenstaat m.
~**lord** n Wirt m; (of land) Grundbesitzer m; (of building) Haus-
besitzer m. ~**mark** n Erkennungs-
zeichen nt; (fig) Meilenstein
m. ~**owner** n Grundbesitzer m.
~**scape** /-skeıp/ n Landschaft f.
~**slide** n Erdrutsch m

lane /leın/ n kleine Landstraße f;
(Auto) Spur f; (Sport) Bahn f; '**get in**
~' (Auto) 'bitte einordnen'

language /'læŋgwıdʒ/ n Sprache f;
(speech, style) Ausdrucksweise f. ~
laboratory n Sprachlabor nt

languid /'læŋgwıd/ a, **-ly** adv träge

languish /'læŋgwıʃ/ vi schmachten

lank /læŋk/ a (hair) strähnig

lanky /'læŋkı/ a (**-ier, -iest**) schlaksig

lantern /'læntən/ n Laterne f

lap¹ /læp/ n Schoß m

lap² n (Sport) Runde f; (of journey)
Etappe f ● vi (pt/pp lapped) plätschern (**against** gegen)

lap³ vt (pt/pp lapped) ~ **up** auf-
schlecken

lapel /lə'pel/ n Revers nt

lapse /læps/ n Fehler m; (moral)
Fehltritt m; (of time) Zeitspanne f
● vi (expire) erlöschen; ~ **into** verfallen in (+ acc)

larceny /'lɑ:sənı/ n Diebstahl m

lard /lɑ:d/ n [Schweine]schmalz nt

larder /'lɑ:də(r)/ n Speisekammer f

large /lɑ:dʒ/ a (**-r, -st**) & adv groß; **by**
and ~ im großen und ganzen; **at** ~
auf freiem Fuß; (in general) im
allgemeinen. ~**ly** adv größenteils

lark¹ /lɑ:k/ n (bird) Lerche f

lark² n (joke) Jux m ● vi ~ **about** herumalbern

larva /'lɑ:və/ n (pl **-vae** /-vi:/) Larve f

laryngitis /lærın'dʒaıtıs/ n Kehl-
kopfentzündung f

larynx /'lærıŋks/ n Kehlkopf m

lascivious /lə'sıvıəs/ a lüstern

laser /'leızə(r)/ n Laser m

lash /læʃ/ n Peitschenhieb m; (eye-
lash) Wimper f ● vt peitschen; (tie)
festbinden (**to** an + acc). ~ **out** vi um
sich schlagen; (spend) viel Geld ausgeben (**on** für)

lashings /'læʃıŋz/ npl ~ **of** (fam) eine
Riesenmenge von

lass /læs/ n Mädchen nt

lasso /lə'su:/ n Lasso nt

last¹ /lɑ:st/ n (for shoe) Leisten m

last² a & n letzte(r,s); ~ **night** od
gestern nacht; (evening) gestern abend;
at ~ endlich; **the** ~ **time** das letztemal;
for the ~ **time** zum letztenmal; **the** ~
but one der/die/das letzte; **that's**
the ~ **straw** (fam) das schlägt dem Faß
den Boden aus ● adv zuletzt; (last time)
das letztemal; **do sth** ~ etw zuletzt od
als letztes machen; **he/she went** ~ er/
sie ging als letzter/letzte ● vi dauern;

⟨*weather:*⟩ sich halten; ⟨*relationship:*⟩ halten. ~**ing** *a* dauerhaft. ~**ly** *adv* schließlich, zum Schluß

latch /lætʃ/ *n* [einfache] Klinke *f*; **on the** ~ nicht verschlossen

late /leɪt/ *a & adv* (**-r, -st**) spät; (*delayed*) verspätet; (*deceased*) verstorben; **the** ~**st news** die neuesten Nachrichten; **stay up** ~ bis spät aufbleiben; **of** ~ in letzter Zeit; **arrive** ~ zu spät ankommen; **I am** ~ ich komme zu spät *od* habe mich verspätet; **the train is** ~ der Zug hat Verspätung. ~**comer** *n* Zuspätkommende(r) *m/f.* ~**ly** *adv* in letzter Zeit. ~**ness** *n* Zuspätkommen *nt*; (*delay*) Verspätung *f*

latent /'leɪtnt/ *a* latent

later /'leɪtə(r)/ *a & adv* später; ~ **on** nachher

lateral /'lætərəl/ *a* seitlich

lathe /leɪð/ *n* Drehbank *f*

lather /'lɑ:ðə(r)/ *n* [Seifen]schaum *m* ● *vt* einseifen ● *vi* schäumen

Latin /'lætɪn/ *a* lateinisch ● *n* Latein *nt.* ~ **A'merica** *n* Lateinamerika *nt*

latitude /'lætɪtju:d/ *n* (*Geog*) Breite *f*; (*fig*) Freiheit *f*

latter /'lætə(r)/ *a & n* **the** ~ der/die/das letztere. ~**ly** *adv* in letzter Zeit

lattice /'lætɪs/ *n* Gitter *nt*

Latvia /'lætvɪə/ *n* Lettland *nt*

laudable /'lɔ:dəbl/ *a* lobenswert

laugh /lɑ:f/ *n* Lachen *nt*; **with a** ~ lachend ● *vi* lachen (**at/about** über + *acc*); ~ **at s.o.** (*mock*) jdn auslachen. ~**able** /-əbl/ *a* lachhaft, lächerlich. ~**ing-stock** *n* Gegenstand *m* des Spottes

laughter /'lɑ:ftə(r)/ *n* Gelächter *nt*

launch[1] /'lɔ:ntʃ/ *n* (*boat*) Barkasse *f*

launch[2] *n* Stapellauf *m*; (*of rocket*) Abschuß *m*; (*of product*) Lancierung *f* ● *vt* vom Stapel lassen ⟨*ship*⟩; zu Wasser lassen ⟨*lifeboat*⟩; abschießen ⟨*rocket*⟩; starten ⟨*attack*⟩; (*Comm*) lancieren ⟨*product*⟩

launder /'lɔ:ndə(r)/ *vt* waschen. ~**ette** /-'dret/ *n* Münzwäscherei *f*

laundry /'lɔ:ndrɪ/ *n* Wäscherei *f*; (*clothes*) Wäsche *f*

laurel /'lɒrl/ *n* Lorbeer *m*

lava /'lɑ:və/ *n* Lava *f*

lavatory /'lævətrɪ/ *n* Toilette *f*

lavender /'lævəndə(r)/ *n* Lavendel *m*

lavish /'lævɪʃ/ *a*, **-ly** *adv* großzügig; (*wasteful*) verschwenderisch; **on a** ~

scale mit viel Aufwand ● *vt* ~ **sth on s.o.** jdn mit etw überschütten

law /lɔ:/ *n* Gesetz *nt*; (*system*) Recht *nt*; **study** ~ Jura studieren; ~ **and order** Recht und Ordnung

law: ~**-abiding** *a* gesetzestreu. ~**court** *n* Gerichtshof *m.* ~**ful** *a* rechtmäßig. ~**less** *a* gesetzlos

lawn /lɔ:n/ *n* Rasen *m.* ~**-mower** *n* Rasenmäher *m*

'**law suit** *n* Prozeß *m*

lawyer /'lɔ:jə(r)/ *n* Rechtsanwalt *m*/ -anwältin *f*

lax /læks/ *a* lax, locker

laxative /'læksətɪv/ *n* Abführmittel *nt*

laxity /'læksətɪ/ *n* Laxheit *f*

lay[1] /leɪ/ *a* Laien-

lay[2] *see* **lie**[2]

lay[3] *vt* (*pt/pp* **laid**) legen; decken ⟨*table*⟩; ~ **a trap** eine Falle stellen. ~ **down** *vt* hinlegen; festlegen ⟨*rules, conditions*⟩. ~ **off** *vt* entlassen ⟨*workers*⟩ ● *vi* (*fam: stop*) aufhören. ~ **out** *vt* hinlegen; aufbahren ⟨*corpse*⟩; anlegen ⟨*garden*⟩; (*Typ*) gestalten

lay: ~**about** *n* Faulenzer *m.* ~**-by** *n* Parkbucht *f*; (*on motorway*) Rastplatz *m*

layer /'leɪə(r)/ *n* Schicht *f*

layette /leɪ'et/ *n* Babyausstattung *f*

lay: ~**man** *n* Laie *m.* ~**out** *n* Anordnung *f*; (*design*) Gestaltung *f*; (*Typ*) Layout *nt.* ~ '**preacher** *n* Laienprediger *m*

laze /leɪz/ *vi* ~ [**about**] faulenzen

laziness /'leɪzɪnɪs/ *n* Faulheit *f*

lazy /'leɪzɪ/ *a* (**-ier, -iest**) faul. ~**-bones** *n* Faulenzer *m*

lb /paʊnd/ *abbr* (**pound**) Pfd.

lead[1] /led/ *n* Blei *nt*; (*of pencil*) [Bleistift]mine *f*

lead[2] /li:d/ *n* Führung *f*; (*leash*) Leine *f*; (*flex*) Schnur *f*; (*clue*) Hinweis *m*, Spur *f*; (*Theat*) Hauptrolle *f*; (*distance ahead*) Vorsprung *m*; **be in the** ~ in Führung liegen ● *vt/i* (*pt/pp* **led**) führen; leiten ⟨*team*⟩; (*induce*) bringen; (*at cards*) ausspielen; ~ **the way** vorangehen; ~ **up to sth** (*fig*) etw (*dat*) vorangehen. ~ **away** *vt* wegführen

leaded /'ledɪd/ *a* verbleit

leader /'li:də(r)/ *n* Führer *m*; (*of expedition, group*) Leiter(in) *m(f)*; (*of orchestra*) Konzertmeister *m*; (*in newspaper*) Leitartikel *m.* ~**ship** *n* Führung *f*; Leitung *f*

leading

legislature

leading /'li:dɪŋ/ *a* führend; ~ **lady** Hauptdarstellerin *f*; ~ **question** Suggestivfrage *f*

leaf /li:f/ *n* (*pl* **leaves**) Blatt *nt*; (*of table*) Ausziehplatte *f* ● *vi* ~ **through** sth etw durchblättern. **~let** *n* Merkblatt *nt*; (*advertising*) Reklameblatt *nt*; (*political*) Flugblatt *nt*

league /li:g/ *n* Liga *f*; **be in** ~ **with** unter einer Decke stecken mit

leak /li:k/ *n* (*hole*) undichte Stelle *f*; (*Naut*) Leck *nt*; (*of gas*) Gasausfluß *m* ● *vi* undicht sein; ⟨*ship*:⟩ leck sein, lecken; ⟨*liquid*:⟩ auslaufen; ⟨*gas*:⟩ ausströmen ● *vt* auslaufen lassen; ~ **sth to s.o.** (*fig*) jdm etw zuspielen. **~y** *a* undicht; (*Naut*) leck

lean¹ /li:n/ *a* (**-er, -est**) mager

lean² *v* (*pt/pp* **leaned** *or* **leant** /lent/) ● *vt* lehnen (**against/on** an + *acc*) ● *vi* ⟨*person*:⟩ sich lehnen (**against/on** an + *acc*); (*not be straight*) sich neigen; **be ~ing against** lehnen an (+ *dat*); ~ **on s.o.** (*depend*) bei jdm festen Halt finden. ~ **back** *vi* sich zurücklehnen. ~ **forward** *vi* sich vorbeugen. ~ **out** *vi* sich hinauslehnen. ~ **over** *vi* sich vorbeugen

leaning /'li:nɪŋ/ *a* schief ● *n* Neigung *f*

leap /li:p/ *n* Sprung *m* ● *vi* (*pt/pp* **leapt** /lept/ *or* **leaped**) springen; **he leapt at it** (*fam*) er griff sofort zu. **~-frog** *n* Bockspringen *nt*. ~ **year** *n* Schaltjahr *nt*

learn /lɜːn/ *vt/i* (*pt/pp* **learnt** *or* **learned**) lernen; (*hear*) erfahren; ~ **to swim** schwimmen lernen

learn|ed /'lɜːnɪd/ *a* gelehrt. **~er** *n* Anfänger *m*; **~er [driver]** Fahrschüler(in) *m(f)*. **~ing** *n* Gelehrsamkeit *f*

lease /li:s/ *n* Pacht *f*; (*contract*) Mietvertrag *m*; (*Comm*) Pachtvertrag *m* ● *vt* pachten; ~ **[out]** verpachten

leash /li:ʃ/ *n* Leine *f*

least /li:st/ *a* geringste(r,s); **have ~ time** am wenigsten Zeit haben ● *n* the ~ das wenigste; **at ~** wenigstens, mindestens; **not in the ~** nicht im geringsten ● *adv* am wenigsten

leather /'leðə(r)/ *n* Leder *nt*. **~y** *a* ledern; (*tough*) zäh

leave /li:v/ *n* Erlaubnis *f*; (*holiday*) Urlaub *m*; **on ~** auf Urlaub; **take one's ~** sich verabschieden ● *v* (*pt/pp* **left**) ● *vt* lassen; (*go out of, abandon*) verlassen; (*forget*) liegenlassen; (*bequeath*) vermachen (**to** *dat*); ~ **it to me!**

überlassen Sie es mir! **there is nothing left** es ist nichts mehr übrig ● *vi* [weg]gehen/-fahren; ⟨*train, bus*:⟩ abfahren. ~ **behind** *vt* zurücklassen; (*forget*) liegenlassen. ~ **out** *vt* liegenlassen; (*leave outside*) draußen lassen; (*omit*) auslassen

leaves /li:vz/ *see* **leaf**

Lebanon /'lebənən/ *n* Libanon *m*

lecherous /'letʃərəs/ *a* lüstern

lectern /'lektɜːn/ *n* [Lese]pult *nt*

lecture /'lektʃə(r)/ *n* Vortrag *m*; (*Univ*) Vorlesung *f*; (*reproof*) Strafpredigt *f* ● *vi* einen Vortrag/eine Vorlesung halten (**on** über + *acc*) ● *vt* ~ **s.o.** eine Strafpredigt halten. **~r** *n* Vortragende(r) *m/f*; (*Univ*) Dozent(in) *m(f)*

led /led/ *see* **lead²**

ledge /ledʒ/ *n* Leiste *f*; (*shelf, of window*) Sims *m*; (*in rock*) Vorsprung *m*

ledger /'ledʒə(r)/ *n* Hauptbuch *nt*

lee /li:/ *n* (*Naut*) Lee *f*

leech /li:tʃ/ *n* Blutegel *m*

leek /li:k/ *n* Stange *f* Porree; **~s** *pl* Porree *m*

leer /lɪə(r)/ *n* anzügliches Grinsen *nt* ● *vi* anzüglich grinsen

lee|ward /'li:wəd/ *adv* nach Lee. **~way** *n* (*fig*) Spielraum *m*

left¹ /left/ *see* **leave**

left² *a* linke(r,s) ● *adv* links; ⟨*go*⟩ nach links ● *n* linke Seite *f*; **on the ~** links; **from/to the ~** von/nach links; **the ~** (*Pol*) die Linke

left: **~-'handed** *a* linkshändig. **~-'luggage [office]** *n* Gepäckaufbewahrung *f*. **~overs** *npl* Reste *pl*. **~-'wing** *a* (*Pol*) linke(r,s)

leg /leg/ *n* Bein *nt*; (*Culin*) Keule *f*; (*of journey*) Etappe *f*

legacy /'legəsɪ/ *n* Vermächtnis *nt*, Erbschaft *f*

legal /'li:gl/ *a*, **-ly** *adv* gesetzlich; ⟨*matters*⟩ rechtlich; ⟨*department, position*⟩ Rechts-; **be ~** [gesetzlich] erlaubt sein; **take ~ action** gerichtlich vorgehen

legality /lɪ'gælətɪ/ *n* Legalität *f*

legalize /'li:gəlaɪz/ *vt* legalisieren

legend /'ledʒənd/ *n* Legende *f*. **~ary** *a* legendär

legible /'ledʒəbl/ *a*, **-bly** *adv* leserlich

legion /'li:dʒn/ *n* Legion *f*

legislat|e /'ledʒɪsleɪt/ *vi* Gesetze erlassen. **~ion** /-'leɪʃn/ *n* Gesetzgebung *f*; (*laws*) Gesetze *pl*

legislat|ive /'ledʒɪslətɪv/ *a* gesetzgebend. **~ure** /-leɪtʃə(r)/ *n* Legislative *f*

legitimate /lɪ'dʒɪtɪmət/ a rechtmäßig; (justifiable) berechtigt;
⟨child⟩ ehelich

leisure /'leʒə(r)/ n Freizeit f; **at your
~** wenn Sie Zeit haben. **~ly** a gemächlich

lemon /'lemən/ n Zitrone f. **~ade**
/-'neɪd/ n Zitronenlimonade f

lend /lend/ vt (pt/pp lent) leihen; **~
s.o. sth** jdm etw leihen; **~ a hand**
(fam) helfen. **~ing library** n Leih-
bücherei f

length /leŋθ/ n Länge f; (piece) Stück
nt; (of wallpaper) Bahn f; (of time)
Dauer f; **at ~** ausführlich; (at last)
endlich

length|en /'leŋθən/ vt länger
machen ● vi länger werden. **~ways**
adv der Länge nach, längs

lengthy /'leŋθɪ/ a (-ier, -iest) lang-
wierig

lenien|ce /'liːnɪəns/ n Nachsicht f.
~t a, **-ly** adv nachsichtig

lens /lenz/ n Linse f; (Phot) Objektiv
nt; (of spectacles) Glas nt

lent /lent/ see lend

Lent n Fastenzeit f

lentil /'lentl/ n (Bot) Linse f

Leo /'liːəʊ/ n (Astr) Löwe m

leopard /'lepəd/ n Leopard m

leotard /'liːətɑːd/ n Trikot nt

leper /'lepə(r)/ n Leprakranke(r)
m/f; n (Bible & fig) Aussätzige(r)
m/f

leprosy /'leprəsɪ/ n Lepra f

lesbian /'lezbɪən/ a lesbisch ● n Les-
bierin f

lesion /'liːʒn/ n Verletzung f

less /les/ a, adv, n & prep weniger; **~
and ~** immer weniger; **not any the ~**
um nichts weniger

lessen /'lesn/ vt verringern ● vi
nachlassen; ⟨value:⟩ abnehmen

lesser /'lesə(r)/ a geringere(r,s)

lesson /'lesn/ n Stunde f; (in text-
book) Lektion f; (Relig) Lesung f;
teach s.o. a ~ (fig) jdm eine Lehre erteilen

lest /lest/ conj (liter) damit ... nicht

let /let/ vt (pt/pp let, pres p letting)
lassen; (rent) vermieten; **~ alone** (not
to mention) geschweige denn; **'to ~'** 'zu
vermieten'; **~ us go** gehen wir; **~ me
know** sagen Sie mir Bescheid; **~ him
do it** laß ihn das machen; **just ~ him!**
soll er doch! **~ s.o. sleep/win** jdn
schlafen/gewinnen lassen; **~ oneself**

in for sth (fam) sich (dat) etw ein-
brocken. **~ down** vt hinunter-/
herunterlassen; (lengthen) länger
machen; **~ s.o. down** (fam) jdn im
Stich lassen; (disappoint) jdn enttäuschen. **~ in** vt hereinlassen. **~ off** vt
abfeuern ⟨gun⟩; hochgehen lassen
⟨firework, bomb⟩; (emit) ausstoßen;
(excuse from) befreien von; (not punish) frei ausgehen lassen. **~ out** vt
hinaus-/ herauslassen; (make larger)
auslassen. **~ through** vt durchlassen. **~ up** vi (fam) nachlassen

'let-down n Enttäuschung f, (fam)
Reinfall m

lethal /'liːθl/ a tödlich

letharg|ic /lɪ'θɑːdʒɪk/ a lethargisch.
~y /'leθədʒɪ/ n Lethargie f

letter /'letə(r)/ n Brief m; (of alphabet) Buchstabe m; **by ~** brieflich.
~-box n Briefkasten m. **~-head** n
Briefkopf m. **~ing** n Beschriftung f

lettuce /'letɪs/ n [Kopf]salat m

'let-up n (fam) Nachlassen nt

leukaemia /luː'kiːmɪə/ n Leukämie f

level /'levl/ a eben; (horizontal)
waagerecht; (in height) auf glei-
cher Höhe; ⟨spoonful⟩ gestrichen;
draw ~ with gleichziehen mit; **one's
~ best** sein möglichstes ● n Höhe f;
(fig) Ebene f, Niveau nt; (stage) Stufe
f; **on the ~** (fam) ehrlich ● vt (pt/pp
levelled) einebnen; (aim) richten (at
auf + acc)

level: **~ 'crossing** n Bahnübergang
m. **~-'headed** a vernünftig

lever /'liːvə(r)/ n Hebel m ● vt **~ up**
mit einem Hebel anheben. **~age**
/-rɪdʒ/ n Hebelkraft f

levity /'levətɪ/ n Heiterkeit f;
(frivolity) Leichtfertigkeit f

levy /'levɪ/ vt (pt/pp levied) erheben
⟨tax⟩

lewd /ljuːd/ a (-er, -est) anstößig

liab|ility /laɪə'bɪlətɪ/ n Haftung f;
~ies pl Verbindlichkeiten pl

liable /'laɪəbl/ a haftbar; **be ~ to do
sth** etw leicht tun können

liaise /lɪ'eɪz/ vi (fam) Verbin-
dungsperson sein

liaison /lɪ'eɪzɒn/ n Verbindung f; (affair) Verhältnis nt

liar /'laɪə(r)/ n Lügner(in) m(f)

libel /'laɪbl/ n Verleumdung f ● vt
(pt/pp libelled) verleumden. **~ous** a
verleumderisch

liberal /'lɪbərl/ a, **-ly** adv tolerant;
(generous) großzügig. **L~** a (Pol) liberal ● n Liberale(r) m/f

liberat|e /'lɪbəreɪt/ vt befreien. **~ed** a ⟨woman⟩ emanzipiert. **~ion** /-'reɪʃn/ n Befreiung f. **~or** n Befreier m

liberty /'lɪbətɪ/ n Freiheit f; **take the ~ of doing sth** sich (dat) erlauben, etw zu tun; **take liberties** sich (dat) Freiheiten erlauben

Libra /'liːbrə/ n (Astr) Waage f

librarian /laɪ'breərɪən/ n Bibliothekar(in) m(f)

library /'laɪbrərɪ/ n Bibliothek f

Libya /'lɪbɪə/ n Libyen nt

lice /laɪs/ see **louse**

licence /'laɪsns/ n Genehmigung f; (Comm) Lizenz f; (for TV) ≈ Fernsehgebühr f; (for driving) Führerschein m; (for alcohol) Schankkonzession f; (freedom) Freiheit f

license /'laɪsns/ vt eine Genehmigung/(Comm) Lizenz erteilen (+ dat); **be ~d** ⟨car:⟩ zugelassen sein; ⟨restaurant:⟩ Schankkonzession haben. **~-plate** n Nummernschild nt

licentious /laɪ'senʃəs/ a lasterhaft

lichen /'laɪkən/ n (Bot) Flechte f

lick /lɪk/ n Lecken nt; **a ~ of paint** ein bißchen Farbe ● vt lecken; (fam: defeat) schlagen

lid /lɪd/ n Deckel m; (of eye) Lid nt

lie[1] /laɪ/ n Lüge f; **tell a ~** lügen ● vi (pt/pp **lied**, pres p **lying**) lügen; **~ to** belügen

lie[2] vi (pt **lay**, pp **lain**, pres p **lying**) liegen; **here ~s** ... hier ruht ... **~ down** vi sich hinlegen

Liège /lɪ'eɪʒ/ n Lüttich nt

'lie-in n **have a ~** [sich] ausschlafen

lieu /ljuː/ n **in ~ of** statt (+ gen)

lieutenant /lef'tenənt/ n Oberleutnant m

life /laɪf/ n (pl **lives**) Leben nt; (biography) Biographie f; **lose one's ~** ums Leben kommen

life: **~belt** n Rettungsring m. **~boat** n Rettungsboot nt. **~buoy** n Rettungsring m. **~guard** n Lebensretter m. **~jacket** n Schwimmweste f. **~less** a leblos. **~like** a naturgetreu. **~line** n Rettungsleine f. **~long** a lebenslang. **~preserver** n (Amer) Rettungsring m. **~-size(d)** a ... in Lebensgröße. **~time** n Leben nt; **in s.o.'s ~time** zu jds Lebzeiten; **the chance of a ~time** eine einmalige Gelegenheit

lift /lɪft/ n Aufzug m, Lift m; **give s.o. a ~** jdn mitnehmen; **get a ~** mitgenommen werden ● vt heben; aufheben ⟨restrictions⟩ ● vi ⟨fog:⟩ sich lichten. **~ up** vt hochheben

'lift-off n Abheben nt

ligament /'lɪgəmənt/ n (Anat) Band nt

light[1] /laɪt/ a (-er, -est) (not dark) hell; **~ blue** hellblau ● n Licht nt; (lamp) Lampe f; **in the ~ of** (fig) angesichts (+ gen); **have you [got] a ~?** haben Sie Feuer? ● vt (pt/pp **lit** or **lighted**) anzünden ⟨fire, cigarette⟩; anmachen ⟨lamp⟩; (illuminate) beleuchten. **~ up** vi ⟨face:⟩ sich erhellen

light[2] a (-er, -est) (not heavy) leicht; **~ sentence** milde Strafe f ● adv **travel ~** mit wenig Gepäck reisen

'light-bulb n Glühbirne f

lighten[1] /'laɪtn/ vt heller machen ● vi heller werden

lighten[2] vt leichter machen ⟨load⟩

lighter /'laɪtə(r)/ n Feuerzeug nt

light: **~-'headed** a benommen. **~-'hearted** a unbekümmert. **~house** n Leuchtturm m. **~ing** n Beleuchtung f. **~ly** adv leicht; (casually) leichthin; **get off ~ly** glimpflich davonkommen

lightning /'laɪtnɪŋ/ n Blitz m. **~-conductor** n Blitzableiter m

'lightweight a leicht ● n (Boxing) Leichtgewicht nt

like[1] /laɪk/ a ähnlich; (same) gleich ● prep wie; (similar to) ähnlich (+ dat); **~ this** so; **a man ~ that** so ein Mann; **what's he ~?** wie ist er denn? ● conj (fam: as) wie; (Amer: as if) als ob

like[2] vt mögen; **I should/would ~** ich möchte; **I ~ the car** das Auto gefällt mir; **I ~ chocolate** ich esse gern Schokolade; **~ dancing/singing** gern tanzen/singen; **I ~ that!** (fam) das ist doch die Höhe! ● n **~s and dislikes** pl Vorlieben und Abneigungen pl

like|able /'laɪkəbl/ a sympathisch. **~lihood** /-lɪhʊd/ n Wahrscheinlichkeit f. **~ly** a (-ier, -iest) & adv wahrscheinlich; **not ~ly!** (fam) auf gar keinen Fall!

'like-minded a gleichgesinnt

liken /'laɪkən/ vt vergleichen (**to** mit)

like|ness /'laɪknɪs/ n Ähnlichkeit f. **~wise** adv ebenso

liking /'laɪkɪŋ/ n Vorliebe f; **is it to your ~?** gefällt es Ihnen?

lilac /'laɪlək/ n Flieder m ● a fliederfarben

lily /'lɪlɪ/ n Lilie f. ~ **of the valley** n Maiglöckchen nt

limb /lɪm/ n Glied nt

limber /'lɪmbə(r)/ vi ~ **up** Lockerungsübungen machen

lime¹ /laɪm/ n (fruit) Limone f; (tree) Linde f

lime² n Kalk m. ~**light** n be in the ~**light** im Rampenlicht stehen. ~**stone** n Kalkstein m

limit /'lɪmɪt/ n Grenze f; (limitation) Beschränkung f; **that's the ~!** (fam) das ist doch die Höhe! ● vt beschränken (**to** auf + acc). ~**ation** /-'teɪʃn/ n Beschränkung f. ~**ed** a beschränkt; ~**ed company** Gesellschaft f mit beschränkter Haftung

limousine /'lɪməziːn/ n Limousine f

limp¹ /lɪmp/ n Hinken nt; **have a ~** hinken ● vi hinken

limp² a (-er, -est), **-ly** adv schlaff

limpet /'lɪmpɪt/ n **like a ~** (fig) wie eine Klette

limpid /'lɪmpɪd/ a klar

linctus /'lɪŋktəs/ n [cough] ~ Hustensirup m

line¹ /laɪn/ n Linie f; (length of rope, cord) Leine f; (Teleph) Leitung f; (of writing) Zeile f; (row) Reihe f; (wrinkle) Falte f; (of business) Branche f; (Amer: queue) Schlange f; **in ~ with** gemäß (+ dat) ● vt säumen (street). ~ **up** vi sich aufstellen ● vt aufstellen

line² vt füttern (garment); (Techn) auskleiden

lineage /'lɪnɪɪdʒ/ n Herkunft f

linear /'lɪnɪə(r)/ a linear

lined¹ /laɪnd/ a (wrinkled) faltig; (paper) liniert

lined² a (garment) gefüttert

linen /'lɪnɪn/ n Leinen nt; (articles) Wäsche f

liner /'laɪnə(r)/ n Passagierschiff nt

linesman n (Sport) Linienrichter m

linger /'lɪŋgə(r)/ vi [zurück]bleiben

lingerie /'læʒərɪ/ n Damenunterwäsche f

linguist /'lɪŋgwɪst/ n Sprachkundige(r) m/f

linguistic /lɪŋ'gwɪstɪk/ a, **-ally** adv sprachlich. ~**s** n Linguistik f

lining /'laɪnɪŋ/ n (of garment) Futter nt; (Techn) Auskleidung f

link /lɪŋk/ n (of chain) Glied nt; (fig) Verbindung f ● vt verbinden; ~ **arms** sich unterhaken

links /lɪŋks/ n or npl Golfplatz m

lino /'laɪnəʊ/ n, **linoleum** /lɪ'nəʊlɪəm/ n Linoleum nt

lint /lɪnt/ n Verbandstoff m

lion /'laɪən/ n Löwe m; ~'s share (fig) Löwenanteil m. ~**ess** n Löwin f

lip /lɪp/ n Lippe f; (edge) Rand m; (of jug) Schnabel m

lip: ~-**reading** n Lippenlesen nt. ~-**service** n pay ~-**service** ein Lippenbekenntnis ablegen (**to** zu). ~**stick** n Lippenstift m

liquefy /'lɪkwɪfaɪ/ vt (pt/pp -ied) verflüssigen ● vi sich verflüssigen

liqueur /lɪ'kjʊə(r)/ n Likör m

liquid /'lɪkwɪd/ n Flüssigkeit f ● a flüssig

liquidat|e /'lɪkwɪdeɪt/ vt liquidieren. ~**ion** /-'deɪʃn/ n Liquidation f

liquidize /'lɪkwɪdaɪz/ vt [im Mixer] pürieren. ~**r** n (Culin) Mixer m

liquor /'lɪkə(r)/ n Alkohol m; (juice) Flüssigkeit f

liquorice /'lɪkərɪs/ n Lakritze f

'**liquor store** n (Amer) Spirituosengeschäft nt

lisp /lɪsp/ n Lispeln nt ● vt/i lispeln

list¹ /lɪst/ n Liste f ● vt aufführen

list² vi (ship:) Schlagseite haben

listen /'lɪsn/ vi zuhören (**to** dat); ~ **to the radio** Radio hören. ~**er** n Zuhörer(in) m(f); (Radio) Hörer(in) m(f)

listless /'lɪstlɪs/ a, **-ly** adv lustlos

lit /lɪt/ see **light**

litany /'lɪtənɪ/ n Litanei f

literacy /'lɪtərəsɪ/ n Lese- und Schreibfertigkeit f

literal /'lɪtərl/ a wörtlich. ~**ly** adv buchstäblich

literary /'lɪtərərɪ/ a literarisch

literate /'lɪtərət/ a **be ~** lesen und schreiben können

literature /'lɪtrətʃə(r)/ n Literatur f; (fam) Informationsmaterial nt

lithe /laɪð/ a geschmeidig

Lithuania /lɪθjʊ'eɪɪə/ n Litauen nt

litigation /lɪtɪ'geɪʃn/ n Rechtsstreit m

litre /'liːtə(r)/ n Liter m & nt

litter /'lɪtə(r)/ n Abfall m; (Zool) Wurf m ● vt be ~**ed with** übersät sein mit. ~-**bin** n Abfalleimer m

little /'lɪtl/ a klein; (not much) wenig ● adv & n wenig; **a ~** ein bißchen; wenig; ~ **by** ~ nach und nach

liturgy /'lɪtədʒɪ/ n Liturgie f
live[1] /laɪv/ a lebendig; ⟨ammunition⟩ scharf; ~ **broadcast** Live-Sendung f; **be** ~ (Electr) unter Strom stehen ● adv (Radio, TV) live
live[2] /lɪv/ vi leben; (reside) wohnen; ~ **up to** gerecht werden (+ dat). ~ **on** vt leben von; (eat) sich ernähren von ● vi weiterleben
liveli|hood /'laɪvlɪhʊd/ n Lebensunterhalt m. ~**ness** n Lebendigkeit f
lively /'laɪvlɪ/ a (-ier, -iest) lebhaft, lebendig
liven /'laɪvn/ v ~ **up** vt beleben ● vi lebhaft werden
liver /'lɪvə(r)/ n Leber f
lives /laɪvz/ see **life**
livestock /'laɪv-/ n Vieh nt
livid /'lɪvɪd/ a (fam) wütend
living /'lɪvɪŋ/ a lebend ● n **earn one's** ~ seinen Lebensunterhalt verdienen; **the** ~ pl die Lebenden. ~-**room** n Wohnzimmer nt
lizard /'lɪzəd/ n Eidechse f
load /ləʊd/ n Last f; (quantity) Ladung f; (Electr) Belastung f; ~**s of** (fam) jede Menge ● vt laden ⟨goods, gun⟩; beladen ⟨vehicle⟩; ~ **a camera** einen Film in eine Kamera einlegen. ~**ed** a beladen; (fam: rich) steinreich; ~**ed question** Fangfrage f
loaf[1] /ləʊf/ n (pl **loaves**) Brot nt
loaf[2] vi faulenzen
loan /ləʊn/ n Leihgabe f; (money) Darlehen nt; **on** ~ geliehen ● vt leihen (**to** dat)
loath /ləʊθ/ a **be** ~ **to do sth** etw ungern tun
loath|e /ləʊð/ vt verabscheuen. ~**ing** n Abscheu m. ~**some** a abscheulich
loaves /ləʊvz/ see **loaf**[1]
lobby /'lɒbɪ/ n Foyer nt; (anteroom) Vorraum m; (Pol) Lobby f
lobe /ləʊb/ n (of ear) Ohrläppchen nt
lobster /'lɒbstə(r)/ n Hummer m
local /'ləʊkl/ a hiesig; ⟨time, traffic⟩ Orts-; **under** ~ **anaesthetic** unter örtlicher Betäubung; **I'm not** ~ ich bin nicht von hier ● n Hiesige(r) m/f; (fam: public house) Stammkneipe f. ~ **au'thority** n Kommunalbehörde f. ~ **call** n (Teleph) Ortsgespräch nt
locality /ləʊ'kælətɪ/ n Gegend f
localized /'ləʊkəlaɪzd/ a lokalisiert
locally /'ləʊkəlɪ/ adv am Ort

locat|e /ləʊ'keɪt/ vt ausfindig machen; **be** ~**ed** sich befinden. ~**ion** /-'keɪʃn/ n Lage f; **filmed on** ~**ion** als Außenaufnahme gedreht
lock[1] /lɒk/ n (hair) Strähne f
lock[2] n (on door) Schloß nt; (on canal) Schleuse f ● vt abschließen ● vi sich abschließen lassen. ~ **in** vt einschließen. ~ **out** vt aussschließen. ~ **up** vt abschließen; einsperren ⟨person⟩ ● vi zuschließen
locker /'lɒkə(r)/ n Schließfach nt; (Mil) Spind m; (in hospital) kleiner Schrank m
locket /'lɒkɪt/ n Medaillon nt
lock: ~-**out** n Aussperrung f. ~**smith** n Schlosser m
locomotion /ləʊkə'məʊʃn/ n Fortbewegung f
locomotive /ləʊkə'məʊtɪv/ n Lokomotive f
locum /'ləʊkəm/ n Vertreter(in) m(f)
locust /'ləʊkəst/ n Heuschrecke f
lodge /lɒdʒ/ n (porter's) Pförtnerhaus nt; (masonic) Loge f ● vt (submit) einreichen; (deposit) deponieren ● vi zur Untermiete wohnen (**with** bei); (become fixed) steckenbleiben. ~**r** n Untermieter(in) m(f)
lodging /'lɒdʒɪŋ/ n Unterkunft f; ~**s** npl möbliertes Zimmer nt
loft /lɒft/ n Dachboden m
lofty /'lɒftɪ/ a (-ier, -iest) hoch; (haughty) hochmütig
log /lɒg/ n Baumstamm m; (for fire) [Holz]scheit nt; **sleep like a** ~ (fam) wie ein Murmeltier schlafen
logarithm /'lɒgərɪðm/ n Logarithmus m
'**log-book** n (Naut) Logbuch nt
loggerheads /'lɒgə-/ npl **be at** ~ (fam) sich in den Haaren liegen
logic /'lɒdʒɪk/ n Logik f. ~**al** a, -**ly** adv logisch
logistics /lə'dʒɪstɪks/ npl Logistik f
logo /'ləʊgəʊ/ n Symbol nt, Logo nt
loin /lɔɪn/ n (Culin) Lende f
loiter /'lɔɪtə(r)/ vi herumlungern
loll /lɒl/ vi sich lümmeln
loll|ipop /'lɒlɪpɒp/ n Lutscher m. ~**y** n Lutscher m; (fam: money) Moneten pl
London /'lʌndən/ n London nt ● attrib Londoner. ~**er** n Londoner(in) m(f)

lone /ləʊn/ *a* einzeln. **~liness** *n* Einsamkeit *f*

lonely /'ləʊnlɪ/ *a* (**-ier, -iest**) einsam

lone|r /'ləʊnə(r)/ *n* Einzelgänger *m*. **~some** *a* einsam

long[1] /lɒŋ/ *a* (**-er** /'lɒŋɡə(r)/, **-est** /'lɒŋɡɪst/) lang; (*journey*) weit; **a ~ time** lange; **a ~ way** weit; **in the ~ run** auf lange Sicht; (*in the end*) letzten Endes ● *adv* lange; **all day ~** den ganzen Tag; **not ~ ago** vor kurzem; **before ~** bald; **no ~er** nicht mehr; **as** *or* **so ~ as** solange; **so ~!** (*fam*) tschüs! **will you be ~?** dauert es noch lange [bei dir]? **it won't take ~** es dauert nicht lange

long[2] *vi* **~ for** sich sehnen nach

long-'distance *a* Fern-; (*Sport*) Langstrecken-

longevity /lɒn'dʒevətɪ/ *n* Langlebigkeit *f*

'longhand *n* Langschrift *f*

longing /'lɒŋɪŋ/ *a*, **-ly** *adv* sehnsüchtig ● *n* Sehnsucht *f*

longitude /'lɒŋɡɪtjuːd/ *n* (*Geog*) Länge *f*

long: ~ jump *n* Weitsprung *m*. **~-life 'milk** *n* H-Milch *f*. **~-lived** /-lɪvd/ *a* langlebig. **~-range** *a* (*Mil, Aviat*) Langstrecken-; (*forecast*) langfristig. **~-sighted** *a* weitsichtig. **~-sleeved** *a* langärmelig. **~-suffering** *a* langmütig. **~-term** *a* langfristig. **~ wave** *n* Langwelle *f*. **~-winded** /-'wɪndɪd/ *a* langatmig

loo /luː/ *n* (*fam*) Klo *nt*

look /lʊk/ *n* Blick *m*; (*appearance*) Aussehen *nt*; **[good] ~s** *pl* [gutes] Aussehen *nt*; **have a ~** sich (*dat*) ansehen; **go and have a ~** sieh mal nach ● *vi* sehen; (*search*) nachsehen; (*seem*) aussehen; **don't ~** sieh nicht hin; **~ here!** hören Sie mal! **~ at** ansehen; **~ for** suchen; **~ forward to** sich freuen auf (+ *acc*); **~ in on** vorbeischauen bei; **~ into** (*examine*) nachgehen (+ *dat*); **~ like** aussehen wie; **~ on to** ⟨*room:*⟩ gehen auf (+ *acc*). **~ after** *vt* betreuen. **~ down** *vi* hinuntersehen; **~ down on s.o.** (*fig*) auf jdn herabsehen. **~ out** *vi* hinaus-/heraussehen; (*take care*) aufpassen; **~ out for** Ausschau halten nach; **~ out!** Vorsicht! **~ round** *vi* sich umsehen. **~ up** *vi* aufblicken; **~ up to s.o.** (*fig*) zu jdm aufsehen ● *vt* nachschlagen ⟨*word*⟩

'look-out *n* Wache *f*; (*prospect*) Aussicht *f*; **be on the ~ for** Ausschau halten nach

loom[1] /luːm/ *n* Webstuhl *m*

loom[2] *vi* auftauchen; (*fig*) sich abzeichnen

loony /'luːnɪ/ *a* (*fam*) verrückt

loop /luːp/ *n* Schlinge *f*; (*in road*) Schleife *f*; (*on garment*) Aufhänger *m* ● *vt* schlingen. **~hole** *n* Hintertürchen *nt*; (*in the law*) Lücke *f*

loose /luːs/ *a* (**-r, -st**), **-ly** *adv* lose; (*not tight enough*) locker; (*inexact*) frei; **be at a ~ end** nichts zu tun haben; **set ~** freilassen; **run ~** frei herumlaufen. **~ 'change** *n* Kleingeld *nt*. **~ 'chippings** *npl* Rollsplit *m*

loosen /'luːsn/ *vt* lockern ● *vi* sich lockern

loot /luːt/ *n* Beute *f* ● *vt/i* plündern. **~er** *n* Plünderer *m*

lop /lɒp/ *vt* (*pt/pp* lopped) stutzen. **~ off** *vt* abhacken

lop'sided *a* schief

loquacious /lə'kweɪʃəs/ *a* redselig

lord /lɔːd/ *n* Herr *m*; (*title*) Lord *m*; **House of L~s** ≈ Oberhaus *nt*; **the L~'s Prayer** das Vaterunser; **good L~!** du liebe Zeit!

lore /lɔː(r)/ *n* Überlieferung *f*

lorry /'lɒrɪ/ *n* Last[kraft]wagen *m*

lose /luːz/ *v* (*pt/pp* lost) ● *vt* verlieren; (*miss*) verpassen ● *vi* verlieren; ⟨*clock:*⟩ nachgehen; **get lost** verlorengehen; ⟨*person:*⟩ sich verlaufen. **~r** *n* Verlierer *m*

loss /lɒs/ *n* Verlust *m*; **be at a ~** nicht mehr weiter wissen; **be at a ~ for words** nicht wissen, was man sagen soll

lost /lɒst/ *see* lose. **~ 'property office** *n* Fundbüro *nt*

lot[1] /lɒt/ *n* Los *nt*; (*at auction*) Posten *m*; **draw ~s** losen (**for** um)

lot[2] *n* **the ~** alle; (*everything*) alles; **a ~ [of]** viel; (*many*) viele; **~s of** (*fam*) eine Menge; **it has changed a ~** es hat sich sehr verändert

lotion /'ləʊʃn/ *n* Lotion *f*

lottery /'lɒtərɪ/ *n* Lotterie *f*. **~ ticket** *n* Los *nt*

loud /laʊd/ *a* (**-er, -est**), **-ly** *adv* laut; ⟨*colours*⟩ grell ● *adv* [out] **~** laut. **~ 'hailer** *n* Megaphon *nt*. **~'speaker** *n* Lautsprecher *m*

lounge /laʊndʒ/ *n* Wohnzimmer *nt*; (*in hotel*) Aufenthaltsraum *m*. ● *vi* sich lümmeln. **~ suit** *n* Straßenanzug *m*

louse /laʊs/ *n* (*pl* lice) Laus *f*

lousy /'laʊzɪ/ *a* (**-ier, -iest**) (*fam*) lausig

lout /laʊt/ *n* Flegel *m*, Lümmel *m*. **~ish** *a* flegelhaft

lovable /'lʌvəbl/ *a* liebenswert

love /lʌv/ *n* Liebe *f*; (*Tennis*) null; **in ~** verliebt ● *vt* lieben; **~ doing sth** etw sehr gerne machen; **I ~ chocolate** ich esse sehr gerne Schokolade. **~-affair** *n* Liebesverhältnis *nt*. **~ letter** *n* Liebesbrief *m*

lovely /'lʌvlɪ/ *a* (**-ier, -iest**) schön; **we had a ~ time** es war sehr schön

lover /'lʌvə(r)/ *n* Liebhaber *m*

love: ~ song *n* Liebeslied *nt*. **~ story** *n* Liebesgeschichte *f*

loving /'lʌvɪŋ/ *a*, **-ly** *adv* liebevoll

low /ləʊ/ *a* (**-er, -est**) niedrig; ⟨cloud, note⟩ tief; ⟨voice⟩ leise; (*depressed*) niedergeschlagen ● *adv* niedrig; ⟨fly, sing⟩ tief; ⟨speak⟩ leise; **feel ~** deprimiert sein ● *n* (*Meteorol*) Tief *nt*; (*fig*) Tiefstand *m*

low: ~brow *a* geistig anspruchslos. **~-cut** *a* ⟨dress⟩ tief ausgeschnitten

lower /'ləʊə(r)/ *a* & *adv* see **low** ● *vt* niedriger machen; (*let down*) herunterlassen; (*reduce*) senken; **~ oneself** sich herabwürdigen

low: ~-'fat *a* fettarm. **~-'grade** *a* minderwertig. **~lands** /-ləndz/ *npl* Tiefland *nt*. **~ 'tide** *n* Ebbe *f*

loyal /'lɔɪəl/ *a*, **-ly** *adv* treu. **~ty** *n* Treue *f*

lozenge /'lɒzɪndʒ/ *n* Pastille *f*

Ltd *abbr* (**Limited**) GmbH

lubricant /'luːbrɪkənt/ *n* Schmiermittel *nt*

lubricat|e /'luːbrɪkeɪt/ *vt* schmieren. **~ion** /-'keɪʃn/ *n* Schmierung *f*

lucid /'luːsɪd/ *a* klar. **~ity** /-'sɪdətɪ/ *n* Klarheit *f*

luck /lʌk/ *n* Glück *nt*; **bad ~** Pech *nt*; **good ~!** viel Glück! **~ily** *adv* glücklicherweise, zum Glück

lucky /'lʌkɪ/ *a* (**-ier, -iest**) glücklich; ⟨day, number⟩ Glücks-; **be ~** Glück haben; ⟨thing:⟩ Glück bringen. **~ 'charm** *n* Amulett *nt*

lucrative /'luːkrətɪv/ *a* einträglich

ludicrous /'luːdɪkrəs/ *a* lächerlich

lug /lʌg/ *vt* (*pt/pp* **lugged**) (*fam*) schleppen

luggage /'lʌgɪdʒ/ *n* Gepäck *nt*

luggage: ~-rack *n* Gepäckablage *f*. **~ trolley** *n* Kofferkuli *m*. **~-van** *n* Gepäckwagen *m*

lugubrious /luː'guːbrɪəs/ *a* traurig

lukewarm /'luːk-/ *a* lauwarm

lull /lʌl/ *n* Pause *f* ● *vt* **~ to sleep** einschläfern

lullaby /'lʌləbaɪ/ *n* Wiegenlied *nt*

lumbago /lʌm'beɪgəʊ/ *n* Hexenschuß *m*

lumber /'lʌmbə(r)/ *n* Gerümpel *nt*; (*Amer: timber*) Bauholz *nt* ● *vt* **~ s.o. with sth** jdm etw aufhalsen. **~jack** *n* (*Amer*) Holzfäller *m*

luminous /'luːmɪnəs/ *a* leuchtend; **be ~** leuchten

lump[1] /lʌmp/ *n* Klumpen *m*; (*of sugar*) Stück *nt*; (*swelling*) Beule *f*; (*in breast*) Knoten *m*; (*tumour*) Geschwulst *f*; **a ~ in one's throat** (*fam*) ein Kloß im Hals ● *vt* **~ together** zusammentun

lump[2] *vt* **~ it** (*fam*) sich damit abfinden

lump: ~ sugar *n* Würfelzucker *m*. **~ 'sum** *n* Pauschalsumme *f*

lumpy /'lʌmpɪ/ *a* (**-ier, -iest**) klumpig

lunacy /'luːnəsɪ/ *n* Wahnsinn *m*

lunar /'luːnə(r)/ *a* Mond-

lunatic /'luːnətɪk/ *n* Wahnsinnige(r) *m/f*

lunch /lʌntʃ/ *n* Mittagessen *nt* ● *vi* zu Mittag essen

luncheon /'lʌntʃn/ *n* Mittagessen *nt*. **~ meat** *n* Frühstücksfleisch *nt*. **~ voucher** *n* Essensbon *m*

lunch: ~-hour *n* Mittagspause *f*. **~-time** *n* Mittagszeit *f*

lung /lʌŋ/ *n* Lungenflügel *m*; **~s** *pl* Lunge *f*. **~ cancer** *n* Lungenkrebs *m*

lunge /lʌndʒ/ *vi* sich stürzen (**at** auf + *acc*)

lurch[1] /lɜːtʃ/ *n* **leave in the ~** (*fam*) im Stich lassen

lurch[2] *vi* schleudern; ⟨person:⟩ torkeln

lure /lʊə(r)/ *n* Lockung *f*; (*bait*) Köder *m* ● *vt* locken

lurid /'lʊərɪd/ *a* grell; (*sensational*) reißerisch

lurk /lɜːk/ *vi* lauern

luscious /'lʌʃəs/ *a* lecker, köstlich

lush /lʌʃ/ *a* üppig

lust /lʌst/ *n* Begierde *f* ● *vi* **~ after** gieren nach. **~ful** *a* lüstern

lustre /'lʌstə(r)/ *n* Glanz *m*

lusty /'lʌstɪ/ *a* (**-ier, -iest**) kräftig

lute /luːt/ *n* Laute *f*

luxuriant /lʌg'zʊərɪənt/ *a* üppig

luxurious /lʌg'zʊərɪəs/ *a*, **-ly** *adv* luxuriös

luxury /'lʌkʃərɪ/ *n* Luxus *m* ● *attrib* Luxus-

lying /'laɪɪŋ/ *see* **lie**[1], **lie**[2]

lymph gland /'lımf-/ n Lymphdrüse f

lynch /lıntʃ/ vt lynchen

lynx /lıŋks/ n Luchs m

lyric /'lırık/ a lyrisch. ~al a lyrisch; (fam: enthusiastic) schwärmerisch. ~ poetry n Lyrik f. ~s npl [Lied]text m

M

mac /mæk/ n (fam) Regenmantel m

macabre /mə'kɑ:br/ a makaber

macaroni /mækə'rəʊnɪ/ n Makkaroni pl

macaroon /mækə'ru:n/ n Makrone f

mace[1] /meɪs/ n Amtsstab m

mace[2] n (spice) Muskatblüte f

machinations /mækɪ'neɪʃnz/ pl Machenschaften pl

machine /mə'ʃi:n/ n Maschine f ● vt (sew) mit der Maschine nähen; (Techn) maschinell bearbeiten. ~-gun n Maschinengewehr nt

machinery /mə'ʃi:nərɪ/ n Maschinerie f

machine tool n Werkzeugmaschine f

machinist /mə'ʃi:nɪst/ n Maschinist m; (on sewing machine) Maschinennäherin f

mackerel /'mækrl/ n inv Makrele f

mackintosh /'mækɪntɒʃ/ n Regenmantel m

mad /mæd/ a (madder, maddest) verrückt; (dog) tollwütig; (fam: angry) böse (at auf + acc)

madam /'mædəm/ n gnädige Frau f

madden /'mædn/ vt (make angry) wütend machen

made /meɪd/ see make; ~ to measure maßgeschneidert

Madeira cake /mə'dɪərə-/ n Sandkuchen m

mad|ly /'mædlɪ/ adv (fam) wahnsinnig. ~man n Irre(r) m. ~ness n Wahnsinn m

madonna /mə'dɒnə/ n Madonna f

magazine /mægə'zi:n/ n Zeitschrift f; (Mil, Phot) Magazin nt

maggot /'mægət/ n Made f. ~y a madig

Magi /'meɪdʒaɪ/ npl the ~ die Heiligen Drei Könige

magic /'mædʒɪk/ n Zauber m; (tricks) Zauberkunst f ● a magisch; (word, wand, flute) Zauber-. ~al a zauberhaft

magician /mə'dʒɪʃn/ n Zauberer m; (entertainer) Zauberkünstler m

magistrate /'mædʒɪstreɪt/ n ≈ Friedensrichter m

magnanim|ity /mægnə'nɪmətɪ/ n Großmut f. ~ous /-'nænɪməs/ a großmütig

magnesia /mæg'ni:ʃə/ n Magnesia f

magnet /'mægnɪt/ n Magnet m. ~ic /-'netɪk/ a magnetisch. ~ism n Magnetismus m. ~ize vt magnetisieren

magnification /mægnɪfɪ'keɪʃn/ n Vergrößerung f

magnificen|ce /mæg'nɪfɪsəns/ n Großartigkeit f. ~t a, -ly adv großartig

magnify /'mægnɪfaɪ/ vt (pt/pp -ied) vergrößern; (exaggerate) übertreiben. ~ing glass n Vergrößerungsglas nt

magnitude /'mægnɪtju:d/ n Größe f; (importance) Bedeutung f

magpie /'mægpaɪ/ n Elster f

mahogany /mə'hɒgənɪ/ n Mahagoni nt

maid /meɪd/ n Dienstmädchen nt; (liter: girl) Maid f; **old** ~ (pej) alte Jungfer f

maiden /'meɪdn/ n (liter) Maid f ● a (speech, voyage) Jungfern-. ~ 'aunt n unverheiratete Tante f. ~ name n Mädchenname m

mail[1] /meɪl/ n Kettenpanzer m

mail[2] n Post f ● vt mit der Post schicken; (send off) abschicken

mail: ~-bag n Postsack m. ~box n (Amer) Briefkasten m. ~ing list n Postversandliste f. ~man n (Amer) Briefträger m. ~-order firm n Versandhaus nt

maim /meɪm/ vt verstümmeln

main[1] /meɪn/ n (water, gas, electricity) Hauptleitung f

main[2] a Haupt- ● n **in the** ~ im großen und ganzen

main: ~land /-lənd/ n Festland nt. ~ly adv hauptsächlich. ~stay n (fig) Stütze f. ~ street n Hauptstraße f

maintain /meɪn'teɪn/ vt aufrechterhalten; (keep in repair) instand halten; (support) unterhalten; (claim) behaupten

maintenance /'meɪntənəns/ n Aufrechterhaltung f; (care) Instandhaltung f; (allowance) Unterhalt m

maisonette /meɪzə'net/ n Wohnung f [auf zwei Etagen]

maize /meɪz/ n Mais m

majestic /mə'dʒestɪk/ a, **-ally** adv majestätisch

majesty /'mædʒəstɪ/ n Majestät f

major /'meɪdʒə(r)/ a größer ● n (Mil) Major m; (Mus) Dur nt ● vi (Amer) ~ **in** als Hauptfach studieren

Majorca /mə'jɔːkə/ n Mallorca nt

majority /mə'dʒɒrətɪ/ n Mehrheit f; **in the** ~ in der Mehrzahl

major road n Hauptverkehrsstraße f

make /meɪk/ n (brand) Marke f ● v (pt/pp **made**) ● vt machen; (force) zwingen; (earn) verdienen; halten ⟨speech⟩; treffen ⟨decision⟩; erreichen ⟨destination⟩ ● vi ~ **as if to** Miene machen zu. ~ **do** vi zurechtkommen (**with** mit). ~ **for** vi zusteuern auf (+ acc). ~ **off** vi sich davonmachen (**with** mit). ~ **out** vt (distinguish) ausmachen; (write out) ausstellen; (assert) behaupten. ~ **over** vt überschreiben (**to** auf + acc). ~ **up** vt (constitute) bilden; (invent) erfinden; (apply cosmetics to) schminken; ~ **up one's mind** sich entschließen ● vi sich versöhnen; ~ **up for sth** etw wiedergutmachen; ~ **up for lost time** verlorene Zeit aufholen

'make-believe n Phantasie f

maker /'meɪkə(r)/ n Hersteller m

make: ~**shift** a behelfsmäßig ● n Notbehelf m. ~-**up** n Make-up nt

making /'meɪkɪŋ/ n **have the** ~**s of** das Zeug haben zu

maladjusted /mælə'dʒʌstɪd/ a verhaltensgestört

malaise /mə'leɪz/ n (fig) Unbehagen nt

male /meɪl/ a männlich ● n Mann m; (animal) Männchen nt. ~ **nurse** n Krankenpfleger m. ~ **voice 'choir** n Männerchor m

malevolen|ce /mə'levələns/ n Bosheit f. ~**t** a boshaft

malfunction /mæl'fʌŋkʃn/ n technische Störung f; (Med) Funktionsstörung f ● vi nicht richtig funktionieren

malice /'mælɪs/ n Bosheit f; **bear s.o.** ~ einen Groll gegen jdn hegen

malicious /mə'lɪʃəs/ a, **-ly** adv böswillig

malign /mə'laɪn/ vt verleumden

malignan|cy /mə'lɪgnənsɪ/ n Bösartigkeit f. ~**t** a bösartig

malinger /mə'lɪŋɡə(r)/ vi simulieren, sich krank stellen. ~**er** n Simulant m

malleable /'mælɪəbl/ a formbar

mallet /'mælɪt/ n Holzhammer m

malnu'trition /mæl-/ n Unterernährung f

mal'practice n Berufsvergehen nt

malt /mɔːlt/ n Malz nt

mal'treat /mæl-/ vt mißhandeln. ~**ment** n Mißhandlung f

mammal /'mæml/ n Säugetier nt

mammoth /'mæməθ/ a riesig ● n Mammut nt

man /mæn/ n (pl **men**) Mann m; (mankind) der Mensch; (chess) Figur f; (draughts) Stein m ● vt (pt/pp **manned**) bemannen ⟨ship⟩; bedienen ⟨pump⟩; besetzen ⟨counter⟩

manacle /'mænəkl/ vt fesseln (**to an** + acc); ~**d** in Handschellen

manage /'mænɪdʒ/ vt leiten; verwalten ⟨estate⟩; (cope with) fertig werden mit; ~ **to do sth** es schaffen, etw zu tun ● vi zurechtkommen; ~ **on** auskommen mit. ~**able** /-əbl/ a ⟨tool⟩ handlich; ⟨person⟩ fügsam. ~**ment** /-mənt/ n **the** ~**ment** die Geschäftsleitung f

manager /'mænɪdʒə(r)/ n Geschäftsführer m; (of bank) Direktor m; (of estate) Verwalter m; (Sport) [Chef]trainer m. ~**ess** n Geschäftsführer(in) f. ~**ial** /-'dʒɪərɪəl/ a ~**ial staff** Führungskräfte pl

managing /'mænɪdʒɪŋ/ a ~ **director** Generaldirektor m

mandarin /'mændərɪn/ n ~ [**orange**] Mandarine f

mandat|e /'mændeɪt/ n Mandat nt. ~**ory** /-dətrɪ/ a obligatorisch

mane /meɪn/ n Mähne f

manful /'mænfl/ a, **-ly** adv mannhaft

manger /'meɪndʒə(r)/ n Krippe f

mangle[1] /'mæŋgl/ n Wringmaschine f; (for smoothing) Mangel f

mangle[2] vt (damage) verstümmeln

mango /'mæŋɡəʊ/ n (pl **-es**) Mango f

mangy /'meɪndʒɪ/ a ⟨dog⟩ räudig

man: ~'**handle** vt grob behandeln ⟨person⟩. ~**hole** n Kanalschacht m. ~**hole cover** n Kanaldeckel m. ~**hood** n Mannesalter nt; (quality) Männlichkeit f. ~-**hour** n Arbeitsstunde f. ~-**hunt** n Fahndung f

man|ia /'meɪnɪə/ n Manie f. **~iac** /-ræk/ n Wahnsinnige(r) m/f

manicur|e /'mænɪkjʊə(r)/ n Maniküre f ● vt maniküren. **~ist** n Maniküre f

manifest /'mænɪfest/ a, **-ly** adv offensichtlich ● vt ~ **itself** sich manifestieren

manifesto /mænɪ'festəʊ/ n Manifest nt

manifold /'mænɪfəʊld/ a mannigfaltig

manipulat|e /mə'nɪpjʊleɪt/ vt handhaben; (pej) manipulieren. **~ion** /-'leɪʃn/ n Manipulation f

man'kind n die Menschheit

manly /'mænlɪ/ a männlich

'man-made a künstlich. **~ fibre** n Kunstfaser f

manner /'mænə(r)/ n Weise f; (kind, behaviour) Art f; **in this ~** auf diese Weise; **[good/bad] ~s** [gute/schlechte] Manieren pl. **~ism** n Angewohnheit f

mannish /'mænɪʃ/ a männlich

manœuvrable /mə'nu:vrəbl/ a manövrierfähig

manœuvre /mə'nu:və(r)/ n Manöver nt ● vt/i manövrieren

manor /'mænə(r)/ n Gutshof m; (house) Gutshaus nt

man: **~power** n Arbeitskräfte pl. **~servant** n (pl menservants) Diener m

mansion /'mænʃn/ n Villa f

manslaughter n Totschlag m

mantelpiece /'mæntl-/ n Kaminsims m & nt

manual /'mænjʊəl/ a Hand- ● n Handbuch nt

manufacture /mænjʊ'fæktʃə(r)/ vt herstellen ● n Herstellung f. **~r** n Hersteller m

manure /mə'njʊə(r)/ n Mist m

manuscript /'mænjʊskrɪpt/ n Manuskript nt

many /'menɪ/ a viele; **~ a time** oft ● n **a good/great ~** sehr viele

map /mæp/ n Landkarte f; (of town) Stadtplan m ● vt (pt/pp mapped) **~ out** (fig) ausarbeiten

maple /'meɪpl/ n Ahorn m

mar /mɑ:(r)/ vt (pt/pp marred) verderben

marathon /'mærəθən/ n Marathon m

marauding /mə'rɔ:dɪŋ/ a plündernd

marble /'mɑ:bl/ n Marmor m; (for game) Murmel f

March /mɑ:tʃ/ n März m

march n Marsch m ● vi marschieren ● vt marschieren lassen; **~ s.o. off** jdn abführen

mare /'meə(r)/ n Stute f

margarine /mɑ:dʒə'ri:n/ n Margarine f

margin /'mɑ:dʒɪn/ n Rand m; (leeway) Spielraum m; (Comm) Spanne f. **~al** a, **-ly** adv geringfügig

marigold /'mærɪgəʊld/ n Ringelblume f

marijuana /mærɪ'hwɑ:nə/ n Marihuana nt

marina /mə'ri:nə/ n Jachthafen m

marinade /mærɪ'neɪd/ n Marinade f ● vt marinieren

marine /mə'ri:n/ a Meeres- ● n Marine f; (sailor) Marineinfanterist m

marionette /mærɪə'net/ n Marionette f

marital /'mærɪtl/ a ehelich. **~ status** n Familienstand m

maritime /'mærɪtaɪm/ a See-

marjoram /'mɑ:dʒərəm/ n Majoran m

mark[1] /mɑ:k/ n (currency) Mark f

mark[2] n Fleck m; (sign) Zeichen nt; (trace) Spur f; (target) Ziel nt; (Sch) Note f ● vt markieren; (spoil) beschädigen; (characterize) kennzeichnen; (Sch) korrigieren; (Sport) decken; **~ time** (Mil) auf der Stelle treten; (fig) abwarten; **~ my words** das [eine] will ich dir sagen. **~ out** vt markieren

marked /mɑ:kt/ a, **-ly** /-kɪdlɪ/ adv deutlich; (pronounced) ausgeprägt

marker /'mɑ:kə(r)/ n Marke f; (of exam) Korrektor(in) m(f)

market /'mɑ:kɪt/ n Markt m ● vt vertreiben; (launch) auf den Markt bringen. **~ing** n Marketing nt. **~re-'search** n Marktforschung f

marking /'mɑ:kɪŋ/ n Markierung f; (on animal) Zeichnung f

marksman /'mɑ:ksmən/ n Scharfschütze m

marmalade /'mɑ:məleɪd/ n Orangenmarmelade f

marmot /'mɑ:mət/ n Murmeltier nt

maroon /mə'ru:n/ a dunkelrot

marooned /mə'ru:nd/ a (fig) von der Außenwelt abgeschnitten

marquee /mɑ:'ki:/ n Festzelt nt; (Amer: awning) Markise f

marquetry /'mɑːkɪtrɪ/ n Einlegearbeit f
marquis /'mɑːkwɪs/ n Marquis m
marriage /'mærɪdʒ/ n Ehe f; (wedding) Hochzeit f. **~able** /-əbl/ a
heiratsfähig
married /'mærɪd/ see **marry** ● a
verheiratet. ~ **life** n Eheleben nt
marrow /'mærəʊ/ n (Anat) Mark nt;
(vegetable) Kürbis m
marr|y /'mærɪ/ vt/i (pt/pp **married**)
heiraten; (unite) trauen; **get ~ied** heiraten
marsh /mɑːʃ/ n Sumpf m
marshal /'mɑːʃl/ n Marschall m;
(steward) Ordner m ● vt (pt/pp **mar-
shalled**) (Mil) formieren; (fig) ordnen
marshy /'mɑːʃɪ/ a sumpfig
marsupial /mɑː'suːpɪəl/ n Beuteltier
nt
martial /'mɑːʃl/ a kriegerisch. ~
'**law** n Kriegsrecht nt
martyr /'mɑːtə(r)/ n Märtyrer(in)
m(f) ● vt zum Märtyrer machen.
~dom /-dəm/ n Martyrium nt
marvel /'mɑːvl/ n Wunder nt ● vi
(pt/pp **marvelled**) staunen (**at** über
+ acc). **~lous** /-vələs/ a, **-ly** adv wunderbar
Marxis|m /'mɑːksɪzm/ n Marxismus
m. **~t** a marxistisch ● n Marxist(in)
m(f)
marzipan /'mɑːzɪpæn/ n Marzipan
nt
mascara /mæ'skɑːrə/ n Wimpern-
tusche f
mascot /'mæskət/ n Maskottchen nt
masculin|e /'mæskjʊlɪn/ a männlich
● n (Gram) Maskulinum nt. **~ity**
/-'lɪnətɪ/ n Männlichkeit f
mash /mæʃ/ n (fam, Culin) Kartoffelpüree nt ● vt stampfen. **~ed
potatoes** npl Kartoffelpüree nt
mask /mɑːsk/ n Maske f ● vt maskieren
masochis|m /'mæsəkɪzm/ n Ma-
sochismus m. **~t** /-ɪst/ n Masochist
m
mason /'meɪsn/ n Steinmetz m
Mason n Freimaurer m. **~ic** /mə's-
ɒnɪk/ a freimaurerisch
masonry /'meɪsnrɪ/ n Mauerwerk nt
masquerade /mæskə'reɪd/ n (fig)
Maskerade f ● vi ~ **as** (pose) sich ausgeben als
mass[1] /mæs/ n (Relig) Messe f
mass[2] n Masse f ● vi sich sammeln;
(Mil) sich massieren

massacre /'mæsəkə(r)/ n Massaker
nt ● vt niedermetzeln
massage /'mæsɑːʒ/ n Massage f ● vt
massieren
masseu|r /mæ'sɜː(r)/ n Masseur m.
~se /-'sɜːz/ n Masseuse f
massive /'mæsɪv/ a massiv; (huge)
riesig
mass: ~ **media** npl Massenmedien
pl. **~-pro'duce** vt in Massenproduktion herstellen. ~ **pro-
'duction** n Massenproduktion f
mast /mɑːst/ n Mast m
master /'mɑːstə(r)/ n Herr m;
(teacher) Lehrer m; (craftsman,
artist) Meister m; (of ship) Kapitän m
● vt meistern; beherrschen (language)
master: **~-key** n Hauptschlüssel m.
~ly a meisterhaft. **~-mind** n
führender Kopf m ● vt der führende
Kopf sein von. **~piece** n Meister-
werk nt. **~y** n (of subject) Beherrschung f
masturbat|e /'mæstəbeɪt/ vi
masturbieren. **~ion** /-'beɪʃn/ n
Masturbation f
mat /mæt/ n Matte f; (on table)
Untersatz m
match[1] /mætʃ/ n Wettkampf m; (in
ball games) Spiel nt; (Tennis) Match
nt; (marriage) Heirat f; **be a good ~**
⟨colours:⟩ gut zusammenpassen; **be no
~ for s.o.** jdm nicht gewachsen sein
● vt (equal) gleichkommen (+ dat); (be
like) passen zu; (find sth similar) etwas
Passendes finden zu ● vi zusammenpassen
match[2] n Streichholz nt. **~box** n
Streichholzschachtel f
matching /'mætʃɪŋ/ a [zusammen]-
passend
mate[1] /meɪt/ n Kumpel m; (assistant)
Gehilfe m; (Naut) Maat m; (Zool)
Männchen nt; (female) Weibchen nt
● vi sich paaren ● vt paaren
mate[2] n (Chess) Matt nt
material /mə'tɪərɪəl/ n Material nt;
(fabric) Stoff m; **raw ~s** Rohstoffe pl
● a materiell
material|ism /mə'tɪərɪəlɪzm/ n
Materialismus m. **~istic** /-'lɪstɪk/ a
materialistisch. **~ize** /-laɪz/ vi sich
verwirklichen
maternal /mə'tɜːnl/ a mütterlich
maternity /mə'tɜːnətɪ/ n Mutterschaft f. ~ **clothes** npl Umstands-

kleidung f. **~ ward** n Entbindungs-
station f

matey /'meɪtɪ/ a (fam) freundlich

mathematic|al /mæθə'mætɪkl/ a,
-ly adv mathematisch. **~ian**
/-mə'tɪʃn/ n Mathematiker(in) m(f)

mathematics /mæθə'mætɪks/ n
Mathematik f

maths /mæθs/ n (fam) Mathe f

matinée /'mætɪneɪ/ n (Theat)
Nachmittagsvorstellung f

matriculat|e /mə'trɪkjʊleɪt/ vi sich
immatrikulieren. **~ion** /-'leɪʃn/ n
Immatrikulation f

matrimon|ial /mætrɪ'məʊnɪəl/ a
Ehe-. **~y** /'mætrɪmənɪ/ n Ehe f

matrix /'meɪtrɪks/ n (pl matrices
/-siːz/) n (Techn: mould) Matrize f

matron /'meɪtrən/ n (of hospital)
Oberin f; (of school) Hausmutter f.
~ly a matronenhaft

matt /mæt/ a matt

matted /'mætɪd/ a verfilzt

matter /'mætə(r)/ n (affair) Sache f;
(pus) Eiter m; (Phys: substance)
Materie f; **money ~s** Geld-
angelegenheiten pl; **as a ~ of fact**
eigentlich; **what is the ~?** was ist los?
● vi wichtig sein; **~ to s.o.** jdm etwas
ausmachen; **it doesn't ~** es macht
nichts. **~-of-fact** a sachlich

matting /'mætɪŋ/ n Matten pl

mattress /'mætrɪs/ n Matratze f

matur|e /mə'tjʊə(r)/ a reif; (Comm)
fällig ● vi reifen; (person:) reifer
werden; (Comm) fällig werden ● vt
reifen lassen. **~ity** n Reife f; (Comm)
Fälligkeit f

maul /mɔːl/ vt übel zurichten

Maundy /'mɔːndɪ/ n **~ Thursday**
Gründonnerstag m

mauve /məʊv/ a lila

mawkish /'mɔːkɪʃ/ a rührselig

maxim /'mæksɪm/ n Maxime f

maximum /'mæksɪməm/ a maximal
● n (pl -ima) Maximum nt. **~ speed** n
Höchstgeschwindigkeit f

may /meɪ/ v aux (nur Präsens) (be
allowed to) dürfen; (be possible)
können; **may I come in?** darf ich
reinkommen? **may he succeed** möge
es ihm gelingen; **I may as well stay** am
besten bleibe ich hier; **it may be true**
es könnte wahr sein

May n Mai m

maybe /'meɪbiː/ adv vielleicht

'May Day n der Erste Mai

mayonnaise /meɪə'neɪz/ n Mayonnaise f

mayor /'meə(r)/ n Bürgermeister m.
~ess n Bürgermeisterin f; (wife of
mayor) Frau Bürgermeister f

maze /meɪz/ n Irrgarten m; (fig)
Labyrinth nt

me /miː/ pron (acc) mich; (dat) mir;
he knows ~ er kennt mich; **give ~ the
money** gib mir das Geld; **it's ~** (fam)
ich bin es

meadow /'medəʊ/ n Wiese f

meagre /'miːgə(r)/ a dürftig

meal¹ /miːl/ n Mahlzeit f; (food) Essen
nt

meal² n (grain) Schrot m

mealy-mouthed /miːlɪ'maʊðd/ a
heuchlerisch

mean¹ /miːn/ a (-er, -est) geizig;
(unkind) gemein; (poor) schäbig

mean² a mittlere(r,s) ● n (average)
Durchschnitt m; **the golden ~** die
goldene Mitte

mean³ vt (pt/pp meant) heißen; (signify) bedeuten; (intend) beabsichtigen; **I
~ it** das ist mein Ernst; **~ well** es gut
meinen; **be meant for** ⟨present:⟩ bestimmt sein für; ⟨remark:⟩ gerichtet
sein an (+ acc)

meander /mɪ'ændə(r)/ vi sich
schlängeln; ⟨person:⟩ schlendern

meaning /'miːnɪŋ/ n Bedeutung f.
~ful a bedeutungsvoll. **~less** a be-
deutungslos

means /miːnz/ n Möglichkeit f, Mittel nt; **~ of transport** Verkehrsmittel
nt; **by ~ of** durch; **by all ~!** aber
natürlich! **by no ~** keineswegs ● npl
(resources) [Geld]mittel pl. **~ test** n Be-
dürftigkeitsnachweis m

meant /ment/ see **mean³**

'meantime n **in the ~** in der Zwischenzeit ● adv inzwischen

'meanwhile adv inzwischen

measles /'miːzlz/ n Masern pl

measly /'miːzlɪ/ a (fam) mickerig

measurable /'meʒərəbl/ a meßbar

measure /'meʒə(r)/ n Maß nt; (action) Maßnahme f ● vt/i messen; **~
up to** (fig) herankommen an (+ acc).
~d a gemessen. **~ment** /-mənt/ n
Maß nt

meat /miːt/ n Fleisch nt. **~ball** n
(Culin) Klops m. **~ loaf** n falscher
Hase m

mechan|ic /mɪ'kænɪk/ n Mecha-
niker m. **~ical** a, **-ly** adv mechanisch.
~ical engineering Maschinenbau

m. ~**ics** *n* Mechanik *f* ● *n pl* Mech-anismus *m*

mechan|ism /'mekənızm/ *n* Mecha-nismus *m*. ~**ize** *vt* mechanisieren

medal /'medl/ *n* Orden *m*; (*Sport*) Medaille *f*

medallion /mɪ'dælɪən/ *n* Medaillon *nt*

medallist /'medəlɪst/ *n* Medaillen-gewinner(in) *m*(*f*)

meddle /'medl/ *vi* sich einmischen (**in** in + *acc*); (*tinker*) herumhantieren (**with** an + *acc*)

media /'miːdɪə/ *see* **medium** ● *n pl* **the ~** die Medien *pl*

median /'miːdɪən/ *a* ~ **strip** (*Amer*) Mittelstreifen *m*

mediat|e /'miːdɪeɪt/ *vi* vermitteln. ~**or** *n* Vermittler(in) *m*(*f*)

medical /'medɪkl/ *a* medizinisch; (*treatment*) ärztlich ● *n* ärztliche Untersuchung *f*. ~ **insurance** *n* Krankenversicherung *f*. ~ **student** *n* Medizinstudent *m*

medicat|ed /'medɪkeɪtɪd/ *a* medi-zinisch. ~**ion** /-'keɪʃn/ *n* (*drugs*) Medikamente *pl*

medicinal /mɪ'dɪsɪnl/ *a* medizinisch; (*plant*) heilkräftig

medicine /'medsən/ *n* Medizin *f*; (*preparation*) Medikament *nt*

medieval /medɪˈiːvl/ *a* mittel-alterlich

mediocr|e /miːdɪˈəʊkə(r)/ *a* mittel-mäßig. ~**ity** /-'ɒkrətɪ/ *n* Mittel-mäßigkeit *f*

meditat|e /'medɪteɪt/ *vi* nach-denken (**on** über + *acc*); (*Relig*) medi-tieren. ~**ion** /-'teɪʃn/ *n* Meditation *f*

Mediterranean /medɪtə'reɪnɪən/ *n* Mittelmeer *nt* ● *a* Mittelmeer-

medium /'miːdɪəm/ *a* mittlere(r,s); (*steak*) medium; **of** ~ **size** von mitt-lerer Größe ● *n* (*pl* **media**) Medium *nt*; (*means*) Mittel *nt* ● (*pl* **-s**) (*person*) Medium *nt*

medium: ~**-sized** *a* mittelgroß. ~ **wave** *n* Mittelwelle *f*

medley /'medlɪ/ *n* Gemisch *nt*; (*Mus*) Potpourri *nt*

meek /miːk/ *a* (**-er**, **-est**), **-ly** *adv* sanftmütig; (*unprotesting*) wider-spruchslos

meet /miːt/ *v* (*pt/pp* **met**) ● *vt* treffen; (*by chance*) begegnen (+ *dat*); (*at sta-tion*) abholen; (*make the acquaintance of*) kennenlernen; stoßen auf (+ *acc*)

(*problem*); bezahlen (*bill*); erfüllen (*re-quirements*) ● *vi* sich treffen; (*for the first time*) sich kennenlernen; ~ **with** stoßen auf (+ *acc*) (*problem*); sich tref-fen mit (*person*) ● *n* Jagdtreffen *nt*

meeting /'miːtɪŋ/ *n* Treffen *nt*; (*by chance*) Begegnung *f*; (*discussion*) Be-sprechung *f*; (*of committee*) Sitzung *f*; (*large*) Versammlung *f*

megalomania /megələ'meɪnɪə/ *n* Größenwahnsinn *m*

megaphone /'megəfəʊn/ *n* Mega-phon *nt*

melancholy /'melənkəlɪ/ *a* melan-cholisch ● *n* Melancholie *f*

mellow /'meləʊ/ *a* (**-er**, **-est**) (*fruit*) ausgereift; (*sound, person*) sanft ● *vi* reifer werden

melodic /mɪ'lɒdɪk/ *a* melodisch

melodious /mɪ'ləʊdɪəs/ *a* melodiös

melodrama /'melə-/ *n* Melodrama *nt*. ~**tic** /-drə'mætɪk/ *a*, **-ally** *adv* melodramatisch

melody /'melədɪ/ *n* Melodie *f*

melon /'melən/ *n* Melone *f*

melt /melt/ *vt/i* schmelzen. ~ **down** *vt* einschmelzen. ~**ing-pot** *n* (*fig*) Schmelztiegel *m*

member /'membə(r)/ *n* Mitglied *nt*; (*of family*) Angehörige(r) *m/f*; **M~ of Parliament** Abgeordnete(r) *m/f*. ~**ship** *n* Mitgliedschaft *f*; (*members*) Mitgliederzahl *f*

membrane /'membreɪn/ *n* Mem-bran *f*

memento /mɪ'mentəʊ/ *n* Andenken *nt*

memo /'meməʊ/ *n* Mitteilung *f*

memoirs /'memwɑːz/ *n pl* Me-moiren *pl*

memorable /'memərəbl/ *a* denk-würdig

memorandum /memə'rændəm/ *n* Mitteilung *f*

memorial /mɪ'mɔːrɪəl/ *n* Denkmal *nt*. ~ **service** *n* Gedenkfeier *f*

memorize /'meməraɪz/ *vt* sich (*dat*) einprägen

memory /'memərɪ/ *n* Gedächtnis *nt*; (*thing remembered*) Erinnerung *f*; (*of computer*) Speicher *m*; **from** ~ aus-wendig; **in** ~ **of** zur Erinnerung an (+ *acc*)

men /men/ *see* **man**

menac|e /'menɪs/ *n* Drohung *f*; (*nuisance*) Plage *f* ● *vt* bedrohen. ~**ing** *a*, **-ly** *adv* drohend

mend /mend/ vt reparieren; (patch) flicken; ausbessern ⟨clothes⟩ ● n **on the** ~ auf dem Weg der Besserung

'**menfolk** n pl Männer pl

menial /'miːnɪəl/ a niedrig

meningitis /menɪn'dʒaɪtɪs/ n Hirnhautentzündung f, Meningitis f

menopause /'menə-/ n Wechseljahre pl

menstruat|e /'menstrʊeɪt/ vi menstruieren. ~**ion** /-'eɪʃn/ n Menstruation f

mental /'mentl/ a, -ly adv geistig; (fam: mad) verrückt. ~ **a'rithmetic** n Kopfrechnen nt. ~ '**illness** n Geisteskrankheit f

mentality /men'tælətɪ/ n Mentalität f

mention /'menʃn/ n Erwähnung f ● vt erwähnen; **don't** ~ **it** keine Ursache; bitte

menu /'menjuː/ n Speisekarte f

mercantile /'mɜːkəntaɪl/ a Handels-

mercenary /'mɜːsɪnərɪ/ a geldgierig ● n Söldner m

merchandise /'mɜːtʃəndaɪz/ n Ware f

merchant /'mɜːtʃənt/ n Kaufmann m; (dealer) Händler m. ~ '**navy** n Handelsmarine f

merci|ful /'mɜːsɪfl/ a barmherzig. ~**fully** adv (fam) glücklicherweise. ~**less** a, -ly adv erbarmungslos

mercury /'mɜːkjʊrɪ/ n Quecksilber nt

mercy /'mɜːsɪ/ n Barmherzigkeit f, Gnade f; **be at s.o.'s** ~ jdm ausgeliefert sein

mere /mɪə(r)/ a, -ly adv bloß

merest /'mɪərɪst/ a kleinste(r,s)

merge /mɜːdʒ/ vi zusammenlaufen; (Comm) fusionieren ● vt (Comm) zusammenschließen

merger /'mɜːdʒə(r)/ n Fusion f

meridian /mə'rɪdɪən/ n Meridian m

meringue /mə'ræŋ/ n Baiser nt

merit /'merɪt/ n Verdienst nt; (advantage) Vorzug m; (worth) Wert m ● vt verdienen

mermaid /'mɜːmeɪd/ n Meerjungfrau f

merri|ly /'merɪlɪ/ adv fröhlich. ~**ment** /-mənt/ n Fröhlichkeit f; (laughter) Gelächter nt

merry /'merɪ/ a (-ier, -iest) fröhlich; ~ **Christmas!** fröhliche Weihnachten!

merry: ~**-go-round** n Karussell nt. ~**-making** n Feiern nt

mesh /meʃ/ n Masche f; (size) Maschenweite f; (fig: network) Netz nt

mesmerize /'mezməraɪz/ vt hypnotisieren. ~**d** a (fig) [wie] gebannt

mess /mes/ n Durcheinander nt; (trouble) Schwierigkeiten pl; (something spilt) Bescherung f (fam); (Mil) Messe f; **make a** ~ **of** (botch) verpfuschen ● vt ~ **up** in Unordnung bringen; (botch) verpfuschen ● vi ~ **about** herumalbern; (tinker) herumspielen (**with** mit)

message /'mesɪdʒ/ n Nachricht f; **give s.o. a** ~ jdm etwas ausrichten

messenger /'mesɪndʒə(r)/ n Bote m

Messiah /mɪ'saɪə/ n Messias m

Messrs /'mesəz/ n pl see **Mr**; (on letter) ~ **Smith** Firma Smith

messy /'mesɪ/ a (-ier, -iest) schmutzig; (untidy) unordentlich

met /met/ see **meet**

metabolism /mɪ'tæbəlɪzm/ n Stoffwechsel m

metal /'metl/ n Metall nt ● a Metall-. ~**lic** /mɪ'tælɪk/ a metallisch. ~**lurgy** /mɪ'tælədʒɪ/ n Metallurgie f

metamorphosis /metə'mɔːfəsɪs/ n (pl -**phoses** /-siːz/) Metamorphose f

metaphor /'metəfə(r)/ n Metapher f. ~**ical** /-'fɒrɪkl/ a, -ly adv metaphorisch

meteor /'miːtɪə(r)/ n Meteor m. ~**ic** /-'ɒrɪk/ a kometenhaft

meteorological /miːtɪərə'lɒdʒɪkl/ a Wetter-

meteorolog|ist /miːtɪə'rɒlədʒɪst/ n Meteorologe m/-gin f. ~**y** n Meteorologie f

meter[1] /'miːtə(r)/ n Zähler m

meter[2] n (Amer) = **metre**

method /'meθəd/ n Methode f; (Culin) Zubereitung f

methodical /mɪ'θɒdɪkl/ a, -ly adv systematisch, methodisch

Methodist /'meθədɪst/ n Methodist(in) m(f)

meths /meθs/ n (fam) Brennspiritus m

methylated /'meθɪleɪtɪd/ a ~ **spirit[s]** Brennspiritus m

meticulous /mɪ'tɪkjʊləs/ a, -ly adv sehr genau

metre /'miːtə(r)/ n Meter m & nt; (rhythm) Versmaß nt

metric /'metrɪk/ a metrisch

metropolis /mɪ'trɒpəlɪs/ n Metropole f

metropolitan /metrə'pɒlɪtən/ *a* hauptstädtisch; *(international)* weltstädtisch

mettle /'metl/ *n* Mut *m*

mew /mju:/ *n* Miau *nt* ● *vi* miauen

Mexican /'meksɪkən/ *a* mexikanisch ● *n* Mexikaner(in) *m(f)*. **'Mexico** *n* Mexiko *nt*

miaow /mɪ'aʊ/ *n* Miau *nt* ● *vi* miauen

mice /maɪs/ *see* **mouse**

microbe /'maɪkrəʊb/ *n* Mikrobe *f*

micro /'maɪkrəʊ/: **~chip** *n* Mikrochip *nt*. **~computer** *n* Mikrocomputer *m*. **~film** *n* Mikrofilm *m*. **~phone** *n* Mikrophon *nt*. **~processor** *n* Mikroprozessor *m*. **~scope** /-skəʊp/ *n* Mikroskop *nt*. **~scopic** /-'skɒpɪk/ *a* mikroskopisch. **~wave** *n* Mikrowelle *f*. **~wave [oven]** *n* Mikrowellenherd *m*

mid /mɪd/ *a* **~ May** Mitte Mai; **in ~ air** in der Luft

midday /mɪd'deɪ/ *n* Mittag *m*

middle /'mɪdl/ *a* mittlere(r,s); **the M~ Ages** das Mittelalter; **the ~ class[es]** der Mittelstand; **the M~ East** der Nahe Osten ● *n* Mitte *f*; **in the ~ of the night** mitten in der Nacht

middle: **~-aged** *a* mittleren Alters. **~-class** *a* bürgerlich. **~man** *n* *(Comm)* Zwischenhändler *m*

middling /'mɪdlɪŋ/ *a* mittelmäßig

midge /mɪdʒ/ *n* [kleine] Mücke *f*

midget /'mɪdʒɪt/ *n* Liliputaner(in) *m(f)*

Midlands /'mɪdləndz/ *npl* **the ~** Mittelengland *n*

'midnight *n* Mitternacht *f*

midriff /'mɪdrɪf/ *n (fam)* Taille *f*

midst /mɪdst/ *n* **in the ~ of** mitten in (+ *dat*); **in our ~** unter uns

mid: **~summer** *n* Hochsommer *m*; *(solstice)* Sommersonnenwende *f*. **~way** *adv* auf halbem Wege. **~wife** *n* Hebamme *f*. **~wifery** /-wɪfrɪ/ *n* Geburtshilfe *f*. **~'winter** *n* Mitte *f* des Winters

might¹ /maɪt/ *v aux* **I ~** vielleicht; **it ~ be true** es könnte wahr sein; **I ~ as well stay** am besten bleibe ich hier; **he asked if he ~ go** er fragte, ob er gehen dürfte; **you ~ have drowned** du hättest ertrinken können

might² *n* Macht *f*

mighty /'maɪtɪ/ *a* (**-ier, -iest**) mächtig

migraine /'mi:greɪn/ *n* Migräne *f*

migrant /'maɪgrənt/ *a* Wander- ● *n* *(bird)* Zugvogel *m*

migrat|e /maɪ'greɪt/ *vi* abwandern; *(birds:)* ziehen. **~ion** /-'greɪʃn/ *n* Wanderung *f*; *(of birds)* Zug *m*

mike /maɪk/ *n (fam)* Mikrophon *nt*

mild /maɪld/ *a* (**-er, -est**) mild

mildew /'mɪldju:/ *n* Schimmel *m*; *(Bot)* Mehltau *m*

mild|ly /'maɪldlɪ/ *adv* leicht; **to put it ~ly** gelinde gesagt. **~ness** *n* Milde *f*

mile /maɪl/ *n* Meile *f* (= 1,6 km); **~s too big** *(fam)* viel zu groß

mile|age /-ɪdʒ/ *n* Meilenzahl *f*; *(of car)* Meilenstand *m*. **~stone** *n* Meilenstein *m*

militant /'mɪlɪtənt/ *a* militant

military /'mɪlɪtrɪ/ *a* militärisch. **~ service** *n* Wehrdienst *m*

militate /'mɪlɪteɪt/ *vi* **~ against** sprechen gegen

militia /mɪ'lɪʃə/ *n* Miliz *f*

milk /mɪlk/ *n* Milch *f* ● *vt* melken

milk: **~man** *n* Milchmann *m*. **~ shake** *n* Milchmixgetränk *nt*

milky /'mɪlkɪ/ *a* (**-ier, -iest**) milchig. **M~ Way** *n (Astr)* Milchstraße *f*

mill /mɪl/ *n* Mühle *f*; *(factory)* Fabrik *f* ● *vt/i* mahlen; *(Techn)* fräsen. **~ about, ~ around** *vi* umherlaufen

millennium /mɪ'leniəm/ *n* Jahrtausend *nt*

miller /'mɪlə(r)/ *n* Müller *m*

millet /'mɪlɪt/ *n* Hirse *f*

milli|gram /'mɪlɪ-/ *n* Milligramm *nt*. **~metre** *n* Millimeter *m & nt*

milliner /'mɪlɪnə(r)/ *n* Modistin *f*; *(man)* Hutmacher *m*. **~y** *n* Damenhüte *pl*

million /'mɪljən/ *n* Million *f*; **a ~ pounds** eine Million Pfund. **~aire** /-'neə(r)/ *n* Millionär(in) *m(f)*

'millstone *n* Mühlstein *m*

mime /maɪm/ *n* Pantomime *f* ● *vt* pantomimisch darstellen

mimic /'mɪmɪk/ *n* Imitator *m* ● *vt* *(pt/pp* **mimicked)** nachahmen. **~ry** *n* Nachahmung *f*

mimosa /mɪ'məʊzə/ *n* Mimose *f*

mince /mɪns/ *n* Hackfleisch *nt* ● *vt* *(Culin)* durchdrehen; **not ~ words** kein Blatt vor den Mund nehmen

mince: **~meat** *n* Masse *f* aus Korinthen, Zitronat *usw*; **make ~meat of** *(fig)* vernichtend schlagen. **~'pie** *n* mit 'mincemeat' gefülltes Pastetchen *nt*

mincer /'mɪnsə(r)/ *n* Fleischwolf *m*

mind /maɪnd/ n Geist m; (sanity) Verstand m; **to my ~** meiner Meinung nach; **give s.o. a piece of one's ~** jdm gehörig die Meinung sagen; **make up one's ~** sich entschließen; **be out of one's ~** nicht bei Verstand sein; **have sth in ~** etw im Sinn haben; **bear sth in ~** an etw (acc) denken; **have a good ~ to** große Lust haben, zu; **I have changed my ~** ich habe es mir anders überlegt ● vt aufpassen auf (+ acc); **I don't ~ the noise** der Lärm stört mich nicht; **~ the step!** Achtung Stufe! ● vi (care) sich kümmern (**about** um); **I don't ~** mir macht es nichts aus; never **~!** macht nichts! **do you ~ if?** haben Sie etwas dagegen, wenn? **~ out** vi aufpassen

mind|ful a **~ful of** eingedenk (+ gen). **~less** a geistlos

mine[1] /maɪn/ poss pron meine(r), meins; **a friend of ~** ein Freund von mir; **that is ~** das gehört mir

mine[2] n Bergwerk nt; (explosive) Mine f ● vt abbauen; (Mil) verminen. **~ detector** n Minensuchgerät nt. **~field** n Minenfeld nt

miner /'maɪnə(r)/ n Bergarbeiter m

mineral /'mɪnərl/ n Mineral nt. **~ogy** /-'rælədʒɪ/ n Mineralogie f. **~ water** n Mineralwasser nt

minesweeper /'maɪn-/ n Minenräumboot nt

mingle /'mɪŋgl/ vi **~ with** sich mischen unter (+ acc)

miniature /'mɪnɪtʃə(r)/ a Klein- ● n Miniatur f

mini|bus /'mɪnɪ-/ n Kleinbus m. **~cab** n Taxi nt

minim /'mɪnɪm/ n (Mus) halbe Note f

minim|al /'mɪnɪməl/ a minimal. **~ize** vt auf ein Minimum reduzieren. **~um** n (pl -ima) Minimum nt ● a Mindest-

mining /'maɪnɪŋ/ n Bergbau m

miniskirt /'mɪnɪ-/ n Minirock m

minist|er /'mɪnɪstə(r)/ n Minister m; (Relig) Pastor m. **~erial** /-'stɪərɪəl/ a ministeriell

ministry /'mɪnɪstrɪ/ n (Pol) Ministerium nt; **the ~** (Relig) das geistliche Amt

mink /mɪŋk/ n Nerz m

minor /'maɪnə(r)/ a kleiner; (less important) unbedeutend ● n Minderjährige(r) m/f; (Mus) Moll nt

minority /maɪ'nɒrətɪ/ n Minderheit f; (age) Minderjährigkeit f

minor road n Nebenstraße f

mint[1] /mɪnt/ n Münzstätte f ● a ⟨stamp⟩ postfrisch; **in ~ condition** wie neu ● vt prägen

mint[2] n (herb) Minze f; (sweet) Pfefferminzbonbon m & nt

minuet /mɪnjʊ'et/ n Menuett nt

minus /'maɪnəs/ prep minus, weniger; (fam: without) ohne ● n **~ [sign]** Minuszeichen nt

minute[1] /'mɪnɪt/ n Minute f; **in a ~** (shortly) gleich; **~s** pl (of meeting) Protokoll nt

minute[2] /maɪ'njuːt/ a winzig; (precise) genau

mirac|le /'mɪrəkl/ n Wunder nt. **~ulous** /-'rækjʊləs/ a wunderbar

mirage /'mɪrɑːʒ/ n Fata Morgana f

mire /'maɪə(r)/ n Morast m

mirror /'mɪrə(r)/ n Spiegel m ● vt widerspiegeln

mirth /mɜːθ/ n Heiterkeit f

misad'venture /mɪs-/ n Mißgeschick nt

misanthropist /mɪ'zænθrəpɪst/ n Menschenfeind m

misappre'hension n Mißverständnis nt; **be under a ~** sich irren

misbe'hav|e vi sich schlecht benehmen. **~iour** n schlechtes Benehmen nt

mis'calcu|late vt falsch berechnen ● vi sich verrechnen. **~'lation** n Fehlkalkulation f

'miscarriage n Fehlgeburt f; **~ of justice** Justizirrtum m. **mis'carry** vi eine Fehlgeburt haben

miscellaneous /mɪsə'leɪnɪəs/ a vermischt

mischief /'mɪstʃɪf/ n Unfug m; (harm) Schaden m

mischievous /'mɪstʃɪvəs/ a, **-ly** adv schelmisch; (malicious) boshaft

miscon'ception n falsche Vorstellung f

mis'conduct n unkorrektes Verhalten nt; (adultery) Ehebruch m

miscon'strue vt mißdeuten

mis'deed n Missetat f

misde'meanour n Missetat f

miser /'maɪzə(r)/ n Geizhals m

miserable /'mɪzrəbl/ a, **-bly** adv unglücklich; (wretched) elend

miserly /'maɪzəlɪ/ adv geizig

misery /'mɪzərɪ/ n Elend nt; (fam: person) Miesepeter m

mis'fire vi fehlzünden; (go wrong) fehlschlagen

'**misfit** *n* Außenseiter(in) *m*(*f*)
mis'fortune *n* Unglück *nt*
mis'givings *npl* Bedenken *pl*
mis'guided *a* töricht
mishap /'mɪshæp/ *n* Mißgeschick *nt*
misin'form *vt* falsch unterrichten
misin'terpret *vt* mißdeuten
mis'judge *vt* falsch beurteilen; (*estimate wrongly*) falsch einschätzen
mis'lay *vt* (*pt*/*pp* -**laid**) verlegen
mis'lead *vt* (*pt*/*pp* -**led**) irreführen.
~**ing** *a* irreführend
mis'manage *vt* schlecht verwalten.
~**ment** *n* Mißwirtschaft *f*
misnomer /mɪs'nəʊmə(r)/ *n* Fehlbezeichnung *f*
'**misprint** *n* Druckfehler *m*
mis'quote *vt* falsch zitieren
misrepre'sent *vt* falsch darstellen
miss /mɪs/ *n* Fehltreffer *m* ● *vt* verpassen; (*fail to hit or find*) verfehlen; (*fail to attend*) versäumen; (*fail to notice*) übersehen; (*feel the loss of*) vermissen ● *vi* (*fail to hit*) nicht treffen. ~ **out** *vt* auslassen
Miss *n* (*pl* -**es**) Fräulein *nt*
misshapen /mɪs'ʃeɪpən/ *a* mißgestaltet
missile /'mɪsaɪl/ *n* [Wurf]geschoß *nt*; (*Mil*) Rakete *f*
missing /'mɪsɪŋ/ *a* fehlend; (*lost*) verschwunden; (*Mil*) vermißt; **be ~** fehlen
mission /'mɪʃn/ *n* Auftrag *m*; (*Mil*) Einsatz *m*; (*Relig*) Mission *f*
missionary /'mɪʃənrɪ/ *n* Missionar(in) *m*(*f*)
mis'spell *vt* (*pt*/*pp* -**spelt** *or* -**spelled**) falsch schreiben
mist /mɪst/ *n* Dunst *m*; (*fog*) Nebel *m*; (*on window*) Beschlag *m* ● *vi* ~ **up** beschlagen
mistake /mɪ'steɪk/ *n* Fehler *m*; **by ~** aus Versehen ● *vt* (*pt* **mistook**, *pp* **mistaken**) mißverstehen; ~ **for** verwechseln mit
mistaken /mɪ'steɪkən/ *a* falsch; **be ~** sich irren; ~ **identity** Verwechslung *f*.
~**ly** *adv* irrtümlicherweise
mistletoe /'mɪsltəʊ/ *n* Mistel *f*
mistress /'mɪstrɪs/ *n* Herrin *f*; (*teacher*) Lehrerin *f*; (*lover*) Geliebte *f*
mis'trust *n* Mißtrauen *nt* ● *vt* mißtrauen (+ *dat*)
misty /'mɪstɪ/ *a* (-**ier**, -**iest**) dunstig; (*foggy*) neblig; (*fig*) unklar

misunder'stand *vt* (*pt*/*pp* -**stood**) mißverstehen. ~**ing** *n* Mißverständnis *nt*
misuse[1] /mɪs'juːz/ *vt* mißbrauchen
misuse[2] /mɪs'juːs/ *n* Mißbrauch *m*
mite /maɪt/ *n* (*Zool*) Milbe *f*; **little ~** (*child*) kleines Ding *nt*
mitigat|e /'mɪtɪgeɪt/ *vt* mildern.
~**ing** *a* mildernd
mitten /'mɪtn/ *n* Fausthandschuh *m*
mix /mɪks/ *n* Mischung *f* ● *vt* mischen ● *vi* sich mischen; ~ **with** (*associate with*) verkehren mit. ~ **up** *vt* mischen; (*muddle*) durcheinanderbringen; (*mistake for*) verwechseln (**with** mit)
mixed /mɪkst/ *a* gemischt; **be ~ up** durcheinander sein
mixer /'mɪksə(r)/ *n* Mischmaschine *f*; (*Culin*) Küchenmaschine *f*
mixture /'mɪkstʃə(r)/ *n* Mischung *f*; (*medicine*) Mixtur *f*; (*Culin*) Teig *m*
'**mix-up** *n* Durcheinander *nt*; (*confusion*) Verwirrung *f*; (*mistake*) Verwechslung *f*
moan /məʊn/ *n* Stöhnen *nt* ● *vi* stöhnen; (*complain*) jammern
moat /məʊt/ *n* Burggraben *m*
mob /mɒb/ *n* Horde *f*; (*rabble*) Pöbel *m*; (*fam: gang*) Bande *f* ● *vt* (*pt*/*pp* **mobbed**) herfallen über (+ *acc*); belagern ⟨*celebrity*⟩
mobile /'məʊbaɪl/ *a* beweglich ● *n* Mobile *nt*. ~ '**home** *n* Wohnwagen *m*
mobility /mə'bɪlətɪ/ *n* Beweglichkeit *f*
mobi|lization /məʊbɪlaɪ'zeɪʃn/ *n* Mobilisierung *f*. ~**lize** /'məʊbɪlaɪz/ *vt* mobilisieren
mocha /'mɒkə/ *n* Mokka *m*
mock /mɒk/ *a* Schein- ● *vt* verspotten ● *vi* spotten. ~**ery** *n* Spott *m*
'**mock-up** *n* Modell *nt*
modal /'məʊdl/ *a* ~ **auxiliary** Modalverb *nt*
mode /məʊd/ *n* [Art und] Weise *f*; (*fashion*) Mode *f*
model /'mɒdl/ *n* Modell *nt*; (*example*) Vorbild *nt*; [**fashion**] ~ Mannequin *nt* ● *a* Modell-; (*exemplary*) Muster- ● *v* (*pt*/*pp* **modelled**) ● *vt* formen, modellieren; vorführen ⟨*clothes*⟩ ● *vi* Mannequin sein; (*for artist*) Modell stehen
moderate[1] /'mɒdəreɪt/ *vt* mäßigen ● *vi* sich mäßigen

moderate² /'mɒdərət/ *a* mäßig; ⟨*opinion*⟩ gemäßigt ● *n* (*Pol*) Gemäßigte(r) *m/f.* ∼**ly** *adv* mäßig; (*fairly*) einigermaßen

moderation /mɒdə'reɪʃn/ *n* Mäßigung *f*; **in** ∼ mit Maß[en]

modern /'mɒdn/ *a* modern. ∼**ize** *vt* modernisieren. ∼ **languages** *npl* neuere Sprachen *pl*

modest /'mɒdɪst/ *a* bescheiden; (*decorous*) schamhaft. ∼**y** *n* Bescheidenheit *f*

modicum /'mɒdɪkəm/ *n* **a** ∼ **of** ein bißchen

modif|ication /mɒdɪfɪ'keɪʃn/ *n* Abänderung *f.* ∼**y** /'mɒdɪfaɪ/ *vt* (*pt/pp* -**fied**) abändern

modulate /'mɒdjʊleɪt/ *vt/i* modulieren

moist /mɔɪst/ *a* (-**er,** -**est**) feucht

moisten /'mɔɪsn/ *vt* befeuchten

moistur|e /'mɔɪstʃə(r)/ *n* Feuchtigkeit *f.* ∼**izer** *n* Feuchtigkeitscreme *f*

molar /'məʊlə(r)/ *n* Backenzahn *m*

molasses /mə'læsɪz/ *n* (*Amer*) Sirup *m*

mole¹ /məʊl/ *n* Leberfleck *m*

mole² *n* (*Zool*) Maulwurf *m*

mole³ *n* (*breakwater*) Mole *f*

molecule /'mɒlɪkjuːl/ *n* Molekül *m*

'molehill *n* Maulwurfshaufen *m*

molest /mə'lest/ *vt* belästigen

mollify /'mɒlɪfaɪ/ *vt* (*pt/pp* -**ied**) besänftigen

mollusc /'mɒləsk/ *n* Weichtier *nt*

mollycoddle /'mɒlɪkɒdl/ *vt* verzärteln

molten /'məʊltən/ *a* geschmolzen

mom /mɒm/ *n* (*Amer fam*) Mutti *f*

moment /'məʊmənt/ *n* Moment *m*, Augenblick *m*; **at the** ∼ im Augenblick, augenblicklich. ∼**ary** *a* vorübergehend

momentous /mə'mentəs/ *a* bedeutsam

momentum /mə'mentəm/ *n* Schwung *m*

monarch /'mɒnək/ *n* Monarch(in) *m*(*f*). ∼**y** *n* Monarchie *f*

monast|ery /'mɒnəstrɪ/ *n* Kloster *nt.* ∼**ic** /mə'næstɪk/ *a* Kloster-

Monday /'mʌndeɪ/ *n* Montag *m*

money /'mʌnɪ/ *n* Geld *nt*

money: ∼-**box** *n* Sparbüchse *f.* ∼-**lender** *n* Geldverleiher *m.* ∼ **order** *n* Zahlungsanweisung *f*

mongrel /'mʌŋgrəl/ *n* Promenadenmischung *f*

monitor /'mɒnɪtə(r)/ *n* (*Techn*) Monitor *m* ● *vt* überwachen (*progress*); abhören ⟨*broadcast*⟩

monk /mʌŋk/ *n* Mönch *m*

monkey /'mʌŋkɪ/ *n* Affe *m.* ∼-**nut** *n* Erdnuß *f.* ∼-**wrench** *n* (*Techn*) Engländer *m*

mono /'mɒnəʊ/ *n* Mono *nt*

monocle /'mɒnəkl/ *n* Monokel *nt*

monogram /'mɒnəgræm/ *n* Monogramm *nt*

monologue /'mɒnəlɒg/ *n* Monolog *m*

monopol|ize /mə'nɒpəlaɪz/ *vt* monopolisieren. ∼**y** *n* Monopol *nt*

monosyll|abic /mɒnəsɪ'læbɪk/ *a* einsilbig. ∼**able** /'mɒnəsɪləbl/ *n* einsilbiges Wort *nt*

monotone /'mɒnətəʊn/ *n* **in a** ∼ mit monotoner Stimme

monoton|ous /mə'nɒtənəs/ *a*, -**ly** *adv* eintönig, monoton; (*tedious*) langweilig. ∼**y** *n* Eintönigkeit *f*, Monotonie *f*

monsoon /mɒn'suːn/ *n* Monsun *m*

monster /'mɒnstə(r)/ *n* Ungeheuer *nt*; (*cruel person*) Unmensch *m*

monstrosity /mɒn'strɒsətɪ/ *n* Monstrosität *f*

monstrous /'mɒnstrəs/ *a* ungeheuer; (*outrageous*) ungeheuerlich

montage /mɒn'tɑːʒ/ *n* Montage *f*

month /mʌnθ/ *n* Monat *m.* ∼**ly** *a* & *adv* monatlich ● *n* (*periodical*) Monatszeitschrift *f*

monument /'mɒnjʊmənt/ *n* Denkmal *nt.* ∼**al** /-'mentl/ *a* (*fig*) monumental

moo /muː/ *n* Muh *nt* ● *vi* (*pt/pp* **mooed**) muhen

mooch /muːtʃ/ *vi* ∼ **about** (*fam*) herumschleichen

mood /muːd/ *n* Laune *f*; **be in a good/bad** ∼ gute/schlechte Laune haben

moody /'muːdɪ/ *a* (-**ier,** -**iest**) launisch

moon /muːn/ *n* Mond *m*; **over the** ∼ (*fam*) überglücklich

moon: ∼-**light** *n* Mondschein *m.* ∼-**lighting** *n* (*fam*) ≈ Schwarzarbeit *f.* ∼-**lit** *a* mondhell

moor¹ /mʊə(r)/ *n* Moor *nt*

moor² *vt* (*Naut*) festmachen ● *vi* anlegen. ∼**ings** *npl* (*chains*) Verankerung *f*; (*place*) Anlegestelle *f*

moose /muːs/ *n* Elch *m*

moot /muːt/ *a* it's a ~ point darüber läßt sich streiten ● *vt* aufwerfen ⟨question⟩

mop /mɒp/ *n* Mop *m*; ~ of hair Wuschelkopf *m* ● *vt* (*pt/pp* **mopped**) wischen. ~ **up** *vt* aufwischen

mope /məʊp/ *vi* Trübsal blasen

moped /'məʊped/ *n* Moped *nt*

moral /'mɒrl/ *a*, **-ly** *adv* moralisch, sittlich; (*virtuous*) tugendhaft ● *n* Moral *f*; ~s *pl* Moral *f*

morale /mə'rɑːl/ *n* Moral *f*

morality /mə'rælətɪ/ *n* Sittlichkeit *f*

moralize /'mɒrəlaɪz/ *vi* moralisieren

morbid /'mɔːbɪd/ *a* krankhaft; (*gloomy*) trübe

more /mɔː(r)/ *a*, *adv* & *n* mehr; (*in addition*) noch; **a few** ~ noch ein paar; **any** ~ noch etwas; **once** ~ noch einmal; ~ **or less** mehr oder weniger; **some** ~ **tea?** noch etwas Tee? ~ **interesting** interessanter; ~ [**and** ~] **quickly** [immer] schneller; **no** ~, **thank you**, nichts mehr, danke; **no** ~ **bread** kein Brot mehr; **no** ~ **apples** keine Äpfel mehr

moreover /mɔː'rəʊvə(r)/ *adv* außerdem

morgue /mɔːg/ *n* Leichenschauhaus *nt*

moribund /'mɒrɪbʌnd/ *a* sterbend

morning /'mɔːnɪŋ/ *n* Morgen *m*; **in the** ~ morgens, am Morgen; (*tomorrow*) morgen früh

Morocco /mə'rɒkəʊ/ *n* Marokko *nt*

moron /'mɔːrɒn/ *n* (*fam*) Idiot *m*

morose /mə'rəʊs/ *a*, **-ly** *adv* mürrisch

morphine /'mɔːfiːn/ *n* Morphium *nt*

Morse /mɔːs/ *n* ~ [**code**] Morsealphabet *nt*

morsel /'mɔːsl/ *n* (*food*) Happen *m*

mortal /'mɔːtl/ *a* sterblich; (*fatal*) tödlich ● *n* Sterbliche(r) *m/f*. ~**ity** /mɔː'tælətɪ/ *n* Sterblichkeit *f*. ~**ly** *adv* tödlich

mortar /'mɔːtə(r)/ *n* Mörtel *m*

mortgage /'mɔːgɪdʒ/ *n* Hypothek *f* ● *vt* hypothekarisch belasten

mortify /'mɔːtɪfaɪ/ *vt* (*pt/pp* **-ied**) demütigen

mortuary /'mɔːtjʊərɪ/ *n* Leichenhalle *f*; (*public*) Leichenschauhaus *nt*; (*Amer: undertaker's*) Bestattungsinstitut *nt*

mosaic /məʊ'zeɪɪk/ *n* Mosaik *nt*

Moscow /'mɒskəʊ/ *n* Moskau *nt*

Moselle /məʊ'zel/ *n* Mosel *f*; (*wine*) Moselwein *m*

mosque /mɒsk/ *n* Moschee *f*

mosquito /mɒs'kiːtəʊ/ *n* (*pl* **-es**) [Stech]mücke *f*, Schnake *f*; (*tropical*) Moskito *m*

moss /mɒs/ *n* Moos *nt*. ~**y** *a* moosig

most /məʊst/ *a* der/die/das meiste; (*majority*) die meisten; **for the** ~ **part** zum größten Teil ● *adv* am meisten; (*very*) höchst; **the** ~ **interesting day** der interessanteste Tag; ~ **unlikely** höchst unwahrscheinlich ● *n* das meiste; ~ **of them** die meisten [von ihnen]; **at [the]** ~ höchstens; ~ **of the time** die meiste Zeit. ~**ly** *adv* meist

MOT *n* ≈ TÜV *m*

motel /məʊ'tel/ *n* Motel *nt*

moth /mɒθ/ *n* Nachtfalter *m*; [**clothes-**]~ Motte *f*

moth: ~**ball** *n* Mottenkugel *f*. ~**-eaten** *a* mottenzerfressen

mother /'mʌðə(r)/ *n* Mutter *f*; **M**~'s **Day** Muttertag *m* ● *vt* bemuttern

mother: ~**hood** *n* Mutterschaft *f*. ~**-in-law** *n* (*pl* ~s-**in-law**) Schwiegermutter *f*. ~**land** *n* Mutterland *nt*. ~**ly** *a* mütterlich. ~**-of-pearl** *n* Perlmutter *f*. ~**-to-be** *n* werdende Mutter *f*. ~**tongue** *n* Muttersprache *f*

mothproof /'mɒθ-/ *a* mottenfest

motif /məʊ'tiːf/ *n* Motiv *nt*

motion /'məʊʃn/ *n* Bewegung *f*; (*proposal*) Antrag *m* ● *vt/i* ~ [**to**] **s.o.** jdm ein Zeichen geben (**to** zu). ~**less** *a*, **-ly** *adv* bewegungslos

motivate /'məʊtɪveɪt/ *vt* motivieren. ~**ion** /-'veɪʃn/ *n* Motivation *f*

motive /'məʊtɪv/ *n* Motiv *nt*

motley /'mɒtlɪ/ *a* bunt

motor /'məʊtə(r)/ *n* Motor *m*; (*car*) Auto *nt* ● *a* Motor-; (*Anat*) motorisch ● *vi* [mit dem Auto] fahren

Motorail /'məʊtəreɪl/ *n* Autozug *m*

motor: ~ **bike** *n* (*fam*) Motorrad *nt*. ~ **boat** *n* Motorboot *nt*. ~**cade** /-keɪd/ *n* (*Amer*) Autokolonne *f*. ~ **car** *n* Auto *nt*, Wagen *m*. ~ **cycle** *n* Motorrad *nt*. ~**cyclist** *n* Motorradfahrer *m*. ~**ing** *n* Autofahren *nt*. ~**ist** *n* Autofahrer(in) *m(f)*. ~**ize** *vt* motorisieren. ~ **vehicle** *n* Kraftfahrzeug *nt*. ~**way** *n* Autobahn *f*

mottled /'mɒtld/ *a* gesprenkelt

motto /'mɒtəʊ/ *n* (*pl* **-es**) Motto *nt*

mould¹ /məʊld/ *n* (*fungus*) Schimmel *m*

mould² n Form f ● vt formen (**into** zu). ~**ing** n (Archit) Fries m

mouldy /ˈmoʊldɪ/ a schimmelig; (fam: worthless) schäbig

moult /moʊlt/ vi (bird:) sich mausern; (animal:) sich haaren

mound /maʊnd/ n Hügel m; (of stones) Haufen m

mount¹ /maʊnt/ n Berg m

mount² n (animal) Reittier nt; (of jewel) Fassung f; (of photo, picture) Passepartout nt ● vt (get on) steigen auf (+ acc); (on pedestal) montieren auf (+ acc); besteigen (horse); fassen (jewel); aufziehen (photo, picture) ● vi aufsteigen; (tension:) steigen. ~ **up** vi sich häufen; (add up) sich anhäufen

mountain /ˈmaʊntɪn/ n Berg m

mountaineer /maʊntɪˈnɪə(r)/ n Bergsteiger(in) m(f). ~**ing** n Bergsteigen nt

mountainous /ˈmaʊntɪnəs/ a bergig, gebirgig

mourn /mɔːn/ vt betrauern ● vi trauern (**for** um). ~**er** n Trauernde(r) m/f. ~**ful** a, **-ly** adv trauervoll. ~**ing** n Trauer f

mouse /maʊs/ n (pl mice) Maus f. ~**trap** n Mausefalle f

mousse /muːs/ n Schaum m; (Culin) Mousse f

moustache /məˈstɑːʃ/ n Schnurrbart m

mousy /ˈmaʊsɪ/ a graubraun; (person) farblos

mouth¹ /maʊð/ vt ~ sth etw lautlos mit den Lippen sagen

mouth² /maʊθ/ n Mund m; (of animal) Maul nt; (of river) Mündung f

mouth: ~**ful** n Mundvoll m; (bite) Bissen m. ~**-organ** n Mundharmonika f. ~**piece** n Mundstück nt; (fig: person) Sprachrohr nt. ~**wash** n Mundwasser nt

movable /ˈmuːvəbl/ a beweglich

move /muːv/ n Bewegung f; (fig) Schritt m; (moving house) Umzug m; (in board-game) Zug m; **on the** ~ unterwegs; **get a** ~ **on** (fam) sich beeilen ● vt bewegen; (emotionally) rühren; (move along) rücken; (in board-game) ziehen; (take away) wegnehmen; wegfahren (car); (rearrange) umstellen; (transfer) versetzen (person); verlegen (office); (propose) beantragen; ~ **house** umziehen ● vi sich bewegen; (move house) umziehen; **don't** ~! stillhalten!

(stop) stillstehen! ~ **along** vt/i weiterrücken. ~ **away** vt/i wegrücken; (move house) wegziehen. ~ **forward** vt/i vorrücken; (vehicle:) vorwärts fahren. ~ **in** vi einziehen. ~ **off** vi (vehicle:) losfahren. ~ **out** vi ausziehen. ~ **over** vt/i [zur Seite] rücken. ~ **up** vi aufrücken

movement /ˈmuːvmənt/ n Bewegung f; (Mus) Satz m; (of clock) Uhrwerk nt

movie /ˈmuːvɪ/ n (Amer) Film m; **go to the** ~**s** ins Kino gehen

moving /ˈmuːvɪŋ/ a beweglich; (touching) rührend

mow /moʊ/ vt (pt mowed, pp mown or mowed) mähen. ~ **down** vt (destroy) niedermähen

mower /ˈmoʊə(r)/ n Rasenmäher m

MP abbr see **Member of Parliament**

Mr /ˈmɪstə(r)/ n (pl **Messrs**) Herr m

Mrs /ˈmɪsɪz/ n Frau f

Ms /mɪz/ n Frau f

much /mʌtʃ/ a, adv & n viel; **as** ~ **as** soviel wie; **very** ~ **loved/interested** sehr geliebt/interessiert

muck /mʌk/ n Mist m; (fam: filth) Dreck m. ~ **about** vi herumalbern; (tinker) herumspielen (**with** mit). ~ **in** vi (fam) mitmachen. ~ **out** vt ausmisten. ~ **up** vt (fam) vermasseln; (make dirty) schmutzig machen

mucky /ˈmʌkɪ/ a (**-ier, -iest**) dreckig

mucus /ˈmjuːkəs/ n Schleim m

mud /mʌd/ n Schlamm m

muddle /ˈmʌdl/ n Durcheinander nt; (confusion) Verwirrung f ● vt ~ [**up**] durcheinanderbringen

muddy /ˈmʌdɪ/ a (**-ier, -iest**) schlammig; (shoes) schmutzig

'mudguard n Kotflügel m; (on bicycle) Schutzblech nt

muesli /ˈmuːzlɪ/ n Müsli nt

muff /mʌf/ n Muff m

muffle /ˈmʌfl/ vt dämpfen (sound); ~ [**up**] (for warmth) einhüllen (**in** in + acc)

muffler /ˈmʌflə(r)/ n Schal m; (Amer, Auto) Auspufftopf m

mufti /ˈmʌftɪ/ n **in** ~ in Zivil

mug¹ /mʌg/ n Becher m; (for beer) Bierkrug m; (fam: face) Visage f; (fam: simpleton) Trottel m

mug² vt (pt/pp mugged) überfallen. ~**ger** n Straßenräuber m. ~**ging** n Straßenraub m

muggy /ˈmʌgɪ/ a (**-ier, -iest**) schwül

mule¹ /ˈmjuːl/ n Maultier nt

mule[2] n (slipper) Pantoffel m

mull /mʌl/ vt ~ **over** nachdenken über (+acc)

mulled /mʌld/ a ~ **wine** Glühwein m

multi /'mʌltı/: ~**coloured** a vielfarbig, bunt. ~**lingual** /-'lıŋgwəl/ a mehrsprachig. ~'**national** a multinational

multiple /'mʌltıpl/ a vielfach; (with pl) mehrere ● n Vielfache(s) nt

multiplication /mʌltıplı'keıʃn/ n Multiplikation f

multiply /'mʌltıplaı/ v (pt/pp -ied) ● vt multiplizieren (**by** mit) ● vi sich vermehren

multi-storey a ~ **car park** Parkhaus nt

mum[1] /mʌm/ a **keep** ~ (fam) den Mund halten

mum[2] n (fam) Mutti f

mumble /'mʌmbl/ vt/i murmeln

mummy[1] /'mʌmı/ n (fam) Mutti f

mummy[2] n (Archaeol) Mumie f

mumps /mʌmps/ n Mumps m

munch /mʌntʃ/ vt/i mampfen

mundane /mʌn'deın/ a banal; (worldly) weltlich

municipal /mju:'nısıpl/ a städtisch

munitions /mju:'nıʃnz/ npl Kriegsmaterial nt

mural /'mjʊərəl/ n Wandgemälde nt

murder /'mɜːdə(r)/ n Mord m ● vt ermorden; (fam: ruin) verhunzen. ~**er** n Mörder m. ~**ess** n Mörderin f. ~**ous** /-rəs/ a mörderisch

murky /'mɜːkı/ a (-ier, -iest) düster

murmur /'mɜːmə(r)/ n Murmeln nt ● vt/i murmeln

muscle /'mʌsl/ n Muskel m

muscular /'mʌskjʊlə(r)/ a Muskel-; (strong) muskulös

muse /mju:z/ vi nachsinnen (**on** über + acc)

museum /mju:'zıəm/ n Museum nt

mush /mʌʃ/ n Brei m

mushroom /'mʌʃrʊm/ n [eßbarer] Pilz m, esp Champignon m ● vi (fig) wie Pilze aus dem Boden schießen

mushy /'mʌʃı/ a breiig

music /'mju:zık/ n Musik f; (written) Noten pl; **set to** ~ vertonen

musical /'mju:zıkl/ a musikalisch ● n Musical nt. ~ **box** n Spieldose f. ~ **instrument** n Musikinstrument nt

'**music-hall** n Varieté nt

musician /mju:'zıʃn/ n Musiker(in) m(f)

'**music-stand** n Notenständer m

Muslim /'mʊzlım/ a mohammedanisch ● n Mohammedaner(in) m(f)

muslin /'mʌzlın/ n Musselin m

mussel /'mʌsl/ n [Mies]muschel f

must /mʌst/ v aux (nur Präsens) müssen; (with negative) dürfen ● n a ~ (fam) ein Muß nt

mustard /'mʌstəd/ n Senf m

muster /'mʌstə(r)/ vt versammeln; aufbringen (strength) ● vi sich versammeln

musty /'mʌstı/ a (-ier, -iest) muffig

mutation /mju:'teıʃn/ n Veränderung f; (Biol) Mutation f

mute /mju:t/ a stumm

muted /'mju:tıd/ a gedämpft

mutilat|e /'mju:tıleıt/ vt verstümmeln. ~**ion** /-'leıʃn/ n Verstümmelung f

mutin|ous /'mju:tınəs/ a meuterisch. ~**y** n Meuterei f ● vi (pt/pp -ied) meutern

mutter /'mʌtə(r)/ n Murmeln nt ● vt/i murmeln

mutton /'mʌtn/ n Hammelfleisch nt

mutual /'mju:tjʊəl/ a gegenseitig; (fam: common) gemeinsam. ~**ly** adv gegenseitig

muzzle /'mʌzl/ n (of animal) Schnauze f; (of firearm) Mündung f; (for dog) Maulkorb m ● vt einen Maulkorb anlegen (+ dat)

my /maı/ a mein

myopic /maı'ɒpık/ a kurzsichtig

myself /maı'self/ pron selbst; (refl) mich; **by** ~ allein; **I thought to** ~ ich habe mir gedacht

mysterious /mı'stıərıəs/ a, -**ly** adv geheimnisvoll; (puzzling) mysteriös, rätselhaft

mystery /'mıstərı/ n Geheimnis nt; (puzzle) Rätsel nt; ~ [**story**] Krimi m

mysti|c[al] /'mıstık[l]/ a mystisch. ~**cism** /-sızm/ n Mystik f

mystification /mıstıfı'keıʃn/ n Verwunderung f

mystified /'mıstıfaıd/ a **be** ~ vor einem Rätsel stehen

mystique /mı'sti:k/ n geheimnisvoller Zauber m

myth /mıθ/ n Mythos m; (fam: untruth) Märchen nt. ~**ical** a mythisch; (fig) erfunden

mythology /mɪ'θɒlədʒɪ/ n Mythologie f

N

nab /næb/ vt (pt/pp **nabbed**) (fam) erwischen

nag¹ /næg/ n (horse) Gaul m

nag² vt/i (pt/pp **nagged**) herumnörgeln (s.o. an jdm). **~ging** a ⟨pain⟩ nagend ● n Nörgelei f

nail /neɪl/ n (Anat, Techn) Nagel m; **on the ~** (fam) sofort ● vt nageln (**to** an +acc). **~ down** vt festnageln; (close) zunageln

nail: ~-brush n Nagelbürste f. **~-file** n Nagelfeile f. **~ polish** n Nagellack m. **~ scissors** npl Nagelschere f. **~ varnish** n Nagellack m

naive /naɪ'i:v/ a, **-ly** adv naiv. **~ty** /-əti/ n Naivität f

naked /'neɪkɪd/ a nackt; ⟨flame⟩ offen; **with the ~ eye** mit bloßem Auge. **~ness** n Nacktheit f

name /neɪm/ n Name m; (reputation) Ruf m; **by ~** dem Namen nach; **by the ~ of** namens; **call s.o. ~s** (fam) jdn beschimpfen ● vt nennen; (give a name to) einen Namen geben (+dat); (announce publicly) den Namen bekanntgeben von. **~less** a namenlos. **~ly** adv nämlich

name: ~-plate n Namensschild nt. **~sake** n Namensvetter m/ Namensschwester f

nanny /'nænɪ/ n Kindermädchen nt. **~-goat** n Ziege f

nap /næp/ n Nickerchen nt; **have a ~** ein Nickerchen machen ● vi **catch s.o. ~ping** jdn überrumpeln

nape /neɪp/ n **~ [of the neck]** Nacken m

napkin /'næpkɪn/ n Serviette f; (for baby) Windel f

nappy /'næpɪ/ n Windel f

narcotic /nɑ:'kɒtɪk/ a betäubend ● n Narkotikum nt; (drug) Rauschgift nt

narrat|e /nə'reɪt/ vt erzählen. **~ion** /-eɪʃn/ n Erzählung f

narrative /'nærətɪv/ a erzählend ● n Erzählung f

narrator /nə'reɪtə(r)/ n Erzähler(in) m(f)

narrow /'nærəʊ/ a (-er, -est) schmal; (restricted) eng; ⟨margin, majority⟩ knapp; (fig) beschränkt; **have a ~ escape**, adv **~ly escape** mit knapper Not

davonkommen ● vi sich verengen. **~-'minded** a engstirnig

nasal /'neɪzl/ a nasal; (Med & Anat) Nasen-

nastily /'nɑ:stɪlɪ/ adv boshaft

nasturtium /nə'stɜ:ʃəm/ n Kapuzinerkresse f

nasty /'nɑ:stɪ/ a (-ier, -iest) übel; (unpleasant) unangenehm; (unkind) boshaft; (serious) schlimm; **turn ~** gemein werden

nation /'neɪʃn/ n Nation f; (people) Volk nt

national /'næʃənl/ a national; ⟨newspaper⟩ überregional; ⟨campaign⟩ landesweit ● n Staatsbürger(in) m(f)

national: ~ 'anthem n Nationalhymne f. **N~ 'Health Service** n staatlicher Gesundheitsdienst m. **N~ In'surance** n Sozialversicherung f

nationalism /'næʃənəlɪzm/ n Nationalismus m

nationality /næʃə'nælətɪ/ n Staatsangehörigkeit f

national|ization /næʃənəlaɪ'zeɪʃn/ n Verstaatlichung f. **~ize** /'næʃənə- laɪz/ vt verstaatlichen. **~ly** /'næʃə-nəlɪ/ adv landesweit

'nation-wide a landesweit

native /'neɪtɪv/ a einheimisch; (innate) angeboren ● n Eingeborene(r) m/f; (local inhabitant) Einheimische(r) m/f; **a ~ of Vienna** ein gebürtiger Wiener

native: ~ 'land n Heimatland nt. **~ 'language** n Muttersprache f

Nativity /nə'tɪvɪtɪ/ n **the ~** Christi Geburt f. **~ play** n Krippenspiel nt

natter /'nætə(r)/ n **have a ~** (fam) einen Schwatz halten ● vi (fam) schwatzen

natural /'nætʃrəl/ a, **-ly** adv natürlich; **~-[coloured]** naturfarben

natural: ~ 'gas n Erdgas nt. **~ 'history** n Naturkunde f

naturalist /'nætʃrəlɪst/ n Naturforscher m

natural|ization /nætʃrəlaɪ'zeɪʃn/ n Einbürgerung f. **~ize** /'nætʃrəlaɪz/ vt einbürgern

nature /'neɪtʃə(r)/ n Natur f; (kind) Art f; **by ~** von Natur aus. **~ reserve** n Naturschutzgebiet nt

naturism /'neɪtʃərɪzm/ n Freikörperkultur f

naught /nɔ:t/ n = **nought**

naughty /'nɔ:tɪ/ a (**-ier, -iest**), **-ily** adv
unartig; (slightly indecent) gewagt

nausea /'nɔ:zɪə/ n Übelkeit f

nause|ate /'nɔ:zɪeɪt/ vt anekeln.
~**ating** a ekelhaft. ~**ous** /-ɪəs/ a
I feel ~**ous** mir ist übel

nautical /'nɔ:tɪkl/ a nautisch. ~
mile n Seemeile f

naval /'neɪvl/ a Marine-

nave /neɪv/ n Kirchenschiff nt

navel /'neɪvl/ n Nabel m

navigable /'nævɪgəbl/ a schiffbar

navigat|e /'nævɪgeɪt/ vi navigieren
● vt befahren ⟨river⟩. ~**ion** /-'geɪʃn/
n Navigation f. ~**or** n Navigator m

navvy /'nævɪ/ n Straßenarbeiter m

navy /'neɪvɪ/ n [Kriegs]marine f ● a
~ **[blue]** marineblau

near /nɪə(r)/ a (**-er, -est**) nah[e]; the
~**est bank** die nächste Bank ● adv
nahe; ~ **by** nicht weit weg; ~ **at hand**
in der Nähe; **draw** ~ sich nähern
● prep nahe an (+ dat/acc); in der Nähe
von; ~ **to tears** den Tränen nahe; **go** ~
[to] sth nahe an etw (acc) herangehen
● vt sich nähern (+ dat)

near: ~**by** a nahegelegen. ~**ly** adv
fast, beinahe; **not** ~**ly** bei weitem
nicht. ~**ness** n Nähe f. ~ **side** n
Beifahrerseite f. ~**-sighted** a
(Amer) kurzsichtig

neat /ni:t/ a (**-er, -est**), **-ly** adv adrett;
(tidy) ordentlich; (clever) geschickt;
(undiluted) pur. ~**ness** n Ordentlichkeit f

necessarily /'nesəserəlɪ/ adv not-
wendigerweise; **not** ~ nicht unbedingt

necessary /'nesəsərɪ/ a nötig, notwendig

necessit|ate /nɪ'sesɪteɪt/ vt not-
wendig machen. ~**y** n Notwendigkeit f; **she works from** ~**y** sie
arbeitet, weil sie es nötig hat

neck /nek/ n Hals m; ~ **and** ~ Kopf
an Kopf

necklace /'neklɪs/ n Halskette f

neck: ~**line** n Halsausschnitt m.
~**tie** n Schlips m

nectar /'nektə(r)/ n Nektar m

née /neɪ/ a ~ **Brett** geborene Brett

need /ni:d/ n Bedürfnis nt; (misfortune) Not f; **be in** ~ Not leiden; **be
in** ~ **of** brauchen; **in case of** ~ notfalls;
if ~ **be** wenn nötig; **there is a** ~ **for** es
besteht ein Bedarf an (+ dat); **there is
no** ~ **for that** das ist nicht nötig; **there
is no** ~ **for you to go** du brauchst

nicht zu gehen ● vt brauchen; **you** ~
not go du brauchst nicht zu gehen; ~ **I
come?** muß ich kommen? **I** ~ **to know**
ich muß es wissen; **it** ~**s to be done** es
muß gemacht werden

needle /'ni:dl/ n Nadel f ● vt (annoy)
ärgern

needless /'ni:dlɪs/ a, **-ly** adv unnötig;
~ **to say** selbstverständlich, natürlich

'needlework n Nadelarbeit f

needy /'ni:dɪ/ a (**-ier, -iest**) bedürftig

negation /nɪ'geɪʃn/ n Verneinung f

negative /'negətɪv/ a negativ ● n
Verneinung f; (photo) Negativ nt

neglect /nɪ'glekt/ n Vernach-
lässigung f; **state of** ~ verwahrloster
Zustand m ● vt vernachlässigen; (omit)
versäumen (**to** zu). ~**ed** a verwahrlost. ~**ful** a nachlässig; **be** ~**ful
of** vernachlässigen

negligen|ce /'neglɪdʒəns/ n Nach-
lässigkeit f; (Jur) Fahrlässigkeit f.
~**t** a, **-ly** adv nachlässig; (Jur) fahr-
lässig

negligible /'neglɪdʒəbl/ a unbedeutend

negotiable /nɪ'gəʊʃəbl/ a (road) befahrbar; (Comm) unverbindlich; **not**
~ nicht übertragbar

negotiat|e /nɪ'gəʊʃɪeɪt/ vt aus-
handeln; (Auto) nehmen ⟨bend⟩ ● vi
verhandeln. ~**ion** /-'eɪʃn/ n Verhandlung f. ~**or** n Unterhändler(in)
m(f)

Negro /'ni:grəʊ/ a Neger- ● n (pl **-es**)
Neger m

neigh /neɪ/ vi wiehern

neighbour /'neɪbə(r)/ n Nachbar(in)
m(f). ~**hood** n Nachbarschaft f; **in
the** ~**hood of** in der Nähe von; (fig)
um … herum. ~**ing** a Nachbar-. ~**ly**
a [gut]nachbarlich

neither /'naɪðə(r)/ a & pron keine-
(r,s) [von beiden] ● adv ~ … **nor**
weder … noch ● conj auch nicht

neon /'ni:ɒn/ n Neon nt. ~ **light** n
Neonlicht nt

nephew /'nevju:/ n Neffe m

nepotism /'nepətɪzm/ n Vettern-
wirtschaft f

nerve /nɜ:v/ n Nerv m; (fam: courage) Mut m; (fam: impudence)
Frechheit f; **lose one's** ~ den Mut
verlieren. ~**-racking** a nerven-
aufreibend

nervous /'nɜ:vəs/ a, **-ly** adv (afraid)
ängstlich; (highly-strung) nervös;
(Anat, Med) Nerven-; **be** ~ Angst

haben. ~ **'breakdown** n Nerven-
zusammenbruch m. ~**ness** Ängst-
lichkeit f; (Med) Nervosität f

nervy /'nɜːvɪ/ a (**-ier, -iest**) nervös;
(Amer: impudent) frech

nest /nest/ n Nest nt ● vi nisten.
~**-egg** n Notgroschen m

nestle /'nesl/ vi sich schmiegen
(**against** an + acc)

net /net/ n Netz nt; (curtain) Store m
● vt (pt/pp **netted**) (catch) [mit dem
Netz] fangen

net² a netto; (salary, weight) Netto- ● vt
(pt/pp **netted**) netto einnehmen;
(yield) einbringen

'netball n / Korbball m

Netherlands /'neðələndz/ npl the ~
die Niederlande pl

netting /'netɪŋ/ n [**wire**] ~ Maschendraht m

nettle /'netl/ n Nessel f

'network n Netz nt

neuralgia /njʊə'rældʒə/ n Neuralgie
f

neurolog|ist /njʊə'rɒlədʒɪst/ n
Neurologe m /-gin f. ~**y** n Neurologie
f

neur|osis /njʊə'rəʊsɪs/ n (pl **-oses**
/-siːz/) Neurose f. ~**otic** /-'rɒtɪk/ a
neurotisch

neuter /'njuːtə(r)/ a (Gram) sächlich
● n (Gram) Neutrum nt ● vt
kastrieren; (spay) sterilisieren

neutral /'njuːtrl/ a neutral ● n **in** ~
(Auto) im Leerlauf. ~**ity** /-'trælətɪ/ n
Neutralität f. ~**ize** vt neutralisieren

never /'nevə(r)/ adv nie, niemals;
(fam: not) nicht; ~ **mind** macht
nichts; **well I** ~! ja so was! ~**-ending**
a endlos

nevertheless /nevəðə'les/ adv
dennoch, trotzdem

new /njuː/ a (**-er, -est**) neu

new: ~**born** a neugeboren. ~**comer**
n Neuankömmling m. ~**fangled**
/-'fæŋgld/ a (pej) neumodisch.
~**-laid** a frisch gelegt

'newly adv frisch. ~**-weds** npl
jungverheiratetes Paar nt

new: ~ **'moon** n Neumond m.
~**ness** n Neuheit f

news /njuːz/ n Nachricht f; (Radio,
TV) Nachrichten pl; **piece of** ~
Neuigkeit f

news: ~**agent** n Zeitungshändler m.
~ **bulletin** n Nachrichtensendung f.
~**caster** n Nachrichtensprecher(in)
m(f). ~**flash** n Kurzmeldung f.

~**letter** n Mitteilungsblatt nt.
~**paper** n Zeitung f; (material)
Zeitungspapier nt. ~**reader** n
Nachrichtensprecher(in) m(f)

newt /njuːt/ n Molch m

New: ~ **Year's 'Day** n Neujahr nt. ~
Year's 'Eve n Silvester m. ~ **Zealand** /'ziːlənd/ n Neuseeland nt

next /nekst/ a & n nächste(r,s);
who's ~? wer kommt als nächster
dran? **the** ~ **best** das nächstbeste; ~
door nebenan; **my** ~ **of kin** mein
nächster Verwandter; ~ **to nothing**
fast gar nichts; **the week after** ~
übernächste Woche ● adv als nächstes;
~ **to** neben

NHS abbr see **National Health Service**

nib /nɪb/ n Feder f

nibble /'nɪbl/ vt/i knabbern (**at** an
+ dat)

nice /naɪs/ a (**-r, -st**) nett; (day,
weather) schön; (food) gut; (distinction)
fein. ~**ly** adv nett; (well) gut. ~**ties**
/'naɪsətɪz/ npl Feinheiten pl

niche /niːʃ/ n Nische f; (fig) Platz m

nick /nɪk/ n Kerbe f; (fam: prison)
Knast m; (fam: police station) Revier
nt; **in the** ~ **of time** (fam) gerade noch
rechtzeitig; **in good** ~ (fam) in gutem
Zustand ● vt einkerben; (steal) klauen;
(fam: arrest) schnappen

nickel /'nɪkl/ n Nickel nt; (Amer)
Fünfcentstück nt

'nickname n Spitzname m

nicotine /'nɪkətiːn/ n Nikotin nt

niece /niːs/ n Nichte f

Nigeria /naɪ'dʒɪərɪə/ n Nigeria nt.
~**n** a nigerianisch ● n Nigeria-
ner(in) m(f)

niggardly /'nɪgədlɪ/ a knauserig

niggling /'nɪglɪŋ/ a gering; (petty)
kleinlich; (pain) quälend

night /naɪt/ n Nacht f; (evening)
Abend m; **at** ~ nachts; **Monday** ~
Montag nacht/abend

night: ~**cap** n Schlafmütze f; (drink)
Schlaftrunk m. ~**-club** n Nachtklub
m. ~**dress** n Nachthemd nt. ~**fall** n
at ~**fall** bei Einbruch der Dunkelheit.
~**-gown** n, (fam) ~**ie** /'naɪtɪ/ n
Nachthemd nt

nightingale /'naɪtɪŋgeɪl/ n Nachtigall f

night: ~**-life** n Nachtleben nt. ~**ly** a
nächtlich ● adv jede Nacht. ~**mare**
n Alptraum m. ~**shade** n (Bot)
deadly ~**shade** Tollkirsche f.

~-**time** *n* at ~-time bei Nacht.
~-'**watchman** *n* Nachtwächter *m*
nil /nɪl/ *n* null
nimble /'nɪmbl/ *a* (-**r**, -**st**), -**bly** *adv*
flink
nine /naɪn/ *a* neun ● *n* Neun *f*.
~'**teen** *a* neunzehn. ~'**teenth** *a*
neunzehnte(r,s)
ninetieth /'naɪntɪɪθ/ *a* neunzigste-
(r,s)
ninety /'naɪntɪ/ *a* neunzig
ninth /naɪnθ/ *a* neunte(r,s)
nip /nɪp/ *n* Kniff *m*; (*bite*) Biß *m* ● *vt*
kneifen; (*bite*) beißen; ~ **in the bud**
(*fig*) im Keim ersticken ● *vi* (*fam: run*)
laufen
nipple /'nɪpl/ *n* Brustwarze *f*; (*Amer:
on bottle*) Sauger *m*
nippy /'nɪpɪ/ *a* (-**ier**, -**iest**) (*fam*) (*cold*)
frisch; (*quick*) flink
nitrate /'naɪtreɪt/ *n* Nitrat *nt*
nitrogen /'naɪtrədʒən/ *n* Stickstoff
m
nitwit /'nɪtwɪt/ *n* (*fam*) Dummkopf
m
no /nəʊ/ *adv* nein ● *n* (*pl* **noes**) Nein
nt ● *a* kein(e); (*pl*) keine; **in no time**
[sehr] schnell; **no parking/smoking**
Parken/Rauchen verboten; **no one** =
nobody
nobility /nəʊ'bɪlətɪ/ *n* Adel *m*
noble /'nəʊbl/ *a* (-**r**, -**st**) edel; (*aris-
tocratic*) adlig. ~**man** *n* Adlige(r) *m*
nobody /'nəʊbədɪ/ *pron* niemand,
keiner; **he knows** ~ er kennt nie-
manden *od* keinen ● *n* **a** ~ ein Niemand *m*
nocturnal /nɒk'tɜ:nl/ *a* nächtlich;
(*animal, bird*) Nacht-
nod /nɒd/ *n* Nicken *nt* ● *v* (*pt/pp*
nodded) ● *vi* nicken ● *vt* ~ **one's head**
mit dem Kopf nicken. ~ **off** *vi* einnicken
nodule /'nɒdju:l/ *n* Knötchen *nt*
noise /nɔɪz/ *n* Geräusch *nt*; (*loud*)
Lärm *m*. ~**less** *a*, -**ly** *adv* geräuschlos
noisy /'nɔɪzɪ/ *a* (-**ier**, -**iest**), -**ily** *adv*
laut; (*eater*) geräuschvoll
nomad /'nəʊmæd/ *n* Nomade *m*.
~**ic** /-'mædɪk/ *a* nomadisch; (*life,
tribe*) Nomaden-
nominal /'nɒmɪnl/ *a*, -**ly** *adv* nominell
nominat|e /'nɒmɪneɪt/ *vt* nomi-
nieren, aufstellen; (*appoint*) ernennen. ~**ion** /-'neɪʃn/ *n* Nominierung
f; Ernennung *f*

nominative /'nɒmɪnətɪv/ *a* & *n*
(*Gram*) ~ [**case**] Nominativ *m*
nonchalant /'nɒnʃələnt/ *a*, -**ly** *adv*
nonchalant; (*gesture*) lässig
non-com'missioned /nɒn-/ *a* ~
officer Unteroffizier *m*
non-com'mittal *a* unverbindlich;
be ~ sich nicht festlegen
nondescript /'nɒndɪskrɪpt/ *a* unbe-
stimmbar; (*person*) unscheinbar
none /nʌn/ *pron* keine(r)/keins; ~
of us keiner von uns; ~ **of it/this**
nichts davon ● *adv* ~ **too** nicht gerade;
~ **too soon** [um] keine Minute zu früh;
~ **the wiser** um nichts klüger; ~ **the
less** dennoch
nonentity /nɒ'nentətɪ/ *n* Null *f*
non-ex'istent *a* nichtvorhanden;
be ~ nicht vorhanden sein
non-'fiction *n* Sachliteratur *f*
non-'iron *a* bügelfrei
nonplussed /nɒn'plʌst/ *a* verblüfft
nonsens|e /'nɒnsəns/ *n* Unsinn *m*.
~**ical** /-'sensɪkl/ *a* unsinnig
non-'smoker *n* Nichtraucher *m*;
(*compartment*) Nichtraucherabteil
nt
non-'stop *adv* ununterbrochen; (*fly*)
nonstop; ~ '**flight** Nonstopflug *m*
non-'swimmer *n* Nichtschwimmer
m
non-'violent *a* gewaltlos
noodles /'nu:dlz/ *npl* Bandnudeln *pl*
nook /nʊk/ *n* Eckchen *nt*, Winkel *m*
noon /nu:n/ *n* Mittag *m*; **at** ~ um 12
Uhr mittags
noose /nu:s/ *n* Schlinge *f*
nor /nɔ:(r)/ *adv* noch ● *conj* auch
nicht
Nordic /'nɔ:dɪk/ *a* nordisch
norm /nɔ:m/ *n* Norm *f*
normal /'nɔ:ml/ *a* normal. ~**ity**
/-'mælətɪ/ *n* Normalität *f*. ~**ly** *adv*
normal; (*usually*) normalerweise
north /nɔ:θ/ *n* Norden *m*; **to the** ~
of nördlich von ● *a* Nord-, nord- ● *adv*
nach Norden
north: N~ **America** *n* Nordamerika
nt. ~-**east** *a* Nordost- ● *n* Nordosten
m
norther|ly /'nɔ:ðəlɪ/ *a* nördlich. ~**n**
a nördlich. **N**~**n Ireland** *n* Nord-
irland *nt*
north: N~ '**Pole** *n* Nordpol *m*. **N**~
'**Sea** *n* Nordsee *f*. ~**ward[s]**
/-wəd[z]/ *adv* nach Norden. ~-**west**
a Nordwest- ● *n* Nordwesten *m*

Nor|way /'nɔːweɪ/ n Norwegen nt. **~wegian** /-'wiːdʒn/ a norwegisch ● n Norweger(in) m(f)

nose /nəʊz/ n Nase f ● vi ~ **about** herumschnüffeln

nose: **~bleed** n Nasenbluten nt. **~dive** n (Aviat) Sturzflug m

nostalg|ia /nɒ'stældʒɪə/ n Nostalgie f. **~ic** a nostalgisch

nostril /'nɒstrəl/ n Nasenloch nt; (of horse) Nüster f

nosy /'nəʊzɪ/ a (-ier, -iest) (fam) neugierig

not /nɒt/ adv nicht; ~ **a** kein(e); **if** ~ wenn nicht; ~ **at all** gar nicht; ~ **a bit** kein bißchen; ~ **even** nicht mal; ~ **yet** noch nicht; **he is** ~ **a German** er ist kein Deutscher

notab|le /'nəʊtəbl/ a bedeutend; (remarkable) bemerkenswert. **~ly** adv insbesondere

notary /'nəʊtərɪ/ n ~ **'public /** Notar

notation /nəʊ'teɪʃn/ n Notation f; (Mus) Notenschrift f

notch /nɒtʃ/ n Kerbe f. ~ **up** vt (score) erzielen

note /nəʊt/ n (written comment) Notiz f, Anmerkung f; (short letter) Briefchen nt, Zettel m; (bank~) Banknote f, Schein m; (Mus) Note f; (sound) Ton m; (on piano) Taste f; **eighth/quarter** ~ (Amer) Achtel-/ Viertelnote f; **half/whole** ~ (Amer) halbe/ganze Note f; **of** ~ von Bedeutung; **make a** ~ **of** notieren ● vt beachten; (notice) bemerken (**that** daß). ~ **down** vt notieren

'notebook n Notizbuch nt

noted /'nəʊtɪd/ a bekannt (**for** für)

note: **~paper** n Briefpapier nt. **~worthy** a beachtenswert

nothing /'nʌθɪŋ/ n, pron & adv nichts; **for** ~ umsonst; ~ **but** nichts als; ~ **much** nicht viel; ~ **interesting** nichts Interessantes; **it's** ~ **to do with you** das geht dich nichts an

notice /'nəʊtɪs/ n (on board) Anschlag m, Bekanntmachung f; (announcement) Anzeige f; (review) Kritik f; (termination of lease, employment) Kündigung f; **[advance]** ~ Bescheid m; **give [in one's]** ~ kündigen; **give s.o.** ~ jdm kündigen; **take no** ~ **of** keine Notiz nehmen von; **take no** ~! ignoriere es! ● vt bemerken. **~able** /-əbl/ a, **-bly** adv merklich. **~-board** n Anschlagbrett nt

noti|fication /nəʊtɪfɪ'keɪʃn/ n Benachrichtigung f. **~fy** /'nəʊtɪfaɪ/ vt (pt/pp -ied) benachrichtigen

notion /'nəʊʃn/ n Idee f; **~s** pl (Amer: haberdashery) Kurzwaren pl

notorious /nəʊ'tɔːrɪəs/ a berüchtigt

notwith'standing prep trotz (+ gen) ● adv trotzdem, dennoch

nought /nɔːt/ n Null f

noun /naʊn/ n Substantiv nt

nourish /'nʌrɪʃ/ vt nähren. **~ing** a nahrhaft. **~ment** n Nahrung f

novel /'nɒvl/ a neu[artig] ● n Roman m. **~ist** n Romanschriftsteller(in) m(f). **~ty** n Neuheit f; **~ties** pl kleine Geschenkartikel pl

November /nəʊ'vembə(r)/ n November m

novice /'nɒvɪs/ n Neuling m; (Relig) Novize m/Novizin f

now /naʊ/ adv & conj jetzt; ~ **[that]** jetzt, wo; **just** ~ gerade, eben; **right** ~ sofort; ~ **and again** hin und wieder; **now, now!** na, na!

'nowadays adv heutzutage

nowhere /'nəʊ-/ adv nirgendwo, nirgends

noxious /'nɒkʃəs/ a schädlich

nozzle /'nɒzl/ n Düse f

nuance /'njuːɑ̃s/ n Nuance f

nuclear /'njuːklɪə(r)/ a Kern-. ~ **de'terrent** n nukleares Abschreckungsmittel nt

nucleus /'njuːklɪəs/ n (pl -lei /-lɪaɪ/) Kern m

nude /njuːd/ a nackt ● n (Art) Akt m; **in the** ~ nackt

nudge /nʌdʒ/ n Stups m ● vt stupsen

nud|ist /'njuːdɪst/ n Nudist m. **~ity** n Nacktheit f

nugget /'nʌgɪt/ n [Gold]klumpen m

nuisance /'njuːsns/ n Ärgernis nt; (pest) Plage f; **be a** ~ ärgerlich sein; (person:) lästig sein; **what a** ~! wie ärgerlich!

null /nʌl/ a ~ **and void** null und nichtig. **~ify** /'nʌlɪfaɪ/ vt (pt/pp -ied) für nichtig erklären

numb /nʌm/ a gefühllos, taub; ~ **with cold** taub vor Kälte ● vt betäuben

number /'nʌmbə(r)/ n Nummer f; (amount) Anzahl f; (Math) Zahl f ● vt numerieren; (include) zählen (**among** zu). **~-plate** n Nummernschild nt

numeral /'njuːmərl/ n Ziffer f

numerate /'njuːmərət/ a **be** ~ rechnen können

numerical /njuːˈmerɪkl/ *a*, **-ly** *adv* numerisch; **in ∼ order** zahlenmäßig geordnet

numerous /ˈnjuːmərəs/ *a* zahlreich

nun /nʌn/ *n* Nonne *f*

nuptial /ˈnʌpʃl/ *a* Hochzeits-. **∼s** *npl* (*Amer*) Hochzeit *f*

nurse /nɜːs/ *n* [Kranken]schwester *f*; (*male*) Krankenpfleger *m*; **children's ∼** Kindermädchen *nt* ● *vt* pflegen. **∼maid** *n* Kindermädchen *nt*

nursery /ˈnɜːsərɪ/ *n* Kinderzimmer *nt*; (*Hort*) Gärtnerei *f*; **[day] ∼** Kindertagesstätte *f*. **∼ rhyme** *n* Kinderreim *m*. **∼ school** *n* Kindergarten *m*

nursing /ˈnɜːsɪŋ/ *n* Krankenpflege *f*. **∼ home** *n* Pflegeheim *nt*

nurture /ˈnɜːtʃə(r)/ *vt* nähren; (*fig*) hegen

nut /nʌt/ *n* Nuß *f*; (*Techn*) [Schrauben]mutter *f*; (*fam: head*) Birne *f* (*fam*); **be ∼s** (*fam*) spinnen (*fam*). **∼crackers** *npl* Nußknacker *m*. **∼meg** *n* Muskat *m*

nutrient /ˈnjuːtrɪənt/ *n* Nährstoff *m*

nutrit|ion /njuːˈtrɪʃn/ *n* Ernährung *f*. **∼ious** /-ʃəs/ *a* nahrhaft

'nutshell *n* Nußschale *f*; **in a ∼** (*fig*) kurz gesagt

nuzzle /ˈnʌzl/ *vt* beschnüffeln

nylon /ˈnaɪlɒn/ *n* Nylon *nt*; **∼s** *pl* Nylonstrümpfe *pl*

nymph /nɪmf/ *n* Nymphe *f*

O

O /əʊ/ *n* (*Teleph*) null

oaf /əʊf/ *n* (*pl* **oafs**) Trottel *m*

oak /əʊk/ *n* Eiche *f* ● *attrib* Eichen-

OAP *abbr* (**old-age pensioner**) Rentner(in) *m*(*f*)

oar /ɔː(r)/ *n* Ruder *nt*. **∼sman** *n* Ruderer *m*

oasis /əʊˈeɪsɪs/ *n* (*pl* **oases** /-siːz/) Oase *f*

oath /əʊθ/ *n* Eid *m*; (*swear-word*) Fluch *m*

oatmeal /ˈəʊt-/ *n* Hafermehl *nt*

oats /əʊts/ *npl* Hafer *m*; (*Culin*) **[rolled] ∼** Haferflocken *pl*

obedien|ce /əˈbiːdɪəns/ *n* Gehorsam *m*. **∼t** *a*, **-ly** *adv* gehorsam

obes|e /əʊˈbiːs/ *a* fettleibig. **∼ity** *n* Fettleibigkeit *f*

obey /əˈbeɪ/ *vt/i* gehorchen (+ *dat*); befolgen ⟨*instructions, rules*⟩

obituary /əˈbɪtjʊərɪ/ *n* Nachruf *m*; (*notice*) Todesanzeige *f*

object[1] /ˈɒbdʒɪkt/ *n* Gegenstand *m*; (*aim*) Zweck *m*; (*intention*) Absicht *f*; (*Gram*) Objekt *nt*; **money is no ∼** Geld spielt keine Rolle

object[2] /əbˈdʒekt/ *vi* Einspruch erheben (**to** gegen); (*be against*) etwas dagegen haben

objection /əbˈdʒekʃn/ *n* Einwand *m*; **have no ∼** nichts dagegen haben. **∼able** /-əbl/ *a* anstößig; ⟨*person*⟩ unangenehm

objectiv|e /əbˈdʒektɪv/ *a*, **-ly** *adv* objektiv ● *n* Ziel *nt*. **∼ity** /-ˈtɪvətɪ/ *n* Objektivität *f*

objector /əbˈdʒektə(r)/ *n* Gegner *m*

obligation /ɒblɪˈgeɪʃn/ *n* Pflicht *f*; **be under an ∼** verpflichtet sein; **without ∼** unverbindlich

obligatory /əˈblɪɡətrɪ/ *a* obligatorisch; **be ∼** Vorschrift sein

oblig|e /əˈblaɪdʒ/ *vt* verpflichten; (*compel*) zwingen; (*do a small service*) einen Gefallen tun (+ *dat*); **much ∼ed!** vielen Dank! **∼ing** *a* entgegenkommend

oblique /əˈbliːk/ *a* schräg; ⟨*angle*⟩ schief; (*fig*) indirekt. **∼ stroke** *n* Schrägstrich *m*

obliterate /əˈblɪtəreɪt/ *vt* auslöschen

oblivion /əˈblɪvɪən/ *n* Vergessenheit *f*

oblivious /əˈblɪvɪəs/ *a* **be ∼** sich (*dat*) nicht bewußt sein (**of** *or* **to** *gen*)

oblong /ˈɒblɒŋ/ *a* rechteckig ● *n* Rechteck *nt*

obnoxious /əbˈnɒkʃəs/ *a* widerlich

oboe /ˈəʊbəʊ/ *n* Oboe *f*

obscen|e /əbˈsiːn/ *a* obszön; (*atrocious*) abscheulich. **∼ity** /-ˈsenətɪ/ *n* Obszönität *f*; Abscheulichkeit *f*

obscur|e /əbˈskjʊə(r)/ *a* dunkel; (*unknown*) unbekannt ● *vt* verdecken; (*confuse*) verwischen. **∼ity** *n* Dunkelheit *f*; Unbekanntheit *f*

obsequious /əbˈsiːkwɪəs/ *a* unterwürfig

observa|nce /əbˈzɜːvns/ *n* (*of custom*) Einhaltung *f*. **∼nt** *a* aufmerksam. **∼tion** /ɒbzəˈveɪʃn/ *n* Beobachtung *f*; (*remark*) Bemerkung *f*

observatory /əbˈzɜːvətrɪ/ *n* Sternwarte *f*; (*weather*) Wetterwarte *f*

observe /əb'zɜːv/ vt beobachten; (say, notice) bemerken; (keep, celebrate) feiern; (obey) einhalten. **~r** n Beobachter m

obsess /əb'ses/ vt **be ~ed by** besessen sein von. **~ion** /-eʃn/ n Besessenheit f; (persistent idea) fixe Idee f. **~ive** /-ɪv/ a, **-ly** adv zwanghaft

obsolete /'ɒbsəliːt/ a veraltet

obstacle /'ɒbstəkl/ n Hindernis nt

obstetrician /ɒbstə'trɪʃn/ n Geburtshelfer m. **obstetrics** /-'stetrɪks/ n Geburtshilfe f

obstina|cy /'ɒbstɪnəsɪ/ n Starrsinn m. **~te** /-nət/ a, **-ly** adv starrsinnig; (refusal) hartnäckig

obstreperous /əb'strepərəs/ a widerspenstig

obstruct /əb'strʌkt/ vt blockieren; (hinder) behindern. **~ion** /-ʌkʃn/ n Blockierung f; Behinderung f; (obstacle) Hindernis nt. **~ive** /-ɪv/ a **be ~ive** Schwierigkeiten bereiten

obtain /əb'teɪn/ vt erhalten, bekommen ● vi gelten. **~able** /-əbl/ a erhältlich

obtrusive /əb'truːsɪv/ a aufdringlich; (thing) auffällig

obtuse /əb'tjuːs/ a (Geom) stumpf; (stupid) begriffsstutzig

obviate /'ɒbvɪeɪt/ vt beseitigen

obvious /'ɒbvɪəs/ a, **-ly** adv offensichtlich, offenbar

occasion /ə'keɪʒn/ n Gelegenheit f; (time) Mal nt; (event) Ereignis nt; (cause) Anlaß m, Grund m; **on ~** gelegentlich, hin und wieder; **on the ~ of** anläßlich (+ gen) ● vt veranlassen

occasional /ə'keɪʒənl/ a gelegentlich; **he has the ~ glass of wine** er trinkt gelegentlich ein Glas Wein. **~ly** adv gelegentlich, hin und wieder

occult /ɒ'kʌlt/ a okkult

occupant /'ɒkjʊpənt/ n Bewohner(in) m(f); (of vehicle) Insasse m

occupation /ɒkjʊ'peɪʃn/ n Beschäftigung f; (job) Beruf m; (Mil) Besetzung f; (period) Besatzung f. **~al** a Berufs-. **~al therapy** n Beschäftigungstherapie f

occupier /'ɒkjʊpaɪə(r)/ n Bewohner(in) m(f)

occupy /'ɒkjʊpaɪ/ vt (pt/pp occupied) besetzen (seat, (Mil) country); einnehmen (space); in Anspruch nehmen (time); (live in) bewohnen; (fig)

bekleiden (office); (keep busy) beschäftigen; **~ oneself** sich beschäftigen

occur /ə'kɜː(r)/ vi (pt/pp occurred) geschehen; (exist) vorkommen, auftreten; **it ~red to me that** es fiel mir ein, daß. **~rence** /ə'kʌrəns/ n Auftreten nt; (event) Ereignis nt

ocean /'əʊʃn/ n Ozean m

o'clock /ə'klɒk/ adv **[at] 7~** [um] 7 Uhr

octagonal /ɒk'tægənl/ a achteckig

octave /'ɒktɪv/ n (Mus) Oktave f

October /ɒk'təʊbə(r)/ n Oktober m

octopus /'ɒktəpəs/ n (pl **-puses**) Tintenfisch m

odd /ɒd/ a (**-er, -est**) seltsam, merkwürdig; (number) ungerade; (not of set) einzeln; **forty ~** über vierzig; **~ jobs** Gelegenheitsarbeiten pl; **the ~ one out** die Ausnahme; **at ~ moments** zwischendurch; **have the ~ glass of wine** gelegentlich ein Glas Wein trinken

odd|ity /'ɒdɪtɪ/ n Kuriosität f. **~ly** adv merkwürdig; **~ly enough** merkwürdigerweise. **~ment** n (of fabric) Rest m

odds /ɒdz/ npl (chances) Chancen pl; **at ~** uneinig; **~ and ends** Kleinkram m; **it makes no ~** es spielt keine Rolle

ode /əʊd/ n Ode f

odious /'əʊdɪəs/ a widerlich, abscheulich

odour /'əʊdə(r)/ n Geruch m. **~less** a geruchlos

oesophagus /iː'sɒfəgəs/ n Speiseröhre f

of /ɒv, unbetont əv/ prep von (+ dat); (made of) aus (+ dat); **the two of us** wir zwei; **a child of three** ein dreijähriges Kind; **the fourth of January** der vierte Januar; **a pound of butter** ein Pfund Butter; **a cup of tea/coffee** eine Tasse Tee/Kaffee; **a bottle of wine** eine Flasche Wein; **half of it** die Hälfte davon; **the whole of the room** das ganze Zimmer

off /ɒf/ prep von (+ dat); **£10 ~ the price** £10 Nachlaß; **~ the coast** vor der Küste; **get ~ the ladder/bus** von der Leiter/aus dem Bus steigen; **take/leave the lid ~ the saucepan** den Topf abdecken/nicht zudecken ● adv weg; (button, lid, handle) ab; (light) aus; (brake) los; (machine) abgeschaltet; (tap) zu; (on appliance) **'off'** 'aus'; **2 kilometres ~** 2 Kilometer entfernt; **a**

long way ~ weit weg; (*time*) noch lange
hin; ~ **and on** hin und wieder; **with
his hat/coat** ~ ohne Hut/Mantel; **with
the light/lid** ~ ohne Licht/Deckel;
20% ~ 20% Nachlaß; **be** ~ (*leave*) [weg]-
gehen; (*Sport*) starten; ⟨*food:*⟩ schlecht/
(*all gone*) alle sein; **be better/
worse** ~ besser/schlechter dran
sein; **be well** ~ gut dran sein;
(*financially*) wohlhabend sein; **have a
day** ~ einen freien Tag haben; **go/
drive** ~ weggehen/-fahren; **turn/take
sth** ~ etw abdrehen/-nehmen

offal /'ɒfl/ n (*Culin*) Innereien pl

offence /ə'fens/ n (*illegal act*) Vergehen nt; **give/take** ~ Anstoß er-
regen/nehmen (**at** an + *dat*)

offend /ə'fend/ vt beleidigen. ~**er** n
(*Jur*) Straftäter m

offensive /ə'fensɪv/ a anstößig;
(*Mil, Sport*) offensiv ● n Offensive f

offer /'ɒfə(r)/ n Angebot nt; **on special** ~ im Sonderangebot ● vt anbieten
(**to** *dat*); leisten ⟨*resistance*⟩; ~ **s.o. sth**
jdm etw anbieten; ~ **to do sth** sich
anbieten, etw zu tun. ~**ing** n Gabe f

off'hand a brüsk; (*casual*) lässig
● adv so ohne weiteres

office /'ɒfɪs/ n Büro nt; (*post*) Amt
nt; **in** ~ im Amt; ~ **hours** pl
Dienststunden pl

officer /'ɒfɪsə(r)/ n Offizier m;
(*official*) Beamte(r) m/Beamtin f;
(*police*) Polizeibeamte(r) m/
-beamtin f

official /ə'fɪʃl/ a offiziell, amtlich ● n
Beamte(r) m/Beamtin f; (*Sport*)
Funktionär m. ~**ly** adv offiziell

officiate /ə'fɪʃɪeɪt/ vi amtieren

officious /ə'fɪʃəs/ a, **-ly** adv über-
eifrig

'offing n **in the** ~ in Aussicht

'off-licence n Wein- und Spiri-
tuosenhandlung f

off-'load vt ausladen

'off-putting a (*fam*) abstoßend

off'set vt (*pt/pp* -**set**, *pres p* -**setting**)
ausgleichen

'offshoot n Schößling m; (*fig*)
Zweig m

'offshore a offshore-. ~ **rig** n
Bohrinsel f

off'side a (*Sport*) abseits

'offspring n Nachwuchs m

off'stage adv hinter den Kulissen

off-'white a fast weiß

often /'ɒfn/ adv oft; **every so** ~ von
Zeit zu Zeit

ogle /'əʊgl/ vt beäugeln

ogre /'əʊgə(r)/ n Menschenfresser m

oh /əʊ/ int oh! ach! **oh dear!** o weh!

oil /ɔɪl/ n Öl nt; (*petroleum*) Erdöl nt
● vt ölen

oil: ~**cloth** n Wachstuch nt. ~**field** n
Ölfeld nt. ~-**painting** n Ölgemälde
nt. ~ **refinery** n [Erd]ölraffinerie f.
~**skins** npl Ölzeug nt. ~-**slick** n Ölteppich m. ~-**tanker** n Öltanker m.
~ **well** n Ölquelle f

oily /'ɔɪlɪ/ a (-**ier, -iest**) ölig

ointment /'ɔɪntmənt/ n Salbe f

OK /əʊ'keɪ/ a & int (*fam*) in Ordnung;
okay ● adv (*well*) gut ● vt (*auch
okay*) (*pt/pp* okayed) genehmigen

old /əʊld/ a (-**er, -est**) alt; (*former*)
ehemalig

old: ~ '**age** n Alter nt. ~-**age 'pensioner** n Rentner(in) m(f). ~ **boy** n
ehemaliger Schüler. ~-'**fashioned**
a altmodisch. ~ **girl** ehemalige
Schülerin f. ~ '**maid** n alte Jungfer f

olive /'ɒlɪv/ n Olive f; (*colour*) Oliv nt
● a olivgrün. ~ **branch** n Ölzweig m;
(*fig*) Friedensangebot nt. ~ '**oil** n
Olivenöl m

Olympic /ə'lɪmpɪk/ a olympisch ● n
the ~**s** die Olympischen Spiele pl

omelette /'ɒmlɪt/ n Omelett nt

omen /'əʊmən/ n Omen nt

ominous /'ɒmɪnəs/ a bedrohlich

omission /ə'mɪʃn/ n Auslassung f;
(*failure to do*) Unterlassung f

omit /ə'mɪt/ vt (*pt/pp* omitted) auslassen; ~ **to do sth** es unterlassen, etw
zu tun

omnipotent /ɒm'nɪpətənt/ a allmächtig

on /ɒn/ prep auf (+ *dat*/(*on to*)
+ *acc*); (*on vertical surface*) an
(+ *dat*/(*on to*) + *acc*); (*about*) über
(+ *acc*); **on Monday** [am] Montag; **on
Mondays** montags; **on the first of
May** am ersten Mai; **on arriving** als ich
ankam; **on one's finger** am Finger; **on
the right/left** rechts/links; **on the
Rhine/Thames** am Rhein/an der
Themse; **on the radio/television** im
Radio/Fernsehen; **on the bus/train** im
Bus/Zug; **go on the bus/train** mit dem
Bus/Zug fahren; **get on the bus/train**
in den Bus/Zug einsteigen; **on me** (*with
me*) bei mir; **it's on me** (*fam*) das spen-
diere ich ● adv (*further on*) weiter;
(*switched on*) an; ⟨*brake*⟩ angezogen;
⟨*machine*⟩ angeschaltet; (*on appliance*)
'**on**' 'ein'; **with/without his hat/coat**

on mit/ohne Hut/Mantel; **with/ without the lid on** mit/ohne Deckel; **be on** ⟨*film:*⟩ laufen; ⟨*event:*⟩ stattfinden; **be on at** (*fam*) bedrängen (**zu** to); **it's not on** (*fam*) das geht nicht; **on and on** immer weiter; **on and off** hin und wieder; **and so on** und so weiter; **later on** später; **move/drive on** weitergehen/-fahren; **stick/sew on** ankleben/-nähen

once /wʌns/ *adv* einmal; (*formerly*) früher; **at ~** sofort; (*at the same time*) gleichzeitig; **~ and for all** ein für allemal ● *conj* wenn; (*with past tense*) als. **~-over** *n* (*fam*) **give s.o./sth the ~-over** sich (*dat*) jdn/etw kurz ansehen

'**oncoming** *a* **~ traffic** Gegenverkehr *m*

one /wʌn/ *a* ein(e); (*only*) einzig; **not ~** kein(e); **~ day/evening** eines Tages/Abends **~ Eins** *f* ● *pron* eine(r)/eins; (*impersonal*) man; **which ~** welche(r,s); **~ another** einander; **~ by ~** einzeln; **~ never knows** man kann nie wissen

one: ~-eyed *a* einäugig. **~-parent 'family** *n* Einelternfamilie *f*. **~'self** *pron* selbst; (*refl*) sich; **by ~self** allein. **~-sided** *a* einseitig. **~-way** *a* ⟨*street*⟩ Einbahn-; ⟨*ticket*⟩ einfach

onion /'ʌnjən/ *n* Zwiebel *f*

'**onlooker** *n* Zuschauer(in) *m(f)*

only /'əʊnlɪ/ *a* einzige(r,s); **an ~ child** ein Einzelkind *nt* ● *adv* & *conj* nur; **~ just** gerade erst; (*barely*) gerade noch

'**onset** *n* Beginn *m*; (*of winter*) Einsetzen *nt*

onslaught /'ɒnslɔːt/ *n* heftiger Angriff *m*

onus /'əʊnəs/ *n* **the ~ is on me** es liegt an mir (**to** zu)

onward[s] /'ɒnwəd[z]/ *adv* vorwärts; **from then ~** von der Zeit an

ooze /uːz/ *vi* sickern

opal /'əʊpl/ *n* Opal *m*

opaque /əʊ'peɪk/ *a* undurchsichtig

open /'əʊpən/ *a*, **-ly** *adv* offen; **be ~** ⟨*shop:*⟩ geöffnet sein; **in the ~ air** im Freien ● *n* **in the ~** im Freien ● *vt* öffnen, aufmachen; (*start, set up*) eröffnen ● *vi* sich öffnen; ⟨*flower:*⟩ aufgehen; ⟨*shop:*⟩ öffnen, aufmachen; (*be started*) eröffnet werden. **~ up** *vt* öffnen, aufmachen; (*fig*) eröffnen ● *vi* sich öffnen; (*fig*) sich eröffnen

open: ~-air 'swimming pool *n* Freibad *nt*. **~ day** *n* Tag *m* der offenen Tür

opener /'əʊpənə(r)/ *n* Öffner *m*

opening /'əʊpənɪŋ/ *n* Öffnung *f*; (*beginning*) Eröffnung *f*; (*job*) Einstiegsmöglichkeit *f*. **~ hours** *npl* Öffnungszeiten *pl*

open: ~-'minded *a* aufgeschlossen. **~-plan** *a* **~-plan office** Großraumbüro *nt*. **~ 'sandwich** *n* belegtes Brot *nt*

opera /'ɒpərə/ *n* Oper *f*

operable /'ɒpərəbl/ *a* operierbar

opera: ~-glasses *npl* Opernglas *nt*. **~-house** *n* Opernhaus *nt*. **~-singer** *n* Opernsänger(in) *m(f)*

operate /'ɒpəreɪt/ *vt* bedienen ⟨*machine, lift*⟩; betätigen ⟨*lever, brake*⟩; (*fig: run*) betreiben ● *vi* (*Techn*) funktionieren; (*be in action*) in Betrieb sein; (*Mil & fig*) operieren; **~ [on]** (*Med*) operieren

operatic /ɒpə'rætɪk/ *a* Opern-

operation /ɒpə'reɪʃn/ *n* (*see operate*) Bedienung *f*; Betätigung *f*; Operation *f*; **in ~** (*Techn*) in Betrieb; **come into ~** (*fig*) in Kraft treten; **have an ~** (*Med*) operiert werden. **~al** *a* **be ~al** in Betrieb sein; ⟨*law:*⟩ in Kraft sein

operative /'ɒpərətɪv/ *a* wirksam

operator /'ɒpəreɪtə(r)/ *n* (*user*) Bedienungsperson *f*; (*Teleph*) Vermittlung *f*

operetta /ɒpə'retə/ *n* Operette *f*

opinion /ə'pɪnjən/ *n* Meinung *f*; **in my ~** meiner Meinung nach. **~ated** *a* rechthaberisch

opium /'əʊpɪəm/ *n* Opium *nt*

opponent /ə'pəʊnənt/ *n* Gegner(in) *m(f)*

opportune /'ɒpətjuːn/ *a* günstig. **~ist** /-'tjuːnɪst/ *a* opportunistisch ● *n* Opportunist *m*

opportunity /ɒpə'tjuːnətɪ/ *n* Gelegenheit *f*

oppos|e /ə'pəʊz/ *vt* Widerstand leisten (+ *dat*); (*argue against*) sprechen gegen; **be ~ed to sth** gegen etw sein; **as ~ed to** im Gegensatz zu. **~ing** *a* gegnerisch; (*opposite*) entgegengesetzt

opposite /'ɒpəzɪt/ *a* entgegengesetzt; ⟨*house, side*⟩ gegenüberliegend; **~ number** (*fig*) Gegenstück *nt*; **the ~ sex** das andere Geschlecht ● *n* Gegenteil *nt* ● *adv* gegenüber ● *prep* gegenüber (+ *dat*)

opposition /ɒpə'zɪʃn/ *n* Widerstand *m*; (*Pol*) Opposition *f*

oppress /ə'pres/ vt unterdrücken.
~ion /-eʃn/ n Unterdrückung f.
~ive /-ɪv/ a tyrannisch; (heat)
drückend. **~or** n Unterdrücker m

opt /ɒpt/ vi **~ for** sich entscheiden für;
~ out ausscheiden (of aus)

optical /'ɒptɪkl/ a optisch; **~ illusion**
optische Täuschung f

optician /ɒp'tɪʃn/ n Optiker m

optics /'ɒptɪks/ n Optik f

optimis|m /'ɒptɪmɪzm/ n Opti-
mismus m. **~t** /-mɪst/ n Optimist m.
~tic /-'mɪstɪk/ a, **-ally** adv opti-
mistisch

optimum /'ɒptɪməm/ a optimal ● n
(pl **-ima**) Optimum nt

option /'ɒpʃn/ n Wahl f; (Comm) Option f. **~al** a auf Wunsch erhältlich;
(subject) wahlfrei; **~al extras** pl
Extras pl

opu|lence /'ɒpjʊləns/ n Prunk m;
(wealth) Reichtum m. **~lent** a
prunkvoll; (wealthy) sehr reich

or /ɔː(r)/ conj oder; (after negative)
noch; **or [else]** sonst; **in a year or two**
in ein bis zwei Jahren

oracle /'ɒrəkl/ n Orakel nt

oral /'ɔːrl/ a, **-ly** adv mündlich; (Med)
oral ● n (fam) Mündliche(s) nt

orange /'ɒrɪndʒ/ n Apfelsine f,
Orange f; (colour) Orange nt ● a
orangefarben. **~ade** /-'dʒeɪd/ n
Orangeade f

oration /ə'reɪʃn/ n Rede f

orator /'ɒrətə(r)/ n Redner m

oratorio /ɒrə'tɔːrɪəʊ/ n Oratorium
nt

oratory /'ɒrətərɪ/ n Redekunst f

orbit /'ɔːbɪt/ n Umlaufbahn f ● vt
umkreisen. **~al** a **~al road** Ring-
straße f

orchard /'ɔːtʃəd/ n Obstgarten m

orches|tra /'ɔːkɪstrə/ n Orchester
nt. **~tral** /-'kestrəl/ a Orchester-.
~trate vt orchestrieren

orchid /'ɔːkɪd/ n Orchidee f

ordain /ɔː'deɪn/ vt bestimmen; (Relig)
ordinieren

ordeal /ɔː'diːl/ n (fig) Qual f

order /'ɔːdə(r)/ n Ordnung f;
(sequence) Reihenfolge f; (condition)
Zustand m; (command) Befehl m; (in
restaurant) Bestellung f; (Comm)
Auftrag m; (Relig, medal) Orden m;
out of ~ (machine) außer Betrieb; **in ~
that** damit; **in ~ to help** um zu helfen;
take holy ~s Geistlicher werden ● vt
(put in ~) ordnen; (command) befehlen

(+ dat); (Comm, in restaurant) bestellen; (prescribe) verordnen

orderly /'ɔːdəlɪ/ a ordentlich; (not
unruly) friedlich ● n (Mil, Med)
Sanitäter m

ordinary /'ɔːdmərɪ/ a gewöhnlich,
normal; (meeting) ordentlich

ordination /ɔːdɪ'neɪʃn/ n (Relig)
Ordination f

ore /ɔː(r)/ n Erz nt

organ /'ɔːgən/ n (Biol & fig) Organ nt;
(Mus) Orgel f

organic /ɔː'gænɪk/ a, **-ally** adv organisch; (without chemicals) bio-
dynamisch; (crop) biologisch angebaut;
(food) Bio-; **~ally grown** biologisch angebaut. **~ farm** n Biohof m. **~ farm-
ing** n biologischer Anbau m

organism /'ɔːgənɪzm/ n Organismus
m

organist /'ɔːgənɪst/ n Organist m

organization /ɔːgənar'zeɪʃn/ n Or-
ganisation f

organize /'ɔːgənaɪz/ vt organisieren;
veranstalten (event). **~r** n Orga-
nisator m; Veranstalter m

orgasm /'ɔːgæzm/ n Orgasmus m

orgy /'ɔːdʒɪ/ n Orgie f

Orient /'ɔːrɪənt/ n Orient m. **o~al**
/-'entl/ a orientalisch; **~al carpet**
Orientteppich m ● n Orientale m/
Orientalin f

orient|ate /'ɔːrɪənteɪt/ vt **~ate one-
self** sich orientieren. **~ation** /-'teɪʃn/
n Orientierung f

orifice /'ɒrɪfɪs/ n Öffnung f

origin /'ɒrɪdʒɪn/ n Ursprung m; (of
person, goods) Herkunft f

original /ə'rɪdʒənl/ a ursprünglich;
(not copied) original; (new) originell
● n Original nt. **~ity** /-'nælɪtɪ/ n
Originalität f. **~ly** adv ursprünglich

originat|e /ə'rɪdʒɪneɪt/ vi entstehen
● vt hervorbringen. **~or** n Urheber
m

ornament /'ɔːnəmənt/ n Zier-
gegenstand m; (decoration) Verzierung f. **~al** /-'mentl/ a dekorativ.
~ation /-'teɪʃn/ n Verzierung f

ornate /ɔː'neɪt/ a reich verziert

ornithology /ɔːnɪ'θɒlədʒɪ/ n Vogel-
kunde f

orphan /'ɔːfn/ n Waisenkind nt,
Waise f ● vt zur Waise machen; **~ed**
verwaist. **~age** /-ɪdʒ/ n Waisenhaus
nt

orthodox /'ɔːθədɒks/ a orthodox

orthography /ɔ:'θɒgrəfɪ/ n Rechtschreibung f

orthopaedic /ɔ:θə'pi:dɪk/ a orthopädisch

oscillate /'ɒsɪleɪt/ vi schwingen

ostensible /ɒ'stensəbl/ a, **-bly** adv angeblich

ostentat|ion /ɒsten'teɪʃn/ n Protzerei f (fam). **~ious** /-ʃəs/ a protzig (fam)

osteopath /'ɒstɪəpæθ/ n Osteopath m

ostracize /'ɒstrəsaɪz/ vt ächten

ostrich /'ɒstrɪtʃ/ n Strauß m

other /'ʌðə(r)/ a, pron & n andere(r, s); **the ~ [one]** der/die/das andere; **the ~ two** die zwei anderen; **two ~s** zwei andere; (more) noch zwei; **no ~s** sonst keine; **any ~ questions?** sonst noch Fragen? **every ~ day** jeden zweiten Tag; **the ~ day** neulich; **the ~ evening** neulich abends; **someone/ something or ~** irgend jemand/etwas ● adv anders; **~ than him** außer ihm; **somehow/somewhere or ~** irgendwie/ irgendwo

'**otherwise** adv sonst; (differently) anders

otter /'ɒtə(r)/ n Otter m

ouch /aʊtʃ/ int autsch

ought /ɔ:t/ v aux **I/we ~ to stay** ich sollte/wir sollten eigentlich bleiben; **he ~ not to have done it** er hätte es nicht machen sollen; **that ~ to be enough** das sollte eigentlich genügen

ounce /aʊns/ n Unze f (28,35 g)

our /'aʊə(r)/ a unser

ours /'aʊəz/ poss pron unsere(r,s); **a friend of ~** ein Freund von uns; **that is ~** das gehört uns

ourselves /aʊə'selvz/ pron selbst; (refl) uns; **by ~** allein

oust /aʊst/ vt entfernen

out /aʊt/ adv (not at home) weg; (outside) draußen; (not alight) aus; (unconscious) bewußtlos; **be ~** (sun:) scheinen; (flower:) blühen; (workers:) streiken; (calculation:) nicht stimmen; (Sport) aus sein; (fig: not feasible) nicht in Frage kommen; **~ and about** unterwegs; **have it ~ with s.o.** (fam) jdn zur Rede stellen; **get ~!** (fam) raus! **~ with it!** (fam) heraus damit! **go/send ~** hinausgehen/-schicken; **come/ bring ~** herauskommen/-bringen ● prep **~ of** aus (+ dat); **go ~ of the door** zur Tür hinausgehen; **be ~ of bed/the room** nicht im Bett/im Zimmer sein; **~ of breath/ danger** außer Atem/Gefahr; **~ of work** arbeitslos; **nine ~ of ten** neun von zehn; **be ~ of sugar/bread** keinen Zucker/ kein Brot mehr haben ● prep aus (+ dat); **go ~ the door** zur Tür hinausgehen

out'bid vt (pt/pp **-bid**, pres p **-bidding**) überbieten

'**outboard** a **~ motor** Außenbordmotor m

'**outbreak** n Ausbruch m

'**outbuilding** n Nebengebäude nt

'**outburst** n Ausbruch m

'**outcast** n Ausgestoßene(r) m/f

'**outcome** n Ergebnis nt

'**outcry** n Aufschrei m [der Entrüstung]

out'dated a überholt

out'do vt (pt **-did**, pp **-done**) übertreffen, übertrumpfen

'**outdoor** a (life, sports) im Freien; **~ shoes** pl Straßenschuhe pl; **~ swimming pool** Freibad nt

out'doors adv draußen; **go ~** nach draußen gehen

'**outer** a äußere(r,s)

'**outfit** n Ausstattung f; (clothes) Ensemble nt; (fam: organization) Betrieb m; (fam) Laden m. **~ter** n **men's ~ter's** Herrenbekleidungsgeschäft nt

'**outgoing** a ausscheidend; (mail) ausgehend; (sociable) kontaktfreudig. **~s** npl Ausgaben pl

out'grow vt (pt **-grew**, pp **-grown**) herauswachsen aus

'**outhouse** n Nebengebäude nt

outing /'aʊtɪŋ/ n Ausflug m

outlandish /aʊt'lændɪʃ/ a ungewöhnlich

'**outlaw** n Geächtete(r) m/f ● vt ächten

'**outlay** n Auslagen pl

'**outlet** n Abzug m; (for water) Abfluß m; (fig) Ventil nt; (Comm) Absatzmöglichkeit f

'**outline** n Umriß m; (summary) kurze Darstellung f ● vt umreißen

out'live vt überleben

'**outlook** n Aussicht f; (future prospect) Aussichten pl; (attitude) Einstellung f

'**outlying** a entlegen; **~ areas** pl Außengebiete pl

out'moded a überholt

out'number vt zahlenmäßig überlegen sein (+ dat)

'**out-patient** *n* ambulanter Patient *m*; ~**s' department** Ambulanz *f*

'**outpost** *n* Vorposten *m*

'**output** *n* Leistung *f*, Produktion *f*

'**outrage** *n* Greueltat *f*; (*fig*) Skandal *m*; (*indignation*) Empörung *f* ● *vt* empören. ~**ous** /-'reidʒəs/ *a* empörend

'**outright**[1] *a* völlig, total; ⟨*refusal*⟩ glatt

out'**right**[2] *adv* ganz; (*at once*) sofort; (*frankly*) offen

'**outset** *n* Anfang *m*; **from the** ~ von Anfang an

'**outside**[1] *a* äußere(r,s); ~ **wall** Außenwand *f* ● *n* Außenseite *f*; **from the** ~ von außen; **at the** ~ höchstens

out'**side**[2] *adv* außen; (*out of doors*) draußen; **go** ~ nach draußen gehen ● *prep* außerhalb (+ *gen*); (*in front of*) vor (+ *dat/acc*)

out'**sider** *n* Außenseiter *m*

'**outsize** *a* übergroß

'**outskirts** *npl* Rand *m*

out'**spoken** *a* offen; **be** ~ kein Blatt vor den Mund nehmen

out'**standing** *a* hervorragend; (*conspicuous*) bemerkenswert; (*not settled*) unerledigt; (*Comm*) ausstehend

'**outstretched** *a* ausgestreckt

out'**strip** *vt* (*pt/pp* -**stripped**) davonlaufen (+ *dat*); (*fig*) übertreffen

out'**vote** *vt* überstimmen

'**outward** /-wəd/ *a* äußerlich; ~ **journey** Hinreise *f* ● *adv* nach außen; **be** ~ **bound** ⟨*ship:*⟩ auslaufen. ~**ly** *adv* nach außen hin, äußerlich. ~**s** *adv* nach außen

out'**weigh** *vt* überwiegen

out'**wit** *vt* (*pt/pp* -**witted**) überlisten

oval /'əʊvl/ *a* oval ● *n* Oval *nt*

ovary /'əʊvəri/ *n* (*Anat*) Eierstock *m*

ovation /əʊ'veiʃn/ *n* Ovation *f*

oven /'ʌvn/ *n* Backofen *m*. ~-**ready** *a* bratfertig

over /'əʊvə(r)/ *prep* über (+ *acc/dat*); ~ **dinner** beim Essen; ~ **the weekend** übers Wochenende; ~ **the phone** am Telefon; ~ **the page** auf der nächsten Seite; **all** ~ **Germany** in ganz Deutschland; ⟨*travel*⟩ durch ganz Deutschland; **all** ~ **the place** (*fam*) überall ● *adv* (*remaining*) übrig; (*ended*) zu Ende; ~ **again** noch einmal; ~ **and** ~ immer wieder; ~ **here/there** hier/da drüben; **all** ~ (*everywhere*) überall; **it's all** ~ es ist vorbei; **I ache all** ~ mir tut alles weh; **go/drive** ~

hinübergehen/-fahren; **come/bring** ~ herüberkommen/-bringen; **turn** ~ herumdrehen

overall[1] /'əʊvərɔːl/ *n* Kittel *m*; ~**s** *pl* Overall *m*

overall[2] /əʊvər'ɔːl/ *a* gesamt; (*general*) allgemein ● *adv* insgesamt

over'**awe** *vt* (*fig*) überwältigen

over'**balance** *vi* das Gleichgewicht verlieren

over'**bearing** *a* herrisch

'**overboard** *adv* (*Naut*) über Bord

'**overcast** *a* bedeckt

over'**charge** *vt* ~ **s.o.** jdm zu viel berechnen ● *vi* zu viel verlangen

'**overcoat** *n* Mantel *m*

over'**come** *vt* (*pt* -**came**, *pp* -**come**) überwinden; **be** ~ **by** überwältigt werden von

over'**crowded** *a* überfüllt

over'**do** *vt* (*pt* -**did**, *pp* -**done**) übertreiben; (*cook too long*) zu lange kochen; ~ **it** (*fam: do too much*) sich übernehmen

'**overdose** *n* Überdosis *f*

'**overdraft** *n* [Konto]überziehung *f*; **have an** ~ sein Konto überzogen haben

over'**draw** *vt* (*pt* -**drew**, *pp* -**drawn**) (*Comm*) überziehen

over'**due** *a* überfällig

over'**estimate** *vt* überschätzen

'**overflow**[1] *n* Überschuß *m*; (*outlet*) Überlauf *m*

over'**flow**[2] *vi* überlaufen

over'**grown** *a* ⟨*garden*⟩ überwachsen

'**overhang**[1] *n* Überhang *m*

over'**hang**[2] *vt/i* (*pt/pp* -**hung**) überhängen (über + *acc*)

'**overhaul**[1] *n* Überholung *f*

over'**haul**[2] *vt* (*Techn*) überholen

over'**head**[1] *adv* oben

'**overhead**[2] *a* Ober-; (*ceiling*) Decken-. ~**s** *npl* allgemeine Unkosten *pl*

over'**hear** *vt* (*pt/pp* -**heard**) mit anhören ⟨*conversation*⟩; **I overheard him saying it** ich hörte zufällig, wie er das sagte

over'**heat** *vi* zu heiß werden ● *vt* zu stark erhitzen

over'**joyed** *a* überglücklich

'**overland** *a* & *adv* /-'-/ auf dem Landweg; ~ **route** Landroute *f*

over'**lap** *v* (*pt/pp* -**lapped**) ● *vi* sich überschneiden ● *vt* überlappen

over'**leaf** *adv* umseitig

over'load vt überladen; (*Electr*) überlasten

'overlook[1] n (*Amer*) Aussichtspunkt m

over'look[2] vt überblicken; (*fail to see, ignore*) übersehen

overly /'əʊvəlɪ/ adv übermäßig

over'night[1] adv über Nacht; **stay ~** übernachten

'overnight[2] a Nacht-; **~ stay** Übernachtung f

'overpass n Überführung f

over'pay vt (*pt/pp* **-paid**) überbezahlen

over'populated a übervölkert

over'power vt überwältigen. **~ing** a überwältigend

over'priced a zu teuer

overpro'duce vt überproduzieren

over'rate vt überschätzen. **~d** a überbewertet

over'reach vt **~ oneself** sich übernehmen

overre'act vi überreagieren. **~ion** n Überreaktion f

over'rid|e vt (*pt* **-rode**, *pp* **-ridden**) sich hinwegsetzen über (+ *acc*). **~ing** a Haupt-

over'rule vt ablehnen; **we were ~d** wir wurden überstimmt

over'run vt (*pt* **-ran**, *pp* **-run**, *pres p* **-running**) überrennen; überschreiten ⟨*time*⟩; **be ~ with** überlaufen sein von

over'seas[1] adv in Übersee; **go ~** nach Übersee gehen

'overseas[2] a Übersee-

over'see vt (*pt* **-saw**, *pp* **-seen**) beaufsichtigen

'overseer /-sɪə(r)/ n Aufseher m

over'shadow vt überschatten

over'shoot vt (*pt/pp* **-shot**) hinausschießen über (+ *acc*)

'oversight n Versehen nt

over'sleep vi (*pt/pp* **-slept**) [sich] verschlafen

over'step vt (*pt/pp* **-stepped**) überschreiten

over'strain vt überanstrengen

overt /əʊ'vɜːt/ a offen

over'tak|e vt/i (*pt* **-took**, *pp* **-taken**) überholen. **~ing** n Überholen nt; **no ~ing** Überholverbot nt

over'tax vt zu hoch besteuern; (*fig*) überfordern

'overthrow[1] n (*Pol*) Sturz m

over'throw[2] vt (*pt* **-threw**, *pp* **-thrown**) (*Pol*) stürzen

'overtime n Überstunden pl ● adv **work ~** Überstunden machen

over'tired a übermüdet

'overtone n (*fig*) Unterton m

overture /'əʊvətjʊə(r)/ n (*Mus*) Ouvertüre f; **~s** pl (*fig*) Annäherungsversuche pl

over'turn vt umstoßen ● vi umkippen

over'weight a übergewichtig; **be ~** Übergewicht haben

overwhelm /-'welm/ vt überwältigen. **~ing** a überwältigend

over'work n Überarbeitung f ● vt überfordern ● vi sich überarbeiten

over'wrought a überreizt

ovulation /ɒvjʊ'leɪʃn/ n Eisprung m

ow|e /əʊ/ vt schulden/(*fig*) verdanken (**[to] s.o.** jdm); **~e s.o. sth** jdm etw schuldig sein; **be ~ing** ⟨*money:*⟩ ausstehen. **'~ing to** prep wegen (+ *gen*)

owl /aʊl/ n Eule f

own[1] /əʊn/ a & pron eigen; **it's my ~** es gehört mir; **a car of my ~** mein eigenes Auto; **on one's ~** allein; **hold one's ~** sich behaupten; **get one's ~ back** (*fam*) sich revanchieren

own[2] vt besitzen; (*confess*) zugeben; **I don't ~ it** es gehört mir nicht. **~ up** vi es zugeben

owner /'əʊnə(r)/ n Eigentümer(in) m(f), Besitzer(in) m(f); (*of shop*) Inhaber(in) m(f). **~ship** n Besitz m

ox /ɒks/ n (*pl* **oxen**) Ochse m

oxide /'ɒksaɪd/ n Oxyd nt

oxygen /'ɒksɪdʒən/ n Sauerstoff m

oyster /'ɔɪstə(r)/ n Auster f

ozone /'əʊzəʊn/ n Ozon nt. **~-'friendly** a ≈ ohne FCKW. **~ layer** n Ozonschicht f

P

pace /peɪs/ n Schritt m; (*speed*) Tempo nt; **keep ~ with** Schritt halten mit ● vi **~ up and down** auf und ab gehen. **~-maker** n (*Sport & Med*) Schrittmacher m

Pacific /pə'sɪfɪk/ a & n **the ~ [Ocean]** der Pazifik

pacifier /'pæsɪfaɪə(r)/ n (*Amer*) Schnuller m

pacifist /'pæsɪfɪst/ n Pazifist m

pacify /'pæsɪfaɪ/ vt (*pt/pp* **-ied**) beruhigen

pack /pæk/ n Packung f; (*Mil*) Tornister m; (*of cards*) [Karten]spiel nt;

(*gang*) Bande *f*; (*of hounds*) Meute *f*;
(*of wolves*) Rudel *nt*; **a ~ of lies** ein
Haufen Lügen ● *vt/i* packen; einpacken
⟨*article*⟩; **be ~ed** (*crowded*) [gedrängt]
voll sein; **send s.o. ~ing** (*fam*) jdn weg-
schicken. **~ up** *vt* einpacken ● *vi*
(*fam*) ⟨*machine*:⟩ kaputtgehen; ⟨*person*:⟩ einpacken (*fam*)

package /'pækɪdʒ/ *n* Paket *nt* ● *vt*
verpacken. **~ holiday** *n* Pau-
schalreise *f*

packed 'lunch *n* Lunchpaket *nt*

packet /'pækɪt/ *n* Päckchen *nt*; **cost a
~** (*fam*) einen Haufen Geld kosten

packing /'pækɪŋ/ *n* Verpackung *f*

pact /pækt/ *n* Pakt *m*

pad[1] /pæd/ *n* Polster *nt*; (*for writing*)
[Schreib]block *m*; (*fam: home*)
Wohnung *f* ● *vt* (*pt/pp* **padded**) pol-
stern

pad[2] *vi* (*pt/pp* **padded**) tappen

padding /'pædɪŋ/ *n* Polsterung *f*; (*in
written work*) Füllwerk *nt*

paddle[1] /'pædl/ *n* Paddel *nt* ● *vt* (*row*)
paddeln

paddle[2] *vi* waten

paddock /'pædək/ *n* Koppel *f*

padlock /'pædlɒk/ *n* Vorhängeschloß *nt* ● *vt* mit einem Vorhängeschloß verschließen

paediatrician /pi:dɪə'trɪʃn/ *n*
Kinderarzt *m*/-ärztin *f*

pagan /'peɪɡən/ *a* heidnisch ● *n*
Heide *m*/Heidin *f*

page[1] /peɪdʒ/ *n* Seite *f*

page[2] *n* (*boy*) Page *m* ● *vt* ausrufen (*person*)

pageant /'pædʒənt/ *n* Festzug *m*.
~ry *n* Prunk *m*

paid /peɪd/ *see* **pay** ● *a* bezahlt; **put ~
to** (*fam*) zunichte machen

pail /peɪl/ *n* Eimer *m*

pain /peɪn/ *n* Schmerz *m*; **be in ~**
Schmerzen haben; **take ~s** sich (*dat*)
Mühe geben; **~ in the neck** (*fam*)
Nervensäge *f* ● *vt* (*fig*) schmerzen

pain: **~ful** *a* schmerzhaft; (*fig*)
schmerzlich. **~-killer** *n* schmerz-
stillendes Mittel *nt*. **~less** *a*, **-ly** *adv*
schmerzlos

painstaking /'peɪnzteɪkɪŋ/ *a* sorgfältig

paint /peɪnt/ *n* Farbe *f* ● *vt/i* streichen; ⟨*artist*:⟩ malen. **~brush** *n* Pinsel *m*. **~er** *n* Maler *m*; (*decorator*)
Anstreicher *m*. **~ing** *n* Malerei *f*;
(*picture*) Gemälde *nt*

pair /peə(r)/ *n* Paar *nt*; **~ of trousers**
Hose *f*; **~ of scissors** Schere *f* ● *vt*
paaren ● *vi* **~ off** Paare bilden

pajamas /pə'dʒɑːməz/ *npl* (*Amer*)
Schlafanzug *m*

Pakistan /pɑːkɪ'stɑːn/ *n* Pakistan *nt*.
~i *a* pakistanisch ● *n* Pakista-
ner(in) *m(f)*

pal /pæl/ *n* Freund(in) *m(f)*

palace /'pælɪs/ *n* Palast *m*

palatable /'pælətəbl/ *a* schmackhaft

palate /'pælət/ *n* Gaumen *m*

palatial /pə'leɪʃl/ *a* palastartig

palaver /pə'lɑːvə(r)/ *n* (*fam: fuss*)
Theater *nt* (*fam*)

pale[1] /peɪl/ *n* (*stake*) Pfahl *m*; **beyond
the ~** (*fam*) unmöglich

pale[2] *a* (**-r, -st**) blaß ● *vi* blaß werden.
~ness *n* Blässe *f*

Palestin|e /'pælɪstaɪn/ *n* Palästina
nt. **~ian** /pælə'stɪnɪən/ *a* palästinen-
sisch ● *n* Palästinenser(in) *m(f)*

palette /'pælɪt/ *n* Palette *f*

pall /pɔːl/ *n* Sargtuch *nt*; (*fig*) Decke
f ● *vi* an Reiz verlieren

pall|id /'pælɪd/ *a* bleich. **~or** *n*
Blässe *f*

palm /pɑːm/ *n* Handfläche *f*; (*tree,
symbol*) Palme *f* ● *vt* **~ sth off on
s.o.** jdm etw andrehen. **P~ 'Sunday**
n Palmsonntag *m*

palpable /'pælpəbl/ *a* tastbar; (*perceptible*) spürbar

palpitat|e /'pælpɪteɪt/ *vi* klopfen.
~ions /-'teɪʃnz/ *npl* Herzklopfen *nt*

paltry /'pɔːltrɪ/ *a* (**-ier, -iest**) armselig

pamper /'pæmpə(r)/ *vt* verwöhnen

pamphlet /'pæmflɪt/ *n* Broschüre *f*

pan /pæn/ *n* Pfanne *f*; (*saucepan*)
Topf *m*; (*of scales*) Schale *f* ● *vt* (*pt/
pp* **panned**) (*fam*) verreißen

panacea /pænə'siːə/ *n* Allheilmittel
nt

panache /pə'næʃ/ *n* Schwung *m*

'pancake *n* Pfannkuchen *m*

pancreas /'pæŋkrɪəs/ *n* Bauch-
speicheldrüse *f*

panda /'pændə/ *n* Panda *m*. **~ car** *n*
Streifenwagen *m*

pandemonium /pændɪ'məʊnɪəm/ *n*
Höllenlärm *m*

pander /'pændə(r)/ *vi* **~ to s.o.** jdm
zu sehr nachgeben

pane /peɪn/ *n* [Glas]scheibe *f*

panel /'pænl/ *n* Tafel *f*, Platte *f*; **~ of
experts** Expertenrunde *f*; **~ of judges**
Jury *f*. **~ling** *n* Täfelung *f*

pang /pæŋ/ n ~s of hunger Hungergefühl nt; ~s of conscience Gewissensbisse pl

panic /'pænɪk/ n Panik f ● vi (pt/pp panicked) in Panik geraten. ~-stricken a von Panik ergriffen

panoram|a /pænə'rɑ:mə/ n Panorama nt. ~ic /-'ræmɪk/ a Panorama-

pansy /'pænzɪ/ n Stiefmütterchen nt

pant /pænt/ vi keuchen; ⟨dog:⟩ hecheln

pantechnicon /pæn'teknɪkən/ n Möbelwagen m

panther /'pænθə(r)/ n Panther m

panties /'pæntɪz/ npl [Damen]slip m

pantomime /'pæntəmaɪm/ n [zu Weihnachten aufgeführte] Märchenvorstellung f

pantry /'pæntrɪ/ n Speisekammer f

pants /pænts/ npl Unterhose f; (woman's) Schlüpfer m; (trousers) Hose f

'pantyhose n (Amer) Strumpfhose f

papal /'peɪpl/ a päpstlich

paper /'peɪpə(r)/ n Papier nt; (wall~) Tapete f; (newspaper) Zeitung f; (exam ~) Testbogen m; (exam) Klausur f; (treatise) Referat nt; ~s pl (documents) Unterlagen pl; (for identification) [Ausweis]papiere pl; on ~ schriftlich ● vt tapezieren

paper: ~back n Taschenbuch nt. ~-clip n Büroklammer f. ~-knife n Brieföffner m. ~weight n Briefbeschwerer m. ~work n Schreibarbeit f

par /pɑ:(r)/ n (Golf) Par nt; on a ~ gleichwertig (with dat); feel below ~ sich nicht ganz auf der Höhe fühlen

parable /'pærəbl/ n Gleichnis nt

parachut|e /'pærəʃu:t/ n Fallschirm m ● vi [mit dem Fallschirm] abspringen. ~ist n Fallschirmspringer m

parade /pə'reɪd/ n Parade f; (procession) Festzug m ● vi marschieren ● vt (show off) zur Schau stellen

paradise /'pærədaɪs/ n Paradies nt

paradox /'pærədɒks/ n Paradox nt. ~ical /-'dɒksɪkl/ paradox

paraffin /'pærəfɪn/ n Paraffin nt

paragon /'pærəgən/ n ~ of virtue Ausbund m der Tugend

paragraph /'pærəgrɑ:f/ n Absatz m

parallel /'pærəlel/ a & adv parallel ● n (Geog) Breitenkreis m; (fig) Parallele f

paralyse /'pærəlaɪz/ vt lähmen; (fig) lahmlegen

paralysis /pə'ræləsɪs/ n (pl -ses /-si:z/) Lähmung f

paramount /'pærəmaʊnt/ a überragend; be ~ vorgehen

paranoid /'pærənɔɪd/ a [krankhaft] mißtrauisch

parapet /'pærəpɪt/ n Brüstung f

paraphernalia /pærəfə'neɪlɪə/ n Kram m

paraphrase /'pærəfreɪz/ n Umschreibung f ● vt umschreiben

paraplegic /pærə'pli:dʒɪk/ a querschnittsgelähmt ● n Querschnittsgelähmte(r) m/f

parasite /'pærəsaɪt/ n Parasit m, Schmarotzer m

parasol /'pærəsɒl/ n Sonnenschirm m

paratrooper /'pærətru:pə(r)/ n Fallschirmjäger m

parcel /'pɑ:sl/ n Paket nt

parch /pɑ:tʃ/ vt austrocknen; be ~ed ⟨person:⟩ einen furchtbaren Durst haben

parchment /'pɑ:tʃmənt/ n Pergament nt

pardon /'pɑ:dn/ n Verzeihung f; (Jur) Begnadigung f; ~? (fam) bitte? I beg your ~ wie bitte? (sorry) Verzeihung! ● vt verzeihen; (Jur) begnadigen

pare /peə(r)/ vt (peel) schälen

parent /'peərənt/ n Elternteil m; ~s pl Eltern pl. ~al /pə'rentl/ a elterlich

parenthesis /pə'renθəsɪs/ n (pl -ses /-si:z/) Klammer f

parish /'pærɪʃ/ n Gemeinde f. ~ioner /pə'rɪʃənə(r)/ n Gemeindemitglied nt

parity /'pærətɪ/ n Gleichheit f

park /pɑ:k/ n Park m ● vt/i parken

parking /'pɑ:kɪŋ/ n Parken nt; 'no ~' 'Parken verboten'. ~-lot n (Amer) Parkplatz m. ~-meter n Parkuhr f. ~ space n Parkplatz m

parliament /'pɑ:ləmənt/ n Parlament nt. ~ary /-'mentərɪ/ a parlamentarisch

parlour /'pɑ:lə(r)/ n Wohnzimmer nt

parochial /pə'rəʊkɪəl/ a Gemeinde-; (fig) beschränkt

parody /'pærədɪ/ n Parodie f ● vt (pt/pp -ied) parodieren

parole /pə'rəʊl/ n on ~ auf Bewährung

paroxysm /'pærəksɪzm/ n Anfall m

parquet /'pɑ:keɪ/ n ~ floor Parkett nt

parrot /'pærət/ n Papagei m

parry /'pærɪ/ vt (pt/pp **-ied**) abwehren ⟨blow⟩; (Fencing) parieren

parsimonious /pɑːsɪ'məʊnɪəs/ a geizig

parsley /'pɑːslɪ/ n Petersilie f

parsnip /'pɑːsnɪp/ n Pastinake f

parson /'pɑːsn/ n Pfarrer m

part /pɑːt/ n Teil m; (Techn) Teil nt; (area) Gegend f; (Theat) Rolle f; (Mus) Part m; **spare** ~ Ersatzteil nt; **for my** ~ meinerseits; **on the** ~ **of** von Seiten (+ gen); **take s.o.'s** ~ für jdn Partei ergreifen; **take** ~ **in** teilnehmen an (+ dat) ● adv teils ● vt trennen; scheiteln ⟨hair⟩ ● vi ⟨people:⟩ sich trennen; ~ **with** sich trennen von

partake /pɑː'teɪk/ vt (pt **-took**, pp **-taken**) teilnehmen; ~ **of** ⟨eat⟩ zu sich nehmen

part-ex'change n take in ~ in Zahlung nehmen

partial /'pɑːʃl/ a Teil-; **be** ~ **to** mögen. ~**ity** /pɑːʃɪ'ælətɪ/ n Voreingenommenheit f; (liking) Vorliebe f. ~**ly** adv teilweise

particip|ant /pɑː'tɪsɪpənt/ n Teilnehmer(in) m(f). ~**ate** /-peɪt/ vi teilnehmen (**in** an + dat). ~**ation** /-'peɪʃn/ n Teilnahme f

participle /'pɑːtɪsɪpl/ n Partizip nt; **present/past** ~ erstes/zweites Partizip nt

particle /'pɑːtɪkl/ n Körnchen nt; (Phys) Partikel nt; (Gram) Partikel f

particular /pə'tɪkjʊlə(r)/ a besondere(r,s); (precise) genau; (fastidious) penibel; **in** ~ besonders. ~**ly** adv besonders. ~**s** npl nähere Angaben pl

parting /'pɑːtɪŋ/ n Abschied m; (in hair) Scheitel m ● attrib Abschieds-

partition /pɑː'tɪʃn/ n Trennwand f; (Pol) Teilung f ● vt teilen. ~ **off** vt abtrennen

partly /'pɑːtlɪ/ adv teilweise

partner /'pɑːtnə(r)/ n Partner(in) m(f); (Comm) Teilhaber m. ~**ship** n Partnerschaft f; (Comm) Teilhaberschaft f

partridge /'pɑːtrɪdʒ/ n Rebhuhn nt

part-'time a & adv Teilzeit-; **be** ● **work** ~ Teilzeitarbeit machen

party /'pɑːtɪ/ n Party f, Fest nt; (group) Gruppe f; (Pol, Jur) Partei f; **be** ~ **to** sich beteiligen an (+ dat)

'party line¹ n (Teleph) Gemeinschaftsanschluß m

party 'line² n (Pol) Parteilinie f

pass /pɑːs/ n Ausweis m; (Geog, Sport) Paß m; (Sch) ≈ ausreichend; **get a** ~ bestehen ● vt vorbeigehen/-fahren an (+ dat); (overtake) überholen; ⟨hand⟩ reichen; (Sport) abgeben, abspielen; (approve) annehmen; (exceed) übersteigen; bestehen ⟨exam⟩; machen ⟨remark⟩; fällen ⟨judgement⟩; (Jur) verhängen ⟨sentence⟩; ~ **water** Wasser lassen; ~ **the time** sich ⟨dat⟩ die Zeit vertreiben; ~ **sth off as sth** etw als etw ausgeben; ~ **one's hand over sth** mit der Hand über etw ⟨acc⟩ fahren ● vi vorbeigehen/-fahren; (get by) vorbeikommen; (overtake) überholen; ⟨time:⟩ vergehen; (in exam) bestehen; **let sth** ~ (fig) etw übergehen; **[I]** ~! [ich] passe! ~ **away** vi sterben. ~ **down** vt herunterreichen; (fig) weitergeben. ~ **out** vi ohnmächtig werden. ~ **round** vt herumreichen. ~ **up** vt heraufreichen; (fam: miss) vorübergehen lassen

passable /'pɑːsəbl/ a ⟨road⟩ befahrbar; (satisfactory) passabel

passage /'pæsɪdʒ/ n Durchgang m; (corridor) Gang m; (voyage) Überfahrt f; (in book) Passage f

passenger /'pæsɪndʒə(r)/ n Fahrgast m; (Naut, Aviat) Passagier m; (in car) Mitfahrer m. ~ **seat** n Beifahrersitz m

passer-by /pɑːsə'baɪ/ n (pl **-s-by**) Passant(in) m(f)

'passing place n Ausweichstelle f

passion /'pæʃn/ n Leidenschaft f. ~**ate** /-ət/ a, **-ly** adv leidenschaftlich

passive /'pæsɪv/ a passiv ● n Passiv nt

Passover /'pɑːsəʊvə(r)/ n Passah nt

pass: ~**port** n [Reise]paß m. ~**word** n Kennwort nt; (Mil) Losung f

past /pɑːst/ a vergangene(r,s); (former) ehemalig; **in the** ~ **few days** in den letzten paar Tagen; **that's all** ~ das ist jetzt vorbei ● n Vergangenheit f ● prep an (+ dat) … vorbei; (after) nach; **at ten** ~ **two** um zehn nach zwei ● adv vorbei; **go/come** ~ vorbeigehen/-kommen

pasta /'pæstə/ n Nudeln pl

paste /peɪst/ n Brei m; (dough) Teig m; (fish-, meat-) Paste f; (adhesive) Kleister m; (jewellery) Straß m ● vt kleistern

pastel /'pæstl/ n Pastellfarbe f; (crayon) Pastellstift m; (drawing) Pastell nt ● attrib Pastell-

pasteurize /'pɑːstʃəraɪz/ vt pasteurisieren

pastille /'pæstɪl/ n Pastille f

pastime /'pɑːstaɪm/ n Zeitvertreib m

pastoral /'pɑːstərl/ a ländlich; ⟨care⟩ seelsorgerisch

pastr|y /'peɪstrɪ/ n Teig m; **cakes and** ~ies Kuchen und Gebäck

pasture /'pɑːstʃə(r)/ n Weide f

pasty[1] /'pæstɪ/ n Pastete f

pasty[2] /'peɪstɪ/ a blaß, (fam) käsig

pat /pæt/ n Klaps m; (of butter) Stückchen nt ● adv **have sth off** ~ etw aus dem Effeff können ● vt (pt/pp patted) tätscheln; ~ **s.o. on the back** jdm auf die Schulter klopfen

patch /pætʃ/ n Flicken m; (spot) Fleck m; **not a** ~ **on** (fam) gar nicht zu vergleichen mit ● vt flicken. ~ **up** vt [zusammen]flicken; beilegen ⟨quarrel⟩

patchy /'pætʃɪ/ a ungleichmäßig

pâté /'pæteɪ/ n Pastete f

patent /'peɪtnt/ a, **-ly** adv offensichtlich ● n Patent nt ● vt patentieren. ~ **leather** n Lackleder nt

patern|al /pə'tɜːnl/ a väterlich. ~ity n Vaterschaft f

path /pɑːθ/ n (pl ~s /pɑːðz/) [Fuß]weg m, Pfad m; (orbit, track) Bahn f; (fig) Weg m

pathetic /pə'θetɪk/ a mitleidregend; ⟨attempt⟩ erbärmlich

patholog|ical /pæθə'lɒdʒɪkl/ a pathologisch. ~ist /pə'θɒlədʒɪst/ n Pathologe m

pathos /'peɪθɒs/ n Rührseligkeit f

patience /'peɪʃns/ n Geduld f; (game) Patience f

patient /'peɪʃnt/ a, **-ly** adv geduldig ● n Patient(in) m(f)

patio /'pætɪəʊ/ n Terrasse f

patriot /'pætrɪət/ n Patriot(in) m(f). ~ic /-'ɒtɪk/ a patriotisch. ~ism n Patriotismus m

patrol /pə'trəʊl/ n Patrouille f ● vt/i patrouillieren [in (+ dat)]; ⟨police:⟩ auf Streife gehen/fahren [in (+ dat)]. ~ **car** n Streifenwagen m

patron /'peɪtrən/ n Gönner m; (of charity) Schirmherr m; (of the arts) Mäzen m; (customer) Kunde m/Kundin f; (Theat) Besucher m. ~age /'pætrənɪdʒ/ n Schirmherrschaft f

patroniz|e /'pætrənaɪz/ vt (fig) herablassend behandeln. ~ing a, **-ly** adv gönnerhaft

patter[1] /'pætə(r)/ n Getrippel nt; (of rain) Plätschern nt ● vi trippeln; plätschern

patter[2] n (speech) Gerede nt

pattern /'pætn/ n Muster nt

paunch /pɔːntʃ/ n [Schmer]bauch m

pauper /'pɔːpə(r)/ n Arme(r) m/f

pause /pɔːz/ n Pause f ● vi innehalten

pave /peɪv/ vt pflastern; ~ **the way** den Weg bereiten (**for** dat). ~ment n Bürgersteig m

pavilion /pə'vɪljən/ n Pavillon m; (Sport) Klubhaus nt

paw /pɔː/ n Pfote f; (of large animal) Pranke f, Tatze f

pawn[1] /pɔːn/ n (Chess) Bauer m; (fig) Schachfigur f

pawn[2] vt verpfänden ● n **in** ~ verpfändet. ~broker n Pfandleiher m. ~shop n Pfandhaus nt

pay /peɪ/ n Lohn m; (salary) Gehalt nt; **be in the** ~ **of** bezahlt werden von ● v (pt/pp paid) ● vt bezahlen; zahlen ⟨money⟩; ~ **s.o. a visit** jdm einen Besuch abstatten; ~ **s.o. a compliment** jdm ein Kompliment machen ● vi zahlen; (be profitable) sich bezahlt machen; (fig) sich lohnen; ~ **for sth** etw bezahlen. ~ **back** vt zurückzahlen. ~ **in** vt einzahlen. ~ **off** vt abzahlen ⟨debt⟩ ● vi (fig) sich auszahlen. ~ **up** vi zahlen

payable /'peɪəbl/ a zahlbar; **make** ~ **to** ausstellen auf (+ acc)

payee /peɪ'iː/ n [Zahlungs]empfänger m

payment /'peɪmənt/ n Bezahlung f; (amount) Zahlung f

pay: ~ **packet** n Lohntüte f; ~ **phone** n Münzfernsprecher m

pea /piː/ n Erbse f

peace /piːs/ n Frieden m; **for my** ~ **of mind** zu meiner eigenen Beruhigung

peace|able /'piːsəbl/ a friedlich. ~ful a, **-ly** adv friedlich. ~maker n Friedensstifter m

peach /piːtʃ/ n Pfirsich m

peacock /'piːkɒk/ n Pfau m

peak /piːk/ n Gipfel m; (fig) Höhepunkt m. ~ed 'cap n Schirmmütze f. ~ **hours** npl Hauptbelastungszeit f; (for traffic) Hauptverkehrszeit f

peaky /'piːkɪ/ a kränklich

peal /piːl/ n (of bells) Glockengeläut nt; ~s **of laughter** schallendes Gelächter nt

'peanut n Erdnuß f; **for** ~s (fam) für einen Apfel und ein Ei

pear /peə(r)/ n Birne f

pearl /pɜːl/ n Perle f
peasant /'peznt/ n Bauer m
peat /piːt/ n Torf m
pebble /'pebl/ n Kieselstein m
peck /pek/ n Schnabelhieb m; (kiss)
flüchtiger Kuß m ● vt/i picken/(nip)
hacken (**at** nach). **~ing order** n
Hackordnung f
peckish /'pekɪʃ/ a **be ~** (fam) Hunger
haben
peculiar /pɪ'kjuːlɪə(r)/ a eigenartig,
seltsam; **~ to** eigentümlich (+ dat).
~ity /-'ærətɪ/ n Eigenart f
pedal /'pedl/ n Pedal nt ● vt fahren
⟨bicycle⟩ ● vi treten. **~ bin** n
Treteimer m
pedantic /pɪ'dæntɪk/ a, **-ally** adv
pedantisch
peddle /'pedl/ vt handeln mit
pedestal /'pedɪstl/ n Sockel m
pedestrian /pɪ'destrɪən/ n Fuß-
gänger(in) m(f) ● a (fig) prosaisch.
~ 'crossing n Fußgängerüberweg
m. **~ 'precinct** n Fußgängerzone f
pedicure /'pedɪkjʊə(r)/ n Pediküre f
pedigree /'pedɪgriː/ n Stammbaum
m ● attrib ⟨animal⟩ Rasse-
pedlar /'pedlə(r)/ n Hausierer m
pee /piː/ vi (pt/pp **peed**) (fam) pinkeln
peek /piːk/ vi (fam) gucken
peel /piːl/ n Schale f ● vt schälen ● vi
⟨skin:⟩ sich schälen; ⟨paint:⟩ abblättern. **~ings** npl Schalen pl
peep /piːp/ n kurzer Blick m ● vi
gucken. **~-hole** n Guckloch nt. **P~-
ing 'Tom** n (fam) Spanner m
peer¹ /pɪə(r)/ vi **~ at** forschend
ansehen
peer² n Peer m; **his ~s** pl seines-
gleichen
peev|ed /piːvd/ a (fam) ärgerlich.
~ish a reizbar
peg /peg/ n (hook) Haken m; (for
tent) Pflock m, Hering m; (for
clothes) [Wäsche]klammer f; **off the
~** (fam) von der Stange ● vt (pt/pp
pegged) anpflocken; anklammern
⟨washing⟩
pejorative /pɪ'dʒɒrətɪv/ a, **-ly** adv
abwertend
pelican /'pelɪkən/ n Pelikan m
pellet /'pelɪt/ n Kügelchen nt
pelt¹ /pelt/ n ⟨skin⟩ Pelz m, Fell nt
pelt² vt bewerfen ● vi (fam: run fast)
rasen; **~ [down]** ⟨rain:⟩ [hernieder]-
prasseln
pelvis /'pelvɪs/ n ⟨Anat⟩ Becken nt

pen¹ /pen/ n (for animals) Hürde f
pen² n Federhalter m; (ball-point) Kugelschreiber m
penal /'piːnl/ a Straf-. **~ize** vt bestrafen; (fig) benachteiligen
penalty /'penltɪ/ n Strafe f; (fine)
Geldstrafe f; (Sport) Strafstoß m;
(Football) Elfmeter m
penance /'penəns/ n Buße f
pence /pens/ see **penny**
pencil /'pensl/ n Bleistift m ● vt (pt/
pp **pencilled**) mit Bleistift schreiben.
~-sharpener n Bleistiftspitzer m
pendant /'pendənt/ n Anhänger m
pending /'pendɪŋ/ a unerledigt
● prep bis zu
pendulum /'pendjʊləm/ n Pendel nt
penetrat|e /'penɪtreɪt/ vt durch-
dringen; **~e [into]** eindringen in
(+ acc). **~ing** a durchdringend.
~ion /-'treɪʃn/ n Durchdringen nt
'penfriend n Brieffreund(in) m(f)
penguin /'peŋgwɪn/ n Pinguin m
penicillin /penɪ'sɪlɪn/ n Penizillin nt
peninsula /pə'nɪnsʊlə/ n Halbinsel f
penis /'piːnɪs/ n Penis m
peniten|ce /'penɪtəns/ n Reue f. **~t**
a reuig ● n Büßer m
penitentiary /penɪ'tenʃərɪ/ n
(Amer) Gefängnis nt
pen: ~knife n Taschenmesser nt.
~name n Pseudonym nt
pennant /'penənt/ n Wimpel m
penniless /'penɪlɪs/ a mittellos
penny /'penɪ/ n (pl **pence**; single coins
pennies) Penny m; (Amer) Centstück
nt; **spend a ~** (fam) mal verschwinden; **the ~'s dropped** (fam) der
Groschen ist gefallen
pension /'penʃn/ n Rente f; (of civil
servant) Pension f. **~er** n Rent-
ner(in) m(f); Pensionär(in) m(f)
pensive /'pensɪv/ a nachdenklich
Pentecost /'pentɪkɒst/ n Pfingsten
nt
pent-up /'pentʌp/ a angestaut
penultimate /pe'nʌltɪmət/ a vor-
letzte(r,s)
penury /'penjʊrɪ/ n Armut f
peony /'pɪənɪ/ n Pfingstrose f
people /'piːpl/ npl Leute pl, Menschen pl; (citizens) Bevölkerung f;
the ~ das Volk; **English ~** die Engländer; **~ say** man sagt; **for four ~** für
vier Personen ● vt bevölkern
pep /pep/ n (fam) Schwung m
pepper /'pepə(r)/ n Pfeffer m; (vegetable) Paprika m ● vt (Culin)
pfeffern

pepper: ~**corn** n Pfefferkorn nt. ~**mint** n Pfefferminz nt; (Bot) Pfefferminze f. ~**pot** n Pfefferstreuer m

per /pɜː(r)/ prep pro; ~ **cent** Prozent nt

perceive /pə'siːv/ vt wahrnehmen

percentage /pə'sentɪdʒ/ n Prozentsatz m; (part) Teil m

perceptible /pə'septəbl/ a wahrnehmbar

percept|ion /pə'sepʃn/ n Wahrnehmung f. ~**ive** /-tɪv/ a feinsinnig

perch[1] /pɜːtʃ/ n Stange f ● vi (bird:) sich niederlassen

perch[2] n inv (fish) Barsch m

percolat|e /'pɜːkəleɪt/ vi durchsickern. ~**or** n Kaffeemaschine f

percussion /pə'kʌʃn/ n Schlagzeug nt. ~ **instrument** n Schlaginstrument nt

peremptory /pə'remptərɪ/ a herrisch

perennial /pə'renɪəl/ a (problem) immer wiederkehrend ● n (Bot) mehrjährige Pflanze f

perfect[1] /'pɜːfɪkt/ a perfekt, vollkommen; (fam: utter) völlig ● n (Gram) Perfekt nt

perfect[2] /pə'fekt/ vt vervollkommnen. ~**ion** /-ekʃn/ n Vollkommenheit f; **to** ~**ion** perfekt

perfectly /'pɜːfɪktlɪ/ adv perfekt; (completely) vollkommen, völlig

perforate /'pɜːfəreɪt/ vt perforieren; (make a hole in) durchlöchern. ~**d** a perforiert

perform /pə'fɔːm/ vt ausführen; erfüllen (duty); (Theat) aufführen (play); spielen (role) ● vi (Theat) auftreten; (Techn) laufen. ~**ance** n Aufführung f; (at theatre, cinema) Vorstellung f; (Techn) Leistung f. ~**er** n Künstler(in) m(f)

perfume /'pɜːfjuːm/ n Parfüm nt; (smell) Duft m

perfunctory /pə'fʌŋktərɪ/ a flüchtig

perhaps /pə'hæps/ adv vielleicht

peril /'perəl/ n Gefahr f. ~**ous** /-əs/ a gefährlich

perimeter /pə'rɪmɪtə(r)/ n [äußere] Grenze f; (Geom) Umfang m

period /'pɪərɪəd/ n Periode f; (Sch) Stunde f; (full stop) Punkt m ● attrib (costume) zeitgenössisch; (furniture) antik. ~**ic** /-'ɒdɪk/ a, -**ally** adv periodisch. ~**ical** /-'ɒdɪkl/ n Zeitschrift f

peripher|al /pə'rɪfərl/ a nebensächlich. ~**y** n Peripherie f

periscope /'perɪskəʊp/ n Periskop nt

perish /'perɪʃ/ vi (rubber:) verrotten; (food:) verderben; (die) ums Leben kommen. ~**able** /-əbl/ a leicht verderblich. ~**ing** a (fam: cold) eiskalt

perjur|e /'pɜːdʒə(r)/ vt ~**e oneself** einen Meineid leisten. ~**y** n Meineid m

perk[1] /pɜːk/ n (fam) [Sonder]vergünstigung f

perk[2] vi ~ **up** munter werden

perky /'pɜːkɪ/ a munter

perm /pɜːm/ n Dauerwelle f ● vt ~ **s.o.'s hair** jdm eine Dauerwelle machen

permanent /'pɜːmənənt/ a ständig; (job, address) fest. ~**ly** adv ständig; (work, live) dauernd, permanent; (employed) fest

permeable /'pɜːmɪəbl/ a durchlässig

permeate /'pɜːmɪeɪt/ vt durchdringen

permissible /pə'mɪsəbl/ a erlaubt

permission /pə'mɪʃn/ n Erlaubnis f

permissive /pə'mɪsɪv/ a (society) permissiv

permit[1] /pə'mɪt/ vt (pt/pp -mitted) erlauben (s.o. jdm); ~ **me!** gestatten Sie!

permit[2] /'pɜːmɪt/ n Genehmigung f

pernicious /pə'nɪʃəs/ a schädlich; (Med) perniziös

perpendicular /pɜːpən'dɪkjʊlə(r)/ a senkrecht ● n Senkrechte f

perpetrat|e /'pɜːpɪtreɪt/ vt begehen. ~**or** n Täter m

perpetual /pə'petjʊəl/ a, -**ly** adv ständig, dauernd

perpetuate /pə'petjʊeɪt/ vt bewahren; verewigen (error)

perplex /pə'pleks/ vt verblüffen. ~**ed** a verblüfft. ~**ity** n Verblüffung f

persecut|e /'pɜːsɪkjuːt/ vt verfolgen. ~**ion** /-'kjuːʃn/ n Verfolgung f

perseverance /pɜːsɪ'vɪərəns/ n Ausdauer f

persever|e /pɜːsɪ'vɪə(r)/ vi beharrlich weitermachen. ~**ing** a ausdauernd

Persia /'pɜːʃə/ n Persien nt

Persian /'pɜːʃn/ a persisch; (cat, carpet) Perser-

persist /pə'sɪst/ vi beharrlich weitermachen; (continue) anhalten;

⟨*view:*⟩ weiter bestehen; ~ **in doing sth** dabei bleiben, etw zu tun. **~ence** *n* Beharrlichkeit *f*. **~ent** *a*, **-ly** *adv* beharrlich; (*continuous*) anhaltend

person /'pɜːsn/ *n* Person *f*; **in** ~ persönlich

personal /'pɜːsənl/ *a*, **-ly** *adv* persönlich. ~ '**hygiene** *n* Körperpflege *f*

personality /pɜːsə'nælətɪ/ *n* Persönlichkeit *f*

personify /pə'sɒnɪfaɪ/ *vt* (*pt/pp* **-ied**) personifizieren, verkörpern

personnel /pɜːsə'nel/ *n* Personal *nt*

perspective /pə'spektɪv/ *n* Perspektive *f*

perspicacious /pɜːspɪ'keɪʃəs/ *a* scharfsichtig

persp|iration /pɜːspɪ'reɪʃn/ *n* Schweiß *m*. **~ire** /-'spaɪə(r)/ *vi* schwitzen

persua|de /pə'sweɪd/ *vt* überreden; (*convince*) überzeugen. **~sion** /-eɪʒn/ *n* Überredung *f*; (*powers of* ~*sion*) Überredungskunst *f*; (*belief*) Glaubensrichtung *f*

persuasive /pə'sweɪsɪv/ *a*, **-ly** *adv* beredsam; (*convincing*) überzeugend

pert /pɜːt/ *a*, **-ly** *adv* keß

pertain /pə'teɪn/ *vi* ~ **to** betreffen; (*belong*) gehören zu

pertinent /'pɜːtɪnənt/ *a* relevant (**to** für)

perturb /pə'tɜːb/ *vt* beunruhigen

peruse /pə'ruːz/ *vt* lesen

perva|de /pə'veɪd/ *vt* durchdringen. **~sive** /-sɪv/ *a* durchdringend

pervers|e /pə'vɜːs/ *a* eigensinnig. **~ion** /-ɜːʃn/ *n* Perversion *f*

pervert[1] /pə'vɜːt/ *vt* verdrehen; verführen ⟨*person*⟩

pervert[2] /'pɜːvɜːt/ *n* Perverse(r) *m*

perverted /pə'vɜːtɪd/ *a* abartig

pessimis|m /'pesɪmɪzm/ *n* Pessimismus *m*. **~t** /-mɪst/ *n* Pessimist *m*. **~tic** /-'mɪstɪk/ *a*, **-ally** *adv* pessimistisch

pest /pest/ *n* Schädling *m*; (*fam: person*) Nervensäge *f*

pester /'pestə(r)/ *vt* belästigen; ~ **s.o. for sth** jdm wegen etw in den Ohren liegen

pesticide /'pestɪsaɪd/ *n* Schädlingsbekämpfungsmittel *nt*

pet /pet/ *n* Haustier *nt*; (*favourite*) Liebling *m* ● *vt* (*pt/pp* **petted**) liebkosen

petal /'petl/ *n* Blütenblatt *nt*

peter /'piːtə(r)/ *vi* ~ **out** allmählich aufhören; ⟨*stream:*⟩ versickern

petite /pə'tiːt/ *a* klein und zierlich

petition /pə'tɪʃn/ *n* Bittschrift *f* ● *vt* eine Bittschrift richten an (+ *acc*)

pet 'name *n* Kosename *m*

petrif|y /'petrɪfaɪ/ *vt/i* (*pt/pp* **-ied**) versteinern; **~ied** (*frightened*) vor Angst wie versteinert

petrol /'petrl/ *n* Benzin *nt*

petroleum /pɪ'trəʊlɪəm/ *n* Petroleum *nt*

petrol: **~-pump** *n* Zapfsäule *f*. ~ **station** *n* Tankstelle *f*. ~ **tank** *n* Benzintank *m*

'pet shop *n* Tierhandlung *f*

petticoat /'petɪkəʊt/ *n* Unterrock *m*

petty /'petɪ/ *a* (**-ier, -iest**) kleinlich. ~ '**cash** *n* Portokasse *f*

petulant /'petjʊlənt/ *a* gekränkt

pew /pjuː/ *n* [Kirchen]bank *f*

pewter /'pjuːtə(r)/ *n* Zinn *nt*

phantom /'fæntəm/ *n* Gespenst *nt*

pharmaceutical /fɑːmə'sjuːtɪkl/ *a* pharmazeutisch

pharmac|ist /'fɑːməsɪst/ *n* Apotheker(in) *m(f)*. **~y** *n* Pharmazie *f*; (*shop*) Apotheke *f*

phase /feɪz/ *n* Phase *f* ● *vt* ~ **in/out** allmählich einführen/abbauen

Ph.D. (*abbr of* **Doctor of Philosophy**) Dr. phil.

pheasant /'feznt/ *n* Fasan *m*

phenomen|al /fɪ'nɒmɪnl/ *a* phänomenal. **~on** *n* (*pl* **-na**) Phänomen *nt*

phial /'faɪəl/ *n* Fläschchen *nt*

philanderer /fɪ'lændərə(r)/ *n* Verführer *m*

philanthrop|ic /fɪlən'θrɒpɪk/ *a* menschenfreundlich. **~ist** /fɪ'lænθrəpɪst/ *n* Philanthrop *m*

philately /fɪ'lætəlɪ/ *n* Philatelie *f*, Briefmarkenkunde *f*

philharmonic /fɪlɑː'mɒnɪk/ *n* (*orchestra*) Philharmoniker *pl*

Philippines /'fɪlɪpiːnz/ *npl* Philippinen *pl*

philistine /'fɪlɪstaɪn/ *n* Banause *m*

philosoph|er /fɪ'lɒsəfə(r)/ *n* Philosoph *m*. **~ical** /fɪlə'sɒfɪkl/ *a*, **-ly** *adv* philosophisch. **~y** *n* Philosophie *f*

phlegm /flem/ *n* (*Med*) Schleim *m*

phlegmatic /fleg'mætɪk/ *a* phlegmatisch

phobia /'fəʊbɪə/ *n* Phobie *f*

phone /fəʊn/ *n* Telefon *nt*; **be on the** ~ Telefon haben; (*be phoning*) telefonieren ● *vt* anrufen ● *vi* telefonieren.

~ **back** vt/i zurückrufen. ~ **book** n
Telefonbuch nt. ~ **box** n Telefonzelle
f. ~ **card** n Telefonkarte f. ~**in** n
(Radio) Hörersendung f. ~ **number**
n Telefonnummer f
phonetic /fə'netɪk/ a phonetisch. ~**s**
n Phonetik f
phoney /'fəʊnɪ/ a (-ier, -iest) falsch;
(forged) gefälscht
phosphorus /'fɒsfərəs/ n Phosphor
m
photo /'fəʊtəʊ/ n Foto nt, Aufnahme
f. ~**copier** n Fotokopiergerät nt.
~**copy** n Fotokopie f ● vt fotokopieren
photogenic /fəʊtəʊ'dʒenɪk/ a foto-
gen
photograph /'fəʊtəgrɑːf/ n Fotografie f, Aufnahme f ● vt fotogra-
fieren
photograph|er /fə'tɒgrəfə(r)/ n
Fotograf(in) m(f). ~**ic** /fəʊtə
'græfɪk/ a, **-ally** adv fotografisch. ~**y** n
Fotografie f
phrase /freɪz/ n Redensart f ● vt formulieren. ~**book** n Sprachführer
m
physical /'fɪzɪkl/ a, **-ly** adv körperlich;
(geography, law) physikalisch. ~ **edu-
'cation** n Turnen nt
physician /fɪ'zɪʃn/ n Arzt m/Ärztin f
physic|ist /'fɪzɪsɪst/ n Physiker(in)
m(f). ~**s** n Physik f
physiology /fɪzɪ'ɒlədʒɪ/ n Physiolo-
gie f
physio'therap|ist /fɪzɪəʊ-/ n
Physiotherapeut(in) m(f). ~**y** n
Physiotherapie f
physique /fɪ'ziːk/ n Körperbau m
pianist /'pɪənɪst/ n Klavier-
spieler(in) m(f); (professional)
Pianist(in) m(f)
piano /pɪ'ænəʊ/ n Klavier nt
pick[1] /pɪk/ n Spitzhacke f
pick[2] n Auslese f; **take one's** ~ sich
(dat) aussuchen ● vt/i (pluck)
pflücken; (select) wählen, sich (dat) aussuchen; ~ **and choose** wählerisch
sein; ~ **one's nose** in der Nase bohren; ~ **a quarrel** einen Streit anfangen;
~ **a hole in sth** ein Loch in etw
(acc) machen; ~ **holes in** (fam) kritisieren; ~ **at one's food** im Essen her-
umstochern. ~ **on** vt wählen; (fam:
find fault with) herumhacken auf
(+ dat). ~ **up** vt in die Hand nehmen;
(off the ground) aufheben; hoch-
nehmen (baby); (learn) lernen;

(acquire) erwerben; (buy) kaufen;
(Teleph) abnehmen (receiver); auf-
fangen (signal); (collect) abholen;
aufnehmen (passengers); (police:)
aufgreifen (criminal); sich holen (illness); (fam) aufgabeln (girl); ~ **oneself up** aufstehen ● vi (improve) sich
bessern
'**pickaxe** n Spitzhacke f
picket /'pɪkɪt/ n Streikposten m ● vt
Streikposten aufstellen vor (+ dat).
~ **line** n Streikpostenkette f
pickle /'pɪkl/ n (Amer: gherkin)
Essiggurke f; ~**s** pl [Mixed] Pickles pl
● vt einlegen
pick: ~**pocket** n Taschendieb m.
~**-up** n (truck) Lieferwagen m; (on
record-player) Tonabnehmer m
picnic /'pɪknɪk/ n Picknick nt ● vi
(pt/pp -**nicked**) picknicken
pictorial /pɪk'tɔːrɪəl/ a bildlich
picture /'pɪktʃə(r)/ n Bild nt; (film)
Film m; **as pretty as a** ~ bildhübsch;
put s.o. in the ~ (fig) jdn ins Bild
setzen ● vt (imagine) sich (dat) vorstellen
picturesque /pɪktʃə'resk/ a malerisch
pie /paɪ/ n Pastete f; (fruit) Kuchen
m
piece /piːs/ n Stück nt; (of set) Teil nt;
(in game) Stein m; (Journ) Artikel m;
a ~ **of bread/paper** ein Stück Brot/
Papier; **a** ~ **of news/advice** eine
Nachricht/ein Rat; **take to** ~**s** auseinandernehmen ● vt ~ **together** zusammensetzen; (fig) zusammen-
stückeln. ~**meal** adv stückweise.
~**work** n Akkordarbeit f
pier /pɪə(r)/ n Pier m; (pillar) Pfeiler
m
pierc|e /pɪəs/ vt durchstechen; ~**e a
hole in sth** ein Loch in etw (acc) stechen. ~**ing** a durchdringend
piety /'paɪətɪ/ n Frömmigkeit f
piffle /'pɪfl/ n (fam) Quatsch m
pig /pɪg/ n Schwein nt
pigeon /'pɪdʒɪn/ n Taube f. ~**-hole** n
Fach nt
piggy /'pɪgɪ/ n (fam) Schweinchen
nt. ~**back** n **give s.o. a** ~**back** jdn
huckepack tragen. ~ **bank** n Sparschwein nt
pig'headed a (fam) starrköpfig
pigment /'pɪgmənt/ n Pigment nt.
~**ation** /-men'teɪʃn/ n Pigmentie-
rung f

pig: ~**skin** *n* Schweinsleder *nt*. ~**sty** *n* Schweinestall *m*. ~**tail** *n* (*fam*) Zopf *m*

pike /paɪk/ *n inv* (*fish*) Hecht *m*

pilchard /'pɪltʃəd/ *n* Sardine *f*

pile¹ /paɪl/ *n* (*of fabric*) Flor *m*

pile² *n* Haufen *m* ● *vt* ~ sth on to sth etw auf etw (*acc*) häufen. ~ **up** *vt* häufen ● *vi* sich häufen

piles /paɪlz/ *npl* Hämorrhoiden *pl*

'pile-up *n* Massenkarambolage *f*

pilfer /'pɪlfə(r)/ *vt/i* stehlen

pilgrim /'pɪlgrɪm/ *n* Pilger(in) *m(f)*. ~**age** /-ɪdʒ/ *n* Pilgerfahrt *f*, Wallfahrt *f*

pill /pɪl/ *n* Pille *f*

pillage /'pɪlɪdʒ/ *vt* plündern

pillar /'pɪlə(r)/ *n* Säule *f*. ~**box** *n* Briefkasten *m*

pillion /'pɪljən/ *n* Sozius[sitz] *m*

pillory /'pɪlərɪ/ *n* Pranger *m* ● *vt* (*pt/pp* -**ied**) anprangern

pillow /'pɪləʊ/ *n* Kopfkissen *nt*. ~**case** *n* Kopfkissenbezug *m*

pilot /'paɪlət/ *n* Pilot *m*; (*Naut*) Lotse *m* ● *vt* fliegen (*plane*); lotsen ⟨*ship*⟩. ~**light** *n* Zündflamme *f*

pimp /pɪmp/ *n* Zuhälter *m*

pimple /'pɪmpl/ *n* Pickel *m*

pin /pɪn/ *n* Stecknadel *f*; (*Techn*) Bolzen *m*, Stift *m*; (*Med*) Nagel *m*; **I have ~s and needles in my leg** (*fam*) mein Bein ist eingeschlafen ● *vt* (*pt/pp* **pinned**) anstecken (**to/on** an +*acc*); (*sewing*) stecken; (*hold down*) festhalten; ~ **sth on s.o.** (*fam*) jdm etw anhängen. ~ **up** *vt* hochstecken; (*on wall*) anheften, anschlagen

pinafore /'pɪnəfɔ:(r)/ *n* Schürze *f*. ~ **dress** *n* Kleiderrock *m*

pincers /'pɪnsəz/ *npl* Kneifzange *f*; (*Zool*) Scheren *pl*

pinch /pɪntʃ/ *n* Kniff *m*; (*of salt*) Prise *f*; **at a ~** (*fam*) zur Not ● *vt* kneifen, zwicken; (*fam: steal*) klauen; ~ **one's finger** sich (*dat*) den Finger klemmen ● *vi* sich (*shoe.*) drücken

'pincushion *n* Nadelkissen *nt*

pine¹ /paɪn/ *n* (*tree*) Kiefer *f*

pine² *vi* ~ **for** sich sehnen nach; ~ **away** sich verzehren

pineapple /'paɪn-/ *n* Ananas *f*

ping /pɪŋ/ *n* Klingeln *nt*

'ping-pong *n* Tischtennis *nt*

pink /pɪŋk/ *a* rosa

pinnacle /'pɪnəkl/ *n* Gipfel *m*; (*on roof*) Turmspitze *f*

pin: ~**point** *vt* genau festlegen. ~**stripe** *n* Nadelstreifen *m*

pint /paɪnt/ *n* Pint *nt* (*0,57 l, Amer: 0, 47 l*)

'pin-up *n* Pin-up-Girl *nt*

pioneer /paɪə'nɪə(r)/ *n* Pionier *m* ● *vt* bahnbrechende Arbeit leisten für

pious /'paɪəs/ *a*, -**ly** *adv* fromm

pip¹ /pɪp/ *n* (*seed*) Kern *m*

pip² *n* (*sound*) Tonsignal *nt*

pipe /paɪp/ *n* Pfeife *f*; (*for water, gas*) Rohr *nt* ● *vt* in Rohren leiten; (*Culin*) spritzen. ~ **down** *vi* (*fam*) den Mund halten

pipe: ~**dream** *n* Luftschloß *nt*. ~**line** *n* Pipeline *f*; **in the ~line** (*fam*) in Vorbereitung

piper /'paɪpə(r)/ *n* Pfeifer *m*

piping /'paɪpɪŋ/ *a* ~ **hot** kochend heiß

piquant /'pi:kənt/ *a* pikant

pique /pi:k/ *n* **in a fit of** ~ beleidigt

pirate /'paɪərət/ *n* Pirat *m*

Pisces /'paɪsi:z/ *n* (*Astr*) Fische *pl*

piss /pɪs/ *vi* (*sl*) pissen

pistol /'pɪstl/ *n* Pistole *f*

piston /'pɪstən/ *n* (*Techn*) Kolben *m*

pit /pɪt/ *n* Grube *f*; (*for orchestra*) Orchestergraben *m* ● *vt* (*pt/pp* **pitted**) (*fig*) messen (**against** mit)

pitch¹ /pɪtʃ/ *n* (*steepness*) Schräge *f*; (*of voice*) Stimmlage *f*; (*of sound*) [Ton]höhe *f*; (*Sport*) Feld *nt*; (*of street-trader*) Standplatz *m*; (*fig: degree*) Grad *m* ● *vt* werfen; aufschlagen ⟨*tent*⟩ ● *vi* fallen

pitch² *n* (*tar*) Pech *nt*. ~**'black** *a* pechschwarz. ~**'dark** *a* stockdunkel

pitcher /'pɪtʃə(r)/ *n* Krug *m*

'pitchfork *n* Heugabel *f*

piteous /'pɪtɪəs/ *a* erbärmlich

'pitfall *n* (*fig*) Falle *f*

pith /pɪθ/ *n* (*Bot*) Mark *nt*; (*of orange*) weiße Haut *f*; (*fig*) Wesentliche(s) *nt*

pithy /'pɪθɪ/ *a* (-**ier, -iest**) (*fig*) prägnant

piti|ful /'pɪtɪfl/ *a* bedauernswert. ~**less** *a* mitleidslos

pittance /'pɪtns/ *n* Hungerlohn *m*

pity /'pɪtɪ/ *n* Mitleid *nt*, Erbarmen *nt*; **[what a] ~!** [wie] schade! **take ~ on** sich erbarmen über (+*acc*) ● *vt* bemitleiden

pivot /'pɪvət/ *n* Drehzapfen *m*; (*fig*) Angelpunkt *m* ● *vi* sich drehen (**on** um)

pixie /'pɪksɪ/ *n* Kobold *m*

pizza /'pi:tsə/ *n* Pizza *f*

placard /'plækɑːd/ n Plakat nt

placate /plə'keɪt/ vt beschwichtigen

place /pleɪs/ n Platz m; (spot) Stelle f; (town, village) Ort m; (fam: house) Haus nt; **out of ~** fehl am Platze; **take ~** stattfinden; **all over the ~** überall • vt setzen; (upright) stellen; (flat) legen; (remember) unterbringen (fam); **~ an order** eine Bestellung aufgeben; **be ~d** (in race) sich plazieren. **~-mat** n Set nt

placid /'plæsɪd/ a gelassen

plagiar|ism /'pleɪdʒərɪzm/ n Plagiat nt. **~ize** vt plagiieren

plague /pleɪg/ n Pest f • vt plagen

plaice /pleɪs/ n inv Scholle f

plain /pleɪn/ a (-er, -est) klar; (simple) einfach; (not pretty) nicht hübsch; (not patterned) einfarbig; (chocolate) zartbitter; **in ~ clothes** in Zivil • adv (simply) einfach • n Ebene f; (Knitting) linke Masche f. **~ly** adv klar, deutlich; (simply) einfach; (obviously) offensichtlich

plaintiff /'pleɪntɪf/ n (Jur) Kläger(in) m(f)

plaintive /'pleɪntɪv/ a, **-ly** adv klagend

plait /plæt/ n Zopf m • vt flechten

plan /plæn/ n Plan m • vt (pt/pp planned) planen; (intend) vorhaben

plane¹ /pleɪn/ n (tree) Platane f

plane² n Flugzeug nt; (Geom & fig) Ebene f

plane³ n (Techn) Hobel m • vt hobeln

planet /'plænɪt/ n Planet m

plank /plæŋk/ n Brett nt; (thick) Planke f

planning /'plænɪŋ/ n Planung f. **~ permission** n Baugenehmigung f

plant /plɑːnt/ n Pflanze f; (Techn) Anlage f; (factory) Werk nt • vt pflanzen; (place in position) setzen; **~ oneself in front of s.o.** sich vor jdn hinstellen. **~ation** /plæn'teɪʃn/ n Plantage f

plaque /plɑːk/ n [Gedenk]tafel f; (on teeth) Zahnbelag m

plasma /'plæzmə/ n Plasma nt

plaster /'plɑːstə(r)/ n Verputz m; (sticking ~) Pflaster nt; **~ [of Paris]** Gips m • vt verputzen (wall); (cover) bedecken mit. **~ed** a (sl) besoffen. **~er** n Gipser m

plastic /'plæstɪk/ n Kunststoff m, Plastik nt • a Kunststoff-, Plastik-; (malleable) formbar, plastisch

Plasticine (P) /'plæstɪsiːn/ n Knetmasse f

plastic 'surgery n plastische Chirurgie f

plate /pleɪt/ n Teller m; (flat sheet) Platte f; (with name, number) Schild nt; (gold and silverware) vergoldete/versilberte Ware f; (in book) Tafel f • vt (with gold) vergolden; (with silver) versilbern

plateau /'plætəʊ/ n (pl ~x /-əʊz/) Hochebene f

platform /'plætfɔːm/ n Plattform f; (stage) Podium nt; (Rail) Bahnsteig m; **~ 5** Gleis 5

platinum /'plætɪnəm/ n Platin nt

platitude /'plætɪtjuːd/ n Platitüde f

platonic /plə'tɒnɪk/ a platonisch

platoon /plə'tuːn/ n (Mil) Zug m

platter /'plætə(r)/ n Platte f

plausible /'plɔːzəbl/ a plausibel

play /pleɪ/ n Spiel nt; [Theater]stück nt; (Radio) Hörspiel nt; (TV) Fernsehspiel nt; **~ on words** Wortspiel nt • vt/i spielen; ausspielen (card); **~ safe** sichergehen. **~ down** vt herunterspielen. **~ up** vi (fam) Mätzchen machen

play: ~boy n Playboy m. **~er** n Spieler(in) m(f). **~ful** a, **-ly** adv verspielt. **~ground** n Spielplatz m; (Sch) Schulhof m. **~group** n Kindergarten m

playing: ~-card n Spielkarte f. **~-field** n Sportplatz m

play: ~mate n Spielkamerad m. **~-pen** n Laufstall m, Laufgitter nt. **~thing** n Spielzeug nt. **~wright** /-raɪt/ n Dramatiker m

plc abbr (public limited company) ≈ GmbH

plea /pliː/ n Bitte f; **make a ~ for** bitten um

plead /pliːd/ vt vorschützen; (Jur) vertreten (case) • vi flehen (for um); **~ guilty** sich schuldig bekennen; **~ with s.o.** jdn anflehen

pleasant /'plezənt/ a angenehm; (person) nett. **~ly** adv angenehm; (say, smile) freundlich

pleas|e /pliːz/ adv bitte • vt gefallen (+ dat); **~e s.o.** jdm eine Freude machen; **~e oneself** tun, was man will. **~ed** a erfreut; **be ~ed with/about sth** sich über etw (acc) freuen. **~ing** a erfreulich

pleasurable /'pleʒərəbl/ a angenehm

pleasure /'pleʒə(r)/ n Vergnügen nt; (joy) Freude f; **with** ~ gern[e]

pleat /pli:t/ n Falte f ● vt fälteln. ~ed 'skirt n Faltenrock m

plebiscite /'plebɪsɪt/ n Volksabstimmung f

pledge /pledʒ/ n Pfand nt; (promise) Versprechen nt ● vt verpfänden; versprechen

plentiful /'plentɪfl/ a reichlich; **be** ~ reichlich vorhanden sein

plenty /'plentɪ/ n eine Menge; (enough) reichlich; ~ **of money/people** viel Geld/viele Leute

pleurisy /'pluərəsɪ/ n Rippenfellentzündung f

pliable /'plaɪəbl/ a biegsam

pliers /'plaɪəz/ npl [Flach]zange f

plight /plaɪt/ n [Not]lage f

plimsolls /'plɪmsəlz/ npl Turnschuhe pl

plinth /plɪnθ/ n Sockel m

plod /plɒd/ vi (pt/pp plodded) trotten; (work hard) sich abmühen

plonk /plɒŋk/ n (fam) billiger Wein m

plot /plɒt/ n Komplott nt; (of novel) Handlung f; ~ **of land** Stück nt Land ● vt einzeichnen ● vi ein Komplott schmieden

plough /plaʊ/ n Pflug m ● vt/i pflügen. ~ **back** vt (Comm) wieder investieren

ploy /plɔɪ/ n (fam) Trick m

pluck /plʌk/ n Mut m ● vt zupfen; rupfen (bird); pflücken (flower); ~ **up courage** Mut fassen

plucky /'plʌkɪ/ a (-ier, -iest) tapfer, mutig

plug /plʌg/ n Stöpsel m; (wood) Zapfen m; (cotton wool) Bausch m; (Electr) Stecker m; (Auto) Zündkerze f; (fam: advertisement) Schleichwerbung f ● vt zustopfen; (fam: advertise) Schleichwerbung machen für. ~ **in** vt (Electr) einstecken

plum /plʌm/ n Pflaume f

plumage /'plu:mɪdʒ/ n Gefieder nt

plumb /plʌm/ n Lot nt ● adv lotrecht ● vt loten. ~ **in** vt installieren

plumb|er /'plʌmə(r)/ n Klempner m. ~**ing** n Wasserleitungen pl

'plumb-line n [Blei]lot nt

plume /plu:m/ n Feder f

plummet /'plʌmɪt/ vi herunterstürzen

plump /plʌmp/ a (-er, -est) mollig, rundlich ● vt ~ **for** wählen

plunder /'plʌndə(r)/ n Beute f ● vt plündern

plunge /plʌndʒ/ n Sprung m; **take the** ~ (fam) den Schritt wagen ● vt/i tauchen

plu'perfect /plu:-/ n Plusquamperfekt nt

plural /'pluərl/ a pluralisch ● n Mehrzahl f, Plural m

plus /plʌs/ prep plus (+ dat) ● a Plus- ● n Pluszeichen nt; (advantage) Plus nt

plush[y] /'plʌʃ[ɪ]/ a luxuriös

ply /plaɪ/ vt (pt/pp plied) ausüben (trade); ~ **s.o. with drink** jdm ein Glas nach dem anderen eingießen. ~**wood** n Sperrholz nt

p.m. adv (abbr of post meridiem) nachmittags

pneumatic /nju:'mætɪk/ a pneumatisch. ~ **'drill** n Preßlufthammer m

pneumonia /nju:'məʊnɪə/ n Lungenentzündung f

poach /pəʊtʃ/ vt (Culin) pochieren; (steal) wildern. ~**er** n Wilddieb m

pocket /'pɒkɪt/ n Tasche f; ~ **of resistance** Widerstandsnest nt; **be out of** ~ [an einem Geschäft] verlieren ● vt einstecken. ~**-book** n Notizbuch nt; (wallet) Brieftasche f. ~**-money** n Taschengeld nt

pock-marked /'pɒk-/ a pockennarbig

pod /pɒd/ n Hülse f

podgy /'pɒdʒɪ/ a (-ier, -iest) dick

poem /'pəʊɪm/ n Gedicht nt

poet /'pəʊɪt/ n Dichter(in) m(f). ~**ic** /-'etɪk/ a dichterisch

poetry /'pəʊɪtrɪ/ n Dichtung f

poignant /'pɔɪnjənt/ a ergreifend

point /pɔɪnt/ n Punkt m; (sharp end) Spitze f; (meaning) Sinn m; (purpose) Zweck m; (Electr) Steckdose f; ~**s** pl (Rail) Weiche f; ~ **of view** Standpunkt m; **good/bad** ~**s** gute/schlechte Seiten; **what is the** ~? wozu? **the** ~ **is** es geht darum; **I don't see the** ~ das sehe ich nicht ein; **up to a** ~ bis zu einem gewissen Grade; **be on the** ~ **of doing sth** im Begriff sein, etw zu tun ● vt richten (**at** auf + acc); ausfugen (brickwork) ● vi deuten (**at/to** auf + acc); (with finger) mit dem Finger zeigen. ~ **out** vt zeigen auf (+ acc); ~ **sth out to s.o.** jdn auf etw (acc) hinweisen

point-'blank a aus nächster Entfernung; (fig) rundweg

point|ed /'pɔmtɪd/ *a* spitz; ⟨*question*⟩ gezielt. **~er** *n* (*hint*) Hinweis *m*. **~less** *a* zwecklos, sinnlos

poise /pɔɪz/ *n* Haltung *f*. **~d** *a* (*confident*) selbstsicher; **~d to** bereit zu

poison /'pɔɪzn/ *n* Gift *nt* ● *vt* vergiften. **~ous** *a* giftig

poke /pəʊk/ *n* Stoß *m* ● *vt* stoßen; schüren ⟨*fire*⟩; ⟨*put*⟩ stecken; **~ fun at** sich lustig machen über (+ *acc*)

poker¹ /'pəʊkə(r)/ *n* Schüreisen *nt*

poker² *n* (*Cards*) Poker *nt*

poky /'pəʊkɪ/ *a* (**-ier, -iest**) eng

Poland /'pəʊlənd/ *n* Polen *nt*

polar /'pəʊlə(r)/ *a* Polar-. **~ 'bear** *n* Eisbär *m*. **~ize** *vt* polarisieren

Pole /pəʊl/ *n* Pole *m*/Polin *f*

pole¹ *n* Stange *f*

pole² *n* (*Geog, Electr*) Pol *m*

'polecat *n* Iltis *m*

'pole-star *n* Polarstern *m*

'pole-vault *n* Stabhochsprung *m*

police /pə'liːs/ *npl* Polizei *f* ● *vt* polizeilich kontrollieren

police: ~man *n* Polizist *m*. **~ state** *n* Polizeistaat *m*. **~ station** *n* Polizeiwache *f*. **~woman** *n* Polizistin *f*

policy¹ /'pɒlɪsɪ/ *n* Politik *f*

policy² *n* (*insurance*) Police *f*

polio /'pəʊlɪəʊ/ *n* Kinderlähmung *f*

Polish /'pəʊlɪʃ/ *a* polnisch

polish /'pɒlɪʃ/ *n* (*shine*) Glanz *m*; (*for shoes*) [Schuh]creme *f*; (*for floor*) Bohnerwachs *m*; (*for furniture*) Politur *f*; (*for silver*) Putzmittel *nt*; (*for nails*) Lack *m*; (*fig*) Schliff *m* ● *vt* polieren; bohnern ⟨*floor*⟩. **~ off** *vt* (*fam*) verputzen ⟨*food*⟩; erledigen ⟨*task*⟩

polisher /'pɒlɪʃə(r)/ *n* (*machine*) Poliermaschine *f*; (*for floor*) Bohnermaschine *f*

polite /pə'laɪt/ *a*, **-ly** *adv* höflich. **~ness** *n* Höflichkeit *f*

politic /'pɒlɪtɪk/ *a* ratsam

politic|al /pə'lɪtɪkl/ *a*, **-ly** *adv* politisch. **~ian** /pɒlɪ'tɪʃn/ *n* Politiker(in) *m*(*f*)

politics /'pɒlətɪks/ *n* Politik *f*

polka /'pɒlkə/ *n* Polka *f*

poll /pəʊl/ *n* Abstimmung *f*; (*election*) Wahl *f*; [**opinion**] **~** [Meinungs]umfrage *f*; **go to the ~s** wählen ● *vt* erhalten ⟨*votes*⟩

pollen /'pɒlən/ *n* Blütenstaub *m*, Pollen *m*

polling /'pəʊlɪŋ/: **~-booth** *n* Wahlkabine *f*. **~-station** *n* Wahllokal *nt*

'poll tax *n* Kopfsteuer *f*

pollutant /pə'luːtənt/ *n* Schadstoff *m*

pollut|e /pə'luːt/ *vt* verschmutzen. **~ion** /-'uːʃn/ *n* Verschmutzung *f*

polo /'pəʊləʊ/ *n* Polo *nt*. **~-neck** *n* Rollkragen *m*. **~ shirt** *n* Polohemd *nt*

polyester /pɒlɪ'estə(r)/ *n* Polyester *m*

polystyrene /pɒlɪ'staɪriːn/ *n* Polystyrol *nt*; (*for packing*) Styropor (P) *nt*

polytechnic /pɒlɪ'teknɪk/ *n* ≈ technische Hochschule *f*

polythene /'pɒlɪθiːn/ *n* Polyäthylen *nt*. **~ bag** *n* Plastiktüte *f*

polyun'saturated *a* mehrfachungesättigt

pomegranate /'pɒmɪgrænɪt/ *n* Granatapfel *m*

pomp /pɒmp/ *n* Pomp *m*

pompon /'pɒmpɒn/ *n* Pompon *m*

pompous /'pɒmpəs/ *a*, **-ly** *adv* großspurig

pond /pɒnd/ *n* Teich *m*

ponder /'pɒndə(r)/ *vi* nachdenken

ponderous /'pɒndərəs/ *a* schwerfällig

pong /pɒŋ/ *n* (*fam*) Mief *m*

pony /'pəʊnɪ/ *n* Pony *nt*. **~-tail** *n* Pferdeschwanz *m*. **~-trekking** *n* Ponyreiten *nt*

poodle /'puːdl/ *n* Pudel *m*

pool¹ /puːl/ *n* [Schwimm]becken *nt*; (*pond*) Teich *m*; (*of blood*) Lache *f*

pool² *n* (*common fund*) [gemeinsame] Kasse *f*; **~s** *pl* [Fußball]toto *nt* ● *vt* zusammenlegen

poor /pʊə(r)/ *a* (**-er, -est**) arm; (*not good*) schlecht; **in ~ health** nicht gesund ● *npl* **the ~** die Armen. **~ly** *a* **be ~ly** krank sein ● *adv* ärmlich; (*badly*) schlecht

pop¹ /pɒp/ *n* Knall *m*; (*drink*) Brause *f* ● *v* (*pt/pp* **popped**) ● *vt* (*fam: put*) stecken (**in** in + *acc*) ● *vi* knallen; (*burst*) platzen. **~ in** *vi* (*fam*) reinschauen. **~ out** *vi* (*fam*) kurz rausgehen

pop² *n* (*fam*) Popmusik *f*, Pop *m* ● *attrib* Pop-

'popcorn *n* Puffmais *m*

pope /pəʊp/ *n* Papst *m*

poplar /'pɒplə(r)/ *n* Pappel *f*

poppy /'pɒpɪ/ *n* Mohn *m*

popular /'pɒpjʊlə(r)/ *a* beliebt, populär; ⟨*belief*⟩ volkstümlich. ~**ity** /-'lærəti/ *n* Beliebtheit *f*, Popularität *f*

populat|e /'pɒpjʊleɪt/ *vt* bevölkern. ~**ion** /-'leɪʃn/ *n* Bevölkerung *f*

porcelain /'pɔ:səlɪn/ *n* Porzellan *nt*

porch /pɔ:tʃ/ *n* Vorbau *m*; (*Amer*) Veranda *f*

porcupine /'pɔ:kjʊpaɪn/ *n* Stachelschwein *nt*

pore[1] /pɔ:(r)/ *n* Pore *f*

pore[2] *vi* ~ **over** studieren

pork /pɔ:k/ *n* Schweinefleisch *nt*

porn /pɔ:n/ *n* (*fam*) Porno *m*

pornograph|ic /pɔ:nə'græfɪk/ *a* pornographisch. ~**y** /-'nɒgrəfi/ *n* Pornographie *f*

porous /'pɔ:rəs/ *a* porös

porpoise /'pɔ:pəs/ *n* Tümmler *m*

porridge /'pɒrɪdʒ/ *n* Haferbrei *m*

port[1] /pɔ:t/ *n* Hafen *m*; (*town*) Hafenstadt *f*

port[2] *n* (*Naut*) Backbord *nt*

port[3] *n* (*wine*) Portwein *m*

portable /'pɔ:təbl/ *a* tragbar

porter /'pɔ:tə(r)/ *n* Portier *m*; (*for luggage*) Gepäckträger *m*

portfolio /pɔ:t'fəʊlɪəʊ/ *n* Mappe *f*; (*Comm*) Portefeuille *nt*

'**porthole** *n* Bullauge *nt*

portion /'pɔ:ʃn/ *n* Portion *f*; (*part, share*) Teil *nt*

portly /'pɔ:tlɪ/ *a* (**-ier, -iest**) beleibt

portrait /'pɔ:trɪt/ *n* Porträt *nt*

portray /pɔ:'treɪ/ *vt* darstellen. ~**al** *n* Darstellung *f*

Portug|al /'pɔ:tjʊgl/ *n* Portugal *nt*. ~**uese** /-'gi:z/ *a* portugiesisch ● *n* Portugiese *m*/-giesin *f*

pose /pəʊz/ *n* Pose *f* ● *vt* aufwerfen ⟨*problem*⟩; stellen ⟨*question*⟩ ● *vi* posieren; (*for painter*) Modell stehen; ~ **as** sich ausgeben als

posh /pɒʃ/ *a* (*fam*) feudal

position /pə'zɪʃn/ *n* Platz *m*; (*posture*) Haltung *f*; (*job*) Stelle *f*; (*situation*) Lage *f*, Situation *f*; (*status*) Stellung *f* ● *vt* plazieren; ~ **oneself** sich stellen

positive /'pɒzətɪv/ *a*, **-ly** *adv* positiv; (*definite*) eindeutig; (*real*) ausgesprochen ● *n* Positiv *nt*

possess /pə'zes/ *vt* besitzen. ~**ion** /pə'zeʃn/ *n* Besitz *m*; ~**ions** *pl* Sachen *pl*

possess|ive /pə'zesɪv/ *a* Possessiv-; **be** ~**ive** zu sehr an jdm hängen. ~**or** *n* Besitzer *m*

possibility /pɒsə'bɪlətɪ/ *n* Möglichkeit *f*

possib|le /'pɒsəbl/ *a* möglich. ~**ly** *adv* möglicherweise; **not** ~**ly** unmöglich

post[1] /pəʊst/ *n* (*pole*) Pfosten *m* ● *vt* anschlagen ⟨*notice*⟩

post[2] *n* (*place of duty*) Posten *m*; (*job*) Stelle *f* ● *vt* postieren; (*transfer*) versetzen

post[3] *n* (*mail*) Post *f*; **by** ~ mit der Post ● *vt* aufgeben ⟨*letter*⟩; ⟨*send by* ~⟩ mit der Post schicken; **keep s.o.** ~**ed** jdn auf dem laufenden halten

postage /'pəʊstɪdʒ/ *n* Porto *nt*. ~ **stamp** *n* Briefmarke *f*

postal /'pəʊstl/ *a* Post-. ~ **order** *n* ≈ Geldanweisung *f*

post: ~**-box** *n* Briefkasten *m*. ~**card** *n* Postkarte *f*; (*picture*) Ansichtskarte *f*. ~**code** *n* Postleitzahl *f*. ~**-'date** *vt* vordatieren

poster /'pəʊstə(r)/ *n* Plakat *nt*

posterior /pɒ'stɪərɪə(r)/ *a* hintere(r,s) ● *n* (*fam*) Hintern *m*

posterity /pɒ'sterətɪ/ *n* Nachwelt *f*

posthumous /'pɒstjʊməs/ *a*, **-ly** *adv* postum

post: ~**man** *n* Briefträger *m*. ~**mark** *n* Poststempel *m*

post-mortem /-'mɔ:təm/ *n* Obduktion *f*

'**post office** *n* Post *f*

postpone /pəʊst'pəʊn/ *vt* aufschieben; ~ **until** verschieben auf (+ *acc*). ~**ment** *n* Verschiebung *f*

postscript /'pəʊstskrɪpt/ *n* Nachschrift *f*

posture /'pɒstʃə(r)/ *n* Haltung *f*

post-'war *a* Nachkriegs-

posy /'pəʊzɪ/ *n* Sträußchen *nt*

pot /pɒt/ *n* Topf *m*; (*for tea, coffee*) Kanne *f*; ~**s of money** (*fam*) eine Menge Geld; **go to** ~ (*fam*) herunterkommen

potassium /pə'tæsɪəm/ *n* Kalium *nt*

potato /pə'teɪtəʊ/ *n* (*pl* **-es**) Kartoffel *f*

poten|cy /'pəʊtənsɪ/ *n* Stärke *f*. ~**t** *a* stark

potential /pə'tenʃl/ *a*, **-ly** *adv* potentiell ● *n* Potential *nt*

pot: ~**-hole** *n* Höhle *f*; (*in road*) Schlagloch *nt*. ~**-holer** *n* Höhlenforscher *m*. ~**-shot** *n* take a ~**-shot at** schießen auf (+ *acc*)

potted /'pɒtɪd/ *a* eingemacht; (*shortened*) gekürzt. ~ '**plant** *n* Topfpflanze *f*

potter[1] /'pɒtə(r)/ *vi* ~ **[about]** herumwerkeln

potter[2] *n* Töpfer(in) *m(f)*. **~y** *n* Töpferei *f*; (*articles*) Töpferwaren *pl*

potty /'pɒtɪ/ *a* (**-ier, -iest**) (*fam*) verrückt ● *n* Töpfchen *nt*

pouch /paʊtʃ/ *n* Beutel *m*

pouffe /puːf/ *n* Sitzkissen *nt*

poultry /'pəʊltrɪ/ *n* Geflügel *nt*

pounce /paʊns/ *vi* zuschlagen; **~ on** sich stürzen auf (+ *acc*)

pound[1] /paʊnd/ *n* (*money & 0,454 kg*) Pfund *nt*

pound[2] *vt* hämmern ● *vi* ⟨*heart:*⟩ hämmern; (*run heavily*) stampfen

pour /pɔː(r)/ *vt* gießen; einschenken ⟨*drink*⟩ ● *vi* strömen; (*with rain*) gießen. **~ out** *vi* ausströmen ● *vt* ausschütten; einschenken ⟨*drink*⟩

pout /paʊt/ *vi* einen Schmollmund machen

poverty /'pɒvətɪ/ *n* Armut *f*

powder /'paʊdə(r)/ *n* Pulver *nt*; (*cosmetic*) Puder *m* ● *vt* pudern. **~y** *a* pulverig

power /'paʊə(r)/ *n* Macht *f*; (*strength*) Kraft *f*; (*Electr*) Strom *m*; (*nuclear*) Energie *f*; (*Math*) Potenz *f*. **~ cut** *n* Stromsperre *f*. **~ed** *a* betrieben (**by** mit); **~ed by electricity** mit Elektroantrieb. **~ful** *a* mächtig; (*strong*) stark. **~less** *a* machtlos. **~-station** *n* Kraftwerk *nt*

practicable /'præktɪkəbl/ *a* durchführbar, praktikabel

practical /'præktɪkl/ *a*, **-ly** *adv* praktisch. **~ 'joke** *n* Streich *m*

practice /'præktɪs/ *n* Praxis *f*; (*custom*) Brauch *m*; (*habit*) Gewohnheit *f*; (*exercise*) Übung *f*; (*Sport*) Training *nt*; **in ~** (*in reality*) in der Praxis; **out of ~** außer Übung; **put into ~** ausführen

practise /'præktɪs/ *vt* üben; (*carry out*) praktizieren; ausüben ⟨*profession*⟩ ● *vi* üben; ⟨*doctor:*⟩ praktizieren. **~d** *a* geübt

pragmatic /præg'mætɪk/ *a*, **~ally** *adv* pragmatisch

praise /preɪz/ *n* Lob *nt* ● *vt* loben. **~worthy** *a* lobenswert

pram /præm/ *n* Kinderwagen *m*

prance /prɑːns/ *vi* herumhüpfen; ⟨*horse:*⟩ tänzeln

prank /præŋk/ *n* Streich *m*

prattle /'prætl/ *vi* plappern

prawn /prɔːn/ *n* Garnele *f*, Krabbe *f*. **~ 'cocktail** *n* Krabbencocktail *m*

pray /preɪ/ *vi* beten. **~er** /preə(r)/ *n* Gebet *nt*; **~ers** *pl* (*service*) Andacht *f*

preach /priːtʃ/ *vt/i* predigen. **~er** *n* Prediger *m*

preamble /priː'æmbl/ *n* Einleitung *f*

pre-ar'range /priː-/ *vt* im voraus arrangieren

precarious /prɪ'keərɪəs/ *a*, **-ly** *adv* unsicher

precaution /prɪ'kɔːʃn/ *n* Vorsichtsmaßnahme *f*; **as a ~** zur Vorsicht. **~ary** *a* Vorsichts-

precede /prɪ'siːd/ *vt* vorangehen (+ *dat*)

preceden|ce /'presɪdəns/ *n* Vorrang *m*. **~t** *n* Präzedenzfall *m*

preceding /prɪ'siːdɪŋ/ *a* vorhergehend

precinct /'priːsɪŋkt/ *n* Bereich *m*; (*traffic-free*) Fußgängerzone *f*; (*Amer: district*) Bezirk *m*

precious /'preʃəs/ *a* kostbar; ⟨*style*⟩ preziös ● *adv* (*fam*) **~ little** recht wenig

precipice /'presɪpɪs/ *n* Steilabfall *m*

precipitate[1] /prɪ'sɪpɪtət/ *a* voreilig

precipitat|e[2] /prɪ'sɪpɪteɪt/ *vt* schleudern; (*fig: accelerate*) beschleunigen. **~ion** /-'teɪʃn/ *n* (*Meteorol*) Niederschlag *m*

précis /'preɪsiː/ *n* (*pl* **précis** /-siːz/) Zusammenfassung *f*

precis|e /prɪ'saɪs/ *a*, **-ly** *adv* genau. **~ion** /-'sɪʒn/ *n* Genauigkeit *f*

preclude /prɪ'kluːd/ *vt* ausschließen

precocious /prɪ'kəʊʃəs/ *a* frühreif

pre|con'ceived /priː-/ *a* vorgefaßt. **~con'ception** *n* vorgefaßte Meinung *f*

precursor /priː'kɜːsə(r)/ *n* Vorläufer *m*

predator /'predətə(r)/ *n* Raubtier *nt*

predecessor /'priːdɪsesə(r)/ *n* Vorgänger(in) *m(f)*

predicament /prɪ'dɪkəmənt/ *n* Zwangslage *f*

predicat|e /'predɪkət/ *n* (*Gram*) Prädikat *nt*. **~ive** /prɪ'dɪkətɪv/ *a*, **-ly** *adv* prädikativ

predict /prɪ'dɪkt/ *vt* voraussagen. **~able** /-əbl/ *a* voraussehbar; (*person*) berechenbar. **~ion** /-'dɪkʃn/ *n* Voraussage *f*

pre'domin|ant /prɪ-/ *a* vorherrschend. **~antly** *adv* hauptsächlich, überwiegend. **~ate** *vi* vorherrschen

pre-'eminent /priː-/ *a* hervorragend

pre-empt /pri:'empt/ *vt* zuvorkommen (+ *dat*)

preen /pri:n/ *vt* putzen; ~ **oneself** (*fig*) selbstgefällig tun

pre|fab /'pri:fæb/ *n* (*fam*) [einfaches] Fertighaus *nt*. ~'**fabricated** *a* vorgefertigt

preface /'prefɪs/ *n* Vorwort *nt*

prefect /'pri:fekt/ *n* Präfekt *m*

prefer /prɪ'fɜ:(r)/ *vt* (*pt/pp* **preferred**) vorziehen; **I** ~ **to walk** ich gehe lieber zu Fuß; **I** ~ **wine** ich trinke lieber Wein

prefera|ble /'prefərəbl/ *a* **be** ~**ble** vorzuziehen sein (**to** *dat*). ~**bly** *adv* vorzugsweise

preferen|ce /'prefərəns/ *n* Vorzug *m*. ~**tial** /-'renʃl/ *a* bevorzugt

prefix /'pri:fɪks/ *n* Vorsilbe *f*

pregnan|cy /'pregnənsɪ/ *n* Schwangerschaft *f*. ~**t** *a* schwanger; ⟨animal⟩ trächtig

prehi'storic /pri:-/ *a* prähistorisch

prejudice /'predʒʊdɪs/ *n* Vorurteil *nt*; (*bias*) Voreingenommenheit *f* ● *vt* einnehmen (**against** gegen). ~**d** *a* voreingenommen

preliminary /prɪ'lɪmɪnərɪ/ *a* Vor-

prelude /'prelju:d/ *n* Vorspiel *nt*

pre-'marital *a* vorehelich

premature /'premətjʊə(r)/ *a* vorzeitig; ⟨birth⟩ Früh-. ~**ly** *adv* zu früh

pre'meditated /pri:-/ *a* vorsätzlich

premier /'premɪə(r)/ *a* führend ● *n* (*Pol*) Premier[minister] *m*

première /'premɪeə(r)/ *n* Premiere *f*

premises /'premɪsɪz/ *npl* Räumlichkeiten *pl*; **on the** ~ im Haus

premiss /'premɪs/ *n* Prämisse *f*

premium /'pri:mɪəm/ *n* Prämie *f*; **be at a** ~ hoch im Kurs stehen

premonition /premə'nɪʃn/ *n* Vorahnung *f*

preoccupied /prɪ'ɒkjʊpaɪd/ *a* [in Gedanken] beschäftigt

prep /prep/ *n* (*Sch*) Hausaufgaben *pl*

pre-'packed /pri:-/ *a* abgepackt

preparation /prepə'reɪʃn/ *n* Vorbereitung *f*; (*substance*) Präparat *nt*

preparatory /prɪ'pærətrɪ/ *a* Vor- ● *adv* ~ **to** vor (+ *dat*)

prepare /prɪ'peə(r)/ *vt* vorbereiten; anrichten ⟨meal⟩ ● *vi* sich vorbereiten (**for** auf + *acc*); ~**d to** bereit zu

pre'pay /pri:-/ *vt* (*pt/pp* **-paid**) im voraus bezahlen

preposition /prepə'zɪʃn/ *n* Präposition *f*

prepossessing /pri:pə'zesɪŋ/ *a* ansprechend

preposterous /prɪ'pɒstərəs/ *a* absurd

prerequisite /pri:'rekwɪzɪt/ *n* Voraussetzung *f*

prerogative /prɪ'rɒgətɪv/ *n* Vorrecht *nt*

Presbyterian /prezbɪ'tɪərɪən/ *a* presbyterianisch ● *n* Presbyterianer(in) *m(f)*

prescribe /prɪ'skraɪb/ *vt* vorschreiben; (*Med*) verschreiben

prescription /prɪ'skrɪpʃn/ *n* (*Med*) Rezept *nt*

presence /'prezns/ *n* Anwesenheit *f*, Gegenwart *f*; ~ **of mind** Geistesgegenwart *f*

present[1] /'preznt/ *a* gegenwärtig; **be** ~ anwesend sein; (*occur*) vorkommen ● *n* Gegenwart *f*; (*Gram*) Präsens *nt*; **at** ~ zur Zeit; **for the** ~ vorläufig

present[2] *n* ⟨gift⟩ Geschenk *nt*

present[3] /prɪ'zent/ *vt* überreichen; (*show*) zeigen; vorlegen ⟨cheque⟩; (*introduce*) vorstellen; ~ **s.o. with sth** jdm etw überreichen. ~**able** /-əbl/ *a* **be** ~**able** sich zeigen lassen können

presentation /prezn'teɪʃn/ *n* Überreichung *f*. ~ **ceremony** *n* Verleihungszeremonie *f*

presently /'prezntlɪ/ *adv* nachher; (*Amer: now*) zur Zeit

preservation /prezə'veɪʃn/ *n* Erhaltung *f*

preservative /prɪ'zɜ:vətɪv/ *n* Konservierungsmittel *nt*

preserve /prɪ'zɜ:v/ *vt* erhalten; (*Culin*) konservieren; (*bottle*) einmachen ● *n* (*Hunting & fig*) Revier *nt*; (*jam*) Konfitüre *f*

preside /prɪ'zaɪd/ *vi* den Vorsitz haben (**over** bei)

presidency /'prezɪdənsɪ/ *n* Präsidentschaft *f*

president /'prezɪdənt/ *n* Präsident *m*; (*Amer: chairman*) Vorsitzende(r) *m/f*. ~**ial** /-'denʃl/ *a* Präsidenten-; (*election*) Präsidentschafts-

press /pres/ *n* Presse *f* ● *vt/i* drücken; drücken auf (+ *acc*) ⟨button⟩; pressen ⟨flower⟩; (*iron*) bügeln; (*urge*) bedrängen; ~ **for** drängen auf (+ *acc*); **be** ~**ed for time** in Zeitdruck sein. ~ **on** *vi* weitergehen/-fahren; (*fig*) weitermachen

press: ~ **cutting** *n* Zeitungsausschnitt *m*. ~**ing** *a* dringend. ~**-stud**

n Druckknopf *m*. ∼**-up** *n* Liegestütz *m*

pressure /'preʃə(r)/ *n* Druck *m* ● *vt* = **pressurize**. ∼**-cooker** *n* Schnellkochtopf *m*. ∼ **group** *n* Interessengruppe *f*

pressurize /'preʃəraɪz/ *vt* Druck ausüben auf (+ *acc*). ∼**d** *a* Druck-

prestige /pre'sti:ʒ/ *n* Prestige *nt*. ∼**ious** /-'stɪdʒəs/ *a* Prestige-

presumably /prɪ'zju:məblɪ/ *adv* vermutlich

presume /prɪ'zju:m/ *vt* vermuten; ∼ **to do sth** sich (*dat*) anmaßen, etw zu tun ● *vi* ∼ **on** ausnutzen

presumpt|ion /prɪ'zʌmpʃn/ *n* Vermutung *f*; (*boldness*) Anmaßung *f*. ∼**uous** /-'zʌmptjʊəs/ *a*, **-ly** *adv* anmaßend

presup'pose /pri:-/ *vt* voraussetzen

pretence /prɪ'tens/ *n* Verstellung *f*; (*pretext*) Vorwand *m*; **it's all** ∼ das ist alles gespielt

pretend /prɪ'tend/ *vt* (*claim*) vorgeben; ∼ **that** so tun, als ob; ∼ **to be** sich ausgeben als

pretentious /prɪ'tenʃəs/ *a* protzig

pretext /'pri:tekst/ *n* Vorwand *m*

pretty /'prɪtɪ/ *a* (**-ier, -iest**), ∼**ily** *adv* hübsch ● *adv* (*fam: fairly*) ziemlich

pretzel /'pretsl/ *n* Brezel *f*

prevail /prɪ'veɪl/ *vi* siegen; (*custom:*) vorherrschen; ∼ **on s.o. to do sth** jdn dazu bringen, etw zu tun

prevalen|ce /'prevələns/ *n* Häufigkeit *f*. ∼**t** *a* vorherrschend

prevent /prɪ'vent/ *vt* verhindern, verhüten; ∼ **s.o. [from] doing sth** jdn daran hindern, etw zu tun. ∼**able** /-əbl/ *a* vermeidbar. ∼**ion** /-enʃn/ *n* Verhinderung *f*, Verhütung *f*. ∼**ive** /-ɪv/ *a* vorbeugend

preview /'pri:vju:/ *n* Voraufführung *f*

previous /'pri:vɪəs/ *a* vorhergehend; ∼ **to** vor (+ *dat*). ∼**ly** *adv* vorher, früher

pre-'war /pri:-/ *a* Vorkriegs-

prey /preɪ/ *n* Beute *f*; **bird of** ∼ Raubvogel *m* ● *vi* ∼ **on** Jagd machen auf (+ *acc*); ∼ **on s.o.'s mind** jdm schwer auf der Seele liegen

price /praɪs/ *n* Preis *m* ● *vt* (*Comm*) auszeichnen. ∼**less** *a* unschätzbar; (*fig*) unbezahlbar

prick /prɪk/ *n* Stich *m* ● *vt/i* stechen; ∼ **up one's ears** die Ohren spitzen

prickl|e /'prɪkl/ *n* Stachel *m*; (*thorn*) Dorn *m*. ∼**y** *a* stachelig; (*sensation*) stechend

pride /praɪd/ *n* Stolz *m*; (*arrogance*) Hochmut *m*; (*of lions*) Rudel *nt* ● *vt* ∼ **oneself on** stolz sein auf (+ *acc*)

priest /pri:st/ *n* Priester *m*

prig /prɪg/ *n* Tugendbold *m*

prim /prɪm/ *a* (**primmer, primmest**) prüde

primarily /'praɪmərɪlɪ/ *adv* hauptsächlich, in erster Linie

primary /'praɪmərɪ/ *a* Haupt-. ∼ **school** *n* Grundschule *f*

prime[1] /praɪm/ *a* Haupt-; (*first-rate*) erstklassig ● *n* **be in one's** ∼ **in den besten Jahren sein**

prime[2] *vt* scharf machen (*bomb*); grundieren (*surface*); (*fig*) instruieren

Prime Minister /praɪ'mɪnɪstə(r)/ *n* Premierminister(in) *m(f)*

primeval /praɪ'mi:vl/ *a* Ur-

primitive /'prɪmɪtɪv/ *a* primitiv

primrose /'prɪmrəʊz/ *n* gelbe Schlüsselblume *f*

prince /prɪns/ *n* Prinz *m*

princess /prɪn'ses/ *n* Prinzessin *f*

principal /'prɪnsəpl/ *a* Haupt- ● *n* (*Sch*) Rektor(in) *m(f)*

principality /prɪnsɪ'pælətɪ/ *n* Fürstentum *nt*

principally /'prɪnsəplɪ/ *adv* hauptsächlich

principle /'prɪnsəpl/ *n* Prinzip *nt*, Grundsatz *m*; **in/on** ∼ im/aus Prinzip

print /prɪnt/ *n* Druck *m*; (*Phot*) Abzug *m*; **in** ∼ gedruckt; (*available*) erhältlich; **out of** ∼ vergriffen ● *vt* drucken; (*write in capitals*) in Druckschrift schreiben; (*Computing*) ausdrucken; (*Phot*) abziehen. ∼**ed matter** *n* Drucksache *f*

print|er /'prɪntə(r)/ *n* Drucker *m*. ∼**ing** *n* Druck *m*

'**printout** *n* (*Computing*) Ausdruck *m*

prior /'praɪə(r)/ *a* frühere(r,s); ∼ **to** vor (+ *dat*)

priority /praɪ'ɒrətɪ/ *n* Priorität *f*, Vorrang *m*; (*matter*) vordringliche Sache *f*

prise /praɪz/ *vt* ∼ **open/up** aufstemmen/hochstemmen

prism /'prɪzm/ *n* Prisma *nt*

prison /'prɪzn/ *n* Gefängnis *nt*. ∼**er** *n* Gefangene(r) *m/f*

pristine /'prɪsti:n/ *a* tadellos

privacy /'prɪvəsɪ/ n Privatsphäre f;
have no ∼ nie für sich sein

private /'praɪvət/ a, **-ly** adv privat;
(confidential) vertraulich; ⟨car, secretary, school⟩ Privat- ● n (Mil) [ein-
facher] Soldat m; **in ∼** privat;
(confidentially) vertraulich

privation /praɪ'veɪʃn/ n Entbehrung f

privatize /'praɪvətaɪz/ vt privati-
sieren

privilege /'prɪvəlɪdʒ/ n Privileg nt.
∼d a privilegiert

privy /'prɪvɪ/ a **be ∼ to** wissen

prize /praɪz/ n Preis m ● vt schätzen.
∼-giving n Preisverleihung f.
∼-winner n Preisgewinner(in) m(f)

pro /prəʊ/ n (fam) Profi m; **the ∼s
and cons** das Für und Wider

probability /prɒbə'bɪlətɪ/ n Wahr-
scheinlichkeit f

probable /'prɒbəbl/ a, **-bly** adv
wahrscheinlich

probation /prə'beɪʃn/ n (Jur) Bewährung f. **∼ary** a Probe-; **∼ary
period** Probezeit f

probe /prəʊb/ n Sonde f; (fig: investigation) Untersuchung f ● vt/i ∼
[into] untersuchen

problem /'prɒbləm/ n Problem nt;
(Math) Textaufgabe f. **∼atic**
/-'mætɪk/ a problematisch

procedure /prə'siːdʒə(r)/ n Verfahren nt

proceed /prə'siːd/ vi gehen; (in
vehicle) fahren; (continue) weiter-
gehen/-fahren; (speaking) fortfahren; (act) verfahren ● vt **∼ to do
sth** anfangen, etw zu tun

proceedings /prə'siːdɪŋz/ npl Verfahren nt; (Jur) Prozeß m

proceeds /'prəʊsiːdz/ npl Erlös m

process /'prəʊses/ n Prozeß m; (procedure) Verfahren nt; **in the ∼** dabei
● vt verarbeiten; (Admin) bearbeiten;
(Phot) entwickeln

procession /prə'seʃn/ n Umzug m,
Prozession f

proclaim /prə'kleɪm/ vt ausrufen

proclamation /prɒklə'meɪʃn/ n
Proklamation f

procure /prə'kjʊə(r)/ vt beschaffen

prod /prɒd/ n Stoß m ● vt stoßen;
(fig) einen Stoß geben (+ dat)

prodigal /'prɒdɪgl/ a verschwenderisch

prodigious /prə'dɪdʒəs/ a gewaltig

prodigy /'prɒdɪdʒɪ/ n **[infant]** ∼
Wunderkind nt

produce[1] /'prɒdjuːs/ n landwirt-
schaftliche Erzeugnisse pl

produce[2] /prə'djuːs/ vt erzeugen,
produzieren; (manufacture) herstellen; (bring out) hervorholen;
(cause) hervorrufen; inszenieren
⟨play⟩; (Radio, TV) redigieren. **∼r** n
Erzeuger m, Produzent m; Hersteller
m; (Theat) Regisseur m; (Radio, TV)
Redakteur(in) m(f)

product /'prɒdʌkt/ n Erzeugnis nt,
Produkt nt. **∼ion** /prə'dʌkʃn/ n Produktion f; (Theat) Inszenierung f

productiv|**e** /prə'dʌktɪv/ a pro-
duktiv; ⟨land, talks⟩ fruchtbar.
∼ity /-'tɪvətɪ/ n Produktivität f

profan|**e** /prə'feɪn/ a weltlich; (blas-
phemous) [gottes]lästerlich. **∼ity**
/-'fænətɪ/ n (oath) Fluch m

profess /prə'fes/ vt behaupten; bekennen ⟨faith⟩

profession /prə'feʃn/ n Beruf m.
∼al a, **-ly** adv beruflich; (not amateur)
Berufs-; (expert) fachmännisch; (Sport)
professionell ● n Fachmann m; (Sport)
Profi m

professor /prə'fesə(r)/ n Professor
m

proficien|**cy** /prə'fɪʃnsɪ/ n Können
nt. **∼t** a **be ∼t in** beherrschen

profile /'prəʊfaɪl/ n Profil nt; (character study) Porträt nt

profit /'prɒfɪt/ n Gewinn m, Profit m
● vi **∼ from** profitieren von. **∼able**
/-əbl/ a, **-bly** adv gewinnbringend;
(fig) nutzbringend

profound /prə'faʊnd/ a, **-ly** adv tief

profus|**e** /prə'fjuːs/ a, **-ly** adv üppig;
(fig) überschwenglich. **∼ion** /-juːʒn/
n **in ∼ion** in großer Fülle

progeny /'prɒdʒənɪ/ n Nachkom-
menschaft f

program /'prəʊgræm/ n Programm
nt ● vt (pt/pp **programmed**) pro-
grammieren

programme /'prəʊgræm/ n Programm nt; (Radio, TV) Sendung f. **∼r**
n (Computing) Programmierer(in)
m(f)

progress[1] /'prəʊgres/ n Vorankommen nt; (fig) Fortschritt m; **in ∼**
im Gange; **make ∼** (fig) Fortschritte
machen

progress[2] /prə'gres/ vi vorankommen; (fig) fortschreiten. **∼ion**

/-eʃn/ n Folge f; (development) Entwicklung f

progressive /prə'gresɪv/ a fortschrittlich; (disease) fortschreitend. ~ly adv zunehmend

prohibit /prə'hɪbɪt/ vt verbieten (s.o. jdm). ~ive /-ɪv/ a unerschwinglich

project[1] /'prɒdʒekt/ n Projekt nt; (Sch) Arbeit f

project[2] /prə'dʒekt/ vt projizieren (film); (plan) planen ● vi (jut out) vorstehen

projectile /prə'dʒektaɪl/ n Geschoß nt

projector /prə'dʒektə(r)/ n Projektor m

proletariat /prəʊlɪ'teərɪət/ n Proletariat nt

prolific /prə'lɪfɪk/ a fruchtbar; (fig) produktiv

prologue /'prəʊlɒg/ n Prolog m

prolong /prə'lɒŋ/ vt verlängern

promenade /prɒmə'nɑːd/ n Promenade f ● vi spazierengehen

prominent /'prɒmɪnənt/ a vorstehend; (important) prominent; (conspicuous) auffällig; (place) gut sichtbar

promiscu|ity /prɒmɪ'skjuːɪtɪ/ n Promiskuität f. ~ous /prə'mɪskjʊəs/ a be ~ous häufig den Partner wechseln

promis|e /'prɒmɪs/ n Versprechen nt ● vt/i versprechen (s.o. jdm); the P~ed Land das Gelobte Land. ~ing a vielversprechend

promot|e /prə'məʊt/ vt befördern; (advance) fördern; (publicize) Reklame machen für; be ~ed (Sport) aufsteigen. ~ion /-əʊʃn/ n Beförderung f; (Sport) Aufstieg m; (Comm) Reklame f

prompt /prɒmpt/ a prompt, unverzüglich; (punctual) pünktlich ● adv pünktlich ● vt/i veranlassen (to zu); (Theat) soufflieren (+ dat). ~er n Souffleur m/Souffleuse f. ~ly adv prompt

prone /prəʊn/ a be/lie ~ auf dem Bauch liegen; be ~ to neigen zu; be ~ to do sth dazu neigen, etw zu tun

prong /prɒŋ/ n Zinke f

pronoun /'prəʊnaʊn/ n Fürwort nt, Pronomen nt

pronounce /prə'naʊns/ vt aussprechen; (declare) erklären. ~d a ausgeprägt; (noticeable) deutlich. ~ment n Erklärung f

pronunciation /prənʌnsɪ'eɪʃn/ n Aussprache f

proof /pruːf/ n Beweis m; (Typ) Korrekturbogen m ● a ~ against water/theft wasserfest/diebessicher. ~-reader n Korrektor m

prop[1] /prɒp/ n Stütze f ● vt (pt/pp propped) ~ open offenhalten; ~ against (lean) lehnen an (+ acc). ~ up vt stützen

prop[2] n (Theat, fam) Requisit nt

propaganda /prɒpə'gændə/ n Propaganda f

propagate /'prɒpəgeɪt/ vt vermehren; (fig) verbreiten, propagieren

propel /prə'pel/ vt (pt/pp propelled) [an]treiben. ~ler n Propeller m. ~ling 'pencil n Drehbleistift m

propensity /prə'pensətɪ/ n Neigung f (for zu)

proper /'prɒpə(r)/ a, -ly adv richtig; (decent) anständig. ~ 'name, ~ 'noun n Eigenname m

property /'prɒpətɪ/ n Eigentum nt; (quality) Eigenschaft f; (Theat) Requisit nt; (land) [Grund]besitz m; (house) Haus nt. ~ market n Immobilienmarkt m

prophecy /'prɒfəsɪ/ n Prophezeiung f

prophesy /'prɒfɪsaɪ/ vt (pt/pp -ied) prophezeien

prophet /'prɒfɪt/ n Prophet m. ~ic /prə'fetɪk/ a prophetisch

proportion /prə'pɔːʃn/ n Verhältnis nt; (share) Teil m; ~s pl Proportionen; (dimensions) Maße. ~al a, -ly adv proportional

proposal /prə'pəʊzl/ n Vorschlag m; (of marriage) [Heirats]antrag m

propose /prə'pəʊz/ vt vorschlagen; (intend) vorhaben; einbringen (motion); ausbringen (toast) ● vi einen Heiratsantrag machen

proposition /prɒpə'zɪʃn/ n Vorschlag m

propound /prə'paʊnd/ vt darlegen

proprietor /prə'praɪətə(r)/ n Inhaber(in) m(f)

propriety /prə'praɪətɪ/ n Korrektheit f; (decorum) Anstand m

propulsion /prə'pʌlʃn/ n Antrieb m

prosaic /prə'zeɪɪk/ a prosaisch

prose /prəʊz/ n Prosa f

prosecut|e /'prɒsɪkjuːt/ vt strafrechtlich verfolgen. ~ion /-'kjuːʃn/ n strafrechtliche Verfolgung f; the

~ion die Anklage. ~or n [Public]
P~or Staatsanwalt m
prospect[1] /'prɒspekt/ n Aussicht f
prospect[2] /prə'spekt/ vi suchen (for
nach)
prospect|ive /prə'spektɪv/ a
(future) zukünftig. ~or n Pro-
spektor m
prospectus /prə'spektəs/ n Prospekt m
prosper /'prɒspə(r)/ vi gedeihen,
florieren; ⟨person⟩ Erfolg haben.
~ity /-'sperətɪ/ n Wohlstand m
prosperous /'prɒspərəs/ a wohlhabend
prostitut|e /'prɒstɪtjuːt/ n Prosti-
tuierte f. ~ion /-'tjuːʃn/ n Prostitution f
prostrate /'prɒstreɪt/ a ausgestreckt; ~ with grief (fig) vor
Kummer gebrochen
protagonist /prəʊ'tægənɪst/ n
Kämpfer m; (fig) Protagonist m
protect /prə'tekt/ vt schützen (from
vor + dat); beschützen ⟨person⟩. ~ion
/-ekʃn/ n Schutz m. ~ive /-ɪv/ a
Schutz-; (fig) beschützend. ~or n Be-
schützer m
protégé /'prɒtɪʒeɪ/ n Schützling m,
Protegé m
protein /'prəʊtiːn/ n Eiweiß nt
protest[1] /'prəʊtest/ n Protest m
protest[2] /prə'test/ vi protestieren
Protestant /'prɒtɪstənt/ a prote-
stantisch, evangelisch ● n Prote-
stant(in) m(f), Evangelische(r) m/f
protester /prə'testə(r)/ n Prote-
stierende(r) m/f
protocol /'prəʊtəkɒl/ n Protokoll nt
prototype /'prəʊtə-/ n Prototyp m
protract /prə'trækt/ vt verlängern.
~or n Winkelmesser m
protrude /prə'truːd/ vi [her]vor-
stehen
proud /praʊd/ a, -ly adv stolz (of auf
+ acc)
prove /pruːv/ vt beweisen ● vi ~ to
be sich erweisen als
proverb /'prɒvɜːb/ n Sprichwort nt.
~ial /prə'vɜːbɪəl/ a sprichwörtlich
provide /prə'vaɪd/ vt zur Verfügung
stellen; spenden ⟨shade⟩; ~ s.o. with
sth jdn mit etw versorgen od versehen
● vi ~ for sorgen für
provided /prə'vaɪdɪd/ conj ~ [that]
vorausgesetzt [daß]
providen|ce /'prɒvɪdəns/ n Vor-
sehung f. ~tial /-'denʃl/ a be ~tial
ein Glück sein

providing /prə'vaɪdɪŋ/ conj = provided
provinc|e /'prɒvɪns/ n Provinz f;
(fig) Bereich m. ~ial /prə'vɪnʃl/ a
provinziell
provision /prə'vɪʒn/ n Versorgung f
(of mit); ~s pl Lebensmittel pl. ~al a,
-ly adv vorläufig
proviso /prə'vaɪzəʊ/ n Vorbehalt m
provocat|ion /prɒvə'keɪʃn/ n Pro-
vokation f. ~ive /prə'vɒkətɪv/ a, -ly
adv provozierend; (sexually) aufreizend
provoke /prə'vəʊk/ vt provozieren;
(cause) hervorrufen
prow /praʊ/ n Bug m
prowess /'praʊɪs/ n Kraft f
prowl /praʊl/ vi herumschleichen
● n be on the ~ herumschleichen
proximity /prɒk'sɪmətɪ/ n Nähe f
proxy /'prɒksɪ/ n Stellvertreter(in)
m(f); (power) Vollmacht f
prude /pruːd/ n be a ~ prüde sein
pruden|ce /'pruːdns/ n Umsicht f.
~t a, -ly adv umsichtig; (wise) klug
prudish /'pruːdɪʃ/ a prüde
prune[1] /pruːn/ n Backpflaume f
prune[2] vt beschneiden
pry /praɪ/ vi (pt/pp pried) neugierig
sein
psalm /sɑːm/ n Psalm m
pseudonym /'sjuːdənɪm/ n Pseudonym nt
psychiatric /saɪkɪ'ætrɪk/ a psych-
iatrisch
psychiatr|ist /saɪ'kaɪətrɪst/ n Psych-
iater(in) m(f). ~y n Psychiatrie f
psychic /'saɪkɪk/ a übersinnlich; I'm
not ~ ich kann nicht hellsehen
psycho|analyse /saɪkəʊ-/ vt psy-
choanalysieren. ~a'nalysis n Psy-
choanalyse f. ~'analyst Psycho-
analytiker(in) m(f)
psychological /saɪkə'lɒdʒɪkl/ a, -ly
adv psychologisch; ⟨illness⟩ psychisch
psycholog|ist /saɪ'kɒlədʒɪst/ n Psy-
chologe m/-login f. ~y n Psychologie
f
psychopath /'saɪkəpæθ/ n Psy-
chopath(in) m(f)
PTO abbr (please turn over) b.w.
pub /pʌb/ n (fam) Kneipe f
puberty /'pjuːbətɪ/ n Pubertät f
public /'pʌblɪk/ a, -ly adv öffentlich;
make ~ publik machen ● n the ~ die
Öffentlichkeit; **in** ~ in aller Öffentlichkeit
publican /'pʌblɪkən/ n [Gast]wirt m

publication /pʌblɪ'keɪʃn/ n Veröffentlichung f

public: ~ **con'venience** n öffentliche Toilette f. ~ **'holiday** n gesetzlicher Feiertag m. ~ **'house** n [Gast]wirtschaft f

publicity /pʌb'lɪsətɪ/ n Publicity f; (advertising) Reklame f

publicize /'pʌblɪsaɪz/ vt Reklame machen für

public: ~ **'library** n öffentliche Bücherei f. ~ **'school** n Privatschule f; (Amer) staatliche Schule f. ~-'spirited a be ~-spirited Gemeinsinn haben. ~ **'transport** n öffentliche Verkehrsmittel pl

publish /'pʌblɪʃ/ vt veröffentlichen. ~er n Verleger(in) m(f); (firm) Verlag m. ~ing n Verlagswesen nt

pucker /'pʌkə(r)/ vt kräuseln

pudding /'pʊdɪŋ/ n Pudding m; (course) Nachtisch m

puddle /'pʌdl/ n Pfütze f

puerile /'pjʊəraɪl/ a kindisch

puff /pʌf/ n (of wind) Hauch m; (of smoke) Wölkchen nt; (for powder) Quaste f ● vt blasen, pusten; ~ **out** ausstoßen. ● vi keuchen; ~ **at** paffen an (+ dat) ⟨pipe⟩. ~ed a (out of breath) aus der Puste. ~ **pastry** n Blätterteig m

puffy /'pʌfɪ/ a geschwollen

pugnacious /pʌg'neɪʃəs/ a, -ly adv aggressiv

pull /pʊl/ n Zug m; (jerk) Ruck m; (fam: influence) Einfluß m ● vt ziehen; ziehen an (+ dat) ⟨rope⟩; ~ **a muscle** sich ⟨dat⟩ einen Muskel zerren; ~ **oneself together** sich zusammennehmen; ~ **one's weight** tüchtig mitarbeiten; ~ **s.o.'s leg** (fam) jdn auf den Arm nehmen. ~ **down** vt herunterziehen; (demolish) abreißen. ~ **in** vt hereinziehen ● vi (Auto) einscheren. ~ **off** vt abziehen; (fam) schaffen. ~ **out** vt herausziehen ● vi (Auto) ausscheren. ~ **through** vt durchziehen ● vi (recover) durchkommen. ~ **up** vt heraufziehen; ausziehen ⟨plant⟩; (reprimand) zurechtweisen ● vi (Auto) anhalten

pulley /'pʊlɪ/ n (Techn) Rolle f

pullover /'pʊləʊvə(r)/ n Pullover m

pulp /pʌlp/ n Brei m; (of fruit) [Frucht]fleisch nt

pulpit /'pʊlpɪt/ n Kanzel f

pulsate /pʌl'seɪt/ vi pulsieren

pulse /pʌls/ n Puls m

pulses /'pʌlsɪz/ npl Hülsenfrüchte pl

pulverize /'pʌlvəraɪz/ vt pulverisieren

pumice /'pʌmɪs/ n Bimsstein m

pummel /'pʌml/ vt (pt/pp **pummelled**) mit den Fäusten bearbeiten

pump /pʌmp/ n Pumpe f ● vt pumpen; (fam) aushorchen. ~ **up** vt hochpumpen; (inflate) aufpumpen

pumpkin /'pʌmpkɪn/ n Kürbis m

pun /pʌn/ n Wortspiel nt

punch[1] /pʌntʃ/ n Faustschlag m; (device) Locher m ● vt boxen; lochen ⟨ticket⟩; stanzen ⟨hole⟩

punch[2] n (drink) Bowle f

punch: ~ **line** n Pointe f. ~-**up** n Schlägerei f

punctual /'pʌŋktjʊəl/ a, -ly adv pünktlich. ~ity /-'ælətɪ/ n Pünktlichkeit f

punctuat|e /'pʌŋktjʊeɪt/ vt mit Satzzeichen versehen. ~ion /-'eɪʃn/ n Interpunktion f. ~ion mark n Satzzeichen nt

puncture /'pʌŋktʃə(r)/ n Loch nt; (tyre) Reifenpanne f ● vt durchstechen

pundit /'pʌndɪt/ n Experte m

pungent /'pʌndʒənt/ a scharf

punish /'pʌnɪʃ/ vt bestrafen. ~**able** /-əbl/ a strafbar. ~**ment** n Strafe f

punitive /'pjuːnɪtɪv/ a Straf-

punnet /'pʌnɪt/ n Körbchen nt

punt /pʌnt/ n (boat) Stechkahn m

punter /'pʌntə(r)/ n (gambler) Wetter m; (client) Kunde m

puny /'pjuːnɪ/ a (-ier, -iest) mickerig

pup /pʌp/ n = **puppy**

pupil /'pjuːpl/ n Schüler(in) m(f); (of eye) Pupille f

puppet /'pʌpɪt/ n Puppe f; (fig) Marionette f

puppy /'pʌpɪ/ n junger Hund m

purchase /'pɜːtʃəs/ n Kauf m; (leverage) Hebelkraft f ● vt kaufen. ~r n Käufer m

pure /pjʊə(r)/ a (-r, -st), -ly adv rein

purée /'pjʊəreɪ/ n Püree nt, Brei m

purgatory /'pɜːgətrɪ/ n (Relig) Fegefeuer nt; (fig) Hölle f

purge /pɜːdʒ/ n (Pol) Säuberungsaktion f ● vt reinigen; (Pol) säubern

puri|fication /pjʊərɪfɪ'keɪʃn/ n Reinigung f. ~**fy** /'pjʊərɪfaɪ/ vt (pt/pp -ied) reinigen

puritanical /pjʊərɪˈtænɪkl/ a puritanisch

purity /ˈpjʊərɪtɪ/ n Reinheit f

purl /pɜːl/ n (Knitting) linke Masche f ● vt/i links stricken

purple /ˈpɜːpl/ a [dunkel]lila

purport /pəˈpɔːt/ vt vorgeben

purpose /ˈpɜːpəs/ n Zweck m; (intention) Absicht f; (determination) Entschlossenheit f; **on** ~ absichtlich; **to no** ~ unnützerweise. ~**ful** a, **-ly** adv entschlossen. ~**ly** adv absichtlich

purr /pɜː(r)/ vi schnurren

purse /pɜːs/ n Portemonnaie nt; (Amer: handbag) Handtasche f ● vt schürzen (lips)

pursue /pəˈsjuː/ vt verfolgen; (fig) nachgehen (+ dat). ~**r** /-ə(r)/ n Verfolger m

pursuit /pəˈsjuːt/ n Verfolgung f; Jagd f; (pastime) Beschäftigung f; **in** ~ hinterher

pus /pʌs/ n Eiter m

push /pʊʃ/ n Stoß m, (fam) Schubs m; **get the** ~ (fam) hinausfliegen ● vt/i schieben; (press) drücken; (roughly) stoßen; **be** ~**ed for time** (fam) unter Zeitdruck stehen. ~ **off** vt hinunterstoßen ● vi (fam: leave) abhauen. ~ **on** vi (continue) weitergehen/-fahren; (with activity) weitermachen. ~ **up** vt hochschieben; hochtreiben (price)

push: ~**-button** n Druckknopf m. ~**-chair** n [Kinder]sportwagen m. ~**-over** n (fam) Kinderspiel nt. ~**-up** n (Amer) Liegestütz m

pushy /ˈpʊʃɪ/ a (fam) aufdringlich

puss /pʊs/ n, **pussy** /ˈpʊsɪ/ n Mieze f

put /pʊt/ vt (pt/pp put, pres p putting) tun; (place) setzen; (upright) stellen; (flat) legen; (express) ausdrücken; (say) sagen; (estimate) schätzen (**at** auf + acc); ~ **aside** or **by** beiseite legen; ~ **one's foot down** (fam) energisch werden; (Auto) Gas geben ● vi ~ **to sea** auslaufen ● a **stay** ~ dableiben. ~ **away** vt wegräumen. ~ **back** vt wieder hinsetzen/-stellen/-legen; zurückstellen (clock). ~ **down** vt hinsetzen/-stellen/-legen; (suppress) niederschlagen; (kill) töten; (write) niederschreiben; (attribute) zuschreiben (**to** dat). ~ **forward** vt vorbringen; vorstellen (clock). ~ **in** vt hineinsetzen/-stellen/-legen; (insert) einstecken; (submit) einreichen ● vi ~ **in for** beantragen. ~

off vt ausmachen (light); (postpone) verschieben; ~ **s.o. off** jdn abbestellen; (disconcert) jdn aus der Fassung bringen; ~ **s.o. off sth** jdm etw verleiden. ~ **on** vt anziehen (clothes, brake); sich (dat) aufsetzen (hat); (Culin) aufsetzen; anmachen (light); aufführen (play); annehmen (accent); ~ **on weight** zunehmen. ~ **out** vt hinaussetzen/-stellen/-legen; ausmachen (fire, light); ausstrecken (hand); (disconcert) aus der Fassung bringen; ~ **s.o./oneself out** jdm/sich Umstände machen. ~ **through** vt durchstecken; (Teleph) verbinden (**to** mit). ~ **up** vt errichten (building); aufschlagen (tent); aufspannen (umbrella); anschlagen (notice); erhöhen (price); unterbringen (guest); ~ **s.o. up to sth** jdn zu etw anstiften ● vi (at hotel) absteigen in (+ dat); ~ **up with sth** (dat) etw bieten lassen

putrefy /ˈpjuːtrɪfaɪ/ vi (pt/pp -ied) verwesen

putrid /ˈpjuːtrɪd/ a faulig

putty /ˈpʌtɪ/ n Kitt m

put-up /ˈpʊtʌp/ a a ~ **job** ein abgekartetes Spiel nt

puzzl|e /ˈpʌzl/ n Rätsel nt; (jig-saw) Puzzlespiel nt ● vt **it** ~**es me** es ist mir rätselhaft ● vi ~**e over** sich (dat) den Kopf zerbrechen über (+ acc). ~**ing** a rätselhaft

pyjamas /pəˈdʒɑːməz/ npl Schlafanzug m

pylon /ˈpaɪlən/ n Mast m

pyramid /ˈpɪrəmɪd/ n Pyramide f

python /ˈpaɪθn/ n Pythonschlange f

Q

quack[1] /kwæk/ n Quaken nt ● vi quaken

quack[2] n (doctor) Quacksalber m

quad /kwɒd/ n (fam: court) Hof m; ~**s** pl = **quadruplets**

quadrangle /ˈkwɒdræŋgl/ n Viereck nt; (court) Hof m

quadruped /ˈkwɒdrʊped/ n Vierfüßer m

quadruple /ˈkwɒdrʊpl/ a vierfach ● vt vervierfachen ● vi sich vervierfachen. ~**ts** /-plɪts/ npl Vierlinge pl

quagmire /ˈkwɒgmaɪə(r)/ n Sumpf m

quaint /kweɪnt/ a (-er, -est) malerisch; (odd) putzig

quake /kweɪk/ n (fam) Erdbeben nt ● vi beben; (with fear) zittern

Quaker /'kweɪkə(r)/ n Quäker(in) m(f)

qualif|ication /ˌkwɒlɪfɪ'keɪʃn/ n Qualifikation f; (reservation) Einschränkung f. **~ied** /-faɪd/ a qualifiziert; (trained) ausgebildet; (limited) bedingt

qualify /'kwɒlɪfaɪ/ v (pt/pp -ied) ● vt qualifizieren; (entitle) berechtigen; (limit) einschränken ● vi sich qualifizieren

quality /'kwɒlətɪ/ n Qualität f; (characteristic) Eigenschaft f

qualm /kwɑːm/ n Bedenken pl

quandary /'kwɒndərɪ/ n Dilemma nt

quantity /'kwɒntətɪ/ n Quantität f, Menge f; **in ~** in großen Mengen

quarantine /'kwɒrəntiːn/ n Quarantäne f

quarrel /'kwɒrl/ n Streit m ● vi (pt/pp **quarrelled**) sich streiten. **~some** a streitsüchtig

quarry[1] /'kwɒrɪ/ n (prey) Beute f

quarry[2] n Steinbruch m

quart /kwɔːt/ n Quart nt

quarter /'kwɔːtə(r)/ n Viertel nt; (of year) Vierteljahr nt; (Amer) 25-Cent-Stück nt; **~s** pl Quartier nt; **at [a] ~ to six** um Viertel vor sechs; **from all ~s** aus allen Richtungen ● vt vierteln; (Mil) einquartieren (**on** bei). **~-'final** n Viertelfinale nt

quarterly /'kwɔːtəlɪ/ a & adv vierteljährlich

quartet /kwɔː'tet/ n Quartett nt

quartz /kwɔːts/ n Quarz m. **~ watch** n Quarzuhr f

quash /kwɒʃ/ vt aufheben; niederschlagen (rebellion)

quaver /'kweɪvə(r)/ n (Mus) Achtelnote f ● vi zittern

quay /kiː/ n Kai m

queasy /'kwiːzɪ/ a **I feel ~** mir ist übel

queen /kwiːn/ n Königin f; (Cards, Chess) Dame f

queer /kwɪə(r)/ a (-er, -est) eigenartig; (dubious) zweifelhaft; (ill) unwohl; (fam: homosexual) schwul ● n (fam) Schwule(r) m

quell /kwel/ vt unterdrücken

quench /kwentʃ/ vt löschen

query /'kwɪərɪ/ n Frage f; (question mark) Fragezeichen nt ● vt (pt/pp -ied) in Frage stellen; reklamieren (bill)

quest /kwest/ n Suche f (**for** nach)

question /'kwestʃn/ n Frage f; (for discussion) Thema nt; **out of the ~** ausgeschlossen; **without ~** ohne Frage; **the person in ~** die fragliche Person ● vt in Frage stellen; **~ s.o.** jdn ausfragen; (police:) jdn verhören. **~able** /-əbl/ a zweifelhaft. **~ mark** n Fragezeichen nt

questionnaire /kwestʃə'neə(r)/ n Fragebogen m

queue /kjuː/ n Schlange f ● vi **~ [up]** Schlange stehen, sich anstellen (**for** nach)

quibble /'kwɪbl/ vi Haarspalterei treiben

quick /kwɪk/ a (-er, -est), **-ly** adv schnell; **be ~!** mach schnell! **have a ~ meal** schnell etwas essen ● adv schnell ● n **cut to the ~** (fig) bis ins Mark getroffen. **~en** vt beschleunigen ● vi sich beschleunigen

quick: ~sand n Treibsand m. **~-tempered** a aufbrausend

quid /kwɪd/ n inv (fam) Pfund nt

quiet /'kwaɪət/ a (-er, -est), **-ly** adv still; (calm) ruhig; (soft) leise; **keep ~ about** (fam) nichts sagen von ● n Stille f; Ruhe f; **on the ~** heimlich

quiet|en /'kwaɪətn/ vt beruhigen ● vi **~en down** ruhig werden. **~ness** n (see quiet) Stille f; Ruhe f

quill /kwɪl/ n Feder f; (spine) Stachel m

quilt /kwɪlt/ n Steppdecke f. **~ed** a Stepp-

quince /kwɪns/ n Quitte f

quins /kwɪnz/ npl (fam) = **quintuplets**

quintet /kwɪn'tet/ n Quintett nt

quintuplets /'kwɪntjʊplɪts/ npl Fünflinge pl

quip /kwɪp/ n Scherz m ● vi (pt/pp **quipped**) scherzen

quirk /kwɜːk/ n Eigenart f

quit /kwɪt/ v (pt/pp **quitted** or quit) ● vt verlassen; (give up) aufgeben; **~ doing sth** aufhören, etw zu tun ● vi gehen; **give s.o. notice to ~** jdm die Wohnung kündigen

quite /kwaɪt/ adv ganz; (really) wirklich; **~ [so]!** genau! **~ a few** ziemlich viele

quits /kwɪts/ a quitt

quiver /'kwɪvə(r)/ vi zittern

quiz /kwɪz/ n Quiz nt ● vt (pt/pp **quizzed**) ausfragen. **~zical** a, **-ly** adv fragend

quorum /'kwɔːrəm/ n **have a** ~ beschlußfähig sein

quota /'kwəʊtə/ n Anteil m; (Comm) Kontingent nt

quotation /kwəʊ'teɪʃn/ n Zitat nt; (price) Kostenvoranschlag m; (of shares) Notierung f. ~ **marks** npl Anführungszeichen pl

quote /kwəʊt/ n (fam) = **quotation;** **in** ~**s** in Anführungszeichen ● vt/i zitieren

R

rabbi /'ræbaɪ/ n Rabbiner m; (title) Rabbi m

rabbit /'ræbɪt/ n Kaninchen nt

rabble /'ræbl/ n **the** ~ der Pöbel

rabid /'ræbɪd/ a fanatisch; ⟨animal⟩ tollwütig

rabies /'reɪbiːz/ n Tollwut f

race[1] /reɪs/ n Rasse f

race[2] n Rennen nt; (fig) Wettlauf m ● vi [am Rennen] teilnehmen; ⟨athlete, horse:⟩ laufen; (fam: rush) rasen ● vt um die Wette laufen mit; an einem Rennen teilnehmen lassen ⟨horse⟩

race: ~**course** n Rennbahn f. ~**horse** n Rennpferd nt. ~**track** n Rennbahn f

racial /'reɪʃl/ a, **-ly** adv rassisch; ⟨discrimination, minority⟩ Rassen-

racing /'reɪsɪŋ/ n Rennsport m; ⟨horse-⟩ Pferderennen nt. ~ **car** n Rennwagen m. ~ **driver** n Rennfahrer m

racis|m /'reɪsɪzm/ n Rassismus m. ~**t**/-ɪst/ a rassistisch ● n Rassist m

rack[1] /ræk/ n Ständer m; (for plates) Gestell nt ● vt ~ **one's brains** sich (dat) den Kopf zerbrechen

rack[2] n **go to** ~ **and ruin** verfallen; (fig) herunterkommen

racket[1] /'rækɪt/ n (Sport) Schläger m

racket[2] n (din) Krach m; (swindle) Schwindelgeschäft nt

racy /'reɪsɪ/ a (**-ier, -iest**) schwungvoll; (risqué) gewagt

radar /'reɪdɑː(r)/ n Radar m

radian|ce /'reɪdɪəns/ n Strahlen nt. ~**t** a, **-ly** adv strahlend

radiat|e /'reɪdɪeɪt/ vt ausstrahlen ● vi ⟨heat:⟩ ausgestrahlt werden; ⟨roads:⟩ strahlenförmig ausgehen. ~**ion** /-'eɪʃn/ n Strahlung f

radiator /'reɪdɪeɪtə(r)/ n Heizkörper m; (Auto) Kühler m

radical /'rædɪkl/ a, **-ly** adv radikal ● n Radikale(r) m/f

radio /'reɪdɪəʊ/ n Radio nt; **by** ~ über Funk ● vt funken ⟨message⟩

radio|'active a radioaktiv. ~**ac-'tivity** n Radioaktivität f

radiography /reɪdɪ'ɒgrəfɪ/ n Röntgenographie f

'radio ham n Hobbyfunker m

radio'therapy n Strahlenbehandlung f

radish /'rædɪʃ/ n Radieschen nt

radius /'reɪdɪəs/ n (pl **-dii** /-dɪaɪ/) Radius m, Halbmesser m

raffle /'ræfl/ n Tombola f ● vt verlosen

raft /rɑːft/ n Floß nt

rafter /'rɑːftə(r)/ n Dachsparren m

rag[1] /ræg/ n Lumpen m; (pej: newspaper) Käseblatt nt; **in** ~**s** in Lumpen

rag[2] vt (pt/pp **ragged**) (fam) aufziehen

rage /reɪdʒ/ n Wut f; **all the** ~ (fam) der letzte Schrei ● vi rasen; ⟨storm:⟩ toben

ragged /'rægɪd/ a zerlumpt; ⟨edge⟩ ausgefranst

raid /reɪd/ n Überfall m; (Mil) Angriff m; (police) Razzia f ● vt überfallen; (Mil) angreifen; ⟨police:⟩ eine Razzia durchführen in (+ dat); (break in) eindringen in (+ acc). ~**er** n Eindringling m; (of bank) Bankräuber m

rail /reɪl/ n Schiene f; (pole) Stange f; (hand~) Handlauf m; (Naut) Reling f; **by** ~ mit der Bahn

railings /'reɪlɪŋz/ npl Geländer nt

'railroad n (Amer) = **railway**

'railway n [Eisen]bahn f. ~**man** n Eisenbahner m. ~ **station** n Bahnhof m

rain /reɪn/ n Regen m ● vi regnen

rain: ~**bow** n Regenbogen m. ~**check** n (Amer) **take a** ~**check on** aufschieben. ~**coat** n Regenmantel m. ~**fall** n Niederschlag m

rainy /'reɪnɪ/ a (**-ier, -iest**) regnerisch

raise /reɪz/ n (Amer) Lohnerhöhung f ● vt erheben; (upright) aufrichten; (make higher) erhöhen; (lift) [hoch]heben; lüften ⟨hat⟩; [auf]ziehen ⟨children, animals⟩; aufwerfen ⟨question⟩; aufbringen ⟨money⟩

raisin /'reɪzn/ n Rosine f

rake /reɪk/ n Harke f, Rechen m ● vt harken, rechen. ~ **up** vt zusammenharken; (fam) wieder aufführen

'rake-off n (fam) Prozente pl

rally /'rælɪ/ n Versammlung f; (Auto) Rallye f; (Tennis) Ballwechsel m ● vt sammeln ● vi sich sammeln; (recover strength) sich erholen

ram /ræm/ n Schafbock m; (Astr) Widder m ● vt (pt/pp **rammed**) rammen

rambl|e /'ræmbl/ n Wanderung f ● vi wandern; (in speech) irrereden. **~er** n Wanderer m; (rose) Kletterrose f. **~ing** a weitschweifig; ⟨club⟩ Wander-

ramp /ræmp/ n Rampe f; (Aviat) Gangway f

rampage[1] /'ræmpeɪdʒ/ n **be/go on the ~** randalieren

rampage[2] /ræm'peɪdʒ/ vi randalieren

rampant /'ræmpənt/ a weit verbreitet; (in heraldry) aufgerichtet

rampart /'ræmpɑːt/ n Wall m

ramshackle /'ræmʃækl/ a baufällig

ran /ræn/ see **run**

ranch /rɑːntʃ/ n Ranch f

rancid /'rænsɪd/ a ranzig

rancour /'ræŋkə(r)/ n Groll m

random /'rændəm/ a willkürlich; **~ sample** eine Stichprobe ● n **at ~** aufs Geratewohl; ⟨choose⟩ willkürlich

randy /'rændɪ/ a (-ier, -iest) (fam) geil

rang /ræŋ/ see **ring**[2]

range /reɪndʒ/ n Serie f, Reihe f; (Comm) Auswahl f, Angebot nt (**of an** + dat); (of mountains) Kette f; (Mus) Umfang m; (distance) Reichweite f; (for shooting) Schießplatz m; (stove) Kohlenherd m; **at a ~ of** auf eine Entfernung von ● vi reichen; **~ from ... to** gehen von ... bis. **~r** n Aufseher m

rank[1] /ræŋk/ n (row) Reihe f; (Mil) Rang m; (social position) Stand m; **the ~ and file** die breite Masse; **the ~s** pl die gemeinen Soldaten ● vt/i einstufen; **~ among** zählen zu

rank[2] a (bad) übel; ⟨plants⟩ üppig; (fig) kraß

ransack /'rænsæk/ vt durchwühlen; (pillage) plündern

ransom /'rænsəm/ n Lösegeld nt; **hold s.o. to ~** Lösegeld für jdn fordern

rant /rænt/ vi rasen

rap /ræp/ n Klopfen nt; (blow) Schlag m ● v (pt/pp **rapped**) ● vt klopfen auf (+ acc) ● vi **~ at/on** klopfen an/auf (+ acc)

rape[1] /reɪp/ n (Bot) Raps m

rape[2] n Vergewaltigung f ● vt vergewaltigen

rapid /'ræpɪd/ a, **-ly** adv schnell. **~ity** /rə'pɪdətɪ/ n Schnelligkeit f

rapids /'ræpɪdz/ npl Stromschnellen pl

rapist /'reɪpɪst/ n Vergewaltiger m

rapport /ræ'pɔː(r)/ n [innerer] Kontakt m

rapt /ræpt/ a, **-ly** adv gespannt; ⟨look⟩ andächtig; **~ in** versunken in (+ acc)

raptur|e /'ræptʃə(r)/ n Entzücken nt. **~ous** /-rəs/ a, **-ly** adv begeistert

rare[1] /reə(r)/ a (**-r, -st**), **-ly** adv selten

rare[2] a (Culin) englisch gebraten

rarefied /'reərɪfaɪd/ a dünn

rarity /'reərətɪ/ n Seltenheit f

rascal /'rɑːskl/ n Schlingel m

rash[1] /ræʃ/ n (Med) Ausschlag m

rash[2] a (**-er, -est**), **-ly** adv voreilig

rasher /'ræʃə(r)/ n Speckscheibe f

rasp /rɑːsp/ n Raspel f

raspberry /'rɑːzbərɪ/ n Himbeere f

rat /ræt/ n Ratte f; (fam: person) Schuft m; **smell a ~** (fam) Lunte riechen

rate /reɪt/ n Rate f; (speed) Tempo nt; (of payment) Satz m; (of exchange) Kurs m; **~s** pl (taxes) ≈ Grundsteuer f; **at any ~** auf jeden Fall; **at this ~** auf diese Weise ● vt einschätzen; **~ among** zählen zu ● vi **~ as** gelten als

rather /'rɑːðə(r)/ adv lieber; (fairly) ziemlich; **~!** und ob!

rati|fication /rætɪfɪ'keɪʃn/ n Ratifizierung f. **~fy** /'rætɪfaɪ/ vt (pt/pp -ied) ratifizieren

rating /'reɪtɪŋ/ n Einschätzung f; (class) Klasse f; (sailor) [einfacher] Matrose m; **~s** pl (Radio, TV) ≈ Einschaltquote f

ratio /'reɪʃɪəʊ/ n Verhältnis nt

ration /'ræʃn/ n Ration f ● vt rationieren

rational /'ræʃənl/ a, **-ly** adv rational. **~ize** vt/i rationalisieren

'rat race n (fam) Konkurrenzkampf m

rattle /'rætl/ n Rasseln nt; (of china, glass) Klirren nt; (of windows) Klappern nt; (toy) Klapper f ● vi rasseln; klirren; klappern ● vt rasseln mit; (shake) schütteln. **~ off** vt herunterrasseln

'rattlesnake n Klapperschlange f

raucous /'rɔːkəs/ a rauh

ravage /'rævɪdʒ/ vt verwüsten, verheeren

rave /reɪv/ *vi* toben; ~ **about** schwärmen von

raven /'reɪvn/ *n* Rabe *m*

ravenous /'rævənəs/ *a* heißhungrig

ravine /rə'viːn/ *n* Schlucht *f*

raving /'reɪvɪŋ/ *a* ~ **mad** (*fam*) total verrückt

ravishing /'rævɪʃɪŋ/ *a* hinreißend

raw /rɔː/ *a* (**-er, -est**) roh; (*not processed*) Roh-; ⟨*skin*⟩ wund; ⟨*weather*⟩ naßkalt; (*inexperienced*) unerfahren; **get a ~ deal** (*fam*) schlecht wegkommen. ~ **ma'terials** *npl* Rohstoffe *pl*

ray /reɪ/ *n* Strahl *m*; ~ **of hope** Hoffnungsschimmer *m*

raze /reɪz/ *vt* ~ **to the ground** dem Erdboden gleichmachen

razor /'reɪzə(r)/ *n* Rasierapparat *m*. ~ **blade** *n* Rasierklinge *f*

re /riː/ *prep* betreffs (+ *gen*)

reach /riːtʃ/ *n* Reichweite *f*; (*of river*) Strecke *f*; **within/out of** ~ in/außer Reichweite; **within easy** ~ leicht erreichbar ● *vt* erreichen; (*arrive at*) ankommen in (+ *dat*); (~ *as far as*) reichen bis zu; kommen zu ⟨*decision, conclusion*⟩; (*pass*) reichen ● *vi* reichen (**to** bis zu); ~ **for** greifen nach; **I can't** ~ ich komme nicht daran

re'act /rɪ-/ *vi* reagieren (**to** auf + *acc*)

re'action /rɪ-/ *n* Reaktion *f*. ~**ary** *a* reaktionär

reactor /rɪ'æktə(r)/ *n* Reaktor *m*

read /riːd/ *vt/i* (*pt/pp* **read** /red/) lesen; (*aloud*) vorlesen (**to** *dat*); ⟨*Univ*⟩ studieren; ablesen ⟨*meter*⟩. ~ **out** *vt* vorlesen

readable /'riːdəbl/ *a* lesbar

reader /'riːdə(r)/ *n* Leser(in) *m(f)*; (*book*) Lesebuch *nt*

readi|ly /'redɪlɪ/ *adv* bereitwillig; (*easily*) leicht. ~**ness** *n* Bereitschaft *f*; **in** ~**ness** bereit

reading /'riːdɪŋ/ *n* Lesen *nt*; (*Pol, Relig*) Lesung *f*

rea'djust /riː-/ *vt* neu einstellen ● *vi* sich umstellen (**to** auf + *acc*)

ready /'redɪ/ *a* (**-ier, -iest**) fertig; (*willing*) bereit; (*quick*) schnell; **get** ~ sich fertigmachen; (*prepare to*) sich bereitmachen

ready: ~**-'made** *a* fertig. ~**-'money** *n* Bargeld *nt*. ~**-to-'wear** *a* Konfektions-

real /rɪəl/ *a* wirklich; (*genuine*) echt; (*actual*) eigentlich ● *adv* (*Amer, fam*) echt. ~ **estate** *n* Immobilien *pl*

realis|m /'rɪəlɪzm/ *n* Realismus *m*. ~**t** /-lɪst/ *n* Realist *m*. ~**tic** /-'lɪstɪk/ *a*, **-ally** *adv* realistisch

reality /rɪ'ælətɪ/ *n* Wirklichkeit *f*, Realität *f*

realization /rɪəlaɪ'zeɪʃn/ *n* Erkenntnis *f*

realize /'rɪəlaɪz/ *vt* einsehen; (*become aware*) gewahr werden; verwirklichen ⟨*hopes, plans*⟩; (*Comm*) realisieren; einbringen ⟨*price*⟩; **I didn't** ~ das wußte ich nicht

really /'rɪəlɪ/ *adv* wirklich; (*actually*) eigentlich

realm /relm/ *n* Reich *nt*

realtor /'riːəltə(r)/ *n* (*Amer*) Immobilienmakler *m*

reap /riːp/ *vt* ernten

reap'pear /riː-/ *vi* wiederkommen

rear[1] /rɪə(r)/ *a* Hinter-; (*Auto*) Heck- ● *n* **the** ~ der hintere Teil; **from the** ~ von hinten

rear[2] *vt* aufziehen ● *vi* ~ **[up]** ⟨*horse:*⟩ sich aufbäumen

'rear-light *n* Rücklicht *nt*

re'arm /riː-/ *vi* wieder aufrüsten

rear'range /riː-/ *vt* umstellen

rear-view 'mirror *n* (*Auto*) Rückspiegel *m*

reason /'riːzn/ *n* Grund *m*; (*good sense*) Vernunft *f*; (*ability to think*) Verstand *m*; **within** ~ in vernünftigen Grenzen ● *vi* argumentieren; ~ **with** vernünftig reden mit. ~**able** /-əbl/ *a* vernünftig; (*not expensive*) preiswert. ~**ably** /-əblɪ/ *adv* (*fairly*) ziemlich

reas'sur|ance /riː-/ *n* Beruhigung *f*; Versicherung *f*. ~**e** *vt* beruhigen; ~**e s.o. of sth** jdm etw ⟨*gen*⟩ versichern

rebate /'riːbeɪt/ *n* Rückzahlung *f*; (*discount*) Nachlaß *m*

rebel[1] /'rebl/ *n* Rebell *m*

rebel[2] /rɪ'bel/ *vi* (*pt/pp* **rebelled**) rebellieren. ~**lion** /-ɪən/ *n* Rebellion *f*. ~**lious** /-ɪəs/ *a* rebellisch

re'bound[1] /rɪ-/ *vi* abprallen

'rebound[2] /riː-/ *n* Rückprall *m*

rebuff /rɪ'bʌf/ *n* Abweisung *f* ● *vt* abweisen; eine Abfuhr erteilen (**s.o.** jdm)

re'build /riː-/ *vt* (*pt/pp* **-built**) wieder aufbauen; (*fig*) wiederaufbauen

rebuke /rɪ'bjuːk/ *n* Tadel *m* ● *vt* tadeln

rebuttal /rɪ'bʌtl/ *n* Widerlegung *f*

re'call /rɪ-/ n Erinnerung f; **beyond** ∼ unwiderruflich ● vt zurückrufen; abberufen ⟨diplomat⟩; vorzeitig einberufen ⟨parliament⟩; (remember) sich erinnern an (+ acc)

recant /rɪˈkænt/ vi widerrufen

recap /ˈriːkæp/ vt/i (fam) = **recapitulate**

recapitulate /riːkəˈpɪtjʊleɪt/ vt/i zusammenfassen; rekapitulieren

re'capture /riː-/ vt wieder gefangennehmen ⟨person⟩; wieder einfangen ⟨animal⟩

reced|e /rɪˈsiːd/ vi zurückgehen. ∼**ing** a ⟨forehead, chin⟩ fliehend; ∼**ing hair** Stirnglatze f

receipt /rɪˈsiːt/ n Quittung f; (receiving) Empfang m; ∼**s** pl (Comm) Einnahmen pl

receive /rɪˈsiːv/ vt erhalten, bekommen; empfangen ⟨guests⟩. ∼**r** n (Teleph) Hörer m; (Radio, TV) Empfänger m; (of stolen goods) Hehler m

recent /ˈriːsənt/ a kürzlich erfolgte(r,s). ∼**ly** adv in letzter Zeit; (the other day) kürzlich, vor kurzem

receptacle /rɪˈseptəkl/ n Behälter m

reception /rɪˈsepʃn/ n Empfang m; ∼ **[desk]** (in hotel) Rezeption f. ∼**ist** n Empfangsdame f

receptive /rɪˈseptɪv/ a aufnahmefähig; ∼ **to** empfänglich für

recess /rɪˈses/ n Nische f; (holiday) Ferien pl; (Amer, Sch) Pause f

recession /rɪˈseʃn/ n Rezession f

re'charge /riː-/ vt [wieder] aufladen

recipe /ˈresəpɪ/ n Rezept nt

recipient /rɪˈsɪpɪənt/ n Empfänger m

recipro|cal /rɪˈsɪprəkl/ a gegenseitig. ∼**cate** /-keɪt/ vt erwidern

recital /rɪˈsaɪtl/ n (of poetry, songs) Vortrag m; (on piano) Konzert nt

recite /rɪˈsaɪt/ vt aufsagen; (before audience) vortragen; (list) aufzählen

reckless /ˈreklɪs/ a, -ly adv leichtsinnig; (careless) rücksichtslos. ∼**ness** n Leichtsinn m; Rücksichtslosigkeit f

reckon /ˈrekən/ vt rechnen; (consider) glauben ● vi ∼ **on/with** rechnen mit

re'claim /rɪ-/ vt zurückfordern; zurückgewinnen ⟨land⟩

reclin|e /rɪˈklaɪn/ vi liegen. ∼**ing seat** n Liegesitz m

recluse /rɪˈkluːs/ n Einsiedler(in) m(f)

recognition /rekəgˈnɪʃn/ n Erkennen nt; (acknowledgement) Anerkennung f; **in** ∼ als Anerkennung (**of** gen); **be beyond** ∼ nicht wiederzuerkennen sein

recognize /ˈrekəgnaɪz/ vt erkennen; (know again) wiedererkennen; (acknowledge) anerkennen

re'coil /rɪ-/ vi zurückschnellen; (in fear) zurückschrecken

recollect /rekəˈlekt/ vt sich erinnern an (+ acc). ∼**ion** /-ekʃn/ n Erinnerung f

recommend /rekəˈmend/ vt empfehlen. ∼**ation** /-ˈdeɪʃn/ n Empfehlung f

recompense /ˈrekəmpens/ n Entschädigung f ● vt entschädigen

recon|cile /ˈrekənsaɪl/ vt versöhnen; ∼**cile oneself to** sich abfinden mit. ∼**ciliation** /-sɪlɪˈeɪʃn/ n Versöhnung f

recon'dition /riː-/ vt generalüberholen. ∼**ed engine** n Austauschmotor m

reconnaissance /rɪˈkɒnɪsns/ n (Mil) Aufklärung f

reconnoitre /rekəˈnɔɪtə(r)/ vi (pres p -tring) auf Erkundung ausgehen

recon'sider /riː-/ vt sich (dat) noch einmal überlegen

recon'struct /riː-/ vt wieder aufbauen; rekonstruieren ⟨crime⟩. ∼**ion** n Wiederaufbau m; Rekonstruktion f

record[1] /rɪˈkɔːd/ vt aufzeichnen; (register) registrieren; (on tape) aufnehmen

record[2] /ˈrekɔːd/ n Aufzeichnung f; (Jur) Protokoll nt; (Mus) [Schall]platte f; (Sport) Rekord m; ∼**s** pl Unterlagen pl; **keep a** ∼ **of** sich (dat) notieren; **off the** ∼ inoffiziell; **have a** [**criminal**] ∼ vorbestraft sein

recorder /rɪˈkɔːdə(r)/ n (Mus) Blockflöte f

recording /rɪˈkɔːdɪŋ/ n Aufzeichnung f, Aufnahme f

'record-player n Plattenspieler m

recount /rɪˈkaʊnt/ vt erzählen

re-'count[1] /riː-/ vt nachzählen

're-count[2] /riː-/ n (Pol) Nachzählung f

recoup /rɪˈkuːp/ vt wiedereinbringen; ausgleichen ⟨losses⟩

recourse /rɪˈkɔːs/ n **have** ∼ **to** Zuflucht nehmen zu

re-'cover /riː-/ vt neu beziehen

recover /rɪˈkʌvə(r)/ vt zurückbekommen; bergen ⟨wreck⟩ ● vi sich

erholen. **~y** *n* Wiedererlangung *f*;
Bergung *f*; (*of health*) Erholung *f*
recreation /rekrɪ'eɪʃn/ *n* Erholung
f; (*hobby*) Hobby *nt*. **~al** *a* Freizeit-;
be ~al erholsam sein
recrimination /rɪkrɪmɪ'neɪʃn/ *n* Ge-
genbeschuldigung *f*
recruit /rɪ'kruːt/ *n* (*Mil*) Rekrut *m*;
new ~ (*member*) neues Mitglied *nt*;
(*worker*) neuer Mitarbeiter *m* ● *vt* re-
krutieren; anwerben ⟨*staff*⟩. **~ment** *n*
Rekrutierung *f*; Anwerbung *f*
rectang|le /'rektæŋgl/ *n* Rechteck
nt. **~ular** /-'tæŋgjʊlə(r)/ *a* rechteckig
rectify /'rektɪfaɪ/ *vt* (*pt/pp* -ied) be-
richtigen
rector /'rektə(r)/ *n* Pfarrer *m*; (*Univ*)
Rektor *m*. **~y** *n* Pfarrhaus *nt*
recuperat|e /rɪ'kjuːpəreɪt/ *vi* sich
erholen. **~ion** /-'reɪʃn/ *n* Erholung *f*
recur /rɪ'kɜː(r)/ *vi* (*pt/pp* recurred)
sich wiederholen; (*illness:*) wieder-
kehren
recurren|ce /rɪ'kʌrəns/ *n* Wieder-
kehr *f*. **~t** *a* wiederkehrend
recycle /riː'saɪkl/ *vt* wieder-
verwerten. **~d paper** *n*
Umweltschutzpapier *nt*
red /red/ *a* (**redder, reddest**) rot ● *n*
Rot *nt*. **~'currant** *n* rote Johannisbeere *f*
redd|en /'redn/ *vt* röten ● *vi* rot
werden. **~ish** *a* rötlich
re'decorate /riː-/ *vt* renovieren;
(*paint*) neu streichen; (*wallpaper*)
neu tapezieren
redeem /rɪ'diːm/ *vt* einlösen; (*Relig*)
erlösen
redemption /rɪ'dempʃn/ *n* Erlösung *f*
rede'ploy /riː-/ *vt* an anderer Stelle
einsetzen
red: ~-haired *a* rothaarig. **~-
'handed** *a* **catch s.o. ~-handed** jdn
auf frischer Tat ertappen. **~ 'herring**
n falsche Spur *f*. **~-hot** *a* glühend
heiß. **R~ 'Indian** *n* Indianer(in)
m(f)
redi'rect /riː-/ *vt* nachsenden ⟨*letter*⟩; umleiten ⟨*traffic*⟩
red: ~ 'light *n* (*Auto*) rote Ampel *f*.
~ness *n* Röte *f*
re'do /riː-/ *vt* (*pt* -did, *pp* -done) noch
einmal machen
re'double /riː-/ *vt* verdoppeln
redress /rɪ'dres/ *n* Entschädigung *f*
● *vt* wiedergutmachen; wiederherstellen ⟨*balance*⟩

red 'tape *n* (*fam*) Bürokratie *f*
reduc|e /rɪ'djuːs/ *vt* verringern, ver-
mindern; (*in size*) verkleinern; er-
mäßigen (*costs*); herabsetzen ⟨*price,
goods*⟩; (*Culin*) einkochen lassen.
~tion /-'dʌkʃn/ *n* Verringerung *f*;
(*in price*) Ermäßigung *f*; (*in size*) Ver-
kleinerung *f*
redundan|cy /rɪ'dʌndənsɪ/ *n* Be-
schäftigungslosigkeit *f*; (*payment*)
Abfindung *f*. **~t** *a* überflüssig; **make
~t** entlassen; **be made ~t** be-
schäftigungslos werden
reed /riːd/ *n* [Schilf]rohr *nt*; **~s** *pl*
Schilf *nt*
reef /riːf/ *n* Riff *nt*
reek /riːk/ *vi* riechen (**of** nach)
reel /riːl/ *n* Rolle *f*, Spule *f* ● *vi* (*stagger*) taumeln ● *vt* **~ off** (*fig*) herunterrasseln
refectory /rɪ'fektərɪ/ *n* Refektorium
nt; (*Univ*) Mensa *f*
refer /rɪ'fɜː(r)/ *v* (*pt/pp* referred) ● *vt*
verweisen (**to** an + *acc*); übergeben,
weiterleiten ⟨*matter*⟩ (**to** an + *acc*) ● *vi*
~ to sich beziehen auf (+ *acc*); (*mention*) erwähnen; (*concern*) betreffen;
(*consult*) sich wenden an (+ *acc*);
nachschlagen in (+ *dat*) ⟨*book*⟩; **are
you ~ring to me?** meinen Sie mich?
referee /refə'riː/ *n* Schiedsrichter
m; (*Boxing*) Ringrichter *m*; (*for job*)
Referenz *f* ● *vt/i* (*pt/pp* refereed)
Schiedsrichter/Ringrichter sein (bei)
reference /'refərəns/ *n* Erwähnung
f; (*in book*) Verweis *m*; (*for job*) Referenz *f*; (*Comm*) **'your ~'** 'Ihr Zeichen';
with ~ to in bezug auf (+ *acc*); (*in letter*) unter Bezugnahme auf (+ *acc*);
make [a] ~ to erwähnen. **~ book** *n*
Nachschlagewerk *nt*. **~ number** *n*
Aktenzeichen *nt*
referendum /refə'rendəm/ *n* Volksabstimmung *f*
re'fill[1] /riː-/ *vt* nachfüllen
'refill[2] /riː-/ *n* (*for pen*) Ersatzmine *f*
refine /rɪ'faɪn/ *vt* raffinieren. **~d** *a*
fein, vornehm. **~ment** *n* Vor-
nehmheit *f*; (*Techn*) Verfeinerung *f*.
~ry /-ərɪ/ *n* Raffinerie *f*
reflect /rɪ'flekt/ *vt* reflektieren;
⟨*mirror:*⟩ [wider]spiegeln; **be ~ed in**
sich spiegeln in (+ *dat*) ● *vi* nachdenken (**on** über + *acc*); **~ badly upon
s.o.** (*fig*) jdn in ein schlechtes
Licht stellen. **~ion** /-ekʃn/ *n* Refle-
xion *f*; (*image*) Spiegelbild *nt*; **on
~ion** nach nochmaliger Überlegung.

~ive /-ɪv/ *a*, **-ly** *adv* nachdenklich.
~or *n* Rückstrahler *m*
reflex /'ri:fleks/ *n* Reflex *m* ● *attrib* Reflex-
reflexive /rɪ'fleksɪv/ *a* reflexiv
reform /rɪ'fɔ:m/ *n* Reform *f* ● *vt* reformieren ● *vi* sich bessern. **R~ation** /refə'meɪʃn/ *n* (*Relig*) Reformation *f*. ~er *n* Reformer *m*; (*Relig*) Reformator *m*
refract /rɪ'frækt/ *vt* (*Phys*) brechen
refrain[1] /rɪ'freɪn/ *n* Refrain *m*
refrain[2] *vi* ~ **from doing sth** etw nicht tun
refresh /rɪ'freʃ/ *vt* erfrischen. ~ing *a* erfrischend. ~ments *npl* Erfrischungen *pl*
refrigerat|e /rɪ'frɪdʒəreɪt/ *vt* kühlen. ~or *n* Kühlschrank *m*
re'fuel /ri:-/ *v* (*pt/pp* **-fuelled**) *vt/i* auftanken
refuge /'refju:dʒ/ *n* Zuflucht *f*; **take** ~ **in** Zuflucht nehmen in (+ *dat*)
refugee /refjʊ'dʒi:/ *n* Flüchtling *m*
'refund[1] /ri:-/ **get a** ~ sein Geld zurückbekommen
re'fund[2] /rɪ-/ *vt* zurückerstatten
refurbish /ri:'fɜ:bɪʃ/ *vt* renovieren
refusal /rɪ'fju:zl/ *n* (*see* **refuse**[1]) Ablehnung *f*; Weigerung *f*
refuse[1] /rɪ'fju:z/ *vt* ablehnen; (*not grant*) verweigern; ~ **to do sth** sich weigern, etw zu tun ● *vi* ablehnen; sich weigern
refuse[2] /'refju:s/ *n* Müll *m*, Abfall *m*. ~ **collection** *n* Müllabfuhr *f*
refute /rɪ'fju:t/ *vt* widerlegen
re'gain /rɪ-/ *vt* wiedergewinnen
regal /'ri:gl/ *a*, **-ly** *adv* königlich
regalia /rɪ'geɪlɪə/ *npl* Insignien *pl*
regard /rɪ'gɑ:d/ *n* (*heed*) Rücksicht *f*; (*respect*) Achtung *f*; ~s *pl* Grüße *pl*; **with** ~ **to** in bezug auf (+ *acc*) ● *vt* ansehen, betrachten (**as** als); **as** ~s in bezug auf (+ *acc*). ~ing *prep* bezüglich (+ *gen*). ~less *adv* ohne Rücksicht (**of** auf + *acc*)
regatta /rɪ'gætə/ *n* Regatta *f*
regenerate /rɪ'dʒenəreɪt/ *vt* regenerieren ● *vi* sich regenerieren
regime /reɪ'ʒi:m/ *n* Regime *nt*
regiment /'redʒɪmənt/ *n* Regiment *nt*. ~al /-'mentl/ *a* Regiments-. ~ation /-teɪʃn/ *n* Reglementierung *f*
region /'ri:dʒən/ *n* Region *f*; **in the** ~ **of** (*fig*) ungefähr. ~al *a*, **-ly** *adv* regional

register /'redʒɪstə(r)/ *n* Register *nt*; (*Sch*) Anwesenheitsliste *f* ● *vt* registrieren; (*report*) anmelden; einschreiben (*letter*); aufgeben (*luggage*) ● *vi* (*report*) sich anmelden; **it didn't** ~ (*fig*) ich habe es nicht registriert
registrar /redʒɪ'strɑ:(r)/ *n* Standesbeamte(r) *m*
registration /redʒɪ'streɪʃn/ *n* Registrierung *f*; Anmeldung *f*. ~ **number** *n* Autonummer *f*
registry office /'redʒɪstrɪ-/ *n* Standesamt *nt*
regret /rɪ'gret/ *n* Bedauern *nt* ● *vt* (*pt/pp* **regretted**) bedauern. ~fully *adv* mit Bedauern
regrettab|le /rɪ'gretəbl/ *a* bedauerlich. ~ly *adv* bedauerlicherweise
regular /'regjʊlə(r)/ *a*, **-ly** *adv* regelmäßig; (*usual*) üblich; (*Mil*) Berufs- ● *n* Berufssoldat *m*; (*in pub*) Stammgast *m*; (*in shop*) Stammkunde *m*. ~ity /-'lærətɪ/ *n* Regelmäßigkeit *f*
regulat|e /'regjʊleɪt/ *vt* regulieren. ~ion /-'leɪʃn/ *n* (*rule*) Vorschrift *f*
rehabilitat|e /ri:hə'bɪlɪteɪt/ *vt* rehabilitieren. ~ion /-'teɪʃn/ *n* Rehabilitation *f*
rehears|al /rɪ'hɜ:sl/ *n* (*Theat*) Probe *f*. ~e *vt* proben
reign /reɪn/ *n* Herrschaft *f* ● *vi* herrschen, regieren
reimburse /ri:ɪm'bɜ:s/ *vt* ~ **s.o. for sth** jdm etw zurückerstatten
rein /reɪn/ *n* Zügel *m*
reincarnation /ri:ɪnkɑ:'neɪʃn/ *n* Reinkarnation *f*, Wiedergeburt *f*
reindeer /'reɪndɪə(r)/ *n inv* Rentier *nt*
reinforce /ri:ɪn'fɔ:s/ *vt* verstärken. ~d **'concrete** *n* Stahlbeton *m*. ~ment *n* Verstärkung *f*; **send** ~ments Verstärkung schicken
reinstate /ri:ɪn'steɪt/ *vt* wiedereinstellen; (*to office*) wiedereinsetzen
reiterate /ri:'ɪtəreɪt/ *vt* wiederholen
reject /rɪ'dʒekt/ *vt* ablehnen. ~ion /-ekʃn/ *n* Ablehnung *f*
rejects /'ri:dʒekts/ *npl* (*Comm*) Ausschußware *f*
rejoic|e /rɪ'dʒɔɪs/ *vi* (*liter*) sich freuen. ~ing *n* Freude *f*
re'join /rɪ-/ *vt* sich wieder anschließen (+ *dat*); wieder beitreten (+ *dat*) (*club, party*); (*answer*) erwidern

rejuvenate /rɪ'dʒu:vəneɪt/ vt verjüngen

relapse /rɪ'læps/ n Rückfall m ● vi einen Rückfall erleiden

relate /rɪ'leɪt/ vt (tell) erzählen; (connect) verbinden ● vi zusammenhängen (to mit). ~d a verwandt (to mit)

relation /rɪ'leɪʃn/ n Beziehung f; (person) Verwandte(r) m/f. ~ship n Beziehung f; (link) Verbindung f; (blood tie) Verwandtschaft f; (affair) Verhältnis nt

relative /'relətɪv/ n Verwandte(r) m/ f ● a relativ; (Gram) Relativ-. ~ly adv relativ, verhältnismäßig

relax /rɪ'læks/ vt lockern, entspannen ● vi sich lockern, sich entspannen. ~ation /-'seɪʃn/ n Entspannung f. ~ing a entspannend

relay[1] /'ri:'leɪ/ vt (pt/pp -layed) weitergeben; (Radio, TV) übertragen

relay[2] /'ri:leɪ/ n (Electr) Relais nt; work in ~s sich bei der Arbeit ablösen. ~ [race] n Staffel f

release /rɪ'li:s/ n Freilassung f, Entlassung f; (Techn) Auslöser m ● vt freilassen; (let go of) loslassen; (Techn) auslösen; veröffentlichen (information)

relegate /'relɪgeɪt/ vt verbannen; be ~d (Sport) absteigen

relent /rɪ'lent/ vi nachgeben. ~less a, -ly adv erbarmungslos; (unceasing) unaufhörlich

relevan|ce /'reləvəns/ n Relevanz f. ~t a relevant (to für)

reliab|ility /rɪlaɪə'bɪlətɪ/ n Zuverlässigkeit f. ~le /-'laɪəbl/ a, -ly adv zuverlässig

relian|ce /rɪ'laɪəns/ n Abhängigkeit f (on von). ~t a angewiesen (on auf + acc)

relic /'relɪk/ n Überbleibsel nt; (Relig) Reliquie f

relief /rɪ'li:f/ n Erleichterung f; (assistance) Hilfe f; (distraction) Abwechslung f; (replacement) Ablösung f; (Art) Relief nt; in ~ im Relief. ~ map n Reliefkarte f. ~ train n Entlastungszug m

relieve /rɪ'li:v/ vt erleichtern; (take over from) ablösen; ~ of entlasten von

religion /rɪ'lɪdʒən/ n Religion f

religious /rɪ'lɪdʒəs/ a religiös. ~ly adv (conscientiously) gewissenhaft

relinquish /rɪ'lɪŋkwɪʃ/ vt loslassen; (give up) aufgeben

relish /'relɪʃ/ n Genuß m; (Culin) Würze f ● vt genießen

relo'cate /ri:-/ vt verlegen

reluctan|ce /rɪ'lʌktəns/ n Widerstreben nt. ~t a widerstrebend; be ~t zögern (to zu). ~tly adv ungern, widerstrebend

rely /rɪ'laɪ/ vi (pt/pp -ied) ~ on sich verlassen auf (+ acc); (be dependent on) angewiesen sein auf (+ acc)

remain /rɪ'meɪn/ vi bleiben; (be left) übrigbleiben. ~der n Rest m. ~ing a restlich. ~s npl Reste pl; [mortal] ~s [sterbliche] Überreste pl

remand /rɪ'mɑ:nd/ n on ~ in Untersuchungshaft ● vt ~ in custody in Untersuchungshaft schicken

remark /rɪ'mɑ:k/ n Bemerkung f ● vt bemerken. ~able /-əbl/ a, -bly adv bemerkenswert

re'marry /ri:-/ vi wieder heiraten

remedial /rɪ'mi:dɪəl/ a Hilfs-; (Med) Heil-

remedy /'remədɪ/ n [Heil]mittel nt (for gegen); (fig) Abhilfe f ● vt (pt/pp -ied) abhelfen (+ dat); beheben (fault)

rememb|er /rɪ'membə(r)/ vt sich erinnern an (+ acc); ~er to do sth daran denken, etw zu tun; ~er me to him grüßen Sie ihn von mir ● vi sich erinnern. ~rance n Erinnerung f

remind /rɪ'maɪnd/ vt erinnern (of an + acc). ~er n Andenken nt; (letter, warning) Mahnung f

reminisce /remɪ'nɪs/ vi sich seinen Erinnerungen hingeben. ~nces /-ənsɪs/ npl Erinnerungen pl. ~nt a be ~nt of erinnern an (+ acc)

remiss /rɪ'mɪs/ a nachlässig

remission /rɪ'mɪʃn/ n Nachlaß m; (of sentence) [Straf]erlaß m; (Med) Remission f

remit /rɪ'mɪt/ vt (pt/pp remitted) überweisen (money). ~tance n Überweisung f

remnant /'remnənt/ n Rest m

remonstrate /'remənstreɪt/ vi protestieren; ~ with s.o. jdm Vorhaltungen machen

remorse /rɪ'mɔ:s/ n Reue f. ~ful a, -ly adv reumütig. ~less a, -ly adv unerbittlich

remote /rɪ'məʊt/ a fern; (isolated) abgelegen; (slight) gering. ~ con'trol n Fernsteuerung f; (for TV) Fernbedienung f. ~-con'trolled a ferngesteuert; fernbedient

remotely /rɪ'məʊtlɪ/ *adv* entfernt; **not** ~ nicht im entferntesten

re'movable /rɪ-/ *a* abnehmbar

removal /rɪ'muːvl/ *n* Entfernung *f*; *(from house)* Umzug *m.* ~ **van** *n* Möbelwagen *m*

remove /rɪ'muːv/ *vt* entfernen; *(take off)* abnehmen; *(take out)* herausnehmen

remunerat|e /rɪ'mjuːnəreɪt/ *vt* bezahlen. ~**ion** /-'reɪʃn/ *n* Bezahlung *f*. ~**ive** /-ətɪv/ *a* einträglich

render /'rendə(r)/ *vt* machen; erweisen *(service)*; *(translate)* wiedergeben; *(Mus)* vortragen

renegade /'renɪgeɪd/ *n* Abtrünnige(r) *m/f*

renew /rɪ'njuː/ *vt* erneuern; verlängern *(contract)*. ~**al** *n* Erneuerung *f*; Verlängerung *f*

renounce /rɪ'naʊns/ *vt* verzichten auf *(+ acc)*; *(Relig)* abschwören *(+ dat)*

renovat|e /'renəveɪt/ *vt* renovieren. ~**ion** /-'veɪʃn/ *n* Renovierung *f*

renown /rɪ'naʊn/ *n* Ruf *m.* ~**ed** *a* berühmt

rent /rent/ *n* Miete *f* ● *vt* mieten; *(hire)* leihen; ~ **[out]** vermieten; verleihen. ~**al** *n* Mietgebühr *f*; Leihgebühr *f*

renunciation /rɪnʌnsɪ'eɪʃn/ *n* Verzicht *m*

re'open /riː-/ *vt/i* wieder aufmachen

re'organize /riː-/ *vt* reorganisieren

rep /rep/ *n* *(fam)* Vertreter *m*

repair /rɪ'peə(r)/ *n* Reparatur *f*; **in good/bad** ~ in gutem/schlechtem Zustand ● *vt* reparieren

repartee /repɑː'tiː/ *n* **piece of** ~ schlagfertige Antwort *f*

repatriat|e /riː'pætrɪeɪt/ *vt* repatriieren. ~**ion** /-'eɪʃn/ *n* Repatriierung *f*

re'pay /riː-/ *vt* (*pt/pp* **-paid**) zurückzahlen; ~ **s.o. for sth** jdm etw zurückzahlen. ~**ment** *n* Rückzahlung *f*

repeal /rɪ'piːl/ *n* Aufhebung *f* ● *vt* aufheben

repeat /rɪ'piːt/ *n* Wiederholung *f* ● *vt/i* wiederholen; ~ **after me** sprechen Sie mir nach. ~**ed** *a*, **-ly** *adv* wiederholt

repel /rɪ'pel/ *vt* (*pt/pp* **repelled**) abwehren; *(fig)* abstoßen. ~**lent** *a* abstoßend

repent /rɪ'pent/ *vi* Reue zeigen. ~**ance** *n* Reue *f*. ~**ant** *a* reuig

repercussions /riːpə'kʌʃnz/ *npl* Auswirkungen *pl*

repertoire /'repətwɑː(r)/ *n* Repertoire *nt*

repertory /'repətrɪ/ *n* Repertoire *nt*

repetit|ion /repɪ'tɪʃn/ *n* Wiederholung *f*. ~**ive** /rɪ'petɪtɪv/ *a* eintönig

re'place /rɪ-/ *vt* zurücktun; *(take the place of)* ersetzen; *(exchange)* austauschen, auswechseln. ~**ment** *n* Ersatz *m.* ~**ment part** *n* Ersatzteil *nt*

'replay /riː-/ *n* *(Sport)* Wiederholungsspiel *nt*; **[action]** ~ Wiederholung *f*

replenish /rɪ'plenɪʃ/ *vt* auffüllen *(stocks)*; *(refill)* nachfüllen

replete /rɪ'pliːt/ *a* gesättigt

replica /'replɪkə/ *n* Nachbildung *f*

reply /rɪ'plaɪ/ *n* Antwort *f* (**to** auf *+ acc*) ● *vt/i* (*pt/pp* **replied**) antworten

report /rɪ'pɔːt/ *n* Bericht *m*; *(Sch)* Zeugnis *nt*; *(rumour)* Gerücht *nt*; *(of gun)* Knall *m* ● *vt* berichten; *(notify)* melden; ~ **s.o. to the police** jdn anzeigen ● *vi* berichten (**on** über *+ acc*); *(present oneself)* sich melden (**to** bei). ~**er** *n* Reporter(in) *m(f)*

repose /rɪ'pəʊz/ *n* Ruhe *f*

repos'sess /riː-/ *vt* wieder in Besitz nehmen

reprehensible /reprɪ'hensəbl/ *a* tadelnswert

represent /reprɪ'zent/ *vt* darstellen; *(act for)* vertreten, repräsentieren. ~**ation** /-'teɪʃn/ *n* Darstellung *f*; **make** ~**ations** to vorstellig werden bei

representative /reprɪ'zentətɪv/ *a* repräsentativ (**of** für) ● *n* Bevollmächtigte(r) *m/f*; *(Comm)* Vertreter(in) *m(f)*; *(Amer, Pol)* Abgeordnete(r) *m/f*

repress /rɪ'pres/ *vt* unterdrücken. ~**ion** /-eʃn/ *n* Unterdrückung *f*. ~**ive** /-ɪv/ *a* repressiv

reprieve /rɪ'priːv/ *n* Begnadigung *f*; *(postponement)* Strafaufschub *m*; *(fig)* Gnadenfrist *f* ● *vt* begnadigen

reprimand /'reprɪmɑːnd/ *n* Tadel *m* ● *vt* tadeln

'reprint[1] /riː-/ *n* Nachdruck *m*

re'print[2] /riː-/ *vt* neu auflegen

reprisal /rɪ'praɪzl/ *n* Vergeltungsmaßnahme *f*

reproach /rɪˈprəʊtʃ/ n Vorwurf m
● vt Vorwürfe pl machen (+ dat).
~ful a, -ly adv vorwurfsvoll

repro'duc|e /riː-/ vt wiedergeben,
reproduzieren ● vi sich fortpflanzen.
~tion /-ˈdʌkʃn/ n Reproduktion f;
(Biol) Fortpflanzung f. ~tion furniture n Stilmöbel pl. ~tive
/-ˈdʌktɪv/ a Fortpflanzungs-

reprove /rɪˈpruːv/ vt tadeln

reptile /ˈreptaɪl/ n Reptil nt

republic /rɪˈpʌblɪk/ n Republik f.
~an a republikanisch ● n Re-
publikaner(in) m(f)

repudiate /rɪˈpjuːdɪeɪt/ vt zurückweisen

repugnan|ce /rɪˈpʌgnəns/ n Wider-
wille m. ~t a widerlich

repuls|e /rɪˈpʌls/ vt abwehren; (fig)
abweisen. ~ion /-ˈʌlʃn/ n Widerwille
m. ~ive /-ɪv/ a abstoßend, widerlich

reputable /ˈrepjʊtəbl/ a (firm) von
gutem Ruf; (respectable) anständig

reputation /repjʊˈteɪʃn/ n Ruf m

repute /rɪˈpjuːt/ n Ruf m. ~d /-ɪd/ a,
-ly adv angeblich

request /rɪˈkwest/ n Bitte f ● vt
bitten. ~ stop n Bedarfshaltestelle f

require /rɪˈkwaɪə(r)/ vt (need) brauchen; (demand) erfordern; be ~d to
do sth etw tun müssen. ~ment n Bedürfnis nt; (condition) Erfordernis nt

requisite /ˈrekwɪzɪt/ a erforderlich
● n toilet/travel ~s pl Toiletten-/
Reiseartikel pl

requisition /rekwɪˈzɪʃn/ n ~ [order]
Anforderung f ● vt anfordern

re'sale /riː-/ n Weiterverkauf m

rescind /rɪˈsɪnd/ vt aufheben

rescue /ˈreskjuː/ n Rettung f ● vt
retten. ~r n Retter m

research /rɪˈsɜːtʃ/ n Forschung f ● vt
erforschen; (Journ) recherchieren
● vi ~ into erforschen. ~er n Forscher m; (Journ) Rechercheur m

resem|blance /rɪˈzembləns/ n Ähn-
lichkeit f. ~ble /-bl/ vt ähneln
(+ dat)

resent /rɪˈzent/ vt übelnehmen;
einen Groll hegen gegen (person).
~ful a, -ly adv verbittert. ~ment n
Groll m

reservation /rezəˈveɪʃn/ n Reservie-
rung f; (doubt) Vorbehalt m; (enclosure) Reservat nt

reserve /rɪˈzɜːv/ n Reserve f; (for
animals) Reservat nt; (Sport) Re-
servespieler(in) m(f) ● vt reservieren; (client:) reservieren lassen;

(keep) aufheben; sich (dat) vor-
behalten (right). ~d a reserviert

reservoir /ˈrezəvwɑː(r)/ n Reservoir
nt

re'shape /riː-/ vt umformen

re'shuffle /riː-/ n (Pol) Umbildung f
● vt (Pol) umbilden

reside /rɪˈzaɪd/ vi wohnen

residence /ˈrezɪdəns/ n Wohnsitz m;
(official) Residenz f; (stay) Aufenthalt m. ~ permit n Aufent-
haltsgenehmigung f

resident /ˈrezɪdənt/ a ansässig (in in
+ dat); (housekeeper, nurse) im Haus
wohnend ● n Bewohner(in) m(f); (of
street) Anwohner m. ~ial /-ˈdenʃl/ a
Wohn-

residue /ˈrezɪdjuː/ n Rest m; (Chem)
Rückstand m

resign /rɪˈzaɪn/ vt ~ oneself to sich
abfinden mit ● vi kündigen; (from
public office) zurücktreten. ~ation
/rezɪgˈneɪʃn/ n Resignation f; (from
job) Kündigung f; Rücktritt m. ~ed
a, -ly adv resigniert

resilient /rɪˈzɪlɪənt/ a federnd; (fig)
widerstandsfähig

resin /ˈrezɪn/ n Harz nt

resist /rɪˈzɪst/ vt/i sich widersetzen
(+ dat); (fig) widerstehen (+ dat).
~ance n Widerstand m. ~ant a
widerstandsfähig

resolut|e /ˈrezəluːt/ a, -ly adv ent-
schlossen. ~ion /-ˈluːʃn/ n Entschlossenheit f; (intention) Vorsatz
m; (Pol) Resolution f

resolve /rɪˈzɒlv/ n Entschlossenheit
f; (decision) Beschluß m ● vt
beschließen; (solve) lösen. ~d a entschlossen

resonan|ce /ˈrezənəns/ n Resonanz
f. ~t a klangvoll

resort /rɪˈzɔːt/ n (place) Urlaubsort
m; as a last ~ wenn alles andere
fehlschlägt ● vi ~ to (fig) greifen zu

resound /rɪˈzaʊnd/ vi widerhallen.
~ing a widerhallend; (loud) laut;
(notable) groß

resource /rɪˈsɔːs/ n ~s pl Ressourcen
pl. ~ful a findig. ~fulness n Fin-
digkeit f

respect /rɪˈspekt/ n Respekt m, Achtung f (for vor + dat); (aspect) Hinsicht f; with ~ to in bezug auf (+ acc)
● vt respektieren, achten

respectability /rɪspektəˈbɪlətɪ/ n
(see respectable) Ehrbarkeit f; An-
ständigkeit f

respect|able /rɪ'spektəbl/ *a*, **-bly** *adv* ehrbar; (*decent*) anständig; (*considerable*) ansehnlich. ~**ful** *a*, **-ly** *adv* respektvoll

respective /rɪ'spektɪv/ *a* jeweilig. ~**ly** *adv* beziehungsweise

respiration /respə'reɪʃn/ *n* Atmung *f*

respite /'respaɪt/ *n* [Ruhe]pause *f*; (*delay*) Aufschub *m*

resplendent /rɪ'splendənt/ *a* glänzend

respond /rɪ'spɒnd/ *vi* antworten; (*react*) reagieren (**to** auf +*acc*); (*patient:*) ansprechen (**to** auf +*acc*)

response /rɪ'spɒns/ *n* Antwort *f*; Reaktion *f*

responsibility /rɪspɒnsɪ'bɪlətɪ/ *n* Verantwortung *f*; (*duty*) Verpflichtung *f*

responsib|le /rɪ'spɒnsəbl/ *a* verantwortlich; (*trustworthy*) verantwortungsvoll. ~**ly** *adv* verantwortungsbewußt

responsive /rɪ'spɒnsɪv/ *a* **be** ~ reagieren

rest[1] /rest/ *n* Ruhe *f*; (*holiday*) Erholung *f*; (*interval & Mus*) Pause *f*; **have a** ~ eine Pause machen; (*rest*) sich ausruhen ● *vt* ausruhen; (*lean*) lehnen (**on** an/auf +*acc*) ● *vi* ruhen; (*have a rest*) sich ausruhen

rest[2] *n* **the** ~ der Rest; (*people*) die Übrigen *pl* ● *vi* **it** ~**s with you** es ist an Ihnen (**to** zu)

restaurant /'restərɒnt/ *n* Restaurant *nt*, Gaststätte *f*. ~ **car** *n* Speisewagen *m*

restful /'restfl/ *a* erholsam

restitution /restɪ'tjuːʃn/ *n* Entschädigung *f*; (*return*) Rückgabe *f*

restive /'restɪv/ *a* unruhig

restless /'restlɪs/ *a*, **-ly** *adv* unruhig

restoration /restə'reɪʃn/ *n* (*of building*) Restaurierung *f*

restore /rɪ'stɔː(r)/ *vt* wiederherstellen; restaurieren (*building*); (*give back*) zurückgeben

restrain /rɪ'streɪn/ *vt* zurückhalten; ~ **oneself** sich beherrschen. ~**ed** *a* zurückhaltend. ~**t** *n* Zurückhaltung *f*

restrict /rɪ'strɪkt/ *vt* einschränken; ~ **to** beschränken auf (+*acc*). ~**ion** /-ɪkʃn/ *n* Einschränkung *f*; Beschränkung *f*. ~**ive** /-ɪv/ *a* einschränkend

'rest room *n* (*Amer*) Toilette *f*

result /rɪ'zʌlt/ *n* Ergebnis *nt*, Resultat *nt*; (*consequence*) Folge *f*; **as a** ~ als Folge (**of** *gen*) ● *vi* sich ergeben (**from** aus); ~ **in** enden in (+*dat*); (*lead to*) führen zu

resume /rɪ'zjuːm/ *vt* wiederaufnehmen; wieder einnehmen (*seat*) ● *vi* wieder beginnen

résumé /'rezʊmeɪ/ *n* Zusammenfassung *f*

resumption /rɪ'zʌmpʃn/ *n* Wiederaufnahme *f*

resurgence /rɪ'sɜːdʒəns/ *n* Wiederaufleben *nt*

resurrect /rezə'rekt/ *vt* (*fig*) wiederbeleben. ~**ion** /-ekʃn/ *n* **the R~ion** (*Relig*) die Auferstehung

resuscitat|e /rɪ'sʌsɪteɪt/ *vt* wiederbeleben. ~**ion** /-'teɪʃn/ *n* Wiederbelebung *f*

retail /'riːteɪl/ *n* Einzelhandel *m* ● *a* Einzelhandels- ● *adv* im Einzelhandel ● *vt* im Einzelhandel verkaufen ● *vi* ~ **at** im Einzelhandel kosten. ~**er** *n* Einzelhändler *m*. ~ **price** *n* Ladenpreis *m*

retain /rɪ'teɪn/ *vt* behalten

retaliat|e /rɪ'tælɪeɪt/ *vi* zurückschlagen. ~**ion** /-'eɪʃn/ *n* Vergeltung *f*; **in** ~**ion** als Vergeltung

retarded /rɪ'tɑːdɪd/ *a* zurückgeblieben

retentive /rɪ'tentɪv/ *a* (*memory*) gut

reticen|ce /'retɪsns/ *n* Zurückhaltung *f*. ~**t** *a* zurückhaltend

retina /'retɪnə/ *n* Netzhaut *f*

retinue /'retɪnjuː/ *n* Gefolge *nt*

retire /rɪ'taɪə(r)/ *vi* in den Ruhestand treten; (*withdraw*) sich zurückziehen. ~**d** *a* im Ruhestand. ~**ment** *n* Ruhestand *m*; **since my** ~**ment** seit ich nicht mehr arbeite

retiring /rɪ'taɪərɪŋ/ *a* zurückhaltend

retort /rɪ'tɔːt/ *n* scharfe Erwiderung *f*; (*Chem*) Retorte *f* ● *vt* scharf erwidern

re'touch /riː-/ *vt* (*Phot*) retuschieren

re'trace /rɪ-/ *vt* zurückverfolgen; ~ **one's steps** denselben Weg zurückgehen

retract /rɪ'trækt/ *vt* einziehen; zurücknehmen (*remark*) ● *vi* widerrufen

re'train /riː-/ *vt* umschulen ● *vi* umgeschult werden

retreat /rɪ'triːt/ *n* Rückzug *m*; (*place*) Zufluchtsort *m* ● *vi* sich zurückziehen

re'trial /riː-/ n Wiederaufnahme-verfahren nt

retribution /retrɪ'bjuː.ʃn/ n Vergel-tung f

retrieve /rɪ'triːv/ vt zurückholen; (from wreckage) bergen; (Computing) wiederauffinden; ⟨dog:⟩ ap-portieren

retrograde /'retrəgreɪd/ a rück-schrittlich

retrospect /'retrəspekt/ n in ~ rück-blickend. ~ive /-ɪv/ a, -ly adv rück-wirkend; (looking back) rückblickend

return /rɪ'tɜːn/ n Rückkehr f; (giving back) Rückgabe f; (Comm) Ertrag m; (ticket) Rückfahrkarte f; (Aviat) Rückflugschein m; by ~ [of post] postwendend; in ~ dafür; in ~ for für; many happy ~s! herzlichen Glück-wunsch zum Geburtstag! ● vi zurück-gehen/-fahren; (come back) zurückkommen ● vt zurückgeben; (put back) zurückstellen/-legen; (send back) zurückschicken; (elect) wählen

return: ~ **flight** n Rückflug m. ~ **match** n Rückspiel nt. ~ **ticket** n Rückfahrkarte f; (Aviat) Rückflug-schein m

reunion /riː'juːnɪən/ n Wieder-vereinigung f; (social gathering) Treffen nt

reunite /riːjuː'naɪt/ vt wieder-vereinigen ● vi sich wieder-vereinigen

re'us|able /riː-/ a wieder-verwendbar. ~e vt wieder-verwenden

rev /rev/ n (Auto, fam) Umdrehung f ● vt/i ~ [up] den Motor auf Touren bringen

reveal /rɪ'viːl/ vt zum Vorschein bringen; (fig) enthüllen. ~ing a (fig) aufschlußreich

revel /'revl/ vi (pt/pp revelled) ~ in sth etw genießen

revelation /revə'leɪʃn/ n Offen-barung f, Enthüllung f

revelry /'revlrɪ/ n Lustbarkeit f

revenge /rɪ'vendʒ/ n Rache f; (fig & Sport) Revanche f ● vt rächen

revenue /'revənjuː/ n [Staats]-einnahmen pl

reverberate /rɪ'vɜːbəreɪt/ vi nach-hallen

revere /rɪ'vɪə(r)/ vt verehren. ~nce /'revərəns/ n Ehrfurcht f

Reverend /'revərənd/ a the ~ X Pfarrer X; (Catholic) Hochwürden X

reverent /'revərənt/ a, -ly adv ehrfürchtig

reverie /'revərɪ/ n Träumerei f

revers /rɪ'vɪə/ n (pl revers /-z/) Re-vers nt

reversal /rɪ'vɜːsl/ n Umkehrung f

reverse /rɪ'vɜːs/ a umgekehrt ● n Ge-genteil nt; (back) Rückseite f; (Auto) Rückwärtsgang m ● vt umkehren; (Auto) zurücksetzen; ~ the charges (Teleph) ein R-Gespräch führen ● vi zurücksetzen

revert /rɪ'vɜːt/ vi ~ to zurückfallen an (+ acc); zurückkommen auf (+ acc) ⟨topic⟩

review /rɪ'vjuː/ n Rückblick m (of auf + acc); (re-examination) Über-prüfung f; (Mil) Truppenschau f; (of book, play) Kritik f, Rezension f ● vt zurückblicken auf (+ acc); überprüfen ⟨situation⟩; (Mil) besichtigen; kriti-sieren, rezensieren ⟨book, play⟩. ~er n Kritiker m, Rezensent m

revile /rɪ'vaɪl/ vt verunglimpfen

revis|e /rɪ'vaɪz/ vt revidieren; (for exam) wiederholen. ~ion /-'vɪʒn/ n Revision f; Wiederholung f

revival /rɪ'vaɪvl/ n Wiederbelebung f

revive /rɪ'vaɪv/ vt wiederbeleben; (fig) wieder aufleben lassen ● vi wieder aufleben

revoke /rɪ'vəʊk/ vt aufheben; wider-rufen ⟨command, decision⟩

revolt /rɪ'vəʊlt/ n Aufstand m ● vi rebellieren ● vt anwidern. ~ing a widerlich, eklig

revolution /revə'luːʃn/ n Revo-lution f; (Auto) Umdrehung f. ~ary /-ərɪ/ a revolutionär. ~ize vt revo-lutionieren

revolve /rɪ'vɒlv/ vi sich drehen; ~ around kreisen um

revolv|er /rɪ'vɒlvə(r)/ n Revolver m. ~ing a Dreh-

revue /rɪ'vjuː/ n Revue f; (satirical) Kabarett nt

revulsion /rɪ'vʌlʃn/ n Abscheu m

reward /rɪ'wɔːd/ n Belohnung f ● vt belohnen. ~ing a lohnend

re'write /riː-/ vt (pt rewrote, pp re-written) noch einmal [neu] schreiben; (alter) umschreiben

rhapsody /'ræpsədɪ/ n Rhapsodie f

rhetoric /'retərɪk/ n Rhetorik f. ~al /rɪ'tɒrɪkl/ a rhetorisch

rheuma|tic /ruː'mætɪk/ a rheuma-tisch. ~tism /'ruː'mətɪzm/ n Rheuma-tismus m, Rheuma nt

Rhine /raɪn/ n Rhein m
rhinoceros /raɪ'nɒsərəs/ n Nashorn nt, Rhinozeros nt
rhubarb /'ru:bɑ:b/ n Rhabarber m
rhyme /raɪm/ n Reim m ● vt reimen ● vi sich reimen
rhythm /'rɪðm/ n Rhythmus m. ~ic[al] a, -ally adv rhythmisch
rib /rɪb/ n Rippe f ● vt (pt/pp ribbed) (fam) aufziehen (fam)
ribald /'rɪbld/ a derb
ribbon /'rɪbən/ n Band nt; (for typewriter) Farbband nt; in ~s in Fetzen
rice /raɪs/ n Reis m
rich /rɪtʃ/ a (-er, -est), -ly adv reich; ⟨food⟩ gehaltvoll; ⟨heavy⟩ schwer ● n the ~ pl die Reichen; ~es pl Reichtum m
rickets /'rɪkɪts/ n Rachitis f
rickety /'rɪkəti/ a wackelig
ricochet /'rɪkəʃeɪ/ vi abprallen
rid /rɪd/ vt (pt/pp rid, pres p ridding) befreien (of von); get ~ of loswerden
riddance /'rɪdns/ n good ~! auf Nimmerwiedersehen!
ridden /'rɪdn/ see ride
riddle /'rɪdl/ n Rätsel nt
riddled /'rɪdld/ a ~ with durchlöchert mit
ride /raɪd/ n Ritt m; (in vehicle) Fahrt f; take s.o. for a ~ (fam) jdn reinlegen ● v (pt rode, pp ridden) ● vt reiten ⟨horse⟩; fahren mit ⟨bicycle⟩ ● vi reiten; (in vehicle) fahren. ~r n Reiter(in) m(f); (on bicycle) Fahrer(in) m(f); (in document) Zusatzklausel f
ridge /rɪdʒ/ n Erhebung f; (on roof) First m; (of mountain) Grat m, Kamm m; (of high pressure) Hochdruckkeil m
ridicule /'rɪdɪkju:l/ n Spott m ● vt verspotten, spotten über (+ acc)
ridiculous /rɪ'dɪkjʊləs/ a, -ly adv lächerlich
riding /'raɪdɪŋ/ n Reiten nt ● attrib Reit-
rife /raɪf/ a be ~ weit verbreitet sein
riff-raff /'rɪfræf/ n Gesindel nt
rifle /'raɪfl/ n Gewehr nt ● vt plündern; ~ through durchwühlen
rift /rɪft/ n Spalt m; (fig) Riß m
rig[1] /rɪg/ n Ölbohrturm m; (at sea) Bohrinsel f ● vt (pt/pp rigged) ~ out ausrüsten; ~ up aufbauen
rig[2] vt (pt/pp rigged) manipulieren
right /raɪt/ a richtig; (not left) rechte(r,s); be ~ ⟨person:⟩ recht haben; ⟨clock:⟩ richtig gehen; put ~ wieder in

Ordnung bringen; (fig) richtigstellen; that's ~! das stimmt! ● adv richtig; (directly) direkt; (completely) ganz; (not left) rechts; (go) nach rechts; ~ away sofort ● n Recht nt; (not left) rechte Seite f; on the ~ rechts; from/to the ~ von/nach rechts; be in the ~ recht haben; by ~s eigentlich; the R~ (Pol) die Rechte. ~ angle n rechter Winkel m
righteous /'raɪtʃəs/ a rechtschaffen
rightful /'raɪtfl/ a, -ly adv rechtmäßig
right: ~-'handed a rechtshändig. ~-hand 'man n (fig) rechte Hand f
rightly /'raɪtlɪ/ adv mit Recht
right: ~ of way n Durchgangsrecht nt; (path) öffentlicher Fußweg m; (Auto) Vorfahrt f. ~-'wing a (Pol) rechte(r,s)
rigid /'rɪdʒɪd/ a starr; (strict) streng. ~ity /-'dʒɪdətɪ/ n Starrheit f; Strenge f
rigmarole /'rɪgmərəʊl/ n Geschwätz nt; (procedure) Prozedur f
rigorous /'rɪgərəs/ a, -ly adv streng
rigour /'rɪgə(r)/ n Strenge f
rile /raɪl/ vt (fam) ärgern
rim /rɪm/ n Rand m; (of wheel) Felge f
rind /raɪnd/ n (on fruit) Schale f; (on cheese) Rinde f; (on bacon) Schwarte f
ring[1] /rɪŋ/ n Ring m; (for circus) Manege f; stand in a ~ im Kreis stehen ● vt umringen; ~ in red rot einkreisen
ring[2] n Klingeln nt; give s.o. a ~ (Teleph) jdn anrufen ● v (pt rang, pp rung) ● vt läuten; ~ [up] (Teleph) anrufen ● vi läuten, klingeln. ~ back vt/i (Teleph) zurückrufen. ~ off vi (Teleph) auflegen
ring: ~leader n Rädelsführer m. ~ road n Umgehungsstraße f
rink /rɪŋk/ n Eisbahn f
rinse /rɪns/ n Spülung f; (hair colour) Tönung f ● vt spülen; tönen ⟨hair⟩. ~ off vt abspülen
riot /'raɪət/ n Aufruhr m; ~s pl Unruhen pl; ~ of colours bunte Farbenpracht f; run ~ randalieren ● vi randalieren. ~er n Randalierer m. ~ous /-əs/ a aufrührerisch; (boisterous) wild
rip /rɪp/ n Riß m ● vt/i (pt/pp ripped) zerreißen; ~ open aufreißen. ~ off vt (fam) neppen
ripe /raɪp/ a (-r, -st) reif
ripen /'raɪpn/ vi reifen ● vt reifen lassen

ripeness /'raɪpnɪs/ n Reife f
'rip-off n (fam) Nepp m
ripple /'rɪpl/ n kleine Welle f ● vt
kräuseln ● vi sich kräuseln
rise /raɪz/ n Anstieg m; (fig) Aufstieg
m; (increase) Zunahme f; (in wages)
Lohnerhöhung f; (in salary) Gehalts-
erhöhung f; **give ~ to** Anlaß geben
zu ● vi (pt **rose,** pp **risen**) steigen;
(ground:) ansteigen; (sun, dough:) aufgehen; (river:) entspringen; (get up) aufstehen; (fig) aufsteigen (**to** zu); (rebel)
sich erheben; (court:) sich vertagen. **~r**
n **early ~r** Frühaufsteher m
rising /'raɪzɪŋ/ a steigend; (sun) auf-
gehend; **the ~ generation** die her-
anwachsende Generation ● n (revolt)
Aufstand m
risk /rɪsk/ n Risiko nt; **at one's own**
~ auf eigene Gefahr ● vt riskieren
risky /'rɪskɪ/ a (**-ier, -iest**) riskant
risqué /'rɪskeɪ/ a gewagt
rissole /'rɪsəʊl/ n Frikadelle f
rite /raɪt/ n Ritus m; **last ~s** Letzte
Ölung f
ritual /'rɪtjʊəl/ a rituell ● n Ritual nt
rival /'raɪvl/ a rivalisierend ● n Ri-
vale m/Rivalin f; **~s** pl (Comm) Kon-
kurrenten pl ● vt (pt/pp **rivalled**)
gleichkommen (+ dat); (compete with)
rivalisieren mit. **~ry** n Rivalität f;
(Comm) Konkurrenzkampf m
river /'rɪvə(r)/ n Fluß m. **~-bed** n
Flußbett m
rivet /'rɪvɪt/ n Niete f ● vt [ver]-
nieten; **~ed by** (fig) gefesselt von
road /rəʊd/ n Straße f; (fig) Weg m
road: **~-block** n Straßensperre f.
~-hog n (fam) Straßenschreck m.
~-map n Straßenkarte f. **~ safety** n
Verkehrssicherheit f. **~ sense** n Ver-
kehrssinn m. **~side** n Straßenrand
m. **~way** n Fahrbahn f. **~-works**
npl Straßenarbeiten pl. **~worthy** a
verkehrssicher
roam /rəʊm/ vi wandern
roar /rɔː(r)/ n Gebrüll nt; **~s of**
laughter schallendes Gelächter nt ● vi
brüllen; (with laughter) schallend lachen; (fire) prasseln; **do a**
~ing trade (fam) ein Bombengeschäft
machen
roast /rəʊst/ a gebraten, Brat-; **~**
beef/pork Rinder-/Schweinebraten m
● n Braten m ● vt/i braten; rösten (coffee, chestnuts)
rob /rɒb/ vt (pt/pp **robbed**) berauben
(**of** gen); ausrauben (bank). **~ber** n
Räuber m. **~bery** n Raub m

robe /rəʊb/ n Robe f; (Amer: bathrobe) Bademantel m
robin /'rɒbɪn/ n Rotkehlchen nt
robot /'rəʊbɒt/ n Roboter m
robust /rəʊ'bʌst/ a robust
rock[1] /rɒk/ n Fels m; **stick of ~**
Zuckerstange f; **on the ~s** (ship) auf-
gelaufen; (marriage) kaputt; (drink) mit
Eis
rock[2] vt/i schaukeln
rock[3] n (Mus) Rock m
rock-'bottom n Tiefpunkt m
rockery /'rɒkərɪ/ n Steingarten m
rocket /'rɒkɪt/ n Rakete f ● vi in die
Höhe schießen
rocking: **~-chair** n Schaukelstuhl m.
~-horse n Schaukelpferd nt
rocky /'rɒkɪ/ a (**-ier, -iest**) felsig; (unsteady) wackelig
rod /rɒd/ n Stab m; (stick) Rute f; (for
fishing) Angel[rute] f
rode /rəʊd/ see **ride**
rodent /'rəʊdnt/ n Nagetier nt
roe[1] /rəʊ/ n Rogen m; (soft) Milch f
roe[2] n (pl **roe** or **roes**) **~[-deer]** Reh m
rogue /rəʊg/ n Gauner m
role /rəʊl/ n Rolle f
roll /rəʊl/ n Rolle f; (bread) Brötchen
nt; (list) Liste f; (of drum) Wirbel m
● vi rollen; **be ~ing in money** (fam)
Geld wie Heu haben ● vt rollen; walzen
(lawn); ausrollen (pastry). **~ over** vi
sich auf die andere Seite rollen. **~ up**
vt aufrollen; hochkrempeln (sleeves)
● vi (fam) auftauchen
'roll-call n Namensaufruf m; (Mil)
Appell m
roller /'rəʊlə(r)/ n Rolle f; (lawn,
road) Walze f; (hair) Lockenwickler
m. **~ blind** n Rollo nt. **~-coaster** n
Berg-und-Talbahn f. **~-skate** n
Rollschuh m
'rolling-pin n Teigrolle f
Roman /'rəʊmən/ a römisch ● n Rö-
mer(in) m(f)
romance /rə'mæns/ n Romantik f;
(love-affair) Romanze f; (book)
Liebesgeschichte f
Romania /rəʊ'meɪnɪə/ n Rumänien
nt. **~n** a rumänisch ● n Rumäne m/
-nin f
romantic /rəʊ'mæntɪk/ a, **-ally**
adv romantisch. **~ism** /-tɪsɪzm/ n Romantik f
Rome /rəʊm/ n Rom m
romp /rɒmp/ n Tollen nt ● vi
[herum]tollen. **~ers** npl Stram-
pelhöschen nt

roof /ruːf/ n Dach nt; (of mouth) Gaumen m ● vt ~ **over** überdachen. ~-**rack** n Dachgepäckträger m. ~-**top** n Dach nt

rook /rʊk/ n Saatkrähe f; (Chess) Turm m ● vt (fam: swindle) schröpfen

room /ruːm/ n Zimmer nt; (for functions) Saal m; (space) Platz m. ~**y** a geräumig

roost /ruːst/ n Hühnerstange f ● vi schlafen

root[1] /ruːt/ n Wurzel f; **take** ~ anwachsen ● vi Wurzeln schlagen. ~ **out** vt (fig) ausrotten

root[2] vi ~ **about** zu wühlen; ~ **for s.o.** (Amer, fam) für jdn sein

rope /rəʊp/ n Seil nt; **know the** ~**s** (fam) sich auskennen. ~ **in** vt (fam) einspannen

rope-'ladder n Strickleiter f

rosary /'rəʊzərɪ/ n Rosenkranz m

rose[1] /rəʊz/ n Rose f; (of watering-can) Brause f

rose[2] see **rise**

rosemary /'rəʊzmərɪ/ n Rosmarin m

rosette /rəʊ'zet/ n Rosette f

roster /'rɒstə(r)/ n Dienstplan m

rostrum /'rɒstrəm/ n Podest nt, Podium nt

rosy /'rəʊzɪ/ a (-ier, -iest) rosig

rot /rɒt/ n Fäulnis f; (fam: nonsense) Quatsch m ● vi (pt/pp **rotted**) [ver]faulen

rota /'rəʊtə/ n Dienstplan m

rotary /'rəʊtərɪ/ a Dreh-; (Techn) Rotations-

rotat|e /rəʊ'teɪt/ vt drehen; im Wechsel anbauen (crops) ● vi sich drehen; (Techn) rotieren. ~**ion** /-eɪʃn/ n Drehung f; (of crops) Fruchtfolge f; **in** ~**ion** im Wechsel

rote /rəʊt/ n **by** ~ auswendig

rotten /'rɒtn/ a faul; (fam) mies; (person) fies

rotund /rəʊ'tʌnd/ a rundlich

rough /rʌf/ a (-er, -est) rauh; (uneven) uneben; (coarse, not gentle) grob; (brutal) roh; (turbulent) stürmisch; (approximate) ungefähr ● adv **sleep** ~ im Freien übernachten; **play** ~ holzen ● n **do sth in** ~ etw ins unreine schreiben ● vt ~ **it** primitiv leben. ~ **out** vt im Groben entwerfen

roughage /'rʌfɪdʒ/ n Ballaststoffe pl

rough 'draft n grober Entwurf m

rough|ly /'rʌflɪ/ adv (see **rough**) rauh; grob; roh; ungefähr. ~**ness** n Rauheit f

'rough paper n Konzeptpapier nt

round /raʊnd/ a (-er, -est) rund ● n Runde f; (slice) Scheibe f; **do one's** ~**s** seine Runde machen ● prep um (+ acc). ~ **the clock** rund um die Uhr ● adv **all** ~ ringsherum; ~ **and** ~ im Kreis; **ask s.o.** ~ jdn einladen; **turn/look** ~ sich umdrehen/umsehen ● vt biegen um (corner) ● vi ~ **on s.o.** jdn anfahren. ~ **off** vt abrunden. ~ **up** vt aufrunden; zusammentreiben (animals); festnehmen (criminals)

roundabout /'raʊndəbaʊt/ a ~ **route** Umweg m ● n Karussell nt; (for traffic) Kreisverkehr m

round: ~-'**shouldered** a mit einem runden Rücken. ~ '**trip** n Rundreise f

rous|e /raʊz/ vt wecken; (fig) erregen. ~**ing** a mitreißend

route /ruːt/ n Route f; (of bus) Linie f

routine /ruː'tiːn/ a, -**ly** adv routinemäßig ● n Routine f; (Theat) Nummer f

roux /ruː/ n Mehlschwitze f

rove /rəʊv/ vi wandern

row[1] /rəʊ/ n (line) Reihe f; **in a** ~ (one after the other) nacheinander

row[2] vt/i rudern

row[3] /raʊ/ n (fam) Krach m ● vi (fam) sich streiten

rowan /'rəʊən/ n Eberesche f

rowdy /'raʊdɪ/ a (-ier, -iest) laut

rowing boat /'rəʊɪŋ-/ n Ruderboot nt

royal /'rɔɪəl/ a, -**ly** adv königlich

royal|ty /'rɔɪəltɪ/ n Königtum nt; (persons) Mitglieder pl der königlichen Familie; -**ies** pl (payments) Tantiemen pl

rub /rʌb/ n **give sth a** ~ etw reiben/(polish) polieren ● vt (pt/pp **rubbed**) reiben; (polish) polieren; **don't** ~ **it in** (fam) reib es mir nicht unter die Nase. ~ **off** vt abreiben ● vi abgehen; ~ **off on** abfärben auf (+ acc). ~ **out** vt ausradieren

rubber /'rʌbə(r)/ n Gummi m; (eraser) Radiergummi m. ~ **band** n Gummiband nt. ~**y** a gummiartig

rubbish /'rʌbɪʃ/ n Abfall m, Müll m; (fam: nonsense) Quatsch m; (fam: junk) Plunder m, Kram m ● vt (fam) schlechtmachen. ~ **bin** n Mülleimer m, Abfalleimer m. ~ **dump** n Abfallhaufen m; (official) Müllhalde f

rubble /'rʌbl/ n Trümmer pl, Schutt m

ruby /'ru:bɪ/ n Rubin m

rucksack /'rʌksæk/ n Rucksack m

rudder /'rʌdə(r)/ n [Steuer]ruder nt

ruddy /'rʌdɪ/ a (-ier, -iest) rötlich; (sl) verdammt

rude /ru:d/ a (-r, -st), -ly adv unhöflich; (improper) unanständig. ∼ness n Unhöflichkeit f

rudiment /'ru:dɪmənt/ n ∼s pl Anfangsgründe pl. ∼ary /-'mentərɪ/ a elementar; (Biol) rudimentär

rueful /'ru:fl/ a, -ly adv reumütig

ruffian /'rʌfɪən/ n Rüpel m

ruffle /'rʌfl/ n Rüsche f ● vt zerzausen

rug /rʌg/ n Vorleger m, [kleiner] Teppich m; (blanket) Decke f

rugged /'rʌgɪd/ a (coastline) zerklüftet

ruin /'ru:ɪn/ n Ruine f; (fig) Ruin m ● vt ruinieren. ∼ous /-əs/ a ruinös

rule /ru:l/ n Regel f; (control) Herrschaft f; (government) Regierung f; (for measuring) Lineal nt; **as a** ∼ in der Regel ● vt regieren, herrschen über (+ acc); (fig) beherrschen; (decide) entscheiden; ziehen (line) ● vi regieren, herrschen. ∼ **out** vt ausschließen

ruled /ru:ld/ a (paper) liniert

ruler /'ru:lə(r)/ n Herrscher(in) m(f); (measure) Lineal nt

ruling /'ru:lɪŋ/ a herrschend; (factor) entscheidend; (Pol) regierend ● n Entscheidung f

rum /rʌm/ n Rum m

rumble /'rʌmbl/ n Grollen nt ● vi grollen; (stomach:) knurren

ruminant /'ru:mɪnənt/ n Wiederkäuer m

rummage /'rʌmɪdʒ/ vi wühlen; ∼ **through** durchwühlen

rummy /'rʌmɪ/ n Rommé nt

rumour /'ru:mə(r)/ n Gerücht nt ● vt **it is** ∼ed that es geht das Gerücht, daß

rump /rʌmp/ n Hinterteil nt. ∼ **steak** n Rumpsteak nt

rumpus /'rʌmpəs/ n (fam) Spektakel m

run /rʌn/ n Lauf m; (journey) Fahrt f; (series) Serie f, Reihe f; (Theat) Laufzeit f; (Skiing) Abfahrt f; (enclosure) Auslauf m; (Amer: ladder) Laufmasche f; **at a** ∼ im Laufschritt; ∼ **of bad luck** Pechsträhne f; **be on the** ∼ flüchtig sein; **have the** ∼ **of sth** etw zu seiner freien Verfügung haben; **in**

the long ∼ auf lange Sicht ● v (pt ran, pp run, pres p running) ● vi laufen; (flow) fließen; (eyes:) tränen; (bus:) verkehren, fahren; (butter, ink:) zerfließen; (colours:) [ab]färben; (in election) kandidieren; ∼ **across s.o./sth** auf jdn/etw stoßen ● vt laufen lassen; einlaufen lassen (bath); (manage) führen, leiten; (drive) fahren; eingehen (risk); (Journ) bringen (article); ∼ **one's hand over sth** mit der Hand über etw (acc) fahren.

∼ **away** vi weglaufen. ∼ **down** vi hinunter-/herunterlaufen; (clockwork:) ablaufen; (stocks:) sich verringern ● vt (run over) überfahren; (reduce) verringern; (fam: criticize) heruntermachen. ∼ **in** vi hinein-/hereinlaufen. ∼ **off** vi weglaufen ● vt abziehen (copies). ∼ **out** vi hinaus-/herauslaufen; (supplies, money:) ausgehen; **I've** ∼ **out of sugar** ich habe keinen Zucker mehr. ∼ **over** vi hinüber-/herüberlaufen; (overflow) überlaufen ● vt überfahren. ∼ **through** vi durchlaufen. ∼ **up** vi hinauf-/herauflaufen; (towards) hinlaufen ● vt machen (debts); auflaufen lassen (bill); (sew) schnell nähen

'runaway n Ausreißer m

run-'down a (area) verkommen

rung[1] /rʌŋ/ n (of ladder) Sprosse f

rung[2] see **ring**[2]

runner /'rʌnə(r)/ n Läufer m; (Bot) Ausläufer m; (on sledge) Kufe f. ∼ **bean** n Stangenbohne f. ∼**-up** n Zweite(r) m/f

running /'rʌnɪŋ/ a laufend; (water) fließend; **four times** ∼ viermal nacheinander ● n Laufen nt; (management) Führung f, Leitung f; **be/not be in the** ∼ eine/keine Chance haben. ∼ **'commentary** n fortlaufender Kommentar m

runny /'rʌnɪ/ a flüssig

run: ∼-of-the-'mill a gewöhnlich. ∼-up n (Sport) Anlauf m; (to election) Zeit f vor der Wahl. ∼**way** n Start- und Landebahn f, Piste f

rupture /'rʌptʃə(r)/ n Bruch m ● vt/i brechen; ∼ **oneself** sich (dat) einen Bruch heben

rural /'rʊərəl/ a ländlich

ruse /ru:z/ n List f

rush[1] /rʌʃ/ n (Bot) Binse f

rush[2] n Hetze f; **in a** ∼ in Eile ● vi sich hetzen; (run) rasen; (water:) rauschen

● *vt* hetzen, drängen; ~ **s.o. to hospital** jdn schnellstens ins Krankenhaus bringen. ~**-hour** *n* Hauptverkehrszeit *f*, Stoßzeit *f*

rusk /rʌsk/ *n* Zwieback *m*

Russia /'rʌʃə/ *n* Rußland *nt*. ~**n** *a* russisch ● *n* Russe *m*/Russin *f*; (*Lang*) Russisch *nt*

rust /rʌst/ *n* Rost *m* ● *vi* rosten

rustic /'rʌstɪk/ *a* bäuerlich; (*furniture*) rustikal

rustle /'rʌsl/ *vi* rascheln ● *vt* rascheln mit; (*Amer*) stehlen (*cattle*). ~ **up** *vt* (*fam*) improvisieren

'**rustproof** *a* rostfrei

rusty /'rʌstɪ/ *a* (**-ier, -iest**) rostig

rut /rʌt/ *n* Furche *f*; **be in a** ~ (*fam*) aus dem alten Trott nicht herauskommen

ruthless /'ru:θlɪs/ *a*, **-ly** *adv* rücksichtslos. ~**ness** *n* Rücksichtslosigkeit *f*

rye /raɪ/ *n* Roggen *m*

S

sabbath /'sæbəθ/ *n* Sabbat *m*

sabbatical /sə'bætɪkl/ *n* (*Univ*) Forschungsurlaub *m*

sabot|age /'sæbətɑːʒ/ *n* Sabotage *f* ● *vt* sabotieren. ~**eur** /-'tɜː(r)/ *n* Saboteur *m*

sachet /'sæʃeɪ/ *n* Beutel *m*; (*scented*) Kissen *nt*

sack[1] /sæk/ *vt* (*plunder*) plündern

sack[2] *n* Sack *m*; **get the** ~ (*fam*) rausgeschmissen werden ● *vt* (*fam*) rausschmeißen. ~**ing** *n* Sackleinen *nt*; (*fam: dismissal*) Rausschmiß *m*

sacrament /'sækrəmənt/ *n* Sakrament *nt*

sacred /'seɪkrɪd/ *a* heilig

sacrifice /'sækrɪfaɪs/ *n* Opfer *nt* ● *vt* opfern

sacrilege /'sækrɪlɪdʒ/ *n* Sakrileg *nt*

sad /sæd/ *a* (**sadder, saddest**) traurig; (*loss, death*) schmerzlich. ~**den** *vt* traurig machen

saddle /'sædl/ *n* Sattel *m* ● *vt* satteln; ~ **s.o. with sth** (*fam*) jdm etw aufhalsen

sadis|m /'seɪdɪzm/ *n* Sadismus *m*. ~**t** /-dɪst/ *n* Sadist *m*. ~**tic** /sə'dɪstɪk/ *a*, **-ally** *adv* sadistisch

sad|ly /'sædlɪ/ *adv* traurig; (*unfortunately*) leider. ~**ness** *n* Traurigkeit *f*

safe /seɪf/ *a* (**-r, -st**) sicher; (*journey*) gut; (*not dangerous*) ungefährlich; ~ **and sound** gesund und wohlbehalten ● *n* Safe *m*. ~**guard** *n* Schutz *m* ● *vt* schützen. ~**ly** *adv* sicher; (*arrive*) gut

safety /'seɪftɪ/ *n* Sicherheit *f*. ~**-belt** *n* Sicherheitsgurt *m*. ~**-pin** *n* Sicherheitsnadel *f*. ~**-valve** *n* [Sicherheits]ventil *nt*

sag /sæg/ *vi* (*pt/pp* **sagged**) durchhängen

saga /'sɑːgə/ *n* Saga *f*; (*fig*) Geschichte *f*

sage[1] /seɪdʒ/ *n* (*herb*) Salbei *m*

sage[2] *a* weise ● *n* Weise(r) *m*

Sagittarius /sædʒɪ'teərɪəs/ *n* (*Astr*) Schütze *m*

said /sed/ *see* **say**

sail /seɪl/ *n* Segel *nt*; (*trip*) Segelfahrt *f* ● *vi* segeln; (*on liner*) fahren; (*leave*) abfahren (**for** nach) ● *vt* segeln mit

'**sailboard** *n* Surfbrett *nt*. ~**ing** *n* Windsurfen *nt*

sailing /'seɪlɪŋ/ *n* Segelsport *m*. ~**-boat** *n* Segelboot *nt*. ~**-ship** *n* Segelschiff *nt*

sailor /'seɪlə(r)/ *n* Seemann *m*; (*in navy*) Matrose *m*

saint /seɪnt/ *n* Heilige(r) *m*/*f*. ~**ly** *a* heilig

sake /seɪk/ *n* **for the** ~ **of** ... um ... (*gen*) willen; **for my/your** ~ um meinet-/deinetwillen

salad /'sæləd/ *n* Salat *m*. ~ **cream** *n* ≈ Mayonnaise *f*. ~**-dressing** *n* Salatsoße *f*

salary /'sælərɪ/ *n* Gehalt *nt*

sale /seɪl/ *n* Verkauf *m*; (*event*) Basar *m*; (*at reduced prices*) Schlußverkauf *m*; **for** ~ zu verkaufen

sales|man *n* Verkäufer *m*. ~**woman** *n* Verkäuferin *f*

salient /'seɪlɪənt/ *a* wichtigste(r,s)

saliva /sə'laɪvə/ *n* Speichel *m*

sallow /'sæləʊ/ *a* (**-er, -est**) bleich

salmon /'sæmən/ *n* Lachs *m*. ~**-pink** *a* lachsrosa

saloon /sə'luːn/ *n* Salon *m*; (*Auto*) Limousine *f*; (*Amer: bar*) Wirtschaft *f*

salt /sɔːlt/ *n* Salz *nt* ● *a* salzig; (*water, meat*) Salz- ● *vt* salzen; (*cure*) pökeln; streuen (*road*). ~**-cellar** *n* Salzfaß *nt*. ~ '**water** *n* Salzwasser *nt*. ~**y** *a* salzig

salutary /'sæljʊtərɪ/ *a* heilsam

salute /sə'lu:t/ n (Mil) Gruß m ● vt/i (Mil) grüßen

salvage /'sælvɪdʒ/ n (Naut) Bergung f ● vt bergen

salvation /sæl'veɪʃn/ n Rettung f; (Relig) Heil nt. **S~ 'Army** n Heilsarmee f

salvo /'sælvəʊ/ n Salve f

same /seɪm/ a & pron the ~ der/die/das gleiche; (pl) die gleichen; (identical) der-/die-/dasselbe; (pl) dieselben ● adv the ~ gleich; **all the** ~ trotzdem; **the ~ to you** gleichfalls

sample /'sɑ:mpl/ n Probe f; (Comm) Muster nt ● vt probieren, kosten

sanatorium /sænə'tɔ:rɪəm/ n Sanatorium nt

sanctify /'sæŋktɪfaɪ/ vt (pt/pp -fied) heiligen

sanctimonious /sæŋktɪ'məʊnɪəs/ a, -ly adv frömmlerisch

sanction /'sæŋkʃn/ n Sanktion f ● vt sanktionieren

sanctity /'sæŋktətɪ/ n Heiligkeit f

sanctuary /'sæŋktjʊərɪ/ n (Relig) Heiligtum nt; (refuge) Zuflucht f; (for wildlife) Tierschutzgebiet nt

sand /sænd/ n Sand m ● vt ~ **[down]** [ab]schmirgeln

sandal /'sændl/ n Sandale f

sand: ~**bank** n Sandbank f. ~**paper** n Sandpapier nt ● vt [ab]schmirgeln. ~**-pit** n Sandkasten m

sandwich /'sænwɪdʒ/ n ≈ belegtes Brot nt; Sandwich m ● vt ~**ed between** eingeklemmt zwischen

sandy /'sændɪ/ a (-ier, -iest) sandig; (beach, soil) Sand-; (hair) rotblond

sane /seɪn/ a (-r, -st) geistig normal; (sensible) vernünftig

sang /sæŋ/ see **sing**

sanitary /'sænɪtərɪ/ a hygienisch; (system) sanitär. ~ **napkin** n (Amer), ~ **towel** n [Damen]binde f

sanitation /sænɪ'teɪʃn/ n Kanalisation und Abfallbeseitigung pl

sanity /'sænɪtɪ/ n [gesunder] Verstand m

sank /sæŋk/ see **sink**

sap /sæp/ n (Bot) Saft m ● vt (pt/pp sapped) schwächen

sapphire /'sæfaɪə(r)/ n Saphir m

sarcas|m /'sɑ:kæzm/ n Sarkasmus m. ~**tic** /-'kæstɪk/ a, -ally adv sarkastisch

sardine /sɑ:'di:n/ n Sardine f

Sardinia /sɑ:'dɪnɪə/ n Sardinien nt

sardonic /sɑ:'dɒnɪk/ a, -ally adv höhnisch; (smile) sardonisch

sash /sæʃ/ n Schärpe f

sat /sæt/ see **sit**

satanic /sə'tænɪk/ a satanisch

satchel /'sætʃl/ n Ranzen m

satellite /'sætəlaɪt/ n Satellit m. ~ **dish** n Satellitenschüssel f. ~ **television** n Satellitenfernsehen nt

satin /'sætɪn/ n Satin m

satire /'sætaɪə(r)/ n Satire f

satirical /sə'tɪrɪkl/ a, -ly adv satirisch

satir|ist /'sætərɪst/ n Satiriker(in) m(f). ~**ize** vt satirisch darstellen; (book:) eine Satire sein auf (+ acc)

satisfaction /sætɪs'fækʃn/ n Befriedigung f; **to my** ~ zu meiner Zufriedenheit

satisfactory /sætɪs'fæktərɪ/ a, -ily adv zufriedenstellend

satisf|y /'sætɪsfaɪ/ vt (pt/pp -fied) befriedigen; zufriedenstellen (customer); (convince) überzeugen; **be** ~**ied** zufrieden sein. ~**ying** a befriedigend; (meal) sättigend

saturat|e /'sætʃəreɪt/ vt durchtränken; (Chem & fig) sättigen. ~**ed** a durchnäßt; (fat) gesättigt

Saturday /'sætədeɪ/ n Samstag m, Sonnabend m

sauce /sɔ:s/ n Soße f; (cheek) Frechheit f. ~**pan** n Kochtopf m

saucer /'sɔ:sə(r)/ n Untertasse f

saucy /'sɔ:sɪ/ a (-ier, -iest) frech

Saudi Arabia /saʊdɪə'reɪbɪə/ n Saudi-Arabien nt

sauna /'sɔ:nə/ n Sauna f

saunter /'sɔ:ntə(r)/ vi schlendern

sausage /'sɒsɪdʒ/ n Wurst f

savage /'sævɪdʒ/ a wild; (fierce) scharf; (brutal) brutal ● n Wilde(r) m/f ● vt anfallen. ~**ry** n Brutalität f

save /seɪv/ n (Sport) Abwehr f ● vt retten (**from** vor + dat); (keep) aufheben; (not waste) sparen; (collect) sammeln; (avoid) ersparen; (Sport) verhindern (goal) ● vi ~ **[up]** sparen ● prep außer (+ dat), mit Ausnahme (+ gen)

saver /'seɪvə(r)/ n Sparer m

saving /'seɪvɪŋ/ n (see **save**) Rettung f; Sparen nt; Ersparnis f; ~**s** pl (money) Ersparnisse pl. ~**s account** n Sparkonto nt. ~**s bank** n Sparkasse f

saviour /'seɪvjə(r)/ n Retter m

savour /'seɪvə(r)/ n Geschmack m ● vt auskosten. ~**y** a herzhaft, würzig; (fig) angenehm

saw[1] /sɔː/ *see* **see**[1]

saw[2] *n* Säge *f* ● *vt/i* (*pt* **sawed**, *pp* **sawn** *or* **sawed**) sägen. **~dust** *n* Sägemehl *nt*

saxophone /'sæksəfəʊn/ *n* Saxophon *nt*

say /seɪ/ *n* Mitspracherecht *nt*; **have one's ~** seine Meinung sagen ● *vt/i* (*pt/pp* **said**) sagen; sprechen ⟨*prayer*⟩; **that is to ~** das heißt; **that goes without ~ing** das versteht sich von selbst; **when all is said and done** letzten Endes; **I ~!** ⟨*attracting attention*⟩ hallo! **~ing** *n* Redensart *f*

scab /skæb/ *n* Schorf *m*; (*pej*) Streikbrecher *m*

scaffold /'skæfəld/ *n* Schafott *nt*. **~ing** *n* Gerüst *nt*

scald /skɔːld/ *vt* verbrühen

scale[1] /skeɪl/ *n* (*of fish*) Schuppe *f*

scale[2] *n* Skala *f*; (*Mus*) Tonleiter *f*; (*ratio*) Maßstab *m*; **on a grand ~** in großem Stil ● *vt* (*climb*) erklettern. **~ down** *vt* verkleinern

scales /skeɪlz/ *npl* (*for weighing*) Waage *f*

scalp /skælp/ *n* Kopfhaut *f* ● *vt* skalpieren

scalpel /'skælpl/ *n* Skalpell *nt*

scam /skæm/ *n* (*fam*) Schwindel *m*

scamper /'skæmpə(r)/ *vi* huschen

scan /skæn/ *n* (*Med*) Szintigramm *nt* ● *v* (*pt/pp* **scanned**) ● *vt* absuchen; (*quickly*) flüchtig ansehen; (*Med*) szintigraphisch untersuchen ● *vi* ⟨*poetry:*⟩ das richtige Versmaß haben

scandal /'skændl/ *n* Skandal *m*; (*gossip*) Skandalgeschichten *pl*. **~ize** /-dəlaɪz/ *vt* schockieren. **~ous** /-əs/ *a* skandalös

Scandinavia /skændɪ'neɪvɪə/ *n* Skandinavien *nt*. **~n** *a* skandinavisch ● *n* Skandinavier(in) *m(f)*

scant /skænt/ *a* wenig

scanty /'skæntɪ/ *a* (**-ier, -iest**), **-ily** *adv* spärlich; ⟨*clothing*⟩ knapp

scapegoat /'skeɪp-/ *n* Sündenbock *m*

scar /skɑː(r)/ *n* Narbe *f* ● *vt* (*pt/pp* **scarred**) eine Narbe hinterlassen auf (+ *dat*)

scarc|e /skeəs/ *a* (**-r, -st**) knapp; **make oneself ~e** (*fam*) sich aus dem Staub machen. **~ely** *adv* kaum. **~ity** *n* Knappheit *f*

scare /skeə(r)/ *n* Schreck *m*; (*panic*) [allgemeine] Panik *f*; (*bomb* **~**) Bombendrohung *f* ● *vt* Angst machen (+ *dat*); **be ~d** Angst haben (**of** vor + *dat*)

'scarecrow *n* Vogelscheuche *f*

scarf /skɑːf/ *n* (*pl* **scarves**) Schal *m*; (*square*) Tuch *nt*

scarlet /'skɑːlət/ *a* scharlachrot. **~ 'fever** *n* Scharlach *m*

scary /'skeərɪ/ *a* unheimlich

scathing /'skeɪðɪŋ/ *a* bissig

scatter /'skætə(r)/ *vt* verstreuen; (*disperse*) zerstreuen ● *vi* sich zerstreuen. **~-brained** *a* (*fam*) schusselig. **~ed** *a* verstreut; ⟨*showers*⟩ vereinzelt

scatty /'skætɪ/ *a* (**-ier, -iest**) (*fam*) verrückt

scavenge /'skævɪndʒ/ *vi* [im Abfall] Nahrung suchen; ⟨*animal:*⟩ Aas fressen. **~r** *n* Aasfresser *m*

scenario /sɪ'nɑːrɪəʊ/ *n* Szenario *nt*

scene /siːn/ *n* Szene *f*; (*sight*) Anblick *m*; (*place of event*) Schauplatz *m*; **behind the ~s** hinter den Kulissen; **~ of the crime** Tatort *m*

scenery /'siːnərɪ/ *n* Landschaft *f*; (*Theat*) Szenerie *f*

scenic /'siːnɪk/ *a* landschaftlich schön; (*Theat*) Bühnen-

scent /sent/ *n* Duft *m*; (*trail*) Fährte *f*; (*perfume*) Parfüm *nt*. **~ed** *a* parfümiert

sceptic|al /'skeptɪkl/ *a*, **-ly** *adv* skeptisch. **~ism** /-tɪsɪzm/ *n* Skepsis *f*

schedule /'ʃedjuːl/ *n* Programm *nt*; (*of work*) Zeitplan *m*; (*timetable*) Fahrplan *m*; **behind ~** im Rückstand; **according to ~** planmäßig ● *vt* planen. **~d flight** *n* Linienflug *m*

scheme /skiːm/ *n* Programm *nt*; (*plan*) Plan *m*; (*plot*) Komplott *nt* ● *vi* Ränke schmieden

schizophren|ia /skɪtsə'friːnɪə/ *n* Schizophrenie *f*. **~ic** /-'frenɪk/ *a* schizophren

scholar /'skɒlə(r)/ *n* Gelehrte(r) *m/f*. **~ly** *a* gelehrt. **~ship** *n* Gelehrtheit *f*; (*grant*) Stipendium *nt*

school /skuːl/ *n* Schule *f*; (*Univ*) Fakultät *f* ● *vt* schulen; dressieren ⟨*animal*⟩

school: ~boy *n* Schüler *m*. **~girl** *n* Schülerin *f*. **~ing** *n* Schulbildung *f*. **~master** *n* Lehrer *m*. **~mistress** *n* Lehrerin *f*. **~teacher** *n* Lehrer(in) *m(f)*

sciatica /saɪ'ætɪkə/ *n* Ischias *m*

scien|ce /'saɪəns/ *n* Wissenschaft *f*. **~tific** /-'tɪfɪk/ *a* wissenschaftlich. **~tist** *n* Wissenschaftler *m*

scintillating /'sɪntɪleɪtɪŋ/ a sprühend

scissors /'sɪzəz/ npl Schere f; **a pair of** ~ eine Schere

scoff[1] /skɒf/ vi ~ **at** spotten über (+acc)

scoff[2] vt (fam) verschlingen

scold /skəʊld/ vt ausschimpfen

scoop /sku:p/ n Schaufel f; (Culin) Portionierer m; (Journ) Exklusivmeldung f ● vt ~ **out** aushöhlen; (remove) auslöffeln; ~ **up** schaufeln; schöpfen (liquid)

scoot /sku:t/ vi (fam) rasen. ~**er** n Roller m

scope /skəʊp/ n Bereich m; (opportunity) Möglichkeiten pl

scorch /skɔ:tʃ/ vt versengen. ~**ing** a glühend heiß

score /skɔ:(r)/ n [Spiel]stand m; (individual) Punktzahl f; (Mus) Partitur f; (Cinema) Filmmusik f; **a** ~ **[of]** (twenty) zwanzig; **keep [the]** ~ zählen; (written) aufschreiben; **on that** ~ was das betrifft ● vt erzielen; schießen (goal); (cut) einritzen ● vi Punkte erzielen; (Sport) ein Tor schießen; (keep score) Punkte zählen. ~**r** n Punktezähler m; (of goals) Torschütze m

scorn /skɔ:n/ n Verachtung f ● vt verachten. ~**ful** a, -**ly** adv verächtlich

Scorpio /'skɔ:pɪəʊ/ n (Astr) Skorpion m

scorpion /'skɔ:pɪən/ n Skorpion m

Scot /skɒt/ n Schotte m/Schottin f

Scotch /skɒtʃ/ a schottisch ● n (whisky) Scotch m

scotch vt unterbinden

scot-'free a **get off** ~ straffrei ausgehen

Scot|land /'skɒtlənd/ n Schottland nt. ~**s**, ~**tish** a schottisch

scoundrel /'skaʊndrl/ n Schurke m

scour[1] /'skaʊə(r)/ vt (search) absuchen

scour[2] vt (clean) scheuern

scourge /skɜ:dʒ/ n Geißel f

scout /skaʊt/ n (Mil) Kundschafter m ● vi ~ **for** Ausschau halten nach
Scout n [Boy] ~ Pfadfinder m

scowl /skaʊl/ n böser Gesichtsausdruck m ● vi ein böses Gesicht machen

scraggy /'skrægɪ/ a (-ier, -iest) (pej) dürr, hager

scram /skræm/ vi (fam) abhauen

scramble /'skræmbl/ n Gerangel nt ● vi klettern; ~ **for** sich drängen nach

● vt (Teleph) verschlüsseln. ~**d 'egg[s]** n[pl] Rührei nt

scrap[1] /skræp/ n (fam: fight) Rauferei f ● vi sich raufen

scrap[2] n Stückchen nt; (metal) Schrott m; ~**s** pl Reste; **not a** ~ kein bißchen ● vt (pt/pp scrapped) aufgeben

'scrap-book n Sammelalbum nt

scrape /skreɪp/ vt schaben; (clean) abkratzen; (damage) [ver]schrammen. ~ **through** vi gerade noch durchkommen. ~ **together** vt zusammenkriegen

scraper /'skreɪpə(r)/ n Kratzer m

'scrap iron n Alteisen nt

scrappy /'skræpɪ/ a lückenhaft

'scrap-yard n Schrottplatz m

scratch /skrætʃ/ n Kratzer m; **start from** ~ von vorne anfangen; **not be up to** ~ zu wünschen übriglassen ● vt/i kratzen; (damage) zerkratzen

scrawl /skrɔ:l/ n Gekrakel nt ● vt/i krakeln

scrawny /'skrɔ:nɪ/ a (-ier, -iest) (pej) dürr, hager

scream /skri:m/ n Schrei m ● vt/i schreien

screech /skri:tʃ/ n Kreischen nt ● vt/i kreischen

screen /skri:n/ n Schirm m; (Cinema) Leinwand f; (TV) Bildschirm m ● vt schützen; (conceal) verdecken; vorführen (film); (examine) überprüfen; (Med) untersuchen. ~**ing** n (Med) Reihenuntersuchung f. ~**play** n Drehbuch nt

screw /skru:/ n Schraube f ● vt schrauben; ~ **up** vt festschrauben; (crumple) zusammenknüllen; zusammenkneifen (eyes); (sl: bungle) vermasseln; ~ **up one's courage** seinen Mut zusammennehmen

'screwdriver n Schraubenzieher m

screwy /'skru:ɪ/ a (-ier, -iest) (fam) verrückt

scribble /'skrɪbl/ n Gekritzel nt ● vt/i kritzeln

script /skrɪpt/ n Schrift f; (of speech, play) Text m; (Radio, TV) Skript nt; (of film) Drehbuch nt

Scripture /'skrɪptʃə(r)/ n (Sch) Religion f; **the** ~**s** pl die Heilige Schrift f

scroll /skrəʊl/ n Schriftrolle f; (decoration) Volute f

scrounge /skraʊndʒ/ vt/i schnorren. ~**r** n Schnorrer m

scrub[1] /skrʌb/ n (land) Buschland nt, Gestrüpp nt

scrub[2] *vt/i* (*pt/pp* **scrubbed**) schrubben; (*fam: cancel*) absagen; fallenlassen ⟨*plan*⟩

scruff /skrʌf/ *n* **by the ~ of the neck** beim Genick

scruffy /'skrʌfɪ/ *a* (**-ier, -iest**) vergammelt

scrum /skrʌm/ *n* Gedränge *nt*

scruple /'skruːpl/ *n* Skrupel *m*

scrupulous /'skruːpjʊləs/ *a*, **-ly** *adv* gewissenhaft

scrutin|ize /'skruːtɪnaɪz/ *vt* [genau] ansehen. **~y** *n* (*look*) prüfender Blick *m*

scuff /skʌf/ *vt* abstoßen

scuffle /'skʌfl/ *n* Handgemenge *nt*

scullery /'skʌlərɪ/ *n* Spülküche *f*

sculpt|or /'skʌlptə(r)/ *n* Bildhauer(in) *m(f)*. **~ure** /-tʃə(r)/ *n* Bildhauerei *f*; (*piece of work*) Skulptur *f*, Plastik *f*

scum /skʌm/ *n* Schmutzschicht *f*; (*people*) Abschaum *m*

scurrilous /'skʌrɪləs/ *a* niederträchtig

scurry /'skʌrɪ/ *vi* (*pt/pp* **-ied**) huschen

scuttle[1] /'skʌtl/ *n* Kohleneimer *m*

scuttle[2] *vt* versenken ⟨*ship*⟩

scuttle[3] *vi* schnell krabbeln

scythe /saɪð/ *n* Sense *f*

sea /siː/ *n* Meer *nt*, See *f*; **at ~** auf See; **by ~** mit dem Schiff. **~board** *n* Küste *f*. **~food** *n* Meeresfrüchte *pl*. **~gull** *n* Möwe *f*

seal[1] /siːl/ *n* (*Zool*) Seehund *m*

seal[2] *n* Siegel *nt*; (*Techn*) Dichtung *f* ● *vt* versiegeln; (*Techn*) abdichten; (*fig*) besiegeln. **~ off** *vt* abriegeln

'sea-level *n* Meeresspiegel *m*

seam /siːm/ *n* Naht *f*; (*of coal*) Flöz *nt*

'seaman *n* Seemann *m*; (*sailor*) Matrose *m*

seamless /'siːmlɪs/ *a* nahtlos

seance /'seɪɑːns/ *n* spiritistische Sitzung *f*

sea: ~plane *n* Wasserflugzeug *nt*. **~port** *n* Seehafen *m*

search /sɜːtʃ/ *n* Suche *f*; (*official*) Durchsuchung *f* ● *vt* durchsuchen; absuchen ⟨*area*⟩ ● *vi* suchen (**for** nach). **~ing** *a* prüfend, forschend

search: ~light *n* [Such]scheinwerfer *m*. **~-party** *n* Suchmannschaft *f*

sea: ~sick *a* seekrank. **~side** *n* **at/to the ~side** am/ans Meer

season /'siːzn/ *n* Jahreszeit *f*; (*social, tourist, sporting*) Saison *f* ● *vt* (*flavour*) würzen. **~able** /-əbl/ *a* der Jahreszeit gemäß. **~al** *a* Saison-. **~ing** *n* Gewürze *pl*

'season ticket *n* Dauerkarte *f*

seat /siːt/ *n* Sitz *m*; (*place*) Sitzplatz *m*; (*bottom*) Hintern *m*; **take a ~** Platz nehmen ● *vt* setzen; (*have seats for*) Sitzplätze bieten (+ *dat*); **remain ~ed** sitzen bleiben. **~-belt** *n* Sicherheitsgurt *m*; **fasten one's ~-belt** sich anschnallen

sea: ~weed *n* [See]tang *m*. **~worthy** *a* seetüchtig

secateurs /sekə'tɜːz/ *npl* Gartenschere *f*

seclu|de /sɪ'kluːd/ *vt* absondern. **~ded** *a* abgelegen. **~sion** /-ʒn/ *n* Zurückgezogenheit *f*

second[1] /'sɪkɒnd/ *vt* (*transfer*) [vorübergehend] versetzen

second[2] /'sekənd/ *a* zweite(r,s); **on ~ thoughts** nach weiterer Überlegung ● *n* Sekunde *f*; (*Sport*) Sekundant *m*; **~s** *pl* (*goods*) Waren zweiter Wahl; **the ~** der/die/das zweite ● *adv* (*in race*) an zweiter Stelle ● *vt* unterstützen ⟨*proposal*⟩

secondary /'sekəndrɪ/ *a* zweitrangig; (*Phys*) Sekundär-. **~ school** *n* höhere Schule *f*

second: ~-best *a* zweitbeste(r,s). **~ 'class** *adv* (*travel, send*) zweiter Klasse. **~-class** *a* zweitklassig

'second hand *n* (*on clock*) Sekundenzeiger *m*

second-'hand *a* gebraucht ● *adv* aus zweiter Hand

secondly /'sekəndlɪ/ *adv* zweitens

second-'rate *a* zweitklassig

secrecy /'siːkrəsɪ/ *n* Heimlichkeit *f*

secret /'siːkrɪt/ *a* geheim; (*agent, police*) Geheim-; (*drinker, lover*) heimlich ● *n* Geheimnis *nt*

secretarial /sekrə'teərɪəl/ *a* Sekretärinnen-; (*work, staff*) Sekretariats-

secretary /'sekrətərɪ/ *n* Sekretär(in) *m(f)*

secret|e /sɪ'kriːt/ *vt* absondern. **~ion** /-iːʃn/ *n* Absonderung *f*

secretive /'siːkrətɪv/ *a* geheimtuerisch. **~ness** *n* Heimlichtuerei *f*

secretly /'siːkrɪtlɪ/ *adv* heimlich

sect /sekt/ *n* Sekte *f*

section /'sekʃn/ *n* Teil *m*; (*of text*) Abschnitt *m*; (*of firm*) Abteilung *f*; (*of organization*) Sektion *f*

sector /'sektə(r)/ *n* Sektor *m*

secular /'sekjulə(r)/ *a* weltlich

secure /sɪ'kjʊə(r)/ *a*, **-ly** *adv* sicher; (*firm*) fest; (*emotionally*) geborgen ● *vt* sichern; (*fasten*) festmachen; (*obtain*) sich (*dat*) sichern

securit|y /sɪ'kjʊərətɪ/ *n* Sicherheit *f*; (*emotional*) Geborgenheit *f*; **~ies** *pl* Wertpapiere *pl*; (*Fin*) Effekten *pl*

sedan /sɪ'dæn/ *n* (*Amer*) Limousine *f*

sedate[1] /sɪ'deɪt/ *a*, **-ly** *adv* gesetzt

sedate[2] *vt* sedieren

sedation /sɪ'deɪʃn/ *n* Sedierung *f*; **be under ~** sediert sein

sedative /'sedətɪv/ *a* beruhigend ● *n* Beruhigungsmittel *nt*

sedentary /'sedəntərɪ/ *a* sitzend

sediment /'sedɪmənt/ *n* [Boden]satz *m*

seduce /sɪ'djuːs/ *vt* verführen

seduct|ion /sɪ'dʌkʃn/ *n* Verführung *f*. **~ive** /-tɪv/ *a*, **-ly** *adv* verführerisch

see[1] /siː/ *v* (*pt* **saw**, *pp* **seen**) ● *vt* sehen; (*understand*) einsehen; (*imagine*) sich (*dat*) vorstellen; (*escort*) begleiten; **go and ~** nachsehen; (*visit*) besuchen; **~ you later!** bis nachher! **~ing that** da ● *vi* sehen; (*check*) nachsehen; **~ about** sich kümmern um. **~ off** *vt* verabschieden; (*chase away*) vertreiben. **~ through** *vi* durchsehen ● *vt* (*fig*) **~ through s.o.** jdn durchschauen

see[2] *n* (*Relig*) Bistum *nt*

seed /siːd/ *n* Samen *m*; (*of grape*) Kern *m*; (*fig*) Saat *f*; (*Tennis*) gesetzter Spieler *m*; **go to ~** Samen bilden; (*fig*) herunterkommen. **~ed** *a* (*Tennis*) gesetzt. **~ling** *n* Sämling *m*

seedy /'siːdɪ/ *a* (**-ier**, **-iest**) schäbig; (*area*) heruntergekommen

seek /siːk/ *vt* (*pt/pp* **sought**) suchen

seem /siːm/ *vi* scheinen. **~ingly** *adv* scheinbar

seemly /'siːmlɪ/ *a* schicklich

seen /siːn/ *see* **see**[1]

seep /siːp/ *vi* sickern

see-saw /'siːsɔː/ *n* Wippe *f*

seethe /siːð/ *vi* **~ with anger** vor Wut schäumen

'see-through *a* durchsichtig

segment /'segmənt/ *n* Teil *m*; (*of worm*) Segment *nt*; (*of orange*) Spalte *f*

segregat|e /'segrɪgeɪt/ *vt* trennen. **~ion** /-'geɪʃn/ *n* Trennung *f*

seize /siːz/ *vt* ergreifen; (*Jur*) beschlagnahmen; **~ s.o. by the arm** jdn

am Arm packen. **~ up** *vi* (*Techn*) sich festfressen

seizure /'siːʒə(r)/ *n* (*Jur*) Beschlagnahme *f*; (*Med*) Anfall *m*

seldom /'seldəm/ *adv* selten

select /sɪ'lekt/ *a* ausgewählt; (*exclusive*) exklusiv ● *vt* auswählen; aufstellen ⟨team⟩. **~ion** /-ekʃn/ *n* Auswahl *f*. **~ive** /-ɪv/ *a*, **-ly** *adv* selektiv; (*choosy*) wählerisch

self /self/ *n* (*pl* **selves**) Ich *nt*

self: **~-ad'dressed** *a* adressiert. **~-ad'hesive** *a* selbstklebend. **~-as'surance** *n* Selbstsicherheit *f*. **~-as'sured** *a* selbstsicher. **~-'catering** *n* Selbstversorgung *f*. **~-'centred** *a* egozentrisch. **~-'confidence** *n* Selbstbewußtsein *nt*, Selbstvertrauen *nt*. **~-'confident** *a* selbstbewußt. **~-'conscious** *a* befangen. **~-con'tained** *a* ⟨flat⟩ abgeschlossen. **~-con'trol** *n* Selbstbeherrschung *f*. **~-de'fence** *n* Selbstverteidigung *f*; (*Jur*) Notwehr *f*. **~-de'nial** *n* Selbstverleugnung *f*. **~-determi'nation** *n* Selbstbestimmung *f*. **~-em'ployed** *a* selbständig. **~-e'steem** *n* Selbstachtung *f*. **~-'evident** *a* offensichtlich. **~-'governing** *a* selbstverwaltet. **~-'help** *n* Selbsthilfe *f*. **~-in'dulgent** *a* maßlos. **~-'interest** *n* Eigennutz *m*

self|ish /'selfɪʃ/ *a*, **-ly** *adv* egoistisch, selbstsüchtig. **~less** *a*, **-ly** *adv* selbstlos

self: **~-'pity** *n* Selbstmitleid *nt*. **~-'portrait** *n* Selbstporträt *nt*. **~-pos'sessed** *a* selbstbeherrscht. **~-preser'vation** *n* Selbsterhaltung *f*. **~-re'spect** *n* Selbstachtung *f*. **~-'righteous** *a* selbstgerecht. **~-'sacrifice** *n* Selbstaufopferung *f*. **~-'satisfied** *a* selbstgefällig. **~-'service** *n* Selbstbedienung *f* ● *attrib* Selbstbedienungs-. **~-suf'ficient** *a* selbständig. **~-'willed** *a* eigenwillig

sell /sel/ *v* (*pt/pp* **sold**) ● *vt* verkaufen; **be sold out** ausverkauft sein ● *vi* sich verkaufen. **~ off** *vt* verkaufen

seller /'selə(r)/ *n* Verkäufer *m*

Sellotape (P) /'seləʊ-/ *n* ≈ Tesafilm (P) *m*

'sell-out *n* **be a ~** ausverkauft sein; (*fam: betrayal*) Verrat sein

selves /selvz/ *see* **self**

semblance /'sembləns/ *n* Anschein *m*

semen /'si:mən/ n (Anat) Samen m

semester /sɪ'mestə(r)/ n (Amer) Semester nt

semi|breve /'semɪbri:v/ n (Mus) ganze Note f. ~**circle** n Halbkreis m. ~'**circular** a halbkreisförmig. ~'**colon** n Semikolon nt. ~-**de'tached** a & n ~-**detached** [**house**] Doppelhaushälfte f. ~'**final** n Halbfinale nt

seminar /'semɪnɑ:(r)/ n Seminar nt. ~**y** /-nərɪ/ n Priesterseminar nt

'**semitone** n (Mus) Halbton m

semolina /semə'li:nə/ n Grieß m

senat|e /'senət/ n Senat m. ~**or** n Senator m

send /send/ vt/i (pt/pp **sent**) schicken; ~ **one's regards** grüßen lassen; ~ **for** kommen lassen ⟨person⟩; sich (dat) schicken lassen ⟨thing⟩. ~**er** n Absender m. ~-**off** n Verabschiedung f

senil|e /'si:naɪl/ a senil. ~**ity** /sɪ'nɪlətɪ/ n Senilität f

senior /'si:nɪə(r)/ a älter; (in rank) höher ● n Ältere(r) m/f; (in rank) Vorgesetzte(r) m/f. ~ '**citizen** n Senior(in) m(f)

seniority /si:nɪ'ɒrətɪ/ n höheres Alter nt; (in rank) höherer Rang m

sensation /sen'seɪʃn/ n Sensation f; (feeling) Gefühl nt. ~**al** a, -**ly** adv sensationell

sense /sens/ n Sinn m; (feeling) Gefühl nt; (common ~) Verstand m; **in a** ~ in gewisser Hinsicht; **make** ~ Sinn ergeben ● vt spüren. ~**less** a, -**ly** adv sinnlos; (unconscious) bewußtlos

sensible /'sensəbl/ a, -**bly** adv vernünftig; ⟨suitable⟩ zweckmäßig

sensitiv|e /'sensətɪv/ a, -**ly** adv empfindlich; ⟨understanding⟩ einfühlsam. ~**ity** /-'tɪvətɪ/ Empfindlichkeit f

sensory /'sensərɪ/ a Sinnes-

sensual /'sensjʊəl/ a sinnlich. ~**ity** /-'ælətɪ/ n Sinnlichkeit f

sensuous /'sensjʊəs/ a sinnlich

sent /sent/ see **send**

sentence /'sentəns/ n Satz m; (Jur) Urteil nt; (punishment) Strafe f ● vt verurteilen

sentiment /'sentɪmənt/ n Gefühl nt; (opinion) Meinung f; (sentimentality) Sentimentalität f. ~**al** /-'mentl/ a sentimental. ~**ality** /-'tælətɪ/ n Sentimentalität f

sentry /'sentrɪ/ n Wache f

separable /'sepərəbl/ a trennbar

separate[1] /'sepərət/ a, -**ly** adv getrennt, separat

separat|e[2] /'sepəreɪt/ vt trennen ● vi sich trennen. ~**ion** /-'reɪʃn/ n Trennung f

September /sep'tembə(r)/ n September m

septic /'septɪk/ a vereitert; **go** ~ vereitern

sequel /'si:kwl/ n Folge f; (fig) Nachspiel nt

sequence /'si:kwəns/ n Reihenfolge f

sequin /'si:kwɪn/ n Paillette f

serenade /serə'neɪd/ n Ständchen nt ● vt ~ s.o. jdm ein Ständchen bringen

seren|e /sɪ'ri:n/ a, -**ly** adv gelassen. ~**ity** /-'renətɪ/ n Gelassenheit f

sergeant /'sɑ:dʒənt/ n (Mil) Feldwebel m; (in police) Polizeimeister m

serial /'sɪərɪəl/ n Fortsetzungsgeschichte f; (Radio, TV) Serie f. ~**ize** vt in Fortsetzungen veröffentlichen/ (Radio, TV) senden

series /'sɪəri:z/ n inv Serie f

serious /'sɪərɪəs/ a, -**ly** adv ernst; (illness, error) schwer. ~**ness** n Ernst m

sermon /'sɜ:mən/ n Predigt f

serpent /'sɜ:pənt/ n Schlange f

serrated /se'reɪtɪd/ a gezackt

serum /'sɪərəm/ n Serum nt

servant /'sɜ:vənt/ n Diener(in) m(f)

serve /sɜ:v/ n (Tennis) Aufschlag m ● vt dienen (+ dat); bedienen ⟨customer, guest⟩; servieren ⟨food⟩; (Jur) zustellen (**on s.o.** jdm); verbüßen ⟨sentence⟩; ~ **its purpose** seinen Zweck erfüllen; **it** ~**s you right!** das geschieht dir recht! ~**s two** für zwei Personen ● vi dienen; (Tennis) aufschlagen

service /'sɜ:vɪs/ n Dienst m; (Relig) Gottesdienst m; (in shop, restaurant) Bedienung f; (transport) Verbindung f; (maintenance) Wartung f; (set of crockery) Service nt; (Tennis) Aufschlag m; ~**s** pl Dienstleistungen pl; (on motorway) Tankstelle und Raststätte f; **in the** ~**s** beim Militär; **be of** ~ nützlich sein; **out of/in** ~ ⟨machine:⟩ außer/in Betrieb ● vt (Techn) warten. ~**able** /-əbl/ a nützlich; (durable) haltbar

service: ~ **area** n Tankstelle und Raststätte f. ~ **charge** n Bedienungszuschlag m. ~**man** n Soldat m. ~ **station** n Tankstelle f

serviette /sɜ:vɪ'et/ n Serviette f

servile /'sɜːvaɪl/ a unterwürfig

session /'seʃn/ n Sitzung f; (Univ) Studienjahr nt

set /set/ n Satz m; (of crockery) Service n; (of cutlery) Garnitur f; (TV, Radio) Apparat m; (Math) Menge f; (Theat) Bühnenbild nt; (Cinema) Szenenaufbau m; (of people) Kreis m; **shampoo and ~** Waschen und Legen ● a (ready) fertig, bereit; (rigid) fest; ⟨book⟩ vorgeschrieben; **be ~ on doing sth** entschlossen sein, etw zu tun; **be ~ in one's ways** in seinen Gewohnheiten festgefahren sein ● v (pt/pp set, pres p setting) ● vt setzen; (adjust) einstellen; stellen ⟨task, alarm clock⟩; festsetzen, festlegen ⟨date, limit⟩; aufgeben ⟨homework⟩; zusammenstellen ⟨questions⟩; [ein]fassen ⟨gem⟩; einrichten ⟨bone⟩; legen ⟨hair⟩; decken ⟨table⟩ ● vi (sun:) untergehen; (become hard) fest werden; **~ about** sich an etw (acc) machen; **~ about doing sth** sich daranmachen, etw zu tun. **~ back** vt zurücksetzen; (hold up) aufhalten; (fam: cost) kosten. **~ off** vi losgehen; (in vehicle) losfahren ● vt auslösen ⟨alarm⟩; explodieren lassen ⟨bomb⟩. **~ out** vi losgehen; (in vehicle) losfahren; **~ out to do sth** sich vornehmen, etw zu tun ● vt auslegen; (state) darlegen. **~ up** vt aufbauen; (fig) gründen

set 'meal n Menü nt

settee /se'tiː/ n Sofa nt, Couch f

setting /'setɪŋ/ n Rahmen m; (surroundings) Umgebung f; (of sun) Untergang m; (of jewel) Fassung f

settle /'setl/ vt (decide) entscheiden; (agree) regeln; (fix) festsetzen; (calm) beruhigen; (pay) bezahlen ● vi sich niederlassen; ⟨snow, dust:⟩ liegenbleiben; (subside) sich senken; ⟨sediment:⟩ sich absetzen. **~ down** vi sich beruhigen; (permanently) seßhaft werden. **~ up** vi abrechnen

settlement /'setlmənt/ n (see settle) Entscheidung f; Regelung f; Bezahlung f; (Jur) Vergleich m; (colony) Siedlung f

settler /'setlə(r)/ n Siedler m

'set-to n (fam) Streit m

'set-up n System nt

seven /'sevn/ a sieben. **~teen** a siebzehn. **~teenth** a siebzehnte(r,s)

seventh /'sevnθ/ a siebte(r,s)

seventieth /'sevntɪɪθ/ a siebzigste(r,s)

seventy /'sevntɪ/ a siebzig

sever /'sevə(r)/ vt durchtrennen; abbrechen ⟨relations⟩

several /'sevrl/ a & pron mehrere, einige

sever|e /sɪ'vɪə(r)/ a (-r, -st), **-ly** adv streng; ⟨pain⟩ stark; ⟨illness⟩ schwer. **~ity** /-'verətɪ/ n Strenge f; Schwere f

sew /səʊ/ vt/i (pt sewed, pp sewn or sewed) nähen. **~ up** vt zunähen

sewage /'suːɪdʒ/ n Abwasser nt

sewer /'suːə(r)/ n Abwasserkanal m

sewing /'səʊɪŋ/ n Nähen nt; (work) Näharbeit f. **~ machine** n Nähmaschine f

sewn /səʊn/ see sew

sex /seks/ n Geschlecht nt; (sexuality, intercourse) Sex m. **~ist** a sexi stisch. **~ offender** n Triebverbrecher m

sexual /'seksjʊəl/ a, **-ly** adv sexuell. **~ 'intercourse** n Geschlechtsverkehr m

sexuality /seksjʊ'ælətɪ/ n Sexualität f

sexy /'seksɪ/ a (-ier, -iest) sexy

shabby /'ʃæbɪ/ a (-ier, -iest), **-ily** adv schäbig

shack /ʃæk/ n Hütte f

shackles /'ʃæklz/ npl Fesseln pl

shade /ʃeɪd/ n Schatten m; (of colour) [Farb]ton m; (for lamp) [Lampen]schirm m; (Amer: window-blind) Jalousie f ● vt beschatten; (draw lines on) schattieren

shadow /'ʃædəʊ/ n Schatten m ● vt (follow) beschatten. **~y** a schattenhaft

shady /'ʃeɪdɪ/ a (-ier, -iest) schattig; (fam: disreputable) zwielichtig

shaft /ʃɑːft/ n Schaft m; (Techn) Welle f; (of light) Strahl m; (of lift) Schacht m; **~s** pl (of cart) Gabeldeichsel f

shaggy /'ʃægɪ/ a (-ier, -iest) zottig

shake /ʃeɪk/ n Schütteln nt ● v (pt shook, pp shaken) ● vt schütteln; (cause to tremble, shock) erschüttern; **~ hands with s.o.** jdm die Hand geben ● vi wackeln; (tremble) zittern. **~ off** vt abschütteln

shaky /'ʃeɪkɪ/ a (-ier, -iest) wackelig; ⟨hand, voice⟩ zittrig

shall /ʃæl/ v aux I **~ go** ich werde gehen; **we ~ see** wir werden sehen; **what ~ I do?** was soll ich machen? **I'll come too, ~ I?** ich komme mit, ja? **thou shalt not kill** (liter) du sollst nicht töten

shallow /'ʃæləʊ/ *a* (**-er, -est**) seicht; ⟨*dish*⟩ flach; (*fig*) oberflächlich

sham /ʃæm/ *a* unecht ● *n* Heuchelei *f*; (*person*) Heuchler(in) *m(f)* ● *vt* (*pt/pp* **shammed**) vortäuschen

shambles /'ʃæmblz/ *n* Durcheinander *nt*

shame /ʃeɪm/ *n* Scham *f*; (*disgrace*) Schande *f*; **be a** ∼ schade sein; **what a** ∼**!** wie schade! ∼**- faced** *a* betreten

shame|ful /'ʃeɪmfl/ *a*, **-ly** *adv* schändlich. ∼**less** *a*, **-ly** *adv* schamlos

shampoo /ʃæm'pu:/ *n* Shampoo *nt* ● *vt* schamponieren

shandy /'ʃændɪ/ *n* Radler *m*

shan't /ʃɑ:nt/ = **shall not**

shape /ʃeɪp/ *n* Form *f*; (*figure*) Gestalt *f*; **take** ∼ Gestalt annehmen ● *vt* formen (**into** zu) ● *vi* ∼ **up** sich entwickeln. ∼**less** *a* formlos; ⟨*clothing*⟩ unförmig

shapely /'ʃeɪplɪ/ *a* (**-ier, -iest**) wohlgeformt

share /ʃeə(r)/ *n* [An]teil *m*; (*Comm*) Aktie *f* ● *vt/i* teilen. ∼**holder** *n* Aktionär(in) *m(f)*

shark /ʃɑ:k/ *n* Hai[fisch] *m*

sharp /ʃɑ:p/ *a* (**-er, -est**), **-ly** *adv* scharf; (*pointed*) spitz; (*severe*) heftig; (*sudden*) steil; (*alert*) clever; (*unscrupulous*) gerissen ● *adv* scharf; (*Mus*) zu hoch; **at six o'clock** ∼ Punkt sechs Uhr; **look** ∼**!** beeil dich! ● *n* (*Mus*) Kreuz *nt*. ∼**en** *vt* schärfen; [an]spitzen ⟨*pencil*⟩

shatter /'ʃætə(r)/ *vt* zertrümmern; (*fig*) zerstören; **be** ∼**ed** ⟨*person:*⟩ erschüttert sein ● *vi* zersplittern

shave /ʃeɪv/ *n* Rasur *f*; **have a** ∼ sich rasieren ● *vt* rasieren ● *vi* sich rasieren. ∼**r** *n* Rasierapparat *m*

shaving /'ʃeɪvɪŋ/ *n* Rasieren *nt*. ∼**-brush** *n* Rasierpinsel *m*

shawl /ʃɔ:l/ *n* Schultertuch *nt*

she /ʃi:/ *pron* sie

sheaf /ʃi:f/ *n* (*pl* **sheaves**) Garbe *f*; (*of papers*) Bündel *nt*

shear /ʃɪə(r)/ *vt* (*pt* **sheared**, *pp* **shorn** *or* **sheared**) scheren

shears /ʃɪəz/ *npl* [große] Schere *f*

sheath /ʃi:θ/ *n* (*pl* ∼**s** /ʃi:ðz/) Scheide *f*

sheaves /ʃi:vz/ *see* **sheaf**

shed¹ /ʃed/ *n* Schuppen *m*; (*for cattle*) Stall *m*

shed² *vt* (*pt/pp* **shed**, *pres p* **shedding**) verlieren; vergießen ⟨*blood, tears*⟩; ∼ **light on** Licht bringen in (+ *acc*)

sheen /ʃi:n/ *n* Glanz *m*

sheep /ʃi:p/ *n inv* Schaf *nt*. ∼**-dog** *n* Hütehund *m*

sheepish /'ʃi:pɪʃ/ *a*, **-ly** *adv* verlegen

'sheepskin *n* Schaffell *nt*

sheer /ʃɪə(r)/ *a* rein; (*steep*) steil; (*transparent*) hauchdünn ● *adv* steil

sheet /ʃi:t/ *n* Laken *nt*, Bettuch *nt*; (*of paper*) Blatt *nt*; (*of glass, metal*) Platte *f*

sheikh /ʃeɪk/ *n* Scheich *m*

shelf /ʃelf/ *n* (*pl* **shelves**) Brett *nt*, Bord *nt*; (*set of shelves*) Regal *nt*

shell /ʃel/ *n* Schale *f*; (*of snail*) Haus *nt*; (*of tortoise*) Panzer *m*; (*on beach*) Muschel *f*; (*of unfinished building*) Rohbau *m*; (*Mil*) Granate *f* ● *vt* pellen; enthülsen ⟨*peas*⟩; (*Mil*) [mit Granaten] beschießen. ∼ **out** *vi* (*fam*) blechen

'shellfish *n inv* Schalentiere *pl*; (*Culin*) Meeresfrüchte *pl*

shelter /'ʃeltə(r)/ *n* Schutz *m*; (*air-raid* ∼) Luftschutzraum *m* ● *vt* schützen (**from** vor + *dat*) ● *vi* sich unterstellen. ∼**ed** *a* geschützt; ⟨*life*⟩ behütet

shelve /ʃelv/ *vt* auf Eis legen; (*abandon*) aufgeben ● *vi* ⟨*slope:*⟩ abfallen

shelves /ʃelvz/ *see* **shelf**

shelving /'ʃelvɪŋ/ *n* ⟨*shelves*⟩ Regale *pl*

shepherd /'ʃepəd/ *n* Schäfer *m*; (*Relig*) Hirte *m* ● *vt* führen. ∼**ess** *n* Schäferin *f*. ∼**'s pie** *n* Auflauf *m* aus mit Kartoffelbrei bedecktem Hackfleisch

sherry /'ʃerɪ/ *n* Sherry *m*

shield /ʃi:ld/ *n* Schild *m*; (*for eyes*) Schirm *m*; (*Techn & fig*) Schutz *m* ● *vt* schützen (**from** vor + *dat*)

shift /ʃɪft/ *n* Verschiebung *f*; (*at work*) Schicht *f*; **make** ∼ sich (*dat*) behelfen (**with** mit) ● *vt* rücken; (*take away*) wegnehmen; (*rearrange*) umstellen; schieben ⟨*blame*⟩ (**on to** auf + *acc*) ● *vi* sich verschieben; (*fam: move quickly*) rasen

'shift work *n* Schichtarbeit *f*

shifty /'ʃɪftɪ/ *a* (**-ier, -iest**) (*pej*) verschlagen

shilly-shally /'ʃɪlɪʃælɪ/ *vi* fackeln (*fam*)

shimmer /'ʃɪmə(r)/ *n* Schimmer *m* ● *vi* schimmern

shin /ʃɪn/ *n* Schienbein *nt*

shine /ʃaɪn/ *n* Glanz *m* ● *v* (*pt/pp* **shone**) ● *vi* leuchten; (*reflect light*) glänzen; ⟨sun:⟩ scheinen ● vt ~ **a light on** beleuchten

shingle /'ʃɪŋgl/ n (pebbles) Kiesel pl

shingles /'ʃɪŋglz/ n (Med) Gürtelrose f

shiny /'ʃaɪnɪ/ a (-ier, -iest) glänzend

ship /ʃɪp/ n Schiff nt ● vt (pt/pp shipped) verschiffen

ship: ~**building** n Schiffbau m. ~**ment** n Sendung f. ~**per** n Spediteur m. ~**ping** n Versand m; (traffic) Schiffahrt f. ~**shape** a & adv in Ordnung. ~**wreck** n Schiffbruch m. ~**wrecked** a schiffbrüchig. ~**yard** n Werft f

shirk /ʃɜːk/ vt sich drücken vor (+ dat). ~**er** n Drückeberger m

shirt /ʃɜːt/ n [Ober]hemd nt; (for woman) Hemdbluse f

shit /ʃɪt/ n (vulg) Scheiße f ● vi (pt/pp shit) (vulg) scheißen

shiver /'ʃɪvə(r)/ n Schauder m ● vi zittern

shoal /ʃəʊl/ n (of fish) Schwarm m

shock /ʃɒk/ n Schock m; (Electr) Schlag m; (impact) Erschütterung f ● vt einen Schock versetzen (+ dat); (scandalize) schockieren. ~**ing** a schockierend; (fam: dreadful) fürchterlich

shod /ʃɒd/ see **shoe**

shoddy /'ʃɒdɪ/ a (-ier, -iest) minderwertig

shoe /ʃuː/ n Schuh m; (of horse) Hufeisen nt ● vt (pt/pp shod, pres p shoeing) beschlagen ⟨horse⟩

shoe: ~**horn** n Schuhanzieher m. ~**lace** n Schnürsenkel m. ~**maker** n Schuhmacher m. ~**string** n on a ~**string** (fam) mit ganz wenig Geld

shone /ʃɒn/ see **shine**

shoo /ʃuː/ vt scheuchen ● int sch!

shook /ʃʊk/ see **shake**

shoot /ʃuːt/ n (Bot) Trieb m; (hunt) Jagd f ● v (pt/pp shot) ● vt schießen; (kill) erschießen; drehen ⟨film⟩ ● vi schießen. ~ **down** vt abschießen. ~ **out** vi (rush) herausschießen. ~ **up** vi (grow) in die Höhe schießen; ⟨prices:⟩ schnellen

'**shooting-range** n Schießstand m

shop /ʃɒp/ n Laden m, Geschäft nt; (workshop) Werkstatt f; **talk** ~ (fam) fachsimpeln ● vi (pt/pp shopped, pres p shopping) einkaufen; **go** ~**ping** einkaufen gehen

shop: ~ **assistant** n Verkäufer(in) m(f). ~**keeper** n Ladenbesitzer(in)

m(f). ~**lifter** n Ladendieb m. ~**lifting** n Ladendiebstahl m

shopping /'ʃɒpɪŋ/ n Einkaufen nt; (articles) Einkäufe pl; **do the** ~ einkaufen. ~ **bag** n Einkaufstasche f. ~ **centre** n Einkaufszentrum nt. ~ **trolley** n Einkaufswagen m

shop: ~-'**steward** n [gewerkschaftlicher] Vertrauensmann m. ~-'**window** n Schaufenster nt

shore /ʃɔː(r)/ n Strand m; (of lake) Ufer nt

shorn /ʃɔːn/ see **shear**

short /ʃɔːt/ a (-er, -est) kurz; ⟨person⟩ klein; (curt) schroff; **a** ~ **time ago** vor kurzem; **be** ~ **of** ... zuwenig ... haben; **be in** ~ **supply** knapp sein ● adv kurz; (abruptly) plötzlich; (curtly) kurz angebunden; **in** ~ kurzum; ~ **of** (except) außer; **go** ~ Mangel leiden; **stop** ~ **of doing sth** davor zurückschrecken, etw zu tun

shortage /'ʃɔːtɪdʒ/ n Mangel m (**of** an + dat); (scarcity) Knappheit f

short: ~**bread** n ≈ Mürbekekse pl. ~ '**circuit** n Kurzschluß m. ~**coming** n Fehler m. ~ '**cut** n Abkürzung f

shorten /'ʃɔːtn/ vt [ab]kürzen; kürzer machen ⟨garment⟩

short: ~**hand** n Kurzschrift f, Stenographie f. ~-'**handed** a **be** ~-**handed** zuwenig Personal haben. ~**hand** '**typist** n Stenotypistin f. ~-**list** n engere Auswahl f. ~-**lived** /-lɪvd/ a kurzlebig

short|ly /'ʃɔːtlɪ/ adv in Kürze; ~**ly before/after** kurz vorher/danach. ~**ness** n Kürze f; (of person) Kleinheit f

shorts /ʃɔːts/ npl kurze Hose f, Shorts pl

short: ~-'**sighted** a kurzsichtig. ~-**sleeved** a kurzärmelig. ~-'**staffed** a **be** ~-**staffed** zuwenig Personal haben. ~ '**story** n Kurzgeschichte f. ~-'**tempered** a aufbrausend. ~-**term** a kurzfristig. ~**wave** n Kurzwelle f

shot /ʃɒt/ see **shoot** ● n Schuß m; (pellets) Schrot m; (person) Schütze m; (Phot) Aufnahme f; (injection) Spritze f; (fam: attempt) Versuch m; **like a** ~ (fam) sofort. ~**gun** n Schrotflinte f. ~-**putting** n (Sport) Kugelstoßen nt

should /ʃʊd/ v aux **you** ~ **go** du solltest gehen; **I** ~ **have seen him** ich hätte ihn sehen sollen; **I** ~ **like** ich möchte;

this ~ be enough das müßte eigentlich reichen; if he ~ be there falls er da
sein sollte

shoulder /'ʃəʊldə(r)/ n Schulter f
● vt schultern; (fig) auf sich (acc)
nehmen. ~-blade n Schulterblatt nt.
~-strap n Tragriemen m; (on
garment) Träger m

shout /ʃaʊt/ n Schrei m ● vt/i
schreien. ~ down vt niederschreien

shouting /'ʃaʊtɪŋ/ n Geschrei nt

shove /ʃʌv/ n Stoß m; (fam) Schubs
m ● vt stoßen; (fam) schubsen; (fam:
put) tun ● vi drängeln. ~ off vi
(fam) abhauen

shovel /'ʃʌvl/ n Schaufel f ● vt (pt/
pp shovelled) schaufeln

show /ʃəʊ/ n (display) Pracht f; (exhibition) Ausstellung f, Schau f;
(performance) Vorstellung f; (Theat,
TV) Show f; on ~ ausgestellt ● v (pt
showed, pp shown) ● vt zeigen; (put
on display) ausstellen; vorführen (film)
● vi sichtbar sein; (film:) gezeigt
werden. ~ in vt hereinführen. ~ off
vi (fam) angeben ● vt vorführen;
(flaunt) angeben mit. ~ up vi
[deutlich] zu sehen sein; (fam: arrive) auftauchen ● vt deutlich
zeigen; (fam: embarrass) blamieren

'show-down n Entscheidungs-
kampf m

shower /'ʃaʊə(r)/ n Dusche f; (of
rain) Schauer m; have a ~ duschen
● vt ~ with überschütten mit ● vi duschen. ~proof a regendicht. ~y a
regnerisch

'show-jumping n Springreiten nt

shown /ʃəʊn/ see show

show: ~-off n Angeber(in) m(f).
~-piece n Paradestück nt. ~room n
Ausstellungsraum m

showy /'ʃəʊi/ a protzig

shrank /ʃræŋk/ see shrink

shred /ʃred/ n Fetzen m; (fig) Spur
f ● vt (pt/pp shredded) zerkleinern;
(Culin) schnitzeln. ~der n Reißwolf
m; (Culin) Schnitzelwerk nt

shrewd /ʃruːd/ a (-er, -est), -ly adv
klug. ~ness n Klugheit f

shriek /ʃriːk/ n Schrei m ● vt/i
schreien

shrift /ʃrɪft/ n give s.o. short ~ jdn
kurz abfertigen

shrill /ʃrɪl/ a, -y adv schrill

shrimp /ʃrɪmp/ n Garnele f, Krabbe f

shrine /ʃraɪn/ n Heiligtum nt

shrink /ʃrɪŋk/ vi (pt shrank, pp
shrunk) schrumpfen; (garment:) einlaufen; (draw back) zurückschrecken
(from vor + dat)

shrivel /'ʃrɪvl/ vi (pt/pp shrivelled)
verschrumpeln

shroud /ʃraʊd/ n Leichentuch nt;
(fig) Schleier m

Shrove /ʃrəʊv/ n ~ 'Tuesday Fast-
nachtsdienstag m

shrub /ʃrʌb/ n Strauch m

shrug /ʃrʌg/ n Achselzucken nt ● vt/
i (pt/pp shrugged) ~ [one's shoul-
ders] die Achseln zucken

shrunk /ʃrʌŋk/ see shrink. ~en a ge-
schrumpft

shudder /'ʃʌdə(r)/ n Schauder m
● vi schaudern; (tremble) zittern

shuffle /'ʃʌfl/ vi schlurfen ● vt mischen (cards)

shun /ʃʌn/ vt (pt/pp shunned) meiden

shunt /ʃʌnt/ vt rangieren

shush /ʃʊʃ/ int sch!

shut /ʃʌt/ v (pt/pp shut, pres p shut-
ting) ● vt zumachen, schließen; ~
one's finger in the door sich (dat) den
Finger in der Tür einklemmen ● vi sich
schließen; (shop:) schließen, zumachen.
~ down vt schließen; stillegen
(factory) ● vi schließen; (factory:)
stillgelegt werden. ~ up vt abschließen; (lock in) einsperren ● vi
(fam) den Mund halten

'shut-down n Stillegung f

shutter /'ʃʌtə(r)/ n [Fenster]laden
m; (Phot) Verschluß m

shuttle /'ʃʌtl/ n (Tex) Schiffchen nt
● vi pendeln

shuttle: ~cock n Federball m. ~ser-
vice n Pendelverkehr m

shy /ʃaɪ/ a (-er, -est), -ly adv schüchtern; (timid) scheu ● vi (pt/pp shied)
(horse:) scheuen. ~ness n Schüch-
ternheit f

Siamese /saɪə'miːz/ a siamesisch

siblings /'sɪblɪŋz/ npl Geschwister pl

Sicily /'sɪsɪlɪ/ n Sizilien nt

sick /sɪk/ a krank; (humour)
makaber; be ~ (vomit) sich übergeben; be ~ of sth (fam) etw satt
haben; I feel ~ mir ist schlecht

sicken /'sɪkn/ vt anwidern ● vi be
~ing for something krank werden

sickle /'sɪkl/ n Sichel f

sick|ly /'sɪklɪ/ a (-ier, -iest) kränklich.
~ness n Krankheit f; (vomiting) Erbrechen nt

'**sick-room** *n* Krankenzimmer *nt*

side /saɪd/ *n* Seite *f*; **on the ~** (*as side-line*) nebenbei; **~ by ~** nebenein-ander; (*fig*) Seite an Seite; **take ~s** Partei ergreifen (**with** für); **to be on the safe ~** vorsichtshalber ● *attrib* Seiten- ● *vi* **~ with** Partei ergreifen für

side: **~board** *n* Anrichte *f*. **~burns** *npl* Koteletten *pl*. **~-effect** *n* Nebenwirkung *f*. **~lights** *npl* Standlicht *nt*. **~line** *n* Neben-beschäftigung *f*. **~-show** *n* Neben-attraktion *f*. **~-step** *vt* ausweichen (+ *dat*). **~-track** *vt* ablenken. **~walk** *n* (*Amer*) Bürgersteig *m*. **~ways** *adv* seitwärts

siding /'saɪdɪŋ/ *n* Abstellgleis *nt*

sidle /'saɪdl/ *vi* sich heranschleichen (**up to** an + *acc*)

siege /si:dʒ/ *n* Belagerung *f*; (*by police*) Umstellung *f*

sieve /sɪv/ *n* Sieb *nt* ● *vt* sieben

sift /sɪft/ *vt* sieben; (*fig*) durchsehen

sigh /saɪ/ *n* Seufzer *m* ● *vi* seufzen

sight /saɪt/ *n* Sicht *f*; (*faculty*) Sehvermögen *nt*; (*spectacle*) Anblick *m*; (*on gun*) Visier *nt*; **~s** *pl* Sehenswürdigkeiten *pl*; **at first ~** auf den ersten Blick; **within/out of ~** in/außer Sicht; **lose ~ of** aus dem Auge verlieren; **know by ~** vom Sehen kennen; **have bad ~** schlechte Augen haben ● *vt* sichten

'**sightseeing** *n* **go ~** die Sehens-würdigkeiten besichtigen

sign /saɪn/ *n* Zeichen *nt*; (*notice*) Schild *nt* ● *vt/i* unterschreiben; (*au-thor, artist:*) signieren. **~ on** *vi* (*as unemployed*) sich arbeitslos melden; (*Mil*) sich verpflichten

signal /'sɪgnl/ *n* Signal *nt* ● *vt/i* (*pt/pp* **signalled**) signalisieren; **~ to s.o.** jdm ein Signal geben (**to** zu). **~-box** *n* Stellwerk *nt*

signature /'sɪgnətʃə(r)/ *n* Unter-schrift *f*; (*of artist*) Signatur *f*. **~ tune** *n* Kennmelodie *f*

signet-ring /'sɪgnɪt-/ *n* Siegelring *m*

significan|ce /sɪg'nɪfɪkəns/ *n* Bedeutung *f*. **~t** *a*, **-ly** *adv* bedeu-tungsvoll; (*important*) bedeutend

signify /'sɪgnɪfaɪ/ *vt* (*pt/pp* -ied) be-deuten

signpost /'saɪn-/ *n* Wegweiser *m*

silence /'saɪləns/ *n* Stille *f*; (*of per-son*) Schweigen *nt* ● *vt* zum Schweigen bringen. **~r** *n* (*on gun*)

Schalldämpfer *m*; (*Auto*) Auspufftopf *m*

silent /'saɪlənt/ *a*, **-ly** *adv* still; (*with-out speaking*) schweigend; **remain ~** schweigen. **~ film** *n* Stummfilm *m*

silhouette /sɪlu:'et/ *n* Silhouette *f*; (*picture*) Schattenriß *m* ● *vt* **be ~d** sich als Silhouette abheben

silicon /'sɪlɪkən/ *n* Silizium *nt*

silk /sɪlk/ *n* Seide *f* ● *attrib* Seiden-. **~worm** *n* Seidenraupe *f*

silky /'sɪlkɪ/ *a* (**-ier, -iest**) seidig

sill /sɪl/ *n* Sims *m* & *nt*

silly /'sɪlɪ/ *a* (**-ier, -iest**) dumm, albern

silo /'saɪləʊ/ *n* Silo *m*

silt /sɪlt/ *n* Schlick *m*

silver /'sɪlvə(r)/ *a* silbern; (*coin, paper*) Silber- ● *n* Silber *nt*

silver: **~-plated** *a* versilbert. **~ware** *n* Tafelsilber *nt*. **~ 'wedding** *n* Silberhochzeit *f*

similar /'sɪmɪlə(r)/ *a*, **-ly** *adv* ähnlich. **~ity** /-'lærətɪ/ *n* Ähnlichkeit *f*

simile /'sɪmɪlɪ/ *n* Vergleich *m*

simmer /'sɪmə(r)/ *vi* leise kochen, ziehen ● *vt* ziehen lassen

simple /'sɪmpl/ *a* (**-r, -st**) einfach; (*person*) einfältig. **~-'minded** *a* ein-fältig. **~ton** /'sɪmpltən/ *n* Einfalts-pinsel *m*

simplicity /sɪm'plɪsətɪ/ *n* Ein-fachheit *f*

simpli|fication /sɪmplɪfɪ'keɪʃn/ *n* Vereinfachung *f*. **~fy** /'sɪmplɪfaɪ/ *vt* (*pt/pp* -ied) vereinfachen

simply /'sɪmplɪ/ *adv* einfach

simulat|e /'sɪmjʊleɪt/ *vt* vor-täuschen; (*Techn*) simulieren. **~ion** /-'leɪʃn/ *n* Vortäuschung *f*; Simulation *f*

simultaneous /sɪml'teɪnɪəs/ *a*, **-ly** *adv* gleichzeitig; (*interpreting*) Simul-tan-

sin /sɪn/ *n* Sünde *f* ● *vi* (*pt/pp* **sinned**) sündigen

since /sɪns/ *prep* seit (+ *dat*) ● *adv* seitdem ● *conj* seit; (*because*) da

sincere /sɪn'sɪə(r)/ *a* aufrichtig; (*heartfelt*) herzlich. **~ly** *adv* auf-richtig; **Yours ~ly** Mit freundlichen Grüßen

sincerity /sɪn'serətɪ/ *n* Aufrichtig-keit *f*

sinew /'sɪnju:/ *n* Sehne *f*

sinful /'sɪnfl/ *a* sündhaft

sing /sɪŋ/ *vt/i* (*pt* **sang**, *pp* **sung**) singen

singe /sɪndʒ/ *vt* (*pres p* **singeing**) versengen

singer /'sɪŋə(r)/ *n* Sänger(in) *m(f)*

single /'sɪŋgl/ *a* einzeln; (*one only*) einzig; (*unmarried*) ledig; (*ticket*) einfach; ⟨*room, bed*⟩ Einzel- ● *n* (*ticket*) einfache Fahrkarte *f*; ⟨*record*⟩ Single *f*; ~**s** *pl* (*Tennis*) Einzel *nt* ● *vt* ~ **out** auswählen

single: ~**-breasted** *a* einreihig. ~**-handed** *a* & *adv* allein. ~**-minded** *a* zielstrebig. ~ '**parent** *n* Alleinerziehende(r) *m/f*

singlet /'sɪŋglɪt/ *n* Unterhemd *nt*

singly /'sɪŋglɪ/ *adv* einzeln

singular /'sɪŋgjʊlə(r)/ *a* eigenartig; (*Gram*) im Singular ● *n* Singular *m*. ~**ly** *adv* außerordentlich

sinister /'sɪnɪstə(r)/ *a* finster

sink /sɪŋk/ *n* Spülbecken *nt* ● *v* (*pt* **sank**, *pp* **sunk**) ● *vi* sinken ● *vt* versenken ⟨*ship*⟩; senken ⟨*shaft*⟩. ~ **in** *vi* einsinken; (*fam: be understood*) kapiert werden

'**sink unit** *n* Spüle *f*

sinner /'sɪnə(r)/ *n* Sünder(in) *m(f)*

sinus /'saɪnəs/ *n* Nebenhöhle *f*

sip /sɪp/ *n* Schlückchen *nt* ● *vt* (*pt/pp* **sipped**) in kleinen Schlucken trinken

siphon /'saɪfn/ *n* ⟨*bottle*⟩ Siphon *m*. ~ **off** *vt* mit einem Saugheber ablassen

sir /sɜː(r)/ *n* mein Herr; **S**~ (*title*) Sir; **Dear S**~**s** Sehr geehrte Herren

siren /'saɪrən/ *n* Sirene *f*

sissy /'sɪsɪ/ *n* Waschlappen *m*

sister /'sɪstə(r)/ *n* Schwester *f*; (*nurse*) Oberschwester *f*. ~**-in-law** *n* (*pl* ~**s-in-law**) Schwägerin *f*. ~**ly** *a* schwesterlich

sit /sɪt/ *v* (*pt/pp* **sat**, *pres p* **sitting**) ● *vi* sitzen; (*sit down*) sich setzen; ⟨*committee:*⟩ tagen ● *vt* setzen; machen ⟨*exam*⟩. ~ **back** *vi* sich zurücklehnen. ~ **down** *vi* sich setzen. ~ **up** *vi* [aufrecht] sitzen; (*rise*) sich aufsetzen; (*not slouch*) gerade sitzen; (*stay up*) aufbleiben

site /saɪt/ *n* Gelände *nt*; (*for camping*) Platz *m*; (*Archaeol*) Stätte *f* ● *vt* legen

sitting /'sɪtɪŋ/ *n* Sitzung *f*; (*for meals*) Schub *m*

situat|e /'sɪtjʊeɪt/ *vt* legen; **be** ~**ed** liegen. ~**ion** /-'eɪʃn/ *n* Lage *f*; (*circumstances*) Situation *f*; (*job*) Stelle *f*

six /sɪks/ *a* sechs. ~**teen** *a* sechzehn. ~**teenth** *a* sechzehnte(r,s)

sixth /sɪksθ/ *a* sechste(r,s)

sixtieth /'sɪkstɪɪθ/ *a* sechzigste(r,s)

sixty /'sɪkstɪ/ *a* sechzig

size /saɪz/ *n* Größe *f* ● *vt* ~ **up** (*fam*) taxieren

sizeable /'saɪzəbl/ *a* ziemlich groß

sizzle /'sɪzl/ *vi* brutzeln

skate[1] /skeɪt/ *n inv* (*fish*) Rochen *m*

skate[2] *n* Schlittschuh *m*; (*roller-*) Rollschuh *m* ● *vi* Schlittschuh/Rollschuh laufen. ~**r** *n* Eisläufer(in) *m(f)*; Rollschuhläufer(in) *m(f)*

skating /'skeɪtɪŋ/ *n* Eislaufen *nt*. ~**-rink** *n* Eisbahn *f*

skeleton /'skelɪtn/ *n* Skelett *nt*. ~ '**key** *n* Dietrich *m*. ~ '**staff** *n* Minimalbesetzung *f*

sketch /sketʃ/ *n* Skizze *f*; (*Theat*) Sketch *m* ● *vt* skizzieren

sketchy /'sketʃɪ/ *a* (**-ier, -iest**), **-ily** *adv* skizzenhaft

skew /skjuː/ *n* **on the** ~ schräg

skewer /'skjʊə(r)/ *n* [Brat]spieß *m*

ski /skiː/ *n* Ski *m* ● *vi* (*pt/pp* **skied**, *pres p* **skiing**) Ski fahren *or* laufen

skid /skɪd/ *n* Schleudern *nt* ● *vi* (*pt/pp* **skidded**) schleudern

skier /'skiːə(r)/ *n* Skiläufer(in) *m(f)*

skiing /'skiːɪŋ/ *n* Skilaufen *nt*

skilful /'skɪlfl/ *a*, **-ly** *adv* geschickt

skill /skɪl/ *n* Geschick *nt*. ~**ed** *a* geschickt; (*trained*) ausgebildet

skim /skɪm/ *vt* (*pt/pp* **skimmed**) entrahmen ⟨*milk*⟩. ~ **off** *vt* abschöpfen. ~ **through** *vt* überfliegen

skimp /skɪmp/ *vt* sparen an (+ *dat*)

skimpy /'skɪmpɪ/ *a* (**-ier, -iest**) knapp

skin /skɪn/ *n* Haut *f*; (*on fruit*) Schale *f* ● *vt* (*pt/pp* **skinned**) häuten; schälen ⟨*fruit*⟩

skin: ~**-deep** *a* oberflächlich. ~**-diving** *n* Sporttauchen *nt*

skinflint /'skɪnflɪnt/ *n* Geizhals *m*

skinny /'skɪnɪ/ *a* (**-ier, -iest**) dünn

skip[1] /skɪp/ *n* Container *m*

skip[2] *n* Hüpfer *m* ● *v* (*pt/pp* **skipped**) *vi* hüpfen; (*with rope*) seilspringen ● *vt* überspringen

skipper /'skɪpə(r)/ *n* Kapitän *m*

'**skipping-rope** *n* Sprungseil *nt*

skirmish /'skɜːmɪʃ/ *n* Gefecht *nt*

skirt /skɜːt/ *n* Rock *m* ● *vt* herumgehen um

skit /skɪt/ *n* parodistischer Sketch *m*

skittle /'skɪtl/ *n* Kegel *m*

skive /skaɪv/ *vi* (*fam*) blaumachen

skulk /skʌlk/ *vi* lauern

skull /skʌl/ *n* Schädel *m*

skunk /skʌŋk/ n Stinktier nt
sky /skaɪ/ n Himmel m. ∼**light** n
Dachluke f. ∼**scraper** n Wolken-
kratzer m
slab /slæb/ n Platte f; (slice) Scheibe
f; (of chocolate) Tafel f
slack /slæk/ a (-er, -est) schlaff,
locker; ⟨person⟩ nachlässig; (Comm)
flau ● vi bummeln
slacken /'slækn/ vi sich lockern;
(diminish) nachlassen; ⟨speed:⟩ sich
verringern ● vt lockern; (diminish)
verringern
slacks /slæks/ npl Hose f
slag /slæg/ n Schlacke f
slain /sleɪn/ see **slay**
slake /sleɪk/ vt löschen
slam /slæm/ v (pt/pp **slammed**) ● vt
zuschlagen; (put) knallen (fam); ⟨fam:
criticize⟩ verreißen ● vi zuschlagen
slander /'slɑːndə(r)/ n Verleumdung
f ● vt verleumden. ∼**ous** /-rəs/ a
verleumderisch
slang /slæŋ/ n Slang m. ∼**y** a salopp
slant /slɑːnt/ n Schräge f; **on the** ∼
schräg ● vt abschrägen; (fig) färben ⟨re-
port⟩ ● vi sich neigen
slap /slæp/ n Schlag m ● vt (pt/pp
slapped) schlagen; (put) knallen (fam)
● adv direkt
slap: ∼**dash** a (fam) schludrig. ∼**-up**
a (fam) toll
slash /slæʃ/ n Schlitz m ● vt aufschlitzen; [drastisch] reduzieren
⟨prices⟩
slat /slæt/ n Latte f
slate /sleɪt/ n Schiefer m ● vt (fam)
heruntermachen; verreißen ⟨per-
formance⟩
slaughter /'slɔːtə(r)/ n Schlachten
nt; (massacre) Gemetzel nt ● vt
schlachten; abschlachten. ∼**house** n
Schlachthaus nt
Slav /slɑːv/ a slawisch ● n Slawe m/
Slawin f
slave /sleɪv/ n Sklave m/Sklavin f
● vi ∼ **[away]** schuften. ∼**-driver** n
Leuteschinder m
slav|ery /'sleɪvərɪ/ n Sklaverei f.
∼**ish** a, **-ly** adv sklavisch
Slavonic /slə'vɒnɪk/ a slawisch
slay /sleɪ/ vt (pt **slew**, pp **slain**) ermorden
sleazy /'sliːzɪ/ a (-ier, -iest) schäbig
sledge /sledʒ/ n Schlitten m.
∼**-hammer** n Vorschlaghammer m.
sleek /sliːk/ a (-er, -est) seidig; (well-
fed) wohlgenährt

sleep /sliːp/ n Schlaf m; **go to** ∼ einschlafen; **put to** ∼ einschläfern ● v (pt/
pp **slept**) ● vi schlafen ● vt (accommodate) Unterkunft bieten für. ∼**er**
n Schläfer(in) m(f); (Rail)
Schlafwagen m; (on track) Schwelle f
sleeping: ∼**-bag** n Schlafsack m.
∼**-car** n Schlafwagen m. ∼**-pill** n
Schlaftablette f
sleep: ∼**less** a schlaflos. ∼**-walking**
n Schlafwandeln nt
sleepy /'sliːpɪ/ a (-ier, -iest), **-ily** adv
schläfrig
sleet /sliːt/ n Schneeregen m ● vi **it is**
∼**ing** es gibt Schneeregen
sleeve /sliːv/ n Ärmel m; (for record)
Hülle f. ∼**less** a ärmellos
sleigh /sleɪ/ n [Pferde]schlitten m
sleight /slaɪt/ n ∼ **of hand**
Taschenspielerei f
slender /'slendə(r)/ a schlank; (fig)
gering
slept /slept/ see **sleep**
sleuth /sluːθ/ n Detektiv m
slew¹ /sluː/ vi schwenken
slew² see **slay**
slice /slaɪs/ n Scheibe f ● vt in
Scheiben schneiden; ∼**d bread**
Schnittbrot nt
slick /slɪk/ a clever ● n (of oil) Ölteppich m
slid|e /slaɪd/ n Rutschbahn f; (for
hair) Spange f; (Phot) Dia nt ● v (pt/
pp **slid**) ● vi rutschen ● vt schieben.
∼**ing** a gleitend; ⟨door, seat⟩ Schiebe-
slight /slaɪt/ a (-er, -est), **-ly** adv
leicht; (importance) gering; (acquaintance) flüchtig; (slender) schlank;
not in the ∼**est** nicht im geringsten;
∼**ly better** ein bißchen besser ● vt
kränken, beleidigen ● n Beleidigung f
slim /slɪm/ a (**slimmer, slimmest**)
schlank; ⟨volume⟩ schmal; (fig) gering
● vi eine Schlankheitskur machen
slim|e /slaɪm/ n Schleim m. ∼**y** a
schleimig
sling /slɪŋ/ n (Med) Schlinge f ● vt
(pt/pp **slung**) (fam) schmeißen
slip /slɪp/ n (mistake) Fehler m, (fam)
Patzer m; (petticoat) Unterrock m;
(for pillow) Bezug m; (paper) Zettel
m; **give s.o. the** ∼ (fam) jdm entwischen; ∼ **of the tongue** Versprecher
m ● v (pt/pp **slipped**) ● vi rutschen;
(fall) ausrutschen; (go quickly)
schlüpfen; (decline) nachlassen ● vt
schieben; ∼ **s.o.'s mind** jdm entfallen.
∼ **away** vi sich fortschleichen;

⟨*time:*⟩ verfliegen. ~ **up** *vi* (*fam*) einen Schnitzer machen

slipped 'disc *n* (*Med*) Bandscheibenvorfall *m*

slipper /'slɪpə(r)/ *n* Hausschuh *m*

slippery /'slɪpərɪ/ *a* glitschig; ⟨*surface*⟩ glatt

slipshod /'slɪpʃɒd/ *a* schludrig

'slip-up *n* (*fam*) Schnitzer *m*

slit /slɪt/ *n* Schlitz *m* ● *vt* (*pt/pp* **slit**) aufschlitzen

slither /'slɪðə(r)/ *vi* rutschen

sliver /'slɪvə(r)/ *n* Splitter *m*

slobber /'slɒbə(r)/ *vi* sabbern

slog /slɒg/ *n* [hard] ~ Schinderei *f* ● *v* (*pt/pp* **slogged**) ● *vi* schuften ● *vt* schlagen

slogan /'sləʊgən/ *n* Schlagwort *nt*; (*advertising*) Werbespruch *m*

slop /slɒp/ *v* (*pt/pp* **slopped**) ● *vt* verschütten ● *vi* ~ **over** überschwappen. ~**s** *npl* Schmutzwasser *nt*

slop|e /sləʊp/ *n* Hang *m*; (*inclination*) Neigung *f* ● *vi* sich neigen. ~**ing** *a* schräg

sloppy /'slɒpɪ/ *a* (**-ier, -iest**) schludrig; (*sentimental*) sentimental

slosh /slɒʃ/ *vi* (*fam*) platschen; ⟨*water:*⟩ schwappen ● *vt* (*fam: hit*) schlagen

slot /slɒt/ *n* Schlitz *m*; (*TV*) Sendezeit *f* ● *v* (*pt/pp* **slotted**) ● *vt* einfügen ● *vi* sich einfügen (**in** in + *acc*)

sloth /sləʊθ/ *n* Trägheit *f*

'slot-machine *n* Münzautomat *m*; (*for gambling*) Spielautomat *m*

slouch /slaʊtʃ/ *vi* sich schlecht halten

slovenly /'slʌvnlɪ/ *a* schlampig

slow /sləʊ/ *a* (**-er, -est**), **-ly** *adv* langsam; **be** ~ ⟨*clock:*⟩ nachgehen; **in** ~ **motion** in Zeitlupe ● *adv* langsam ● *vt* verlangsamen ● *vi* ~ **down**, ~ **up** langsamer werden

slow: ~**coach** *n* (*fam*) Trödler *m*. ~**ness** *n* Langsamkeit *f*

sludge /slʌdʒ/ *n* Schlamm *m*

slug /slʌg/ *n* Nacktschnecke *f*

sluggish /'slʌgɪʃ/ *a*, **-ly** *adv* träge

sluice /sluːs/ *n* Schleuse *f*

slum /slʌm/ *n* (*house*) Elendsquartier *nt*; ~**s** *pl* Elendsviertel *nt*

slumber /'slʌmbə(r)/ *n* Schlummer *m* ● *vi* schlummern

slump /slʌmp/ *n* Sturz *m* ● *vi* fallen; (*crumple*) zusammensacken; ⟨*prices:*⟩ stürzen; ⟨*sales:*⟩ zurückgehen

slung /slʌŋ/ *see* **sling**

slur /slɜː(r)/ *n* (*discredit*) Schande *f* ● *vt* (*pt/pp* **slurred**) undeutlich sprechen

slurp /slɜːp/ *vt/i* schlürfen

slush /slʌʃ/ *n* [Schnee]matsch *m*; (*fig*) Kitsch *m*. ~ **fund** *n* Fonds *m* für Bestechungsgelder

slushy /'slʌʃɪ/ *a* matschig; (*sentimental*) kitschig

slut /slʌt/ *n* Schlampe *f* (*fam*)

sly /slaɪ/ *a* (**-er, -est**), **-ly** *adv* verschlagen ● *n* **on the** ~ heimlich

smack[1] /smæk/ *n* Schlag *m*, Klaps *m* ● *vt* schlagen; ~ **one's lips** mit den Lippen schmatzen ● *adv* (*fam*) direkt

smack[2] *vi* ~ **of** (*fig*) riechen nach

small /smɔːl/ *a* (**-er, -est**) klein; **in the** ~ **hours** in den frühen Morgenstunden ● *adv* **chop up** ~ kleinhacken ● *n* ~ **of the back** Kreuz *nt*

small: ~ **ads** *npl* Kleinanzeigen *pl.* ~ **'change** *n* Kleingeld *nt.* ~**- holding** *n* landwirtschaftlicher Kleinbetrieb *m.* ~**pox** *n* Pocken *pl.* ~ **talk** *n* leichte Konversation *f*

smarmy /'smɑːmɪ/ *a* (**-ier, -iest**) (*fam*) ölig

smart /smɑːt/ *a* (**-er, -est**), **-ly** *adv* schick; (*clever*) schlau, clever; (*brisk*) flott; (*Amer fam: cheeky*) frech ● *vi* brennen

smarten /'smɑːtn/ *vt* ~ **oneself up** mehr auf sein Äußeres achten

smash /smæʃ/ *n* Krach *m*; (*collision*) Zusammenstoß *m*; (*Tennis*) Schmetterball *m* ● *vt* zerschlagen; (*strike*) schlagen; (*Tennis*) schmettern ● *vi* zerschmettern; (*crash*) krachen (**into** gegen). ~**ing** *a* (*fam*) toll

smattering /'smætərɪŋ/ *n* a ~ **of German** ein paar Brocken Deutsch

smear /smɪə(r)/ *n* verschmierter Fleck *m*; (*Med*) Abstrich *m*; (*fig*) Verleumdung *f* ● *vt* schmieren; (*coat*) beschmieren (**with** mit); (*fig*) verleumden ● *vi* schmieren

smell /smel/ *n* Geruch *m*; (*sense*) Geruchssinn *m* ● *v* (*pt/pp* **smelt** *or* **smelled**) ● *vt* riechen; (*sniff*) riechen an (+ *dat*) ● *vi* riechen (**of** nach)

smelly /'smelɪ/ *a* (**-ier, -iest**) übelriechend

smelt[1] /smelt/ *see* **smell**

smelt[2] *vt* schmelzen

smile /smaɪl/ *n* Lächeln *nt* ● *vi* lächeln; ~ **at** anlächeln

smirk /smɜːk/ *vi* feixen

smith /smɪθ/ n Schmied m
smithereens /smɪðə'ri:nz/ npl
smash to ~ in tausend Stücke
schlagen
smitten /'smɪtn/ a ~ **with** sehr angetan von
smock /smɒk/ n Kittel m
smog /smɒg/ n Smog m
smoke /sməʊk/ n Rauch m ● vt/i
rauchen; (Culin) räuchern. ~**less** a
rauchfrei; (fuel) rauchlos
smoker /'sməʊkə(r)/ n Raucher m;
(Rail) Raucherabteil nt
'**smoke-screen** n [künstliche] Ne-
belwand f
smoking /'sməʊkɪŋ/ n Rauchen nt;
'**no** ~' 'Rauchen verboten'
smoky /'sməʊkɪ/ a (-ier, -iest) ver-
raucht; (taste) rauchig
smooth /smu:ð/ a (-er, -est), -ly adv
glatt ● vt glätten. ~ **out** vt glatt-
streichen
smother /'smʌðə(r)/ vt ersticken;
(cover) bedecken; (suppress) unterdrücken
smoulder /'sməʊldə(r)/ vi schwelen
smudge /smʌdʒ/ n Fleck m ● vt verwischen ● vi schmieren
smug /smʌg/ a (smugger, smug-
gest), -ly adv selbstgefällig
smuggl|e /'smʌgl/ vt schmuggeln.
~**er** n Schmuggler m. ~**ing** n
Schmuggel m
smut /smʌt/ n Rußflocke f; (mark)
Rußfleck m; (fig) Schmutz m
smutty /'smʌtɪ/ a · (-ier, -iest)
schmutzig
snack /snæk/ n Imbiß m. ~**-bar** n
Imbißstube f
snag /snæg/ n Schwierigkeit f, (fam)
Haken m
snail /sneɪl/ n Schnecke f; **at a** ~'s
pace im Schneckentempo
snake /sneɪk/ n Schlange f
snap /snæp/ n Knacken nt; (photo)
Schnappschuß m ● attrib (decision)
plötzlich ● v (pt/pp snapped) ● vi
[entzwei]brechen; ~ **at** (bite) schnappen nach; (speak sharply) [scharf] anfahren ● vt zerbrechen; (say) fauchen;
(Phot) knipsen. ~ **up** vt wegschnap-
pen
snappy /'snæpɪ/ a (-ier, -iest) bissig;
(smart) flott; **make it** ~! ein bißchen
schnell!
'**snapshot** n Schnappschuß m
snare /sneə(r)/ n Schlinge f

snarl /snɑ:l/ vi [mit gefletschten
Zähnen] knurren
snatch /snætʃ/ n (fragment) Fetzen
pl; (theft) Raub m; **make a** ~ **at** greifen nach ● vt schnappen; (steal)
klauen; entführen (child); ~ **sth from**
s.o. jdm etw entreißen
sneak /sni:k/ n (fam) Petze f ● vi
schleichen; (fam: tell tales) petzen
● vt (take) mitgehen lassen ● vi ~ **in/**
out sich hinein-/hinausschleichen
sneakers /'sni:kəz/ npl (Amer) Turnschuhe pl
sneaking /'sni:kɪŋ/ a heimlich; (suspicion) leise
sneaky /'sni:kɪ/ a hinterhältig
sneer /snɪə(r)/ vi höhnisch lächeln;
(mock) spotten
sneeze /sni:z/ n Niesen nt ● vi niesen
snide /snaɪd/ a (fam) abfällig
sniff /snɪf/ vi schnüffeln ● vt
schnüffeln an (+ dat); schnüffeln
(glue)
snigger /'snɪgə(r)/ vi [boshaft] kichern
snip /snɪp/ n Schnitt m; (fam: bargain) günstiger Kauf m ● vt/i ~ [at]
schnippeln an (+ dat)
snipe /snaɪp/ vi ~ **at** aus dem Hinterhalt schießen (auf + acc); (fig) an-
schießen. ~**r** n Heckenschütze m
snippet /'snɪpɪt/ n Schnipsel m; (of
information) Bruchstück nt
snivel /'snɪvl/ vi (pt/pp snivelled)
flennen
snob /snɒb/ n Snob m. ~**bery** n
Snobismus m. ~**bish** a snobistisch
snoop /snu:p/ vi (fam) schnüffeln
snooty /'snu:tɪ/ a (fam) hochnäsig
snooze /snu:z/ n Nickerchen nt ● vi
dösen
snore /snɔ:(r)/ vi schnarchen
snorkel /'snɔ:kl/ n Schnorchel m
snort /snɔ:t/ vi schnauben
snout /snaʊt/ n Schnauze f
snow /snəʊ/ n Schnee m ● vi
schneien; ~**ed under with** (fig) üb-
erhäuft mit
snow: ~**ball** n Schneeball m ● vi
lawinenartig anwachsen. ~**drift** n
Schneewehe f. ~**drop** n Schnee-
glöckchen nt. ~**fall** n Schneefall m.
~**flake** n Schneeflocke f. ~ **flurry** n
Schneegestöber nt. ~**man** n
Schneemann m. ~**plough** n
Schneepflug m. ~**storm** n Schneesturm m

snub /snʌb/ n Abfuhr f ● vt (pt/pp **snubbed**) brüskieren

'snub-nosed a stupsnasig

snuff¹ /snʌf/ n Schnupftabak m

snuff² vt ~ **[out]** löschen

snuffle /'snʌfl/ vi schnüffeln

snug /snʌg/ a (**snugger, snuggest**) behaglich, gemütlich

snuggle /'snʌgl/ vi sich kuscheln (**up to** an + acc)

so /səʊ/ adv so; **not so fast** nicht so schnell; **so am I** ich auch; **so does he** er auch; **so I see** das sehe ich; **that is so** das stimmt; **so much the better** um so besser; **so it is** tatsächlich; **if so** wenn ja; **so as to** um zu; **so long!** (fam) tschüs! ● pron **I hope so** hoffentlich; **I think so** ich glaube schon; **I told you so** ich hab's dir gleich gesagt; **because I say so** weil ich es sage; **I'm afraid so** leider ja; **so saying/doing**, he/she ... indem er/sie das sagte/tat, ...; **an hour or so** eine Stunde oder so; **very much so** durchaus ● conj (therefore) also; **so that** damit; **so there!** fertig! **so what!** na und! **so you see** wie du siehst; **so where have you been?** wo warst du denn?

soak /səʊk/ vt naß machen; (steep) einweichen; (fam: fleece) schröpfen ● vi weichen; ⟨liquid:⟩ sickern. ~ **up** vt aufsaugen

soaking /'səʊkɪŋ/ a & adv ~ **[wet]** patschnaß (fam)

soap /səʊp/ n Seife f. ~ **opera** n Seifenoper f. ~ **powder** n Seifenpulver nt

soapy /'səʊpɪ/ a (-ier, -iest) seifig

soar /sɔ:(r)/ vi aufsteigen; ⟨prices:⟩ in die Höhe schnellen

sob /sɒb/ n Schluchzer m ● vi (pt/pp **sobbed**) schluchzen

sober /'səʊbə(r)/ a, -ly adv nüchtern; (serious) ernst; ⟨colour:⟩ gedeckt. ~ **up** vi nüchtern werden

'so-called a sogenannt

soccer /'sɒkə(r)/ n (fam) Fußball m

sociable /'səʊʃəbl/ a gesellig

social /'səʊʃl/ a gesellschaftlich; (Admin, Pol, Zool) sozial

socialis|m /'səʊʃəlɪzm/ n Sozialismus m. ~**t** /-ɪst/ a sozialistisch ● n Sozialist m

socialize /'səʊʃəlaɪz/ vi [gesellschaftlich] verkehren

socially /'səʊʃəlɪ/ adv gesellschaftlich; **know** ~ privat kennen

social: ~ **se'curity** n Sozialhilfe f. ~ **work** n Sozialarbeit f. ~ **worker** n Sozialarbeiter(in) m(f)

society /sə'saɪətɪ/ n Gesellschaft f; (club) Verein m

sociolog|ist /səʊsɪ'ɒlədʒɪst/ n Soziologe m. ~**y** n Soziologie f

sock¹ /sɒk/ n Socke f; (knee-length) Kniestrumpf m

sock² n (fam) Schlag m ● vt (fam) hauen

socket /'sɒkɪt/ n (of eye) Augenhöhle f; (of joint) Gelenkpfanne f; (wall plug) Steckdose f; (for bulb) Fassung f

soda /'səʊdə/ n Soda nt; (Amer) Limonade f. ~ **water** n Sodawasser nt

sodden /'sɒdn/ a durchnäßt

sodium /'səʊdɪəm/ n Natrium nt

sofa /'səʊfə/ n Sofa nt. ~ **bed** n Schlafcouch f

soft /sɒft/ a (-er, -est), -ly adv weich; (quiet) leise; (gentle) sanft; (fam: silly) dumm; **have a** ~ **spot for s.o.** jdn mögen. ~ **drink** n alkoholfreies Getränk nt

soften /'sɒfn/ vt weich machen; (fig) mildern ● vi weich werden

soft: ~ **toy** n Stofftier nt. ~**ware** n Software f

soggy /'sɒgɪ/ a (-ier, -iest) aufgeweicht

soil¹ /sɔɪl/ n Erde f, Boden m

soil² vt verschmutzen

solace /'sɒləs/ n Trost m

solar /'səʊlə(r)/ a Sonnen-

sold /səʊld/ see **sell**

solder /'səʊldə(r)/ n Lötmetall nt ● vt löten

soldier /'səʊldʒə(r)/ n Soldat m ● vi ~ **on** [unbeirrbar] weitermachen

sole¹ /səʊl/ n Sohle f

sole² n (fish) Seezunge f

sole³ a einzig. ~**ly** adv einzig und allein

solemn /'sɒləm/ a, -ly adv feierlich; (serious) ernst. ~**ity** /sə'lemnətɪ/ n Feierlichkeit f; Ernst m

solicit /sə'lɪsɪt/ vt bitten um ● vi ⟨prostitute:⟩ sich an Männer heranmachen

solicitor /sə'lɪsɪtə(r)/ n Rechtsanwalt m/-anwältin f

solicitous /sə'lɪsɪtəs/ a besorgt

solid /'sɒlɪd/ a fest; (sturdy) stabil; (not hollow, of same substance) massiv; (unanimous) einstimmig; (complete) ganz ● n (Geom) Körper m; ~**s** pl (food) feste Nahrung f

solidarity /sɒlɪˈdærətɪ/ n Solidarität f

solidify /səˈlɪdɪfaɪ/ vi (pt/pp -ied) fest werden

soliloquy /səˈlɪləkwɪ/ n Selbstgespräch nt

solitary /ˈsɒlɪtərɪ/ a einsam; (sole) einzig. ~ con'finement n Einzelhaft f

solitude /ˈsɒlɪtjuːd/ n Einsamkeit f

solo /ˈsəʊləʊ/ n Solo nt ● a Solo-; (flight) Allein- ● adv solo. ~ist n Solist(in) m(f)

solstice /ˈsɒlstɪs/ n Sonnenwende f

soluble /ˈsɒljʊbl/ a löslich; (solvable) lösbar

solution /səˈluːʃn/ n Lösung f

solvable /ˈsɒlvəbl/ a lösbar

solve /sɒlv/ vt lösen

solvent /ˈsɒlvənt/ a zahlungsfähig; (Chem) lösend ● n Lösungsmittel nt

sombre /ˈsɒmbə(r)/ a dunkel; (mood) düster

some /sʌm/ a & pron etwas; (a little) ein bißchen; (with pl noun) einige; (a few) ein paar; (certain) manche(r,s); (one or the other) [irgend]ein; ~ day eines Tages; I want ~ ich möchte etwas/(pl) welche; will you have ~ wine? möchten Sie Wein? I need ~ money/books ich brauche Geld/ Bücher; do ~ shopping einkaufen

some: ~body /-bədɪ/ pron & n jemand; (emphatic) irgend jemand. ~how adv irgendwie. ~one pron & n = somebody

somersault /ˈsʌməsɔːlt/ n Purzelbaum m (fam); (Sport) Salto m; turn a ~ einen Purzelbaum schlagen/ einen Salto springen

'something pron & adv etwas; (emphatic) irgend etwas; ~ different etwas anderes; ~ like so etwas wie; see ~ of s.o. jdn mal sehen

some: ~time adv irgendwann ● a ehemalig. ~times adv manchmal. ~what adv ziemlich. ~where adv irgendwo; (go) irgendwohin

son /sʌn/ n Sohn m

sonata /səˈnɑːtə/ n Sonate f

song /sɒŋ/ n Lied nt. ~bird n Singvogel m

sonic /ˈsɒnɪk/ a Schall-. ~ 'boom n Überschallknall m

'son-in-law n (pl ~s-in-law) Schwiegersohn m

soon /suːn/ adv (-er, -est) bald; (quickly) schnell; too ~ zu früh; as ~

as sobald; as ~ as possible so bald wie möglich; ~er or later früher oder später; no ~er had I arrived than ... kaum war ich angekom- men, da ...; I would ~er stay ich würde lieber bleiben

soot /sʊt/ n Ruß m

soothe /suːð/ vt beruhigen; lindern (pain). ~ing a, -ly adv beruhigend; lindernd

sooty /ˈsʊtɪ/ a rußig

sop /sɒp/ n Beschwichtigungsmittel nt

sophisticated /səˈfɪstɪkeɪtɪd/ a weltgewandt; (complex) hochentwickelt

soporific /sɒpəˈrɪfɪk/ a einschläfernd

sopping /ˈsɒpɪŋ/ a & adv ~ [wet] durchnäßt

soppy /ˈsɒpɪ/ a (-ier, -iest) (fam) rührselig

soprano /səˈprɑːnəʊ/ n Sopran m; (woman) Sopranistin f

sordid /ˈsɔːdɪd/ a schmutzig

sore /sɔː(r)/ a (-r, -st) wund; (painful) schmerzhaft; have a ~ throat Halsschmerzen haben ● n wunde Stelle f. ~ly adv sehr

sorrow /ˈsɒrəʊ/ n Kummer m, Leid nt. ~ful a traurig

sorry /ˈsɒrɪ/ a (-ier, -iest) (sad) traurig; (wretched) erbärmlich; I am ~ es tut mir leid; she is or feels ~ for him er tut ihr leid; I am ~ to say leider; ~! Entschuldigung!

sort /sɔːt/ n Art f; (brand) Sorte f; he's a good ~ (fam) er ist in Ordnung; be out of ~s (fam) nicht auf der Höhe sein ● vt sortieren. ~ out vt sortieren; (fig) klären

sought /sɔːt/ see seek

soul /səʊl/ n Seele f. ~ful a gefühlvoll

sound[1] /saʊnd/ a (-er, -est) gesund; (sensible) vernünftig; (secure) solide; (thorough) gehörig ● adv be ~ asleep fest schlafen

sound[2] vt (Naut) loten. ~ out vt (fig) aushorchen

sound[3] n (strait) Meerenge f

sound[4] n Laut m; (noise) Geräusch nt; (Phys) Schall m; (Radio, TV) Ton m; (of bells, music) Klang m; I don't like the ~ of it (fam) das hört sich nicht gut an ● vi [er]tönen; (seem) sich anhören ● vt (pronounce) aussprechen; schlagen (alarm); (Med) abhorchen (chest).

~ **barrier** *n* Schallmauer *f.* ~**less** *a*, -**ly** *adv* lautlos

soundly /'saʊndlɪ/ *adv* solide; ⟨*sleep*⟩ fest; ⟨*defeat*⟩ vernichtend

'**soundproof** *a* schalldicht

soup /su:p/ *n* Suppe *f.* ~**ed-up** *a* (*fam*) ⟨*engine*⟩ frisiert

soup: ~-**plate** *n* Suppenteller *m.* ~-**spoon** *n* Suppenlöffel *m*

sour /'saʊə(r)/ *a* (-**er, -est**) sauer; (*bad-tempered*) griesgrämig, verdrießlich

source /so:s/ *n* Quelle *f*

south /saʊθ/ *n* Süden *m*; **to the ~ of** südlich von ● *a* Süd-, süd- ● *adv* nach Süden

south: S~ 'Africa *n* Südafrika *nt.* **S~ A'merica** *n* Südamerika *nt.* ~-'**east** *n* Südosten *m*

southerly /'sʌðəlɪ/ *a* südlich

southern /'sʌðən/ *a* südlich

South 'Pole *n* Südpol *m*

'**southward[s]** /-wəd[z]/ *adv* nach Süden

souvenir /su:və'nɪə(r)/ *n* Andenken *nt*, Souvenir *nt*

sovereign /'sɒvrɪn/ *a* souverän ● *n* Souverän *m.* ~**ty** *n* Souveränität *f*

Soviet /'səʊvɪət/ *a* sowjetisch; ~ **Union** Sowjetunion *f*

sow[1] /saʊ/ *n* Sau *f*

sow[2] /səʊ/ *vt* (*pt* **sowed,** *pp* **sown** or **sowed**) säen

soya /'sɔɪə/ *n* ~ **bean** Sojabohne *f*

spa /spa:/ *n* Heilbad *nt*

space /speɪs/ *n* Raum *m*; (*gap*) Platz *m*; (*Astr*) Weltraum *m*; **leave/clear a ~** Platz lassen/schaffen ● *vt* ~ [**out**] [in Abständen] verteilen

space: ~**craft** *n* Raumfahrzeug *nt.* ~**ship** *n* Raumschiff *nt*

spacious /'speɪʃəs/ *a* geräumig

spade /speɪd/ *n* Spaten *m*; (*for child*) Schaufel *f*; ~**s** *pl* ⟨*Cards*⟩ Pik *nt*; **call a ~ a ~** das Kind beim rechten Namen nennen. ~**work** *n* Vorarbeit *f*

Spain /speɪn/ *n* Spanien *nt*

span[1] /spæn/ *n* Spanne *f*; (*of arch*) Spannweite *f* ● *vt* (*pt/pp* **spanned**) überspannen; umspannen ⟨*time*⟩

span[2] *see* **spick**

Span|iard /'spænjəd/ *n* Spanier(in) *m(f).* ~**ish** *a* spanisch ● *n* (*Lang*) Spanisch *nt*; **the ~ish** *pl* die Spanier

spank /spæŋk/ *vt* verhauen

spanner /'spænə(r)/ *n* Schraubenschlüssel *m*

spar /spa:(r)/ *vi* (*pt/pp* **sparred**) (*Sport*) sparren; (*argue*) sich zanken

spare /speə(r)/ *a* (*surplus*) übrig; (*additional*) zusätzlich; ⟨*seat, time*⟩ frei; ⟨*room*⟩ Gäste-; ⟨*bed, cup*⟩ Extra- ● *n* (*part*) Ersatzteil *nt* ● *vt* ersparen; (*not hurt*) verschonen; (*do without*) entbehren; (*afford to give*) erübrigen; **to ~** (*surplus*) übrig. ~ '**wheel** *n* Reserverad *nt*

sparing /'speərɪŋ/ *a*, -**ly** *adv* sparsam

spark /spa:k/ *n* Funke *m* ● *vt* ~ **off** zünden; (*fig*) auslösen. ~**ing-plug** *n* (*Auto*) Zündkerze *f*

sparkl|e /'spa:kl/ *n* Funkeln *nt* ● *vi* funkeln. ~**ing** *a* funkelnd; ⟨*wine*⟩ Schaum-

sparrow /'spærəʊ/ *n* Spatz *m*

sparse /spa:s/ *a* spärlich. ~**ly** *adv* spärlich; ⟨*populated*⟩ dünn

Spartan /'spa:tn/ *a* spartanisch

spasm /'spæzm/ *n* Anfall *m*; (*cramp*) Krampf *m.* ~**odic** /-'mɒdɪk/ *a*, -**ally** *adv* sporadisch; (*Med*) krampfartig

spastic /'spæstɪk/ *a* spastisch [gelähmt] ● *n* Spastiker(in) *m(f)*

spat /spæt/ *see* **spit**[2]

spate /speɪt/ *n* Flut *f*; (*series*) Serie *f*; **be in full ~** Hochwasser führen

spatial /'speɪʃl/ *a* räumlich

spatter /'spætə(r)/ *vt* spritzen; ~ **with** bespritzen mit

spatula /'spætjʊlə/ *n* Spachtel *m*; (*Med*) Spatel *m*

spawn /spo:n/ *n* Laich *m* ● *vi* laichen ● *vt* (*fig*) hervorbringen

spay /speɪ/ *vt* sterilisieren

speak /spi:k/ *v* (*pt* **spoke,** *pp* **spoken**) ● *vi* sprechen (**to** mit); ~**ing!** (*Teleph*) am Apparat! ● *vt* sprechen; sagen ⟨*truth*⟩. ~ **up** *vi* lauter sprechen; ~ **up for oneself** seine Meinung äußern

speaker /'spi:kə(r)/ *n* Sprecher(in) *m(f)*; (*in public*) Redner(in) *m(f)*; (*loudspeaker*) Lautsprecher *m*

spear /spɪə(r)/ *n* Speer *m* ● *vt* aufspießen. ~**head** *vt* (*fig*) anführen

spec /spek/ *n* **on ~** (*fam*) auf gut Glück

special /'speʃl/ *a* besondere(r,s), speziell. ~**ist** *n* Spezialist *m*; (*Med*) Facharzt *m*/-ärztin *f.* ~**ity** /-ʃɪ'ælətɪ/ *n* Spezialität *f*

special|ize /'speʃəlaɪz/ *vi* sich spezialisieren (**in** auf + *acc*). ~**ly** *adv* speziell; (*particularly*) besonders

species /'spi:ʃi:z/ *n* Art *f*

specific /spə'sɪfɪk/ *a* bestimmt; (*precise*) genau; (*Phys*) spezifisch. ~**ally** *adv* ausdrücklich

specification /spesɪfɪ'keɪʃn/ n & ~s pl genaue Angaben pl

specify /'spesɪfaɪ/ vt (pt/pp -ied) [genau] angeben

specimen /'spesɪmən/ n Exemplar nt; (sample) Probe f; (of urine) Urinprobe f

speck /spek/ n Fleck m; (particle) Teilchen nt

speckled /'spekld/ a gesprenkelt

specs /speks/ npl (fam) Brille f

spectacle /'spektəkl/ n (show) Schauspiel nt; (sight) Anblick m. ~s npl Brille f

spectacular /spek'tækjʊlə(r)/ a spektakulär

spectator /spek'teɪtə(r)/ n Zuschauer(in) m(f)

spectre /'spektə(r)/ n Gespenst nt; (fig) Schreckgespenst nt

spectrum /'spektrəm/ n (pl -tra) Spektrum nt

speculat|e /'spekjʊleɪt/ vi spekulieren. ~ion /-'leɪʃn/ n Spekulation f. ~or n Spekulant m

sped /sped/ see speed

speech /spiːtʃ/ n Sprache f; (address) Rede f. ~less a sprachlos

speed /spiːd/ n Geschwindigkeit f; (rapidity) Schnelligkeit f; (gear) Gang m; **at** ~ mit hoher Geschwindigkeit ● vi (pt/pp sped) schnell fahren ● (pt/pp speeded) (go too fast) zu schnell fahren. ~ **up** (pt/pp speeded up) ● vt beschleunigen ● vi schneller werden; (vehicle:) schneller fahren

speed: ~**boat** n Rennboot nt. ~**ing** n Geschwindigkeitsüberschreitung f. ~ **limit** n Geschwindigkeitsbeschränkung f

speedometer /spiːˈdɒmɪtə(r)/ n Tachometer m

speedy /'spiːdɪ/ a (-ier, -iest), -ily adv schnell

spell[1] /spel/ n Weile f; (of weather) Periode f

spell[2] v (pt/pp spelled or spelt) ● vt schreiben; (aloud) buchstabieren; (fig: mean) bedeuten ● vi richtig schreiben; (aloud) buchstabieren. ~ **out** vt buchstabieren; (fig) genau erklären

spell[3] n Zauber m; (words) Zauberspruch m. ~**bound** a wie verzaubert

spelling /'spelɪŋ/ n Schreibweise f; (orthography) Rechtschreibung f

spelt /spelt/ see spell[2]

spend /spend/ vt/i (pt/pp spent) ausgeben; verbringen (time)

spent /spent/ see spend

sperm /spɜːm/ n Samen m

spew /spjuː/ vt speien

spher|e /sfɪə(r)/ n Kugel f; (fig) Sphäre f. ~**ical** /'sferɪkl/ a kugelförmig

spice /spaɪs/ n Gewürz nt; (fig) Würze f

spick /spɪk/ a ~ **and span** blitzsauber

spicy /'spaɪsɪ/ a würzig, pikant

spider /'spaɪdə(r)/ n Spinne f

spik|e /spaɪk/ n Spitze f; (Bot, Zool) Stachel m; (on shoe) Spike m. ~**y** a stachelig

spill /spɪl/ v (pt/pp spilt or spilled) ● vt verschütten; vergießen (blood) ● vi überlaufen

spin /spɪn/ v (pt/pp spun, pres p spinning) ● vt drehen; spinnen (wool); schleudern (washing) ● vi sich drehen. ~ **out** vt in die Länge ziehen

spinach /'spɪnɪdʒ/ n Spinat m

spinal /'spaɪnl/ a Rückgrat-. ~ '**cord** n Rückenmark nt

spindl|e /'spɪndl/ n Spindel f. ~**y** a spindeldürr

spin-'drier n Wäscheschleuder f

spine /spaɪn/ n Rückgrat nt; (of book) [Buch]rücken m; (Bot, Zool) Stachel m. ~**less** a (fig) rückgratlos

spinning /'spɪnɪŋ/ n Spinnen nt. ~**wheel** n Spinnrad nt

'**spin-off** n Nebenprodukt nt

spinster /'spɪnstə(r)/ n ledige Frau f

spiral /'spaɪrl/ a spiralig ● n Spirale f ● vi (pt/pp spiralled) sich hochwinden; (smoke:) in einer Spirale aufsteigen. ~ '**staircase** n Wendeltreppe f

spire /'spaɪə(r)/ n Turmspitze f

spirit /'spɪrɪt/ n Geist m; (courage) Mut m; ~s pl (alcohol) Spirituosen pl; **in high** ~s in gehobener Stimmung; **in low** ~s niedergedrückt. ~ **away** vt verschwinden lassen

spirited /'spɪrɪtɪd/ a lebhaft; (courageous) beherzt

spirit: ~-**level** n Wasserwaage f. ~ **stove** n Spirituskocher m

spiritual /'spɪrɪtjʊəl/ a geistig; (Relig) geistlich. ~**ism** /-ɪzm/ n Spiritismus m. ~**ist** /-ɪst/ a spiritistisch ● n Spiritist m

spit[1] /spɪt/ n (for roasting) [Brat]spieß m

spit[2] n Spucke f • vt/i (pt/pp **spat**, pres p **spitting**) spucken; ⟨cat:⟩ fauchen; ⟨fat:⟩ spritzen; **it's ~ting with rain** es tröpfelt; **be the ~ting image of s.o.** jdm wie aus dem Gesicht geschnitten sein

spite /spait/ n Boshaftigkeit f; **in ~ of** trotz (+ gen) • vt ärgern. **~ful** a, **-ly** adv gehässig

spittle /'spitl/ n Spucke f

splash /splæʃ/ n Platschen nt; (fam: drop) Schuß m; **~ of colour** Farbfleck m • vt spritzen; **~ s.o. with sth** jdn mit etw bespritzen • vi spritzen. **~ about** vi planschen

spleen /spli:n/ n Milz f

splendid /'splendid/ a herrlich, großartig

splendour /'splendə(r)/ n Pracht f

splint /splint/ n (Med) Schiene f

splinter /'splintə(r)/ n Splitter m • vi zersplittern

split /split/ n Spaltung f; (Pol) Bruch m; (tear) Riß m • v (pt/pp **split**, pres p **splitting**) • vt spalten; (share) teilen; (tear) zerreißen; **~ one's sides** sich kaputtlachen • vi sich spalten; (tear) zerreißen; **~ on s.o.** (fam) jdn verpfeifen. **~ up** vt aufteilen • vi ⟨couple:⟩ sich trennen

splutter /'splʌtə(r)/ vi prusten

spoil /spoil/ n **~s** pl Beute f • v (pt/pp **spoilt** or **spoiled**) • vt verderben; verwöhnen (person) • vi verderben. **~sport** n Spielverderber m

spoke[1] /spəʊk/ n Speiche f

spoke[2], **spoken** /spəʊkn/ see **speak**

'spokesman n Sprecher m

sponge /spʌndʒ/ n Schwamm m • vt abwaschen • vi **~ on** schmarotzen bei. **~-bag** n Waschbeutel m. **~-cake** n Biskuitkuchen m

spong|er /'spʌndʒə(r)/ n Schmarotzer m. **~y** a schwammig

sponsor /'spɒnsə(r)/ n Sponsor m; (god-parent) Pate m/Patin f; (for membership) Bürge m • vt sponsern; bürgen für

spontaneous /spɒn'teiniəs/ a, **-ly** adv spontan

spoof /spu:f/ n (fam) Parodie f

spooky /'spu:ki/ a (**-ier, -iest**) (fam) gespenstisch

spool /spu:l/ n Spule f

spoon /spu:n/ n Löffel m • vt löffeln. **~-feed** vt (pt/pp **-fed**) (fig) alles vorkauen (+ dat). **~ful** n Löffel m

sporadic /spə'rædik/ a, **-ally** adv sporadisch

sport /spɔ:t/ n Sport m; (amusement) Spaß m • vt [stolz] tragen. **~ing** a sportlich; **a ~ing chance** eine faire Chance

sports: **~ car** n Sportwagen m. **~ coat** n, **~ jacket** n Sakko m. **~man** n Sportler m. **~woman** n Sportlerin f

sporty /'spɔ:ti/ a (**-ier, -iest**) sportlich

spot /spɒt/ n Fleck m; (place) Stelle f; (dot) Punkt m; (drop) Tropfen m; (pimple) Pickel m; **~s** pl (rash) Ausschlag m; **a ~ of** (fam) ein bißchen; **on the ~** auf der Stelle; **be in a tight ~** (fam) in der Klemme sitzen • vt (pt/pp **spotted**) entdecken

spot: **~ 'check** n Stichprobe f. **~less** a makellos; (fam: very clean) blitzsauber. **~light** n Scheinwerfer m; (fig) Rampenlicht nt

spotted /'spɒtid/ a gepunktet

spotty /'spɒti/ a (**-ier, -iest**) fleckig; (pimply) pickelig

spouse /spaʊz/ n Gatte m/Gattin f

spout /spaʊt/ n Schnabel m, Tülle f • vi schießen (from aus)

sprain /sprein/ n Verstauchung f • vt verstauchen

sprang /spræŋ/ see **spring**[2]

sprat /spræt/ n Sprotte f

sprawl /sprɔ:l/ vi sich ausstrecken; (fall) der Länge nach hinfallen

spray[1] /sprei/ n (of flowers) Strauß m

spray[2] n Sprühnebel m; (from sea) Gischt m; (device) Spritze f; (container) Sprühdose f; (preparation) Spray nt • vt spritzen; (with aerosol) sprühen

spread /spred/ n Verbreitung f; (paste) Aufstrich m; (fam: feast) Festessen nt • v (pt/pp **spread**) • vt ausbreiten; streichen (butter, jam); bestreichen (bread, surface); streuen (sand, manure); verbreiten (news, disease); verteilen (payments) • vi sich ausbreiten. **~ out** vt ausbreiten; (space out) verteilen • vi sich verteilen

spree /spri:/ n (fam) **go on a shopping ~** groß einkaufen gehen

sprig /sprig/ n Zweig m

sprightly /'spraitli/ a (**-ier, -iest**) rüstig

spring[1] /spriŋ/ n Frühling m • attrib Frühlings-

spring[2] n (jump) Sprung m; (water) Quelle f; (device) Feder f; (elasticity) Elastizität f • v (pt **sprang**, pp **sprung**) • vi springen; (arise) entspringen

(from *dat*) ● *vt* ~ **sth on s.o.** jdn mit etw überfallen

spring: ~**board** *n* Sprungbrett *nt*. ~**'cleaning** *n* Frühjahrsputz *m*. ~**time** *n* Frühling *m*

sprinkl|e /'sprɪŋkl/ *vt* sprengen; (*scatter*) streuen; bestreuen (*surface*). ~**er** *n* Sprinkler *m*; (*Hort*) Sprenger *m*. ~**ing** *n* dünne Schicht *f*

sprint /sprɪnt/ *n* Sprint *m* ● *vi* rennen; (*Sport*) sprinten. ~**er** *n* Kurzstreckenläufer(in) *m(f)*

sprout /spraut/ *n* Trieb *m*; **[Brussels]** ~**s** *pl* Rosenkohl *m* ● *vi* sprießen

spruce /spru:s/ *a* gepflegt ● *n* Fichte *f*

sprung /sprʌŋ/ *see* **spring²** ● *a* gefedert

spry /spraɪ/ *a* (**-er, -est**) rüstig

spud /spʌd/ *n* (*fam*) Kartoffel *f*

spun /spʌn/ *see* **spin**

spur /spɜ:(r)/ *n* Sporn *m*; (*stimulus*) Ansporn *m*; (*road*) Nebenstraße *f*; **on the** ~ **of the moment** ganz spontan ● *vt* (*pt/pp* **spurred**) ~ **[on]** (*fig*) anspornen

spurious /'spjʊərɪəs/ *a*, **-ly** *adv* falsch

spurn /spɜ:n/ *vt* verschmähen

spurt /spɜ:t/ *n* Strahl *m*; (*Sport*) Spurt *m*; **put on a** ~ spurten ● *vi* spritzen

spy /spaɪ/ *n* Spion(in) *m(f)* ● *vi* spionieren; ~ **on s.o.** jdm nachspionieren ● *vt* (*fam: see*) sehen. ~ **out** *vt* auskundschaften

spying /'spaɪɪŋ/ *n* Spionage *f*

squabble /'skwɒbl/ *n* Zank *m* ● *vi* sich zanken

squad /skwɒd/ *n* Gruppe *f*; (*Sport*) Mannschaft *f*

squadron /'skwɒdrən/ *n* (*Mil*) Geschwader *nt*

squalid /'skwɒlɪd/ *a*, **-ly** *adv* schmutzig

squall /skwɔ:l/ *n* Bö *f* ● *vi* brüllen

squalor /'skwɒlə(r)/ *n* Schmutz *m*

squander /'skwɒndə(r)/ *vt* vergeuden

square /skweə(r)/ *a* quadratisch; (*metre, mile*) Quadrat-; (*meal*) anständig; **all** ~ (*fam*) quitt ● *n* Quadrat *nt*; (*area*) Platz *m*; (*on chessboard*) Feld *nt* ● *vt* (*settle*) klären; (*Math*) quadrieren ● *vi* (*agree*) übereinstimmen

squash /skwɒʃ/ *n* Gedränge *nt*; (*drink*) Fruchtsaftgetränk *nt*; (*Sport*) Squash *nt* ● *vt* zerquetschen; (*suppress*) niederschlagen. ~**y** *a* weich

squat /skwɒt/ *a* gedrungen ● *n* (*fam*) besetztes Haus *nt* ● *vi* (*pt/pp* **squatted**) hocken; ~ **in a house** ein Haus besetzen. ~**ter** *n* Hausbesetzer *m*

squawk /skwɔ:k/ *vi* krächzen

squeak /skwi:k/ *n* Quieken *nt*; (*of hinge, brakes*) Quietschen *nt* ● *vi* quieken; quietschen

squeal /skwi:l/ *n* Schrei *m*; (*screech*) Kreischen *nt* ● *vi* schreien; kreischen

squeamish /'skwi:mɪʃ/ *a* empfindlich

squeeze /skwi:z/ *n* Druck *m*; (*crush*) Gedränge *nt* ● *vt* drücken; (*to get juice*) ausdrücken; (*force*) zwängen; (*fam: extort*) herauspressen (**from** aus) ● *vi* ~ **in/out** sich hinein-/hinauszwängen

squelch /skweltʃ/ *vi* quatschen

squid /skwɪd/ *n* Tintenfisch *m*

squiggle /'skwɪgl/ *n* Schnörkel *m*

squint /skwɪnt/ *n* Schielen *nt* ● *vi* schielen

squire /'skwaɪə(r)/ *n* Gutsherr *m*

squirm /skwɜ:m/ *vi* sich winden

squirrel /'skwɪrl/ *n* Eichhörnchen *nt*

squirt /skwɜ:t/ *n* Spritzer *m* ● *vt/i* spritzen

St *abbr* (**Saint**) St.; (**Street**) Str.

stab /stæb/ *n* Stich *m*; (*fam: attempt*) Versuch *m* ● *vt* (*pt/pp* **stabbed**) stechen; (*to death*) erstechen

stability /stə'bɪlətɪ/ *n* Stabilität *f*

stabilize /'steɪbɪlaɪz/ *vt* stabilisieren ● *vi* sich stabilisieren

stable¹ /'steɪbl/ *a* (**-r, -st**) stabil

stable² *n* Stall *m*; (*establishment*) Reitstall *m*

stack /stæk/ *n* Stapel *m*; (*of chimney*) Schornstein *m*; (*fam: large quantity*) Haufen *m* ● *vt* stapeln

stadium /'steɪdɪəm/ *n* Stadion *nt*

staff /stɑ:f/ *n* (*stick & Mil*) Stab *m* ● (*& pl*) (*employees*) Personal *nt*; (*Sch*) Lehrkräfte *pl* ● *vt* mit Personal besetzen. ~**-room** *n* (*Sch*) Lehrerzimmer *nt*

stag /stæg/ *n* Hirsch *m*

stage /steɪdʒ/ *n* Bühne *f*; (*in journey*) Etappe *f*; (*in process*) Stadium *nt*; **by** *or* **in** ~**s** in Etappen ● *vt* aufführen; (*arrange*) veranstalten

stage: ~ **door** *n* Bühneneingang *m*. ~ **fright** *n* Lampenfieber *nt*

stagger /'stægə(r)/ *vi* taumeln ● *vt* staffeln (*holidays*); versetzt anordnen (*seats*); **I was** ~**ed** es hat mir die

Sprache verschlagen. **~ing** a unglaublich

stagnant /'stægnənt/ a stehend; (fig) stagnierend

stagnat|e /stæg'neɪt/ vi (fig) stagnieren. **~ion** /-'neɪʃn/ n Stagnation f

staid /steɪd/ a gesetzt

stain /steɪn/ n Fleck m; (for wood) Beize f ● vt färben; beizen (wood); (fig) beflecken; **~ed glass** farbiges Glas nt. **~less** a fleckenlos; (steel) rostfrei. **~ remover** n Fleckentferner m

stair /steə(r)/ n Stufe f; **~s** pl Treppe f. **~case** n Treppe f

stake /steɪk/ n Pfahl m; (wager) Einsatz m; (Comm) Anteil m; **be at ~** auf dem Spiel stehen ● vt [an einem Pfahl] anbinden; (wager) setzen; **~ a claim to sth** Anspruch auf etw (acc) erheben

stale /steɪl/ a (-r, -st) alt; (air) verbraucht. **~mate** n Patt nt

stalk[1] /stɔːk/ n Stiel m, Stengel m

stalk[2] vt pirschen auf (+ acc) ● vi stolzieren

stall /stɔːl/ n Stand m; **~s** pl (Theat) Parkett nt ● vi (engine:) stehenbleiben; (fig) ausweichen ● vt abwürgen (engine)

stallion /'stæljən/ n Hengst m

stalwart /'stɔːlwət/ a treu ● n treuer Anhänger m

stamina /'stæmɪnə/ n Ausdauer f

stammer /'stæmə(r)/ n Stottern nt ● vt/i stottern

stamp /stæmp/ n Stempel m; (postage ~) [Brief]marke f ● vt stempeln; (impress) prägen; (put postage on) frankieren; **~ one's feet** mit den Füßen stampfen ● vi stampfen. **~ out** vt [aus]stanzen; (fig) ausmerzen

stampede /stæm'piːd/ n wilde Flucht f; (fam) Ansturm m ● vi in Panik fliehen

stance /stɑːns/ n Haltung f

stand /stænd/ n Stand m; (rack) Ständer m; (pedestal) Sockel m; (Sport) Tribüne f; (fig) Einstellung f ● v (pt/pp stood) ● vi stehen; (rise) aufstehen; (be candidate) kandidieren; (stay valid) gültig bleiben; **~ still** stillstehen; **~ firm** (fig) festbleiben; **~ together** zusammenhalten; **~ to lose/gain** gewinnen/verlieren können; **~ to reason** logisch sein; **~ in for** vertreten; **~ for** (mean) bedeuten; **I won't ~ for that** das lasse ich mir nicht bieten

● vt stellen; (withstand) standhalten (+ dat); (endure) ertragen; vertragen (climate); (put up with) aushalten; haben (chance); **~ one's ground** nicht nachgeben; **~ the test of time** sich bewähren; **~ s.o. a beer** jdm ein Bier spendieren; **I can't ~ her** (fam) ich kann sie nicht ausstehen. **~ by** vi danebenstehen; (be ready) sich bereithalten ● vt **~ by s.o.** (fig) zu jdm stehen. **~ down** vi (retire) zurücktreten. **~ out** vi hervorstehen; (fig) herausragen. **~ up** vi aufstehen; **~ up for** eintreten für; **~ up to** sich wehren gegen

standard /'stændəd/ a Normal-; **be ~ practice** allgemein üblich ● n Maßstab m; (Techn) Norm f; (level) Niveau nt; (flag) Standarte f; **~s** pl (morals) Prinzipien pl; **~ of living** Lebensstandard m. **~ize** vt standardisieren; (Techn) normen

'standard lamp n Stehlampe f

'stand-in n Ersatz m

standing /'stændɪŋ/ a (erect) stehend; (permanent) ständig ● n Rang m; (duration) Dauer f. **~'order** n Dauerauftrag m. **~-room** n Stehplätze pl

stand: ~-offish /stænd'ɒfɪʃ/ a distanziert. **~point** n Standpunkt m. **~still** n Stillstand m; **come to a ~still** zum Stillstand kommen

stank /stæŋk/ see **stink**

staple[1] /'steɪpl/ a Grund- ● n (product) Haupterzeugnis nt

staple[2] n Heftklammer f ● vt heften. **~r** n Heftmaschine f

star /stɑː(r)/ n Stern m; (asterisk) Sternchen nt; (Theat, Sport) Star m ● vi (pt/pp starred) die Hauptrolle spielen

starboard /'stɑːbəd/ n Steuerbord nt

starch /stɑːtʃ/ n Stärke f ● vt stärken. **~y** a stärkehaltig; (fig) steif

stare /steə(r)/ n Starren nt ● vi starren; **~ at** anstarren

'starfish n Seestern m

stark /stɑːk/ a (-er, -est) scharf; (contrast) kraß ● adv **~ naked** splitternackt

starling /'stɑːlɪŋ/ n Star m

'starlit a sternhell

starry /'stɑːrɪ/ a sternklar

start /stɑːt/ n Anfang m, Beginn m; (departure) Aufbruch m; (Sport) Start m; **from the ~** von Anfang an;

for a ∼ erstens ● *vi* anfangen, beginnen; (*set out*) aufbrechen; ⟨*engine:*⟩ anspringen; (*Auto, Sport*) starten; (*jump*) aufschrecken; **to** ∼ **with** zuerst ● *vt* anfangen, beginnen; (*cause*) verursachen; (*found*) gründen; starten ⟨*car, race*⟩; in Umlauf setzen ⟨*rumour*⟩. ∼**er** *n* (*Culin*) Vorspeise *f*; (*Auto, Sport*) Starter *m*. ∼**ing-point** *n* Ausgangspunkt *m*

startle /'stɑːtl/ *vt* erschrecken

starvation /stɑːˈveɪʃn/ *n* Verhungern *nt*

starve /stɑːv/ *vi* hungern; (*to death*) verhungern ● *vt* verhungern lassen

stash /stæʃ/ *vt* (*fam*) ∼ **[away]** beiseite schaffen

state /steɪt/ *n* Zustand *m*; (*grand style*) Prunk *m*; (*Pol*) Staat *m*; ∼ **of play** Spielstand *m*; **be in a** ∼ ⟨*person:*⟩ aufgeregt sein; **lie in** ∼ feierlich aufgebahrt sein ● *attrib* Staats-, staatlich ● *vt* erklären; (*speci-fy*) angeben. ∼**-aided** *a* staatlich gefördert. ∼**less** *a* staatenlos

stately /'steɪtlɪ/ *a* (**-ier, -iest**) stattlich. ∼ '**home** *n* Schloß *nt*

statement /'steɪtmənt/ *n* Erklärung *f*; (*Jur*) Aussage *f*; (*Banking*) Auszug *m*

'**statesman** *n* Staatsmann *m*

static /'stætɪk/ *a* statisch; **remain** ∼ unverändert bleiben

station /'steɪʃn/ *n* Bahnhof *m*; (*police*) Wache *f*; (*radio*) Sender *m*; (*space, weather*) Station *f*; (*Mil*) Posten *m*; (*status*) Rang *m* ● *vt* stationieren; (*post*) postieren. ∼**ary** /-ərɪ/ *a* stehend; **be** ∼**ary** stehen

stationer /'steɪʃənə(r)/ *n* ∼**'s [shop]** Schreibwarengeschäft *nt*. ∼**y** *n* Briefpapier *nt*; (*writing-materials*) Schreibwaren *pl*

'**station-wagon** *n* (*Amer*) Kombi-[wagen] *m*

statistic /stəˈtɪstɪk/ *n* statistische Tatsache *f*. ∼**al** *a*, **-ly** *adv* statistisch. ∼**s** *n & pl* Statistik *f*

statue /'stætjuː/ *n* Statue *f*

stature /'stætʃə(r)/ *n* Statur *f*; (*fig*) Format *nt*

status /'steɪtəs/ *n* Status *m*, Rang *m*. ∼ **symbol** *n* Statussymbol *nt*

statut|e /'stætjuːt/ *n* Statut *nt*. ∼**ory** *a* gesetzlich

staunch /stɔːntʃ/ *a* (**-er, -est**), **-ly** *adv* treu

stave /steɪv/ *vt* ∼ **off** abwenden

stay /steɪ/ *n* Aufenthalt *m* ● *vi* bleiben; (*reside*) wohnen; ∼ **the night** übernachten; ∼ **put** dableiben ● *vt* ∼ **the course** durchhalten. ∼ **away** *vi* wegbleiben. ∼ **behind** *vi* zurückbleiben. ∼ **in** *vi* zu Hause bleiben; (*Sch*) nachsitzen. ∼ **up** *vi* oben bleiben; (*upright*) stehen bleiben; (*on wall*) hängen bleiben; ⟨*person:*⟩ aufbleiben

stead /sted/ *n* **in his** ∼ an seiner Stelle; **stand s.o. in good** ∼ jdm zustatten kommen. ∼**fast** *a*, **-ly** *adv* standhaft

steadily /'stedɪlɪ/ *adv* fest; (*continually*) stetig

steady /'stedɪ/ *a* (**-ier, -iest**) fest; (*not wobbly*) stabil; (*hand*) ruhig; (*regular*) regelmäßig; (*dependable*) zuverlässig

steak /steɪk/ *n* Steak *nt*

steal /stiːl/ *vt/i* (*pt* **stole**, *pp* **stolen**) stehlen (**from** *dat*). ∼ **in/out** *vi* sich hinein-/hinausstehlen

stealth /stelθ/ *n* Heimlichkeit *f*; **by** ∼ heimlich. ∼**y** *a* heimlich

steam /stiːm/ *n* Dampf *m*; **under one's own** ∼ (*fam*) aus eigener Kraft ● *vt* (*Culin*) dämpfen, dünsten ● *vi* dampfen. ∼ **up** *vi* beschlagen

'**steam-engine** *n* Dampfmaschine *f*; (*Rail*) Dampflokomotive *f*

steamer /'stiːmə(r)/ *n* Dampfer *m*

'**steamroller** *n* Dampfwalze *f*

steamy /'stiːmɪ/ *a* dampfig

steel /stiːl/ *n* Stahl *m* ● *vt* ∼ **oneself** allen Mut zusammennehmen

steep[1] /stiːp/ *vt* (*soak*) einweichen

steep[2] *a*, **-ly** *adv* steil; (*fam: exorbitant*) gesalzen

steeple /'stiːpl/ *n* Kirchturm *m*. ∼**chase** *n* Hindernisrennen *nt*

steer /stɪə(r)/ *vt/i* steuern; ∼ **clear of s.o./sth** jdm/etw aus dem Weg gehen. ∼**ing** *n* (*Auto*) Steuerung *f*. ∼**ing-wheel** *n* Lenkrad *nt*

stem[1] /stem/ *n* Stiel *m*; (*of word*) Stamm *m* ● *vi* (*pt/pp* **stemmed**) ∼ **from** zurückzuführen sein auf (+ *acc*)

stem[2] *vt* (*pt/pp* **stemmed**) eindämmen; stillen ⟨*bleeding*⟩

stench /stentʃ/ *n* Gestank *m*

stencil /'stensl/ *n* Schablone *f*; (*for typing*) Matrize *f*

step /step/ *n* Schritt *m*; (*stair*) Stufe *f*; ∼**s** *pl* (*ladder*) Trittleiter *f*; **in** ∼ im Schritt; ∼ **by** ∼ Schritt für Schritt; **take** ∼**s** (*fig*) Schritte unternehmen ● *vi* (*pt/pp* **stepped**) treten; ∼ **in** (*fig*) eingreifen; ∼ **into s.o.'s shoes** an jds

Stelle treten; ~ **out of line** aus der
Reihe tanzen. ~ **up** *vi* hinaufsteigen
● *vt* (*increase*) erhöhen, steigern;
verstärken (*efforts*)

step: ~**brother** *n* Stiefbruder *m*.
~**child** *n* Stiefkind *nt*. ~**daughter** *n*
Stieftochter *f*. ~**father** *n* Stiefvater
m. ~-**ladder** *n* Trittleiter *f*. ~
mother *n* Stiefmutter *f*

'**stepping-stone** *n* Trittstein *m*;
(*fig*) Sprungbrett *nt*

step: ~**sister** *n* Stiefschwester *f*.
~**son** *n* Stiefsohn *m*

stereo /'sterɪəʊ/ *n* Stereo *nt*;
(*equipment*) Stereoanlage *f*; **in** ~ stereo. ~**phonic** /-'fɒnɪk/ *a* stereophon

stereotype /'sterɪətaɪp/ *n* stereotype Figur *f*. ~**d** *a* stereotyp

steril|e /'steraɪl/ *a* steril. ~**ity**
/stə'rɪletɪ/ *n* Sterilität *f*

steriliz|ation /sterəlaɪ'zeɪʃn/ *n*
Sterilisation *f*. ~**e** *vt* sterilisieren

sterling /'stɜːlɪŋ/ *a* Sterling-; (*fig*)
gediegen ● *n* Sterling *m*

stern[1] /stɜːn/ *a* (**-er, -est**), **-ly** *adv*
streng

stern[2] *n* (*of boat*) Heck *nt*

stew /stjuː/ *n* Eintopf *m*; **in a** ~ (*fam*)
aufgeregt ● *vt/i* schmoren; ~**ed fruit**
Kompott *nt*

steward /'stjuːəd/ *n* Ordner *m*; (*on
ship, aircraft*) Steward *m*. ~**ess** *n*
Stewardeß *f*

stick[1] /stɪk/ *n* Stock *m*; (*of chalk*)
Stück *nt*; (*of rhubarb*) Stange *f*;
(*Sport*) Schläger *m*

stick[2] *v* (*pt/pp* **stuck**) ● *vt* stecken; (*stab*)
stechen; (*glue*) kleben; (*fam: put*) tun;
(*fam: endure*) aushalten ● *vi* stecken;
(*adhere*) kleben, haften (**to** an + *dat*);
(*jam*) klemmen; ~ **to sth** (*fig*) bei etw
bleiben; ~ **at it** (*fam*) dranbleiben; ~ **at
nothing** (*fam*) vor nichts zurückschrecken; ~ **up for** (*fam*) eintreten
für; **be stuck** nicht weiterkönnen;
(*vehicle:*) festsitzen, festgefahren sein;
(*drawer:*) klemmen; **be stuck with sth**
(*fam*) etw am Hals haben. ~ **out** *vi* ab-
stehen; (*project*) vorstehen ● *vt* (*fam*)
hinausstrecken; herausstrecken
(*tongue*)

sticker /'stɪkə(r)/ *n* Aufkleber *m*

'**sticking plaster** *n* Heftpflaster *nt*

stickler /'stɪklə(r)/ *n* **be a** ~ **for** es
sehr genau nehmen mit

sticky /'stɪkɪ/ *a* (**-ier, -iest**) klebrig;
(*adhesive*) Klebe-

stiff /stɪf/ *a* (**-er, -est**), **-ly** *adv* steif;
(*brush*) hart; (*dough*) fest; (*difficult*)
schwierig; (*penalty*) schwer; **be**

bored ~ (*fam*) sich zu Tode langweilen.
~**en** *vt* steif machen ● *vi* steif
werden. ~**ness** *n* Steifheit *f*

stifl|e /'staɪfl/ *vt* ersticken; (*fig*)
unterdrücken. ~**ing** *a* **be** ~**ing** zum
Ersticken sein

stigma /'stɪgmə/ *n* Stigma *nt*

stile /staɪl/ *n* Zauntritt *m*

stiletto /str'letəʊ/ *n* Stilett *nt*; (*heel*)
Bleistiftabsatz *m*

still[1] /stɪl/ *n* Destillierapparat *m*

still[2] *a* still; (*drink*) ohne Kohlensäure;
keep ~ stillhalten; **stand** ~ stillstehen
● *n* Stille *f* ● *adv* noch; (*emphatic*) immer noch; (*nevertheless*) trotzdem; ~
not immer noch nicht

'**stillborn** *a* totgeboren

still 'life *n* Stilleben *nt*

stilted /'stɪltɪd/ *a* gestelzt, geschraubt

stilts /stɪlts/ *npl* Stelzen *pl*

stimulant /'stɪmjʊlənt/ *n* An-
regungsmittel *nt*

stimulat|e /'stɪmjʊleɪt/ *vt* anregen.
~**ion** /-'leɪʃn/ *n* Anregung *f*

stimulus /'stɪmjʊləs/ *n* (*pl* **-li** /-laɪ/)
Reiz *m*

sting /stɪŋ/ *n* Stich *m*; (*from nettle,
jellyfish*) Brennen *nt*; (*organ*) Stachel
m ● *v* (*pt/pp* **stung**) ● *vt* stechen ● *vi*
brennen; (*insect:*) stechen. ~**ing
nettle** *n* Brennessel *f*

stingy /'stɪndʒɪ/ *a* (**-ier, -iest**) geizig,
(*fam*) knauserig

stink /stɪŋk/ *n* Gestank *m* ● *vi* (*pt*
stank, *pp* **stunk**) stinken (**of** nach)

stint /stɪnt/ *n* Pensum *nt* ● *vi* ~ **on**
sparen an (+ *dat*)

stipulat|e /'stɪpjʊleɪt/ *vt* vor-
schreiben. ~**ion** /-'leɪʃn/ *n* Bedingung *f*

stir /stɜː(r)/ *n* (*commotion*) Aufregung *f* ● *v* (*pt/pp* **stirred**) *vt* rühren
● *vi* sich rühren

stirrup /'stɪrəp/ *n* Steigbügel *m*

stitch /stɪtʃ/ *n* Stich *m*; (*Knitting*)
Masche *f*; (*pain*) Seitenstechen *nt*; **be
in** ~**es** (*fam*) sich kaputtlachen ● *vt*
nähen

stoat /stəʊt/ *n* Hermelin *nt*

stock /stɒk/ *n* Vorrat *m* (**of** an + *dat*);
(*in shop*) [Waren]bestand *m*; (*livestock*)
Vieh *nt*; (*lineage*) Abstammung *f*; (*Finance*) Wertpapiere *pl*; (*Culin*) Brühe *f*;
(*plant*) Levkoje *f*; **in/out of** ~ vorrätig/
nicht vorrätig; **take** ~ (*fig*) Bilanz
ziehen ● *a* Standard- ● *vt* (*shop:*) führen;

auffüllen ⟨shelves⟩. ~ **up** vi sich eindecken (**with** mit)
stock: ~**broker** n Börsenmakler m.
~ **cube** n Brühwürfel m. **S~ Exchange** n Börse f
stocking /'stɒkɪŋ/ n Strumpf m
stockist /'stɒkɪst/ n Händler m
stock: ~ **market** n Börse f. ~**pile** vt
horten; anhäufen ⟨weapons⟩. ~-
'**still** a bewegungslos. ~**taking** n
(Comm) Inventur f
stocky /'stɒkɪ/ a (**-ier, -iest**)
untersetzt
stodgy /'stɒdʒɪ/ a pappig [und
schwer verdaulich]
stoical /'stəʊɪkl/ a, **-ly** adv stoisch
stoke /stəʊk/ vt heizen
stole[1] /stəʊl/ n Stola f
stole[2], **stolen** /'stəʊln/ see **steal**
stolid /'stɒlɪd/ a, **-ly** adv stur
stomach /'stʌmək/ n Magen m ● vt
vertragen. ~**-ache** n Magen-
schmerzen pl
stone /stəʊn/ n Stein m; (weight)
6,35 kg ● a steinern; ⟨wall, Age⟩
Stein- ● vt mit Steinen bewerfen;
entsteinen ⟨fruit⟩. ~**-cold** a eiskalt. ~-'**deaf** n (fam) stocktaub
stony /'stəʊnɪ/ a steinig
stood /stʊd/ see **stand**
stool /stuːl/ n Hocker m
stoop /stuːp/ n **walk with a** ~ gebeugt gehen ● vi sich bücken; (fig) sich
erniedrigen
stop /stɒp/ n Halt m; (break) Pause
f; (for bus) Haltestelle f; (for train)
Station f; (Gram) Punkt m; (on
organ) Register nt; **come to a** ~
stehenbleiben; **put a** ~ **to sth** etw unterbinden ● v (pt/pp **stopped**) ● vt anhalten, stoppen; (switch off) abstellen;
(plug, block) zustopfen; (prevent)
verhindern; ~ **s.o. doing sth** jdn daran
hindern, etw zu tun; ~ **doing sth** aufhören, etw zu tun; ~ **that!** hör auf damit! laß das sein! ● vi anhalten; (cease)
aufhören; ⟨clock:⟩ stehenbleiben; (fam:
stay) bleiben (**with** bei) ● int halt!
stopp!
stop: ~**gap** n Notlösung f. ~**-over** n
Zwischenaufenthalt m; (Aviat) Zwi-
schenlandung f
stoppage /'stɒpɪdʒ/ n Unterbrechung f; (strike) Streik m; (deduction) Abzug m
stopper /'stɒpə(r)/ n Stöpsel m
stop: ~**-press** n letzte Meldungen pl.
~**-watch** n Stoppuhr f

storage /'stɔːrɪdʒ/ n Aufbewahrung
f; (in warehouse) Lagerung f; (Computing) Speicherung f
store /stɔː(r)/ n (stock) Vorrat m;
(shop) Laden m; (department ~)
Kaufhaus nt; (depot) Lager nt; **in** ~
auf Lager; **put in** ~ lagern; **set great** ~
by großen Wert legen auf (+ acc); **be in**
~ **for s.o.** (fig) jdm bevorstehen ● vt
aufbewahren; (in warehouse) lagern;
(Computing) speichern. ~**-room** n
Lagerraum m
storey /'stɔːrɪ/ n Stockwerk nt
stork /stɔːk/ n Storch m
storm /stɔːm/ n Sturm m; (with thunder) Gewitter nt ● vt/i stürmen. ~**y** a
stürmisch
story /'stɔːrɪ/ n Geschichte f; (in
newspaper) Artikel m; (fam: lie)
Märchen nt
stout /staʊt/ a (**-er, -est**) beleibt;
(strong) fest
stove /stəʊv/ n Ofen m; (for cooking)
Herd m
stow /stəʊ/ vt verstauen. ~**away** n
blinder Passagier m
straddle /'strædl/ vt rittlings sitzen
auf (+ dat); (standing) mit ge-
spreizten Beinen stehen über (+ dat)
straggl|e /'strægl/ vi hinter-
herhinken. ~**er** n Nachzügler m. ~**y**
a strähnig
straight /streɪt/ a (**-er, -est**) gerade;
(direct) direkt; (clear) klar; ⟨hair⟩ glatt;
⟨drink⟩ pur; **be** ~ (tidy) in Ordnung sein
● adv gerade; (directly) direkt, ge-
radewegs; (clearly) klar; ~ **away** sofort;
~ **on** or **ahead** geradeaus; ~ **out** (fig)
geradeheraus; **go** ~ (fam) ein ehr-
liches Leben führen; **put sth** ~ etw in
Ordnung bringen; **sit/stand up** ~ ge-
radesitzen/-stehen
straighten /'streɪtn/ vt gerade-
machen; (put straight) gerade-
richten ● vi gerade werden; ~ [**up**]
⟨person:⟩ sich aufrichten. ~ **out** vt ge-
radebiegen
straight'forward a offen; (simple)
einfach
strain[1] /streɪn/ n Rasse f; (Bot) Sorte
f; (of virus) Art f
strain[2] /streɪn/ n Belastung f; ~**s** pl (of music)
Klänge pl ● vt belasten; (overexert)
überanstrengen; (injure) zerren
⟨muscle⟩; (Culin) durchseihen; abgießen
⟨vegetables⟩ ● vi sich anstrengen. ~**ed**
a ⟨relations⟩ gespannt. ~**er** n Sieb nt

strait /streɪt/ n Meerenge f; **in dire ~s** in großen Nöten. **~-jacket** n Zwangsjacke f. **~-'laced** a puritanisch

strand[1] /strænd/ n (of thread) Faden m; (of beads) Kette f; (of hair) Strähne f

strand[2] vt be **~ed** festsitzen

strange /streɪndʒ/ a (**-r, -st**) fremd; (odd) seltsam, merkwürdig. **~r** n Fremde(r) m/f

strangely /'streɪndʒlɪ/ adv seltsam, merkwürdig; **~ enough** seltsamerweise

strangle /'stræŋgl/ vt erwürgen; (fig) unterdrücken

strangulation /stræŋgjʊ'leɪʃn/ n Erwürgen nt

strap /stræp/ n Riemen m; (for safety) Gurt m; (to grasp in vehicle) Halteriemen m; (of watch) Armband nt; (shoulder-) Träger m ● vt (pt/pp **strapped**) schnallen; **~ in** or **down** festschnallen

strapping /'stræpɪŋ/ a stramm

strata /'strɑːtə/ npl see **stratum**

stratagem /'strætədʒəm/ n Kriegslist f

strategic /strə'tiːdʒɪk/ a, **-ally** adv strategisch

strategy /'strætədʒɪ/ n Strategie f

stratum /'strɑːtəm/ n (pl **strata**) Schicht f

straw /strɔː/ n Stroh nt; (single piece, drinking) Strohhalm m; **that's the last ~** jetzt reicht's aber

strawberry /'strɔːbərɪ/ n Erdbeere f

stray /streɪ/ a streunend ● n streunendes Tier nt ● vi sich verirren; (deviate) abweichen

streak /striːk/ n Streifen m; (in hair) Strähne f; (fig: trait) Zug m ● vi flitzen. **~y** a streifig; (bacon) durchwachsen

stream /striːm/ n Bach m; (flow) Strom m; (current) Strömung f; (Sch) Parallelzug m ● vi strömen; **~ in/out** hinaus-/herausströmen

streamer /'striːmə(r)/ n Luftschlange f; (flag) Wimpel m

'streamline vt (fig) rationalisieren. **~d** a stromlinienförmig

street /striːt/ n Straße f. **~car** n (Amer) Straßenbahn f. **~ lamp** n Straßenlaterne f

strength /streŋθ/ n Stärke f; (power) Kraft f; **on the ~ of** auf Grund (+ gen). **~en** vt stärken; (reinforce) verstärken

strenuous /'strenjʊəs/ a anstrengend

stress /stres/ n (emphasis) Betonung f; (strain) Belastung f; (mental) Streß m ● vt betonen; (put a strain on) belasten. **~ful** a stressig (fam)

stretch /stretʃ/ n (of road) Strecke f; (elasticity) Elastizität f; **at a ~** ohne Unterbrechung; **a long ~** eine lange Zeit; **have a ~** sich strecken ● vt strecken; (widen) dehnen; (spread) ausbreiten; fordern (person); **~ one's legs** sich (dat) die Beine vertreten ● vi sich erstrecken; (become wider) sich dehnen; (person:) sich strecken. **~er** n Tragbahre f

strew /struː/ vt (pp **strewn** or **strewed**) streuen

stricken /'strɪkn/ a betroffen; **~ with** heimgesucht von

strict /strɪkt/ a (**-er, -est**), **-ly** adv streng; **~ly speaking** strenggenommen

stride /straɪd/ n [großer] Schritt m; **make great ~s** (fig) große Fortschritte machen; **take sth in one's ~** mit etw gut fertig werden ● vi (pt **strode**, pp **stridden**) [mit großen Schritten] gehen

strident /'straɪdnt/ a, **-ly** adv schrill; (colour) grell

strife /straɪf/ n Streit m

strike /straɪk/ n Streik m; (Mil) Angriff m; **be on ~** streiken ● v (pt/pp **struck**) ● vt schlagen; (knock against, collide with) treffen; prägen (coin); anzünden (match); stoßen auf (+ acc) (oil, gold); abbrechen (camp); (delete) streichen; (impress) beeindrucken; (occur to) einfallen (+ dat); (Mil) angreifen; **~ s.o. a blow** jdm einen Schlag versetzen ● vi treffen; (lightning:) einschlagen; (clock:) schlagen; (attack) zuschlagen; (workers:) streiken; **~ lucky** Glück haben. **~-breaker** n Streikbrecher m

striker /'straɪkə(r)/ n Streikende(r) m/f

striking /'straɪkɪŋ/ a auffallend

string /strɪŋ/ n Schnur f; (thin) Bindfaden m; (of musical instrument, racket) Saite f; (of bow) Sehne f; (of pearls) Kette f; **the ~s** (Mus) die Streicher pl; **pull ~s** (fam) seine Beziehungen spielen lassen, Fäden ziehen ● vt (pt/pp **strung**) (thread) aufziehen (beads). **~ed** a (Mus) Saiten-; (played with bow) Streich-

stringent /'strɪndʒnt/ a streng

strip /strɪp/ n Streifen m ● v (pt/pp **stripped**) ● vt ablösen; ausziehen ⟨clothes⟩; abziehen ⟨bed⟩; abbeizen ⟨wood, furniture⟩; auseinandernehmen ⟨machine⟩; ⟨deprive⟩ berauben (**of** gen); ~ **sth off** sth etw von etw entfernen ● vi ⟨undress⟩ sich ausziehen. ~ **club** n Stripteaselokal nt

stripe /straɪp/ n Streifen m. ~**d** a gestreift

'**striplight** n Neonröhre f

stripper /'strɪpə(r)/ n Stripperin f; ⟨male⟩ Stripper m

strip-'tease n Striptease m

strive /straɪv/ vi (pt **strove**, pp **striven**) sich bemühen (**to** zu); ~ **for** streben nach

strode /strəʊd/ see **stride**

stroke[1] /strəʊk/ n Schlag m; ⟨of pen⟩ Strich m; ⟨Swimming⟩ Zug m; ⟨style⟩ Stil m; ⟨Med⟩ Schlaganfall m; ~ **of luck** Glücksfall m; **put s.o. off his** ~ jdn aus dem Konzept bringen

stroke[2] a ● vt streicheln

stroll /strəʊl/ n Spaziergang m, ⟨fam⟩ Bummel m ● vi spazieren, ⟨fam⟩ bummeln. ~**er** n ⟨Amer: pushchair⟩ [Kinder]sportwagen m

strong /strɒŋ/ a (-**er** /-gə(r)/, -**est** /-gɪst/), -**ly** adv stark; ⟨powerful, healthy⟩ kräftig; ⟨severe⟩ streng; ⟨sturdy⟩ stabil; ⟨convincing⟩ gut

strong: ~-**box** n Geldkassette f. ~**hold** n Festung f; ⟨fig⟩ Hochburg f. ~-'**minded** a willensstark. ~-'**room** n Tresorraum m

stroppy /'strɒpɪ/ a widerspenstig

strove /strəʊv/ see **strive**

struck /strʌk/ see **strike**

structural /'strʌktʃərl/ a, -**ly** adv baulich

structure /'strʌktʃə(r)/ n Struktur f; ⟨building⟩ Bau m

struggle /'strʌgl/ n Kampf m; **with a** ~ mit Mühe ● vi kämpfen; ~ **for breath** nach Atem ringen; ~ **to do sth** sich abmühen, etw zu tun; ~ **to one's feet** mühsam aufstehen

strum /strʌm/ v (pt/pp **strummed**) ● vt klimpern auf (+ dat) ● vi klimpern

strung /strʌŋ/ see **string**

strut[1] /strʌt/ n Strebe f

strut[2] vi (pt/pp **strutted**) stolzieren

stub /stʌb/ n Stummel m; ⟨counterfoil⟩ Abschnitt m ● vt (pt/pp **stubbed**) ~ **one's toe** sich ⟨dat⟩ den Zeh stoßen (**on** an + dat). ~ **out** vt ausdrücken ⟨cigarette⟩

stubb|le /'stʌbl/ n Stoppeln pl. ~**ly** a stoppelig

stubborn /'stʌbən/ a, -**ly** adv starrsinnig; ⟨refusal⟩ hartnäckig

stubby /'stʌbɪ/ a (-**ier**, -**iest**) kurz und dick

stucco /'stʌkəʊ/ n Stuck m

stuck /stʌk/ see **stick**[2]. ~-'**up** a ⟨fam⟩ hochnäsig

stud[1] /stʌd/ n Nagel m; ⟨on clothes⟩ Niete f; ⟨for collar⟩ Kragenknopf m; ⟨for ear⟩ Ohrstecker m

stud[2] n ⟨of horses⟩ Gestüt nt

student /'stjuːdnt/ n Student(in) m(f); ⟨Sch⟩ Schüler(in) m(f). ~ **nurse** n Lernschwester f

studied /'stʌdɪd/ a gewollt

studio /'stjuːdɪəʊ/ n Studio nt; ⟨for artist⟩ Atelier nt

studious /'stjuːdɪəs/ a lerneifrig; ⟨earnest⟩ ernsthaft

stud|y /'stʌdɪ/ n Studie f; ⟨room⟩ Studierzimmer nt; ⟨investigation⟩ Untersuchung f; ~**ies** pl Studium nt ● v (pt/pp **studied**) ● vt studieren; ⟨examine⟩ untersuchen ● vi lernen; ⟨at university⟩ studieren

stuff /stʌf/ n Stoff m; ⟨fam: things⟩ Zeug nt ● vt vollstopfen; ⟨with padding, Culin⟩ füllen; ausstopfen ⟨animal⟩; ~ **sth into sth** etw in etw ⟨acc⟩ [hinein]stopfen. ~**ing** n Füllung f

stuffy /'stʌfɪ/ a (-**ier**, -**iest**) stickig; ⟨old-fashioned⟩ spießig

stumbl|e /'stʌmbl/ vi stolpern; ~**e across** zufällig stoßen auf (+ acc). ~**ing-block** n Hindernis nt

stump /stʌmp/ n Stumpf m ● vt/i ~ **up** ⟨fam⟩ blechen. ~**ed** a ⟨fam⟩ überfragt

stun /stʌn/ vt (pt/pp **stunned**) betäuben; ~**ned by** ⟨fig⟩ wie betäubt von

stung /stʌŋ/ see **sting**

stunk /stʌŋk/ see **stink**

stunning /'stʌnɪŋ/ a ⟨fam⟩ toll

stunt[1] /stʌnt/ n ⟨fam⟩ Kunststück nt

stunt[2] vt hemmen. ~**ed** a verkümmert

stupendous /stjuː'pendəs/ a, -**ly** adv enorm

stupid /'stjuːpɪd/ a dumm. ~**ity** /-'pɪdətɪ/ n Dummheit f. ~**ly** adv dumm; ~**ly** [**enough**] dummerweise

stupor /'stjuːpə(r)/ n Benommenheit f

sturdy /'stɜːdɪ/ a (-**ier**, -**iest**) stämmig; ⟨furniture⟩ stabil; ⟨shoes⟩ fest

stutter /'stʌtə(r)/ n Stottern nt ● vt/i stottern

sty[1] /staɪ/ n (pl **sties**) Schweinestall m

sty[2], **stye** n (pl **styes**) (Med) Gerstenkorn nt

style /staɪl/ n Stil m; (fashion) Mode f; (sort) Art f; (hair~) Frisur f; **in ~** in großem Stil

stylish /'staɪlɪʃ/ a, **-ly** adv stilvoll

stylist /'staɪlɪst/ n Friseur m/Friseuse f. **~ic** /-'lɪstɪk/ a, **-ally** adv stilistisch

stylized /'staɪlaɪzd/ a stilisiert

stylus /'staɪləs/ n (on record-player) Nadel f

suave /swɑːv/ a (pej) gewandt

sub'conscious /sʌb-/ a, **-ly** adv unterbewußt ● n Unterbewußtsein nt

subcon'tract vt [vertraglich] weitervergeben (**to** an + acc)

'subdivi|de vt unterteilen. **~sion** n Unterteilung f

subdue /səb'djuː/ vt unterwerfen; (make quieter) beruhigen. **~d** a gedämpft; (person) still

subject[1] /'sʌbdʒɪkt/ a **be ~ to** sth etw (dat) unterworfen sein ● n Staatsbürger(in) m(f); (of ruler) Untertan m; (theme) Thema nt; (of investigation) Gegenstand m; (Sch) Fach nt; (Gram) Subjekt nt

subject[2] /səb'dʒekt/ vt unterwerfen (**to** dat); (expose) aussetzen (**to** dat)

subjective /səb'dʒektɪv/ a, **-ly** adv subjektiv

subjugate /'sʌbdʒʊgeɪt/ vt unterjochen

subjunctive /səb'dʒʌŋktɪv/ n Konjunktiv m

sub'let vt (pt/pp **-let**) untervermieten

sublime /sə'blaɪm/ a, **-ly** adv erhaben

subliminal /sʌ'blɪmɪnl/ a unterschwellig

sub-ma'chine-gun n Maschinenpistole f

subma'rine n Unterseeboot nt

submerge /səb'mɜːdʒ/ vt untertauchen; **be ~d** unter Wasser stehen ● vi tauchen

submiss|ion /səb'mɪʃn/ n Unterwerfung f. **~ive** /-sɪv/ a gehorsam; (pej) unterwürfig

submit /səb'mɪt/ v (pt/pp **-mitted**, pres p **-mitting**) ● vt vorlegen (**to** dat); (hand in) einreichen ● vi sich unterwerfen (**to** dat)

subordinate[1] /sə'bɔːdɪnət/ a untergeordnet ● n Untergebene(r) m/f

subordinate[2] /sə'bɔːdɪneɪt/ vt unterordnen (**to** dat)

subscribe /səb'skraɪb/ vi spenden; **~ to** (fig) sich anschließen (+ dat); abonnieren (newspaper). **~r** n Spender m; Abonnent m

subscription /səb'skrɪpʃn/ n (to club) [Mitglieds]beitrag m; (to newspaper) Abonnement nt; **by ~** mit Spenden

subsequent /'sʌbsɪkwənt/ a, **-ly** adv folgend; (later) später

subservient /səb'sɜːvɪənt/ a, **-ly** adv untergeordnet; (servile) unterwürfig

subside /səb'saɪd/ vi sinken; (ground:) sich senken; (storm:) nachlassen

subsidiary /səb'sɪdɪərɪ/ a untergeordnet ● n Tochtergesellschaft f

subsid|ize /'sʌbsɪdaɪz/ vt subventionieren. **~y** n Subvention f

subsist /səb'sɪst/ vi leben (**on** von). **~ence** n Existenz f

substance /'sʌbstəns/ n Substanz f

sub'standard a unzulänglich; (goods) minderwertig

substantial /səb'stænʃl/ a solide; (meal) reichhaltig; (considerable) beträchtlich. **-ly** adv solide; (essentially) im wesentlichen

substantiate /səb'stænʃɪeɪt/ vt erhärten

substitut|e /'sʌbstɪtjuːt/ n Ersatz m; (Sport) Ersatzspieler(in) m(f) ● vt **~e A for B** B durch A ersetzen ● vi **~e for s.o.** jdn vertreten. **~ion** /-'tjuːʃn/ n Ersetzung f

subterfuge /'sʌbtəfjuːdʒ/ n List f

subterranean /sʌbtə'reɪnɪən/ a unterirdisch

'subtitle n Untertitel m

subtle /'sʌtl/ a (**-r, -st**), **-tly** adv fein; (fig) subtil

subtract /səb'trækt/ vt abziehen, subtrahieren. **~ion** /-ækʃn/ n Subtraktion f

suburb /'sʌbɜːb/ n Vorort m; **in the ~s** am Stadtrand. **~an** /sə'bɜːbən/ a Vorort-; (pej) spießig. **~ia** /sə'bɜː- bɪə/ n die Vororte pl

subversive /səb'vɜːsɪv/ a subversiv

'subway n Unterführung f; (Amer: railway) U-Bahn f

succeed /sək'siːd/ vi Erfolg haben; (plan:) gelingen; (follow) nachfolgen (+ dat); **I ~ed** es ist mir gelungen; **he ~ed in escaping** es gelang

ihm zu entkommen ● *vt* folgen
(+ *dat*). ~**ing** *a* folgend

success /sək'ses/ *n* Erfolg *m*. ~**ful** *a*,
-**ly** *adv* erfolgreich

succession /sək'seʃn/ *n* Folge *f*;
⟨*series*⟩ Serie *f*; (*to title, office*)
Nachfolge *f*; (*to throne*) Thronfolge *f*;
in ~ hintereinander

successive /sək'sesɪv/ *a* aufeinanderfolgend. ~**ly** *adv* hintereinander

successor /sək'sesə(r)/ *n* Nach-
folger(in) *m(f)*

succinct /sək'sɪŋkt/ *a*, -**ly** *adv*
prägnant

succulent /'sʌkjʊlənt/ *a* saftig

succumb /sə'kʌm/ *vi* erliegen (**to**
dat)

such /sʌtʃ/ *a* solche(r,s); ~ **a book** ein
solches *od* solch ein Buch; ~ **a thing** so
etwas; ~ **a long time** so lange; **there is
no** ~ **thing** das gibt es gar nicht; **there
is no** ● **person** eine solche Person gibt
es nicht ● *pron* **as** ~ als solche(r,s);
⟨*strictly speaking*⟩ an sich; ~ **as** wie
[zum Beispiel]; **and** ~ und dergleichen.
~**like** *pron* (*fam*) dergleichen

suck /sʌk/ *vt/i* saugen; lutschen
⟨*sweet*⟩. ~ **up** *vt* aufsaugen ● *vi* ~ **up
to s.o.** (*fam*) sich bei jdm einschmeicheln

sucker /'sʌkə(r)/ *n* (*Bot*) Ausläufer
m; (*fam: person*) Dumme(r) *m/f*

suckle /'sʌkl/ *vt* säugen

suction /'sʌkʃn/ *n* Saugwirkung *f*

sudden /'sʌdn/ *a*, -**ly** *adv* plötzlich;
⟨*abrupt*⟩ jäh ● **n all of a** ~ auf einmal

sue /su:/ *vt* ⟨*pres p* **suing**⟩ verklagen
(**for** auf + *acc*) ● *vi* klagen

suede /sweɪd/ *n* Wildleder *nt*

suet /'su:ɪt/ *n* [Nieren]talg *m*

suffer /'sʌfə(r)/ *vi* leiden (**from** an
+ *dat*) ● *vt* erleiden; ⟨*tolerate*⟩ dulden.
~**ance** /-əns/ *n* **on** ~**ance** bloß ge-
duldet. ~**ing** *n* Leiden *nt*

suffice /sə'faɪs/ *vi* genügen

sufficient /sə'fɪʃnt/ *a*, -**ly** *adv* genug,
genügend; **be** ~ genügen

suffix /'sʌfɪks/ *n* Nachsilbe *f*

suffocat|e /'sʌfəkeɪt/ *vt/i* ersticken.
~**ion** /-'keɪʃn/ *n* Ersticken *nt*

sugar /'ʃʊgə(r)/ *n* Zucker *m* ● *vt*
zuckern; (*fig*) versüßen. ~ **basin**,
~-**bowl** *n* Zuckerschale *f*. ~**y** *a* süß;
(*fig*) süßlich

suggest /sə'dʒest/ *vt* vorschlagen;
⟨*indicate, insinuate*⟩ andeuten. ~**ion**
/-estʃn/ *n* Vorschlag *m*; Andeutung *f*;

⟨*trace*⟩ Spur *f*. ~**ive** /-ɪv/ *a*, -**ly** *adv* anzüglich; **be** ~**ive of** schließen las-
sen auf (+ *acc*)

suicidal /su:ɪ'saɪdl/ *a* selbst-
mörderisch

suicide /'su:ɪsaɪd/ *n* Selbstmord *m*

suit /su:t/ *n* Anzug *m*; (*woman's*) Kostüm *nt*; ⟨*Cards*⟩ Farbe *f*; ⟨*Jur*⟩
Prozeß *m*; **follow** ~ (*fig*) das Gleiche
tun ● *vt* ⟨*adapt*⟩ anpassen (**to** *dat*); ⟨*be
convenient for*⟩ passen (+ *dat*); ⟨*go with*⟩
passen zu; ⟨*clothing:*⟩ stehen (**s.o.** jdm);
be ~**ed for** geeignet sein für; ~ **yourself!** wie du willst!

suit|able /'su:təbl/ *a* geeignet;
⟨*convenient*⟩ passend; ⟨*appropriate*⟩
angemessen; ⟨*for weather, activity*⟩
zweckmäßig. ~**ably** *adv* angemessen; zweckmäßig

'suitcase *n* Koffer *m*

suite /swi:t/ *n* Suite *f*; (*of furniture*)
Garnitur *f*

sulk /sʌlk/ *vi* schmollen. ~**y** *a*
schmollend

sullen /'sʌlən/ *a*, -**ly** *adv* mürrisch

sulphur /'sʌlfə(r)/ *n* Schwefel *f*. ~**ic**
/-'fjʊərɪk/ *a* ~**ic acid** Schwefelsäure *f*

sultana /sʌl'tɑ:nə/ *n* Sultanine *f*

sultry /'sʌltrɪ/ *a* ⟨-**ier**, -**iest**⟩ ⟨*weather*⟩
schwül

sum /sʌm/ *n* Summe *f*; ⟨*Sch*⟩ Rechen-
aufgabe *f* ● *vt/i* ⟨*pt/pp* **summed**⟩ ~
up zusammenfassen; ⟨*assess*⟩ einschätzen

summar|ize /'sʌməraɪz/ *vt* zu-
sammenfassen. ~**y** *n* Zusammenfassung *f* ● *a*, -**ily** *adv* summarisch;
⟨*dismissal*⟩ fristlos

summer /'sʌmə(r)/ *n* Sommer *m*.
~-**house** *n* [Garten]laube *f*. ~**time** *n*
Sommer *m*

summery /'sʌmərɪ/ *a* sommerlich

summit /'sʌmɪt/ *n* Gipfel *m*. ~ **conference** *n* Gipfelkonferenz *f*

summon /'sʌmən/ *vt* rufen; holen
⟨*help*⟩; ⟨*Jur*⟩ vorladen. ~ **up** *vt* aufbringen

summons /'sʌmənz/ *n* ⟨*Jur*⟩ Vor-
ladung *f* ● *vt* vorladen

sump /sʌmp/ *n* ⟨*Auto*⟩ Ölwanne *f*

sumptuous /'sʌmptjʊəs/ *a*, -**ly** *adv*
prunkvoll; ⟨*meal*⟩ üppig

sun /sʌn/ *n* Sonne *f* ● *vt* ⟨*pt/pp*
sunned⟩ ~ **oneself** sich sonnen

sun: ~**bathe** *vi* sich sonnen. ~-**bed**
n Sonnenbank *f*. ~**burn** *n* Son-
nenbrand *m*

sundae /'sʌndeɪ/ *n* Eisbecher *m*

Sunday /'sʌndeɪ/ n Sonntag m
'sundial n Sonnenuhr f
sundry /'sʌndrɪ/ a verschiedene pl;
all and ~ alle pl
'sunflower n Sonnenblume f
sung /sʌŋ/ see **sing**
'sun-glasses npl Sonnenbrille f
sunk /sʌŋk/ see **sink**
sunken /'sʌŋkn/ a gesunken; ⟨eyes⟩
eingefallen
sunny /'sʌnɪ/ a (-ier, -iest) sonnig
sun: ~**rise** n Sonnenaufgang m.
~-**roof** n (Auto) Schiebedach nt.
~**set** n Sonnenuntergang m. ~
shade n Sonnenschirm m. ~**shine** n
Sonnenschein m. ~**stroke** n Sonnen-
stich m. ~**tan** n [Sonnen]bräune f.
~-**tanned** a braun[gebrannt].
~-**tan oil** n Sonnenöl nt
super /'su:pə(r)/ a (fam) prima, toll
superb /sʊ'pɜ:b/ a erstklassig
supercilious /su:pə'sɪlɪəs/ a überlegen
superficial /su:pə'fɪʃl/ a, -**ly** adv
oberflächlich
superfluous /sʊ'pɜ:flʊəs/ a überflüssig
super'human a übermenschlich
superintendent /'su:pərɪn'tendənt/
n (of police) Kommissar m
superior /su:'pɪərɪə(r)/ a überlegen;
(in rank) höher ● n Vorgesetzte(r)
m/f. ~**ity** /-'ɒrətɪ/ n Überlegenheit f
superlative /su:'pɜ:lətɪv/ a un-
übertrefflich ● n Superlativ m
'superman n Übermensch m
'supermarket n Supermarkt m
super'natural a übernatürlich
'superpower n Supermacht f
supersede /su:pə'si:d/ vt ersetzen
super'sonic a Überschall-
superstiti|on /su:pə'stɪʃn/ n Aber-
glaube m. ~**ous** /-'stɪʃəs/ a, -**ly** adv
abergläubisch
supervis|e /'su:pəvaɪz/ vt be-
aufsichtigen; überwachen ⟨work⟩.
~**ion** /-'vɪʒn/ n Aufsicht f; Überwachung f. ~**or** n Aufseher(in) m(f)
supper /'sʌpə(r)/ n Abendessen nt
supple /'sʌpl/ a geschmeidig
supplement /'sʌplɪmənt/ n Ergänzung f; (addition) Zusatz m; (to
fare) Zuschlag m; (book) Er-
gänzungsband m; (to newspaper)
Beilage f ● vt ergänzen. ~**ary**
/-'mentərɪ/ a zusätzlich
supplier /sə'plaɪə(r)/ n Lieferant m

supply /sə'plaɪ/ n Vorrat m; **supplies**
pl (Mil) Nachschub m ● vt (pt/pp -ied)
liefern; ~ s.o. with sth jdn mit etw
versorgen
support /sə'pɔ:t/ n Stütze f; (fig)
Unterstützung f ● vt stützen; (bear
weight of) tragen; (keep) ernähren;
(give money to) unterstützen; (speak
in favour of) befürworten; (Sport)
Fan sein von. ~**er** n Anhänger(in)
m(f); (Sport) Fan m. ~**ive** /-ɪv/ a be
~**ive [to s.o.]** [jdm] eine große Stütze
sein
suppose /sə'pəʊz/ vt annehmen;
(presume) vermuten; (imagine) sich
(dat) vorstellen; **be** ~**d to do sth**
etw tun sollen; **nct be** ~**d to** (fam)
nicht dürfen; **I** ~ **so** vermutlich. ~**dly**
/-ɪdlɪ/ adv angeblich
supposition /sʌpə'zɪʃn/ n Vermutung f
suppository /sʌ'pɒzɪtrɪ/ n Zäpfchen
nt
suppress /sə'pres/ vt unterdrücken.
~**ion** /-eʃn/ n Unterdrückung f
supremacy /su:'preməsɪ/ n Vorherr-
schaft f
supreme /su:'pri:m/ a höchste(r,s);
⟨court⟩ oberste(r,s)
surcharge /'sɜ:tʃɑ:dʒ/ n Zuschlag m
sure /ʃʊə(r)/ a (-r, -st) sicher; **make**
~ sich vergewissern (of gen);
(check) nachprüfen; **be** ~ **to do it** sieh
zu, daß du es tust ● adv (Amer, fam)
klar; ~ **enough** tatsächlich. ~**ly** adv
sicher; (for emphasis) doch; (Amer:
gladly) gern
surety /'ʃʊərətɪ/ n Bürgschaft f;
stand ~ **for** bürgen für
surf /sɜ:f/ n Brandung f
surface /'sɜ:fɪs/ n Oberfläche f ● vi
(emerge) auftauchen. ~ **mail** n **by** ~
mail auf dem Land-/Seeweg
'surfboard n Surfbrett nt
surfeit /'sɜ:fɪt/ n Übermaß nt
surfing /'sɜ:fɪŋ/ n Surfen nt
surge /sɜ:dʒ/ n (of sea) Branden nt;
(fig) Welle f ● vi branden; ~ **forward**
nach vorn drängen
surgeon /'sɜ:dʒən/ n Chirurg(in)
m(f)
surgery /'sɜ:dʒərɪ/ n Chirurgie f;
(place) Praxis f; (room) Sprechzimmer nt; (hours) Sprechstunde f;
have ~ operiert werden
surgical /'sɜ:dʒɪkl/ a, -**ly** adv
chirurgisch
surly /'sɜ:lɪ/ a (-ier, -iest) mürrisch

surmise /səˈmaɪz/ vt mutmaßen
surmount /səˈmaʊnt/ vt überwinden
surname /ˈsɜːneɪm/ n Nachname m
surpass /səˈpɑːs/ vt übertreffen
surplus /ˈsɜːpləs/ a überschüssig; **be ~ to requirements** nicht benötigt werden ● n Überschuß m (**of** an + dat)
surpris|e /səˈpraɪz/ n Überraschung f ● vt überraschen; **be ~ed** sich wundern (**at** über + acc). **~ing** a, **-ly** adv überraschend
surrender /səˈrendə(r)/ n Kapitulation f ● vi sich ergeben; (Mil) kapitulieren ● vt aufgeben
surreptitious /sʌrəpˈtɪʃəs/ a, **-ly** adv heimlich, verstohlen
surrogate /ˈsʌrəgət/ n Ersatz m. **~ ˈmother** n Leihmutter f
surround /səˈraʊnd/ vt umgeben; (encircle) umzingeln; **~ed by** umgeben von. **~ing** a umliegend. **~ings** npl Umgebung f
surveillance /səˈveɪləns/ n Überwachung f; **be under ~** überwacht werden
survey[1] /ˈsɜːveɪ/ n Überblick m; (poll) Umfrage f; (investigation) Untersuchung f; (of land) Vermessung f; (of house) Gutachten nt
survey[2] /səˈveɪ/ vt betrachten; vermessen (land); begutachten (building). **~or** n Landvermesser m; Gutachter m
survival /səˈvaɪvl/ n Überleben nt; (of tradition) Fortbestand m
surviv|e /səˈvaɪv/ vt überleben ● vi überleben; (tradition:) erhalten bleiben. **~or** n Überlebende(r) m/f; **be a ~or** (fam) nicht unterzukriegen sein
susceptible /səˈseptəbl/ a empfänglich/(Med) anfällig (**to** für)
suspect[1] /səˈspekt/ vt verdächtigen; (assume) vermuten; **he ~s nothing** er ahnt nichts
suspect[2] /ˈsʌspekt/ a verdächtig ● n Verdächtige(r) m/f
suspend /səˈspend/ vt aufhängen; (stop) [vorläufig] einstellen; (from duty) vorläufig beurlauben. **~er belt** n Strumpfbandgürtel m. **~ers** npl Strumpfbänder pl; (Amer: braces) Hosenträger pl
suspense /səˈspens/ n Spannung f
suspension /səˈspenʃn/ n (Auto) Federung f. **~ bridge** n Hängebrücke f

suspici|on /səˈspɪʃn/ n Verdacht m; (mistrust) Mißtrauen nt; (trace) Spur f. **~ous** /-ɪʃəs/ a, **-ly** adv mißtrauisch; (arousing suspicion) verdächtig
sustain /səˈsteɪn/ vt tragen; (fig) aufrechterhalten; erhalten (life); erleiden (injury)
sustenance /ˈsʌstɪnəns/ n Nahrung f
swab /swɒb/ n (Med) Tupfer m; (specimen) Abstrich m
swagger /ˈswægə(r)/ vi stolzieren
swallow[1] /ˈswɒləʊ/ vt/i schlucken. **~ up** vt verschlucken; verschlingen (resources)
swallow[2] n (bird) Schwalbe f
swam /swæm/ see **swim**
swamp /swɒmp/ n Sumpf m ● vt überschwemmen. **~y** a sumpfig
swan /swɒn/ n Schwan m
swank /swæŋk/ vi (fam) angeben
swap /swɒp/ n (fam) Tausch m ● vt/i (pt/pp swapped) (fam) tauschen (**for** gegen)
swarm /swɔːm/ n Schwarm m ● vi schwärmen; **be ~ing with** wimmeln von
swarthy /ˈswɔːðɪ/ a (**-ier, -iest**) dunkel
swastika /ˈswɒstɪkə/ n Hakenkreuz nt
swat /swɒt/ vt (pt/pp swatted) totschlagen
sway /sweɪ/ n (fig) Herrschaft f ● vi schwanken; (gently) sich wiegen ● vt wiegen; (influence) beeinflussen
swear /sweə(r)/ v (pt swore, pp sworn) ● vt schwören ● vi schwören (**by** auf + acc); (curse) fluchen. **~-word** n Kraftausdruck m
sweat /swet/ n Schweiß m ● vi schwitzen
sweater /ˈswetə(r)/ n Pullover m
sweaty /ˈswetɪ/ a schwitzig
swede /swiːd/ n Kohlrübe f
Swed|e n Schwede m/-din f. **~en** n Schweden nt. **~ish** a schwedisch
sweep /swiːp/ n Schornsteinfeger m; (curve) Bogen m; (movement) ausholende Bewegung f; **make a clean ~** (fig) gründlich aufräumen ● v (pt/pp swept) ● vt fegen, kehren ● vi (go swiftly) rauschen; (wind:) fegen. **~ up** vt zusammenfegen/-kehren
sweeping /ˈswiːpɪŋ/ a ausholend; (statement) pauschal; (changes) weitreichend

sweet /swiːt/ a (-er, -est) süß; **have a ~ tooth** gern Süßes mögen ● n Bonbon m & nt; (*dessert*) Nachtisch m. **~ corn** n [Zucker]mais m

sweeten /'swiːtn/ vt süßen. **~er** n Süßstoff m; (*fam: bribe*) Schmiergeld nt

sweet: ~heart n Schatz m. **~-shop** n Süßwarenladen m. **~ness** n Süße f. **~'pea** n Wicke f

swell /swel/ a (pt swelled, pp swollen or swelled) ● vi [an]schwellen; ⟨sails:⟩ sich blähen; ⟨wood:⟩ aufquellen ● vt anschwellen lassen; (*increase*) vergrößern. **~ing** n Schwellung f

swelter /'sweltə(r)/ vi schwitzen

swept /swept/ see **sweep**

swerve /swɜːv/ vi einen Bogen machen

swift /swift/ a (-er, -est), -ly adv schnell

swig /swig/ n (*fam*) Schluck m, Zug m ● vt (pt/pp swigged) (*fam*) [herunter]kippen

swill /swil/ n (*for pigs*) Schweinefutter nt ● vt ~ [out] [aus]spülen

swim /swim/ n **have a ~** schwimmen ● vi (pt swam, pp swum) schwimmen; **my head is ~ming** mir dreht sich der Kopf. **~mer** n Schwimmer(in) m(f)

swimming /'swimiŋ/ n Schwimmen nt. **~-baths** npl Schwimmbad nt. **~-pool** n Schwimmbecken nt; (*private*) Swimmingpool m

'swim-suit n Badeanzug m

swindle /'swindl/ n Schwindel m, Betrug m ● vt betrügen. **~r** n Schwindler m

swine /swain/ n Schwein nt

swing /swiŋ/ n Schwung m; (*shift*) Schwenk m; (*seat*) Schaukel f; **in full ~** in vollem Gange ● v (pt/pp swung) ● vi schwingen; (*on swing*) schaukeln; (*sway*) schwanken; (*dangle*) baumeln; (*turn*) schwenken ● vt schwingen; (*influence*) beeinflussen. **~-'door** n Schwingtür f

swingeing /'swindʒiŋ/ a hart; (*fig*) drastisch

swipe /swaip/ n (*fam*) Schlag m ● vt (*fam*) knallen; (*steal*) klauen

swirl /swɜːl/ n Wirbel m ● vt/i wirbeln

swish /swiʃ/ a (*fam*) schick ● vi zischen

Swiss /swis/ a Schweizer, schweizerisch ● n Schweizer(in) m(f); **the ~**

pl die Schweizer. **~ 'roll** n Biskuitrolle f

switch /switʃ/ n Schalter m; (*change*) Wechsel m; (*Amer, Rail*) Weiche f ● vt wechseln; (*exchange*) tauschen ● vi wechseln; **~ to** umstellen auf (+ acc). **~ off** vt ausschalten; abschalten (*engine*). **~ on** vt einschalten, anschalten

switch: ~back n Achterbahn f. **~ board** n [Telefon]zentrale f

Switzerland /'switsələnd/ n die Schweiz

swivel /'swivl/ v (pt/pp swivelled) ● vt drehen ● vi sich drehen

swollen /'swəʊlən/ see **swell** ● a geschwollen. **~-'headed** a eingebildet

swoop /swuːp/ n Sturzflug m; (*by police*) Razzia f ● vi **~ down** herabstoßen

sword /sɔːd/ n Schwert nt

swore /swɔː(r)/ see **swear**

sworn /swɔːn/ see **swear**

swot /swɒt/ n (*fam*) Streber m ● vt/i (pt/pp swotted) (*fam*) büffeln

swum /swʌm/ see **swim**

swung /swʌŋ/ see **swing**

syllable /'siləbl/ n Silbe f

syllabus /'siləbəs/ n Lehrplan m; (*for exam*) Studienplan m

symbol /'simbəl/ n Symbol nt (of für). **~ic** /-'bɒlik/ a, -ally adv symbolisch. **~ism** /-izm/ n Symbolik f. **~ize** vt symbolisieren

symmetr|ical /si'metrikl/ a, -ly adv symmetrisch. **~y** /'simətri/ n Symmetrie f

sympathetic /simpə'θetik/ a, -ally adv mitfühlend; (*likeable*) sympathisch

sympathize /'simpəθaiz/ vi mitfühlen. **~r** n (*Pol*) Sympathisant m

sympathy /'simpəθi/ n Mitgefühl nt; (*condolences*) Beileid nt

symphony /'simfəni/ n Sinfonie f

symptom /'simptəm/ n Symptom nt. **~atic** /-'mætik/ a symptomatisch (of für)

synagogue /'sinəgɒg/ n Synagoge f

synchronize /'siŋkrənaiz/ vt synchronisieren

syndicate /'sindikət/ n Syndikat nt

syndrome /'sindrəʊm/ n Syndrom nt

synonym /'sinənim/ n Synonym nt. **~ous** /-'nɒniməs/ a, -ly adv synonym

synopsis /si'nɒpsis/ n (pl -opses /-siːz/) Zusammenfassung f; (of opera, ballet) Inhaltsangabe f

syntax /'sɪntæks/ n Syntax f
synthesis /'sɪnθəsɪs/ n (pl -ses /-siːz/) Synthese f
synthetic /sɪn'θetɪk/ a synthetisch ● n Kunststoff m
Syria /'sɪrɪə/ n Syrien nt
syringe /sɪ'rɪndʒ/ n Spritze f ● vt spritzen; ausspritzen ⟨ears⟩
syrup /'sɪrəp/ n Sirup m
system /'sɪstəm/ n System nt. **~atic** /-'mætɪk/ a, **-ally** adv systematisch

T

tab /tæb/ n (projecting) Zunge f; (with name) Namensschild nt; (loop) Aufhänger m; **keep ~s on** (fam) [genau] beobachten; **pick up the ~** (fam) bezahlen
tabby /'tæbɪ/ n getigerte Katze f
table /'teɪbl/ n Tisch m; (list) Tabelle f; **at [the] ~** bei Tisch ● vt einbringen. **~-cloth** n Tischdecke f, Tischtuch nt. **~spoon** n Servierlöffel m
tablet /'tæblɪt/ n Tablette f; (of soap) Stück nt; (slab) Tafel f
'table tennis n Tischtennis nt
tabloid /'tæblɔɪd/ n kleinformatige Zeitung f; (pej) Boulevardzeitung f
taboo /tə'buː/ a tabu ● n Tabu nt
tacit /'tæsɪt/ a, **-ly** adv stillschweigend
taciturn /'tæsɪtɜːn/ a wortkarg
tack /tæk/ n (nail) Stift m; (stitch) Heftstich m; (Naut & fig) Kurs m ● vt festnageln; (sew) heften ● vi (Naut) kreuzen
tackle /'tækl/ n Ausrüstung f ● vt angehen
tacky /'tækɪ/ a klebrig
tact /tækt/ n Takt m, Taktgefühl nt. **~ful** a, **-ly** adv taktvoll
tactic|al /'tæktɪkl/ a, **-ly** adv taktisch. **~s** npl Taktik f
tactless /'tæktlɪs/ a, **-ly** adv taktlos. **~ness** n Taktlosigkeit f
tadpole /'tædpəʊl/ n Kaulquappe f
tag¹ /tæg/ n (label) Schild nt ● vi (pt/pp **tagged**) **~ along** mitkommen
tag² n (game) Fangen nt
tail /teɪl/ n Schwanz m; **~s** pl (tailcoat) Frack m; **heads or ~s?** Kopf oder Zahl? ● vt (fam: follow) beschatten ● vi **~ off** zurückgehen
tail: **~back** n Rückstau m. **~coat** n Frack m. **~-end** n Ende nt. **~ light** n Rücklicht nt

tailor /'teɪlə(r)/ n Schneider m. **~-made** a maßgeschneidert
'tail wind n Rückenwind m
taint /teɪnt/ vt verderben
take /teɪk/ v (pt **took**, pp **taken**) ● vt nehmen; (with one) mitnehmen; (take to a place) bringen; (steal) stehlen; (win) gewinnen; (capture) einnehmen; (require) brauchen; (last) dauern; (teach) geben; machen ⟨exam, subject, holiday, photograph⟩; messen ⟨pulse, temperature⟩; **~ s.o. home** jdn nach Hause bringen; **~ sth to the cleaner's** etw in die Reinigung bringen; **~ s.o. prisoner** jdn gefangennehmen; **be ~n ill** krank werden; **~ sth calmly** etw gelassen aufnehmen ● vi ⟨plant:⟩ angehen; **~ after s.o.** jdm nachschlagen; (in looks) jdm ähnlich sehen; **~ to** (like) mögen; (as a habit) sich (dat) angewöhnen. **~ away** vt wegbringen; (remove) wegnehmen; (subtract) abziehen; **'to ~ away'** 'zum Mitnehmen'. **~ back** vt zurücknehmen; (return) zurückbringen. **~ down** vt herunternehmen; (remove) abnehmen; (write down) aufschreiben. **~ in** vt hineinbringen; (bring indoors) hereinholen; (to one's home) aufnehmen; (understand) begreifen; (deceive) hereinlegen; (make smaller) enger machen. **~ off** vt abnehmen; ablegen ⟨coat⟩; sich (dat) ausziehen ⟨clothes⟩; (deduct) abziehen; (mimic) nachmachen; **~ time off** sich (dat) frei nehmen; **~ oneself off** [fort]gehen ● vi (Aviat) starten. **~ on** vt annehmen; (undertake) übernehmen; (engage) einstellen; (as opponent) antreten gegen. **~ out** vt hinausbringen; (for pleasure) ausgehen mit; ausführen ⟨dog⟩; (remove) herausnehmen; (withdraw) abheben ⟨money⟩; (from library) ausleihen; **~ out a subscription to sth** etw abonnieren; **~ it out on s.o.** (fam) seinen Ärger an jdm auslassen. **~ over** vt hinüberbringen; übernehmen ⟨firm, control⟩ ● vi **~ over from s.o.** jdn ablösen. **~ up** vt hinaufbringen; annehmen ⟨offer⟩; ergreifen ⟨profession⟩; sich (dat) zulegen ⟨hobby⟩; in Anspruch nehmen ⟨time⟩; einnehmen ⟨space⟩; aufreißen ⟨floorboards⟩; **~ sth up with s.o.** mit jdm über etw (acc) sprechen ● vi **~ up with s.o.** sich mit jdm einlassen

take: ~-**away** n Essen nt zum Mit-nehmen; (restaurant) Restaurant nt mit Straßenverkauf. ~-**off** n (Aviat) Start m, Abflug m. ~-**over** n Übernahme f

takings /'teikiŋz/ npl Einnahmen pl

talcum /'tælkəm/ n ~ [**powder**] Kör-perpuder m

tale /teil/ n Geschichte f

talent /'tælənt/ n Talent nt. ~**ed** a talentiert

talk /tɔ:k/ n Gespräch nt; (lecture) Vortrag m; **make small** ~ Kon-versation machen • vi reden, sprechen (**to/with** mit) • vt reden; ~ **s.o. into sth** jdn zu etw überreden. ~ **over** vt besprechen

talkative /'tɔ:kətiv/ a gesprächig

'talking-to n Standpauke f

tall /tɔ:l/ a (-**er, -est**) groß; (building, tree) hoch; **that's a** ~ **order** das ist ziemlich viel verlangt. ~**boy** n hohe Kommode f. ~**'story** n übertriebene Geschichte f

tally /'tælɪ/ n **keep a** ~ **of** Buch führen über (+ acc) • vi übereinstimmen

talon /'tælən/ n Klaue f

tambourine /tæmbə'ri:n/ n Tam-burin nt

tame /teim/ a (-**r, -st**), -**ly** adv zahm; (dull) lahm (fam) • vt zähmen. ~**r** n Dompteur m

tamper /'tæmpə(r)/ vi ~ **with** sich (dat) zu schaffen machen an (+ dat)

tampon /'tæmpɒn/ n Tampon m

tan /tæn/ a gelbbraun • n Gelbbraun nt; (from sun) Bräune f • v (pt/pp **tanned**) • vt gerben (hide) • vi braun werden

tang /tæŋ/ n herber Geschmack m; (smell) herber Geruch m

tangent /'tændʒənt/ n Tangente f; **go off at a** ~ (fam) vom Thema ab-schweifen

tangible /'tændʒɪbl/ a greifbar

tangle /'tæŋgl/ n Gewirr nt; (in hair) Verfilzung f • vt ~ [**up**] verheddern • vi sich verheddern

tango /'tæŋgəʊ/ n Tango m

tank /tæŋk/ n Tank m; (Mil) Panzer m

tankard /'tæŋkəd/ n Krug m

tanker /'tæŋkə(r)/ n Tanker m; (lorry) Tank[last]wagen m

tantaliz|e /'tæntəlaɪz/ vt quälen. ~**ing** a verlockend

tantamount /'tæntəmaʊnt/ a **be** ~ **to** gleichbedeutend sein mit

tantrum /'tæntrəm/ n Wutanfall m

tap /tæp/ n Hahn m; (knock) Klopfen nt; **on** ~ zur Verfügung • v (pt/pp **tapped**) • vt klopfen an (+ acc); anzapfen (barrel, tree); erschließen (re-sources); abhören (telephone) • vi klop-fen. ~**dance** n Step[tanz] m • vi Step tanzen, steppen

tape /teip/ n Band nt; (adhesive) Klebstreifen m; (for recording) Ton-band nt • vt mit Klebstreifen zukle-ben; (record) auf Band aufnehmen

'tape-measure n Bandmaß nt

taper /'teipə(r)/ n dünne Wachskerze f • vi sich verjüngen

'tape recorder n Tonbandgerät nt

tapestry /'tæpɪstrɪ/ n Gobelin-stickerei f

'tapeworm n Bandwurm m

'tap water n Leitungswasser nt

tar /tɑ:(r)/ n Teer m • vt (pt/pp **tarred**) teeren

tardy /'tɑ:dɪ/ a (-**ier, -iest**) langsam; (late) spät

target /'tɑ:gɪt/ n Ziel nt; (board) [Ziel]scheibe f

tariff /'tærɪf/ n Tarif m; (duty) Zoll m

tarnish /'tɑ:nɪʃ/ vi anlaufen

tarpaulin /tɑ:'pɔ:lɪn/ n Plane f

tarragon /'tærəgən/ n Estragon m

tart¹ /tɑ:t/ a (-**er, -est**) sauer; (fig) scharf

tart² n / Obstkuchen m; (individual) Törtchen nt; (sl: prostitute) Nutte f • vt ~ **oneself up** (fam) sich auftakeln

tartan /'tɑ:tn/ n Schottenmuster nt; (cloth) Schottenstoff m • attrib schottisch kariert

tartar /'tɑ:tə(r)/ n (on teeth) Zahnstein m

tartar 'sauce /tɑ:tə-/ n ≈ Remou-ladensoße f

task /tɑ:sk/ n Aufgabe f; **take s.o. to** ~ jdm Vorhaltungen machen. ~ **force** n Sonderkommando nt

tassel /'tæsl/ n Quaste f

taste /teist/ n Geschmack m; (sample) Kostprobe f • vt kosten, probieren; schmecken (flavour) • vi schmecken (**of** nach). ~**ful** a, -**ly** adv (fig) geschmackvoll. ~**less** a, -**ly** adv geschmacklos

tasty /'teistɪ/ a (-**ier, -iest**) lecker, schmackhaft

tat /tæt/ see **tit²**

tatter|ed /'tætəd/ a zerlumpt; (pages) zerfleddert. ~**s** npl **in** ~**s** in Fetzen

tattoo[1] /tə'tu:/ n Tätowierung f ● vt tätowieren

tattoo[2] n (Mil) Zapfenstreich m

tatty /'tætɪ/ a (-ier, -iest) schäbig; ⟨book⟩ zerfleddert

taught /tɔ:t/ see **teach**

taunt /tɔ:nt/ n höhnische Bemerkung f ● vt verhöhnen

Taurus /'tɔ:rəs/ n (Astr) Stier m

taut /tɔ:t/ a straff

tavern /'tævən/ n (liter) Schenke f

tawdry /'tɔ:drɪ/ a (-ier, -iest) billig und geschmacklos

tawny /'tɔ:nɪ/ a gelbbraun

tax /tæks/ n Steuer f ● vt besteuern; (fig) strapazieren; ~ **with** beschuldigen (+ gen). ~**able** /-əbl/ a steuerpflichtig. ~**ation** /-'seɪʃn/ n Besteuerung f. ~**-free** a steuerfrei

taxi /'tæksɪ/ n Taxi nt ● vi (pt/pp taxied, pres p taxiing) ⟨aircraft:⟩ rollen. ~ **driver** n Taxifahrer m. ~ **rank** n Taxistand m

'**taxpayer** n Steuerzahler m

tea /ti:/ n Tee m. ~**-bag** n Teebeutel m. ~**-break** n Teepause f

teach /ti:tʃ/ vt/i (pt/pp taught) unterrichten; ~ **s.o. sth** jdm etw beibringen. ~**er** n Lehrer(in) m(f)

tea: ~**-cloth** n (for drying) Geschirrtuch nt. ~**cup** n Teetasse f

teak /ti:k/ n Teakholz nt

team /ti:m/ n Mannschaft f; (fig) Team nt; (of animals) Gespann nt ● vi ~ **up** sich zusammentun

'**team-work** n Teamarbeit f

'**teapot** n Teekanne f

tear[1] /teə(r)/ n Riß m ● v (pt tore, pp torn) ● vt reißen; (damage) zerreißen; ~ **open** aufreißen; ~ **oneself away** sich losreißen ● vi [zer]reißen; (run) rasen. ~ **up** vt zerreißen

tear[2] /tɪə(r)/ n Träne f. ~**ful** a weinend. ~**fully** adv unter Tränen. ~**-gas** n Tränengas nt

tease /ti:z/ vt necken

tea: ~**-set** n Teeservice nt. ~ **shop** n Café nt. ~**spoon** n Teelöffel m. ~**-strainer** n Teesieb nt

teat /ti:t/ n Zitze f; (on bottle) Sauger m

'**tea-towel** n Geschirrtuch nt

technical /'teknɪkl/ a technisch; (specialized) fachlich. ~**ity** /-'kælətɪ/ n technisches Detail nt; (Jur) Formfehler m. ~**ly** adv technisch; (strictly) streng genommen. ~ **term** n Fachausdruck m

technician /tek'nɪʃn/ n Techniker m

technique /tek'ni:k/ n Technik f

technological /teknə'lɒdʒɪkl/ a, -**ly** adv technologisch

technology /tek'nɒlədʒɪ/ n Technologie f

teddy /'tedɪ/ n ~ [**bear**] Teddybär m

tedious /'ti:dɪəs/ a langweilig

tedium /'ti:dɪəm/ n Langeweile f

teem /ti:m/ vi (rain) in Strömen gießen; **be** ~**ing with** (full of) wimmeln von

teenage /'ti:neɪdʒ/ a Teenager-; ~ **boy/girl** Junge m/Mädchen nt im Teenageralter. ~**r** n Teenager m

teens /ti:nz/ npl **the** ~ die Teenagerjahre pl

teeny /'ti:nɪ/ a (-ier, -iest) winzig

teeter /'ti:tə(r)/ vi schwanken

teeth /ti:θ/ see **tooth**

teeth|e /ti:ð/ vi zahnen. ~**ing troubles** npl (fig) Anfangsschwierigkeiten pl

teetotal /ti:'təʊtl/ a abstinent. ~**ler** n Abstinenzler m

telecommunications /telɪkəmju:nɪ'keɪʃnz/ npl Fernmeldewesen nt

telegram /'telɪgræm/ n Telegramm nt

telegraph /'telɪgrɑ:f/ n Telegraf m. ~**ic** /-'græfɪk/ a telegrafisch. ~ **pole** n Telegrafenmast m

telepathy /tɪ'lepəθɪ/ n Telepathie f; **by** ~ telepathisch

telephone /'telɪfəʊn/ n Telefon nt; **be on the** ~ Telefon haben; (be telephoning) telefonieren ● vt anrufen ● vi telefonieren

telephone: ~ **book** n Telefonbuch nt. ~ **booth** n, ~ **box** n Telefonzelle f. ~ **directory** n Telefonbuch nt. ~ **number** n Telefonnummer f

telephonist /tɪ'lefənɪst/ n Telefonist(in) m(f)

tele'photo /telɪ-/ a ~ **lens** Teleobjektiv nt

teleprinter /'telɪ-/ n Fernschreiber m

telescop|e /'telɪskəʊp/ n Teleskop nt, Fernrohr nt. ~**ic** /-'skɒpɪk/ a teleskopisch; (collapsible) ausziehbar

televise /'telɪvaɪz/ vt im Fernsehen übertragen

television /'telɪvɪʒn/ n Fernsehen nt; **watch** ~ fernsehen. ~ **set** n Fernsehapparat m, Fernseher m

telex /'teleks/ n Telex nt ● vt telexen

tell /tel/ *vt/i* (*pt/pp* **told**) sagen (**s.o.** jdm); (*relate*) erzählen; (*know*) wissen; (*distinguish*) erkennen; ~ **the time** die Uhr lesen; **time will** ~ das wird man erst sehen; **his age is beginning to** ~ sein Alter macht sich bemerkbar; **don't** ~ **me** sag es mir nicht; **you mustn't** ~ du darfst nichts sagen. ~ **off** *vt* ausschimpfen

teller /'telə(r)/ *n* (*cashier*) Kassierer(in) *m(f)*

telly /'telı/ *n* (*fam*) = **television**

temerity /tı'merətı/ *n* Kühnheit *f*

temp /temp/ *n* (*fam*) Aushilfssekretärin *f*

temper /'tempə(r)/ *n* (*disposition*) Naturell *nt*; (*mood*) Laune *f*; (*anger*) Wut *f*; **lose one's** ~ wütend werden ● *vt* (*fig*) mäßigen

temperament /'temprəmənt/ *n* Temperament *nt*. ~**al** /-'mentl/ *a* temperamentvoll; (*moody*) launisch

temperance /'tempərəns/ *n* Mäßigung *f*; (*abstinence*) Abstinenz *f*

temperate /'tempərət/ *a* gemäßigt

temperature /'temprətʃə(r)/ *n* Temperatur *f*; **have** *or* **run a** ~ Fieber haben

tempest /'tempıst/ *n* Sturm *m*. ~**uous** /-'pestjʊəs/ *a* stürmisch

template /'templıt/ *n* Schablone *f*

temple[1] /'templ/ *n* Tempel *m*

temple[2] *n* (*Anat*) Schläfe *f*

tempo /'tempəʊ/ *n* Tempo *nt*

temporary /'tempərərı/ *a*, **-ily** *adv* vorübergehend; (*measure, building*) provisorisch

tempt /tempt/ *vt* verleiten; (*Relig*) versuchen; herausfordern (*fate*); (*entice*) [ver]locken; **be** ~**ed** versucht sein (**to** zu); **I am** ~**ed by it** es lockt mich. ~**ation** /-'teıʃn/ *n* Versuchung *f*. ~**ing** *a* verlockend

ten /ten/ *a* zehn

tenable /'tenəbl/ *a* (*fig*) haltbar

tenaci|ous /tı'neıʃəs/ *a*, **-ly** *adv* hartnäckig. ~**ty** /-'næsıtı/ *n* Hartnäckigkeit *f*

tenant /'tenənt/ *n* Mieter(in) *m(f)*; (*Comm*) Pächter(in) *m(f)*

tend[1] /tend/ *vt* (*look after*) sich kümmern um

tend[2] *vi* ~ **to do sth** dazu neigen, etw zu tun

tendency /'tendənsı/ *n* Tendenz *f*; (*inclination*) Neigung *f*

tender[1] /'tendə(r)/ *n* (*Comm*) Angebot *nt*; **legal** ~ gesetzliches Zahlungsmittel *nt* ● *vt* anbieten; einreichen (*resignation*)

tender[2] *a* zart; (*loving*) zärtlich; (*painful*) empfindlich. ~**ly** *adv* zärtlich. ~**ness** *n* Zartheit *f*; Zärtlichkeit *f*

tendon /'tendən/ *n* Sehne *f*

tenement /'tenəmənt/ *n* Mietshaus *nt*

tenet /'tenıt/ *n* Grundsatz *m*

tenner /'tenə(r)/ *n* (*fam*) Zehnpfundschein *m*

tennis /'tenıs/ *n* Tennis *nt*. ~**-court** *n* Tennisplatz *m*

tenor /'tenə(r)/ *n* Tenor *m*

tense[1] /tens/ *n* (*Gram*) Zeit *f*

tense[2] *a* (**-r, -st**) gespannt ● *vt* anspannen (*muscle*)

tension /'tenʃn/ *n* Spannung *f*

tent /tent/ *n* Zelt *nt*

tentacle /'tentəkl/ *n* Fangarm *m*

tentative /'tentətıv/ *a*, **-ly** *adv* vorläufig; (*hesitant*) zaghaft

tenterhooks /'tentəhʊks/ *npl* **be on** ~ wie auf glühenden Kohlen sitzen

tenth /tenθ/ *a* zehnte(r,s) ● *n* Zehntel *nt*

tenuous /'tenjʊəs/ *a* (*fig*) schwach

tepid /'tepıd/ *a* lauwarm

term /tɜːm/ *n* Zeitraum *m*; (*Sch*) ≈ Halbjahr *nt*; (*Univ*) *l* Semester *nt*; (*expression*) Ausdruck *m*; ~**s** *pl* (*conditions*) Bedingungen *pl*; ~ **of office** Amtszeit *f*; **in the short/long** ~ kurz-/langfristig; **be on good/bad** ~**s** gut/nicht gut miteinander auskommen; **come to** ~**s with** sich abfinden mit

terminal /'tɜːmınl/ *a* End-; (*Med*) unheilbar ● *n* (*Aviat*) Terminal *m*; (*of bus*) Endstation *f*; (*on battery*) Pol *m*; (*Computing*) Terminal *nt*

terminat|e /'tɜːmıneıt/ *vt* beenden; lösen (*contract*); unterbrechen (*pregnancy*) ● *vi* enden. ~**ion** /-'neıʃn/ *n* Beendigung *f*; (*Med*) Schwangerschaftsabbruch *m*

terminology /tɜːmı'nɒlədʒı/ *n* Terminologie *f*

terminus /'tɜːmınəs/ *n* (*pl* **-ni** /-naı/) Endstation *f*

terrace /'terəs/ *n* Terrasse *f*; (*houses*) Häuserreihe *f*; **the** ~**s** (*Sport*) die [Steh]ränge *pl*. ~**d house** *n* Reihenhaus *nt*

terrain /te'reın/ *n* Gelände *nt*

terrible /'terəbl/ *a*, **-bly** *adv* schrecklich

terrier /'terıə(r)/ *n* Terrier *m*

terrific /tə'rɪfɪk/ a (fam) (excellent) sagenhaft; (huge) riesig

terri|fy /'terɪfaɪ/ vt (pt/pp -ied) angst machen (+ dat); be ~fied Angst haben. ~fying a furchterregend

territorial /terɪ'tɔːrɪəl/ a Territorial-

territory /'terɪtərɪ/ n Gebiet nt

terror /'terə(r)/ n [panische] Angst f; (Pol) Terror m. ~ism /-ɪzm/ n Terrorismus m. ~ist /-ɪst/ n Terrorist m. ~ize vt terrorisieren

terse /tɜːs/ a, -ly adv kurz, knapp

test /test/ n Test m; (Sch) Klassenarbeit f; put to the ~ auf die Probe stellen ● vt prüfen; (examine) untersuchen (for auf + acc)

testament /'testəmənt/ n Testament nt; Old/New T~ Altes/Neues Testament nt

testicle /'testɪkl/ n Hoden m

testify /'testɪfaɪ/ v (pt/pp -ied) ● vt beweisen; ~ that bezeugen, daß ● vi aussagen; ~ to bezeugen

testimonial /testɪ'məʊnɪəl/ n Zeugnis nt

testimony /'testɪmənɪ/ n Aussage f

'test-tube n Reagenzglas nt. ~ 'baby n (fam) Retortenbaby nt

testy /'testɪ/ a gereizt

tetanus /'tetənəs/ n Tetanus m

tetchy /'tetʃɪ/ a gereizt

tether /'teðə(r)/ n be at the end of one's ~ am Ende seiner Kraft sein ● vt anbinden

text /tekst/ n Text m. ~book n Lehrbuch nt

textile /'tekstaɪl/ a Textil- ● n ~s pl Textilien pl

texture /'tekstʃə(r)/ n Beschaffenheit f; (Tex) Struktur f

Thai /taɪ/ a thailändisch. ~land n Thailand nt

Thames /temz/ n Themse f

than /ðən, betont ðæn/ conj als; older ~ me älter als ich

thank /θæŋk/ vt danken (+ dat); ~ you [very much] danke [schön]. ~ful a, -ly adv dankbar. ~less a undankbar

thanks /θæŋks/ npl Dank m; ~! (fam) danke! ~ to dank (+ dat or gen)

that /ðæt/ a & pron (pl those) der/die/das; (pl) die; ~ one der/die/das da; I'll take ~ ich nehme den/die/das; I don't like those die mag ich nicht; ~ is das heißt; is ~ you? bist du es? who is ~? wer ist da? with/after ~ damit/danach; like ~ so; a man like ~ so ein Mann; ~ is why deshalb; ~'s it! genau! all ~ I know alles was ich weiß; the day ~ I saw him an dem Tag, als ich ihn sah ● adv so; ~ good/hot so gut/heiß ● conj daß

thatch /θætʃ/ n Strohdach nt. ~ed a strohgedeckt

thaw /θɔː/ n Tauwetter nt ● vt/i auftauen; it's ~ing es taut

the /ðə, vor einem Vokal ðiː/ def art der/die/das; (pl) die; play ~ piano/violin Klavier/Geige spielen ● adv ~ more ~ better je mehr, desto besser; all ~ better um so besser

theatre /'θɪətə(r)/ n Theater nt; (Med) Operationssaal m

theatrical /θɪ'ætrɪkl/ a Theater-; (showy) theatralisch

theft /θeft/ n Diebstahl m

their /ðeə(r)/ a ihr

theirs /ðeəz/ poss pron ihre(r), ihrs; a friend of ~ ein Freund von ihnen; those are ~ die gehören ihnen

them /ðem/ pron (acc) sie; (dat) ihnen; I know ~ ich kenne sie; give ~ the money gib ihnen das Geld

theme /θiːm/ n Thema nt

them'selves pron selbst; (refl) sich; by ~ allein

then /ðen/ adv dann; (at that time in past) damals; by ~ bis dahin; since ~ seitdem; before ~ vorher; from ~ on von da an; now and ~ dann und wann; there and ~ auf der Stelle ● a damalig

theolog|ian /θɪə'ləʊdʒɪən/ n Theologe m. ~y /-'ɒlədʒɪ/ n Theologie f

theorem /'θɪərəm/ n Lehrsatz m

theoretical /θɪə'retɪkl/ a, -ly adv theoretisch

theory /'θɪərɪ/ n Theorie f; in ~ theoretisch

therapeutic /θerə'pjuːtɪk/ a therapeutisch

therap|ist /'θerəpɪst/ n Therapeut(in) m(f). ~y n Therapie f

there /ðeə(r)/ adv da; (with movement) dahin, dorthin; down/up ~ da unten/oben; ~ is/are da ist/sind; (in existence) es gibt; ~ he/she is da ist er/sie; send/take ~ hinschicken/-bringen ● int there, there! nun, nun!

there: ~abouts adv da [in der Nähe]; or ~abouts (roughly) ungefähr. ~'after adv danach. ~by adv dadurch. ~fore /-fɔː(r)/ adv deshalb, also

thermal /'θɜːml/ a Thermal-; ~ 'underwear n Thermowäsche f

thermometer /θəˈmɒmɪtə(r)/ n Thermometer nt

Thermos (P) /ˈθɜːməs/ n ~ **[flask]** Thermosflasche (P) f

thermostat /ˈθɜːməstæt/ n Thermostat m

these /ðiːz/ see this

thesis /ˈθiːsɪs/ n (pl -ses /-siːz/) Dissertation f; (proposition) These f

they /ðeɪ/ pron sie; ~ **say** (generalizing) man sagt

thick /θɪk/ a (-er, -est), -ly adv dick; (dense) dicht; (liquid) dickflüssig; (fam: stupid) dumm ● adv dick ● n **in the** ~ **of** mitten in (+ dat). ~**en** vt dicker machen; eindicken (sauce) ● vi dicker werden; (fog:) dichter werden; (plot:) kompliziert werden. ~**ness** n Dicke f; Dichte f; Dickflüssigkeit f

thick: ~**set** a untersetzt. ~**-skinned** a (fam) dickfellig

thief /θiːf/ n (pl thieves) Dieb(in) m(f)

thieving /ˈθiːvɪŋ/ a diebisch ● n Stehlen nt

thigh /θaɪ/ n Oberschenkel m

thimble /ˈθɪmbl/ n Fingerhut m

thin /θɪn/ a (thinner, thinnest), -ly adv dünn ● adv dünn ● vi (pt/pp thinned) ● vt verdünnen (liquid) ● vi sich lichten. ~ **out** vt ausdünnen

thing /θɪŋ/ n Ding nt; (subject, affair) Sache f; ~s pl (belongings) Sachen pl; **for one** ~ erstens; **the right** ~ das Richtige; **just the** ~! genau das Richtige! **how are** ~s? wie geht's? **the latest** ~ (fam) der letzte Schrei; **the best** ~ **would be** am besten wäre es

think /θɪŋk/ vt/i (pt/pp thought) denken (about/of an + acc); (believe) meinen; (consider) nachdenken; (regard as) halten für; **I** ~ **so** ich glaube schon; **what do you** ~? was meinen Sie? **what do you** ~ **of it?** was halten Sie davon? ~ **better of it** es sich (dat) anders überlegen. ~ **over** vt sich (dat) überlegen. ~ **up** vt sich (dat) ausdenken

third /θɜːd/ a dritte(r,s) ● n Drittel nt. ~**ly** adv drittens. ~**-rate** a drittrangig

thirst /θɜːst/ n Durst m. ~**y** a, -ily adv durstig; **be** ~**y** Durst haben

thirteen /θɜːˈtiːn/ a dreizehn. ~**th** a dreizehnte(r,s)

thirtieth /ˈθɜːtɪɪθ/ a dreißigste(r,s)

thirty /ˈθɜːtɪ/ a dreißig

this /ðɪs/ a (pl these) diese(r,s); (pl) diese; ~ **one** diese(r,s) da; **I'll take** ~ ich nehme diesen/diese/dieses; ~ **evening/morning** heute abend/morgen; **these days** heutzutage ● pron (pl these) das, dies[es]; (pl) die, diese; ~ **and that** dies und das; ~ **or that** dieses oder das; **like** ~ so; ~ **is Peter** das ist Peter; (Teleph) hier [spricht] Peter; **who is** ~? wer ist das? (Teleph, Amer) wer ist am Apparat?

thistle /ˈθɪsl/ n Distel f

thorn /θɔːn/ n Dorn m. ~**y** a dornig

thorough /ˈθʌrə/ a gründlich

thorough: ~**bred** n reinrassiges Tier nt; (horse) Rassepferd nt. ~**fare** n Durchfahrtsstraße f; **'no** ~**fare'** 'keine Durchfahrt'

thorough|ly /ˈθʌrəlɪ/ adv gründlich; (completely) völlig; (extremely) äußerst. ~**ness** n Gründlichkeit f

those /ðəʊz/ see that

though /ðəʊ/ conj obgleich, obwohl; **as** ~ als ob ● adv (fam) doch

thought /θɔːt/ see think ● n Gedanke m; (thinking) Denken nt. ~**ful** a, -ly adv nachdenklich; (considerate) rücksichtsvoll. ~**less** a, -ly adv gedankenlos

thousand /ˈθaʊznd/ a **one/a** ~ [ein]tausend ● n Tausend nt; ~**s of** Tausende von. ~**th** a tausendste(r,s) ● n Tausendstel nt

thrash /θræʃ/ vt verprügeln; (defeat) [vernichtend] schlagen. ~ **about** vi sich herumwerfen; (fish:) zappeln. ~ **out** vt ausdiskutieren

thread /θred/ n Faden m; (of screw) Gewinde nt ● vt einfädeln; auffädeln (beads); ~ **one's way through** sich schlängeln durch. ~**bare** a fadenscheinig

threat /θret/ n Drohung f; (danger) Bedrohung f

threaten /ˈθretn/ vt drohen (+ dat); (with weapon) bedrohen; ~ **to do sth** drohen, etw zu tun; ~ **s.o. with sth** jdm etw androhen ● vi drohen. ~**ing** a, -ly adv drohend; (ominous) bedrohlich

three /θriː/ a drei. ~**fold** a & adv dreifach. ~**some** /-səm/ n Trio nt

thresh /θreʃ/ vt dreschen

threshold /ˈθreʃəʊld/ n Schwelle f

threw /θruː/ see throw

thrift /θrɪft/ n Sparsamkeit f. ~**y** a sparsam

thrill /θrɪl/ n Erregung f; (fam) Nervenkitzel m ● vt (excite) erregen;

be ~ed with sich sehr freuen über
(+acc). ~er n Thriller m. ~ing a
erregend

thrive /θraɪv/ vi (pt **thrived** or
throve, pp **thrived** or **thriven**
/'θrɪvn/) gedeihen (**on** bei); ⟨business:⟩ florieren

throat /θrəʊt/ n Hals m; **sore** ~
Halsschmerzen pl; **cut s.o.'s** ~ jdm die
Kehle durchschneiden

throb /θrɒb/ n Pochen nt ● vi (pt/pp
throbbed) pochen; ⟨vibrate⟩ vibrieren

throes /θrəʊz/ npl **in the** ~ **of** ⟨fig⟩
mitten in (+dat)

thrombosis /θrɒm'bəʊsɪs/ n Thrombose f

throne /θrəʊn/ n Thron m

throng /θrɒŋ/ n Menge f

throttle /'θrɒtl/ vt erdrosseln

through /θru:/ prep durch (+acc);
⟨during⟩ während (+gen); ⟨Amer: up
to & including⟩ bis einschließlich
● adv durch; **all** ~ die ganze Zeit; ~
and ~ durch und durch; **wet** ~ durch
und durch naß; **read sth** ~ etw
durchlesen; **let/walk** ~ durchlassen/
-gehen ● a ⟨train⟩ durchgehend; **be** ~
⟨finished⟩ fertig sein; ⟨Teleph⟩ durch
sein

throughout /θru:'aʊt/ prep ~ **the
country** im ganzen Land; ~ **the night**
die Nacht durch ● adv ganz; ⟨time⟩ die
ganze Zeit

throve /θrəʊv/ see **thrive**

throw /θrəʊ/ n Wurf m ● vt (pt
threw, pp **thrown**) werfen; schütten
⟨liquid⟩; betätigen ⟨switch⟩; abwerfen
⟨rider⟩; ⟨fam: disconcert⟩ aus der Fassung bringen; ⟨fam⟩ geben ⟨party⟩; ~
sth to s.o. jdm etw zuwerfen; ~ **sth at
s.o.** nach jdm werfen; ⟨pelt with⟩ jdn
mit etw bewerfen. ~ **away** vt wegwerfen. ~ **out** vt hinauswerfen; ⟨~
away⟩ wegwerfen; verwerfen ⟨plan⟩.
~ **up** vt hochwerfen ● vi ⟨fam⟩ sich
übergeben

'**throw-away** a Wegwerf-

thrush /θrʌʃ/ n Drossel f

thrust /θrʌst/ n Stoß m; ⟨Phys⟩ Schub
m ● vt (pt/pp **thrust**) stoßen; ⟨insert⟩
stecken; ~ **[up]on** aufbürden (**s.o.** jdm)

thud /θʌd/ n dumpfer Schlag m

thug /θʌg/ n Schläger m

thumb /θʌm/ n Daumen m; **rule of** ~
Faustregel f; **under s.o.'s** ~ unter jds
Fuchtel ● vt ~ **a lift** ⟨fam⟩ per Anhalter
fahren. ~-**index** n Daumenregister
nt. ~**tack** n ⟨Amer⟩ Reißzwecke f

thump /θʌmp/ n Schlag m; ⟨noise⟩
dumpfer Schlag m ● vt schlagen ● vi
hämmern (**on** an/auf +acc); ⟨heart:⟩
pochen

thunder /'θʌndə(r)/ n Donner m ● vi
donnern. ~**clap** n Donnerschlag m.
~**storm** n Gewitter nt. ~**y** a gewittrig

Thursday /'θɜ:zdeɪ/ n Donnerstag m

thus /ðʌs/ adv so

thwart /θwɔ:t/ vt vereiteln; ~ **s.o.**
jdm einen Strich durch die Rechnung
machen

thyme /taɪm/ n Thymian m

thyroid /'θaɪrɔɪd/ n Schilddrüse f

tiara /tɪ'ɑ:rə/ n Diadem nt

tick[1] /tɪk/ n **on** ~ ⟨fam⟩ auf Pump

tick[2] n ⟨sound⟩ Ticken nt; ⟨mark⟩ Häkchen nt; ⟨fam: instant⟩ Sekunde f ● vi
ticken ● vt abhaken. ~ **off** vt abhaken; ⟨fam⟩ rüffeln. ~ **over** vi ⟨engine:⟩ im Leerlauf laufen

ticket /'tɪkɪt/ n Karte f; ⟨for bus,
train⟩ Fahrschein m; ⟨Aviat⟩ Flugschein m; ⟨for lottery⟩ Los nt; ⟨for
article deposited⟩ Schein m; ⟨label⟩
Schild nt; ⟨for library⟩ Lesekarte f;
⟨fine⟩ Strafzettel m. ~-**collector** n
Fahrkartenkontrolleur m. ~-**office**
n Fahrkartenschalter m; ⟨for entry⟩
Kasse f

tick|**le** /'tɪkl/ n Kitzeln nt ● vt/i kitzeln. ~**lish** /'tɪklɪʃ/ a kitzlig

tidal /'taɪdl/ a ⟨river, harbour⟩ Tide-.
~ **wave** n Flutwelle f

tiddly-winks /'tɪdlɪwɪŋks/ n Flohspiel nt

tide /taɪd/ n Gezeiten pl; ⟨of events⟩
Strom m; **the** ~ **is in/out** es ist Flut/
Ebbe ● vt ~ **s.o. over** jdm über die
Runden helfen

tidiness /'taɪdɪnɪs/ n Ordentlichkeit
f

tidy /'taɪdɪ/ a (-ier, -iest), -ily adv ordentlich ● vt ~ [**up**] aufräumen; ~
oneself up sich zurechtmachen

tie /taɪ/ n Krawatte f, Schlips m;
⟨cord⟩ Schnur f; ⟨fig: bond⟩ Band nt;
⟨restriction⟩ Bindung f; ⟨Sport⟩ Unentschieden nt; ⟨in competition⟩
Punktgleichheit f ● v (pres p **tying**)
● vt binden; machen ⟨knot⟩ ● vi ⟨Sport⟩
unentschieden spielen; ⟨have equal
scores, votes⟩ punktgleich sein; ~ **in
with** passen zu. ~ **up** vt festbinden;
verschnüren ⟨parcel⟩; fesseln ⟨person⟩; **be** ~**d up** ⟨busy⟩ beschäftigt sein

tier /tɪə(r)/ n Stufe f; (of cake) Etage f; (in stadium) Rang m

tiff /tɪf/ n Streit m, (fam) Krach m

tiger /'taɪgə(r)/ n Tiger m

tight /taɪt/ a (-er, -est), -ly adv fest; (taut) straff; (clothes) eng; (control) streng; (fam: drunk) blau; **in a ~ corner** (fam) in der Klemme ● adv fest

tighten /'taɪtn/ vt festerziehen; straffen (rope); anziehen (screw); verschärfen (control) ● vi sich spannen

tight: ~**·'fisted** a knauserig. ~**rope** n Hochseil nt

tights /taɪts/ npl Strumpfhose f

tile /taɪl/ n Fliese f; (on wall) Kachel f; (on roof) [Dach]ziegel m ● vt mit Fliesen auslegen; kacheln (wall); decken (roof)

till[1] /tɪl/ prep & conj = **until**

till[2] n Kasse f

tiller /'tɪlə(r)/ n Ruderpinne f

tilt /tɪlt/ n Neigung f; **at full ~** mit voller Wucht ● vt kippen; [zur Seite] neigen (head) ● vi sich neigen

timber /'tɪmbə(r)/ n [Nutz]holz nt

time /taɪm/ n Zeit f; (occasion) Mal nt; (rhythm) Takt m; ~**s** (Math) mal; **at any ~** jederzeit; **this ~** dieses Mal, diesmal; **at ~s** manchmal; **~ and again** immer wieder; **two at a ~** zwei auf einmal; **on ~** pünktlich; **in ~** rechtzeitig; (eventually) mit der Zeit; **in no ~** im Handumdrehen; **in a year's ~** in einem Jahr; **behind ~** verspätet; **behind the ~s** rückständig; **for the ~ being** vorläufig; **what is the ~?** wie spät ist es? wieviel Uhr ist es? **by the ~ we arrive** bis wir ankommen; **did you have a nice ~?** hat es dir gut gefallen? **have a good ~!** viel Vergnügen! ● vt stoppen (race); **be well ~d** gut abgepaßt sein

time: ~ **bomb** n Zeitbombe f. ~**·lag** n Zeitdifferenz f. ~**less** a zeitlos. ~**ly** a rechtzeitig. ~**·switch** n Zeitschalter m. ~**table** n Fahrplan m; (Sch) Stundenplan m

timid /'tɪmɪd/ a, -ly adv scheu; (hesitant) zaghaft

timing /'taɪmɪŋ/ n Wahl f des richtigen Zeitpunkts; (Sport, Techn) Timing nt

tin /tɪn/ n Zinn nt; (container) Dose f ● vt (pt/pp tinned) in Dosen od Büchsen konservieren. ~ **foil** n Stanniol nt; (Culin) Alufolie f

tinge /tɪndʒ/ n Hauch m ● vt ~**d with** mit einer Spur von

tingle /'tɪŋgl/ vi kribbeln

tinker /'tɪŋkə(r)/ vi herumbasteln (**with** an + dat)

tinkle /'tɪŋkl/ n Klingeln nt ● vi klingeln

tinned /tɪnd/ a Dosen-, Büchsen-

'tin opener n Dosen-/Büchsenöffner m

'tinpot a (pej) (firm) schäbig

tinsel /'tɪnsl/ n Lametta nt

tint /tɪnt/ n Farbton m ● vt tönen

tiny /'taɪnɪ/ a (-ier, -iest) winzig

tip[1] /tɪp/ n Spitze f

tip[2] n (money) Trinkgeld nt; (advice) Rat m, (fam) Tip m; (for rubbish) Müllhalde f ● v (pt/pp **tipped**) ● vt (tilt) kippen; (reward) Trinkgeld geben (**s.o.** jdm) ● vi kippen. ~ **off** vt ~ **s.o. off** jdm einen Hinweis geben. ~ **out** vt auskippen. ~ **over** vt/i umkippen

'tip-off n Hinweis m

tipped /tɪpt/ a Filter-

tipsy /'tɪpsɪ/ a (fam) beschwipst

tiptoe /'tɪptəʊ/ n **on ~** auf Zehenspitzen

tiptop /tɪp'tɒp/ a (fam) erstklassig

tire /'taɪə(r)/ vt/i ermüden. ~**d** a müde; **be ~d of** sth etw satt haben; ~**d out** [völlig] erschöpft. ~**less** a, -ly adv unermüdlich. ~**some** /-səm/ a lästig

tiring /'taɪrɪŋ/ a ermüdend

tissue /'tɪʃuː/ n Gewebe nt; (handkerchief) Papiertaschentuch nt. ~**·paper** n Seidenpapier nt

tit[1] /tɪt/ n (bird) Meise f

tit[2] n ~ **for tat** wie du mir, so ich dir

'titbit n Leckerbissen m

titillate /'tɪtɪleɪt/ vt erregen

title /'taɪtl/ n Titel m. ~**·role** n Titelrolle f

tittle-tattle /'tɪtltætl/ n Klatsch m

titular /'tɪtjʊlə(r)/ a nominell

to /tuː/, unbetont /tə/ prep zu (+ dat); (with place, direction) nach; (to cinema, theatre) in (+ acc); (to wedding, party) auf (+ acc); (address, send, fasten) an (+ acc); (per) pro; (up to, until) bis; **to the station** zum Bahnhof; **to Germany/Switzerland** nach Deutschland/in die Schweiz; **to the toilet/one's room** auf die Toilette/sein Zimmer; **to the office/an exhibition** ins Büro/in eine Ausstellung; **to university** auf die Universität; **twenty/quarter to eight** zwanzig/Viertel vor acht; **5 to 6 pounds** 5 bis 6 Pfund; **to the end** bis zum Schluß; **to this day** bis heute; **to the best of my knowledge**

nach meinem besten Wissen; **give/say sth to s.o.** jdm etw geben/sagen; **go/ come to s.o.** zu jdm gehen/kommen; **I've never been to Berlin** ich war noch nie in Berlin; **there's nothing to it** es ist nichts dabei ● *verbal constructions* **to go** gehen; **to stay** bleiben; **learn to swim** schwimmen lernen; **want to/ have to go** gehen wollen/müssen; **be easy/difficult to forget** leicht/schwer zu vergessen sein; **too ill/tired to go** zu krank/müde, um zu gehen; **he did it to annoy me** er tat es, um mich zu ärgern; **you have to** du mußt; **I don't want to** ich will nicht; **I'd love to** gern; **I forgot to** ich habe es vergessen; **he wants to be a teacher** er will Lehrer werden; **live to be 90** 90 werden; **he was the last to arrive** er kam als letzter; **to be honest** ehrlich gesagt ● *adv* **pull to** anlehnen; **to and fro** hin und her

toad /təud/ n Kröte f. **~stool** n Giftpilz m

toast /təust/ n Toast m ● vt toasten ⟨bread⟩; (drink a ~ to) trinken auf (+ acc). **~er** n Toaster m

tobacco /tə'bækəu/ n Tabak m. **~nist's [shop]** n Tabakladen m

toboggan /tə'bɒgən/ n Schlitten m ● vi Schlitten fahren

today /tə'deɪ/ n & adv heute; **~ week** heute in einer Woche; **~'s paper** die heutige Zeitung

toddler /'tɒdlə(r)/ n Kleinkind nt

to-do /tə'du:/ n (fam) Getue nt, Theater nt

toe /təu/ n Zeh m; (of footwear) Spitze f ● vt **~ the line** spuren. **~nail** n Zehennagel m

toffee /'tɒfɪ/ n Karamelbonbon m & nt

together /tə'geðə(r)/ adv zusammen; (at the same time) gleichzeitig

toil /tɔɪl/ n [harte] Arbeit f ● vi schwer arbeiten

toilet /'tɔɪlɪt/ n Toilette f. **~ bag** n Kulturbeutel m. **~ paper** n Toilettenpapier nt

toiletries /'tɔɪlɪtrɪz/ npl Toilettenartikel pl

toilet: ~ roll n Rolle f Toilettenpapier. **~ water** n Toilettenwasser nt

token /'təukən/ n Zeichen nt; (counter) Marke f; (voucher) Gutschein m ● attrib symbolisch

told /təuld/ see tell ● a all ~ insgesamt

tolerable /'tɒlərəbl/ a, **-bly** adv erträglich; (not bad) leidlich

toleran|ce /'tɒlərəns/ n Toleranz f. **~t** a, **-ly** adv tolerant

tolerate /'tɒləreɪt/ vt dulden, tolerieren; (bear) ertragen

toll¹ /təul/ n Gebühr f; (for road) Maut f (Aust); **death ~** Zahl f der Todesopfer; **take a heavy ~** einen hohen Tribut fordern

toll² vi läuten

tom /tɒm/ n (cat) Kater m

tomato /tə'mɑ:təʊ/ n (pl -es) Tomate f. **~ purée** n Tomatenmark nt

tomb /tu:m/ n Grabmal nt

tomboy n Wildfang m

tombstone n Grabstein m

tom-cat n Kater m

tome /təum/ n dicker Band m

tomfoolery /tɒm'fu:lərɪ/ n Blödsinn m

tomorrow /tə'mɒrəʊ/ n & adv morgen; **~ morning** morgen früh; **the day after ~** übermorgen; **see you ~!** bis morgen!

ton /tʌn/ n Tonne f; **~s of** (fam) jede Menge

tone /təun/ n Ton m; (colour) Farbton m ● vt **~ down** dämpfen; (fig) mäßigen. **~ up** vt kräftigen; straffen ⟨muscles⟩

tongs /tɒŋz/ npl Zange f

tongue /tʌŋ/ n Zunge f; **~ in cheek** (fam) nicht ernst. **~-twister** n Zungenbrecher m

tonic /'tɒnɪk/ n Tonikum nt; (for hair) Haarwasser nt; (fig) Wohltat f; **~ [water]** Tonic nt

tonight /tə'naɪt/ n & adv heute nacht; (evening) heute abend

tonne /tʌn/ n Tonne f

tonsil /'tɒnsl/ n (Anat) Mandel f. **~litis** /-sə'laɪtɪs/ n Mandelentzündung f

too /tu:/ adv zu; (also) auch; **~ much/ little** zuviel/zuwenig

took /tʊk/ see take

tool /tu:l/ n Werkzeug nt; (for gardening) Gerät nt

toot /tu:t/ n Hupsignal nt ● vi tuten; (Auto) hupen

tooth /tu:θ/ n (pl teeth) Zahn m

tooth: ~ache n Zahnschmerzen pl. **~brush** n Zahnbürste f. **~less** a zahnlos. **~paste** n Zahnpasta f. **~pick** n Zahnstocher m

top¹ /tɒp/ n (toy) Kreisel m

top[2] *n* oberer Teil *m*; (*apex*) Spitze *f*; (*summit*) Gipfel *m*; (*Sch*) Erste(r) *m/f*; (*top part or half*) Oberteil *nt*; (*head*) Kopfende *nt*; (*of road*) oberes Ende *nt*; (*upper surface*) Oberfläche *f*; (*lid*) Deckel *m*; (*of bottle*) Verschluß *m*; (*garment*) Top *nt*; **at the/on** ~ oben; **on** ~ **of** oben auf (+ *dat/acc*); **on** ~ **of that** (*besides*) obendrein; **from** ~ **to bottom** von oben bis unten ● *a* oberste(r,s); (*highest*) höchste(r,s); (*best*) beste(r,s) ● *vt* (*pt/pp* **topped**) an erster Stelle stehen auf (+ *dat*) ⟨*list*⟩; (*exceed*) übersteigen; (*remove the* ~ *of*) die Spitze abschneiden von. ~ **up** *vt* nachfüllen, auffüllen

top: ~ **'hat** *n* Zylinder[hut] *m*. ~**-heavy** *a* kopflastig

topic /'tɒpɪk/ *n* Thema *nt*. ~**al** *a* aktuell

top: ~**less** *a* & *adv* oben ohne. ~**most** *a* oberste(r,s)

topple /'tɒpl/ *vt/i* umstürzen. ~ **off** *vi* stürzen

top-'secret *a* streng geheim

topsy-turvy /tɒpsɪ'tɜːvɪ/ *adv* völlig durcheinander

torch /tɔːtʃ/ *n* Taschenlampe *f*; (*flaming*) Fackel *f*

tore /tɔː(r)/ *see* **tear**[1]

torment[1] /'tɔːment/ *n* Qual *f*

torment[2] /tɔː'ment/ *vt* quälen

torn /tɔːn/ *see* **tear**[1] ● *a* zerrissen

tornado /tɔː'neɪdəʊ/ *n* (*pl* -es) Wirbelsturm *m*

torpedo /tɔː'piːdəʊ/ *n* (*pl* -es) Torpedo *m* ● *vt* torpedieren

torrent /'tɒrənt/ *n* reißender Strom *m*. ~**ial** /tə'renʃl/ *a* ⟨*rain*⟩ wolkenbruchartig

torso /'tɔːsəʊ/ *n* Rumpf *m*; (*Art*) Torso *m*

tortoise /'tɔːtəs/ *n* Schildkröte *f*. ~**shell** *n* Schildpatt *nt*

tortuous /'tɔːtjʊəs/ *a* verschlungen; (*fig*) umständlich

torture /'tɔːtʃə(r)/ *n* Folter *f*; (*fig*) Qual *f* ● *vt* foltern; (*fig*) quälen

toss /tɒs/ *vt* werfen; (*into the air*) hochwerfen; (*shake*) schütteln; (*unseat*) abwerfen; mischen ⟨*salad*⟩; wenden ⟨*pancake*⟩; ~ **a coin** mit einer Münze losen ● *vi* ~ **and turn** (*in bed*) sich [schlaflos] im Bett wälzen. ~ **up** *vi* [mit einer Münze] losen

tot[1] /tɒt/ *n* kleines Kind *nt*; (*fam: of liquor*) Gläschen *nt*

tot[2] *vt* (*pt/pp* **totted**) ~ **up** (*fam*) zusammenzählen

total /'təʊtl/ *a* gesamt; (*complete*) völlig, total ● *n* Gesamtzahl *f*; (*sum*) Gesamtsumme *f* ● *vt* (*pt/pp* **totalled**) zusammenzählen; (*amount to*) sich belaufen auf (+ *acc*)

totalitarian /təʊtælɪ'teərɪən/ *a* totalitär

totally /'təʊtəlɪ/ *adv* völlig, total

totter /'tɒtə(r)/ *vi* taumeln; (*rock*) schwanken. ~**y** *a* wackelig

touch /tʌtʃ/ *n* Berührung *f*; (*sense*) Tastsinn *m*; (*Mus*) Anschlag *m*; (*contact*) Kontakt *m*; (*trace*) Spur *f*; (*fig*) Anflug *m*; **get/be in** ~ sich in Verbindung setzen/in Verbindung stehen (**with** mit) ● *vt* berühren; (*get hold of*) anfassen; (*lightly*) tippen auf/an (+ *acc*); (*brush against*) streifen [gegen]; (*reach*) erreichen; (*equal*) herankommen an (+ *acc*); (*fig: move*) rühren; anrühren ⟨*food, subject*⟩; **don't** ~ **that!** faß das nicht an! ● *vi* sich berühren; ~ **on** (*fig*) berühren. ~ **down** *vi* (*Aviat*) landen. ~ **up** *vt* ausbessern

touch|ing /'tʌtʃɪŋ/ *a* rührend. ~**y** *a* empfindlich; ⟨*subject*⟩ heikel

tough /tʌf/ *a* (-er, -est) zäh; (*severe, harsh*) hart; (*difficult*) schwierig; (*durable*) strapazierfähig

toughen /'tʌfn/ *vt* härten; ~ **up** abhärten

tour /tʊə(r)/ *n* Reise *f*, Tour *f*; (*of building, town*) Besichtigung *f*; (*Theat, Sport*) Tournee *f*; (*of duty*) Dienstzeit *f* ● *vt* fahren durch; besichtigen ⟨*building*⟩ ● *vi* herumreisen

touris|m /'tʊərɪzm/ *n* Tourismus *m*, Fremdenverkehr *m*. ~**t** /-rɪst/ *n* Tourist(in) *m(f)* ● *attrib* Touristen-. ~**t office** *n* Fremdenverkehrsbüro *nt*

tournament /'tʊənəmənt/ *n* Turnier *nt*

'tour operator *n* Reiseveranstalter *m*

tousle /'taʊzl/ *vt* zerzausen

tout /taʊt/ *n* Anreißer *m*; (*ticket* ~) Kartenschwarzhändler *m* ● *vi* ~ **for customers** Kunden werben

tow /təʊ/ *n* **give s.o./a car a** ~ jdn/ein Auto abschleppen; **'on** ~ 'wird geschleppt'; **in** ~ (*fam*) im Schlepptau ● *vt* schleppen; ziehen ⟨*trailer*⟩. ~ **away** *vt* abschleppen

toward[s] /tə'wɔːd(z)/ *prep* zu (+*dat*); *(with time)* gegen (+*acc*); *(with respect to)* gegenüber (+*dat*)

towel /'tauəl/ *n* Handtuch *nt*. **~ling** *n* (*Tex*) Frottee *nt*

tower /'tauə(r)/ *n* Turm *m* ● *vi* ~ **above** überragen. **~ block** *n* Hochhaus *nt*. **~ing** *a* hochragend

town /taun/ *n* Stadt *f*. ~ **'hall** *n* Rathaus *nt*

tow: **~-path** *n* Treidelpfad *m*. **~-rope** *n* Abschleppseil *nt*

toxic /'tɒksɪk/ *a* giftig. ~ **'waste** *n* Giftmüll *m*

toxin /'tɒksɪn/ *n* Gift *nt*

toy /tɔɪ/ *n* Spielzeug *nt* ● *vi* ~ **with** spielen mit; stochern in (+*dat*) *(food)*. **~shop** *n* Spielwarengeschäft *nt*

trac|e /treɪs/ *n* Spur *f* ● *vt* folgen (+*dat*); *(find)* finden; *(draw)* zeichnen; *(with tracing-paper)* durchpausen. **~ing-paper** *n* Pauspapier *nt*

track /træk/ *n* Spur *f*; *(path)* [unbefestigter] Weg *m*; *(Sport)* Bahn *f*; *(Rail)* Gleis *nt*; **keep ~ of** im Auge behalten ● *vt* verfolgen. ~ **down** *vt* aufspüren; *(find)* finden

'tracksuit *n* Trainingsanzug *m*

tract[1] /trækt/ *n* (*land*) Gebiet *nt*

tract[2] *n* (*pamphlet*) [Flug]schrift *f*

tractor /'træktə(r)/ *n* Traktor *m*

trade /treɪd/ *n* Handel *m*; *(line of business)* Gewerbe *nt*; *(business)* Geschäft *nt*; *(craft)* Handwerk *nt*; **by ~** von Beruf ● *vt* tauschen; ~ **in** *(give in part exchange)* in Zahlung geben ● *vi* handeln (**in** mit)

'trade mark *n* Warenzeichen *nt*

trader /'treɪdə(r)/ *n* Händler *m*

trade: ~ **'union** *n* Gewerkschaft *f*. ~ **'unionist** *n* Gewerkschaftler(in) *m(f)*

trading /'treɪdɪŋ/ *n* Handel *m*. ~ **estate** *n* Gewerbegebiet *nt*. ~ **stamp** *n* Rabattmarke *f*

tradition /trə'dɪʃn/ *n* Tradition *f*. **~al** *a*, **-ly** *adv* traditionell

traffic /'træfɪk/ *n* Verkehr *m*; *(trading)* Handel *m* ● *vi* handeln (**in** mit)

traffic: ~ **circle** *n* (*Amer*) Kreisverkehr *m*. ~ **jam** *n* [Verkehrs]stau *m*. ~ **lights** *npl* [Verkehrs]ampel *f*. ~ **warden** *n* ≈ Hilfspolizist *m*; *(woman)* Politesse *f*

tragedy /'trædʒədɪ/ *n* Tragödie *f*

tragic /'trædʒɪk/ *a*, **-ally** *adv* tragisch

trail /treɪl/ *n* Spur *f*; *(path)* Weg *m*, Pfad *m* ● *vi* schleifen; *(plant:)* sich ranken; ~ **[behind]** zurückbleiben; *(Sport)* zurückliegen ● *vt* verfolgen, folgen (+*dat*); *(drag)* schleifen

trailer /'treɪlə(r)/ *n* (*Auto*) Anhänger *m*; *(Amer: caravan)* Wohnwagen *m*; *(film)* Vorschau *f*

train /treɪn/ *n* Zug *m*; *(of dress)* Schleppe *f*; ~ **of thought** Gedankengang *m* ● *vt* ausbilden; *(Sport)* trainieren; *(aim)* richten auf (+*acc*); erziehen *(child)*; abrichten *(to do tricks)* dressieren *(animal)*; ziehen *(plant)* ● *vi* eine Ausbildung machen; *(Sport)* trainieren. **~ed** *a* ausgebildet

trainee /treɪ'niː/ *n* Auszubildende(r) *m/f*; *(Techn)* Praktikant(in) *m(f)*

train|er /'treɪnə(r)/ *n* (*Sport*) Trainer *m*; *(in circus)* Dompteur *m*; **~ers** *pl* Trainingsschuhe *pl*. **~ing** *n* Ausbildung *f*; *(Sport)* Training *nt*; *(of animals)* Dressur *f*

traipse /treɪps/ *vi* (*fam*) latschen

trait /treɪt/ *n* Eigenschaft *f*

traitor /'treɪtə(r)/ *n* Verräter *m*

tram /træm/ *n* Straßenbahn *f*. **~-lines** *npl* Straßenbahnschienen *pl*

tramp /træmp/ *n* Landstreicher *m*; *(hike)* Wanderung *f* ● *vi* stapfen; *(walk)* marschieren

trample /'træmpl/ *vt/i* trampeln (**on** auf +*acc*)

trampoline /'træmpəliːn/ *n* Trampolin *nt*

trance /trɑːns/ *n* Trance *f*

tranquil /'træŋkwɪl/ *a* ruhig. **~lity** /-'kwɪlətɪ/ *n* Ruhe *f*

tranquillizer /'træŋkwɪlaɪzə(r)/ *n* Beruhigungsmittel *nt*

transact /træn'zækt/ *vt* abschließen. **~ion** /-ækʃn/ *n* Transaktion *f*

transcend /træn'send/ *vt* übersteigen

transcript /'trænskrɪpt/ *n* Abschrift *f*; *(of official proceedings)* Protokoll *nt*. **~ion** /-'skrɪpʃn/ *n* Abschrift *f*

transept /'trænsept/ *n* Querschiff *nt*

transfer[1] /'trænsfə(r)/ *n* (*see* **transfer**[2]) Übertragung *f*; Verlegung *f*; Versetzung *f*; Überweisung *f*; *(Sport)* Transfer *m*; *(design)* Abziehbild *nt*

transfer[2] /træns'fɜː(r)/ *v* (*pt/pp* **transferred**) ● *vt* übertragen; verlegen *(firm, prisoners)*; versetzen *(employee)*; überweisen *(money)*; *(Sport)* transferieren ● *vi* [über]wechseln; *(when* *travelling*) umsteigen. **~able** /-əbl/ *a* übertragbar

transform /træns'fɔ:m/ *vt* verwandeln. **~ation** /-fə'meɪʃn/ *n* Verwandlung *f*. **~er** *n* Transformator *m*

transfusion /træns'fju:ʒn/ *n* Transfusion*f*

transient /'trænzɪənt/ *a* kurzlebig; ⟨*life*⟩ kurz

transistor /træn'zɪstə(r)/ *n* Transistor *m*

transit /'trænsɪt/ *n* Transit *m*; (*of goods*) Transport *m*; **in ~** ⟨*goods*⟩ auf dem Transport

transition /træn'sɪʒn/ *n* Übergang *m*. **~al** *a* Übergangs-

transitive /'trænsɪtɪv/ *a*, **-ly** *adv* transitiv

transitory /'trænsɪtərɪ/ *a* vergänglich; ⟨*life*⟩ kurz

translat|e /træns'leɪt/ *vt* übersetzen. **~ion** /-'leɪʃn/ *n* Übersetzung *f*. **~or** *n* Übersetzer(in) *m(f)*

translucent /trænz'lu:snt/ *a* durchscheinend

transmission /trænz'mɪʃn/ *n* Übertragung*f*

transmit /trænz'mɪt/ *vt* (*pt/pp* transmitted) übertragen. **~ter** *n* Sender *m*

transparen|cy /træns'pærənsɪ/ *n* (*Phot*) Dia *nt*. **~t** *a* durchsichtig

transpire /træn'spaɪə(r)/ *vi* sich herausstellen; (*fam: happen*) passieren

transplant¹ /'trænsplɑ:nt/ *n* Verpflanzung*f*, Transplantation*f*

transplant² /træns'plɑ:nt/ *vt* umpflanzen; (*Med*) verpflanzen

transport¹ /'trænspɔ:t/ *n* Transport *m*

transport² /træn'spɔ:t/ *vt* transportieren. **~ation** /-'teɪʃn/ *n* Transport *m*

transpose /træns'pəʊz/ *vt* umstellen

transvestite /træns'vestaɪt/ *n* Transvestit *m*

trap /træp/ *n* Falle *f*; (*fam: mouth*) Klappe *f*; **pony and ~** Einspänner *m* ● *vt* (*pt/pp* trapped) [mit einer Falle] fangen; (*jam*) einklemmen; **be ~ped** festsitzen; (*shut in*) eingeschlossen sein; (*cut off*) abgeschnitten sein. **~'door** *n* Falltür *f*

trapeze /trə'pi:z/ *n* Trapez *nt*

trash /træʃ/ *n* Schund *m*; (*rubbish*) Abfall *m*; (*nonsense*) Quatsch *m*.

~can *n* (*Amer*) Mülleimer *m*. **~y** *a* Schund-

trauma /'trɔ:mə/ *n* Trauma *nt*. **~tic** /-'mætɪk/ *a* traumatisch

travel /'trævl/ *n* Reisen *nt* ● *v* (*pt/pp* travelled) ● *vi* reisen; (*go in vehicle*) fahren; ⟨*light, sound:*⟩ sich fortpflanzen; (*Techn*) sich bewegen ● *vt* bereisen; fahren ⟨*distance*⟩. **~ agency** *n* Reisebüro *nt*. **~ agent** *n* Reisebürokaufmann *m*

traveller /'trævələ(r)/ *n* Reisende(r) *m/f*; (*Comm*) Vertreter *m*; **~s** *pl* (*gypsies*) Zigeuner *pl*. **~'s cheque** *n* Reisescheck *m*

trawler /'trɔ:lə(r)/ *n* Fischdampfer *m*

tray /treɪ/ *n* Tablett *nt*; (*for baking*) [Back]blech *nt*; (*for documents*) Ablagekorb *m*

treacher|ous /'tretʃərəs/ *a* treulos; (*dangerous, deceptive*) tückisch. **~y** *n* Verrat *m*

treacle /'tri:kl/ *n* Sirup *m*

tread /tred/ *n* Schritt *m*; (*step*) Stufe *f*; (*of tyre*) Profil *nt* ● *v* (*pt* trod, *pp* trodden) ● *vi* (*walk*) gehen; **~ on/in** treten auf/in (+ *acc*) ● *vt* treten

treason /'tri:zn/ *n* Verrat *m*

treasure /'treʒə(r)/ *n* Schatz *m* ● *vt* in Ehren halten. **~r** *n* Kassenwart *m*

treasury /'treʒərɪ/ *n* Schatzkammer *f*; **the T~** das Finanzministerium

treat /tri:t/ *n* [besonderes] Vergnügen *nt*; **give s.o. a ~** jdm etwas Besonderes bieten ● *vt* behandeln; **~ s.o. to sth** jdm etw spendieren

treatise /'tri:tɪz/ *n* Abhandlung *f*

treatment /'tri:tmənt/ *n* Behandlung *f*

treaty /'tri:tɪ/ *n* Vertrag *m*

treble /'trebl/ *a* dreifach; **~ the amount** dreimal soviel ● *n* (*Mus*) Diskant *m*; (*voice*) Sopran *m* ● *vt* verdreifachen ● *vi* sich verdreifachen. **~ clef** *n* Violinschlüssel *m*

tree /tri:/ *n* Baum *m*

trek /trek/ *n* Marsch *m* ● *vi* (*pt/pp* trekked) latschen

trellis /'trelɪs/ *n* Gitter *nt*

tremble /'trembl/ *vi* zittern

tremendous /trɪ'mendəs/ *a*, **-ly** *adv* gewaltig; (*fam: excellent*) großartig

tremor /'tremə(r)/ *n* Zittern *nt*; **[earth] ~** Beben *nt*

trench /trentʃ/ *n* Graben *m*; (*Mil*) Schützengraben *m*

trend /trend/ n Tendenz f; (fashion) Trend m. **~y** a (**-ier, -iest**) (fam) modisch

trepidation /trepr'deɪʃn/ n Beklommenheit f

trespass /'trespəs/ vi **~ on** unerlaubt betreten. **~er** n Unbefugte(r) m/f

trial /'traɪəl/ n (Jur) [Gerichts]verfahren nt, Prozeß m; (test) Probe f; (ordeal) Prüfung f; **be on ~** auf Probe sein; (Jur) angeklagt sein (**for** wegen); **by ~ and error** durch Probieren

triang|le /'traɪæŋgl/ n Dreieck nt; (Mus) Triangel m. **~ular** /-'æŋgjʊlə(r)/ a dreieckig

tribe /traɪb/ n Stamm m

tribulation /trɪbjʊ'leɪʃn/ n Kummer m

tribunal /traɪ'bju:nl/ n Schiedsgericht nt

tributary /'trɪbjʊtərɪ/ n Nebenfluß m

tribute /'trɪbju:t/ n Tribut m; **pay ~** Tribut zollen (**to** dat)

trice /traɪs/ n **in a ~** im Nu

trick /trɪk/ n Trick m; (joke) Streich m; (Cards) Stich m; (feat of skill) Kunststück nt; **that should do the ~** (fam) damit dürfte es klappen ● vt täuschen, (fam) hereinlegen

trickle /'trɪkl/ vi rinnen

trick|ster /'trɪkstə(r)/ n Schwindler m. **~y** a (**-ier, -iest**) a schwierig

tricycle /'traɪsɪkl/ n Dreirad nt

tried /traɪd/ see **try**

trifl|e /'traɪfl/ n Kleinigkeit f; (Culin) Trifle nt. **~ing** a unbedeutend

trigger /'trɪgə(r)/ n Abzug m; (fig) Auslöser m ● vt **~ [off]** auslösen

trigonometry /trɪgə'nɒmɪtrɪ/ n Trigonometrie f

trim /trɪm/ a (**trimmer, trimmest**) gepflegt ● n (cut) Nachschneiden nt; (decoration) Verzierung f; (condition) Zustand m ● vt schneiden; (decorate) besetzen; (Naut) trimmen. **~ming** n Besatz m; **~mings** pl (accessories) Zubehör nt; (decorations) Verzierungen pl; **with all the ~mings** mit allem Drum und Dran

Trinity /'trɪnətɪ/ n **the [Holy] ~** die [Heilige] Dreieinigkeit f

trinket /'trɪŋkɪt/ n Schmuckgegenstand m

trio /'tri:əʊ/ n Trio nt

trip /trɪp/ n Reise f; (excursion) Ausflug m ● v (pt/pp **tripped**) ● vt **~ s.o.**

up jdm ein Bein stellen ● vi stolpern (**on/over** über + acc)

tripe /traɪp/ n Kaldaunen pl; (nonsense) Quatsch m

triple /'trɪpl/ a dreifach ● vt verdreifachen ● vi sich verdreifachen

triplets /'trɪplɪts/ npl Drillinge pl

triplicate /'trɪplɪkət/ n **in ~** in dreifacher Ausfertigung

tripod /'traɪpɒd/ n Stativ nt

tripper /'trɪpə(r)/ n Ausflügler m

trite /traɪt/ a banal

triumph /'traɪʌmf/ n Triumph m ● vi triumphieren (**over** über + acc). **~ant** /-'ʌmfnt/ a, **-ly** adv triumphierend

trivial /'trɪvɪəl/ a belanglos. **~ity** /-'ælətɪ/ n Belanglosigkeit f

trod, trodden /trɒd, 'trɒdn/ see **tread**

trolley /'trɒlɪ/ n (for serving food) Servierwagen m; (for shopping) Einkaufswagen m; (for luggage) Kofferkuli m; (Amer: tram) Straßenbahn f. **~ bus** n O-Bus m

trombone /trɒm'bəʊn/ n Posaune f

troop /tru:p/ n Schar f; **~s** pl Truppen pl ● vi **~ in/out** hinein-/hinausströmen

trophy /'trəʊfɪ/ n Trophäe f; (in competition) ≈ Pokal m

tropic /'trɒpɪk/ n Wendekreis m; **~s** pl Tropen pl. **~al** a tropisch; (fruit) Süd-

trot /trɒt/ n Trab m ● vi (pt/pp **trotted**) traben

trouble /'trʌbl/ n Ärger m; (difficulties) Schwierigkeiten pl; (inconvenience) Mühe f; (conflict) Unruhe f; (Med) Beschwerden pl; (Techn) Probleme pl; **get into ~** Ärger bekommen; **take ~** sich (dat) Mühe geben ● vt (disturb) stören; (worry) beunruhigen ● vi sich bemühen. **~-maker** n Unruhestifter m. **~some** /-səm/ a schwierig; (flies, cough) lästig

trough /trɒf/ n Trog m

trounce /traʊns/ vt vernichtend schlagen; (thrash) verprügeln

troupe /tru:p/ n Truppe f

trousers /'traʊzəz/ npl Hose f

trousseau /'tru:səʊ/ n Aussteuer f

trout /traʊt/ n inv Forelle f

trowel /'traʊəl/ n Kelle f; (for gardening) Pflanzkelle f

truant /'tru:ənt/ n **play ~** die Schule schwänzen

truce /truːs/ n Waffenstillstand m
truck /trʌk/ n Last[kraft]wagen m; (Rail) Güterwagen m
truculent /'trʌkjʊlənt/ a aufsässig
trudge /trʌdʒ/ n [mühseliger] Marsch m ● vi latschen
true /truː/ a (-r, -st) wahr; (loyal) treu; (genuine) echt; **come ~** in Erfüllung gehen; **is that ~?** stimmt das?
truism /'truːɪzm/ n Binsenwahrheit f
truly /'truːlɪ/ adv wirklich; (faithfully) treu; **Yours ~** Hochachtungsvoll
trump /trʌmp/ n (Cards) Trumpf m ● vt übertrumpfen. **~ up** vt (fam) erfinden
trumpet /'trʌmpɪt/ n Trompete f. **~er** n Trompeter m
truncheon /'trʌntʃn/ n Schlagstock m
trundle /'trʌndl/ vt/i rollen
trunk /trʌŋk/ n [Baum]stamm m; (body) Rumpf m; (of elephant) Rüssel m; (for travelling) [Übersee]koffer m; (for storage) Truhe f; (Amer: of car) Kofferraum m; **~s** pl Badehose f
truss /trʌs/ n (Med) Bruchband nt
trust /trʌst/ n Vertrauen nt; (group of companies) Trust m; (organization) Treuhandgesellschaft f; (charitable) Stiftung f ● vt trauen (+ dat), vertrauen (+ dat); (hope) hoffen ● vi vertrauen (**in/to** auf + acc)
trustee /trʌs'tiː/ n Treuhänder m
'trust|ful /'trʌstfl/ a, **-ly** adv vertrauensvoll. **~ing** a vertrauensvoll. **~worthy** a vertrauenswürdig
truth /truːθ/ n (pl **-s** /truːðz/) Wahrheit f. **~ful** a, **-ly** adv ehrlich
try /traɪ/ n Versuch m ● v (pt/pp **tried**) ● vt versuchen; (sample, taste) probieren; (be a strain on) anstrengen; (Jur) vor Gericht stellen; verhandeln (case) ● vi versuchen; (make an effort) sich bemühen. **~ on** vt anprobieren; aufprobieren (hat). **~ out** vt ausprobieren
trying /'traɪɪŋ/ a schwierig
T-shirt /'tiː-/ n T-Shirt nt
tub /tʌb/ n Kübel m; (carton) Becher m; (bath) Wanne f
tuba /'tjuːbə/ n (Mus) Tuba f
tubby /'tʌbɪ/ a (-ier, -iest) rundlich
tube /tjuːb/ n Röhre f; (pipe) Rohr nt; (flexible) Schlauch m; (of toothpaste) Tube f; (Rail, fam) U-Bahn f
tuber /'tjuːbə(r)/ n Knolle f
tuberculosis /tjuːbɜːkjʊ'ləʊsɪs/ n Tuberkulose f

tubing /'tjuːbɪŋ/ n Schlauch m
tubular /'tjuːbjʊlə(r)/ a röhrenförmig
tuck /tʌk/ n Saum m; (decorative) Biese f ● vt (put) stecken. **~ in** vt hineinstecken; **~ s.o. in** jdn zudecken ● vi (fam: eat) zulangen. **~ up** vt hochkrempeln (sleeves); (in bed) zudecken
Tuesday /'tjuːzdeɪ/ n Dienstag m
tuft /tʌft/ n Büschel nt
tug /tʌg/ n Ruck m; (Naut) Schleppdampfer m ● v (pt/pp **tugged**) ● vt ziehen ● vi zerren (**at** an + dat). **~ of war** n Tauziehen nt
tuition /tjuː'ɪʃn/ n Unterricht m
tulip /'tjuːlɪp/ n Tulpe f
tumble /'tʌmbl/ n Sturz m ● vi fallen; **~ to sth** (fam) etw kapieren. **~down** a verfallen. **~-drier** n Wäschetrockner m
tumbler /'tʌmblə(r)/ n Glas nt
tummy /'tʌmɪ/ n (fam) Magen m; (abdomen) Bauch m
tumour /'tjuːmə(r)/ n Geschwulst f, Tumor m
tumult /'tjuːmʌlt/ n Tumult m. **~uous** /-'mʌltjʊəs/ a stürmisch
tuna /'tjuːnə/ n Thunfisch m
tune /tjuːn/ n Melodie f; **out of ~** (instrument) verstimmt; **to the ~ of** (fam) in Höhe von ● vt stimmen; (Techn) einstellen. **~ in** vt einstellen ● vi **~ in to a station** einen Sender einstellen. **~ up** vi (Mus) stimmen
tuneful /'tjuːnfl/ a melodisch
tunic /'tjuːnɪk/ n (Mil) Uniformjacke f; (Sch) Trägerkleid nt
Tunisia /tjuː'nɪzɪə/ n Tunesien nt
tunnel /'tʌnl/ n Tunnel m ● vi (pt/pp **tunnelled**) einen Tunnel graben
turban /'tɜːbən/ n Turban m
turbine /'tɜːbaɪn/ n Turbine f
turbot /'tɜːbət/ n Steinbutt m
turbulen|ce /'tɜːbjʊləns/ n Turbulenz f. **~t** a stürmisch
tureen /tjʊə'riːn/ n Terrine f
turf /tɜːf/ n Rasen m; (segment) Rasenstück nt. **~ out** vt (fam) rausschmeißen
'turf accountant n Buchmacher m
Turk /tɜːk/ n Türke m/Türkin f
turkey /'tɜːkɪ/ n Pute f, Truthahn m
Turk|ey n die Türkei. **~ish** a türkisch
turmoil /'tɜːmɔɪl/ n Aufruhr m; (confusion) Durcheinander nt

turn /tɜːn/ n (rotation) Drehung f; (in road) Kurve f; (change of direction) Wende f; (short walk) Runde f; (Theat) Nummer f; (fam: attack) Anfall m; **do s.o. a good ~** jdm einen guten Dienst erweisen; **take ~s** sich abwechseln; **in ~** der Reihe nach; **out of ~** außer der Reihe; **it's your ~** du bist an der Reihe ● vt drehen; (~ over) wenden; (reverse) umdrehen; (Techn) drechseln (wood); **~ the page** umblättern; **~ the corner** um die Ecke biegen ● vi sich drehen; (~ round) sich umdrehen; (car:) wenden; (leaves:) sich färben; (weather:) umschlagen; (become) werden; **~ right/left** nach rechts/links abbiegen; **~ to s.o.** sich an jdn wenden; **have ~ed against s.o.** gegen jdn sein. **~ away** vt abweisen ● vi sich abwenden. **~ down** vt herunterschlagen (collar); herunterdrehen (heat, gas); leiser stellen (sound); (reject) ablehnen; abweisen (person). **~ in** vt einschlagen (edges) ● vi (car:) einbiegen; (fam: go to bed) ins Bett gehen. **~ off** vt zudrehen (tap); ausschalten (light, radio); abstellen (water, gas, engine, machine) ● vi abbiegen. **~ on** vt aufdrehen (tap); einschalten (light, radio); anstellen (water, gas, engine, machine). **~ out** vt (expel) vertreiben; (fam) hinauswerfen; ausschalten (light); abdrehen (gas); (produce) produzieren; (empty) ausleeren; [gründlich] aufräumen (room, cupboard) ● vi (go out) hinausgehen; (transpire) sich herausstellen; **~ out well/badly** gut/schlecht gehen. **~ over** vt umdrehen ● vi sich umdrehen. **~ up** vt hochschlagen (collar); aufdrehen (heat, gas); lauter stellen (sound, radio) ● vi auftauchen

turning /'tɜːnɪŋ/ n Abzweigung f. **~-point** n Wendepunkt m

turnip /'tɜːnɪp/ n weiße Rübe f

turn: **~-out** n (of people) Teilnahme f, Beteiligung f; (of goods) Produktion f. **~over** n (Comm) Umsatz m; (of staff) Personalwechsel m. **~pike** n (Amer) gebührenpflichtige Autobahn f. **~stile** n Drehkreuz nt. **~table** n Drehscheibe f; (on record-player) Plattenteller m. **~-up** n [Hosen]aufschlag m

turpentine /'tɜːpəntaɪn/ n Terpentin nt

turquoise /'tɜːkwɔɪz/ a türkis[farben] ● n (gem) Türkis m

turret /'tʌrɪt/ n Türmchen nt

turtle /'tɜːtl/ n Seeschildkröte f

tusk /tʌsk/ n Stoßzahn m

tussle /'tʌsl/ n Balgerei f; (fig) Streit m ● vi sich balgen

tutor /'tjuːtə(r)/ n [Privat]lehrer m

tuxedo /tʌk'siːdəʊ/ n (Amer) Smoking m

TV abbr of **television**

twaddle /'twɒdl/ n Geschwätz nt

twang /twæŋ/ n (in voice) Näseln nt ● vt zupfen

tweed /twiːd/ n Tweed m

tweezers /'twiːzəz/ npl Pinzette f

twelfth /twelfθ/ a zwölfte(r,s)

twelve /twelv/ a zwölf

twentieth /'twentɪθ/ a zwanzigste(r,s)

twenty /'twentɪ/ a zwanzig

twerp /twɜːp/ n (fam) Trottel m

twice /twaɪs/ adv zweimal

twiddle /'twɪdl/ vt drehen an (+ dat)

twig[1] /twɪg/ n Zweig m

twig[2] vt/i (pt/pp **twigged**) (fam) kapieren

twilight /'twaɪ-/ n Dämmerlicht nt

twin /twɪn/ n Zwilling m ● attrib Zwillings-. **~ beds** npl zwei Einzelbetten pl

twine /twaɪn/ n Bindfaden m ● vi sich winden; (plant:) sich ranken

twinge /twɪndʒ/ n Stechen nt; **~ of conscience** Gewissensbisse pl

twinkle /'twɪŋkl/ n Funkeln nt ● vi funkeln

twin 'town n Partnerstadt f

twirl /twɜːl/ vt/i herumwirbeln

twist /twɪst/ n Drehung f; (curve) Kurve f; (unexpected occurrence) überraschende Wendung f ● vt drehen; (distort) verdrehen; (fam: swindle) beschummeln; **~ one's ankle** sich (dat) den Knöchel verrenken ● vi sich drehen; (road:) sich winden. **~er** n (fam) Schwindler m

twit /twɪt/ n (fam) Trottel m

twitch /twɪtʃ/ n Zucken nt ● vi zucken

twitter /'twɪtə(r)/ n Zwitschern nt ● vi zwitschern

two /tuː/ a zwei

two: **~-faced** a falsch. **~-piece** a zweiteilig. **~some** /-səm/ n Paar nt. **~-way** a **~-way traffic** Gegenverkehr m

tycoon /taɪ'kuːn/ n Magnat m

tying /'taɪɪŋ/ *see* **tie**
type /taɪp/ *n* Art *f*, Sorte *f*; (*person*)
Typ *m*; (*printing*) Type *f* • *vt* mit der
Maschine schreiben, (*fam*) tippen
• *vi* maschinenschreiben, (*fam*)
tippen. ~**writer** *n* Schreibmaschine
f. ~**written** *a* maschinegeschrieben
typhoid /'taɪfɔɪd/ *n* Typhus *m*
typical /'tɪpɪkl/ *a*, **-ly** *adv* typisch (**of**
für)
typify /'tɪpɪfaɪ/ *vt* (*pt/pp* **-ied**) typisch
sein für
typing /'taɪpɪŋ/ *n* Maschine-
schreiben *nt*. ~ **paper** *n* Schreib-
maschinenpapier *nt*
typist /'taɪpɪst/ *n* Schreibkraft *f*
typography /taɪ'pɒɡrəfɪ/ *n* Typographie *f*
tyrannical /tɪ'rænɪkl/ *a* tyrannisch
tyranny /'tɪrənɪ/ *n* Tyrannei *f*
tyrant /'taɪrənt/ *n* Tyrann *m*
tyre /'taɪə(r)/ *n* Reifen *m*

U

ubiquitous /juː'bɪkwɪtəs/ *a* all-
gegenwärtig; **be** ~ überall zu finden
sein
udder /'ʌdə(r)/ *n* Euter *nt*
ugl|iness /'ʌɡlɪnɪs/ *n* Häßlichkeit *f*.
~**y** *a* (**-ier**, **-iest**) häßlich; (*nasty*) übel
UK *abbr see* **United Kingdom**
ulcer /'ʌlsə(r)/ *n* Geschwür *nt*
ulterior /ʌl'tɪərɪə(r)/ *a* ~ **motive**
Hintergedanke *m*
ultimate /'ʌltɪmət/ *a* letzte(r,s);
(*final*) endgültig; (*fundamental*)
grundlegend, eigentlich. ~**ly** *adv*
schließlich
ultimatum /ʌltɪ'meɪtəm/ *n* Ultimatum *nt*
ultrasound /'ʌltrə-/ *n* (*Med*) Ultraschall *m*
ultra'violet *a* ultraviolett
umbilical /ʌm'bɪlɪkl/ *a* ~ **cord**
Nabelschnur *f*
umbrella /ʌm'brelə/ *n* [Regen]-
schirm *m*
umpire /'ʌmpaɪə(r)/ *n* Schiedsrichter *m* • *vt/i* Schiedsrichter sein
(bei)
umpteen /ʌmp'tiːn/ *a* (*fam*) zig.
~**th** *a* (*fam*) zigste(r,s); **for the** ~**th**
time zum zigsten Mal
un'able /ʌn-/ *a* **be** ~ **to do sth** etw
nicht tun können
una'bridged *a* ungekürzt

unac'companied *a* ohne Be-
gleitung; (*luggage*) unbegleitet
unac'countabl|e *a* unerklärlich.
~**y** *adv* unerklärlicherweise
unac'customed *a* ungewohnt; **be** ~
to sth etw nicht gewohnt sein
una'dulterated *a* unverfälscht,
rein; (*utter*) völlig
un'aided *a* ohne fremde Hilfe
unalloyed /ʌnə'lɔɪd/ *a* (*fig*) ungetrübt
unanimity /juːnə'nɪmətɪ/ *n* Ein-
stimmigkeit *f*
unanimous /juː'nænɪməs/ *a*, **-ly** *adv*
einmütig; (*vote, decision*) einstimmig
un'armed *a* unbewaffnet; ~ **combat**
Kampf *m* ohne Waffen
unas'suming *a* bescheiden
unat'tached *a* nicht befestigt; (*person*) ungebunden
unat'tended *a* unbeaufsichtigt
un'authorized *a* unbefugt
una'voidable *a* unvermeidlich
una'ware *a* **be** ~ **of sth** sich (*dat*) etw
(*gen*) nicht bewußt sein. ~**s** /-eəz/ *adv*
catch s.o. ~**s** jdn überraschen
un'balanced *a* unausgewogen;
(*mentally*) unausgeglichen
un'bearable *a*, **-bly** *adv* unerträglich
unbeat|able /ʌn'biːtəbl/ *a* un-
schlagbar. ~**en** *a* ungeschlagen; (*record*) ungebrochen
unbeknown /ʌnbɪ'nəʊn/ *a* (*fam*) ~
to me ohne mein Wissen
unbe'lievable *a* unglaublich
un'bend *vi* (*pt/pp* **-bent**) (*relax*) aus
sich herausgehen
un'biased *a* unvoreingenommen
un'block *vt* frei machen
un'bolt *vt* aufriegeln
un'breakable *a* unzerbrechlich
unbridled /ʌn'braɪdld/ *a* ungezügelt
un'burden *vt* ~ **oneself** (*fig*) sich
aussprechen
un'button *vt* aufknöpfen
uncalled-for /ʌn'kɔːldfɔː(r)/ *a* unangebracht
un'canny *a* unheimlich
un'ceasing *a* unaufhörlich
uncere'monious *a*, **-ly** *adv* formlos;
(*abrupt*) brüsk
un'certain *a* (*doubtful*) ungewiß;
(*origins*) unbestimmt; **be** ~ nicht
sicher sein; **in no** ~ **terms** ganz eindeutig. ~**ty** *n* Ungewißheit *f*
un'changed *a* unverändert
un'charitable *a* lieblos
uncle /'ʌŋkl/ *n* Onkel *m*

un'comfortable *a*, **-bly** *adv* unbequem; **feel ~** (*fig*) sich nicht wohl fühlen

un'common *a* ungewöhnlich

un'compromising *a* kompromißlos

uncon'ditional *a*, **-ly** *adv* bedingungslos

un'conscious *a* bewußtlos; (*unintended*) unbewußt; **be ~ of sth** sich (*dat*) etw (*gen*) nicht bewußt sein. **~ly** *adv* unbewußt

uncon'ventional *a* unkonventionell

unco'operative *a* nicht hilfsbereit

un'cork *vt* entkorken

uncouth /ʌn'ku:θ/ *a* ungehobelt

un'cover *vt* aufdecken

unctuous /'ʌŋktjʊəs/ *a*, **-ly** *adv* salbungsvoll

unde'cided *a* unentschlossen; (*not settled*) nicht entschieden

undeniable /ʌndɪ'naɪəbl/ *a*, **-bly** *adv* unbestreitbar

under /'ʌndə(r)/ *prep* unter (*+ dat/acc*); **~ it** darunter; **~ there** da drunter; **~ repair** in Reparatur; **~ construction** im Bau; **~ age** minderjährig; **~ way** unterwegs; (*fig*) im Gange ● *adv* darunter

'undercarriage *n* (*Aviat*) Fahrwerk *nt*, Fahrgestell *nt*

'underclothes *npl* Unterwäsche *f*

under'cover *a* geheim

'undercurrent *n* Unterströmung *f*; (*fig*) Unterton *m*

under'cut *vt* (*pt/pp* **-cut**) (*Comm*) unterbieten

'underdog *n* Unterlegene(r) *m*

under'done *a* nicht gar; (*rare*) nicht durchgebraten

under'estimate *vt* unterschätzen

under'fed *a* unterernährt

under'foot *adv* am Boden; **trample ~** zertrampeln

under'go *vt* (*pt* **-went**, *pp* **-gone**) durchmachen; sich unterziehen (*+ dat*) (*operation, treatment*); **~ repairs** repariert werden

under'graduate *n* Student(in) *m(f)*

under'ground¹ *adv* unter der Erde; (*mining*) unter Tage

'underground² *a* unterirdisch; (*secret*) Untergrund- ● *n* (*railway*) U-Bahn *f*. **~ car park** *n* Tiefgarage *f*

'undergrowth *n* Unterholz *nt*

'underhand *a* hinterhältig

'underlay *n* Unterlage *f*

under'lie *vt* (*pt* **-lay**, *pp* **-lain**, *pres p* **-lying**) (*fig*) zugrundeliegen (*+ dat*)

under'line *vt* unterstreichen

underling /'ʌndəlɪŋ/ *n* (*pej*) Untergebene(r) *m/f*

under'lying *a* (*fig*) eigentlich

under'mine *vt* (*fig*) unterminieren, untergraben

underneath /ʌndə'ni:θ/ *prep* unter (*+ dat/acc*); **~ it** darunter ● *adv* darunter

'underpants *npl* Unterhose *f*

'underpass *n* Unterführung *f*

under'privileged *a* unterprivilegiert

under'rate *vt* unterschätzen

'underseal *n* (*Auto*) Unterbodenschutz *m*

'undershirt *n* (*Amer*) Unterhemd *nt*

under'staffed /-'sta:ft/ *a* unterbesetzt

under'stand *vt/i* (*pt/pp* **-stood**) verstehen; **I ~ that ...** (*have heard*) ich habe gehört, daß ... **~able** /-əbl/ *a* verständlich. **~ably** /-əblɪ/ *adv* verständlicherweise

under'standing *a* verständnisvoll ● *n* Verständnis *nt*; (*agreement*) Vereinbarung *f*; **reach an ~** sich verständigen; **on the ~ that** unter der Voraussetzung, daß

'understatement *n* Untertreibung *f*

'understudy *n* (*Theat*) Ersatzspieler(in) *m(f)*

under'take *vt* (*pt* **-took**, *pp* **-taken**) unternehmen; **~ to do sth** sich verpflichten, etw zu tun

'undertaker *n* Leichenbestatter *m*; **[firm of] ~s** Bestattungsinstitut *nt*

under'taking *n* Unternehmen *nt*; (*promise*) Versprechen *nt*

'undertone *n* (*fig*) Unterton *m*; **in an ~** mit gedämpfter Stimme

under'value *vt* unterbewerten

'underwater¹ *a* Unterwasser-

under'water² *adv* unter Wasser

'underwear *n* Unterwäsche *f*

'underweight *a* untergewichtig; **be ~** Untergewicht haben

'underworld *n* Unterwelt *f*

'underwriter *n* Versicherer *m*

unde'sirable *a* unerwünscht

undies /'ʌndɪz/ *npl* (*fam*) [Damen]unterwäsche *f*

un'dignified *a* würdelos

un'do vt (pt **-did**, pp **-done**) aufmachen; (fig) ungeschehen machen; (ruin) zunichte machen

un'done a offen; (not accomplished) unerledigt

un'doubted a unzweifelhaft. **~ly** adv zweifellos

un'dress vt ausziehen; **get ~ed** sich ausziehen ● vi sich ausziehen

un'due a übermäßig

undulating /'ʌndjʊleɪtɪŋ/ a Wellen-; ⟨country⟩ wellig

un'duly adv übermäßig

un'dying a ewig

un'earth vt ausgraben; (fig) zutage bringen. **~ly** a unheimlich; **at an ~ly hour** (fam) in aller Herrgottsfrühe

un'eas|e n Unbehagen nt. **~y** a unbehaglich; **I feel ~y** mir ist unbehaglich zumute

un'eatable a ungenießbar

uneco'nomic a, **-ally** adv unwirtschaftlich

uneco'nomical a verschwenderisch

unem'ployed a arbeitslos ● npl **the ~** die Arbeitslosen

unem'ployment n Arbeitslosigkeit f. **~ benefit** n Arbeitslosenunterstützung f

un'ending a endlos

un'equal a unterschiedlich; ⟨struggle⟩ ungleich; **be ~ to a task** einer Aufgabe nicht gewachsen sein. **~ly** adv ungleichmäßig

unequivocal /ʌnɪ'kwɪvəkl/ a, **-ly** adv eindeutig

unerring /ʌn'ɜːrɪŋ/ a unfehlbar

un'ethical a unmoralisch; **be ~** gegen das Berufsethos verstoßen

un'even a uneben; (unequal) ungleich; (not regular) ungleichmäßig; ⟨number⟩ ungerade. **~ly** adv ungleichmäßig

unex'pected a, **-ly** adv unerwartet

un'failing a nie versagend

un'fair a, **-ly** adv ungerecht, unfair. **~ness** n Ungerechtigkeit f

un'faithful a untreu

unfa'miliar a ungewohnt; (unknown) unbekannt

un'fasten vt aufmachen; (detach) losmachen

un'favourable a ungünstig

un'feeling a gefühllos

un'finished a unvollendet; ⟨business⟩ unerledigt

un'fit a ungeeignet; (incompetent) unfähig; (Sport) nicht fit; **~ for work** arbeitsunfähig

unflinching /ʌn'flɪntʃɪŋ/ a unerschrocken

un'fold vt auseinanderfalten, entfalten; (spread out) ausbreiten ● vi sich entfalten

unfore'seen a unvorhergesehen

unforgettable /ʌnfə'getəbl/ a unvergeßlich

unforgivable /ʌnfə'gɪvəbl/ a unverzeihlich

un'fortunate a unglücklich; (unfavourable) ungünstig; (regrettable) bedauerlich; **be ~** ⟨person:⟩ Pech haben. **~ly** adv leider

un'founded a unbegründet

unfurl /ʌn'fɜːl/ vt entrollen ● vi sich entrollen

un'furnished a unmöbliert

ungainly /ʌn'geɪnlɪ/ a unbeholfen

ungodly /ʌn'gɒdlɪ/ a gottlos; **at an ~ hour** (fam) in aller Herrgottsfrühe

un'grateful a, **-ly** adv undankbar

un'happi|ly adv unglücklich; (unfortunately) leider. **~ness** n Kummer m

un'happy a unglücklich; (not content) unzufrieden

un'harmed a unverletzt

un'healthy a ungesund

un'hook vt vom Haken nehmen; aufhaken ⟨dress⟩

un'hurt a unverletzt

unhy'gienic a unhygienisch

unicorn /'juːnɪkɔːn/ n Einhorn nt

unification /juːnɪfɪ'keɪʃn/ n Einigung f

uniform /'juːnɪfɔːm/ a, **-ly** adv einheitlich ● n Uniform f

unify /'juːnɪfaɪ/ vt (pt/pp **-ied**) einigen

uni'lateral /juːnɪ-/ a, **-ly** adv einseitig

uni'maginable a unvorstellbar

unim'portant a unwichtig

unin'habited a unbewohnt

unin'tentional a, **-ly** adv unabsichtlich

union /'juːnɪən/ n Vereinigung f; (Pol) Union f; (trade ~) Gewerkschaft f. **~ist** n (Pol) Unionist m

unique /juː'niːk/ a einzigartig. **~ly** adv einmalig

unison /'juːnɪsn/ n **in ~** einstimmig

unit /'juːnɪt/ n Einheit f; (Math) Einer m; (of furniture) Teil nt, Element nt

unite /juːˈnaɪt/ vt vereinigen ● vi sich vereinigen

united /juːˈnaɪtɪd/ a einig. **U~ 'Kingdom** n Vereinigtes Königreich nt. **U~ 'Nations** n Vereinte Nationen pl. **U~ States [of America]** n Vereinigte Staaten pl [von Amerika]

unity /ˈjuːnətɪ/ n Einheit f; (harmony) Einigkeit f

universal /juːnɪˈvɜːsl/ a, **-ly** adv allgemein

universe /ˈjuːnɪvɜːs/ n [Welt]all nt, Universum nt

university /juːnɪˈvɜːsətɪ/ n Universität f ● attrib Universitäts-

unjust a, **-ly** adv ungerecht

unkempt /ʌnˈkempt/ a ungepflegt

unkind a, **-ly** adv unfreundlich; (harsh) häßlich. **~ness** n Unfreundlichkeit f; Häßlichkeit f

unknown a unbekannt

unlawful a, **-ly** adv gesetzwidrig

unleaded /ʌnˈledɪd/ a bleifrei

unleash vt (fig) entfesseln

unless /ənˈles/ conj wenn … nicht; **~ I am mistaken** wenn ich mich nicht irre

unlike a nicht ähnlich, unähnlich; (not the same) ungleich ● prep im Gegensatz zu (+ dat)

unlikely a unwahrscheinlich

unlimited a unbegrenzt

unload vt entladen; ausladen (luggage)

unlock vt aufschließen

unlucky a unglücklich; (day, number) Unglücks-; **be ~** Pech haben; (thing:) Unglück bringen

unmanned a unbemannt

unmarried a unverheiratet. **~ 'mother** n ledige Mutter f

unmask vt (fig) entlarven

unmistakable /ʌnmɪˈsteɪkəbl/ a, **-bly** adv unverkennbar

unmitigated a vollkommen

unnatural a, **-ly** adv unnatürlich; (not normal) nicht normal

unnecessary a, **-ily** adv unnötig

unnoticed a unbemerkt

unobtainable a nicht erhältlich

unobtrusive a, **-ly** adv unaufdringlich; (thing) unauffällig

unofficial a, **-ly** adv inoffiziell

unpack vt/i auspacken

unpaid a unbezahlt

unpalatable a ungenießbar

unparalleled a beispiellos

unpick vt auftrennen

unpleasant a, **-ly** adv unangenehm. **~ness** n (bad feeling) Ärger m

unplug vt (pt/pp **-plugged**) den Stecker herausziehen von

unpopular a unbeliebt

unprecedented a beispiellos

unpredictable a unberechenbar

unpremeditated a nicht vorsätzlich

unprepared a nicht vorbereitet

unprepossessing a wenig attraktiv

unpretentious a bescheiden

unprincipled a skrupellos

unprofessional a **be ~** gegen das Berufsethos verstoßen; (Sport) unsportlich sein

unprofitable a unrentabel

unqualified a unqualifiziert; (fig: absolute) uneingeschränkt

unquestionable a unbezweifelbar; (right) unbestreitbar

unravel /ʌnˈrævl/ vt (pt/pp **-ravelled**) entwirren; (Knitting) aufziehen

unreal a unwirklich

unreasonable a unvernünftig; **be ~** zuviel verlangen

unrelated a unzusammenhängend; **be ~** nicht verwandt sein; (events:) nicht miteinander zusammenhängen

unreliable a unzuverlässig

unrequited /ʌnrɪˈkwaɪtɪd/ a unerwidert

unreservedly /ʌnrɪˈzɜːvɪdlɪ/ adv uneingeschränkt; (frankly) offen

unrest n Unruhen pl

unrivalled a unübertroffen

unroll vt aufrollen ● vi sich aufrollen

unruly /ʌnˈruːlɪ/ a ungebärdig

unsafe a nicht sicher

unsaid a ungesagt

unsalted a ungesalzen

unsatisfactory a unbefriedigend

unsavoury a unangenehm; (fig) unerfreulich

unscathed /ʌnˈskeɪðd/ a unversehrt

unscrew vt abschrauben

unscrupulous a skrupellos

unseemly a unschicklich

unselfish a selbstlos

unsettled a ungeklärt; (weather) unbeständig; (bill) unbezahlt

unshakeable /ʌnˈʃeɪkəbl/ a unerschütterlich

unshaven /ʌnˈʃeɪvn/ a unrasiert

unsightly /ʌnˈsaɪtlɪ/ a unansehnlich

un'skilled *a* ungelernt; ⟨*work*⟩ un-qualifiziert

un'sociable *a* ungesellig

unso'phisticated *a* einfach

un'sound *a* krank, nicht gesund; ⟨*building*⟩ nicht sicher; ⟨*advice*⟩ unzuverlässig; ⟨*reasoning*⟩ nicht stichhaltig; **of ~ mind** unzurechnungsfähig

unspeakable /ʌn'spi:kəbl/ *a* unbeschreiblich

un'stable *a* nicht stabil; ⟨*mentally*⟩ labil

un'steady *a*, **-ily** *adv* unsicher; ⟨*wobbly*⟩ wackelig

un'stuck **a come ~** sich lösen; ⟨*fam: fail*⟩ scheitern

unsuc'cessful *a*, **-ly** *adv* erfolglos; **be ~** keinen Erfolg haben

un'suitable *a* ungeeignet; ⟨*inappropriate*⟩ unpassend; ⟨*for weather, activity*⟩ unzweckmäßig

unsu'specting *a* ahnungslos

un'sweetened *a* ungesüßt

unthinkable /ʌn'θɪŋkəbl/ *a* unvorstellbar

un'tidiness *n* Unordentlichkeit *f*

un'tidy *a*, **-ily** *adv* unordentlich

un'tie *vt* aufbinden; losbinden ⟨*person, boat, horse*⟩

until /ən'tɪl/ *prep* bis (+ *acc*); **not ~** erst; **~ the evening** bis zum Abend; **~ his arrival** bis zu seiner Ankunft ● *conj* bis; **not ~** erst wenn; ⟨*in past*⟩ erst als

untimely /ʌn'taɪmlɪ/ *a* ungelegen; ⟨*premature*⟩ vorzeitig

un'tiring *a* unermüdlich

un'told *a* unermeßlich

unto'ward *a* ungünstig; ⟨*unseemly*⟩ ungehörig; **if nothing ~ happens** wenn nichts dazwischenkommt

un'true *a* unwahr; **that's ~** das ist nicht wahr

unused[1] /ʌn'ju:zd/ *a* unbenutzt; ⟨*not utilized*⟩ ungenutzt

unused[2] /ʌn'ju:st/ *a* **be ~ to sth** etw nicht gewohnt sein

un'usual *a*, **-ly** *adv* ungewöhnlich

un'veil *vt* enthüllen

un'versed *a* nicht bewandert (**in** in + *dat*)

un'wanted *a* unerwünscht

un'warranted *a* ungerechtfertigt

un'welcome *a* unwillkommen

un'well *a* **be** *or* **feel ~** sich nicht wohl fühlen

unwieldy /ʌn'wi:ldɪ/ *a* sperrig

un'willing *a*, **-ly** *adv* widerwillig; **be ~ to do sth** etw nicht tun wollen

un'wind *v* (*pt/pp* **unwound**) ● *vt* abwickeln ● *vi* sich abwickeln; ⟨*fam: relax*⟩ sich entspannen

un'wise *a*, **-ly** *adv* unklug

unwitting /ʌn'wɪtɪŋ/ *a*, **-ly** *adv* unwissentlich

un'worthy *a* unwürdig

un'wrap *vt* (*pt/pp* **-wrapped**) auswickeln; auspacken ⟨*present*⟩

un'written *a* ungeschrieben

up /ʌp/ *adv* oben; ⟨*with movement*⟩ nach oben; ⟨*not in bed*⟩ auf; ⟨*collar*⟩ hochgeklappt; ⟨*road*⟩ aufgerissen; ⟨*price*⟩ gestiegen; ⟨*curtains*⟩ aufgehängt; ⟨*shelves*⟩ angebracht; ⟨*notice*⟩ angeschlagen; ⟨*tent*⟩ aufgebaut; ⟨*building*⟩ gebaut; **be up for sale** zu verkaufen sein; **up there** da oben; **up to** (*as far as*) bis; **time's up** die Zeit ist um; **what's up?** ⟨*fam*⟩ was ist los? **what's he up to?** ⟨*fam*⟩ was hat er vor? **I don't feel up to it** ich fühle mich dem nicht gewachsen; **be one up on s.o.** ⟨*fam*⟩ jdm etwas voraushaben; **go up** hinaufgehen; **come up** heraufkommen ● *prep* **be up on sth** [oben] auf etw (*dat*) sein; **up the mountain** oben am Berg; ⟨*movement*⟩ den Berg hinauf; **be up the tree** oben im Baum sein; **up the road** die Straße entlang; **up the river** stromaufwärts; **go up the stairs** die Treppe hinaufgehen; **be up the pub** ⟨*fam*⟩ in der Kneipe sein

'upbringing *n* Erziehung *f*

up'date *vt* auf den neuesten Stand bringen

up'grade *vt* aufstufen

upheaval /ʌp'hi:vl/ *n* Unruhe *f*; ⟨*Pol*⟩ Umbruch *m*

up'hill *a* ⟨*fig*⟩ mühsam ● *adv* bergauf

up'hold *vt* (*pt/pp* **upheld**) unterstützen; bestätigen ⟨*verdict*⟩

upholster /ʌp'həʊlstə(r)/ *vt* polstern. **~er** *n* Polsterer *m*. **~y** *n* Polsterung *f*

'upkeep *n* Unterhalt *m*

up-'market *a* anspruchsvoll

upon /ə'pɒn/ *prep* auf (+ *dat/acc*)

upper /'ʌpə(r)/ *a* obere(r,s); ⟨*deck, jaw, lip*⟩ Ober-; **have the ~ hand** die Oberhand haben ● *n* (*of shoe*) Obermaterial *nt*

upper: ~ circle *n* zweiter Rang *m*. **~ class** *n* Oberschicht *f*. **~most** *a* oberste(r,s)

'upright *a* aufrecht ● *n* Pfosten *m*

'**uprising** *n* Aufstand *m*

'**uproar** *n* Aufruhr *m*

up'root *vt* entwurzeln

up'set[1] *vt* (*pt/pp* **upset**, *pres p* **upsetting**) umstoßen; (*spill*) verschütten; durcheinanderbringen (*plan*); (*distress*) erschüttern; (*food:*) nicht bekommen (+ *dat*); **get ~ about sth** sich über etw (*acc*) aufregen; **be very ~** sehr bestürzt sein

'**upset**[2] *n* Aufregung *f*; **have a stomach ~** einen verdorbenen Magen haben

'**upshot** *n* Ergebnis *nt*

upside 'down *adv* verkehrt herum; **turn ~** umdrehen

up'stairs[1] *adv* oben; (*go*) nach oben

'**upstairs**[2] *a* im Obergeschoß

'**upstart** *n* Emporkömmling *m*

up'stream *adv* stromaufwärts

'**upsurge** *n* Zunahme *f*

'**uptake** *n* **slow on the ~** schwer von Begriff; **be quick on the ~** schnell begreifen

up'tight *a* nervös

'**upturn** *n* Aufschwung *m*

upward /'ʌpwəd/ *a* nach oben; (*movement*) Aufwärts-; **~ slope** Steigung *f* ● **~[s]** aufwärts, nach oben

uranium /jʊ'reɪnɪəm/ *n* Uran *nt*

urban /'ɜːbən/ *a* städtisch

urbane /ɜː'beɪn/ *a* weltmännisch

urge /ɜːdʒ/ *n* Trieb *m*, Drang *m* ● *vt* drängen; **~ on** antreiben

urgen|cy /'ɜːdʒənsɪ/ *n* Dringlichkeit *f*. **~t** *a*, **-ly** *adv* dringend

urinate /'jʊərɪneɪt/ *vi* urinieren

urine /'jʊərɪn/ *n* Urin *m*, Harn *m*

urn /ɜːn/ *n* Urne *f*; (*for tea*) Teemaschine *f*

us /ʌs/ *pron* uns; **it's us** wir sind es

US[A] *abbr* USA *pl*

usable /'juːzəbl/ *a* brauchbar

usage /'juːzɪdʒ/ *n* Brauch *m*; (*of word*) [Sprach]gebrauch *m*

use[1] /juːs/ *n* (*see* **use**[2]) Benutzung *f*; Verwendung *f*; Gebrauch *m*; **be of ~** nützlich sein; **be of no ~** nichts nützen; **make ~ of** Gebrauch machen von; (*exploit*) ausnutzen; **it is no ~** es hat keinen Zweck; **what's the ~?** wozu?

use[2] /juːz/ *vt* benutzen (*implement, room, lift*); verwenden (*ingredient, method, book, money*); gebrauchen (*words, force, brains*); **~ [up]** aufbrauchen

used[1] /juːzd/ *a* benutzt; (*car*) Gebraucht-

used[2] /juːst/ *pt/pp* **be ~ to sth** an etw (*acc*) gewöhnt sein; **get ~ to** sich gewöhnen an (+ *acc*); **he ~ to say** er hat immer gesagt; **he ~ to live here** er hat früher hier gewohnt

useful /'juːsfl/ *a* nützlich. **~ness** *n* Nützlichkeit *f*

useless /'juːslɪs/ *a* nutzlos; (*not usable*) unbrauchbar; (*pointless*) zwecklos

user /'juːzə(r)/ *n* Benutzer(in) *m(f)*. **~-'friendly** *a* benutzerfreundlich

usher /'ʌʃə(r)/ *n* Platzanweiser *m*; (*in court*) Gerichtsdiener *m* ● *vt* **~ in** hineinführen

usherette /ʌʃə'ret/ *n* Platzanweiserin *f*

USSR *abbr* UdSSR *f*

usual /'juːʒʊəl/ *a* üblich. **~ly** *adv* gewöhnlich

usurp /juː'zɜːp/ *vt* sich (*dat*) widerrechtlich aneignen

utensil /juː'tensl/ *n* Gerät *nt*

uterus /'juːtərəs/ *n* Gebärmutter *f*

utilitarian /juːtɪlɪ'teərɪən/ *a* zweckmäßig

utility /juː'tɪlɪtɪ/ *a* Gebrauchs- ● *n* Nutzen *m*. **~ room** *n* Waschküche *f*

utiliz|ation /juːtɪlaɪ'zeɪʃn/ *n* Nutzung *f*. **~e** /'juː'tɪlaɪz/ *vt* nutzen

utmost /'ʌtməʊst/ *a* äußerste(r,s), größte(r,s) ● *n* **do one's ~** sein möglichstes tun

utter[1] /'ʌtə(r)/ *a*, **-ly** *adv* völlig

utter[2] *vt* von sich geben (*sigh, sound*); sagen (*word*). **~ance** /-əns/ *n* Äußerung *f*

U-turn /'juː-/ *n* (*fig*) Kehrtwendung *f*; **'no ~s'** (*Auto*) 'Wenden verboten'

V

vacan|cy /'veɪkənsɪ/ *n* (*job*) freie Stelle *f*; (*room*) freies Zimmer *nt*; **'no ~cies'** 'belegt'. **~t** *a* frei; (*look*) [gedanken]leer

vacate /və'keɪt/ *vt* räumen

vacation /və'keɪʃn/ *n* (*Univ & Amer*) Ferien *pl*

vaccinat|e /'væksɪneɪt/ *vt* impfen. **~ion** /-'neɪʃn/ *n* Impfung *f*

vaccine /'væksiːn/ *n* Impfstoff *m*

vacuum /'vækjʊəm/ *n* Vakuum *nt*, luftleerer Raum *m* ● *vt* saugen. **~ cleaner** *n* Staubsauger *m*.

~ **flask** n Thermosflasche (P) f.
~**-packed** a vakuumverpackt
vagaries /'veɪɡərɪz/ npl Launen pl
vagina /və'dʒaɪnə/ n (Anat) Scheide f
vagrant /'veɪɡrənt/ n Landstreicher m
vague /veɪɡ/ a (-r, -st), -ly adv vage; ⟨outline⟩ verschwommen
vain /veɪn/ a (-er, -est) eitel; ⟨hope, attempt⟩ vergeblich; **in** ~ vergeblich. ~**ly** adv vergeblich
vale /veɪl/ n (liter) Tal nt
valet /'væleɪ/ n Kammerdiener m
valiant /'væliənt/ a, -ly adv tapfer
valid /'vælɪd/ a gültig; ⟨claim⟩ berechtigt; ⟨argument⟩ stichhaltig; ⟨reason⟩ triftig. ~**ate** vt (confirm) bestätigen. ~**ity** /və'lɪdətɪ/ n Gültigkeit f
valley /'vælɪ/ n Tal nt
valour /'vælə(r)/ n Tapferkeit f
valuable /'væljʊəbl/ a wertvoll. ~s npl Wertsachen pl
valuation /vælju'eɪʃn/ n Schätzung f
value /'vælju:/ n Wert m; (usefulness) Nutzen m ● vt schätzen. ~ '**added tax** n Mehrwertsteuer f
valve /vælv/ n Ventil nt; (Anat) Klappe f; (Electr) Röhre f
vampire /'væmpaɪə(r)/ n Vampir m
van /væn/ n Lieferwagen m
vandal /'vændl/ n Rowdy m. ~**ism** /-ɪzm/ n mutwillige Zerstörung f. ~**ize** vt demolieren
vanilla /və'nɪlə/ n Vanille f
vanish /'vænɪʃ/ vi verschwinden
vanity /'vænətɪ/ n Eitelkeit f. ~ **bag** n Kosmetiktäschchen nt
vantage-point /'vɑ:ntɪdʒ-/ n Aussichtspunkt m
vapour /'veɪpə(r)/ n Dampf m
variable /'veərɪəbl/ a unbeständig; (Math) variabel; (adjustable) regulierbar
variance /'veərɪəns/ n **be at** ~ nicht übereinstimmen
variant /'veərɪənt/ n Variante f
variation /veərɪ'eɪʃn/ n Variation f; (difference) Unterschied m
varicose /'værɪkəʊs/ a ~ **veins** pl Krampfadern pl
varied /'veərɪd/ a vielseitig; ⟨diet⟩ abwechslungsreich
variety /və'raɪətɪ/ n Abwechslung f; (quantity) Vielfalt f; (Comm) Auswahl f; (type) Art f; (Bot) Abart f; (Theat) Varieté nt

various /'veərɪəs/ a verschiedene. ~**ly** adv unterschiedlich
varnish /'vɑ:nɪʃ/ n Lack m ● vt lackieren
vary /'veərɪ/ v (pt/pp -ied) ● vi sich ändern; (be different) verschieden sein ● vt [ver]ändern; (add variety to) abwechslungsreicher gestalten. ~**ing** a wechselnd; (different) unterschiedlich
vase /vɑ:z/ n Vase f
vast /vɑ:st/ a riesig; ⟨expanse⟩ weit. ~**ly** adv gewaltig
vat /væt/ n Bottich m
VAT /vi:eɪ'ti:, væt/ abbr (value added tax) Mehrwertsteuer f, MwSt.
vault[1] /vɔ:lt/ n (roof) Gewölbe nt; (in bank) Tresor m; (tomb) Gruft f
vault[2] n Sprung m ● vt/i ~ [over] springen über
VDU abbr (visual display unit) Bildschirmgerät nt
veal /vi:l/ n Kalbfleisch nt ● attrib Kalbs-
veer /vɪə(r)/ vi sich drehen; (Naut) abdrehen; (Auto) ausscheren
vegetable /'vedʒtəbl/ n Gemüse nt; ~s pl Gemüse nt ● attrib Gemüse-; (oil, fat) Pflanzen-
vegetarian /vedʒɪ'teərɪən/ a vegetarisch ● n Vegetarier(in) m(f)
vegetat|e /'vedʒɪteɪt/ vi dahinvegetieren. ~**ion** /-'teɪʃn/ n Vegetation f
vehemen|ce /'vi:əməns/ n Heftigkeit f. ~**t** a, -ly adv heftig
vehicle /'vi:ɪkl/ n Fahrzeug nt; (fig: medium) Mittel nt
veil /veɪl/ n Schleier m ● vt verschleiern
vein /veɪn/ n Ader f; (mood) Stimmung f; (manner) Art f; ~s **and arteries** Venen und Arterien. ~**ed** a geädert
Velcro (P) /'velkrəʊ/ n ~ **fastening** Klettverschluß m
velocity /vɪ'lɒsətɪ/ n Geschwindigkeit f
velvet /'velvɪt/ n Samt m. ~**y** a samtig
vending-machine /'vendɪŋ-/ n [Verkaufs]automat m
vendor /'vendə(r)/ n Verkäufer(in) m(f)
veneer /və'nɪə(r)/ n Furnier nt; (fig) Tünche f. ~**ed** a furniert
venerable /'venərəbl/ a ehrwürdig

venereal /vɪ'nɪərɪəl/ *a* ~ **disease** Geschlechtskrankheit *f*

Venetian /və'ni:ʃn/ *a* venezianisch. **v~blind** *n* Jalousie *f*

vengeance /'vendʒəns/ *n* Rache *f*; **with a** ~ (*fam*) gewaltig

Venice /'venɪs/ *n* Venedig *nt*

venison /'venɪsn/ *n* (*Culin*) Wild *nt*

venom /'venəm/ *n* Gift *nt*; (*fig*) Haß *m*. **~ous** /-əs/ *a* giftig

vent¹ /vent/ *n* Öffnung *f*; (*fig*) Ventil *nt*; **give** ~ **to** Luft machen (+ *dat*) ● *vt* Luft machen (+ *dat*)

vent² *n* (*in jacket*) Schlitz *m*

ventilat|e /'ventɪleɪt/ *vt* belüften. **~ion** /-'leɪʃn/ *n* Belüftung *f*; (*installation*) Lüftung *f*. **~or** *n* Lüftungsvorrichtung *f*; (*Med*) Beatmungsgerät *nt*

ventriloquist /ven'trɪləkwɪst/ *n* Bauchredner *m*

venture /'ventʃə(r)/ *n* Unternehmung *f* ● *vt* wagen ● *vi* sich wagen

venue /'venju:/ *n* Treffpunkt *m*; (*for event*) Veranstaltungsort *m*

veranda /və'rændə/ *n* Veranda *f*

verb /vɜ:b/ *n* Verb *nt*. **~al** *a*, **-ly** *adv* mündlich; (*Gram*) verbal

verbatim /vɜ:'beɪtɪm/ *a & adv* [wort]wörtlich

verbose /vɜ:'bəus/ *a* weitschweifig

verdict /'vɜ:dɪkt/ *n* Urteil *nt*

verge /vɜ:dʒ/ *n* Rand *m*; **be on the ~ of doing sth** im Begriff sein, etw zu tun ● *vi* ~ **on** (*fig*) grenzen an (+ *acc*)

verger /'vɜ:dʒə(r)/ *n* Küster *m*

verify /'verɪfaɪ/ *vt* (*pt/pp* **-ied**) überprüfen; (*confirm*) bestätigen

vermin /'vɜ:mɪn/ *n* Ungeziefer *nt*

vermouth /'vɜ:məθ/ *n* Wermut *m*

vernacular /və'nækjʊlə(r)/ *n* Landessprache *f*

versatil|e /'vɜ:sətaɪl/ *a* vielseitig. **~ity** /-'tɪlətɪ/ *n* Vielseitigkeit *f*

verse /vɜ:s/ *n* Strophe *f*; (*of Bible*) Vers *m*; (*poetry*) Lyrik *f*

version /'vɜ:ʃn/ *n* Version *f*; (*translation*) Übersetzung *f*; (*model*) Modell *nt*

versus /'vɜ:səs/ *prep* gegen (+ *acc*)

vertebra /'vɜ:tɪbrə/ *n* (*pl* **-brae** /-bri:/) (*Anat*) Wirbel *m*

vertical /'vɜ:tɪkl/ *a*, **-ly** *adv* senkrecht ● *n* Senkrechte *f*

vertigo /'vɜ:tɪgəu/ *n* (*Med*) Schwindel *m*

verve /vɜ:v/ *n* Schwung *m*

very /'verɪ/ *adv* sehr; ~ **much** sehr; (*quantity*) sehr viel; ~ **little** sehr wenig; ~ **probably** höchstwahrscheinlich; **at the** ~ **most** allerhöchstens ● *a* (*mere*) bloß; **the** ~ **first** der/die/das allererste; **the** ~ **thing** genau das Richtige; **at the** ~ **end/beginning** ganz am Ende/Anfang; **only a** ~ **little** nur ein ganz kleines bißchen

vessel /'vesl/ *n* Schiff *nt*; (*receptacle & Anat*) Gefäß *nt*

vest /vest/ *n* [Unter]hemd *nt*; (*Amer: waistcoat*) Weste *f* ● *vt* ~ **sth in s.o.** jdm etw verleihen; **have a** ~**ed interest in sth** ein persönliches Interesse an etw (*dat*) haben

vestige /'vestɪdʒ/ *n* Spur *f*

vestment /'vestmənt/ *n* (*Relig*) Gewand *nt*

vestry /'vestrɪ/ *n* Sakristei *f*

vet /vet/ *n* Tierarzt *m*/-ärztin *f* ● *vt* (*pt/pp* **vetted**) überprüfen

veteran /'vetərən/ *n* Veteran *m*. ~ **car** *n* Oldtimer *m*

veterinary /'vetərɪnərɪ/ *a* tierärztlich. ~ **surgeon** *n* Tierarzt *m* / -ärztin *f*

veto /'vi:təu/ *n* (*pl* **-es**) Veto *nt* ● *vt* sein Veto einlegen gegen

vex /veks/ *vt* ärgern. **~ation** /-'seɪʃn/ *n* Ärger *m*. **~ed** *a* verärgert; **~ed question** vieldiskutierte Frage *f*

VHF *abbr* (**very high frequency**) UKW

via /'vaɪə/ *prep* über (+ *acc*)

viable /'vaɪəbl/ *a* lebensfähig; (*fig*) realisierbar; (*firm*) rentabel

viaduct /'vaɪədʌkt/ *n* Viadukt *nt*

vibrant /'vaɪbrənt/ *a* (*fig*) lebhaft

vibrat|e /vaɪ'breɪt/ *vi* vibrieren. **~ion** /-'breɪʃn/ *n* Vibrieren *nt*

vicar /'vɪkə(r)/ *n* Pfarrer *m*. **~age** /-rɪdʒ/ *n* Pfarrhaus *nt*

vicarious /vɪ'keərɪəs/ *a* nachempfunden

vice¹ /vaɪs/ *n* Laster *nt*

vice² *n* (*Techn*) Schraubstock *m*

vice 'chairman *n* stellvertretender Vorsitzender *m*

vice 'president *n* Vizepräsident *m*

vice versa /vaɪsɪ'vɜ:sə/ *adv* umgekehrt

vicinity /vɪ'sɪnətɪ/ *n* Umgebung *f*; **in the** ~ **of** in der Nähe von

vicious /'vɪʃəs/ *a*, **-ly** *adv* boshaft; (*animal*) bösartig. ~ **'circle** *n* Teufelskreis *m*

victim /'vɪktɪm/ *n* Opfer *nt*. **~ize** *vt* schikanieren

victor /'vɪktə(r)/ *n* Sieger *m*
victor|ious /vɪk'tɔːrɪəs/ *a* siegreich.
~y /'vɪktərɪ/ *n* Sieg *m*
video /'vɪdɪəʊ/ *n* Video *nt*; *(recorder)*
Videorecorder *m* ● *attrib* Video- ● *vt*
[auf Videoband] aufnehmen
video: ~ **cas'sette** *n* Videokassette
f. ~ **game** *n* Videospiel *nt*. ~'**nasty**
n Horrorvideo *nt*. ~ **recorder** *n*
Videorecorder *m*
vie /vaɪ/ *vi (pres p* **vying)** wetteifern
Vienn|a /vɪ'enə/ *n* Wien *nt*. ~**ese**
/vɪə'niːz/ *a* Wiener
view /vjuː/ *n* Sicht *f*; *(scene)* Aussicht
f, Blick *m*; *(picture, opinion)* Ansicht
f; **in my** ~ meiner Ansicht nach; **in** ~
of angesichts (+ *gen)*; **keep/have sth**
in ~ etw im Auge behalten/haben; **be**
on ~ besichtigt werden können ● *vt*
sich *(dat)* ansehen; besichtigen *(house)*;
(consider) betrachten ● *vi* (TV) fernsehen. ~**er** *n* (TV) Zuschauer(in)
m(f); *(Phot)* Diabetrachter *m*
view: ~**finder** *n* (Phot) Sucher *m*.
~**point** *n* Standpunkt *m*
vigil /'vɪdʒɪl/ *n* Wache *f*
vigilan|ce /'vɪdʒɪləns/ *n* Wach-
samkeit *f*. ~**t** *a*, -**ly** *adv* wachsam
vigorous /'vɪgərəs/ *a*, -**ly** *adv* kräftig;
(fig) heftig
vigour /'vɪgə(r)/ *n* Kraft *f*; *(fig)* Heftigkeit *f*
vile /vaɪl/ *a* abscheulich
villa /'vɪlə/ *n (for holidays)* Ferien-
haus *nt*
village /'vɪlɪdʒ/ *n* Dorf *nt*. ~**r** *n*
Dorfbewohner(in) *m(f)*
villain /'vɪlən/ *n* Schurke *m*; *(in
story)* Bösewicht *m*
vim /vɪm/ *n (fam)* Schwung *m*
vindicat|e /'vɪndɪkeɪt/ *vt* recht-
fertigen. ~**ion** /-'keɪʃn/ *n* Recht-
fertigung *f*
vindictive /vɪn'dɪktɪv/ *a* nach-
tragend
vine /vaɪn/ *n* Weinrebe *f*
vinegar /'vɪnɪgə(r)/ *n* Essig *m*
vineyard /'vɪnjɑːd/ *n* Weinberg *m*
vintage /'vɪntɪdʒ/ *a* erlesen ● *n
(year)* Jahrgang *m*. ~ '**car** *n* Oldtimer
m
viola /vɪ'əʊlə/ *n (Mus)* Bratsche *f*
violat|e /'vaɪəleɪt/ *vt* verletzen;
(break) brechen; *(disturb)* stören;
(defile) schänden. ~**ion** /-'leɪʃn/ *n*
Verletzung *f*; Schändung *f*
violen|ce /'vaɪələns/ *n* Gewalt *f*;
(fig) Heftigkeit *f*. ~**t** *a* gewalttätig;

(fig) heftig. ~**tly** *adv* brutal; *(fig)*
heftig
violet /'vaɪələt/ *a* violett ● *n (flower)*
Veilchen *nt*
violin /vaɪə'lɪn/ *n* Geige *f*, Violine *f*.
~**ist** *n* Geiger(in) *m(f)*
VIP *abbr* **(very important person)** Pro-
minente(r) *m/f*
viper /'vaɪpə(r)/ *n* Kreuzotter *f*; *(fig)*
Schlange *f*
virgin /'vɜːdʒɪn/ *a* unberührt ● *n*
Jungfrau *f*. ~**ity** /-'dʒɪnətɪ/ *n* Unschuld *f*
Virgo /'vɜːgəʊ/ *n (Astr)* Jungfrau *f*
viril|e /'vɪraɪl/ *a* männlich. ~**ity**
/-'rɪlətɪ/ *n* Männlichkeit *f*
virtual /'vɜːtjʊəl/ *a* **a** ~ ... praktisch
ein ... ~**ly** *adv* praktisch
virtu|e /'vɜːtjuː/ *n* Tugend *f*; *(ad-
vantage)* Vorteil *m*; **by** *or* **in** ~**e of** auf
Grund (+ *gen)*
virtuoso /vɜːtjʊ'əʊzəʊ/ *n (pl* -**si** /-ziː/)
Virtuose *m*
virtuous /'vɜːtjʊəs/ *a* tugendhaft
virulent /'vɪrʊlənt/ *a* bösartig;
(poison) stark; *(fig)* scharf
virus /'vaɪərəs/ *n* Virus *nt*
visa /'viːzə/ *n* Visum *nt*
vis-à-vis /viːzɑː'viː/ *adv & prep*
gegenüber (+ *dat)*
viscous /'vɪskəs/ *a* dickflüssig
visibility /vɪzə'bɪlətɪ/ *n* Sichtbarkeit
f; *(Meteorol)* Sichtweite *f*
visible /'vɪzəbl/ *a*, -**bly** *adv* sichtbar
vision /'vɪʒn/ *n* Vision *f*; *(sight)* Sehkraft *f*; *(foresight)* Weitblick *m*
visit /'vɪzɪt/ *n* Besuch *m* ● *vt* besuchen; besichtigen *(town, building)*.
~**ing hours** *npl* Besuchszeiten *pl*.
~**or** *n* Besucher(in) *m(f)*; *(in hotel)*
Gast *m*; **have** ~**ors** Besuch haben
visor /'vaɪzə(r)/ *n* Schirm *m*; *(on
helmet)* Visier *nt*; *(Auto)* [Sonnen]-
blende *f*
vista /'vɪstə/ *n* Aussicht *f*
visual /'vɪzjʊəl/ *a*, -**ly** *adv* visuell; ~**ly**
handicapped sehbehindert. ~ **aids**
npl Anschauungsmaterial *nt*. ~ **dis-
'play unit** *n* Bildschirmgerät *nt*
visualize /'vɪzjʊəlaɪz/ *vt* sich *(dat)*
vorstellen
vital /'vaɪtl/ *a* unbedingt notwendig;
(essential to life) lebenswichtig.
~**ity** /vaɪ'tælətɪ/ *n* Vitalität *f*. ~**ly**
/'vaɪtlɪ/ *adv* äußerst
vitamin /'vɪtəmɪn/ *n* Vitamin *nt*

vitreous /'vɪtrɪəs/ *a* glasartig; ⟨*enamel*⟩ Glas-

vivaci|ous /vɪ'veɪʃəs/ *a*, **-ly** *adv* lebhaft. **~ty** /-'væsətɪ/ *n* Lebhaftigkeit *f*

vivid /'vɪvɪd/ *a*, **-ly** *adv* lebhaft; ⟨*description*⟩ lebendig

vixen /'vɪksn/ *n* Füchsin *f*

vocabulary /və'kæbjʊlərɪ/ *n* Wortschatz *m*; ⟨*list*⟩ Vokabelverzeichnis *nt*; **learn ~** Vokabeln lernen

vocal /'vəʊkl/ *a*, **-ly** *adv* stimmlich; ⟨*vociferous*⟩ lautstark. **~ cords** *npl* Stimmbänder *pl*

vocalist /'vəʊkəlɪst/ *n* Sänger(in) *m(f)*

vocation /və'keɪʃn/ *n* Berufung *f*. **~al** *a* Berufs-

vociferous /və'sɪfərəs/ *a* lautstark

vodka /'vɒdkə/ *n* Wodka *m*

vogue /vəʊg/ *n* Mode *f*; **in ~** in Mode

voice /vɔɪs/ *n* Stimme *f* ● *vt* zum Ausdruck bringen

void /vɔɪd/ *a* leer; ⟨*not valid*⟩ ungültig; **~ of** ohne ● *n* Leere *f*

volatile /'vɒlətaɪl/ *a* flüchtig; ⟨*person*⟩ sprunghaft

volcanic /vɒl'kænɪk/ *a* vulkanisch

volcano /vɒl'keɪnəʊ/ *n* Vulkan *m*

volition /və'lɪʃn/ *n* **of one's own ~** aus eigenem Willen

volley /'vɒlɪ/ *n* ⟨*of gunfire*⟩ Salve *f*; ⟨*Tennis*⟩ Volley *m*

volt /vəʊlt/ *n* Volt *nt*. **~age** /-ɪdʒ/ *n* ⟨*Electr*⟩ Spannung *f*

voluble /'vɒljʊbl/ *a*, **-bly** *adv* redselig; ⟨*protest*⟩ wortreich

volume /'vɒljuːm/ *n* ⟨*book*⟩ Band *m*; ⟨*Geom*⟩ Rauminhalt *m*; ⟨*amount*⟩ Ausmaß *nt*; ⟨*Radio, TV*⟩ Lautstärke *f*. **~ control** *n* Lautstärkeregler *m*

voluntary /'vɒləntərɪ/ *a*, **-ily** *adv* freiwillig

volunteer /vɒlən'tɪə(r)/ *n* Freiwillige(r) *m/f* ● *vt* anbieten; geben ⟨*information*⟩ ● *vi* sich freiwillig melden

voluptuous /və'lʌptjʊəs/ *a* sinnlich

vomit /'vɒmɪt/ *n* Erbrochene(s) *nt* ● *vt* erbrechen ● *vi* sich übergeben

voracious /və'reɪʃəs/ *a* gefräßig; ⟨*appetite*⟩ unbändig

vot|e /vəʊt/ *n* Stimme *f*; ⟨*ballot*⟩ Abstimmung *f*; ⟨*right*⟩ Wahlrecht *nt*; **take a ~e on** abstimmen über (+ *acc*) ● *vi* abstimmen; ⟨*in election*⟩ wählen ● *vt* **~e s.o. president** jdn zum Präsidenten wählen. **~er** *n* Wähler(in) *m(f)*

vouch /vaʊtʃ/ *vi* **~ for** sich verbürgen für. **~er** *n* Gutschein *m*

vow /vaʊ/ *n* Gelöbnis *nt*; ⟨*Relig*⟩ Gelübde *nt* ● *vt* geloben

vowel /'vaʊəl/ *n* Vokal *m*

voyage /'vɔɪɪdʒ/ *n* Seereise *f*; ⟨*in space*⟩ Reise *f*, Flug *m*

vulgar /'vʌlgə(r)/ *a* vulgär, ordinär. **~ity** /-'gærətɪ/ *n* Vulgarität *f*

vulnerable /'vʌlnərəbl/ *a* verwundbar

vulture /'vʌltʃə(r)/ *n* Geier *m*

vying /'vaɪɪŋ/ *see* **vie**

W

wad /wɒd/ *n* Bausch *m*; ⟨*bundle*⟩ Bündel *nt*. **~ding** *n* Wattierung *f*

waddle /'wɒdl/ *vi* watscheln

wade /weɪd/ *vi* waten; **~ through** ⟨*fam*⟩ sich durchackern durch ⟨*book*⟩

wafer /'weɪfə(r)/ *n* Waffel *f*; ⟨*Relig*⟩ Hostie *f*

waffle[1] /'wɒfl/ *vi* ⟨*fam*⟩ schwafeln

waffle[2] *n* ⟨*Culin*⟩ Waffel *f*

waft /wɒft/ *vt/i* wehen

wag /wæg/ *v* (*pt/pp* **wagged**) ● *vt* wedeln mit; **~ one's finger at s.o.** jdm mit dem Finger drohen ● *vi* wedeln

wage[1] /weɪdʒ/ *vt* führen

wage[2] *n*, & **~s** *pl* Lohn *m*. **~ packet** *n* Lohntüte *f*

wager /'weɪdʒə(r)/ *n* Wette *f*

waggle /'wægl/ *vt* wackeln mit ● *vi* wackeln

wagon /'wægən/ *n* Wagen *m*; ⟨*Rail*⟩ Waggon *m*

wail /weɪl/ *n* [klagender] Schrei *m* ● *vi* heulen; ⟨*lament*⟩ klagen

waist /weɪst/ *n* Taille *f*. **~coat** /'weɪskəʊt/ *n* Weste *f*. **~line** *n* Taille *f*

wait /weɪt/ *n* Wartezeit *f*; **lie in ~ for** auflauern (+ *dat*) ● *vi* warten (**for** auf + *acc*); ⟨*at table*⟩ servieren; **~ on** bedienen ● *vt* **~ one's turn** warten, bis man an der Reihe ist

waiter /'weɪtə(r)/ *n* Kellner *m*; **~!** Herr Ober!

waiting: ~-list *n* Warteliste *f*. **~-room** *n* Warteraum *m*; ⟨*doctor's*⟩ Wartezimmer *nt*

waitress /'weɪtrɪs/ *n* Kellnerin *f*

waive /weɪv/ *vt* verzichten auf (+ *acc*)

wake[1] /weɪk/ *n* Totenwache *f* ● *v* (*pt* **woke**, *pp* **woken**) ~ [**up**] ● *vt* [auf]wecken ● *vi* aufwachen

wake[2] *n* (*Naut*) Kielwasser *nt*; **in the** ~ **of** im Gefolge (+ *gen*)

waken /'weɪkn/ *vt* [auf]wecken ● *vi* aufwachen

Wales /weɪlz/ *n* Wales *nt*

walk /wɔːk/ *n* Spaziergang *m*; (*gait*) Gang *m*; (*path*) Weg *m*; **go for a** ~ spazierengehen ● *vi* gehen; (*not ride*) laufen, zu Fuß gehen; (*ramble*) wandern; **learn to** ~ laufen lernen ● *vt* ausführen ⟨*dog*⟩. ~ **out** *vi* hinausgehen; ⟨*workers:*⟩ in den Streik treten; ~ **out on s.o.** jdn verlassen

walker /'wɔːkə(r)/ *n* Spaziergänger(in) *m(f)*; (*rambler*) Wanderer *m*/Wanderin *f*

walking /'wɔːkɪŋ/ *n* Gehen *nt*; (*rambling*) Wandern *nt*. ~**-stick** *n* Spazierstock *m*

walk: ~**-out** *n* Streik *m*. ~**-over** *n* (*fig*) leichter Sieg *m*

wall /wɔːl/ *n* Wand *f*; (*external*) Mauer *f*; **go to the** ~ (*fam*) eingehen; **drive s.o. up the** ~ (*fam*) jdn auf die Palme bringen ● *vt* ~ **up** zumauern

wallet /'wɒlɪt/ *n* Brieftasche *f*

'**wallflower** *n* Goldlack *m*

wallop /'wɒləp/ *n* (*fam*) Schlag *m* ● *vt* (*pt/pp* **walloped**) (*fam*) schlagen

wallow /'wɒləʊ/ *vi* sich wälzen; (*fig*) schwelgen

'**wallpaper** *n* Tapete *f* ● *vt* tapezieren

walnut /'wɔːlnʌt/ *n* Walnuß *f*

waltz /wɔːlts/ *n* Walzer *m* ● *vi* Walzer tanzen; **come** ~**ing up** (*fam*) angetanzt kommen

wan /wɒn/ *a* bleich

wand /wɒnd/ *n* Zauberstab *m*

wander /'wɒndə(r)/ *vi* umherwandern, (*fam*) bummeln; (*fig: digress*) abschweifen. ~ **about** *vi* umherwandern. ~**lust** *n* Fernweh *nt*

wane /weɪn/ *n* **be on the** ~ schwinden; ⟨*moon:*⟩ abnehmen ● *vi* schwinden; abnehmen

wangle /'wæŋgl/ *vt* (*fam*) organisieren

want /wɒnt/ *n* Mangel *m* (**of** an + *dat*); (*hardship*) Not *f*; (*desire*) Bedürfnis *nt* ● *vt* wollen; (*need*) brauchen; ~ [**to do sth**] etw haben wollen; ~ **to do sth** etw tun wollen; **we** ~ **to stay** wir wollen bleiben; **I** ~ **you to go** ich will, daß du gehst; **it** ~**s painting** es

müßte gestrichen werden; **you** ~ **to learn to swim** du solltest schwimmen lernen ● *vi* **he doesn't** ~ **for anything** ihm fehlt es an nichts. ~**ed** *a* gesucht. ~**ing** *a* be ~**ing** fehlen; **he is** ~**ing in** ihm fehlt es an (+ *dat*)

wanton /'wɒntən/ *a*, **-ly** *adv* mutwillig

war /wɔː(r)/ *n* Krieg *m*; **be at** ~ sich im Krieg befinden

ward /wɔːd/ *n* [Kranken]saal *m*; (*unit*) Station *f*; (*of town*) Wahlbezirk *m*; (*child*) Mündel *nt* ● *vt* ~ **off** abwehren

warden /'wɔːdn/ *n* Heimleiter(in) *m(f)*; (*of youth hostel*) Herbergsvater *m*; (*supervisor*) Aufseher(in) *m(f)*

warder /'wɔːdə(r)/ *n* Wärter(in) *m(f)*

wardrobe /'wɔːdrəʊb/ *n* Kleiderschrank *m*; (*clothes*) Garderobe *f*

warehouse /'weəhaʊs/ *n* Lager *nt*; (*building*) Lagerhaus *nt*

wares /weəz/ *npl* Waren *pl*

war: ~**fare** *n* Krieg *m*. ~**head** *n* Sprengkopf *m*. ~**like** *a* kriegerisch

warm /wɔːm/ *a* (**-er, -est**), **-ly** *adv* warm; (*welcome*) herzlich; **I am** ~ mir ist warm ● *vt* wärmen. ~ **up** *vt* aufwärmen ● *vi* warm werden; (*Sport*) sich aufwärmen. ~**-hearted** *a* warmherzig

warmth /wɔːmθ/ *n* Wärme *f*

warn /wɔːn/ *vt* warnen (**of** vor + *dat*). ~**ing** *n* Warnung *f*; (*advance notice*) Vorwarnung *f*; (*caution*) Verwarnung *f*

warp /wɔːp/ *vt* verbiegen ● *vi* sich verziehen

'**war-path** *n* **on the** ~ auf dem Kriegspfad

warrant /'wɒrənt/ *n* (*for arrest*) Haftbefehl *m*; (*for search*) Durchsuchungsbefehl *m* ● *vt* (*justify*) rechtfertigen; (*guarantee*) garantieren

warranty /'wɒrəntɪ/ *n* Garantie *f*

warrior /'wɒrɪə(r)/ *n* Krieger *m*

'**warship** *n* Kriegsschiff *nt*

wart /wɔːt/ *n* Warze *f*

'**wartime** *n* Kriegszeit *f*

wary /'weərɪ/ *a* (**-ier, -iest**), **-ily** *adv* vorsichtig; (*suspicious*) mißtrauisch

was /wɒz/ *see* **be**

wash /wɒʃ/ *n* Wäsche *f*; (*Naut*) Wellen *pl*; **have a** ~ sich waschen ● *vt* waschen; spülen ⟨*dishes*⟩; aufwischen ⟨*floor*⟩; (*flow over*) bespülen; ~ **one's**

hands sich (dat) die Hände waschen ● vi sich waschen; ⟨fabric:⟩ sich waschen lassen. ~ **out** vt auswaschen; ausspülen ⟨mouth⟩. ~ **up** vt abwaschen, spülen ● vi (Amer) sich waschen

washable /'wɒʃəbl/ a waschbar

wash: ~-**basin** n Waschbecken nt. ~**cloth** n (Amer) Waschlappen m

washed 'out a (faded) verwaschen; (tired) abgespannt

washer /'wɒʃə(r)/ n (Techn) Dichtungsring m; (machine) Waschmaschine f

washing /'wɒʃɪŋ/ n Wäsche f. ~-**machine** n Waschmaschine f. ~-**powder** n Waschpulver nt. ~-'**up** n Abwasch m; **do the** ~-**up** abwaschen, spülen. ~-'**up liquid** n Spülmittel nt

wash: ~-**out** n Pleite f; (person) Niete f. ~-**room** n Waschraum m

wasp /wɒsp/ n Wespe f

wastage /'weɪstɪdʒ/ n Schwund m

waste /weɪst/ n Verschwendung f; (rubbish) Abfall m; ~**s** pl Öde f; **of time** Zeitverschwendung f ● a (product) Abfall-; **lay** ~ verwüsten ● vt verschwenden ● vi ~ **away** immer mehr abmagern

waste: ~-**di'sposal unit** n Müllzerkleinerer m. ~**ful** a verschwenderisch. ~**land** n Ödland nt. ~ '**paper** n Altpapier nt. ~'**paper basket** n Papierkorb m

watch /wɒtʃ/ n Wache f; (timepiece) [Armband]uhr f; **be on the** ~ aufpassen ● vt beobachten; sich (dat) ansehen ⟨film, match⟩; **be careful of, look after**) achten auf (+ acc); ~ **television** fernsehen ● vi zusehen. ~ **out** vi Ausschau halten (**for** nach); (be careful) aufpassen

watch: ~-**dog** n Wachhund m. ~**ful** a, -**ly** adv wachsam. ~**maker** n Uhrmacher m. ~**man** n Wachmann m. ~-**strap** n Uhrarmband nt. ~-**tower** n Wachturm m. ~**word** n Parole f

water /'wɔːtə(r)/ n Wasser nt; ~**s** pl Gewässer nt ● vt gießen ⟨garden, plant⟩; (dilute) verdünnen; (give drink to) tränken ● vi ⟨eyes:⟩ tränen; **my mouth was** ~**ing** mir lief das Wasser im Munde zusammen. ~ **down** vt verwässern

water: ~-**colour** n Wasserfarbe f; (painting) Aquarell nt. ~**cress** n Brunnenkresse f. ~**fall** n Wasserfall m

'**watering-can** n Gießkanne f

water: ~-**lily** n Seerose f. ~**logged** a **be** ~**logged** ⟨ground:⟩ unter Wasser stehen. ~-**main** n Hauptwasserleitung f. ~**mark** n Wasserzeichen nt. ~ **polo** n Wasserball m. ~-**power** n Wasserkraft f. ~**proof** a wasserdicht. ~**shed** n Wasserscheide f; (fig) Wendepunkt m. ~-**skiing** n Wasserskilaufen nt. ~**tight** a wasserdicht. ~**way** n Wasserstraße f

watery /'wɔːtərɪ/ a wäßrig

watt /wɒt/ n Watt nt

wave /weɪv/ n Welle f; (gesture) Handbewegung f; (as greeting) Winken nt ● vt winken mit; (brandish) schwingen; (threateningly) drohen mit; wellen ⟨hair⟩; ~ **one's hand** winken ● vi winken (**to** dat); ⟨flag:⟩ wehen. ~**length** n Wellenlänge f

waver /'weɪvə(r)/ vi schwanken

wavy /'weɪvɪ/ a wellig

wax[1] /wæks/ vi ⟨moon:⟩ zunehmen; (fig: become) werden

wax[2] n Wachs nt; (in ear) Schmalz m ● vt wachsen. ~**works** n Wachsfigurenkabinett nt

way /weɪ/ n Weg m; (direction) Richtung f; (respect) Hinsicht f; (manner) Art f; (method) Art und Weise f; ~**s** pl Gewohnheiten pl; **in the** ~ im Weg; **on the** ~ auf dem Weg (**to** nach/zu); (under way) unterwegs; **a little/long** ~ ein kleines/ganzes Stück; **a long** ~ **off** weit weg; **this** ~ hierher; (like this) so; **which** ~ in welche Richtung; (how) wie; **by the** ~ übrigens; **in some** ~**s** in gewisser Hinsicht; **either** ~ so oder so; **in this** ~ auf diese Weise; **in a** ~ in gewisser Weise; **in a bad** ~ ⟨person⟩ in schlechter Verfassung; **lead the** ~ vorausgehen; **make** ~ Platz machen (**for** dat); '**give** ~' (Auto) 'Vorfahrt beachten'; **go out of one's** ~ (fig) sich (dat) besondere Mühe geben (**to** zu); **get one's [own]** ~ seinen Willen durchsetzen ● adv weit; ~ **behind** weit zurück. ~ '**in** n Eingang m

way'lay vt (pt/pp -**laid**) überfallen; (fam: intercept) abfangen

way 'out n Ausgang m; (fig) Ausweg m

way-'out a (fam) verrückt

wayward /'weɪwəd/ a eigenwillig

WC abbr WC nt

we /wi:/ *pron* wir

weak /wi:k/ *a* (**-er, -est**), **-ly** *adv* schwach; ⟨*liquid*⟩ dünn. ∼**en** *vt* schwächen ● *vi* schwächer werden. ∼**ling** *n* Schwächling *m*. ∼**ness** *n* Schwäche *f*

wealth /welθ/ *n* Reichtum *m*; ⟨*fig*⟩ Fülle *f* (**of** an + *dat*). ∼**y** *a* (**-ier, -iest**) reich

wean /wi:n/ *vt* entwöhnen

weapon /'wepən/ *n* Waffe *f*

wear /weə(r)/ *n* ⟨*clothing*⟩ Kleidung *f*; ∼ **and tear** Abnutzung *f*, Verschleiß *m* ● *v* (*pt* **wore**, *pp* **worn**) ● *vt* tragen; ⟨*damage*⟩ abnutzen; ∼ **a hole in sth** etw durchwetzen; **what shall I ∼?** was soll ich anziehen? ● *vi* sich abnutzen; ⟨*last*⟩ halten. ∼ **off** *vi* abgehen; ⟨*effect:*⟩ nachlassen. ∼ **out** *vt* abnutzen; ⟨*exhaust*⟩ erschöpfen ● *vi* sich abnutzen

wearable /'weərəbl/ *a* tragbar

weary /'wɪərɪ/ *a* (**-ier, -iest**), **-ily** *adv* müde ● *v* (*pt/pp* **wearied**) ● *vt* ermüden ● *vi* ∼ **of sth** etw ⟨*gen*⟩ überdrüssig werden

weasel /'wi:zl/ *n* Wiesel *nt*

weather /'weðə(r)/ *n* Wetter *nt*; **in this ∼** bei diesem Wetter; **under the ∼** ⟨*fam*⟩ nicht ganz auf dem Posten ● *vt* abwettern ⟨*storm*⟩, ⟨*fig*⟩ überstehen

weather: ∼**-beaten** *a* verwittert; wettergegerbt ⟨*face*⟩. ∼**cock** *n* Wetterhahn *m*. ∼ **forecast** *n* Wettervorhersage *f*. ∼**-vane** *n* Wetterfahne *f*

weave[1] /wi:v/ *vi* (*pt/pp* **weaved**) sich schlängeln (**through** durch)

weave[2] *n* ⟨*Tex*⟩ Bindung *f* ● *vt* (*pt* **wove**, *pp* **woven**) weben; ⟨*plait*⟩ flechten; ⟨*fig*⟩ einflechten (**in** in + *acc*). ∼**r** *n* Weber *m*

web /web/ *n* Netz *nt*. ∼**bed feet** *npl* Schwimmfüße *pl*

wed /wed/ *vt/i* (*pt/pp* **wedded**) heiraten. ∼**ding** *n* Hochzeit *f*; ⟨*ceremony*⟩ Trauung *f*

wedding: ∼ **day** *n* Hochzeitstag *m*. ∼ **dress** *n* Hochzeitskleid *nt*. ∼**-ring** *n* Ehering *m*, Trauring *m*

wedge /wedʒ/ *n* Keil *m*; ⟨*of cheese*⟩ [keilförmiges] Stück *nt* ● *vt* festklemmen

wedlock /'wedlɒk/ *n* ⟨*liter*⟩ Ehe *f*; **in/ out of ∼** ehelich/unehelich

Wednesday /'wenzdeɪ/ *n* Mittwoch *m*

wee /wi:/ *a* ⟨*fam*⟩ klein ● *vi* Pipi machen

weed /wi:d/ *n* & ∼**s** *pl* Unkraut *nt* ● *vt/i* jäten. ∼ **out** *vt* ⟨*fig*⟩ aussieben

'weed-killer *n* Unkrautvertilgungsmittel *nt*

weedy /'wi:dɪ/ *a* ⟨*fam*⟩ spillerig

week /wi:k/ *n* Woche *f*. ∼**day** *n* Wochentag *m*. ∼**end** *n* Wochenende *nt*

weekly /'wi:klɪ/ *a* & *adv* wöchentlich ● *n* Wochenzeitschrift *f*

weep /wi:p/ *vi* (*pt/pp* **wept**) weinen. ∼**ing 'willow** *n* Trauerweide *f*

weigh /weɪ/ *vt/i* wiegen; ∼ **anchor** den Anker lichten. ∼ **down** *vt* ⟨*fig*⟩ niederdrücken. ∼ **up** *vt* ⟨*fig*⟩ abwägen

weight /weɪt/ *n* Gewicht *nt*; **put on/ lose ∼** zunehmen/abnehmen. ∼**ing** *n* ⟨*allowance*⟩ Zulage *f*

weight: ∼**lessness** *n* Schwerelosigkeit *f*. ∼**-lifting** *n* Gewichtheben *nt*

weighty /'weɪtɪ/ *a* (**-ier, -iest**) schwer; ⟨*important*⟩ gewichtig

weir /wɪə(r)/ *n* Wehr *nt*

weird /wɪəd/ *a* (**-er, -est**) unheimlich; ⟨*bizarre*⟩ bizarr

welcome /'welkəm/ *a* willkommen; **you're ∼!** nichts zu danken! **you're ∼ to have it** das können Sie gerne haben ● *n* Willkommen *nt* ● *vt* begrüßen

weld /weld/ *vt* schweißen. ∼**er** *n* Schweißer *m*

welfare /'welfeə(r)/ *n* Wohl *nt*; ⟨*Admin*⟩ Fürsorge *f*. **W∼ State** *n* Wohlfahrtsstaat *m*

well[1] /wel/ *n* Brunnen *m*; ⟨*oil* ∼⟩ Quelle *f*; ⟨*of staircase*⟩ Treppenhaus *nt*

well[2] *adv* (**better, best**) gut; **as ∼** auch; **as ∼ as** ⟨*in addition*⟩ sowohl ... als auch; ∼ **done!** gut gemacht! ● *a* gesund; **he is not ∼** es geht ihm nicht gut; **get ∼ soon!** gute Besserung! ● *int* nun, na

well: ∼**-behaved** *a* artig. ∼**-being** *n* Wohl *nt*. ∼**-bred** *a* wohlerzogen. ∼**-heeled** *a* ⟨*fam*⟩ gut betucht

wellingtons /'welɪŋtənz/ *npl* Gummistiefel *pl*

well: ∼**-known** *a* bekannt. ∼**-meaning** *a* wohlmeinend. ∼**-meant** *a* gutgemeint. ∼**-off** *a* wohlhabend; **be ∼-off** gut dran sein. ∼**-read** *a* belesen. ∼**-to-do** *a* wohlhabend

Welsh /welʃ/ a walisisch ● n (Lang) Walisisch nt; **the** ~ pl die Waliser. ~**man** n Waliser m. ~ **rabbit** n überbackenes Käsebrot nt

went /went/ see **go**

wept /wept/ see **weep**

were /wɜ:(r)/ see **be**

west /west/ n Westen m; **to the** ~ **of** westlich von ● a West-, west- ● adv nach Westen; **go** ~ (fam) flötengehen. ~**erly** a westlich. ~**ern** a westlich ● n Western m

West: ~ '**Germany** n Westdeutschland nt. ~ '**Indian** a westindisch ● n Westinder(in) m(f). ~ '**Indies** /-'ɪndɪz/ npl Westindische Inseln pl

'**westward[s]** /-wəd[z]/ adv nach Westen

wet /wet/ a (**wetter, wettest**) naß; ⟨fam: person⟩ weichlich, lasch; '~ **paint**' 'frisch gestrichen' ● vt (pt/pp **wet** or **wetted**) naß machen. ~ '**blanket** n Spaßverderber m

whack /wæk/ n (fam) Schlag m ● vt (fam) schlagen. ~**ed** a (fam) kaputt

whale /weɪl/ n Wal m; **have a** ~ **of a time** (fam) sich toll amüsieren

wharf /wɔːf/ n Kai m

what /wɒt/ pron & int was; ~ **for?** wozu? ~ **is it like?** wie ist es? ~ **is your name?** wie ist Ihr Name? ~ **is the weather like?** wie ist das Wetter? ~'**s he talking about?** wovon redet er? ● a welche(r,s); ~ **kind of a** was für ein(e); **at** ~ **time?** um wieviel Uhr?

what'ever a [egal] welche(r,s) ● pron was ... auch; ~ **is it?** was ist das bloß? ~ **he does** was er auch tut; ~ **happens** was auch geschieht; **nothing** ~ überhaupt nichts

whatso'ever pron & a ≈ **whatever**

wheat /wiːt/ n Weizen m

wheedle /'wiːdl/ vt gut zureden (+ dat); ~ **sth out of s.o.** jdm etw ablocken

wheel /wiːl/ n Rad nt; (pottery) Töpferscheibe f; (steering ~) Lenkrad nt; **at the** ~ am Steuer ● vt (push) schieben ● vi kehrtmachen; (circle) kreisen

wheel: ~**barrow** n Schubkarre f. ~**chair** n Rollstuhl m. ~-**clamp** n Parkkralle f

wheeze /wiːz/ vi keuchen

when /wen/ adv wann; **the day** ~ der Tag, an dem ● conj wenn; (in the past) als; (although) wo ... doch; ~

swimming/reading beim Schwimmen/Lesen

whence /wens/ adv (liter) woher

when'ever conj & adv [immer] wenn; (at whatever time) wann immer; ~ **did it happen?** wann ist das bloß passiert?

where /weə(r)/ adv & conj wo; ~ **[to]** wohin; ~ **[from]** woher

whereabouts[1] /weərə'baʊts/ adv wo

'**whereabouts**[2] n Verbleib m; (of person) Aufenthaltsort m

where'as conj während; (in contrast) wohingegen

where'by adv wodurch

whereu'pon adv worauf[hin]

wher'ever conj & adv wo immer; (to whatever place) wohin immer; (from whatever place) woher immer; (everywhere) überall wo; ~ **is he?** wo ist er bloß? ~ **possible** wenn irgend möglich

whet /wet/ vt (pt/pp **whetted**) wetzen; anregen ⟨appetite⟩

whether /'weðə(r)/ conj ob

which /wɪtʃ/ a & pron welche(r,s); ~ **one** welche(r,s) ● rel pron der/die/das, (pl) die; (after clause) was; **after** ~ wonach; **on** ~ worauf

which'ever a & pron [egal] welche(r, s); ~ **it is** was es auch ist

whiff /wɪf/ n Hauch m

while /waɪl/ n Weile f; **a long** ~ lange; **be worth** ~ sich lohnen; **it's worth my** ~ es lohnt sich für mich ● conj während; (as long as) solange; (although) obgleich ● vt ~ **away** sich (dat) vertreiben

whilst /waɪlst/ conj während

whim /wɪm/ n Laune f

whimper /'wɪmpə(r)/ vi wimmern; ⟨dog:⟩ winseln

whimsical /'wɪmzɪkl/ a skurril

whine /waɪn/ n Winseln nt ● vi winseln

whip /wɪp/ n Peitsche f; (Pol) Einpeitscher m ● vt (pt/pp **whipped**) peitschen; (Culin) schlagen; (snatch) reißen; (fam: steal) klauen. ~ **up** vt (incite) anheizen; (fam) schnell hinzaubern ⟨meal⟩. ~**ped** '**cream** n Schlagsahne f

whirl /wɜːl/ n Wirbel m; **I am in a** ~ mir schwirrt der Kopf ● vt/i wirbeln. ~**pool** n Strudel m. ~**wind** n Wirbelwind m

whirr /wɜː(r)/ vi surren

whisk /wɪsk/ n (Culin) Schneebesen m ● vt (Culin) schlagen. ~ **away** vt wegreißen

whisker /'wɪskə(r)/ n Schnurrhaar nt; **~s** pl (on man's cheek) Backenbart m

whisky /'wɪskɪ/ n Whisky m

whisper /'wɪspə(r)/ n Flüstern nt; (rumour) Gerücht nt; **in a ~** im Flüsterton ● vt/i flüstern

whistle /'wɪsl/ n Pfiff m; (instrument) Pfeife f ● vt/i pfeifen

white /waɪt/ a (**-r, -st**) weiß ● n Weiß nt; (of egg) Eiweiß nt; (person) Weiße(r) m/f

white: **~ 'coffee** n Kaffee m mit Milch. **~-'collar worker** n Angestellte(r) m. **~'lie** n Notlüge f

whiten /'waɪtn/ vt weiß machen ● vi weiß werden

whiteness /'waɪtnɪs/ n Weiß nt

'whitewash n Tünche f; (fig) Schönfärberei f ● vt tünchen

Whitsun /'wɪtsn/ n Pfingsten nt

whittle /'wɪtl/ vt **~ down** reduzieren; kürzen (list)

whiz[z] /wɪz/ vi (pt/pp **whizzed**) zischen. **~-kid** n (fam) Senkrechtstarter m

who /hu:/ pron wer; (acc) wen; (dat) wem ● rel pron der/die/das, (pl) die

who'ever pron wer [immer]; **~ he is** wer er auch ist; **~ is it?** wer ist das bloß?

whole /həʊl/ a ganz; (truth) voll ● n Ganze(s) nt; **as a ~** als Ganzes; **on the ~** im großen und ganzen; **the ~ lot** alle; (everything) alles; **the ~ of Germany** ganz Deutschland; **the ~ time** die ganze Zeit

whole: **~food** n Vollwertkost f. **~-'hearted** a rückhaltlos. **~meal** a Vollkorn-

'wholesale a Großhandels- ● adv en gros; (fig) in Bausch und Bogen. **~r** n Großhändler m

wholesome /'həʊlsəm/ a gesund

wholly /'həʊlɪ/ adv völlig

whom /hu:m/ pron wen; **to ~** wem ● rel pron den/die/das, (pl) die; (dat) dem/der/dem, (pl) denen

whooping cough /'hu:pɪŋ-/ n Keuchhusten m

whopping /'wɒpɪŋ/ a (fam) Riesen-

whore /hɔ:(r)/ n Hure f

whose /hu:z/ pron wessen; **~ is that?** wem gehört das? ● rel pron dessen/deren/dessen, (pl) deren

why /waɪ/ adv warum; (for what purpose) wozu; **that's ~** darum ● int na

wick /wɪk/ n Docht m

wicked /'wɪkɪd/ a böse; (mischievous) frech, boshaft

wicker /'wɪkə(r)/ n Korbgeflecht nt ● attrib Korb-

wide /waɪd/ a (**-r, -st**) weit; (broad) breit; (fig) groß; **be ~** (far from target) danebengehen ● adv weit; (off target) daneben; **~ awake** hellwach; **far and ~** weit und breit. **~ly** adv weit; (known, accepted) weithin; (differ) stark

widen /'waɪdn/ vt verbreitern; (fig) erweitern ● vi sich verbreitern

'widespread a weitverbreitet

widow /'wɪdəʊ/ n Witwe f. **~ed** a verwitwet. **~er** n Witwer m

width /wɪdθ/ n Weite f; (breadth) Breite f

wield /wi:ld/ vt schwingen; ausüben (power)

wife /waɪf/ n (pl **wives**) [Ehe]frau f

wig /wɪg/ n Perücke f

wiggle /'wɪgl/ vi wackeln ● vt wackeln mit

wild /waɪld/ a (**-er, -est**), **-ly** adv wild; (animal) wildlebend; (flower) wildwachsend; (furious) wütend; **be ~ about** (keen on) wild sein auf (+ acc) ● adv wild; **run ~** frei herumlaufen ● n **in the ~** wild; **the ~s** pl die Wildnis f

'wildcat strike n wilder Streik m

wilderness /'wɪldənɪs/ n Wildnis f; (desert) Wüste f

wild: **~'goose chase** n aussichtslose Suche f. **~life** n Tierwelt f

wilful /'wɪlfl/ a, **-ly** adv mutwillig; (self-willed) eigenwillig

will[1] /wɪl/ v aux wollen; (forming future tense) werden; **he ~ arrive tomorrow** er wird morgen kommen; **~ you go?** gehst du? **you ~ be back soon, won't you?** du kommst doch bald wieder, nicht? **he ~ be there, won't he?** er wird doch da sein? **she ~ be there by now** sie wird jetzt schon da sein; **~ you be quiet!** willst du wohl ruhig sein! **~ you have some wine?** möchten Sie Wein? **the engine won't start** der Motor will nicht anspringen

will[2] n Wille m; (document) Testament nt

willing /'wɪlɪŋ/ a willig; (eager) bereitwillig; **be ~** bereit sein. **~ly** adv bereitwillig; (gladly) gern. **~ness** n Bereitwilligkeit f

willow /'wɪləʊ/ n Weide f

'will-power n Willenskraft f

willy-'nilly *adv* wohl oder übel

wilt /wɪlt/ *vi* welk werden, welken

wily /'waɪlɪ/ *a* (**-ier, -iest**) listig

wimp /wɪmp/ *n* Schwächling *m*

win /wɪn/ *n* Sieg *m*; **have a** ~ gewinnen ● *v* (*pt/pp* **won**; *pres p* **winning**) ● *vt* gewinnen; bekommen ⟨*scholarship*⟩ ● *vi* gewinnen; (*in battle*) siegen. ~ **over** *vt* auf seine Seite bringen

wince /wɪns/ *vi* zusammenzucken

winch /wɪntʃ/ *n* Winde *f* ● *vt* ~ **up** hochwinden

wind[1] /wɪnd/ *n* Wind *m*; (*breath*) Atem *m*; (*fam: flatulence*) Blähungen *pl*; **have the** ~ **up** (*fam*) Angst haben ● *vt* ~ s.o. jdm den Atem nehmen

wind[2] /waɪnd/ *v* (*pt/pp* **wound**) ● *vt* (*wrap*) wickeln; (*move by turning*) kurbeln; aufziehen ⟨*clock*⟩ ● *vi* (*road:*) sich winden. ~ **up** *vt* aufziehen ⟨*clock*⟩; schließen ⟨*proceedings*⟩

wind /wɪnd/: ~**fall** *n* unerwarteter Glücksfall *m*; ~**falls** *pl* (*fruit*) Fallobst *nt*. ~ **instrument** *n* Blasinstrument *nt*. ~**mill** *n* Windmühle *f*

window /'wɪndəʊ/ *n* Fenster *nt*; (*of shop*) Schaufenster *nt*

window: ~**-box** *n* Blumenkasten *m*. ~**-cleaner** *n* Fensterputzer *m*. ~**-dresser** *n* Schaufensterdekorateur(in) *m(f)*. ~**-dressing** *n* Schaufensterdekoration *f*; (*fig*) Schönfärberei *f*. ~**-pane** *n* Fensterscheibe *f*. ~**-shopping** *n* Schaufensterbummel *m*. ~**-sill** *n* Fensterbrett *nt*

'windpipe *n* Luftröhre *f*

'windscreen *n*, (*Amer*) **'windshield** *n* Windschutzscheibe *f*. ~ **washer** *n* Scheibenwaschanlage *f*. ~**-wiper** *n* Scheibenwischer *m*

wind: ~**surfing** *n* Windsurfen *nt*. ~**swept** *a* windgepeitscht; ⟨*person*⟩ zersaust

windy /'wɪndɪ/ *a* (**-ier, -iest**) windig; **be** ~ (*fam*) Angst haben

wine /waɪn/ *n* Wein *m*

wine: ~**-bar** *n* Weinstube *f*. ~**glass** *n* Weinglas *nt*. ~**-list** *n* Weinkarte *f*

winery /'waɪnərɪ/ *n* (*Amer*) Weingut *nt*

'wine-tasting *n* Weinprobe *f*

wing /wɪŋ/ *n* Flügel *m*; (*Auto*) Kotflügel *m*; ~**s** *pl* (*Theat*) Kulissen *pl*

wink /wɪŋk/ *n* Zwinkern *nt*; **not sleep a** ~ kein Auge zutun ● *vi* zwinkern; ⟨*light:*⟩ blinken

winner /'wɪnə(r)/ *n* Gewinner(in) *m(f)*; (*Sport*) Sieger(in) *m(f)*

winning /'wɪnɪŋ/ *a* siegreich; ⟨*smile*⟩ gewinnend. ~**-post** *n* Zielpfosten *m*. ~**s** *npl* Gewinn *m*

wint|er /'wɪntə(r)/ *n* Winter *m*. ~**ry** *a* winterlich

wipe /waɪp/ *n* **give sth a** ~ etw abwischen ● *vt* abwischen; aufwischen ⟨*floor*⟩; (*dry*) abtrocknen. ~ **off** *vt* abwischen; (*erase*) auslöschen. ~ **out** *vt* (*cancel*) löschen; (*destroy*) ausrotten. ~ **up** *vt* aufwischen; abtrocknen ⟨*dishes*⟩

wire /waɪə(r)/ *n* Draht *m*. ~**-haired** *a* rauhhaarig

wireless /'waɪəlɪs/ *n* Radio *nt*

wire 'netting *n* Maschendraht *m*

wiring /'waɪərɪŋ/ *n* [elektrische] Leitungen *pl*

wiry /'waɪərɪ/ *a* (**-ier, -iest**) drahtig

wisdom /'wɪzdəm/ *n* Weisheit *f*; (*prudence*) Klugheit *f*. ~ **tooth** *n* Weisheitszahn *m*

wise /waɪz/ *a* (**-r, -st**), **-ly** *adv* weise; (*prudent*) klug

wish /wɪʃ/ *n* Wunsch *m* ● *vt* wünschen; ~ **s.o. well** jdm alles Gute wünschen; **I** ~ **you could stay** ich wünschte, du könntest hierbleiben ● *vi* sich (*dat*) etwas wünschen. ~**ful** *a* ~**ful thinking** Wunschdenken *nt*

wishy-washy /'wɪʃɪwɒʃɪ/ *a* labberig; ⟨*colour*⟩ verwaschen; ⟨*person*⟩ lasch

wisp /wɪsp/ *n* Büschel *nt*; (*of hair*) Strähne *f*; (*of smoke*) Fahne *f*

wisteria /wɪs'tɪərɪə/ *n* Glyzinie *f*

wistful /'wɪstfl/ *a*, **-ly** *adv* wehmütig

wit /wɪt/ *n* Geist *m*, Witz *m*; (*intelligence*) Verstand *m*; (*person*) geistreicher Mensch *m*; **be at one's** ~**s' end** sich (*dat*) keinen Rat mehr wissen; **scared out of one's** ~**s** zu Tode erschrocken

witch /wɪtʃ/ *n* Hexe *f*. ~**craft** *n* Hexerei *f*. ~**-hunt** *n* Hexenjagd *f*

with /wɪð/ *prep* mit (+ *dat*); ~ **fear/ cold** vor Angst/Kälte; ~ **it** damit; **I'm going** ~ **you** ich gehe mit; **take it** ~ **you** nimm es mit; **I haven't got it** ~ **me** ich habe es nicht bei mir; **I'm not** ~ **you** (*fam*) ich komme nicht mit

with'draw *v* (*pt* **-drew**, *pp* **-drawn**) ● *vt* zurückziehen; abheben ⟨*money*⟩ ● *vi* sich zurückziehen. ~**al** *n* Zurückziehen *nt*; (*of money*) Abhebung

f; (*from drugs*) Entzug *m*. **~al symptoms** *npl* Entzugserscheinungen *pl*
with'drawn *see* **withdraw** ● *a* ⟨*person*⟩ verschlossen
wither /'wɪðə(r)/ *vi* [ver]welken
with'hold *vt* (*pt/pp* **-held**) vorenthalten (**from s.o.** jdm)
with'in *prep* innerhalb (+ *gen*); **~ the law** im Rahmen des Gesetzes ● *adv* innen
with'out *prep* ohne (+ *acc*); **~ my noticing it** ohne daß ich es merkte
with'stand *vt* (*pt/pp* **-stood**) standhalten (+ *dat*)
witness /'wɪtnɪs/ *n* Zeuge *m*/Zeugin *f*; (*evidence*) Zeugnis *nt* ● *vt* Zeuge/Zeugin sein (+ *gen*); bestätigen ⟨*signature*⟩. **~-box** *n*, (*Amer*) **~-stand** *n* Zeugenstand *m*
witticism /'wɪtɪsɪzm/ *n* geistreicher Ausspruch *m*
wittingly /'wɪtɪŋlɪ/ *adv* wissentlich
witty /'wɪtɪ/ *a* (**-ier, -iest**) witzig, geistreich
wives /waɪvz/ *see* **wife**
wizard /'wɪzəd/ *n* Zauberer *m*. **~ry** *n* Zauberei *f*
wizened /'wɪznd/ *a* verhutzelt
wobb|le /'wɒbl/ *vi* wackeln. **~ly** *a* wackelig
woe /wəʊ/ *n* (*liter*) Jammer *m*; **~ is me!** wehe mir!
woke, woken /wəʊk, 'wəʊkn/ *see* **wake¹**
wolf /wʊlf/ *n* (*pl* **wolves** /wʊlvz/) Wolf *m* ● *vt* **~ [down]** hinunterschlingen
woman /'wʊmən/ *n* (*pl* **women**) Frau *f*. **~izer** *n* Schürzenjäger *m*. **~ly** *a* fraulich
womb /wuːm/ *n* Gebärmutter *f*
women /'wɪmɪn/ *npl see* **woman**; **W~'s Libber** /'lɪbə(r)/ *n* Frauenrechtlerin *f*. **W~'s Liberation** *n* Frauenbewegung *f*
won /wʌn/ *see* **win**
wonder /'wʌndə(r)/ *n* Wunder *nt*; (*surprise*) Staunen *nt* ● *vt/i* sich fragen; (*be surprised*) sich wundern; **I ~ da frage ich mich; I ~ whether she is ill** ob sie wohl krank ist? **~ful** *a*, **-ly** *adv* wunderbar
won't /wəʊnt/ = **will not**
woo /wuː/ *vt* (*liter*) werben um; (*fig*) umwerben
wood /wʊd/ *n* Holz *nt*; (*forest*) Wald *m*; **touch ~!** unberufen!

wood: ~cut *n* Holzschnitt *m*. **~ed** /-ɪd/ *a* bewaldet. **~en** *a* Holz-; (*fig*) hölzern. **~pecker** *n* Specht *m*. **~wind** *n* Holzbläser *pl*. **~work** *n* (*wooden parts*) Holzteile *pl*; (*craft*) Tischlerei *f*. **~worm** *n* Holzwurm *m*. **~y** *a* holzig
wool /wʊl/ *n* Wolle *f* ● *attrib* Woll-. **~len** *a* wollen. **~lens** *npl* Wollsachen *pl*
woolly /'wʊlɪ/ *a* (**-ier, -iest**) wollig; (*fig*) unklar
word /wɜːd/ *n* Wort *nt*; (*news*) Nachricht *f*; **by ~ of mouth** mündlich; **have a ~ with** sprechen mit; **have ~s** einen Wortwechsel haben. **~ing** *n* Wortlaut *m*. **~ processor** *n* Textverarbeitungssystem *nt*
wore /wɔː(r)/ *see* **wear**
work /wɜːk/ *n* Arbeit *f*; (*Art, Literature*) Werk *nt*; **~s** *pl* (*factory, mechanism*) Werk *nt*; **at ~** bei der Arbeit; **out of ~** arbeitslos ● *vi* arbeiten; ⟨*machine, system*⟩ funktionieren; (*have effect*) wirken; (*study*) lernen; **it won't ~** (*fig*) es klappt nicht ● *vt* arbeiten lassen; bedienen ⟨*machine*⟩; betätigen ⟨*lever*⟩; **~ one's way through sth** sich durch etw hindurcharbeiten. **~ off** *vt* abarbeiten. **~ out** *vt* ausrechnen; (*solve*) lösen ● *vi* gutgehen, (*fam*) klappen. **~ up** *vt* aufbauen; sich (*dat*) holen ⟨*appetite*⟩; **get ~ed up** sich aufregen
workable /'wɜːkəbl/ *a* (*feasible*) durchführbar
workaholic /wɜːkə'hɒlɪk/ *n* arbeitswütiger Mensch *m*
worker /'wɜːkə(r)/ *n* Arbeiter(in) *m*(*f*)
working /'wɜːkɪŋ/ *a* berufstätig; ⟨*day, clothes*⟩ Arbeits-; **be in ~ order** funktionieren. **~ 'class** *n* Arbeiterklasse *f*. **~-class** *a* Arbeiter-; **be ~-class** zur Arbeiterklasse gehören
work: ~man *n* Arbeiter *m*; (*craftsman*) Handwerker *m*. **~manship** *n* Arbeit *f*. **~-out** *n* [Fitneß]training *nt*. **~shop** *n* Werkstatt *f*
world /wɜːld/ *n* Welt *f*; **in the ~** auf der Welt; **a ~ of difference** ein himmelweiter Unterschied; **think the ~ of s.o.** große Stücke auf jdn halten. **~ly** *a* weltlich; ⟨*person*⟩ weltlich gesinnt. **~-wide** *a* & *adv* /-'-/ weltweit
worm /wɜːm/ *n* Wurm *m* ● *vt* **~ one's way into s.o.'s confidence** sich in jds

Vertrauen einschleichen. **~-eaten** *a* wurmstichig

worn /wɔːn/ *see* wear ● *a* abgetragen. **~-out** *a* abgetragen; ⟨*carpet*⟩ abgenutzt; ⟨*person*⟩ erschöpft

worried /'wʌrɪd/ *a* besorgt

worry /'wʌrɪ/ *n* Sorge *f* ● *v* (*pt/pp* **worried**) ● *vt* beunruhigen, Sorgen machen (+ *dat*); ⟨*bother*⟩ stören ● *vi* sich beunruhigen, sich (*dat*) Sorgen machen. **~ing** *a* beunruhigend

worse /wɜːs/ *a* & *adv* schlechter; ⟨*more serious*⟩ schlimmer ● *n* Schlechtere(s) *nt*; Schlimmere(s) *nt*

worsen /'wɜːsn/ *vt* verschlechtern ● *vi* sich verschlechtern

worship /'wɜːʃɪp/ *n* Anbetung *f*; ⟨*service*⟩ Gottesdienst *m*; **Your/His W~** Euer/Seine Ehren ● *v* (*pt/pp* **-shipped**) ● *vt* anbeten ● *vi* am Gottesdienst teilnehmen

worst /wɜːst/ *a* schlechteste(r,s); ⟨*most serious*⟩ schlimmste(r,s) ● *adv* am schlechtesten; am schlimmsten ● *n* the ~ das Schlimmste; **get the ~ of it** den kürzeren ziehen

worsted /'wʊstɪd/ *n* Kammgarn *m*

worth /wɜːθ/ *n* Wert *m*; **£10's ~ of petrol** Benzin für £10 ● *a* **be ~ £5** £5 wert sein; **be ~ it** (*fig*) sich lohnen. **~less** *a* wertlos. **~while** *a* lohnend

worthy /'wɜːðɪ/ *a* würdig

would /wʊd/ *v aux* **I ~ do it** ich würde es tun, ich täte es; **~ you go?** würdest du gehen? **he said he ~n't** er sagte, er würde es nicht tun; **what ~ you like?** was möchten Sie?

wound[1] /wuːnd/ *n* Wunde *f* ● *vt* verwunden

wound[2] /waʊnd/ *see* wind[2]

wove, woven /wəʊv, 'wəʊvn/ *see* weave[2]

wrangle /'ræŋgl/ *n* Streit *m* ● *vi* sich streiten

wrap /ræp/ *n* Umhang *m* ● *vt* (*pt/pp* **wrapped**) ~ **[up]** wickeln; einpacken ⟨*present*⟩ ● *vi* ~ **up warmly** sich warm einpacken; **be ~ped up in** (*fig*) aufgehen in (+ *dat*). **~per** *n* Hülle *f*. **~ping** *n* Verpackung *f*. **~ping paper** *n* Einwickelpapier *nt*

wrath /rɒθ/ *n* Zorn *m*

wreak /riːk/ *vt* ~ **havoc** Verwüstungen anrichten

wreath /riːθ/ *n* (*pl* ~**s** /-ðz/) Kranz *m*

wreck /rek/ *n* Wrack *nt* ● *vt* zerstören; zunichte machen ⟨*plans*⟩;

zerrütten ⟨*marriage*⟩. **~age** /-ɪdʒ/ *n* Wrackteile *pl*; (*fig*) Trümmer *pl*

wren /ren/ *n* Zaunkönig *m*

wrench /rentʃ/ *n* Ruck *m*; ⟨*tool*⟩ Schraubenschlüssel *m*; **be a ~** (*fig*) weh tun ● *vt* reißen; ~ **sth from s.o.** jdm etw entreißen

wrest /rest/ *vt* entwinden (**from s.o.** jdm)

wrestl|e /'resl/ *vi* ringen. **~er** *n* Ringer *m*. **~ing** *n* Ringen *nt*

wretch /retʃ/ *n* Kreatur *f*. **~ed** /-ɪd/ *a* elend; ⟨*very bad*⟩ erbärmlich

wriggle /'rɪgl/ *n* Zappeln *nt* ● *vi* zappeln; ⟨*move forward*⟩ sich schlängeln; ~ **out of sth** (*fam*) sich vor etw (*dat*) drücken

wring /rɪŋ/ *vt* (*pt/pp* **wrung**) wringen; (~ **out**) auswringen; umdrehen ⟨*neck*⟩; ringen ⟨*hands*⟩; **be ~ing wet** tropfnaß sein

wrinkle /'rɪŋkl/ *n* Falte *f*; (*on skin*) Runzel *f* ● *vt* kräuseln ● *vi* sich kräuseln, sich falten. **~d** *a* runzlig

wrist /rɪst/ *n* Handgelenk *nt*. **~-watch** *n* Armbanduhr *f*

writ /rɪt/ *n* (*Jur*) Verfügung *f*

write /raɪt/ *vt/i* (*pt* **wrote**, *pp* **written**, *pres p* **writing**) schreiben. ~ **down** *vt* aufschreiben. ~ **off** *vt* abschreiben; zu Schrott fahren ⟨*car*⟩

'write-off *n* ≈ Totalschaden *m*

writer /'raɪtə(r)/ *n* Schreiber(in) *m(f)*; ⟨*author*⟩ Schriftsteller(in) *m(f)*

'write-up *n* Bericht *m*; ⟨*review*⟩ Kritik *f*

writhe /raɪð/ *vi* sich winden

writing /'raɪtɪŋ/ *n* Schreiben *nt*; ⟨*handwriting*⟩ Schrift *f*; **in ~** schriftlich. **~-paper** *n* Schreibpapier *nt*

written /'rɪtn/ *see* write

wrong /rɒŋ/ *a*, **-ly** *adv* falsch; ⟨*morally*⟩ unrecht; (*not just*) ungerecht; **be ~** nicht stimmen; ⟨*person:*⟩ unrecht haben; **what's ~?** was ist los? ● *adv* falsch; **go ~** ⟨*person:*⟩ etwas falsch machen; ⟨*machine:*⟩ kaputtgehen; ⟨*plan:*⟩ schiefgehen ● *n* Unrecht *nt* ● *vt* Unrecht tun (+ *dat*). **~ful** *a* ungerechtfertigt. **~fully** *adv* ⟨*accuse*⟩ zu Unrecht

wrote /rəʊt/ *see* write

wrought 'iron /rɔːt-/ *n* Schmiedeeisen *nt* ● *attrib* schmiedeeisern

wrung /rʌŋ/ *see* wring

wry /raɪ/ a (**-er, -est**) ironisch;
⟨humour⟩ trocken

X

xerox (P) /'zɪərɒks/ vt fotokopieren
Xmas /'krɪsməs, 'eksməs/ n (fam)
Weihnachten nt
'X-ray n (picture) Röntgenaufnahme
f; ~s pl Röntgenstrahlen pl; **have an ~**
geröntgt werden ● vt röntgen;
durchleuchten ⟨luggage⟩

Y

yacht /jɒt/ n Jacht f; (for racing)
Segelboot nt. ~**ing** n Segeln nt
yank /jæŋk/ vt (fam) reißen
Yank n (fam) Amerikaner(in) m(f),
(fam) Ami m
yap /jæp/ vi (pt/pp yapped) ⟨dog:⟩
kläffen
yard[1] /jɑ:d/ n Hof m; (for storage)
Lager nt
yard[2] n Yard nt (= 0,91 m). ~**stick** n
(fig) Maßstab m
yarn /jɑ:n/ n Garn nt; (fam: tale)
Geschichte f
yawn /jɔ:n/ n Gähnen nt ● vi
gähnen. ~**ing** a gähnend
year /jɪə(r)/ n Jahr nt; (of wine)
Jahrgang m; **for** ~s jahrelang.
~**-book** n Jahrbuch nt. ~**ly** a & adv
jährlich
yearn /jɜ:n/ vi sich sehnen (**for** nach).
~**ing** n Sehnsucht f
yeast /ji:st/ n Hefe f
yell /jel/ n Schrei m ● vi schreien
yellow /'jeləʊ/ a gelb ● n Gelb nt.
~**ish** a gelblich
yelp /jelp/ vi jaulen
yen /jen/ n Wunsch m (**for** nach)
yes /jes/ adv ja; (contradicting) doch
● n Ja nt
yesterday /'jestədeɪ/ n & adv
gestern; ~**'s paper** die gestrige Zeitung; **the day before** ~ vorgestern
yet /jet/ adv noch; (in question)
schon; (nevertheless) doch; **as** ~ bisher; **not** ~ noch nicht; **the best** ~ das
bisher beste ● conj doch
yew /ju:/ n Eibe f
Yiddish /'jɪdɪʃ/ n Jiddisch nt

yield /ji:ld/ n Ertrag m ● vt bringen;
abwerfen ⟨profit⟩ ● vi nachgeben;
(Amer, Auto) die Vorfahrt beachten
yodel /'jəʊdl/ vi (pt/pp yodelled)
jodeln
yoga /'jəʊgə/ n Yoga m
yoghurt /'jɒgət/ n Joghurt m
yoke /jəʊk/ n Joch nt; (of garment)
Passe f
yokel /'jəʊkl/ n Bauerntölpel m
yolk /jəʊk/ n Dotter m, Eigelb nt
yonder /'jɒndə(r)/ adv (liter) dort
drüben
you /ju:/ pron du; (acc) dich; (dat)
dir; (pl) ihr; (acc, dat) euch; (formal)
(nom & acc, sg & pl) Sie; (dat, sg & pl)
Ihnen; (one) man; (acc) einen; (dat)
einem; **all of** ~ ihr/Sie alle; **I know**
~ ich kenne dich/euch/Sie; **I'll give** ~
the money ich gebe dir/euch/Ihnen
das Geld; **it does** ~ **good** es tut gut; **it's**
bad for ~ es ist ungesund
young /jʌŋ/ a (**-er** /-gə(r)/, **-est**
/-gɪst/) jung ● npl (animals) Junge
pl; **the** ~ die Jugend f. ~**ster** n
Jugendliche(r) m/f; (child) Kleine(r)
m/f
your /jɔ:(r)/ a dein; (pl) euer;
(formal) Ihr
yours /jɔ:z/ poss pron deine(r), deins;
(pl) eure(r), euers; (formal, sg & pl)
Ihre(r), Ihr[e]s; **a friend of** ~ ein
Freund von dir/Ihnen/euch; **that is** ~
das gehört dir/Ihnen/euch
your'self pron (pl **-selves**) selbst;
(refl) dich; (dat) dir; (pl) euch; (formal)
sich; **by** ~ allein
youth /ju:θ/ n (pl **youths** /-ðz/ Jugend f; (boy) Jugendliche(r) m. ~**ful**
a jugendlich. ~ **hostel** n Jugend-
herberge f
Yugoslav /'ju:gəslɑ:v/ a jugosla-
wisch. ~**ia** /-'slɑ:vɪə/ n Jugoslawien
nt

Z

zany /'zeɪnɪ/ a (**-ier, -iest**) närrisch,
verrückt
zeal /zi:l/ n Eifer m
zealous /'zeləs/ a, **-ly** adv eifrig
zebra /'zebrə/ n Zebra nt. ~**'cross-**
ing n Zebrastreifen m
zenith /'zenɪθ/ n Zenit m; (fig) Gipfel
m
zero /'zɪərəʊ/ n Null f
zest /zest/ n Begeisterung f

zigzag /'zɪgzæg/ n Zickzack m ● vi (pt/pp -zagged) im Zickzack laufen/ (in vehicle) fahren

zinc /zɪŋk/ n Zink nt

zip /zɪp/ n ~ [fastener] Reißverschluß m ● vt ~ [up] den Reißverschluß zuziehen an (+ dat)

'Zip code n (Amer) Postleitzahl f

zipper /'zɪpə(r)/ n Reißverschluß m

zither /'zɪðə(r)/ n Zither f

zodiac /'zəʊdɪæk/ n Tierkreis m

zombie /'zɒmbɪ/ n (fam) like a ~ ganz benommen

zone /zəʊn/ n Zone f

zoo /zu:/ n Zoo m

zoological /zəʊə'lɒdʒɪkl/ a zoologisch

zoolog|ist /zəʊ'ɒlədʒɪst/ n Zoologe m/ -gin f. ~y Zoologie f

zoom /zu:m/ vi sausen. ~ lens n Zoomobjektiv nt

Englische unregelmäßige Verben

Ein Sternchen (*) weist darauf hin, daß die korrekte Form von der jeweiligen Bedeutung abhängt.

Infinitive *Infinitiv*	Past Tense *Präteritum*	Past Participle *2. Partizip*
arise	arose	arisen
awake	awoke	awoken
be	was *sg*, were *pl*	been
bear	bore	borne
beat	beat	beaten
become	became	become
begin	began	begun
behold	beheld	beheld
bend	bent	bent
beseech	beseeched, besought	beseeched, besought
bet	bet, betted	bet, betted
bid	*bade, bid	*bidden, bid
bind	bound	bound
bite	bit	bitten
bleed	bled	bled
blow	blew	blown
break	broke	broken
breed	bred	bred
bring	brought	brought
build	built	built
burn	burnt, burned	burnt, burned
burst	burst	burst
bust	busted, bust	busted, bust
buy	bought	bought
cast	cast	cast
catch	caught	caught
choose	chose	chosen
cling	clung	clung
come	came	come
cost	*cost, costed	*cost, costed
creep	crept	crept
cut	cut	cut
deal	dealt	dealt
dig	dug	dug
do	did	done
draw	drew	drawn
dream	dreamt, dreamed	dreamt, dreamed
drink	drank	drunk
drive	drove	driven
dwell	dwelt	dwelt
eat	ate	eaten
fall	fell	fallen
feed	fed	fed
feel	felt	felt
fight	fought	fought
find	found	found
flee	fled	fled

Infinitive *Infinitiv*	Past Tense *Präteritum*	Past Participle *2. Partizip*
fling	flung	flung
fly	flew	flown
forbid	forbade	forbidden
forget	forgot	forgotten
forgive	forgave	forgiven
forsake	forsook	forsaken
freeze	froze	frozen
get	got	got, gotten
give	gave	given
go	went	gone
grind	ground	ground
grow	grew	grown
hang	*hung, hanged	*hung, hanged
have	had	had
hear	heard	heard
hew	hewed	hewed, hewn
hide	hid	hidden
hit	hit	hit
hold	held	held
hurt	hurt	hurt
keep	kept	kept
kneel	knelt	knelt
know	knew	known
lay	laid	laid
lead	led	led
lean	leaned, lent	leaned, lent
leap	leapt, leaped	leapt, leaped
learn	learned, learnt	learned, learnt
leave	left	left
lend	lent	lent
let	let	let
lie²	lay	lain
light	lit, lighted	lit, lighted
lose	lost	lost
make	made	made
mean	meant	meant
meet	met	met
mow	mowed	mown, mowed
overhang	overhung	overhung
pay	paid	paid
put	put	put
quit	quitted, quit	quitted, quit
read /riːd/	read /red/	read /red/
rid	rid	rid
ride	rode	ridden
ring²	rang	rung
rise	rose	risen
run	ran	run
saw	sawed	sawn, sawed
say	said	said
see	saw	seen
seek	sought	sought
sell	sold	sold
send	sent	sent

Infinitive *Infinitiv*	Past Tense *Präteritum*	Past Participle *2. Partizip*
set	set	set
sew	sewed	sewn, sewed
shake	shook	shaken
shear	sheared	shorn, sheared
shed	shed	shed
shine	shone	shone
shit	shit	shit
shoe	shod	shod
shoot	shot	shot
show	showed	shown
shrink	shrank	shrunk
shut	shut	shut
sing	sang	sung
sink	sank	sunk
sit	sat	sat
slay	slew	slain
sleep	slept	slept
slide	slid	slid
sling	slung	slung
slit	slit	slit
smell	smelled, smelt	smelled, smelt
sow	sowed	sown, sowed
speak	spoke	spoken
speed	*sped, speeded	*sped, speeded
spell	spelled, spelt	spelled, spelt
spend	spent	spent
spill	spilled, spilt	spilled, spilt
spin	spun	spun
spit	spat	spat
split	split	split
spoil	spoiled, spoilt	spoiled, spoilt
spread	spread	spread
spring	sprang	sprung
stand	stood	stood
steal	stole	stolen
stick	stuck	stuck
sting	stung	stung
stink	stank	stunk
strew	strewed	strewn, strewed
stride	strode	stridden
strike	struck	struck
string	strung	strung
strive	strove	striven
swear	swore	sworn
sweep	swept	swept
swell	swelled	swollen, swelled
swim	swam	swum
swing	swung	swung
take	took	taken
teach	taught	taught
tear	tore	torn
tell	told	told
think	thought	thought
thrive	thrived, throve	thrived, thriven
throw	threw	thrown

Infinitive *Infinitiv*	Past Tense *Präteritum*	Past Participle *2. Partizip*
thrust	thrust	thrust
tread	trod	trodden
understand	understood	understood
undo	undid	undone
wake	woke	woken
wear	wore	worn
weave[2]	wove	woven
weep	wept	wept
wet	wet, wetted	wet, wetted
win	won	won
wind[2] /waɪnd/	wound /waʊnd/	wound /waʊnd/
wring	wrung	wrung
write	wrote	written

Phonetic symbols used for German words

a	Hand	hant		ŋ	lang	laŋ
a:	Bahn	ba:n		o	moral	mo'ra:l
ɐ	Ober	'o:bɐ		o:	Boot	bo:t
ɐ̯	Uhr	u:ɐ̯		o̯	Foyer	fo̯a'je:
ã	Conférencier	kõferã'sje:		õ	Konkurs	kõ'kʊrs
ã:	Abonnement	abɔnə'mã:		õ:	Ballon	ba'lõ:
a̯i	weit	va̯it		ɔ	Post	pɔst
a̯u	Haut	ha̯ut		ø	Ökonom	øko'no:m
b	Ball	bal		ø:	Öl	ø:l
ç	ich	ɪç		œ	göttlich	'gœtlɪç
d	dann	dan		ɔ̯y	heute	'hɔ̯ytə
dʒ	Gin	dʒɪn		p	Pakt	pakt
e	Metall	me'tal		r	Rast	rast
e:	Beet	be:t		s	Hast	hast
ɛ	mästen	'mɛstən		ʃ	Schal	ʃa:l
ɛ:	wählen	'vɛ:lən		t	Tal	ta:l
ɛ̃:	Cousin	ku'zɛ̃:		ts	Zahl	tsa:l
ə	Nase	'na:zə		tʃ	Couch	ka̯utʃ
f	Faß	fas		u	kulant	ku'lant
g	Gast	gast		u:	Hut	hu:t
h	haben	'ha:bən		u̯	aktuell	ak'tu̯ɛl
i	Rivale	ri'va:lə		ʊ	Pult	pʊlt
i:	viel	fi:l		v	was	vas
i̯	Aktion	ak'tsi̯o:n		x	Bach	bax
ɪ	Birke	'bɪrkə		y	Physik	fy'zi:k
j	ja	ja:		y:	Rübe	'ry:bə
k	kalt	kalt		ỹ	Nuance	'nỹã:sə
l	Last	last		ʏ	Fülle	'fʏlə
m	Mast	mast		z	Nase	'na:zə
n	Naht	na:t		ʒ	Regime	re'ʒi:m

ˀ Glottal stop, e.g. Koordination /koˀɔrdina'tsi̯o:n/.
: Length sign after a vowel, e.g. Chrom /kro:m/.
' Stress mark before stressed syllable, e.g. Balkon /bal'kõ:/.

Die für das Englische verwendeten Zeichen der Lautschrift

ɑː	barn	bɑːn		l	lot	lɒt
ɑ̃	nuance	'njuːɑ̃s		m	mat	mæt
æ	fat	fæt		n	not	nɒt
æ̃	lingerie	'læʒərɪ		ŋ	sing	sɪŋ
aɪ	fine	faɪn		ɒ	got	gɒt
aʊ	now	naʊ		ɔː	paw	pɔː
b	bat	bæt		ɔɪ	boil	bɔɪl
d	dog	dɒg		p	pet	pet
dʒ	jam	dʒæm		r	rat	ræt
e	met	met		s	sip	sɪp
eɪ	fate	feɪt		ʃ	ship	ʃɪp
eə	fairy	'feərɪ		t	tip	tɪp
əʊ	goat	gəʊt		tʃ	chin	tʃɪn
ə	ago	ə'gəʊ		θ	thin	θɪn
ɜː	fur	fɜː(r)		ð	the	ðə
f	fat	fæt		uː	boot	buːt
g	good	gʊd		ʊ	book	bʊk
h	hat	hæt		ʊə	tourism	'tʊərɪzm
ɪ	bit, happy	bɪt, 'hæpɪ		ʌ	dug	dʌg
ɪə	near	nɪə(r)		v	van	væn
iː	meet	miːt		w	win	wɪn
j	yet	jet		z	zip	zɪp
k	kit	kɪt		ʒ	vision	'vɪʒn

:   bezeichnet Länge des vorhergehenden Vokals, z. B. boot [buːt].

'   Betonung, steht unmittelbar vor einer betonten Silbe, z. B. ago [ə'gəʊ].

(r)   Ein „r" in runden Klammern wird nur gesprochen, wenn im Text-zusammenhang ein Vokal unmittelbar folgt, z. B. fire /'faɪə(r); fire at /'faɪər æt/.

Guide to German pronunciation

Consonants are pronounced as in English with the following exceptions:

b	as	p	
d	as	t	*at the end of a word or syllable*
g	as	k	
ch	as in Scottish lo<u>ch</u> *after a, o, u, au*		
	like an exaggerated h as in <u>h</u>uge		
			after i, e, ä, ö, ü, eu, ei
-chs	as	x	(as in bo<u>x</u>)
-ig	as	-ich /ɪç/	*when a suffix*
j	as	y	(as in <u>y</u>es)
ps			
			the p is pronounced
pn			
qu	as	k+v	
s	as	z	(as in <u>z</u>ero) *at the beginning of a word*
	as	s	(as in bu<u>s</u>) *at the end of a word or syllable, before a consonant, or when doubled*
sch	as	sh	
sp	as	shp	*at the beginning of a*
st	as	sht	*word*
v	as	f	(as in <u>f</u>or)
	as	v	(as in <u>v</u>ery) *within a word*
w	as	v	(as in <u>v</u>ery)
z	as	ts	

Vowels are approximately as follows:

a	short	as	u	(as in b<u>u</u>t)
	long	as	a	(as in c<u>a</u>r)
e	short	as	e	(as in p<u>e</u>n)
	long	as	a	(as in p<u>a</u>per)
i	short	as	i	(as in b<u>i</u>t)
	long	as	ee	(as in qu<u>ee</u>n)
o	short	as	o	(as in h<u>o</u>t)
	long	as	o	(as in p<u>o</u>pe)

u	short	as	oo	(as in f<u>oo</u>t)
	long	as	oo	(as in b<u>oo</u>t)

Vowels are always short before a double consonant, and long when followed by an h or when double

ie	is pronounced ee		(as in k<u>ee</u>p)

Diphthongs

au		as	ow	(as in h<u>ow</u>)
ei				
ai		as	y	(as in m<u>y</u>)
eu				
äu		as	oy	(as in b<u>oy</u>)

German irregular verbs

1st, 2nd and 3rd person present are given after the infinitive, and past subjunctive after the past indicative, where there is a change of vowel or any other irregularity.

Compound verbs are only given if they do not take the same forms as the corresponding simple verb, e.g. *befehlen*, or if there is no corresponding simple verb, e.g. *bewegen*.

An asterisk (*) indicates a verb which is also conjugated regularly.

Infinitive *Infinitiv*	Past Tense *Präteritum*	Past Participle *2. Partizip*
abwägen	wog (wöge) ab	abgewogen
ausbedingen	bedang (bedänge) aus	ausbedungen
*backen (du bäckst, er bäckt)	buk (büke)	gebacken
befehlen (du befiehlst, er befiehlt)	befahl (beföhle, befähle)	befohlen
beginnen	begann (begänne)	begonnen
beißen (du/er beißt)	biß (bisse)	gebissen
bergen (du birgst, er birgt)	barg (bärge)	geborgen
bersten (du/er birst)	barst (bärste)	geborsten
bewegen²	bewog (bewöge)	bewogen
biegen	bog (böge)	gebogen
bieten	bot (böte)	geboten
binden	band (bände)	gebunden
bitten	bat (bäte)	gebeten
blasen (du/er bläst)	blies	geblasen
bleiben	blieb	geblieben
*bleichen	blich	geblichen
braten (du brätst, er brät)	briet	gebraten
brechen (du brichst, er bricht)	brach (bräche)	gebrochen
brennen	brannte (brennte)	gebrannt
bringen	brachte (brächte)	gebracht
denken	dachte (dächte)	gedacht
dreschen (du drischst, er drischt)	drosch (drösche)	gedroschen
dringen	drang (dränge)	gedrungen
dürfen (ich/er darf, du darfst)	durfte (dürfte)	gedurft
empfehlen (du empfiehlst, er empfiehlt)	empfahl (empföhle)	empfohlen
erlöschen (du erlischst, er erlischt)	erlosch (erlösche)	erloschen
*erschallen	erscholl (erschölle)	erschollen
*erschrecken (du erschrickst, er erschrickt)	erschrak (erschräke)	erschrocken

Infinitive *Infinitiv*	Past Tense *Präteritum*	Past Participle *2. Partizip*
erwägen	erwog (erwöge)	erwogen
essen (du/er ißt)	aß (äße)	gegessen
fahren (du fährst, er fährt)	fuhr (führe)	gefahren
fallen (du fällst, er fällt)	fiel	gefallen
fangen (du fängst, er fängt)	fing	gefangen
fechten (du fichtst, er ficht)	focht (föchte)	gefochten
finden	fand (fände)	gefunden
flechten (du flichtst, er flicht)	flocht (flöchte)	geflochten
fliegen	flog (flöge)	geflogen
fliehen	floh (flöhe)	geflohen
fließen (du/er fließt)	floß (flösse)	geflossen
fressen (du/er frißt)	fraß (fräße)	gefressen
frieren	fror (fröre)	gefroren
*gären	gor (göre)	gegoren
gebären (du gebierst, sie gebiert)	gebar (gebäre)	geboren
geben (du gibst, er gibt)	gab (gäbe)	gegeben
gedeihen	gedieh	gediehen
gehen	ging	gegangen
gelingen	gelang (gelänge)	gelungen
gelten (du giltst, er gilt)	galt (gölte, gälte)	gegolten
genesen (du/er genest)	genas (genäse)	genesen
genießen (du/er genießt)	genoß (genösse)	genossen
geschehen (es geschieht)	geschah (geschähe)	geschehen
gewinnen	gewann (gewönne, gewänne)	gewonnen
gießen (du/er gießt)	goß (gösse)	gegossen
gleichen	glich	geglichen
gleiten	glitt	geglitten
glimmen	glomm (glömme)	geglommen
graben (du gräbst, er gräbt)	grub (grübe)	gegraben
greifen	griff	gegriffen
haben (du hast, er hat)	hatte (hätte)	gehabt
halten (du hältst, er hält)	hielt	gehalten
hängen[2]	hing	gehangen
hauen	haute	gehauen
heben	hob (höbe)	gehoben
heißen (du/er heißt)	hieß	geheißen
helfen (du hilfst, er hilft)	half (hülfe)	geholfen
kennen	kannte (kennte)	gekannt
klingen	klang (klänge)	geklungen
kneifen	kniff	gekniffen
kommen	kam (käme)	gekommen
können (ich/er kann, du kannst)	konnte (könnte)	gekonnt
kriechen	kroch (kröche)	gekrochen
laden (du lädst, er lädt)	lud (lüde)	geladen
lassen (du/er läßt)	ließ	gelassen
laufen (du läufst, er läuft)	lief	gelaufen

Infinitive *Infinitiv*	Past Tense *Präteritum*	Past Participle *2. Partizip*
leiden	litt	gelitten
leihen	lieh	geliehen
lesen (du/er liest)	las (läse)	gelesen
liegen	lag (läge)	gelegen
lügen	log (löge)	gelogen
mahlen	mahlte	gemahlen
meiden	mied	gemieden
melken	molk (mölke)	gemolken
messen (du/er mißt)	maß (mäße)	gemessen
mißlingen	mißlang (mißlänge)	mißlungen
mögen (ich/er mag, du magst)	mochte (möchte)	gemocht
müssen (ich/er muß, du mußt)	mußte (müßte)	gemußt
nehmen (du nimmst, er nimmt)	nahm (nähme)	genommen
nennen	nannte (nennte)	genannt
pfeifen	pfiff	gepfiffen
preisen (du/er preist)	pries	gepriesen
quellen (du quillst, er quillt)	quoll (quölle)	gequollen
raten (du rätst, er rät)	riet	geraten
reiben	rieb	gerieben
reißen (du/er reißt)	riß	gerissen
reiten	ritt	geritten
rennen	rannte (rennte)	gerannt
riechen	roch (röche)	gerochen
ringen	rang (ränge)	gerungen
rinnen	rann (ränne)	geronnen
rufen	rief	gerufen
*salzen (du/er salzt)	salzte	gesalzen
saufen (du säufst, er säuft)	soff (söffe)	gesoffen
*saugen	sog (söge)	gesogen
schaffen[1]	schuf (schüfe)	geschaffen
scheiden	schied	geschieden
scheinen	schien	geschienen
scheißen (du/er scheißt)	schiß	geschissen
schelten (du schiltst, er schilt)	schalt (schölte)	gescholten
scheren[1]	schor (schöre)	geschoren
schieben	schob (schöbe)	geschoben
schießen (du/er schießt)	schoß (schösse)	geschossen
schinden	schindete	geschunden
schlafen (du schläfst, er schläft)	schlief	geschlafen
schlagen (du schlägst, er schlägt)	schlug (schlüge)	geschlagen
schleichen	schlich	geschlichen
schleifen[2]	schliff	geschliffen
schließen (du/er schließt)	schloß (schlösse)	geschlossen
schlingen	schlang (schlänge)	geschlungen

Infinitive *Infinitiv*	Past Tense *Präteritum*	Past Participle *2. Partizip*
schmeißen (du/er schmeißt)	schmiß (schmisse)	geschmissen
schmelzen (du/er schmilzt)	schmolz (schmölze)	geschmolzen
schneiden	schnitt	geschnitten
*schrecken (du schrickst, er schrickt)	schrak (schräke)	geschreckt
schreiben	schrieb	geschrieben
schreien	schrie	geschrie[e]n
schreiten	schritt	geschritten
schweigen	schwieg	geschwiegen
schwellen (du schwillst, er schwillt)	schwoll (schwölle)	geschwollen
schwimmen	schwamm (schwömme)	geschwommen
schwinden	schwand (schwände)	geschwunden
schwingen	schwang (schwänge)	geschwungen
schwören	schwor (schwüre)	geschworen
sehen (du siehst, er sieht)	sah (sähe)	gesehen
sein (ich bin, du bist, er ist, wir sind, ihr seid, sie sind)	war (wäre)	gewesen
senden[1]	sandte (sendete)	gesandt
sieden	sott (sötte)	gesotten
singen	sang (sänge)	gesungen
sinken	sank (sänke)	gesunken
sinnen	sann (sänne)	gesonnen
sitzen (du/er sitzt)	saß (säße)	gesessen
sollen (ich/er soll, du sollst)	sollte	gesollt
*spalten	spaltete	gespalten
speien	spie	gespie[e]n
spinnen	spann (spönne, spänne)	gesponnen
sprechen (du sprichst, er spricht)	sprach (spräche)	gesprochen
sprießen (du/er sprießt)	sproß (sprösse)	gesprossen
springen	sprang (spränge)	gesprungen
stechen (du stichst, er sticht)	stach (stäche)	gestochen
stehen	stand (stünde, stände)	gestanden
stehlen (du stiehlst, er stiehlt)	stahl (stähle)	gestohlen
steigen	stieg	gestiegen
sterben (du stirbst, er stirbt)	starb (stürbe)	gestorben
stinken	stank (stänke)	gestunken
stoßen (du/er stößt)	stieß	gestoßen
streichen	strich	gestrichen
streiten	stritt	gestritten
tragen (du trägst, er trägt)	trug (trüge)	getragen
treffen (du triffst, er trifft)	traf (träfe)	getroffen

Infinitive *Infinitiv*	Past Tense *Präteritum*	Past Participle *2. Partizip*
treiben	trieb	getrieben
treten (du trittst, er tritt)	trat (träte)	getreten
*triefen	troff (tröffe)	getroffen
trinken	trank (tränke)	getrunken
trügen	trog (tröge)	getrogen
tun (du tust, er tut)	tat (täte)	getan
verderben (du verdirbst, er verdirbt)	verdarb (verdürbe)	verdorben
vergessen (du/er vergißt)	vergaß (vergäße)	vergessen
verlieren	verlor (verlöre)	verloren
verschleißen (du/er verschleißt)	verschliß	verschlissen
verzeihen	verzieh	verziehen
wachsen[1] (du/er wächst)	wuchs (wüchse)	gewachsen
waschen (du wäschst, er wäscht)	wusch (wüsche)	gewaschen
weichen[2]	wich	gewichen
weisen (du/er weist)	wies	gewiesen
*wenden[2]	wandte (wendete)	gewandt
werben (du wirbst, er wirbt)	warb (würbe)	geworben
werden (du wirst, er wird)	wurde (würde)	geworden
werfen (du wirfst, er wirft)	warf (würfe)	geworfen
wiegen[1]	wog (wöge)	gewogen
winden	wand (wände)	gewunden
wissen (ich/er weiß, du weißt)	wußte (wüßte)	gewußt
wollen (ich/er will, du willst)	wollte	gewollt
wringen	wrang (wränge)	gewrungen
ziehen	zog (zöge)	gezogen
zwingen	zwang (zwänge)	gezwungen

The last word in reference.
The first name in reference.

OXFORD
BERKLEY

THE OXFORD DESK DICTIONARY
AND THESAURUS: AMERICAN EDITION

The only reference of its kind available in paperback—combines a dictionary and a thesaurus in a single, integrated A-to-Z volume with 150,000 entries, definitions, and synonyms.

___0-425-16008-4/$6.99

Also available— outstanding foreign-language dictionaries for travelers, students, and businesspeople:

THE OXFORD SPANISH DICTIONARY   0-425-16009-2
THE OXFORD FRENCH DICTIONARY   0-425-16010-6
THE OXFORD GERMAN DICTIONARY   0-425-16011-4
THE OXFORD ITALIAN DICTIONARY   0-425-16012-2
THE OXFORD RUSSIAN DICTIONARY   0-425-16013-0

All books $4.99

Payable in U.S. funds. No cash accepted. Postage & handling: $1.75 for one book, 75¢ for each additional. Maximum postage $5.50. Prices, postage and handling charges may change without notice. Visa, Amex, MasterCard call 1-800-788-6262, ext. 1, or fax 1-201-933-2316; refer to ad #736

Or, check above books   Bill my: ☐ Visa ☐ MasterCard ☐ Amex _____ (expires)
and send this order form to:
The Berkley Publishing Group Card#_____

P.O. Box 12289, Dept. B   Daytime Phone #_____ ($10 minimum)
Newark, NJ 07101-5289   Signature_____
Please allow 4-6 weeks for delivery.   Or enclosed is my: ☐ check ☐ money order
Foreign and Canadian delivery 8-12 weeks.

Ship to:

Name_____   Book Total $_____
Address_____   Applicable Sales Tax $_____
    (NY, NJ, PA, CA, GST Can.)
City_____   Postage & Handling $_____
State/ZIP_____   Total Amount Due $_____

Bill to: Name_____

Address_____City_____
State/ZIP_____